ENCYCLOPEDIA OF WORLD BIOGRAPHY

SUPPLEMENT

24

ENCYCLOPEDIA OF WORLD BIOGRAPHY

SUPPLEMENT

$$\frac{A}{Z}$$ **24**

Detroit • New York • San Francisco • San Diego • New Haven, Conn. • Waterville, Maine • London • Munich

Encyclopedia of World Biography Supplement, Volume 24

Project Editors
Andrea Kovacs Henderson, Tracie Ratiner

Editorial
Julie Bedard

Editorial Support Services
Andrea Lopeman

Rights and Acquisitions Management
Margaret A. Chamberlain, Lori Hines,
Shalice Shah-Caldwell

Imaging and Multimedia
Leitha Etheridge-Sims, Lezlie Light,
Dan Newell

Manufacturing
Lori Kessler

LIBRARY OF CONGRESS CATALOGING-IN-PUBLICATION DATA

ISBN 0-7876-6903-2
ISSN 1099-7326

This title is also available as an e-book.
ISBN 7876-9345-6

Printed in the United States of America

10 9 8 7 6 5 4 3 2 1

CONTENTS

INTRODUCTION

The study of biography has always held an important, if not explicitly stated, place in school curricula. The absence in schools of a class specifically devoted to studying the lives of the giants of human history belies the focus most courses have always had on people. From ancient times to the present, the world has been shaped by the decisions, philosophies, inventions, discoveries, artistic creations, medical breakthroughs, and written works of its myriad personalities. Librarians, teachers, and students alike recognize that our lives are immensely enriched when we learn about those individuals who have made their mark on the world we live in today.

Encyclopedia of World Biography Supplement, Volume 24, provides biographical information on 200 individuals not covered in the 17-volume second edition of *Encyclopedia of World Biography (EWB)* and its supplements, Volumes 18, 19, 20, 21, 22, and 23. Like other volumes in the *EWB* series, this supplement represents a unique, comprehensive source for biographical information on those people who, for their contributions to human culture and society, have reputations that stand the test of time. Each original article ends with a bibliographic section. There is also an index to names and subjects, which cumulates all persons appearing as main entries in the *EWB* second edition, the Volume 18, 19, 20, 21, 22, and 23 supplements, and this supplement—more than 8,000 people!

Articles. Arranged alphabetically following the letter-by-letter convention (spaces and hyphens have been ignored), articles begin with the full name of the person profiled in large, bold type. Next is a boldfaced, descriptive paragraph that includes birth and death years in parentheses. It provides a capsule identification and a statement of the person's significance. The essay that follows is approximately 2,000 words in length and offers a substantial treatment of the person's life. Some of the essays proceed chronologically while others con-

fine biographical data to a paragraph or two and move on to a consideration and evaluation of the subject's work. Where very few biographical facts are known, the article is necessarily devoted to an analysis of the subject's contribution.

Following the essay is a bibliographic section arranged by source type. Citations include books, periodicals, and online Internet addresses for World Wide Web pages, where current information can be found.

Portraits accompany many of the articles and provide either an authentic likeness, contemporaneous with the subject, or a later representation of artistic merit. For artists, occasionally self-portraits have been included. Of the ancient figures, there are depictions from coins, engravings, and sculptures; of the moderns, there are many portrait photographs.

Index. The *EWB Supplement* index is a useful key to the encyclopedia. Persons, places, battles, treaties, institutions, buildings, inventions, books, works of art, ideas, philosophies, styles, movements—all are indexed for quick reference just as in a general encyclopedia. The index entry for a person includes a brief identification with birth and death dates *and* is cumulative so that any person for whom an article was written who appears in the second edition of *EWB* (volumes 1-16) and its supplements (volumes 18-24) can be located. The subject terms within the index, however, apply only to volume 24. Every index reference includes the title of the article to which the reader is being directed as well as the volume and page numbers.

Because *EWB Supplement,* Volume 24, is an encyclopedia of biography, its index differs in important ways from the indexes to other encyclopedias. Basically, this is an index of people, and that fact has several interesting consequences. First, the information to which the index refers the reader on a particular topic is always about people associated with that topic. Thus the entry "Quantum theory (physics)" lists articles on people associated with quantum theory. Each article may discuss a person's contribution to quantum theory, but no single article or group of articles is intended to provide a comprehensive treatment of quantum theory as such. Second, the index is rich in classified entries. All persons who are subjects of articles in the encyclopedia, for example, are listed in one or more classifications in the index—abolitionists, astronomers, engineers, philosophers, zoologists, etc.

The index, together with the biographical articles, make *EWB Supplement* an enduring and valuable source for biographical information. As school course work changes to reflect advances in technology and fur-ther revelations about the universe, the life stories of the people who have risen above the ordinary and earned a place in the annals of human history will continue to fascinate students of all ages.

We Welcome Your Suggestions. Mail your comments and suggestions for enhancing and improving the *Encyclopedia of World Biography Supplement* to:

The Editors
Encyclopedia of World Biography Supplement
Thomson Gale
27500 Drake Road
Farmington Hills, MI 48331-3535
Phone: (800) 347-4253

ADVISORY BOARD

ACKNOWLEDGMENTS

Photographs and illustrations appearing in the *Encyclopedia of World Biography Supplement*, Volume 24, have been used with the permission of the following sources:

AMERICAN INSTITUTE OF PHYSICS: Katherine Burr Blodgett

AP/WIDE WORLD PHOTOS: Toshiko Akiyoshi, Ivo Andric, German Arciniegas, Meher Baba, Romana Acosta Banuelos, Sir John Barbirolli, Sir Thomas Beecham, Gerd Binnig, Fernando Botero, Sir Adrian Boult, Sir Francis Chichester, John Cornforth, Howard Cosell, James Cronin, Doris Duke, Tan Dun, Gerald Durrell, Leo Esaki, Rene Geronimo Favaloro, Sally Field, Peggy Fleming, Mingxia Fu, Eric Heiden, Keisuke Kinoshita, Olga Korbut, Julie Krone, Chuan Leekpai, Sugar Ray Leonard, Bob Marley, Paul McCartney, Franco Modigliani, Alva Myrdal, Jean Negulesco, Aristotle Onassis, Cyril Northcote Parkinson, Aristides Maria Pereira, Seewoosagur Ramgoolam, Dan Rather, Sir Michael Redgrave, Sir Ralph Richardson, Rozanne Ridgway, Augusto Antonio Roa Bastos, Romy Schneider, Tex Schramm, Richard Sears, Amartya Sen, Sobhuza II, Bruce Springsteen, Standing Bear, Jackie Stewart, Dame Sybil Thorndike, Susumu Tonegawa, Grete Waitz

JERRY BAUER: Breyten Breytenbach

THE BRIDGEMAN ART LIBRARY: Roberto Matta

CORBIS: Alexander III, Alicia Alonso, Yehuda Amichai, Evelyn Ashford, Benny Carter, Feodor Chaliapin, Celia Cruz, Tamara de Lempicka, Christine de Pisan, Grazia Deledda, A.J. Foyt, Maria Grever, Herbert A. Hauptman, Ofra Haza, John William Heisman, Johns Hopkins, Johannes Vilhelm Jensen, Serge Koussevitzky, John

James Rickard Macleod, Vincent Massey, Jose Medina, Nellie Melba, Ernest Oppenheimer, Andrzej Panufnik, Annie Peck Smith, Ilya Repin, Abdus Salam, Sheba, Margaret Smith Court, Vivienne Tam, Maria Telkes, Leon Theremin, Cy Young, Raul Yzaguirre, Nathan Zach

FISK UNIVERSITY LIBRARY: Rube Foster, Henry Highland Garnet

MARK GERSON PHOTOGRAPHY: William Plomer

GETTY IMAGES: Saint Agnes, Richard Burbage, Richard M. Daley, Ferdinand de Saussure, Peter Hall, Innocent X, Mary Magdalene, Carl Wilhelm Emil Milles, Ismael Montes, Jelly Roll Morton, Dolly Parton, Philip, Nina Simone, Dame Ellen Alicia Terry, Rosetta Tharpe, Sippie Wallace

THE GRANGER COLLECTION, NEW YORK: Susan La Flesche Picotte, Sonia Sanchez

ILLINOIS STATE HISTORICAL LIBRARY: Myra Bradwell

THE KOBAL COLLECTION: Vera Chytilova

THE LIBRARY OF CONGRESS: Val Logsdon Fitch, Nancy Reagan

MATHEMATISCHES FORSCHUNGSINSTITUT OBERWOLFACH: Erik Ivar Fredholm

MOUNT HOLYOKE COLLEGE ARCHIVES AND SPECIAL COLLECTIONS: Ann Morgan

PGA TOUR, INC.: Lee Trevino

KEN SETTLE: Bono

MILDRED D. TAYLOR: Mildred D. Taylor

JACK VARTOOGIAN: Ali Akbar Khan

OBITUARIES

The following people, appearing in volumes 1-23 of the *Encyclopedia of World Biography*, have died since the publication of the second edition and its supplements. Each entry lists the volume where the full biography can be found.

AMIN DADA, IDI (born circa 1926), president of Uganda, died from kidney failure in Saudi Arabia, on August 16, 2003 (Vol. 1).

BLANKERS-KOEN, FANNY (born 1918), Dutch track and field athlete, died in Amsterdam, Netherlands, on January 25, 2004 (Vol. 20).

BOORSTIN, DANIEL (born 1914), American historian, died of pneumonia in Washington, D.C., on February 28, 2004 (Vol. 2).

BRANDO, MARLON (born 1924), American actor, died in Los Angeles, California, on July 1, 2004 (Vol. 2).

CARTIER-BRESSON, HENRI (born 1908), French photographer and painter, died in l'Ile-sur-Sorgue, France, on August 2, 2004 (Vol. 19).

CASH, JOHNNY (born 1932), American singer and songwriter, died of complications from diabetes that lead to respiratory failure in Nashville, Tennessee, on September 12, 2003 (Vol. 3).

CHARLES, RAY (born 1932), American jazz musician-singer, pianist, and composer, died of acute liver disease in Beverly Hills, California, on June 10, 2004 (Vol. 3).

CONABLE, BARBER B., JR. (born 1922), head of the World bank, died of complications from a staph infection in Sarasota, Florida, on November 30, 2003 (Vol. 4).

COX, ARCHIBALD (born 1912), American lawyer, educator, author, labor arbitrator, and public servant, died of natural causes in Brooksville, Maine, on May 29, 2004 (Vol. 4).

DELLINGER, DAVID (born 1915), American pacifist, died of complications from Alzheimer's disease in Montpelier, Vermont, on May 25, 2004 (Vol. 4).

DUGAN, ALAN (born 1923), American poet, died of pneumonia in Hyannis, Massachusetts, on September 3, 2003 (Vol. 5).

EDERLE, GERTRUDE (born 1906), American swimmer, died of natural causes in Wycoff, New Jersey, on November 30, 2003 (Vol. 19).

FACKENHEIM, EMIL LUDWIG (bon 1916), liberal post World War II Jewish theologian, died in Jerusalem, Israel, on September 19, 2003 (Vol. 5).

GIBSON, ALTHEA (born 1927), African American tennis player, died in East Orange, New Jersey, on September 28, 2003 (Vol. 6).

GOLD, THOMAS (born 1920), American astronomer and physicist, died of heart disease in Ithaca, New York, on June 22, 2004 (Vol. 18).

GRAHAM, OTTO (born 1921), American football player and coach, died of an aneurysm to the heart in Sarasota, Florida, on December 17, 2003 (Vol. 21).

GUNN, THOM (born 1929), English poet, died in San Francisco, California, on April 25, 2004 (Vol. 18).

HAGEN, UTA THYRA (born 1919), American actress, died in Manhattan, New York, on January 14, 2004 (Vol. 18).

HEPBURN, KATHARINE (born 1907), American actress, died in Old Saybrook, Connecticut, on June 29, 2003 (Vol. 7).

HOPE, BOB (born 1903), entertainer in vaudeville, radio, television, and movies, died of pneumonia in Toluca Lake, California, on July 27, 2003 (Vol. 7).

IZETBEGOVIC, ALIJA (born 1926), president of the eight-member presidency of the Republic of Bosnia-

Herzegovina, died due to complications following a fall in Sarajevo, Bosnia, on October 19, 2003 (Vol. 8).

JACKSON, MAYNARD HOLBROOK, JR. (born 1938), first African American mayor of Atlanta, Georgia, died of a heart attack in Arlington, Virgina, on June 23, 2003 (Vol. 8).

JULIANA (born 1909), queen of the Netherlands, died of pneumonia in Baarn, Netherlands, on March 20, 2004 (Vol. 8).

KAZAN, ELIA (born 1909), American film and stage director, died in New York, New York, on September 28, 2003 (Vol. 8).

KERR, CLARK (born 1911), American economist, labor/management expert, and university president, died in El Cerrito, California, on December 1, 2003 (Vol. 8).

LAUDER, ESTEE (born circa 1908), founder of an international cosmetics empire, died of cardiopulmonary arrest in Manhattan, New York, on April 24, 2004 (Vol. 9).

LOPEZ, PROTILLO JOSE (born 1920), president of Mexico (1976-1982), died of pneumonia in Mexico City, Mexico, on February 17, 2004 (Vol. 9).

NIN-CULMELL, JOAQUIN MARIA (born 1908), American composer, pianist, and conductor, died from complications of a heart attack, in Berkeley, California, on January 14, 2004 (Vol. 11).

REAGAN, RONALD W. (born 1911), governor of California and U.S. president, died of pneumonia in Los Angeles, California, on June 5, 2004 (Vol. 13).

REGAN, DONALD (born 1918), American Secretary of the Treasury and White House chief of staff under President Ronald Reagan, died of cancer in Virginia, on June 10, 2003 (Vol. 13).

RIEFENSTAHL, LENI (born 1902), German film director, died in Poecking, Germany, on September 8, 2003 (Vol. 13).

SHOEMAKER, WILLIE (born 1931), American jockey and horse trainer, died of natural causes in San Marino, California, on October 12, 2003 (Vol. 21).

SIMON, PAUL (born 1928), newspaper publisher, Illinois state legislator, lieutenant governor, and U.S. representative and senator, died after undergoing heart surgery in Springfield, Illinois, on December 9, 2003 (Vol. 14).

TELLER, EDWARD (born 1908), Hungarian American physicist, died in Palo Alto, California, on September 9, 2003 (Vol. 15).

THURMOND, JAMES STROM (born 1902), American lawyer and statesman, died in Edgefield, South Carolina, on June 26, 2003 (Vol. 15).

WERNER, HELMUT (born 1936), German business executive, died in Berlin, Germany, on February 6, 2004 (Vol. 19).

Faye Glenn Abdellah

Faye Glenn Abdellah (born 1919) dedicated her life to nursing and, as a researcher and educator, helped change the profession's focus from a disease-centered approach to a patient-centered approach. She served as a public health nurse for 40 years, helping to educate Americans about the needs of the elderly and the dangers posed by AIDS, addiction, smoking, and violence. As a nursing professor, she developed teaching methods based on scientific research. Abdellah continued to work as a leader in the nursing profession into her eighties.

Abdellah was born on March 13, 1919, in New York City. Years later, on May 6, 1937, the German hydrogen-fueled airship *Hindenburg* exploded over Lakehurst, New Jersey, where 18-year-old Abdellah and her family then lived, and Abdellah and her brother ran to the scene to help. In an interview with a writer for *Advance for Nurses,* Abdellah recalled: "I could see people jumping from the zeppelin and I didn't know how to take care of them, so it was then that I vowed that I would learn nursing."

Abdellah earned a nursing diploma from Fitkin Memorial Hospital's School of Nursing (now Ann May School of Nursing). In the 1940s, this was sufficient for practicing nursing, but Abdellah believed that nursing care should be based on research, not hours of care. She went on to earn three degrees from Columbia University: a bachelor of science degree in nursing in 1945, a master of arts degree in

physiology in 1947 and a doctor of education degree in 1955.

With her advanced education, Abdellah could have chosen to become a doctor. However, as she explained in her *Advance for Nurses* interview, "I never wanted to be an M.D. because I could do all I wanted to do in nursing, which is a caring profession." As a practicing nurse, Abdellah managed a primary care clinic at the Child Education Foundation in New York City and managed the obstetrics-gynecology floor at Columbia University's Presbyterian Medical Center.

Transformed Nursing Profession

Abdellah went on to become a nursing instructor and researcher and helped transform the focus of the profession from disease centered to patient centered. She expanded the role of nurses to include care of families and the elderly. She researched nursing practices and taught research methods and theory at several universities, including schools in Washington, Colorado, Minnesota, and South Carolina. She also held several administrative positions in medical facilities. In 1993 she founded and served as the first dean of the Graduate School of Nursing at the Uniformed Services University of Health Sciences in Bethesda, Maryland.

Abdellah's first teaching job was at Yale University School of Nursing, where she worked when she was in her early twenties. At that time she was required to teach a class called "120 Principles of Nursing Practice," using a standard nursing textbook published by the National League for Nursing. The book included guidelines that had no scientific basis and, as Abdellah told Maura S. McAuliffe in an interview for *Image:* "Those Yale students were just brilliant and challenged me to explain why they were required to follow procedures without questioning the science behind them.'' After a year Abdellah became so frustrated that she gathered her colleagues in the Yale courtyard and burned the textbooks. The next morning the school's dean told her she would have to pay for the destroyed texts. It took a year for Abdellah to settle the debt, but she never regretted her actions. As she told *Image:* ''Of the 120 principles I was required to teach, I really spent the rest of my life undoing that teaching, because it started me on the long road in pursuit of the scientific basis of our practice.''

Abdellah was an advocate of degree programs for nursing. Diploma programs, she believes, were never meant to prepare nurses at the professional level. Nursing education, she argued, should be based on research; she herself became among the first in her role as an educator to focus on theory and research. Her first studies were qualitative; they simply described situations. As her career progressed, her research evolved to include physiology, chemistry, and behavioral sciences.

In 1957 Abdellah headed a research team in Manchester, Connecticut, that established the groundwork for what became known as progressive patient care. In this framework, critical care patients were treated in an intensive care unit, followed by a transition to immediate care, and then home care. The first two segments of the care program proved very popular within the caregiver profession. Abdellah is also credited with developing the first nationally tested coronary care unit as an outgrowth of her work in Manchester.

The third phase of the progressive patient care equation—home care—was not widely accepted in the mid-twentieth century. Abdellah explained in her *Image* interview that ''Short-sighted people at the time kept saying home care would mean having a maid (nurse) in everyone's home. They could not understand that home care with nurses teaching self care would be a way of helping patients regain independent function.'' Forty years later home care had become an essential part of long-term health care.

Established Standards

In another innovation within her field, Abdellah developed the Patient Assessment of Care Evaluation (PACE), a system of standards used to measure the relative quality of individual health-care facilities that was still used in the health care industry into the 21st century. She was also one of the first people in the health care industry to develop a classification system for patient care and patient-oriented records. Classification systems have evolved in different ways within in the health-care industry, and Abdellah's work was foundational in the development of the most widely used form: Diagnostic related groups, or DRGs. DRGs, which became the standard coding system used by Medicare, categorize patients according to particular primary and secondary diagnoses. This system keeps health-care costs down because each DRG code includes the maximum amount Medicare will pay out for a specific diagnosis or procedure, while also taking into account patient age and length of stay in a health care facility. Providers are given an incentive to keep costs down because they only realize a profit if costs are less than the amount specified by the relevant DRG category.

In addition to leading to the DRG system, Abdellah's work with classification has been instrumental in the ongoing development of an international classification system for nursing practice. As she explained in *Image,* ''There is a major effort ongoing to develop an international classification for nursing practice—to provide a unifying framework for nursing.''

Served in Military

Abdellah served for 40 years in the U.S. Public Health Service (PHS) Commissioned Corps, a branch of the military. She served on active duty during the Korean War and was the first nurse officer to achieve the rank of two-star rear admiral. Outside her wartime work, as a public health nurse, she focused much of her attention on care of the elderly. She was one of the first to talk about gerontological nursing, to conduct research in that area, and to influence public policy regarding nursing homes. During the 1970s she was responsible for establishing nursing-home standards in the United States. Abdellah checked on nursing homes by making unannounced visits and wandering throughout the facility checking areas visitors rarely saw. She found many fire hazards and also discovered that it was often hard to trace ownership of nursing homes. Abdellah's scrutiny was not welcomed, even by the licensing boards charged with looking out for their elderly patients, and some states prohibited Abdellah and others from making unannounced visits.

Abdellah has frequently stated that she believes nurses should be more involved in public-policy discussions concerning nursing home regulations. As she told *Image,* ''Our general attitude is let someone else do it. We need to make inroads in counties, states, and regions before we get to the federal level. Then we can have more of a voice at the national level. . . . I am convinced that if we want to have an effect on legislators, the most important way is to get nurses assigned as congressional fellows . . . 'they' are the ones who actually draft the legislation.''

In 1981 U.S. Surgeon General C. Everett Koop named Abdellah deputy surgeon general, making her the first nurse and the first woman to hold the position. She served under the U.S. surgeon general for eight years and retired from the military in 1989. As deputy surgeon general, it was Abdellah's responsibility to educate Americans about public-health issues, and she worked diligently in the areas of AIDS, hospice care, smoking, alcohol and drug addiction, the mentally handicapped, and violence.

In her government position, Abdellah also continued her efforts to improve the health and safety of America's elderly. She prepared and distributed a series of leaflets designed to inform people about Alzheimer's disease, arthritis, the safe use of medicines, influenza, high blood pressure, and other threats to elderly health. Under her guidance, the PHS also worked with physicians to make them aware of the latest research on health issues regarding older patients. For instance, physicians were warned that ordinary drug dosages may not be appropriate for elderly patients.

International Contributions

As a consultant and educator, Abdellah shared her nursing theories with caregivers around the world. She led seminars in France, Portugal, Israel, Japan, China, New Zealand, Australia, and the former Soviet Union. She also served as a research consultant to the World Health Organization. From her global perspective, Abdellah learned to appreciate nontraditional and complementary medical treatments and developed the belief such non-Western treatments deserved scientific research.

Abdellah has written many articles in professional journals as well as several books, including *Effect of Nurse Staffing on Satisfactions with Nursing Care* (1959), *Patient-centered Approaches to Nursing* (1960), *Better Patient Care through Nursing Research* (1965; revised 1986), and *Intensive Care, Concepts and Practices for Clinical Nurse Specialists* (1969). She is the recipient of over 70 awards and honorary degrees and is a fellow of the American Academy of Nursing. Abdellah was named to the Nursing Hall of Fame at Columbia University in 1999.

In 2000 Abdellah was inducted into the National Women's Hall of Fame in Seneca, New York. During her Hall of Fame induction speech, Abdellah said, "We cannot wait for the world to change. . . . Those of us with intelligence, purpose, and vision must take the lead and change the world. Let us move forward together! . . . I promise never to rest until my work has been completed!"

Periodicals

Advance for Nurses, November 20, 2000.
American Psychologist, January, 1984.
Image, Fall 1998.
Uniformed Services University Quarterly, May 2000.

Online

National Womens's Hall of Fame, http://www.greatwomen.org/ (February 4, 2004). □

Eduardo Acevedo Diaz

Uruguayan author and political activist Eduardo Acevedo Diaz (1851–1924) is considered by literary experts to be the founder of the "gauchismo" movement, which came to define the cultural identity of the country's insurgent nationalist movement in the years prior to the turn of the 20th century. Acevedo Diaz was also Uruguay's first major novelist: Among his best-known works is the 1888 novel *Ismael.*

Acevedo Diaz was born in the small town of Villa de la Union, Uruguay, on April 20, 1851. He was highly educated and eventually earned a doctoral degree. By the time he reached his 20s, he had also become an accomplished writer, and the idealistic young man frequently used his talent to voice his strong political opinions in the newspapers and other periodicals of the day. Banished from his country for his radical partisan journalism in the 1870s, Acevedo Diaz spent many years in exile in Buenos Aires, Argentina.

First Novels Inspired Blanco Rebels

Since declaring independence from Brazil in 1828, Uruguay had been home to two political parties: the conservative and predominately Catholic *Blancos* were nationalists, while the redshirts or *Colorados* were liberal federalists. The Colorados, supported by the French and British fleets, had their power base in the port city of Montevideo, while the Blancos controlled the rest of Uruguay with the help of Argentine dictator Juan Manuel de Rosas. This was a lawless epoch in the Uruguayan countryside.

While he was in exile, Acevedo Diaz wrote a trilogy of historical novels based on the *patriadas,* the first wars of independence in Uruguay. However, he recycled and rebuilt the *patriadas* into a myth designed to inspire the discouraged Blancos into rising once again against the Colorados. Even from exile, Acevedo Diaz had vociferously criticized the Blancos for losing their masculinity and becoming degenerates during their long years of political oppression under Colorado tyrants. His books offered the Blancos a vision of their glorious, war-like forefathers and spurred them to turn back their moral regeneration.

In his books, Acevedo Diaz cultivated a sense of nostalgia for the great old days of the Blancos that came to be known as "gauchismo." The single word evoked a sense of identity in those who subscribed to it, and there were many; it became something of a cult in Uruguay and was organized formally in hundreds of local clubs that revered ranch life, traditional folk dance, and the old-time Farrapo rancher cowboys. Acevedo Diaz's books were solemn, brutal, and reverential. His "Hymn of Hate" trilogy was comprised of his first novel, *Ismael* (1888), and by *Nativa* (1890) and *Grito de Gloria* (1894; translated as *Shout of Glory*). The 1894 novel *Soledad,* however, is considered by many to be Acevedo Diaz's finest work as well as his most realistic. It was *Soledad,* in fact, that likely served as the primary model of "gauchismo" for the author's literary successors, among them Uruguayan writers Javier de Viana, Carlos Reyles, and Justino Zavala Muniz.

Brought Back by Nationalists

In 1895 some young members of Uruguay's nationalist Blanco movement urged Acevedo Diaz to return to his homeland from exile in Argentina. At their request, the author founded the newspaper *El Nacional,* which quickly began publishing vicious verbal attacks on Uruguay's highly unpopular Colorado President Idiarte Borda. In addition, Acevedo Diaz used his formidable oratorical skills and his stern, gravelly voice to prepare reactionary Blancos for an imminent revolt against the Colorados. In a speech given in 1895 and transcribed in *Latin American Research Review,* Acevedo Diaz urged his followers to overthrow the ruling party, intoning: "Rise up from the past, oh venerated ghosts, who gave all before the altars of our political religion: I call on you now, not in ignoble vengeance, but as emblems of supreme valor . . . in hand-to-hand combat between the holy aspirations of the people and the iniquitous habits of corruption and decadence."

In this appeal for masculine self-sacrifice on the eve of civil war, Acevedo Diaz further inflamed his listeners in a characteristically turgid manner, using the *patriada* he had created earlier. After reminding the Blancos that they were descended from "the fiercest and most valiant caudillos" or military leaders, he whipped up their indignation and will to fight by telling them that the Colorados viewed Blancas as effeminate, passive, unpatriotic, and ineffectual. When addressing mothers whose sons would soon go off fight in the civil war, Acevedo Diaz expertly evoked the image of a Spartan woman of Rome tearlessly preparing her offspring to die proudly in battle.

Due in large part to Acevedo Diaz's ability to stir up a crowd, the Blancos were able to quickly accept a relative newcomer, Aparicio Saravia, as their leader in 1896. Historians believe that Saravia's sudden influence over the group was thanks to Acevedo Diaz's portrayal of the newcomer as a gaucho, since Saravia had a number of strikes against him as a leader: lack of experience, little education, and Brazilian origins. Meanwhile, in November of 1896 Acevedo Diaz threatened the somewhat complacent Blancos that he would quit his political pep talks if no uprising occurred by the end of the month, or if the elections scheduled for November—and the Colorados' traditional manipulation of them—did not at least incite a public uproar. One of the Blanco leaders, who likely believed that Acevedo Diaz embodied the true revolutionary spirit fueling the nationalist rebellion, traveled to Montevideo to assure the 45-year-old journalist that the Blancos planned to disrupt the elections at locations throughout the country. During the unrest that followed, Uruguayan president Borda was assassinated.

Disappointed in Desire to Lead Blancos

Through their efforts, the Blancos succeeded in winning a minority representation in Uruguay's national elections, the first to be held using secret ballots. Despite his integral role in the Blancos' successful revolution against the oppressive Colorado rulers, Acevedo Diaz was not asked to become a member of the party's leadership. Instead, Saravia rewarded the venerable middle-aged agitator only a symbolic position, disappointing Acevedo Diaz in his dream of helping to lead his newly empowered party.

During this time Acevedo Diaz served as a senator and led a small group of Blancos legislators in opposition to interim President Juan Lindolfo Cuestas, who had taken over after the 1897 assassination of Borda and retained power by violently overthrowing the legislature and declaring himself dictator. Although Cuestas allowed democratic elections, the Blancos and the Colorados agreed to an accord instead, believing the situation was too unstable for elections. In 1899, the resulting legislature appointed Cuestas as president.

Acevedo Diaz and a longtime ally, Colorado senator and presidential hopeful José Batlle y Ordóñez, worked to prevent further accords and lobbied for true elections to be held. Although it was unusual for Acevedo Diaz to side with a Colorado, the writer believed that Batlle's election would injure the Colorados by insulting Cuestas, thus bringing Acevedo Diaz added standing with the Blancos. Through such Machiavellian political machinations, Acevedo Diaz accomplished his goal, and Batlle was elected president in 1903. The following year civil war again broke out in Uruguay, and during nine months of fighting the Blancos, led by Saravia, attempted to undermine the Batlle y Ordóñez government. Ultimately Saravia was killed, and the civil war ended with the Treaty of Aceguá, which also ended Blanco hopes for true representational elections.

Acevedo Diaz's work as an author remains well known in South America, but his successors—especially Viana—have enjoyed more widespread popularity. The author was awarded two posthumous awards for his novels: the Buenos Aires Literary Prize in 1932 for *Ramon Hazaa* and the Argentine National Prize for Literature in 1940 for *Cancha larga*. Acevedo Diaz died in Buenos Aires, Argentina, on June 18, 1924. His biography, *La vida de batalla de Eduardo Acevedo Diaz* ("Eduardo Acevedo Diaz's Life of Battle"), was published in 1941.

Books

Chasteen, John Charles, *Heroes on Horseback: A Life and Times of the Last Gaucho Caudillos,* University of New Mexico Press, 1995.

Jones, Willis Knapp, ed., *Spanish-American Literature in Translation,* Frederick Ungar, 1963.

Vanger, Milton I., *Jose Batlle y Ordóñez of Uruguay: The Creator of His Times,* Harvard University Press, 1963.

Periodicals

Latin American Research Review, Volume 28, 1993. □

Aerosmith

Aerosmith, the Boston-based band that became America's version of the Rolling Stones, has been making music for nearly 40 years. The band essentially has had two careers: one before they kicked drugs and alcohol and an even bigger one after rehabilitation.

One of the longest-running, top 10 best-selling bands in American hard rock history, Aerosmith was formed in late 1969 in Sunapee, New Hampshire. Two bands, Chain Reaction, led by Steven Tallarico, and the Jam Band, featuring Joe Perry and Tom Hamilton, had often played at a local club called The Barn. At a Jam Band gig at The Barn, Tallarico decided that he should front this sloppy, blues-based band, and that they needed another guitarist and a new drummer.

The new band formed, and Aerosmith played its first gig at Nipmuc Regional High School in Mendon, Massachusetts, in autumn 1970. The lineup: Steven Tallarico (born March 26, 1948) on vocals, Joe Perry (born September 10, 1950) on lead guitar, Ray Tabano on rhythm guitar, Tom Hamilton (born December 31, 1951) on bass, and Joey Kramer (born June 21, 1950) on drums.

The group moved into a three-bedroom apartment together on Commonwealth Avenue in Boston. The band played at high school and fraternity parties and began writing their own material. Kramer had come up with the band's name back in high school and insists it had nothing to do with Sinclair Lewis' novel, *Arrowsmith*.

Tabano was replaced by Brad Whitford (born February 23, 1952) in 1971 after some artistic differences. Tabano later came back to work on Aerosmith's road crew and then as the band's marketing director.

First Record Contract

In 1972, Steven Tallarico changed his name to Steven Tyler. Big things were about to happen for the band. At a summer gig at Max's Kansas City in New York that year, record industry mogul Clive Davis saw the band perform. Aerosmith, managed by David Krebs and Steve Leber, was offered a $125,000 contract with Columbia Records.

"We weren't too ambitious when we started out," Tyler said in their autobiography, *Walk This Way*. "We just wanted to be the biggest thing that ever walked the planet, the greatest rock band that ever was. We just wanted everything. We wanted it all."

Moving quickly, the band's self-titled debut album was released in January 1973. Aerosmith went on tour in support of the album, opening for big acts like Mott the Hoople and The Kinks. Stardom would be a relatively short climb for the band from this point.

The following year, a second album, *Get Your Wings,* was released. A single, "Same Old Song And Dance"/ "Pandora's Box" made a small splash and the album went gold. In April 1975, *Toys In The Attic* was released and hit the Billboard Top 20 Album Chart. "Sweet Emotion" was released on a single and became the band's first Top 40 hit.

On June 12, 1976, Aerosmith headlined their first stadium show at the Pontiac Silverdome in Pontiac, Michigan, to a crowd of 80,000. The show had sold out within 12 hours. It was only the first in a series of successful stadium tours to follow.

Tyler later reflected, "The stage was so high and so far from the audience, you couldn't even see any kids, just lines of bullet-head security guys with their backs to us. The whole thing was too abstract. We were in, like, surrealism shock."

An Army of Fans

The band started calling their fans "The Blue Army" for the blue jeans that they all wore. In *Walk This Way*, "We were America's band," Joe Perry said. "We were the guys you could actually see. Back then in the Seventies, it wasn't like Led Zeppelin was out there on the road in America all of the time. The Stones weren't always coming to your town. We were. You could count on us to come by."

In 1976, the band released the platinum-selling *Rocks* album. Earlier songs, "Walk This Way" and "Dream On"/ "Sweet Emotion" were re-released and garnered the band Top 40 hits. "Dream On," re-released from their first album, peaked at number three on the charts. In March 1977, "Back In The Saddle"/"Nobody's Fault" was released as a single. In October of that year, "Draw the Line" was released on a single, previewing tracks from their fifth album of the same name, to be released in December of that year. The album went platinum.

In October 1978, the band made a movie appearance in Robert Stigwood's flop, *Sgt. Pepper's Lonely Hearts Club Band,* as the Future Villain Band. (Stigwood had produced '70s movie hits *Grease* and *Saturday Night Fever*.) The band recorded a cover of The Beatles' "Come Together" for the film, and the song made it to the top 30 on the charts. Kramer later remarked, "It was a disaster. A real debacle. The Stones refused to do the part that was offered to us. Now we know why. It was just a pretty silly movie." That same month, *Live Bootleg,* featuring live versions of the band's hits was released.

The End of Aerosmith

Disagreements between band members and ego clashes tore at the lineup in 1979 as their seventh album, *Night in the Ruts,* was recorded. Perry left, and Jimmy Crespo replaced him as lead guitarist. Aerosmith toured briefly with new lineup, but fans yelled for Perry.

Perry had formed the Joe Perry Project, rounding up a band of relatively unknown musicians. They released an album of covers and Perry originals called *Let the Music Do the Talking*. The group released three albums between 1980 and 1983, doing small tours, as well.

By 1980, the year Aerosmith's *Greatest Hits* was released, Whitford left the band as well. Rick Dufay replaced Whitford in the Aerosmith lineup. Whitford joined forces with Derek St. Holmes, from Ted Nugent's band, on an album, *Whitford/St. Holmes*. That summer, Tyler took a forced sabbatical after a motorcycle accident. Drugs and alcohol were involved, and the singer spent six months in a hospital.

Rock In A Hard Place, recorded with the new lineup, was released in August 1982. The follow-up tour was hit and miss. In the meantime, Whitford was on tour with The Joe Perry Project.

Aerosmith Reformed

On Valentine's Day in 1984, after a long and publicly infamous estrangement between Tyler and Perry, the two, along with Whitford, were reunited backstage after an Aerosmith show at The Orpheum Theater in Boston. Conversations continued between Tyler and Perry, and by April of that year, the original band was back together. They began this new phase with the aptly titled "Back In The Saddle Tour" and a new manager, Tim Collins.

In November 1985, the band released *Done With Mirrors* on a new label, Geffen. The album, produced by Ted Templeman, who had produced the early Van Halen albums, was not a platinum-selling comeback.

In 1986, up-and-coming rappers Run DMC gave Aerosmith the push back into the spotlight they needed with their cover of "Walk This Way" on their album, *Raising Hell*. The song hit the charts, and the video, featuring Tyler and Perry dueling with the rappers through a thin wall, played frequently on MTV.

Over the years, the band had become infamous for their alcohol and drug abuse. The press dubbed Tyler and Perry "The Toxic Twins." In September 1986, Collins called a 6 a.m. band meeting and included New York psychiatrist Dr. Lou Cox. It was an intervention for Tyler, but the whole band needed help.

In the band's 1997 autobiography, *Walk This Way*, Collins recounted that he had told the band, "You guys need to change your lives and get sober and I'll *promise* you this: We will turn this group around and make it the biggest band in the world by 1990." Tyler and Perry went through rehab. The band worked together to become—and to stay—sober.

Aerosmith released *Permanent Vacation* in August 1987. For the first time, the band had songwriting help. Desmond Child, who had written hit songs for Bon Jovi, was called in and helped finish "Dude Looks Like A Lady" and "Angel." The songs garnered the band their first hits in years. In September 1988, Aerosmith received their first MTV Music Award for "Best Group Video" for "Dude Looks Like a Lady." Single "Angel" peaked at number three on the Billboard charts.

Tyler's Famous Children

Tyler's former girlfriend, Bebe Buell, and her daughter, Liv, went to see Aerosmith in August 1988. "She was eleven years old," Buell said. "We were the only ones allowed in Steven's dressing room, and Steven took her around and introduced her to everybody. She met her sister Mia for the first time. . . . This was when everything finally clicked for her."

Liv Tyler, to that point, had been brought up believing that her father was performer/producer Todd Rundgren. Rundgren had been involved in her life and contributed support. Her younger sister, Mia, was born to Tyler and his first wife, Cyrinda Foxe. Tyler's two daughters made names for themselves in acting and modeling, respectively.

Hit the Charts, Won Grammys

Pump was released in September 1989 and produced multi-platinum album sales and numerous awards. In 1990, Aerosmith won MTV's Best Metal/Hard Rock Video and Viewers' Choice Awards, as well as their first Grammy Award, for "Janie's Got A Gun," a song about child abuse.

Their success continued in 1993 with *Get A Grip*, which shot up the charts to number one. Four tracks from the album, "Livin' On the Edge," "Cryin,'" "Crazy" and "Amazing" hit the charts. "Livin' On the Edge" won the 1993 Grammy for "Best Rock Performance by a Duo or Group With Vocal." "Crazy" also won a Grammy in 1994.

Nine Lives debuted at number one on the album charts in 1997 and spawned the hit single, "Falling In Love (Is Hard On The Knees)." The following year, the band contributed a track for the movie *Armageddon*, "I Don't Want to Miss a Thing" (written by Diane Warren). It was the band's first number one hit. Aerosmith continued recording for film in 2003, with a track called "Lizard Love," on the soundtrack of the movie *Rugrats Go Wild!* Perry wrote score music for the 2003 Small Planet Pictures film, *This Thing of Ours*, as well.

In March 2001, *Just Push Play* was released, debuting at number two on the charts. "Jaded," the single from the album, hit number seven on the charts that year. The album was unusual in that it was recorded without the band being in the same room together. Joe Perry told *The Tennessean*, "We were making the record on ProTools and massaging everything, polishing everything up. . . . I couldn't make another record like that and call it an Aerosmith record."

The new century saw Aerosmith gaining awards and recognition. On March 19, 2001, Aerosmith was inducted into the Rock and Roll Hall of Fame. Boston's Berklee College of Music awarded Steven Tyler an honorary doctoral degree in music in May 2003. The band also has an "Aerosmith Endowment Award" recognizing outstanding musical and academic achievement, at Berklee.

Aerosmith was one of the few bands in rock history to come back as strong as they had started. One reviewer from *The Times of London* summed up the Aerosmith concert experience: "Tyler, a glamorous stick insect, brought the band out dancing through a two-hour set which took in all the best tunes of their career. . . . They saved "Walk This Way" for the last encore as the sunset grew to a distant purple glow. Tyler strutted and pouted until a giant fireworks display signaled the end. The shimmering brilliance belonged, however, to Aerosmith alone, a band who retain the power to astound."

In August 2003 Aerosmith once again, 30 years later, joined forces with Kiss to launch a summer tour called the Rocksimus Maximus Tour. This nation-wide tour was a huge success producing a gross of approximately $50 million. With some time on their hands before the tour with Kiss took off, Aerosmith decided to produce an all-blues album. "Honkin' on Bobo," the album's title, was released March 30, 2004. This album got back to Aerosmith's earlier sound of the 1970's making it appeal to past fans as well as new. According to Jim Farber from the Knight Ridder/Tribune News Service the new album "treats blues as slamming party music rather than as the soul-searching stuff of legend."

Books

Aerosmith and Stephen Davis, *Walk This Way*, Avon Books, 1997.

Huxley, Martin, *Aerosmith: The Fall and the Rise of Rock's Greatest Band*, St. Martin's Press, 1995.

Periodicals

Associated Press Newswires, May 10, 2003.

Billboard, August 16, 2003; April 4, 2004.

Billboard Bulletin, January 20, 2004.

Business Wire, September 8, 2003.

Finance Wire, October 8, 2003.

Knight Ridder/Tribune News Service, March 30, 2004.

Pittsburgh Post-Gazette, May 22, 2003.

Plain Dealer, September 6, 2002.

Press-Enterprise, November 1, 2002.

Reuters News, September 4, 2003.

Rocky Mountain News, December 6, 2002.

San Antonio Express-News, October 4, 2003.

State Journal-Register, October 19, 2003.

Tennessean, September 19, 2003.

Times Union, November 27, 2003.

Wilkes-Barre Times Leader, September 6, 2002.

Online

"Aerosmith" *46th Grammy Awards,* http://www.grammy.com (January 19, 2004).

"Aerosmith: Bio," *MTV.com,* http://www.mtv.com (January 12, 2004).

"Aerosmith: History," *Aerosmith.com,* http://www.aerosmith .com (January 12, 2004). □

Aesop

Little is known about the ancient Greek writer Aesop (c. 620 B.C.E.–c. 560 B.C.E.), whose stories of clever animals and foolish humans are considered Western civilization's first morality tales. He was said to have been a slave who earned his freedom through his storytelling and went on to serve as advisor to a king. Both his name and the animist tone of his tales have led some scholars to believe he may have been Ethiopian in origin.

Freed from Slavery

Aesop never wrote down any of the tales himself; he merely recited them orally. The first recorded mention of his life came about a hundred years after he died, in a work by the eminent Greek historian Herodotus, who noted that he was a slave of one Iadmon of Samos and died at Delphi. In the first century C.E., Plutarch, another Greek historian, also speculated on Aesop's origins and life. Plutarch placed Aesop at the court of immensely weighty Croesus, the king of Lydia (now northwestern Turkey). A source from Egypt dating back to this same century also described Aesop as a slave from the Aegean island of Samos, near the Turkish mainland. The source claims that after he was released from bondage he went to Babylon. Aesop has also been referred to as Phrygian, pointing to origins in central Turkey settled by Balkan tribes around 1200 B.C.E. They spoke an Indo-European language and their communities were regularly raided for slaves to serve in Greece.

The name "Aesop" is a variant of "Acthiop," which is a reference to Ethiopia in ancient Greek. This and the trickster nature of some of his stories, where humans are regularly outwitted by a cleverer animal figure, has led some scholars to speculate that Aesop may have been from Africa. The link was discussed in a *Spectator* essay from 1932 by the critic J. H. Driberg. There are two tales from Aesop in which a man tries to come to the aid of a serpent, and Driberg noted that such acts mirror "the habitual kindness shown to snakes by many tribes: for snakes are the repositories of the souls of ancestors and they are cherished therefore and invited to live in the houses of men by daily gifts of milk."

Tales Reflected Human Folly

Anthropomorphism, or animals with human capabilities, is the common thread throughout Aesop's fables. The most famous among them are "The Tortoise and the Hare," in which the plodding turtle and the energetic rabbit hold a race. The arrogant hare is so confident that he rests and falls asleep halfway; the wiser tortoise plods past and wins. "Slow but steady wins the race," the fable concludes. These and other Aesop fables, wrote Peter Jones in the *Spectator* in 2002, often pit "the rich and powerful against the poor and weak. They stress either the folly of taking on a stronger power, or the cunning which the weaker must deploy if he is to stand any chance of success; and they often warn that nature never changes."

Several phrases are traced back to the fables of Aesop, such as "don't count your chickens before they are hatched," which concludes the tale of the greedy "Milkmaid and Her Pail." In "The Fox and the Grapes," a fox ambles through the forest and spies a bunch of grapes. Thirsty, he tries in vain to reach them but finally gives up and walks off muttering that they were likely sour anyway. From this comes the term "sour grapes."

Thrown from Cliff

According to myth, Aesop won such fame throughout Greece for his tales that he became the target of resentment and perhaps even a political witch-hunt. He was accused of stealing a gold cup from Delphi temple to the god Apollo and was supposedly tossed from the cliffs at Delphi as punishment for the theft. His tales told of human folly and the abuses of power, and he lived during a period of tyrannical rule in Greece. His defense, it is said, was the fable "The Eagle and the Beetle," in which a hare, being preyed upon by an eagle, asks the beetle for protection. The small insect agrees, but the eagle fails to see it and strikes the hare, killing it. From then on, the beetle watched the eagle's nest and shook it when there were eggs inside, which then fell to the ground. Worried about her inability to reproduce, the eagle asks a god for help, and the deity offers to store the eggs in its lap. The beetle learns of this and puts a ball of dirt there among the eggs, and the god—in some accounts Zeus, in others Jupiter—rises, startled, and the eggs fall out. For this reason, it is said, eagles never lay their eggs during the season when beetles flourish. "No matter how powerful one's position may be, there is nothing that can protect the oppressor from the vengeance of the oppressed" is the moral associated with this particular fable.

The first written compilation of Aesop's tales came from Demetrius of Phaleron around 320 B.C.E., *Assemblies of Aesopic Tales*, but it disappeared in the ninth century. The first extant version of the fables is thought to be from Phaedrus, a former slave from Macedonia who translated the tales into Latin in the first century C.E. in what became known as the Romulus collection. Valerius Babrius, a Greek living in Rome, translated these and other fables of the day into Greek in the first half of the 200s C.E. Forty-two of those, in turn, were translated into Latin by Avianus around 400 C.E. There is also a link between Aesop and Islam. The prophet Mohamed mentioned "Lokman," said to be the wisest man in the east, in the 31st sura of the Koran. In Arab folklore, Lokman supposedly lived around 1100 B.C.E. and was an Ethiopian. His father, it was said, was descended from the biblical figure Job. Some of his tales may have been adapted by Aesop some five centuries after his death.

Censored for Children's Sake

The Latin translation of Aesop's fables helped them survive the ages. Their enduring appeal, wrote English poet and critic G. K. Chesterton in an introduction to a 1912 Doubleday edition, might lead back to a primeval allure. "These ancient and universal tales are all of animals; as the latest discoveries in the oldest prehistoric caverns are all of animals," Chesterton wrote. "Man, in his simpler states, always felt that he himself was something too mysterious to be drawn. But the legend he carved under these cruder symbols was everywhere the same; and whether fables began with Æsop or began with Adam . . . the upshot is everywhere essentially the same: that superiority is always insolent, because it is always accidental; that pride goes before a fall; and that there is such a thing as being too clever by half."

Aesop's tales were known in medieval Europe, and a German edition brought back to England by William Caxton, along with the first printing press in England, was translated by Caxton and became one of the first books ever printed in the English language. A 1692 version from English pamphleteer Roger L'Estrange *A Hundred Fables of Aesop* was popular for a number of years, and the Aesop fables began to be promoted as ideal for teaching children to read. A discovery by contemporary scholar Robert Temple and his wife Olivia, a translator, resulted in a 1998 Penguin edition that contained some ribald original tales they found in a 1927 Greek-language text. As David Lister explained in an article for London's *Independent* newspaper, "many of the never before translated fables were coarse and brutal. And even some of the most famous ones had been mistranslated to give them a more comforting and more moral tone. What the Temples began to realise was that the Victorians had simply suppressed the fables which shocked them and effectively changed others."

Books

Chesterton, G.K., in an introduction to *Aesop Fables*, translated by V.S. Verson Jones, Doubleday & Co., 1912, reprinted in *Classical and Medieval Literature Criticism*, Vol 24.
Major Authors and Illustrators for Children and Young Adults, 2nd ed., 8 vols. Gale Group, 2002.
Richardson, Samuel, in a preface to *Aesop Fables*, 1740, edited by Samuel Richardson, Garland Publishing, Inc., 1975, reprinted in *Classical and Medieval Literature Criticism*, Vol 24.

Periodicals

Independent (London, England), January 15, 1998.
Spectator, June 18, 1932; March 16, 2002. □

Saint Agnes

St. Agnes (c. 292–c. 304) is one of the first women venerated in the Roman Catholic Church's hierarchy of saints. She was believed to have been martyred at the age of 12 because she refused to marry the son of a Roman official, instead declaring herself committed to Christ during an era when Christianity was still an underground religion. In the decades after her death, Agnes's tomb became a place of pilgrimage.

There is little reliable evidence giving the specific dates of Agnes's life, but it is thought that she died in the last wave of persecutions of Christians that took place in the Roman Empire, a surge of terrorism known as the Persecution of Diocletian which occurred in 304. After this point, Agnes's name appears several times in the historical written record. Seven decades after her purported death, St. Ambrose, Bishop of Milan and a former lawyer, mentions that when Agnes appeared before authorities to answer charges of practicing Christianity, she was still a minor and therefore according to Roman law of that time not yet of an age to bear witness in court, or even be tried. Other sources refer to Agnes's nurse; in Roman times nurses for girls from affluent families usually remained with their charges until the girls were of marriageable age, which was twelve. St. Augustine, another early Father of the Church, claimed Agnes was 13 at the time of her death in his *Agnes puella tredecim annorum*.

Died under Diocletian's Edict

Agnes may have been the daughter of a Roman noble family, and one surname that has been ventured is that of the Clodia Crescentiana. The story surrounding her life asserts that she consecrated her life to Christ at the age of ten, which brought with that a commitment to remain a virgin. Her parents would have had to consent to this, and they may have been practicing Christians as well. In the years following Christ's death in 33 C.E., the religion had grown in numbers, and its adherents refused to venerate either the Roman emperor or the Roman state, claiming allegiance

instead to Christ, the son of a supreme being worshiped in the Jewish religion, and his father. The new religion, initially condemned as a cult, had by now spread from Palestine, where Christ was put to death by Roman colonial officials, through the Middle East and into Europe. Roman officials, who controlled much of that part of the world, treated Christianity's practitioners harshly, and there were periodic crackdowns. In these persecutions, Christians were brought before tribunals and strongly urged to renounce their beliefs. Many chose the alternative, which was a death sentence often carried out before large crowds under the most horrific of circumstances.

Thought to Have Spurned Marriage

It is thought that a young Roman, also the son of high-ranking official, wanted to marry Agnes. This may have been a son of either the prefect Maximum Herculeus or the prefect Sempronius. The preteen reportedly replied, "The one to whom I am betrothed is Christ whom the angels serve," according to *Three Ways of Love,* by Frances Parkinson Keyes. Agnes may have been taken by Roman soldiers from her family home and brought before a panel of judges. Other sources say she was forcibly removed and placed in a house of prostitution.

There is another version of the events surrounding Agnes's martyrdom, and it is found in an inscription at the foot of a marble staircase leading to a sepulcher located in the Roman church erected over her burial site in her honor and named Sant' Agnese fuori le muri ("St. Agnes outside the Walls"). It is known that Pope Damasus wrote the inscription, and that it was carved before 384. According to Louis André-Delastre in his book *Saint Agnes,* the inscription reads: "Tradition tells us that her holy parents used to tell the story of how the young Agnes, when she heard the mournful notes of the trumpet, ran from her nurse's side and defied the threats and ragings of the cruel tyrant, who wished to have her noble body burnt in flames." Damasus also reports that an imperial edict had been issued against Christians, and when Agnes learned of it, she publicly announced that she was one herself.

Pleaded for Death

The account of Prudentius, a Spanish poet whose 405 work *Peristephanon* also provides a version of Agnes's story, was the first to mention that she had been taken to a brothel. If so, it may have been one known to have been located under the arch in the Stadium of Domitian (now Rome's Piazza Navona). This also may have been the location of the forum where Agnes's death occurred. It is reported that in the eighth century an oratory was built over the site where Agnes met her death, and that this oratory was consecrated as a church in 1123 by Pope Calixtus II.

Church histories note that Agnes refused to renounce her religion before the judges, and as punishment she may have been sentenced to serve as a virgin sacrifice to pagan deities. The Roman goddess Minerva has been mentioned in some reports of the martyrdom of Agnes, and the ceremonial fire from Minerva's temple, located on the Aventine Hill, may have been brought to the forum where Agnes was being tried, or she may have been taken there. The official church story asserts that while on trial, Agnes repeatedly appealed to Christ, which angered the tribunal. One judge reportedly asked the crowd that had gathered to watch the trial whether anyone among them wished to marry her, and that some young men came forward, hoping to spare Agnes's life. Most sources also note that one spectator who looked at her with lust instead was blinded, but this detail is also found in the reports of her being taken to a brothel. According to André-Delastre's translation of the Ambrose account, Agnes told the judges, "It is wrong for the bride to keep the bridegroom waiting. He who chose me first shall be the only one to have me. What are you waiting for, executioner? Destroy this body, for unwanted eyes may desire it."

Legend has it that Agnes went unshackled to her death because all the irons were too large for her wrists. There are various reports of how she died. Some accounts say she was burned at the stake, while Ambrose claims her death came by sword. Beheading has also been mentioned, or the judges may have taken some pity on her and ordered what was called a gentle death, usually reserved for women in the Roman era. In this, the head was held back and the throat slit at the base of the neck.

Devotional Cult Grew

Because Agnes's body was not thrown into the river Tiber, which was common practice for martyred Christians at the time, it is thought that her family may have intervened, which yields evidence that they were indeed well connected. She was buried on cemetery land owned by her parents, and a week later they came to pray at the grave. There, according to the church history, they saw a vision of her surrounded by other virgins and with a lamb at her side. Others also came to visit the burial site, but it was thought to have been reached by an underground passageway for a time.

In 313, with the conversion of the Emperor Constantine to Christianity and his issue of the Edict of Milan, Agnes's religion was officially tolerated throughout the Empire. There is a story that his daughter, Constantina, was cured of leprosy when she visited the shrine to Agnes, and that she urged her father to have a basilica erected over the grave, which became the church of St. Agnes outside the Walls. The church, which dates from 364, stands on via Nomentana and contains Damasus's inscription. It was renovated during the reign of Pope Honorius in the seventh century. Ambrose's writings on Agnes, *De Virginibus,* probably came from a sermon he delivered in Milan in 376 on her feast day, which had likely been the urging of his sister Marcellina, a devout woman who is also thought to have visited Agnes's shrine.

Inspired Keats Poem

Agnes's feast day is January 21, the day she is thought to have been martyred. The first mention of this comes in the *Depositio Martyrum,* a list of martyrs, from 354. In the Roman Catholic iconography, she is usually depicted holding a lamb, a symbol of virginity. She is the patron saint of engaged couples, gardeners, Girl Scouts, and victims of sexual assault. During medieval times rituals linked to virginity and marriage arose surrounding her name and feast day. A young woman could forego supper on the night of January 20, it was said, and she would dream of her future husband thanks to the saint's intervention. Other customs involved sewing one's stockings together, or putting rosemary in one's shoes, also to glean a vision of one's future mate. In parts of Scotland grain was scattered in cornfields by unwed men and women, who recited a poem as they did so asking for guidance to "let me see/The lad (or lass) who is to marry me." Nineteenth-century Romantic poet John Keats wrote an epic poem, "The Eve of St. Agnes," linked to these superstitions.

On Agnes's feast day, two lambs from the Trappist monastery at Tre Fontaine outside Rome are adorned with crowns and ribbons of red and white and blessed at her church by the pope. They are then taken to the abbey of St. Cecilia in Trastavere, also in Rome, where Benedictine nuns raise them. Their wool is shorn on Holy Thursday, and palliums are then made from it. These are circular ceremonial bands worn over the shoulders in Roman Catholic ecclesiastical dress and signify one of the highest church offices. The pope bestows a dozen or so annually to his archbishops.

Books

André-Delastre, Louis, *Saint Agnes,* translated by Rosemary Sheed, Macmillan, 1962.

Catholic Encyclopedia, Appleton, 1907.

Keyes, Frances Parkinson, *Three Ways of Love,* Hawthorn Books, 1963.

Online

"St. Agnes," Domestic-Church.com, http://www.domestic-church.com/content.dcc/19990101/saints/stagnes.htm (January 9, 2004). ☐

Toshiko Akiyoshi

One of the first Asian-born musicians to succeed in the jazz and big band arenas, Toshiko Akiyoshi (born 1929) is also a pioneering woman in these traditionally male-dominated arts. Her jazz orchestra has become one of the most popular of its kind and has received 14 Grammy Award nominations since 1976.

A truly international music star, Akiyoshi was born of well-to-do Japanese Buddhist parents in Darien, Manchuria Province (now part of China), on December 12, 1929. Her father, the owner of an import-export textile business and a practitioner of classic Japanese *Noh* drama, encouraged Akiyoshi and her three sisters to take music, acting, and dance lessons. Akiyoshi later recalled feeling a strong affinity for the piano by the age of six, and her early training was exclusively in classical music.

Early Interest in Music Interrupted by War

By the early 1930s the ancient kingdom of Manchuria had become a furiously contested piece of land as Japan, the Soviet Union, and China battled over its sovereignty. The conflict worsened during World War II, as one country's domination quickly gave way to that of another. Soldiers commandeered the Akiyoshi home several times, eventually prompting the family to flee to the resort town of Beppu, Japan. Financially ruined, they were met at Beppu by American occupation troops who deloused the entire family with DDT.

When asked if she remembers the American atomic bombs dropped in nearby Hiroshima and Nagasaki, Japan, that put an end to World War II in August of 1945, Akiyoshi, who was then age 15, recalled in a *Down Beat* interview with Michael Bourne: "All I knew was that the war was ended. We knew that a bomb was dropped, but we didn't know the effect. People at that time tried to avoid speaking about it. Even the victims didn't want to talk about it."

Living in Japan during her teen years, Akiyoshi heard for the first time the jazz rhythms popular with the American GI's occupying the country after the war. Although she had begun to consider a career in medicine during the tumult of wartime, by the time she was 16, Akiyoshi had found a job as a jazz pianist for four dollars an hour at one of the many new dance halls being set up for occupation troops. Her

and TV wearing a kimono, because people were amazed to see an Oriental woman playing jazz." She soon met saxophonist Charlie Mariano while playing in a quartet. They fell in love and married in 1959 and had a daughter, Michiru, together. Akiyoshi finished her studies at Berklee in 1959.

Began Band with Second Husband

During the 1960s Akiyoshi often traveled to Japan for extended periods, and she also worked with bassists Charles Mingus and Oscar Pettfried in small combos in New York City and around Japan. She made her debut as a conductor-composer in 1967 in the Town Hall in New York in a concert for which she had raised funds by playing the Holiday Inn circuit for seven months. She had by now divorced Mariano, and now she met Lew Tabackin, a Jewish saxophonist and flautist. Marrying in 1969, the couple formed a group they thought of as a rehearsal band that designed to showcase Akiyoshi's new jazz and big band compositions.

Moving to Los Angeles in 1972, the couple transformed their rehearsal band into the wildly successful Toshiko Akiyoshi Jazz Orchestra in 1973. Following the death of jazz great Duke Ellington in 1974, Akiyoshi read an article about how proud he had always been of his heritage. This prompted her to begin studying Japanese music for the first time, looking for ways to, as she put it, "return to the jazz tradition something that might make it a little bit richer." In the meantime, the awards poured in as the band began recording albums such as *Long Yellow Road* (1976), *Insights* (1977), *Minamata* (1978), and *Kogun* (1978), the last which included her first Japanese jazz pieces. Meanwhile, Akiyoshi and Tabackin received increasing kudos for what had become one of the most innovative and accomplished big bands in the jazz world.

In 1982 Akiyoshi and Tabackin moved to New York, where Akiyoshi recreated her band with local musicians. The following year the new Jazz Orchestra received high critical praise during its debut at the Kool Jazz Festival. Also in 1983, Renee Cho released a documentary film about Akiyoshi titled *Jazz Is My Native Language.* Unlike others before them, the husband-and-wife team impressed people with their equality. Akiyoshi composed, conducted, and played piano, emulating such greats as Fletcher Henderson, Ellington, Earl Hines, and Count Basie, while Tabackin served as the ensemble's principal soloist.

Japanese Heritage Integral to Music

Once she accepted her Japanese heritage as an asset, rather than fighting it as a liability in a world of prejudice and racism, Akiyoshi decided to make Japanese themes and cultural elements part of her music. The 1976 album *Tales of a Courtesan,* for instance, was reportedly inspired by Akiyoshi's interest in the courtesans of the Edo period in 18th-century Japan. Other pieces, for both small groups and big band, incorporated elements of traditional Japanese folk songs, such as susumi and taiko drumming and vocal cries from Noh dramas, to evoke Japanese grace and delicacy. In addition, Akiyoshi and Tabackin liked to emphasize the juxtaposition of what they call the "vertical" rhythmic syn-

parents initially disapproved but told her she could play until school started in March. The musician later remembered, "March came and went, and no one noticed. I just kept playing!" A young admirer and record collector also introduced Akiyoshi to the music of Teddy Wilson. She fell in love with the song "Sweet Lorraine" and swore that she would one day play "like that."

Started New Life

Akiyoshi eventually tired of the dance-hall scene and in 1952, at age 23, got permission from her parents to move to Tokyo. After playing with ten jazz groups and three symphonies, she started her first band in Tokyo and quickly became the highest-paid studio musician in Japan and within a year was discovered by popular American pianist Oscar Peterson. At Peterson's request, Akiyoshi made a recording in 1953 for entrepreneur Norman Granz, who was running the Jazz at the Philharmonic tour of Japan. Peterson was very impressed by the young woman's work, telling Granz that she was "the greatest female jazz pianist" ever. Peterson recommended Akiyoshi for a full scholarship to the Berklee School of Music (now Berklee College of Music) in Boston, Massachusetts. She won the scholarship, moved to the United States, and began attending Berklee as a full-time student in 1956.

In the United States Akiyoshi's passion for music continued to build. She quickly developed a reputation as a fierce bebop pianist but had to deal with constant sexual and racial prejudice. As she told *Downbeat,* "I played clubs copation of jazz music with the "sideways" way Japanese music is played. Playing these elements against each other produced what many critics call an unparalleled sound in jazz. Despite its quality, however, much of Akiyoshi's music (like many of her predecessors in jazz) was given short shrift in the United States, finding appreciative audiences instead in Japan, Brazil, Germany, and France.

Main Influences

When asked who has influenced her career the most, Akiyoshi has frequently cited Ellington as her main inspiration. From the way she composed pieces to highlight the virtuosity of particular bandmembers—usually Tabackin—to how she has led and conducted the band, Akiyoshi clearly showed her admiration for the late bandleader. Other musicians she credited in helping shape her musical development include Roy Haynes, Charles Mingus, Miles Davis, and Sonny Rollins, while her big-band compositions often paid tribute to such artists as Thad Jones, Mel Lewis, and Gil Evans. Akiyoshi even recalled her piano teacher at the Berklee School who insisted that she learn pieces backward and forward in order to create an intimate familiarity with the music. This practice may have led to Akiyoshi's unique multi-meter compositions in which accents are often placed in unusual spots and forms are extended beyond what the listener expects.

Akiyoshi and her band continued to produce powerful and popular music throughout the 1980s and 1990s, including such milestone albums as *Farewell to Mingus* (1980), *European Memoirs* (1982), *Wishing Peace* (1986), and *Four Seasons in a Morita Village* (1996). Her 2001 work, *Hiroshima: Rising from the Abyss,* received a great deal of attention from critics everywhere, not only because of its quality, but for its subject matter. The album was recorded in Hiroshima on the anniversary of the bombing of that city, and reviewers and fans alike found the work haunting and evocative. Akiyoshi was reportedly inspired to write the piece, after a lifetime of avoiding the subject, by the wish of a Buddhist priest and jazz fan from Hiroshima.

Closed down the Big Band

On October 17, 2003, Akiyoshi, then age 73, and Tabackin played a farewell concert with their Jazz Orchestra at New York's Carnegie Hall, recording the event live for their last album. The event marked the end of three decades' work and 30 years of Akiyoshi composing for and holding a band together—an unprecedented accomplishment. Akiyoshi told reporters at the concert, "I started my career as a pianist, and I want to devote my remaining years to composing and playing in solo and small-group formats. I am artistically challenged by this decision and want to become a better pianist, and for me this is the way."

Akiyoshi never formally became an American citizen. She and Tabackin live in New York City, where they own a brownstone on the upper West Side, Akiyoshi reportedly writing and practicing upstairs while Tabackin works in the basement. They both enjoy collecting wine and keeping track of baseball, their favorite sport. Their last gig at Birdland, the famous New York City nightclub where the Jazz Orchestra once performed every Monday, took place in December of 2003. Akiyoshi published her autobiography, *Life with Jazz,* in 1996.

Books

Commire, Anne, editor, *Women in World History,* Yorkin Publications, 2001.

Periodicals

Down Beat, July 2003.

Online

"Akiyoshi, Toshiko," *MusicWeb,* http://www.musicweb.uk.net/ (December 10, 2003).
"Jazz Profiles: Toshiko Akiyoshi," *British Broadcasting Corporation Web site,* http://www.bbc.co.uk/ (December 10, 2003).
"Toshiko Akiyoshi," *Alice M. Wang's Home page,* http://www.duke.edu/~amw6/akio.htm (December 10, 2003).
"Toshiko Akiyoshi," *Berkeley Agency Web site,* http://www.berkeleyagency.com/ (December 10, 2003).
"Toshiko Akiyoshi Ends Big Band," *JazzTimes.com,* http://www.jazztimes.com/ (December 10, 2003).
"Toshiko Akiyoshi Jazz Orchestra," *University of Southern California Web site,* http://www.usc.edu/ (December 10, 2003). □

Alexander III

Considered one of the great medieval popes, Alexander III (c. 1100–1181) held the pontificate from September 7, 1159, until his death in 1181. He is remembered for instituting the two-thirds majority rule for papal elections, championing the universities, and endorsing ecclesiastical independence. A man of courage and conviction, Alexander, often forced to reign in exile, stood up to the emperor Frederick I and his antipopes. It was during Alexander's papacy that St. Thomas Becket was martyred.

Alexander III was born as Orlando (also known as Roland, Rolandus, and Laurentius) Bandinelli around 1100 to a respected Tuscan family with political roots. He became a celebrated professor of Holy Scripture at the University of Bologna, where most likely he had studied under Gratian, the "father of the science of canon law." Through Gratian's scholarship, the study of church law first became a discipline quite apart from theology; his *Concordantia discordantium canonum* became the basic text on canon law.

Prudent, Merciful, Chaste

The *Summa Magistri Rolandi,* a commentary on Gratian's treatise, is thought to have enhanced Alexander's reputation among the curia, though some scholars contest the attribution. Canon regular at Pisa from 1142 to 1147, Alexander was summoned to Rome in 1148 by Pope Eu-

genius III, who named him cardinal deacon in 1150, then cardinal priest of St. Mark's in 1151. It is possible that during this period Alexander completed a manuscript, *Sententie Rodlandi Bononiensis magistri,* based on the work of French canon and scholastic philosopher Abelard. In 1153 Alexander became vice-chancellor of the Holy Roman Church. In 1153, he was appointed chancellor, a position in the curia responsible for diplomatic relations. He would hold the post through the pontificates of Eugenius III (1145–1153), Anastasius IV (1154), and Adrian IV (1154–1159), remaining a trusted advisor to Adrian throughout his reign.

Alexander's contemporary and biographer, Boso, characterized his subject as "a man of letters, fluent with polished eloquence, a prudent, kind, patient, merciful, gentle, sober, chaste man." These traits helped ensure his success in Rome. Adrian frequently chose Alexander to lead negotiations on numerous missions between the papacy and secular monarchies in an ongoing battle to wrest power from one another. Alexander's unwavering anti-imperialist stance during these early conventions would have far-reaching effects on his own papacy.

Frederick and the Antipopes

In 1152, Pope Adrian IV crowned Frederick I of Germany Holy Roman Emperor. It was an alliance formed for the mutual support and protection of the Church and the sovereign king against their enemies, especially the Normans. But within two years, the pope had befriended the Normans and no longer needed the protection of Frederick.

The pope's relationship with the emperor gradually deteriorated until finally, at the Diet of Besançon in 1157, as the pope's representative Alexander challenged Frederick I's supremacy.

The convention had been called by Frederick to hear complaints from the papal legation on his treatment of Archbishop of Scandinavia, an outspoken anti-imperialist whom he had arrested. The historical fracas ensued over the papal legate's use of the Latin word *beneficium,* which could connote either personal benefit or feudal concession. Frederick insisted that his authority was God-given, not something conferred on him by the pope. But Alexander remained firm among the cardinals in opposing the supremacy of Frederick I.

With an eye to influencing the succeeding pope, Frederick plotted to undermine the cardinals who opposed him. He sent two anti-papist emissaries to Rome: Otto, Count of Wittelsbach, and archbishop-elect of Cologne, Rainald von Dassel, whose appointment was never confirmed by the Holy See. The emissaries' work became evident when it came time for the twenty-two cardinals to elect the pope's successor: Alexander, though favored by a majority after three days of deliberations, was opposed by three imperialist cardinals, who voted for Victor IV. The conclave, or gathering of cardinals for the express purpose of choosing a pope, was disbursed by a horde sympathetic to the antipope Victor IV, and Alexander fled south, where he was consecrated pope at the monastery of Farfa.

Frederick believed, as protector of Christendom, that it was his duty to solve the controversy among the cardinals over the papal election. But Alexander refused to cede such authority over to the earthly jurisdiction of the emperor. After refusing to acknowledge Alexander III as true pope, Frederick was excommunicated in 1160. The schism this created would last for seventeen years, with Frederick installing succeeding antipopes Paschal III (1164–1168) and Calixtus III (1168–1178) in Rome. With Alexander in exile in France from 1162 to 1165, and in Gaeta, Benevento, Anagni, and Venice in 1167, he became the West's symbol of resistance to German domination. Frederick, meanwhile, busy defending his sovereignty, fell to the Lombard League, an alliance of the northern cities of Verona, Vicenza, and Padua, along with Venice, Constantinople, and Sicily. In 1176, after numerous attempts to overthrow the League and the pope, and after seeing his army destroyed in Rome by a fatal fever, Frederick surrendered at the battle of Legnano. At the treaty of Venice the following year, Frederick submitted and recognized Alexander as pope.

Trouble in Canterbury

While in exile in France, Alexander met Thomas Becket, Archbishop of Canterbury. Becket had been chancellor to Henry II of England, and when appointed archbishop he was hesitant to accept the position, fearing his duties as archbishop would require him to take positions unfavorable to the king. This indeed was the case, especially on issues that pitted church and crown against one another. In 1164, Becket was forced to flee England.

Alexander III, having received support from England, was hesitant to criticize Henry II, even as the king tried to shape the relationship between the church and state in such a way that the state would have precedence in certain legal issues and could weigh in on matters of excommunication. Alexander, still the quintessential diplomat, advised Becket in 1165 that he should "not act hastily or rashly" and that he ought to attempt to "regain the favor and goodwill of the illustrious English king." Scholars have both scrutinized and censured Alexander for his failure to defend Becket against Henry. Many believe the conflict did not have much resonance for the pope at the time, while others suggest that twelfth-century canon law did not support Becket's legal arguments. Still other scholars marvel at Alexander's diplomatic skills, adding that his vast experience with secular leaders told him persuasion generally yielded better results than confrontation.

In 1170, after an escalation in the conflicts between the archbishop and Henry II, the archbishop was murdered at the altar of his cathedral by four knights. Alexander canonized the saint two years later, and in 1174 humbled the British king by receiving his penance and securing from Henry II all the rights for which Becket had fought.

A Serene Sun

In an effort to repair the schism that tore at the church with Frederick's appointment of the antipopes, Alexander convoked the Third Lateran Council in 1179. Before hundreds of bishops and abbots, twenty-one cardinals, and laymen from all corners of the Earth, the pope issued a number of regulations that sealed his reputation as a gifted ecclesiastical legislator. The bishop of Assisi opened the council by praising the pontiff, declaring, "The great pontiff—who recently rose from the ocean of raging waves of persecution like a serene sun—illuminates not only the present church but the entire world with his worthy brilliance of shining splendor."

Among the pope's decrees at the council was the institution of the two-thirds majority rule for papal elections, a law extant today. Other improvements to the church included establishing procedures for canonizing saints to avoid numerous abuses of canonization, setting minimum age limits for bishops, and recommending they stress simplicity in their lifestyles and refrain from hunting.

Even Alexander's enemies recognized his intellectual and moral virtues. His legacy as an adherent of the movement to build and support universities, which became the great centers of learning in the Middle Ages, and as a champion of ecclesiastical independence are among his most outstanding accomplishments. His epitaph referred to him as "the Light of the Clergy, the Ornament of the Church, the Father of his City and of the World." Voltaire, the eighteenth-century French writer and opponent of organized religion, commemorated the pontiff by writing, "If men have regained their rights, it is chiefly to Pope Alexander III that they are indebted for it; it is to him that so many cities owe their splendor." Upon the death of Alexander III in 1181, Lucius III succeeded to the papacy.

Books

Columbia Encyclopedia, 2001.
Encyclopedia Britannica, 1965.

Online

Camelot Village, www.camelotintl.com/ (October 26, 2002).
Catholic Encyclopedia, www.newadvent.org/ (October 25, 2002; October 26, 2002).
Catholic University of America, http://faculty.cua.edu/ (October 25, 2002).
Christians Unite, http://bible.christiansunite.com/ (October 27, 2002).
Papal Library, www.saint-mike.org/ (October 25, 2002).
Patron Saint Index, www.catholic-forum.com/ (October 25, 2002).
Who's Who in Medieval History, http://historymedren.about .com/ (October 26, 2002).
Wikipedia, www.wikipedia.org (October 25, 2002). □

Alicia Alonso

Overcoming near blindness and numerous other obstacles that would have crippled lesser people, Cuban dancer Alicia Alonso (born 1921) became one of the greatest ballerinas in history and has starred in the most famous ballets all over the world. She later founded and directed the Alicia Alonso Ballet Company, which eventually became the Cuban National Ballet.

Began Dancing as a Little Girl

Born Alicia Ernestina de la Caridad dei Cobre Martinez Hoya on December 21, 1921, in Havana, Cuba, Alonso was the daughter of an army officer and his wife. The family was financially comfortable and lived in a fashionable section of the then-vibrant capital. Alonso indicated at a very early age an affinity for music and dance—her mother could occupy her happily for long periods with just a phonograph, a scarf, and some records. Alonso took her first ballet lessons at age nine at Havana's Escuela de Sociedad Pro-Arte Musical and a year later performed publicly for the first time in Tchaikovsky's *Sleeping Beauty.*

The dancer's rapid progress in her lessons came to an abrupt halt in 1937, when the 16-year-old fell in love with and married a fellow ballet student, Fernando Alonso. The new couple moved to New York City, hoping to begin their professional careers there and found a home with relatives in the Spanish Harlem section of the city. Alonso soon gave birth to a daughter, Laura, but managed to continue her training at the School of American Ballet and take private classes with Leon Fokine, Alexandra Fedorova, Enrico Zanfretta, and Anatole Vilzak. She even arranged to travel to London to study for a time with the renowned Vera Volkova.

Meanwhile, her husband had joined the new Mordkin Ballet Company in New York.

Made Professional Debut

Surprisingly, Alonso debuted not as a ballerina, but in the chorus line of the musical comedies *Great Lady* (1938), which only ran for 20 shows, and *Stars in Your Eyes* (1939), with Ethel Merman and Jimmy Durante and choreography by George Balanchine.

Perhaps discouraged by this less-than-auspicious beginning, Alonso sent Laura back to her family in Cuba, determined to remove all distractions from her training. She and Fernando embarked upon a stringent and unrelenting physical regime and vigilantly scoured all opportunities for their big break into the world of ballet. Dancer Agnes de Mille had become a friend of the couple at this point and later recalled wondering how the Alonsos could put themselves through such grueling pain and sacrifice. Meanwhile, the dancer joined the American Ballet Caravan as a soloist in 1939 and stayed with the company when it became the New York City Ballet in 1940. Occasionally, Alonso would return to Cuba to dance as prima ballerina with Havana's Teatro Pro-Arte. (Alonso did all this traveling prior to the chilling of relations between the United States and Cuba.) She created her own works for the company during this period, including *La Tinaja* (1943), *Lidia,* and *Ensayos Sinfonicos.*

In 1941, the new Ballet Theater chose Alonso as a dancer for its corps de ballet, a group of dancers who per-

formed together in a company. As part of this job, she had to do 90 minutes of demanding exercises every morning in the company class, but Alonso chose to take a second class at another school later in the day as well. Each night before her performance, she would do an elaborate warm-up routine coached by Fernando, after which she would go to her dressing room, dry off, and get into her costume. Accounts from this period say that Alonso would go on to give brilliant performances, but de Mille eventually chastised her friend for continuing the harsh regimen. Alonso reportedly replied that she had to continue in order to "get strong." In fact, the intense work had changed the dancer's body so that her immense strength and capability were obvious. Critics began to take notice and wrote rave reviews of the ballerina they called a rising star.

Vision Problems

After seeing the doctor for worsening vision problems, Alonso was diagnosed in 1941 with a detached retina. She had surgery to correct the problem and was ordered to lie in bed motionless for three months to allow her eyes to heal. Unable to comply completely, Alonso practiced with her feet alone, pointing and stretching to, as she put it, "keep my feet alive." When the bandages came off, Alonso was dismayed to find that the operation had not been completely successful. The doctors performed a second surgery, but its failure caused them to conclude that the dancer would never have peripheral vision. Finally, Alonso consented to a third procedure in Havana, but this time was ordered to lay completely motionless in bed for an entire year. She was not permitted to play with Laura, chew food too hard, laugh or cry, or move her head. Her husband sat with her every day, using their fingers to teach her the great dancing roles of classical ballet. From *Women in World History,* Alonso later recalled of that period, "I danced in my mind. Blinded, motionless, flat on my back, I taught myself to dance Giselle."

Finally, she was allowed to leave her bed, although dancing was still out of the question. Instead, she walked with her dogs and, against doctor's orders, went to the ballet studio down the street every day to begin practicing again. Then, just as her hope was returning, Alonso was injured when a hurricane shattered a door in her home, spraying glass splinters onto her head and face. Amazingly, her eyes were not injured. When her doctor saw this, he cleared Alonso to begin dancing, figuring that if she could survive an explosion of glass, dancing would do no harm.

Back to Work at Last

Nearly mad with impatience and still partially blind, Alonso traveled back to New York in 1943 to begin rebuilding her skills. However, before she had barely settled, out of the blue she was asked to dance *Giselle* to replace the ballet Theater's injured prima ballerina. Alonso accepted and gave such a performance that the critics immediately declared her a star. She was promoted to principal dancer of the company in 1946 and danced the role of Giselle until 1948, also performing in *Swan Lake,* Anthony Tudor's *Undertow* (1943), Balanchine's *Theme and Varia-*

tions (1947), and in such world premieres as de Mille's dramatic ballet *Fall River Legend* (1948), in which she starred as the Accused. By this time in her career, she had developed a reputation as an intensely dramatic dancer, as well as an ultra-pure technician and a supremely skilled interpreter of classical and romantic repertories.

Alonso's longtime dance partnership with the Ballet Theater's Igor Youskevitch has been compared to that of Fred Astaire and Ginger Rogers. Youskevitch and her other partners quickly became expert at helping Alonso conceal her handicap. To compensate for only partial sight in one eye and no peripheral vision, the ballerina trained her partners to be exactly where she needed them without exception. She also had the set designers install strong spotlights in different colors to serve as guides for her movements. Alonso knew, for instance, that if she stepped into the glow of the spotlights near the front of the stage, she was getting too close to the orchestra pit. There was also a thin wire stretched across the edge of the stage at waist height as another marker for her, but in general she danced within the encircling arms of her partners and was led by them from point to point. Audiences were reportedly never the wiser as they watched the prima ballerina.

A New Endeavor in Havana

In 1948, Alonso returned to Havana to found her own company, the Alicia Alonso Ballet Company. Fernando was general director of the company, which was at that time composed mainly of Ballet Theater dancers temporarily out of work due to a reorganization in the New York company. Fernando's brother Alberto, a choreographer, served as artistic director for the company.

The company debuted briefly in the capital and then departed for a tour of South America. The performances were a hit with audiences everywhere, but Alonso found herself funding the company with her savings to keep it going despite donations from wealthy families and a modest subsidy from the Cuban Ministry of Education. Meanwhile, she commuted between Havana and New York to recruit the world's best teachers to train her new students. She remained a sought-after prima ballerina during this hectic time, dancing twice in Russia in 1952 and then producing and starring in *Giselle* for the Paris Opera in 1953.

Political Change in Cuba

By the mid-1950s, the Alicia Alonso Ballet Company was in dire straights financially and politically. A dictator, Fulgencio Batista, had taken control and was determined to quash the heavy opposition to his rule. Supported by the island's financial infrastructure, the Mafia, and American business interests, he mercilessly repressed anyone who stood in his path. Declaring that all artists and intellectuals were left-wing sympathizers, he drastically cut what little funding the government had given Alonso's ballet school and touring group. Forced to work in nightclubs to earn a living, the dancers often had no energy to perform for Alonso. As the dancer became increasingly vocal in her disdain for Batista, the regime offered her five hundred dollars a month in perpetuity to stop her criticism.

Disgusted, she folded her school in 1956 and joined the Ballet Rousse de Monte Carlo with Yousevitch.

Alonso worked with the Ballet Rousse until 1959, during which time she performed in a 10-week tour of the Soviet Union, dancing in *Giselle,* the Leningrad Opera Ballet's *Path of Thunder,* and other pieces. Her performances earned her the coveted *Dance Magazine* Award in 1958.

Castro Lured Her Back Home

When he took power from the Batista dictatorship on January 1, 1959, Fidel Castro also vowed to increase funding to the nation's languishing cultural programs. Encouraged by this sudden change and eager to see her homeland again, Alonso returned to Cuba and in March 1959 received $200,000 in funding to form a new dance school, to be called the Ballet Nacional de Cuba, along with a guarantee of annual financial support. She officially founded the school in 1960, and within several years her dancers were winning international dance competitions.

Alonso felt strongly that she and her ballet school were "very much part of the Cuban revolution." She wanted her dancers to bring the beauty and excitement of ballet to the island nation's workers and farmers who had virtually no experience with artistic expression. She and her dancers even helped to bring in the crops from the fields, Alonso wearing a wide Vietnamese worker's hat as a political statement.

Disappeared from American Artistic Scene

Because of her intense and passionate affiliation with the new communist government in Havana, American audiences turned their backs on the prima ballerina and she vanished from the country's cultural radar. However, her company continued to build its prowess and achievements in both Eastern and Western Europe. In 1967 and 1971 she performed in Canada, where reviewers noted that Alonso was still the greatest ballerina of her time. When the Vietnam War ended and Richard Nixon left the presidency, Alonso was permitted to perform again in the United States in 1975 and 1976. An American reviewer said of the dancer, then 54 years old and a grandmother, "she creates more sexual promise than ballerinas half her age." The state-run Cuban film industry made a film containing all of Alonso's repertoire, but in American ballet circles she had been all but forgotten.

Ended Days of Dancing

Alonso danced solos in Europe and elsewhere well into her 70s, although her near blindness became increasingly apparent. In 1995, she and a number of other aging National Ballet members performed in San Francisco in a piece called *In the Middle of the Sunset.* Reviewers deemed the work an allegory about the crushed dreams of the Cuban revolution and lamented that so many of the superstar's productive years had been spent under the isolating umbrella of communism.

Alonso continued to serve as the director of the Ballet Nacional de Cuba in the early twenty-first century. Numerous books have been written on the ballerina, including *Alicia Alonso: At Home and Abroad* (1970), *Alicia Alonso: The Story of a Ballerina* (1979), *Alicia Alonso: A Passionate Life of Dance* (1984), and *Alicia Alonso: First Lady of the Ballet* (1993). During a November 2003 on-stage interview prior to a Cuban National Ballet performance in San Diego, California, she exclaimed, "I'm so happy to be here. And I'm happy whenever I'm on the stage. The stage is where a dancer should be, even if it's only to walk or sit. I am at home on the stage."

Books

Commire, Anne, ed., *Women in World History,* Yorkin Publications, 2001.

Online

"Alicia Alonso," *AllRefer.com Reference website,* http://reference.allrefer.com (December 10, 2003).
"Alicia Alonso," *Andros on Ballet website,* http://androsdance .tripod.com (December 10, 2003).
"Alicia Alonso," *Ballerina Gallery website,* http://www .ballerinagallery.com (December 10, 2003).
"Alicia Alonso: Biografia," *Portalatino.com website,* http://www .portalatino.com (December 10, 2003).
"Alicia Alonso, Director of the Cuban Ballet," *Cuban Journeys website,* http://www.cubanjourneys.com (December 10, 2003).
"Alicia Alonso, Prima Ballerina, Ballet Nacional de Cuba Interview," *Ballet.co website,* http://www.ballet.co.uk (December 10, 2003).
"Biography of Alicia Alonso," *United Nations Educational, Scientific, and Cultural Organization website,* http://portal .unesco.org (December 10, 2003). □

Natan Alterman

One of the national poets of Israel, Natan Alterman (1910–1970) was widely considered the literary spokesperson for pronationalist Israelis in the years just prior to and following Israel's statehood.

Early Life

Natan Alterman was born in Warsaw, Poland, in 1910. His parents were both teachers, and his father, Yitzhak, was one of the founders of the Hebrew kindergarten in Warsaw. Alterman received a traditional Hebrew education beginning at a young age. The family fled Warsaw at the start of World War I, moving to Moscow and then Kishinev. They finally settled in Tel Aviv in 1925.

Alterman attended Herzliya Gymnasia, a college preparatory school, in Tel Aviv, and then moved to France, where he studied at universities in Nancy and Paris. He graduated with a degree in agricultural engineering in 1932.

A year earlier, he had begun publishing politically oriented pieces.

Became Zionist Spokesperson

Returning to Palestine in 1934, Alterman decided to make a career of writing. His literary talents would prove to be wide ranging, but he started with poetry. After joining the staff of the newspaper *Ha'aretz* in 1934, he started a weekly political column called "Moments." The column became a showcase for his poetry, in which he used satire to discuss the tumult surrounding Israeli's settlement in Palestine (called Yishuv), which then was controlled by Britain and, later, its quest for statehood. Alterman soon became known as the poet of the Yishuv and the literary spokesperson for the Zionist (nationalist) movement. Although often censored by British officials during the final two years of Britain's mandate in Palestine (1946–1947), the poet's works, which he collectively called "Poems of the Time and the Tabloid," became anthems for the Jews' struggle.

Far from being merely a political writer, Alterman showed an astonishing range of talent, regularly publishing theatrical works, children's books, and plays. He was also a highly skilled translator and transformed works by Shakespeare, Racine, and Moliere into Hebrew in translations that were unsurpassed in their sensitivity and nuance.

Poetry Expanded Beyond Politics

Alterman's lyrical poetry is among his most highly acclaimed work. Publishing his first book of poetry, *Kohavim BaHutz* (Stars Outside) in 1938, he received strong reviews for his meditative work. The book was a collection of poems he had written between 1935 and 1938, but he assembled them into a cycle using common elements. A second collection in 1941, titled *Joy of the Poor,* spoke of the torture of love and the tension between life and death. Some reviewers suggested that the Holocaust, which killed millions of Jews and other innocent people, might have inspired the work.

Alterman married an actress, Rachel Markus, in 1935. In 1941 they had a son named Tirzah. By this time, he had consolidated his poetic style into a unique form. Alterman's lyrical work was influenced by the French and Russian symbolists and contained complex references to Jewish history. Descriptive and symbolic, many pieces also featured a tension between natural forces and the increasingly urban, mechanized world he saw evolving around him. Love played a prominent role in Alterman's lyrical poems, often centering on women to whom he assigned opposing roles in the conflict between man and nature. He wrote a popular song called "Shir Ha'amek" (Song of the Valley), a haunting, lullaby-like piece about the Jezerel Valley. Written from the viewpoint of a pioneer, the song was typical of the popular Land of Israel genre that developed in the 1930s and 1940s.

In 1943, Alterman moved from the *Ha'aretz* to a competing Hebrew daily newspaper, *Davar.* He continued to use the press to engage in skilled polemics about the issue of Israeli statehood. He also published several more books of poetry in the 1940s, including *Shirei Makkot Mitzrayim*

(*Poems of the Plagues of Egypt*), in 1944. The book employs the biblical narrative to suggest the repetitive and cyclical nature of sin and judgment.

Also during the 1940s, Alterman became strongly affiliated with and influenced by Avraham Shlonsky, a Hebrew poet living in Palestine. Together, they led what became known as the second radical wave of artistic expression in Hebrew poetry. They scoffed at the figurative hyperbole popular in earlier forms of poetry and avoided idioms and religious allusions as passé. His affiliation with Shlonsky gave rise to speculation that Alterman sympathized with the Arab quest to keep Palestine. Alterman was a man of myriad contradictions, and neither his supporters nor his critics could ever pin him down for certain on many issues.

Focus on Israeli Statehood

When Israel declared independence in 1948, Alterman's work began to focus more closely on the political and social issues facing the country. One of Alterman's most famous poems, "Silver Platter," was published soon after Israel achieved statehood. The poem suggests that miracles are not the result of divine intervention, but rather human effort, and it provided the image of Israeli soldiers and fighters as "the silver platter upon which the Jewish state was served" to its people. The vision stirred controversy in some circles, since being handed something on a silver platter usually connotes that the receiver did nothing to earn it.

Beginning in the 1950s, Alterman wrote a column, known as "The Seventh Column," in *Davar* that became a key gauge of the political atmosphere in the new country. He was so much a part of Israel's political scene that Defense Minister Shimon Peres dragged Alterman out of bed late one night in 1956 to show him shipments of French weapons being secretly unloaded at Haifa Port to support Israel in its new offense against the Palestinians. Alterman later wrote of the event in *Davar*, recalling his impression of a cargo container dangling from a crane: "With the first touch of the land it becomes the expression of the Jews' power."

Alterman wrote *Wailing City*, for which he won the Bialik Prize, in 1957 and—in another example of his astonishing diversity as an author—produced an anthology of children's verse in 1958. The 1960s were productive: he published his collected works in a four-volume set in 1961–1962; released a collection of works, *Summer Festival*, in 1965; wrote five plays, staging four of them in Israel with great success; and published a satirical prose narrative, *Hamasikhah ha'aharonah*, which targeted the ideological failure of Zionism and the Israeli state, in 1969.

Alterman's political involvement remained intense even in his last decade. After the Six-Day War of 1967, triggered by conflict over territory between Israel and its Arab neighbors (Egypt, Syria, and Jordon), Israel occupied the Gaza Strip and began creating Jewish settlements in former exclusively Palestinian areas. Alterman became a member of the Land of Israel Movement and was closely involved with the Israeli settlement campaign, visiting the settlers on several occasions.

Recognition for Literary Work

For his contributions to Hebrew literature, Alterman received the Israel Prize in 1968. He died in 1970, but more than 30 years later his work was still among the most widely read in Israel. In 2001, director Eli Cohen made a film about him, *Altermania,* which won the prestigious Wolgin Award at that year's Israeli Film Festival. In the promotional materials for the film, Alterman is described as a "double personality" who was by turns "charismatic, clever, rational, and bright" and a "gloomy skeptic," a man perhaps "bedeviled by a death wish," a fighter "for justice" who nonetheless abused "those closest to him." The film asks the question, "Did he fight for the rights of Arabs or did he believe in a Greater Israel?" calling him a "tortured man full of contradictions." The only answers lie somewhere in the works Alterman left behind.

Books

Abramson, Glenda, ed., *The Blackwell Companion to Jewish Literature,* Blackwell Reference, 1991.

Online

"Altermania," *The 18th Israel Film Festival,* http://www.israelfilmfestival.com (December 10, 2003).
"Alterman, Natan (1910–1970)," *The Jewish Agency for Israel,* http://www.jafi.org.il (December 10, 2003).
"Different Strokes for Different Folks," *The Jerusalem Post Internet Edition,* http://www.jpost.com (December 10, 2003).
"Hebrew Poetry in the New Millennium," *The Israeli Government,* http://www.mfa.gov.il (December 10, 2003).
"Hebron: The Jewish People's Deepest Roots (Part II)," *Our Jerusalem,* http//:www.ourjerusalem.com (December 10, 2003).
"Intermediate Course in Hebrew Literature," *The Open University of Israel,* http://www-e.openu.ac.il (December 10, 2003).
"Israeli Popular Music," *My Jewish Learning,* http://www.myjewishlearning.com (December 10, 2003).
"A Literary Blank Ballot," *The Jerusalem Post Internet Edition,* http://www.jpost.com (December 10, 2003).
"Natan Alterman," *The Drunken Boat,* http//:www.thedrunkenboat.com (December 31, 2003).
"A Silver Platter," *Association of Jewish 6th Formers,* http://www.aj6.org (December 10, 2003). □

Calin Alupi

The works of Romanian artist Calin Alupi (1906–1988) remain sought after as representative of Romanian post-impressionism in contemporary art. His most critically acclaimed works were done in pastel and oil.

Calinic "Calin" Alupi was born on July 20, 1906, in the small village of Vancicauti, Hotin Department, Bessarabia (eventually to become part of the USSR). His parents, Teodoro and Antonina, were farmers. Tragically, Alupi lost his father in 1917 when Teodoro died in Galicia while fighting as a soldier of the Russian Imperial Army during World War I.

Headed to School

In 1919 Alupi seized the opportunity to begin studying at a school in Sendriceni-Dorohoi. Drawing, taught by painter Nicolae Popovici Lespezi, quickly became one of the young teen's favorite subjects. After six years at the school his passion for art and his promise as an artist grew, and in 1925 the 19-year-old Alupi became a student at the Fine Arts Academy of Iasi, Romania. Among his teachers were folk artist Stefan Dimitrescu, who taught painting, and Jean Cosmovici, who taught drawing. To pay his way, Alupi worked in the school library, but still met with early success as an aspiring artist, winning both the academy's Schiller grant and its Grigorovici prize. Between 1925 and 1926 Alupi was a student at the Officer of the Reserve School in Bacau.

Alupi graduated from the Fine Arts Academy in 1932 with high honors in painting. By the following year he was exhibiting his work at an official show of Moldavian art staged in Iasi (Moldavia was a principality of Romania at that time), and by 1934 he was holding his first personal exhibition in Iasi.

From Art Student to Professional Artist

In 1935 Alupi found a job as a teacher in the drawing and calligraphy department of his old school at Sendriceni-Dorohoi. He worked there for a year, then returned to Iasi to show his work at local exhibitions. It was from this point forward that Alupi began painting under the tutelage of Nicolae Tonitza and other locally renowned artists at the Durau Monastery. The monastery, located at the foot of Ceahlau Mountain in the Romanian Carpathian Mountains, was home to hermits, monks, and nuns and provided a quiet and beautiful space for Alupi to continue developing his artistic style. The region is now a nature preserve.

An important art show took place in 1938 in Bucharest, and Alupi exhibited there at the city's Dalles Hall along with several other notable local artists. The *Bucharest Arts and Literature Review* printed a favorable critique of his work, leading to increased exposure for the artist. The following year he participated in the official art exhibit of Moldavia, which was staged in Iasi.

War Arrived, but Art Continued

At the beginning of World War II Alupi, like many of his friends and colleagues, was sent to the front lines to fight. He spent his entire tour of duty, which lasted until 1944, at the front as a lieutenant. The army capitalized on Alupi's well-known skill and put him in charge of drawing maps of enemy positions. He would later receive the Order of the Romanian Crown and the country's prestigious Military Virtue ribbon for his service.

After leaving the Russian army, Alupi created more pieces for a large painting and sculpture showcase in Bucharest. Another Bucharest exhibit followed in 1946, and in 1947 he became an assistant in the drawing department of

the Fine Arts Academy. Popular with the students and a talented teacher, Alupi received a promotion to professor within the year.

Married and Continued Teaching and Showing

After taking part in two key shows in 1948, one in Bucharest and the other in Iasi, Alupi married Sanda Constantinescu Ballif. They had their only daughter, Antonina, in 1950. Meanwhile, he had become an instructor at the school of Plastic Art in Iasi. Despite the new demands of fatherhood, Alupi's showings at local art exhibitions continued at a steady pace throughout the 1950s and 1960s, and art fans came from around Europe to see his shows in Bucharest, Sofia, Iasi, and Varsovia. In 1954 the Plastic Art School rewarded his increasing notoriety with a promotion to full professor.

Alupi began working at the Pedagogical Institute in Iasi at some point during the 1960s, and he was reported to have been promoted to painting teacher at the school in 1968. In 1971, for perhaps the first time, Alupi exhibited his work outside Romania, staging personal shows in Trieste and Roma, Italy. He also showed in Paris in 1972 and 1973. Then, on February 19, 1975, the National Museum of Romania threw what it called an "homage party" for the artist.

A Decade Filled with Work and Honors

For the last ten years of his life Alupi continued to create new art and maintained a steady schedule of exhibitions and shows in both Romania and France. In 1978 his country's national art museum staged a retrospective of his work and honored Alupi with another gala. According to records, his last shows were held in 1986 in Iasi.

Alupi died at age 82 on September 19, 1988. He was buried in Iasi's Eternitate Cemetery. His daughter Antonina became a respected artist in her own right. She escaped from communist Romania on foot in 1972, fled to France, and went on to become a teacher like her father.

Online

"Calin Alupi," *Artists Online Web site,* http://artistsonline.biz/ (December 31, 2003).

"Calin Alupi," *Atelier Alupi Web site,* http://www.atelieralupi .com/ (January 1, 2004).

Cultural Pastoral Center St. Daniil the Hermit Web site, http://www.ccpdurau.go.ro/ (January 1, 2004). □

Yehuda Amichai

Nominated many times for the Nobel Prize for Literature, Yehuda Amichai (1924–2000) was often considered the national poet of Israel for his generation. Many critics consider his final work, a collection of poetry titled *Open Closed Open,* to be Amichai's finest work. His poetry, which portrays life in modern Israel as life with war and insecurity while simul-

taneously addressing the everyday human issues of any Western society, has been translated into 37 languages.

Born in Germany, Immigrated to Israel

On May 3, 1924, in Würzburg in the Bavarian region of Germany, Yehuda Amichai was born to Orthodox Jewish merchants whose ancestors had lived there since the Middle Ages. His original last name was Pfeuffer, but when the family immigrated to Palestine in 1936 to escape the Nazis, his parents changed their surname to Amichai (Hebrew for "my people lives"). They finally settled in Israel, having avoided the Holocaust that killed more than 6 million Jews.

From his early childhood, Amichai studied Hebrew and later attended religious schools that propounded the Orthodox faith. Once the family moved to Jerusalem, by which time he was fluent in Hebrew, he was enrolled at the Ma'aleh high school. As Amichai reached adolescence, he began to reject the Orthodoxy of his parents, to their great dismay. However, he later recalled that they forgave their wayward son because he spent three years during World War II in North Africa with the Jewish Brigade of the British Army and became a member of the Zionist underground in 1946 to fight with the Palmach (an elite commando section

of the Israeli defense force) in the Negev during the Arab-Israeli War of 1948.

From Soldier to Teacher and Back Again

When the fighting ended, Amichai began attending Hebrew University in Jerusalem, concentrating on Biblical texts and Hebrew literature. However, he also read widely among the works of English poets T. S. Eliot, Dylan Thomas, and W. H. Auden, who would later strongly influence his writing. (In fact, Amichai would later become friends with Auden.) When he had completed his university degree in about 1955, he found work as a teacher of biblical and Hebrew writings in Jerusalem's secondary schools. Furthermore, the young man had begun to develop his writing abilities and had started writing poetry in 1949. In 1955, he published his first book of poetry, *Akhshav u-ve-yamim aherim* (Now and in Other Days), which was among the first to contain colloquial Israeli Hebrew and marked the emergence of an entirely new style in Hebrew poetry. The following year, Amichai fought again in the Arab-Israeli War of 1956.

Amichai's intense patriotism and commitment to the State of Israel are apparent even in his earliest work, which contained numerous biblical images and references to Jewish history. As more of his writings appeared, critics began to note his lyrical use of ordinary language and the deceptive simplicity of his work—an effect, perhaps, of the English poets' influence.

Established as Important Poet

With his publication in 1958 of his second collection of poetry, *Bemerhak shtei tikvot* (Two Hopes Apart), Amichai established himself as one of the leading poets of the generally disillusioned "Palmach generation," (writers who surfaced from Israel's war for Independence). The poems were revolutionary in their use of such workday images as tanks, fuel, and airplanes and the appearance of technological terms—all of which had been considered inappropriate for use in poetry. Amichai's use of them reflected his strong belief that modern poetry must not avoid dealing with and contemplating modern issues. In addition, literary critics noticed Amichai's propensity for word play, citing his innovative use of both classical and colloquial Hebrew. He often coined new phrases and slang for his work, adding to his fans' delight in reading the poet's new largely autobiographical collections. Amichai's passion for life and sense of the underlying profundity of day-to-day experiences, which are intrinsic to his work, also endeared him to many readers.

Amichai wrote a play titled *Journey to Nineveh,* in 1962 and several novels, including *Not of This Time, Not of This Place,* (1963), about the search for identity of a Jewish immigrant to Israel. His *Jerusalem* (1967) and *Poems* (1969) were both met with critical acclaim as well. Even as he became widely recognized as the country's leading poet and thus something of a celebrity in Jerusalem, Amichai continued to live a simple life and remained highly accessible. Although he generally stayed away from active politics and literary societies, he was often seen walking in the city or lecturing in classrooms.

Body of Work Grew Rapidly

Amichai was a prolific author. He wrote poems, plays, children's books, essays, radio shows, and short stories. Despite continuing his work as an educator (serving as a visiting professor at the University of California, Berkeley, in 1971 and 1976) and serving in the army again in 1973, he published numerous works in quick succession: *Mi Yitneni Malon* (Hotel in the Wilderness, 1971—his second novel); *Poems of Jerusalem and of Myself* (1973); *Amen* (1977); *Time* (1979); *Love Poems* (1981); *The Great Tranquility: Questions and Answers* (1983); *The World Is a Room and Other Stories* (1984); *Poems of Jerusalem* (1988); and *Even a Fist Was Once an Open Palm with Fingers* (1989). For initiating and encouraging what the award committee termed "the revolutionary change in poetry's language," Amichai received the Israel Prize, the country's highest honor, in 1982.

Amichai's works were especially popular in English, and his readings in the United States, France, and England drew large crowds. However, admirers of his original Hebrew works often claim that the poet's innovative and refreshing use of the language—one of the main charms of his work—is lost in translation. Likewise, the subtle layers of meaning that Amichai achieved using the complexity of the 3,000-year-old language (for instance, using an ancient word rather than its modern synonym to impart a biblical connotation to a phrase or scene) vanished when translated into a comparatively younger language. Some literary experts say this factor belies the legendary accessibility of Amichai's work.

In a 1994 article in *Modern Hebrew Literature* commemorating Amichai's 70th birthday, author Robert Alter illustrates this difficulty with a phrase from Amichai's love poem *In the Middle of This Century*. The poem mentions "the linsey-woolsey of our being together," which Alter concedes may sound funny to an English reader, but explains that the Hebrew term, *sha'atnez,* means the biblically taboo interweaving of linen and wool. Alter suggests that any informed Hebrew reader would immediately grasp that Amichai means to evoke an image of a forbidden union of too different entities in a Romeo and Juliet-like scenario.

Amichai continued to write and do readings throughout the 1990s. His 1998 work, *Open Closed Open,* written just before his death and published in English in 2000, was considered by many to be Amichai's crowning literary achievement. Comprising 25 sequential poems, he continues in his use of the rich Jewish spiritual tradition and Israel's current anxieties as overarching structures through which he offers thoughts on human nature at large: religious insecurity, the love of children, commitment to creating a better world, and other universal concerns.

Although nominated for the Nobel Prize for Literature several times, Amichai never won the coveted award. He reportedly believed, along with his millions of devotees, that he deserved the prize but that, as an author of such politically charged work, would never receive it. Amichai also repeatedly rejected the notion that he was the national poet of Israel, saying that unlike such "mobilized" poets as Natan Alterman, he spoke for no one but himself. Amichai

died of cancer in Jerusalem on September 22, 2000. He had married twice and was the father of three children.

Books

Abramson, Glenda, ed., *The Blackwell Companion to Jewish Literature,* Blackwell Reference, 1991.
Contemporary Authors, Gale, 2003.

Online

"Amichai," *Academy of American Poets website,* http://www.poets.org (December 16, 2003).
"Amichai, Yehuda," *Encyclopedia Britannica Online website,* http://www.britannica.com (December 16, 2003).
"Amichai, Yehuda," *The Drunken Boat website,* http://www.drunkenboat.com (December 31, 2003).
"Amichai, Yehuda," *World Zionist Organization website,* http://wzo.org.il (December 16, 2003).
"The Most Accessible Poet, Yehuda Amichai, 1924–2000," *Jerusalem Report Magazine website,* http://www.jrep.com (December 16, 2003).
"The Untranslatable Amichai," *Institute for Translation of Hebrew Literature website,* http://www.ithl.org.il (December 16, 2003).
"Yehuda Amichai," *Jewish Virtual Library website,* http://us-israel.org (December 16, 2003).
"Yehuda Amichai (1924–2000)," *Pegasos: A Literature-Related Resource Site website,* http://www.kirjasto.sci.fr (December 16, 2003). □

Ivo Andrić

Ivo Andrić (1892–1975) was a great writer of the twentieth century. His work reflected the historical turmoil of his Yugoslav homeland and emphasized the humanity of the people caught in the political unrest. Andrić began his public career as a diplomat and by the time he retired from the Yugoslav diplomatic service he was already a well-respected author. In the years following the Second World War, Andrić published his masterpiece and his reputation spread throughout the world. He was awarded the Nobel Prize in Literature in 1962.

From Prison to the Foreign Ministry

Ivo Andrić was born to Croatian parents on October 10, 1892, in the Bosnian village of Dolac, near the town of Travnik, at a time when Bosnia was part of the Austro-Hungarian Empire. Andrić's father, a silversmith, died when Andrić was three years old. Andrić then went to live with his aunt and uncle in the town of Višegrad, the town that he associated the most with his childhood. In 1903 Andrić moved to Sarajevo where he attended the Great Sarajevo Gymnasium for eight years. In 1911 Andrić published his first poem, "U sumrak." In 1912 he received a scholarship from the cultural-educational society Napredak to attend

the University of Zagreb, where his course load was heavy in science. In 1913, when he transferred to the University of Vienna, his academic interest shifted from science to the humanities. In 1914, Andrić entered the University of Kraków; that same year the Croatian Writers Society published six of Andrić's prose poems in their anthology, *Hrvatska mlada lirika* (Young Croatian Lyricists). Prior to attending university, Andrić had become involved with one of the many Bosnian underground resistance groups whose secondary goal was to unify Serbs and Croats. One of the members of Andrić's group, "Mlada Bosna" (Young Bosna), was Gavrilo Princip, who assassinated Archduke Franz Ferdinand and his wife in Sarajevo on June 28, 1914—an action that triggered a chain of events that led to the outbreak of the First World War.

Andrić returned to Yugoslavia from Kraków after the assassination, but because of his underground political activities he was imprisoned for three years during the First World War. He spent his prison years reading Fedor Dostoevsky and Søren Kierkegaard. Upon his release he worked as an editor at the literary journal *Književni Jug* (The Literary South). In 1918 Andrić reregistered at the University of Zagreb where he completed the coursework but withdrew before the exams because of ill health. Andrić had planned to complete the exams as soon as he recovered but was diverted from this plan because of his family's dire financial circumstances. Consequently, he wrote a letter to a former teacher who had become a cabinet minister in the postwar Kingdom of the Serbs, Croats and Slovenes, applying for a government position. In September 1919 Andrić became a

junior minister in the ministry of faith and moved to Belgrade. Andrić remained at the ministry of faith until February 1920 when he transferred to the ministry of foreign affairs. Andrić's first foreign posting was to the Vatican in Rome, Italy, as a vice-consul.

By 1923 Andrić was in Graz, Austria, again serving as vice-consul. However, a new law was declared that required all civil service personnel serving in positions of responsibility to hold university degrees. Due to Andrić's recognized diplomatic ability his immediate superiors tried to have an exception made for him but to no avail. However, he was retained at the consulate as a temporary worker (at his old salary) during the time he resumed his studies for a doctorate at the University of Graz. Andrić received his Ph.D. in 1924; his dissertation was titled, "Die Entwicklung des geistigen Lebens in Bosnien unter der Einwirkung dur Türkischen Herrschaft" (The Development of Spiritual Life in Bosnia Under the Influence of Turkish Rule). With a degree in hand, Andrić was soon reinstated as a vice-consul. Over the course of his diplomatic career Andrić served in Rome, Italy; Graz, Austria; Bucharest, Romania; Madrid, Spain; Geneva, Switzerland; Brussels, Belgium; and Trieste, Italy. His diplomatic service culminated in Berlin, Germany.

In 1939, with a change in government in Yugoslavia (as the Kingdom of Serbs, Croats, and Slovenes officially became known in 1929), there was a vacancy in Berlin for the post of royal Yugoslav minister or ambassador when the previous minister, Aleksander Cincar-Marković, became the foreign minister. Cincar-Marković's appointment was an attempt to mollify the Nazi regime in Germany, which was pushing for Yugoslavia's alliance with the Axis (principally Germany, Italy, and Japan). Andrić was clearly the most qualified candidate for the post, and so it was that he presented his credentials to Adolf Hitler (as called for by diplomatic protocol) on April 19, 1939. Andrić served as ambassador to Germany for just under two years; he resigned his post on April 5, 1941, after Yugoslavia had signed the Tripartite Pact, aligning that country with the Axis, and just hours before Germany sent troops into Yugoslavia. Andrić returned to Belgrade were he spent the entire war. He resigned from the foreign ministry on November 15, 1941, and never resumed his diplomatic career.

Early Work

Throughout Andrić's diplomatic career, he continued to write and his literary reputation in Yugoslavia was formidable at the time of his retirement from diplomatic service. In addition to his earlier published prose poems, Andrić translated works by Walt Whitman and August Strindberg. In the years just after the First World War, Andrić published *Ex Ponto* (From the Bridge) in 1918 and *Nemiri* (Troubles) in 1920, both collections of prose poems. He wrote part of *Ex Ponto* while in prison. Thereafter Andrić concentrated on prose, in the beginning short stories, and by the end of the 1920s he no longer wrote poetry. Andrić's first short story was "Put Alije Djerzeleza" (The Journey of Ali Djerzelez), written in 1920. The protagonist is a mythic Muslim hero in the modern world. In the 1920s and 1930s Andrić's literary reputation rested on three powerful collections of short stories; each collection was simply titled *Pripovetke*. Originally appearing in newspapers and journals, these stories included: "Mustafa Madjar" (Mustafa Magyar), "Lyubav u kasbi" (Love in a Small Town), "U musafirhani" (In the Guest House), "Mara milosnica" (The Pasha's Concubine), "Cudo u Olovu" (Miracle I Olovo), and "Most na Žepi" (The Bridge on the Zepa). The last two stories were written in 1926, the year Andrić became an associate member of the Serbian Academy of Science and Art. In 1930 he published "Anikina vremena."

Andrić's work as a diplomat and his brief time in "Mlada Bosna" undoubtedly influenced his outlook regarding his fellow southern Slavs. Andrić was committed to the idea of Yugoslavia. In 1933 he refused publication in the anthology *Antologija novije hrvatske lirike* (Anthology of New Croatian Writers) because of its underlying philosophy of separation. In 1934 he became editor of the *Serbian Literary Gazette*. By the end of the 1930s, Andrić's literary reputation in his country was such that he was the subject of a monograph.

Postwar Masterpieces

During the war years, Andrić wrote some of his finest works including his masterpiece *Na Drini Cuprija* (The Bridge on the Drina), but it was not until 1945 that he published these novels. Returning to the settings of his youth, albeit in a historical period, Andrić placed *Travnicka Chronika* (Bosnian Chronicle, also titled in English as The Days of the Consuls) in Travnik, the town of his birth during the years 1806–1813. The bridge in *Na Drini Cuprija* is an actual landmark in Višegrad. Both novels were published in Belgrade. Andrić also published a psychological novel, *Gospodjica* (The Woman from Sarajevo), in Sarajevo, in 1945.

Na Drini Cuprija gained Andrić worldwide attention that culminated in his receiving the Nobel Prize for Literature. It tells the story of four centuries of Bosnian history, from 1516 to the onset of the First World War. Andrić's narrative power within the novel created something far richer than a metaphor for the connection of separate generations and religious beliefs. The bridge, in *Na Drini Cuprija*, is nothing less than the novel's protagonist, an inanimate, lifeless, and therefore static object that nevertheless carries hope and change. Andrić returned to the image of the bridge more than once. He later wrote an essay titled "Bridges" in which he declared: "Of all that a man is impelled to build in this life, nothing is in my eyes finer than a bridge. . . . Belonging to everyone and the same for everyone, useful, built always rationally, in a place in which the greatest number of human needs coincide, they are more enduring than other buildings and serve nothing which is secret or evil."

In 1948 Andrić published *Nove Pripovetke* (New Stories). While the stories in this collection had contemporary settings, Andrić returned to an historical setting with the 1954 publication of *Prokleta Avlija* (The Devil's Yard). A collection of intertwined short stories set primarily in a Turkish prison.

The Nobel Prize

Andrić was very active in the postwar years. He served as president of the Yugoslav Writers Association and as vice-president of the Society for Cultural Cooperation with the Soviet Union. He also attended the third meeting of the Antifascist Liberation Council of Bosnia and Herzegovina. In 1946 he became a full member of the Serbian Academy of Science and Art and in 1947 was a member of the Presidium of the People's Assembly of NR Bosnia and Herzegovina. Also that year, he published the novella *Prica o vezirovom slonu* (The Story of the Vizier's Elephant). Andrić also traveled extensively. In 1949 he served in the Yugoslav Federal Assembly. Andrić joined the Yugoslav Communist Party in 1954 and was the first signer of the Novi Sad Agreement concerning the Serbo-Croatian language. He was also instrumental in maintaining Yugoslavia's cultural independence (as it had its political independence) from the Soviet Union. Thus, socialist realism was never a major literary or artistic force in Yugoslavia. In 1958 Andrić married costume designer Milica Babić; she died in 1968.

Andrić earned numerous awards and honors, but the high point of his international recognition came when he was awarded (in 1962) the 1961 Nobel Prize for Literature. Following this award, Andrić's international reputation grew enormously. For his part, the now 70-year-old donated all of his prize money to the library fund in Bosnia and Herzegovina. In 1963, his first Collected Works published in 10 volumes, and in 1964, the University of Jagiellonian in Kraków awarded Andrić an honorary doctorate degree. In the 1960s and 1970s his literary output slowed as his health deteriorated, especially after the death of his wife. Ivo Andrić died in Belgrade on March 13, 1975.

In addition to his short stories and novels, Andrić published several essays on writers and artists. Andrić especially admired Goya and in 1935 published the essay "Razgovor s Gojom" (Conversation with Goya). Also in 1935, he published one of his most important piece of literary criticism: "Njegoš kao tragnīni junak kosovske misli" (Njegoš as Tragic hero of the Kosovo Idea). Andrić's last four books were published posthumously. They include: the short-story collection *Kuća no osami* (The House on Its Own) and the novel *Omerpaša Latas* (Omer Pasha, Latas), both published in 1976. The other two books were *Znakovi pored puta* (Signs by the Roadside) and *Sveske* (Notebooks). In conjunction with the revival of Andrić's work, which occurred after his death, a number of his stories including "Anikina vremena," were made into films during the 1980s and 1990s for theatrical distribution and television in Yugoslavia.

Books

Andrić, Ivo, *The Bridge on the Drina* translated by Lovett F. Edwards, Signet Books, 1960.

——, *Conversation with Goya/Bridges/Signs by the Roadside*, translated by Celia Hawkesworth and Andre Harvey, The Menard Press, 1992.

——, *Devil's Yard*, translated by Kenneth Johnstone, Grove Press, 1962.

Juričlć, Želimir B., *The Man and the Artist: Essays on Ivo Andrić*, University Press of America, 1986.

Online

"Biography of Ivo Andrić," http://www.ivoAndrić.org.yu/html/body_biography.html (January 5, 2004).
"Ivo Andrić (1892–1975)," http://kirjasto.sci.fi/Andrić.htm (January 5, 2004).
"Ivo Andrić—Biography," Nobel e-Museum, http://www.nobel.se/cgi-bin/print (January 4, 2004). □

Constance Applebee

English coach Constance Applebee (1873–1981) introduced field hockey to the United States. A native of England, Applebee became athletic director at Bryn Mawr College in Pennsylvania. Under her direction, the college's athletic program became a model for the rest of the country. She encouraged young women to compete in sports during a time when they were considered too fragile to participate in physical activities. Through her advocacy, the perception of women in sports changed forever.

Constance Mary Katherine Applebee was born in Chigwall, Essex, England, on June 4, 1873. She suffered from poor health as a child and was not allowed to attend school. Instead she was tutored at home by a cleric.

As Applebee grew older, she discovered that her health improved if she remained active. Women were considered too delicate to exercise at the time, but Applebee became convinced that physical activity could improve women's strength and overall health.

Applebee graduated from the British College of Physical Education. In 1901, at the age of 29, she traveled to the United States for a summer course in anthropometry (the measurement of the human body) at Harvard University. While she was there, she used makeshift equipment to demonstrate the sport of field hockey for her classmates. The women's sport had been very popular in England for some 20 years, but it was unknown in the United States, where women's fitness was largely confined to croquet, golf, and bicycling. Classmates were enthusiastic about the new sport and Harriet Ballintine, director of athletics at Vassar College, asked Applebee to remain in the United States and teach field hockey to American women students.

For the next two years Applebee traveled to Vassar, Smith, Wellesley, Mt. Holyoke, Radcliffe, and Bryn Mawr Colleges to demonstrate field hockey to women students. At first, she had trouble even finding equipment. She finally located 22 hockey sticks and a cricket ball in New York and carried it with her as she traveled from campus to campus. Thus began Applebee's 80-year career as a champion of field hockey and other women's sports.

Changed Perception of Women's Sports

Until Applebee introduced field hockey to American colleges, the only team sport for women was basketball, which had recently been introduced by Senda Berenson and quickly became the most popular women's sport.

Sports rules were modified for women because it was believed that the men's rules were too rough. For instance, in basketball, modified rules divided the court into three sections and players had to stay in their designated area to prevent overexertion. Also, players could not grab the ball from another player's hands and could only dribble three times before they were required to pass or shoot.

Women were introduced to basketball and other team sports in the nation's female colleges and seminaries. By the turn of the century, all colleges taught physical education. Initially, students competed on an intraclass and intramural basis. Faculty believed extramural competition would cause young women emotional and physical stress they could not handle.

While many women were enthusiastic about sports, they found it difficult to compete in the tight corsets and long skirts that were the fashion of the day. Janet Woolum quoted a turn-of-the-century athlete in *Outstanding Women Athletes: Who They Are and How They Influenced Sports in America:* "No girl would appear unless upholstered with a corset, a starched petticoat, a starched skirt, heavily button-trimmed blouse, a starched shirtwaist with long sleeves and cuff links, a high collar and four-in-hand necktie; a belt with silver buckle; and sneakers with large silk bows."

Applebee was one of several women who advocated a change in dress for women's athletics. She required participants to wear shorter skirts (6 inches from the ground). She suggested that petticoats be replaced with knickerbockers fastened at the knee. As women realized the advantages of more comfortable clothing in athletics, they began demanding changes to their everyday clothing as well.

Established Field Hockey Rules

By the turn of the century, when Applebee introduced field hockey, women's sports were beginning to gain acceptance and rules were being standardized. In 1901, Applebee co-founded the American Field Hockey Association to establish rules for the sport and promote it. Applebee worked with Senda Berenson, physical education director at Smith College, and Lucille Eaton Hill, physical education director at Wellesley. The three established rules of field hockey and promoted and monitored its play, just as Berenson had previously done for women's basketball.

In 1904, Applebee was named athletic director at Bryn Mawr College in Pennsylvania. Under her direction, the college's athletic program became a model for the rest of the country. She also founded the school's Department of Health. Applebee fought a continuous battle with people who believed women were too frail for participation in organized sports. She believed women could benefit from sports participation in the same way men did. In *Women in Sports: The Complete Book on the World's Greatest Female Athletes,* Joe Layden reports that Applebee told Bryn Mawr president M. Carey Thomas, "You want all these students to go out and do something in the world, to get the vote. What's the good of their having the vote if they're too ill to use it?"

Applebee founded 25 hockey teams and 50 basketball teams at Bryn Mawr. She also introduced water polo, track, tennis, swimming, fencing, archery, and badminton. She encouraged students to play hard at all levels. Applebee coached at Bryn Mawr until 1971 when she was 97. She was a stern coach, but her students loved her and affectionately called her "The Apple."

Applebee was involved in other campus activities as well. She trained students in dance and served as festival director of the school's Elizabethan May Day program. As director, she organized the event's plays and made sure hundreds of costumes were sewn. She was faculty advisor to the school's *College News* for five years. She negotiated a compromise among two rival religious groups and encouraged them to form a united Christian Association.

Applebee pulled back from her many campus activities between 1929 and 1936 when her devoted friend and secretary to the Department of Athletics and Gymnastics Mary Warren Taylor became ill. Applebee cared for her friend until her death in 1936.

Founded USFHA

Women's enthusiasm for field hockey spread beyond Bryn Mawr. By the 1920s, women in several colleges, high schools and junior high schools played field hockey. The sport also attracted some 50,000 club sports players. In 1922, Applebee saw a need for a new organization to promote the game and sponsor tournaments. She founded the United States Field Hockey Association (USFHA), which replaced the American Field Hockey Association. The USFHA promoted the game internationally, but did not recognize champions because Applebee believed such competition "might destroy the friendly atmosphere among players and nations," reported Karin Loewen Haag in *Women in World History*. The USFHA continues to preside over the sport to this day.

Applebee regularly traveled to her native England to coach field hockey teams there. In 1923, Applebee founded a field hockey camp called The Pocono Hockey Camp in Mt. Pocono, Pennsylvania. She recruited British players and coaches to teach the game to high school and college field hockey players, coaches, and physical education teachers. In 1923, she led a field hockey camp in Peru.

In 1922, Applebee founded *The Sportswoman*, the country's first magazine for women athletes. The magazine covered women's participation in field hockey, swimming, lacrosse, fencing, archery, skating, and bowling. She published the magazine for ten years.

Close Ties with England

Applebee became a naturalized American citizen but she maintained close ties to England, coaching teams in both countries. During World War II, travel to her native country was restricted. Applebee rallied the United States

Field Hockey Association to help her homeland during the Battle of Britain. She spearheaded a fundraising campaign to purchase an ambulance for her homeland. Her efforts were so successful that three ambulances were sent. Written on their doors was "Donated by the Women Hockey Players of the USA."

Applebee remained active as a hockey coach into her 90s. At age 94, during one of her annual visits to Britain, her doctor ordered her to stay because of failing eyesight. She moved to a cottage in Burley. At the end of her life, she was confined to an electric wheelchair, but continued to live alone and care for herself. She died on January 26, 1981, at the age of 107 in Burley, England.

Applebee was recognized many times for her contributions to women's athletics. She received a Distinguished Service Award from the American Association for Health, Physical Education and Recreation; was inducted into the College of William & Mary Hall of Fame; was an Honorary Life Member of the All-England Women's Hockey Association; and received the Award of Merit from the Association of Intercollegiate Athletics. She was also inducted into the U.S. Field Hockey Association Hall of Fame and the International Women's Sports Hall of Fame.

Books

Layden, Joe, *Women in Sports: The Complete Book on the World's Greatest Female Athletes*, General Publishing Group, 1997.

Women in World History: A Biographical Encyclopedia, edited by Anne Commire, Yorkin Publications, 1999.

Woolum, Janet, *Outstanding Women Athletes: Who They Are and How They Influenced Sports in America*, 2nd ed., Oryx Press, 1988.

Periodicals

New York Times, January 28, 1981.

Online

"Constance M.K. Applebee," *Biography Resource Center*, The Gale Group (November 8, 2003). □

Abbas Mahmud al-Aqqad

Egyptian Abbas Mahmud al-Aqqad (1889–1964) was a largely self-educated writer, historian, poet, philosopher, translator, and journalist. Known for his patriotism toward the country of his birth, he used his writing to spread his pro-democratic beliefs and was known as a leading innovator in 20th-century Arabic criticism and poetry. His biographies of 14 religious figures are perhaps his most famous works.

Born on June 28, 1889, in Aswan, Upper Egypt, al-Aqqad was the son of an archivist. He began attending the village *kuttab*, a religious preschool where the principal subjects were the Qu'ran and Arabic, at age six. Al-Aqqad advanced to a nearby elementary school in 1899, where he spent just four years; whether because of economic pressures or other factors, he then ended his formal education. That he went on to become an important figure in 20th-century intellectual life is testimony to his ambition, discipline, and natural talent. Historical records report that al-Aqqad was an avid reader in numerous fields.

Quit Government Work to Write Full Time

Al-Aqqad was hired, while still in his teens, to work in a government office, but resigned in 1906, at age 17, to dedicate himself to a writing career. He is said to have settled permanently in Cairo at that point, having until now lived and worked in various cities throughout Egypt. His first professional writing work was reportedly as a journalist; he became an editor with the newspapers *Al Doustour* (The Constitution) in 1907 and *Al Bayan* (The Clarification) in 1911 and in 1908 became the first Egyptian journalist to interview Saad Zaghloul, a nationalist leader who would one day become the country's prime minister. Al-Aqqad also wrote critical essays for a magazine called *Oukaz* in 1912.

First Literary Works Published

Al-Aqqad was perhaps driven to writing as a primary method of intellectual self-expression. One of the earliest themes of his written works was freedom of thought and expression, which were under constant threat from political and religious repressive forces in Egypt in the early 1900s. Although he worked as a writer for a living, he wrote during his spare time as well, and in 1915 he published his first *diwans,* or collections of poems, titled *Bits and Pieces* and *Shazarat.* The following year the 37-year-old al-Aqqad published *Yaqazat al-Sabah* (The Morning Awakening), a political commentary in poetic form, and *A Compound of the Living,* which discusses the issue of good versus evil. Also, as a philosopher, al-Aqqad crystallized his own strain of existentialism, which he would come to call "Universal Consciousness." According to al-Aqqad, this comprises the integration of the senses, reason, and spirituality.

During the 1920s al-Aqqad wrote a book called *A Daily Resume,* which was an autobiographical account of his experiences. He tried his hand at script writing in 1931, producing *The Song of the Heart,* which became the fourteenth film to be produced in Egypt. He began writing biographies of great thinkers and religious leaders, the work for which he remains best known, in 1932. In these biographical accounts al-Aqqad sought to identify the "key to greatness" within each of his subjects, among who were included Benjamin Franklin, Ibn Rushd, Saad Zaghlool, and Francis Bacon.

Outspokenness

As the repressive Egyptian political regime sought to tighten control, al-Aqqad was jailed for several months in 1930–1931 for defending parliamentary democracy in interviews he gave as a member of the House of Representatives. Also that year, he was appointed to the Arabic

Language Academy. In 1938 al-Aqqad wrote the novel *Sarah,* in which he related his experience with a woman— reportedly the only woman he ever loved. Mainly, however, the writer concentrated his efforts on poetry, believing that it was the best medium through which to express his emotions and broadcast his message about the importance of free speech.

In 1942 al-Aqqad began his famous 14-volume "geniuses" series on great historical religious figures, publishing *The Ingenuity of Christ, The Ingenuity of Abraham,* and *The Ingenuity of Mohamed* in quick succession. Next to his biographical series, these would be the most popular of all his publications. In addition, al-Aqqad completed a critical biography of the Arab poet ibn el Roumy that offers insight into that author's life, personality, and works. Also in 1942, he released one of his several studies on Islam, *The Arab Impact on European Civilization.*

Al-Aqqad's outspokenness in support of freedom of expression and his strong pro-democratic views extended also to his condemnation of German Chancellor Adolph Hitler as the Nazis expanded their control over Europe and the Middle East. In fact, the writer fled Egypt in 1942 as German troops advanced on his homeland, moving temporarily to Sudan to escape any retribution for his repeated criticism. His books on the subject include *Hitler in the Balance* and *Nazism and Religions.*

Historical documentation on al-Aqqad's life refers to "literary troubles" that began for him in 1944 and which reportedly center on his poetic works and perhaps refer to government efforts to silence the writer. The "troubles" were no doubt caused by his liberal views on literary criticism and freedom of speech. No doubt contributing to the strife was al-Aqqad's publication of his controversial *Allah or God* in 1947.

An Icon of Arab Culture

Beginning in the early 1950s, al-Aqqad established a salon in his home that met every Friday. Its participants, who included some of the leading Egyptian intellectuals and artists of the day, discussed literature, philosophy, science, history, and other subjects. One of the most contentious topics of the salon was the role of Muslim women in society. Al-Aqqad, who reportedly had great respect for women, wrote three books on the subject, insisting in each of them that women should have the right to participate fully in society, as opposed to the severely restricted role they were relegated to orthodox Islam. He argued that women should enjoy freedom of thought as well.

In 1954 al-Aqqad published a two-volume collection of his translations of world literature, including what he considered to be the best American short stories of the period. Two years later, he was appointed to the Egyptian Higher Council of Literature and the Arts. He released one of his 11 books of literary criticism, *An Introduction to Shakespeare,* in 1958, along with works titled *Eblees or the Devil* and *Poetic Language.*

Near the end of his life, critics hailed al-Aqqad as a "human encyclopedia" of modern Arab culture. He received the prestigious State Recognition Award in 1960 and published one of his last works, *The Diaries,* in 1963. Al-Aqqad died at age 85 on March 12, 1964, in Cairo, Egypt. In more recent years, many scholars have made his life and works the subject of in-depth study.

Online

"Abbas Mahmoud Al-Aqqad," *Egyptian State Information Service Web site,* http://www.sis.gov.eg/ (January 2, 2004). □

German Arciniegas

Colombian educator and historian German Arciniegas (1900–1999) was a noted intellectual and journalist whose criticism of Latin-American dictators forced him to live in exile in the United States for almost two decades beginning in the 1940s.

Educator, historian, and civil servant German Arciniegas represented his native Colombia as ambassador to several countries, while also serving in the Colombian Ministry of Education and as a member of the Colombian Parliament for three terms. The author of 1986's *America in Europe: A History of the New World in Reverse* and many other books, he promoted a non-Eurocentric view of world history in which the Americas played a positive role. Arciniegas also became a noted journalist and lived abroad from 1942 through 1960 because of his strong criticism of the military dictatorships then in power throughout Latin America.

Arciniegas was born in a rural area near Bogota, Colombia, on December 6, 1900, to dairy owners Rafael and Aurora (Angueyra) Arciniegas, and as a child he developed a great love for the countryside. He came from a long line of political agitators: his great grandfather, Pedro Figueredo, was executed by Spanish officials for leading a rebel Cuban force and penning that country's national anthem, "La Bayamesa." Columbia, at the time of Arciniegas's birth, was undergoing recurrent political turmoil, and the discussions of family and friends made the young man keenly aware of local and national politics. Fourteen years before Arciniegas's birth, in 1886, the Republic of Columbia had been established under a new constitution, but within a decade the nation found itself in a futile war against U.S.-backed insurgents who successfully liberated Panama from the republic during the War of a Thousand Days. By the time Arciniegas reached age two the war was over, and his childhood was spent working on his family's dairy farm in a nation where agriculture was the chief source of income.

Began Intellectual Pursuits

Despite the fact that the country was enjoying a period of relative peace following the War of a Thousand Days, during the early twentieth century Columbians retained a strong anti-U.S. sentiment as well as resentments against the Roman Catholic Church. Schooled in such views, Arciniegas began his studies at the Universidad Republi-

cana de Bogota, and, in the family tradition, he soon gained a reputation as an outspoken political liberal. In 1920 he enrolled in the law program at Bogota's Universidad Nacional, earning his LL.D. in 1924. While a law student Arciniegas continued to be a campus agitator, marching to protest Jesuit control of Columbia's schools and to protest various actions by the government that he viewed as oppressive. At one point, he was shot at and almost died while delivering a speech on a Bogota street. Two years later, in November of 1926, he married Gabriela Vieira, with whom he would have two daughters, Aurora and Gabriela Mercedes.

Joining the faculty of the Universidad Nacional in 1925, Arciniegas served as a professor of sociology from 1925 to 1928. He then left academia, joining the staff of Bogota newspaper *El Tiempo* as an editor in 1928. During law school he had already gained journalism experience through his founding of a political reformist campus newspaper; now he expanded that experience and became a voice for such activists as Victor Raul Haya de la Torre and others who sought to overhaul Colombia's unresponsive and unrepresentative political system. Two years later he left South America and relocated to England, working as *El Tiempo*'s London correspondent from 1930 through 1933. While in London he was also appointed vice-consul by the Columbian government, thereby beginning his civil service career. In 1933 Arciniegas was promoted to editor-in-chief of *El Tiempo,* becoming director in 1939. Leaving the paper later that same year after being offered a higher position within the government, he continued to contribute columns containing his analysis of local politics throughout the remainder of his life.

From 1930 to 1946, beginning with the administration of President Enrique Olaya, Columbia enjoyed a period of peace under a liberal republican administration. While progress had been made on many fronts, there was much work to do, as Arciniegas noted in his first published book, 1932's *El estudiante de la mesa redonda.* Due to his role as a prominent intellectual and political voice, the government of Colombia appointed Arciniegas charge d'affaires in Buenos Aires, Argentina, in 1939, and he was named minister of education in 1941. He remained in the ministry from 1941 to 1942, and again from 1945 to 1946, working to advance educational opportunities among Colombians of all social and economic classes. His friendships with thinkers such as John Dewey, Aldous Huxley, and John Dos Pasos greatly influenced his efforts to liberalize education amid poverty and inequality.

Rise of Militarism Prompted Exile

World War II found the country on the side of the Allies, and Columbia was among the 41 nations to join the United Nations in 1945. Unfortunately, the war years threw the country into turmoil, the violence spreading from the cities and college campuses into the countryside. Despite a Pan-American conference held in Bogota in April 1948, a military government was instituted under Jorge Eliecer Gaitan. Between 1953 and 1958 military juntas alternated power, but their power ended after the formation of a quasi-representative democracy under the National Front that was able to stabilize the government during the 1960s.

In 1942 Arciniegas left Colombia for the United States, serving as visiting professor at several schools, among them the University of Chicago; Mills College; the University of California, Berkeley; and Columbia University, where he taught in 1943 and again from 1948 to 1957. The desire to teach abroad soon became a necessity, as Arciniegas's outspoken writings condemning the increasing violence of the military governments not only in Columbia but also elsewhere in Latin America gave rise to concerns for his own safety. His book *Entre la libertad y el miedo,* published in ten editions beginning in 1952 and translated as *The State of Latin America,* chronicles the tortures, jailings, and oppression of military dictatorships, its author boldly stating: "The increasing withdrawal of representative forms of government in our America places us ever more outside the democratic world. Sixty million inhabitants live in ten nations where some or all of the rights consecrated in the charter of human rights are ignored." Not surprisingly, books such as *The State of Latin America* were banned and its author targeted by government officials. For much of the 1950s Arciniegas remained in exile in New York, writing constantly and maintaining a strong voice in that city's vibrant intellectual community.

Righted the Historical Record

Through his teaching and his journalism, Arciniegas dedicated his life to not only advancing civil rights, but also broadening the view of both Hispanics and Westerners about the role of the Americas. His efforts in this regard became well known in 1947, when he took umbrage at a series of writings by Italian historian Giovanni Papini. Papini argued that the efforts of European governments to settle the New World had resulted in failure; after all, many Western hemisphere governments were in turmoil, the region's countries were economically backward, and the Americas had produced no great talent on the order of Michelangelo or Beethoven. Papini's accusations crystallized Arciniegas's thought, and in a great wave of essays, columns, and speeches the Columbian historian argued that the value of the Americas was not in its institutions or its ability to foster exceptional individuals. Rather, it was in its ability to allow all men the freedom to advance in society and contribute in ways that would never be allowed in Europe. America's great wealth was the vision of individual men and women and each person's efforts to attain that vision unconstrained.

Arciniegas authored more than forty books, many of which were translated into English, beginning with *The Knight of the El Dorado: The Tale of Don Gonzalo Jiménez de Quesada and His Conquest of New Granada, Now Called Colombia,* which was published in 1939. Concerned over the Eurocentric approach taken by most historians when examining the role of Europeans and their role in the "New World," Arciniegas published several other biographies, among them *America magica: los hombres y los meses* and three books focusing on Simon Bolivar, including 1980's *Bolivar, de Cartagena a Santa Marta.* In these works, according to *Américas* contributor Steven Ambrus, Arciniegas hoped to educate the masses. He devised a "colorful history" combining fantasy and realism and "intended to instruct the everyday person in the distinctiveness of his past. He crafted a singular 'historical journalism,' which transports the reader into the eyes and minds of the fisherman, candle maker, or tailor of distinct epochs, honoring the common man as the hero of his own vast drama."

According to Barbara Mujica in *Americas,* in Arciniegas's view Latin America is "quintessentially Indian, not European. The Spanish veneer concealed a collective psyche . . . forged from centuries of proximity to nature. The Spanish language, Catholicism, private property, and Renaissance notions of selfhood were imported from abroad and imposed on the Indian populations, . . . but beneath the surface, Latin America was never 'Latin' at all." America allowed Europeans fleeing oppression a *tabula rasa* of sorts: a place to rework social structures, develop new forms of government, and flee racial and class restrictions in order to more fully develop human potential. Such freedoms allowed intellectual and artistic abilities full reign, the combination of Indian, African, and European peoples generating scientific, political, and social advances that would never have coalesced in Europe.

Arciniegas devoted much of his career to studying the Age of Exploration, and books such as 1955's *Americo and the New World: The Life and Times of Amerigo Vespucci* and 1941's *Germans in the Conquest of America* reflect this interest. His most well-known works encompass 1965's *El continente de siete colores: historia de la cultura en la*

America Latina and Biografia del Caribe, the latter a 1945 work translated as Caribbean, Sea of the New World that presents a colorful, inventive, and panoramic history of the region from Columbus's arrival through modern times. Other translated books include The State of Latin America and The Twilight of the Tyrants, which he wrote with John S. Knight in the mid-1970s. In 1944 he edited The Green Continent: A Comprehensive View of Latin America by Its Leading Writers, an anthology of essays by the region's leading twentieth-century intellectuals that has since been reprinted.

First published in 1975 as America en Europa, Arciniegas's America in Europe: A History of the New World in Reverse is considered among his best-known books. Released in an English translation completed with the help of the author's wife in 1986, the work reflects its author's multicultural world view. "Everything from the time of the revelation of America on back seems to us today as fictional as a novel, as mythical as a painting," he writes in the book's English translation. "With America, the modern world begins. Scientific progress begins, philosophy thrives. By means of America, Europe acquires a new dimension and emerges from its shadows." The book was praised by many reviewers, an Atlantic Monthly contributor dubbing it "impressively presented and impossible to ignore."

In 1959 Arciniegas assumed a series of ambassadorial positions. Arciniegas became ambassador to Italy from 1959 to 1962, to Israel from 1960 to 1962, to Venezuela from 1967 to 1970, and to the Vatican City from 1976 to 1978. Arciniegas balanced his journalism and ambassadorial duties with a political calling. He was elected a member of the Colombian Parliament for several terms: 1933–34, 1939–40, and 1957–58. In the realm of the arts, he also founded Bogota's Museo de Arte Colonial as a way to provide Colombians with a visual sense of their non-Western cultural heritage.

Even while teaching and working for the Colombian government, Arciniegas continued to speak out on political matters. He worked as director of the Paris-based Cuadernos from 1963 to 1965 and also wrote for France's Revue des Deux Mondes. His contributions to Americas, Cuadernos Americanos, La Republica, and Sur were considered insightful and enlightening, and despite his intellect he expressed himself in a manner that did not alienate the general reader. Arciniegas also served as director of the publishers Ediciones Colombia and as co-director of Revista de America.

Due to his contributions to Latin America's intellectual life, in 1947 Arciniegas was elected a correspondent to the Academia Española. Twenty years later, in 1967, he was awarded the Hammarsjkold Prize; he also received an honorary doctorate from Mills College. A member of the Academia Colombiana de la Lengua, he was also president of the Colombian Academy of History from 1980 until his death and was a corresponding member of the academy of letters in Cuba, Mexico, Spain, and Venezuela.

Returned to Academia

Retiring from his ambassadorship in 1978, Arciniegas moved back to the academic realm he had worked in five decades before. At Bogota's Universidad de los Andes, he joined the faculty of Philosophy and Letters as dean, a position he held for the remainder of his life. In addition to his academic position, he continued to write columns for El Tiempo as well as for Miami, Florida's Diario las Americas and Argentina's La Nación. Introductions and prologues to books by other Latin authors also took up much of Arciniegas's time.

Restricted by blindness during his final years, Arciniegas was nonetheless encouraged to see Colombia's economy stabilize and with it the country's government. The late 1980s brought the first popularly elected president in Columbia in Luis Carlos Gallant. Unfortunately, political advances were increasingly threatened by drug cartels and guerilla factions, and Arciniegas fought back in his columns. In July of 1991 he was able to write of a major success as the country's Constituent National Assembly created a new constitution ensuring fundamental liberties and rights to all Colombians. Ever vigilant, he remained outspoken about the United States' restrictive immigration policies and worked to inform the world about the ecological threat to the Amazon region.

Arciniegas died of lung failure on December 5, 1999, just one day before he would have celebrated his hundredth birthday, in Bogota. He died a widower, his wife, Gabriela, having passed away three years before. At his death he was remembered as one of the most inspired political reformists of his century, and his efforts to provide Latin Americans with a renewed respect for their contributions to world history continue to bear fruit. As Mujica noted of Arciniegas: "His passing signals the end of an epoch; his influence will be felt well into the future."

Books

Arciniegas, German, Memorias de un congresista, Editorial Cromos, 1933.
Cobo Borda, Juan Gustavo, Arciniegas de cuerpo entero, Planeta, 1987.
Cordova, Federico, Vida y obra de German Arciniegas, [Havana, Cuba], 1950.

Periodicals

Américas, May–June, 1997; April, 2000.
Atlantic Monthly, March 1986.
New York Times, December 5, 1999.
Times Literary Supplement, December 4, 1969; March 25, 1977.
□

Evelyn Ashford

Over a sixteen year period, American sprinter Evelyn Ashford (born 1957) won five Olympic medals. It is likely that she would have won more medals if the United States had not boycotted the 1980 Olympics

when she was in her prime. She participated in the Olympics in 1976, 1984, 1988, and 1992. She raced not only against seconds, but also against years, as she raced in her fourth Olympics at age 35.

Ashford was born on April 15, 1957, in Shreveport, Louisiana. Her father, Samuel Ashford, was a career Air Force man, and so the family, which also included a brother and three sisters, moved often, following him from post to post. Her mother, Vietta, told *People,* about her daughter, "She was a start-and-stop sort of child. She only had two speeds, either she was running full tilt or sitting quietly, reading."

When Ashford was a young adolescent, her father was sent to Vietnam to fight in the war, and the rest of the family moved to Athens, Alabama. Then, while Ashford was in high school, her father was stationed at McClellan Air Force Base, and the family moved to Roseville, California, where she attended Roseville High School. "My father was in the Air Force, so we moved around a lot, and my high school didn't have a girls' track team," she explained, according to Frederick C. Klein of the *Wall Street Journal.* "One day the football coach saw me running with the other girls in P.E. class and noticed I was fast. He got me to run against some of his players, to motivate them, I guess. I beat 'em all. Pretty soon, watching the boys try to run against Evelyn at lunch time was the thing to do for the rest of the kids." She regularly beat the school's star football running back in the

50-yard dash. Even competing against boys from other schools, she was winning. In 1975, she placed third in the Junior National Track Championships. She was one of the first women offered an athletic scholarship to the University of California at Los Angeles (UCLA) and she accepted.

Became Olympian

One of the coaches at UCLA, three-time Olympian Pat Connolly, took an interest in Ashford. One day, she asked Ashford to run the 100-yard dash. The time was so fast that Connolly thought she had made a mistake using the stopwatch and asked Ashford to run it again. She told Ashford that she had a good chance of making the 1976 United States Olympic Team. "I thought the lady was nuts," said Ashford, as reported in *A to Z of American Women in Sports.* Connolly helped Ashford develop her speed, as well as her self-esteem and belief in her ability to win. Ashford placed third at the Olympic trials and earned herself a spot on the team. At the Olympics, in Montreal, Canada, Ashford finished fifth in the 100-yard dash, beating her more experienced teammate Chandra Cheeseborough, as well as East German Marlies Gohr, who through the years would become a chief rival.

Ashford had quickly been drawn into the world of competitive sprinting, and after her taste of the Olympics, she wanted more. She wanted to win a gold medal. In 1977, she dominated, winning sprint titles in both collegiate and national women's competitions. Then, when she went to the Dusseldorf World Cup, she continued to beat the American sprinters but was beaten by other runners. Ashford felt humiliated and determined. She said, "I had to find out if I had what it took to become a true world class sprinter," reported *Great Athletes.*

In 1978, Ashford married Ray Washington, a basketball coach at San Jacinto College, and in 1979, she decided to leave UCLA and take a job at a Nike shoe store in order to concentrate on her athletic training. Connolly agreed to continue to coach her, even though she was no longer at UCLA. Ashford set the American record for the 100-meters at 10.97 seconds. At the 1979 Montreal World Cup, Ashford took the world by storm, beating her rival, Gohr, who was the current world record holder and favorite to win, in the 100-meter race. She also beat another rival, Marita Koch, in the 200-meter race, with a time of 21.83 seconds. This established her as the favorite to win the 100-meter race at the 1980 Olympics in Moscow in the Soviet Union.

Olympic Dream Catastrophe

Politics shattered Ashfrod's world. The Soviet Union invaded Afghanistan, and in protest, United States President Jimmy Carter and the Unites States Olympic Committee (USOC) announced that the United States athletes would not be attending the Moscow Olympics. Over 50 other countries also participated in the boycott. Ashford was devastated—she had trained so hard. She was in prime condition and she was so upset that she considered leaving the sport. Ashford also suffered an injury, so she ran very little in 1980. That summer, she and her husband, Washington, went on a car trip across the United States. Ashford used the time to re-evaluate her career and determine what her goals were. By the end of the trip, she had made some decisions. She would continue to train with the hopes of attaining two gold medals in the 1984 Olympics. She also decided to have her husband become her head coach.

Her determination to succeed showed in her successes. In 1981, she won the 100-meter and the 200-meter events at the World Cup. At the National Sports Festival in Colorado Springs, Colorado, in 1983, Ashford ran in the 100-meters. "I wasn't thinking about anything; I just ran," she said in *Sports Illustrated* reported by Kenny Moore. "I didn't seem to wake up until the last 20 meters. When I crossed the line, I thought, 'That was nothing special. Maybe 11.1.'" But it was something special. Ashford had set a world record in 10.79 seconds. When she heard the time, she was very surprised, "I'm stunned," she said. "Just stunned . . . stunned." Colorado Springs is at 7,200 feet above sea level, providing slightly less air resistance. "Hey, it was a world record," she replied when asked about the air. "Nobody ever got through 100 meters faster. I finally got perfect conditions; I realize that. A pretty day, nice mountains, nice people. Sure, altitude helps. I can't deny that my two best times were done up here [her previous American record of 10.90 was set in Colorado Springs at the Olympic Training Center two years earlier], but I can run as well at low altitude." In 1984, she was chosen as Athlete of the Year.

Olympic Gold

During the quarterfinals in the 100-meter dash at the 1984 Olympic trials, Ashford felt a pull in her leg with only ten minutes before the gun would go off for the start of the race. Worried about possible injury, she went to the trainer's tent where her leg was taped in a rush. She had to place in the top three in order to make the cut onto the team. The gun went off, and Ashford raced to a third place finish, making the team despite her injury. She went on to become the fastest woman in the world; winning two gold medals at the Los Angeles Olympics. First, she raced in the 100-meters. "I didn't feel that much in control," she reportedly said in the August 13, 1984, edition of *Sports Illustrated.* "I felt that my legs were moving too fast for my body." She won with an Olympic Record of 10.97. As Ashford stood on the platform to receive her first gold medal, she burst into tears of joy and relief. She had worked long and hard to get there. "The response in the Olympic stadium today tells me that I'm very much appreciated. Running fast and being good at what I do are reward enough for me right now," she said in *Sports Illustrated.* The other gold medal was for racing as part of the 4x100 relay team, which also included Alice Brown, Jeanette Bolden, and Chandra Cheeseborough. The only thing that could have made the experience better for Ashford was if she were racing against some of her toughest rivals. In 1984, the Soviet Union and 13 communist allies boycotted the Olympics, so Ashford had not yet had an Olympic competition against some of her toughest opponents. However, later in the year, Ashford beat Gohr with a world record time of 10.76.

Then, Ashford took some time off to have a baby. Raina Ashley Washington was born on May 30, 1985. It was Ashford's first time off from racing in a long time, and she took advantage of it. "I slept late, watched the soap operas and ate what I wanted," she told the *Wall Street Journal.* "I gained 40 pounds while I was having my baby." A month after the birth, Ashford was back to training, and in 1986, she won the 55-meter dash in the Vitalis Olympic Invitational in 6.6 seconds.

Training continued to pay off, and in 1988, she won another gold in the 4x100 meter relay. However, Florence Griffith Joyner edged her out of the race for gold in the 100-meter dash, and she accepted the silver medal. At the time, she was one of only three women to win three Olympic gold medals, sharing the honor with Wyomia Tyus and Wilma Rudolph.

Defied Age

Amazingly, after 12 years of Olympic competition, Ashford did not stop. Her body did not seem aware that it was supposed to age. Ashford placed third at the qualifying trials for the 1992 Olympic team, granting her a ticket to her fourth Olympics. "I don't know about you guys, but I'm excited!" Ashford told the press, as reported in *Runners World.* "I'm 35. I'm not supposed to be running like this." She was honored by her teammates by being chosen to carry the United States flag in the Olympic opening ceremonies. Ashford went on to participate in the 1992 Olympics in Barcelona, Spain, and at age 35, she won her final gold medal, again in the 4x100 relay.

Following the Barcelona Olympics, Ashford retired from sprinting after 16 years of Olympic competition. She worked occasionally as a television commentator and served as a co-chairperson of Athletes for Literacy.

In 1989, the Flo Hyman Award was presented to Ashford in one of President George H. W. Bush's first official receptions as president in conjunction with the third annual National Girls and Women in Sports Day, sponsored by the Women's Sports Foundation. The award is named for Flo Hyman, an Olympic volleyball star, who worked to develop Title IX, a bill that forbids sexual discrimination in educational institutions. Ashford spoke at a luncheon on Capital Hill in conjunction with receiving the award. "I'm a product of Title IX," she said, according to the *Washington Post.* "Because Title IX had passed, they had to let me run on the boys track team. Because of that, I was able to go to college." She also used her time at the podium to denounce the rampant use of drugs and steroids among track and field competitors. Ashford has inspired many people with her determination and enthusiasm, and in 1997, she was named to the International Women's Hall of Fame.

Books

Edelson, Paula, *A to Z of American Women in Sports,* Facts on File, Inc., 2002.
Great Athletes, Salem Press/Magill Books, 2001.
Molzahn, Arlene Bourgeois, *Top 10 American Women Sprinters,* Enslow Publishers, Inc., 1998.
Plowden, Martha Ward, *Olympic Black Women,* Pelican Publishing Company, 1996.

Periodicals

People, August 6, 1984.
Runner's World, September 1992.
Sports Illustrated, July 11, 1983; August 13, 1984.
Wall Street Journal, February 7, 1986.
Washington Post, February 2, 1989; February 3, 1989. □

Mary Astell

**British writer Mary Astell (1666–1731) is considered
one of the first British feminists. A devout Christian
who possessed strong reasoning skills and an interest
in philosophy, Astell set forth her thoughts upon the
inequities of the "woman's sphere" in such works as
1697's *A Serious Proposal to the Ladies* and *Some
Reflections upon Marriage,* the latter published in
1700.**

Although she was not of high birth, Astell gained the
learning and skill to match wits, in print, with some
of the intellects of her age. In addition to expressing
her conservative opinion regarding political and theological
matters in a published forum, Astell also gained a popular
following through her writings on the status of women. In *A
Serious Proposal to the Ladies* she reflects on the education
of women, while *Some Reflections upon Marriage* exhorts
women to make marriage matches based on reason rather
than necessity.

Rendered Unmarriageable by Family Setback

Astell was born on November 12, 1666, in the English
coal-mining town of Newcastle on Tyne. The daughter of
Peter and Mary (Errington) Astell, she grew up in a strict
Anglican household, despite the fact that her mother had
been raised a Catholic. Although her Tory family was of the
middle class, Astell did not attend school; instead, she was
taught at home, at first by her uncle, Ralph Astell. A clergyman loyal to the crown who was heavily involved in Newcastle's St. Nicholas Church, Ralph Astell was also a
Neoplatonist–a member of the Cambridge-based philosophical school that espoused a rationalist belief system
centering around the teachings of Aristotle, Plato, and
Pythagoras–and he inspired his young niece through his
intellectually challenging instruction. Unfortunately, Ralph
Astell died when Mary was thirteen, leaving her on her own
in pursuit of further education. During her teenage years she
continued to read in many subjects, kept abreast of the
political debates of the day, and began an in-depth study of
political philosophy.

Ralph Astell's death was not the first setback young
Astell faced; the previous year, in March of 1678, her father
had died, leaving the girl in the care of her widowed
mother. Mrs. Astell moved with her daughter and son Peter
to the home of Mary's aunt, thus allowing the family to

avoid poverty. Still, finances were severely constrained
from this point on, particularly after Mrs. Astell's widow's
pension was curtailed in 1679. Such circumstances made it
unlikely that Mary would be a suitable wife for someone of
her social class, as her dowry prospects were dim. Perhaps it
was this knowledge that spurred the intelligent young
woman's interest in intellectual pursuits.

In early October of 1684 Astell's mother died, and
within a few years Mary moved to the Chelsea district of
London. A relatively rural suburb, Chelsea was home to
many artists and intellectuals, as well as to wealthy families
who sought to escape the stress and grime of the city. By
1688 the 22-year-old Astell had fallen on hard times, but
she rallied with the help of the Archbishop of Canterbury.
Fortunately for Astell, she was also befriended by Lady
Catherine Jones, who introduced the budding intellectual to
many in her educated and high-born social circle. The pious
Astell proved to be a charming companion whose well-
reasoned, challenging conversation made her popular, and
she collected a number of friends whose discussions helped
her to hone her thoughts regarding philosophy and the
status of women in society. Lady Elizabeth Hastings, Lady
Ann Coventry, Elizabeth Thomas, Lady Mary Chudleigh,
and Lady Mary Wortley Montagu numbered among Astell's
friends, patrons, and admirers.

Gained Respect as Intellectual Despite Gender

The close of the 1600s brought to an end a tumultuous
century that had witnessed civil war, the subsequent Protectorate of Oliver and Richard Cromwell, the restoration of the
monarchy under King Charles in 1660, and the Glorious
Revolution of 1688 that removed unpopular Stuart monarch
James II and brought William of Orange and Queen Mary to
the English throne. Despite such political upheaval, little
had changed regarding the political or social status of
women. In an era where the ideas of political philosophers
Thomas Hobbes and John Locke were causing intellectual
foment, Astell provided a voice for intellectually engaged
women and, through her outspokenness and persuasive
writings, gained a significant following among other members of her sex. However, she did not limit herself to issues
relevant to women; her passion lay in critiquing contemporary theories according to her rational Platonist world view.
Beginning in September of 1693, she exchanged several
letters with Cambridge scholar Reverend John Norris, and
this year-long exchange was published in 1695 as *Letters
Concerning the Love of God, Between the Author of the
Proposal to the Ladies and Mr. John Norris. Wherein His
Late Discourse Shewing That It Ought to Be Intire and
Exclusive of All Other Loves, Is Further Cleared and Justified.* Dedicated to Lady Catherine Jones, the volume provides clear evidence of Astell's insight and analytical ability
as she takes issue with fellow Platonist Norris over his arguments relating to the role of pain in God's plan. Norris,
while surprised that a woman would argue so forcefully,
graciously acknowledged Astell's points and ultimately
modified his *Practical Discourses upon Several Divine
Subjects.*

Although Astell went on to publish such works as 1703's pro-royalist *An Impartial Inquiry into the Causes of Rebellion and Civil War in This Kingdom* as well as a barbed attack on Daniel Defoe titled *A Fair Way with the Dissenters and Their Patrons. Not Writ by Mr. L—y, or any Other Furious Jacobite Whether Clergyman or Layman; But by a Very Moderate Person and Dutiful Subject to the Queen* in 1704, she remains best known for her feminist writings. *A Serious Proposal to the Ladies for the Advancement of Their True and Greatest Interest. By a Lover of Her Sex* was printed by London publisher Richard Wilkin in 1694, and *Some Reflections upon Marriage* followed six years later, when its author was in her mid-thirties. As was the case with all her writings, Astell never published under her own name; instead her works appeared either anonymously or under the pseudonyms Tom Single or Mr. Wooton.

In *A Serious Proposal to the Ladies* Astell addresses herself directly to women readers, encouraging them to study and gain knowledge in order to better serve God and be more productive friends and companions to their husbands and families. As a means to this end she outlines a detailed plan for a religious community of women. Astell maintains that the seventeenth-century system of education relegates women to a state of ignorance in which they are "Tulips in a Garden," useful only "to make a fine show and be good for nothing."

In 1687 she expanded upon her first book by publishing *A Serious Proposal to the Ladies, Part II. Wherein a Method Is Offer'd for the Improvement of Their Minds.* In this work—her most popular tract—Astell provides detailed instructions on how to develop logic and clarity of thought. In true Neoplatonist fashion, she argues that one should evaluate all issues in an organized, rational manner, beginning with basic assumptions and moving from there to more complex issues, and accepting as truth nothing that cannot be proven or otherwise objectively demonstrated.

Advocated Women's Intellectual Advancement

The belief that not only men but also all women can master clarity of thought is an important element in the most reactionary of Astell's writings, *Some Reflections upon Marriage, Occasion'd by the Duke and Duchess of Mazarine's Case,* published in 1700. Written in response to witnessing the divorce of a friend of Lady Catharine Jones, this work argues that a sound education is a requirement for any woman wishing to enter a healthy marriage. In addition to criticizing men who marry for money, power, or out of the vain desire to display an attractive wife, Astell paints marriage as an unhealthy state for most women, and therefore a state sought only by the irrational: "A Woman has no mighty Obligations to the Man who makes Love to her; she has no Reason to be fond of being a Wife, or to reckon it a Piece of Preferment when she is taken to be a Man's Upper-Servant; it is no Advantage to her in this World; if rightly managed it may prove one as to the next." While economic necessity and social constraints might force a woman into such an injurious institution as marriage, according to Astell

a sound education would arm her with the skills necessary to turn the situation to her favor.

In 1706 Astell released a third edition of *Some Reflections upon Marriage,* responding to critics of her work and urging England's womenfolk to strive for a marriage based on true friendship rather than necessity or pride. "Let us learn to pride ourselves in something more excellent than the invention of a Fashion," she counsels readers, "and not entertain such a degrading thought of our own worth as to imagine that . . . the best improvement we can make of these is to attract the Eyes of men." In the Appendix of this work is her most-quoted line among feminists: "If all men are born free, how is it that women are born slaves? as they must be if the being subjected to the inconstant, uncertain, unknown, arbitrary Will of Men, be the perfect Condition of Slavery?"

Perhaps because it was not overtly defiant of male authority, *A Serious Proposal to the Ladies* was immensely popular among women readers, and through its wide circulation Astell won many fans. Perhaps not surprisingly, it also won its share of detractors. In June and again in September of 1709 the popular *Tatler* included essays by writers Jonathan Swift and Richard Steele that attacked Astell's idea of a women's school. Dubbing Astell "Madonella," the essays satirized her so-called "Order of Platonics" by imagining this order of reclusive, fragile nuns hiding while their nunnery is rudely entered by a group of rough gentlemen. Flattering Madonella by praising her writing skill, the men gain mastery over the situation; in short, they hold these educated women to their "inconstant, uncertain, unknown, arbitrary Will."

The proposal for a quasi-religious college for women that Astell first outlined in *A Serious Proposal to the Ladies* was revived in *The Christian Religion as Profess'd by a Daughter of the Church of England,* a plea for furthering women's education that was addressed to England's Queen Ann, who had taken the throne in 1702. Although because of this work the school was reported to have been at least considered by Anne, it never came to fruition due to rumors by Anne's Protestant advisors that it would result in the reestablishment of Catholic nunneries. After 1709, perhaps partially in response to the ridiculing she received in the *Tatler,* Astell ceased writing. Her last published book was a revised edition of *Bart'lemy Fair; or, an Enquiry after Wit; In Which Due Respect Is Had to a Letter concerning Enthusiasm,* which appeared in 1722. Now in middle age, Astell refocused her attention toward opening a charity school. With the help of her patrons, she succeeded, and a school for girls was established at London's Chelsea Hospital that remained operational until the late 1800s. Ultimately succumbing to breast cancer, Astell died on May 9, 1731, at the age of sixty-four in Chelsea, England.

Books

Dictionary of Literary Biography, Volume 252: British Philosophers, 1500–1799, Gale, 2001.

Feminist Writers, edited by Pamela Kester-Shelton, St. James Press, 1996.

Ferguson, Moira, *First Feminists: British Women Writers 1578–1799,* University of Indiana Press, 1985.

Fraser, Antonia, *The Weaker Vessel,* Knopf, 1984.
Perry, Ruth, *The Celebrated Mary Astell: An Early English Feminist,* University of Chicago Press, 1986.
Smith, Florence M., *Mary Astell,* Columbia University Press, 1916.

Periodicals

Eighteenth-Century Studies, Summer 1985.
Journal of British Studies, Autumn 1979.
Political Science Review, September 1995. □

B

Meher Baba

Generally known by the name of Meher Baba or The Awakener, Indian mystic Merwan Sheriar Irani (1894–1969) attracted many followers around the world throughout his lifetime. "Baba-lovers," as they are known, believe that Meher Baba (along with Jesus Christ, Buddha, Mohammed, Krishna, and Zoroaster) was the Avatar, an extraordinary soul who periodically takes a human form as the incarnation of God.

Ordinary Beginnings

The son of Persians, Meher Baba was born on February 25, 1894, in Poona, Maharashtra, India. As fervent Zoroastrians, his parents centered their spiritual life around the Avesta, which describes the religious system founded by Zoroaster and espouses the worship of Ahura Mazda in the context of a universal struggle between the forces of darkness and light. In fact, Baba's father had been a wandering Sufi dervish—the equivalent of a monk—in his younger years and had only been persuaded by "a voice" to return to his home in Poona, where he would find a wife and bear a child. This child, he was told, would "complete his search for God." He continued to live as an ascetic for another decade, until 1883, when he announced that he would marry the then-five-year-old Shireen. Her parents permitted the girl to marry Irani when she was 14 and he was 39. He would later run a teashop in Poona.

Despite their religious beliefs, the Iranis (a common surname of the period meaning "from Iran") sent their son to St. Vincent's High School, a Jesuit Catholic school in Poona. Beginning in 1911, Baba attended Poona's Deccan College.

Accounts of his early life suggest that Baba led a happy, active and normal childhood. His mother, Shireen, who had one other son, called Baba her "most beautiful child," and, when he was a little older, friends nicknamed the charismatic young man "Electricity." He reportedly had an interest in mystical topics and the occult from an early age, although he also enjoyed sports such as cricket. In college, Baba became a talented musician and poet and enjoyed reading Shakespeare, Shelley, and Wordsworth, as well as Sufi poets such as Hafiz.

A Momentous Event

Baba's life is said to have changed abruptly in 1913, when at the age of 19 he was bicycling to his classes at college and felt compelled to stop and sit with an old woman who was a fixture in Poona. Named Hazrat Babajan, the Mohammedan woman lived under a neem tree and was thought to be at least 100 years old. She was also believed to be one of the five *Sadgurus* (Perfect Masters of the Age), those beings who are responsible for the birth of the Avatar ("first soul" or "ancient one") in each Avataric age. The day they met, she briefly embraced Baba and sat with him for a time silently.

After a number of such meetings, one night in January 1914 she kissed Baba on the forehead, thereby transferring to him what he later termed "God-realization," or the knowledge that he was the Avatar. This state of being, Baba later explained, was a permanent one which consisted of a

continuous experience of infinite bliss, knowledge, and power.

The awareness of his true identity caused Baba to appear to lose his mind. Much to his family's and friends' dismay, he stopped eating and sleeping and wandered randomly throughout the area. Baba's parents took him to doctors and put him on medications, but despite their efforts the young man spent most of his time sitting and staring. During this period he was reportedly led to each of the other four Perfect Masters. Mrs. Irani even went to Babajan to see what she had done to her son. The old woman merely told the distraught mother that Baba was not insane but that he "was destined to shake the world into wakefulness." Meanwhile, as he later recalled, Baba was completely involved in "experiencing God" and was so unconscious of the world that he kept a stone in his room to knock his head against in order to bring an awareness of his surroundings to his mind.

As legend has it, after nine months Baba began sleeping and eating again. He offered to teach Persian to a friend, Behramji, who became Baba's first disciple. In April 1915, Baba announced that he would be traveling for a time, and—although he was still considered insane by most—he departed Poona for the first time.

Then Baba was guided to another Perfect Master in Kedgaon, Narayan Maharaj, who did "spiritual work" with him and helped him back to "more normal consciousness." Baba then returned to Poona for some time but ventured forth again to seek out the third Perfect Master, Tajuddin Baba, who helped him become more aware of his divine

nature. In December 1915 Baba met the fourth Perfect Master, Sai Baba, who lived in Shirdi and who reportedly exclaimed *Parvardigar!* ("God Almighty Sustainer!") upon seeing Baba. Sai Baba sent Baba on to the fifth Perfect Master, a hermit named Upasni Maharaj, who threw a rock at the approaching man that hit him exactly where Hazrat Babajan had once kissed him on the forehead. Upon sustaining this blow, Baba reportedly became even more aware of his divine purpose.

Returned to Everyday Life

From 1915 to approximately 1922, Baba held a series of jobs, including managing a theater and working in his father's tea shop. The elder Irani decided to sell alcohol at one point to improve business, but his son frequently chastised customers to quit drinking. Eventually, Baba and Behramji took over the shop, but their mismanagement of it combined with the Noncooperation Movement (a civilian protest against goods made in Britain) soon forced them to close the business.

Meanwhile, Baba was working with Upasni Maharaj to integrate his consciousness of God with everyday human existence. At the end of 1921, Upasni was so impressed with Baba's progress that he declared him to be a Perfect Master as well as the Avatar. In 1922, Baba began to attract a small group of dedicated followers who began to call him "Meher Baba," or "Compassionate Father." Although his disciples considered him to be a Perfect Master and some even began to call him a messiah, Baba did not openly state what he believed to be his destiny. In the next several years, people from all over India came to see him as word spread of his presence, and eventually he announced to his growing body of followers, "I am infinite power, knowledge and bliss. I am the Ancient One, come to redeem the modern world."

Established as Spiritual Leader

Baba next established an ashram (the secluded residence of a guru and his or her religious community) in Bombay (now Mumbai) named Manzil-e-Meem (House of the Master). There, he trained his disciples. He insisted that his followers live under strict discipline, giving up "selfish thoughts" and all possessions, as well as obeying Baba in all matters. The ashram dissolved in about 1923, and Baba relocated with his most dedicated followers, the *mandali*, to another ashram in Arangaon, outside Ahmednagar.

In 1923–1924, Baba fasted, traveled around India, and held spiritual discussions. The new ashram was named Meherabad after its leader, and under its guru's watchful eye, an entire city developed there by 1925, complete with a post office, free school, and free hospital. Because many people of all different backgrounds lived there, getting the community to run smoothly was especially challenging in such a religion- and caste-conscious society. Nevertheless, Meherabad would become Baba's spiritual base.

Began Decades of Silence

On July 10, 1925, Baba began what he initially said would be a short period of silence "to save mankind from monumental ignorance." The leader assured his followers that he would end his silence when "suffering on earth was at its height" and would be linked to "the universal awareness of God on earth." His controversial silence would last 44 years—for the remainder of his long life.

At the beginning of his vow of silence, Baba would communicate through writing and promised that he would soon speak again. He and his *mandali* fasted and worked intensively together. Meanwhile, Baba began writing a book of spiritual thoughts. It would never be published. In 1927, he began using an alphabet board to communicate and also established a school for boys of all religions and castes to teach them secular and spiritual subjects. The school closed in 1929.

Introduced to the West

By 1930, news of Baba had begun to reach the West. He traveled to England in 1931 and 1932, meeting there with Indian political and spiritual leader Mahatma Gandhi. Baba gave many interviews to curious reporters, and when asked if he was the Messiah did not deny that the salvation of mankind was his purpose. In one of these interviews, he reportedly declared, "I have not come to establish any cult, society, or organization, nor to establish a new religion. The religion I shall give teaches the knowledge of the One behind the many." He also spoke of a book that he would write that would hold "the key to the mystery of life." His claims prompted contempt, hostility, and amusement, and many skeptics called him a false prophet. Baba refused demands to perform miracles, saying that the only miracles he could cause were the "awakening of the heart" and the breaking of his silence.

Baba visited the United States in 1932, where he was especially well received in Hollywood. Top celebrities of the day, including Douglas Fairbanks, Tallulah Bankhead, and Mary Pickford, attended a large reception there for him. From 1932 to 1936, Baba traveled to Europe and Asia several times. Beginning in 1936, he initiated a campaign to gather together all of the *mast-Allah* ("God-intoxicated ones") that he and his disciples could find. (According to Baba's accounts, these individuals appear insane but are actually in such blissful states that they cannot relate to the everyday world in any meaningful way. He believed that these people are found only in Eastern countries.) Baba set up special ashrams for the *masts,* as he called them, where he personally bathed, fed, and clothed them.

Near the end of the 1930s, Baba founded a new ashram in Nasik, India, for his Western followers. The discipline there was much less rigorous and had more Western-style conveniences than the ashram at Meherabad. Apparently the most difficult aspect of life there was learning to get along with other Baba devotees, but the guru preached, "If you cannot love each other, then learn to give in."

Baba divided his time among the *mast* ashrams and the Nasik ashram until 1941, when he shut down all but the Meherabad group because of Word War II. However, he continued with his search for *masts* throughout India until 1948.

Start of "New Life"

In 1949, Baba shocked and dismayed his followers by announcing that he would immediately begin a "new life," saying that all his ashrams except Meherabad would be closed down or would have to operate without his guidance. Baba said that from this point on he would "rely solely upon God" and would renounce his role of Perfect Master, instead calling himself a common man, or Perfect Seeker. He permitted only a few of his closest devotees to remain with him as he entered this phase of his life, which he said comprised "complete renunciation of falsehood, lies, hatred, greed, and lust" and which would "live by itself eternally, even if there is no one to live it."

Baba and his small circle of followers began to wander throughout Nepal and India in what would become a severe test of their devotion. Baba personally bathed lepers, washed the feet of many poor people, and handed out grain and clothing to the needy. He called his existence during this period "Helplessness and Hopelessness," but insisted that his followers "wholeheartedly face all hardships with 100 percent cheerfulness." After several years of this strict regimen, Baba secluded himself in order to achieve *mano-nash,* or "annihilation of the mind," saying, "We must lose ourselves to find ourselves. . . . We must die to self to live in God; thus death means life. . . . Being is dying by loving."

"Fiery Free Life"

In 1952 Baba entered a new phase of his life that he called the "Fiery Free Life." The goal of this period, he said, was to "dissolve the bindings of every soul, and establish to the world that everyone and everything is one with God." Later that year, he announced publicly for the first time that he was the Messiah. . .God in human form. Baba said that injuries he sustained in automobile accidents in 1952 and 1956 were the modern equivalent of the physical traumas suffered by the world's great spiritual leaders. He proclaimed that his "physical bones were broken so as to break the backbone of the material aspect of the machine age, while keeping intact its spiritual aspect." By now, thousands of worshippers, sometimes as many as 100,000 in one day, were traveling from all over India just to see Baba from a distance.

In 1954, Baba had stopped using the alphabet board and was communicating with his closest subjects using their sign language. By then, he had dictated his 1954 book *God Speaks* using the English-alphabet board. Starting in 1957, he held many *darshan* (divine blessings or viewings), one of which united his Eastern and Western followers for the first time. A year later, his *mandali* issued "Meher Baba's Universal Message," which comprised all the leader's sayings and teachings that they had gathered together. In it, Baba pronounced, "I have not come to teach, but to awaken. . . . Because man has been deaf to the principles and precepts laid down by God in the past, in this present Avataric Form I observe silence. . . . My present [form] is the last Incarnation of the cycle of time. Hence, my manifestation will be the greatest. When I break my silence, the impact of my love will be universal and all life in creation will know, feel, and receive of it. . . . I had to come, and I have come. I am the Ancient One."

Baba's last trip to the United States was in 1958, when he visited the Meher Spiritual Center in Myrtle Beach, South Carolina. The center had been established to study his teachings. Baba's popularity surged in the 1960s with the rise of the hippie culture in the United States and Australia. Young people experimenting with drugs were especially attracted to the leader, but when Baba sternly warned against the dangers of drug use, these followers left him in droves. However, many devotees felt even more strongly attached to him because of this message. It was also around this time that Baba is credited with coining the now popular phrase, "Don't worry, be happy."

Seclusion Again

Baba went into strict seclusion again in 1967 despite strong demands from his audience. Only a select few of his closest associates were permitted to see him during this phase, which he said was part of his "universal work," the results of which would be "intensely felt by all the people of the world." He pledged that he would give a public *darshan* in 1969, although the 75-year-old Baba's health was quickly declining.

By January 1969, the guru was reportedly in chronic major pain from a hip that he had broken in one of the automobile accidents in the 1950s, but he announced that he had finished his "universal work." On January 31, 1969, in Pimplegaon, India, to the great dismay of his many followers, Baba died without breaking his long silence, only signing to a disciple the message "Do not forget that I am God." Over the following week, mourners came from all over the world to pass through Baba's tomb prior to his burial in Meherabad. From April through June 1969, his followers carried out the final *darshan* that their leader had promised. Thousands attended the ceremonies in Poona and at Baba's tomb.

After his death, Baba retained a strong following all over the world. Baba-lovers observe "Silence Day" every year on July 10, and dozens of Internet sites are dedicated to disseminating information by and about him. Pilgrims continued to frequent several sites at which Baba's spirit is thought to be especially strong: the ashram at Meherabad, Avatar's Abode in Australia, Meher Mount in California and the Meher Spiritual Center.

Online

"The Life of Meher Baba," *The Northern California Meher Baba Center,* http://www.meherbabameherbaba.org (December 16, 2003).

"Meher Baba," *Meta-Religion,* http://www.met-religion.com (December 16, 2003).

"Meher Baba," *Wikipedia,* http://en2.wikipedia.org (December 16, 2003).

"Meher Baba, Avatar of the Age, Biography," *Avatar Meher Baba,* http://www.avatarmeherbaba.org (December 16, 2003). □

Ban Zhao

The first female Chinese historian, Ban Zhao (c. 45–120) wrote *Nu Jie* (Lessons for Women), a treatise on how women of the period should behave, which became central to the Chinese gender system for two millennia. The book made Ban one of the most respected female authors in China until social mores changed dramatically in the 20th Century.

Prominent Literary Parents

Ban Zhao was born in the town of An-ling, Ku-Fang Province, China, around the year 45. (The town is now the city of Hsien-yang, and the province has been renamed Shensi.) She had two brothers, Ban Gu and Ban Chao, both of whom were at least 13 years older than her and who would go on to become famous in different areas.

Her father, Ban Biao, was a noted scholar and an administrator of the extensive and powerful Ban family, who traced their lineage back to the time of Confucius (551–479 B.C.). He spent much of his time working on the *Han shu (History of the Han),* a history of the first 200 years of the Han Dynasty. Her mother and great-aunt, Ban Jieyu, were highly educated women and literary figures.

Ban's parents hired well-known tutors to educate their daughter, who at an early age demonstrated a love for reading. She was taught both Confucianism (the hierarchy- and order-based system that had recently come into favor and that would remain the dominant value system of China and its people for the next 2,000 years) and the more traditional Chinese belief system of Taoism, which stresses man's place within nature.

Born at a time of great reform in China, Ban was witness to and participated in the early days of the replacement of the ancient feudal system with the imperial system. Powerful families with thousands of acres of land had ruled the country for many eras, but over several centuries they gradually yielded to government centered in the imperial court. The Han court had adopted Confucianism as its central value system. Ban was fortunate that the Han court's interpretation of Confucianism was far more liberal during her lifetime than it was later,when it became more rigidly codified.

In Chinese feudal society, women had often been powerful influences in politics and sometimes even rulers. Later on, women became distinctly inferior to men in the eyes of Confucians, who believed the father or husband was the absolute authority in the family and the core of Chinese society. However, the new system was beneficial because, unlike feudalism, it provided a degree of social mobility. Those with ambition and sufficient leisure time to study, mainly men could rise through the system by proving their knowledge. Learning and scholarly accomplishment were handsomely rewarded under the Confucian system, so the incentive to become highly educated was strong.

Married, Widowed, Began Writing

Ban's father died when she was eight years old. In about the year 76, the royal court of the Eastern Han emperor summoned her brother, Ban Gu, to finish the monumental job of writing the *Han shu,* giving him Ban Biao's post as royal historian. In the meantime, Ban married Cao Shishu at age 14 and went to live with her husband's family. He died within a short time, and Ban remained a widow for the remainder of her long life. She reportedly had at least one child with her husband, although historical accounts greatly differ as to which gender and how many. There are also reports that Ban's husband had been frustrated by his young wife's desire to "write all day."

Although still living with her husband's family as tradition required, and presumably carrying out all the chores and rituals required of the lowest-positioned member of the household, Ban found time to continue her writing and studying. Unlike widows of later generations, who were required by more stringent Confucian social standards to remain virtually secluded, Ban becqme an active participant in politics at several Han courts and an admired member of literary circles.

Call from Han Court

In about 92, Ban's brother Ban Gu died in prison. He had chosen the wrong side among competing cliques at Dowager Empress Dou's court. Ban's son, who had become a soldier, was assigned to a faraway post, which may have been part of the court's reprisal against his involvement in the royal feud, and she may have gone with him. However, the court eventually summoned her back to the capital and ordered her to continue her brother's work as imperial historian. The authorities apparently put her in charge of the royal Tuan Kuan Library and the other historians working on the important document. Some historians believe that Ban is responsible for about one-quarter of the final *Han shu,* which was completed 14 years after the court ordered her to finish it.

Close to Royal Family

In addition to her duties on the Han manuscript, Ban was appointed to be a teacher of the ladies of the court, including all the concubines. One of them, Deng, was an apt student to whom Ban taught mathematics, history, the Confucian classics and astronomy. When the emperor tired of his empress, he promoted Deng to that position in 102, and Ban became her lady-in-waiting and companion.

The emperor had two sons with Empress Deng. After his death in 106, the boys ruled briefly before they died at a very young age. Dowager Empress Deng served as acting leader during these short reigns, and Ban was said to have a powerful influence. She was known in the court as "Mother Ban." Historian and translator Nancy Lee Swann wrote that, during a conflict at the court, "at a word from [Ban], the whole [royal] family resigned." Ban was so important to the royal family that the Dowager reportedly mourned her death — and for a member of the Han court to mourn a commoner's passing was highly unusual.

Ban's work on the *Han shu* contributed to what historians have called the second most famous of all of China's many formal dynastic histories, after the works of Sima Qian. Although her efforts were not acknowledged for many years because later Confucian scholars refer to her brother as the official editor, some scholars deem Ban to be the primary author. Regardless of the amount of her authorship of the *Han shu,* she was the most famous female historian in her country's history.

Ban was also a respected poet and produced many volumes during her life. However, only a few poems, such as "The Needle and Thread" and "Traveling Eastward," still exist.

Lessons for Women

The work for which Ban is most remembered was her *Nu Jie (Lessons for Women),* a treatise on how women of the period should behave. Part etiquette guide and part moral compass, the book became a key influence on the Chinese gender system for 2,000 years. Ban is believed to have begun writing it in about 106, during the period when she was tutoring and later consulting with Empress Dengt.

Lessons for Women was published at a time when China's Confucian society desperately needed a way to impose order on its often complex and unruly families. Expected to serve as models of decorum and order, the typical Chinese family often consisted of multiple wives and concubines and many children. Conflicts were common, and chaos was the norm in many households. The existing Confucian documents did not offer specific and practical information for women's everyday lives.

Ban's book served to codify easily learned rules of behavior, which centered on her advice to women to subjugate themselves to the men in the family. With her husband at the top of the pyramid of authority (or her father if she was unmarried), a woman was supposed to accord the appropriate amount of respect to her brothers, brothers-in-law, father, father-in-law and other male relatives. Ban also declared that widows should never remarry, that women must "think of themselves last in all situations" and that in general, "the Way of respect and acquiescence is woman's most important principle of conduct."

Although many women began to scoff at Ban's outdated rules at the beginning of the 19th Century, it is important to recognize that in Ban's time it was of paramount importance to establish and support the Confucian way of life. Indeed, her family had been working toward that goal for generations. In contrast to the often violent and volatile feudal times from which the country was still emerging, the political order and social stability of Confucianism was important for Chinese women to support. Ban also insisted that women receive a good education, although Confucian scholars of later generations would largely ignore that injunction.

Ban lived into her 70s and died in about 120. Her literary works, which Ban's daughter-in-law collected after her death, filled at least 16 volumes. It was not until the 800s that Ban came to be most famous for writing *Lessons for Women*. Her influence continued into the 21st Century in a new *Kunqu* opera titled *Ban Zhao* by the Shanghai-based writer Luo Huaizhen. The author explained, ''I wanted to express my respect for the intellectuals in this society who work hard to realize their ideals without caring for material benefits.''

Books

Commire, Anne, ed., *Women in World History*, Yorkin Publications, 2001.

Online

''Ban Zhao,'' *FactMonster.com*, http://www.factmonster.com (December 16, 2003).

''Ban Zhao/Pan Chao/Cao Dagu,'' *Other Women's Voices*, http://home.infionline.net/~ddisse/banzhao.html (December 16, 2003).

''Chinese Cultural Studies: Ban Zhao,'' *City University of New York at Brooklyn*, http://www.academic.Brooklyn.cuny.edu (December 16, 2003).

''Chronicler of China: Historian Ban Zhao,'' *Heroines in History*, http://www.heroinesinhistory.com (December 16, 2003).

''Millennial Women: Women of the Han Dynasty,'' *Sino: China at the Millennium*, http://www.sinorama.com.tw/Millennium/en/Millennium-en-02.html (December 16, 2003).

''Modern *Kunqu* Opera Tells Historian's Story,'' *China.org: Culture and Science,/i]* http://www.china.org.cn/English/9551.htm (December 16, 2003).

''Pan Chao,'' *Britannica Encyclopedia Online*, http://www.britannica.com (December 16, 2003). □

Romana Acosta Bañuelos

The story of Romana Acosta Bañuelos (born 1925) is a traditional American rags-to-riches adventure. Born into a poor family of Mexican Americans, she became the first Latina treasurer of the United States (1971–1974) and owner of a multimillion-dollar business, Ramona's Mexican Food Products, Inc.

Early Life

Bañuelos, the daughter of poor Mexican immigrants, was born in the tiny mining town of Miami, Arizona, on March 20, 1925. In 1933, during the Great Depression, the U.S. government deported the family, along with thousands of other Mexican Americans, even though many of the deportees, like Bañuelos, had been born in the United States. The Bañueloses believed the deportation officials' statement that they could return as soon as the country's economy had improved, so they accepted the government's offer to pay for their moving expenses and left their home peacefully.

They moved in with relatives who owned a small ranch in Sonora, Mexico. Along with her parents, Bañuelos began rising early to tend the crops that her father and other male relatives had planted. She helped her mother in the kitchen as well, making *empanadas* that her mother sold to bakeries and restaurants to make extra money. Bañuelos later recalled that her mother, who also raised chickens for their eggs, ''was the type of woman who taught us how to live in any place and work with what we have.'' She called her mother a resourceful businesswoman who presented a strong role model for what a woman could do economically with very little.

Disaster into Opportunity

Bañuelos married in Mexico at age 16, not an unusually young age in that time and culture. She had two sons, Carlos and Martin, by age 18, but her husband deserted the family in 1943. She returned to the United States with her children. Some reports speculate she worked in an El Paso, Texas, laundromat for a time, while others say she followed an aunt to Los Angeles. Most accounts describe Bañuelos arriving in Los Angeles with her children, unable to speak English and with only seven dollars to her name.

Quickly finding jobs as a dishwasher during the day and as a tortilla maker from midnight to 6 a.m., Bañuelos soon began making enough money to save a little. At 21, she married a man named Alejandro and saved about $500, which she used to start her own tortilla factory in downtown Los Angeles. Bañuelos bought a tortilla machine, a fan, and a corn grinder, and with her aunt helping her she made $36 on the factory's first day of business in 1949.

Ambitious, young, and driven, Bañuelos looked constantly for opportunities to sell her tortillas to local businesses. As sales volumes increased, she incorporated the company and named it Ramona's Mexican Food Products, Inc. There is some discrepancy as to how the business' name came about: some say the sign painters made a mistake when spelling "Romana"; others insist "Ramona" was an early California folk hero; and still others believe it was a product of people's unfamiliarity with the name "Romana." Regardless, by the mid-1960s, Ramona's Mexican Food Products, Inc. was thriving and Bañuelos had a daughter, whom she named Ramona after the business.

Helped Other Poor Latinos

In 1963, looking for ways to help the struggling Latinos in her neighborhood, Bañuelos and some businessmen founded the Pan-American National Bank in East Los Angeles. The men had initially approached Alejandro with the proposal, but he was busy with political work and suggested the men talk to Bañuelos. The bank's main purpose was to bankroll Latinos who wanted to start their own businesses. Bañuelos also believed that if Hispanics could increase their financial base they would have more political influence and be able to improve their standard of living.

In 1969 Bañuelos was appointed chairperson of the bank's board of directors and received the city's Outstanding Business Woman of the Year Award. Later that year, Mayor Sam Yorty presented her with a commendation from the County Board of Supervisors, and Bañuelos established a college scholarship fund, the Ramona Mexican Food Products Scholarship, for poor Mexican American students.

U.S. Treasurer

With bank assets already in the millions and deposits climbing rapidly, Pan-American National's huge success caught the attention of the Richard Nixon administration. The president was seeking to repay the Hispanic Republic Assembly, which had played a strong role in his election. Bañuelos agreed to throw her name into the hat when asked in 1970 if she would consider the post of U.S. treasurer. Not believing she had a chance to be nominated and confirmed, Bañuelos went about her daily life. She was stunned, then, when Nixon personally chose her as his candidate.

During the ensuing nomination process, Bañuelos was even more taken aback by a sudden raid on her tortilla factory by U.S. Immigration Service agents. The agents, contrary to their usual methods, reportedly carried out a loud, disruptive raid through the facility, attracting a lot of press attention and apparently hurting Bañuelos's chances of securing the treasurer nomination. However, Nixon sided with her and called the raid politically motivated, charging the Democratic Party with instigating it. She was later vindicated when a Senate investigation ruled that the raid was carried out solely to cause embarrassment to the Nixon administration.

Despite the ugly affair, Bañuelos sailed through the confirmation process to become the nation's 34th treasurer and the first Latina in the position in U.S. history. She took office on December 17, 1971, becoming the highest-ranking Mexican American in the government.

As treasurer, Bañuelos was in charge of writing checks for money spent by government agencies and replacing worn-out currency. Her signature also appeared on all U.S. paper currency. Her daughter would later say of Bañuelos's performance as treasurer, "My mother's legacy is that she ran the place as a business, not just as another wing of the government."

Bañuelos served as treasurer for one term, until 1974, when she resigned to spend more time with her businesses, family, and philanthropic pursuits. She said during a 1979 interview with *Nuestro* magazine, "It was a beautiful experience. I will always be grateful to President Nixon." Later that year, Bañuelos was a founding member of Executive Women in Government.

Ramona's Growth

By 1979, Ramona's was making and distributing 22 different food products. It had more than 400 employees and sales of $12 million a year. The company's success was instrumental in the popularization of Mexican cuisine in the United States. As the Hispanic population of the country grew, of course, so did sales of tortillas, empanadas, and many other traditional favorites. However, other races began to favor the inexpensive, delicious foods as well, boosting the company's profits. Ramona's continued to grow throughout the 1980s, when it became the one of the largest Mexican food distributors and manufacturers in California.

Throughout the 1980s and 1990s, Bañuelos continued to serve as president of Ramona's and Pan-American National, and by 1992, she had served three terms as chair of the bank's board of directors. However, in the late 1990s, she allowed her three children to take over daily operations of Ramona's and to play large roles in the bank's operations.

Bañuelos remained CEO at Pan-American National and president of Ramona's, running both businesses from her Los Angeles home. The privately held company distributed nationwide. Her daughter was chief financial officer of the bank, which had 30 bilingual employees and three branches. The Bañuelos family owned two-thirds of the shares in the publically traded bank. Pan-American National was credited with helping economically troubled East Los Angeles develop a sense of community and with being a vital factor in the economic improvement of its Latino population.

Books

Dictionary of Hispanic Biography, Gale Research, 1996.

Periodicals

Nuestro, June–July 1979.

Online

"Bañuelos, Romana" *Worldbook,* http://www2.worldbook.com (December 17, 2003).

"East-LA-Based Bank Has Strong Ties to Community," *Findarticles.com,* http://www.findarticles.com (January 7, 2004).

"Founding Members," *Executive Women in Government,* http://www.execwomeningov.org (January 7, 2004).

"Pan-American National Bank: Corporate Profile," *SNL Financial,* http://www.snl.com (December 17, 2003).

"Romana Acosta Bañuelos," *Biography Resource Center,* http://galenet.galegroup.com (January 5, 2004).

"Romana Bañuelos," *Wit and Wisdom,* http://www.witandwisdom.com (December 17, 2003).

"Romana Bañuelos, U.S. Treasurer and Business Executive," *Women of Achievement,* http://www.undelete.or/woa (December 17, 2003). ☐

Marius Barbeau

Dedicating his life to preserving the traditional cultures of northernmost America, Marius Barbeau (1883–1969) was perhaps the most noted Canadian ethnographer of the twentieth century. Through his efforts, thousands of folk songs, tales, and other art forms reflecting the unique culture of Canada were recorded, catalogued, and preserved for future generations.

Ethnographer, anthropologist, and author Marius Barbeau devoted his life to preserving the cultural heritage of his native Canada, a country divided by language, heritage, and a vast terrain. Working under the auspices of the National Museum of Man in Canada after 1911, Barbeau recorded the songs, stories, and languages of the native peoples inhabiting northernmost North America at the turn of the twentieth century, while also devoting his attention to collecting the stories and songs unique to his own French-Canadian culture. A prolific author, he penned nonfiction, biographies, and novels such as 1928's *The Downfall of Temlaham,* 1944's *Mountain Cloud,* and *Le Rêve de Kamalmouk,* published in Montreal in 1948. His many nonfiction works include 1928's *Folk Songs of French Canada,* which he coedited with fellow anthropologist Edward Sapir, as well as *The Tsimshian, Their Arts and Music, Quebec, Where Ancient France Lingers,* and *I Have Seen Quebec.* Barbeau was fluent in French and English and authored a number of books in his native French; several of his books for general readers, such as 1936's *Quebec, Where Ancient France Lingers* and 1957's *I Have Seen Quebec,* were published in bilingual editions.

Barbeau's most noteworthy contributions to anthropology consist of the relationships he unearthed between contemporary culture and cultures of the distant past. In eastern Canada, he linked modern cultural practices to more ancient cultures—for instance, he revealed relationships between French- Canadian social habits and customs and those of medieval France, while the Tsimshian people were shown to retain cultural attributes dating from their Asian forbears. While spending much of his time in fieldwork in remote areas of Canada, Barbeau was not a reserved, closeted academic; he was enthusiastic about sharing his knowledge and discoveries with the general public through radio and television programs as well as through his many books and his frequent lectures at schools and other assemblies. In addition to anthropological advances, Barbeau's published contribution to the body of Canadian folk music—contained in *Le rossignol y chante, En roulant ma boule* and *Le roi boit*—can be considered on a par with the contributions to British balladry made by American musicologist James Francis Child in the mid-nineteenth century.

Inspired by Cultural Heritage

Frédéric Charles Joseph Marius Barbeau was born in Sainte-Marie-de-la-Beauce, Quebec, Canada, on March 5, 1883. His mother, Marie Virginie Morency, was an educated woman who introduced him to folksongs through her love of music; his father, farmer and horseman Charles Barbeau, was a ready source of folk stories and tall tales who also performed a vast repertoire of old-time fiddle tunes. Barbeau was a good student who exhibited a keen intellect and intense curiosity, and his parents realized by the time their son was eleven that his potential lay beyond life on the family farm. Consequently, they planned for him to one day attend college.

In 1899 Barbeau left home and enrolled at the College of Sainte-Anne-de-la Pocatièe, earning his bachelor's degree in 1903. From there he moved to Laval University, where he first planned to become a lawyer or a notary and return to his hometown to set up a law practice. Completing his studies in four years and admitted to the Canadian Bar in 1907, the twenty-three-year-old Barbeau unexpectedly won a Rhodes scholarship to study law at Oxford University in England. Although he arrived at Oxford with the intent of studying criminal law, Barbeau found the law lectures dull and cast about for a subject of greater interest. He found it in anthropology and for the next three years took classes in archaeology, anthropology, and ethnology at Oxford's Oriel College. Completing his thesis, *The Totemic System of the North-Western Tribes of North America,* in 1910, he earned a B.S. from Oxford, although his desire to learn continued.

While at Oxford, Barbeau's interest in the study of mankind had taken him across the English Channel to the École d'anthropologie and the Sorbonne at the University of Paris. At the Sorbonne Barbeau met Professor Marcel Mauss, an anthropologist who greatly influenced the young man's budding career. Returning home to Canada with his Oxford degree in 1911, Barbeau followed the advice of one of his teachers, Sir William Osler, who advised the young French Canadian to seek out Professor Fisher at the University of Ottawa. Osler encouraged Barbeau to pursue his calling creatively, as anthropology was a young field and there were few constraints on scholarship.

Began Lifetime of Study

Shortly after his return to Canada, with Professor Fisher's advice 26-year-old Barbeau joined the National

Museum of Man, which was then a branch of the Canadian Geological Survey. He remained at the National Museum after it became an independent institution in 1927, serving as its staff anthropologist and ethnologist until his retirement in 1948 and continuing to work in its Ottawa offices until his death. In addition, he was an active member of many organizations dedicated to promoting and preserving the Canadian cultural heritage, such as the American Folklore Society, the Royal Society of Canada, the International Folk Music Council, the Academie cannadienne-française, and the Canadian Folk Music Society, the last which he helped organize in 1956. At Laval University he also helped to establish a folklore archive to serve future scholarship.

Although he had loved the songs and stories of French Canada since childhood, Barbeau's major interest lay in the tribal culture of Canada, particularly the Huron people living in the eastern region. Barbeau's first study for the Canadian Geological Survey involved the Huron and Wyandot tribes who lived near the Detroit River near Amherstburg, in southern Ontario. In order to prepare himself to communicate with these people, he traveled south to Oklahoma, spending three months living among the people of the Cayuga nation and recording clan names, stories, and tribal customs while learning the Huron language. Back in Canada, he began fieldwork at the Huron reservation in Notre-Dame-de-Lorette, a small town near Quebec City, where he spent many hours with an aged Huron named Prosper Vincent, recording the man's singing and storytelling on wax cylinders and in the shorthand he had learned as a student in Beauce. The wax cylinder gramophone had been invented by Thomas Edison and was at that time the only means of capturing speech while in the field. In 1912 Barbeau returned again to Oklahoma, spending four more months completing his work. Boas oversaw the publication of some of Barbeau's findings in the *Journal of American Folklore;* a more extensive representation, the book *Huron and Wyandot Mythology,* was published by Canada's Government Printing Bureau in 1915, and was based on Barbeau's first three years in the field.

Meeting with Boas Proved Influential

In 1912 Barbeau broke away from studying the Huron culture of the eastern North American woodlands and traveled west to British Columbia. There he spent time among the Salish, adding to his growing collection of songs. In 1914, noted Columbia University anthropology professor Franz Boas inspired Barbeau with a new channel for his work. Meeting while in Washington, D.C., attending a gathering of the Anthropological Association, the two lunched together and discussed the fact that many of the Huron stories incorporated elements from French folklore. Fascinated by this cultural exchange, Barbeau realized that the 1865 collection of French-Canadian songs compiled by Ernest Gagnon was limited by a Eurocentric attitude.

Determined to expand on Gagnon's historical record, in 1916 Barbeau traveled down the St. Lawrence River through Charlevois, Kamouraska, and Beauce counties and recorded hundreds of new songs and stories on wax cylinders. This was the first of many trips Barbeau would undertake in his dedication to broaden general understanding and appreciation of French-Canadian culture, and his findings were published in such books as *Contes populaires Canadiens.* His method for studying and classifying his findings required complex systematization and vast amounts of time: each recording was transcribed and then grouped with those determined to be variants due to similarities in refrains, melodies, and storylines. Versions were made in both English and French, and further interrelationships then established. Each variant was classified according to a numbering system devised by Barbeau to differentiate among the 13,000 different texts he assembled over his career.

Fueled by a ceaseless curiosity, Barbeau characterized himself as "an inveterate collector" who was "always grabbing." And the object of his search was never-ending. As quoted on the *Canadian Museum of Civilization Web site,* he once observed of his calling: "There are plenty of folk songs everywhere. We have only to turn, to go to a village, a concession somewhere and enquire, and we find that there are more folksongs, more folktale tellers all the time. It is surprising how they have been preserved in the memory of the old people. . . . you only have to gather these people together and start them in a *veillée du bon vieux temps* and they give you a good evening of old folksongs."

While French influences on eastern Canada continued to interest Barbeau, his position at the National Museum of Man demanded that his focus be on Canadian culture as a whole. Barbeau viewed social interaction as of equal importance as scholarship, and his personal interest in the people he interviewed contributed greatly to the esteem with which native Canadians held him. His fascination with their beliefs, their customs, their opinions, their morality, and their personal philosophy of life was not merely scholarly, and his visits among the tribes became anticipated events. Barbeau's novels, which he began writing in the 1920s, also promoted native culture by depicting Indian societies as thriving, self-sufficient communities with strong moral foundations and little need for the social and material trappings of Western civilization.

During his decades studying the country's music, legends, crafts, and social customs and structures, Barbeau spanned the continent, traveling from its east coast through the central prairies to points west. Moving north and westward, in 1915 he worked among the Gitksan and Haida tribes and spent eight seasons among the Tsimshian, a tribe making its home near the Alaskan border. Folk art became an interest in the 1920s, and he amassed a valuable collection of pottery, weavings, and paintings during his travels. In addition to native American artists, Barbeau promoted the works of Canadians such as sculptor Louis Jobin, painters Emily Carr and Cornelius Krieghoff, and Quebec wood carver Jean-Baptiste Côté.

Early in his career with the Canadian Geological Survey, Barbeau had the chance to interview members of a delegation of over a dozen tribal chiefs from western Alberta and the Rocky Mountain region, who had assembled in the Canadian capitol city to discuss tribal lands. During three weeks of interviews in Ottawa, Barbeau recorded and transcribed over sixty songs, establishing lifelong friendships with several of the chiefs in the process. The wax-cylinder recordings made of these sessions, as well as those from his other fieldwork, number approximately 3,000 and are now housed at the Canadian Museum of Civilization in Gatineau, near Ottawa.

In 1949 66-year-old Barbeau led a group of anthropologists to the village of Oshwegan, located in the Grand River Reserve near Hamilton, Ontario. There, over three seasons, he oversaw the study of Iroquois dialects and with the help of interpreter Charles Cook created the first comprehensive dictionary of Iroquois language variants, while also adding a number of songs to his collection during the tribe's White Dog music festival.

Created Archive for Posterity

Over his lifetime Barbeau is credited with amassing over 400 folk tales and 8,000 songs and recorded for posterity the native ceremonies, myths, languages and dialects, architecture, handicrafts, and other manifestations of the many unique native cultures of northern America. Not content with mere scholarship, he encouraged the use of his research by other scholars and made available many recordings of native and French-Canadian songs as a way of preserving the music from extinction. At his death his related collection of Canadian artifacts numbered over 2,000 pieces.

A prolific author, Barbeau shared his knowledge in over thirty books and hundreds of articles, some published in scholarly journals and many others appearing in magazines and newspapers for the enjoyment of the general reading public. As associate editor of the *Journal of American Folklore* from 1916 to 1950, he spread information regarding Canadian folk songs and myths throughout the whole of North America and edited ten issues of the journal that focused almost wholly on Canadian folklore. In his publications, he often called upon the talents of Canadian artists such as Emily Carr, A. Y. Jackson, and Ernest MacMillan in illustrating his many books.

Considered a pioneer in his field, Barbeau was honored on many occasions. He received the Prix David from the Quebec government on three separate occasions, earned the Gold Medal from the Royal Society of Canada, and was named a Companion of the Order of Canada. Barbeau was also honored with honorary degrees from his alma maters, the universities of Montreal—from which he earned a Ph.D.—Laval, and Oxford.

Following Barbeau's death on March 27, 1969, in Ottawa, Canada, at age 86, the Canadian Museum of Civilization celebrated the centennial of Barbeau's birth with a special exhibition, and two years later Canada's Historic Sites and Monuments Board named him a "person of national historic importance." A mountain on Ellesmere Island, the highest point in the Canadian Arctic, was dubbed Barbeau Peak in his honor. Barbeau's work has also been commemorated by the Marius Barbeau Museum, located in Quebec near where Barbeau was born and raised. Focusing on local history, the museum houses a collection of traditional crafts, religious objects, and items relating to maple syrup production, the area's chief product. His papers are archived at Canada's National Museum of Civilization, located in the capital city of Ottawa.

Books

Dictionary of Literary Biography, Volume 92: *Canadian Writers, 1890–1920,* Gale, 1990.
Nowry, Lawrence, *Man of Mana: Marius Barbeau,* N.C. Press (Toronto, Ontario, Canada), 1995.

Periodicals

Canadian Folklore Canadien, Volume 17, number 1, 1995.
Journal of American Folklore, Volume 82, 1969.

Online

Canadian Museum of Civilization Web site, http://www .civilization.ca/ (July 18, 2001). □

John Barbirolli

British conductor Sir John Barbirolli (1899–1970) led the Hallé Orchestra of Manchester, England, from 1943 to 1968 and was one of classical music's most compelling figures of his era. His London *Times* obituary termed him "a virtuoso conductor in the tradition of those spellbinding artists who made the conductor the centre of popular devotion for concertgoers in the twentieth century."

Child Prodigy on Cello

Of Italian and French parentage, Barbirolli was baptized with the name Giovanni Battista Barbirolli after his birth in London on December 2, 1899. The family lived above a baker's shop in a south London neighborhood. His father, Filippo Lorenzo Barbirolli, an orchestra violinist, had met his wife, Louise Ribèyrol, in Paris while working as a musician and brought her to London when he and his father settled in the city in the 1890s. Both men were musicians who had played in the orchestra pit for the world premiere of Giuseppe Verdi's *Otello* at the La Scala opera house in Milan in 1887.

Young Barbirolli's musically inclined home was also a crowded one. In addition to his parents and older sister, his paternal grandparents and an aunt lived in the flat. From a young age, Barbirolli accompanied his father when he went to rehearsals, and Barbirolli loved watching the conductor. He began imitating the time-keeping movements at home, even donning white gloves like conductors wore in those days. Though his family hoped that he would become a doctor, his parents allowed him to learn the violin. But when he wandered from room to room in the apartment while practicing, it irked the rest of the household. His father bought him a cello instead, so that he would have to sit in one place to play music.

As a cellist, Barbirolli became a child prodigy. At the age of 11 he won a scholarship to Trinity College of Music in London. The following year he made his public debut on December 16, 1911, at Trinity College's annual concert at Queen's Hall, playing a Saint-Saëns solo. Soon after he won a scholarship to the prestigious Royal Academy of Music, where he studied from 1912 to 1917. He made a series of recordings with his sister Rosa accompanying him on piano. Because World War I led to a shortage of musicians, he won a permanent slot with the Queen's Hall Orchestra in 1916, and the following July delivered his first solo performance at Aeolian Hall, one of London's main recital venues, launching his professional career as a concert cellist.

In 1917 Barbirolli played with the Royal Philharmonic Orchestra before entering the British Army to serve in the Suffolks Regiment as an instructor on defending against gas attacks. The unit was stationed on the Isle of Grain, a parcel of land at the mouth of the Thames River that housed a military base. Once the armistice was signed there was little to do, so he and some other musicians formed a small orchestra. His got his first chance to conduct when the superior officer who served as bandmaster fell ill before a performance.

An Egalitarian Career

Decommissioned from the army in 1919, Barbirolli took work where he could find it over the next few years. He played with small opera companies and even in the theater, a venue that some working classical musicians disdained as

popular entertainment beneath their training. "In fact I scorned no avenue that would teach me something about my job," Barbirolli wrote in the October 1936 issue of *Gramophone.* "In those days mechanical music was unknown in the theatre; wherever plays were performed there would be a small theatre orchestra. I played in one of these. There was not much to do, incidental music to plays had fallen into disuse.... In the long waits between the act intervals I studied scores."

In 1924, Barbirolli founded a Chelsea chamber orchestra with members of the Guild of Singers and Players and served as its conductor. It quickly garnered acclaim, and the group made some recordings for the National Gramophonic Society. In 1926, the British National Opera Company invited him to conduct its orchestra on a provincial tour. He would remain with the company off and on until 1929, gaining experience with such classics as *Madama Butterfly, Aïda,* and *Romeo et Juliette.* In a 1947 article titled "The Art of Conducting" that reappeared in the *Barbirolli Society Journal,* the conductor noted that opera performances, though somewhat nerve-wracking, provided the best training for a would-be orchestra leader. "The number of little things that can happen for which the conductor is technically responsible are, I am sure, not realised by the audience. For instance, a character has to rush in and sing something and the door sticks—a little delay ensues, and yet all must be made to seem as if everything is proceeding smoothly."

Replaced Toscanini

Barbirolli's star rose on one fortuitous night in December 1927 when he stepped in for the famed Sir Thomas Beecham, conductor of the London Symphony Orchestra. He had just two days to rehearse a concert program that included Edward Elgar's Second Symphony, and the renowned cellist Pablo Casals was present at one of the rehearsals. After Barbiroll, then 28 years old, made some comments, Casals leaned in his chair and enjoined his fellow musicians, "Listen to him. He knows," Barbirolli recalled in the 1936 *Gramophone* article. "I was only a boy, and those few words coming from such a great artist touched me deeply. It was a wonderful thing for a man of his greatness to do: I shall never forget it."

Barbirolli spent several years working in opera. He debuted at Covent Garden in 1928, working regularly with the Royal Opera until 1933, when he became the regular conductor of the Scottish Orchestra in Glasgow. There he started to tackle the canon of major symphonic works, from Beethoven to Stravinsky and began to display great flair at the podium. A recording contract helped launch his career across the Atlantic, and in November 1936 he was invited to make his American debut with the New York Philharmonic. Its esteemed leader, Arturo Toscanini, had recently retired, and Philharmonic management decided to offer Barbirolli a three-year contract. The announcement caused a stir in New York classical music circles, for Barbirolli was just 36 and critics and Toscanini-lovers contended he was too inexperienced for the post. The music writer for the *New York Times,* Olin Downes, observed that "Barbirolli may conceivably reveal unexpected and phenomenal capacities, but there is nothing in the available records to indicate such a likelihood," according to *John Barbirolli: A Musical Biography* by John Reid.

Homesick for England

Over the next few years, Downs occasionally granted Barbirolli a grudgingly favorable comment, but rival music journalist Virgil Thomson of the *New York Herald Tribune* was usually brutal. One example of his vitriol came after the opening night of the 1940 Philharmonic season, in which Barbirolli led the group in a program that included Beethoven and Elgar. "The concert as a whole, both as to programme and as to playing, was anything but a memorable experience," Thomson asserted, according to the Reid biography. "The music itself was soggy, the playing dull and brutal." Other writers judged Barbirolli less harshly. A *New York Times* profile by S. J. Woolf noted: "One instinctively knows as the maestro leans over his stand and asks for more volume, as he crouches low with bent knees in subdued passages, as he shifts his baton to his left hand and with his right wheedles greater feeling into the music, that he is working harder than any member of his orchestra."

Barbirolli was under contract to the New York Philharmonic when Britain and Germany went to war in 1939, the year he wed Evelyn Rothwell, a renowned oboist in her own right. He was still with them when the United States entered World War II in 1941. The American Musicians' Union urged him to take U.S. citizenship, but he was homesick for England, which was being attacked regularly by German bombers. Despite his Italian and French heritage, Barbirolli considered himself thoroughly English and was a follower of cricket. He went back for a ten-week tour in 1942, making a perilous Atlantic crossing, and decided to return permanently when the Hallé Society of Manchester, a northern industrial city, asked him to become its permanent conductor.

Revitalized Orchestra

The Hallé Orchestra had lost many players to the British Broadcasting Corporation's Northern Orchestra and was in dire financial trouble. Some members had joined the armed forces, and there was a shortage of skilled musicians. Arriving in mid-1943, Barbirolli found a bare minimum of players, as he recollected in an interview from 1963 reprinted in the *Barbirolli Society Journal*. "I had been led to believe I would find an orchestra of 70 or so and I found 26," he said. "I arrived on 2nd June, the first concert was booked for 5th July, so I had a month to find and train players at a time when many of the best were in the Services." He went to work immediately, and the result was impressive, asserted his *Times* of London obituary. "The story of how, in a couple of months of endless auditions, he rebuilt the Hallé, accepting any good player whatever his musical background—he found himself with a schoolboy first flute, a school mistress hornist, and various brass players recruited from brass and military bands in the Manchester area—deservedly ranks as a wartime epic," the paper noted.

Barbirolli gained a reputation for taking the Hallé group through the paces of the Romantic canon with his typical verve and along the way helped it become a respected, income-producing orchestra. He championed works by British composers like Elgar and Benjamin Britten as well. Regularly offered more prestigious posts elsewhere, he turned them down, remaining conductor of the Manchester cultural institution on a full-time schedule until 1958, when he became its conductor-in-chief. His schedule after that required just 70 concerts a year, and he began to take more international work. From 1961 to 1967 he was the conductor of the Houston Symphony Orchestra, and he spent twelve weeks of the year in Texas. He also appeared with the Vienna and Berlin philharmonics and at Austria's prestigious Salzburg Festival.

Barbirolli retired from Hallé in 1968, though he was given the title of Conductor Laureate for Life. Knighted in 1949, he was elevated to Companion of Honour in 1969. His retirement from Hallé did not bring a less taxing schedule, however. He conducted at the King's Lynn Festival on July 25, 1970, and four days later rehearsed with the Philharmonia Orchestra in preparation for a planned tour of Japan. He died of a heart attack later that day, on July 29, 1970, in London.

Books

Reid, John, *John Barbirolli: A Musical Biography,* Taplinger Publishing, 1971.
Slonimsky, Nicolas, editor emeritus, *Baker's Biographical Dictionary of Musicians,* Centennial Edition, Schirmer, 2001.

Periodicals

Barbirolli Society Journal, February 1997.
Gramophon, October 1936.
New York Times, December 27, 1936.
Observer (London), July 6, 1947.
Times (London, England), May 20, 1960; July 30, 1970. □

Thomas Beecham

English conductor Thomas Beecham's (1879–1961) influence on classical music during a span of several decades across the twentieth century was unparalleled. Founder and principal conductor of the London Philharmonic Orchestra, Beecham depleted much of his own fortune to present before British audiences orchestral works and operas that had been considered daring, avant-garde, or even too "foreign"; as a result, he introduced a generation of London music-lovers to some outstanding composers, especially the lighter French artists of the previous century.

Beecham was born in St. Helens, a town in the Lancashire area of England, on April 29, 1879. He was the namesake of his grandfather, who had created a tremendous family fortune with his own brand of digestive pills that also bore the name Beecham. The young boy enjoyed close ties with the elder Beecham; relations with his own parents were never wholly amiable during his adult life. His gift for music was evident at a young age to his father, a collector of rare musical instruments, and formal instruction at the piano began at the age of six. For several years he attended a Lancashire school where he was also able to indulge in his second love—athletics—but enrolled in Wadham College at Oxford University to study music in 1897. He considered becoming a concert pianist.

Made Surprise Debut

That same year, Beecham had founded the St. Helens Orchestral Society, where he first practiced the art of conducting. When in 1899 the Hallé Society Orchestra appeared in St. Helens for a scheduled engagement, its conductor became unavailable, and Beecham took the podium instead. This debut was deemed a success, though he and the musicians had not been able to rehearse the program beforehand. The following year, he moved to London and began to study music composition privately with a series of teachers.

Beecham was still working toward a career as a pianist, but a 1904 injury to his wrist ended these hopes. Though still in his mid-twenties, Beecham had already traveled ex-

tensively in Europe to further his musical education, attending opera performances at some of the continent's most famous venues. He made his London conducting debut with the Queen's Hall Orchestra in December 1905, but the performance was given mixed reviews by critics. Beecham had been disheartened by the difficulty of the experience as well. With the support of a clarinetist named Charles Draper, he founded the New Symphony Orchestra in 1906, and Beecham began selecting its sixty-five members according to his own high standards.

Performances of the New Symphony Orchestra, with Beecham at the podium, met with a more favorable reception from critics. His newfound acclaim brought him into contact with the relatively unknown English composer Frederick Delius, and Beecham began to debut new orchestral works written by Delius with the New Symphony. Delius, of German parentage, was influenced by Norwegian composer Edvard Grieg and created works that blended the styles of Romanticism and Impressionism beginning with his first success, 1907's *Brigg Fair.*

The Covent Garden Years

In 1903, during a period of family strife, Beecham wed the daughter of an American diplomat, Utica Celestia Welles. Together they had two sons and traveled across Europe but the union disintegrated within a few short years. They did not divorce, however, until 1943. By 1910, Beecham and his father had mended their differences, and the latter provided financial backing for the son's plan to mount a program of operas at London's Covent Garden. Over the next several years, Beecham and his British National Opera Company presented some striking, altogether grand productions of works from the canon of European composers, some of which had not yet been performed in Britain. Richard Strauss's *Elektra, Feuersnot,* and *Der Rosenkavalier,* Richard Wagner's *Tristan und Isolde,* and even Sergei Diaghilev's famed Ballets Russes from Paris all appeared before London audiences, led by Beecham's baton.

The Covent Garden seasons were annual financial losses, however, and the outbreak of World War I and England's belligerent relationship with Germany further curtailed Beecham's plans. So Beecham founded a small touring company and with it staged operas across the British Isles during the war years; the programs were notable for their affordable ticket prices, making the whole endeavor quite an egalitarian one. In 1916, Beecham's father died, and he inherited a baronetcy, but financial woes began to plague him. His 1920 season of Covent Garden operas sustained heavy losses, and he nearly went bankrupt. As the *British Dictionary of National Biography* noted, "until 1923 he was almost absent from the musical scene. From then until 1929 his life seems to have been a gradual climb back to the pinnacle he had achieved so early."

The composer Delius, who suffered from paralysis and encroaching vision problems with age, was feted with a festival in his honor presented by Beecham in 1929; the series, which became an annual event, marked the beginning of a more widespread recognition for Delius's works. By 1932, after several years of exacting negotiations,

Beecham entered into an agreement with the British Broadcasting Corporation and the London Symphony Orchestra to create the London Philharmonic Orchestra. Several seasons of distinguished performances followed, but the onset of world war once more brought an abrupt change to Beecham's fortunes.

Performance for Hitler

Beecham spent much of the war years touring the United States and Australia, perhaps the result of lingering problems in Britain as a result of his 1936 tour of Nazi Germany with the orchestra group. Furthermore, an expatriate German woman, Berta Geissmar, served as his personal secretary at both home and on tour. At one performance, German chancellor Adolf Hitler was the guest of honor, and as customary, the entire hall was expected to rise and salute him upon his entrance. Beecham avoided this by adamantly entering the concert hall after the Führer had been seated. On another night, Beecham and the Philharmonic played at a concert hall in Ludwigshafen belonging to the chemical giant BASF, who also manufactured recording equipment. The evening's program was recorded, the first time in history that a live orchestra's performance was duplicated on tape.

Beginning in 1940, Beecham, like other European masters, made a number of guest appearances with the Metropolitan Opera of New York. Divorced in 1943, he remarried pianist Betty Humby Thomas and wrote an autobiography of his early life, *A Mingled Chime,* that was published in 1944. He returned to London in 1944 and became immersed in artistic and other arguments with the London Philharmonic. As a result, he broke with the organization and formed the Royal Philharmonic Orchestra in 1946. With that body he honored Strauss with a momentous London festival in 1947. In 1950, the Royal Philharmonic made a successful tour of North America, and Beecham led the orchestra through several stellar recordings as well. He also wrote a biography of Delius that appeared in 1958.

Among the recordings that preserve Beecham's legacy, critics have cited *Puccini: La Bohéme* with Jussi Bjoerling and Victoria De Los Angeles, issued on RCA in 1956 and reissued by the EMI's Seraphim label, as exemplary. As with the lighthearted operatic romp of *La Bohéme,* Beecham was partial to the works of French composers such as Bizet, Debussy, and Saint-Saëns; the entire Mozart repertoire was also a personal favorite.

Beecham's second wife died in 1957, the same year he received the Companion of Honour designation from the British crown. He married his personal secretary, Shirley Hudson, in 1959, but fell ill the following year while touring the United States with the Royal Philharmonic. He died in London on March 8, 1961. As a conductor and orchestra director, Beecham had a reputation for a rather formidable style of management. He left behind an extensive musical library, which in 1997 was acquired by England's University of Sheffield.

Books

Williams, E. T., and C. S. Nicholls, editors, *British Dictionary of National Biography, 1961–1970,* Oxford University Press.

Periodicals

American Record Guide, May/June 1999.
Opera News, March 18, 1995; July 1, 1995. □

Giaconda Belli

Nicaraguan Gianconda Belli (born 1948), a respected author and poet, also took part in the overthrow of dictator Anastasio Somoza as a Sandinista rebel.

Early Life and Education

On December 9, 1948, in Managua, Nicaragua, Giaconda Belli was born to a wealthy family. Her father, Humberto, was an industrialist, and her mother, the former Gloria Pereira, was the founder of the city's Experimental Theater. Belli had two brothers and two sisters. Since their parents wanted them to have a European education, all the children attended Catholic primary school at the School of Asunción in Managua and Catholic secondary school at the Royal School of Santa Isabel in Madrid, Spain. Belli did not enjoy either school, later calling them "cold and austere."

In the summers, Belli and her siblings visited England to learn English. She finished secondary school in 1964 and followed her father's advice to give up her ambition to become a doctor in favor of the "more feminine" career of advertising. She was accepted at the Charles Morris Price School in Philadelphia, Pennsylvania, where she took classes in advertising and journalism in 1965.

Belli returned to Nicaragua at age 17 and soon became the first woman advertising account executive in the country, working at the Alpha Omega Advertising Company. Having discovered her love of and talent for writing, Belli went on to study advertising management at INCAE, the new Harvard University school of business administration with campuses throughout Central America, and later took courses in literature and philosophy at Georgetown University in Washington, D.C. In 1967, Belli married Mariano A. Downing and hosted the reception at the local country club. She had her first child (Maryam) with him in 1969.

First Poetry Published

Belli's first poems appeared in the Managuan cultural newspaper *La Prensa* in 1970. Sensual and with many erotic references to the female body, the pieces caused considerable consternation in some circles (one critic from a report in *The Guardian* called the poetry "shameless pornography"), although most critics deemed the poems revolutionary. Also in 1970, she joined the Sandinista National

Volume 24

LIBRARY
ALLEGANY COLLEGE OF MARYLAND
12401 Willowbrook Road, SE
Cumberland. MD 21502-2596

BELLI **49**

Liberation Front (SNLF), like many artists and intellectuals of her generation. She had been introduced to the rebel group, whose goal was to overthrow the repressive and corrupt dictatorship of Anastasio Samoza, through a poet friend several years earlier. She would remember in a 2003 interview with Barbara Liss of *The Houston Chronicle,* "It was as if the guilt of privilege had suddenly been lifted from my shoulders." Despite her upper-class background, Belli enthusiastically joined in weapons training and other drills with her fellow comandantes, although one teased her that she "carried her submachinegun like a handbag." In 1973 she had her second child, Melissa, with Downing.

Her first book of poetry, *Sobre la Grama* (On the Grass), appeared in 1974. It won the first and most prestigious poetry award in the country at the time, the Mariano Fiallos Gil Award from the Universidad Nacional Autónoma de Nicaragua. Also that year, as written in *Hispanic Literary Criticism* Belli later recalled, "I lived in constant fear of being discovered." In addition to her duties of transporting arms, carrying illegal mail, and broadcasting news of the Sandinista struggle throughout Latin America and Europe, the SNLF assigned Belli to the "clandestine intelligence" section of a logistics team that would carry out a commando action against the Samoza regime. She was in charge of stealing blueprints of the mansion where a key official was to attend a party. The plan was to kidnap the official and hold him hostage in exchange for the release of political prisoners. However, the plan went awry when Belli was spotted and followed. To prevent her imprisonment, she went into exile in 1975. (She was later tried in absentia, found guilty, and sentenced to seven years in prison.) In the *Chronical* interview, Belli recalled of this period, "It was exhilarating because you felt you were doing something important, yet on the other hand, it was very scary. But we were young and fear was quite manageable."

Lived in Exile

Belli lived in exile in Mexico and Costa Rica without her family for four years but continued her writing at a steady pace. Her marriage did not survive this trying period, and in 1976 she was divorced from Downing. She later described the union as "stifling." However, a new relationship followed quickly in its footsteps, and in 1977, Belli married Sergio de Castro, a fellow SNLF member, in Costa Rica. They would soon have a son, Camilo, together. Meanwhile, in 1976 she had taken a job as creative director at Garnier Advertising in San Jose, Costa Rica, where she would work until 1978.

In 1978 Belli published *Linea de Fuego* (Line of Fire), a collection of 54 poems that is perhaps her most acclaimed work. In the collection, she experiments with combinations of poetry and prose, surreal metaphor, and conventional imagery. The book won the coveted Casa de las Americas Prize in Poetry and launched Belli's reputation as a respected author. It also showcased her linkage of women's struggle for sexual, political, and personal freedom with the Sandinista revolution, often using each as a metaphor to describe the other. Critics of the period added Belli to a group of bourgeois female authors of about the same age

who were all writing political poetry centered on exalted sensuality, disdain of society's treatment of women, celebration of the human body, and glorification of political revolution. They were known collectively as "the Six."

Returned to Homeland, Continued Writing and SNLF Work

Belli would not return to Nicaragua until 1979, when the SNLF finally succeeded in toppling Samoza. Later that year she and de Castro divorced, and he won a bitter custody dispute for their son. Belli had been working as a member of the Front's Political-Diplomatic Commission since 1978 and continued to do so upon her return. However, in 1979, the Sandinista government, led by the Ortega brothers (Humberto and Daniel), appointed her as director of communications and public relations for its new Economic Planning Ministry. She served in that post until 1982, when she became the group's international press liaison.

Belli's cosmopolitan background gave her natural confidence during her liaison work. However, she was disappointed and appalled by how the male politicians treated her—especially those who supposedly supported the Sandinista credo of sexual equality. While in Panama, for instance, Panamanian General Omar Torrijos pursued her constantly, and Cuban dictator Fidel Castro asked her suggestively, "Where have the Sandinistas been hiding you?" and repeatedly tried to seduce her. The "cult of machismo," as Belli called it, was pervasive and resistant to change among the revolutionaries. She would later chafe at the government's refusal to let women actively serve in the military, demanding, "How could they think such a thing when women had already proven themselves to be as able fighters as men during the war?"

Left Government to Write Full-Time, Married Third Husband

Belli published another collection of poems, *Truenos y Arco Iris* (Thunder and Rainbows), in 1982. She continued as SNLF liaison until 1983, when she joined the Nicaragua Writer's Union as its foreign affairs secretary. (She would hold that post until 1988.) From 1983 to1984, Belli also served as executive secretary and spokesperson for the SNLF. She was appointed managing director of the National Publicity System in 1984, but that position eventually proved to be too time-consuming, and she resigned in 1986 to devote herself to writing full-time. Meanwhile, she had published *Amor Insurrecto* (Insurgent Love) in 1984 and cofounded the literary journal *Ventana.*

Freed from her SNLF professional obligations, Belli began writing and publishing at a faster pace. She proposed to American Charles Castaldi, a National Public Radio producer whom she had met during a previous trip to Washington, D.C., in 1987. The Sandinista government strongly disapproved of the relationship, since Washington was at the time supporting Nicaragua's counterrevolutionary Contras in violent attempts to oust the Ortegas. However, Belli rebelled somewhat against her old allies, having become somewhat disillusioned with the double standard she perceived—it was common practice then for Sandinista officials to conduct open affairs with American women. She had also been long concerned about what she termed the "unscrupulous policies" of the Ortega brothers and wondered if the revolution had been for naught.

In 1988 she produced *De la Costilla de Eva* (translated in 1989 as *From Eve's Rib*), and in 1989 released her first novel, *La Mujer Habitada* (translated in 1994 as *The Inhabited Woman*). The latter, a semi-autobiographical story about a professional, politically ignorant, Latin-American woman suddenly possessed by an ancient spirit seeking an end to oppression, immediately received critical acclaim in Europe and Latin America. It received both the 1989 Friedrich Ebhert Foundation's Book Sellers, Editors, and Publishers Best Political Novel of the Year Award and the 1989 Anna Seghers Prize.

Belli published a second novel, *Sofia de la Presagios* (Sophia of the Prophecies), in 1990, writing about her disillusionment with the Sandinistas on feminist issues. Also that year, she and her husband moved temporarily to the United States so he could run his business more closely and she could begin research for another novel. *El Oto de la Mujer* (Through a Woman's Eye) appeared in 1991, followed by the poetry collection *Sortilegio Contra el Frio* (A Spell Against the Cold) in 1992. She also tried her hand at writing for children in 1994, with *The Workshop of the Butterflies.* Then her third novel, *Waslala*, a cautionary tale of environmental doom inspired by a 1988 toxic waste accident in Brazil, was released in 1996. During this time, Belli and Castaldi's daughter Adriana, was born in 1995.

Wrote *El Pais Bajo mi Piel*

While splitting her time between Nicaragua and her home in Santa Monica, California, Belli next began to write an autobiography. *The Country Under My Skin: A Memoir of Love and War* was released in 2001 in Dutch, German, and Italian. The book debuted in the United States in English in 2002. It received rave reviews, earning the comment from fellow author Salman Rushdie, "The best autobiography I've read in years." Belli calls the book "an ode to romanticism, to believing that great dreams are possible," and laments, "The one thing lacking right now is imagination. There is no crazy dreaming anymore. The world has always gone forward when people have dared to have crazy ideas."

Books

Contemporary Authors, Gale Group, 1997.
Hispanic Literature Criticism, Gale Group, 1994.

Periodicals

Houston Chronicle, January 17, 2003.

Online

"Author Q&A: A Conversation with Gioconda Belli," *Random House Publishers website,* http://www.randomhouse.com (December 17, 2003).
"Belli, Giaconda," *Giaconda Belli website,* http://www .giacondabelli.com (December 17, 2003).

Campbell, Duncan, "Daughter of the Revolution," *The Guardian Unlimited website,* http://www.guardian.co.uk (December 17, 2003).
"Daughter of the Revolution," *The Guardian Unlimited website,* http://www.guardian.co.uk (December 17, 2003).
"Gioconda Belli," *Pinoleros.com website,* http://www.pinoleros .com (December 17, 2003).
"Gioconda Belli," *Time Warner Bookmark website,* http://www .twbook.com (December 17, 2003).
"Gioconda Belli: Bio," *Las Mujeres website,* http://www .lasmujeres.com (December 17, 2003). □

Gerd Karl Binnig

German physicist Gerd Binnig (born 1947) won a portion of the Nobel Prize for Physics in 1986 for his part in the invention of the scanning tunneling microscope (STM). He also invented the atomic force microscope, which launched a new field of microscopy, in 1985. Without Binnig's contributions, there would be no nanotechnology as we know it today.

Born A Scientist

B orn in Frankfurt, West Germany, on July 20, 1947, Binnig was the son of Ruth Bracke Binnig, a drafter, and Karl Franz Binnig, a machine engineer. World War II was so newly over that Binnig and his friends played among the ruins of buildings in his demolished neighborhood. Precocious and bright, Binnig had decided on a career in physics by age ten, although he recalls not really knowing what that entailed. He went to primary and secondary public schools in Frankfurt, where he first began to learn what physics was all about.

As a young man, Binnig pursued a strong interest in music, having been exposed to classical music at an early age. He began playing violin at age 15 and although he did not develop a great talent, he enjoyed playing in the school orchestra nonetheless. Influenced by his older brother's immersion in such bands as the Rolling Stones and the Beatles, Binnig played in a rock band with friends and even wrote some of his own music. However, as time passed, he went back to his early interest in physics and became more serious about studying the subject. He eventually earned a diploma and a doctorate in physics from Johann Wolfgang Goethe University in Frankfurt.

Got First Job at IBM, Met Rohrer

Immediately after receiving his doctorate for work on superconductivity in 1978, Binnig joined the staff of the research laboratory operated by International Business Machines (IBM) in Zurich, Switzerland. Rohrer had been at the IBM lab since 1963 and also had a background in superconductivity. Together Binnig and Rohrer, who Binnig later credited with "fully restoring my somewhat lost curiosity in

physics," became interested in exploring the characteristics of the surface of materials.

At first they tried using spectroscopy, a specialized tool that allows the identification of matter by the way its molecules emitted or absorbed radiation, to look at miniscule areas on extremely thin films. This was a challenging proposition: the atomic structure of the surface of a solid differs from the atomic structure of the solid's interior in that atoms on the surface can interact only with atoms at, on, and immediately below the surface, making surface structures astoundingly complex. In the words of physicist Wolfgang Pauli, quoted by Binnig and Rohrer in the introduction to their description of the STM in *Scientific American* (August 1985), "The surface was invented by the devil." Frustrated, the scientists turned to another possibility.

Binnig and Rohrer began to explore a phenomenon of quantum mechanics known as tunneling. Quantum mechanics had earlier revealed that the wavelike nature of electrons permits them to escape the surface boundary of a solid—they "smear out" beyond the surface and form an electron cloud around the solid. Electrons can "tunnel" through touching and overlapping clouds between two surfaces. Ivar Giaever of General Electric verified this experimentally in 1960. Binnig had investigated tunneling in superconductors during his graduate studies. Now he and Rohrer decided to make electrons tunnel through a vacuum from a sample solid surface to a sharp, needlelike probe. This proved surprisingly easy to accomplish: as the needle tip approaches within a nanometer (one billionth of a me-

ter) of the sample, their electron clouds touch and a tunneling current starts to flow. The probe's tip follows this current at a constant height above the surface atoms, producing a three-dimensional map of the solid's surface, atom by atom.

STM Became a Reality

In order to insulate their microscope against the serious problem of distorting vibration and noise, Binnig and Rohrer made a series of technical advances that included the creation of a probe tip consisting of a single atom. The colleagues and their research team soon demonstrated practical uses of the STM, revealing the surface structure of crystals, observing chemical interactions, and scanning the surface of DNA (deoxyribonucleic acid) chains. Using the STM, Binnig became the first person to observe a virus escape from a living cell. They soon realized that they had invented the first microscope powerful enough to let scientists see individual atoms. The tremendous importance of the STM lies in its many applications—for basic research in chemistry, physics, and biology and for applied research in semiconductor physics, microelectronics, metallurgy, and bioengineering.

Developed Atomic Force Microscope, Received Nobel Prize

Binnig continued to research while he was on leave at Stanford University in California in 1985. Freed from his constant work on the STM, he had time to contemplate using the atomic force between atoms, rather than tunneling current, to move the scanning tip over a solid's surface. Binnig shared his ideas with Christoph Gerber of IBM Zurich and Calvin Quate of Stanford, and soon they had produced a prototype of a new type of scanner, the atomic force microscope (AFM), which started a new field of microscopy. The AFM made it possible for the first time to image materials that were not electrically conductive.

Binnig became group leader at IBM's Zurich lab in 1984, and was working there in 1986 when he and Rohrer received half of the Nobel Prize for Physics for their invention of the STM. The Royal Swedish Academy of Sciences had found the STM so important that it awarded Binnig and Rohrer the prize just five years after the STM's first successful test. The academy stated that although development of the tool was in its infancy, it was already clear that "entirely new fields are opening up for the study of the structure of matter."

Unlike the vast majority of Nobel Prize winners who wait until their waning years for the honor, Binnig was only 39 years old at that point. In his Nobel speech, he recalled of his early experiences with the STM, "I couldn't stop looking at the images. It was entering a new world." He was quoted in the *New York Times* as having mixed emotions, saying, "It was beautiful and terrible at the same time"—beautiful because it signaled a great success but terrible because it concluded "an exciting story of discovery."

Binnig was appointed an IBM fellow in 1987, when he took over as head of the IBM physics group at the University of Munich. He also worked as visiting professor at Stanford from 1986 to 1988. In 1990, he joined the board of Daimler Benz Holdings and began exploring an interest in politics. Also that year, scientists at IBM used the STM to actually move and rearrange individual atoms, bringing to fruition physicist Richard Feynman's 1959 prediction that one day we would be "manipulating and controlling things on a small scale."

Started Research Company

In 1994 Binnig started his own company and named it Delphi Creative Technologies GmbH. The Munich-based firm, which eventually became Definiens Cognition Network Technology and is now a subsidiary of Definiens AG, develops knowledge-based systems. Binnig served as the company's chief researcher and scientific coordinator. Still an extremely productive scientist, he and his team developed what they call the "Cognition Network," which used technology that closely simulates the patterns of human thought. Binnig stepped down from leadership of the IBM physics group in Munich in 1995.

Working as a permanent consultant to Definiens AG, Binnig works closely on the Cognition Network, whose goal is to "integrate human models of perception into software to enable industry to analyze complex biological systems." The company won the 2002 European Information Society Technologies Prize for its eCognition product, a new technology that can analyze satellite and aerial images. Meanwhile, Binnig serves as a research staff member at IBM's Zurich Research Laboratory. Among his fields of research is his theory of "Fractal Darwinism," which he developed to describe complex systems. In a 2002 paper on the subject for *Europhysics News,* he explained, "Machines that are able to handle this complexity can be regarded as intelligent tools that support our thinking capabilities. The need for such intelligent tools will grow as new forms of complexity evolve; for example, those of our increasingly global networked information society."

In the spring of 2003, Binnig delivered the plenary lecture at the annual Electrochemical Society meeting in Paris, where he discussed his work on IBM's new "Millipede" project. A program concentrating on increasing the density of data-storage capacity, Millipede uses thousands of nanoscale needles to make indentations that represent individual pieces of information into thin plastic films. Binnig is optimistic about the project, saying, "While current storage technologies may be approaching their fundamental limits, this nanomechanical approach is potentially valid for a thousand-fold increase in data-storage density."

Binnig married Lore Wagler in 1969. They had a daughter in 1984 and a son in 1986. Binnig is athletic and enjoys a number of outdoor pursuits, including sailing, golf, tennis, soccer, and skiing. After taking a break from many of his hobbies to help raise his children, he has renewed his involvement in music as a composer, guitar and violin player, and singer.

The scientist wrote a popular German book on human creativity and chaos titled *Aus dem Nichts (Out of Nothing)* in 1990, which argued that creativity arises from disordered

thoughts. Binnig and Rohrer have shared a number of prestigious international awards for their pioneering research in microscopy, including the German Physics Prize, the Hewlett Packard Prize, the Otto Klung Prize, and the King Faisal Prize.

Online

"About Definiens Imaging," *Definiens Imaging website,* http://www.definiens.com (January 8, 2004).
"Binnig, Gerd," *Britannica Online website,* http://www.britannica.com (January 8, 2004).
"Binnig's Explorations in Microscopy Opened a New Science, a 'New World,' " *Small Times website,* http://www.smalltimes.com (December 18, 2003).
"Definiens Imaging GmbH Is Awarded with the European IST Prize," *European Information Societies Technologies website,* http://www.it-prize.org (December 18, 2003).
"Gerd Binnig," *The Gale Group Biography Resource Center website,* http://galenet.galegroup.com (January 8, 2004).
"Gerd Binnig-Autobiography," *The Nobel e-Museum website,* http://www.nobel.se (January 8, 2004).
"Gerd K. Binnig," *IBM Research website,* http://www.research.ibm.com (January 8, 2004).
"Gerd K. Binnig," *IBM website,* http://www.ibm.com (January 8, 2004).
"STM Inventor to Address ECS Paris Meeting on Nanotechnology: The Path to Handling Complexity?," *Electrochemical Society, Interface Winter 2002, website,* http://www.electrochem.org/publications/interface (January 8, 2004). □

Lucian Blaga

A poet, philosopher, translator, and dramatist, Romanian writer Lucian Blaga (1895–1961) narrowly missed winning the 1956 Nobel Prize for Literature because of Soviet government interference. Blaga created the field of philosophy of culture and the concept of Mioritic Space, both of which became key concepts in the development of a Romanian national identity.

Blaga was born on May 9, 1895, in Lâncrâm, Transylvania, in what was then part of the vast Austro-Hungarian Empire but which became Romania. He was the ninth child born to a Romanian Orthodox priest and his wife. Interestingly, the future poet did not speak until he was four years old, but once he did, any concerns raised as to his intelligence were quickly put to rest. His education was a predominantly German one, and he was especially influenced by the philosophical texts of Friedrich Nietzsche, Gotthold Lessing, and Henri Bergson. Blaga attended primary school in his native village, but after his family became destitute upon the death of his father in 1908, he was forced to withdraw from secondary school. He resumed his schooling in Sebeş, where his family moved in 1909, and completed his secondary schooling in Braşov.

Blaga published his first poems in 1910, and two years later he traveled to Italy, where he scoured libraries for books on philosophy and visited historical sites. In 1914 he published "Notes on Intuition in Bergson," his first philosophical article. From 1914 to 1917 he avoided serving in the Austro-Hungarian army by taking theology courses at the Sibiu Orthodox Seminary, then moved to Vienna, Austria, where he studied philosophy and biology at the University of Vienna. In 1919 his first volume of poetry, *Poemele luminii* (Poems of Light), was published. His thesis titled "Culture and Cognition" earned him a Ph.D. in philosophy in 1920, the same year he married.

Nominated for Nobel Prize for Literature

Blaga moved back to Romania in 1920 and published plays and more poems. He and a group of prominent Romanian writers established the journal *Gîndirea* (Thought) which was devoted to exploring Romanian national identity and which became the most influential literary magazine of its day. In 1921 the Romanian Academy presented Blaga with the Adamachi Award and in 1922 his thesis was published.

In 1926 Blaga began a career as a diplomat and journalist as the press attaché to the Romanian legation in Warsaw. A year later he was transferred to Prague, where his daughter, Dorli, was born. Another transfer in 1932 took Braga and his family back to Vienna. He made his first speech, "Eulogy to the Romanian Village," before the Romanian Academy in 1937. One year later his diplomatic career took him to Bucharest, Romania, and then to Lisbon, Portugal.

In 1939 Blaga returned to Romania to become a professor of the philosophy of culture, a position created specifically for him, at the University of Cluj. The Romanian Students' Union published *On Philosophical Cognition,* the first part of Blaga's course, in 1947, followed by his *Anthropological Aspects* the next year.

The 1949 Communist takeover of Romania forced Blaga to give up his academic chair at the University of Cluj, and he was also banned from further publishing. He found work as a librarian and resigned himself to publishing translations of German authors such as Friedrich Schiller/Schelling and Johann Wolfgang von Goethe. He became the Romanian Academy's head librarian in 1951. In 1956 he was nominated for the Nobel Prize for Literature, on the proposal of Italy's Rosa del Conte and France's Brazil Munteanu. Blaga was on the verge of receiving the award when the communist regime in Bucharest dispatched emissaries to Sweden to make false political allegations in protest of his nomination.

Silenced as a writer and intellectual, Blaga died of cancer on May 6, 1961, in Cluj, Romania, and was buried three days later, on his birthday, in the Lâncrâm church garden, near Sebeş. In 1962 his writings began to be published once more, many of them edited by his daughter, and in 1995 the University of Sibiu changed its name to Lucian Blaga University.

Formulated Philosophy of Culture

Blaga was known as both poet and social philosopher, and his poetry is often examined in relation to his philoso-

phy. The two are inseparable, linked "like Siamese twins, with the same blood running in their veins," according to Dumitru Ghise in *Romanian Review*. In his work, Blaga investigated day-to-day village life and its mythical traditions and devised an original philosophy of culture, distilled the essence of Romania, and fixed the nation's position in the world. In his poetry he reworked Romanian folklore to illuminate the relationship between the individual and his society. For instance, Blaga proposed that the pastoral folk ballad "Miorita" (The Little Ewe Lamb), of which there are over 900 variations, are mirrored in the Romanian landscape and portray nature and man as two inseparable entities. He felt the layout of the Romanian environment to be represented by the ballad's alternating accented and unaccented syllables, the unaccented syllables reflected the distinctive arrangement of peasant houses alternating with green fields.

Blaga applied his philosophy to religion as well. He believed that Protestantism and Catholicism encouraged the development of cities while Orthodoxy contributed to the growth of villages: Western villages were miniature cities no longer possessing their creative originality and rural character, while Eastern cites were overgrown villages that retained their primitive creativity. Therefore, the uniqueness of the Romanian national character was born of Orthodox dogma resulting from semi-pagan folklore, and the elements that distinguished Romanians from Serbs and Bulgarians were manifested most obviously in the output of folk artists and poets. As a result, self-definition through the Romanian cultural unconscious established an original perception of "Romanianness."

Blaga's Theory of Mioritic Space

Blaga asserted that mystery is the tenet behind all creation, an elusive principle he called the "Great Anonymous" because it can only be ascertained residually in nature and not seen directly. For Blaga, the Great Anonymous forms the collective ethnic consciousness, or cultural soul, of the Romanian people. This collective consciousness functions as the cornerstone of his theory of "Spatiul Mioritic" or Mioritic Space, which offers a definition of Romanian national identity by means of the characteristics that distinguish cultures from one another, including differences in environment and landscape. He envisioned life as a search for the origin of all creation and mystery and believed that each unique culture, born of its environment, is humankind's creative reaction to that search. As environment contributed to shaping the Romanian lifestyle and the Romanian lifestyle helped shape the environment, collective experiences occurring within the environment over time caused a unique culture to develop. As a consequence, national identity defines itself and can only be fashioned by the members of a specific nation.

Blaga argued that factors such as history, politics, and geography all influence the development of national identity. Considering the impact of such diversity and constant change of identity led Blaga to advance his theory of "style," a concept essential to his understanding of the roots of national identity. To Blaga, style comprised the complete number of categories employed by a people to distinguish historical periods, ethnic communities, and works of art from each other. He believed style emerges from unconscious primary and secondary groupings in the mind—a stylistic matrix—and that these serve as a nation's roots. Many matrix combinations exist and, consequently, there are various interpretations of the style of national identity. Primary categories contain prime instincts, such as the desire to form order, while secondary categories contain preferences for massive or delicate movement or calm. Blaga's theory of the stylistic matrix holds that it is the complex fusion of the characteristics of a community and its individuals that determines national identity, and that since experience is ongoing and new elements are incorporated into the community, this identity is constantly changing. It is in this manner that cultures develop regionally while occurring inside the same general context.

Blaga, as a humanist, did not subscribe to the view of German philosopher Oswald Spengler that culture is a parasitical result of a soul alienated from man and thus a means of suppressing him. He argued the contrary: that regional culture and mankind's creative destiny are entwined; that culture is a means by which an individual is able to transcend his mortality, endure the moment, and experience fulfillment.

Reflecting his philosophical beliefs, shadow and light, naive candor and wisdom, spontaneity and restraint constantly crisscross in Blaga's poetic work. The poetry simultaneously affirms and denies, with the poet reaching out toward transcendence, stirred by the spectacle of nature and cosmic grandeur yet suffering from an inner exile. This personal experience mirrors a universal condition: that creation attempts to find and reunite with its source, but encounters obstacles in nature established by the Great Anonymous.

Books

Contemporary Authors, Volume 157, Gale, 1997.
Contemporary Literary Criticism, Volume 75, Gale, 1993.

Periodicals

Central Europe Review, October 25, 1999.

Online

English-Language Web site for Lucian Blaga, http://homepage
.ntlworld.com/rt.allen/life.html (December 22, 2003).
"Lucian Blaga (1895–1961)," Welcome to Romania Web site,
http://www.ici.ro/romania/culture/l_blaga.html (December
22, 2003).
"Lucian Blaga: Romanian Poet and Philosopher," Simply Romania Web site, http://www.simplyromania.com/ (December
22, 2003). □

Katharine Burr Blodgett

**American physicist Katharine Burr Blodgett (1898–
1979), the first woman scientist ever hired by Gen-**

eral Electric, is credited as the inventor of nonreflective glass. She spent her entire career with General Electric, where through her work she made significant contributions to the field of industrial chemistry. Blodgett's invention of invisible nonreflective glass went on to find utility in the nascent photographic, optics, and automotive industries. She was also the first woman to earn a Ph.D. in physics from England's Cambridge University.

A Worldly Education

Blodgett was born on January 10, 1898, in Schenectady, New York. Her mother was Katharine Buchanan Blodgett; her father, patent attorney George Bedington Blodgett, was director of the patent department at General Electric's Schenectady-based research facility. He died several weeks before young Katharine was born, leaving his widow with a young son and the newborn Katharine.

The grieving family moved to New York where Mrs. Blodgett hoped to find more opportunity than in a small town. After three years, she moved her family to France and then to Germany, because she wanted her children to learn languages while they were young. The family then returned to the United States, where Katharine started school at the age of eight. She attended a public school in Saranac Lake, New York, for one year before entering the exclusive Rayson School in New York City. There she learned precise English speaking patterns and excelled in science.

Upon completing her studies at Rayson, Blodgett earned a scholarship to Bryn Mawr, where she studied under mathematician Dr. Charlotte Scott and physicist Dr. James Barnes. It was while at Bryn Mawr that Blodgett was inspired to pursue a career in science. During the early 20th century the most logical career for women interested in science was teaching, but Blodgett wanted a greater challenge. She hoped the increased job opportunities for women as a result of the World War I labor shortage would benefit her.

Found Mentor in Irving Langmuir

At the age of 18, Blodgett visited the General Electric research laboratories where her father had worked. She met the laboratory's assistant director, Irving Langmuir, a distinguished physicist who was impressed by Blodgett's interest and intellect. He gave the young woman a tour of the lab and advised her that she would find greater job opportunities with General Electric if she obtained a master's degree in physics.

Blodgett obtained her master's degree in physics from the University of Chicago in 1918. It took her only one year to complete the postgraduate work. Her master's thesis was on the chemical structure of gas masks—a timely topic during World War I.

Langmuir came through with his promise of employment, and when Blodgett returned to Schenectady at the age of 20, she became the first woman research scientist at the General Electric laboratories. Though she never knew her father, she worked in the same facility he once had and met many of his former colleagues. As Langmuir's assistant, she gained the advice of a valuable mentor. Langmuir had been working at General Electric since 1909. His early work included research on vacuum pumps and light bulbs and resulted in many patents in his name. In 1932 he would be awarded the Nobel Prize in chemistry. Blodgett collaborated with him on many projects leading up to this award.

During her first six years at the General Electric labs, Blodgett assisted Langmuir on projects related to electric current flow under restricted conditions. The two scientists published many papers on the subject in scientific journals. Blodgett excelled at communication and she became known for her clear presentation of scientific ideas.

Earned Ph.D. from Cambridge University

Langmuir encouraged Blodgett to continue her education in order to advance her career and in 1924 was able to get his protégé into the Cavendish Laboratory at Cambridge University in England. Cavendish was an exclusive laboratory, and it was only through Langmuir's influence that administrators allowed a woman to study there. Blodgett studied under world-renowned physicists, including Nobel Prize winner Sir Ernest Rutherford. In 1926 she became the first woman to earn a Ph.D. in physics from Cambridge University.

When Blodgett returned to the General Electric labs in Schenectady, she became a member of Langmuir's core research group. She worked on perfecting tungsten filaments in electric light bulbs. Later Langmuir assigned her to work on surface chemistry. Langmuir had previously discovered that oily substances form a one-molecule thin surface film when added to water. He asked Blodgett to find an application for this phenomenon.

Blodgett found that when she dipped a metal plate in water containing oil, the oily substance formed a layer on it, as it did on the water's surface. She inserted the plate into the water repeatedly and found that additional molecular layers formed. Each layer exhibited a different color, and these colors could be used to gauge the thickness of the coating. From these experiments, Blodgett invented a gauge for measuring the thickness of film within one micro-inch. General Electric marketed her color gauge for use by physicists, chemists, and metallurgists. It was simple, accurate, and more affordable than that attainable through existing instruments. Blodgett and Langmuir published a paper on depositing successive monomolecular layers of stearic acid on glass in the February 1935 *Journal of the American Chemical Society*. Two additional papers on the topic followed.

Invented Non-reflecting Glass

Blodgett continued to work on applications for her discovery. Within five years she discovered that coating sheets of glass with 44 one-molecule-thick layers of liquid soap resulted in an invisible glass that neutralizes light rays. The coated glass allows 99 percent of light to pass through and no light is reflected. Blodgett had invented non-reflecting glass, and in 1938 General Electric happily credited Blodgett with her invention. However, only two days later, two physicists at Massachusetts Institute of Technology announced that they, too, had manufactured non-reflecting glass by using another method: evaporating calcium fluoride in a vacuum and applying it to glass. Both Blodgett's method and the MIT scientists' methods resulted in coatings that easily rubbed off. Later scientists perfected the methods, making durable coatings that are used in many products such as telescopes, camera lenses, automobile windows, eyeglasses, pictures frames, and periscopes.

When World War II broke out, Blodgett began work on military applications. She devised improvements in a generator that produced smokescreens on the battlefield, an invention that saved thousands of lives during the Allied invasions of France and Italy. She also did experiments that led to better methods of de-icing the wings of airplanes.

Her research for military applications continued after the war. In 1947 she used her thin film knowledge to create an instrument for measuring humidity in the upper atmosphere that was then used by the U.S. Army Signal Corps in its weather balloons. Blodgett worked with Vincent J. Shaefer in devising a technique to create artificial rain by dropping dry ice pellets into clouds from airplanes. She also helped devise a high-resistance electrical material.

Recognized for Achievements

Blodgett was recognized worldwide for her scientific discoveries and received numerous honorary degrees. She won the 1945 Annual Achievement Award from the American Association of University Women and the 1951 American Chemical Society's Francis P. Garvan Medal for her research in surface chemistry. Named a fellow of the American Physical Society and a member of the Optical Society of America, she was also the only scientist honored in Boston's First Assembly of American Women of Achievement. Blodgett presented two James Mapes Dodge Lectures at the Franklin Institute and also was awarded the Photographic Society of America Progress Medal.

Blodgett continued her work with Langmuir until his death in 1957. She spent leisure time with Langmuir's family, often visiting them at their summer home at Lake George, in upstate New York. She also wrote a biographical sketch of Langmuir that was published in the *Journal of Chemical Education* in 1933.

Blodgett, who never married, lived in her Schenectady home, near the house where she was born, for her entire adult life. Her hometown honored her with the celebration of Katharine Blodgett Day. Blodgett was active in civic affairs and served as treasurer of the Travelers Aid Society and president of the General Electric employee's club. She enjoyed gardening, playing bridge, astronomy, antiquing, and attending the Presbyterian church. Retiring from General Electric in 1963, she continued to enjoy gardening and conducted several horticultural experiments. She died at home on October 12, 1979, at the age of 81.

Books

Notable Scientists: From 1900 to the Present, Gale, 2001.
Women in World History: A Biographical Encyclopedia, Anne Commire, editor, Yorkin Publications, 1999.

Periodicals

New York Times, September 24, 1939; October 19, 1979.
Physics Today, March 1980. □

Bono

Bono (born 1960), the Irish-born lead singer and guitarist of the rock band U2, has also gained acclaim—and sometimes criticism—for his many efforts on behalf of humanitarian causes that range from the AIDS crisis in Africa to debt reduction in impoverished Third World nations.

As lead singer in one of the most popular rock bands of all time, Irish-born guitarist Bono has become familiar to the general public as much for his support of social causes as for his trademark blue sunglasses and his energetic performances as lead singer in the musical group U2. Bono went from wowing concert audiences with

songs such as "Sunday, Bloody Sunday" during the 1980s to spearheading benefit tours during the 1990s to speaking about Africa's AIDS epidemic before a church congregation in Lincoln, Nebraska, in 2002.

Grew up in a Fragile World

Born Paul Hewson, in Dublin, Ireland, on May 10, 1960, Bono was the second son of Robert and Iris Hewson. His father was Catholic, his mother Protestant, and the religious differences their relationship represented played themselves out almost daily, not in the Hewson household, but in the violence erupting nearby in Northern Ireland. This turmoil was not lost on young Bono. Coming to embrace the Christian faith while in his 20s, the musician was quoted on *World Faith News* online as revealing to talk-show host Larry King: "I learned [as a child] that religion is often the enemy of God.... Religion is [actually] the artifice—you know, the building—after God has left it.... You hold onto religion, you know, rules, regulations, traditions. I think what God is interested in is people's heart."

When he reached school age, Bono adjusted well to the new routine of attending school, receiving high marks from his teachers and making many friends. Things changed when he reached St. Patrick's secondary school, however. Working for good grades no longer seemed important and neither did chess, or several other activities he dabbled in. Bored, the teen began cutting classes, and as the years passed he developed antagonistic relationships with several of his teachers. Having earned the label of "problem student," he was removed from St. Patrick's by his parents and transferred to a non-Catholic school, Mount Temple. There, the Hewsons hoped, their son would find his niche.

The move to Mount Temple was indeed where Bono found his niche, although it was not in academics. Although he got good grades in English, history, and art, his true calling lay in his popularity among his fellow students. The teen's outspokenness, charisma, and ability to spin a good story earned him the nickname "Bono Vox," which is schoolboy Latin for "good voice." Rather than identifying his singing talent, the nickname stuck because of Bono's outspokenness and his penchant for embroidering the truth.

Unfortunately, tragedy struck the Hewson family in September 1974, when Bono's mother suffered a brain hemorrhage and died within days. Iris Hewson's death left her younger son devastated. Depressed, feeling alone, and realizing that he had no clear plans for a future, the teen cast about for something to give his life meaning and a sense of purpose. That he found it in music surprised everyone who knew him.

Helped Form Band U2

It was one of Bono's Mount Temple classmates, Larry Mullen, Jr., who sparked Bono's interest in forming a musical group. One day in 1976 16-year-old Mullen put up a notice on the school bulletin board, welcoming any interested musicians to show up at his house for a jam session. Five teens—including Bono, brothers David "the Edge" and Dick Evans, and Adam Clayton—showed up, and by the time the meeting was over it was decided that the Edge would make the best guitarist, Clayton could find his way around a bass guitar, and Mullen could keep the beat on drums. While he had not yet developed his vocal abilities and was a rudimentary guitarist, Bono had something else the band needed: enthusiasm, energy, and the drive to make them a success. As U2 manager Paul McGuinness later admitted to a *Time* contributor, he was at first lukewarm about taking on the group. "They were very bad," McGuiness recalled. "But it wasn't the songs that were the attraction. It was the energy and commitment to performance that were fantastic even then. Bono would run around looking for people to meet his eyes." The five teens from Dublin decided to call their band Feedback.

During the late 1970s the music scene was veering from the disco era to the punk scene due to the popularity of such bands as the Sex Pistols. Feedback followed suit, adopting a hard-edged sound and playing covers in Dublin clubs. After Dick Evans left, the group renamed itself, first the Hype, and then U2. In 1978 the group won a talent contest and an audition for CBS Ireland. On the strength of their sound and the large following they had by this time developed in Ireland, CBS signed the band and released the three-song EP *U2-3*. When, despite the band's sold-out shows and chart-topping success, the record company opted not to distribute U2's EP beyond Ireland's borders, Bono began sending tapes to journalists and radio stations. He finally attracted interest at England's Island Records, which signed the band in 1980 and quickly released U2's debut album, *Boy*.

In 1980 Bono and U2 took off from Dublin for their first tour of Europe and the U.S., traveling up the east coast. They returned in early 1981, and, on the strength of *Boy* played to packed houses in New York City and Santa Monica. Soon London crowds got the news, and U2 swept the English pop charts as well.

As Bono took his turn before larger and larger crowds, he reaped the rewards of his success, as did his fellow band members. In the early 1980s his role as a rock idol and sex symbol began to conflict with his reawakened Christian faith. Joined by the Edge and Mullen, Bono began questioning whether he could reconcile his life of rock-stardom with his responsibilities as a Christian. Meanwhile, Clayton, whose faith *was* rock 'n' roll, began to feel estranged from his bandmates. *October*, U2's 1981 album, reflects this state of affairs in being less cohesive than *Boy*. Fortunately, Bono's issues of faith resolved themselves, and 1983's *War*, which contains such songs as "New Year's Day" and "Sunday, Bloody Sunday," reflects the songwriter's new politically conscious morality.

War was a powerful statement, made more powerful when videos of the single "New Year's Day" appeared on the newly-minted MTV. Airplay of the album increased following the band's video exposure, which showcased U2's handsome, energetic, and charismatic lead singer. *Under a Blood Red Sky*, a live 1983 album, further solidified the band's standing as the best-selling live album to date.

Band Developed New Direction

The Unforgettable Fire, released in 1984, signaled a departure for U2. Changing producers from Steve Lillywhite to Talking Heads band member Brian Eno and producer Daniel Lanois, the new collaboration yielded the hit "Pride (In the Name of Love)," a tribute to U.S. civil rights leader Martin Luther King, Jr. The tour that followed ended with Bono strutting on stage at the Live Aid concert to earn funds for Ethiopian famine relief. A single from U2's rendition of "Do They Know It's Christmas" also went to feed the victims of Africa's drought.

U2's transition to making "serious" music addressing social and political issues reflected the will of its frontman. While continuing to turn in a gritty, noisy performance, he also began to channel the band in a crusading direction. He also worked on a number of side projects, including spending time in the studio with Steven Van Zandt on the anti-apartheid *Sun City*, where he absorbed some blues influences while working with Keith Richards and Ron Wood of the Rolling Stones. 1986 found Bono and U2 joined by fellow musical philanthropists Sting, Peter Gabriel, and Lou Reed as headliners during the six-city Conspiracy of Hope tour benefiting Amnesty International.

While U2's reputation as an "important" band grew, Bono discounted his crusading efforts to the press. "We're a noisy rock 'n' roll band," he asserted to *Time* contributor Jay Cocks. "If we got on stage, and instead of going 'Yeow!' the audience all went 'Ummmmm' or started saying the rosary, it would be awful." While U2 audiences continued to yell and clap and shout, they were also more educated, activists, and older-than-average, and for them being a fan of U2 held a special meaning. It was the band's role as crusaders that propelled their sixth album, 1987's *The Joshua Tree,* into the Top Ten. Focusing on problems ranging from drug addiction to homelessness to political turmoil, the album was unique among its pop predecessors for being more intellectual than commercial. During the tour following its release, Bono performed for some of the largest crowds in the band's history.

U2 was, by the late 1980s, the most successful musical group in the world. With sales of *The Joshua Tree* cresting at eight million copies, the group's four members found their picture on the cover of a 1987 issue of *Time* magazine. However, by this point *Time* was behind the times; two years before, *Rolling Stone* had already proclaimed U2 the Band of the '80s. 1988's *Rattle and Hum* confirmed the *Rolling Stone* pronouncement, producing the singles ''Desire'' and ''When Love Comes to Town.''

Although their sound became more experimental during the 1990s, U2 remained popular. Albums such as *Achtung Baby* (1991) and *Zooropa* (1993), with their Grammy Award-winning performances, retained the group's loyal following, and the band's *Best of 1980–1990,* released by Island in 1998, cemented U2's roots and earned them new fans among younger listeners. Bono and his bandmates also continued to pinpoint areas of humanitarian concern. In 1990 U2 contributed to a Cole Porter anthology to benefit AIDS education, released as *Red Hot + Blue.* Two years later U2 ended a tour with a benefit for Greenpeace during which they protested the construction of a U.K. nuclear power plant. Their transition album into the next century, 2000's *All That You Can't Leave Behind,* took Bono and the band back to their '80s roots, particularly the song ''Beautiful Day.'' Following the terrorist attacks against U.S. soil in September of 2001, the album's ''Walk On'' became, for many, an anthem of hope for a safer future. Other actions in response to the terror earned Bono and U2 four awards at the 2002 Grammys as well as an invitation to perform before crowds at the February 3, 2002, NFL Super Bowl.

Committed Frontman for Activism

Bono's activism began in earnest in the summer of 1983, when he accepted an invitation from Irish Prime Minister Garrett Fitzgerald to join a Select Government Action Committee on Unemployment. Two years later, in 1985, he and his wife, Alison, visited Ethiopia and spent seven weeks working alongside other humanitarian relief workers to improve housing and sanitation in a crowded refugee camp. During a visit to El Salvador, he witnessed a military attack on a village. These experiences found voice in the album *The Joshua Tree.* Other causes he has supported, both on and off the stage, include gun control, Jamaican hurricane relief efforts, and the forgiveness, by the world's superpowers, of Third World debt.

While Bono's activist efforts have drawn praise from many quarters, and inspired thousands of his fans to become involved in social change, they have also drawn some criticism. Among his colleagues, rock group Black Flag's former lead Henry Rollins was quoted in *Launch* as ques-

tioning how Bono could shift from one social cause to the next so frequently. ''If he's using all that rock-star power, well, right on,'' but ''how did you go from Third World debt to AIDS?'' Other, more cynical pundits questioned whether the singer's activism was perhaps just another way to promote the band's music.

Acting apart from the band, Bono continued to appear on world stages as part of celebrity gatherings and musical events supporting relief and humanitarian causes. In 2003 he was awarded the King Centre Humanitarian Award, presented by the fallen civil rights leader's widow, Coretta Scott King. He also traveled to Rome to meet with Pope John Paul II regarding ways to ease the financial strain of poor nations and has appeared before the U.S. Congress and legislative bodies in Europe. In 2002 he established the nonprofit advocacy group Debt, Aid, Trade for Africa (DATA), in a continuing effort to aid the world's most impoverished and threatened populations. In May of 2004 Bono was a guest speaker at the University of Pennsylvania commencement ceremony where he encouraged graduates to get involved with the fight against the AIDS epidemic in Africa. He also received an honorary doctor of laws degree. Also in May 2004 Bono helped launch a new campaign called the ONE Campaign. The goal of the campaign is to get Americans to come together and fight against poverty and AIDS.

Throughout his career, Bono has eschewed the ''pop star'' crown and attempted to live a normal life as possible for one whose face is known to millions around the world. He has been known to invite fans into his home in Bray, just outside Dublin. Married to his childhood sweetheart, Alison Stewart, in 1983, he announced the birth of his fourth child, a son, in May of 2001. The couple's three other children include daughters Jordan and Eve and son Elijah.

Books

Dunphy, Eamon, *Unforgettable Fire,* Warner Books, 1988.
Newsmakers, Gale, 2002.
Rees, Dafydd, and Luke Crampton, *Rock Movers and Shakers,* ABC-Clio, 1991.

Periodicals

America's Intelligence Wire, May 20, 2004.
Entertainment Weekly, May 9, 1997; November 3, 2000; February 15, 2002.
Knight Ridder/Tribune News Service, May 19, 2004.
Launch, August 1, 2003.
Musician, March 1992; September 1992.
People, April 1, 1985; July 8, 2002.
Rolling Stone, October 1, 1984; March 14, 1985; May 7, 1987; September 8, 1988; May 10, 2001.
Spin, August 1993.
Time, April 27, 1987; March 10, 1997; March 4, 2002.
Village Voice, December 10, 1991; December 22, 1992.

Online

''One Campaign,'' *The One Campaign,* http://www.the onecampaign.org (June 10, 2004).
''U2,'' *J.A.M.,* http://www.ascap.com/jam/feature/artists/u2.cfm (January 17, 2004).

"U2's Bono Launches AIDS Awareness Tour from Church,"
World Faith News online, http://www.wfn.org/2002/12/
msg00088.html (December 10, 2003).

U2 News Service, http://www.u2world.com/news/ (January 17,
2004). □

Fernando Botero

Known for his enormous metal sculptures and vibrantly colorful paintings of robust human and animal shapes, Colombian artist Fernando Botero (born 1932) was one of the most popular modern artists.

Studied Bullfighting

Fernando Botero was born in Medellin, in the Colombian Andes, on April 19, 1932. His parents, David and Flora Angulo de Botero, had been raised in the remote highlands of the Andes. His father, a traveling salesman who journeyed on horseback to outlying areas of the city, died when Botero was four, and his mother supported the family as a seamstress.

The second of three boys, Botero attended a Jesuit secondary school on a scholarship starting at age 12. His uncle also enrolled him in matador school, which he attended for two years, and the images in his first drawings come from the world of bullfighting (a watercolor of a matador is his first known work). Until he discovered a book of modern art at the age of 15 he "didn't even know this thing called art existed," he says.

In 1948 Botero decided he wanted to become an artist and first exhibited his work in a joint show in his native town. He began working at *El Colombiano,* Medellin's leading newspaper, illustrating the Sunday magazine. At this time a period of civil unrest began in Colombia, and there was a low tolerance for nonconformity and radicalism. Some of Botero's teachers began to express disapproval of his work, and he received several warnings about nudity in his newspaper illustrations. In response he published an article called "Picasso and Nonconformity in Art" and was subsequently expelled from the school. He completed his secondary education at the Liceo de la Universidad de Antioquia in Medellin, graduating in 1950, and continued to publish articles on modern art.

Joined Avant Garde

Botero worked for two months for a traveling theater group as a set designer, then moved to Bogota, where he met some avant-garde intellectuals and artists and was influenced by the work of such Mexican muralists as Diego Rivera, Josè Clemente Orozco, and David Alfaro Siqueiros. Botero's large watercolor paintings, such as 1949's *Donna Che Piange* (The Crying Woman), are from this period. In 1951 he had his first one-man exhibition—consisting of 25 oils, drawings, watercolors, and gouaches—at the Galerias de Arte Foto-Estudio Leo Matiz. All the pieces sold, and he

took the proceeds from the exhibit and moved to a small coastal town to work.

In 1952 he moved back to Bogota and mounted his second show, which earned him 7,000 pesos. He won an additional 7,000 pesos when his 1952 painting *Sulla Costa* (On the Coast) took second place in the IX Salon Annual de Artistas Colombianos, sponsored by the Bogota National Library. He used these funds to move to Europe and study art. He spent a year in Madrid, enrolled in the San Ferdinando Academy, and earned a living by copying paintings by Francisco de Goya, Titian, Diego Velasquez, and Tintoretto and selling them to tourists. From there he moved to Paris, where he spent a summer studying old masters at the Louvre. From 1953 to 1954 he lived in Italy, attending the San Marco Academy in Florence, where he studied fresco techniques and copied works by Andrea del Castagno and Giotto, in addition to creating his own oil paintings. He studied with Roberto Longhi, who further stimulated his enthusiasm for the Italian Renaissance.

Developed Distinctive Style

In 1955, he returned to Bogota with his new paintings, 20 of which he exhibited at the National Library. His work was harshly criticized for not having a style of its own. Few paintings sold, and Botero was compelled to work at non-artistic employment. This included an attempt to sell automobile tires and a position doing magazine layout. At the end of the year, Botero married Gloria Zea and they moved to Mexico City, where their son, Fernando, was born.

In Mexico City Botero began developing his own style. In 1956, while at work on a painting called *Still Life with Mandolin,* he had a revelation that would change his art. As he sketched a mandolin, he placed a small dot where a larger sound hole should have been, making the mandolin suddenly seem enormous. He began to experiment with size and proportion in his work and eventually developed his trademark style. The people and objects in his paintings were inflated, giving them presence, weight, and a round sensuality. This style, combined with his paintings' Latin American-influenced flatness, bright colors and boldly outlined shapes, made him one of the 20th Century's most recognizable artists.

Gained Worldwide Recognition

Botero's art began to gain recognition outside Latin America. In 1957 he went to New York City, where the abstract expressionist movement was thriving. On that trip, he sold most of the paintings he exhibited at the Pan-American Union in Washington, D.C. He returned to Bogota in 1958, and his daughter, Lina, was born. He became a professor of painting at the Bogota Academy of Art, a post he held for two years. By this time he was renowned as one of the country's most promising artists.

He designed a portion of the illustrations for the writer Gabriel Garcia Marquez's *La Siesta del Martes,* and the work also appeared in an important Colombian daily newspaper, *El Tiempo.* Amid some controversy, his painting *Camera degli Sposi* (The Bride's Chamber) won first prize in that year's Colombian salon and was exhibited the same year at the Gres Gallery in Washington, D.C. The Washington show was hugely successful, with nearly all his work selling on the first day. His work was also shown in 1958's Guggenheim International Award show in New York.

In 1959, following more exposure to abstract expressionism in the United States and a phase of personal tumult during which his marriage was dissolving, Botero's style began to change. He started painting in a monochromatic palette and using looser brushstrokes. His *El Nino de Vallecas,* painted in this style, was not as popular as his other work at a third Washington exhibit in October 1960. His son, Juan Carlos, was born that year, and Botero was nominated to represent Colombia at the II Mexico Biennial Exhibition.

In 1960, Botero moved to Greenwich Village in New York and began working at a feverish pace. His work, which celebrated volume and voluptuousness, received a generally tepid American response at a time when flatness was the craze, although in 1961 the Museum of Modern Art did buy his painting *Monna Lisa all'età di Dodici Anni* (Mona Lisa, Age 12). Despite the cool response, he kept painting work that was outside the mainstream. His 1962 exhibit at The Contemporaries Gallery in New York was harshly attacked in what Botero felt was a personal manner. In 1964, he married a second time, to Cecilia Zambrano.

Botero became fascinated by the art of the Flemish master Rubens and created a number of paintings inspired by him. By 1965, his painting had acquired greater sophistication. He began to concentrate on forms rather than individual brushstrokes, and the surfaces of objects appeared almost sculptural. His figures used subtle tones and were both monumental and plastic. He began to apply thin pastel-colored glazes to his canvases.

In 1966, Botero's work had its first European exhibition in Baden-Baden, Germany. He had begun to receive more American recognition, yet he felt at once that he was more tuned into the European sensibility. From 1966 to 1975, he divided his time among Europe, New York, and Colombia. On a visit to Germany, he became enamored of Albrecht Dürer's work, which inspired him to create a series of large charcoal drawings, "Dureroboteros," mimicking the German artist's famous paintings. He also painted works in which he interpreted the styles of Manet and Bonnard. In 1969, he mounted his first Paris exhibition and had become a full-fledged member of Europe's avant-garde by the early 1970s. His third son, Pedro, was born in New York in 1970.

During this period, Botero's painting moved beyond its focus on sensuous, sculptural, Latin forms and became harder and more sparkling, with an underlying darkness. An example from this period includes *War,* with its images of corpses. In 1973, he moved from New York to Paris and began to sculpt. His son, Pedro, was killed in an automobile accident in which the artist was also seriously injured, losing a finger and some motion in his right arm. Botero had painted his son repeatedly and continued to do so after the boy's death, working him into various paintings. Three years after his son's death, he dedicated a suite of galleries housed in Medellin's art museum to his son's memory. He and his second wife separated in 1975.

Sculpting and Politics

Botero devoted himself to sculpting from 1975 to 1977, putting his painting temporarily on hold. He created 25 metal sculptures that began from sketches. The subjects were huge animals (including bulls), human torsos, reclining women, and massive objects, including a gigantic coffee pot. His sculpture was exhibited at the Paris Art Fair in 1977, the year he also began to paint again (he paid homage to Velasquez in paintings depicting the Infantas—Spanish or Portuguese princesses). His work continued to be shown in galleries worldwide. In 1983 he established a workshop in an area of Tuscany renowned for its metalworks, which allowed him to spend several months each year creating his increasingly large sculptures, which weighed an average of 3,000 pounds. He also revisited bullfighting as subject matter for his painting, aspiring to become the definitive artist on the subject.

Botero became disturbed that his birthplace, Medellin, had become associated with the drug-trafficking cartel run by Colombian drug kingpin Pablo Escobar. Botero was said to be incensed that two of his paintings were discovered in Escobar's home after the druglord was killed in 1993. Despite Escobar's death, the violence continued in Medellin, and Botero was the target of a failed kidnapping in 1994.

In 1995 a guerrilla group blew up a sculpture of a dove, *The Bird,* that Bonero had donated to the city. The explosion occurred during a downtown street festival, and 23 people were killed while 200 others were wounded. When taking responsibility for the blast, the guerrillas called Botero a symbol of oppression. Botero cast a new dove for the plaza but insisted the remnants of the original remain so that the sculptures could represent peace and violence.

In 1996 Botero's son Fernando was convicted of accepting drug money to finance former Colombian President Ernesto Samper's campaign. Botero did not speak to his son for three years, but they later reconciled. In 2000, Botero began exhibiting paintings that reflected the violence in Colombia—images of massacres, torture, and car bombings, and one depicting Escobar's killing—a distinct departure from his usual domestic style. In a 2001 article in the *Christian Science Monitor,* Botero said, "Art should be an oasis, a. . .refuge from the hardness of life. But the Colombian drama is so out of proportion that today you can't ignore the violence, the thousands displaced and dead, the processions of coffins."

Donated Work to Colombian Museums

In 2000 Botero donated artwork valued at $200 million to two Colombian museums, the renovated Museum of Antioquia in Medellin and the cultural wing of the Banco de la Republica in Bogota. The Medellin site includes an area that was razed to create a sculpture garden, while the Bogota gift is housed in a 12-room gallery prepared for the collection. Botero's donation consisted of dozens of his own paintings and sculptures, as well as some 90 pieces from his private collection, including 14 impressionist paintings (including oils by Monet, Renoir, Degas, and Pissarro), four Picassos, and works by Dali, Miro, Chagall, Ernst, de Kooning, Klimt, Rauschenberg, Giacometti, and Calder.

Botero estimated that by the mid-1990s he had created 1,000 paintings and 100 sculptures. His work had become very popular in the 1980s and commanded high sums. In 1992 a brothel scene sold for $1.5 million at auction. His pencil and watercolor canvases have carried on his familiar themes—portrait-style images of people, brothel scenes, nudes, and still lifes. He married for a third time, to Greek sculptor Sophia Vari, and divided his time among Paris, New York City, Italy, and Colombia.

In January 2002 the French ambassador to Columbia inducted Botero into the Legion of Honor. Botero was honored by this since France had lent aid to help boost peace between Columbia's government and the Revolutionary Armed Forces of Colombia (FARC) guerrillas.

Books

Newsmakers, Gale Research, 1994.

Periodicals

EFE World News Service, January 24, 2002.

Online

"Colombia gets $200 million gift of art: Botero makes gesture for homeland," *Miami Herald,* http://www.miami.com (December 22, 2003).
"Fernando Botero," *Britannica Online,* http://www.brittanica.com (December 22, 2003).
"Fernando Botero," *The Gale Group Biography Research Center,* http://galenet.gale.com (January 2, 2004).
"Fernando Botero Art," *Fernando Botero,* http://www.fernandobotero.biz (December 22, 2003). □

Adrian Cedric Boult

Music director of the British Broadcasting Corporation (BBC) beginning in 1930 and conductor of the London Philharmonic Orchestra from 1950 to 1957, English conductor Sir Adrian Boult (1889–1983) became something of a national icon in Great Britain due to his continued efforts to boost national morale through music during World War II. In addition to his work as a conductor, he championed the work of British composers and performers throughout the world, including composers Ralph Vaughn Williams and Edward Elgar.

An Early Interest in Music

Adrian Cedric Boult, born in Chester, England, on April 8, 1889, was the second and youngest child born to oil merchant and justice of the peace Cedric Randal Boult and his wife, Katherine, whose promising career as a pianist was thwarted by illness. Katherine Boult exposed her young son to music beginning in infancy. Young Boult responded, demonstrating remarkable musical talent: he startled his parents by picking out tunes on the piano at age 18 months and was composing music at seven years of age. A family friend introduced the youngster to British composer Sir Edward Elgar (1857–1934), whose music the boy would later conduct. The family attended the nearby Unitarian church during much of Boult's childhood.

Boult attended the Westminster School as a boy, studying harmony and counterpoint with his science teacher there. One of his favorite activities was to attend concerts at Queen's Hall in London, where he liked to study the score as he listened. Boult went on to Christ Church, Oxford, where he studied under Sir Hugh Allen (1869–1946), a distinguished conductor and one of the leading figures in British cultural life. In college Boult continued to develop his talents as a musician, singing in the Oxford Bach Choir and serving as president of the University Musical Club in 1910.

Boult earned a "pass degree"—a lower-level university or equivalent degree—in 1912 but was disappointed to learn that the school required him to wait five years before he could begin his doctoral work. Forced to put his formal education at Oxford on hold, Boult traveled to the Leipzig Conservatorium in Germany, where in 1912 he studied under composer Max Reger and eminent conductor Arthur Nikisch. He returned to Oxford to take his bachelor's in music examination in 1913 and received his master's degree from the school in 1914.

cluded works by Liszt, Bach, Hayden, and several contemporary composers. This and other of the young conductor's performances prompted composer Gustav Holst to request Boult to conduct the first private performance of Holst's new orchestral suite, *The Planets.* Boult showcased the piece in a performance at the Queen's Hall in London in 1918.

Teaching Added to Responsibilities

Boult became a teacher at the Royal College of Music in 1919, although he continued his work as a conductor and welcomed his growing popularity among London's musical elite. The following year, he accepted an appointment as conductor of the City of Birmingham Orchestra (later known as the City of Birmingham Symphony Orchestra), where he worked for a number of years. He conducted first performances of the revised *London Symphony* by Ralph Vaughn Williams in 1922, followed by Elgar's four-movement Symphony No. 2 in E-flat Major, which boosted the latter composer's flagging popularity. Elgar wrote the young conductor, telling him that he felt confident that the fate of classical music was safe with Boult. This confidence was well placed, since Boult became known for his authoritative interpretation of many new pieces and his strong championship of 20th-century English music. Boult published *The Point of the Stick: A Handbook on the Technique of Conducting* in 1920 and received a doctorate in music from Oxford University in 1921.

As his renown increased, Boult began to conduct orchestras and symphonies all over the world. He kept England as his home base, however, and in 1924 accepted the directorship of the Birmingham Festival Chorus. After working for the first time as an opera conductor with the British National Opera Company, Boult became assistant musical director back at Covent Garden in 1926. Then, in 1927 he conducted the London Bach Choir and from 1928 to 1931 he conducted BBC-Radio's Bach choir. In the meantime, he left his position as teacher at the Royal College of Music in 1930.

Asked to Conduct BBC Orchestra

Boult not only left the Royal College, where he had happily taught for 11 years, but also his position with the City of Birmingham Orchestra to accept a new job as director of music for the BBC Symphony Orchestra. This conductorship brought Boult true international fame and marked the beginning of the most important phase of his career, since the British Broadcasting Corporation's reach was far and its pockets deep. However, Boult remained involved in the world of opera, and his conducting of *Fidelio* at Sadler's Wells Theater in 1930 and *Die Walküre* at Covent Gardens in 1931 are considered among his finest performances.

After a somewhat controversial romance, Boult married a divorcee, the former Ann Mary Grace Bowles, in 1933. While Bowles had four children from her previous marriage to tenor singer Sir James Steuart Wilson, she and Boult had no children together.

Having replaced Percy Pitt as conductor of the BBC Symphony Orchestra, Boult rose to the challenge of work-

Launched Musical Career Despite World War I

Boult began his professional musical career in 1914 when he joined the music staff at the Royal Opera House in Covent Garden, one of the cultural centers of London. There, in February and March of that year, he helped to stage the first British performances of *Parsifal,* an opera by German composer Richard Wagner, playing the off-stage bells that the work called for. In 1915 he became the youngest conductor ever to work with the Liverpool Philharmonic Society.

When World War I broke out later that year, the 25-year-old Boult was spared from being sent to the front because of a pre-existing heart condition that disqualified him from active duty. However, he spent 1914 to 1916 as an orderly officer in Cheshire and North Wales, helping to drill new recruits. From 1916 to 1918 he worked as a translator for MI-5—the British Secret Service—helped out at the Commission for Foreign Supplies and assisted Food Minister Frederick Marquis in the war office. Meanwhile, in his spare time, Boult gathered musicians from the Liverpool Philharmonic Society to form a small wartime orchestra, conducting the group in concerts to entertain the area's war-weary residents.

The local musicians were impressed by Boult's obvious conducting talent and reported this to leaders of the local musical scene. As a result, Boult was invited to conduct the full orchestra in Liverpool in January 1916. The performance, which constituted Boult's debut as a conductor, in-

ing with some of the world's finest musicians and soon proved that his talent and tireless nature could make even the best orchestra even better. His directorship of the orchestra entailed his recruitment of musicians and other administrative duties, as well as serving as chief conductor of the group.

Under Boult's directorship, the BBC Symphony Orchestra gave public concerts throughout Great Britain and broadcast performances from the BBC studios. Boult also launched a successful world tour with the orchestra, performing in Vienna, Paris, Budapest, Zurich, Brussels, Salzburg, Boston, and New York City. He also accepted invitations to be a guest conductor for orchestras in Vienna, Boston, New York, and Salzburg. By 1936 his fame had become so great that he was asked to conduct during the coronation of King George VI.

Boult developed a distinctive style of conducting. He was quite restrained on the platform, guiding his musicians through his natural authority and innate musicianship. He preferred to carry out meticulous rehearsals but was also known for producing excellent results with few practices. Tall, erect, and commanding, Boult could explode into a violent temper during difficult rehearsals, but he was generally known for his genteel, courteous manner and understated, old-fashioned speaking style. The conductor's ultimate goal was to preserve a composer's original conceptions and he strove to avoid "interpreting" the music as a means to impose his own personality on a piece. Critics believed that Boult was a master of both 19th-century classical music and the works of his British contemporaries.

Became Preeminent Conductor

Boult became the conductor-of-choice among nervous composers whose works were being publically performed for the first time, since the conductor's capability and sensitivity with new and unfamiliar music had become legendary. As a result, he conducted many pieces in their first public performances, including Arthur Bliss's *Music for String* (1935) and Concert for Piano and Orchestra (1939); Vaughn Williams' Symphony No. 4 (1935); and Paul Hindemith's *Trauermusik* (1936). He also premiered Arnold Schoenberg's Variations, opus 31; Alban Berg's tragic opera *Wozzeck* (1934); and Ferrucio Busoni's *Doktor Faust* (1937), garnering praise from critics for his willingness to introduce new pieces. These were considered some of his most notable operatic achievements.

Boult's reputation and standing as an icon of the British musical world was cemented in 1937 when he received a knighthood from the British royal family. He left his position as music director of the BBC in 1942 but continued as the BBC Symphony Orchestra's conductor. World War II began in 1939 and quickly interrupted the BBC's formerly hectic schedule. To escape the German bombing of London, the orchestra was evacuated to Bristol, then Bedford. Boult worked to maintain the orchestra's high standards, although morale became a problem as more and more key musicians left. Nevertheless, even during these trying years, he made several significant recordings. He also served as deputy director of the popular London promenade concerts—

where part of the audience stood in a promenade area of the hall—from 1942 to 1950. When the war finally ended in 1945, Boult presided over BBC-Radio's *Third Programme*, introducing such revolutionary new composers as Gustav Mahler to the country.

Resurrected London Philharmonic after Losing BBC

Boult published *The Saint Matthew Passion: Its Preparation and Performance* in 1949. He remained with the BBC Symphony Orchestra until 1950, when at age 60, he was forced to retire by newly appointed director of music. It was alleged that the reason for Boult's removal was that the BBC Symphony Orchestra's quality had sunk to unacceptable levels, an assertion that remains controversial. Boult quickly rebounded from this setback and immediately accepted a position as musical director of the world-famous but flagging London Philharmonic Orchestra. He rebuilt the group and toured West Germany with it in 1951.

During his years with the London Philharmonic, Boult led the orchestra through the recordings of nine Vaughan Williams symphonies and many Elgar works. He also helped the group's resurrection by winning recording contracts with several American companies, for which the Philharmonic recorded works by Brahms, Hector Berlioz, Sibelius, and others.

Boult retired from the London Philharmonic in 1957 at age 68 and from then on worked only as a guest conductor. He remained much sought after, though, because of his sterling reputation for being impartial and reliable. He also found time to teach at the Royal College of Music from 1962 to 1966 and published his third book, *Thoughts on Conducting*, in 1963. Boult resumed recording in 1966 for the EMI label. His work during this short period, which included his direction of a televised performance of Elgar's *Dream of Gerontius* filmed at Canterbury Cathedral in 1968, is still considered among his finest. Chronic back pain finally slowed the energetic conductor in 1978, forcing him to do only seated studio work for several years.

Retired from conducting entirely in 1981, Boult died at a nursing home in Tunbridge Wells, Kent, England on February 22, 1983. A documentary, *The Point of the Stick*, was released in 1971, and his autobiography, the popular *My Own Trumpet*, was published in 1973. Numerous books were written about the conductor, including *Sir Adrian Boult: A Tribute* (1980); Malcolm Walker's *Sir Adrian Boult* (1984); Michael Kennedy's *Adrian Boult* (1987); *Sir Adrian Boult: Companion of Honour* (1989); and the publication *A Portrait of Sir Adrian Boult* (1999).

Books

Boult, Adrian, *Boult on Music: Words from a Lifetime's Communication,* Toccata Press, 1983.

Contemporary Authors, Volume 114, Gale, 1985.

Dictionary of National Biography, 1981–1985, Oxford University Press, 1986.

Online

"Adrian Boult (Conductor)," *Bach Cantatas Web site,* http://www.bach-cantatas.com/ (December 20, 2003).
"Sir Adrian Boult Papers," *Archives Hub,* http://www .archiveshub.ac.uk/ (December 20, 2003). □

Myra Bradwell

America's first woman lawyer, Myra Bradwell (1831–1894), never practiced law, yet she became one of the most influential people in the legal profession. Through her publication of the monthly *Chicago Legal News,* she initiated many legal and social reforms. Bradwell eventually was offered admittance to the Illinois bar, making her the first woman attorney in the United States.

Myra Bradwell was born Myra Colby on February 12, 1831, in Manchester, Vermont. She was the youngest of five children of Eben and Abigail Willey Colby. Both parents were descendents of Boston settlers and were active abolitionists.

Shortly after Bradwell's birth, the family moved to Portage, New York, where they lived until 1843. They then moved to Shaumberg, Illinois, near Chicago. Education for young girls in the nineteenth century often meant attendance at a finishing school or female seminary, which provided a broad education in literature and the arts and trained girls for their roles as wives and mothers. Bradwell attended finishing school in Kenosha, Wisconsin, where she lived with a married sister. She completed her education at the Elgin Female Seminary in Illinois, and later taught at the seminary for one year.

Met James Bradwell

While attending the seminary, Bradwell met James Bolesworth Bradwell, a Tennessee law student who was visiting Elgin. James Bradwell came from a family of poor English immigrants. He financed his education by doing manual labor, a fact that led the Colby family to disapprove of him as a suitor for Myra. When the couple eloped a few months after meeting, Myra's brother pursued them with a shotgun in an attempt to stop the marriage. Nevertheless, they were married in Chicago on May 18, 1852.

The Bradwells moved to Memphis, Tennessee, where they opened a private school. James continued to study law and was admitted to the Tennessee bar. Bradwell had their first child, a daughter named Myra, in 1854. The couple subsequently had three other children: Thomas in 1856, Bessie in 1858, and James in 1862. Young Myra died at the age of 7 and James died at 2.

After Myra's birth, the Bradwells returned to Chicago, where James continued to study law. He was admitted to the Illinois bar in 1855 and formed a law partnership with Myra's brother, Frank Colby.

Studied Law

In 1861, James Bradwell was elected a Cook County judge. He served one term and returned to his law practice a few years later. Bradwell wanted to work with her husband in his law practice. During the mid-nineteenth century, there were two ways to learn law: attend law school or study law under the supervision of a practicing attorney. As a woman, Bradwell was prohibited from attending law school, so she read law with James. According to biographer Jane M. Friedman in *America's First Woman Lawyer: The Biography of Myra Bradwell,* Bradwell said in an 1889 *Chicago Tribune* article, "I acquired the idea [of studying law] from helping my husband in his office. I was always with him, helping in whatever way I could. . . . I believe that married people should share the same toil and the same interests and be separated in no way. It is the separation of interests and labor that develops people in opposite directions and makes them grow apart. If they worked side by side and thought side by side we would need no divorce courts."

Bradwell's studies were put on hold when the Civil War began. During the war, Bradwell became involved with charitable endeavors that raised funds for the sick and wounded Union soldiers. Bradwell and suffragist Mary Livermore organized the Northwestern Sanitary Fair in Chicago in 1865. As secretary of the Arms, Trophies and Curiosities Committee, Bradwell was in charge of one of the fair's two exhibits, which featured a collection of Union flags, captured Confederate flags, trophies, and war curios.

Bradwell also served as president of the Chicago Soldiers' Aid Society, which sponsored two other fairs to raise funds for soldiers' families.

At the conclusion of the war, Bradwell returned to her studies and in 1869, when she was 38 years old, she passed the Illinois bar exam with high honors and applied to practice law in Illinois. At the time, women were prohibited from practicing law in the United States. However, an Iowa teacher, Arabella Mansfield, had recently been granted a law license, although she did not practice. Mansfield's admittance to the profession did not cause a stir, so Bradwell hoped her attempt would not attract attention. However, the Illinois Supreme Court denied her request, stating that as a married woman, she was unfit to practice law.

Bradwell filed a brief challenging the court's decision and the court responded, this time denying her admittance simply because she was a woman. Friedman reported that the court argued, among other things, that if it allowed women to practice law, "every civil office in this state may be filled by women—that is . . . [would follow] that women should be made governors and sheriffs."

Bradwell appealed the decision to the United States Supreme Court. She hired Senator Matthew H. Carpenter of Wisconsin to represent her. He was one of the country's best constitutional lawyers and an advocate of women's rights. However, the court denied her appeal in 1873.

Published *Chicago Legal News*

By the time the Supreme Court ruled on Bradwell's appeal, she was already well known as a lawyer, despite the Illinois bar's denial. Bradwell gained her reputation in the legal community through a publication she founded in 1868 called the *Chicago Legal News*. The newspaper offered synopses of legal opinions and news for the Chicago legal community. Bradwell was the paper's publisher, business manager, and editor-in-chief. In addition to legal news and synopses of legal opinions, the paper contained Bradwell's writings advocating a number of issues. The paper was popular throughout the country and for two decades was the most widely circulated legal newspaper in the United States. Through the *Chicago Legal News,* Bradwell was instrumental in enacting legislation granting many rights to women. Among these rights was the right to pursue any occupation a woman chose.

The *Chicago Legal News* began publication on October 3, 1868. According to Friedman, Bradwell outlined the purpose of the publication in the first issue: "The News will be . . . devoted to legal information, general news, the publication of new and important decisions, and of other matters useful to the practicing lawyer or man of business." This brief description falls short of articulating the value of the *Chicago Legal News*. Bradwell made sure that the publication was indispensable to every lawyer in Illinois, and eventually the nation. She did this by publishing newly enacted statutes before the Illinois legislature did, making the *Chicago Legal News* the only source of this information for lawyers and judges. The statutes printed in the *Chicago Legal News* were valid as evidence in court, making a subscription to the publication an essential tool for lawyers.

Within fourteen months of its inception, the *Chicago Legal News* was the official medium for reporting actions of the state legislature.

After the newspaper had earned its reputation in Illinois, Bradwell expanded its subject matter to judicial decisions of the United States Supreme Court and all lower federal courts in the country. Thus, it became the most widely read legal newspaper in the United States. Bradwell also founded the Chicago Legal News Company, which printed legal forms, stationery and briefs.

Bradwell's company was thriving when the great Chicago fire occurred in 1871. Despite the destruction of her offices and most of the city, Bradwell saved the subscription book for the newspaper and when she resumed publishing from a temporary office in Milwaukee, she capitalized on the losses caused by the fire. Recognizing that lawyers in Chicago would have to replace their lost law libraries, she solicited advertisements from legal book publishers. In addition, Bradwell printed and sold back copies of the *Chicago Legal News* to replace those that were lost in the fire. The Illinois legislature designated the *Chicago Legal News* as the official publisher of all legal records lost in the fire.

Legal news was not the only component of the newspaper. Bradwell used the paper to advocate many social and legal reforms and women's issues. She started out with local reform. She decried conditions at the county poor house, encouraged the investigation of jury bribery, and printed humiliating accounts of judges' behavior to weed out heavy drinkers. She also criticized the filthy conditions at the Cook County Courthouse. Bradwell often used humor to get her point across.

Bradwell never again requested entry into the Illinois bar, but in 1890, the Illinois Supreme Court granted her a law license. Two years later, the U.S. Supreme Court followed suit. Since both courts granted the license as of the date of her original application, Bradwell is known as the first woman lawyer in the United States. Bradwell was also the first woman to join a bar association.

Advocated Women's Rights

Women's issues were very important to Bradwell. Having been denied her law license, she was keen on gaining the right for women to practice the profession of their choice. James Bradwell served for some time in the Illinois state legislature, and Myra often drafted legislation that he ushered into law. While Bradwell waited for the Supreme Court to rule on her request to be admitted to the bar, she and another woman who had been refused a law license drafted a statute that gave all people, men and women, the right to select any profession or occupation. Bradwell initially drafted the legislation in order to help other women become lawyers, but the legislation served to help women gain entry into all professions. The *Chicago Legal News* served as her mouthpiece in urging passage of the legislation.

In 1873, she drafted a bill that James introduced that gave women the right to run for office in the Illinois public school system. The bill passed, allowing women to be elected to an office for which they themselves could not vote. Other legislation James Bradwell ushered through the state legislature allowed women to become notaries public, a right Myra had been denied; allowed women to keep their own earnings; and gave them equal rights to the custody of their children. At the time, men had absolute custody of their minor unmarried children, even if they were unfit fathers. In the case of divorce, women were never granted custody. Fathers could even dispose of the custody and give the child to someone other than the mother.

Bradwell also advocated for the rights of people in institutions, including women, children, the mentally ill, and inmates. In Illinois and other states, a married woman could be declared insane by her husband and put in an asylum without a hearing. Elizabeth Parsons Ware Packard was responsible for passage of two laws that prohibited men from institutionalizing their wives without a jury trial and order of a court. A "private madhouse" bill was introduced to nullify the Packard bill and reintroduced in various forms for twenty years. Bradwell campaigned against the bill in the *Chicago Legal News*. She was largely responsible for the bill never being enacted.

A similar issue that Bradwell was involved in was the confinement of her friend Mary Todd Lincoln, widow of President Abraham Lincoln. Mary Lincoln was incarcerated in an insane asylum in 1875 by her son, Robert, who claimed she was insane. Some historians believe that Mary Lincoln's commitment was the result of a conspiracy orchestrated by Robert, who feared she would become his financial charge someday.

When Bradwell learned of her friend's confinement, she immediately tried to secure her release. Bradwell's advocacy helped secure Lincoln's release after about four months.

Worked for Women's Suffrage

Bradwell was very involved in the women's suffrage movement and was one of the Midwest's most notable suffragists. Friedman speculated that Bradwell has been ignored as a leader of the suffrage movement because of differences with Susan B. Anthony, the movement's leading historical figure. But Bradwell's audience of lawyers, judges, and lawmakers gave her enormous influence as a women's rights advocate. The rift between Anthony and Elizabeth Cady Stanton and other suffragists occurred over a disagreement about supporting the 14th and 15th amendments. Anthony and Stanton, of the National Women's Suffrage Association, did not support the amendments that gave black people the right to vote because they felt the amendment should also have included women. Lucy Stone, Bradwell, and other suffragists disagreed and urged a break with Anthony and Stanton. They formed a second women's suffrage organization, the American Women's Suffrage Association. Bradwell served as corresponding secretary of the group's first convention. James was temporary chair.

In 1876, Bradwell was appointed a member of the Illinois Centennial Association, to represent the state in the Centennial Exposition in Philadelphia. In 1888, she helped secure the 1892 World's Fair for Chicago. In 1891, she was

diagnosed with cancer, but continued to work for the fair, which she visited in a wheelchair, despite her illness. She died February 14, 1894, at the age of 63, in Chicago, Illinois.

Bradwell was survived by her husband James and her grown children, Bessie and Thomas. Both children lived with their parents even after marrying and having children of their own. Both became lawyers. Bessie Helmer continued the *Chicago Legal News* until 1925 and also followed in her mother's footsteps as an advocate for women's rights.

Books

Bird, Caroline, *Enterprising Women,* W.W. Norton & Co., 1976.
Friedman, Jane M., *America's First Woman Lawyer: The Biography of Myra Bradwell,* Prometheus Books, 1993.
Women in World History: A Biographical Encyclopedia, edited by Anne Commire, Yorkin Publications, 1999.

Online

"Myra Bradwell," *Biography Resource Center,* Gale Group, 2003. □

Breyten Breytenbach

Widely recognized as South Africa's finest Afrikaner poet, Breyten Breytenbach (born 1939) wrote poems characterized by lush, evocative visuals; commanding use of metaphor; and interwoven elements such as Buddhist references, memories of South African landscapes, and Afrikaans idiomatic speech.

Staunch Opponent of Apartheid

Breytenbach was born into an eminent family of humble means on September 16, 1939, in Bonnievale, South Africa. His ancestors were among 17th-century South Africa's first white settlers who called themselves Afrikaners. The year after his birth, the Breytenbachs moved to the small town of Wellington. After graduation from high school, he developed an interest in poetry and art and enrolled in the English-language University of Cape Town's fine arts program.

Wishing to escape the increasingly repressive environment of apartheid, he withdrew from school at age 20 and left for Europe, where he held various jobs. In 1961 he moved to Paris and began painting, writing, and teaching English. Among his first African friends there were members of the banned African National Congress anti-apartheid group who were living in exile. In 1962 he married a French woman of Vietnamese descent, Yolande Ngo Thi Hoang Lien.

Breytenbach published his first book of poems *Die Ysterkoei Moet Sweet* (The Iron Cow Must Sweat) in 1964, the same year he published his first volume of prose, *Katastrofes* (Catastrophes), and had his first art exhibition, at

wrote its platform. They devised a plan for Breytenbach to travel to South Africa in disguise and contact some black spokespeople and sympathetic whites to funnel money from European religious organizations to South African black trade unionists.

In 1975 a French anti-apartheid group provided a forged French passport to Breytenbach, who flew to Johannesburg under another name. The French organization had apparently been breached, however, and Breytenbach was under the surveillance of South African security police from the moment he acquired his visa. He was followed, his contacts were noted, and he was arrested and charged under the Terrorist Act. Breytonbach was sentenced to nine years in prison. The court considered anti-apartheid trade union campaigns to be a threat to state security.

A few months later, Breytenbach began a period of solitary confinement in the maximum security section of Pretoria's prison. In June 1977 he was again accused of terrorism, tried a second time, and acquitted of all charges other than smuggling letters from prison, for which he paid a fine equivalent to 50 dollars. Breytenbach was transported to Pollsmoor Prison, where he was held as a political prisoner for five years.

The French government exerted diplomatic pressure on South Africa and increased its efforts once France's socialist government came to power under Francois Mitterand. In late 1982, Pretoria finally acquiesced and commuted the poet's sentence to seven years, stipulating only that he leave the country. He was permitted a short visit with his father, then he and his wife flew back to Paris. Breytenbach became a French citizen in 1983 and alternated living in Paris and Gorée, Senegal.

During his imprisonment, Breytenbach wrote a semifictional account of his mental state as a prisoner *Mouroir: Bespieelende notas van 'n roman* (Mouroir: Mirror-notes of a Novel). The book is a group of loosely connected stories presented in a surreal, imagistic style. While critics widely praised the book, they also noted the complex fragmentation and obscurity that made it difficult to digest, though in general the challenging work was considered beautifully written and unforgettable.

Once freed from prison, Breytenbach wrote a more direct account of his incarceration, *The True Confessions of an Albino Terrorist* (1986). In his best-known work, the author describes being ensnared by his captors and subjected to years of psychological and physical deprivation and gives his vision of South Africa's future prospects. This disturbing book, with its detailed depiction of a horrifying penal system, was critically acclaimed as an important contribution to South African prison literature, as well as a work of great artistry.

Completed Four-Volume Memoir

Breytenbach, who maintained that his experiences in prison forever scarred him, returned to South Africa in 1986 to accept the Rapport Prize for Literature from *Rapport,* an Afrikaans newspaper, for his volume of poetry *YK* (1985). He returned again in 1991, a journey chronicled in the 1993 memoir *Return to Paradise.* In it he describes the national

the Galerie Espace in Amsterdam. He followed up by publishing *Die Huis van die Dowe* (House of the Deaf, 1967) and *Kouevuur* (Gangrene) in 1969. In 1970 he published *Lotus* under the pseudonym Jan Blom.

Breytenbach wanted to go back to South Africa to accept poetry awards he had won in 1967 and 1969, but the government refused his wife an entry visa as a "non-white" and Breytenbach faced arrest for violating the Immorality Act, apartheid legislation that made interracial marriage a crime. His poetry collection *Met Ander Woorde* was published in 1973, and the Breytenbachs were both able to obtain three-month visitor's visas to return to South Africa.

After 12 years of exile, his return to South Africa elicited tender childhood memories and bolstered his fury over the injustice and violence of the apartheid system. His strenuous public criticism of the Afrikaner nationalist government so annoyed authorities that at the end of his stay officials told Breytenbach not to return to South Africa. The poet's feelings about his homecoming were published in a 1976 book mixing poetry and prose that came out in a censored version in South Africa called *'N Seisoen in die Paradys.* A later English translation, *A Season in Paradise,* appeared in 1980.

Held as Political Prisoner

Once he returned to Paris, Breytenbach quickly renewed links with anti-apartheid groups. With other exiled white South Africans he founded his own anti-apartheid organization, Okhela (Zulu for "ignite the flame") and turmoil during the transitional period following the fall of the white-controlled government of F.W. De Klerk. The work met with mixed reviews, praised for its narrative, rhythm, and passion, but criticized as unoriginal in its analysis and uninspired in its reporting.

In 1992, Breytenbach co-founded a cultural center in Senegal, the Gorée institute. He co-founded the University of Natal's Center for Creative Arts in 1995. In 1996, a collection of Breytenbach's talks on South Africa, apartheid, and writing was published as *The Memory of Birds in Times of Revolution.* Criticism was again varied. Some felt it was outdated, lacking in insight, clichéd and didactic; others called it another important contribution to his body of work and commented on its admirable sentiments. The 1989 novel *Memory of Snow and Dust* portrayed a semiautobiographical account of Breytenbach's arrest to illuminate his personal struggle between spiritual hunger and his need to be politically useful.

In *Dog Heart: A Memoir* (1999), Breytenbach told about a post-apartheid visit to Bonnieville, his hometown, and his attempts to reconcile his childhood memories with the reality of South African life after apartheid. He did this with a fractured narrative that incorporated snippets of his own personal history, ruminations on the nation's history, pieces of folk tales, and lists of past and present atrocities artfully woven together and beautifully written. In 2000, Breytenbach published *Lady One: Of Love and Other Poems,* a collection of poems for his wife that includes images of east Asia, southern Africa, and Morocco. The combination of the personal and the global in the poems reflects a marriage that, because it was considered taboo under South African apartheid laws, led to the poet's original exile. A dramatic piece, *The Play,* premiered in his homeland in the spring of 2001.

In addition to writing, Breytenbach was an award-winning painter. Many of his paintings depict surreal humans and animals, often in captivity. He first exhibited his visual art in 1962 in Edinburgh and exhibited in 34 solo shows and several group exhibitions in numerous countries, including Belgium, France, Sweden, Germany, the Netherlands, Hong Kong, Scotland, and South Africa. He received honorary doctorates from the University of Cape Town and the University of Natal, Durban. He taught as a visiting professor at both institutions, as well as at Princeton University in New Jersey. He became a global distinguished professor of creative writing at New York University.

Despite the deprivation he suffered from his willingness to speak out against injustice, Breytenbach continued to voice his outrage at matters that stirred his indignation. In 2002, he was one of a number of prominent social, cultural, and political leaders, including Nelson Mandela and Desmond Tutu, who chastised the Israeli government for its occupation of Palestine, calling it disturbingly similar to apartheid South Africa.

Books

Contemporary Authors, Vol. 61, Gale, 1976.

Online

"Breyten Breytenbach," *AllRefer Encyclopedia,* http://reference.allrefer.com (December 27, 2003).

"Breyten Breytenbach," *Biography Resource Center,* http://galenet.gale.com (January 4, 2004).

"Breyten Breytenbach," *Contemporary Africa Database,* http://people.africadatabase.org (December 27, 2003).

"Breyten Breytenbach," *Counterbalance Poetry,* http://counterbalancepoetry.org (December 27, 2003).

"Breyten Breytenbach," *Culturebase,* http://www.culturebase.net (January 3, 2004).

"Breyten Breytenbach," *New York University,* http://nyu.edu/fas/Faculty/Global/BreytonBreytenbach.html (December 27, 2003).

"Breyten Breytenbach," *Stellenbosch Writers,* http://stellenboschwriters.com (December 27, 2003).

"Breyten Breytenbach," *Sun Valley Writers Conference,* http://svwc.com (December 27, 2003).

"The Need for Campus Divestment," *The Palestine Chronicle,* http://www.palestinechronicle.com (January 15, 2004). □

Tony Brown

One of the most sought-after and controversial speakers in the United States, Tony Brown (born 1933) also hosts "Tony Brown's Journal," one of the Public Broadcasting Station's longest-running shows. He hosts the syndicated radio call-in show "Tony Brown" at WLIB AM New York and his books include *Empower the People* and *Black Lies, White Lies.* Most of his efforts are geared toward encouraging African Americans to improve their economic destiny by helping themselves.

Rough Beginnings Gave Rise to Ambition

On April 11, 1933, in Charleston, West Virginia, William Anthony (Tony) Brown became the fifth child born to Royal Brown and the former Katherine Davis. His mother had been having children since the age of 16. There was tension in the marriage from early on due to the different complexions of Royal, a light-skinned mulatto, and Katherine, a dark-skinned beauty. (At that time, the lighter the skin of an African American, the higher his or her rank in society, and vice versa.) Royal's parents had opposed the union, despite the abundant accomplishments of Katherine's family. In addition, the ferocious racism of the small Southern town drove a wedge between the young couple. Unemployed and increasingly frustrated, Royal left with another woman for Philadelphia two months before his last child arrived.

It was into this turbulent world that Tony was born. Katherine was crushed by the desertion and may have suffered from postpartum depression after his birth. Virtually unable to care for the baby, she allowed a concerned neighbor, Elizabeth Sanford, and her daughter, Mabel, to take the starving two-month-old Tony to live with them. Although poor and uneducated, Elizabeth, whom Brown would always call "Mama," and Mabel cared for and raised the boy lovingly as though he were their own until they died within months of each other when he was 12 years old. Brown still credits them not only with saving his life, but with giving him confidence and a sense of self-worth.

Forced to rely on his mother again for support, Brown moved in with her in a housing project in a decrepit area of Charleston known as the Minor. Meanwhile, his parents had divorced. Although he had grown accustomed to poverty, Brown always dreamed of having enough food and clothes. He demonstrated his developing ambition and resourcefulness early on when he started selling soft drink bottles around the neighborhood. Through hard work and determination, he earned enough to buy a rooster and a hen and started a little poultry farm. Soon he was able to sell fresh chicken and eggs to his neighbors at a great profit. He also got paid for putting on shows with his friends at the nearby Furgerson Theater.

Excelled in School, Developed Love of Performing

Brown started in Charleston's public school system in 1939, when he was six. His first school was Boyd Elementary, and from there he graduated to Boyd Junior High. When he entered Garnet High School as a teenager, he joined the track team, running the 220- and 440-yard races and relays. An eager and attentive student, Brown did well in school but particularly in English and drama. His teachers in those subjects encouraged him enormously, realizing his potential. Despite a slight shyness and natural reserve, he won a leading role in the play Our Town, and just before graduation in 1951 he performed parts of Shakespeare's Julius Caesar on the local radio station.

After working for two years after graduation, Brown joined the army in 1953. He eventually made the rank of corporal before leaving in 1955 to study psychology and sociology at Wayne State University in Detroit, Michigan. He graduated with a degree in 1959 despite having worked part-time at a warehouse to pay for his education. Brown had become convinced that he could help fellow African Americans improve their generally dire economic circumstances and remained at Wayne State until 1961 to earn his masters degree in social work. His educational focus, psychiatric social work, meant that he was assigned some of the most tragic and difficult cases in the city, and by 1962 he had had enough.

Career in Social Work Yielded to Media Involvement

In the meantime, Brown had protested racial segregation during massive marches that he organized and that were led by Martin Luther King, Jr. Based on these experiences, Brown decided that the media would be the conveyor of his messages to black Americans. He found a job as a drama critic with the Detroit Courier and quickly moved up the ladder to city editor. In 1968 he left the paper to take a job as public affairs programmer for Detroit's public tele-

vision station, WTVS. He soon became producer of the station's first show specifically for African Americans, "CPT," or "Colored People's Time." Meanwhile, Brown also tried his hand at hosting for the first time on the station's community program "Free Play."

While Brown worked at WTVS for the remainder of the 1960s, a program called "Black Journal" began airing in New York City. Funded by the Corporation for Public Broadcasting (CPB), the show investigated political and social issues relevant to African Americans through interviews, surveys, documentaries, and editorial commentaries. "Black Journal" had won the Emmy, Peabody, and Russwurm awards by 1970.

Later that year, Brown was invited to work as executive producer and host of "Black Journal." He accepted, but within months his candor and unflattering commentaries on the government were igniting controversy and criticism from people at all levels of the broadcasting industry. His allegations of racism in public broadcasting were especially ill-received. The controversy, however, sparked interest in the show and its ratings skyrocketed. The station expanded "Black Journal" from its original once-a-month feature to a weekly, 30-minute show.

Aggressive Style Sparked Controversy

Although his goal was to emphasize the positive aspects of African Americanism, Brown occasionally ran into trouble with his viewers, who perceived him as arrogant, condescending, and out of touch with the experiences of the average black person. Brown's emphasis on self-help may have caused this reaction, but his purpose, to give African Americans self-respect, remained firm.

Brown was one of the first people to encourage blacks to enter the television industry, and most of his staff came from the local community. He located production companies willing to teach his trainees and help them find jobs in the field. His work led to his appointment as the founding dean of the Howard University School of Communications, and he used this position to launch the Careers in Communications Conference. This became an annual event that still helps students find work in the communications industry. Brown resigned as dean in 1974.

When the CPB withdrew its funding of "Black Journal" for the 1973–1974 season, the African American community responded with outrage. The corporation relented and agreed to fund the show but instead reduced its airtime. Brown took matters into his own hands in 1977. Determined to keep the faltering show alive and frustrated with the limits imposed by the CPB, he negotiated a contract with the Pepsi Cola Company to sponsor the show. Brown changed the program's name to "Tony Brown's Journal" and left the relatively sheltered world of public television. The syndicated show began airing in 85 cities nationwide, and he also started doing a successful segment called "Tony Brown at Daybreak" on WRC-TV in Washington, D.C. However, Brown soon became dissatisfied with the odd viewing times commercial stations offered "Tony Brown's Journal," so in 1982 he moved the show back to public television.

Campaigned Hard for Black Education and Economic Empowerment

Throughout the 1980s, Brown was instrumental in improving the outlook and atmosphere for African Americans in the academic world. He launched "Black College Day" in 1982, in what was called a one-man effort to save and support colleges dedicated to serving blacks. In 1985, he founded the Council for the Economic Development of Black Americans, whose motto is "Buy Freedom." The group's main platform is that blacks should patronize businesses displaying the "Freedom Seal," which signified a black owner who had agreed to be courteous, offer competitive prices, provide employment, give discounts, and stay involved in the community.

Brown's most inspired attempt to reach African Americans through the media came in 1988, when he released a cautionary film about cocaine abuse titled *The White Girl.* He wrote, directed, produced, and distributed the film himself, and while it was panned by the critics, it gave Brown a medium in which to address what he perceived as "two destructive trends in society: drug addiction and self-hate." Ignoring the negative reviews, he circulated the film throughout the black community for the next 18 months. Local groups showed it for a small profit, benefiting both Brown and charitable causes.

Became an Author to Reach Audience

In the 1990s, Brown began writing books to broadcast his message of self-help and self-respect to African Americans. His first book, *Black Lies, White Lies: The Truth According to Tony Brown,* came out in 1995. With its innovative approach to making the United State more economically competitive and suggestions of ways to solve the country's racial issues, the book was well received among blacks, although not reviewers. His next book, *Empower the People: A 7-Step Plan to Overthrow the Conspiracy That Is Stealing Your Money,* was published in 1999 and presented, as his publisher put it, as "a practical plan to reclaim our resources and institutions from a selfish and exclusive power elite." It has also enjoyed steady success despite some less than positive reviews. Brown's *What Mama Taught Me: The Seven Core Values of Life* appeared on bookshelves in 2003. Literally the story of his life, Brown uses himself as an example of what people can overcome and achieve with the help of self-empowerment.

Brown, a prominent and influential member of the Republican Party, lives in New York City, where he hosts a call-in radio program on WLIB AM and continues to host the now-syndicated "Tony Brown's Journal." He is an occasional commentator on the popular National Public Radio show "All Things Considered" and appears regularly on C-Span, CNBC, and other major networks. He is also the founder of Tony Brown Productions, Inc., which produces television programs and movies and markets videotapes from a collection called "The Library of Black History." Brown is a member of numerous boards and advisory committees, including the Shaw Divinity School, The Harvard Foundation for Intercultural and Race Relations, and the Association for the Study of Afro-American Life and History.

Talkers, the premiere radio trade magazine, has named Brown one of the top 100 most important talk show hosts in the country, and *USA Today* chose him as one of the top five U.S. experts on the status of African Americans.

Brown married in 1970 and had a son, Byron Anthony Brown, in 1971. The marriage ended in divorce in 1974.

Books

Contemporary Black Biography, Gale Research, 1992.

Online

"Tony Brown," *The Gale Group Biography Resource Center,* http://galenet.gale.com (January 4, 2004).
"Tony Brown," *Lordly & Dame, Inc. website,* http://www.lordly .com (December 27, 2003).
"What Mama Taught Me: The Seven Core Values of Life, Introduction" *Tony Brown Sites website,* http://www.tony brownsites.com (December 27, 2003). □

Richard Burbage

Richard Burbage (c. 1567-1619) was a well-known actor in Elizabethan England. A friend and business associate of the playwright William Shakespeare, Burbage was the first actor to utter some of the Bard's most famous lines on stage, including *Hamlet*'s lament, "to be or not to be, that is the question."

Acting Considered Disreputable Profession

Burbage was probably born around 1567, in an area northeast of London called Shoreditch. Shoreditch was a bustling quarter just outside of the city boundaries, and the family lived on the main thoroughfare, Holywell Street. Nearby was the former site of Holywell Priory, which stood from the mid-twelfth century until the early 1540s. Some of the outbuildings still stood, and in 1576 Burbage's father, James, leased its Great Barn. By then his father was listed as head of the Earl of Leicester's acting company. Sometimes called Leicester's Men, it was the first organized Elizabethan acting troupe and dated back to 1559; it took its name from the fact that its initial founders were members of the Earl of Leicester's household. Though plays were becoming wildly popular among Londoners of all classes, acting was not legally considered a profession at the time. According to the Tudor Poor Law of 1572, actors could be targeted as "rogues" or "vagabonds" for being without an occupation, and such offenses were punishable by whipping or even death. Thus actors in Elizabethan England, who played both male and female roles, skirted the law by forming troupes that enjoyed the patronage of a noble or royal.

Theater performances were a relatively new and novel form of entertainment still in late sixteenth-century England. Drama emerged in classical Greek and Roman times, but by the early centuries of the Christian church, public performances had descended into a more bawdy form of popular amusement, and leading theologians condemned the theater as licentious and immoral. Church fathers eventually banned most theater performances altogether, save for works of a religious theme. The stricture carried on until the Renaissance era of Burbage's day, but the rediscovery of the classical Greek and Roman plays had brought a renewal of interest in drama across Europe, and new playwrights were emerging who adopted events of English history into entertaining tales that also served as social or political commentary for the times. These were usually performed by traveling troupes of actors, most of whom were patronized by wealthy nobles.

Joined Lord Chamberlain's Company

The forward-thinking English queen, Elizabeth I, encouraged drama, and the 1574 Licensing Act stipulated that only nobles with the rank of baron or higher were permitted to sponsor an acting troupe. Two years later, she established a Master of Revels office, which licensed theatrical productions and levied a fee on each performance. London itself, however, was administered by a Privy Council with a strong Puritan streak. Puritanism was a religious reform movement in England based on some of the more ascetic doctrines of Calvinism. Austere and dogmatic, the Puritans banned theater performances during Burbage's day. Shoreditch, how-

ever, stood just outside the Council's jurisdiction, and the elder Burbage used the Great Barn land and materials for what became London's first permanent venue for drama, the Theatre in Shoreditch. Young Burbage likely took his first roles on its stage with the Earl of Leicester's company. It is known he was with another company, Lord Chamberlain's Men, after 1588, and the Admiral's Men company after 1590.

Among Burbage's first known roles was that of King Gorboduc in *The Seven Deadliest Sins* by Thomas Norton and Thomas Sackville, two young nobles, around 1590, which is considered English drama's first genuine tragedy. Shakespeare arrived on the London theater scene about 1592, and began writing plays that were performed by Lord Chamberlain's Men the following year; he also acted with the troupe. In 1594, Burbage appeared in a performance before Elizabeth I along with Shakespeare and fellow thespian Will Kemp. He was listed as a joint-payee of Lord Chamberlain's Men by 1595.

Carted Theater Across Thames

In 1597, after the death of his father, Burbage and his brother Cuthbert inherited the Theatre in Shoreditch, but the landlord of the site was a Puritan, and tried to raise the rent exorbitantly to shut the venue down. The lease did state, however, that the building itself belonged to the Burbages, and so on a late December day in 1598, Burbage and the men of the company dismantled the Theatre and took the timber across the Thames River to Southwark, a half-mile west of the London Bridge. There, the materials were used to build a new theatre, called the Globe, which opened for business in 1599. Besides Cuthbert Burbage and their sister, Alice, the other partners in the venture were Shakespeare and Kemp. The venue would stage the first performances of many of Shakespeare's plays. It had a thatched gallery roof and may have been cylindrical in form, but little concrete information survives regarding its design.

Burbage's rise as the leading actor of his day was linked to the growing popularity of Shakespeare's plays with London audiences and even royal audiences. Though the exact chronology of the Shakespeare canon is unknown, their order can be surmised from dates when they were published or from secondary sources in which they were mentioned. It is known that Burbage played the title role in one of the earliest, *Richard III*, in which he uttered the famous opening line: "Now is the winter of our discontent /Made glorious summer by this sun of York."

Debuted in Appealing, Enduring Roles

Burbage went on to appear as Berowne in the more lighthearted *Love's Labour's Lost,* which is also thought by scholars to be the first that Shakespeare wrote with him in mind. "It is a part well suited to the versatility that we know to have been Burbage's particular characteristic," declared Martin Holmes in his *Shakespeare and Burbage*. "He has to be, in succession, the shrewd, dry commentator on other men's ideas, the smart society conversationalist, the serious, self-confessed, self-criticising, reluctantly self-tormenting lover, and finally the champion of love."

The first years of the seventeenth century became known as the Jacobean period of English drama, after the accession of a new English monarch to the throne, James I, in 1603. That same year, Burbage's Chamberlain's Men players were renamed the King's Men company after winning royal patronage. Burbage remained its principal actor, and Shakespeare its playwright. By this point both were well-known figures in London, and the Globe proved a profitable enterprise for them. Shakespeare's plays were proven money-makers, and while the financial links between the two men enriched both, Shakespeare's talent for writing for Burbage gave rise to some of the choicest dramatic parts in the history of drama. "It appears that Shakespeare either felt obliged to tailor roles to suit Burbage's particular capacities or else, far more likely, perceived that his gifts and style offered the possibility of exploring more rounded, more inward-looking personalities in a more profound fashion," noted the *International Dictionary of Theatre* essay.

Portrayed Increasingly Complex Characters

In his day Burbage was deemed a skilled orator, which likely meant that he possessed an excellent memory for lines, as well as clear enunciation and believable gestures. He probably moved about on the stage as he spoke his lines, which was considered unusual at the time. His great rival was another London actor, Edward Alleyn, but Burbage's close association with Shakespeare enhanced his reputation. "Burbage's voice, it would seem, was not a trumpet like Alleyn's," noted Holmes, "but had more the quality of a stringed instrument, and Shakespeare wrote for it with consideration and full understanding of its potentialities."

As Shakespeare and Burbage matured, the roles offered to the actor grew more contemplative in character. Burbage appeared in the title roles of Shakespeare's great tragedies, *Hamlet, King Lear,* and *Othello.* These were compelling figures from history, and delivered memorable turns of phrase that became commonplace in the English language. Yet these and others from Shakespeare's pen were also compelling and relatively novel portrayals of human nature on the stage at the time: the characters were neither wholly good nor entirely evil. With his wealth of experience on the stage that dated back to his youth, Burbage was ideally suited to the nuances of such parts. "Without him, Shakespeare would most likely have had less opportunity to develop his talents," asserted the *International Dictionary of Theatre* of the actor, "and it is at least arguable that creating parts to suit Burbage's particular characteristics and temperament inspired him to explore more complex dramatic characters than might otherwise have been the case."

Opened Second Profitable Venue

In 1608 Burbage, Shakespeare, and some other partners opened the Blackfriars Theatre, between Ludgate Hill and the Thames, as a new home for the King's Men when not performing at Court. Burbage's father had leased part of an old Dominican friary (hence the term "black" friar because of the dark cloak its members wore) to stage plays back in 1596, but since the building was still within the boundaries of London proper and the neighbors objected as well, he instead leased it for performances of a children's theater company. When Burbage and his partners took it over, they added a solid roof to it so that it could serve as an all-season venue, which was another London theater first. The Globe, meanwhile, caught fire during a performance of *Henry VIII* one night in 1613 when a cannon shot to mark the king's entrance misfired. Burbage barely escaped alive, but rebuilt the theater the next year. It is known that this design was indeed circular in shape, and had a tiled gallery roof.

Burbage is thought to have acted in a long list of other roles from Shakespeare's pen, but these are not reliably documented. They include Angelo in *Measure for Measure,* Bassanio in *The Merchant of Venice,* Claudio in *Much Ado About Nothing,* Demetrius in *A Midsummer Night's Dream,* Ford in *The Merry Wives of Windsor,* Orsino in *Twelfth Night,* Prospero in *The Tempest,* and the title roles of *Coriolanus, Macbeth,* and *Timon of Athens.* He also acted in the plays of other leading dramatists of the era as well, including John Webster and Ben Jonson. He appeared in the latter's *Every Man in his Humour* in 1598 and *Every Man out of his Humour* the following year. For certain he appeared in Jonson's works *Sejanus His Fall* in 1603, *Volpone* in 1605, *The Alchemist* in 1610, and *Catiline His Conspiracy* in 1611. He also appeared as Ferdinand in Webster's *The Duchess of Malfi* in 1616, and may have acted in *The White Devil,* another work from Webster's pen.

Burbage lived in the same Holywell Street of his childhood, and is thought to have married his wife, Winifred, around 1601. They had six daughters and two sons. A painter as well as actor and theater manager, Burbage is thought to have done the Felton portrait of Shakespeare. A self-portrait hangs at Dulwich College. He died in London on March 13, 1619, leaving a small estate of 300 pounds. He is buried in the parish cemetery of St. Leonard's, the landmark Shoreditch church that dates back to the twelfth century. His Globe theater closed in 1642 during a renewal of Puritan religious fervor in England, and was torn down two years later. The Blackfriars theater also closed during this period, and was demolished in 1655. London's "Playhouse Yard" commemorates the latter theater's site.

Books

Holmes, Martin, *Shakespeare and Burbage,* Chichester, 1978.
International Dictionary of Theatre, Volume 3: *Actors, Directors, and Designers,* St. James Press, 1996.

Periodicals

Times (London, England), March 13, 1919.

Online

"Shoreditch, *Tudor Hackney Welcome Page,* http://learningcurve .pro.gov.uk/tudorhackney/localhistory/lochsh.asp (January 10, 2004).
"The Globe Theater of 1599," *Online Shakespeare,* http://www .onlineshakespeare.com/globe1.htm (January 7, 2004). □

C

Benny Carter

Award-winning jazz musician and arranger Benny Carter (1907–2003) had a distinctive sound that was showcased most famously in his 1937 "Honeysuckle Rose." His 1961 album *Further Definitions,* which critics consider a masterpiece, remains one of jazz's most influential recordings.

Influential Arranger

Carter was born as Bennett Carter on August 8, 1907, in New York City, the only son and the youngest of three children in his family. He grew up in one of the roughest Manhattan neighborhoods at that time, San Juan Hill, near what is now Lincoln Center. His formal education ceased after the eighth grade. His mother taught him piano and, through his cousin, Theodore (Cuban) Bennett (who never recorded but who influenced numerous musicians with his highly developed musical ideas), and Bubber Miley, a neighbor who played with Duke Ellington, Carter developed an interest in the trumpet. He saved for months and bought a trumpet at a pawn shop when he was 13, but, when he failed to master it after a weekend's effort, he traded it for a C-melody saxophone (having been told, erroneously, that that instrument was easier to learn). Carter, who was for the most part self-taught, counted Frankie Trumbauer as an early inspiration. By the age of 15 he was sitting in at night spots around Harlem.

In 1925, Carter married his first wife, who died of pneumonia three years later. That same year he briefly at-tended Wilberforce College in Ohio, where he played with the Wilberforce Collegians, then toured with Horace Henderson. After brief stints with James P. Johnson, Earl Hines, and Ellington, he worked for more than a year with the Charlie Johnson Orchestra, his first full-time job.

Carter formed his own group for New York's Arcadia ballroom in 1928 and somehow managed to teach himself to arrange music. That same year he recorded his first records, with the Charlie Johnson group, including two of his own arrangements. Later that year, he began working in a band led by pioneering big band arranger Fletcher Henderson, Horace Henderson's brother. The band was revitalized by Carter's innovative writing, especially his scores for the saxophone section, and he became an influential arranger who also wrote for Ellington and Benny Goodman. Shortly after joining the band, the 21-year-old Carter was chosen by its members to replace the leader, who had walked out during a tour.

Codified Swing Music's Sound

In 1931, Carter became the musical director for the Detroit-based McKinney's Cotton Pickers. Having mastered the alto sax, he now took up the trumpet and within a couple of years was recording trumpet parts that rivaled his alto work. On both instruments, he became known for envisioning a solo as a whole while still retaining spontaneity.

The next year he returned to New York and began assembling his own orchestra, which eventually included swing stars such as Teddy Wilson, Dicky Wells, Chu Berry, and Sid Catlett. As was true of all the bands Carter led, the group, with its high musical standards, became known as a "musicians' band." He was helping to codify what would become the style and essence of swing music, stripping

(a novelty song called "Cow-Cow Boogie," sung by Ella Mae Morse), during the 1930s Carter composed and/or arranged many of the pieces that became Swing Era classics, such as "When Lights Are Low," "Blues in My Heart," and "Lonesome Nights."

In 1941, Carter stripped down to a sextet that included bebop groundbreakers Kenny Clarke and Dizzy Gillespie. He also wrote arrangements for a radio show, "Your Hit Parade." In 1942 he reorganized his band and moved to California, settling in Hollywood, where he would live for the rest of his life. In the mid-1940s, Carter's band included such leading modernists as Miles Davis, Art Pepper, Max Roach, and J.J. Johnson, all of whom have expressed a debt to Carter as an important mentor.

Worked in Films and Teaching

In Hollywood, Carter moved steadily into studio work. He was among the first black arrangers for films and in the 1950s led the integration of white and black musicians unions. In 1943 he wrote arrangements for and played on the soundtrack of the film *Stormy Weather,* although he did not receive a screen credit. From 1946, when he surrendered full-time work as leader of a big band, until 1970, he was virtually out of the public eye. He arranged scores for dozens of movies and, beginning in 1959, television programs. Among his film credits are *The Snows of Kilamanjaro, The Five Pennies, The Gene Krupa Story, The Flower Drum Song, The View From Pompeii's Head,* and Martin Scorcese's *Too Late Blues.* Among his television credits are *M Squad,* the Alfred Hitchcock series, *Banyon, Ironside,* and the *Chrysler Theater.*

He also toured occasionally as a soloist and with the Jazz at the Philharmonic ensemble. Carter's arrangements were used by almost every significant popular jazz and blues singer of the era, including Billie Holiday, Ray Charles, Louis Armstrong, Ella Fitzgerald, Peggy Lee, Sarah Vaughan, Billy Eckstine, Pearl Bailey, Lou Rawls, and Mel Tormé.

In 1969, Carter was persuaded by Morroe Berger, a sociology professor at Princeton University who had done his master's thesis on jazz, to spend a weekend at the college as part of some classes, seminars, and a concert. This led to a new outlet for Carter's talent: teaching. For the next nine years he visited Princeton five times, most of them brief stays except for one in 1973 when he spent a semester there as a visiting professor. In 1974 Princeton awarded him an honorary master of humanities degree. He conducted workshops and seminars at several other universities and was a visiting lecturer at Harvard for a week in 1987.

Carter's touring career was revitalized by his academic work. The U.S. State Department sponsored a tour of the Middle East in 1975, and the following year he played in a nightclub in New York City for the first time in more than three decades. Over the next twenty years Carter made dozens of new records, and much of his early work was reissued. He continued touring in America, Europe, and Japan. On his 82nd birthday, in 1989, he played a concert at Alice Tully Hall in Lincoln Center, returning the next year to introduce a new extended composition.

away the elaborate embellishment of dance bands, streamlining rhythm, and making improvisation and composition equal. Unfortunately, the band struggled for commercial success, especially during the Depression, and Carter was compelled to disband it.

At this time, an opportune invitation sent Carter to Paris to play with the Willie Lewis Orchestra at a club called Chez Florence. After nine months, at the instigation of music critic Leonard Feather, he moved to England to work as an arranger for the BBC dance orchestra, writing a prodigious three to six arrangements weekly for a period of ten months. As he spent the next three years traveling throughout Europe, Carter became pivotal in spreading jazz abroad and changing its face permanently. He visited with U.S. musicians such as his friend Coleman Hawkins and played and recorded with leading French, British, and Scandinavian jazz musicians. He also led the first international interracial group in Holland. Carter credited Doc Cheatham, with whom he played during this period, as his greatest influence on trumpet. He did not own a trumpet at the time, so Carter would use Cheatham's.

In 1938 Carter returned to New York to find the big band sound that he had helped to craft sweeping the nation. He recorded with Lionel Hampton and quickly formed another orchestra, which spent two years playing the Savoy Ballroom in Harlem. His arrangements were much in demand and appeared on recordings by Ellington, Goodman, Count Basie, Glenn Miller, Tommy Dorsey, and Gene Krupa. Though he only had one major hit in the big band era

Won Several Awards

Carter received numerous accolades. In 1978, Carter was invited to the White House to lead a band as part of President Jimmy Carter's commemoration of the Newport Jazz Festival's 25th anniversary. He was also leader of a band that played at Ronald Reagan's 1984 inaugural, played the White House again during the administration of George H.W. Bush in 1989, and in 2000 was presented with the National Medal of Arts by President Bill Clinton.

In 1982, when Carter turned 75, New York's WKCR radio station commemorated his birthday by playing his music for 177 hours. In 1984 the Kool Festival honored him with a retrospective concert. Carter received a Grammy Lifetime Achievement Award in 1987 from the National Academy of Recording Arts and Sciences. In 1988, his *Central City Sketches,* recorded with the American Jazz Orchestra in 1987, was nominated for a Grammy. In a 1989 critics' poll conducted by *Down Beat* magazine, Carter placed first in the arranger's category. In 1990, both *Jazz Times* and *Down Beat* magazines ranked Carter the jazz artist of the year in their international critics' polls. In 1994, he won a Grammy for "Elegy in Blue."

In 1996, Carter was among five recipients of the Kennedy Center Honors in Washington, D.C. In March of that year he played with the Lincoln Center Jazz Orchestra in an evening of Carter's music conducted by Wynton Marsalis. The band debuted a new suite, "Echoes of San Juan Hill," as well as playing some of his classics. Also in 1996, the lauded documentary on Carter, *Symphony in Riffs,* was released on home video. When Carter celebrated his 90th birthday in 1997, a concert tribute was held at the Hollywood Bowl (it was held two days prior to his birthday, since Carter was slated to give a concert in Oslo on his actual birthday).

Carter was married five times, with three of the marriages ending in divorce. He married his fifth wife, Hilma Ollila Arons, whom he had met in 1940 when she went to the Savoy Ballroom to hear his band, in 1979. He had a daughter, Joyce Mills, and a granddaughter and grandson. He died at a Los Angeles hospital on July 12, 2003, just a month shy of his 96th birthday.

Carter's long career was consistently characterized by high musical achievement, and he developed a unique and readily identifiable style as both an alto saxophonist and an arranger. He was able to double on trumpet and was also proficient on clarinet, piano, and trombone. His saxophone playing was pure-toned, fluid, and flawlessly phrased. One of the trademark sounds of his arrangements was four saxes harmonizing one of his sinuous, swooping melodies as if they were one instrument improvising. He also created the big-band model of contending brass and reed sections, anticipated harmonic trends that would later appear in bebop, and transformed a clunky Western notion of musical time into something more buoyant and fresh.

Two recordings that showcase his sound most famously are 1937's "Honeysuckle Rose," recorded with Django Reinhardt and Coleman Hawkins in Europe, and the same tune reprised on his 1961 album *Further Definitions,*

an album considered a masterpiece and one of jazz's most influential recordings. As Jay Weiser said in his farewell to Carter on salon.com, "Nobody in the history of jazz ever did as many things as well." Nicknamed The King by fellow musicians early in his career, Carter was beloved not only for his musical genius, but also for his reserved, dignified, and modest personality. He eschewed flamboyance in his playing and was known as a gracious, warm and witty man. Unlike some of his contemporaries, in the 1940s Carter welcomed saxophonist Charlie Parker as an innovator rather than a threat, an example of his generous spirit.

Online

"Benny Carter," *Riverwalk: Live from the Landing,* http://riverwalk .org (January 5, 2004).
"Benny Carter: Biography," *Benny Carter,* http://bennycarter .com (January 5, 2004).
"Benny Carter 1907–2003," *ASCAP,* http://ascap.com (January 5, 2004).
"Benny Carter, 1907–2003," *Village Voice,* http://villagevoice .com (January 5, 2004).
"Benny Carter, 95, Musician and Arranger Who Shaped 8 Decades of Jazz, Dies," *New York Times,* http://www.nytimes .com (January 5, 2004).
"Farewell to a Jazz Cosmopolitan," *Salon.com,* http://salon.com (January 5, 2004).
"Virtual Exhibit: Benny Carter," *Rutgers University at Newark,* http://newarkwww.rutgers.edu (January 5, 2004). □

Laura Cereta

Renaissance scholar, writer, and feminist Laura Cereta (1469–1499) wrote letters throughout her short adult life, the contents of which formed the basis of feminism that surfaced during the Enlightenment of the 18th century.

Education Began at Convent, Continued at Home

Cereta was born to noble parents in Brescia, Italy, in 1469. She was the eldest of six children born to Veronica di Leno and Silvestro Cereta and, by her own account, the favorite child, even in comparison to her three younger brothers (a noteworthy occurrence in a male-oriented society). She claimed to have been named for a laurel tree in her family's garden that had withstood the severe blows of a violent storm. She was a sickly child and suffered from insomnia. Her father, a member of Brescia's governing elite and a humanist, staunchly supported his daughter's scholarship during a time when it was rare for a woman to be educated and the status of women was a hotly disputed topic.

At the age of seven, Cereta went to live among nuns in a convent, where she learned to read, write, and embroider, as well as learning the basics of Latin. She became increasingly devoted to a contemplative life characterized by humility and humble obedience to God. After two years Cereta was brought home, where, according to a letter she wrote later in life, she felt constricted by her mother's model of femininity (and, typical for the time, the attendant lack of education). Her father apparently sensed her boredom and unhappiness, and within months he returned her to the convent to continue her instruction in Latin (and, presumably, Greek). She was summoned home again at age 11 to help care for her younger siblings, and at the age of 12 she assumed the task of running the household. Her lifelong thirst for knowledge endured, and she studied religion, mathematics, physical sciences, and astrology under her father's capable tutelage. She attended lectures when possible and usually worked late at night reading the ancient authors after her family members had gone to bed.

Scholarship Unimpeded by Marriage, Strengthened in Widowhood

From an early age, Cereta was involved in public debates, orations, and argumentation. This was not unusual for learned women of the time. The focus of this philosophizing was primarily ethics, rather than epistemology (the study of the nature of knowledge) or metaphysics (the study of the fundamental nature of being and reality), as was also standard for her time. She exalted learning as characteristically human and desired to seek truth. Her intellectual pursuits were also driven by a longing for immortality that circulation of her work would eventually bring to her.

When she was 15 years old, Cereta married Pietro Serina, a merchant who owned a shop in Venice and shared her love of learning. While not absent of conflict, the marriage seems to have been a happy one. Cereta began to meet and correspond with local humanist scholars who also studied, imitated, and adapted classical sources. She was widowed after only 18 months of marriage when Serina died of a form of plague. The loss of her husband deeply wounded her. Her contacts with scholars increased after her husband's death, particularly through her correspondence, and it is presumed that the bulk of Cereta's writing—letters, orations, and essays written in Latin—were penned sometime during this period.

Rather than remarry or enter a convent, Cereta overcame her profound grief by becoming more devoted scholar. Being childless and widowed in her youth left her ample opportunity to pursue an intellectual course without the burdens of child-rearing and running a household. She was fortunate to have the respectability and social position of one who had married, without the responsibilities of the union. Her correspondence suggests that she had regular meetings with groups of scholars in Chiari and Brescia and conducted readings from her "disputations," a popular form of essay at the time. She was temporarily recognized as a leading intellectual, but was harshly criticized when she tried to support herself by publishing her compositions. A manuscript of Cereta's letters (including a parody of a funeral oration, on the death of an ass, written in a classical style), *Epistolae Familiares,* circulated in Verona, Venice, and Brescia in 1488 under the patronage of Cardinal Maria Ascanius Sforza. Her father, who was her strongest sup-

porter, died six months after her volume was disseminated. The combination of his passing and attacks on her work by women and men alike conspired to keep Cereta from publishing again.

Letters Laid Groundwork for Feminism of the Enlightenment

A passionate feminist, Cereta's letters (mostly to family and local professionals) are generally secular and explore many enduring feminist issues, including marital oppression, a woman's right to higher education, and the contributions made by women to history, politics, culture, and intellectual life. She staunchly defends womanhood and pleads with women to better their lives through bettering themselves. She routinely exhorts women to forsake materialism and seek joy in the development of their character— their virtue, their honor, and their minds.

In an epistle entitled "Curse against the Ornamentation of Women," she denounces women who find more interest in jewelry, cosmetics, and attire than in enriching their minds. Many of the topics that surface in Cereta's work are associated with the Enlightenment's early feminist critics, such as Ann Finch (1661–1720), Anna Barbauld (1743–1825), Mary Wollstonecraft (1759–1797), Joanna Baillie (1762–1851), and Germaine de Stael (1766–1817). These include the attempt to rebuild and redefine the idea of gender; the establishment of women's writing in mainstream genres and venues once open to only men; women's mutual support of women and the notion of a women's community; housework as an obstacle to women's literary ambitions; and employment of the salon culture (or the convent, in Cereta's time) to span the public and private spheres so often prohibited to women. Cereta's work helped lay the groundwork for the 16th century's call for substantial institutional change in the economic, social, and legal status of women.

Cereta's letters also discuss war, death, fate, chance, malice, the importance of living an active life, the happiness brought by self-control, and contemporary political problems. She provides a detailed picture of the private experience of an early modern woman, delineating such personal concerns as her challenging relationships with her husband and her mother. Some of the epistles served as a forum for her mourning following the death of her husband, and Cereta claimed that through the process of mourning (and, presumably, the act of writing about it) she came to know herself better.

Despite her original ideas, Cereta's letters, especially those focused on classical themes, are completely grounded in the humanism of her time and of her predecessors. She was familiar with the ancient Roman authors at the center of the humanist school's curriculum—such as Cicero, Rome's greatest orator, the poet Virgil, and second-century authors Apuleius and Pliny—but she was also influenced by the early humanist classics scholars Petrarch, Salutati, and Valla.

Used Male-Dominated Format to Express Feminist Sentiments

It is significant that Cereta elected to demonstrate her intellect and to present feminist issues by participating in the predominantly male tradition of epistolography (letter-writing). The letter was not only a means of exchanging information, but a vital way to establish intellectual and social position. Unlike most women of her day, Cereta had the social contacts to participate. In fact, she even attempted to develop a friendship with the most famous female scholar in Italy at the time, Cassandra Fedele, but her efforts were unsuccessful. Still, she seems to have sustained numerous intellectual friendships with other women, including suora Veneranda, the abbess at Chiari (a prestigious boarding school attended by her brothers); the nun Nazaria Olympica; and Cereta's sister suora Deodata de Leno.

It is believed that Cereta was a philosophy teacher at the University of Padua for seven years. She is said to have felt isolated as a woman scholar. She considered her studies to have suffered from both a lack of time and the harassment of those who envied her intellect. Near the end of her life she was pressured to forsake scholarship and join a religious order. It is unclear whether she did so. She died prematurely in 1499, at the age of 30 in Brescia, Italy. She was buried at Brescia's Church of San Domenico. In a 1505 history of Brescia called *Chronica de rebus Brixianorum*, M. Helius Capriolus describes a great throng of mourners who were present at her funeral. Her complete letters were first published in English in 1997. No writings from the last years of her life (1489–1499) survive.

Books

Cereta, Laura, *Collected Letters of a Renaissance Feminist,* Diana Robin, ed., 1997.
Commire, Anne, ed. *Women in World History,* Yorkin Publishers, 2001.

Online

"Laura Cereta," www.pinn.net/ sunshine/march99/cereta3.html (December 20, 2003). □

Fedor Ivanovich Chaliapin

Decades after his death, Fedor Chaliapin (1873–1938) is still considered Russia's greatest opera singer. The dynamism of Chaliapin's acting perfectly complemented his voice, which, being a bass, was best suited for the role of the "villain." In this Chaliapin, who for the most part was self-taught, created such memorable characters on stage as Mephistopheles, Ivan the Terrible, Boris Godonov, and Holofernes.

Fedor Ivanovich Chaliapin (also spelled Fyodor and Feodor—Shalyapin, Shaliapin, and Chaliapine) was born in Kazan in eastern European Russia on February 13, 1873. He was the son of a clerk, and as a young man was apprenticed to first a cobbler then a lathe turner. He also worked as a copyist, though he had very little formal education. Simultaneous to this Chaliapin sang in the church choir and served as an extra in various local theatrical performances. In 1890 Chaliapin made his professional debut when he joined the chorus of the opera company in Ufa. He also sang bit parts such as Stolnik in Moniuszko's *Halka*. In 1891 he joined a Ukrainian opera company and went on tour throughout Russia. The years 1892 and 1893 found the ubiquitous young man in Tbilisi, Georgia, where he studied with the opera singer D. A. Usatov. It was Usatov who introduced Chaliapin to the music of Modest Mussorgsky. During these years Chaliapin began to emerge from the shadows of the chorus. During the 1893–1894 season he first assayed the role of Mephistopheles in Charles Gounod's *Faust*.

Joins the Mariinsky Theatre

Chaliapin's first major career move came in 1895 when he joined the opera company of the Mariinsky Theatre in St. Petersburg. Despite the good reviews he received by the St. Petersburg critics, Chaliapin was unsatisfied with his treatment by the company's management and in 1896 decided to accept the invitation of Savva Mamontov to sing with the Moscow Private Opera. It was here that Chaliapin came into his own as an artist. His first performances for the Private

Opera took place at the All-Russian Trade, Industry, and Arts Fair held in Nizhny-Novgorod. This was actually provisional, summer work as Chaliapin was still under contract to the Mariinsky. At the fair Chaliapin met and fell in love with his first wife, the Italian ballet dancer Iola Tornaghi, publicly declaring his love to her during a performance of Tchaikovsky's *Eugene Onegin,* in which he sang the role of Prince Gremin. When the summer season ended Chaliapin returned to St. Petersburg but was soon persuaded to relocate to Moscow by Mamontov and Tornaghi, who had signed a contract to dance in Mamontov's company. Chaliapin and Tornaghi were married on July 27, 1898.

Perhaps the first great influence on Chaliapin's career was composer Sergei Rachmaninov, whom he met during this period. In *Chaliapin: A Critical Biography* by Victor Borovsky, Chaliapin is quoted as saying that Rachmaninov: "was a great artist, a magnificent musician and a pupil of Tchaikovsky: it was he who urged me to study Mussorgsky and Rimsky-Korsakov. He taught me some of the basic principles of harmony. He tried, generally speaking, to give me a musical education." Operas by Modest Mussorgsky, Nikolai Rimsky-Korsakov, and other Russians would eventually make up the heart of Chaliapin's repertoire.

Triumphs in Moscow and Abroad

From 1896 to 1898 Chaliapin cemented his artistic reputation with the Moscow Private Opera. He sang such great roles as Varlaam in Mussorgsky's *Boris Godunov,* Ivan the Terrible in Rimsky-Korsakov's *The Maid of Pskov,* and Holofernes in Valentin Serov's *Judith.* This latter was the role he was rehearsing for the Mariinsky when he decided to leave that company. In 1898 Chaliapin made a triumphant return to St. Petersburg with the Moscow Private Opera. It was during this tour that the critic Vladimir Stasov took notice of Chaliapin; over the years Stasov would prove to be one of Chaliapin's most ardent champions.

In 1914 an English admirer published this assessment in a newspaper (quoted by Borovsky): "[Chaliapin] differs from most of his colleagues in insisting that the actor's first duty is personation. He is not content to show himself in the limelight in easy contempt of the part which he pretends to be playing. He knows that the material of an actor's art is himself, his voice and his gesture, and he handles this material with a courage and variety which place him high above his fellows." In 1927, near the end of Chaliapin's career, the newspaper *Wiener Zeitung* (also quoted by Borovsky) declared: "It is almost impossible to separate Chaliapin the singer from Chaliapin the actor. Each works for the other. Where the singer ends, the actor begins and vice-versa. They are usually both on stage at the same time. . . ." These assessments show not only that Chaliapin took all aspects of his art seriously, but that he was staunchly in the modern camp of Konstantin Stanislavsky, cofounder of the Moscow Art Theatre and developer of the acting technique known as "the method." Stanislavsky praised Chaliapin for his ability to synthesize his talents into a character's persona. This was evident back in 1898 when Chaliapin took on the title role in the Rimsky-Korsakov version of *Boris Godunov.*

By 1899 Chaliapin was viewed practically as a national treasure, and he signed contracts to sing at both the Mariinsky Theatre in St. Petersburg and the Bolshoi Theatre in Moscow. He would soon become an international figure, as well known as the Italian tenor Enrico Caruso. In 1901 he made his debut at Teatro La Scala in Milan in the title role of Arrigo Boito's *Mefistofole.* Rachmaninov assisted him in preparing for the role. This was the first of many tours in Europe and the United States. In France Chaliapin was especially beloved and did much to promote Russian culture in that country in the early part of the twentieth century.

Friendship with Gorky

1901 was another fateful year for Chaliapin; not only did it mark his first tour abroad, but also the beginning of his friendship with the writer Maxim Gorky (originally Alexei Maximovich Peshkov). It was Gorky who "wrote" Chaliapin's autobiography (published in English as *Chaliapin, an Autobiography as told to Maxim Gorky,* translated by Nina Froud). The idea for the "autobiography" was actually Gorky's; he convinced Chaliapin to come to Capri (where he was staying) to relate his life story. While Gorky certainly introduced Chaliapin to radical political thought, the latter was never a revolutionary in the sense Gorky was. Nevertheless Chaliapin performed for workers and sang revolutionary songs. After the Russian Revolution of October 1918 Chaliapin had at best lukewarm support for the Soviet Union. Yet he admired Gorky and though he thought his friend "quixotic" never wavered in his support.

The first fifteen years of the twentieth century was the apex of Chaliapin's career. During these years he created many memorable roles including the title characters in Anton Rubinstein's *The Demon,* Rachmaninov's *Aleko,* Jules Massenet's *Don Quixote* (considered his last great role), and the aforementioned *Mefistofole.* Chaliapin's other roles during this period included King Philip II in Giuseppe Verdi's *Don Carlos,* Tonio in Ruggierio Leoncavallo's *I Pagliacci,* Salieri in Rimsky-Korsakov's *Mozart and Salieri,* and Dosifei in Mussorgsky's *Khovanshchina.* One composer whom Chaliapin did not sing was Richard Wagner. Although he made polite excuses for his decision throughout his career, these have been deemed weak and disingenuous by Chaliapin's biographers. Nevertheless, this period marked one triumph after another for Chaliapin, both at home and abroad. On January 6, 1911, Tsar Nicholas II conferred on Chaliapin—who was no supporter of the Romanov dynasty—the title of "Soloist to His Majesty," the highest honor for a singer in tsarist Russia. Following his successful La Scala performance Chaliapin made his debut at the Metropolitan Opera in New York City in 1907 and at the Paris Opera in 1908. His return to the Metropolitan Opera in 1921 in the role of Boris Godunov was so successful that it sparked an eight-year run there. He made his debut at London's Covent Garden in 1926.

An Expatriate in France

Following the 1918 Bolshevik takeover, Chaliapin became the artistic director of the Mariinsky Theatre and in 1919 became a member of its managing board. However, despite being named a People's Artist of the Soviet Union in 1918, Chaliapin grew more disenchanted with the way the country was being run, particularly the restrictions on artistic freedom that were creeping in. Following a 1921 tour that took him to the United Kingdom and the United States, in which his family was not allowed to join him, Chaliapin made up his mind to leave the Soviet Union. He left for good on June 29, 1922. Soviet authorities tried many times to entice him to return but to no avail. In 1927 he was stripped of his title of People's Artist of the Soviet Union. In the early 1930s Gorky, who too had gone abroad partly out of disillusionment but returned to the Soviet Union, tried to convince Chaliapin to return also. In 1936 Stalin himself, through an intermediary (Chaliapin's American manager, Sol Hurok) made a plea for Chaliapin's return. He eventually settled in Paris.

By this time Chaliapin had divorced Iola Tornaghi and married Maria Valentinovna Petzold, with whom he had several children. His effort to support two households was another incentive for remaining abroad and especially to return to the Metropolitan Opera. Yet Chaliapin's years in exile were not without personal anguish for a man so strongly identified with Russia.

Chaliapin was also an outstanding chamber singer and gave many concert performances both in Russia and abroad. Before his break with the Soviet Union he gave numerous concerts in Russia for workers; in Europe he sang in benefits to raise money for starving Russians during the Civil War. From the beginning of his career Chaliapin made recordings; in the late nineteenth and early twentieth centuries these were wax cylinders. His first recording abroad was in Milan in 1907 and again in 1912. He also recorded in New York, Paris, and London. In 1926 the live performance of Boito's *Mefistofele,* with Chaliapin in the title role, was recorded at Covent Garden. And in 1927 a recording was made of the concert performance of *Mozart and Salieri* at London's Royal Albert Hall. Chaliapin's final recordings were made in 1936 in Tokyo. Chaliapin also tried his hand at directing opera: *Khovanshchina* and *Don Quixote.* In addition to his singing and acting Chaliapin was a man whose creative outlets were exhibited in painting, drawing, and sculpture. Besides the "autobiography," Chaliapin wrote *Pages from My Life* and *Man and Mask* (the proper translation for the latter work is *Mask and Soul).* Chaliapin also appeared in the title role in the 1933 film *Don Quixote,* directed by G.W. Pabst.

Chaliapin died of leukemia in Paris on April 12, 1938. His old friend, advisor, and fellow expatriate Sergei Rachmaninov had visited Chaliapin two days before his death but could not bear to attend the funeral. The enormous cortège passed by the Paris Opera House before arriving at the Batignolles Cemetery, where Chaliapin was buried. His body remained there until 1984 when he was disinterred and reburied in Moscow's Novodevichy Cemetery.

Books

Borovsky, Victor, *Chaliapin: A Critical Biography,* Alfred A. Knopf, 1988.

Great Soviet Encyclopedia, trans. of Third Ed., Vol. 29, Macmillan, 1982.

Online

Borovsky, Victor, "Feodor Chaliapin," Nimbus Records, Prima Voce, http://www.wyastone.co.uk/nrl/pvoce/7823c.html (December 27, 2003).

"Feodor Chaliapin (1873–1938)," http://www.russia-in-us.com/Music/Opera/Chaliapin/ (December 27, 2003).

"Feodor Ivanovich Shaliapin (1873–1938)," http://www.planet.satto.co.yu/slavbasses/english/sal1a.htm (December 27, 2003). □

Mary Agnes Chase

Mary Agnes Chase (1869–1963) devoted her life to the study of grasses, working in the field as well through the Smithsonian Institution's National Herbarium to expand existing knowledge about the plant she claimed "holds the world together."

Botanist, author, and agrostologist—specialist in grasses—Chase traveled the world to collect and catalogue more than 10,000 species of grasses, many of which she also discovered. Beginning her career in a Chicago museum, she eventually gained positions at the U.S. Department of Agriculture and went on to oversee the National Museum Herbarium, now a part of the Smithsonian Institution. An active prohibitionist and feminist, Chase was also an enthusiastic mentor to many young women attempting to establish careers in botany during the early 20th Century.

An Independent Student

Chase was born Mary Agnes Meara in Iroquois County, Illinois, on April 20, 1869, the second child born to Martin Meara and Mary Cassidy Brannick Meara. Her father, born in Ireland and a blacksmith for the railroad, died when she was only two. To support her five children, Mary Meara moved her family north to Chicago, to live with her own mother.

Chase was a small-boned child. Even in adulthood she was under five feet and never weighed more than 98 pounds. Chase was nonetheless robust and energetic. After finishing grammar school, she had to get work to help support her family. A scholarly child, she found a job suitable to her meticulous, single-minded nature: working as a proofreader and typesetter at a small magazine for country schoolteachers called the *School Herald.* This job led to her meeting William Ingraham Chase, the magazine's 34-year-old editor, and a romance quickly followed. In January 1888 the couple was married. Tragically, William Chase contracted tuberculosis and was dead within the year, leaving 19-year-old Chase a widow saddled with debt.

No stranger to tough times, Chase found a night job proofreading copy for the *Inter-Ocean* newspaper. She lived a no-frills life in Chicago and survived on a modest diet that often consisted of beans and oatmeal. When her time allowed it, she moonlighted at a general store owned by her brother-in-law. At the store she struck up a strong friendship with her nephew, Virginius Chase, and discovered that she shared the boy's interest in plant identification. Chase became increasingly fascinated by botany and read voraciously on the subject. She also went out into more rural areas around Chicago whenever she could, keeping notebooks in which she sketched plants and wrote about what she observed. When she could afford to, she also enrolled in extension courses in botany at the University of Chicago and the Lewis Institute.

During one of her trips into the country Chase encountered a fellow plant lover in the Reverend Ellsworth Hill. Hill, who was interested in mosses, was impressed by Chase's botanical drawings as well as by the woman's enthusiasm. He suggested that she meet with Charles Frederick Millspaugh, director of Chicago's Field Museum of Natural History. In 1901 Millspaugh offered Chase a part-time job as an illustrator for two museum publications, one of them being *Plantae Yucatanae*. Because these drawings often required the rendering of minute botanical details, Chase learned how to use a microscope, a skill she quickly capitalized on by getting a full-time position as a meat inspector for a Chicago stockyard.

Chase and Hill maintained their friendship for many years, and she illustrated several of his scientific reports on mosses. Realizing that working in a stockyard was no way for a woman of Chase's talents to spend her life, in 1903 Hill encouraged his friend to apply for a position as a botanical illustrator at the U.S. Department of Agriculture (USDA) Bureau of Plant Sciences, located in Washington, D.C. Awarded the job, Chase set about providing botanical illustrations for the bureau's many publications and took advantage of her position to spent much of her free time at the USDA's herbarium, where she pursued a growing interest in the study of grasses.

Professional Collaboration

While working on botanical renderings at the USDA's herbarium, Chase met scientist Albert Spear Hitchcock, and in 1907 she went to work as Hitchcock's scientific assistant in his study of systematic agrostology—the study of grass culture. In her working relationship with Hitchcock, which lasted until his death in December 1935, Chase was able to fully indulge her curiosity about plant life, and the many thousands of specimens she collected during her field expeditions contributed to the veteran scientist's magnum opus, 1935's *A Manual of the Grasses of the United States.* Chase would later update this work by Hitchcock, publishing a revised edition in 1951.

An energetic woman, Chase was not content to remain in the laboratory. The first field work she performed for the USDA led her to the southeastern United States and resulted in two books coauthored with Hitchcock: 1910's *The North American Species of Panicum* and 1915's *Tropical North American Species of Panicum.*

Even though she was employed by a government department, the federal budget did not include many frills, so Chase covered many of the expenses resulting from her plant-hunting expeditions on her own. Her independent study had already resulted in one published paper—on the genera Paniceae—and other writing opportunities also came her way, enabling her to survive financially while also traveling. In 1913 she journeyed south to Puerto Rico, collected various grasses, and discovered a new species of fern, among other things; her work there led to 1917's *Grasses of the West Indies,* coauthored with Hitchcock.

As an agrostologist working for the federal government, Chase's duties extended beyond research, writing, and classification. The USDA had developed a large grass collection under its first director, George Vasey. While Chase and Hitchcock contributed wild species, commercially developed strains were also catalogued and studied. Chase spent much of her time performing such tasks to ensure that these newly introduced commercial grasses and other forage plants were not marketed using fraudulent claims. She also made recommendations regarding feed grass for livestock. Beginning in 1923 Chase also served as assistant custodian of the grass herbarium, which had been transferred from the USDA to the United States National Museum (USNM; now the Smithsonian Institution) in October 1912.

Chase published her self-illustrated *A First Book of Grasses: The Structure of Grasses Explained for Beginners* in 1922; the 127-page book was twice revised, was translated into Spanish in 1960 by Zoraida Luces de Febres, and is now considered a classic. "Grass is what holds the earth together," she wroted in the book. "Grass made it possible for the human race to abandon his cave life and follow herds. . . . Grasses have been so successful in the struggle for existence that they have a wider geographic range than any other plant family, and they occupy all parts of the earth." Released while its author was in Europe visiting plant collections, *A First Book of Grasses* resulted in her promotion a year later to assistant botanist.

Two years later, in November 1924, the 56-year-old Chase joined Brazilian botanists Paulo Campos Porto and María Bandeira and embarked on her first trip to eastern Brazil, where for six months she traveled by foot, donkey, and train throughout the mountainous rain forest region near Mt. Itatiaia, collecting 500 new species of grass and more than 19,000 other specimens. Four years later, in 1929, she returned to the Brazilian jungle, this time as associate botanist, and spent a year exploring the terrain and discovering more new species. Through her efforts, thousands of Brazil's grasses were discovered and classified; Chase is also credited by some as being the first woman to climb the region's highest mountain. Many years later, in 1940, the 71-year-old Chase would accept an invitation from the Venezuelan government to come to that country and assist in developing a range management program.

In early 1936 Chase was promoted to senior botanist in charge of systematic agrostology at the USDA's Bureau of Plant Industry, taking over the role of her late mentor, Hitchcock. Her duties at the USNM also expanded when, in 1937, she was appointed custodian of the Grass Herbarium.

Although she retired from her position at the USDA in April 1939, she continued working long hours as a herbarium research associate at the USNM's plant division and retained her custodial duties at the herbarium under the title honorary custodian until near her death.

A Dedicated Feminist

In addition to her passion for grasses, Chase was passionate about woman's rights. Once she was established in her field, she aided the careers of many young botanists with encouraging correspondence. She even offered some the chance to board temporarily at her home, which she affectionately called "Casa Contenta." From 1918 until ratification of the 14th Amendment guaranteeing women the right to vote in August 1920, Chase was active in the suffragist movement. In January 1915 she was among those arrested for maintaining a continuous fire fed by copies of all of President Woodrow Wilson's speeches that referred to liberty or freedom. In the summer of 1918 she was arrested for picketing in front of the White House and in another case had to be force-fed during a hunger strike protest. Chase's radicalism sometimes proved problematic, and at one point it resulted in a threat of dismissal from the USDA.

A committed socialist and activist, Chase worked for the ratification of the amendment supporting Prohibition. She was a member of the National Association for the Advancement of Colored People, The Fellowship for Reconciliation, the National Woman's Party, and the Women's International League for Peace and Freedom.

In her own field, Chase's efforts were rewarded in 1956 by the Botanical Society of America, which presented her with a certificate honoring her as "one of the world's outstanding agrostologists and preeminent among American students in this field." Two years later the 89-year-old botanist received an honorary degree from the University of Illinois, a meaningful gesture for a woman who never earned a college degree. In the late 1950s she was also made a fellow of both the Smithsonian Institution and the Linnean Society.

Chase died at age 94, on September 24, 1963, shortly after being admitted to a nursing home in Bethesda, Maryland. At her death she left a three-volume annotated index to the thousand of grass species she had identified and classified for the USDA. Her 1951 revision of Hitchcock's *Manual of the Grasses of the United States* remains the definitive source on the subject. Chase's papers are collected at the Hunt Institute for Biological Documentation at Carnegie Mellon University, and her field notebooks are housed at the Hitchcock-Chase Library of the Smithsonian Institution.

Books

Bonta, Marcia Myers, *Women in the Field: America's Pioneering Women Naturalists,* Texas A & M University Press, 1991.
Chase, Agnes, *A First Book of Grasses: The Structure of Grasses Explained for Beginners,* Macmillan, 1922, 3rd revised edition, 1968, revised by Lynn G. Clark and Richard W. Pohl, Smithsonian Institution, 2001.
Dictionary of American Biography, Seventh Supplement, 1961– 1965, American Council of Learned Societies, 1981.

Notable Women Scientists, Gale, 2000.

Periodicals

Annual Report of the Smithsonian Institution, 1926.
New York Times, June 12, 1956.

Online

Museum of Natural History, http://www.mnh.si.edu/anthro/ (December 6, 2003). □

Linda Chavez-Thompson

In 1995 American labor activist Linda Chavez-Thompson (born 1944) became the first woman appointed as an executive vice president of the American Federation of Labor-Congress of Industrial Organizations (AFL-CIO). Born to a family of Mexican-American field workers, Chavez-Thompson pursued her dedication to advancing the quality of life for American workers and by the late 20th century had become one of the foremost labor leaders in the United States.

Picked Cotton in Fields as a Girl

Chavez-Thompson was born to sharecropper Felipe Chavez and his wife on August 3, 1944, in Lubbock, Texas. Her grandparents had immigrated to the United States from Mexico, making her a second-generation American. All eight of the Chavez children worked in the fields to earn money for the family; Chavez herself began picking cotton for 30 cents an hour in Lorenzo when she was ten years old. Her grandfather, meanwhile, encouraged her to be proud of her Hispanic heritage and to do the best she could at any endeavor.

The course of Chavez's life would perhaps have been much different had she not resisted her father's demands that she leave school at age 13 to work for the family full-time by cleaning the house and making meals. The family was facing a financial crisis at the time, and her father believed that it was more important that his sons receive a proper education, since Chavez's likely destiny was to get married and become a housewife. Thus, she remained in school through the ninth grade and left at age 16.

As a teen Chavez offered an early demonstration of her soon-to-be legendary labor-negotiating skills when she petitioned her brothers and sisters to join her in quitting fieldwork if their overworked mother was not allowed to stay home and rest. The ploy worked, and Mrs. Chavez left her job and got the rest she needed at home. The incident no doubt made a strong impression on Chavez, proving the increased power of united workers.

In 1963, at age 19, Chavez married a city employee named Robert Thompson. In a move that was unconventional for the time but somewhat reflective of her Mexican heritage, she insisted on keeping her maiden name and hyphenating her husband's with it. She left her family and the cotton fields and found work as a house cleaner for the wage of one dollar an hour. She tired of the backbreaking work by 1967 and, determined to find a better job, applied for and got a secretarial position with the Lubbock local chapter of the Laborers' International Union, to which her father also belonged. She had no real idea what a labor union was but enjoyed the work and the increase in pay to $1.40 an hour.

Clerical Job Brought out Natural Talents

Chavez-Thompson was the only person in the local who could speak both English and Spanish. This increased her value to the office, since many of its members were Spanish speakers, and soon she took on more responsibilities. Before long she was serving as the union representative to all the local's Spanish-speaking members. She wrote up grievances and spoke for them at administrative meetings while taking organizational classes in her spare time. Chavez-Thompson educated herself so well in labor-related issues that she was even mistaken for a lawyer at one hearing.

Chavez-Thompson left the union in 1971 to take a new job as an international representative with the American Federation of State, County, and Municipal Employees Union (AFSCME) in Austin, Texas. This was demanding work and, with a new baby, she was exhausted much of the time. Finally Chavez-Thompson decided to accept a less-demanding position with the San Antonio 2399 Local in 1973. This new job proved an excellent fit, and by 1977 she had been promoted to executive director.

Chavez-Thompson later recalled that these were some of the most difficult but rewarding days of her professional life. At the time, Texas was a hostile environment for union workers and anyone attempting to organize local laborers. She later recalled that sometimes workers would not even speak with her, not only because she was from a union, but because she was a woman and a Latina. In addition, government workers, whom AFSCME represented, were not permitted to join unions under Texas law. Thus, Chavez-Thompson found that much of her work required persuading state officials—and even bullying them a bit—to see things the union's way. Hardened by privation and grueling physical labor, the five-foot-one-inch Latina was more than a worthy opponent for predominantly white male State of Texas administrators. Her experiences as a youth also meant that she knew exactly how the workers she represented felt when their meager livelihood was threatened. As a result of her efforts, AFSCME saw its membership rise rapidly during this period.

Word quickly spread of the powerhouse Latina who was winning battles for workers throughout the state, and soon Chavez-Thompson was in demand for her negotiation and organizational skills. She saved the jobs of 33 community college workers by bringing about the public ouster of three trustees whose financial abuses the workers had reported. Chavez-Thompson organized emergency drivers to cover for workers on a wildcat strike, driving one of the trucks herself, and became known as a union representative who would risk arrest at protests and on picket lines to help the people she represented.

Work Led to High-ranking Labor Positions

By the mid-1980s Chavez-Thompson had become recognized as one of Texas's finest labor negotiators as well as a rising star on the national labor scene. The Labor Council for Latin-American Advancement, a subsidiary of the AFL-CIO, elected her as its national vice president in 1986, and in 1988 she was appointed vice president of AFSCME's seven-state region comprising Utah, Texas, Colorado, Nevada, New Mexico, Arizona, and Oklahoma.

Despite criticism from some quarters that her appointment had been merely a gesture to invigorate the "male, pale, stale" organization, Chavez-Thompson was thrilled to accept the AFSCME position. However, she was also realistic about the challenges she faced. At 13 million people, the group's membership was at a historic low, and there were no funds earmarked for new-member recruitment. In addition, there was a pervasive feeling among many workers that unions were corrupt—a sentiment that effectively kept them from joining—and little loyalty among workers who did belong. Chavez-Thompson decided that these issues were serious enough to warrant dramatic measures.

Her first action was to begin setting aside 30 percent of AFL-CIO funds for recruiting new members, and she determined that such efforts should be focused on minorities and women, neither of which group was well represented in the union. Chavez-Thompson also initiated an education program aimed at young people to teach them about the benefits of labor activism and organization. Among her successes was a recruiting drive that brought in 5,000 new members and passage of a new collective bargaining law for New Mexico public employees. In an interview with *NEA Today*, she explained: "We've lost a couple generations of children who don't realize what their parents have done to build the workplace in America. Forty hours a week didn't just come automatically. Overtime didn't come automatically. Labor Day is more than just the last holiday before you go back to school."

Praised for Saving Flagging AFL-CIO

Chavez-Thompson's drastic measures achieved good results, both in terms of increasing membership and electing more labor-friendly national leaders. In conjunction with these efforts, she also developed a campaign to get grassroots communities—places of worship, schools, women's groups, and civil rights groups—to share a stake in the health of their local unions, reasoning that unions consist of workers who live in these other social communities. In other words, she wanted to show communities that union interests overlap with community interests. This revolutionary approach showed itself to be extremely successful in solving labor disputes, including helping K-Mart workers trying to get their first labor contract and Solomon Smith Barney cafeteria workers who were suffering retaliation for organizing a union. Nationwide, community groups that witnessed such unfair treatment were now more likely, thanks to Chavez-Thompson's efforts, to join with local labor unions to make the offending companies back down.

Chavez-Thompson was elected to the AFL-CIO Executive Council in 1993. Two years later, after almost 20 years of service, she gave up her position as executive director of San Antonio Local 2399 to accept her election as executive vice president of the AFL-CIO. In doing so, she again became the first woman and the first person of color to hold that position.

Known by now throughout the country for her skill and energy, Chavez-Thompson was appointed to serve on President Bill Clinton's Race Advisory Board in 1997 and on the President's Committee on Employment of People with Disabilities in 1998. Chosen for a second four-year term as AFL-CIO executive vice president in 1997, Chavez-Thompson was also elected in 2001 as president of the Inter-American Regional Organization of Workers ORIT. The latter group had more than 45 million members in South, Central, and North America.

Chavez-Thompson, who had two children with her husband before his death, moved from San Antonio to Washington, D.C. in 1998. The labor leader remained active professionally, serving as vice chairperson for the Democratic National Committee; as a member of the board of directors of the United Way and the Institute for Women's Policy Research; a selection committee member for the International Laborer's Hall of Fame; an executive committee member for the Congressional Hispanic Caucus Institute; and a member of the board of trustees for the Labor Heritage Foundation. When asked during an interview with the *Seattle Post-Intelligencer* whether she has any aspirations for political office, Chavez-Thompson replied, "I love being the kingmaker. I don't like being the king." By 2000 her top challenge as a labor leader was to get equal pay for women and people of color. In March 2004 at the American Association of People with Disabilities' (AAPD) Leadership Gala, Chavez-Thompson was awarded with an award named after her, the Linda Chavez-Thompson Award as quoted from *PR Newswire,* "in recognition of her longstanding leadership toward the inclusion of people with disabilities and their families within the labor movement."

Books

Newsmakers, Gale, 1999.

Periodicals

NEA Today, May 1997.
PR Newswire, March 4, 2004.
Seattle Post-Intelligencer, October 10, 2003.

Online

"Linda Chavez-Thompson: A Woman Pioneering the Future," *National Women's History Project Web site,* http://www.nwhp.org/ (December 21, 2003).
"Linda Chavez-Thompson: DNC Vice Chair," *Democratic National Party Web site,* http://www.democrats.org/ (December 21, 2003).
" Linda Chavez-Thompson, Executive Vice President," *AFL-CIO Web site,* http://www.aflcio.org/ (January 12, 2004).
"Linda Chavez-Thompson: Executive Vice President, AFL-CIO," *In These Times.com,* http://www.inthesetimes.com/ (December 21, 2003).
"Spotlight on Linda Chavez-Thompson," *Soy Unica Web site,* http://www.soyunica.gov/ (December 21, 2003). □

Francis Chichester

British adventurer Sir Francis Chichester (1901–1972) gained worldwide fame in the summer of 1967 when he completed an around-the-world solo trip in his yacht, the *Gipsy Moth IV*. His voyage set a new world circumnavigation record of 274 days for its arduous, 28,500-mile journey. Throughout his life, Chichester was an adventurer in the air and on the sea, setting records as an aviator and a seaman.

Chichester had previously won fame for flying around the world in his single-engine *Gipsy Moth* plane during the 1930s. The author of several books that chronicled his years of solo escapades, Chichester asserted that "the only way to live life to the full is to do something that depends on both the brain and on physical sense and action," according to the *New York Times.*

Search for a Calling

Chichester was born September 17, 1901, in Shirwell, Devon, England, the second of four children in a family headed by an austere, Anglican-minister father. Charles Chichester, his son later recalled, "seemed to be disapproving of everything I did, and waiting to squash any enthusiasm," according to his *Times* obituary. On one occasion, the young Chichester was bitten by a snake near the family home, and his father instructed him to ride his bicycle to the nearest hospital, some four miles away, for treatment.

Expected to follow in his father's career footsteps, Chichester was sent to a rigorous boarding school, Marlborough College in Wiltshire, where he endured corporal punishment from the masters and brutal hazing rituals at the hands of the older students. He dropped out at age 17, hoping to join the British colonial administration in India, but his father nixed that plan and instead found him a place as a farmhand. When his workhorse bucked and ruined some dairy equipment, the farmer flogged him and sent him back home. At that point, Chichester's father agreed to buy him passage on board a ship bound for New Zealand.

Arriving on the other side of the world in 1919 with just ten British pounds to his name, Chichester vowed never to return to England until he had turned the ten into 20,000. He failed in a series of jobs, from coal miner to lumberjack to gold prospector but did earn enough as a door-to-door newspaper subscription salesman to finance a small foray into real estate. That venture quickly proved profitable, and

and Australia. He added pontoons to his plane for the journey, but when he capsized once he had to convince aboriginal islanders who came to greet him to help him right his craft. Later that year, he began his next trek, a solo seaplane trip around the world. His plane was unable to avoid telegraph wires near the Katsuura harbor in Japan and crashed into a retaining wall. He woke up in the hospital after surgery with 13 broken bones, and it took him five years to fully recuperate.

Undaunted, Chichester bought a new plane, the *Puss Moth,* and made a 1936 Sydney-to-London flight across Asia. In 1937, he married Sheila Craven, who wholeheartedly supported his quest for new adventures. But the onset of World War II grounded Chichester and his plane in 1939. The skilled pilot tried in vain to join the Royal Air Force but was rejected three times because of his nearsightedness and astigmatism. Instead, he served as chief navigation instructor at Empire Central Flying School in England and wrote navigation materials for the British Air Ministry. On the day he returned to civilian life in 1945, he established a map and guide business, Francis Chichester Ltd., with his wife.

Atlantic Voyage

With the onset of the jet age, and feeling that the skies were now conquered, Chichester looked elsewhere for the thrill that running a business failed to provide for him. He settled on sailing, buying his first boat, the *Gipsy Moth II,* in 1953, and taking part in ocean races. In 1958, he was diagnosed with lung cancer, and doctors suggested that his lung be removed; he refused the surgery and instead went to the south of France for holistic therapy. He remained a vegetarian for the rest of his life, which lasted 14 years beyond the six-month sentence the doctors had given him when he refused the surgery.

One day at the Royal Ocean Racing Club, a fellow member suggested a transatlantic race, and Chichester agreed. The wager amount was a half crown. "On looking back I am astonished how ignorant I was when I started ocean racing," his *New York Times* obituary quoted him as saying. "My only experience with the seamanship needed and the sea was what I had learned in seaplane handling." On June 11, 1960, he and his competitors set sail from Plymouth, England, and Chichester reached the New York harbor on July 21, a week ahead of the others. At 40 days, it was a new world record for a solo Atlantic voyage, beating the previous one by an astonishing 16 days.

Global Trip by Yacht

The transatlantic course became Chichester's new proving ground. He made another east-to-west crossing in June 1962 in 33 days, 15 hours, and took his son along for another two years later and completed the trip in just 25 days, 9 hours. Then Chichester found a new challenge: an around-the-world solo trip. The quickest route was via South America's Cape Horn, but this was one of the world's deadliest passages. He needed a much more solid boat for the feat and found a sponsor in England's Whitbread Brewery, which funded the construction of the $70,000 *Gipsy Moth IV* and then provided him with enough ale for the

a tract of land he acquired and planted trees on provided him with steady income from lumber later in his life. Married in 1923, he became a father, but his wife died in 1929. By then, Chichester and a business partner had established a small aviation firm that took passengers for their first airplane rides. Fascinated by the new method of transport, Chichester decided to return to England and enroll in flight school.

Plane Crash in Japan

Chichester trained as a pilot for three months and bought a de Havilland Gipsy Moth plane, which he named the *Madame Elijah.* He made practice runs for another month, following the railroad line from London to his boyhood home in Devon, and took a few jaunts to the European continent to practice landings and takeoffs. On December 20, 1929, he stunned the ground crew at the Croydon airfield with an announcement that he was going to fly solo back to Australia. Only one other person had ever done so, taking 15 days. The trip was perilous, and he survived a crash landing in Libya, which delayed his trip for days while he waited for a replacement propeller to be sent from London. In the end, he completed the 12,600-mile trip in 180 hours.

Chichester touched down in Sydney to find that he had become a minor celebrity for his feat, and he wrote a book about his experience, *Solo to Sydney,* published in 1930. The following year, he became the first pilot to fly solo across the treacherous Tasman Sea between New Zealand journey. Equipped with state-of-the-art navigational equipment, it boasted an auto-steer device that would allow him sleep for a few hours while the ship sailed on.

Chichester set off from Plymouth in August 1966 with an itinerary that included only one stop on land. He rounded the Cape of Good Hope, on the tip of the African continent, on October 20, and had more than one hazardous high-seas moment. In a *New York Times Magazine* interview with Harry Gordon, he recalled an incident when his boat suddenly picked up incredible speed. "What had happened was that we had been picked up by a surfing wave, about 30 feet high, and the whole boat was being carried along broadside on and horizontally, with the mizzenmast parallel to the water," he told the magazine. "It just stayed like that for a time as we skidded along at about 30 knots sideways. All I could do was watch dumbfounded."

After 107 days, Chichester had logged 13,750 miles but nearly abandoned his adventure when the auto-steering device broke and could not be fixed. He headed for the Sydney harbor anyway and was stunned to see it crowded with boats and planes to greet him. Irked at the traffic after so many isolated days on the open seas, he snarled at the "bloody Sunday drivers" over the radio and then docked to find he had become a celebrity once more. A debate in the press raged over whether or not it was safe for him, at 65 years of age, to continue, but Chichester refused to bend to conventional wisdom and rested for the next six weeks, waiting for modifications to be made to his boat. He was knighted in absentia by Queen Elizabeth II on the day before he set sail once more.

The *Gipsy Moth IV*'s passage across the Pacific continued apace, but Chichester was a few weeks behind schedule when he rounded Cape Horn at the tip of South America in mid-March, just in time for the fierce storms that have wrecked much larger ships than his. Five times his cockpit flooded with water, but he bailed and kept on, with a *Times* of London photographer flying overhead and a Royal Navy frigate following at a courteous distance. He arrived back in Plymouth on May 28, 1967, having set the new around-the-world solo record of 274 days. His Sydney-to-Plymouth leg, at 119 days, was the longest ever by a yacht of its class without stopping at a port of call.

Knighted with Drake's Sword

A crowd estimated at a quarter-million Britons greeted Chichester when he sailed into the harbor, and a Royal Navy ship fired its guns in salute. A few weeks later, the Queen knighted him in person using the sword of Sir Francis Drake, the world-famous navigator. Chichester sailed his *Gipsy Moth IV* up the Thames River for the occasion, which again brought an immense turnout of well-wishers. It one of the few times when the knighthood ceremony was not performed in private. The *Gipsy Moth IV* was donated to England's National Maritime Museum in Greenwich.

After writing two more books, Chichester had a new boat built, the 57-foot *Gipsy Moth V*, and made a 22-day run from Bissau, a port in what is now Guinea-Bissau, to Nicaragua in 1971. He was forced to drop out of another solo Atlantic race in June 1972 when he became ill and

returned to England. He died on August 26, 1972, in Plymouth, England. His books included a 1964 autobiography, *The Lonely Sea and the Sky,* and *Gipsy Moth Circles the World* in 1967. When the *New York Times Magazine*'s Gordon asked Chichester what drove him to take on such desolate solitary voyages, he replied that he took "tremendous satisfaction out of being the first man to various things, and I like to do them alone . . . when I'm alone I perform twice as efficiently as at other times—maybe even four times as efficiently. I don't have to defer to other people's opinions. I'm just a loner, I suppose."

Periodicals

Daily Telegraph (Surrey Hills, Australia), October 28, 2000.
Life, Fall 1986.
New York Times, August 27, 1972.
New York Times Magazine, January 22, 1967.
Times (London, England), January 18, 1967; February 1, 1967; February 8, 1967; February 15, 1967; February 22, 1967; March 1, 1967; March 22, 1967; March 29, 1967; April 26, 1967; May 3, 1967; May 18, 1967; May 24, 1967; May 27, 1967; May 30, 1967; August 28, 1972; July 8, 1998; May 29, 2000.

Online

"Francis Chichester," *Contemporary Authors Online,* http://galenet.galegroup.com/servlet/BioRC (December 7, 2003). □

Vera Chytilová

Innovative and controversial, Vera Chytilová (born 1929) is the only significant Czech woman filmmaker and Czech cinema's first feminist director. She was a prominent member of the early 1960s Czech New Wave, which was influenced by cinema verite's objectivity and French New Wave's subjectivity and employed such techniques as improvised dialogue, amateur actors, allegory, surreal content, and choppy editing. In her work she has explored the troubles of contemporary society and has been harshly critical of human failings. Her inexorable call for morality makes her unique within the Czech film community.

A Latecomer to the Film Industry

Vera Chytilová was born February 2, 1929, in Ostrava, Czechoslovakia (now the Czech Republic). She was an architecture and philosophy student at Charles University in Brno for two years, followed by stints as a technical draftsperson for a chemical laboratory, a fashion model, and a photo retoucher. She worked at Barrandov Film Studios in Prague and, having discovered her passion for filmmaking, decided to enroll at FAMU, the

state film academy, which she did in 1957. Barrandov refused to recommend her for admission to film school or a scholarship, but Chytilová tested without a recommendation and was accepted, even in the face of a daunting rejection rate. She studied with veteran director Otakar Vavra, who was instrumental in the founding of the film academy. Vavra, whose students included Milos Forman and Ivan Passer, nurtured an environment of open artistic growth. Chytilová attended FAMU with others who would become renowned Czech directors, including Jiri Menzel, Jan Nemec, and Evald Schorm, and they became friends who often worked on one another's films.

Chytilová made *Strop* (Ceiling), her graduation project, in 1962. Mixing cinema verite and formalism, it taps Chytilová's own experience to recount the story of a model who encounters exploitation and empty materialism in the world of fashion, and establishes Chytilová's feminist voice and outlook. Initially banned for its criticism of women's roles in Czech society, it won a prize at the Oberhausen Film Festival the following year. She completed her first feature film in 1963, *O necem jinem* (Something Different), which contrasted the lives of a housewife and gymnast through use of parallel narratives that boldly combined documentary and fiction. She was 34 years old at the time, making her a latecomer to the film industry. Some of her more experimental works are *Sedmikrasky* (Daisies, 1966), which follows two girls whose reckless pranks result in complete ruin, and *Ovoce Stromu Rajskych Jime* (Fruit of Paradise, 1969), an allegory about male-female relationships that won an award from the Chicago Film Festival.

These films employ techniques such as tinting, montage, unusual camera angles, film trickery, and visual deformation.

Career Stymied by Soviet Invasion

Daisies established Chytilová's international reputation and, while it won international critical acclaim (winning the Grand Prix at the International Film Festival in Bergamo, Italy), it was officially banned in her native country until 1967 because, as a National Assembly deputy complained about scenes in which a banquet setting is demolished, it depicted a waste of food ("the fruit of the work of our toiling farmers"). In *Daisies,* Chytilová challenged her audience by abandoning cinematic conventions such as smooth visual style, chronology, and sympathetic protagonists. She used visual puns and witty imagery in the spirit of the artists of the Dada movement of the 1920s and made good use of the striking cinematography of her second husband, Jaroslav Kucera. The film has inspired various interpretations, parallel but not necessarily contradictory. This is true of many of Chytilová's films. Many of their conclusions are inconclusive, encouraging the audience to participate in the creation of truth and meaning.

The era of liberalization that paved the way for pioneering and radical Czech filmmaking came to an end with the 1968 Soviet invasion of Czechoslovakia. The film industry was restructured, centralized, and tightly controlled. Unorthodox art was discouraged. Allegory and avant-garde experimentation in film were distrusted, linked with elitism and intellectualism by bureaucrats and politicians who were now in control of the film industry. Several New Wave filmmakers—including Milos Forman, Jan Nemic, and Ivan Passer—went into exile. Chytilová and other New Wave directors who stayed in Czechoslovakia had their projects "shelved," never completed or released due to political censorship. In the 1970s the film industry added a new obstacle, the "literary advisor," whose role was to prevent the making or release of problematic films. Stricter censorship, combined with the practice of shelving, obliterated the Czech New Wave.

Though not officially blacklisted, Chytilová was unable to direct or work with foreign producers for seven years from 1969 to 1976. Her scripts were either shelved or outright rejected, and she was prevented from attending numerous women's film festivals worldwide. In 1975, Chytilová sent a letter to Czech President Gustav Husák in which she explained her movies and the problems she encountered in making them. She also reiterated her socialist conviction. Because of the letter, coupled with some help from surreptitious influences, Chytilová was permitted to resume filmmaking. In 1976 she made a more conventional, feminist comedy about gender wars called *Hra o Jablko* (Apple Game). *Hra o Jablko* was followed by a film with an unflinching portrayal of contemporary morality called *Panelstory Aneb Jak se Rodi Sidiste* (Prefabstory) in 1979, and 1981's *Kalamita (Calamity)*. All of these films caused Chytilová problems with government authorities upon their releases: the first raised eyebrows for the documentary-styled scenes of childbirth, the second depicted socialist life in an unflattering light, and the third was seen as a parable on the Soviet takeover. *Prefabstory* and *Calamity* were harshly attacked by establishment critics and were practically withdrawn from circulation because of their controversial content.

The political changes of the late 1980s and early 1990s changed the Czech film industry into one that relied on a market economy. Though the upside of the political shift was curtailed censorship, production dropped drastically in the face of severe cuts in government subsidy. The survival of Czech cinema came to depend on outside industries, including those from western nations.

Work Continued to Generate Controversy

Chytilová was inspired by theater in the 1980s. She directed a movie version of a mime play called *Sasek a Královna* (The Jester and the Queen) in 1987, then followed up with 1988's AIDS tragicomedy *Kopytem Sem, Kopytem Sam* (Tainted Horseplay), in which she worked with Sklep (The Celler), an avant-garde theater group. In addition to these satires of political and social problems, Chytilová directed numerous artistic documentaries, including *Praha—neklidné Srdce Evropy* (Prague: The Restless Heart of Europe, 1984); *T.G.M.—osvoboditel* (Tomas Garrigue Masaryk—Liberator, 1990); and *Vzlety a pá (Flights and Falls, 2000).* In 1983, Chytilová collaborated with Esther Krumbachova, her co-screenwriter from *Daisies,* on a story about a middle-aged womanizer, *Faunovo Velmi Pozdni Odpoledne (The Very Late Afternoon of a Faun).*

Subsequent to 1989's "Velvet Revolution," she became an active participant in public and political life and has been a staunch campaigner for state subsidization of the Czech film industry. She has completed numerous television documentary films and a 1992 comedy about the pitfalls of sudden wealth. The latter was well received by the public but scorned by the critics. Her 1998 black comedy *Pasti, Pasti, Pasticky* (Traps), though embraced by a small number of hardcore feminists, was largely considered a cruel portrayal of post-Communist Czech life. Chytilová continued to attract controversy: In 2000, while filming a sequence for the film *Vyhnáni z ráje* (Expulsion from Paradise, 2001), she, her cinematographer, and a technician were arrested by German police on charges of suspected pedophilia. The film, based on *The Naked Ape* by Desmond Morris, is set on a nude beach and features Chytilová's school-age granddaughter frolicking naked in the surf. A police spokesperson explained that German law prevents filming of children on the beach.

Chytilová teaches at FAMU, the national film academy in Prague. She has attempted to find a source of funding so that she can make *Face of Hope,* a pet project about the 19th-century writer Bozena Nemcova, but she has thus far been unsuccessful. In 2000 she was honored at the 35th Karlovy Vary film festival for her exceptional contribution to world cinema. Although Chytilová's later films are not as experimental as those from her days as a prominent force in the Czech New Wave, she is regarded as a director who managed to retain her artistic integrity while surviving the most destructive political and social upheavals, and *Daisies* continues to be a relevant example of the Czech New Wave at its finest.

Books

Thomas, Nicholas, "Vera Chytilova," *International Dictionary of Films and Filmmakers, Vol. 2: Directors,* St. James Press, 2000.

Online

"Biography: Vera Chytilova," *Prague on Film website,* http://pragueonfilm.co.uk (December 27, 2003).
"Bohemian Rhapsodist," *Guardian Unlimited website,* http://guardian.co.uk (December 27, 2003).
"Interview from 'Closely Watched Films,'" *Czech Cinema website,* http://maxpages.com/czechcinema/Interview (December 27, 2003).
"Vera Chytilova," *Gale Group Biography Resource Center website,* http://galenet.gale.com (January 2, 2004).
"Vera Chytilova," *Internet Movie Database website,* http://us.imdb.com (December 27, 2003).
"Vera Chytilova," *Yahoo Movies website,* http://movies.yahoo.com (December 27, 2003).
"Vera Chytilova: Permanent Rebel" *Kinoeye website,* http://www.kinoeye.org (December 27, 2003). □

Rebecca Thacher Clarke

Englishwoman and modern classical composer Rebecca Thacher Clarke (1886–1979) was one of the most talented viola players of her generation and worked during the renaissance of English music that occurred between the two World Wars. Critics have called her compositions for voice and instruments far ahead of her time, as many of them employ a technique that verges on atonality. Because Clarke was reticent by nature, many of her compositions were not even discovered and performed until the late 1970s.

Early Life Dominated by Abusive Father

Born in Harrow, England, on August 27, 1886, Rebecca Thacher Clarke was the daughter of the former Agnes Helferich of Munich and Joseph Thacher Clarke of Boston. She had a sister, Vanessa, who would become a sculptor, and two brothers. Her upper-middle-class family lived in a Victorian home dominated by the tyrannical and abusive Joseph, who made his daughters virtual servants. Distant and discouraging, Clarke's father often beat the children with a two-foot steel architect's rule at the slightest sign of disobedience, including biting their nails. Their mother would stand by and cry, watching helplessly. After Mrs. Clarke died, Mr. Clarke expected his teenage daughters to run the household and became murderously angry if he felt they made any errors. Clarke would later write in her diary about one of these incidents, saying, "Never have I felt such rage and frustration. For not a word of my feeling could be expressed. . . . Even now I can find nothing to say of his behavior save that it was brutal."

Clarke likely developed a form of low-grade but persistent depression called "dysthymia" from these early formative experiences, or the treatment exacerbated a predisposition to the illness. She described her feelings of sorrow and hopelessness in detailed diary entries, giving insight into a condition that even today is not well understood. Clarke's mental state would come into play throughout her life, both shaping and thwarting her creative impulse, and causing her to doubt profoundly her talent as an artist. She seems to have taken her father's abuse personally and later blamed herself intensely for any professional difficulties or failures. To Clarke, her father reportedly represented a cultural authority, so his disapproval, which was apparently constant and brutal, meant that the world disapproved as well.

Clarke found refuge from the chaos of her home life in her early musical interest, which began with violin lessons in 1894, when she was eight. In 1900, she traveled to the World's Fair in Paris and heard a performance by a Javanese gamelan, an Indonesian instrumental ensemble that features gongs, drums, woodwinds, and string instruments. The experience sparked in her a desire to become a musician, and when Clarke returned to England she began petitioning her parents to let her study at the prestigious Royal Academy of Music in London. They agreed, and she began studying violin there in 1902, composing her first pieces of music (mainly solo songs with English and German texts) in 1905. Clarke's father removed her from the school in 1905 for reasons that remain unclear, although they traveled to Europe together in 1906.

In 1907, Clarke traveled to Boston alone and stayed with family friends. In 1908, she began studying musical composition at London's Royal College of Music; she was Sir Charles Stanford's first female student. Clarke remained there until completing her formal studies in 1910, publishing her first piece, *Violin Sonata,* in 1909. In 1908, she had made the decision to abandon the violin in favor of the viola, which is slightly larger than a violin but tuned a fifth lower. The instrument provides a deeper, richer sound, versus the higher range and tonality of the violin. Clarke was fortunate to be able to study briefly with Lionel Tertis (1876–1975), who was arguably the top viola player in the world at the time and who reportedly influenced the young musician in her choice.

Clarke immediately felt an affinity for the viola, which gave her subsequent compositions, as a 2002 review in the *American Record Guide* put it, "that blend of melancholy, nostalgia, and dreaminess that makes the British music written at this time the best ever composed for the instrument."

Started Professional Music Career

In 1912, Sir Henry Wood admitted Clarke to his Queen's Hall Orchestra in London at the urging of Ethyl Smith, a musician and a major influence on the young

woman. Clarke, thereafter, played chamber music with a number of the most famous musicians of the 1910s and 1920s, including cellist Pablo Casals, pianist Artur Schnabel, violinist Jacques Thibaud, pianist and composer Percy Grainger, and conductor and pianist George Szell. It is important to keep in mind that as a woman trying to work in an area traditionally dominated by men—especially as one raised during Victorian times—Clarke felt that her creativity was in direct opposition to her femininity.

Clarke visited the United States again in 1916, visiting her brothers in Rochester, New York. Also that year, she toured the country with her close friend, cellist May Mukle, performing alone and in ensembles. The following year, she composed *Morpheus* for viola and piano, which would many years later become known as one of her finest pieces. However, the 1917 work, with its reference to the Roman god of sleep, seems to have been a metaphor for Clarke's frequent bouts of depression-related despair and her desire to be free of its pain, whether through sleep or, perhaps, even death. Reflecting her ambivalent thoughts about her career as a composer, and also aware of the sexual prejudices of the period, Clarke published the work under the pseudonym "Anthony Trent."

Clarke attended the first Berkshire Festival of Chamber Music in Pittsfield, Massachusetts, founded in 1918 by wealthy American music patron Elizabeth Sprague Coolidge. As Clarke's musical talent developed, she benefited from being away from her father on travels all around the United States, playing in concerts and composing in Detroit, New York, and Hawaii. She entered her superb new *Viola Sonata* in the 1919 Berkshire Festival and won second place. Afterward, she played in numerous concerts and earned a teaching position in New York in 1920.

Clarke's father died the same year, but as she had never expressed anger toward him in life, nor did she in death. In fact, as with many other things, the composer blamed herself for Mr. Clarke's violent outbursts and voiced pity for him many times, since he had to deal with her, "the naughtiest" of his children.

Produced Most Work in 1920s

With her composition and release of the *Trio for Violin, Cello, and Piano* in 1920, Clarke emerged as a clear leader among the composers of the day. She submitted the work as her entry in the 1921 Berkshire Festival, receiving second place. Her other notable works that year included *Epilogue* for cello and piano and *Chinese Puzzle* for violin and piano. In 1922, Clarke embarked on a world tour but arrived back in Massachusetts in time for the 1923 Berkshire event. Mrs. Coolidge, impressed by the young woman's talent and passion for music, commissioned Clarke to compose a piece for her. Clarke finished the resulting *Rhapsody for Cello and Piano* later in 1923.

The 1920s would be the most productive decade of Clarke's musical life. After returning to her hometown of Harrow in 1924, she composed *Midsummer Moon* for violin and piano (1924), *3 Old English Songs* for voice and piano (1924), and *3 Irish Country Songs* for voice and piano (1926), among many others. She favored the use of English musical themes, as well as texts by William Shakespeare, William Yeats, and William Blake. Modern critics have also been impressed by Clarke's use of elements that border on atonality, a technique in which the composer avoids harmonic or melodic reference to tonal centers. (Atonality is the deliberate rejection of tonality, which mandates a clear distinction between consonant and dissonant sounds.) Atonality was only just becoming a subject of experiment with some of the more advanced composers of the time—a group to which Clarke apparently belonged.

During the last half of the 1920s, Clarke used Harrow and London as her home base and did all of her concertizing and composing there. In 1927, she began an illicit affair that would have lasting consequences for her, both emotionally and professionally. John Goss was a respected baritone singer and a married man, and Clarke's hopeless love for him seems to have had an unhealthily obsessive quality. In her diaries of 1928–1931, she lamented her inability to work because of thoughts of the singer, which combined with restlessness and chronic sorrow to produce what became a suicidal anguish at least once during this period.

Romances Put Damper on Brilliant Career

Clarke's dalliance with Ross, which lasted at least until 1933, all but ended her work as a composer during the 1930s. Her more modern fans would later look back on her actions as evidence that, rather than fighting the cultural bias against creative women, she acquiesced and conformed to it. In some ways, she lived a stereotype—the empty, forlorn woman waiting endlessly for the unattainable man—and let her preoccupation with Ross ruin her career, rather than resisting and learning from the creative block she was experiencing.

However, Clarke continued to play the viola and established an all-woman piano quartet, the English Ensemble, in 1928 with friends Kathleen Long, May Mukle, and Marjorie Hayward. She played with the group until 1929. In the meantime, although she was not composing much music, Clarke toured extensively, performed with numerous ensembles, and broadcast performances over BBC radio. By now, she had become known as much for her stellar viola playing as for her compositions.

Despite the outbreak of World War II in 1939, when she was stranded in New York City as fighting raged in Europe, Clarke's musical output increased dramatically. In 1941, she composed some of her last pieces of music, including *Prelude, Allegro, and Pastorale* for clarinet and viola; *Passacaglia on an Old English Tune* for piano and viola; and *Combined Carols* for viola and piano.

Clarke took a job as a governess (nanny) for a family in Connecticut in 1942. Later that year, she was also the only female composer among 30 represented at the International Society of Contemporary Music's meeting in Berkeley, California. Her *Prelude, Allegro, and Pastorale* debuted at the meeting, to rave reviews. Around this time, Clarke met a pianist and renowned Julliard School teacher, James Friskin, who had been a student with her at the Royal College of Music. They fell in love and married in 1944, afterward moving to the cosmopolitan island of Manhattan in New York City.

Later Years Passed Happily

Many accounts state that Clarke and Friskin had a happy marriage, and that Clarke managed to reconcile herself with her creative demons through compromise. They toured the country playing together, with Clarke as the duo's concert violinist. She virtually abandoned all efforts to compose at this point, despite gentle encouragement from her husband. She would write only three more pieces of music during the last three decades of her life, including her last song, "God Made a Tree," in 1954. In total, she had written an estimated 12 choral works, 55 songs, and 25 pieces of chamber music.

Friskin died in 1967. In 1969, Clarke began writing an autobiography and titled it *I Had a Father, Too,* also known as, *The Mustard Spoon.* She completed the book in 1973, but it would never be published. In it, she described her traumatic childhood and the love of music that would stay with her throughout her life.

Such was Clarke's reticence on the subject of her former career that when friends held a 90th birthday party for her in 1976 on New York's classical music radio station WQXR, many of them were astounded to learn that she had been an accomplished and respected composer in her youth. In fact, it was only at that point that many of Clark's compositions, some 40 and 50 years old by then, were brought to light and published for the first time. As she explained in a 1976 newspaper interview, "I never was much good at blowing my own horn." The composer died in New York at age 93 on October 13, 1976.

Books

Commire, Anne, ed., *Women in World History,* The Gale Group, 2001.

Online

"Atonality," *Bartleby.com website,* http://www.bartleby.com (January 11, 2004).

Callus, Helen, "Clarke: Viola Sonata, Morpheus, etc.," *Findarticles.com website,* http://www.findarticles.com (January 10, 2004).

"Clarke, Rebecca," *U.S. Oxford University Press website,* http://www.us.oup.com (December 12, 2003).

"Rebecca Clarke," *Guild Music website,* http://www.guildmusic .com (December 21, 2003).

"Rebecca Clarke," *Wikipedia website,* http://en2.wikipedia.org (December 21, 2003).

"Rebecca Clarke (1886–1979)," *Royal Holloway University of London website,* http://www.sun.rhbnc.ac.uk (December 21,2003).

"Rebecca Thacher Clarke (1886–1979)," *The Gale Group Biography Resource Center website,* http://www.galenet.gale .com (January 10, 2004).

"Recent Events," *The Rebecca Clarke Society website,* http://www.rebeccaclarke.org (January 10, 2004).

"Timeline," *The Rebecca Clarke Society website,* http://www .rebeccaclarke.org (January 10, 2004). □

Clement XI

Regarded as a scholar as well as a patron of letters and science, Clement XI (1649–1721) served as pope of the Roman Catholic Church from 1700 to 1721. Initially reluctant to serve as pontiff, he is remembered for essentially destroying Christianity in China but also for establishing the feast of the Immaculate Conception of Mary as a major church holiday.

Noted Scholar

Pope Clement XI was born Giovanni Francesco Albani on July 22, 1649, in Urbino, a province in central Italy. In his book *The Oxford Dictionary of Popes*, author J.N.D. Kelly noted that the Albani family was of "aristocratic Umbrian stock." His grandfather had been a Roman senator, and his uncle served as a prefect (a high-ranking official) of the Vatican Library.

It was recognized early that young Giovanni was of exceptional intelligence. At the age of 11, he was sent to study at the Roman College where, Kelly noted, he "received a thorough classical education." By the age of 18, his writings received recognition for their scholarly merit, and he attracted the attention of Queen Christina of Sweden. At her personal invitation, he went to study at the Royal Accademia in Sweden. He studied theology and law and ultimately earned doctorates in both civil and canon (church) law.

Rose Through the Church Ranks

As Albani rose to the ranks of the prelates (high-ranking clergy), he was sent to govern in Rieti, Sabina, and then Orvieto. He was recalled to Rome and was named the Vicar of St. Peter's. Upon the death of Cardinal Slusio, Albani succeeded to the important position of Secretary of Papal Briefs, a position he held for thirteen years. On February 13, 1690, he was created a Cardinal-deacon, and ten years later, received the holy order of priesthood.

Elected Pope

After the death of Pope Innocent XII on September 27, 1700, the cardinals convened a conclave to elect the new pope. In the book *Saints & Sinners: A History of the Popes*, Eamon Duffy commented, "At every conclave, there was a strong party of *zelanti* who deplored all political interference. They were rarely able to secure their first choice for pope, but they were often decisive in preventing mere political appointments. Their interventions were admirable in principle, but not always happy in their outcome." The *zelanti* would be key players at this conclave.

The early 18th century was a critical time for Europe and the papacy. During the conclave, Charles II, the last of the Spanish Hapsburgs who was the ruler of Spain, had died childless. This left his realm vulnerable to attack by other countries. The will of Charles II named Philip of Anjou, grandson of King Louis XIV of France, as sole heir to the Spanish Empire.

Some royalty were against this plan of succession, as they believed they had a right to the Spanish empire, for themselves and their heirs. As retold on the *Catholic Encyclopedia* website, what many did not know was that Charles II had secretly met with Pope Innocent XII and three trusted cardinals about who should be his heir. These men aided Charles in deciding a plan of succession. Cardinal Albani had been one of those three cardinals. This decision would have ramifications for both the next pope and feuding European kingdoms over the next several years.

After deliberating and discussing for 46 days, the conclave of cardinals, led by the support of the *zelanti*, selected Cardinal Albani to be the next pope, even though some considered him too young to be pontiff. Kelly wrote, "Only 51, devout, austere, but lacking political flair, he [Albani] accepted with genuine reluctance after several days' anxious reflection, although his elevation was enthusiastically received even in Protestant countries." Duffy noted that the "pious and dedicated" Albani took the papal throne as Pope Clement XI in December of 1700.

A Man of Integrity

Clement was regarded as hard working and genuinely concerned for the poor. He was a patron of the arts and contributed generously to the Vatican Library. His reputation for integrity won him popularity even among Protestants, while Catholic reformers were concerned about this new pope's conservative policies.

As noted by the *Catholic Encyclopedia* website, some Catholic reformers believed that Clement's accession would be the end of papal nepotism. His predecessor had placed friends and relatives into high positions, and it was known that Clement had written a severe condemnation of that abuse. In fact, he appointed the most qualified person to various positions and titles and asked family members to keep their distance.

When it came to governing the church, Clement was a capable administrator. He provided for his subjects, bettered the condition of the prisons, and found food for the people when it was scarce. The *Catholic Encyclopedia* website stated that the dedicated Clement ate and slept very little. In addition, he went to confession and celebrated Mass every day.

However, Duffy noted, "A splendid administrator and a likeable man, he [Clement XI] turned out to lack judgment and plunged the papacy into conflict with Spain and with the church in France."

Trouble With the Spanish Throne

Immediately after becoming pope, Clement faced his first crisis, over the Spanish throne. Charles II had died during the conclave and had named Philip of Anjou his heir. Both Austrian King Leopold and Archduke Charles of Spain protested this plan of succession. In his book, Kelly reflected, "the War of the Spanish Succession (1701–1714), which filled much of his [Clement's] reign, soon exposed his and the papacy's ineffectiveness"

Although Clement sympathized with Philip, he tried to remain neutral. However, that changed when, as Kelly noted, "In January 1709, when the troops of Leopold's successor Joseph I had invaded the papal states, conquered Naples, and threatened Rome." Kelly continued, "Clement had to accept the new emperor's harsh terms, which included his abandonment of Philip V and recognition of Archduke Charles as the Spanish king."

As noted on the *Catholic Encyclopedia* website, "though the Bourbon monarchs had done nothing to aid the pope in his unequal struggle, both Louis and Philip became very indignant and retaliated by every means in their power." In 1713, as the key points for the Peace of Utrecht were negotiated, the rights of the pope and the Catholic Church were disregarded.

Even though the dispute over the Spanish throne was now over, Clement's troubles were not. As recounted on the *Catholic Encyclopedia* website, the new king re-established "the so-called *Monarchia Sicula,* an ancient but much-disputed and abused privilege of pontifical origin which practically excluded the pope from any authority over the church in Sicily." Clement responded with an interdict (a decree that prohibits something). In turn, the new Spanish king banished all the clergy, approximately 3,000 in number, who remained loyal to the pope. The pope was forced to find a means to give them food, water, and shelter. The

interdict was lifted in 1718, but the tactic of *Monarchia Sicula,* would continue over the years.

While all the fighting between the kingdoms and the pope were going on, the Turks decided to take advantage of the situation and invaded Europe by land and sea. The threat of the Turks was over quickly, but damage had been done. As Duffy noted, "Clement XI was the last Pope before the French Revolution to play a major role in European politics as a prince in his own right, and that role was an unqualified calamity for the papacy."

Missionary Work and Church Policy

Many agree that Clement's efforts to keep peace and sustain the rights of the Church among the powers of Europe were not successful. However, many concur that he had more prosperous results with his missionary endeavors. Author Kelly wrote, "Clement was keenly interested in missionary work, and not only founded missionary colleges but promoted missions overseas, notably in India, the Philippines, and China."

However, one decision Clement made regarding missionary work had far-reaching ramifications. Duffy commented, "His decision to outlaw the so-called Chinese Rites, by which Chinese missionaries had accommodated Christian practice to Chinese culture, effectively destroyed Christianity in China." This decree led to hostilities between the Church and the Chinese people, and resulted in the closure of many Catholic missions. This policy remained in effect for over 200 years, before it was retracted by Pope Pius XII in 1939.

The "Jansenism" Debate

A major religious challenge that Clement and many of his predecessors had faced was "Jansenism." Named for its founder, the Dutch theologian Cornelius Jansen (1585–1638), Jansenism was a reform movement among Roman Catholics that thrived during the sixteenth and seventeenth centuries.

Jansenism had many traits in common with Calvinism. Among the principle beliefs were predestination, loss of free will, and the inability to resist God's grace. Duffy added that it also rejected Protestantism and also "took a gloomy view of the average man or woman's chances of salvation."

Kelly reflected, "Clement played a decisive role, largely at the instigation of Louis XIV of France in the repression of Jansenism." In a papal bull (an official document or decree, usually issued by the pope) entitled *Vineam Domini,* written in 1705, Clement rejected the Jansenist views that deny the existence of human free will.

In his book, Duffy wrote, "The Jansenist quarrel came to a disastrous climax in 1713, when Clement XI issued the bull *Unigenitus,* condemning 101 propositions taken from the best-selling devotional treatise by the Jansenist Pasquier Quesnel, *Moral Reflections of the Gospels.* In addition, Clement took the extreme step of excommunicating (barring someone from participating in the Catholic Church) many Jansenist leaders in 1718.

The Legacy

Pope Clement XI died on March 19, 1721, and was succeeded by Pope Innocent XIII. Many of his official papers, letters, and homilies were later collected and published by his nephew, Cardinal Albani. Like many of his papal predecessors, Clement, considered a man with good intentions, is remembered for both positive and negative decisions and policies made during his reign as pontiff.

Books

Duffy, Eamon, *Saints and Sinners-A History of the Popes,* Yale University Press in association with S4C, 1997.

Kelly, J.N.D., *The Oxford Dictionary of Popes,* Oxford University Press, 1991.

Online

"Catholic Encyclopedia: Pope Clement XI," *New Advent* website, http://newadvent.org/cathen/04029a.htm (November 15, 2003).

"Clement XI," *The Gale Group Biography Resource Center website,* http://galenet.galegroup.com (November 15, 2003).

"Patron Saints Index: Pope Clement XI," *Catholic Community Forum* website, http://www.catholic-forum.com (November 15, 2003).

"Pope Clement XI (Giovanni Francesco Albani)," *Catholic Hierarchy* website, http://www.catholic-hierarchy.org (November 15, 2003).

"Pope Clement XI—Wikipedia," *From Wikipedia, the free encyclopedia* website, http://en.wikipedia.org/wiki/Pope_Clement XI (November 15, 2003). □

John Warcup Cornforth

Australian John Warcup Cornforth (born 1917) received a portion of the 1975 Nobel Prize for Chemistry for his research on the stereochemistry of enzyme-catalyzed reactions. Stereochemistry deals with the architecture (shapes) of molecules and the way their three-dimensional structure affects chemical properties.

Scientist's Early Life

The second of four children, John Warcup Cornforth was born in Sydney, Australia, on September 7, 1917. His father, J. W. Cornforth, was an Oxford University graduate, and his mother, Hilda Eipper Cornforth, came from a German family who had immigrated to Australia in the mid-1800s.

Cornforth, who began practicing chemistry in his teens at an improvised home laboratory, spent part of his childhood in Sydney and part in Armidale, New South Wales. He was diagnosed with otosclerosis when he was almost 12, having suffered from increasing hearing loss since age 10. However, he was able to attend regular classes at the Sydney Boys' High School, where he did well. By the time Cornforth entered Sydney University at age 16, he was completely deaf.

Cornforth was unable to hear any of his college lectures but demonstrated to his professors a marked talent for laboratory work in organic chemistry. By dint of this hands-on lab work and close attention to his college textbooks, he completed his undergraduate work at Sydney University in 1937 with first-class honors and a university medal. Cornforth spent a year doing post-graduate research, received a master's degree in 1938, and then in 1939 won one of two annual scholarships to study chemistry with 1947 Nobel Prize winner Robert Robinson at England's Oxford University. The other scholarship winner was fellow organic chemist Rita Harradence, whom he would marry in 1941—the same year they received their doctorates from Oxford.

Began Professional Life as Chemist with Wife

During World War II, the new couple worked with Robinson at Oxford to determine the central molecule of the life-saving antibiotic penicillin. (Although Cornforth would like to have returned to his native Australia to do research, the country at that time did not offer any work to chemists unable to lecture.) The Cornforths also began investigating the problem of chemical synthesis in steroids (compounds that are integral to plants' and animals' cellular structures). Rita, equally brilliant in organic chemistry, helped her husband communicate with others and collaborated closely with him at all times, since Cornforth depended completely on lip-reading and written communication by 1945.

While continuing his work with Robinson, Cornforth began working in 1946 for the National Institute of Medical Research (NIMR) at Hampstead and then at its Mill Hill Research Laboratories in London. During this period, he developed his technique for studying the stereochemical processes of enzymes, whereby he was able to show the pathways of biochemical processes. (The study of stereochemistry is considered vital to understanding the organic world at its most basic biochemical level. It has been called a "point of view" in chemistry, which shows how things fit together at the molecular level and how they affect taste and smell.)

Studied Origins of Cholesterol and Other Steroids

In 1949, Cornforth helped Robinson write *The Chemistry of Penicillin,* which detailed the huge international effort that went into the important wartime project. Cornforth and his NIMR team, simultaneously with chemist Robert Wood, succeeded in their goal of completing the first total synthesis of the cholesterol molecule in 1951. At the NIMR, Cornforth also began what would become a 20-year collaboration with George Popják, who was also interested in the cholesterol molecule. Cornforth wanted to find out how cells actually synthesized cholesterol, so he used labeled isotopes of hydrogen to trace the chemical steps of the process from its originals in acetic acid. (It was for this ingenious technique that he won a portion of the 1975 Nobel Prize.) Historical records show that Rita actually carried out many of the experiments during this project.

Meanwhile, Cornforth continued his work on the synthesis and description of the structure of many natural products, including plant hormones and olefins, synthetic substances used in textiles. He completed the biosynthesis of many other steroids and was able to trace more than a dozen stereochemical steps in the biosynthesis of squalene, a precursor of cholesterol that is widely distributed in nature. Cornforth published his findings in the *Journal of the Chemical Society* in 1959.

In 1962, Cornforth and Popják left the NIMR together and became joint directors of the Milstead Laboratory of Chemical Enzymology of Shell Research Limited at Sittingbourne in Kent. The first project they worked on was an effort to understand the stereochemistry of enzymatic reactions by using isotopic substitution to artificially introduce asymmetry. In 1967 Cornforth had also begun collaborating on the asymmetrical methyl group with Hermann Eggerer. Popják left Milstead in 1968 for new work in California, leaving Cornforth as the sole director at Milstead. Later that year, Cornforth published the results of his latest study in the *Journal of the American Chemical Society.*

Despite his heavy research schedule, Cornforth agreed in 1965 to take on the added responsibility of a post as associate professor in molecular sciences at the University of Warwick in Coventry, England. He remained in that post until 1971, when he accepted a similar position at the University of Sussex in Brighton, England. During his stints

as professor at the schools, the scientist discovered a love of teaching the subject about which he was so passionate. In fact, he decided in 1975 to teach at the University of Sussex full-time as a Royal Society Research Professor, leaving Milstead at age 58. Also that year, he shared the Nobel Prize for Chemistry with Swiss chemist Vladimir Prelog.

By this time, Cornforth had received numerous awards for his contributions to chemistry, including the Corday-Morgan Medal of the Chemical Society of London (1953); the Biochemical Society's CIBA Medal (1965); the Davy Medal of the Royal Society (1968); the Guenther Award of the American Chemical Society (1969); the Royal Society Award in 1976; and a knighthood in 1977. In his acceptance speech for the Australian of the Year award in 1975, Cornfield addressed the issue of science as a business, saying scientists must require of themselves "not to believe, but to test, check and balance all theories, including their own."

Cornforth taught regular classes at the University of Sussex until 1982, when he was granted emeritus status. He also won the prestigious Royal Society's Copley Medal in 1982. Cornforth remained at Sussex following his emeritus status, and despite his intimidating resume is affectionately known as "Kappa" Cornforth. He is an active researcher at the university labs. In 2000, an interview with Cornforth appeared in a 2000 book by Istvan Hargittai titled *Candid Science: Conversations with Famous Chemists.* Cornforth and his wife lent their name to a new foundation at the University of Sydney in 2002: the Cornforth Foundation will support teaching in the field of organic chemistry. The scientist and his wife spend part of their time in Saxon Down, Cuilfail, Lewes, in England. He holds memberships in many scientific academies in Australia, the United States, the Netherlands, Germany, and England.

Cornforth, whose colleagues have described him as having a warm and outgoing personality, excels in numerous leisure activities, notably chess, which he reportedly plays in a manner comparable to his approach to stereochemistry. He has also become somewhat more political in his later years and occasionally speaks out on environmental and societal issues, using his status as a Nobel Prize winner to add weight to his statements. In 2003, Cornforth and many other Nobel Prize winners signed a widely publicized petition affirming the truth of global warming and demanding action to remedy its effects—especially on the "poor and disenfranchised, [who]. . .live a marginal existence in equatorial climates. Global warming, not of their making but originating with the wealthy few, will affect their fragile ecologies most." In signing the missive, Cornforth expressed his belief that, ". . .we must persist in the quest for united action to counter both global warming and a weaponized world. These twin goals will constitute vital components of stability as we move toward the wider degree of social justice that alone gives hope of peace." Cornforth also plays tennis well and still enjoys gardening. He and his wife have three children: a son, John, and two daughters, Brenda and Philippa, as well as several grandchildren.

Books

American Men and Women of Science, The Gale Group, 2003.
Biographical Encyclopedia of Scientists, Institute of Physics Publishing, 1994.

Online

"Cornforth, John Warcup" University of Melbourne Bright SPARCS website, http://www.asap.unimelb.edu.au (December 21, 2003).
"Cornforth, Sir John," Britannica Online website, http://www.britannica.com (December 21, 2003).
"Face2Face with John Cornforth," Vega Science Trust website, http://www.vega.org.uk (December 21, 2003).
"John Cornforth—Autobiography," Nobel e-Museum website, http://www.nobel.se (December 21, 2003).
"John Cornforth," The Gale Group Biography Resource Center website, http://galenet.galegroup.com (January 8, 2004).
"Sir John Cornforth," Australian of the Year website, http://www.australianoftheyear.com (January 8, 2004).
"Sir John Cornforth: Emeritus Professor," University of Sussex website, http://www.sussex.ac.uk/chemistry (December 21, 2003).
"Social Justice Alone Gives Hope of Peace," Wordless.com website, http://www.wordless.com (January 9, 2004). □

Howard Cosell

Despite obvious drawbacks—a nasal Brooklyn accent, an obvious toupé, and a propensity for prolix pronouncements—American sportscaster Howard Cosell (1920–1995) changed the face—and voice— of sports broadcasting forever, replacing bland, sycophantic, sanitized commentary with hard-nosed observations and often-unpopular stands on principle. "History will reflect that Howard Cosell was easily the dominant sportscaster of all time," wrote colleague Al Michaels in the foreword to Cosell's book What's Wrong with Sports, "and certainly the most famous." Cosell was "a broadcasting pioneer who changed the way people listen to and watch sports," recalled ABC radio sports director Shelby Whitfield in People magazine. In his book I Never Played the Game, Cosell summed himself up in his typically self-aggrandizing style: "I'm one helluva communicator."

Born Howard William Cohen on March 25, 1920, in Winston-Salem, North Carolina, Cosell was the son of Isidore and Nellie Cohen. "For the record," Cosell noted in Cosell, "Cosell—once spelled with a K—is the family name. . . . As a Polish refugee, my grandfather had been unable to make his name clear to a harried immigration inspector. The official simply compromised on Cohen and waved him through."

Isidore Cohen, an accountant for a clothing company, moved his family to Brooklyn shortly before Howard turned three. He aspired to a middle-class existence, but, like millions of others, struggled—often unsuccessfully—to provide for his family when the Depression hit and jobs dried up. "I remember the electricity being turned off in our house for nonpayment of rent and my dad fighting with the janitor to try and get it turned back on," Cosell recalled. Always on the ragged outer edges of prosperity, Cohen wanted the security of a profession for his son.

Entered Law Profession to Honor Family Request

Howard's intelligence was apparent early on, his mother claiming that he started talking at age nine months. An excellent student, he attended Brooklyn public schools, including P.S. 9 and Alexander Hamilton High School, where he wrote a sports column for the school newspaper called "Speaking of Sports"—he later gave the same title to his radio program. He went on to New York University, where he earned a degree in English literature and a membership in Phi Beta Kappa. Bowing to his parents wishes, he then earned a law degree at the same university, editing NYU's law review and passing the bar exam at age twenty-one. "I'd never really wanted to become a lawyer," he told Playboy interviewer Lawrence Linderman. "I guess the only reason I went through with it was because my father worked so hard to have a son who'd be a professional."

Before he could settle into a practice, however, World War II intervened and Cosell enlisted in the U.S. Army. Following a pattern he would often repeat, he began as a private and left four and a half years later as a major. After his discharge, Cosell tried to forgo the legal future his parents had ordained for him by auditioning as a radio announcer at WOR. The station flatly rejected him, saying his nasal Brooklyn-inflected voice made him completely unsuitable for radio.

Cosell returned to the law in 1946, opening an office in Manhattan. His practice included many sports and entertainment figures, among them Willie Mays, and it came about that he was asked to oversee the incorporation of Little League Baseball in New York. This brought Cosell to the attention of ABC Radio, which asked him to host a fifteen-minute Saturday-morning show in which Little Leaguers interviewed sports pros. Cosell took the ball and ran with it, getting far more than the network had expected—in one episode New York Yankee baseball player Hank Bauer aired his beefs with team manager Casey Stengel. Nearly 20 years later Cosell was still chuckling about it, telling Linderman: "We made news with that show!"

ABC then signed Cosell to do ten five-minute weekend sports broadcasts, paying him the below-scale sum of $250 a week for the privilege. Lugging a 30-pound tape recorder on his back, Cosell took every interview he could get. As he recalled in Cosell, "There was nothing being done in depth, a total absence of commentary and little in the way of actuality." He wanted to change the status quo: "I was infected with my desire, my resolve, to make it in broadcasting. I knew exactly what I wanted to do, and how." Determined to succeed, Cosell quit his $30,000-a-year law practice.

Out on a Limb for Broadcast Excellence

In 1961 Cosell began his daily *Speaking of Sports* broadcasts for ABC News, a radio staple that ran until 1992. Each show began with Cosell's familiar staccato delivery, which Dave Kindred of the *Sporting News* described as "to voices what the Grand Canyon is to ditches. . . . 'HELLO AGAIN, EVERYBODY, THIS IS HOWARD COSELL SPEAKING OF SPORTS.'" Cosell's penchant for polysyllabism prompted Kindred to quote sportswriter Jim Murray, who said Cosell "has the vocabulary of an Oxford don and the delivery of a Dead End kid." Cosell always closed with another of his famous tag lines: "This is Howard Cosell telling it like it is."

Cosell was determined to get into television as well as radio. His less-than-glamorous looks and grating voice, however, made ABC executives equally determined to keep him off the air. Undeterred, he formed a production company and filmed a well-received documentary titled *Babe Ruth: A Look behind the Legend.* His followup effort was *Run to Daylight,* a look at Vince Lombardi and the Green Bay Packers that Linderman called "still the most highly acclaimed TV sports documentary ever made." Unable to ignore Cosell's talent, ABC began to include him on their popular *Wide World of Sports* broadcasts.

In 1962 Cosell met the great boxer Muhammad Ali, then known as Cassius Clay, and began to cover Ali's fights. Thus began a series of interviews and dialogs that brought both fighter and sportscaster into the national limelight for the first time. Dick Heller noted in the *Washington Times* that Cosell "discovered Muhammad Ali and vice versa—a marriage surely made in athletic heaven." The two developed an enduring friendship, despite the mock arguments that permeated their on-air banter. Their relationship was firmly cemented when Cosell openly supported Ali's name change and entry into the Nation of Islam. Cosell was "angry and finally furious" at those who opposed Ali's decision: "they wanted . . . another Joe Louis," he wrote in *Cosell.* "A white man's black man. . . . Didn't these idiots realize that Cassius Clay was the name of a slave owner? . . . Had I been black and my name Cassius Clay, I damned well would have changed it!"

Cosell also voiced his disapproval in 1967 when Ali was stripped of his title and convicted of evading the draft after declaring himself a conscientious objector to the Vietnam War. (Ali's conviction was later overturned on procedural grounds by the U.S. Supreme Court.) As Tom Callahan noted in *Time* magazine, "Cosell knew that Muslim Ali stood on firm legal ground in conscientiously objecting to the draft. But he also felt Ali was right." Cosell was equally vociferous in his support for John Carlos and Tommie Smith when they silently supported the Black Power movement with upraised fists on the medals dais at the 1968 Mexico City Olympics.

Joined *Monday Night Football* Lineup

Monday Night Football was the brainchild of National Football League commissioner Pete Rozelle and Roone Arledge, Cosell's mentor at ABC. Its debut, on September 21, 1970, featured veteran commentator Keith Jackson, former Dallas Cowboy "Dandy" Don Meredith, and Cosell. Unfortunately, Cosell's open support for Ali unleashed a firestorm of criticism directed at both ABC and Cosell himself. Others were skeptical that anyone who had never played the game could cover it adequately. And there were plenty who raged at his trademark delivery—"the tone of someone describing battles in World War II," claimed Ralph Novak in *People*—and his pompous verbosity and biting commentary.

Stung but undaunted, Cosell continued to persevere, and by the time *Monday Night Football* covered the Packers at San Diego, Cosell's popularity began to rebound. His knowledge of the Packers, accumulated during the Lombardi documentary, was impressive, and viewers voted with their television sets: the program began to earn sky-high ratings, much of it due to Cosell. As Cosell quoted the *Encyclopedia Britannica* 1973 yearbook in his book *Cosell:* "sportscaster Howard Cosell made pro football addicts of more than 25 million viewers on Monday nights"—despite having "a voice that had all the resonance of a clogged Dristan bottle."

During the 1970s Cosell became a national icon, one survey showing that 96 percent of those questioned recognized his name. Some people loved him, others just loved to hate him. A *TV Guide* poll of viewers in 1978 named him both the most- *and* least-liked sportscaster on the air. His trademark style was instantly recognizable and often parodied. He played himself in numerous film and television appearances, including a role in Woody Allen's 1971 film *Bananas* and a turn as host on *Saturday Night Live.*

Cosell's hard-edged criticism of certain athletes was well known, but his views on the corporate organizations running professional sports were equally harsh. In *I Never Played the Game* he accuses baseball's "carpetbagging owners" of taking established teams like the Dodgers and Braves to new cities and lashes out at the sport's iron grip on its players. Cosell also publically applauded Curt Flood's attempt to strike down baseball's reserve clause as a violation of antitrust laws and even testified before Congress in favor of free agency. (The reserve clause was effectively abolished in 1975.) Despite these stands against team owners, so powerful was Cosell's draw that ABC assigned him to *Monday Night Baseball* as a sportscaster.

Sports Arena Reflected Increased Social, Political Conflicts

Sports and history had a gruesome collision in the summer of 1972 when Palestinian terrorists hijacked the Munich Olympics and murdered eleven Israeli athletes. The tragedy had a searing impact on Cosell. As he recalled in *Cosell,* it was "the most trying and dramatic . . . [time] of my life. . . . I had never felt so intensely Jewish." Although his grandfather had been a rabbi, the family was not religious; Cosell had not even been bar mitzvahed. The Munich massacre, however, led him to a deeper recognition and appreciation of his Jewish heritage, one outgrowth of which was the Cosell Center for Physical Education at the Hebrew University of Jerusalem.

In September 1983 Cosell started another firestorm after innocently commenting on a play by Redskins wide receiver Alvin Garrett. As he recalled in *I Never Played the Game,* he remarked, "That little monkey gets loose, doesn't he?" after a particularly good run by Garrett, who is black. Despite Cosell's sterling record on racial and civil-rights issues, and his insistence that the remark was not only laudatory but one he used affectionately with his own grandchildren, many were quick to denounce him. Cosell refused to apologize and defended himself against the charge of racism. Despite support from celebrities like Bill Cosby and Willie Mays, furor continued to rage around him. The incident eventually faded, but Cosell was disgusted. He left *Monday Night Football* two months later, at the end of the season. Nor was he surprised when the show's ratings fell during the 1984 season: "Without me," he claimed in *I Never Played the Game,* "the nature of the telecasts was entirely altered. I had commanded attention. I had a palpable impact on the show, giving it a sense of moment. . . . If that sounds like ego, what can I say? I'm telling it like it is."

A year earlier Cosell had turned his back on professional boxing as well. "For almost a quarter of a century, I was ABC's boxing specialist," Cosell explained, going on to add that: "Boxing gave me my first glimpse of media stardom, and I'd be less than honest if I didn't admit that I was gripped by a spellbinding attraction to the sport." He had known for years that "corruption was all around" boxing and its promoters, and he had tried hard to "expose the dirty underbelly of the sport." The Holmes-Cobb fight on November 26, 1982—a lopsided match-up designed to ensure a Holmes victory—was Cosell's breaking point. The fight, he wrote, was "an unholy mess" and "a bloodbath." Holmes landed twenty-six unanswered blows and inflicted merciless punishment on Cobb, yet the fight was not stopped. Cosell declared then and there that he would never cover another professional boxing match.

During his long career, Cosell wrote four books: *Cosell,* 1973; *Like It Is,* 1974; *I Never Played the Game,* 1985; and *What's Wrong with Sports,* 1991. Like his sports broadcasts, each is filled with unvarnished appraisals of players, teams, and other broadcasters. His third book, in particular, written after he left ABC, contains harsh, even savage, assessments of colleagues such as Roone Arledge, his mentor at ABC, and *Monday Night Football* alums Frank Gifford and Don Meredith. Ralph Novak, in a review of the book for *People,* called *I Never Played the Game* "full of paranoia, condescension and hypocrisy."

When Cosell's beloved wife Emmy died in 1990 after 46 years of marriage, much of the fire seemed to go out of him. He had a cancerous tumor removed from his chest the following year but continued to do his daily radio broadcasts until 1992. Inducted into the American Sportscasters Hall of Fame in 1993, Cosell died of a heart embolism on April 23, 1995, at New York University's Hospital for Joint Diseases in New York City; he was awarded a posthumous Emmy for lifetime achievement the following year.

So powerful was Cosell's legend, however, that the media would not let him go. In 1999 HBO broadcast the cable television documentary *Howard Cosell: Telling It like It Is,* borrowing Cosell's ubiquitous tag line for its title. TNT aired the movie *Monday Night Mayhem* in 2002, with John Turturro portraying Cosell. Edward Achorn, writing in the *Providence Journal,* noted that the film "treats Cosell almost reverently, depicting him, for all his many quirks and faults, as a loyal and loving husband and family man, a quietly generous fellow, a crusader against racial prejudice, a dazzlingly talented professional who happened to be tormented by his insecurities. How many of today's glib sportscasters will stir this kind of attention 20 years from now? It's not going out on a limb to venture the answer: none."

Books

Cosell, Howard, and Mickey Herskowitz, *Cosell,* Playboy Press, 1973.

Cosell, Howard, and Peter Bonventre, *I Never Played the Game,* G. K. Hall, 1986.

Cosell, Howard, and Shelby Whitfield, *What's Wrong with Sports,* Simon & Schuster, 1991.

Periodicals

People, December 9, 1985; May 8, 1995.

Playboy, May 1972.

Providence Journal (Providence, RI), January 15, 2002.

Sporting News, March 27, 1995.

Time, January 6, 1986.
Washington Times, October 31, 1999.

Online

"Put Howard Cosell in the Hall of Fame," *Seconds Out,* http://www.secondsout.com/usa/column_47595.asp (January 9, 2004). ☐

James Watson Cronin

American astrophysicist James Watson Cronin (born 1931) is a pioneer in ultrahigh-energy gamma ray astronomy as well as a professor emeritus at the University of Chicago. Cronin won the 1980 Nobel Prize with colleague Val Logsdon Fitch for their discovery of violations of fundamental symmetry principles in the decay of neutral K-mesons. Through their work, Cronin and Fitch proved that the reactions of subatomic particles are not indifferent to time. In addition to his research in the physical sciences, Cronin taught for many years at the University of Chicago.

Born into World of Academia

Cronin was born on September 29, 1931, in Chicago, Illinois. His father, James Farley Cronin, was a graduate student in classical languages at the University of Chicago, and his mother, the former Dorothy Watson, attended Northwestern University. After receiving his degree, the senior Cronin moved his family briefly to Alabama to take a teaching job but soon settled in Dallas, Texas, to teach Greek and Latin at Southern Methodist University.

As a child Cronin attended local public elementary and high schools in the Highland Park system near Dallas and recalled that his natural interest in science was guided to physics by an outstanding high school teacher. He enrolled as a physics major at Southern Methodist University in 1947, receiving his bachelor's degree in science in 1951. However, it was not until he began graduate studies at the University of Chicago in September 1951 that what Cronin considered his "real education" began. His professors were among the most stellar in the field of physics and included Enrico Fermi, Murray Gell-Mann, Edward Teller, and Maria Mayer.

Cronin earned a master's degree in 1953, writing his thesis on experimental nuclear physics under the guidance of Samuel K. Allison. Meanwhile, a class he was taking from Gell-Mann, who was even then developing his theory of Strangeness, proved crucial in Cronin's eventual decision to study in the new field of particle physics. Also in 1953, the young scientist met Annette Martin. The couple had a whirlwind romance and were married less than a year later. The scientist later credited his wife with providing an oasis of calm and encouragement during the chaos of difficult experiments and looming deadlines.

Began Career as Physicist

The completion of Cronin's doctoral studies led to his receiving a Ph.D. from the University of Chicago in 1955. He immediately accepted a job as a research physicist at the Brookhaven National Laboratory on Long Island, New York. His work at Brookhaven made use of one of the world's most powerful particle accelerators, the three-billion-electron-volt (GeV) Cosmotron. Cronin later recalled these days as some of the most exciting of his long career. His work was not performed without difficulty, however. In early 1958 the Cosmotron had to be shut down after a catastrophic magnet failure rendered it useless. Disappointed and frustrated, the team moved their experiment to the University of California at Berkeley, which owned the Bevatron particle accelerator. Meanwhile, one of Cronin's colleagues at Brookhaven, Val Fitch, had invited him to join him in a teaching position at elite Princeton University in New Jersey. Cronin accepted and was appointed assistant professor of physics at Princeton in the fall of 1958.

At Princeton, Cronin was delighted to find an enthusiastic sponsor for his esoteric atomic research, which, prior to his teaming with Fitch, initially focused on hyperon decays. Laboratory Director George Reynolds assented to Cronin's request to work independently, and over the next decade he strongly supported the physicist's work. During this time, Cronin quickly became involved in the research that would win him and Fitch the Nobel Prize. The roots of that research can be found in a classic experiment suggested in 1956 by physicists Tsung-Dao Lee and Chen Ning Yang on the conservation of parity during certain nuclear reactions. One of the most fundamental laws adhered to by physicists of the mid-20th century was the principle of conservation. Students of high-school physics are familiar with laws dealing with the conservation of mass, energy, charge, momentum, and other qualities. Such laws state that there is a symmetry between the amount of each property prior to and following any change within in a closed system. In 1956 Lee and Yang found reason to believe that a property known as parity (P)—a kind of "left-handedness" versus "right-handedness"—is not conserved in certain types of nuclear changes. Reactions might be possible, they theorized, in which an excess of left-handed or right-handed particles might be observed. Shortly after this theory was announced, another researcher, Chien-Shiung Wu, found the precise violation of parity which had been anticipated by Lee and Yang.

This revolutionary discovery raised a number of new issues for theoretical physicists. Was it possible that other types of symmetry could also be violated? Were there ways of "explaining away" the failure of parity symmetry in the Shiung experiment? Lee and Yang themselves suggested one such system. Perhaps it is possible, they said, that the combination of parity and another property, charge conjugation (C), is conserved even if each alone is not. (The term "charge conjugation" refers to the balance between positively and negatively charged particles in a reaction.) Specifically, the combination CP might remain symmetrical, Lee and Yang said, even if neither C nor P did in a particular reaction.

In June and July 1963, Cronin and Fitch began a series of experiments that soon provided supporting evidence for the concept of CP violation. The original purpose of these experiments was somewhat more modest, however—namely, to investigate the behavior of elementary particles known as neutral K-mesons. The investigators wanted to know more about the process by which a beam of neutral K-mesons could be separated into two parts, one consisting of short-lived neutral K-mesons that decay into two pi-mesons and another consisting of long-lived neutral K-mesons that decay into three pi-mesons.

Hard Work Aided by Luck

The kind of experiments conducted by Cronin and Fitch in 1964 would, given the advanced technology available in later decades, be able to be analyzed at lightning speed by computers. At the time, however, the process was much more laborious and involved the careful, frame-by-frame study of dozens of rolls of film taken in spark chambers which Cronin had helped to develop. Only six months after the process had begun and the primary focus of the research on neutral K-meson decay had been completed did Cronin and Fitch suddenly realize that they also had evidence for violation of CP conservation. Ultimately, they found 45 examples of CP violation in more than 23,000 of the frames studied. Yet to make absolutely certain of their

astounding assertion, Cronin and Fitch spent another six months looking for alternative explanations of their findings. Discovering none, they announced their results in *Physical Review Letters* on July 27, 1964. For their work, Cronin and Fitch each received half of the 1980 Nobel Prize for Physics.

Elated and exhausted, Cronin and his wife left for a year and traveled to France, during which time the physicist worked at the Center for Nuclear Studies in Saclay. He learned French and enjoyed soaking up the culture of another country. Cronin later remarked that giving a lecture on physics at the College de France was one of the "great joys" of his life.

Began Teaching but Continued Experiments

Cronin returned to the United States and Princeton University in 1965, having been promoted to associate professor in 1962 and full professor by 1964. With a fresh batch of graduate students, he began a series of experiments to investigate the neutral CP-violating modes of neutral K-meson particles. He and his team worked on these experiments until 1971, when Cronin left Princeton to accept an appointment as professor of physics at his alma mater, the University of Chicago. His decision was reportedly at least partly based on his eagerness to be near the new Fermilab 400 GeV particle accelerator, located just outside Chicago.

Once he had settled in at the university, Cronin assembled a new team of talented associates to help him carry out experiments on the production of direct leptons and particles at high transverse momentum. Far from writing off CP violation as a fait accompli, he investigated with greater accuracy some of the neutral K-meson's CP-violating parameters. Outside the laboratory Cronin was a popular and effective teacher, believing strongly that his highest purpose as a professor was to develop within his students "a sense of the value of exploring nature experimentally," as he told Paula Huff on the *University of Utah College of Science Web site.*

In 1997 Cronin began dividing his time between the University of Chicago and a new position as physics professor at the University of Utah. He is a professor emeritus in the University of Chicago's departments of physics and astronomy/astrophysics and holds parallel posts at the Enrico Fermi Institute in Chicago.

Made High-Energy Cosmic Rays Focus of Work

Cronin and University of Leeds Professor Alan Watson also headed the international Auger Project to study the nature and origin of rare but extremely powerful high-energy cosmic rays that periodically bombard Earth with the force of a fast-ball pitch. To do so, the scientists used a new form of astronomy based on particle physics. Argentina's Pierre Auger Observatory, which contains a giant detector array, was established in October 2003, and an area near the University of Utah was chosen as the site for a similar facility. Cronin, who became spokesperson emeritus for the

Utah project in 2002, works on its behalf, declaring simply, "I want to find out the answer to cosmic rays." He published an article on the topic, "Cosmic Rays: The Most Energetic Particles in the Universe," in a 1999 issue of *Review of Modern Physics.*

In addition to his Nobel prize, Cronin has been awarded the 1968 Research Corporation Award, the 1975 John Price Wetherill Medal of the Franklin Institute, and the 1977 Ernest O. Lawrence Award. He and his wife have a son, David, and two daughters, Emily and Cathryn.

Books

American Men and Women of Science, Gale Group, 2003.
Biographical Encyclopedia of Scientists, Institute of Physics Publishing, 1994.

Online

Huff, Paula, "Cosmic Rays Keep Cronin Happy," *University of Utah College of Science Web site,* http://www.science.utah .edu/ (December 21, 2003).
"James Cronin—Autobiography," *Nobel e-Museum,* http://www .nobel.se/ (December 21, 2003).
"James W. Cronin," *University of Chicago Experimental Astrophysics Department Web site,* http://physics.uchicago .edu/ (December 21, 2003). □

Celia Cruz

Cuban-born singing star Celia Cruz (1925–2003) has been hailed as the queen of salsa, the queen of rumba, the queen of Latin music, and an inadvertent symbol of the Cuban American community's exile spirit. Cruz, who fled the Caribbean island nation in 1960, became a world-famous singer with an energetic, flamboyant stage presence that brought audiences to their feet. "Cruz is undisputedly the best-known and most influential female figure in the history of Afro-Cuban music," declared *Billboard*'s Leila Cobo.

Sang Lullabies

Though sometimes evasive about her age, it is believed that Cruz was born on October 21, 1925, in Havana, Cuba. Cruz grew up in the Santo Suárez area of Havana in a household headed by her father, a railroad stoker. The family was of Afro-Cuban heritage, descendants of the Africans who were forcibly brought to the island nation to work in its vast sugar fields in centuries past, and eventually grew to include 14 children, some of them Cruz's cousins. As the second eldest child, she would often have to put the younger ones to bed and would sing them to sleep. The adults in the household, hearing her voice, began to gather outside the door to listen themselves.

In her teens, Cruz entered and won first prize in a radio contest, "La hora del té," by singing a tango song. She began entering other amateur contests, and though her mother was encouraging, her father strongly disapproved of her ambitions to become a singer in Cuba's strong salsa scene. This musical style merged elements from traditional Spanish music with the African rhythms that came from the island's former slave population and exemplified national character traits of both exuberance and a penchant for romantic melancholy. Cruz's father hoped instead that she would become a teacher, and so to placate him Cruz entered the local teachers' college for a time, but quit when her singing career began to take off in earnest. From 1947 to 1950 she studied music theory, voice, and piano at the National Conservatory of Music in Havana, but even a teacher there suggested that she pursue stardom full-time.

Fled Castro Regime

Cruz's break came when La Sonora Matancera, a popular Cuban band, hired her as their lead vocalist in 1950. She had a tough time at first, for female singers were a relative rarity in Cuban music—the stage was considered an unseemly place for a woman—and she replaced a singer with a popular following. Irate fans even wrote to the radio station that broadcast La Sonora Matancera performances, but as Cruz told Cobo in *Billboard,* she was unfazed. "I could care less. This was my job—the job of my dreams and the job that fed me." Even an American record company executive that signed the band was uneasy with the proposition of a rumba track with a female singer, so the band's leader, Rogelio Martínez, promised to pay Cruz out of his own pocket for the session if the record failed to catch on, but the song was a hit.

Both La Sonora Matancera and Cruz became stars in Cuba. Throughout the 1950s, they played regularly at Havana's famed Tropicana nightclub, appeared in films, and toured extensively throughout Latin America. These heady years ended in 1959 when Communist leader Fidel Castro seized power and Cuba became a socialist state. A year and a half later, Cruz was with La Sonora Matancera on a Mexican tour when they defected en masse on July 15, 1960. The band settled in the United States, and Cruz soon became a naturalized citizen. Castro was irate that one of his country's most popular musical acts had made such a public statement against his regime and vowed that none would ever be granted entry back into Cuba again. Cruz tried to return when her mother died in 1962 but was unable to secure government permission. That same year, she wed Pedro Knight, La Sonora Matancera's trumpet player, who would eventually become her manager and musical director for much of her career.

Teamed with Puente

For much of the decade, Cruz remained relatively unknown in the United States outside of the Cuban exile community, but that changed when she joined the Tito Puente Orchestra in the mid-1960s. The popular percussionist and bandleader from Puerto Rico had a large following across Latin America, and as frontperson Cruz again became a dynamic focus for the act. Puente, who died in 2000, once told *New York Times* writer Elizabeth Llorente, "She keeps the musicians on their toes. . . . We'll be huffing, exhausted, and she'll be on a roll, with more Tina Turner energy left in her than all of us together."

Cruz recorded several albums with Puente, including *Cuba Y Puerto Rico Son* in 1966. But it was her stage presence that made her such a compelling figure in Latin music. She had a strong, husky voice that could hold its own against a hard-working rhythm section and was a tireless dancer, storyteller, and audience-rouser. Fans adored her glitzy stage outfits, often sewn from yards of fabric and embellished with sequins, feathers, or lace. Reportedly she never wore the same one twice. High heels and towering wigs only added to the diminutive singer's allure. Her signature shout, "Azucar!" (Sugar!), came from a dining experience at a Miami restaurant, when her Cuban waiter asked if she took sugar in her coffee. As she recalled in the *Billboard* interview with Cobo, "I said, 'Chico, you're Cuban. How can you even ask that? With sugar!' And that evening during my show—I always talk during the show so the horn players can rest their mouths—I told the audience the story and they laughed. And one day, instead of telling the story, I simply walked down the stairs and shouted 'Azucar!'"

Latin Music's Own Tina Turner

By the 1970s, the salsa sound had caught on with a new generation of Latin Americans, riding a resurgence of ethnic pride and interest in the music of their parents' era. Cruz even appeared at Carnegie Hall for a 1973 staging of *Hommy–A Latin Opera,* the Spanish-language adaptation of the hit rock opera from the Who's *Tommy.* For a number of years, she was signed to the Fania label, a salsa-source powerhouse co-owned by trombonist Willie Colón, with whom she recorded an acclaimed 1974 work, *Celia and Johnny.* She performed regularly with the Fania All-Stars, including a 1976 concert at Yankee Stadium in the Bronx that was recorded and released as a double album. The singer also appeared annually at a New York City salsa-fest held at Madison Square Garden. "Onstage, she leaps, dances, flaunts, flirts and teases to the gyrating beat of salsa," wrote Llorente in a 1987 *New York Times* article. "She improvises playfully, trading riffs with the chorus and instruments. And just when she seems deeply lost in a song about a doomed love affair—microphone clutched, eyes closed, tears imminent—she looks out at the audience and tosses them an aside ('The man was a jerk, anyway')."

Cruz lived in the New York City area but was also a star in Miami and performed there often. For Cuban Americans, she seemed to symbolize the trajectory of its large exile community centered in southern Florida—many of whom, like her, had fled the Castro regime and then achieved personal and professional success in their adopted homeland. Most were avowed foes of Castro and asserted, as Cruz had also done, that they would never to return to Cuba unless it became a democracy. One song in her repertoire, "Canto a la Habana" (Song to Havana), featured the line, "Cuba que lindos son tus paisajes" (Cuba, what beautiful vistas you have), which would incite an emotional eruption from her audiences. Cruz even gained a following among the second generation of Cuban Americans, noted *New York Times* writer Mirta Ojito. To those "who left Cuba as children or were born in the United States," Ojito wrote, "Cruz embodied the Cuba of the 1950's, an era that, through the prism of exile and the passing of decades, has become mythic for them."

Won Several Grammys

Over the years, Cruz worked with a roster of performers that proved her crossover appeal, though she never sang in anything but her native Spanish language. She recorded or collaborated with Brazilian star Caetano Veloso, Patti LaBelle, Wyclef Jean of the Fugees, producer Emilio Estefan, the tenor Luciano Pavarotti, and even former Talking Heads singer David Byrne. With him she sang a duet, "Loco de Amor," that appeared on the soundtrack to the 1986 film *Something Wild.* In the 1992 film *The Mambo Kings Play Songs of Love,* she was cast as a nightclub owner, and she also appeared in 1995's *The Perez Family.* Her awards included a Grammy for best tropical Latin album of 1989 for *Ritmo en el corazón,* a collaboration with conga player Ray Barretto, and she took three consecutive Latin Grammy awards when the honors were established in 2000, including best salsa album of 2002 for *La Negra Tiene Tumbao,* which spawned a hit single of the same name.

Cruz was not slowed by age and still toured heavily and recorded well into her seventies. "My life is singing," she told Knight-Ridder/Tribune News Service reporter Mario Tarradell in 2002. "I don't plan on retiring. I plan to die on a stage. I can have a headache. But when it's time to sing and I step on that stage, there's no more headache. As long as I'm doing what I want to do, I feel good." Her final album was *Regalo de Alma* ("Gift from the Soul"), recorded in early 2003 when she was already suffering from cancer. She died on July 16, 2003, at her home in Fort Lee, New Jersey. She had requested that her funeral include two public viewings—one in New York City and a second in Miami. Thousands turned out for each, including a woman dressed as a patron saint in Roman Catholic iconography who stood outside the Madison Avenue funeral home the entire day holding a Cuban flag and a Colombian man who was a regular performer on New York city subway platforms, dancing to Cruz's repertoire with a foam doll.

In Miami, Cruz's casket stood inside a building known as the Freedom Tower, once an immigration-processing center that was the first stop in the United States for some half a million Cuban exiles in the 1960s and 1970s. "For the almost two million Cubans who live outside the island," noted Ojito in the *New York Times,* "Cruz was an icon. . . .

She embodied what Cubans view as some of their best qualities, strong family ties, an impeccable work ethic and a joy in living, even in the face of calamity." Many of the fans who stood in line for hours in both cities, however, carried the flags of Puerto Rico, Venezuela, Ecuador, and even Jamaica, a testament to Cruz's immense appeal throughout the Latin and Caribbean world.

Books

Contemporary Hispanic Biography, Volume 1, Gale, 2002.

Periodicals

Billboard, October 28, 2000; July 26, 2003.
Economist, July 26, 2003.
Entertainment Weekly, August 1, 2003.
Knight-Ridder/Tribune News Service, September 13, 2002; July 16, 2003; July 19, 2003; July 22, 2003.
New York Times, August 30, 1987; July 17, 2003; July 20, 2003; July 22, 2003.
People, August 4, 2003.
Time, July 11, 1998. □

D

Richard M. Daley

Known for his efforts to create community-based programs that address Chicago's educational, public safety, and neighborhood development concerns, Mayor Richard M. Daley (born 1942) continued the political dynasty forged by his father, a political institution in that Midwest city for more than two decades.

A Democrat by birth and by conviction, Daley was born into a well-known political clan on April 24, 1942, in Chicago. The fourth of seven children, he was also the first son born to Richard J. Daley and wife Eleanor. The Daley children were raised in Bridgeport, a working-class neighborhood in the city, while the elder Daley worked to further his political aspirations. He became the mayor of Chicago in 1955 and remained in office for six terms until his death in 1976.

The senior Daley guarded the privacy of his family fiercely and worked hard to provide his children with a normal upbringing. He still required them to do chores around the house, but he also indulged them in some of the opportunities his position allowed, such as taking them to White Sox games in his private box at Comiskey Park. Although he was busy due to his responsibilities as mayor of Chicago, he was also actively involved with his family and would come home for lunch most days. "I have great memories of my father," the younger Daley recalled in *People,* "sitting around the dinner table on Sunday talking about politics."

From very early in his life, young Daley followed in his father's footsteps. He was an alter boy at the Nativity of Our Lord Catholic Church and attended De la Salle Academy, just like his father had before him. He completed his bachelor's degree at De Paul University, his father's alma mater, in 1964. While in college he learned a valuable lesson when he ran a stop sign and found himself on the front pages of the Chicago papers the next day. From then on, Daley was extremely cautious of the media. During this time, he also served in the Marine Reserves, which his father considered good training. Young Daley continued at De Paul University and received his law degree in 1968.

Witnessed Chaos at 1968 Democratic Convention

The year 1968 is memorable to many Chicagoans as a result of events that occurred at the Democratic National Convention held in the city that year. The Mayor Daley had fought hard to keep the convention in Chicago, despite a great deal of public debate about safety concerns due to civil unrest and planned Vietnam War protests. Unfortunately, when the convention began, these concerns materialized; what started out as protests to the ongoing war turned violent and there was rioting in the streets for five days. The Chicago police were sent into the mobs of protestors, armed with billy clubs and tear gas, and the Mayor Daley took the blame for allowing the police to use what the federal commission would later condemn as excessive force.

The atmosphere was also volatile inside the convention walls, where the younger Daley—at 26 years of age a contemporary of many of the protesters gathered outside the walls—stood next to his father as the elder Daley shouted obscenities at U.S. Senator Abraham Ribicoff when the Con-

necticut senator criticized the mayor for his police actions. The television cameras were rolling, and the event, with Mayor Daley shouting, made national news and startled the American public. It was a large blemish on the mayor's office, but not large enough to prevent Daley's re-election in 1971 and 1975.

Following the completion of law school, the young Daley passed his bar exam on the third attempt. In 1969 he started on a path of public service when he was named as a delegate to the Illinois Constitutional Convention. A year later, he met Maggie Corbett, a 26-year-old executive at Xerox Corporation, during a Christmas party. Daley asked her to go out with him on New Year's Eve, and she accepted. Fifteen months later, the two were married.

An Elected Official

In 1972 Daley won his first elective office, to serve in the Illinois State Senate representing the 23rd district. He remained a state senator until 1980, working to remove the sales tax from food and medicine, sponsoring landmark mental-health legislation, and establishing rights for nursing-home residents. During this time, the Daley's had their first three children: Nora, Patrick, and Kevin. Sadly, Kevin was born with spina bifida, a birth defect involving the central nervous system, and only survived until 1981.

On December 20, 1976, when the senior Daley passed away while in office, many thought that Senator Daley would step directly into his father's footsteps. However, he did not. In 1980 Daley was elected as state's attorney for

Cook County, where he pushed for tougher narcotics laws, helped to overhaul rape laws, and developed programs to battle drunk driving, domestic violence, and child-support delinquencies. He also became the first official in Cook County to sign a decree eliminating politically motivated hiring and firing. He was re-elected as state's attorney in 1984 and again in 1988. In the mid-eighties, the Daley also had a fourth child, their daughter Elizabeth.

In 1983 Daley made his first run for mayor. However, in a racially charged election, the vote in the Democratic primary was split between Daley and Jane Byrne, which allowed Harold Washington, Chicago's first black mayor, to win the election. Six years later, in 1989, Mayor Washington passed away while in office, and this time Daley was ready. He was elected on April 4, 1989, winning out over two other candidates to complete Washington's term.

Began Era of Fiscal Responsibility

Daley wanted to run Chicago like a business. When he took over the helm as mayor the city was running at a deficit, but by the end of his first term in office he had turned that deficit into a surplus. Largely on the basis of his ability to manage the financial affairs of the large city, he was re-elected mayor in 1991, 1995, 1999, and 2003, winning a greater percentage of votes at each election.

Upon entering the same wood-paneled office that his father had once inhabited, Daley immediately set about cleaning up the city. Shortly after being sworn into office, he griped to an aide about a filthy window. "If this place isn't clean," he said at a press conference, according to *People*, "what does that say about our city?" He took more crucial steps to clean up the city, ridding its streets of abandoned cars, removing graffiti, repairing roads, and planting trees. "Rich has been on that tree kick for years," quipped brother Bill Daley to *People*. "He believes that greenery makes life a little more enjoyable for people." On the social front, Daley encouraged the awarding of city contracts to minority-owned businesses and created the Office of Sexual Harassment to investigate complaints and stiffened penalties for hate crimes. He tripled the number of beds available to the city's homeless and developed a community policing program which joined police officers with city agencies and neighborhood residents to solve problems that cause crime. He worked with the Chicago Police Department to develop an aggressive anti-gang program that seized and destroyed up to 12,000 to 15,000 illegal weapons each year. According to information provided by the mayor's office, under Daley's watch the crime rate dropped every year beginning in 1992.

Among other things, Daley became known for his "drive-by jottings"; he would take notes while on drives through the city, recording eyesores or other issues that needed action. His notes were then written up by his staff and included in appropriate directives.

Daley worked to present himself as a manager rather than a politician. He sought the advice of local business executives and developers and drew on the expertise of key area businesspeople for ways to run the city more efficiently. Despite a great deal of criticism over Daley's efforts to "privatize" city functions, the positive results from his efforts were quickly evident. By turning over many city functions to private contractors, as well as by implementing programs to make city employees more accountable, he saved taxpayers more than $50 million a year by 2002.

Welcomed More Orderly DNC

In 1996 Daley successfully hosted the Democratic National Convention (DNC) in Chicago, where President Bill Clinton received the nomination for his final term in office. The event was held at the United Center, the city's newly constructed sports and convention complex. During the convention the mayor was also the primary spokesperson for the nation's cities and their problems in his capacity as the incoming president of the U.S. Conference of Mayors. Unlike the DNC of 1968, the 1996 convention saw no riots; events proceeded smoothly and professionally.

In an effort to stop the flow of guns into the city of Chicago, officials from both the mayor's office and Cook County joined forces in 1998 to bring a lawsuit against the U.S. gun industry in which the plaintiff sued for damages of $443 million and accused the gun industry of creating a public nuisance by manufacturing and distributing its product. The suit was filed against 22 gun manufacturers, 12 gun shop owners, and 4 gun distributors. Efforts such as this, to improve the quality of life for the people of Chicago and the region, did not go unnoticed. In 1999 Mayor Daley received the Education Excellence Award from the National Conference for Community and Justice, the Public Service Leadership Award from the National Council for Urban Economic Development, the J. Sterling Morton Award from the National Arbor Day Foundation, and the Keystone Award from the American Architectural Foundation, as well as the Martin Luther King, Jr./Robert F. Kennedy Award from the Coalition to Stop Gun Violence/Education Fund to End Handgun Violence. As an *Economist* writer noted in 2002: "The city center is cleaner, greener and more vibrant than ever before. The public schools, though still worse than they ought to be, have shown signs of improvement since Mr. Daley took them under his own control in 1995. Tourist attractions . . . have opened up on Mr. Daley's watch such as the grand opening of Millennium Park in May 2004. Many residential areas have been reinvigorated by immigrants from Latin America, eastern Europe and Asia."

Family traditions run deep in the Daley family, and the study of the law and political service are two such traditions. Daley's brother, Michael Daley, is a lawyer who served as cochair of the 1996 Democratic National convention. The mayor's youngest brother, William Daley, became U.S. secretary of commerce under President Bill Clinton and helped to persuade Congress to pass the North American Free Trade Agreement (NAFTA) in 1993. Although Daley himself started out even more rigidly in the footsteps of his father, he developed his own style and way of doing business. While the basic values of family, education, safe neighborhoods, and economic development remain the same for both men, the younger Richard Daley was definitely considered an "updated version."

Apart from the duties assigned to him as mayor, Daley enjoys bike riding, attending movies, and country-western line dancing. But mostly, he enjoys his work. "I believe today, as I have from the start, that we can only achieve . . . progress together as one city, united in our mission to make our schools, our streets safer, and all of our neighborhoods better places in which to live and raise our families," Daley stated in a speech made following his fifth mayoral win in March of 2003 and reported by *CNN.com.* "That's why I take particular pride in the fact that Chicago is united today, and that our victory was built in every community."

Periodicals

Economist, March 1, 2003.
National Review, September 11, 1995.
People, September 2, 1996.
U.S. World & News Report, March 23, 1992.

Online

"Best Summer Ever," *City of Chicago Web site,* http://egov .cityofchicago.org/ (May 21, 2004).
"Chicago Mayor Daley Wins Fifth Term," *CNN.com,* http://www.cnn.com/2003/ALLPOLITICS/02/26/chicago .daley (December 12, 2003).
"Mayor Richard M. Daley," *City of Chicago Web site,* http://egov.cityofchicago.org/ (December 8, 2003). ☐

Maurice de Hirsch

Baron Maurice de Hirsch (1831–1896), a wealthy German financier, founded the Jewish Colonization Association in 1891. The nonprofit venture sponsored the first organized mass migrations in history. His project to settle thousands of beleaguered Russian Jews onto the vast Argentine pampas had only limited success, but through this and other philanthropic ventures, the Baron helped change the immigration policies of several nations.

From Bavaria

D e Hirsch was born in Munich, Germany, on December 9, 1831, into an affluent and well-connected Jewish family who served as bankers to the Bavarian king. His grandfather had been the first Jewish landowner in Bavaria and was granted a title of nobility, "auf Gereuth," in 1818, which meant the family could add the prefix "von" to its surname. The "baron" that de Hirsch later used was another title, bestowed on his banker father Joseph in 1869 for services to the king. Care was taken by his mother, Caroline Wertheimer von de Hirsch, to see that her son learned Hebrew and was familiar with the religion of his birth; there was even a small synagogue inside their home.

De Hirsch first attended school in Munich and went on to study in Brussels at age 14, where he proved a somewhat indifferent student. At age 17, he took an entry-level position with the Brussels firm of Bischoffsheim & Goldschmidt, a powerful banking enterprise with branches in London and Paris. He rose quickly through its ranks, but his keen business mind was believed too prone to risk-taking by the firm's senior management; thus though he did well in the job, he was never made partner. He did, however, win the hand of Clara Bischoffsheim, the earnest daughter of the firm's chief, and the pair wed in 1855. He eventually left Bischoffsheim & Goldschmidt to set up his own private banking firm.

Made Railroad Investments

With a store of capital that came in part from his wife's fortune as well as via money inherited when his father died, de Hirsch began making investments in sugar plantations and copper mining. He moved into the lucrative world of railroads when he learned that a Brussels financier had landed a contract with the Turkish government to construct a rail route from Europe into the country via the Balkans. But de Hirsch's rival had since engaged in risky speculative ventures, and his businesses collapsed; de Hirsch managed to obtain the contract himself and then negotiated with the Turkish government to start the project. He financed the venture by floating Turkish government bonds on Europe's financial markets, and the construction firm he had established to carry out the work had part of the line completed by 1874. The last link was delayed when the Turkish government suffered financial setbacks, but the Vienna-Constantinople railroad was finally completed in 1883, making it the historic first route from Europe to the East.

The railroad enriched de Hirsch's personal fortunes immensely, and he became one of the Continent's leading financiers and social figures. He was on friendly terms with the Prince of Wales, later England's King Edward VII, but as he entered middle age his interests turned elsewhere. Though he was sometimes the victim of anti-Semitism—he was turned down for membership by the French Jockey Club, for instance—his experiences in Turkey awakened him to the plight of Jews outside of Western Europe. Many lived in dire poverty, and in some places government laws severely restricted their employment opportunities. His father-in-law had been active in the Alliance Israélite Universelle, a Paris organization founded in 1860 to aid Jews living under such severe restrictions. In 1873, de Hirsch donated the sum of one million French francs ($200,000) to the Alliance so that they could establish trade schools in Turkey and the Balkans for Jews there.

De Hirsch became increasingly involved with the Alliance. After 1880, the charity experienced regular annual shortfalls, and de Hirsch paid these for a number of years. In 1889, he set up an endowment fund that gave it an annual income of 400,000 francs, and he was by then also donating heavily to a relief fund to aid refugees fleeing religious persecution in Imperial Russia. The plight of Russia's five million Jews roused de Hirsch's philanthropic sympathies, and he came to believe more dedicated measures were necessary.

Millions Lived in Dire Poverty

At the time, Russia also included much of Poland as well as Lithuania; this area, along with parts of the Ukraine Byelorussia, was called the Pale of Settlement, and Jews in Russia were restricted to it. Even within the bounds of the Pale, they suffered tremendous discrimination: Jews paid double taxes, were forbidden to own land, and could not live in some larger towns without a difficult-to-obtain residency permit. At times, waves of pogroms swept the countryside, in which mobs attacked and destroyed Jewish homes, businesses, and synagogues. Often, local police or military authorities witnessed the violence but did little to stop it. After a new tsar, Alexander III, began a renewal of official anti-Semitic policies in 1881 and even added new restrictions, thousands began to flee. They arrived in the Ukrainian city of Brody, on the border of the Austro-Hungarian empire, which had far more liberal policies toward its Jewish population, and pleaded to be granted entry. Many of them arrived in Brody destitute, and the Alliance provided aid for them, helped in part by the Baron's generous underwriting.

An 1887 imperial edict in Russia limited Jews' access to secondary education within the Pale: they were to make up just ten percent of a given school's student body, though they constituted about one-half to three-quarters of the population. In response, de Hirsch devised a plan in which he would provide Russia with 50 million francs ($10,000,000) to establish a separate school system for Jewish youth in the Pale. The government rejected the offer, however, because of the stipulations that de Hirsch insisted upon in order to prevent the fund from vanishing into the pockets of the Imperial Russia civil servants who ran it. He even met with K. P. Pobedonostsev, the lay head of Russian Orthodox Church and influential adviser to Tsar Alexander, and reportedly gave him one million francs for his help in the negotiations, but the plan fell through.

Precursor to the Kibbutz

Emigration, de Hirsch then came to believe, was the only way to solve the plight of Russia's Jews, and he stepped up his philanthropic efforts accordingly. In 1891, he incorporated the Jewish Colonization Association (JCA) in England to help re-settle Russian Jews on the vastly under populated Argentine pampas. According to the *Jewish Encyclopedia*, de Hirsch claimed that his goal in establishing the JCA was "to assist and promote the emigration of Jews from any part of Europe or Asia—and principally from countries in which they may for the time being be subjected to any special taxes or political or other disabilities—to any parts of the world, and to form and establish colonies in various parts of North and South America and other countries, for agricultural, commercial, and other purposes."

De Hirsch sent emissaries to acquire large swaths of land in Argentina for his project, and others to parts of the globe that he thought might be receptive to the idea of a Jewish colony as well, such as Canada. He also had to negotiate with the Russian government so that it would grant the Jews permission to emigrate, which was forbidden at the time. He secured a deal that would allow 20,000 of them to leave annually in the first years of the project. Local JCA offices were established in the cities of the Pale; there, candidates were interviewed and, if approved, granted the necessary passport, which de Hirsch's organization issued. The JCA also paid their travel costs, including passage to South America. The Argentina experiment was not entirely successful, but de Hirsch was convinced that Jews were ideally suited to till the soil, believing that they had been among the world's first successful pastoral civilizations. He once said in an interview that in the end he hoped ''my efforts shall show that the Jews have not lost the agricultural qualities that their forefathers possessed,'' the *Jewish Encyclopedia.* quoted him as saying. ''I shall try to make for them a new home in different lands, where, as free farmers, on their own soil, they can make themselves useful to the country.''

Founded New Jersey Colony

The plight of Jews in other parts of Europe was also of concern to de Hirsch. He set up the Galician Foundation in 1888 on the occasion of Emperor Francis Joseph's fortieth year on the throne of Austria and through it donated large sums to establish schools in Austro-Hungary's heavily Jewish areas of southeastern Poland and the western Ukraine, which were known as Galicia at the time; this largesse was also earmarked to aid Jews in Bukovina, later subsumed into the Ukraine and Romania. The Foundation set up primary schools there and also provided money for teachers' salaries as well as books, food, and clothing for the students. The Baron's philanthropic efforts also extended to welfare offices to help Jews in Krakow, Budapest, and other Eastern European cities.

The Baron took an active role in helping Russian Jews settle in the United States as well. In 1891 the Baron de Hirsch Fund was incorporated in New York State. It set up trade and English-language schools, offered relief aid to newly arrived immigrants, and also helped resettlement efforts to places that were less crowded than the epicenter of Jewish life in New York City, the Lower East Side. In 1891, the Fund set up an agricultural colony with the purchase of some 5,000 acres in Cape May County, New Jersey. A few years later, the Baron de Hirsch Agricultural College was established there as well, the first secondary school in the United States exclusively for the study of the agricultural sciences. The colony later evolved into the town of Woodbine, New Jersey.

Fund Received Millions

De Hirsch owned thoroughbreds and was an ardent horseracing fan. He often claimed that his horses ran for charity, for he donated all his winnings to London hospital charities. He and his wife had two children, but their daughter died in infancy, and 31-year-old Lucien died of pneumonia in 1887. They had homes in Paris and outside Versailles and an estate in Hungary called Schloss St. Johann. When the Baron died there on April 21, 1896, he left a bequest of $45 million in his will to the Jewish Colonization Association. Over the course of his life, he likely donated a personal fortune of some $100 million in all. His wife was also

devoted philanthropist and worked alongside him for most of their marriage. Generous in spirit as well, she even provided in her will for two children her husband had fathered with a mistress. The JCA received the bulk of her estate after her 1899 death, and for decades was thought to be the world's richest charitable trust.

More than a hundred years after his death, the Baron de Hirsch Fund was still helping Jewish immigrants from Russia and Romania via the United Hebrew Charities of New York. ''In relieving human suffering I never ask whether the cry of necessity comes from a being who belongs to my faith or not,'' he once said, according to the *Jewish Encyclopedia,* ''but what is more natural than that I should find my highest purpose in bringing to the followers of Judaism, who have been oppressed for a thousand years, who are starving in misery, the possibilities of a physical and moral regeneration?''

Books

Norman, Theodore, *An Outstretched Arm: A History of the Jewish Colonization Association,* Routledge & Kegan Paul, 1985.

Periodicals

New York Times, May 23, 1897.
Times (London, England), November 6, 1891.

Online

''Baron de Hirsch Fund,'' *Jewish Encyclopedia.com,* http://www .jewishencyclopedia.com/view.jsp?artid = 763&letter = H (January 8, 2004).
''Baron Maurice de Hirsch,'' *Jewish Encyclopedia.com,* http://www.jewishencyclopedia.com/view.jsp?artid = 771 &letter = &letterH (January 8, 2004). □

Tamara de Lempicka

The most famous painter of the Art Deco period, Tamara de Lempicka (1898–1980), was born in Poland and emigrated to the United States as an adult. De Lempicka was a socialite, wife, refugee, mother, and painter. Her portraits, including her self portraits, appealed to the rich because of her bold use of color, unique style, and the sense of elegance that permeated her work.

Growing Up

Tamara de Lempicka was born Maria Gorska in Warsaw, Poland, in 1898. She had an older brother named Stanczyk and a younger sister named Adrienne. Her parents, Boris and Lavina Gorska, were wealthy socialites. Boris Gorska was a lawyer and Lavina Gorska came from a well-to-do family. The Gorskas treated their children to a luxurious life—a life de Lempicka would soon believe she deserved.

De Lempicka was introduced to art at the age of 12, when her mother paid a famous painter to paint her daughter's portrait. The girl's strong will and dominant personality made it difficult for her to be still for the sittings. When the portrait was finished, she hated the result and knew that she could do a better job. To prove herself right, she made Adrienne, her younger sister, sit for a portrait as she tried painting for the first time. De Lempicka was so pleased with her work that she soon began her life-long love affair with art.

During this time, de Lempicka's parents divorced and she became spoiled by her wealthy grandmother and Aunt Stefa (Stephanie). At the age of 13, she decided that she was bored with school and invented an illness so that she could stay home. Instead of keeping her home, however, her grandmother took her on a tour of Italy. It was there that de Lempicka's love for art intensified. Upon her return home, de Lempicka's mother decided to remarry despite her daughter's protest. Now 14 years old, the teenager was unhappy with her mother's decision. She rebelled by going to stay with her aunt in St. Petersburg (Petrograd) when she was on holiday from her school in Lausanne, Switzerland. Between school and her travels to St. Petersburg, de Lempicka still managed to travel home to Warsaw from time to time. During one of her trips home in 1914, shortly after Russia and Germany declared war, she met a handsome lawyer and ladies' man named Taduesz Lempicki. Lempicki was modestly well-off as a lawyer, but he did not come from money. Still, Tamara fell in love with him, and two years later, in 1916, the couple married in St. Petersburg at the

Chapel of the Knights of Malta. De Lempicka was 17 years old and her millionaire banker uncle provided the dowry.

Life as a Refugee

In December of 1918, in the midst of the Russian Revolution, Taduesz Lempicki was arrested by the Cheka (the Bolshevik secret police). De Lempicka escaped to Copenhagen and used her striking beauty to charm favors from members of the Swedish consul. Her seductive gestures worked well and her husband was released. The couple fled to Paris, changed their names to de Lempicka and tried to resume their glamorous lifestyle. Unfortunately, their marriage had been tarnished by the results of Tamara's sultry, seductive ways with other men.

Life in Paris was far from glamorous for the de Lempickas. Tadeusz had become a womanizer and was bitter from his ordeal with the Cheka. The couple lived in a small room in a cheap hotel and Tadeusz could not find a job. Then Tamara found out she was pregnant. By the time she gave birth to a baby girl, Kizette, money was so scarce that de Lempicka was forced to sell her jewels to support the family. Determined to resume her wealthy lifestyle, she turned to art to make a living.

The Art That Influenced Her Style

De Lempicka took her first painting lesson from Maurice Denis at the Académie Ranson. Denis was a post-symbolist French Nabi painter. Nabi art was developed by Les Nabis, a group of Parisian post-Impressionist artists. It was best identified by an artist's emphasis on graphic art and design. De Lempicka's second teacher, Andreé Lhote, had the most influence on her spare, simple Art Deco style. Lhote was a mute French Cubist painter and sculptor. (Cubism was developed in the early 1900s as a collaboration between Pablo Picasso and Georges Braque.) Cubist art was identified by an artist's ability to capture the essence of an object by showing it from multiple points of view simultaneously. Lhote taught de Lempicka how to modify Cubism by retaining "its commercially acceptable aspects but leaving forms of objects intact" (*Women in World History*). De Lempicka's art combined the styles from her two teachers and she soon became known as one of the best portrait artists in Paris.

Fame and Fortune

De Lempicka's first paintings caught the eye of Collette Weill, owner of Gallerie Colette Weill. Weill displayed de Lempicka's work in her gallery and patrons seemed to fall in love with the sensual, shocking portraits that boldly identified de Lempicka's unique style. She was rewarded with immediate financial success and soon became a celebrity in the art world. Once again, de Lempicka was able to live lavishly. She purchased a diamond bracelet for every two paintings that sold, and before long both of her arms were drenched in gems from wrist to shoulder. As she moved into the upper strata, the artist traveled more, stayed in the finest hotels, and surrounded herself with the cultural elite.

In 1925, de Lempicka established her reputation as a leading Art Deco artist at the Exposition Internationale des

Artes Décoratifs et Industriels Moderne. A form of art that combined Cubism and design, Art Deco had begun to become wildly popular, and this was the first Art Deco exhibition in Paris. From that moment on, her career as an artist took off. She painted portraits of the people she associated herself with: the rich, the famous, the elite. Galleries began to hang her work in their best rooms and critics raved over her erotic portraits. Between the 1920s and 1930s, de Lempicka produced paintings that would become quite famous. One of her most sought-after pieces, *Auto-Portrait (Tamara in the Green Bugatti)* was completed in 1925. In this self-portrait, which she painted for the cover of *Die Dame,* de Lempicka presented herself as "a dazzling and independent woman who looks like she might fly away in her aquamarine car." In 1927, she won first prize at the Exposition Internationale des Beaux-Arts in Bordeaux for a painting of her daughter entitled *Kizette on the Balcony.* Four years later, she would win a bronze medal at the Exposition Internationale in Poznan, Poland, for another portrait of her daughter, *Kizette's First Communion.*

Upon achieving fame and fortune, de Lempicka began to have affairs with wealthy art patrons. Her noted affairs included Marquis Sommi Picenardi, a lover she took during a tour of Italy; Rafaela, the model for her painting *Beautiful Rafaela;* and Gabriele d'Annunzio, Italy's premiere poet and playwright. Her affair with Rafaela lasted one year and her affair with d'Annunzio was a mere flirtation. De Lempicka was more interested in completing his portrait than she was in consummating the affair. Unfortunately, the relationship ended before the portrait was finished.

By 1928, de Lempicka was living an aristocratic life. She divorced Tadeusz and met Baron Raoul Kuffner, an Austro-Hungarian royal who collected many of her paintings. Kuffner hired her to paint a portrait of his mistress, Nana de Herrera. While working on the piece, de Lempicka became one of Kuffner's mistresses. In 1933, the Baroness Kuffner died of leukemia and de Lempicka stepped in to take the baron as her husband. Her new husband gave her everything she wanted: a title, money, culture, and stature. De Lempicka became more popular as an artist and continued to work. She was so popular, in fact, that wealthy people and royalty would stand in line to have the honor of their portrait being painted by the famous Tamara de Lempicka. But with another war on the horizon, the glamorous life did not last.

Moved to America

In 1939, the Nazi influence had spread across Europe and the wealthy were faced with the threat of World War II. Unemployment was high and the world was in a state of chaos. It was no longer acceptable to paint expensive paintings for a rich audience. Instead, galleries were looking for surrealist and abstract art that appealed to common people. Having fled from war once before during the Russian Revolution, de Lempicka knew all too well about the financial insecurity that would ensue when war finally broke. As a result, she encouraged Kuffner to sell parts of his Hungarian estate, and in 1939, the couple sought refuge in America. They moved into a film director's former house in Beverly Hills, and de Lempicka, eager to boost her publicity, held a contest at the University of California-Los Angeles (UCLA) to find a model for her painting *Susannah and the Elders.* She also sponsored her own solo exhibitions at the Paul Reinhart Gallery in Los Angeles, the Julian Levy Gallery in New York, the Courvoisier Galleries in San Francisco, and the Milwaukee Institute of Art. Soon, de Lempicka became friends with such Hollywood stars as Dolores del Rio, Tyrone Power, and George Sanders. They gave her a nickname: "The Baroness with a Brush."

In 1943, the Kuffners moved to New York. By this time, de Lempicka's social life had begun to corrupt her art. Tamara de Lempicka, an artist who had married a baron, was a woman of the past. De Lempicka was now known as Baroness Kuffner, a dilettante who had taken up painting as a hobby. With America's attraction to titles, the latter was far more intriguing to the upper class. No longer taken seriously as an artist, de Lempicka painted less. As her production slowed, she disappeared from the art world for nearly 20 years. Then, in 1960, she ventured into abstract art and tried to reclaim her artistic reputation. Unfortunately, when her work was exhibited in 1962 at New York's Iolas Gallery it was met with a critical yawn. Unable to cope with such disrespect and trying to deal with her husband's sudden death from a heart attack, de Lempicka gave up on painting as a career and never exhibited again.

De Lempicka's Last Travels

Distraught, de Lempicka moved to Houston in 1962 to live near Kizette and her two granddaughters. (Kizette had moved to America in 1941 and married a Texas geologist). Then in 1966, the Musee des Arts Decoratifs commemorated Art Deco in a special exhibition, resurrecting interest and appreciation for this 1920s-1930s art form. Inspired by the exhibit, Alain Blondel opened the Galeire du Luxembourg and launched a major retrospective of Tamara de Lempicka. As a result, de Lempicka's art enjoyed a renaissance in the 1970s and her work was rediscovered by the art world. Unfortunately, de Lempicka would not live to see the enormous surge in popularity her work experienced in the 1990s. (In 1994, Barbara Streisand sold the artist's *Adam and Eve* for $1.8 million, a painting she had purchased in 1984 for $135,000.).

In 1974, de Lempicka decided to move to Cuernavaca, Mexico. She bought a beautiful house called Tres Bambus in a chic neighborhood in 1978, and Kizette joined her in 1979 after her husband died. By this time, de Lempicka was quite ill. She spent her last days with her daughter at her bedside and died in her sleep on March 18, 1980. According to her mother's will, Kizette scattered de Lempicka's ashes over the crater of Mt. Popocatépetl, an active volcano.

Books

Commire, Anne, ed., *Women in World History,* Yorkin Publications, 2001.
Néret, Gilles, *Tamara de Lempicka,* Verlag, 1990.

Online

"An Artist Whose Portraits Symbolize the Wild Ride of the Jazz Age. . .Tamara de Lempicka," *Techniquelle website,* http://www.techniquelle.com (December 22, 2003).

"Artist: Tamara de Lempicka," *SOHO Art website,* http://www.soho-art.com (December 22, 2003).

"Bio: Tamara de Lempicka," *CGFA: A Virtual Art Musuem website,* http://cgfa.sunsite.dk (December 22, 2003).

"Tamara de Lempicka (1898–1980)," *Good Art website,* http://www.goodart.org (December 22, 2003).

"Tamara de Lempicka: Biography, History," *Art City website,* http://www.artcity.com (December 22, 2003). ☐

Christine de Pisan

French poet, scholar, and essayist Christine de Pisan (1363–1431) remains known more than five centuries after her death for her writings defending women, among which *La cité de dames* and *Le livre du trésor de la cité de dames* are most respected.

De Pisan ranks among the most important intellectuals of her day and certainly the most noted woman writer of the medieval period. In her philosophical writings and commentaries she was resolute in her support of a woman's right to pursue education and attain prominence within society in relation to her accomplishments. Her many poems, essays, and books, widely distributed and read during her lifetime, have influenced readers throughout Europe and Britain through the many translated editions that have since been produced. Among her most notable works in defense of women's role in medieval European society, de Pisan's *La cité de dames* recounts for readers the accomplishs of women from history, providing medieval men and women with a sense of the possibilities that can be attained by women when allowed education and social freedoms.

An Education at Court

Born in Venice in 1363, de Pisan was the daughter of Italian scholar Tommaso di Benvenuto da Pizzano, a highly educated man who had been appointed astrologer to the court of Charles V of France. In 1369 the five-year-old de Pisan traveled from Venice to the French court, where she was educated by her father in such academic subjects as literature, Greek, and Latin, as well as becoming schooled in the habits of the French court. Because of her father's many intellectual interests, the young de Pisan had full run of a vast family library that included books on not only literature, history, classics, and astrology, but also scientific advancements, religion, and works engaged in the philosophical arguments underway in France at the time.

In 1380, the same year France's King Charles V died, fifteen-year-old de Pisan married Étienne du Castel, a 24-year-old notary and member of the French court who had been reared in Picardy. The couple, who had three children, enjoyed a relationship in which mutual respect played a large part; Castel encouraged his young wife's intelligence and penchant for poetry and self-expression, while she appreciated his gentle demeanor and loyalty. Tragically, during a wave of bubonic plague that was then ravaging Europe, in 1389 Castel died while on a trip to Beauvais with the king, leaving twenty-five-year-old de Pisan to raise her daughter and two sons on her own. Unfortunately, de Pisan's responsibilities did not end there: she also had to shoulder her husband's financial debts, which were the subject of a prolonged dispute, as well as support her now-widowed and debt-ridden mother and a niece. Because her father's death in 1386 had severed family ties to the new French monarch, King Charles VI, there was little family support to draw on. Although English monarch Henry IV and Milanese ruler Galeazzo Visconti both offered de Pisan a place within their courts, the poetess had no wish to leave her beloved France. Instead, she decided to rely on her wit, her intelligence, and her love of words and write poetry, becoming in the process one of France's first professional writers.

Patronage

Fortunately for de Pisan, many in positions of power knew of and respected her talents, and she was able to gain the patronage of the French queen, Isabella of Bavaria, and several nobles, among them the earl of Salisbury and Philip the Bold, duke of Burgundy, which enabled her to support her family. For Philip—who was rearing her eldest son as his own child—she penned the moral guidebook *Le livre des faitz et bonnes moeurs du Saige Roy Charles.* This work, while appropriate for its time, did not prove as useful to subsequent generations due to its overt moralizing and intricate style. More popular was her *Le livre de paix*, which discusses the proper manner in which princes should be educated. The medieval view of society was that, rather than upward mobility, people were born into a particular station, and their duty was to fulfill the duties that particular station required. De Pisan believed in an orderly society and, unlike the vision Italian political philosopher Niccolò Machiavelli would put forth in *The Prince* a century later, argued that men of power—particularly princes—have an obligation to lead an honest and moral life, support the Catholic Church, and otherwise maintain the status quo. Other long writings include a biography of Charles V published in Paris in 1404 as *Le livre des faicts et bonnes meurs du sage roi Charles V.*

During her lifetime, de Pisan gained renown throughout Europe and England for her writings in verse, such as the long poem ''Le livre des mutations de Fortune,'' ''Le chemin de longue etude,'' and ''Le livre des cent histoires de Troie.'' Intricate, heavily stylized, and verbose, these longer works were eclipsed in popularity by the many shorter poems, ballads, and rondeaux she penned during her early career, most between 1393 and 1400. Expressing her emotions—particularly the sadness, uncertainty, and desolation she endured after her beloved husband's death—many of de Pisan's shorter works have been republished for successive generations of new readers in the centuries following her death.

In the longer, more broadly focused verses de Pisan wrote during her writing life, she gained in sophistication where she lost in popular appeal. She experimented with literary themes and style, creating multi-layered poems with meanings often obscure to a reader unschooled in the social milieu and intellectual issues of her day. Pisan's prose is not for the general reader; it is stylistically intricate, intellectually challenging, and reflects her wide-ranging knowledge and interests. In contrast, her prose histories, her biography of Charles V, and her political essays have been praised by generations of critics. Among her contemporaries, de Pisan was often compared to the classical authors Virgil, Cicero, and Cato due to her technical ability and the intelligence that is revealed throughout her body of work.

In the eyes of modern feminist scholars, de Pisan is most remembered for her *Trésor de la cité des dames*, published in 1405 and translated into English by London publisher Wynkyn de Word as *The City of Ladies. La cité des dames* has preserved for modern readers and historians the life story of a number of women from both history and mythology; for de Pisan's contemporaries it provided women with inspiration. In this work she also examines the source of women's diminished social status and includes advice for readers regarding how to improve education and social standing. Now considered one of the foundational works of feminist literature, the book has served as a source for all those who would argue that women deserved the same right to educational opportunities as men because they were capable of attaining similar accomplishments. For some, her argument that women were socially and intel-

lectually the equals of men was seen as a threat, and efforts—eventually discredited—were made to show that *La cité des dames* was a plagiarized rewrite of an earlier work by Italian writer Giovanni Boccaccio titled *De claris mulieribus.*

De Pisan's 1405 work, *Le livre du trèsor de la cité de dames*—translated as *The Treasure of the City of Ladies; or, The Book of Three Virtues*—continues her arguments on behalf of the gentler sex. In this work she takes her argument to her own age, laying forth what she sees as three basic classes of women: noble and aristocratic women, women of the court and lesser nobility, and women of the growing merchant and artisan classes. Common women were not included because their lack of basic literacy excluded them from the reading public. It is all women's right, she argues, to obtain schooling sufficient to allow them to use their natural talents to benefit themselves and society, and especially to become educated, sophisticated citizens able to recognize corruption among political figures. In the prologue to *Le livre du trèsor de la cité de dames* she wrote: ''If it were customary to send little girls to school and to teach them the same subjects that are taught to boys, they would learn just as fully and would understand the subtleties of all arts and sciences. Indeed, maybe they would understand them better . . . for just as women's bodies are softer than men's, so their understanding is sharper.''

Other works by de Pisan include *Le livre des fais d'armes et de checaleries*—translated and printed by William Caxton in London in 1489 as *The Book of Fayettes of Armes and of Chivalrye*—and 1407's *Le livre du duc des vrais amants*—translated as *The Book of the Duke of True Lovers.* Her *Lettre à Isabeau de Bavière*, a work written in response to a popular satirical parody of the classic *Roman de la rose*, began her multi-volume attack on the writings of Ovid and Jean de Meun. In her poetic *Epistre au dieu d'amour*, which she published in 1399, de Pisan expresses her unhappiness over women's lot within Medieval society and argues against the underlying misogynism in popular literary works. She continues such arguments on behalf of women in *Epistres du délbat sur le Roman de la rose*, which was released to French readers in 1401. In *Avision–Christine*, which was published in 1405 and later translated as *Christine's Vision*, she writes that a man once stated to her that educated women were unbecoming because they were so uncommon. Her quick wit is reflected in her response to him: that ignorant men are more offensive; they are even more unbecoming because they are so very common.

Prolific Writer

Because of her need to support herself and her children following her husband's death, de Pisan was a remarkably prolific writer. By the writer's own account, from 1397 to 1403 she competed 15 major works in addition to a number of essays and shorter verses. Her devotion to her craft of writing accounts, perhaps, for the fact that she did not take the path of many women of her era and station and remarry. She arranged for the copying and illuminating of her own texts in copybooks, a project she closely oversaw, and also founded the Order of the Rose.

Throughout much of de Pisan's life her adopted France had drained its economy to pursue an elusive victory against England in a series of battles that became collectively known as the Hundred Years' War. In her prose writings de Pisan often expressed her frustration with politicians and nobles who supported this war, and she grew even more upset after the assassination of Louis of Orleans in 1407, penning *Lamentations on the Civil War* in response. When, in 1415, English King Henry V at the Battle of Agincourt roundly defeated the French army, she took the setback hard. Three years later, in 1418, she retired to Poissy, entering the same convent her daughter had joined. At Poissy she set aside her pen for 11 years in protest. Her last written work, *Ditié de Jehanne d'Arc,* was a song inspired by the heroism of young Joan of Arc, who de Pisan viewed as embodying the moral and intellectual virtues of all women. This work, which was published in 1429, was the last de Pisan would write; she died at Poissy two years later, in 1431 at the age of ninety-six.

Books

Feminist Writers, St. James Press, 1996.
Kennedy, Angus, *Christine de Pizan: A Bibliographical Guide,* Grant & Cutler, 1994.
The Reception of Christine de Pisan from the 15th through the 19th Centuries, edited by Glenda K. McLeod, Edwin Mellen Press, 1991.
Reinterpreting Christine de Pizan, edited by Earl Jeffrey Richards, University of Georgia Press, 1992.
Willard, Charity Cannon, *Christine de Pizan: Her Life and Works,* Persea Press, 1984.

Periodicals

Review of Metaphysics, September 1996.
Shakespeare Studies, January 1, 1997. □

Ferdinand de Saussure

Swiss linguist Ferdinand de Saussure (1857–1913) is generally recognized as the creator of the modern theory of structuralism and the father of modern linguistics. His best-known book, *A Course in General Linguistics,* was published posthumously in 1916. The book transformed 19th-century comparative and historical philology into 20th-century contemporary linguistics.

Born into Scientific Family

F erdinand de Saussure was born on November 26, 1857, in Geneva, Switzerland, to a family with a long history of contributions to the sciences. A bright and eager student, de Saussure showed an early promise in the area of languages and learned Sanskrit, Greek, German,

Latin, French, and English. He had a mentor, the eminent linguist Adolphe Pictet, who encouraged the young man in his growing passion for languages.

Inclined to follow his ancestors' footsteps into the physical sciences, he began attending the prestigious University of Geneva in 1875 to study chemistry and physics. However, by 1876 he had returned to the study of linguistics. De Saussure studied at the University of Berlin from 1878 to 1879 and then enrolled at the University of Leipzig to study comparative grammar and Indo-European languages. He published his first full-length book, *Memoire sur le systeme primitive des voyelles dans les langues indo-europeennes* (Thesis on the original system of vowels in Indo-European Languages), in 1878. Hailed by critics as a brilliant work, the book launched de Saussure's reputation as a new expert, contributing as it did to the field of comparative linguistics. The work also revealed an important discovery in the area of Indo-European languages that came to be known as de Saussure's laryngeal theory, which explained perplexing characteristics of some of the world's oldest languages. The theory would not enjoy widespread acceptance until the mid-20th century.

De Saussure also published *Remarques de grammaire et de phonetique* (Comments on Grammar and Phonetics) in 1878. He completed his doctoral dissertation, on the use of the absolute genitive in Sanskrit, and finished *summa cum laude* at the University of Leipzig in 1880.

Began Professional Career as Linguist

De Saussure's first professional work in his field was as a teacher at the École Practique des Hautes Études in Paris. He taught numerous languages there, including Lithuanian and Persian, which he had added to his immense repertoire. Meanwhile, he became an active member of the Linguistic Society of Paris and served as its secretary in 1882. He remained at the École Practique for 10 years, finally leaving in 1891 to accept a new position as professor of Indo-European languages and comparative grammar at the University of Geneva.

Historical records indicate that de Saussure had a great fear of publishing any of his studies until they were proven absolutely accurate. Thus, many of his works were not released during his lifetime and many of his theories have been explained in books by other authors. According to Robert Godel in an essay in *Cahiers Ferdinand de Saussure,* de Saussure was also said to be "terrified" when in 1906 the University of Geneva asked him to teach a course on linguistics, believing himself unequal to the job. Godel explained that de Saussure "did not feel up to the task, and had no desire to wrestle with the problems once more. However, he undertook what he believed to be his duty."

Course Notes Became Classic Linguistics Book

Between 1906 and 1911, de Saussure taught his course in general linguistics three times, remaining at the school until 1912. The class would become the basis for his classic and influential *A Course in General Linguistics,* which was published in 1916—three years after his death. Edited entirely by two of his students, Charles Bally and Albert Sechehaye, and based on de Saussure's class notes, the book received good reviews. However, the editors have been criticized for failing to show how their professor's ideas evolved and for not making clear that de Saussure rarely believed his innovative concepts to be fully formed.

Further controversy over the book has been generated by scholars who cite evidence that de Saussure was strongly influenced by his academic peers, W. D. Whitney and Michel Breal, suggesting that de Saussure's theories were not as original as they were once believed to be. Nevertheless, *A Course in General Linguistics* has become recognized as the basis of the modern theory of structuralism, and it established de Saussure as a founder of modern linguistics. Roy Harris, who published a 1983 translation of the *Course,* wrote in its introduction that the book is undoubtedly "one of the most far-reaching works concerning the study of cultural activities to have been published at any time since the Renaissance."

Proposed Revolutionary Theory of Language

A Course in General Linguistics sets out de Saussure's idea of language as a system of signs that evolves constantly, in which particular words do not have meaning. Rather, he explained, meaning happens only when people agree that a certain sound combination indicates an object or idea. This agreement, then, creates a "sign" for the object or idea. De Saussure believed that such signs comprise two parts: the signifier (what it sounds or looks like in vocal or graphic form) and the signified (the object the signifier represents). The relationship between the two parts of the sign, he explained, is hazy and the parts can be impossible to separate because of their arbitrary relationship. In other words, the representation of an object does not define it, and the relationship between signs changes constantly.

De Saussure argued that these signs "are unrelated to what they designate, and that therefore *a* cannot designate anything without the aid of *b* and vice versa, or in other words, that both have value only by the differences between them, or that neither has value, in any of its constituents, except through this same network of forever negative differences." One of the main tenets of the book was that often implicit agreement of meaning occurs at all levels of language, and that in order to achieve successful communication, speakers must be able to distinguish between both nuances of meaning and signs.

Explained Science of Language

Another relationship de Saussure examined in his book was that of *langue* and *parole,* in which *langue* is the conception of language as more than a system of names without social meaning and *parole* is simply the graphic or vocal manifestation of an utterance. A further dichotomy that he discusses is synchronic versus diachronic linguistics, where the former entails the study of language at a certain point and the latter looks at the changing state of language over time. After de Saussure's work became public, linguists, who had traditionally studied language from a historical (diachronic) perspective, were more inclined to experiment with synchronic studies. De Saussure had believed strongly in the value of the synchronic perspective for its ability to facilitate the analysis of language as more than a series of descriptive changes.

Despite his outstanding contributions to his field, de Saussure has been criticized for narrowing his studies to the social aspects of language, omitting the ability of people to manipulate and create new meanings. However, his application of science to his examination of the nature of language has had impacts on a wide range of areas related to linguistics, including contemporary literary theory; deconstructionism (a theory of literary criticism that asserts that words can only refer to other words and that tries to show how statements about any words subvert their own meaning); and structuralism (a method of analyzing a word by contrasting its basic structures in a system of binary opposition).

De Saussure is regarded by many as the creator of the modern theory of structuralism, to which his *langue* and *parole* ideas are integral. He believed that a word's meaning is based less on the object it refers to and more on its structure. In simpler terms, he suggested that when a person chooses a word, he does so in the context of having had the chance to choose other words. This adds another dimension to the chosen word's meaning, since humans instinctively base a word's meaning on its difference from the other words not chosen. De Saussure's theories on this subject, which flew in the face of the positivist research method of his day, laid the foundations for the structuralist schools in both social theory and linguistics.

Although by studying languages he at first seemed to have veered off the path established for him by his scientific ancestors, de Saussure was and still is widely regarded as a scientist. He perceived linguistics as a branch of science that he dubbed semiology (the theory and study of signs and symbols) and, through his *Course,* encouraged other linguists to view language not "as an organism developing of its own accord, but . . . as a product of the collective mind of a linguistic community."

De Saussure died from cancer at age 56 on February 22, 1913. Filling the void that de Saussure's dislike of publishing and early death caused, many of his works have been released posthumously, including *Recueil des publications scientifiques* (1921), *Manoscritti di Harvard* (1994), *Phonetique* (1995), *Linguistik und Semiologie*(1997), *Ecrits de linguistique generale* (2002), and *Theorie de sonantes: Il manoscritto de Ginevra* (2002).

Books

Contemporary Authors, Vol. 168, The Gale Group, 1999.
de Saussure, Ferdinand, *Course in General Linguistics,* translation, introduction, and annotation by Roy Harris, edited by Bally and Sechehaye and Riedlinger, Duckworth, 1983.
Malmkjaer, Kirsten, ed., *The Linguistics Encyclopedia,* 2nd ed., Routledge, 2002.

Periodicals

Cahiers Ferdinand de Saussure, Vol. 38, 1984; Vol. 39, 1985.

Online

"Ferdinand de Saussure," *Wikipedia Encyclopedia website,* http://en.wikipedia.org (December 27, 2003).
"Laryngeal Theory," *Wikipedia Encyclopedia website,* http://en .wikipedia.org (January 16, 2004).
"Saussure, Ferdinand de," *Marxists.org Internet Archive website,* http://www.Marxists.org (December 27, 2003). □

Grazia Deledda

A very popular writer in Italy in her time, Grazia Deledda (1871–1936) was a practitioner of Italian *verismo* or "realist" fiction in the late nineteenth and early twentieth centuries as well as a winner of the Nobel Prize for Literature. The setting for Deledda's novels and stories was her native Sardinia, and she is credited with singlehandedly creating a Sardinian literature out of the island's myths and stories.

Absorbed Family Stories and Island Legends

Grazia Maria Cosima Damiana Deledda was born on September 27, 1871 (some sources cite 1875), in Nuoro, a village on the island of Sardinia, the daughter of Giovanni and Francesca Cambosu Deledda. By Sardinian standards Giovanni Deledda, a landowner and miller, was well to do. Also a poet and a bibliophile, he briefly published his own newspaper. Yet it was Deledda's maternal uncle, a clergyman named Sebastiano Cambosu, who taught her to read and write before she was of school age; her first spoken language was Logudorese Sardo, an island dialect. Deledda's formal education ended in 1882 and thereafter she was largely self-taught through reading. The stories told by family and friends became Deledda's inspiration, and the myths, superstitions, and religious and civil rituals she grew up with later shaped her writing. However, the greatest influences on her writing were her close family and her understanding of the cycles of nature: its cycles of life and death, beauty and decay. Unlike many writers of her generation Deledda was not influenced by writer Gabriele D'Annunzio (1863–1938). If anything, her work harkens back to even older writers, such as Sicilians Luigi Capuana (1813–1915) and Giovanni Verga (1840–1922). The naturalism of Deledda's fiction was a direct descendant of their work. In fact Deledda admired Verga so much that, toward the end of her career, when she was awarded the Nobel Prize, she felt the Nobel committee had slighted him, and that he, not she, deserved the award. Among Deledda's other literary influences must be included Nestor Alessandro Manzoni (1785–1873), the first great Italian novelist; the decadent writer Ogo Tarchetti (1839–1869), and Antonio Fogazarro (1942–1911), in whose work psychology and metaphysics played an important role.

Deledda began writing at an early age. In about 1886 she submitted a short story, "Sangue Sardo" ("Sardinian Blood") to the Rome fashion magazine *Ultima Moda,* which published the piece. The story is about a love triangle involving a teenage girl, and when word got out that Deledda had written such a tale neighbors in her conservative village scorned her and even attacked her mother. Consequently, from this point, if Deledda's work appeared in Sardinian literary and political journals it was published under the pseudonyms G. Razia and Ilia di Sant' Ismael.

Deledda continued to submit work to *Ultima Moda* and published her first short-story collection, *Nell'azzurro,* in 1890. By then her first novel, 1888's *Memorie di Fernanda* ("Recollections of Fernanda"), was being read and reviewed. In quick succession followed the novels *Stella d'oriente* ("Star of the East"), 1890; *Amore regale* ("Regal Love") 1891; *Amori fatali* ("Fatal Loves"), 1892; and *Fior di Sardegna* ("The Flower of Sardinia"), 1892. *Fior di Sardegna* made Deledda famous, though her work—perhaps because it hit too close to home—was still shunned in her native Sardinia.

Moved to Rome

It has been said that Deledda's fatalism sprang from the experiences of her family. Her older sister, having become pregnant out of wedlock, hemorrhaged to death during a miscarriage, and one brother became a thief and a wastrel and the other, disappointed by his failures as an inventor, an alcoholic. The last blow was too much for Deledda's mother who sank into depression. Consequently, Deledda took charge of the family business. This lasted until January of 1900 when she married Palmiro Madesani. Deledda had met Madesani the previous fall on her first trip away from home, to Cagliari, the capital of Sardinia. Madesani was a civil servant and after their marriage he and Deledda lived in Rome.

In 1895 Deledda did research for, and contributed to, the scholarly publication *Tradizioni popolari di Nuoro* ("Popular Traditions of Nuoro"), a collection of the folklore of her native area. The year before she had published the novel *Anime oneste* ("Honest Souls"), a tale of two brothers, one of whom left Sardinia to study law and returned with a sense of unfulfilled entitlement, while the other stayed behind and made sacrifices for his brother's benefit. In 1896 Deledda published *La via del male* ("The Way of Evil"), which novelist Capuana read and praised highly. Her final works written in Sardinia were *La giustizia* ("Justice") and *Le tentazioni,* both published in 1899.

Moving to Rome, Deledda led something of a dual life. A shy and retiring woman by nature—the opposite of her tempestuous siblings—she was both a homemaker dedicated to raising a family and a successful writer. Yet some-

times these two roles clashed in the view of those who felt Deledda had never shed her provincialism. This was made clear when fellow Sicilian Luigi Pirandello penned the scandalous 1911 novel *Suo marito* ("Her Husband"), which satirized Deledda and Madesani. However, even Pirandello regretted his "joke," and was working on a revision 25 years later, near the end of his life.

Two Prolific Decades

In 1900 Deledda published *Il vecchio della montagna* ("The Old Man of the Mountain"). This was followed in 1902 by *Dopo il divozio* (*After the Divorce*), reissued in 1920 as *Naufraghi in porto.* The novel Deledda considered to be her breakthrough work was *Elias Portolú,* published in 1903. The popular book, translated into numerous European languages, brought Deledda a measure of fame outside her own country. *Elias Portolú* revolves around the Portolú family and the eponymous protagonist who has returned to Sardinia from two years in prison for cattle rustling only to fall in love with his brother's fiancée. The conflicts within Elias and the men he seeks out for advice are metaphors for the conflicts and divisions of Sardinia at the turn of the twentieth century. The novel, as Deledda's contemporary Joseph Spencer Kennard wrote in his 1906 study *Italian Romance Writers* "is an interesting study of religious sentiment in the primitive minds of the Sardinians, and a careful analysis of the relation between the mode of interpreting the Christian dogma and the patriarchal compactness of the household."

Deledda produced her best work between the years 1903 and 1920. It was also her most prolific period, and the body of work she produced places her more fully in the verismo tradition. She followed up *Elias Portolú* with the 1904 publication of *Cenere* ("Ashes"). This too was widely translated, affording Deledda a large readership outside of Italy. In 1916 *Cenere* was made into a film by Febo Mari, starring noted Italian stage actress Eleonora Duse (1858–1924). *Cenere* was Deledda's only novel that was made into a film and, coincidentally, the film adaptation of it was the only motion picture in which Duse appeared; she came out of retirement to act in the film, which was shot on location in Sardinia.

The novel *Nostalgie* ("Nostalgia") was published in 1905, the same year its author published her fifth collection of short stories, *I giuochi della vita* ("The Gambles of Life"). In 1907 Deledda published *L'ombra del passato* ("Shadow of the Past") and the following year *L'edera* ("The Ivy"). In 1912 she collaborated with Camillo Antona-Traversi to produce a dramatic version of *L'edera.* This was Deledda's only foray into playwriting, although in 1904 she had authored the dramatic sketch *Odio Vince* ("Hate Wins") and in 1924 wrote another titled *A sinistra* ("To the Left").

In 1913 Deledda published *Canne al vento* ("Reeds in the Wind"), considered among her greatest novels. It tells the story of the three Pintor sisters, impoverished noblewomen who are looked after and whose small farm is tended by their devoted servant, Efix. For his own part, Efix has a sin to atone: the murder of the Pintor sisters' father. Into this climate of stasis comes the sisters' ne'er-do-well nephew Giacinto, the son of a fourth sister who fled from her stifling family culture years before. Giacinto brings chaos, destruction, and change from the outer world, penetrating the calm of the insulated family and their acquaintances while Efix, as protector, watches, powerless to help. *Canne al vento* shows clearly how Deledda combined strands of realism and naturalism, in doing so portraying not only the people of her time but their religious beliefs and practices as well as their mythic—if not pagan— superstitions.

During the years of World War I (1914–1918) the once prolific Deledda published only three novels—*Le cope altrui* ("The Faults of Others"), 1914; *Marianna Sirca*, 1915; and *L'incendio nell'oliveto* ("The Fire in the Olive Grove"), 1918—and a collection of short stories released in 1915 as *Il fanciullo nascosto* ("The Hidden Boy"). In 1920 she released *La madre* (*The Mother*; also translated as *The Woman and the Priest*). In his foreword to the English-language translation of *La Madre*, D. H. Lawrence wrote that "the interest in the book lies, not in plot or characterization, but in the presentation of sheer instinctive life." Deledda's story involves three individuals: a priest and the young woman who falls in love with him, and the priest's mother. It is the mother, from a different generation, who must undergo the greatest change in the book and in the end make the greatest sacrifice.

Honored by Nobel Prize

Deledda's novels of the 1920s include *Il segreto dell'uomo solitario* ("The Secret of the Solitary Man"), 1921; *Il dio dei viventi* ("The God of the Living"), 1922; *La danza della collana* ("The Dance of the Necklace"), 1924; *La fuga in Egitto* ("The Flight into Egypt"), 1925; and *Annalena Bilsini*, 1927.

Deledda was honored with the 1926 Nobel Prize for Literature, becoming the second Italian to win the prize, after poet Giosuè Carducci (1835–1907), and the second woman to win it following Selma Lagerlöf (1858–1940). Among her compatriots who were also nominated that year were D'Annunzio and historian Guglielmo Ferrero. Pirandello would win the award eight years later. Years later it was hinted that Deledda's winning the Prize had to do with the fact that her work was admired by Italian dictator Benito Mussolini, but in fact she had been nominated many times previously, as early as 1913. In keeping with her retiring nature Deledda delivered one of the briefest acceptance speeches in Nobel Prize history.

Deledda's publications during the 1930s included *Il paese del vento* ("Land of the Wind"), 1931; *L'argine* ("The Barrier"), 1934; *Cosima*, 1937; and the 1939 short-story collection *Il cedro di Libano* ("The Cedar of Lebanon"), the last two published posthumously. These works reflect the autobiographical turn Deledda's fiction had taken, none more so than *Cosima*, whose protagonist suffers from breast cancer as did Deledda herself. *Cosima* was originally published in 1937 under the title *La chiesa della solitudine*, which means "The Church of Solitude."

Deledda wrote poetry in her youth, and throughout her adult career she wrote short fiction, publishhed 18 collec-

tions of stories in all. Among her other novels are *Sino al confine* ("Up to the Limit"), 1910; *Nel deserto* ("In the Desert"), 1911; and *Colombi e sparvieri* ("Doves and Falcons"), 1912. She died in Rome on April 15, 1936, and was buried in Sardinia at the foot of Monte Ortobene. A memorial church, la Chiesa della Solitudine, which shares the name of her last novel, was later built at the burial site in Deledda's honor.

Books

Deledda, Grazia, *Reeds in the Wind,* translated by Martha King, Italica Press, 1999.
———, *The Woman and the Priest,* translated by M. G. Steegman, foreword by D. H. Lawrence, Dedalus/Hippocrene, 1987.
Kennard, Joseph Spencer, *Italian Romance Writers,* Brentano's, 1906.

Online

"Grazia Deledda-Autobiography," Nobel e-Museum, http://www.nobel.se/literature/laureates/1926/deledda-autobio.html (December 3, 2003).
Hallgren, Anders, "Grazia Deledda: Voice of Sardinia," Nobel e-Museum, http://www.nobel.se/literature/articles/deledda/index.html (December 3, 2003). □

José Matias Delgado

Widely considered to be the father of El Salvador's independence movement in the early 1800s, José Matias Delgado (1768–1832) was elected president of the national constitutional assembly of the newly established United Provinces of Central America in 1823.

Delgado was born in the city of San Salvador, in what is now El Salvador, on February 24, 1767 (some sources say 1768). His devout parents, Pedro Delgado and Ana Maria de León, encouraged their son's early interest in entering the Roman Catholic priesthood. He attended the seminary in Guatemala and was ordained there in 1797, obtaining a doctoral degree in theology and civil and canonical rights at the same time. In 1797 he was appointed the vicar of San Salvador.

Opposition to Royal Rule Led to Politics

After spending more than a decade in the role for which he was trained, and in which by all accounts he was a commendable example, Delgado was inspired by his intense opposition to the imposition of colonial rule at the hands of the Spanish Empire to organize and lead a rebellion in 1811. In doing so, he became the central figure in the first Central American bid for independence, as well as the founding father of El Salvador's independence movement.

By the late 1700s wars in Europe had reduced the amount of ship traffic to Central America, contributing to a downturn in Salvadoran exports of indigo, one of the region's most lucrative crops. Meanwhile, Spanish control over its colonies in the Americas had weakened as a result of the aggressions against Spain by the French emperor Napoleon Bonaparte, leaving the city of San Salvador free to become an increasingly influential center of liberal—read anticolonial—opinion. The region's Creoles—those who could trace their heritage back to both Spain and native peoples and who were often members of the group of artisans and other businessman who could be considered part of the growing middle class—were at the core of the group agitating for increased economic and political freedom from Spain.

On November 5, 1811, Delgado led a rebellion of Creoles against Spanish rule, but this uprising was swiftly and brutally crushed by a military force sent from the seat of colonial government in Guatemala. Dominated by conservative forces loyal to Spain, Guatemala ruled over not only its own territories but also those of El Salvador, Costa Rica, Honduras, and Nicaragua. With many of his followers severely punished by the Guatemalan authorities, Delgado was temporarily rendered powerless, but the cleric refused to give up hope of an independent El Salvador.

First Failed Uprising Strengthened Resolve

With economic and military aid from the motherland decreasing, Spain's colonies weakened against the growing tide of political unrest. Hostilities between the government in Guatemala and the colony of El Salvador also had intensified as the two entities competed for recognition from religious authorities within the Spanish Church. Guatemala, already the seat of political power, had been elevated from a bishopric to an archdiocese—i.e., an archbishop rather than a bishop now held the country's top religious office—in 1743. San Salvador had neither designation. Following the rebellion of 1811, Delgado, who had become an influential liberal leader, was the top candidate for the position of bishop if it were to be created by Spanish decree. He freely advocated for the separation of El Salvador from Guatemala, believing that in separating from Guatemala in civil matters, San Salvador would more likely gain its own religious power.

Following the end of the Napoleonic Wars, political lines were being redrawn through out Europe, and colonial governments were undergoing fragmentation and collapse around the world. By 1820 the majority of Central Americans in the five-nation group were as adamantly opposed to Guatemalan rule as they were to remaining in the Spanish empire. Delgado was by this time managing San Salvador with fellow liberal Manuel José Arce. On September 29, 1821, Delgado and Arce signed a declaration declaring the independence from Guatemala of the city of San Salvador. They also proposed to two other regions that they should unite in opposition to the efforts of dictator Augustin de Iturbide to bring them under the sway of the newly created government of Mexico. Iturbide had been put in power by the Guatemalan council that also voted to create an independent Mexican empire, and Salvadoran Creoles had as little desire to be ruled by Mexico as they had by Spain via

Guatemala. Delgado's declaration of independence, which helped to ward off that possibility as well, is considered to be the first formal suggestion for a Central American confederation.

Elected Governor, then President

The people of San Salvador elected Delgado governor in 1821 and spent the next several years defending their city from takeover efforts by Mexico. Civil war broke out in 1822 when Guatemala demanded that El Salvador come under Mexican rule. Arce, leading San Salvadoran forces into battle against Guatemalan troops, defeated Guatemala and consolidated power over El Salvador. After the Mexican empire collapsed, on July 1, 1823, Delgado declared the region an independent republic "free and independent" of both Guatemala and Mexico. He and other leaders dubbed the new alliance the "United Provinces of Central America," or the Central American Republic. Acting as president, Delgado established a constituent assembly to frame a constitution for El Salvador and its allies as an independent nation.

Delgado completed the country's constitution on November 22, 1824. Comprising Guatemala, Honduras, Costa Rica, El Salvador, and Nicaragua, the new political union almost immediately encountered difficulties after Guatemala, El Salvador's old enemy, received 18 of the 41 seats in the new congress. Although the distribution was in accordance with the democratic principle of proportional representation, other countries in the alliance were displeased that Guatemala now had the most powerful voice. Such resentments and conflicts built until civil war broke out; one by one the states dropped out of the union, finally causing its collapse in 1838.

Brief Tenure as Bishop

In 1825 Delgado was elected by the constituent assembly to fill the country's newly created bishopric of San Salvador. However, Pope Leo XII, who had not approved of the establishment of a new bishopric in the region, nullified it in 1826. During the last years of his life, Delgado broke with former colleague Arce after Arce moved toward a more conservative political position. Still revered as the most tenacious patriot of his time, Delgado died on November 12, 1832. He was buried at El Rosario Church in the city of San Salvador.

Books

Booth, John A., and Thomas W. Walker, *Understanding Central America,* Westview Press, 1999.

Karnes, Thomas L., *The Failure of Union: Central America,* University of North Carolina Press, 1961.

Olsen, James, editor, *The Historical Dictionary of the Spanish Empire, 1402–1975* Greenwood Press, 1992.

Shepherd, William R., *The Hispanic Nations of the New World: A Chronicle of Our Southern Neighbors,* Yale University Press, 1921.

Online

"José Matias Delgado: Meritorious Founding Father of the Central American Nations," *El Salvador.org,* http://www .elsalvador.org/ (December 27, 2003). □

David Mandessi Diop

David Mandessi Diop (1927–1960), born in France to African parents, was a poet of the Negritude movement, rejecting colonialism and Western values and celebrating African people and culture. Although he died when he was only 33 years old, his poems, described as angry and revolutionary, yet hopeful and optimistic, are read and studied today in Africa and around the world.

Born in Exile

Diop was born in Bordeaux, France, in 1927, the third of five children. His mother was from Cameroon and his father was from Senegal, and as a child Diop traveled often between Europe and Africa. His mother raised the children in German-occupied, World War II France, after his father died. He attended primary school in Senegal and secondary school in France, where one of his teachers was Leopold Sedar Senghor (1906–2001), who would become president of Senegal in 1960.

Diop began to publish poetry while still in school; one of his influences was Aime Cesaire (born 1913), the writer and later statesman from Martinique who, with Senghor and others then in Paris, began the Negritude movement. When barely out of his teenage years, Diop saw several of his poems published in Senghor's *Anthologie de la nouvelle poesie negre at malgache* (1948), described in the Books and Writers website as "an important landmark of modern black writing in French." Most of Diop's poetry was written before he was 21 years old.

Diop spent most of his life in France. He suffered bouts of tuberculosis while growing up and spent months in sanitariums. At one time he planned to study medicine but changed his focus to liberal arts and obtained two baccalaureats and a licence es lettres in order to teach in secondary school. He married in 1950, and his wife, Virginia Kamara, is said to have inspired his poetry.

Returned to Africa in Adulthood

Diop returned to Africa with his wife and children in the 1950s, a time when tabloid publications were playing a sizable role in the development of African poetry. A journal called *Bingo* began publication in Senegal in 1953 and published poems by Diop and Senghor as well as other emerging African writers. Diop was also published in *Presence Africaine,* and he began to call for independence in Africa. His first (and only remaining) book of poems,

Coups de pillon (Hammer Blows and Pounding), was published in 1956.

Died Shortly after Guinea's Independence

Diop taught at the Lycee Delafosse in Dakar, Senegal, and then was a secondary-school principal in Kindia, Guinea. On Guinea's independence in 1958, the French colonial government departed in haste, leaving the country without a civil service. Diop and many other Africans volunteered to work in the new government under Ahmed Sekou Toure (who would remain in power until 1984). Diop was so employed on August 25, 1960, when he and his wife died in a plane crash over the Atlantic in the course of a flight between Dakar and France. The manuscript for his second book of poetry was also lost in the crash, meaning that the twenty-some poems of *Coups de pillon* are all that remain of his work. Even so, he is one of the most widely read poets of the Negritude and anticolonialist movements, and at least one school (le college David Diop in Senegal) bears his name.

Poetry Balanced Bitterness with Hope

The Negritude movement expressed opposition to colonialism and assimilation and lifted up African values and culture, and some of its writers expressed much bitterness and pessimism. Diop, on the other hand, is seen as more inclined to express hopefulness and comfort for exiles (actual and figurative). Wilfred Cartey, in *Whispers From A Continent,* notes, "within the body of each single poem Diop counterpoints notes of exile with recurrent chords of hope and return. Although within each poem harsh and gentle statements, negatives and positives, may alternate, Diop closes, almost without exception, on a note of optimism." Sometimes the return from exile is symbolic. Return may require combat and resistance; it may also be found in memories of Africa. African women represent for Diop the solace to be found in the return. An article in the Encyclopedia Britannica called Diop "the most extreme of the Negritude writers" because he rejected the idea that the colonial experience had done anything good for Africa. He is also said to have believed that political independence had to take place before Africa could come into its own culturally and economically.

Other themes found in Diop's work are "Africa's obstinate endurance and . . . power to survive. Thus in his poems," said Cartey, "there is always a movement away from the negative effects of oppression to the positive possibility of regeneration in the poetic discovery of truth. . . . Hope springs from combat."

Wrote Unsparingly of Colonials

In his poetry, Diop represents separation from Africa with language suggesting agony, monotony, howls, metallic sounds, and machine guns. Among his villains are the Catholic church and Europeans' false promises of friendship, along with their other lies. The colonials are called "mystificateurs," disguising the real effects of their inflicted culture with inflated or pious language. In "Vultures," Diop wrote that "civilization kicked us in the face" and "holy water slapped our cringing brows." The Europeans' efforts to "civilize" Africa are described as "the bloodstained monument of tutelage."

In "Negro Tramp," a poem dedicated to Aime Cesaire and based on Cesaire's description of an old man on a trolley, Diop uses the image of the derelict man as a symbol for Africa under colonial rule. The man is not to blame for his state; he walks "like an old, shattered dream/A dream ripped to shreds. . . . naked in your filthy prison/ . . . offered up to other people's laughter/Other people's wealth/Other people's hideous hunger." He expresses pity for Africans who have submitted to the colonials' will, where they are "squealing and hissing and strutting around in the parlors of condescension." "Africa," which Diop dedicated to his mother, begins with an exile's cry: "I have never known you/But my face is filled with your blood." The continent at first seems to be someone with a bent back breaking "under the weight of humiliation." But the continent reproaches the speaker in the poem, calling him "Impetuous son." Far from bowed and trembling, "this young and robust tree,/This very tree/Splendidly alone . . . /Is Africa, your Africa, growing again/Patiently stubbornly. . . ." The tree's fruit "Bears freedom's bitter flavor," while round about the tree lie "white and wilted flowers," perhaps a reference to the colonials.

Elsewhere, Africa is viewed as enduring forever and offering healing to Africans. In "A Une Danseuse Noire," which some consider his best poem, the black dancing woman represents Africa and its offer of regeneration. She inspires Africans to unchain the whole continent, and Diop promises her "For you we will remake Ghana and Timbuktu." He had already begun that mission when his life was cut short.

Books

Cartey, Wilfred, *Whispers from a Continent: The Literature of Contemporary Black Africa,* Random House, 1969.
The Negritude Poets, edited by Ellen Conroy Kennedy, Thunder's Mouth Press, 1975.

Online

Awhefeada, Sunny, "Development of Modern African Poetry," *The Post Express,* http://allafrica.com/stories/printable/200010210105.html (January 7, 2004).
"David Diop (1927–1960)," *Books and Writers,* www.kirjasto.sci.fi/diop.htm (December 18, 2003).
"Diop," *University of Florida,* http://web.uflib.ufl.edu/cm/africana/diop.htm (December 18, 2003).
"Diop, David," *Encyclopaedia Britannica Library,* http://www.britannica.com/eb/article?eu = 31053&tocid = 0&query = david%20diop&ct = (February 12, 2004).
Lees, Johanna, "A l'ecole David Diop a Liberte VI, la rentree sous le signe du deuil," *Le Soleil,* http://fr.allafrica.com/stories/printable/200210090561.html (January 7, 2004).
Lemmer, Krisjan, "Cultural," *Mail & Guardian,* http://allafrica.com/stories/printable/200103010425.html (January 7, 2004).
"Negritude," *Encyclopaedia Britannica Library,* http://www.britannica.com/eb/article?eu = 31053&tocid = 0&query = david%20diop&ct = (February 12, 2004). □

Doris Duke

American philanthropist and tobacco heiress Doris Duke (1912 –1993) inherited a large family fortune that enabled her to pursue a variety of interests in a lifetime rife with controversy and rumor. Although she lived a lavish lifestyle and was sometimes self-indulgent and eccentric, she was also an astute businesswoman and supported a number of public causes. When she was 21, she established the Independent Aid foundation, which later became the Doris Duke Charitable Foundation. It is estimated that she gave away more than $400 million during her lifetime, often as anonymous contributions. The Doris Duke Charitable Foundation continues to provide grants in programs supporting the arts, environment, medical research, and child welfare.

Early Life

Doris Duke was born on November 22, 1912, in New York City, the only child of James and Nanaline Holt Inman Duke. Her father, James Buchanan "Buck" Duke, founded the American Tobacco Company and, with brother Newton Duke, the Southern Power Company, later known as Duke Power, a Duke Energy Company. A wealthy businessman and philanthropist, James Duke contributed his name and money to various institutions. When he donated $40 million to Trinity College in North Carolina, his native state, the institution changed its name to Duke University.

Duke's family had made its fortune in tobacco in North Carolina. At the end of the Civil War, Duke's grandfather, Washington Duke, formed a cartel of farmers that developed into a thriving business that was inherited by James Duke, who formed the American Tobacco Company in 1890. The company was the largest tobacco trust in the United States until the government forced it to dissolve in 1911. James Duke then invested in real estate and started the Southern Energy Company. By the time Doris Duke was born, her father had amassed a fortune of nearly $80 million, and newspapers called her "the richest little girl in the world" and "million dollar baby."

James Duke doted on his daughter, and Doris Duke led a fairy-tale existence in her early life. She grew up in residences described as "American castles." These included a home on the Upper East Side of Manhattan; the "Rough Point" summer home in Newport, Rhode Island; and the "Duke Farms" in Hillsborough, New Jersey. When she was a child, Duke's chauffer also served as her bodyguard and was with her all of the time, because her very protective father had an obsessive fear that she would be kidnapped.

As a young girl, Doris was physically awkward and emotionally shy. By the time she was 13, she was almost six feet tall. She also had a prominent chin. As a result, she was

nation for the lives of the rich and famous. The newspapers especially liked to report about the extravagant and frivolous lifestyles of wealthy young heiresses to readers who were both captivated and repulsed. Because of their large fortunes, Barbara Hutton ("the poor little rich girl") and Duke were nicknamed the "Gold Dust Twins." Hutton enjoyed the coverage, but Duke loathed it, and she retreated even farther from the spotlight.

But the economic climate did instill in her a sense of philanthropic purpose. As she got older, she kept close tabs on her father's endowment to Duke University, making sure that his wishes were being carried out. The Duke family contributed a great amount to public programs, and Duke later managed the donations. When she was just 21, she established a foundation called Independent Aid, which later became the Doris Duke Foundation. It is estimated that she gave away more than $400 million in anonymous contributions throughout her life.

Married Politician James Cromwell

By the early 1930s, Duke had begun to chafe under the control of her domineering mother. She had wanted to attend college, but her mother would not allow it. Instead, Nanaline took Doris on a grand tour of Europe. In London, she presented her socially withdrawn daughter as a debutante.

In 1935, to free herself from the maternal domination, Duke married James H.R. Cromwell, an aspiring politician. She was 23 years old. News of the hasty marriage shocked everyone. The 39-year-old Cromwell, who was rich, but not as rich as Duke, reputedly was a socialite who had a taste for wealthy women. His ex-wife was Delphine Dodge, heiress to an automobile fortune.

The couple took a two-year honeymoon around the world and then settled in Hawaii, where they built a house that they called Shangri-La, after the mythical paradise made famous in James Hilton's 1933 novel *Lost Horizon*. When Cromwell ran for public office, Duke tried to campaign for him, but the press was more interested in her. This would strain their marriage. Eventually, Cromwell was appointed Minister to Canada, but Duke went back to Hawaii, to the privacy that she cherished so much.

Lost Her Only Child

In 1940, the couple had a child, Arden, who died only 24 hours after being born. Duke would mourn the loss the rest of her life. When doctors told her that she would not be able to have any more children, Duke was so distraught that she consulted with psychics in an attempt to contact the deceased daughter. The death of Arden further weakened her marriage. In three years, Duke and Cromwell would be divorced.

Meanwhile, rumors and speculation about Duke's behaviors and affairs, which would plague her all of her life, had began circulating in the press and high society. When Duke had become pregnant, it was suggested that any number of men besides Cromwell could have been the father.

very self conscious and felt extremely uncomfortable by all of the public attention that the family name drew to her.

Inherited Bulk of Family Fortune

In the winter of 1925, when Doris was 12, James became ill with pneumonia and lingered until October. When he died, he reportedly told her, "Trust no one." It was advice she seemed to ignore often as she grew older.

When James Duke died, he left most of his fortune to his daughter. The family fortune had been significantly reduced by the stock market crash of 1929. Still, Doris inherited $30 million. Doris' mother, Nanaline, only received a modest trust fund, which strained the mother-daughter relationship. The rest went to the Duke Endowment, a foundation James established to serve the people of the Carolinas. When Doris Duke was 14, she sued her mother to stop her from selling family assets.

For years, rumors would circulate about the Duke family and, later, especially about Doris. One that gained currency around this time is that Nanaline, seeking to hasten James' death, left her ill husband locked in the bedroom for days with the windows opened.

Developed Philanthropic Purpose During Depression

Unlike the rest of the country, Duke was unaffected by the deprivations of the Great Depression. She was discomforted however, by the news coverage that families like hers' received. The press and the public developed a fasci-

Went to Work in World War II

During World War II, Doris worked in a canteen for sailors in Egypt. True to her philanthropic instincts, she only took a salary of one dollar a year. Pampered as a child, Duke now found that working was fun. She would later say that she felt that this was the most useful period of her life.

In 1945, she began a short-lived writing career when she became a foreign correspondent for the International News Service, reporting from different cities across the war-ravaged Europe. After the war, she moved to Paris and continued to work, writing for the magazine *Harper's Bazaar*.

By this time, Duke had outgrown her physical awkwardness and was an attractive women. She had relationships with some well-known men. Among them were writer Louis Bromfield, British Parliament member Alec Cunningham-Reid, actor Errol Flynn, United States Army General George Patton, and surfing champion Duke Kahanamoku.

In Europe, she met the man who would become her second husband, Porfirio Rubirosa, a Dominican diplomat and reputed playboy and fortune hunter. Duke was fascinated by his reputation as a great lover. They had an affair that quickly led to a marriage proposal. Before the wedding, the U.S. Government drew up a reportedly iron-clad prenuptial agreement for Duke. Not surprisingly, the marriage lasted only a year. Duke would never marry again.

Pursued Varied Interests

Leaving her bad marriages behind, Duke entered a period in her life when she traveled around the world, pursuing a variety of interests. She traveled to exotic places and mixed with different cultures. She met with Indian mystics and African witch doctors, and wandered with Massai warriors in Africa.

Art became one of her passions and, throughout her travels, she collected treasures from all parts of the world. She acquired priceless collections of Islamic and Southeast Asian art. Her tastes could be rather eccentric. She built a complete Thai village at her 2700-acre New Jersey farm.

She also became interested in the performing arts. She liked music and became an accomplished jazz pianist and wrote songs. Also, she took up belly dancing and even spent weekends singing in a black gospel choir at Southern Baptist meetings in the United States.

While Duke globe trotted, she employed a permanent staff of over 200 to oversee her five homes, which now also included a hillside mansion in Beverly Hills called "Falcon Lair" (the former home of silent movie star Rudolph Valentino).

Although her lifestyle was unconventional and her behavior sometimes eccentric, Duke was very responsible when it came to her inheritance. She had good business sense and, during her lifetime, Duke quadrupled her father's fortune.

In addition to her artistic pursuits, she developed a passion for restoration. Also she became an environmentalist and had a keen interest in conservation and horticulture.

Her homes reflected her interests. At the Jersey farm, she designed elaborate indoor display gardens that reflected various regions of the world. In 1964, she opened them to the public. She also became involved in restoration projects in Newport, one of America's oldest towns.

In 1968, Duke founded the Newport Restoration Foundation to restore some of Newport's oldest structures and to revitalize tourism. It was speculated that this was an appeasement for something that had happened in that town two years before. In October 1966, Duke ran over and killed her interior decorator, Edward Tirella, with her car as he was trying to open the gate to her mansion. Duke claimed her foot accidentally slipped to the accelerator. Tirella was dragged across the street and crushed against a tree. The circumstances were suspicious and the rumors started to fly. According to stories, Duke and Tirella were lovers, and Tirella had planned on leaving her. An investigation into the incident was dropped a week later. Police called it an "unfortunate accident." Fueling more rumors and speculation, the Chief of Police retired a month later and Tirella's family received a large sum of money after a civil suit.

Afterward, Duke became even more reclusive, tending to her charities and supporting the performing arts. She continued buying more art, and her collection became increasingly odd. She bought an old airplane from a Middle Eastern businessman. As part of the deal, Duke had to adopt two camels. She named them "Baby" and "Princess," and the animals lived at Rough Point, where they were free to eat all the vegetation on the grounds.

Adopted Chandi Heffner

As Duke aged, her life became even more bizarre. Her close circle of friends would include a strange cast of characters. In 1985, she met Chandi Heffner, a 32-year-old Hari Krishna devotee. Duke believed that Heffner was the reincarnation of her daughter, Arden. In a peculiar arrangement, in 1988, the 76-year-old Duke legally adopted the 35-year-old Heffner and bought her a $1 million ranch in Hawaii, where the two lived together as mother and daughter. For three years, Duke doted on her "daughter." She even named Heffner in her will. However, the two often fought.

During this period, Heffner's boyfriend, James Burns, became Duke's bodyguard. Also, Heffner introduced Duke to Bernard Lafferty who, according to accounts, was a poor and unintelligent Irishman who liked to drink. Previously, he had worked as a butler for singer Peggy Lee. Now, he became very close to Duke, and he became her butler.

Suffered Declining Health

Duke's friends, family, and acquaintances viewed this as a very disturbing development. Lafferty became very fixated on his new employer and began to isolate her. As Duke's health grew worse in her later years, Lafferty would prevent visitors from seeing her. He also interfered with her staff, preventing them from performing basic functions as he watchfully hovered over Duke.

In 1991, Duke, who was now 79 years old, ended her relationship with Heffner and reversed the adoption. The year before, in a suspicious incident, Duke suffered a fall and was knocked unconscious in her Hawaii home. Lafferty claimed the Heffner and Burns were plotting against Duke. He took his employer to her home in Beverly Hills. At this point, Duke suffered from severe depression.

Back in California, Lafferty encouraged Duke to have several operations, including a face lift and knee replacement surgery. The knee surgery was unsuccessful. Duke suffered constant pain and was confined to a wheelchair. In the months before she died, Duke was in and out of hospitals and was heavily sedated with morphine pain killers.

She died in her bed at Falcon Lair on October 28, 1993, a few weeks short of her 81st birthday. She died without family or friends nearby. Only Lafferty was at her side. Those who knew Duke believed her death came as a result of overmedication. Suspicion was cast on Lafferty, as he had previously dismissed and replaced Duke's physicians. However, no autopsy was performed. Duke was cremated within 24 hours and her ashes scattered into the Pacific Ocean.

At the time she died, Duke's estate was worth over one billion dollars. In her will, she left the majority of her estate to the Doris Duke Charitable Foundation. To everyone's astonishment and displeasure, Lafferty was named trustee of the Foundation. He also was given a payment of over $4 million dollars and a lifetime annuity of $500,000. Although the Foundation's directors carefully gave out the monies as stipulated in Duke's will, Lafferty began to spend money lavishly.

Eventually, he was ousted from control after Duke's lawyers accused him of mishandling her fortune. A California court deemed Lafferty unfit to handle such an important charity. Lafferty died in November 1996, reportedly depressed and bitter.

Suspicions about Duke's death lingered, but, in 1996, after an 18-month investigation, the Los Angeles district attorney's office concluded there was no credible evidence to suggest that Duke had been murdered.

Charitable Legacy

The Doris Duke Charitable Foundation continues to support social, cultural, and health-related programs today. Headquartered in New York and governed by an eight-member Board of Trustees, its mission is "to improve the quality of people's lives through grants supporting the performing arts, wildlife conservation, medical research and the prevention of child maltreatment, and through preservation of the cultural and environmental legacy of Doris Duke's properties." Specifically, it awards grants in four programs: arts, environment, medical research, and child abuse prevention.

By the end of 2002, DDCF had approved 363 grants totaling more than $335 million to nonprofit organizations throughout the United States. The foundation expected to approve approximately $14 million in new grants in 2003.

The foundation also oversees Duke's properties, parts of which are open to the public.

Periodicals

The Associated Press, February 28, 1996.
Rhode Island Roads Magazine, January 2003.

Online

"About Doris Duke," *About.com,* http://gonewengland.about
.com/gi/dynamic/offsite.htm?site = http%3A%2F%2Ffdncenter
.org%2Fgrantmaker%2Fdorisduke%2Fabout.html
%23dorisduke (January 8, 2003).
"Background on Duke Farms—Hillsborough, New Jersey," *The Foundation Center,* http://fdncenter.org/grantmaker/
dorisduke/dukefarmsbgrd.pdf (January 8, 2003).
"Doris Duke," *Biography.com,* http://www.biography.com/
search/article.jsp?aid = 9542083&search = (January 8, 2003).
"Doris Duke," *Divas—The Site,* http://home2.planetinternet.be/
verjans/Society_Divas/doris_duke_a.htm (January 8, 2003).
"Doris Duke," *Gene@star—Famous Geneology,* http://www
.geneastar.org/en/bio.php3?choix = duke (January 8, 2003).
□

Tan Dun

Academy-award winning composer Tan Dun (born 1957) grew up in Communist China during the peak years of Premier Mao Zedong's Cultural Revolution. Although he never had formal music training as a young child, when Dun first heard the music of such Western legends as Bach, Beethoven, and Mozart at the age of 19 his life suddenly gained direction and he began his successful career in the symphony.

Dun was born on August 18, 1957, in Simao, Hunan Province, the son of Tan Xiang Qiu and Fang Qun Ying. When Dun was a teenager he was sent to a commune to work in the rice paddies. Chairman Mao, who now led the country in a communist-inspired cultural reawakening since taking over the government in 1949, determined that all China's educated young people must be given the experience of peasants to better understanding their way of life. While living two years in the peasant village to which he was assigned Dun played the violin, began to collect peasant folk songs and music, and became the village's musical conductor. Recalling that period, Dun explained to Martin Steinberg in *Asian Week:* "For a long time, I would play the violin and have only three strings. That's because I didn't have a violin teacher. During the Cultural Revolution, first of all, it was not allowed to teach Western music. Secondly, I didn't have money to buy the extra string."

Due to a tragic accident that resulted in the death of many musicians affiliated with the Peking opera troupe, Dun was summoned to join the troupe, remaining in Peking for nearly a year and a half. That opportunity gave way to an even greater challenge in 1978 when he was one of 30

students chosen from thousands of applicants to attend the recently reopened Central Conservatory. Mao had died in September of 1976, and life in China was gradually beginning to change as many old-school communists fell from power. Western culture—including music and other arts—was slowly revealed to the Chinese people, and at the conservatory where Dun studied with Zhao Xindao and Li Yinghai, he was finally introduced to the classical music of Europe.

Emerged as a Serious Composer

A visit to China by the Philadelphia Orchestra during the relaxation of cultural barriers in the late 1970s was Dun's first Western-music experience. Exposed to the works of composers such as Bela Bartok, Dun studied with several guest conductors who visited Peking, including Goehr, Crumb, Henze, Takemitsu, and Yun. Tun told Steinberg that, once he started listening to Western music, he "suddenly realized that kind of music should be my future." His talent and passion evident in his 1980 symphony *Li Sao,* Dun stood out from the other students in his class. Unfortunately, he also became embroiled in controversy when his music spawned debates among the government and public officials, who determined in 1983 that it was "spiritual pollution." That same year he won second place in the international Weber prize competition for his "String Quartet: Fen Ya Song." Dun was the first Chinese musician to win that honor since 1949. His 1985 work, "On Taoism," caused even more political controversy, despite being

hailed as one of the most significant classical works ever created by a Chinese composer.

In 1986 Dun moved to New York City to complete his studies in music at Columbia University. Studying alongside classmates Chou Wen-chung, Mario Davidovsky, and George Edwards, Dun also often played his violin on the streets of Greenwich Village to help pay for tuition and rent. He received his doctorate in musical arts from Columbia in 1993. By the time he finished his studies Dun had won several awards, and in 1988 his music had been featured on a British Broadcasting Corporation (BBC)-sponsored Chinese music festival in Glasgow, Scotland. Other honors included an orchestral piece commissioned by the Institute for Development of Intercultural Relations through the Arts in 1988 and Japan's prestigious Suntory Prize in 1992.

Nature Inspired Work

According to Joanna C. Lee in the *New Grove Dictionary of Music and Musicians,* Dun once described himself as a composer "swinging and swimming freely among different cultures." From his childhood making music with found objects and his solid grounding in Chinese philosophy, Lee noted that, in addition to those critical pieces of his genius, it has been the inspiration of nature that has joined forces with Dun's cultural legacy to add the qualities of "timelessness, spirituality, and mysticism" to his musical compositions.

Several of Dun's compositions serve as tributes to the simplicity of nature, among them his 2002 work, "Water Passion after St. Matthew," the fourth and final sequence in a major musical commemoration of the 250th anniversary of Bach's death. Barry Kilpatrick, reviewing the composition in the *American Record Guide,* noted that "Water permeates the work's instrumentation and is a striking visible element of its staging." In performance, a total of 17 lit bowls of water form a cross. A mixed chorus, soprano and bass soloists, violin and cello soloists, and three percussionists are positioned around the cross. The percussionists each play various water instruments, including shakers, tubes, phones, and gongs. Choir members carry Tibetan finger cymbals and smooth stones specified by the composer as coming "preferably from the sea or river." The vocal soloists, according to Kilpatrick, had to master non-Western techniques that included overtone singing, with the bass holding a low C for a significant period of time. The string soloists perform with pitch bending, microtones, and altered tuning systems heard in traditional Chinese orchestras. Dun's two-part "Water Passion," Kilpatrick concluded, is one of the most amazing works of art the critic had ever experienced. On the *Sony Classical Music Web* site a contributor indicated that the composer uses water as a "metaphor for the unity of the eternal and the external, as well as a symbol of baptism, renewal, re-creation and resurrection."

Hollywood Came Calling

Dun's first film score was composed for the 1997 film *Fallen,* starring Denzel Washington. On his second film project, *Crouching Tiger, Hidden Dragon,* Dun worked closely with director Ang Lee to capture the traditional 19th-century Ching dynasty elements that reflect the martial-arts film's themes of love and violence. Following rave reviews at the 2000 Cannes Film Festival, the movie thrilled audiences in cities throughout the world. Lee commented that he created his film as a musical in which Dun's composition is interwoven with the story. In addition to a Academy Award in the United States, the film score won Dun other awards, including a Grammy award and the Anthony Asquith Award of the British Academy of Film and Television Arts.

Dun was also asked to create the film score for director Zhang Yimou's historical action film *The Heroes,* after the two worked together on a project for the Beijing 2008 Olympic Games. For his efforts with Yimou, Dun won an award for best original film score when the 22nd Hong Kong Film Awards were present on April 6, 2003.

Nurtured by Symphonic Music

Although Dun has enjoyed his work for film, symphonic music remains his true love. On July 1, 1997, when Great Britain relinquished control of Hong Kong to mainland China, Dun's commissioned symphony, "Heaven Earth Mankind" joined Eastern and Western traditions. The work featured bianzhong bronze chime bells, an important musical instrument in ancient China. According to a contributor to *China Radio International Online,* the symphony represents a "dramatic montage" that embodies the "panorama of human history and envisages a new global community."

Dun has focused his musical talent in countless ways, and has created a legacy that represents his boundless energy and creativity. Among his original operas are "Nine Songs," 1989; "Marco Polo," 1993–94; "Peony Pavilion," 1998; and "Tea," 2002. His orchestral works include "Feng Ya Song," 1983; "Eight Colors for String Quartet," 1986–88; "Silk Road," 1989; "Soundshape," 1990; "The Pin," 1992; "Death and Fire: Dialogue with Paul Klee (German artist, 1879–1940)," 1992; and the experimental performance work "The Map: Concerto for Cello, Video and Orchestra," 2003.

Chinese Roots Remained Strong

In late November of 2003, Dun made a special trip to his home province in central China for a performance of "The Map: Saving Disappearing Music Traditions." Having premiered the piece earlier that year with the Boston Symphony, the Shanghai Orchestra performed in Hunan for an audience of 3,000, composed mostly of ethnic Miao and Tujia people. Some had never heard an orchestra perform, although they were familiar with the strains of traditional Chinese music that weave throughout the work. The piece itself was inspired by Dun's 1999 tour of Hunan, which is home to many of China's ethnic minorities.

According to Lee, Dun's "Orchestral Theatre" sequence provided "perhaps the best summary" of the composer's concerns in the 1990s. As quoted by Lee, Dun maintained that the cycle aims to "restore music's place 'as an integral part of spiritual life, as ritual as shared participa-tion' through the 'dramatic medium' of the orchestra." In this work, as in other compositions by Dun, the composer reflects on his Chinese roots with the enhanced perspective he has acquired while living in the United States. In an interview for *China Daily online,* in July 2001, Dun said that, "As a Chinese-born musician, I am always willing to cooperate with any outstanding and ambitious Chinese artist to promote Chinese culture. I will surely get my part done best in this mission."

World Travels Continued

In 1994 Dun married Jane Huang, and the couple had one son. While he made his home in New York City and traveled frequently to China, Dun also continued to appear around the United States and throughout the world at music festivals, including the Tanglewood Contemporary Music Festival in Massachusetts, where he served as artistic director; the 2000 Barbican Centre's Fire Crossing Water Festival in London, England; and the 2002 Oregon Bach Festival, where he was composer-in-residence. *Xinhua News Agency* writer Xiao Hong commented that the composer was "born with an enterprising spirit," that had taken him from Hunan to Beijing to Manhattan, "learning to transcend the musical genres of Hunan Drum Opera, Peking Opera and western music." Dun's response to all of this was to note that, "If there is a conservatory on the Moon, I will definitely apply to go there and learn Moon melodies."

Books

New Grove Dictionary of Music and Musicians, Macmillan, 1980.

Periodicals

American Record Guide, March–April 2003; July–August 2003.
AsianWeek, February 16, 2001.
China Daily, July 2, 2001.
China Post, December 25, 2000.
Columbia East Asian Review, Fall 1997.
South China Morning Post, April 7, 2003.
Sydney Morning Herald, August 24, 2003.

Online

"Authentic 'World' Composer," *China Radio International,* http:/web12.cri.com.cn (December 13, 2003).
"Dun," *Sony Classical Web site,* http://www.sonyclassical.com/artists/dun/adhome.html (December 13, 2003).
Grawemeyer Awards Web site, http://www.grawemeyer.org/music/previous/98.htm (December 13, 2003).
"Tan Dun," *G. Schirmer Web site,* http://www.schirmer.com/composers/tan-bio.html (December 13, 2003).
"Tan Dun: Profile," *British Broadcasting Corporation Web site,* http://www.bbc.co.uk/bbcfour/music/features/tan-dun.shtml (December 13, 2003). □

Gerald Malcolm Durrell

British naturalist and conservationist Gerald Malcolm Durrell (1925–1995) devoted his life to the preservation of wild animal species and in 1958

created a wildlife preserve on the Channel Island of Jersey dedicated to scientific research and protecting endangered species.

C alling himself a "champion of small uglies," British naturalist Gerald Durrell had a single goal: to care for and save from extinction as many species of animals as possible. Beginning his career exploring Africa and South America, he went on to organize captive-breeding programs for endangered creatures and find ways of introducing these animals back into the wild.

Advocate for Endangered Wildlife

In 1958, on the Channel Island of Jersey off the coast of England, Durrell founded the Jersey Zoological Park, which remains dedicated to supporting conservation and animal protection efforts while also engaging in scientific research. A prolific and popular author, Durrell wrote many books that reflect his love of animals, although the naturalist often admitted that his main motivation for writing was to fund his work on behalf of endangered species.

In his books and his many radio and television appearances, Durrell was an eloquent spokesman for wildlife. As quoted on the Raptor Conservation website, Durrell once commented: "Year by year, all over the world, various species of animals are being slowly but surely exterminated in their wild state, thanks directly or indirectly to the interference of mankind. . . . In addition . . . a great number of animal species . . . because they are small and generally of no commercial or touristic value, are not receiving adequate protection. To me the extirpation of an animal species is a criminal offence, in the same way as the destruction of anything we cannot recreate or replace, such as . . . a work of art by . . . Rembrandt or the Acropolis.''

Early Love of Animals

Born in Jamshedpur, India, on January 7, 1925, Gerald Malcolm Durrell was the youngest child born to Lawrence Durrell Sr., a British civil engineer hired to help lay out and construct India's first modern bridge and railroad system, and his wife, Louisa Florence (Dixie) Durrell. The affluent Durrell household instilled a creative drive from which each of the Durrell children benefited: brother Lawrence Jr. became a noted writer, brother Leslie an artistr and sister Margot a designer.

The death of Durrell's father in 1927 forced the family to return to Bournemouth, England. Louisa Durrell traveled frequently during the 1930s, exposing her children to life in Great Britain and Europe. Durrell was educated by private teachers as his family settled temporarily in Greece, Italy, France and Switzerland, and his lessons in tedious subjects such as geography were often given out of doors in order to gain the undisciplined boy's attention.

Durrell's love of wild creatures was apparent from an early age, As he later recalled in his book *A Bevy of Beasts,* "at the age of two I made up my mind quite firmly and unequivocally that the only thing I wanted to do was study animals. Nothing else interested me." As a young teen, he spent five years on Corfu, a Greek island, and there developed his skills as a naturalist while accompanying family friend and scientist Theodore Stephanides on many local expeditions. He also spent many days alone among the island's tide pools and hills, searching for new creatures, studying the landscape and often bringing home new "pets"—anything from scorpions, woodlice or birds to tortoises, owls or donkeys. These frequently became part of the family much to the dismay of Durrell's sister. Sensing young Gerald's untamed nature, his older brother Lawrence encouraged Durrell to read and develop his writing by chronicling his discoveries.

Relocated to London after the start of World War II, Durrell discovered the London Zoo and in 1945 became a student keeper at the Whipsnade Zoological Society Park, a zoo located in Bedfordshire that was dedicated to the breeding and preservation of rare species, many of which were almost extinct. During his year at Whipsnade, which would later be immortalized in his book *Beasts in My Belfry,* he fed and groomed animals and cleaned cages and devised a system of recording the behavior of the animals he cared for. He soon began to compare his own observations with those of published research findings. The more he read the findings of biologists and naturalists, the more he realized the threatened status of many of the world's creatures.

In 1946 Durrell inherited his share of the family fortune, 3,000 pounds. Feeling that his work at the zoo was done, he decided to bring to English zoos some of the unusual creatures of the world, so that others may appreciate them. He left Bedfordshire and made the first of many trips into regions where there were many endangered species. Traveling to British-controlled Cameroon, he hiked deep into the west African rain forest and collected so many species of reptiles, birds and mammals that it required over 100 cages and crates to transport them. A second trip to the Bafut region of Cameroon followed, and in 1949 Durrell traveled to South America and hiked into the jungles of mountainous British Guiana (now Guyana).

Writing Supported Work

Durrell quickly spent his inheritance on these expeditions, and zoos were unable to compensate him. In 1951 he married Jacqueline Sonia Rasen and needed a source of regular income, which he found in writing.

Drawing on the advice of his brother Lawrence, who had made a mark as a noted poet and novelist, Durrell completed his first book, a description of his first trip to Cameroon, published in 1953 as *The Overloaded Ark.* Although he had not been formally schooled in writing, Durrell was a natural storyteller, and his passion for his subject was clear in every line.

The success of the book prompted a second effort, *The Bafut Beagles,* which took readers on Durrell's second sojourn into Cameroon, and a third, a chronicle of his South American trip titled *Three Tickets to Adventure.* Popular with English readers, the books were translated into several other languages.

During the remainder of his career, Durrell made many other expeditions, including trips to Argentina, Mexico, Australia and Nigeria, and also wrote several more books, including novels and children's books. He also drew on his own unconventional upbringing in his 1956 best-selling autobiography *My Family and Other Animals,* which was eventually adapted as a 12-part television series that aired in England and the United States in the late 1980s. However, writing was merely a means to an end; as he once admitted to an interviewer for the *Christian Science Monitor,* "I try to get it over with as quickly as possible. . . . I write for money—it provides me with the wherewithal to do the things I really like doing, which is rushing off to Mexico to catch volcano rabbits."

Established Wildlife Preserve

By the mid-1950s Durrell had made major contributions to a number of English zoos, including more than 25 new species for the London Zoo. However, he became increasingly attached to the creatures he collected, and decided to create his own zoo devoted to unusual wildlife. He hoped the zoo would educate the public about the plight facing many species. Although he wanted to locate his zoo in England, local zoning and land-use restrictions made the task impossible.

With a promised advance of 25,000 pounds from his publisher, Rupert Hart-Davis, and while searching for the perfect location, he began accumulating animals, storing creatures at his mother's home until the zoo was completed. Fortunately for Louisa Durrell, her son found 35 acres on the tiny island of Jersey, one of the Channel Islands, British territory located off the coast of northwestern France. The zoo headquarters was located in a large 16th-century house located on the property.

Despite the relative remoteness of its location, the Jersey Zoological Park was everything Durrell hoped it would be. As word spread after it opened in 1958, visitors became more frequent, and by 2000 more than 200,000 people were visiting the zoo each year. In 1963 Durrell founded the Jersey Wildlife Preservation Trust to operate the zoo and oversee efforts dedicated to aiding threatened wildlife. In 1973 he expanded his efforts still further, creating the Wildlife Preservation Trust International, headquartered in Philadelphia.

Durrell remained active as a naturalist for the remainder of his life. After a divorce from Rasen in 1979, he married American zoologist and conservationist Lee Wilson McGeorge. Together they worked to raise threatened creatures in captivity and release them back into the wild to reinforce existing populations. In addition, his involvement in animal care and treatment standards improved the way creatures were treated while in captivity.

Goodbye to Wilderness

In 1990 Durrell set out on his final expedition in search of unique species, making a four-month trip to Madagascar. There he captured a rare species of lemur, the aye-aye. The trip, on which Durrell was accompanied by his wife and a film crew from BBC-TV, resulted in the 1993 book *The Aye-Aye and I: A Rescue Expedition in Madagascar,* as well as an award-winning television film titled *The Island of the Aye-Aye.* By then Durrell had become a fixture on British nature programming. His shows, such as *The Amateur Naturalist,* which focused on wildlife in Malaysia, Australia and New Zealand, resulted in the books *How to Shoot an Amateur Naturalist* and *The Drunken Forest.*

With over 30 best-selling books to his credit, Durrell was both a beloved author and a respected naturalist. He was a member of the Royal Geographical Society, the Fauna Preservation Society, the American Zoo-parks Association, and the Zoological Society of London. Among many honors he received during his lifetime were honorary degrees from Yale University, the University of Kent, and the University of Durham, and he was made an Officer of the Order of the British Empire.

Despite his many successes, Durrell's efforts to alter the course of animal evolution were sometimes controversial. He also came to see the backlash from his efforts. While his book recounting his youth in Greece, *My Family and Other Animals,* provided much-needed funds to operate his island wildlife refuge, its popularity also resulted in an increase of visitors to Corfu, changing forever the character of that island paradise. He also realized that by entering remote wilderness regions he was altering them forever. However, his contributions far outweighed any negative effects; as Robert Rattner noted in *International Wildlife,* Durrell "was a pioneer in captive breeding of endangered wildlife at a time when few zoos even gave the idea lip service." Following a liver transplant, Durrell died on January 30, 1995, at age seventy, in St. Helier on the Chanel Islands, leaving his wife, Lee, to continue his work at the renamed Durrell Conservation Trust.

Books

Durrell, Gerald, *A Bevy of Beasts,* Simon & Schuster, 1973.
———, *Birds, Beasts, and Relatives,* Viking, 1969.
———, *The Garden of the Gods,* Collins, 1978, published as *Fauna and Family,* Simon & Schuster, 1979.
———, *My Family and Other Animals,* Hart-Davies, 1959.
Hughes, David, *Himself and Other Animals: A Portrait of Gerald Durrell,* Hutchinson, 1997.

Periodicals

Geographical, January 2002.
International Wildlife, July–August 1988.
Smithsonian, August 1993.
Spectator, July 6, 1956; October 28, 1960; December 11, 1976.

Online

Durrell Wildlife Conservation Trust, http://www.durrellwildife .org/ (December 6, 2003).
Raptor Conservation, http://www.raptor.uk/com/Features (December 6, 2003). □

E

Leo Esaki

Leo Esaki (born 1925) was one of three winners of the Nobel Prize in Physics in 1973. Esaki was honored for his 1957 pioneering work in electron tunneling in semiconducting materials, which led to his creation of the Esaki diode, or tunnel diode. This technology helped advance research in optical and wireless communication devices. Esaki left Japan in 1960 to conduct research on semiconductor superlattice structures at IBM in the United States, a country more open to scientific research than Japan. He returned to his home country in 1992 to serve as president of Tsukuba University where he encouraged collaborative research between graduate students and industrial research labs.

Turned His Attention to Physics

Reiona "Leo" Esaki was born in Osaka, Japan, the son of Soichiro, an architect, and Niyoko. He attended Third High School, similar to a junior college, in Kyoto. Interestingly, this school produced all three of Japan's Nobel Prize winners in Physics, a testament to its development of scientific talent. Esaki then attended the University of Tokyo, majoring in physics, and earning his MS degree in 1947.

World War II and an interest in understanding how the world works made Esaki first want to do research in nuclear physics. However, Japan, which was rebuilding after the war, did not have the equipment necessary to conduct tests in this field. With a desire to participate in his country's rebuilding, Esaki switched to industrial research and the field of solid-state physics, or the study of semiconductors, which was gaining attention from the accomplishments of pioneer William Shockley.

After he graduated, Esaki joined Kobe Kogyo Corporation as a researcher and stayed for nearly nine years. In 1956, he became chief physicist at Tokyo Tsushin Kogyo, a forerunner of what is today Sony Corporation, serving for four years. At the same time he worked toward his Ph.D. thesis at Tokyo University.

Discovered Tunnel Diode

As part of a small research group at Sony in 1957, Esaki experimented with semiconductor materials and invented what is called the Esaki tunnel diode. By studying p-n junctions, or barriers, made of heavily doped (meaning they have high impurity levels) germanium (Ge) and silicon (Si), Esaki discovered that electric current could be made to cross those junctions. When he applied a voltage to a semiconductor junction, electrons in the current jumped over the junction, resulting in a quantum mechanical "tunneling" effect. He was surprised to learn that the electrons' resistance to the barrier decreased with the intensity of the voltage, the opposite of what was expected.

This tunnel diode allowed electrons to pass through junctions that were only a hundred atoms thick. Tunneling was possible using wave equations of quantum mechanics, rather than approaching the phenomenon using classical theories of physics, in which electrons are thought of as particles.

Esaki published his findings in 1958, answering questions about electron tunneling through solids that scientists

had been asking for decades, and opening a new field in development of solid-state physics that spread to research laboratories around the world. The knowledge of tunneling in semiconductors was useful in practical applications, as super-fast and super-small electrons that could cross barriers would be useful for high-speed circuits. Esaki used his discovery and research for his graduate thesis which earned him a Ph.D. in Physics from Tokyo University in 1959.

The profound impact of the Esaki tunnel diode, in not only his scientific achievement but in creating a basis for other researchers to study, was recognized by a string of accolades. He received Japan's Nishina Memorial Award in 1959; the Asahi Press Award in 1960; the Morris N. Liebmann Memorial Prize from IRE, the Stuart Ballantine Medal from the Franklin Institute, and the Toyo Rayon Foundation Award, all in 1961; the Japan Academy Award in 1965; and the Order of Culture from the Japanese government in 1974.

Joined IBM in United States

In 1960, Esaki was invited to work as a resident consultant at International Business Machines (IBM) in Yorktown, New York, in the United States. His one-year visit soon extended to a 32-year stay after IBM awarded him a fellowship to continue his research in semiconductor physics at the IBM Thomas J. Watson Research Center.

Esaki's departure from Sony was surprising to many. In Japan, companies were known for giving employees lifetime employment; people seldom changed jobs. Now, a

highly regarded scientist was leaving his country to work in the United States, where it was known that scientific research and curiosity were more highly valued. So unprecedented was Esaki's move, that both Sony and IBM released press announcements saying that he was leaving under honorable circumstances.

During his years at the Watson center, Esaki investigated man-made semiconductor superlattice structures to predict quantum mechanical phenomena. He and Raphael Bu published papers in 1969 and 1970 that proposed that single-crystal superlattice structures with unusual electronic properties could be designed using quantum theory and advanced techniques of epitaxy. These lattices are composed of layered thin films which can carry current at discrete voltages. In 1972, Esaki discovered a negative differential conductivity in GaAIAs (gallium aluminum arsenide) superlattice. He confirmed through experimentation, a year later, a resonant tunneling phenomenon between adjacent potential quantum wells in the superlattice structure.

A successful member of IBM, Esaki became director of IBM-Japan in 1976 serving until 1992, and was named to the governing board of the IBM-Tokyo Research Laboratory.

Awarded Nobel Prize in Physics

Esaki was awarded the Nobel Prize in Physics in 1973 for his pioneering work in electron tunneling in semiconducting materials, which led to his creation of the tunnel diode. He shared the award that year with British physicist Brian David Josephson and Norwegian-born American physicist Ivar Giaever.

This technology has been at the core of further research in semiconductor science. In the area of semiconductor lasers, this technology has applications such as optical telecommunications, wireless communication devices, and data readers in computer hard disks. Other applications and research involve nonlinear transport and optical properties on semiconductors, junctions, and thin films.

Esaki's notoriety in his field continued to grow with more scientific recognition. He received the US-Asia Institute Science Achievement Award in 1983. In 1985, he and two others shared the American Physical Society's International Prize for New Materials for pioneering the study of semiconductor quantum structures. The Institute of Electrical and Electronic Engineers awarded him the Medal of Honor for 1991 for his scientific contributions in tunneling, superlattices, and quantum wells.

Over the course of two decades, Esaki joined an impressive number of professional associations and sat on company boards. He served on the board of Yamada Science Foundation, as a member of the Japan Academy, and was adjunct professor of Waseda University in Japan. He was elected a fellow of the American Academy of Arts and Sciences in 1974, and named a foreign associate of both the US National Academy of Sciences in 1976 and US National Academy of Engineering in 1977.

Many international organizations named Esaki as a foreign member, including the Russian Academy of Sciences,

Korean Academy of Science and Technology, Italian National Academy of Science, Max-Planck Gesellschaft, and American Philosophical Society. Esaki was named a Sir John Cass Sr. Visiting Research Fellow at London Polytechnic in 1981.

Named President of Tsukuba University in Japan

In 1992, Esaki retired from IBM and returned to Japan, where he had retained his citizenship. He accepted a position as president of Tsukuba University in Ibaraki, Japan. His selection for president was an unusual one, as he had been living away from Japan for the past thirty years, and had become the first person outside of academia to lead a national university in Japan.

Tsukuba University held an attraction for Esaki for two reasons. Founded in 1973, the year he won the Nobel Prize, the school had been built near Tsukuba Science City, Japan's first government planned high-tech community. Secondly, the school promised to change the stifling Japanese method of learning by rote and suppressing creativity by encouraging original thought and interactions between students and research labs. After nearly two decades, the school had yet to achieve those lofty goals. Several young professors called Esaki to help lead their school in the direction toward scientific research. Esaki noted, "Revitalizing creative activity at University of Tsukuba is the main reason I was invited to become president."

Esaki originally left Japan due to the country's paradoxical approach to science. Despite students garnering traditionally high marks in science, compared to other industrialized countries, Japan placed little emphasis in technological development. That's why the country has produced only five Nobel science and medicine laureates, compared to America's 191. Esaki noted that, "Not many people in Japan appreciated the tunnel diode when I made it in 1957. There was not much commercial application. But the US science community really appreciated it. That is why I went to America first of all and that is why I stayed there." Esaki made his mission at Tsukuba University to create the supportive environment for scientists in Japan that he had craved as a young man.

The transition to Esaki's presidency was not a smooth one. Faculty is traditionally promoted through seniority and elected from within. Esaki was considered an outsider. He told *Science* magazine, "This is almost a 'forbidden transition,' going from industry to academia—especially in Japan." Another concern was that he had become too Americanized and would have a difficult time fitting back into Japanese business. But he had been traveling back to Japan from the US several times a year and keeping close ties to his homeland. Esaki used his experience at IBM to help adjust. "I know how to manage the bureaucracy and politicians," he said.

Urged Research Collaborations for Graduate Students

During his four-year term at Tsukuba University, his goal was to transform the school into a first-rate research institution by encouraging collaborations and scientist exchanges between the school and Tsukuba City's corporate labs and government institutes. He also had to contend with the Japanese government's meager contribution to applied research, which lagged far behind the Research & Development funding of the US. To achieve his goal, he built industry/university relations by establishing the Tsukuba Advanced Research Alliance (TARA) to encourage collaborative Research & Development between private research institutes, Tsukuba University, and national government labs.

Dear to his heart was the desire to expand and strengthen the school's graduate education. Since one quarter of the university's population was graduate students, Esaki created a program that allowed doctoral candidates to work in participating industrial or government labs around Tsukuba Science City. He also negotiated educational exchange programs with universities in the US and Europe. These benefits did not extend strictly to science majors, but also for humanities and social sciences. Other changes he recommended included more interdisciplinary focus, increased use of outside peer review, greater diversity of faculty and students, and increased spending on facilities.

Became President of Shibaura Institute of Technology

In 1998, Esaki received the Japan Prize in the category of "Generation and Design of New Materials Creating Novel Functions" for the creation of the concept of man-made superlattice crystals which lead to new materials with useful applications. The prize came with an award of 50 million yen, about $391,000. That same year, he received the Grand Cordon Order of Rising Sun (First Class), and was named chairman of the Science and Technology Promotion Foundation of Ibaraki, Japan. In 1999, he was named director general of Tsukuba Institute Congress Center.

In 2000, Esaki became president of Shibaura Institute of Technology where he concentrated on the upgrading and internationalization of Japan's education system and academic research program. He also served as director of Open Loop, Inc., a Sapporo-based firm that develops security technology.

Over the years, Esaki earned honorary degrees from schools across the globe, including University of Montpellier in France, University of Athens in Greece, and Universidad Politecnica de Madrid in Spain. Esaki published numerous papers in professional journals and served a time as guest editorial writer for Yomiuri Press. Through clever articles he has helped create a bridge of understanding between Japan and the West. Esaki is married with three children.

Books

Asimov's Biographical Encyclopedia of Science and Technology, Doubleday and Company, 1982.

McGraw Hill's Modern Scientists and Engineers, McGraw Hill, 1980.

World Book Biographical Encyclopedia of Scientists, World Book, 2003.

Periodicals

Physics Today, October 1992.

Science, December 1994; January 9, 1998.

U.S. News & World Report, June 9, 1997.

Online

Institute of Electrical and Electronic Engineers History Center, http://www.ieee.org/organizations/history_center/legacies/esaki.html (December 23, 2003).

Japan Prize, http://www.japanprize.jp/e_1998(esaki).htm (December 12, 2003).

Nobel Museum, http://www.nobel.se/physics/laureates/1973/esaki-bio.html (December 12, 2003).

World of Scientific Discovery, 2nd ed. Gale Group, 1999. □

F

Rene Geronimo Favaloro

Argentinian physician Dr. Rene Favaloro (1923–2000) was a world-renowned heart surgeon who performed the first successful planned bypass surgery of the coronary artery in 1967 at the Cleveland Clinic in Ohio. He later taught his technique for grafting arteries.

Humble Beginnings

Rene Geronimo Favaloro was born on July 14, 1923, in La Plata, Argentina. His father, Juan B. Favaloro, was a carpenter. His mother, Ida Y. Raffaelli, was a dressmaker. Both of his parents were Sicilian immigrants. Favaloro was inspired to become a doctor by an uncle who was a physician.

Favaloro received his bachelor's degree in 1941 and served with the Argentine Army during World War II. In 1946, when Favaloro was discharged as a lieutenant, he began his medical studies at the University of La Plata. In 1949 he received his medical degree and then served an internship at Polyclinic Hospital in La Plata.

When a country surgeon in Jacinto Arauz, a very poor village 300 miles away from La Plata, fell ill and needed a few months away from his practice, Favaloro went to serve in his place. For the rest of his life Favaloro took to heart the lessons he learned in Jacinto Arauz. According to Eric Nagourney, writing Favaloro's obituary for the *New York Times,* the doctor had once said that all doctors in Latin America should be required to work among the poor.

Favaloro had told the *San Diego Union Tribune:* "They would be able to see the combination of dirt and fumes. The people have only one room where they cook, they live, they make love, where they have their children, where they eat." His sojourn in the village also kept him focused all his life on advocating health care for everyone, no matter what their economic situation, and it inspired him to establish his *Fundacion Favaloro* in 1975.

Favaloro's brother, Juan Jose, also became a surgeon, and the two set up a medical practice in La Pampa. They had the only X-ray machine in a 150-kilometer radius. Favaloro spent the next 12 years taking postgraduate courses and performing general surgery at Rawson Hospital in Buenos Aires. Favaloro married his high school sweetheart, Maria Antonia Delgado. The couple had no children.

Bypass Pioneer

In 1962, Dr. Donald Effler invited Favoloro to come to the Cleveland Clinic to observe the work of the Department of Thoracic and Cardiovascular Surgery and serve as an apprentice to Dr. Delos M. Cosgrove, co-chair of the world-famous heart center there. He also studied with Mason Sones, considered to be the father of coronary cineangiography—the reading and interpreting of coronary and ventricular images.

Two other surgeons had already performed heart bypass surgery—Dr. David Sabiston at Duke University in 1962 and Dr. Edward Garrett, an associate of the renowned Dr. Michael DeBakey, in 1964. But both of these surgeries were done in response to deteriorating conditions while the patient was on the operating table, and neither procedure had been reported in a medical journal. Favaloro's heart bypass operation on a 51-year-old woman in 1967 was the first to be planned and reported in a medical journal. His

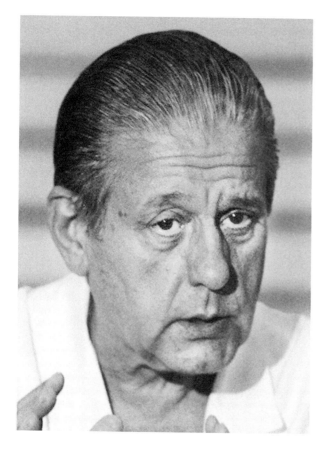

Throughout his career of service Favaloro remained a world figure. He was an active member of numerous professional organizations in the United States, Latin America, Europe, and the world including the American College of Surgeons, the American Association for Thoracic Surgery, the American Medical Association, the International Society of Cardiothoracic Surgeons, the Pan American Medical Association, the Third World Academy of Sciences, and other organizations.

Favaloro had several dozen teaching assignments throughout the international medical world. As an author and editor he wrote several books and served on the editorial boards of the Spanish-language version of the *Journal of the American Medical Association (JAMA)*, the *International Journal of Cardiology*, the *Journal of Cardiac Surgery*, and *Clinical Cardiology*. Favaloro was a prolific author, writing more than 350 scientific papers, and six books, including two that have been translated into English, *Surgical Treatment of Coronary Arteriosclerosis*, published in 1970, and *The Challenging Dream of Heart Surgery: from The Pampas to Cleveland*, published in 1992. The topics of his other books included his personal memoirs of life as a physician.

Favaloro did not limit himself to print media. He developed a television program called "The Great Medical Issues," offering medical information on prevention and treatment of diseases. The program won two awards in Argentina during the mid-1980s. Another television series he created included 24 programs focused on drugs and aimed at young people.

Criticized Economic Policies

Favaloro harbored some discontent at the state of medicine in Argentina, criticizing the social and moral costs of managed health care. In a letter to the editor of *La Nacion*, a Buenos Aires newspaper, he noted that his foundation was owed $18 million from hospitals and state-owned medical centers. Nagourney quoted Favaloro, weeks before his death, writing that "I am going through the saddest period of my life. In the most recent times, I have been turned into a beggar," referring to the increasingly difficult task of finding enough money to perform necessary medical care and surgeries, particularly for the poor.

In a paper Favaloro wrote and presented at Leiden University in the Netherlands in February 1997, and that was reprinted for *Interscientia*, Favaloro explained the nature of cardiosurgery and its advances but also took on the social meaning of such changes. Favaloro noted a direct corollary between socioeconomic status and heart diseases and focused on the widening gap between the rich and the poor in education and health care. He commented that " . . . we are without doubt submerged in a materialistic, hypocritical and dehumanized society that has been developing slowly but steadily and which appears to have no limits to its appetites. All means are justified to increase power and pleasure through economic gains. It is of no importance that the greatest part of the population is excluded and survive in misery and lack of welfare." Favaloro was not referring only to Latin America or to Third World nations. He noted problems in getting adequate health care even in the United

technique was to stop the heart, take a section of vein from the patient's leg, sew one end into the aorta, and attach the other end to the blocked artery. It soon became a standard procedure that continued into the 21st century.

As Favaloro perfected the operation, it popularity spread. Within one year 171 bypasses had been performed at the Cleveland Clinic. Nagourney quoted a friend of Favaloro, Dr. Robert H. Jones of Duke University, who noted that Favaloro was "really the person who should get credit for introducing coronary bypass into the clinical arena." In the past, various methods had been attempted to treat persons with heart disease, but none had succeeded as well as Favaloro's surgical method.

Lifetime of Service

In 1971, Favaloro left Cleveland to return to Argentina, giving up a lucrative career to serve the people of his homeland. There he began to raise funds for a $55 million heart clinic he planned to build. In 1975 he established his foundation for that same purpose. By 1980 he was able to establish a center for cardiovascular surgery, training surgeons and cardiologists in his methods and ideas. The medical center and teaching unit were located in the Guemes private hospital in Buenos Aires. The Society of Distributors of Newspapers and Magazines donated an eight-story building as a private research center. Favoloro's clinic was finally completed in 1992, and his Institute of Cardiology and Cardiovascular Surgery of the Favaloro Foundation had its own home. Favaloro continued as the institute's director.

States. In his closing remarks, Favaloro said, "I did not present you with an indisputable truth. It would be a disgrace to say I am the owner of the truth. I would be gratified if my words only raised some doubts in your minds."

A National Hero

On July 29, 2000, Favaloro shot himself to death at his home in Buenos Aires. Argentina grieved at the loss of a national hero. According to Geoff Olson, writing for the *Vancouver Courier* an article in *La Nacion* "described his death as one more blow to 'the sad land of psychoanalysis and tango.' " Olson also referred to the national money crisis that had plagued Argentina for many years, which some observers blamed on privatization and a global economy that brought lower wages and dire financial conditions for workers. The fiscal downturn meant cutbacks in government funding for Favaloro's foundation. Also, according to Olson, "Two weeks before his death, in a memo to his staff, he excoriated economic globalization, stating that free-market reforms are 'better referred to as a neo-feudalism that is bringing this world toward a social disaster where the rich are getting richer and the poor are getting poorer.' "

Whether Favaloro's suicide was a deliberate statement against the state of the world in which he had to beg for money to cure people, or whether it was simply the act of someone desperately sad, can never be known. What is certain is that Favaloro left behind him a legacy of passion and dedication to serving the human race.

Periodicals

Heart Wire, August 11, 2000.
Interscientia, July 1997.
New York Times, August 1, 2000.
People's Union for Civil Liberties Bulletin (Delhi, India), October 2000.
Perteneser (Argentina), July 2000.
Texas Heart Institute Journal, 2000.
Vancouver Courier, February 11, 2002.

Online

"Altruism," *George Mason University Objectivist Club,* http://129.174.139.240/gmuoc/mt/archives/000071.html (December 31, 2003).
"Dr. Rene Favaloro," *Favaloro Foundation,* http://www.fundacionfavaloro.org (December 31, 2003).
"Dr. Rene Favaloro, Prince Mahidol Awardee," *Prince Mahidol Award Foundation,* http://kanchanapisek.or.th (December 31, 2003).
"Rene G. Favaloro? A great man and a great ideal," *Sociedade Brasileira de Cardiologia (Brazilian Society of Cardiologists),* http://publicaoes.cardiol.br (December 31, 2003).
"The Right to Health: Is it at Risk?" *Canadian Conference on International Health,* http://www.csih.org (October 28, 2003). □

Sally Field

American actress Sally Field (born 1946) vaulted to stardom in the 1960s by playing perky ingénues on the small screen and went on to an equally impressive career in feature film. For nearly three decades, noted *Variety* contributor Charles Isherwood, two-time Academy Award winner Field "has specialized in playing women whose demure exteriors have a way of cracking open to unleash torrents of outsized emotion at times of crisis."

Field grew up in the entertainment business. She was born on November 6, 1946, in Pasadena, California, to Margaret Field, a studio contract player of the era, and a pharmaceutical salesperson. After her parents divorced, her mother remarried Jock Mahoney, a working actor and stuntman whose most noted screen credit came in the 1960s as Tarzan. Both her mother and stepfather, Field later recalled, were "real working-class actors, which was really important to be around, in that I had no illusion about some glorious, glamourous, easy place," she told *Back Stage West* writer Jamie Painter Young.

Cast as Surfer Girl

At Birmingham High School in the San Fernando Valley, Field naturally gravitated toward the drama department, and there she was a standout. Her ebullient personality and wholesome looks landed her a spot in a Columbia Studios workshop for budding screen stars in 1964, and she was ultimately cast as the lead in a new ABC television series, *Gidget,* which reprised the popular surfer-teen movies of the same name. The show ran for one season, and when it ended Field thought about relocating to New York City so that she might try her luck on the stage. "I wanted to study and live on thirty-seven cents in a little apartment, and do off-off-off-off-off-off-Broadway," she said in an interview with Liz Smith for *Good Housekeeping.* "But I was afraid. I had never been outside of California. . . . I was influenced by my family, and they were frightened."

Miserable in Popular Series

ABC had canceled *Gidget,* but it was doing so well in summer reruns that Field was offered another title role in a new sitcom, *The Flying Nun.* She was asked to play Sister Bertrille, a young, irrepressible Roman Catholic nun at a Puerto Rican convent who could actually fly. Field thought the premise was ridiculous, and promptly turned it down. "I hated the whole idea," she later recalled to *Entertainment Weekly* writer Jeff Jensen. But then her stepfather urged her to take it. "He said, 'If you don't do this, you may never work again,' " and so she took the part.

The Flying Nun was a hit and made Field a star. In the show she wore an improbable outfit built around a traditional nun's habit with one of the more extreme, winglike forms of head covering for women's religious orders. The head covering weighed six pounds, and the flying stunts required Field to be strapped to wire contraptions. She was miserable and went through a period of depression and overeating. "I would lose 10 or 15 pounds in a week, eating nothing but cucumbers and working all day," she recalled in an interview with *People* writer Elizabeth Sporkin. "My hands would shake all the time, and sometimes I'd pass out. But then I would go on these enormous binges. I lived alone and was very lonely."

A sympathetic actress from the television series, Madeleine Sherwood, encouraged Field to take classes with renowned drama teacher Lee Strasberg, who held classes in Los Angeles as part of his famed Actors Studio once a year. There, Field blossomed, working alongside Jack Nicholson and Ellen Burstyn, among other young luminaries and future Oscar-winners. Returning to the set of *The Flying Nun* only worsened matters, however, and so on a jaunt to Las Vegas in 1968 Field married her high-school boyfriend, becoming pregnant not long afterward. To her relief, the show was canceled in 1970, and she took a break for a time to concentrate on being a wife and mother.

Moved into Film

Field appeared in the occasional made-for-television movie, but financial pressure from her husband, a carpenter, compelled her to return to work on a more permanent basis. Once again, she accepted a part she loathed: in *The Girl with Something Extra,* a 1973–74 sitcom, she played a newlywed with psychic powers. Not long afterward, Field divorced, fired her manager, and went back to the Actors

Studio. She was eager to move into film, but had a difficult time in the industry, partly because of her high-profile Gidget and Sister Bertrille roles. "It wasn't only that I was typecast or identified with fluffy situation comedy," she explained to Young in her *Back Stage West* interview. "It was that in those days there was a real stigma between television and film, and no one in film wanted anything to do with anyone who came from television." She finally convinced a director to cast her in Jeff Bridges' film *Stay Hungry,* in 1976, but ironically she wound up winning the best actress Emmy that year for her additional work in the television movie *Sybil.* Based on a nonfiction book, the acclaimed project starred Field as a young woman suffering from multiple personality disorder because of childhood abuse.

Field continued to have a tough time landing film roles, and she described this period of her life, during which she was a single mother, as one of the hardest in her life. She recalled in the *Good Housekeeping* interview with Smith that "I really didn't have any money, and I had two kids and a dream and had no real way of knowing that it would ever happen. I was scared." A romance with one of Hollywood's biggest stars of the era, heartthrob Burt Reynolds, began when she appeared in one of Reynolds's *Smokey and the Bandit* films, and the relationship lasted through five years and a few more movies. In the end, intense media scrutiny doomed the relationship, but years later Reynolds often told interviewers that the break-up was the biggest regret of his life.

Two Oscars

Field's sixth movie role gave her the first Oscar nomination of her career: the 1979 drama *Norma Rae.* Here she was cast as an unlikely hero, the scrappy, reluctant union organizer of a small textile mill. In one scene, Field's character shuts off her noisy machine, writes the word "union" on a card, and holds it aloft. One by one, the other workers also turn off their machines in the stirring, three-minute sequence. "It may be the most powerful act of wordless suasion in film: testimony to the fact that in leadership, oratory isn't everything," noted a writer for *Inc.* Field won several best-actress honors for her work in *Norma Rae* and beat out Jane Fonda and Bette Midler for the Academy Award that year.

Field went on to appear in a number of other major Hollywood films of the 1980s, often cast as a plucky fighter who triumphs over sadness and hardship. She won her second Oscar for best actress for 1984's *Places in the Heart,* a 1930s Texas back-country drama. She was cast in the lead as Edna, a woman whose sheriff husband is slain and then must struggle to save the family farm. *New York Times* critic Vincent Canby claimed her character is "beautifully played," and went on to note that Field excels in the part of a woman "whose growth, in the course of the film, reflects an almost 19th-century faith in the possibilities of the American system, not as the system was, but as one wanted to believe it to be."

Infamous Speech

The following March, Field delivered what would become another career-defining performance: her acceptance speech at the Academy Awards ceremony, which is often misquoted as her gushing, "You like me!" What she actually enthused that night, according to *Entertainment Weekly,* was: "The first time, I didn't feel it, but this time I feel it and I can't deny the fact that you like me! Right now, you like me!" Other roles that came her way in the 1980s included *Murphy's Romance,* playing opposite James Garner, and *Steel Magnolias,* in which she played the mother of newcomer Julia Roberts.

In 1991 Field played a diva-like daytime television star in *Soapdish,* and took on another everywoman-heroine role in *Not without My Daughter,* based on the true story of a woman who was forced to smuggle her daughter out of Iran in the early 1980s when her native-born husband refused to let the child return to the United States. She was cast as the soon-to-be ex-wife of Robin Williams's character in 1993's *Mrs. Doubtfire,* playing a woman who does not realize her husband has disguised himself as an elderly female housekeeper in order to spend more time with their children. She was also the oft-quoted "Mama" in *Forrest Gump,* the surprise hit of 1994.

For a time, Field ran her own production company in the hopes of finding better film projects for herself. She produced the 1991 Julia Roberts tearjerker *Dying Young,* and both produced and starred in the 1995 mini-series *A Woman of Independent Means,* which was nominated for two Emmys. Critics mostly assailed her first action-hero role, which came in John Schlesinger's 1996 film *Eye for an Eye.* Field plays a woman whose daughter is murdered and vows to avenge the death when the killer, played by Kiefer Sutherland, goes free on a legal technicality.

Made Directorial Debut

Field was teaching workshops at the invitation of Robert Redford at his Sundance Institute in Utah when she began to explore the possibility of directing. She wrote a teleplay for a holiday fable, *The Christmas Tree,* starring Julie Harris, and her friend Tom Hanks hired her to helm the camera for an episode of his HBO series, *From the Earth to the Moon.* In 2000 she directed the independent film *Beautiful,* which features Minnie Driver as a ruthless beauty pageant contestant determined to win America's top crown. Field went back to television when she was offered a small role on the hit drama *ER* in 2000 and proved so popular as the manic-depressive mother of a series regular that she came back the following season and won an Emmy for her performance. In 2003 Field appeared as a Washington politician who hires Reese Witherspoon's Elle Woods in the popular comedy *Legally Blonde 2.* A much-touted television series which had the veteran actress playing a U.S. Supreme Court justice earned mixed reviews and was not renewed.

Field finally made it onto the New York stage in the fall of 2002, when producers cast her in *The Goat; or, Who Is Sylvia?* The Edward Albee-penned drama centered around an architect who falls in love with his goat, with Field playing his baffled, angry wife. She earned glowing reviews for her performance. Writing in *Variety,* Isherwood noted that Mercedes Ruehl originated the part and had done well, but "Field's touches the heart in a way that brings a new emotional ballast to Stevie's dilemma, and a new emotional equilibrium to the play."

Social-Phobia Sufferer

Field's two sons from her first marriage are grown: Peter Craig is a novelist, while Field's other son has become the third generation in his family to work as an actor. She also has a younger son from her second marriage, with whom she lives in the Brentwood section of Los Angeles. Despite the posh ZIP code, Field eschews the Hollywood party scene. It was her producer husband's love of socializing that ended her second marriage, she told *People* writer Gregory Cerio. "He wanted to go out, to be with people or go to parties," she confessed. "I couldn't take it. I'd have an anxiety attack."

Like many female actresses of her generation, Field maintains that finding mature roles is not an easy task, but she remains sanguine about her years in Hollywood. As she told Smith in the *Good Housekeeping* interview, "I want to be able to look back on my life and my career in the motion picture industry, and say: I'm proud of the work, and I had some significance. I represented women of my generation. I was lucky enough to be part of films that in some way represented me."

Books

International Dictionary of Films and Filmmakers, Volume 3: *Actors and Actresses,* St. James Press, 1996.

Periodicals

Back Stage West, September 14, 2000.
Entertainment Weekly, November 26, 1993; February 17, 1995; September 22, 2000.
Good Housekeeping, March, 1996; October, 1998; June 2001.
Inc., March 2000.
National Review, December 14, 1984.
New Statesman, June 21, 1996.
New York Post, October 2, 2002.
New York Times, September 21, 1984; July 6, 1994; November 4, 2002; July 2, 2003.
People, October 15, 1984; October 17, 1988; July 8, 1991; January 29, 1996; November 27, 2000.
Time, December 24, 1984; November 20, 1989; August 1, 1994.
Variety, October 14, 2002. □

Val Logsdon Fitch

In 1980, American nuclear physicist Val Logsdon Fitch (born 1923) was co-recipient with James Watson Cronin of the Nobel Prize for Physics. The two men received international recognition in the scientific community as a result of an experiment they conducted in 1964 that showed that certain sub-

atomic reactions are not indifferent to time. They did this by studying the decay of particles called K-mesons and demonstrating that reactions run in reserve do not simply follow the backward path of the original reaction. Their results had tremendous impact on world knowledge by disproving long-standing scientific theories.

Early Life

The youngest of three children, Fitch was born March 10, 1923, on a cattle ranch in Cherry County, Nebraska, near the South Dakota border. His father, Fred Fitch, was a cattle rancher and his mother was a school teacher. Fred Fitch bought his four-square-mile ranch when he was only 20 years old.

The family ranch was situated in a sparsely populated part of the United States and far from any large communities. Also, the expanse was located near a site of historical significance: 20 years earlier and only 40 miles away the battle of Wounded Knee had taken place. As such, the Sioux Indians were a large and integral part of the community, and Fred Fitch became friendly with the local Native Americans. He learned their language and eventually was named an honorary chief.

Val Fitch later remarked that the remoteness and vastness of his early environment made a big impression on him. He also commented that his memories of cattle ranching were rather mundane and far removed from the romanticized myths of the American West. Rather than stirring cattle roundups, Fitch remembered rather unexciting chores such as oiling windmills and fixing fences. "E.B. White has defined farming as 10 percent agriculture and 90 percent fixing something that has gotten broken," noted Fitch in the autobiography he penned on the occasion of receiving his Nobel Prize.

Shortly after Val Fitch was born, his father suffered a serious injury in a riding accident. This limited his physical capabilities, and he couldn't perform many of the more arduous activities involved with running a ranch. Because of this, Fred Fitch entered the insurance business and moved his family about 25 miles away to Gordon, Nebraska. The cattle ranch remained within the family, but its operation was left to others. While living in Gordon, Val Fitch began his public schooling. He developed an interest in chemistry, but his scientific pursuits would turn to physics in the 1940s when he entered the U.S. Army in World War II.

Worked on the Manhattan Project

One of the most significant periods in Val Fitch's early adulthood took place during the war. While serving in the Army and stationed in Los Alamos, New Mexico, he worked on the Manhattan Project. The U.S. government began the project in 1942 in response to the growing concern that the Axis powers were close to developing atomic weaponry. The project, operated by the Army Corps of Engineers, was designed to develop an atomic bomb before Germany or Japan. Noted physicist J. Robert Oppenheimer (1904–1967) directed the construction and test of the first A-bomb at the Los Alamos laboratory.

Fitch worked under the direction of nuclear physicist Sir Ernest William Titterton (1916–1990), who was a member of the British Mission. Fitch found his involvement "stimulating." He toiled in a small laboratory as a technician, and had the privilege of working with some of the greatest names in the physics field, including Enrico Fermi, Neils Bohr, James Chadwick, Isidor Rabi, and Richard Tolman. Fitch's experience was recounted as part of a chapter in a book called *All in Our Time,* edited by Jane Wilson and published by the Bulletin of Atomic Scientists.

In all, Fitch spent three years at Los Alamos, learning the techniques of experimental physics. While stationed there, he came to a conclusion that would play a large part in directing his future career. He realized, as he later recalled, that the most successful scientists were the ones who knew the most about electronics. Appropriately, he set about learning all he could about electronic techniques, an educational experience that enabled him to use new technology while measuring new phenomena. More significantly, it opened his mind to a new way of thinking. As he recalled in his Nobel autobiography, he learned how to "allow the mind to wander freely and invent new ways of doing the job."

Studied with Noted Scientists

After being discharged from the Army, Fitch began his formal education at the graduate and post-graduate levels. While at Los Alamos, Fitch also worked with Robert Bacher, the group leader of Weapons and Experimental Physics division. After the war, Bacher offered Fitch a graduate assistantship at Cornell University in Ithaca, New York. However, before he could begin the work, Fitch needed to obtain an undergraduate degree at McGill University in Montreal, Quebec, Canada. He received a bachelor's degree in electrical engineering in 1948.

While at McGill, another graduate opportunity soon presented itself and instead of going to Ithaca, Fitch headed off to Columbia University in New York City, where he worked on his Ph.D. thesis with James Rainwater (1917–1986), another nuclear physicist who worked on the Manhattan Project. (Rainwater would receive the 1975 Nobel Prize in Physics). At Columbia, Fitch made some more valuable academic connections. Rainwater shared his university office with Niels Bohr (1885–1962), whose work on the structure of atoms earned him the 1922 Nobel Prize in Physics. Bohr introduced Fitch to the work of John Wheeler (born 1911), the theoretical physicist who would later increase the understanding of black holes by using the concepts of relativity. Specifically, Fitch became familiar with Wheeler's paper about 5-mesic atoms. Through his exposure to Wheeler's work, Fitch developed his own thesis on 5-mesic atoms.

The opportunity to work with such renowned names in the field proved a pivotal part of Fitch's education. At the same time he was introduced to very new and crucial technical advancements including the Columbia Nevis cyclotron, sodium iodide with thallium activation, and new phototubes. During this period, combining the knowledge gained at Los Alamos with his university education, he designed and built the gamma-ray spectrometer, a multichannel pulse height analyzer. Working with colleagues, Fitch helped develop a technique for precise gamma-ray measurements to obtain a better mass value for the 5-meson. From there, his interests turned to strange particles and K mesons, an area he enjoyed because it was unpredictable and challenging.

Studied K-mesons

Fitch was awarded a Ph.D. in physics by Columbia University in 1954. That same year, he became a faculty member at Princeton University in New Jersey. For the next 20 years, he worked with graduate students researching K-mesons. This eventually resulted in unexpected findings that would eventually lead to the discovery of CP-violation, which earned him the Nobel Prize. The unexpected was what he found most compelling about his work. "At any one time there is a natural tendency among physicists to believe that we already know the essential ingredients of a comprehensive theory," he once wrote. "But each time a new frontier of observation is broached we inevitably discover new phenomena which force us to modify substantially our previous conceptions. I believe this process to be unending, that the delights and challenges of unexpected discovery will continue always."

The unexpected could also be said to apply to his life. Looking back on his early years in Nebraska, he found it remarkable that someone who grew up on a cattle ranch would eventually travel to Stockholm, Sweden to receive the Nobel Prize in physics.

Collaborated with Cronin on Groundbreaking Experiment

Fitch encountered the unexpected most profoundly, perhaps, in the work that led to his Nobel Prize. The experiments that led to the recognition began in 1963. Results were published in 1964. Fitch collaborated with particle physicist James Cronin (born 1931). The two men used the Alternating Gradient Synchroton (AGS) housed at the Brookhaven National Laboratory in New York to study the properties of K0 mesons. Working together, they helped modify the prevailing belief that the laws of symmetry and conservation are unbreakable. According to one of these laws (the principle of time invariance [designated T], particle interactions should be indifferent to the direction of time. For a long time, it had been accepted that this symmetry and two others, those of charge conjugation (C) and parity conservation (P), governed all the laws of physics. In their experiments, Cronin and Fitch showed that in rare instances subatomic particles called K mesons violate CP symmetry during their decay. This was the opposite of what they expected to find. They had originally intended to confirm CP symmetry by demonstrating that two different particles did not decay into the same products. Their data demonstrated the unexpected result that, sometimes, the long-lived neutral K meson does decay into two pi mesons. Thus, decays of K0L mesons sometimes violate the known rules, and so are different from all other known particle interactions. This became known as the CP Violation. This shook the core belief of physics that the universe is symmetrical. Later, their results would be verified in similar experiments conducted at other laboratories by other scientists.

Honored for his Work

Between the publication of the experiment's results and the 1980 Nobel Prize, Cronin and Fitch received the Research Corporation Award for their work on CP violation. In 1968, Fitch received the Ernest Orlando Lawrence Award for his research on mesons. He was recognized for adding to the world's knowledge of both mesons and nuclear structure and for demonstrating the fundamental asymmetry of nature under the combined transformation of charge conjugation and parity. In 1976, Fitch and Cronin were awarded the John Price Witherill Medal of the Franklin Institute.

Fitch would garnered many honors and distinctions during his career. He was named a fellow of the American Physical Society and the American Association for the Advancement of Science, and he became a member of the American Academy of Arts and Sciences and the National Academy of Sciences. In addition, at Princeton University, he garnered the titles of Cyrus Fogg Brackett Professorship of Physics and James S. McDonnell Distinguished University

Professor of Physics. In 1976, he was appointed chairman of the Physics Department. For 50 years (1947–1997), he was actively involved with the Board of Trustees of Associated Universities, Inc., which managed Brookhaven National Laboratory. From 1961–1967 and 1988–1991, he was a trustee. From 1991–1993, he served as Chairman of the Board. In 1993, he returned to the Board as a member. In 2000, he received an honorary degree (Doctor of Science) from Princeton University.

Advocated for Global Reform and Peace

As the 20th Century drew to a close, Fitch grew very concerned about world affairs and he became a sponsor for the Coalition for Peace Action, an grassroots citizens' organization headquartered in Princeton, New Jersey, that advocates global abolition of nuclear weapons, a peace economy, and a halt to weapons trafficking at home and abroad.

In October 1999, he and 31 other Nobel laureates in physics urged the Senate to approve the Comprehensive Test Ban Treaty. In July 2000, he joined 49 other Nobel laureates in signing a letter to President Clinton urging him not to deploy an anti-ballistic missile system during the remaining months of his administration. The signers felt the system was ineffective, would be harmful to the nation's security, and would initiate a new arms race. In December 2001, on the 100th anniversary of the Nobel Prize, Fitch was among the 100 Nobel laureates who issued a written call for environmental and social reform as a means to achieve world peace. In January 2003, he and 40 other Nobel laureates in science and economics issued a declaration opposing United States going to war against Iraq without wide international support. In the brief declaration, the signers wrote: "The undersigned oppose a preventive war against Iraq without broad international support. Military operations against Iraq may indeed lead to a relatively swift victory in the short term. But war is characterized by surprise, human loss and unintended consequences. Even with a victory, we believe that the medical, economic, environmental, moral, spiritual, political and legal consequences of an American preventive attack on Iraq would undermine, not protect, U.S. security and standing in the world.

Fitch has two sons from his first marriage (to Elise Cunningham who died in 1972) and three stepchildren from his second marriage (to Daisy Harper, in 1976).

Online

"James Watson Cronin," *Nobel-winners.com,* http://www .nobel-winners.com/Physics/james_watson_cronin.html (December 10, 2003).

"Nobel Laureates Warn Against Missile Defense Deployment," *Federation of American Scientists,* http://www.fas.org/press/ 000706-letter.htm (December 10, 2003).

"Nobel Winners Urge Halt to Missile Plan," *Yorkshire CND,* http://cndyorks.gn.apc.org/yspace/articles/bmd152.htm (December 10, 2003).

Press Release: The 1980 Nobel Prize in Physics, *Nobel e-Museum,* http://www.nobel.se/physics/laureates/1980/press .html/ (December 10, 2003).

"Val Fitch—Autobiography," *Nobel e-Museum,* http://www .nobel.se/physics/laureates/1980/fitch-autobio.html (December 10, 2003).

"Val Logsdon Fitch," *Bartelby.com,* http://www.bartleby.com/ 65/fi/Fitch-Va.html (December 10, 2003).

"Val Logsdon Fitch," *Nobel-Winners.com,* http://www.nobel-winners.com/Physics/val_logsdon_fitch.html (December 10, 2003). □

Peggy Fleming

American ice skater Peggy Fleming (born 1948) was the only U.S. athlete to win an Olympic gold medal at the 1968 Winter Games in Grenoble, France. One of skating's first bona-fide celebrities, Fleming is credited with luring legions of youth to the sport and for making figure skating a staple of sports broadcasting on network television. "Pretty and balletic, elegant and stylish," noted *Sports Illustrated* writer E. M. Swift, "Fleming took a staid sport that was shackled by its inscrutable compulsory figures and arcane scoring system and, with television as her ally, made it marvelously glamorous."

Unlike many of her homegrown competitors, Peggy Gale Fleming came from a working-class background. She was born on July 27, 1948, in San Jose, California, to Al and Doris Fleming. The family, which would eventually grow to include four daughters, initially lived on a farm in Morgan Hill, California, but began relocating frequently as Fleming's star rose in the junior ranks. Her father was a newspaper-plant press operator who first put his daughter on skates at the age of nine at a Bay Area rink. She proved a natural from the start and began skating daily.

The Flemings went to Cleveland, Ohio, for a time, while Al Fleming took a six-month stint in order to learn how to run a color printing press, and Fleming's supportive mother found a coach for her there. The coach put the young skater through a series of paces and tests and suggested she was already good enough to compete. Fleming was only 11 years old in 1960 when she came in last in Los Angeles at the Pacific Coast Juvenile Figure Skating Championship. As she recalled the event in her autobiography, *The Long Program: Skating toward Life's Victories.* "I was humiliated, especially for my family, who had made the drive down to L.A. The sheer embarrassment of it all gave me a jolt. From that day on I was serious about every competition I entered." Two weeks later, she entered another Pacific Coast event and took first place.

Father Drove Zamboni

Her first-place win began a long winning streak for Fleming in juniors events. Her family moved to Pasadena, and she began working with a new coach there. Her father worked in the printing department of the *Los Angeles Times*

and actually learned how to drive the ice-resurfacing machine—called a Zamboni—because the ice was too rough for the early-morning practice sessions Fleming put in. The cost of renting the ice time in some of the skating arenas where she practiced was more than he sometimes earned per hour as a press operator. Her mother, meanwhile, sewed all her competition costumes at home. As Fleming recalled in her memoir, "We were often made to feel that we were crashing the party. We just weren't from the same world as the more well-off families whose sons and daughters were part of the country club set known as 'the skating world.'"

A tragic event occurred in February 1961 when Fleming's Pasadena coach, Bill Kemp, was killed in a plane crash in Belgium. He and 18 members of the U.S. figure skating team were en route to the World Championships in Prague, Czechoslovakia, when their plane went down. The loss decimated the U.S. figure-skating program. Fleming proved to be a key to the rebuilding of the U.S. figure skating team following the crash. She won the Pacific Coast Women's Championships in 1963 and the U.S. championships the following year, making her, at age 15, the youngest national title-holder in the event's history. In 1964 she won the senior nationals and found herself on the way to the Olympics soon thereafter.

Heralded as Ice Star

In the run-up to the 1964 Winter Olympics in Innsbruck, Austria, Fleming was touted in the press as skating's new star and the potential savior for American figure skating after its tragic loss. "There is a dash of flamboyance to her skating that everyone finds appealing," *New York Times* writer Lincoln A. Werden remarked of her style on the ice. Fleming faced stiff international competition at the Innsbruck Games, however, and harbored no illusions. As she told the *New York Times*, "If I'm among the first 10, I'll be satisfied." Indeed, at the Games she managed only a sixth-place finish, but the experience was a pivotal one for her career. "Seeing the other skaters in Innsbruck was a very important thing for my growth as an athlete and a competitor," Fleming wrote in *The Long Program*. "Being there gave me a different perspective on the European skaters. This was before the days of skating on television, so I really had no idea what the competition looked like or what their style was."

Returning home, Fleming went on to win her second U.S. national title in 1965 and came in third at the 1965 World Championships that year as well. Realizing that the World Championships' high-altitude setting in Colorado Springs, Colorado, had seemed to make her tire more easily, Fleming and her family relocated there so that she might train under such conditions. She spent four hours practicing each morning, then attended classes at Cheyenne Mountain High School, and worked with her coach for another three hours later in the day. She readied for the 1966 World Championships in Davos, Switzerland, which was to take place at an outdoor venue. Before she departed, she told the *New York Times*'s Werden that the Davos event was going to prove more of a challenge for her than the indoor rink in Colorado Springs the previous year. "That makes a big difference," she explained. "You need more physical force, you have the wind to skate against, the rays of the glaring sun and the texture of outdoor ice."

The dedication paid off, and Fleming won the women's World Championship title that year. Skating aficionados were enthused about Fleming's potential. Dick Button, a two-time Olympic gold medalist, called the teen "a delicate lady on ice. She is not a fiery skater, and she shouldn't be made to be," he told the *New York Times*. "With some skaters there is a lot of fuss and feathers, but nothing is happening. With Peggy there's no fuss and feathers, and a great deal is happening. The only other skater in her class since the war has been Tenley Albright."

In 1966 Fleming began classes at Colorado College in Colorado Springs and continued her arduous practice sessions in preparation for the 1968 Olympics. She won another world title in 1967 and arrived in Grenoble early the next year with a chartreuse-colored skating costume her mother had sewed. The unusual green shade was a nod to a monastery near Grenoble at which the odd green liqueur of the same name was made. There were few other American athletes who were predicted to take a gold medal in any of the other Winter Olympic events save for her, and though she appeared nonplussed at the time, Fleming later recalled in an interview with *Winston-Salem Journal* writer Lisa O'Donnell that she was indeed unsettled by the pressure. "My overwhelming memories are of the nerves," she said that day in February of 1968. "When I get nervous, I fiddle with my hair. I kept putting on more and more hair spray. I used a can of Aquanet. I don't think my hair moved for two weeks."

Won Olympic Gold

In her free-skate event, Fleming glided across the ice to a program that featured musical selections by Tchaikovsky, Saint-Saëns, and Rossini and came in first. She was the sole American athlete to win a gold medal at the Games, but the event was historic for another reason as well: it was the first time that the Olympics were broadcast live on television and in color as well. Fleming's verve and grace in her chartreuse-green skating outfit made her a media sensation and awakened television executives to the potential gold in televising figure-skating events. She returned home a celebrity, appearing on the covers of both *Life* magazine and *Sports Illustrated.* Button told *New York Times* journalist Lloyd Garrison that Fleming represented a new, balletic era for figure skating. "You see a lot of Peggy's competition clumping around, skating fast like hockey players, flailing the ice with quick stops, trying to overpower you with gimmicks. The crowd may like it but it's not beautiful and it's not good skating. . . . Position and recovery are just as important in skating. With Peggy, there's not a misplaced move."

Fleming turned professional soon afterward and was signed to a television contract for her own NBC special. The check for that job alone was $35,000, a huge sum of money in those days. She bought a Porsche with it but also provided for her parents, who had sacrificed so much over the years. She went on to appear in four other television specials that pulled in impressive ratings, filmed in such picturesque locales as St. Petersburg, Russia. She also began appearing regularly with the Ice Follies and Holiday on Ice and even performed at the White House—the first skater in history to do so. "I had no idea what lay ahead of me because no one had done the things that I did as a professional . . . ," Fleming said of this era in an interview with *Christian Science Monitor* journalist Ross Atkin. 1960 Olympic champion Carol Heiss "did a movie with Snow White and the Three Stooges, and that was about it, so I had to do kind of groundbreaking things. Television was the tool at that time. There was satellite coverage of the Olympics and color TV."

Skating Commentator for ABC

In 1970 Fleming married Greg Jenkins, and her earnings helped put him through medical school. They had two sons and remained in the San Francisco Bay area. Fleming became a television commentator for ABC Sports in 1980, broadcasting from national, world, and Olympics events alongside Button. She has often been termed the first celebrity athlete that American skating produced in the modern era and was credited with bringing legions of new devotees to the sport in the years after 1968, thanks to the huge ratings her Olympic accomplishment garnered. Fleming, noted *Sports Illustrated*'s Swift in a 1994 issue commemorating the most important athletes of the past four decades, "pulled U.S. skating back to its feet after the 1961 tragedy,

jump-starting a program that for the next 26 years produced an unbroken string of U.S. women stars."

In early 1998, Fleming underwent surgery for breast cancer, almost 30 years to the day after she won her gold medal in Grenoble. The diagnosis was devastating, she told O'Donnell in the *Winston-Salem Journal.* "It was like someone pulled the rug out from me." After her lumpectomy, she endured six weeks of radiation therapy. "My athletic training kicked in," she told *St. Louis Post-Dispatch* writer Ellen Gardner. "I wanted to be the best patient . . . I wanted to win." The experience and the overwhelming outpouring of support she received spurred her to write her 1999 autobiography. She has also become active in breast-cancer awareness issues and speaks publicly on the importance of early detection. The former Olympic champ rarely skates, as she told the *Tampa Tribune.* "I've been doing it all my life, and I just don't have time to do that anymore," Fleming admitted. "And I don't think that's a challenge for me anymore." Fleming did however, put on her skates for SmithKline Beecham Consumer Healthcare's television commercials as their spokeswoman for a calcium supplement called Os-Cal. In March 2003 Fleming was honored with the 13th Vince Lombardi Award of Excellence.

Books

Great Women in Sports, Visible Ink Press, 1996.
Fleming, Peggy, with Peter Kaminsky, *The Long Program: Skating toward Life's Victories,* Pocket Books, 1999.

Periodicals

Christian Science Monitor, February 11, 1998.
Life, February 23, 1968.
M2 Presswire, October 29, 1999.
New York Times, January 19, 1964; February 21, 1965; February 9, 1966; February 28, 1966; February 28, 1967; February 11, 1968; March 2, 1981.
People, March 2, 1998.
PR Newswire, March 11, 2003.
Sports Illustrated, September 19, 1994.
St. Louis Post-Dispatch, October 6, 1998.
Tampa Tribune, March 7, 2002.
Winston-Salem Journal (Winston-Salem, NC), November 26, 2002. □

María Irene Fornés

Cuban-born playwright María Irene Fornés (born 1930) is one of American theater's most acclaimed, yet relatively unknown, talents. Since the early 1960s, Fornés's Off-Broadway plays have raised timely political and philosophical questions with their scathing themes and absurdist touches, but it is her deft touch in writing dialogue in her second language that has made her a favorite with critics for decades. "Fornés' plays," noted an *International Dictionary of Theater,* essay, "locate themselves at that place where the mystery of the human condition

and the enigma of human relationships reveal themselves in sudden, elusive, and often violent spasms.''

Disliked Factory Work

María Fornés was born on May 14, 1930, in Havana, Cuba, in a book-filled home headed by her well-read father, a former bureaucrat. He died when she was in her early teens, and Fornés moved to New York City at the age of 15 with her mother and five sisters, leaving an older brother behind in Havana. As she recalled in a 2000 interview that appeared in the New York Times, ''We had no means of support in Cuba. We came here for economic reasons. It might not be ideal, but you can work here and earn a living. In Cuba, it wasn't so. When we came here, there was no sadness whatsoever. My mother loved it. I thought I was in a Hollywood movie.''

Initially, Fornés could not speak English and was forced to take a job on a ribbon-factory assembly line. Tiring of this rather quickly, she enrolled in English-language courses and eventually found work as a translator. She also worked as a doll maker before she turned her energies to painting, and spent three years in Europe. Her first experiences with the theater came in the late 1950s, when she found work as a costume designer for two local theater and performance groups.

Won Acclaim as Novice

By 1960, Fornés was sharing a New York apartment with Susan Sontag, who would soon emerge as a renowned critic and philosopher. When Sontag suffered a bout of writer's block, Fornés decided to try to write something herself. She spent the next 19 days writing her first play, The Widow, which was produced at New York's Actors' Studio in 1961. She won a John Hay Whitney Foundation fellowship soon afterward that enabled her to devote her time to writing more works for the stage, Her next work was Tango Palace in 1963, a chronicle of the battles between two male lovers before one slays the other in a bullfight. It was the first of her works to hit a nerve with critics, and soon Fornés was one of Off-Broadway's leading new playwrights.

The Successful Life of Three was the first of Fornés's works to deal with a romantic triangle. It was followed by a musical, Promenade, a comic tale of two prison escapees who return to their cells, dissatisfied with the chaos of life on the outside. For both, Fornés won the first of several Obie Awards, given annually by the Village Voice to the best Off-Broadway productions of the year. Granted a Yale University fellowship in 1967, she worked on A Vietnamese Wedding, a commentary on the U.S. war in Southeast Asia at the time. Dr. Kheal was the first of her plays to be seen by a London audience, a solo show in which the eccentric title character expounds his views about the origins of the universe. Critics liked the Surrealist elements in her style, a legacy of her previous career as a painter. ''The dramatic situations of most of Fornés' work are warped and dream-

like,'' noted International Dictionary of Theater essay, ''peppered with vivid, mysterious images.''

Founded Theater Group

Molly's Dream, which debuted at a Boston University workshop in 1968, is one of Fornés's best-known plays. Molly is a saloon waitress whose shift is interrupted by dream sequences of herself as 1930s actress Marlene Dietrich. It appeared in the first published collection of Fornés's drama, Promenade and Other Plays, in 1971. Her reputation firmly established on the more experimental fringes of New York theater, Fornés became a co-founder of New York Theatre Strategy in 1972, which staged the works of rising new voices on the scene. It was home to the debut of another enduring work of hers, Fefu and Her Friends. The 1977 ensemble piece is set in 1935 in a New England home at which eight friends have gathered. Fornés used audience participation to illustrate its themes, and years later a writer for Back Stage, Glenda Frank, asserted that the Obie-winning play ''revolutionized staging and became a feminist classic.''

Around this same time, Fornés began serving as the director for the Hispanic Playwrights in Residence Lab at INTAR, the acronym by which International Arts Relations, a New York City Spanish-language theater group, is known. She continued to produce new works regularly, such as the The Danube from 1982, another favorite of fans of her work. The story is set in Budapest in 1938, and follows the doomed romance between a Hungarian woman and American man. Near the end, they come down with mysterious skin spots—possibly a reference to Acquired Immune Deficiency Syndrome (AIDS)—and the play ends with a blast that might be nuclear. She followed it with Mud, another tale of a trio of lovers. Its lead, Mae, is dispirited by her humdrum life in a small, Middle America town, and spurns one lover for another man; both prove slow-witted and abusive, however.

Delved into Latin American Junta

Fornés wrote another musical, Sarita, which was staged at INTAR, and continued to premier new works at the annual Padua Hills Festival in Claremont, California. In 1985, she won the American Academy and Institute of Arts and Letters Award in Literature, the same year The Conduct of Life was produced at the Theatre for New York City. Another one of her better-known works, the story follows a brutal Latin American army officer whose wife believes his job may be to torture political dissidents. He mistreats her and enslaves a 12-year-old girl in their basement. Again, Fornés won the Obie for the best new play of the year for it, and it is one of the most frequently performed of her works. After seeing a New Orleans revival of it, American Theatre critic Nicole LaPorte found that its ''scenes flow into one another like drifting thoughts. Yet amid these ambiguous spaces, the relations between the women in the play come vividly alive in a melding of realism and idealism that gives the play its force.''

Abingdon Square won Fornés another Obie for the best new work of the season in 1988, and the following she premiered *Hunger,* which dealt with the urban homeless and the nightmarish conditions of the city shelters in which they were forced to live. A 1992 musical, *Terra Incognita,* was staged at INTAR as part of the 500th-anniversary celebrations of Christopher Columbus's voyage to the Caribbean. Yet Fornés's works still remained largely unknown outside of a small New York avant-garde theater scene, but she did become the subject of more than one scholarly tome, including *Fornés: Theater in the Present Tense* a 1996 work by Diane Moroff. "It's not that she's just a ruthless experimenter," asserted *American Theatre* essayist Steven Drukman in a 2000 critique of her work. "It's more that she reinvents the Fornés play each time she writes one. No major playwright who has lasted so long can make the same claim." Yet even Drukman granted that her works were sometimes impenetrable. "The truth is this: Every critic who loves the plays of María Irene Fornés is also, in some small way, stymied by them," he confessed. "For us, too, the intoxication of a Fornés play in production turns to hangover when trying to synopsize the experience in journalistic prose, to provide interpretive closure, to pin each play down in words."

The only play that Fornés ever read before she began writing for the stage was Henrik Ibsen's *Hedda Gabler,* the story of a late nineteenth-century woman who chafes at the boundaries placed on her by marriage and a middle-class life. Fornés made the Ibsen classic the basis for her 1998 play, *The Summer in Gossensass,* in which two actresses in London eagerly await Ibsen's finished manuscript. Both are obsessed with the play, re-reading its scenes and delving into the characters. "The play is less concerned with telling a linear story," noted *Advocate* writer Don Shewey, "than with embodying the essential qualities that drive theater people—their self-dramatization, their restless exploration of ideas, their ecstatic devotion."

Honored by Signature Company

New York's acclaimed Signature Theater Company devoted its 1999–2000 season to Fornés's works, staging several of her plays and debuting a new one. In 1985's *Drowning,* based on a play by Anton Chekhov, Fornés presents a pair of odd, avuncular creatures that were described by *New York Times* critic Peter Marks as "gelatinous mounds of flesh" and resembling "tuskless walruses that have evolved into bipeds." One of them, Pea, has fallen in love with a woman based on her photograph in a newspaper, but when the two meet, she is horrified by his appearance. "The playlet is almost over," wrote Marks, "by the time you recover from the weird effect of the actors' swollen appearances. . . . One leaves the theater wondering where and when Ms. Fornés might next supply such a disturbing moment of emotional clarity."

The Signature Theater Company also staged *Mud* that season, Fornés's 1983 play about Mae and the two deplorable men in her life. Marks wrote favorably of the production in his a *New York Times* review, noting that "the crumbling world in which she slaves—the rooms of the house may be as dank and decrepit as prison cells, but there's always a Beckettesque pair of pants waiting for her to press—is the nightmare domain of martyred women everywhere." Signature's season included the Fornés play *Enter the Night,* which featured a playwright, Jack, who is convinced that he gave his late lover the AIDS virus that killed him. Two female friends struggle to convince him otherwise.

Won Record Ninth Obie

The Signature Theater season wrapped in 2000 with a new play from Fornés, *Letters From Cuba,* in which a New York City dancer, Fran, longs for her home and family back in Cuba. Elsewhere, on a rooftop in Cuba, her brother Luis reads her letters and also rues the political quagmire that separates their family. Fornés utilized some 200 letters from her own brother to write the work, and it won her a ninth Obie Award. Significantly, it was the first of Fornés's works to deal directly with her Cuban heritage, and as she admitted in a *New York Times* interview, "my brother is now 80. Rafael is the oldest and I am the youngest of six brothers and sisters. In the play, he is called Luis. I guess in some ways I have wanted to write about Cuba but I did not know exactly how."

Fornés's impact on a younger generation of writers was summed up by the words of Pulitzer Prize-winning dramatist Paula Vogel. "In the work of every American playwright at the end of the 20th century," the *Advocate's* Shewey quoted Vogel as saying, "there are only two stages: before she or he has read María Irene Fornés—and after." Fornés told the magazine that she has never aspired to genuine commercial success in the theater, and that the "fringe" label is fine with her. Otherwise, she told the *Advocate,* "people put claims on you and expect things of you. I've always liked being on the border." In 2002 Fornés received the PEN/Laura Pels Foundation Award and in 2003 she received the first MACHA Award for her exceptional work mentoring up-and-coming Latina writers.

Books

Contemporary Dramatists, sixth edition, St. James Press, 1999.
Dictionary of Hispanic Biography, Gale, 1996.
International Dictionary of Theater, Volume 2: *Playwrights,* St. James Press, 1993.

Periodicals

Advocate, May 26, 1998; November 9, 1999.
American Theatre, September 2000.
Back Stage, January 24, 1992; July 18, 1997; April 10, 1998; August 27, 1999; March 10, 2000; July 13, 2000; May 11, 2001; May 17, 2002; June 27, 2003.
Nation, April 6, 1985; April 23, 1988.
New York Times, September 27, 1999; December 13, 1999; February 27, 2000; May 29, 2003.
Variety, October 11, 1999; March 6, 2000.

Online

Mackay, Maggie. "Maria Irene Fornes,"*Arts Council England,* http://www.mariairenefornes.com/ (June 7, 2004). □

Rube Foster

For his achievements as a pitcher, manager, and founder and administrator of the first viable black baseball league, the Negro National League (NNL), Rube Foster (1879–1930) became known as "The Father of Black Baseball." He also founded the American Giants—one of the greatest black baseball teams in history.

Foster was born Andrew Foster on September 17, 1879, in Calvert, Texas, a farming community near Waco. He was the son of Andrew, the presiding elder of Calvert's Methodist Episcopal Church, and Sarah Foster. As a child, Foster was asthmatic. He was as devoted to church each Sunday morning as he was to baseball each Sunday afternoon. He showed promise early as an organizer and administrator of the sport and operated a team while a grade school student. After Sarah Foster died, Andrew Sr. remarried and moved to southwest Texas. By then, baseball already drove young Andrew's life. After completing the eighth grade, he left school and ran away to Fort Worth to pursue his love of the sport.

When he was only 17 years old, Foster had already begun to play for the Fort Worth Yellow Jackets. He traveled with the Jackets in Texas and bordering states and was introduced early to the prejudice that existed then toward baseball players. Quoted in *Only the Ball was White,* Foster said that the players "were barred away from homes . . . as baseball and those who played it were considered by Colored as low and ungentlemanly." He also pitched during batting practice when big-league clubs held spring training in Texas.

In 1901, when he was 21 years old, the big, brash, six foot, four inch tall player who weighed over 200 pounds pitched against Connie Mack's Philadelphia Athletics and caught the eye of big-city clubs. He refused an offer to pitch semiprofessional ball in Iowa and joined the black Leland Giants (also called the Chicago Union Giants) owned by Frank Leland, a veteran of black baseball in Chicago.

In 1902 Foster switched to E. B. Lamar's Union Giants, or Cuban Giants—a club from Philadelphia comprised of American blacks—earning $40 a month and 15 cents a meal for "eating money." By then he had become so self-assured about his talent that he called himself the best pitcher in the country. Sources disagree about the outcome of the first few games; however, *Blackball Stars* said that, after losing the first, Foster won 44 straight games. During this period as well, he beat the great Rube Waddell, whose record was 25-7 with the Philadelphia Athletics, and won the nickname "Rube" that was to remain with him for life. Foster led his team to victory over the Philadelphia Giants, the black baseball champions of the previous year. It has been said that the players disliked Foster, primarily because he "engaged in personalities" when he pitched. He was known also as a gunman and always carried his Texas six-shooters with him, which probably sparked the fear that many had of him.

Joined the Cuban X-Giants

Foster joined the Cuban X-Giants in 1903. Also a black American club from across town, they were rivals with the Philadelphia Giants. In the fall of 1903 Foster pitched in black baseball's first World Series, winning four games for the team. The Cuban X-Giants won the championship five games to two. According to legend, that year John McGraw of the New York Giants hired Foster to teach his screwball to Christy Mathewson, Iron Man McGinnity, and Red Ames. The Giants jumped from last place to second.

Nearly the entire Cuban X-Giants team switched to the Philadelphia Giants the next year and led them to victory in the World Series against their former club. Although Foster was sick when the three-game series opened, he won the first game 8–4, with 18 strikeouts, and the third and deciding game 4–2.

While data on Foster for 1904 are lacking, by 1905 he had remarkable power, winning 51 games and losing only 5. According to *Blackball Stars,* Honus Wagner, Pittsburgh's great shortstop, called him "the smoothest pitcher I've ever seen." Foster knew how to unnerve rival players when the bases were loaded. He appeared jolly, unconcerned, and smiled generously; more often than not, he came out victorious. Foster continued a successful career, then about 1906, unable to get a salary increase, left for the Leland Giants as manager and player who would do the booking and run the team as well. He took seven teammates with him. He persuaded Frank Leland to fire his previous players and hire Foster's, resulting in a team so successful that they won the Chicago semipro league title and finished ahead of the City All Stars, who hired big league players.

In 1907 the Lelands won 48 straight games for a total of 110 that year. They lost only ten games and won the pennant in Chicago's otherwise all-white city league. The press as well as baseball managers continued to praise Foster's ability. *Blackball Stars* quotes an undated issue of the *Chicago Inter-Ocean* that commented on Foster's tricks, speed, and coolness, calling him "the greatest baseball pitcher in the country." Willie Powell remembered in *Blackball Stars* that "Rube had a way to grip that ball, throw underhand, and he could hum it. And he was a trick pitcher, always tried to trick you into doing something wrong. If you were a big enough fool to listen to him, he'd have you looking at something else and strike you out."

In 1908 Foster changed the team's name to the American Giants to form what might have been the greatest black baseball team in history. In fact, according to *Blackball Stars,* Foster himself called it "the greatest team he ever assembled." Although there were other good black teams, the American Giants were consistently superior. In 1910 the team won 123 games out of 129. The Giants advertised their star-studded lineup and used heavyweight boxing champion Jack Johnson to hand out souvenirs to the women fans. The team's fame spread widely and rivaled that of the Chicago White Sox, who played two blocks from owner Charlie Comiskey's park. One Sunday in 1911 when the American Giants played, their attendance outdrew the Cubs and the White Sox.

There are conflicting accounts of this period in black baseball. According to *Only the Ball was White,* the American Giants were not formed until 1911, with players from the Leland Giants. Foster had entered a friendly partnership with John M. Schorling, a white tavern owner, who verbally agreed to a 50–50 split of receipts. This was a curious act for Foster, who was a shrewd businessman and should have known the importance of a signed contract.

Both in 1911 and 1912 the American Giants won the Chicago semipro crown. The Giants, who by now traveled by private Pullman, moved across the country for spring training and regular season games. They were an attraction to their fans, who watched them wear a different set of uniforms each day and use a variety of bats and balls. By 1916 when Foster was 35 years old, he had gained considerable weight and pitched less. That fall, however, the American Giants beat the Brooklyn Royal Giants to win the "colored World Series." Foster continued his tricks in the ball game and would do anything to win, including freezing baseballs before a game to spoil the opponent's ability land a good hit. Black baseball star James "Cool Papa" Bell said in *Blackball Stars:* "He built almost imperceptible ridges along the foul lines to insure that any bunted ball would stay fair while his race horses streaked across first base safely." He enticed young players to join his team by flaunting his immense prestige and bragging about the team's elaborate methods of travel.

The race riots of 1919 erupted in several cities. In Chicago alone, 38 people died. When Foster's team returned to their park, they found it occupied by tents of National Guardsmen. As well, during this period eastern black baseball teams threatened to raid Foster's team. By 1918 he paid his players $1,700 a month—more than teachers and mailcarriers earned—yet many of the players were illiterate. Still, the players were attracted by the promise of higher salaries from other owners.

Founded Negro National League

Black organizers had made unsuccessful attempts to form a viable black league in 1887 and again in 1906. In 1919, Foster called a meeting of the best black clubs in the Midwest and proposed the formation of a Negro National League and its governing body, the National Association of Colored Professional Base Ball Clubs. He used the *Chicago Defender* to launch his campaign for the new organization. Meeting on February 13–14, 1920, at the Kansas City YMCA (Young Men's Christian Association), owners of the black clubs drew up a constitution barring player raids and team-jumping, setting fines for unsportsmanlike conduct on and off the field, and other restrictions. Foster wanted an all-black enterprise that would be patterned after the major leagues but would ensure that money earned from the games would stay in black pockets. The group formed an eight–team league comprised of the American Giants, Joe Green's Chicago Giants, the Cuban Stars, the Detroit Stars, the St. Louis Stars, the Indianapolis ABCs, the Kansas City Monarchs, and the Dayton Marcos.

Foster foresaw the time when white and black teams would play each other in a World Series and wanted to be ready to integrate white teams when the time came. According to *Blackball Stars,* Foster told his colleagues, "We are the ship, all else the sea." Club owners criticized Foster, who became president of the league, for the power he had to serve as booking agent and hire umpires for the league since he owned a club himself. The players accused him of hiring umpires who favored the Giants. Foster survived the criticism in part by moving players from one team to another, apparently to effect parity among them. The colorful manager ran the league as a generous and benevolent autocrat, advancing loans to meet payrolls, sometimes from his own pocket. He helped players when they were in financial need. He believed in paying good salaries to keep good players.

The American Giants won the first three pennants in the new league, in 1920, 1921, and 1922. Foster's league prospered and prompted sports leaders in other parts of the country to form leagues. The Southern League was formed around this time, followed by the Eastern Colored League in 1923. Foster was unsuccessful in 1924 in his efforts to merge the NNL and the Eastern Colored League. Each manager wanted to retain his powerful position. When the teams met that year in a World Series, the Kansas City Monarchs of the NNL beat the Hilldale Club of the East. These games showcased some of the best black baseball players of the period.

Foster, who by then owned a barbershop as well as an automobile service shop, continued to oversee both the Negro National League and the American Giants. Throughout his baseball career he manipulated his players like robots and wholly directed his teams. According to *Total Baseball*, "Foster's teams specialized in the bunt, the steal, and the hit and run," which he advocated strongly, and characterized black baseball as well. A man with a remarkable memory who called everyone "darling," he never drank alcohol but puffed on a big pipe. He was both feared and respected by his players and fellow baseball managers. He was often called the greatest baseball manager of any race and shared his talent with others by teaching baseball subtleties to a generation of black managers, including Dave Malarcher, Biz Mackey, and Oscar Charleston. But, according to some writers, he wore himself out.

After being exposed to gas that leaked in his room in Indianapolis in May of 1925, he became unconscious and had to be dragged from his room to safety. Although he recovered, he became prone to illness thereafter. He began to act erratically the following year. Foster was placed in the state insane asylum at Kankakee, Illinois, with baseball still on his mind. He constantly raved about wanting to get out of bed and win another pennant. After his death of a heart attack at age 51 on December 9, 1930, a mammoth funeral drew 3,000 mourners who stood outside the church in the falling snow to watch Foster's final trip to Chicago's Lincoln Cemetery. Unfortunately, Foster's wife was unfamiliar with his business arrangements and realized no benefits from his baseball ventures. Foster's partner, John Schorling, ran the club until 1928, then sold it to a white florist, William E. Trimble. Black business leaders revived the club briefly in the early 1930s, but it never reached its original level of power.

Although Foster's league died with him during the Great Depression, black baseball was reborn in the mid-thirties. By 1945 Jackie Robinson became the first black to enter major league baseball of the modern era. As well, 36 players from the old Negro leagues went to the majors during this early period. Foster's dream of an integrated baseball league was realized. The ultimate recognition for Foster came in 1981, when he was elected to the baseball Hall of Fame in Cooperstown, New York.

Books

Chalk, Ocania, *Pioneers of Black Sport*, Dodd, Mead, 1975.
Holway, John B., *Blackball Stars: Negro League Pioneers*, Meckler Books, 1988.
———, *Voices from the Great Black Baseball Leagues*, Dodd, Mead, 1975.
Logan, Rayford W., and Michael R. Winston, eds., *Dictionary of American Negro Biography*, Norton, 1982.
Peterson, Robert, *Only the Ball Was White*, Prentice-Hall, 1970.
Ribowsky, Mark, *A Complete History of the Negro Leagues 1884 to 1955*, Carol Publishing Group, 1995.
Riley, James A., *The Biographical Encyclopedia of the Negro Baseball Leagues*, Carroll & Graf Publishers, 1994.
Rogosin, Donn, *Invisible Men*, Atheneum, Macmillan, 1983.
Thorn, John, and Peter Palmer, eds., *Total Baseball*, Warner Books, 1989.
Young, A. S., *Negro Firsts in Sports*, Johnson Publishing Co., 1963. □

A. J. Foyt

American race-car driver A. J. Foyt (born 1935), the first driver to have won the Indianapolis 500 four times, captivated both race fans and the general public with his many victories over a racing career that spanned three decades.

Joining Mario Andretti as one of the two best race car driver of the twentieth century according to the Associated Press, A. J. Foyt is the only driver to have won the world's top three professional races: the Indianapolis 500, the Daytona 500, and the 24-Hour LeMans. The only driver to win the Indy 500 four times—in 1961, 1964, 1967, and 1977—Foyt had 34 race starts and logged a record 11,785 miles during an Indy career that earned him $2,448,000 in prize money. Among his other racing victories prior to his retirement in 1993, Foyt took the cup at the Daytona 500 in 1972, won the 24-hour endurance race at LeMans, France, in 1968, 1983, and 1985, and drove over 40 U.S. Auto Club stock cars to victory. His versatility took him from formula one and Indy cars to stock cars, to sprint cars, midgets, sports cars, and dirt cars, and in 1987 he set the world's closed-course speed record for an Oldsmobile, pushing an Olds Aerotech to 257 miles per hour.

Anthony Joseph Foyt, Jr., was born in Houston, Texas on January 16, 1935. His father, A. J. Foyt, Senior, was co-owner of Houston's Burt & Foyt Garage; he knew his way around race cars because he specialized in working on them. Shadowing his dad at the family garage as a child, young Foyt not only learned how to build cars; he also knew by the time he was five that he wanted to race them. With the help of his father, who build his son's first midget racers, and family friends, he honed his driving skills, and during high school began driving a midget racer on the Midwestern race car circuit. Dropping out of high school in 11th grade, Foyt got a job at Burt & Foyt's Garage and began to apprentice as a driver. In 1953 18-year-old Foyt Jr.—who became known for his trademark cowboy boots and competitive spirit—won his first midget race on the quarter-mile dirt track at Houston's Playland Park.

King of the Indy 500

Foyt is unique among race car drivers, not the least because of his successes at Indiana's Indianapolis Motor Speedway. Joining the U.S. Auto Club in 1957, he made his Indy Car debut that same year, and qualified for Formula One's Indy 500 in 1958. In that race, held on Memorial Day, Foyt finished the race—the most difficult open-cockpit competition to run on an oval track in the United States—in the number-16 spot after a 12th-place start, running 148 laps and earning $2,849. Two years later Foyt won four races, including his first Indy Car race, and earned his first

national driving championship. During his first four years racing at the Indianapolis Motor Speedway, Foyt was the youngest driver on the field.

1961 proved to be a banner year for Foyt: it marked his first Indy 500 victory after three previous attempts. Racing at a record 139.13 mph after clocking a qualifying speed of 145.9 mph, he captured a front position after starting in seventh place. Foyt led the race for 71 laps and overcame the setback caused by a late-in-the-race pit stop to take on fuel, barely beating front-runner Eddie Sachs who limped into the pit with a worn tire.

Racing in the Indy 500 became an annual tradition for Foyt, who competed in the Grand Prix event for 35 years in a row, logging 4,909 laps around the two-and-a-half-mile oval track. The first driver to win the race four times, Foyt's winning record has not been beaten, although Al Unser and Rick Mears had it tied as of 2003. He also racked up a record seven Indy Car championships during his career, including those in 1967, 1975, and 1979. He also had his setbacks, however; in 1962, for example, he lost his third-place position after a loose wheel sent him spinning off the track, and four years later, in 1966, he was forced out of the race because of a multi-car accident that occurred shortly after the race start.

In 1964 Foyt swept the U.S. racing field, taking first place in ten out of 13 races. Among those ten victories was his second Indy 500 win, which he claimed after a fifth-position start and an average speed of 147.45 mph, he took the lead in 146 laps from competitors Rodger Ward and

Lloyd Ruby. Starting in fourth place in 1967, he took the Indy cup for the third time, leading the field in his Sheraton Thompson Special for 27 laps with a then-record speed of 151.21 mph. Losing rival driver Parnelli Jones after Jones's turbocharged engine blew in the final laps, and closely tailed by Unser, Foyt avoided a pileup during the final lap to gain the two laps needed to win the race.

Foyt repeated his winning Indy 500 performance one last time in 1977, when, at age 42, he drove to victory from a fourth-place qualifying start; the car that carried him to his legendary fourth win at a top speed of 161.331 mph, is now in the Indianapolis Motor Speedway museum. He earned a total of $2,640,576 for his team by competing in the Indy 500, and because he owned—and sometimes built—the cars he drove, was able to keep much of his race winnings. For this reason, Foyt was the first driver to top earnings of $1 million in the speedway's long and colorful history. He won his last Indy Car race in 1981, winning his ninth 500-mile event at that year's Pocono 500.

Although Foyt continued to return to Indianapolis every year to race in the 500, after 1977 he never again won the event. After more than three decades, in 1992 he made his last run around the legendary track. Qualifying for the 23rd starting position with a speed of 222.798 mph—over 68 mph faster than his qualifying speed in 1964—Foyt held a spot in the top 10 during more than half the race to finish in ninth place. That race proved to be Foyt's final Indy 500 run; although he practiced at the speedway the following season, he retired on the first qualifying day. Although his run for the 500 had ended, Foyt did return to the Indianapolis Motor Speedway to race in 1994's Brickyard 400, running 156 laps to place 30th in the pack, perhaps confirming his decision to retire.

A Versatile Driver

During a stellar career, Foyt has won 67 races on the Indy track—15 more than number-two-ranked driver Mario Andretti—and a total of 172 wins in major competitions. His performance, while rarely flagging, has in some years been amazing, as in 1963 when he won his third national championship by capturing three Indy Car events and finishing in eighth place or better in every race he entered. Besides winning his fourth national title and his second Indy 500 in 1964, Foyt also won the July 4th Firecracker 400 stock car race the following year. He won his fifth national Indy car championship in 1967, coming in 80 points ahead of rival Andretti, and his final national championships came in 1975 and 1979. By career end, he had garnered 12 national titles in the sport.

The mid-1960s were amazing years for Foyt as he became the third race-car driver to win races on an oval speedway, a road course, and a dirt track during a single racing season. On the speedway were his Indy Car victories; the road course was the 24-hour endurance race at LeMans he won in June of 1967, joining fellow driver Dan Gurney in a Ford Mark IV as the first U.S. team to win the grueling race. In the 1980s, with his career in Indy Car racing having already crested, he repeated his victory in the 24 hours at

LeMans in 1983 and 1985, and was victorious at the 12-hour endurance race at Sebring, Florida in 1985.

A versatile racer who competed in as many as 50 races each year at the height of his career, Foyt succeeded not just in Indy car racing, but also in other forms of motor sports, and chalked up a record 20-plus victories in the U.S. Auto Club (USAC)'s Indy Car, USAC stock car (41), sprint car (28) and midget (20) categories. He also had seven victories in sports cars and two in championship dirt cars, earning the USAC dirt car champion title in 1975. Foyt's astonishing record was enhanced even further when he captured the world closed course speed record for an Oldsmobile in 1987, recording a 257-m.p.h. lap in a Quad-4 powered Aerotech.

Surprising to many is the fact that Foyt was capable of chalking up so many wins in stock-car events. Named USAC stock car champion in 1968, 1978, and 1979, in the last-named year he also won the USAC Indy Car championship and became the first driver to win both titles in the same year. Signing up with the Wood Brothers team in the early 1970s, Foyt also competed on the popular NASCAR stock-car circuit, winning seven NASCAR Winston Cup races, the 1972 Daytona 500 his most notable victory.

A True Son of Texas

Foyt, one of the most recognized race-car drivers of his generation as well as of the twentieth century, was able to sustain a career that combined versatility, competitiveness, and leadership, winning him the respect of his peers. Called "Supertex" by fans referring to his Texas roots, the feisty, outspoken, and charismatic Foyt gave racing fans a cause for excitement, especially during his younger years when he was noted for sometimes exhibiting a volatile temper. As Larry Schwartz commented in an essay posted on *ESPN .com,* "Foyt has always believed in God, America and himself—and not necessarily in that order. A man of conviction, he is loyal to his friends and indifferent to his enemies. He is brash and blunt. He expected no quarter on the racetrack, and gave none himself. He knew only one speed—pedal to the floor."

Considered one of Texas's "favorite sons," Foyt has won many fans, not only because of his ability as a driver, but also because of his outgoing, colorful personality. Always working from his home base in Houston, he established A. J. Foyt Enterprises and race shop in that city in 1965. Since his retirement in 1993 at the age of 58, he has shifted gears and moved from race car driving to automobile sales, using his hard-won fortune to open A. J. Foyt Honda, which has become the largest auto dealership in his home state. An astute businessman and a self-made millionaire, he also invested money in oil wells and a hotel chain, and also owns several horse and cattle ranches in his home state. Foyt also serves on the board of directors of Riverway Bank and Service Corporation International, the nation's largest funeral business.

Foyt was the first inductee into the Motor Sports Hall of Fame in 1989, and in 2004 became among the first to be honored in the newly established Texas Motorsports Hall of Fame based in Fort Worth. Not surprisingly, retiring as a driver did not end Foyt's involvement in the racing world; he remains active in motor sports, owning several race cars and fielding two teams in the U.S.-based Indy Racing League he helped establish in 1995 as a competitor with the Formula One Grand Prix. He also continues to be an outspoken proponent of oval-track racing and of maintaining a U.S. presence in a sport that has become increasingly Europeanized. In 1999 he also established A. J. Foyt Racing, a NASCAR team headquartered in North Carolina.

Foyt continues to live in Houston with his wife Lucy, whom he married in 1955. Of Hoyt's four children, Jerry pursued a career in stock car racing, while Larry Foyt drives on the NASCAR circuit as part of Foyt Racing. Beginning with junior dragsters, grandson and Formula One racer A. J. Foyt IV also carries on the family tradition, completing his rookie NASCAR season in 2003. In 1983 Foyt published his autobiography, simply titled *A. J.* Twenty years later he still held the record for the most Indy Car wins, and remained the only driver in the history of the sport to win seven national Indy Car titles.

Books

Foyt, A. J., and Bill Neeley. *A. J.,* Times Books, 1983.
Libby, Bill, *Foyt,* Hawthorn Books, 1974.
St. James Encyclopedia of Popular Culture, St. James Press, 2000.

Periodicals

Saturday Evening Post, November 2, 1963.
Sport, January, 1997.
Sports Illustrated, June 1, 1964; June 13, 1966; June 19, 1967; October 12, 1998.
Time, June 9, 1967.

Online

ABC Sports Online, http://www.espn.go.com/abcsports./wwos/foyt/QandA.html (December 6, 2003).
ESPN.com, http://www.espn.go.com/sportscentury/features/00014199.html (December 6, 2003).
Foyt Racing: The Official Web site, http://www.foytracing.com (December 6, 2003).
Motor Sports Hall of Fame Web site, http://www.mshf.com/hof/foyt.htm (December 14, 2003). □

Erik Ivar Fredholm

Swedish mathematician and educator Erik Ivar Fredholm (1866–1927) proved in early childhood that he was a brilliant student of numerical theory. By the time Fredholm had completed his doctoral studies in 1898, he had also shown himself to be a brilliant theorist by developing the integral equation on which would be built the quantum theory and consequently a future of remarkable discoveries that have altered the way people live.

Fredholm was born on April 7, 1866, in Stockholm, Sweden, the first son of Ludvig Oscar and Catharina Paulina (Stenberg) Fredholm. Ludvig Fredholm, a merchant, amassed a fortune when his business was able to replace gas lamps with electric lamps. His wife was also the daughter of a wealthy merchant, and the couple had married on May 2, 1861, in Arboga, Sweden. In 1875, nine years after Erik's birth, another son, John Oscar was born to the couple. Well-educated themselves and able to afford the best education for their sons that money could buy, the Fredholm's sent their oldest son to the Beskowska School in Stockholm, where he received his diploma on May 16, 1885. As a child he played the flute and maintained a love of music throughout his life, as is characteristic of many mathematicians. The following year he studied at the Polytechnic Institute in Stockholm. According to M. Bernkopf in the *Dictionary of Scientific Biography,* "During this single year he developed an interest in the technical problems of practical mechanics that was to last all his life and that accounted for his continuing interest in applied mathematics."

Pursued Career in Education

Fredholm pursued his education and in 1886 enrolled at the University of Uppsala. At that time, Uppsala was the only institution in Sweden that awarded doctorates. Fredholm received a bachelor of science degree in 1888 and a Ph.D. on May 30, 1893. Ten years later he would receive a Doctor of Science degree from Uppsala, as well. He went to study at the University of Stockholm the same

year he received his bachelor's degree, having heard that teaching in Stockholm was superior. His professor there was Mittag-Leffler, a man well known for his unique brand of instruction. Fredholm remained enrolled at Uppsala in order to obtain his doctorate, but he stayed at Stockholm for the rest of his career, becoming first a lecturer in mathematical physics in 1898 and a professor of rational mechanics and mathematical physics on September 28, 1906. He also served the university as pro-dean beginning in 1909 and then as dean the following year.

Fredholm's responsibilities as an educator at the University of Stockholm did not preclude him from pursuing other careers. In addition to his university affiliation, he worked as a civil servant beginning in 1899 and served as a department head at the Swedish State Insurance Company in 1902. From 1904 until 1907 Fredholm worked as an actuary for the Skandia Insurance Company, and it was while he was there that he developed a formula to determine the surrender value of a life insurance policy. According to J. J. O'Connor and E. F. Robertson, in an essay posted on the *University of St. Andrews School of Mathematics and Statistics Web site,* noted that it is "tempting to think that with two mathematical careers running in parallel, namely applications to physical applied mathematics and applications to actuarial science, Fredholm would have had little time for other interests." In actuality, Fredholm actively pursued music even into his later years, His focus eventually shifted from the flute to the violin, with the compositions of J. S. Bach among his favorites. With an intellect equally at home with music and with mathematics, Fredholm was also actively engaged in the physical world and took time to build machines that could solve differential equations. Fredholm's occupation with mechanics and machines was encompassing enough for him to become a member of the Swedish Society of Engineers, often adding his own expertise in scientific matters to the society.

Began to Publish Research

Fredholm first published in 1890; his paper "A Special Class of Functions" was released under the auspices of the Royal Swedish Academy of Sciences. According to O'Connor and Robertson, "In this paper, he constructed a function which is analytic on the unit disk, is infinitely differentiable on the closed disk, but has no analytic continuation outside the disk. As was always the case with all the deep mathematical results which Fredholm produced, this result was inspired by mathematical physics, in this case by the heat equation." Mittag-Leffler was so impressed that he sent a copy of Fredholm's paper to the well-known French mathematician Jules Henri Poincaré.

Fredholm's doctoral thesis reveals his first major work in partial differential equations. Two years after he received his degree, the paper was published and revealed to the world the solution to the integral equation for which he became famous. The very first equation he completed had already been investigated for nearly a century by U.S. astronomer George Hill, although no satisfactory results had ever been reached by Hill. According to Bernkopf, Niels Abel had solved a different form of it in 1823, but that also had a different function. In 1884 Carl Neuman reached a partial solution to the equation by use of a particular method called an "iteration scheme," but had to add a condition to guarantee the convergence of his solution, noted Bernkopf. An integral equation is a mathematical equation that includes an unknown function, "f." The integral equation solved by Fredholm—which he went on to further study in two algebraic forms—now bears his name and is widely used in quantum mechanics.

Regarding the true significance of Fredholm's work, N. Zeilon noted in his *Obituary of Erik Ivar Fredholm:* "We may ask what in Fredholm's eyes was the essential basis of his work. The answer is immediate: potential theory. Already in 1895 after a seminar lecture in 1895 he had talked about Dirichlet's problem as one of elimination. Two years later in Stockholm a lecture about the 'principal solutions' of Roux and their connections with Volterra's equation led to a vivid discussion. Finally, after a long silence, Fredholm spoke and remarked in his usual slow drawl: 'in potential theory there is also such an equation.'" Fredholm spent several months in Paris in 1899 studying with French mathematicians Poincaré, Emile Picard, and Hadamard, where he was able to reach many of his conclusions that contributed to the success of his work.

Far-reaching Implications

When fellow mathematician Erik Holmgren presented 35-year-old Fredholm's equation to the mathematical world in Göttingen, Germany, in 1901, many were immediately aware of its importance, and for the next 25 years integral equations became a major area of mathematical research. Mathematician David Hilbert eventually extended Fredholm's work and his theory of "Hilbert spaces" became an important step in the development of the quantum theory that describes the behavior of particulate matter—atoms, electrons, and the like—during short intervals.

In *Mathematics and Mathematicians: Mathematics in Sweden before 1950* author Lars Garding explained that "Fredholm's work on integral equations was met with great interest and boosted the morale and self-respect of Swedish mathematicians who so far had been working under the shadow of the continental cultural empires Germany and France. Integral equations had now become a new mathematical tool.... It was developed during several decades and was seen as a universal tool with which it was possible to solve the majority of boundary value problems and physics. But the qualitative insight that the theory gave could also be achieved in a simpler way. The significance of Fredholm's work was more the qualitative insight than the specific formulas."

Gained Family Later in Life

Dedicating much of his early adulthood to education and research, Fredholm finally married in middle age. His wedding occurred in Sankt Olai, Sweden, on May 31, 1911. Fredholm was now 45 years of age; his wife, Agnes Maria Liljeblad, was 33 at the time of the marriage, and was the daughter of members of the Protestant clergy. The couple had several children.

Fredholm's mathematical contributions brought him many honors. His awards include the V. A. Wallmarks prize, awarded to the mathematician in 1903; the Poncelet prize presented him by the French Academy of Sciences in 1908; and an honorary doctorate from the University of Leipzig presented to Fredholm in 1909.

When he died at the age of 61 in 1927, Fredholm was reportedly at work on calculating the mathematics involved in the acoustics of the violin. The papers he left on this project have proven impossible for other to understand, leaving conclusions undetermined. In addition to his work on integral equations, Fredholm also contributed mathematical insights into spectral theory.

Books

Dictionary of Scientific Biography, Volume 5, Charles Scribner's Sons, 1980.
Garding, Lars, *Mathematics and Mathematicians: Mathematics in Sweden before 1950,* American Mathematical Society, 1998.
Zeilon, N. *Obituary of Erik Ivar Fredholm, Oeuvres complete de Ivar Fredholm,* [Malmo, Sweden], 1955.

Periodicals

Physics World, December 1999.

Online

"Erik Ivar Fredholm," *University of St. Andrews School of Mathematics and Statistics Web site,* http://www.-history.mcs.st-andrews.ac.uk/history/Mathematicians/Fredholm.html (December 2002). □

Fu Mingxia

Chinese diver Fu Mingxia (born 1978) won the platform-diving world championship in 1991 at the tender age of 12, making her the youngest diving champ of all time. She also holds the notoriety of being the youngest Olympic-diving champion, having earned a gold at the 1992 Barcelona Games when she was just 13. Throughout the 1990s, Fu dominated the sport with her stunning repertoire of picture-perfect, yet extremely difficult dives. During the 2000 Olympics, held in Sydney, Australia, Fu won her fourth gold, joining Americans Pat McCormick and Greg Louganis as the world's only quadruple Olympic-diving champions. Fu's record speaks for itself—with four Olympic golds and one silver, she is clearly one of the best divers China has ever produced.

On the Beijing 2008 Olympic organizing committee website, Fu described diving as a one-second art. "It takes a diver only 1.7 seconds from the 10-meter-platform to the water surface down below. It requires you to fully display the beauty of the sport in only a second. It's very demanding, but I love the challenge."

Dove Before She Could Swim

Fu Mingxia (pronounced Foo Ming-shah) was born August 16, 1978, into a humble working-class family in the city of Wuhan, located along the Yangtze River in central China. Perhaps Fu's parents knew that she was a diamond in the rough when they named her Mingxia, which translates to "bright rays of tomorrow." Inspired by an older sister, Fu enrolled in gymnastics at a local sports school at the age of 5. From the beginning, it was clear Fu possessed natural athletic grace. Though she was just a child, Fu demonstrated remarkable poise and body control. The coaches, however, felt that she was not flexible enough to make it as a gymnast. Instead, they suggested she pursue diving, though Fu, only about seven years old at the time, could not swim.

"My father would teach me swimming after work by supporting me with his hand in the water," Fu told *Washington Post* writer Lena H. Sun. "When I began to practice diving, the coach would tie a rope around my waist during diving training so she could pull me up after each dive."

Fu easily made the transition from gymnast to springboard diver and before long was noticed by diving coach Yu Fen, who took Fu to Beijing in 1989 to train at a state-sponsored boarding school as a member of the state diving team. China prides itself in churning out athletic prodigies who can win international competitions and bolster the country's reputation. In China, it is common practice for children with athletic promise to be taken away from home at an early age to live at special sports schools where their

talents can be refined. Fu was chosen for such a life. Because of her remarkable talents, she became a part of China's disciplined, but highly successful sports machine.

Once in Beijing, the young Fu began intensive training for the more difficult but dramatic platform-diving event. Coach Yu told the *Washington Post* that many kids who start as young as Fu are afraid to climb to the top of the 10-meter platform, which stands about 33 feet above the water. Fu was scared, too, but she faced her fear head-on, a skill that would help take her to the top of the sport.

Fu recalled her first trip to the top of the platform in an article posted on the Beijing 2008 Olympic organizing committee's website. "It was so high above the water! But we had a professional rule: a diver must leave the platform from the front; that means you have to dive. So I jumped. I was scared to death. My heart was about to come out of my body. But I did it."

Through a strenuous training program, Fu learned to set aside her fears and progressed quickly. Typical of Chinese children at sports schools, her days were highly structured and sheltered, containing little more than diving practice and schooling. Training sessions averaged four to five hours a day, seven days a week, with the occasional nine-hour day. At times, Fu practiced 100 dives a day. In time, she was gliding so close to the platform during her dives that her short hair often touched the end during her descent toward the water.

Fu was clearly on her way to becoming a world-class diver; however, there were drawbacks to the program. Once Fu went to Beijing, she pretty much lost contact with her parents. Fu was allowed visits home only twice a year. Her parents attended her diving competitions when they were close to her hometown of Wuhan. When Fu was competing near her home turf, she would scan the crowd in hopes of locating her parents. In time, however, they became almost unrecognizable. The only way Fu knew they had come to watch was because they would leave care packages for her in the locker room.

Won Olympic Gold at 13

In 1990, Fu made her international diving debut, capturing a gold at the U.S. Open and also at the Goodwill Games, held that summer in Seattle. Her daring dives from the top of the 10-meter platform transformed the teeny 12-year-old into a national treasure. However, with pressure mounting, Fu placed third at the Asian Games held in Beijing in the fall of 1990. Following the loss, she changed her routine, adding moves that were technically more difficult, but which she felt more comfortable performing.

Adding the more difficult moves probably helped her score more points in the long run because the more difficult dives yield higher points. Here is how the scoring works in diving competitions: Judges evaluate dives on several components, including the approach, takeoff, elevation, execution and entry. Dives are rated on a scale of zero to ten. In major competitions, there are typically five to seven judges. After judges determine their ratings, the highest and lowest scores are tossed out. To get the final score, the remaining scores are added. This number is then multiplied by the dive's degree of difficulty, which ranges from 1.0 for an easy dive to 2.9 for the more difficult maneuvers.

By 1991, Fu was talented enough to attend the diving world championships, held in Perth, Australia. The competition was intense, and Fu found herself in eighth place in the final round because she had failed a compulsory dive. Fu pulled herself together, however, and ended up with the title, beating out the Soviet Union's World Cup winner Elena Miroshina by nearly 25 points. At just 12 years old, Fu became the youngest international champ ever. It is a title she will hold forever because after the competition, swimming's national governing body changed the rules, requiring all competitors of international competitions to be at least 14 years old.

While Fu initially made her mark on the 10-meter platform, she also began competing on the three-meter springboard. In April 1992, she won the gold on the springboard at the Chinese international diving tournament in Shanghai.

Fu made her Olympic debut at the 1992 Games, held in Barcelona, Spain. During the competition, the five-foot-half-inch, 94.8-pound Fu used her youthful fearlessness to beat out older, more elegant competitors. Fu easily captured a gold in the platform competition. At 13, she was the youngest medal winner at the Olympics that year-and the second-youngest in the history of the Games. She also qualified as the youngest Olympic diving champion, a title she still holds.

Fu's success in her first Olympics drove her toward her second. In preparing for the 1996 Olympics, held in Atlanta, Fu trained seven hours a day, six days a week. Her only other activities included listening to music, watching television and getting massages. Fu's coaches drilled her hard, but she said she found comfort and peace from the physically and mentally straining regimen through music. The hard work paid off. Fu was in top form at the 1996 Olympics and shined on both the platform and springboard, taking gold in both events. She was the first woman in 36 years to win both events in a single Olympics.

Retired, then Staged a Comeback

Shortly after Atlanta, the triple-gold-medallist quit the sport and enrolled at Beijing's Tsinghua University to study management science. "I want to retire. I am already too old," she said at the time, according to the *South China Morning Post.* "It's like climbing a hill. When you reach the top, there is no way to go other than down." Fu also got involved in politics and in 1997 served as a delegate to the Communist Party's 15th Congress.

Fu spent about two years off the board. By 1998, however, Fu felt a tug toward returning to the sport and began diving with the university team. "Taking a break took the pressure off diving," she told *Time'*s Hannah Beech. "It made me realize that I loved the sport and that I could do it on my own terms."

On her own terms still meant a disciplined training schedule, but she reduced the number of hours per day down to five. Fu told *Time* that she found practicing just for the sake of practicing to be a pointless endeavor.

As a member of the university team, Fu competed in the 1999 World University Games in Palma, Spain, winning both the highboard and springboard titles. Less than a year back into it, she won silver at the Diving World Cup. Fu regained her spot on the national Olympic squad and also took up a new sport—three-meter synchronized diving—as she headed for the 2000 Olympics in Sydney, Australia. Fu and her partner, Guo Jingjing, practiced together for less than six months, yet earned a silver. The Russian pair that beat them had trained together for years. After the synchronized diving event, Fu went on to compete on the springboard. She handily won a gold, nailing her final dive, a reverse one-and-a-half somersault, two-and-a-half twist for nines when eights would have been enough to beat out Guo, her teammate. With her four gold medals and one silver, Fu became one of the most decorated Olympic divers of all time.

Plunged into Marriage, Motherhood

After the Games in Sydney, Fu concentrated on her studies. In 2001, she met Hong Kong Financial Secretary Antony Leung, a popular government official. Born in 1952, the divorced Leung seemed an unlikely suitor. The press reported that the duo met at an awards banquet where he showed her how to play games on his palm pilot. They married within a year. A multi-millionaire, Leung owns properties in Hong Kong, Beijing, Shanghai, Hawaii, and Singapore. Some speculated that Fu was after his money, but Fu also makes plenty of money in advertising deals. For a time, Fu was Sprite's face in China and has also advertised for cosmetics firms, as well as the Chinese mobile phone company Shouxin. Reports have said that Fu is worth more than $3 million from her lucrative contracts. The couple had a daughter in February 2003.

Though Fu is no longer diving, she gave back to her country by helping as a member of the Beijing Olympic bid committee for the 2008 Olympics. Beijing won the bid, and Fu was excited that people from all over the world would see her country in 2008. She was to serve as an ambassador at the event. Fu has said that she hopes that by hosting the Olympics, people from all over the world will become reacquainted with China and recognize the great changes that have occurred in recent years. Her future plans include promoting diving, as well as other sports.

Periodicals

New York Times, May 4, 1992.
South China Morning Post, March 6, 1993; March 24, 2002.
Straits Times (Singapore), February 28, 2003.
Washington Post, May 22, 1991.

Online

"Fu Mingxia," *Time,* http://www.time.com/time/asia/magazine/2000/0911/olys.mingxia.html (November 30, 2003).
"Fu Mingxia, the Diving Queen," Official Website of the Beijing Organizing Committee for the Games of the XXIX Olympiad, http://210.75.208.159/eolympic/ydy/mdmm/mdmm_fmx.htm (December 10, 2003). □

Louis Agassiz Fuertes

Louis Agassiz Fuertes (1874–1927) was one of the most talented illustrators of birds in history. His evocative works remain an influential storehouse of knowledge about avian species.

The Birth of a Great Naturalist

Born in Ithaca, a small upstate New York town, on February 7, 1874, Louis Agassiz Fuertes was named after Louis Agassiz, a renowned 19th-century Harvard naturalist whom his parents admired. His parents were Estevan Antonio Fuertes, a Puerto Rican-born professor of civil engineering at nearby Cornell University, and the former Mary Stone Perry, of Troy, New York. The youngest of six children all educated in the local public schools, Fuertes showed an extraordinary interest in birds at an early age. His parents were finally forced to address their son's growing preoccupation when they found a live owl tied by its leg to the kitchen table. Mr. Fuertes reportedly took his son, then about eight years old, to the Ithaca Public Library and introduced him to John James Audubon's *Birds of America,* which then was regarded as the world's finest compilation of bird illustrations.

Fuertes was strongly influenced by this first exposure to Audubon's works and began drawing birds in earnest. However, perhaps regretting their indulgence of his interest, Fuertes's parents began to discourage their son's passion for illustrating the dozens of birds he killed and brought home to study, believing that he would never be able to support himself as an artist. In 1892, Fuertes went with his parents to Europe, where he attended a preparatory school in Zurich, Switzerland. Upon returning to the United States in 1893, Fuertes was persuaded to enroll at Cornell and take regular courses at the College of Architecture there. However, he did this only to fail virtually all of the classes he entered. A notable exception was a drawing class, in which he excelled.

Fate Took a Hand

Just as it seemed Fuertes might have to consider a future as an engineer, he seized a chance to show his growing portfolio of illustrations to Elliott Coues, who was on the staff of the Smithsonian Institution and then one of the country's top ornithologists, during a school trip to the nation's capital in 1894. Impressed by the young man's talent, Coues made Fuertes his prodigy, convinced him that he could support himself as an artist, introduced him to the world of academia, and showed him how to obtain commissions for his work. In fact, it was Coues who gave Fuertes his first formal commission.

Thus Fuertes launched his career as an artist during college, taking such jobs as doing a series of pen-and-ink drawing's for Florence A. Merriam's *A-Birding on a Bronco* in 1896; four illustrations for *The Osprey,* a new birding

magazine in 1897; and more than 100 drawings for Coues's *Citizen Bird* between 1896 and 1897.

The artist did manage to graduate from Cornell in 1897, but certainly not with any degree of distinction. Fuertes remained busy with illustration jobs throughout this period, doing 18 drawings for the 1897 book *Song Birds and Water Fowl;* a series of illustrations for the American Ornithologists' Union official magazine, *The Auk;* and a color picture for the front of *On the Birds' Highway* (1899). From 1897 to 1898, Fuertes also had his first formal art training with artist Abbott H. Thayer, who had developed theories on the optical characteristics of light and color, and worked toward his artistic goal of depicting live birds authentically. He studied at the artist's summer cottage in New Hampshire and later, in 1898, went on a brief expedition to Florida with Thayer and his son.

Through Coues, Fuertes made the acquaintance of C. Hart Merriman, who in 1899 invited the young artist to accompany him on the Harriman Expedition to Alaska. This was quite an honor, since the other people asked to join the expedition, including landscape painters Frederick Dellenbaugh and Robert Swain Gifford, photographer Edward Curtis, and scientists John Muir and John Burroughs, were older and more accomplished.

Nevertheless, Fuertes was soon in his element in the wilds of Alaska and went with the expedition as far north as Plover Bay in Siberia. There he continued to refine the methods of scientific recording that he had been developing for years. Working almost always with a bird he had shot and sometimes skinned, Fuertes also learned to make rapid sketches of barely glimpsed birds and to retain their songs in his memory until he could add them to his copious field notes back at camp. Friends and associates recall that Fuertes was completely oblivious to everything around him when he was working on an illustration. He was also reportedly a popular member of the expedition, with his never-ending enthusiasm, mischievous sense of humor, and outgoing personality. In a letter to his family written during his travels in Alaska, Fuertes's excitement at coming upon a huge colony of sea birds is apparent when he exclaimed (as quoted on *The Public Broadcasting System website*), "Thousands and thousands of birds—tame to stupidity, seated on every little ledge or projection . . . —all the time coming and going, screaming, croaking, peeping, chuckling, with constant moving of countless heads . . . makes a wonderful sight, and one not soon to be forgotten. . . . "

A Passion Became a Profession

Soon after returning from Alaska, the incredibly detailed, full-color drawings Fuertes had done on the expedition were published. Their reception by the scientific community was such that he was asked to illustrate almost every important bird book published in the country from that point forward. Fuertes's work was distinguished not only by the minute detail of each illustration but by his ability to capture each species' way of acting and holding itself. Every bird he painted seemed to have its own unique and vital personality. This skill, as well as his astounding ability to remember whatever he saw, would grow even stronger as he aged. In fact, many bird lovers who grew up studying the drawings of Fuertes saw birds more as the artist had painted them, rather than as they actually appeared in life.

Fuertes had finally realized his dream of making a living as a bird artist, dedicating himself to preserving on paper what he extolled as "the singular beauty of birds." In 1901, he accepted an invitation from the United States Biological Survey to visit western Texas and New Mexico, and in 1902 he began a long series of trips with the curator of birds at the American Museum in New York City, Dr. Frank M. Chapman. Meanwhile, in 1904 Fuertes married Margaret Sumner, whom he took on another expedition to Jamaica for their honeymoon. (They would later have two children.) Over the next decade, he and Chapman combed the wilds of the Bahamas (1902), Saskatchewan, the Pacific coast of the United States, Florida's Cuthbert Rookery, the Canadian Rockies, eastern Mexico and the Yucatan (1910), and Colombia (1911 and 1913). Fuertes also traveled to the Magdalen Islands and Bird Rock in 1909 with another scientist, adding to the thousands of sketches and drawings he had accumulated.

Some of Fuertes' best-known illustrations appeared in the beautiful *Birds of New York* (1910) and, from 1913 to 1920, *National Geographic* magazine. In addition, in about 1920, the Arm and Hammer Baking Soda Company hired Fuertes to create a large series of bird "collector cards" that were inserted in the boxes of the product and collected by children everywhere throughout the 1920s and 1930s. The cards were widely credited with helping to popularize birdwatching and advance the relatively new concept of conservation. Another of the artist's most critically acclaimed series of illustrations appeared in the lavish, three-volume *Birds of Massachusetts and Other New England States* in 1925.

Having since his late teens spent a good part of every year away from home on birdwatching expeditions, Fuertes began to stay closer to home in the 1920s. In 1923, he accepted a position as a lecturer on ornithology at Cornell and taught such aspiring artists as George Miksch Sutton, who would later be regarded as one of the best bird illustrators in the United States. Fuertes took a leave of absence from his lecturing position to go on what would be his final expedition. In 1926, he accompanied Dr. Wilfred H.

Osgood of Chicago's Field Museum of Natural History to Abyssinia (now Ethiopia). During this trip, he created some of his finest field studies, having honed his talent to the point at which he could render a stunningly lifelike sketch of a bird from just a brief glimpse. Even years after seeing a certain bird, he could reportedly draw the individual in all its complexity without hesitation.

Died in Hometown

Three months after returning home from Abyssinia, Fuertes died on August 22, 1927, in an automobile accident near his home in Ithaca. He was 53 years old. He left behind a collection of 3,500 expertly prepared bird skins and about 1,000 studio and field sketches of more than 400 species of birds from all over the world. At the artist's funeral, according to *American National Biography,* his old friend Dr. Chapman said of Fuertes, ". . . as much as he loved birds, he loved man more. No one could resist the charm of his enthusiasm, his ready wit and whole-souled genuineness . . . If the birds of the world had met to select a human being who could best express to mankind the beauty and charm of their forms . . . they would unquestionably have chosen Louis Fuertes."

Books

Garraty, John A., ed., *American National Biography,* Oxford University Press, 1999.
Johnson, Allen, ed., *Dictionary of American Biography,* Charles Scribner's Sons, 1977.

Online

"Biography for the Artist Fuertes, Louis Agassiz," *AskART.com website,* http://www.askart.com (December 9, 2003).
"Guide to the Louis Agassiz Fuertes Papers, 1892–1954," *The Cornell Institute for Digital Collections website,* http://www.cidc.library.cornell.edu (December 9, 2003).
"Harriman: Louis Agassiz Fuertes," *The Public Broadcasting System website,* http://www.pbs.org (December 9, 2003).
"Louis Agassiz Fuertes," *The Raptor Education Foundation website,* http://www.usaref.org (December 9, 2003).
"Paintings by Louis Agassiz Fuertes," *The New York State Museum website,* http://www.nysm.nysed.gov (December 9, 2003).
"Robert McCracken Peck: A Celebration of Birds: The Life and Art of Louis Agassiz Fuertes," *The Public Broadcasting System website,* http://www.pbs.org (December 9, 2003). □

G

Joseph Galamb

Joseph Galamb (1881–1955), born in Hungary, became a draftsman and designer at the Ford Motor Company in Detroit, Michigan, in 1905. He designed many of the components of the Model T including the planetary gearbox, and he continued design work at Ford until the mid-1940s.

Educated in Hungary

Galamb was born on February 3, 1881, in Mako, Hungary. He graduated from the Budapest Technical University (now Donat Banki Technical College) in 1899 with a diploma in mechanical engineering.

Galamb became a draftsman at the Steel Engineering Factory in Diosgyor, then joined Hungary's largest automobile factory, the Hungarian Automobile Company, in Arad, Transylvania, where he won a scholarship to do postgraduate work in Germany. By 1903 he had worked in several German cities and at the German Adler car factory.

Met Henry Ford

Galamb sailed to the United States to attend the 1903–04 World's Fair in St. Louis, then joined the Westinghouse Corporation as a toolmaker. He traveled to Detroit on December 10, 1905, for a short visit, and he met Henry Ford, who convinced Galamb to work for Ford at the two-year-old Ford Motor Company as a draftsman.

Galamb's ability earned him a quick promotion to the company's experimental factory, where he designed components for the Model M. Soon he was reassigned again to develop a new racing prototype that Ford felt would help publicize and popularize the automobile. Galamb's six-cylinder racer reportedly performed well.

Design on Model T

One day in early 1907, Galamb recalled, as quoted in the Piquette Story website, Ford came to him and said, " 'Joe, I've got an idea to design a new car. . . . At that time we didn't know that it was to be the Model T. It was just a new model.' "

The Model T, whose production continued until 1927, was wildly popular in the United States and is considered the first mass-produced automobile. Working on it, Galamb made drawings on paper and on a blackboard that were photographed next to a calendar every day to avert patent problems later. The planning was a secret. The Model T was developed over a two-year period. Prototypes were tested in a fence-enclosed lot. Galamb is credited with designing the Model T's clutch, transmission, drive shaft, and differential. He also designed much of the chassis. The Model T's design was well-suited to assembly line production. Improvements were ongoing. In March 1919 Galamb made the lives of most Model T Mechanics much more pleasant by changing the design of the pin from a straight pin to a rivet with a cotter pin hole.

Designed Tractors, Trucks

With the Model T under production, Galamb was asked by Ford to design a light tractor for farmers. Galamb used the engine from a Model B coupled with the powertrain from the Model T to create Ford's first gas-powered tractor. Beginning in 1915, Galamb worked on plans for the Fordson tractor and ignition plug. During World War I he worked on Liberty aircraft engines and designed ambulance vans and light trucks. Then in 1927 he began work on the Model A Ford.

Ended Career at Ford

In 1937 Galamb received a formal title, chief of design. He worked with Henry Ford's son, Edsel, and during World War II he designed a small six-cylinder car, completing it in 1942. He retired because of health problems in April 1944. He died on December 4, 1955.

Ford did not consume all Galamb's productive years. He visited Hungary many times, and in 1921 he established a scholarship for poor students in Mako to enable them to pursue higher education. He also lectured at the Association of Hungarian Engineers and Architects. On February 3, 1981, Mako honored Galamb with a plaque memorializing the hundredth anniversary of his birth and describing him as "a mechanical engineer who did pioneering work on the Model T Ford and Fordson tractor."

Books

Lacey, Robert, *Ford: The Men and the Machine,* Little, Brown, 1986.

Online

"Changing Faces of Other Vehicles," *AutomobileIndia.com,* www.automobileindia.com/timeline/time4.html (January 10, 2004).

"Henry Ford's Chief Designer," *Ford's Chief Designer - Joseph Galamb/Haris Bros. Auto Museum,* www.katylon.com/harisauto/x_archyive/galamb/galamb.htm (December 19, 2003).

"Joseph Galamb—(1881–1955) Ford Chief," *The Hungary Page - More Famous Hungarians,* http://hipcat.hungary.org/users/hipcat/sciencemathandtech2.htm (January 10, 2004).

"Jozsef Galamb (1881–1955)," *Jozsef Galamb (1881–1955),* www.hpo.hu/English/inventor/egalamb.html (January 10, 2004).

"The Model T Crank Ratchet and How It Changed," www.mtfca.com/encyclo/ratchets.htm (January 10, 2004).

"Piquette Personalities: Joseph A. Galamb," *The Piquette Story,* www.piquettestory.tplex.org/personsgalamb.htm (December 19, 2003).

"Reminiscences of Joseph Galamb," *The Piquette Story: The Experimental Room,* www.piquettestory.tplex.org/secretroom.htm (December 19, 2003). □

Henry Highland Garnet

Henry Highland Garnet (1815–1882) was a leading member of the generation of black Americans who led the abolition movement away from moral suasion to political action. Garnet urged slaves to act and claim their own freedom. Garnet worked to build up black institutions and was an advocate of colonization in the 1850s and after. Garnet also devoted his life to ministry in the Presbyterian Church.

Garnet was born into slavery near New Market, Kent County, Maryland, on December 23, 1815. His father, George Trusty, was the son of a Mandingo warrior prince, taken prisoner in combat. George and Henny (Henrietta) Trusty had one other child, a girl named Mary. George had learned the trade of shoemaking. The Trusty's owner, William Spencer, died in 1824. A few weeks later 11 members of the Trusty family received permission to attend a family funeral. They never returned. Travelling first in a covered market wagon and then on foot for several days, the family group made its way to Wilmington, Delaware. There they separated; seven went to New Jersey, and Garnet's immediate family went to New Hope, Pennsylvania, where Garnet had his first schooling.

In 1825 the Garnets moved to New York City. There, after earnest prayer, George Trusty gave new names to the family. His wife Henny became Elizabeth, his daughter Mary, Eliza. Although the original first names of George and Henry are unknown, the family name became Garnet. George Garnet found work as a shoemaker and also became a class-leader and exhorter in the African Methodist Episcopal Church.

Garnet entered the African Free School in Mott Street in 1826. There he found an extraordinary group of schoolmates. They included Alexander Crummell, an Episcopal priest and a leading black intellectual, who was Garnet's neighbor and close boyhood friend; Samuel Ringgold Ward, a celebrated abolitionist and a cousin of Garnet; James McCune Smith, the first black to earn a medical degree; Ira Aldridge, the celebrated actor; and Charles Reason, the first black college professor in the United States and long-time educator in black schools. Garnet and his classmates formed their own club, Garrison Literary and Benevolent Association, and soon had occasion to demonstrate their spirit. Garrison's abolitionism had little mass support among whites at this time, and abolition meetings in New York City easily led to mob violence. Thus, even the school authorities feared the use of his name for a club meeting at the school. The boys retained the club's name and moved their activities elsewhere.

As a boy, Garnet was high-spirited and quite different from the sober and quiet adult he later became. In 1828 he made two voyages to Cuba as a cabin boy, and in 1829 he worked as a cook and steward on a schooner from New York to Washington, D.C. On his return from this voyage, he learned that the family had been scattered by the threat of slave catchers. His father had escaped by leaping from the upper floor of the house at 137 Leonard Street—next door to the home of Alexander Crummell. The family of a neighboring grocer had sheltered his mother. His sister was taken but successfully maintained a claim that she had always been a resident of New York and therefore no fugitive slave. All of the family's furniture had been stolen or destroyed. Garnet bought a large clasp-knife to defend himself and wandered on Broadway with ideas of vengeance. Friends found him and sent him to hide at Jericho on Long Island.

Since Garnet had to support himself, he was bound out to Epenetus Smith of Smithtown, Long Island, as a farm worker. While he was there he was tutored by Smith's son Samuel. In the second year there, when he was 15, Garnet injured his knee playing sports so severely that his indentures were canceled. The leg never properly healed, and he used crutches for the rest of his life. (After 13 years of suffering and illness, the leg was finally amputated at the hip in December 1840.) Garnet returned to his family, which had reestablished itself in New York. He then continued his schooling, and in 1831 he entered the newly established high school for blacks, rejoining Alexander Crummell as a fellow student.

The leg injury may have sobered Garnet, who became more studious and turned his thoughts to serious consideration of religion. Sometime between 1833 and 1835 he joined the Sunday school of the First Colored Presbyterian Church, located at the corner of William and Frankfort streets. There Garnet became the protegé of minister and noted abolitionist Theodore Sedgewick Wright, the first black graduate of Princeton's Theological Seminary, who brought about Garnet's conversion and then encouraged him to enter the ministry.

Garnet married Julia Ward Williams in 1841, the year he was ordained an elder. Williams was born in Charleston, South Carolina, but came to Boston at an early age. Williams had studied at Prudence Crandall's school in Canterbury, Connecticut, and also at Noyes Academy. She taught school in Boston for several years and after her marriage was head of the Female Industrial School while the family lived in Jamaica. The couple had three children: James Crummell (1844–1851); Mary Highland (born c. 1845); and a second

son (born 1850). There was also an adopted daughter Stella Weims, a fugitive slave. Julia Garnet died in 1870, and about 1879 he married Susan Smith Thompkins, a noted New York teacher and school principal.

Sought Higher Education

In 1835 Garnet, Alexander Crummell, and Thomas S. Sidney, classmates from New York, made the difficult journey to the newly-established Noyes Academy in Canaan, New Hampshire. Founded by abolitionists, Noyes was open to both blacks and whites and to men and women. (There Garnet met Julia Williams.) The students from New York were in New Hampshire by July 4, when they delivered fiery orations at an abolitionist meeting. A vocal minority of local townspeople was determined to close down the school and drive away the 14 blacks enrolled. In August they attached teams of oxen to the schoolhouse, dragged it away, and burned it. Garnet, Crummell, and Sidney returned to New York.

Fortunately, there was another institution that opened its doors to black students, and this time the local townspeople did not rise up physically to reject them. In early 1836 Garnet joined Crummell and Sidney at Oneida Institute in Whitesboro, New York. In May 1840 Garnet attended the meeting of the American Anti-Slavery Society in New York and delivered a well-received maiden speech. In September, he graduated from Oneida with honors and settled in Troy, New York.

Established a Career

Even though Garnet was not yet ordained, he had been called as minister to the newly established Liberty Street Presbyterian Church at Troy, New York. Garnet studied theology with the noted minister and abolitionist Nathaniel S. S. Beman, taught school, and worked toward the full establishment of the church whose congregation was black. In 1842 Garnet was licensed to preach and in the following year ordained a minister. He thus became the first pastor of the Liberty Street Presbyterian Church in Troy, where he remained until 1848.

Teaching and the ministry hardly filled all of Garnet's time. He assisted in editing *The National Watchman*, an abolitionist paper published in Troy during the latter part of 1842, and later edited *The Clarion*, which combined abolitionist and religious themes. Closely interwoven with Garnet's church work was his work in the Temperance Movement, in which he took a leading part. By 1843 he received a stipend of $100 a year from the American Home Missionary Society for his work for abolition and temperance. When the society expressed its objections to ministers engaging in politics on Sundays, Garnet withdrew his services. His work for temperance was widely recognized. In 1848 one of the two Daughters of Temperance unions in Philadelphia was named for him.

State politics also brought Garnet into prominence. There were black state conventions from 1836 to 1850. Garnet worked for the extension of black male voting rights in New York state, but a property holding qualification was imposed upon blacks. He presented several petitions to the legislature on this subject. However, the state property qualification remained the law until the adoption of the Fifteenth Amendment in 1870.

Urged Rebellion

In 1839 the Liberty Party came into existence with abolition as one of its major planks. Although its vote in the 1840 elections was minuscule, the party set its sights on the 1844 election. Garnet became an early and enthusiastic supporter of this reform party. He delivered a major address at the party's 1842 meeting in Boston. He was also able to secure the endorsement of the revived National Convention of Colored Men, held in Albany in August 1843 for the party. Garnet gave a convincing demonstration of his oratorical powers soon afterwards when he turned around a New York City meeting convened to disavow the convention's action. Much to the organizers' disappointment the meeting ended by endorsing the Liberty Party. The year 1844 marked a peak for the party. Then the Free Soil Party and later the Republican Party began to attract reform-minded voters. Garnet was late and unenthusiastic in supporting the Republicans.

Garnet's turn towards activism marked his break with leading abolitionist William Lloyd Garrison, who rejected politics in favor of moral reform. Garnet's impatience with Garrison's position was expressed publicly as early as 1840 when he was one of the eight black founding members of the American and Foreign Anti-Slavery Society which formalized the split in the ranks of abolitionists.

Just as Garnet was in the vanguard of the blacks who began to seek remedies in political action and even revolution, he also led the way in proposing emigration as a solution for black plight in the United States as proposed by the American Colonization Society. Since 1817 most American blacks condemned the American Colonization Society and were suspicious of the society's aims and of its creation, the nation of Liberia, which became independent in 1847. Garnet, however, was coming to favor black emigration to any area where there might be hope of being treated justly and with dignity. Bitter personal experience soon underlined his position: in the summer of that year he was choked, beaten, and thrown off a train in New York State.

Traveled Abroad

Garnet moved from Troy to Geneva in 1848. Then in 1850 he went to Great Britain at the invitation of the Free Labor Movement, an organization opposing the use of products produced by slave labor. The following year he was joined by his family. There he remained for two and a half years, undertaking a very rigorous schedule of engagements. Both James McCune Smith and Frederick Douglass felt he was doing especially well because he was the first American black of completely African descent to appear there to speak in support of abolition. Douglass did not relax his general hostility to Garnet, however, and gave little attention to Garnet's activities abroad.

In the latter part of 1852, the United Presbyterian Church of Scotland sent Garnet to Jamaica as a missionary. He did effective work there until a severe prolonged illness caused his doctors to order him north. In 1855 he was called to Shiloh Church on Prince Street, where he became the successor of his mentor, Theodore S. Wright.

Although the support for emigration was growing in the black community, Garnet had to face sharp criticism for his position in favor of it, particularly from Frederick Douglass. Douglass commented sharply on a request for American blacks to go to Jamaica made by Garnet before his return.

Alexander Crummell, Garnet's boyhood friend and fellow student who had established himself in Liberia after earning a degree from Cambridge University in England, endorsed the goal, as did the influential West-Indian born educator Edward Wilmot Blyden. Garnet made a trip to England as president of the society in 1861. In conjunction with this trip he established a civil rights breakthrough by insisting that his passport contain the word Negro. Before this time the handful of passports issued to blacks had managed to skirt the issue of whether blacks were or were not citizens of the United States by labeling the bearer with some term such as dark. Although Garnet's and Martin Delany's efforts at colonization at this time were running in parallel and not coordinated, the pair agreed on aims. Garnet proposed a visit to Africa to follow up Delany's 1859 efforts there, but the plan fell through with the outbreak of the Civil War.

Supported Civil War Efforts

With the outbreak of the war, Garnet joined other blacks in urging the formation of black units. When this goal was realized during the beginning of 1863, he traveled to recruit blacks and served as chaplain to the black troops of New York State, who were assembled on Ryker's island for training. He led the work of charitable organizations that worked to overcome the unfavorable conditions initially facing the men due to wide-scale corruption and anti-black sentiments in the city.

In March 1864 Garnet became pastor of the Fifteenth Street Presbyterian Church of Washington. D.C. There he delivered a sermon in the chamber of the House of Representatives on February 12, 1865, the first black to do so, and also one of the first blacks allowed to enter the Capitol. He moved his residence to Washington and became the editor of the Southern Department of the *Anglo-African*. As an assignment Garnet undertook a four month trip to the South at the end of the war, which included a visit to his birthplace. Garnet accepted the presidency of Avery College in Pittsburgh in 1868, but returned to Shiloh Church in New York in 1870.

Crummell reported that Garnet went into a physical and mental decline about 1876. In spite of the discouragement of his friends, Garnet actively lobbied for the position of minister to Liberia, which he obtained. Garnet preached his farewell sermon at Shiloh on November 6, 1881, and landed in Monrovia on December 28. He died on February 13, 1882.

Books

Bell, Howard Holman, ed., *Minutes of the Proceedings of the National Negro Conventions: 1830–1864,* Arno Press and the *New York Times,* 1969.

Crummell, Alexander, *Africa and America,* Willey and Co., 1891.

Litwack, Leon, and August Meier, eds., *Black Leaders of the Nineteenth Century,* University of Illinois Press, 1988.

Moses, Wilson Jeremiah, *Alexander Crummell,* University of Massachusetts Press, 1992.

Ofari, Earl, *"Let Your Motto Be Resistance:" The Life and Thought of Henry Highland Garnet,* Beacon Press, 1972.

Penn, I. Garland, *The Afro-American Press and Its Editors,* Willey and Co., 1891.

Proceedings of the National Convention of the Colored Men of America Held in Washington, D.C., on January 13, 14, 15, and 16, 1869, Great Republic Book and Newspaper Printing Establishment, 1869.

Quarles, Benjamin, *Black Abolitionists,* Oxford, 1969.

Ripley, C. Peter, ed., *The Black Abolitionist Papers,* University of North Carolina Press, 1985.

———, *Witness for Freedom,* University of North Carolina Press, 1993.

Schor, Joel, *Henry Highland Garnet,* Greenwood Press, 1977.

Simmons, William J., *Men of Mark,* George M. Rewell and Co., 1887.

Smith, James McCune, *A Memorial Discourse; Delivered in the Hall of the House of Representatives, Washington City, D.C., on Sabbath, February 12, 1865,* Joseph M. Wilson, 1865.

Sterling, Dorothy, ed., *Speak Out in Thunder,* Doubleday, 1973.

Walker, David, and Henry Highland Garnet, *Walker's Appeal and Garnet's Address to the Slaves of the United States of America,* 1848. Reprint, James C. Winston Publishing, 1994.

Periodicals

Journal of Negro History, January 1928. □

Uri Greenberg

Uri Greenberg (1898–1981) was the founder of Jewish literary Expressionism and the leader of a group of Yiddish and Hebrew expressionist poets. Greenberg's Expressionism, according to *Contemporary Authors Online,* was the view that "Jewish poetry in particular, and literature in general, must be infused with reality, with what people are experiencing at that moment." Because of his radical political views, his poetry fell into disfavor during his lifetime, but his genius was generally acknowledged by the end of the 20th century.

Greenberg was a leading Hebrew poet, politician, journalist, and political activist. His writing comprised a dozen or so volumes of Hebrew poetry as well as works in Yiddish that were collected in two volumes. He also wrote about ideology and Hebrew literature. He chose to leave a good deal of his writing unpublished.

Greenberg's poetry was religious and full of mystical references. It included personal poetry, love poetry, and political verse and had a sense of history and national purpose, as well as expressing a need for self-preservation for the Jewish people.

Childhood in Various Cities

Greenberg was born in the late 1890s (the actual date is disputed between September 22, 1896 and October 17, 1898) in Bilikamin, Eastern Galicia, in the Austro-Hungarian Empire (now Bialykiamien, Ukraine) into a line of distinguished Hasidic Rabbis. He was raised in Lemberg (now Lvov, Ukraine), where he received a traditional education and religious upbringing. By 1912 Greenberg had already published his first Yiddish and Hebrew poetry in periodicals in Lemberg, Warsaw, and Berlin, all cities where he had lived.

War Inspired His Writing

In 1915 Greenberg published his first book of poetry, *Ergits oyf Felder* (Somewhere in the Fields), which told of the horrors of war that he had experienced after being drafted into the Austro-Hungarian army. In 1917 he deserted after observing battle in Serbia. His war experiences had a lasting effect on his future works and life.

Greenberg also witnessed the Polish pogroms of 1918 in Lemberg, watching the destruction of an entire neighborhood. This also was to have a lasting effect on him and it spurred him to become a spokesman for Israel's Zionist Revisionist movement.

Greenberg began partnering with other poets between 1920 and 1923, when he founded the Yiddish literary journal *Kalastrie* (The Gang) with poets Moishe Broderson, Melech Ravich and Peretz Markish. In 1921 he moved to Warsaw, where he wrote *Mefista* (Mephisto), which also echoed his World War I experiences. Between 1922 and 1923, Greenberg edited the *Albatross,* another periodical. In 1923, he relocated again to Berlin, where he continued to write in both Yiddish and Hebrew.

Settled in Palestine

Only a year after his arrival in Berlin, Greenberg settled in Palestine as a part of the third *aliya* (immigration wave) of European Zionist Jews and adopted Hebrew as his almost exclusive poetic language. In that same year, he published his first volume of Hebrew poetry, *Emah G-dolah ve-Yareach,* which presented his ideas of the "Hebrew man" and his relationship to his homeland. From 1925 to 1929, he contributed regularly to *Davar* and *Kunteres,* the official mouthpieces of the Labor movement.

In 1929, Greenberg responded to the British mandate with anger, beginning his movement toward Zionist Revisionism and advocating immediate statehood. He later became one of the most extremist members of the Revisionist Party and represented the Revisionists in Poland and at several Zionist congresses. He also supported the underground in their fight against the British by joining Irgun, a right-wing militant group that fought the British.

In 1930 he published another volume of poetry, *Ezor Magen u-Neum Ben ha-Dam,* and in 1931 Greenberg returned to Warsaw. Immediately, he became an editor for the Revisionist party's weekly *Di Velt,* and remained in that post until 1934. The Revisionist stance became a major theme in his poetry.

Prophesied the Holocaust

In 1934 Greenberg escaped another world war by returning to Palestine, penning prose attacks on moderate socialists and dark poems that warned of the coming destruction in Europe. In 1937 he published *Sefer ha-Kitrug veha-Emunah,* which prophesied the Holocaust. *Sefer ha-Kitrug veha-Emunah* remains one of his most notable collections. Despite Greenberg's prophetic vision and his escaping Europe, the rest of his family perished in the Holocaust.

Joined Extremist Groups

Jerusalem was published in 1939. In the 1940s Greenberg continued to fight as a member of various guerrilla groups that sought to establish an independent Israeli nation in Palestine. From 1949 to 1951, after the formation of the Israeli state, he became a member of the Knesset (Parliament) as a representative of the right-wing Herut party and served for one term. In that year, he published *Rechovot ha-Nachar,* another one of his most notable collections. It won the Bialik Prize in the 1950s and the Israel Prize in 1957, which was also awarded for his general contribution to Hebrew literature.

Following the Six Day War between Israel and Egypt, Greenberg joined the Greater Land of Israel camp and became an extremist spokesman for Jewish settlement and political boundaries that included all of "Greater Israel" (on either side of the Jordan River). In 1976 a special session of the Knesset was called in honor of his eightieth birthday. In 1978 Greenberg won the Manger Prize, and on May 8, 1981, he died in Tel Aviv, Israel.

Jewish Zionism

Throughout Greenberg's life, he was deeply involved with the Jewish Zionist movement, which he believed was the answer to "Jewish blindness." His belief in "Jewish blindness" is what led him to predict the Holocaust. He reprimanded the world for letting the Holocaust happen but also blamed the Jews, who in his view were denying their inherent differences from Gentiles. The Jewish Virtual Library sums up Greenberg's beliefs that "the Holocaust was a tragic but almost inevitable outcome of Jewish indifference to their destiny ... The notion of Jewishness and the essential, inviolable difference between Jews and Gentiles is what underlies his thought."

Greenberg always remained at the fringes even of his own party. And he was not just on the fringe in politics but viewed himself as out of step with the Hebrew literature of the time, which he saw, according to the *Encyclopedia of World Literature in the 20th Century,* as "a trivial marketplace, not truly representing the historical movement." He called himself the Hebrew Walt Whitman and used his

poetry to promote Jewish nationalism, believing Zionism was the way for Jews to realize their promised redemption and that the role of Hebrew poetry was to express a Messianic vision.

Books

Contemporary Authors, Gale, 2002.
Klein, Leonard S., ed., *Encyclopedia of World Literature in the 20th Century,* Vol. 2, Frederick Ungaro Publishing Co., 1985.
Murphy, Bruce, ed., *Benet's Reader's Encyclopedia,* HarperCollins Publishers, 1996.

Online

"Uri Zvi Greenberg,"*The Jewish Virtual Library,* www.us-israel.org (January 10, 2004). □

Maria Grever

Maria Grever (1894–1951), a pioneer in the field of twentieth-century popular music, was the first Mexican woman to become a successful composer. Her romantic songs and ballads, like "Jurame" and "What a Difference a Day Makes," achieved widespread popularity beginning in the 1920s among audiences in Spain, South America, Mexico, and the United States.

Although a few of her songs remain international favorites today, Grever has eluded significant coverage in the pages of music history—she is not even mentioned in most listings and encyclopedias of composers. Yet many of her songs, estimated to number in the hundreds, live on, kept alive by recording stars like Placido Domingo and Aretha Franklin.

Grever was born to a Spanish father and Mexican mother on September 14, 1894, in Mexico City, Mexico. Her maiden name was Maria de la Portilla. She spent much of her childhood in Spain and traveled widely in Europe with her family. At the age of 12, she returned to Mexico. According to a *New York Times* article, Grever composed her first piece of music—a Christmas carol—when she was four years old. Grever settled in New York after marrying Leo A. Grever, an American oil company executive, who was best man in her sister's wedding. She was wed to Grever four days after her sister's nuptials.

Grever studied piano, violin, and voice, although one account of her life suggests that she learned to read music only in her later years. In fact, most of her songs were written in one key. Grever was said to have the gift of perfect pitch. A 1919 review of one of her first New York City concerts in the *New York Times* mentions that Grever, a soprano, performed opera in Madrid early in her career.

Grever was an extraordinarily versatile musician. She frequently wrote both the melodies and lyrics of her pieces and then performed the pieces in live concerts. During her

career, which peaked in the 1930s and 1940s, she wrote film scores and lyrics for Broadway shows and organized concerts combining theatre, music, dance, and song. She was also a voice teacher. But Grever's strongest legacy is her songs. Often based on the folk rhythms and styles of Latin American music, particularly Mexican or Spanish tangos, the lyrics are lushly romantic, full of feeling, and easy to recall. Her message is always direct. For example, her song "Yo No Se" ("I Know Not") begins with the stanza: "When at night my thoughts are winging / To you, my dear, / Then your voice, an old song singing, / I seem to hear; / You are kneeling by me, blending, / Though far away, / Your voice with mine ascending, / In a song of love's first day."

Grever often worked with American lyricists, who translated the songs from Spanish to English to make them accessible to audiences in the United States. In fact, Grever collaborated with three of the leading songwriters of her day—Stanley Adams, Irving Caesar, and Raymond Leveen.

First Hit Became Million-Seller

Grever's first published song, "A una Ola" ("To a Wave"), appeared when she was 18 years old and sold some three million copies, according to a biography on a 1956 retrospective album of Grever's work. Grever published "Besame" ("Kiss Me") in 1921, and in 1926, Grever's Spanish tango "Jurame" ("Promise, Love") found a large audience. Grever's first major hit was "What a Difference a Day Makes," or "Cuando Vuelva a Tu Lado," written in 1934. That song is one of Grever's longest-lasting hits; it is

included on many currently available recordings by artists as diverse as Chet Baker, Ray Conniff, Dinah Washington, and Bobby Darin.

The same year Ella Fitzgerald sang "A-Tisket A-Tasket" and Cole Porter won over the nation with "My Heart Belongs to Daddy," Grever scored one of her biggest sensations, a nonsensical tune entitled "Ti-Pi-Tin." One account of Grever's music claims that "Ti-Pi-Tin," written in 1938, broke with her usual style, and her publisher rejected it. But bandleader Horace Heidt and his orchestra, performing on NBC radio, took the song to the air and contributed to its eventual hit status.

Grever's songs, broadcast frequently on the radio during her time, include "Lamento Gitano," "Lero, Lero from Brazil," "Magic Is the Moonlight," "Make Love with a Guitar," "My First, My Last, My Only," "Rosebud," "Thanks for the Kiss," "My Margarita," "Andalucia," "Cancionera," and many more. Estimates of her musical output range from 200 to 500 songs, depending on the source.

One of the reasons Grever's songs became well known was that leading performers of her era adopted them in their repertoires. Singers like Enrich Caruso, Lawrence Tibbett, Tito Schipa, Nino Martina, and Jessica Dragonette helped popularize Grever's work. Along with other albums which included Grever's tunes, the 1956 album "The Bobby Hackett Horn," a Columbia label, adapted "What a Difference a Day Makes," and the 1959 Columbia Classic album "Happy Session," performed by Benny Goodman and his orchestra, featured "Cuando Vuelva a Tu Lado."

Grever also wrote film scores, including the music for the 1944 movie "Bathing Beauty," featuring her song "Magic Is the Moonlight," or "Te Quiero Dijiste." In 1941, *Viva O'Brien*, a musical with music by Grever and lyrics by Leveen, had 20 performances on a New York stage. Some of the show's songs were entitled "El Matador Terrifico," "Mood of the Moment," "Broken Hearted Romeo," and "Wrap Me in Your Serape."

Enjoyed International Acclaim

Grever apparently enjoyed performing before live audiences and organizing concerts of her work by other musicians. In 1919, one of her earliest New York recitals of Spanish, Italian, and French music, at the Princess Theatre, received positive reviews from critics. During the height of her fame, she made concert tours in Latin America and Europe. In New York, Grever's music was heard live in many of the city's concert halls. In 1927, she organized a concert at the Little Theatre, which featured an Argentine cabaret, song dramas complete with costumes, scenery, dialogue, and dancing, and a short play, *The Gypsy*. The evening opened with performances by a jazz orchestra. One of her first successful New York concerts took place in 1928 at the Pythian Temple before an audience that included the ambassadors of Spain, Mexico, Cuba, and Argentina.

The *New York Times* reviewed a 1939 concert at the Guild Theatre, in which Grever presented popular songs and a miniature opera, entitled "El Cantarito." She performed a few songs, but was assisted by dozens of other singers and musicians, including a large chorus, dance troupe, and orchestra. The *Times* critic praised her "innate gift of spontaneous melody," and commented that, while some of Grever's music is not to be taken too seriously, "her more earnest endeavors were sincere and effective."

In the late 1930s, she was threatened with blindness as a result of an eye infection. In 1942, Grever hosted a benefit for the Spanish-American Association for the Blind, with headquarters in New York City. She served as mistress of ceremonies for a program that included musical performances by students at the New York Institute for the Education of the Blind. The funds raised were to benefit the blind in Spanish-speaking countries.

At the time of her death at the age of 57, on December 15, 1951, following a lengthy illness, she was living in the Wellington Hotel on Manhattan's Seventh Avenue. She was survived by her husband and two children, son Charles Grever, a New York music publisher, and daughter, Carmen Livingston. Following her death, she was honored by a musicale at the Biltmore Hotel by the Union of Women of the Americas. She was named "Woman of the Americas," 1952, by the UWA before her death. Grever was a member of the prestigious American Society of Composers, Authors, and Publishers.

In 1956, RCA released a retrospective album, "Songs of Maria Grever," with 12 songs performed by Argentine singer Libertad Lamarque, accompanied by the orchestras of Chucho Zarzosa and Mario Ruiz Armengol. Along with her more famous songs, the album featured "Volvere" ("I Will Return"), "Eso Es Mentira" ("That Is a Lie"), and "Asi" ("Thus"). The album jacket, written by Bill Zeitung, argues that Grever never enjoyed widespread name recognition, despite the fact that her songs achieved "an immensely deserved run of popularity." Her music "is on every hand," wrote Zeitung. "Yet the name is familiar to only a few."

Books

Lewine, Richard, and Alfred Simon, *Songs of the Theatre,* Wilson, 1984.

Mattfeld, Julius, *Variety Music Cavalcade 1620–1961,* Prentice-Hall.

Spaeth, Sigmund, *A History of Popular Music in America,* Random House, 1962.

Periodicals

New York Times, December 15, 1919; February 14, 1927; February 27, 1928; March 6, 1939; December 16, 1951; May 5, 1952.

Variety, July 31, 1940.

Other

Music research collections, New York Public Library for the Performing Arts at Lincoln Center.

"Songs of Maria Grever," RCA record album, 1956. ☐

Peter Hall

Peter Hall (born 1930) is an award-winning British theatrical director and manager with an impressive list of credits. Over the course of a 50-year career, Hall became one of the world's most renowned directors, received major theatrical awards— including two Antoinette Perry or "Tony" awards— and achieved knighthood. Managing major British theatrical companies before forming his own highly acclaimed company, Hall has directed the production of over 150 plays, operas, and films. Even though his Shakespearean productions are most highly regarded, he exerted enormous influence and impact by introducing the world to the finest examples of modern drama.

The man who would become an internationally renowned director rose from a humble beginning. Peter Reginald Frederick Hall was born on November 22, 1930, in a working-class neighborhood in Bury Saint Edmonds, Suffolk, England. The only child of Grace and Reginald Hall, he grew up in a modest row house that sat among other workers' dwellings. Hall recalled his parents as very loving and despite his family's working-class status he never felt deprived. Reginald Hall, a genial man who enjoyed gardening and liked to grow the family's food, worked as a clerk in a railway station. In his autobiography *Making an Exhibition of Myself,* Hall described his father as a "kind man who did not know the meaning of the word cruelty." Grace Hall had a more forceful nature, and Hall character-

ized his mother as a "genial and quick-witted woman" but something of a "tempest."

Showed Early Ambition, Interests

Hall himself displayed a rather exuberant personality. He recalled that even as a child he tended to be a risk taker and overachiever. This disposition often made his mother anxious, and Hall enjoyed provoking her anxieties and ire. Very much a "Suffolk country woman," Grace Hall responded to her son's antics with cautionary or comforting aphorisms. At the same time, she appreciated her son's character and proved to be an enormous influence in his early life. She had great ambitions for him and made him feel special.

Hall's early interests and ambitions were directed toward the arts, and one of the defining moments in his early life occurred when he saw renowned actor Sir John Gielgud on stage performing William Shakespeare's *Hamlet* in Cambridge. Writing a tribute to Gielgud following the great actor's death in 2000, Hall recalled of that time: "I felt I knew him already, as one does with God." He found an outlet for this newfound interest in the dramatic arts in school. After attending Perse School and then St. Catharine's College, Cambridge, Hall earned his M.A. at Cambridge University in 1953. While at the university, he produced and acted in more than 20 amateur productions, then entered the professional theater.

Hall's industrious nature and enthusiasm for risk-taking was evidenced by his career achievements. While he respected the classics and staged productions of many of Shakespeare's plays, he also took chances on contemporary drama. Hall helped introduce theatregoers around the world to the plays of Howard Pinter, making Pinter one of Britain's most acclaimed post-World War II playwrights. In

Formed Royal Shakespeare Company

In 1960 Hall was named director of the Shakespeare Memorial Theatre, which had been built in 1932 to showcase the Bard's works. During his first year there Hall redesigned the stage and renamed the building the Royal Shakespeare Theatre. He also formed the Royal Shakespeare Company (RSC) and established its home at the Aldwych Theatre in London. Hall expanded the company's repertoire to include both Shakespearean works and modern drama. The company performed at both theaters, and Hall set about developing a distinctive style for types of drama. "The tension between the utterly contemporary and the classical has always been the main spring of my work," Hall later wrote. "It informed my time at the Royal Shakespeare Company and at the Royal National Theatre. It has guided me from *Waiting to Godot* to *King Lear* and back again via [the opera] *Der Ring des Nibelungen*." His innovative Shakespearean productions helped redefine plays such as *Hamlet*—with the "melancholy Dane" portrayed by the young David Warner—and *Twelfth Night* for a new generation of theatergoers.

For the RSC, Hall directed 18 plays at the Stratford theater. His most significant production was *The War of the Roses,* a seven-play history cycle. At the Aldwych Theatre he staged world premiere performances of plays by John Whiting and Edward Albee, the latter who went on to win Pulitzer prizes and Tony awards for such plays as *Who's Afraid of Virginia Woolf* and *A Delicate Balance.* Hall's best-known productions at the Aldwych included the London premiere of Anouilh's *Becket* in 1962 and the 1965 opening of Pinter's *The Homecoming.*

Hall served as managing director of the RSC's theaters until 1968, sharing directorial duties with other accomplished directors, including Peter Brook, Paul Scofield, and Michel Saint-Denis. After his resignation, Hall continued directing plays for the company. In addition, from 1969 to 1971 he was director of the Covent Garden Opera.

Headed Royal National Theatre

In 1973 Hall became managing director of the Royal National Theatre in London, succeeding Lawrence Olivier, who founded the organization. At first Hall staged plays at the Old Vic Theatre, which throughout its 150-plus-year history had included as part of its company such actors as Oliver, Ashcroft, Gielgud, and Sir Ralph Richardson. In 1976 Hall moved the National Theatre company from the Old Vic to a new home on London's South Bank.

Hall held the post of managing director at the National for 15 years, during which time he continued to develop a recognizable style for classical and modern drama. His productions included the 1975 premiere of Pinter's *No Man's Land* and the 1979 premiere of Peter Shaffer's *Amadeus.* Other notable productions included *Volpone*, the classic play by Ben Jonson; *The Oresteia*, the Greek trilogy by Aeschylus; *Animal Farm*, a dramatic adaptation of George Orwell's novel; and *Betrayal*, by Pinter, as well as Shakespeare's *Antony and Cleopatra, Hamlet, The Tempest, Cymbeline,* and *The Winter's Tale.* In his cast he included

all, Hall's credits include more than 80 professional stage productions. However, he also directed opera, television programs, and motion pictures. When his career led him to the United States, he conquered Broadway by staging two enormously successful productions—*The Homecoming* and *Amadeus*—both of which garnered him Tony awards.

At the start of his professional career, Hall worked in repertory and for the Arts Council in England. As newly appointed artistic director of the Elizabethan Theatre Company, he directed his first professional production in 1953, at the Theatre Royal in Windsor. A year later he joined the Arts Theatre in London, first working as an assistant director and then director. Between 1954 and 1956 he staged *The Lesson,* the first play by existential playwright Eugene Ionesco to be performed in England. Hall also directed the premieres of two historically important plays: the English-language premiere of *Waiting for Godot,* an absurdist tragicomedy by Samuel Beckett, and the London premiere of *The Waltz of the Toreadors,* by Jean Anouilh. Hall was only 24 years old when he introduced Beckett's work to the world.

In 1956 Hall staged his first production at the Shakespeare Memorial Theater at Stratford-upon-Avon. The following year he formed his own company, the International Playwrights' Theatre, but returned to Stratford to stage *Cymberline* with Peggy Ashcroft (1957), *Coriolanus* with Laurence Olivier (1958), and *A Midsummer Night's Dream* with Charles Laughton.

established and rising actors such as Albert Finney, Judi Dench, and Anthony Hopkins.

In 1983 Hall published *Peter Hall's Diaries: The Story of a Dramatic Battle,* in which he recounts his time at the Royal National Theatre. He resigned from the theatre in 1988, noting in an interview with the London *Evening Standard:* "I've been lucky. I spent 25 years of my life at the RSC and the National. I made one of them and certainly had quite a big hand in the making of the other. I've worked with all the great dramatists, Beckett, Pinter, Schaffer, Edgar, Ayckbourn."

Formed His Own Company

In 1988 he formed the Peter Hall Company, and the group's first productions included Tennessee Williams's *Orpheus Descending* with Vanessa Redgrave and *The Merchant of Venice* with Dustin Hoffman playing Shylock. The new company worked around the world, appearing in more than 40 productions in London, New York, Europe, and Australia. During this period Hall also worked in other formats. He produced operas and directed films and television productions for the BBC. Though these efforts proved successful, they never reached the heights of his dramatic work. From 1984 to 1990 Hall served as artistic director of Glyndebourne Opera in Sussex, England. He also directed at many of the world's leading opera houses, including the Royal Opera House, Lyric Opera of Chicago, Houston Grand Opera, and Covent Garden. His most celebrated operatic production was the *Der Ring des Nibelungen,* staged at the Bayreuth Opera House in Germany in 1983. His films include *Three into Two Won't Go,* a 1969 film starring Rod Steiger and Claire Bloom. He also directed film adaptations of *A Midsummer Night's Dream, The Homecoming,* and *Orpheus Descending.*

Hall returned to the RSC in 1992 to direct *All's Well That Ends Well* and the world premiere of Shaffer's *The Gift of the Gorgon in the Pit.* In February of that year, he directed the world premiere of John Guare's *Four Baboons Adoring the Sun* and was nominated for a Tony Award. Hall was again nominated for a Tony in 1996, when he took his production of Oscar Wilde's *An Ideal Husband* to Broadway.

Staged Landmark Season

In 1997, at age 66, Hall enjoyed what turned out to be one of the most famous seasons of his career. As artistic director at the Old Vic, he staged a 13-play repertoire that became a landmark in the history of that world-famous institution. The schedule included classics performed from Tuesday to Saturday and new plays on Sunday and Monday. Among the works performed were *Waste* by Harley Granville-Barker, *Cloud Nine* by Caryl Churchill, and *Hurlyburly* by David Rabe. Directors included Michael Pennington, Felicity Kendal, Alan Howard, Anna Carteret, and actor Ben Kingsley. Hall directed Anton Chekhov's *The Seagull* and a new production of *Waiting for Godot,* the play he had introduced 25 years earlier. He also directed, for the first time, Shakespeare's *King Lear.* Hall's aim for the season was not only to present classics and modern works, but also

to provide a venue for new writers and actors. He wanted to provide a fertile ground for aspiring dramatic artists that would allow them to flourish, without restrictive financial concerns or interference from investors and managers. This environment existed for that one glorious season; afterward, the Old Vic's owners decided to sell the theater. The following year the Company moved to the Piccadilly Theatre, where Hall staged productions of *Waiting for Godot, The Misanthrope,* and *Major Barbara.*

In 1999 Hall visited the United States and taught at the University of Houston School of Theatre, having wanted to teach for several years. In addition, in 2000 he worked with the Denver, Colorado, Center for the Performing Arts to develop the ten-hour Greek drama marathon *Tantalus,* which toured the following year. Returning to England, in 2003, his 50th year as a director, Hall and his company collaborated with the Theatre Royal Bath, where he directed the first of three projected summer residencies. That same year he was named artistic director of Kingston University's theatre in London. In addition, Hall lectured regularly in Great Britain and the United States. In 2004 at the age of 73 Hall went back to the Theater Royal Bath for a second summer season where he directed two plays. He also published a book titled *Shakespeare's Advice to the Players,* which consists of three sections. The first section deals with the language of Shakespeare, the second deals with notable speeches, and the third part is a memoir.

Honored for Long Career

Throughout his decades working in the theatre, Hall has received numerous awards and honors. In 1967 he accepted a Tony Award for best director for his production of Pinter's *The Homecoming,* receiving this honor again in 1981 for *Amadeus.* In 1988, he received the first-ever Critic's Circle Award. In 1999 Hall was awarded the Laurence Olivier Award for Lifetime Achievement. Two decades before, in 1977, he was knighted by the Order of the British Empire for his services to British theatre.

Hall, who has been married four times, is the husband of publicist Nicki Frei. He has six children, four of whom work in the theater. Most notably, his son Edward, from Hall's second marriage to Jacky Taylor, became a successful director; and his daughter Rebecca made a name for herself with her acclaimed portrayal of Rosalind in a production of Shakespeare's *As You Like It* directed by her father. Hall published his autobiography, *Making an Exhibition of Myself,* in 1993.

Books

Hall, Peter, *Making an Exhibition of Myself,* Sinclair-Stevenson, 1993.

Periodicals

Daily Variety, March 25, 2004.
Evening Standard, September 6, 1996; March 23, 2000; November 27, 2000.
Library Journal, March 1, 2004.
New Statesman, February 28, 1997.
Theatre Record, August 21, 1997.

Online

"BBC Breakfast with Frost" (interview), *BBC News Web site*, http://news/bbc.co.uk/1/hi/programmes/breakfast_with_frost/3185254.stm (October 12, 2003).

"Finding Rosalind in the Family," *Boston Globe online*, http://www.boston.com/ae/theater_arts/articles/2003/11/09/finding_rosalind_in_the_family/ (November 9, 2003).

"Peter Hall," *Dramaddict*, http://members.aol.com/dramaddict/petrhall.htm (December 27, 2003).

"Sir Peter Hall," *University of Houston School of Theater Web site*, http://www.hfac.uh.edu/theatre/faculty/Hall/hall.htm (December 27, 2003). □

Herbert Hauptman

In 1985, American mathematician Herbert Hauptman (born 1917) won the Nobel Prize in Chemistry, becoming the first non-chemist to win in that category. He shared the honor with a colleague, Jerome Karle, both of whom were honored for their towering discoveries that made mapping the chemical structures of small molecules easy and efficient. Over the years, scientists have used their method to develop new drugs that combat diseases such as cancer, high blood pressure, and heart disease. Shortly after Hauptman won the prize, the *Buffalo News* reported that Hauptman "undoubtedly saved more lives ... than anyone else in recent history," according to the Hauptman-Woodward Medical Research Institute Web site.

Born on February 14, 1917, Hauptman grew up in the Bronx borough of New York City and attended Townsend Harris High School. He was the oldest of three boys born to Israel and Leah (Rosenfeld) Hauptman. Hauptman credits his parents for playing an integral role in his development as a scientist because they gave him the choice to study whatever he wanted. Early on, science caught his eye, and he devoured every scientific book he could find. "My interest in most areas of science and mathematics began at an early age, as soon as I had learned to read, and continues to this day," Hauptman said in his 1985 Nobel acceptance speech, posted on the *Nobel e-Museum Web site.*

Hauptman attended City College of New York during a time when it was common for qualified students to obtain a free education. He later noted that without such financial help, he never would have been able to receive the higher education necessary for his discoveries later on. Hauptman graduated from City College in 1937 with a bachelor of science degree in mathematics. He continued his studies, earning a master of arts degree in mathematics from Columbia University in 1939. On November 10, 1940, he married Edith Citrynell, a teacher, and they settled in the Washington, D.C., area. That same year, Hauptman began working

in Washington as a U.S. Census Bureau statistician. In 1942, with World War II in full swing, and Hauptman found employment as a radar instructor for the U.S. Air Force.

Revealed Breakthrough Research

Following the end of the war in 1945, Hauptman decided to continue his graduate studies, aiming for a career in basic scientific research. By 1947 he was working at the Naval Research Laboratory (NRL) in Washington, D.C., where he teamed up with Jerome Karle, a fellow New Yorker who was also a 1937 graduate of the City College of New York. At the same time, Hauptman enrolled at the University of Maryland and began studies toward his doctorate.

Hauptman's and Karle's backgrounds complemented each other: Hauptman was a mathematician, whereas Karle was an expert in chemistry. Over the next several years the two began the preliminary studies that would ultimately lead to their breakthrough research and which also became a part of Hauptman's doctoral dissertation. Around 1950 the two began research into a technique whereby they could decode the structural makeup of crystals, a dilemma that had daunted scientists for decades.

Since about 1912, scientists had known that when an X-ray beam strikes a substance that has been crystallized, the rays diffract—or scatter—producing fuzzy spots of variable intensities that can be recorded on film. Scientists, however, wanted to be able to work backward, using the diffraction data to determine the atomic arrangement of the substance. The problem was that scientists were basically looking at a molecule's "shadow" and from that attempting to reconstruct the three-dimensional object. Writing for the *Buffalo News,* Henry L. Davis described the task this way: "Imagine yourself on a sandy shoreline as waves move past wooden posts in the water. Depending on the position of the posts, some waves will break on the beach stronger than others. Now, work backwards, and based on the intensity of the waves hitting the shore, figure out the location of the posts in the water."

X-rays, like water, travel in waves, and for years scientists had been stymied trying to work backward looking at the pattern on the film to figure out the position of the atoms from a substance that had been crystallized. Hauptman and Karle took a mathematical approach to the problem. Over several years, they developed a mathematical formula to figure out the location of the atoms in the crystal. This procedure, known as "direct methods" was not understood initially. Decades passed before anyone realized the significance of their work, but by the mid-1980s Hauptman and Karle's discoveries were being used by crystallographers around the world. With the duo's mathematical formula and the correct computer program, crystallographers were able to determine the structures of thousands of molecules for the first time. This new mapping information assisted in the development of many new drugs.

Interestingly, Hauptman's mathematical insights at first had gone virtually unnoticed. By 1954 he had studied the problem for five years and had presented 13 scientific papers on molecular structure determination, yet hardly anyone supported his ideas. "There was a lot of resistance to it, mostly because it wasn't understood," Hauptman explained to *New York Times* writer John Noble Wilford. "It was highly mathematical and crystallographers didn't have the training to understand it. It was not generally accepted until the middle 1960's or so when more and more people began to use it."

Balanced Family, Research, Doctoral Work

While working on his doctorate and researching crystallography, Hauptman balanced studies with parenthood. One daughter, Barbara, was born in 1947, and younger daughter Carol followed in 1950. Hauptman recalled his graduate student years as frantic, as he commuted between campus, his Bethesda, Maryland, home, and the lab where he worked. However, he made it a priority to spend time at home in the evenings to help his wife take care of the children before going back to his studies until the pre-dawn hours.

Hauptman's daughter, now Carol Fullerton, was five years old when her father received his doctorate in 1955. "He would do his work on the dining room table," she told the *Washington Post*'s Barbara Vobejda. Once, she decided to play a joke on him by adding a minus sign to one of his formulas. "But right away, he knew," she added

After receiving his graduate degree, Hauptman continued part-time as a professor at the University of Maryland and later joined the biophysics faculty at the State University of New York at Buffalo. By 1965 he was head of the NRL's mathematical physics branch and began a collaboration on steroids with the Medical Foundation of Buffalo, which eventually lured him to their offices. In 1970, after 20 years at the NRL, he left to join the crystallographic group at the Medical Foundation of Buffalo. He became research director of the foundation in 1972. In 1979 and 1980 he was elected president of the Association of Independent Research Institutes.

Awarded Nobel Prize

Hauptman jumped into the limelight in 1985 when the Royal Swedish Academy of Sciences chose to recognize his long-ago work from the 1950s and award him the Nobel Prize for chemistry. He shared the honor with Karle, and the two split the $225,000 award. Karle explained the lag time this way to *Science News* writer Julie Ann Miller: "Initially it was hard for people to believe that the mathematics would, even in principle, do what it does." William Duax, a colleague of Hauptman's, told the *New York Times* that before the Hauptman-Karle method, it took two years to map out the structure of a simple 15-atom antibiotic molecule. Using Hauptman and Karle's methods, it took only two days to determine the three-dimensional structure of a 50-atom molecule. Over the years, the Hauptman-Karle method has been used to analyze hormones, vitamins, antibiotics, potential anti-cancer drugs, and plant-growth promoters. The U.S. Department of Defense was also interested in the methods as a way to investigate the structure of certain propellants, which could be used for rockets.

In 1986 Hauptman was named president of the Medical Foundation of Buffalo and in 1994 the foundation's name was changed to the Hauptman-Woodward Medical Research Institute (HWI) to honor both Hauptman and foundation benefactor Helen Woodward Rivas. HWI continues as an independent, not-for-profit biomedical research facility located in Buffalo, where one of its missions is to understand diseases at the molecular level.

Discoveries at HWI led to better insulin and a new antibiotic to fight strain-resistant bacterial infections. Under Hauptman's direction, HWI has also developed research experiments that have flown with NASA crews. The institute is also working on a way to determine the chemical interactions that cause polycystic kidney disease and breast cancer, with the hope of determining new treatments or even a cure. "Solving the structures that control our bodies gives us a deeper understanding of how things work, how things go wrong and how we can design drugs that destroy diseases while causing minimal collateral damage," Hauptman told *Buffalo News* writer Davis. At HWI, Hauptman also continued his original, Nobel Prize-winning research, hoping to extend its capabilities. In time, HWI was successful in formulating a new "shake-and-bake" procedure to his original "direct methods" formula, giving scientists the ability to map the structure of even larger molecules than the original breakthrough allowed.

Hauptman's research is recognized by many universities around the world, and the honorary degrees he has received include those from the University of Maryland,

1985; City College of New York, 1996; University of Parma, Italy, 1989; D'Youville College, Buffalo, 1989; Columbia University, 1990; Bar-Ilan University, Israel, 1990; the Technical University of Lodz, Poland, 1992; and Queen's University, Kingston, Canada, 1993. Over the years, he has published his findings in journal articles, research papers, and book chapters.

Continued Research

When he is not working, Hauptman listens to classical music, and in his spare time designs geometric-patterned stained glass. He also swims nearly every day. Although well past retirement age, Hauptman continued his work as a research professor at the State University of New York at Buffalo and also at the research institute, which expanded its state-of-the-art research laboratory in 2003. Though some of the institute's work has gone unnoticed, Hauptman remained unfazed. As he remarked on the HWI website, "When you look at the great strides that were made against polio and tuberculosis, those breakthroughs could not have been made without research that was done 50 or 100 years earlier. . . . And once in a while, with a little luck, lightning strikes."

Books

American Men and Women of Science, Gale, 2003.

Periodicals

Buffalo News, January 30, 2000; November 1, 2003.
New York Times, October 17, 1985.
Science, January 24, 1986.
Science News, October 26, 1985.
Washington Post, December 21, 1985.

Online

Hauptman-Woodward Medical Research Institute Web site, http://www.hwi.buffalo.edu/ (December 19, 2003).
"Herbert A. Hauptman," *SUNY Buffalo Web site,* http://www.cs.buffalo.edu/pub/WWW/faculty/hauptman (December 4, 2003).
Nobel E-Museum, http://www.nobel.se/chemistry/laureates/ (November 30, 2003). □

Ofra Haza

Ofra Haza (1959–2000) was Israel's leading pop music recording artist. Rising from poverty to stardom, Haza left the slums of Tel Aviv to win World Music Awards and to sing at the 1994 Nobel Peace Prize ceremony.

An icon in her country, the mezzo-soprano received international attention for her songs that blended ancient Yemenite-Jewish poetry with western music. After releasing 16 gold and platinum albums in Israel and winning the Israeli equivalent of the Grammy Award for best female singer in 1980, she broke into the European and

North American markets. She died at the age of 41 due to complications from AIDS.

Started in Theater Group

Ofra Haza was born in Tel Aviv, the youngest of nine children in a Jewish family that had escaped religious persecution in Yemen. Growing up in the poor Hatikva district, Haza came from a musical background. Her mother, Shoshana, sang old Yemenite songs around the house and played the tambour drum. Israeli folk songs and songs from the Beatles and Elvis Presley were also among her musical influences during the 1960s.

At age 12, Haza joined the local Hatikva Theater, a protest theater group established by Bezalel Aloni. Aloni, who would manage her career for the next 20 years, made her the star of the show. She participated in the troupe for seven years, singing and gaining a following and appearing on four albums with the members of the Hatikva Theater.

Israel's Top Singer

During her teenage years, Haza performed in a variety of venues. She hit the Israeli charts with songs about poverty and the discrimination faced by Jews who moved to Israel from Arab countries. She won a national singing contest, appeared on television variety shows, and worked in movies with film directors Zalman King and Goran Bregovich. As is mandatory for all Israeli citizens, she joined the army at age 18 for a two-year stint, working as a secretary assigned to the tank corps. After her military service, she released her first solo album in Israel, signing with local label Hed Azri.

Haza's pop albums became best-sellers in Israel. Her 1979 "The Tart's Song" spoke of independent young women defying tradition and social convention. "At that early stage of her career, all Ofra wanted was to forget her ethnic roots and be an Israeli," commented Yoram Rotem, music chief at Israeli broadcaster Galei Zahal, for *Billboard* magazine. "She sang simple songs for the ordinary Israeli. They were largely ignored by radio, but fans bought them."

The mezzo-soprano, who sang in Hebrew and Arabic, easily crossed cultural boundaries and garnered numerous awards. Haza was named Israel's Singer of the Year for five consecutive years and went on to record more than 16 gold and platinum albums in her homeland. In 1983, she was chosen to represent Israel in the Eurovision Song Contest, where she placed second. The experience offered her exposure to the European audience.

Recorded Yemenite Songs

By the mid-1980s, Haza had changed her subject matter, returning to songs learned from her parents. She attracted new audiences with the release of three albums of old Israeli songs that soon earned the attention of radio stations. Record producers who had begun to take notice asked her to make an album for international distribution. She decided to honor her Yemenite Jewish heritage by covering the songs her mother used to sing with a pop beat and modern arrangements.

Haza's first international release came in 1985 with the album, *Fifty Gates of Wisdom: Yemenite Songs.* For the album, Haza created a modern interpretation of a collection of prayers written by 17th-century Rabbi Shalom Shabazi by adding a dance beat that used electronic percussion. She told the *New York Times,* "I wanted to do an album to make my parents happy."

At a time when the World Beat sound was gaining popularity, *Fifty Gates of Wisdom* was an enormous success, hitting the club scenes in Europe, and topping the international pop charts. Haza soon became Israel's most popular international recording artist. Rotem said in *Billboard,* "Ironically, her international success came with the very material from which she wanted to escape. She caught the ethnic wave, and she also had talent, looks, and professionalism."

The album's singles, "Galbi" and "Im Nin'Alu" ("If the Gates of Heaven Closed"), played in dance clubs throughout Europe. "Im Nin'Alu" placed at the top of the singles chart in Germany for nine weeks and ranked number one on the European chart for two weeks. Worldwide, the album sold more than a million copies. In Germany, Haza won the Tigra Award for Singer of the Year in 1989. In 1987, *Fifty Gates of Heaven* reached the United States. Not long after, Haza became the first Israeli singer to be a guest on MTV.

In a circuitous route to fame, the British group Cold Cut heard Haza's voice on a pirated copy of "Im Nin'Alu" and included it on the group's remix of Erik B. and Rakim's rap song, "Paid in Full." M.A.R.R.S.S. also added her voice to

their dance hit, "Pump Up the Volume." Haza commented about her unconventional connection to hip-hop, "That gave my song a big push. People that didn't know me heard my voice on a rap song."

Observed Jewish Tradition

When Haza performed songs from *Fifty Gates of Wisdom,* she added elements of tradition to her style as well as to her music. She proudly wore traditional Yemenite clothing, elaborately beaded and with ornate Yemenite rings and silver bracelets. Devoted to her religion, Haza observed Jewish tradition when she toured and performed. She avoided holding concerts on Friday night to observe Sabbath and requested only kosher meat.

She was living a very different life from the one her parents expected. "I see in front of my eyes my parents who educated me to appreciate what God gave me. I came from a poor neighborhood. Then suddenly I'm staying in first-class hotels, driving in limousines, flying first-class. Every day I say 'Shema Yisrael' and thank God for giving me this opportunity."

Success in English

A German company asked Haza to record an album in English so it could be released in the United States. Few thought a record with Yemenite songs would sell in America. Haza floundered with English and with the conventional subject matter. "He gave me American songs," she said. "You know, 'Love me, love you, need me.' I didn't like the lyrics but I had no choice." The album was abandoned but the idea of an English release was only postponed.

In 1988, Haza signed on with Sire Records, a subsidiary of Warner Bros. A new producer helped her to assemble songs such as "Im Nin'Alu" and Haza's earlier Hebrew songs, translated into English, to create the album, *Shaday.* Released in the United States, Canada, and Japan, it sold a million copies worldwide, and "Im Nin'Alu" won top honors at the Tokyo Music Festival. In New York City, Haza won the New Music Award for the International Album of the Year in 1989.

Two years later, Haza succeeded again with the release of her English album, *Desert Wind.* Haza co-produced four of the songs on the album, which featured her mother chanting Arabic songs. She conducted a U.S. concert tour to promote the album that included 42 cities. Accepted by an audience no longer wary of foreign musicians, Haza commented about her material, "I think people are a little bit tired of the songs they used to hear. They want to listen to something strange and new."

Sang at Nobel Ceremony

Desert Wind brought increased recognition for Haza. She produced a video for MTV and appeared on American talk shows. In 1991, she participated in the Artists of the World for Peace in the World video of John Lennon's "Give Peace a Chance." She was also invited to work with the Sisters of Mercy, Paul Anka, Iggy Pop, and Paula Abdul. Her follow-up album, *Kirya,* featured guest Lou Reed and was nominated for a Grammy Award in the World Beat category.

Her biggest honor came in 1994 when Prime Minister Itzhak Rabin called her Israel's "goodwill ambassador" and invited her to sing at the Nobel Peace Prize ceremony for Rabin, Shimon Peres, and Yasser Arafat. She performed again a year later at Rabin's memorial service following his assassination.

After marrying businessman Doron Ashkenazi in 1997, Haza spent the rest of the 1990s on two movie projects. In 1998, she sang for Steven Spielberg's animated movie *The Prince of Egypt*, voicing Moses' mother Yocheved. For the movie's international release, she sang in 17 languages, including German, Greek, Polish, and Hungarian, from phonetic transcriptions written in Hebrew.

The same year, Haza sang on the Columbia/TriStar film, "The Governess," which portrayed Jewish life in England in the late 19th Century. The soundtrack was released on the Sony Classical label. Also in 1998, Haza joined the late Pakistani virtuoso Ali Akba Khan for *The Prayer Cycle,* inspired by music from Judaic and Muslim traditions.

Succumbed to AIDS

On February 10, 2000, Haza admitted herself to Sheba Hospital in Tel Aviv. Despite her fame, she guarded her privacy and refused to inform the media about her medical condition. She and her family forbade the hospital to leak information about her illness to the press. Some reports claimed she was suffering from influenza and that she was receiving treatment for liver and kidney failure. Fans and well wishers, as well as television crews, gathered daily outside the hospital keeping vigil, praying, and hoping to learn about her condition. On February 23, 2000, 13 days after entering the hospital, Haza was pronounced dead from multiple organ failure.

Her funeral, held on February 27, attracted thousands of mourners. Working-class people and the elite, including Shimon Peres, gathered to eulogize Israel's leading recording artist. Bibi Netanyahu paid public tribute, and Prime Minister Ehud Barak issued a statement, "I was impressed by her shining personality and her great talent. Her voice made its way into the hearts of many in Israel and throughout the world. Her contribution to Israeli culture was great, and the honor she brought this country will never be forgotten."

The daily newspaper *Ha'aretz* had been reporting that Haza was infected with the HIV virus and that AIDS was the cause of her organ failure. The paper was criticized for violating the singer's privacy, yet it defended its decision to report the news, which had existed as a rumor on the Internet and television. In a country where having AIDS was still considered taboo, *Ha'aretz*'s editors believed that secrecy only demonized the disease. Haza's death prompted more discussion in Israel about AIDS and the shame that stills surrounds it.

Some AIDS activists suggested that Ofra Haza could have been her country's Magic Johnson, a celebrity who could have broken down stereotypes and promoted educa-

tion on AIDS prevention and awareness. Bentwich said in the *New York Times,* "In this unfortunate case . . . it appears that Ofra Haza almost died of the embarrassment, from the terrible fear to reveal her illness."

Books

Contemporary Musicians, Volume 29, Gale, 2000.

Periodicals

Billboard, March 11, 2000.
Jerusalem Post, February 24, 2000.
Jewish Journal of Greater Los Angeles, March 3, 2000.
New York Times, February 24, 2000; February 29, 2000.
Wall Street Journal, February 15, 1990.

Online

"Exclusive Interview with Ofra Haza," *Shalom, KakAfonia!* http://kakafonia.hypermart.net/news/ofra.htm (December 23, 2003).
"Secrecy surrounding popular Israeli singer Ofra Haza's death," *National Public Radio: All Things Considered* http://www.npr .org/programs/atc/radio show (December 23, 2003).
Sony Classical, www.sonyclassical.com/artists/haza (December 23, 2003). □

Eric Arthur Heiden

In 1980, American speed skater Eric Heiden (born 1958) became the first athlete ever to win five gold medals in a single Olympics. After his record-setting performance, Heiden went on to compete on the cycling circuit and then became a doctor, enjoying a life of quiet obscurity.

Success Began with Training

Skates were Heiden's first shoes. Being born into a family of skaters—and growing up in Madison, Wisconsin, where winters are long and cold—gave Heiden plenty of opportunities to glide across the ice. Although hockey was his first love, at age 14 he committed all his time and energy to the sport of speed skating.

In 1972, Heiden's training was energized when Dianne Holum, the 1968 and 1972 Olympic speed skating champion, started him on an intensive training regimen. Combining on- and off-the-ice exercises, Heiden's focus became both physical and mental. His physical training concentrated on strengthening the most important muscles for any speed skater—the quadriceps—and included bicycling, weightlifting, and duck walking. His mental training pinpointed how his technique could give him an advantage over his competitors. That advantage would soon lead Heiden to five amazing victories at Lake Placid.

"Turned Ice Into Gold"

Throughout the mid to late 1970s, Heiden's hard work garnered him much success. In 1977, at only 19 years of age, he became the first American to win the World Speed Skating Championships. Thereafter, Heiden dominated every competition, amassing over 15 wins including the World Speed Skating Championships three times.

By 1980, Heiden had become the skater to beat at the Lake Placid Olympics. In fact, some had already accepted defeat. Frode Roenning, Norway's speed skating Olympian, told the *Washington Post*, "Heiden is the biggest, greatest skater there has ever been. The rest of us are waiting for the next Olympics," according to ESPN online. With all the publicity swarming around Heiden, many wondered if he could live up to his potential and to the hype. Heiden was unfazed by it, however. It seemed as if the grandness of the Olympics had no impact on him. In fact, ESPN online noted that Heiden told reporters that he felt that the audience's perception of the games was "overrated" and that the Olympics are "just big in the eyes of the American public."

That public watched in awe as Heiden continued his winning ways. In his next race, the 5,000 meter, no one could match his smooth strokes across the ice. He won his second gold by more than a second. In his third race, the 1,000 meter, Heiden extended his winning margin to one and half seconds. This dominance led *Washington Post* reporter Tom Boswell, as further noted by ESPN online, to comment, "Many athletes have muscles. Few have

Heiden's strength of mind, his mulish will inside a thoroughbred's physique."

Heiden would need that strength of mind in his next race, the 1,500 meter. At the 600 meter mark, he slipped, but escaped catastrophe—"losing only a few hundredths of a second," commented ESPN online—and won his fourth gold medal. With this win, Heiden, as Dave Kindred of the *Washington Post* stated, had become "the first man ever to turn ice into gold." However, his gold medal count had not yet been completed. Heiden still had one more race—the 10,000 meter.

In 1980, the United States was in the midst of a harsh Cold War with their then-enemy the Union of Soviet Socialist Republics (USSR). The country wanted heroes and looked to the Olympics as one place to find them. After winning four gold medals, Heiden had become a national hero. As ESPN online quoted Ken Denlinger from the *Post*, "Heiden is not some Soviet recently emerged from a hidden lab after decades of selective breeding. He is American, from Green Bay Packer country." However, Heiden was not the only hero. The night before Heiden's last race, the American ice hockey team played their miraculous game against the USSR and won. The United States had more heroes to honor. Heiden had attended the game and, too excited about the win, could not fall asleep. Sleep is the body's time to recuperate and prepare for its next challenge. Heiden's body did not get that chance. He overslept, wolfed down some breakfast, and arrived at the track just in time for warm-ups.

Speed skating had never been a popular spectator sport—especially the 10,000 meter race. Overall, the competition is not other skaters, but the clock. At the Olympics, what spectators watched were "two people in funny suits gliding 6.2 miles in little circles with one hand behind their back," commented *Washington Post* reporter Dave Kindred. Gliding for 25 laps over 14 minutes and 12 seconds, Heiden beat the previous world record by six seconds and claimed his fifth gold medal. "That's the last world record I had ever expected to break," Heiden stated as noted by ESPN online. And, as he exited the rink, Heiden had what he would later recall as his "most memorable moment." He told reporter Jo-Ann Barnas of the *Detroit Free Press* that he thought to himself, "I'm never going to be in that kind of shape again."

Yet, much like his attitude towards the games itself, Heiden's attitude about winning a record-setting five gold medals was also blasé. Again, his focus had been skating the best that he could. "Gold, silver and bronze isn't special," he commented at a news conference, according to ESPN online. "It's giving 100 percent." Heiden had not realized the impressiveness of his wins or the worthiness of the medals. "Heck, gold medals, what can you do with them? I'd rather get a nice warmup suit," he told Kindred of the *Washington Post*. "That's something I can use. Gold medals just sit there. When I get old, maybe I could sell them if I need the money."

Rejected Fame for Medical School

Most Olympic medallists have cashed in on their wins by plastering their faces on cereal boxes or by pitching various products on television. Some return for further glory to their sport for the next Olympics. However, Heiden retired. "I didn't get into skating to be famous," he said according to ESPN online. He thought about continuing skating, but only if "I could still be obscure in an obscure sport. . . . I really liked it best when I was a nobody," he further commented.

Yet, Heiden never stopped being an athlete. He just switched sports. In the summer of 1980, he earned a spot as an alternate for the U.S. Olympic cycling team. For the next six years, he continued pedaling and in 1985, won the U.S. professional cycling championship. In 1986, Heiden raced in the prestigious Tour de France. During the race, he suffered what would be his first and only injury, a concussion. "I fell off the bike . . . there was blood coming out of my head," he recalled to *Sports Illustrated*. "That pretty much ended my cycling career."

By 1986, Heiden earned a Bachelor's degree in his premedicine studies, fulfilling his childhood dream. "I can remember in eighth grade making a conscious decision when I was I guess about 14 years old that I wanted to go into medicine," he told an interviewer for the University of California-Davis Medical Center (UCDMC). In 1986, Heiden entered Stanford University Medical School and faded back into an obscure, decidedly non-famous life.

By the late 1990s, Heiden had completed medical school and residency, married, became a father, joined the medical staff for the National Basketball Association's (NBA's) Sacramento Kings, and began working as an orthopedic surgeon for UCDMC. With surgery, Heiden had discovered a connection to sports. "There's a lot of preparation," he told *Sports Illustrated*. "The surgery itself takes maximum concentration and maximum effort, but the competition is with yourself."

Heiden had also discovered a unique connection to his patients, many of whom were injured athletes. "Having been an athlete, I have an idea what the players are going through, the pressures they're under, and what's going on mentally as they try to get back on their feet," he further told *Sports Illustrated*. And, with the passage of time, many of his patients as well as the general public had no idea that Doctor Heiden was Eric Heiden, five-time Olympic gold medallist. Heiden relished that fact: "I love that I can go out in public and only now and then does my face ring a bell for people." Heiden had moved on from the past, never reliving his glory days, but only focusing on the future and "being the best doctor I can be," as he commented to *Sports Illustrated*.

Returned to Olympics

In 2002, another Winter Olympics was being held on American soil and Salt Lake City had decided to honor past American Olympians. Heiden, however, passed on being part of the opening ceremonies after being notified that the U.S. Hockey team, not he, would be the last torch bearers.

He did, however, accept the position as team physician for the American speed skating team. "I've always wanted to give back," Heiden told the *Detroit Free Press*. "And being a sports physician, I looked at that as an opportunity. It's a little strange (being in Salt Lake) but this is pretty rewarding." Also strange was the fact that it had been 22 years since Heiden's record-setting Olympics. "It seems like it was just a few years ago," Heiden said in the *Detroit Free Press*. "People always ask, 'Has it set in?' And I still say, 'It really hasn't. . . . I didn't consider myself a great athlete.' "

Periodicals

Detroit Free Press, February 6, 2002.
Sports Illustrated, November 16, 1998.
Washington Post, February 24, 1980.

Online

"Eric Heiden was a Reluctant Hero," *Sports Century,* http://espn .go.com/sportscentury/features/00014225.html (December 26, 2003).
"Heiden was America's Golden Boy in 1980," ESPN online, http://spots.espn.go.com/oly/winter02/gen/geature?id =1307965 (December 26, 2003).
"Profile: Dr. Eric Heiden," *Pulse,* http://www.ucdmc.ucdavis .edu/pulse/scripts/01_02/dr%20_eric_heiden (December 26, 2003). ☐

John William Heisman

John William Heisman (1869–1936) was the football coach at Georgia Technical University (Georgia Tech) from 1904 until 1919. His teams played 33 games without a defeat including its record-setting win of 222-0 over Cumberland College in 1916. His career in college football lasted 36 years and marked some of the most significant changes in the sport's history.

Born to College Football

John William Heisman was born Johann Wilhelm Heisman, on October 23, 1869, at 183 Bridge Avenue in Cleveland, Ohio, two weeks to the day before the first official intercollegiate football game was played on November 6, between Rutgers and Princeton, both in New Jersey. His parents were Johann "Michael" Heisman and Sarah Lehr Heisman, both German immigrants to America not long before Heisman's birth. The senior Heisman was actually the son of the Baron von Bogart, German nobility, who lost his inheritance and his family when he decided to marry for love instead of title. Heisman's mother's grandfather, the Mater of Knauge, had been an aide to Napoleon, but was not titled. The two young lovers married and took the bride's maiden name of Heisman. By the age of seven, Heisman moved with his family to Titusville, Pennsylvania, at the center of oil country, where his father would practice his

trade as a cooper, or barrel maker. The business supplied barrels to such notables as John D. Rockefeller for his Standard Oil company and prospered quickly to approximately 35 employees. In 1890, the senior Heisman sold out his business and returned to Cleveland. Heisman grew up in a comfortable home, beginning his own love affair with the game of football as a player for Titusville High School.

Heisman first enrolled at Brown University in 1887, where he was active in athletics, especially baseball and football though the school had dropped intercollegiate play until 1889 so his play was limited to a club team within the university. By the time Brown was playing intercollegiately again, Heisman had already transferred to the University of Pennsylvania with the intention of getting a law degree. Throughout the completion of his law studies Heisman continued to play football for the school in that era when transfer restrictions did not exist. In a profile of Heisman included in John T. Brady's book, *The Heisman, a Symbol of Excellence,* writer Gene Griessman wrote an autobiographical chapter on Heisman. He discussed the events surrounding the decision that would change the course of Heisman's life. "There was a Penn player named Pop Thayer, whom Heisman claimed could punt a football 75 yards. Once, when Penn was playing Rutgers in Madison Square Garden, Thayer kicked a ball so high it broke a chandelier in the Garden's arched roof. A later event at the Garden changed Heisman's career forever. According to his widow, during Penn's game with Princeton, which also was played in the Garden, the galvanic lighting system somehow injured Heisman's eyes. The team's physician, Edward Jackson, told

Heisman that he needed to rest his eyes for two years." With that pronouncement, Heisman returned to Ohio in 1892 and accepted the job as Oberlin College's first football coach instead of beginning the practice of law.

Began an Illustrious Career

Oberlin was located just about 20 miles southwest of Cleveland, and was already well-known for its academic excellence, especially in the liberal arts. In addition to joining the football staff, Heisman enrolled in a postgraduate course in art and also played on the football team—a practice, noted Griessman, that was legal at the time. The first team emerged undefeated that season and allowed only 30 points to its own 262 points. In an article for *Campus Life,* of Georgia Tech, Pat Edwards wrote in the fall of 1997, that during those early coaching years in Ohio, something else happened that was worth noting. "With John's career change to coaching, John's father made up for missing his son's high school and college games by attending the game between Oberlin and Western in 1892. At that game the elder Heisman, coming first to see what his son would give up a law practice for, and alter to support a team he saw as an underdog, began to pace up and down the Western sidelines offering $100 bills as bets in favor of Oberlin," noted Edwards. "The elder Heisman made money that day; Oberlin beat Western 38–8."

In a review of Nat Brandt's book, *When Oberlin Was King of the Gridiron: The Heisman Years,* Kevin Kern of the University of Akron noted that it was the author's claim that at Oberlin Heisman began to "revolutionize American football more than almost anyone else in those early years. Heisman's basic innovations and contributions to the college sport (and some that would be translated to the professional play of the game), included displaying downs and yards on the scoreboard, using both guards as blockers for the runner, drawing up a pre-set series of plays to start a game, sending signals in from the sideline, the long count, snapping the ball directly to the quarterback, and, even being the first to use the word "hike" in calling the plays. One move known as the "hidden-ball trick" was later declared illegal. In feats that would be impossible to fathom by mid-twentieth century, Oberlin would beat future powerhouses such as Ohio State and Illinois. In 1892, Oberlin defeated Ohio State twice under Heisman's leadership both times keeping Ohio State scoreless. Other than a year Heisman spent at Buchtel College (later known as the University of Akron) in 1893–94, during which season the Akron team managed to beat Ohio State 12–6, he stayed with Oberlin until 1895. The coach received no regular salary for his job there but received between $400 and $500 when a hat was passed to collect money for him. At Akron, his salary was $750, though the faculty of that college was not very supportive of the sport.

According to Griessman, the attitude of the Akron faculty might have been influenced by the significant differences of the football game then compared to the way the game would come to be known by the end of the twentieth century. Citing those differences, he noted that, "When a team got the ball, it would form a wedge to shield the man carrying the ball and come galloping down the center of the field. Tackling was not allowed below the knees. No forward passes were allowed, substitutions were rare, and if a man was taken out, he could not return to the game. Serous injuries were more common, and the number of deaths was increasing at a troubling rate, as more and more men took up the sport. However, Buchtel was required to play football to qualify for membership in the Ohio Intercollegiate Athletic Association, so the football team was more or less tolerated as a necessary evil."

Heisman left Oberlin for Auburn University, then known as Alabama Polytechnic Institute, where he stayed for five years. Though Heisman followed three previous football coaches at Auburn, he became the school's first full-time head coach. His record during that time was one of 12 wins, 4 losses, and 2 ties. In 1971 Auburn became the only school where Heisman had coached to have any players win the Heisman Trophy: Pat Sullivan won it in 1971 and Bo Jackson, in 1985.

Heisman was coaching at Auburn when he observed what would come to be known as a "forward pass" for the first time. Technically, the play was illegal. During a game between Georgia and North Carolina in 1895, as Griessman described it, "Toward the end of the game, North Carolina, with its back to the goal, was forced to punt. The fullback retreated until the crossbar of his goal was just above his head. Georgia rushed him mercilessly, and in desperation, he lobbed the ball forward to one of his teammates, who caught it and ran for a touchdown." Though Georgia's coach, Pop Warner, disagreed with the decision, the referee held fast to the opinion that the fullback could have fumbled the ball, allowing the touchdown to count. Heisman realized almost immediately that such a pass could open up the field during a game, and wrote to Walter Camp who was then the chair of the rules committee, petitioning him to make it legal. After years of campaigning, and due to the rise of public opinion against football due to the compounding of serious injuries and death, Camp and his committee finally relented. In 1906 the forward pass was confirmed as a legal play in the game of football. In his later years writing for *Collier's,* a popular American magazine, especially during the 1920s and 1930s, Heisman recalled that with the change that one play brought, "American football had come over the line which divides the modern game from the old. Whether it was my contribution to football or Camp's is, perhaps, immaterial. Football had been saved from itself."

Auburn's team lost only once during the 1896 season, and that was to Georgia, the team that Heisman would eventually lead after he left Auburn. When the rematch on Thanksgiving Day 1897 had to be canceled due to the death of one of Georgia's key players, Auburn had to cancel the rest of the season due to the grave financial losses suffered from that one change. The next year's team was small but worthy with an average weight of 148 pounds. Still, the team racked up a season of two wins against Georgia Tech and Georgia and a loss to North Carolina. Heisman maintained throughout his life that his stay at Auburn was highlighted by never having a team there he "did not love,"

quoted Griessman, nor with whom he had any quarrels. He remained friends with all of his players.

From Auburn, Heisman went to Texas briefly to raise tomatoes, investing nearly all of his money. When Walter Riggs, the Clemson University professor, and later its president, founded the school's first football team in 1895, he also served as head coach for the team in 1896 and in 1899. Riggs had played under Heisman at Auburn and urged him out of the tomato fields back into football at Clemson. When he coached at Clemson for the 1901 through 1904 seasons, Heisman enjoyed a 19-3-2 record. His 1900 team had a 6–0 season, the first undefeated season in its history. His players tended to be light but full of speed. His plays were written to make the best of that fact. Griessman noted "he would throw five men into a sweep ahead of the man with the ball, a play subsequently copied widely, but Heisman seem to have originated." One of his best-known tactics was that of using a player in one position for more than simply that one position.

Heisman continued to enjoy dabbling in the theater during his Clemson days and while doing so met his first wife, a widow named Evelyn McCollum Cox who was an actress in a summer stock company. She had one son, Carlisle, who would stay close to Heisman long after his mother and the coach were to divorce. Heisman and Cox married in 1903 when Carlisle was 12. Georgia Tech, whose team Clemson had defeated by 73–0 in the last game of the season, offered Heisman the position as head coach beginning with the 1904 season. The day after the offer had officially expired, he accepted the post at a salary of $2,250 per year, plus 30 percent of net receipts to coach its athletic teams. Heisman and his new family moved to Atlanta where he would coach the best games of his career and stay through 17 football seasons. It was Heisman's 1916 team that entered the *Guinness Book of World Records,* as it beat the once-powerful southern team of Cumberland College with a score of 222–0. By 1918 Heisman and his wife had mutually agreed to a divorce, and he decided that he wanted to prevent any social embarrassment by letting Evelyn choose where she wanted to live, and then he would choose another. When she decided to stay in Atlanta Heisman accepted a job as the head coach at his alma mater, the University of Pennsylvania.

Heisman stayed there for three seasons. He followed that with positions at Washington and Jefferson College in Washington, Pennsylvania, known at the time to be a serious football contender, having played in the Tournament of Roses game in 1921. When he refused to remove a black player for a scheduled game with Washington and Lee College in Virginia, that team backed out of the game. In 1924, he was married a second time, this time to Edith Maora Cole, who had been a student at Buchtel College while Heisman coached at the school. They had been sweethearts but decided not to marry due to Edith's bout with tuberculosis. They met again during the years following his divorce and married. Shortly after that, Heisman took what would be his last coaching position with Rice University in Houston, Texas. His agreement was to be in residence during spring training and for the football season, making him available for a sporting goods business in which he was involved in New York City. He was granted a five-year contract and a salary of $9,000—a cut for him from Washington and Jefferson, but $1,500 higher than the highest paid faculty member. But with the two initial seasons bringing disappointing results, Heisman resigned after a third even more disastrous season. Heisman left college football coaching behind him and headed back to New York.

Final Years

Heisman became the man chosen by a recruiting committee to become the first athletic director of New York's Downtown Athletic Club (DAC), a name that would become synonymous with athletic excellence, particularly in football. In 1933 Heisman helped to organized the first Touchdown Club of New York and, in 1935, inaugurated the first Downtown Athletic Club trophy for the best college football player east of the Mississippi. On December 10, 1936, just over two months after his death on October 3, 1936, in New York City, the trophy was re-named the "Heisman Memorial Trophy," in his honor.

During the years following his coaching career, while at DAC, Heisman wrote and published a book, *The Principles of Football,* wrote magazine columns for various popular magazines, and was at work on another book at the time of his death. Heisman was buried in Rhinelander, Wisconsin, his wife's hometown.

Books

Brady, John T., *The Heisman, A Symbol of Excellence,* Atheneum, 1984.

Periodicals

New York Times, October 4, 1936.

Online

"A Brief History of the Heisman Memorial Trophy," *Heisman .com website,* http://www.heisman.com (January 22, 2004).

Carney, Jim, "Heisman Trophy namesake coached at Buchtel College," *Ohio.com website,* http://www.ohio.com (January 22, 2004).

"College Football History," *College Football History website,* http://www.collegefootballhistory.com (January 22, 2004).

"Creating the Big Game, John W. Heisman and the Invention of American Football," *Greenwood Publishing Group website,* http://info.greenwood.com (January 22, 2004).

"Heisman, John W., Football," *Hickok Sports.com website,* http://www.hickoksports.com (January 22, 2004).

"Heisman Led Jackets to Victory," *Campus Life, Georgia Tech website,* http://cyberbuzz.gatech.edu (January 22, 2004).

"John Heisman," *College Football Hall of Fame website,* http://www.collegefootball.org (January 22, 2004).

"John Heisman," *Find a Grave website,* http://www.findagrave .com (January 22, 2004).

"John Heisman at Auburn," *Rocky Mountain Auburn Club website,* http://www.coloradotigers.com (January 22, 2004).

"John Heisman, Profile," *Fans only, Clemson University,* http://www.fansonly.com (January 22, 2004).

"John William Heisman, Sports, Biographies," *All Refer.com reference website,* http://reference.allrefer.com (January 22, 2004).

Pees, Samuel T., "John Heisman, Football Coach," *Oil History website,* http://www.oilhistory.com (January 22, 2004).

"Principles of Football," *Hill Street Press website,* http://www .hillstreetpress.com (January 22, 2004).

"When Oberlin was King of the Gridiron: The Heisman Years," book review, *Northeast Ohio Journal of History (University of Akron, OH) website,* http://www2.uakron.edu/nojh (January 22, 2004). □

Chang Heng

Chang Heng (78–139) was the leading scientist of the Later (or Eastern) Han Dynasty of first- and second-century China. He was a scholar in many areas, among them astronomy, cartography, mathematics, philosophy, and literature. Also known as Zhang Heng and Pingzhi, Heng is credited with creating the first seismograph to record earthquakes, devised an armillary—or celestial globe—to track the movement of planets and stars, proposed the concept of the lunar eclipse, developed longitude and latitude grids for maps, invented the odometer, and wrote love poems and other literary works.

Chang Heng was born in the Chinese Year of the Horse 2776, or 78 A.D., in the Xie county of Nayang, north of what is today Nanyang County in Henan Province of China. He was born during the Han Dynasty, a golden age of 400 years of enlightenment, scientific discovery, and domestic prosperity. Heng grew up amid literature and learning, becoming a good writer by age twelve. With a desire to travel around China and learn new things, at age 16 he left home to pursue his passion for knowledge. Heng visited the Han capital city of Chang'an where he learned history, current events, and culture, then ventured to the East Han capital of Luoyang and that region's school of higher learning, Taixue. At Taixu Heng spent several years honing his skills in writing and the study of literature.

In 111 the Chinese government asked for Heng's services, so he became an official assigned as the court historian. First serving as a junior officer then as a senior, Heng spent his longest term, 14 years, working under scholar Taishiling. Taishiling oversaw the observation of astronomical phenomena, the compilation of calendars, weather prediction, and meteorological occurrences. Heng studied the astronomical calendar, managed official documents, and became a national historian. Some biographers claim Heng was known for his moral attitude, never taking bribes, and cleaning up government corruption when he encountered it.

In time, Heng became the chief astronomer of the Imperial Chancellery for Astronomical and Calendrical Science and a chief minister under Emperor An'ti. Possessed of the rare talent of interdisciplinary interests, Heng embodied ancient China's reputation for scientific discovery and observation. Although he pursued knowledge in many fields, he is most remembered for devising the first seismograph, which he did in 132 A.D.

Invented the Seismograph: The Dragons and the Toads

Known for excellent record keeping, the Chinese kept accurate records of not only celestial events, but of earthquakes as well. At the time, people believed that seismic events were supernatural in origin: signs from heaven from angry gods designed to punished those below. Heng discounted these superstitions because he had been making careful observations of the symptoms of earthquakes and believed he could explain them by scientific means.

Because news about earthquakes occurring in distant parts of the country took too long to reach the Court, Heng desired a device capable of indicating tremors, their distance from the seismic event, and the event's location. To do so would not only save lives, but raise Heng's status in the Han Court.

Although Heng's original seismograph did not survive time, its description did, and several modern scholars have tried to recreate the device. Called the *houfeng didong yi,* or "instrument for inquiring into the wind and the shaking of the earth," the first seismograph was a cast bronze kettle with a domed lid. The diameter of the device was eight *chhih*—1.8 meters or six feet.

The design of Heng's seismograph was indicative of Chinese artistry. The kettle sported eight dragonheads arranged in eight directions around the outside rim. Each head held a ball in its mouth. At the base of the vessel were eight corresponding toads with their empty mouths open. The "toothed machinery and ingenious constructions" inside the device were hidden. Actually it was an inverted pendulum that reacted to the slightest tremor of the earth. The pendulum swung, tapping a mechanism that ejected one of the balls from the corresponding dragonhead. The ball would fall into the waiting toad's mouth sitting directly under it and make a loud clang. Whichever toad had the ball indicated the direction of the earthquake's location.

Earned Reputation for Accurate Predictions

Heng's reputation was put into question one day in February 138 when a ball fell from a dragon's mouth indicating an earthquake had occurred. No one felt any shocks or tremors and questioned the results of the device. A few days later, a messenger arrived at court announcing that Longxi county in western Gansu Province, 400 miles away, had been struck by an earthquake. The sensitivity and accuracy of Heng's invention solidified his position as chief scientist.

Heng's "scientifically designed" instrument should more accurately be called a seismoscope, since it really measured the direction of ground motion without noting time or amplitude. Nevertheless, it worked on the principle of inertia: the tremor shook the device, causing a displacement between the mass and the kettle. This movement caused the ball to fall out of the dragon's mouth. Heng was able to design the seismoscope to pick up the signals of actual earthquakes and reject false signals.

Heng's machine was in use for four centuries in the form of "earthquake weathercocks." Despite the genius and practicality of the machine, however, exploration in this area of science ended when the Mongols overran China in the 13th century. Some later Chinese historians had doubted that such a device was even possible. Only 1,400 years later in France in 1703, did De la Hautefeuille invent the first modern seismograph.

Created Second Seismograph and Celestial Globe

In competition with another noted scientist of his time, Li Pao, Heng devised another type of seismograph to prove his theory, which was contradictory to Li's. Heng's new machine consisted of a bronze dragon embracing a water driven cylinder covered with porous porcelain plates. In the dragon's mouth was balanced a glass bulb filled with red ink. Many of these machines were placed throughout China. If earthquakes were caused internally in the Earth, as Heng believed, the tremor would dislodge all the ink at the same time. Li believed that earthquakes were caused by meteorites hitting the earth, therefore dislodging only the ink bulb nearest the impact. The bulb would break and ink would flow down the rotating cylinder in a spiral pattern. Unfortunately there is no record of who won the competition.

Heng believed that the Earth was round. In his writing titled *Hun-i chu,* he describes the world: "The sky is like a hen's egg, and is as round as a crossbow pellet; the Earth is like the yolk of the egg, lying alone at the center. The sky is large and the Earth small." To further study his interpretation of the universe, Heng constructed the first rotating celestial globe, or armillary.

The Chinese introduced the first permanently mounted equatorial armillary ring in 52 B.C. Successive astronomers adding rings. In 125 Heng added a ring for the meridian and one for the horizon. He built a wooden sphere at first, then a bronze version nearly five meters in circumference, affixed stars to the device, and made it rotate by water pressure. The water clock, or clepsydra, regulated the rotation of the device so it turned in real time—one circuit in one day, one complete rotation in one year. This allowed people to observe the movements of the sun, moon, and stars as they interrelated. In his book *The Chart and Interpretation of Armillary Sphere,* Heng calculated the year as 365 and a quarter degrees. Heng was the first to add such features as the north and south poles, equator, and elliptics.

Heng's definitive astronomical text is *Lin Xian,* which describes celestial phenomena. In this work he proposes that the moon reflects sunlight rather than being lit on its own. He also sets forth the theory that the moon could be eclipsed by the shadow of the Earth, gives reasons for the shortening and lengthening of the days throughout the year, and argues that the universe is infinite in time and space. He also calculates the angular diameter of the sun and moon as 29'24'' or 1/736 of the celestial globe (the true average angular diameter is 31'59''26). He charted 124 constellations consisting of 2,500 stars he observed while in Luoyang, 320 of which had names. He also explains the optical illusion that makes the sun look bigger at morning and evening and smaller at noon.

A Man of Many Disciplines

Heng was an engineer, meteorologist, geologist, and philosopher. He invented the odometer, or "mileage cart," which carried a figure that struck a drum as each *li*—or 0.5 km—distance was traversed. He is also remembered as being one of the four great painters of his time. A visionary mathematician, Heng computed the value of pi as the square root of 10, or approximately 3.162, not far off from 3.14. He constructed a sundial to measure the position of the sun. In 123 he improved the calendar to coordinate it with the seasons. He invented a compass vehicle in which a wooden figure inside a carriage would always point in the southerly direction due to the specialized gear system. He even created a wooden flying bird.

Many of his efforts focused on geography. Heng invented quantitative cartography, applying a grid system to maps, from which positions, distance, and itineraries could be calculated. His book, *Discourse on New Calculations*, established the basis for the mathematical use of the grid with maps, and he presented one of his maps to the Chinese emperor in 116. He perfected the science of latitude and longitude, and his grids were said to form a "net over the Earth."

Composed Poetry and Literary Works

The Han Dynasty produced narrative poets who described the grandeur of China's imperial court, the region's prosperity, and the lives of the elite. In this climate, Heng wrote more than 20 literary works. His poetry includes verses on such topics as leisure, academics, politics, love, and erotica. In his "Four Stanzas of Sorrow," he earliest known seven-syllabic Chinese poem, Heng writes, "She gives me a sword to my delight;/A jade I give her as requite./ I'm at a loss as she is out of sight;/ Why should I trouble myself all night?"

Heng's other notable poems include "Bones of Zhuang Zi," "Going Back to the Field," "Two Capitals," "A Song of Simultaneous Sounds," and "Thinking about Mysteries," the last in which he describes his astral travels among the solar system. In the prose poem "The Fu" Heng presents a critique of the former emperors of the Han Dynasty.

Not Forgotten

Heng died in the Year of the Tiger 2837, or 139 A.D. in China. Many of the accomplishments of early Chinese scientists have been lost or forgotten, a symptom of the social structure in which academics sought patrons to sponsor their work. Knowledge was localized and spread slowly. Due to his vast number of achievements, however, Heng's work has survived. In the summer of 1980 the People's Republic of China presented an exhibit of science and industrial products in San Francisco, California, that included a model of Heng's ancient seismograph. And more recently, as China announced in 2003 that it planned to build a space telescope fashioned after NASA's Hubble telescope, rumors indicated that the instrument—which was planned for operation in 2008—would be named in honor of Heng. The ancient Chinese inventor has also been honored in space; Heng has a lunar crater on the back side of the moon named after him.

Books

Ross, Frank Jr., *Oracle Bones, Stars, and Wheelbarrows: Ancient and Chinese Science and Technology*, Houghton Mifflin, 1982.

Temple, Robert, *Genius of China*, Simon & Schuster, 1986.

Teresi, Dick, *Lost Discoveries: Ancient Roots of Modern Science—from the Babylonians to the Maya*, Simon & Schuster, 2003.

Online

Albertson College of Idaho Web site, http://www.albertson.edu/math/History/jnewbry/Classical/index.htm (December 22, 2003).

"Ancient Seismometer," *Chinese Historical and Cultural Project Web site*, http://www.chcp.org/seismo.html (December 22, 2003).

"Chinese Seismology," *University of Houston Web site*, http://www.uh.edu/engines/epi324.htm (December 22, 2003).

"The Second Seismograph of Chang Heng," *National Museum of Denmark Web site*, http;//www.natmus.dk/cons/tp/gael/gael.htm (December 22, 2003).

"The Three Wise Men," *University of California Los Angeles Division of Astronomy & Astrophysics Web site*, http://www.astro.ucla.edu/~kaisler/articles/event_horizon/3wisemen.html (December 23, 2003).

Zhang Heng's Cosmology," *Pure Insight.org*, http://www.purinsight.org/pi/articles/2002/7/15/1045.html (December 23, 2003). □

Alonzo Franklin Herndon

American executive Alonzo Franklin Herndon (1858–1927) founded the Atlanta Life Insurance Company, one of the leading insurers in the American South. Born into slavery, he belonged to the first generation of successful African American entrepreneurs of the early twentieth century.

Worked Fields as a Child

Herndon's early life and family history represent a fascinating microcosm of black American life in the pre-and post-Civil War South. Herndon was born on July 21, 1858, to Sophenie Herndon, a slave. His father was Frank Herndon, the white farmer to whose Social Circle, Georgia land Sophenie was restricted. The young Herndon was one of 25 slaves owned by his father, who never acknowledged paternity. He also had a younger brother, Thomas, as well as a number of half-brothers and half-sisters born to other slave women on the Herndon farm.

Herndon was four years old when President Abraham Lincoln's Emancipation Proclamation of January 1, 1863, freed the slaves in the Southern states that had seceded from the Union to join the Confederacy, but was seven when Frank Herndon released them when the war ended. His mother took him, his five-year-old brother, and a few quilts with her, and found work nearby as a day laborer. With the Southern economy wrecked, she was forced to accept payment in molasses, potatoes, or other provisions in order to feed her sons. She eventually went back to work on the Herndon farm, living in a one-room log cabin with four other former slave families and being paid pitifully meager wages. To make ends meet, Herndon and his brother worked in the fields as well alongside their mother and grandparents, and he had very little formal schooling as a result. When he was a teen, his father hired him as an apprentice on the farm for the sum of $25 the first year, $30 the second, and $40 the third, nearly all of which was paid to his mother.

Ran Away from Farm

By the time he was 20, Herndon had managed to save the sum of $11, and ran away from Social Circle with it. "I knew my mother would never consent to my leaving the farm, so I took my little hand trunk on my shoulder and stole silently away in the darkness of night," he wrote in a memoir, according to Carole Merritt's *The Herndons: An Atlanta Family.* On that day in 1878, he walked all the way to Jonesboro, Georgia, but his first stop was a town that had telegraph wires running overhead, something he had never before seen and which unsettled him. "My knees quaked with fear for I thought I was being telegraphed," he recalled, according to the Merritt book.

Herndon trained as a barber, and had his first small shop in Jonesboro. Looking to make his fortune in a place that offered better opportunities for blacks, Herndon relocated to Rome, Georgia, and then Chattanooga, Tennessee, but at one point was so discouraged by his business setbacks that he thought about quitting altogether and taking in a job a plow factory. In 1882, he moved to Atlanta, and found a post with a highly regarded local barber. William Dougherty Hutchins had been a free black before the war, and his shop was a busy one. Herndon eventually bought into a partnership, but it was later dissolved—perhaps due to Hutchins's financial setbacks, which taught Herndon to always be cautious about business expansion. Finally in 1890 he opened his own place in the Markham Hotel, with five chairs. Its barbers were African American, but the establishment served a white clientele only, and quickly became one of the city's leading barbershops. "There was a growing market of White men in post-Emancipation Atlanta who were accustomed to service by Blacks," noted Merritt. "Herndon was eager to capitalize on it."

Black Atlanta's Power Couple

Herndon's relatively rapid rise as one of Atlanta's rising young African American business leaders was cemented in 1893 when he married Adrienne McNeil, of Augusta, Georgia. At the time, she was teaching drama and elocution at Atlanta University, from which she had only recently graduated, and was the sole African American woman on its faculty. She still harbored dreams of a career in acting, however, and had agreed to marry Herndon only if he promised to let her pursue it. Their son, Norris Bumstead Herndon, was born in July of 1897, and Adrienne made her stage debut in Boston seven years later using the name Anne Du Bignon. The publicity materials for the event claimed she was from an old French and Creole family in South Carolina, mentioning nothing about her race, and though she earned good reviews for a recital of Shakespeare's *Antony and Cleopatra,* no other roles came her way.

Twice Herndon's businesses were destroyed by fire: once in 1896 after a gas stove across the street from the Markham ignited its building and leveled the hotel, and again in 1902 when his new place on Marietta Street ignited in a fire that destroyed an entire city block. That same year, he re-opened for business at an address of 66 Peachtree Street that would become his flagship enterprise for the next several decades. Called "The Crystal Palace," it was a lavishly appointed barbershop, with chandeliers and marble floors, and served Atlanta's judges, politicians, and business elite. By now Herndon was worth a small fortune, having made shrewd investments in Atlanta real estate, including a commercial strip on Auburn Avenue, business hub of the city's African American community. He also owned a hundred or so residential rental properties in the city.

Ventured into Insurance Business

Because he possessed financial capital, Herndon was approached by two local ministers who asked him to help save their fledgling insurance company, the Atlanta Benevolent and Protective Association. For dues of 25 cents weekly, a payee's beneficiary would receive a sum up to $50 upon death, which paid for funeral expenses. Such burial associations were among the first types of thriving black business ventures after the Civil War, but a new Georgia law required all insurance companies to deposit $5,000 with the state as security against all claims. Herndon bought the business for $140 in 1905, and when he deposited the sum according to the new state regulatory rules, his company became the first in the state to meet the new requirement.

Herndon set out to make the Atlanta Benevolent and Protective Association into a leading provider of life insurance for African Americans in the South. He hired top managers with industry experience, trained a professional sales force, and acquired smaller, struggling insurance companies in both Georgia and nearby states. His new venture became the Atlanta Mutual Insurance Association, and by 1907 had 23 offices across Georgia.

Struck by Tragedy

Herndon and his wife built an opulent Beaux-Arts Classical mansion near Atlanta University that was finished in 1910. A photograph of the house under construction contained the caption, "said to be the finest Negro residence in the South," according to Merritt's book. Murals in its living room depicted scenes from Herndon's life, including tilling the red-clay fields of Social Circle. "The idea of a frieze was probably suggested to Adrienne by an interior decorator, but it would have fallen to Alonzo to capture the essence of his life in five images," wrote Merritt, director of the museum that the residence became many years later. "Significantly, Alonzo chose field labor rather than barbering to depict his critical path to success." Tragically, Adrienne died the same year the house was completed after a bout with Addison's disease, a glandular condition. Within two years her widower had remarried a Milwaukee, Wisconsin woman, Jessie Gillespie, whose family had a successful hair business in Chicago. An extended European honeymoon was partly spent gathering furnishings to refit his Crystal Palace.

Herndon continued his to expand his insurance empire. In 1913, he signed a partnership agreement with a Kentucky firm, Standard Life. "My aim," he explained in a speech that year delivered at the Tuskegee Institute and quoted in the Merritt book, "has been for several years to try to get as many of our people together to cooperate in business and along all other lines.... The great trouble in establishing insurance companies among our people is that it is difficult for our people to understand the advantage of pulling together for the common and for their own good." In 1915, he ventured into Alabama, and the acquired another Georgia insurance company, Union Mutual, the largest black-owned insurer in the state. A 1916 reorganization made Herndon's company a shareholder-owned one, but he held the majority of stock. A second restructuring in 1922 gave the company, by now operating in several Southern states, the name "Atlanta Life."

Became Leading Philanthropist

Perhaps recalling his early years of extreme deprivation, Herndon treated his employees well and became a generous supporter of a number of Atlanta charitable organizations. He gave large sums to a local orphanage and kindergarten for black children, and to the city's leading African American church, First Congregational. He was also involved in the Southview Cemetery Association, Atlanta Loan and Trust, and the Atlanta State Savings Bank, and was a key investor in Gate City Drug Company, the first black-owned drugstore on Auburn Avenue. In his leisure time, he relaxed at an orange-grove estate he had acquired in Lake County, Florida, which he improved and sold some years later at an impressive profit.

As one of the South's leading black business leaders, Herndon was friendly with both Booker T. Washington and W. E. B. Du Bois. He was even a delegate to the first conference of the National Negro Business League organized by Washington in 1890, and was involved in Du Bois's 1905 Niagara Movement, a conference held in Fort Erie, Ontario that eventually led to the formation of the National Association for the Advancement of Colored People (NAACP). His son was more reluctant to follow in his footsteps, however, for Norris Herndon had inherited Adrienne's passion for the stage. Norris eventually settled down and earned an M.B.A. from Harvard in 1921, where he was one of two blacks in his class.

Extolled as a Pioneer for Other Blacks

Herndon died at home in Atlanta on July 21, 1927, at the age of 69. His funeral was an extraordinary event in the city, and Atlanta Life's Memphis chief, George W. Lee, was one of a lengthy list of eulogists who paid tribute to the company founder. "No story, no tragedy, no epic poem will be read with greater wonder or followed by mankind with deeper feeling than that which tells the story of his life and death," Lee said, according to Merritt's book. Fittingly, Herndon had asked that his pallbearers be drawn from among his barber staff.

In 1933, Jessie and Norris Herndon turned the ownership of the Crystal Palace over to its employees. It remained a segregated establishment until it closed in 1972. Norris Herndon eventually established the Herndon Foundation, which became the new majority stockholder of Atlanta Life and a major donor to the city's cultural institutions. Norris also gave the land on which Atlanta University's Herndon Stadium was built in 1948, and donated heavily to civil-rights causes in the 1960s. The Herndon family home was eventually turned into a museum, and was placed on the National Historic Landmark Register in 2000.

Books

Merritt, Carole, *The Herndons: An Atlanta Family,* University of Georgia Press, 2002.
Notable Black American Men, Gale, 1998.

Periodicals

Atlanta Journal-Constitution, November 22, 1999, p. A1; August 18, 2002, p. G1. □

Johns Hopkins

American financier and philanthropist Johns Hopkins (1795-1873) was the founder of Baltimore, Maryland's Johns Hopkins University, as well as a free hospital to serve the people of the city where he spent his life.

American philanthropist Johns Hopkins made a fortune in banking and real estate by recognizing that Baltimore, Maryland, had a future as a commercial center. Increasing his wealth further by investing in the Baltimore & Ohio Railroad, and inspired by the example of friend and philanthropist George Peabody, Hopkins donated sufficient funds to establish a university and a hospital, both of which bear his name.

From Farm to Baltimore

Johns Hopkins was born May 19, 1795, on his grandparents' 500-acre tobacco plantation in Maryland's Anne Arundel County. He was the second of eleven children born to Samuel and Hannah (Janney) Hopkins. His great grandmother, Margaret Johns, who married into the Hopkins family in 1700, came from a good family that owned a large estate in Maryland's Calvert County, and Hopkins was the second relative to be given his unusual first name in her family's honor, the other being his father's father. The Hopkins family had lived in Maryland since the mid-1600s.

As a boy, Hopkins studied at nearby South River school, where he was taught by a young Oxford University graduate. When he was 12, his grandfather, the first-named Johns Hopkins, a prominent Quaker and a member of the West River Meeting of Friends, decided to act according to his moral beliefs and free the slaves working his land. With no one else to harvest the cotton crop, the task was left to Samuel Hopkins; he pulled young Johns and his older son out of school and quickly trained the boys as field hands. For the remainder of his life, Hopkins regretted the fact that he never finished his education.

When he reached age 17, Hopkins left the family farm and moved to Baltimore, where he was employed by his uncle, Gerard T. Hopkins, to learn the wholesale grocery business. Two years later, in 1814, Gerard Hopkins was forced to leave the business in his nephew's hands when he was called west to Ohio on business. Gone for several

months, Uncle Gerard returned to find that young Johns had kept things running smoothly.

A Head for Business

While Hopkins learned a great deal working alongside his uncle, he was also frustrated by the elder man's rigid and old-fashioned attitudes and unwillingness to modernize some of his business practices. This rigidness was especially counterproductive, it seemed to Hopkins, during the financial upheaval that occurred in 1819 and which caused many cash-poor customers to ask to exchange their personal stock of home-brewed whiskey for food. While the young Hopkins had no problem with such a barter arrangement, his Quaker uncle balked at contributing to the use of strong drink.

Sensing an opportunity, 24-year-old Hopkins decided to go into business for himself. His maternal uncle, John Janney, invested $10,000 toward his nephew's wholesale grocery business, and Hopkins's mother also advanced her son an equal sum. Amenable to exchanging corn whiskey for groceries, the young entrepreneur soon drew customers to his door. Although he was banned from Quaker Meeting for a time, in his first year alone Hopkins and partner Benjamin P. Moore sold $200,000 worth of merchandise.

The partnership between Hopkins and Moore broke up in 1813. After convincing younger brothers Philip and Mahlon to join him in Baltimore, Hopkins changed the name of his firm to Hopkins & Brothers, and soon the brothers had spread their business across Virginia into North Carolina and as far west as Ohio, trading goods for the corn whiskey they marketed as "Hopkins' Best." With his brothers to attend to the day-to-day tasks of mercantilism, Johns had time to build a new career, and he decided to enter the field of banking. Hopkins ended his association with Hopkins & Brothers in 1845, leaving the business to his brothers.

With a natural aptitude for business, Hopkins did not suffer from his lack of formal education, and his career in banking was as successful as his career as a grocer. He served as president of Baltimore's Merchant's Bank, which specialized in loaning money to small business ventures. His practice of buying overdue notes gained him stock in several companies, and with his profits Hopkins built warehouses in the growing city, convinced that Baltimore was well positioned to become a thriving commercial center.

Saw Future of Railroad

In addition to banking, Hopkins involved himself in other business ventures, among them fire and life insurance companies, an iron steamship line and directorships of several other banks within the city. His belief in Baltimore's potential for growth prompted his most lucrative investment, the Baltimore & Ohio Railroad, the first major railroad to form in the United States.

The importance of the development of railroad lines had been made clear to Hopkins by his need to ship and import grocery goods over vast distances as Hopkins Brothers expanded its markets and customer base. Railroads, far more efficient than wagon trains, ensured that a minimum of spoilage and breakage would occur. Appointed director in 1847, Hopkins' role with the railroad expanded in December 1855 when the 60-year-old financier became chairman of the Baltimore & Ohio Railroad's finance committee. His investments in the line made him the largest shareholder after the State of Maryland and the City of Baltimore. At Hopkins' death he held over 15,000 shares of B & O stock.

Hopkins's hopes for the city of Baltimore came to fruition in the mid-1890s, despite financial setbacks resulting from the Civil War. Although Hopkins was not alive to witness it, the city expanded to become a major producer of cotton, milled flour and a variety of other manufactured goods, while shipping and railroad lines made it the second leading grain marketplace in the United States. By 1890 Baltimore served as the financial hub for the southern states.

Importance of Philanthropy

Living his entire adult life in Baltimore, Hopkins made many friends among the city's social elite, many of them members of the Society of Friends. One of these friends was George Peabody, who in 1857 founded the Peabody Institute in Baltimore. Other examples of public giving were evident in the city, as public buildings housing free libraries, schools and foundations sprang up along the city's widening streets. On the advice of Peabody, Hopkins determined to use his great wealth for the public good.

The Civil War had taken its toll on Baltimore, however, as did the yellow fever and cholera epidemics that repeatedly ravaged the nation's cities, killing 853 in Baltimore in the summer of 1832 alone. Hopkins was keenly aware of the city's need for medical facilities, particularly in light of the medical advances made during the war, and in 1870 he made a will setting aside seven million dollars—mostly in B & O stock—for the incorporation of a free hospital and affiliated medical and nurse's training colleges, as well as a university. Each of these institutions would be overseen by a 12-member board of trustees.

Hopkins also willed funds to local agencies for the purpose of educating young people and caring for dependent families. In line with his strong Quaker beliefs, he also earmarked $20,000 per year to fund the Colored Orphans Home, an orphanage for black Americans. He also clearly stipulated that blacks would not be excluded from medical care at his hospital.

Shortly after Hopkins' death in 1874, the required 12-member panels were assembled, and Johns Hopkins University and Johns Hopkins Medical Center were established. The hospital was erected in East Baltimore, on the site of the old Maryland Hospital; the university, established at the Hopkins' family seat at nearby Clifton, opened its doors in 1876. University of California president Daniel C. Gilman was made president of the new university, and he quickly recognized his task—as Stephen Bonsal wrote in *Harper's New Monthly*: "Appreciating . . . the spirit rather than the letter of the bequest which they were charged to execute, the president and trustees determined to give the people of Baltimore the life-giving bread of education rather than the stones and the hollow shell." In "unpretentious but adequate buildings," continued Bonsal, the instructors drawn

to Johns Hopkins University "compared favorably with the faculties of Oxford, Heidelberg, and Paris." Recalling his own childhood and lack of educational opportunity, Hopkins arranged that free scholarships for deserving students from Virginia and Maryland be established.

An Unassuming Life

Hopkins was thrifty in his personal habits—he preferred to walk rather than be driven and never owned an overcoat—but there any similarity to Charles Dickens' character Scrooge ends. Rather than looking after his personal comfort, he amassed a great fortune and willingly spent it when a community need arose. When a financial panic in 1857 resulted in internal disputes, Hopkins underwrote the fledgling Baltimore & Ohio Railroad to keep it sound; its failure would have seriously curtailed trade in the city and the ongoing expansion of the rail line. During the Civil War he advanced $500,000 to the city to keep public services operating. During the financial panic of 1873, as businesses faced bankruptcy, he extended credit to many, often without the expectation of interest, and fronted $900,000 of B & O debt to keep the railroad solvent.

Although he was a well-known public figure, in private Hopkins let a simple, unassuming life. And he lived it in solitude. While he had fallen in love with his cousin, Elizabeth Hopkins, as a young man, Elizabeth's father, Gerard Hopkins, prohibited the two from wedding due to their blood relationship as first cousins. Elizabeth, like Johns Hopkins, never married; instead the pair remained good friends throughout their lives. While intending to travel the world, Hopkins was tied to Baltimore due to his many business interests; instead, he had to be content with connecting with distant places through his railroad and steamship interests and through books—a chronic insomniac, Hopkins became a voracious reader.

Hopkins died on December 24, 1873, at the age of 79. In the Baltimore *Sun* the following morning was a lengthy obituary which closed thus: "In the death of Johns Hopkins a career has been closed which affords a rare example of successful energy in individual accumulations, and of practical beneficence in devoting the gains thus acquired to the public." His contribution to the university that has become his greatest legacy was, by all accounts, the largest philanthropic bequest ever made to an American educational institution.

Books

Dictionary of American Biography, American Council of Learned Societies, 1928-1936.
Thom, Helen Hopkins, *Johns Hopkins: A Silhouette,* 1929.

Periodicals

Harper's New Monthly, February 1896.
Sun (Baltimore), December 25, 1873. □

Hviezdoslav

Slovakian literary great Hviezdoslav (1849-1921) was a genuine Renaissance man; poet, dramatist, journalist, translator, patriot, and Champion of the Slovak language.

Early Life

The Slovakian poet and translator Hviezdoslav was born Pavol Országh on February 2, 1849, at Vysny Kubin. He was the son of a farmer and attended *gymnasium* (high school) in Miskovec, Hungary. He continued his studies in Kezmarok, culminating with law school in Presov. He started out as a lawyer in his native Orava (northwest Slovakia) and quickly entered state service as a judge in Dolny Kubin. While practicing law, he simultaneously studied and wrote poetry under the tutelage of his teacher and mentor, Adolf Medzihradsky. He originally wrote in Hungarian and was a Hungarian patriot. He then wrote in German for a time but switched to the Slovak language on the advice of his teacher in 1868. He quickly became a Slovakian Nationalist and champion of the Slovak language. He published his first poems in 1868 when he was 19 and took the pseudonym Hviezdoslav in 1875 when he was 26. His hope was that the pseudonym would help to separate his identity as a poet from his identity as a lawyer. He presided as a judge for the state for three years and resigned in 1879 to work in private practice in Námestov. He retired in 1899 so that he could devote his life to literature.

Poetry

The Biographical Dictionary of European Literature— European Authors 1000–1900 points out that "Hviezdoslav's poetry combines elements of romanticism and Parnassianism [a French poetic movement emphasizing metrical form rather than emotion]. On one hand he is a patriot whose verse describes his love of country and the beauties of the Slovak landscape; on the other he is an aesthete and accomplished technician who introduced new verse forms such as the sestina and terzina to Slovak poetry." Lauded by the *National Slovak Society* webpage as the "last, brightest star in the Slovak poetical firmament," Hviezdoslav was considered one of the leading artists in the national revival of Slovak literature and language. His dedication to writing in Slovakian supported the people's right to use the Slovak language in schools and public life and helped to develop national consciousness while still managing to publish at least fifteen volumes of original poetry in his lifetime. Much of Hviezdoslav's poetic expression is highly religious. He wrote contemplative lyrical cycles on biblical subjects: *Agar* (Hagar), *Ráchel* (Rachel), and *Kain* (Cain), as well as a biblical play in verse: *Herodes a Herodias*. The lyric cycles *Letorosty* (Off—shoots), *Stesky* (Laments), and *Dozvuky* (Echoes) revived memories of a pleasant childhood while expressing an ever growing dis-

satisfaction with Slovakian dependence. His mature lyric cycles *Growth Rings I, II, & III, Walks Through Spring,* and *Walks Through Summer* were important because they provided the reader with personal contemplations that naturally touched on concerns of the human condition that all people could relate to. His epic compositions *Hájnikova zena* (The Forester's Wife or The Game–Keeper's Wife), *Ezo Vlkolinský* (Ezo Vlkolinský), and *Gábor Vlkolinský* featured a sophisticated use of allegory and native themes to comment on the state of the Slovak nation. *Hájnikova zena* (The Forester's Wife or The Game–Keeper's Wife), published in 1886, told the story of Hanka—the wife of a young gamekeeper—who kills the son of their master when he attempts to rape her. Although epic in scope, the heart of this narrative poem is its sincerity and its sweeping descriptions of the natural beauty of the uplands. In the latter part of his career his focus switched to realism, and he wrote about topics he found in contemporary life rather than in the past. This change was heralded by his infamous collection of anti–war poems *Krvavé sonety* (Bloody Sonnets or Blood– Red Sonnets). This acclaimed sonnet cycle is identified by *The Penguin Companion to European Literature* as "a humanist's passionate protest against the madness of war." It was written during World War I, and projects a dramatic collage of images that showcase the horrors of war. *The World's Lawyer Poets* website notes that Hviezdoslav's poetry "vastly extended the range of possibilities of the Slovak poetic language which he enriched by neologisms and dialect expressions, and which he employed in the most diverse forms of poetic creation." The *Columbia Dictionary of Modern European Literature* notes the way he "developed a new type of reflective lyric, which was both a modern poetic narrative form and a verse play." Critics agree that his work helped to raise Slovak literature from provincialism. He was a humanist by nature and focused on patriotism, evangelical faith, democracy, and social and economic justice. His work has been translated into numerous other languages, and his versatile talents produced an impressive body of work that included verse plays and journalistic pieces as well as poetry. Hviezdoslav's major influences were Andrej Sladkovic, Jan Kollar, Jan Holly and the Czech poets: Jaroslav Vrchlick, Vitezslav Hálek, and Svatopluk Cech. While Jan Holly was known as the father of Slovakian poetry, Hviezdoslav was considered by many to be Slovakia's greatest poet.

A Master of Language

In addition to his accomplishments as a poet and master composer of the Slovak language, Hviezdoslav was also a celebrated translator. He translated English, Russian, German, and Hungarian literature into both Czech and Slovak. It was his desire to translate the world classics into Slovak. He translated William Shakespeare—including *Hamlet* in 1903 and *A Midsummer Night's Dream*—Friedrich Schiller, Alexander Pushkin's *Boris Godunov,* Sandor Petofi, the prologue to Johann Goethe's *Faust,* Adam Mickiewicz's *Crimean Sonnets,* and the work of Juliusz Slowacki.

Servant to His Country

Hviezdoslav was truly a servant to his country, and he supported the Slovak culture outside his substantial literary contributions. He was a vocal advocate of Czech—Slovak cooperation, and he openly supported the Czechoslovak Republic, serving as a delegate to its National Assembly when the new state was founded and as a member of its Parliament. He was rewarded in his lifetime in numerous ways. On August 5, 1919, the Slovak Cultural Institute (Matica Slovenska)—originally opened in 1861 but closed by the Magyars—was re-opened and re-dedicated. Hviezdoslav was honored by being named its new head. It was later enlarged by the addition of a Slovak National Museum. He also served as Poet Laureate of Slovakia for an extended period of time.

Living in Memory

Hviezdoslav died November 8, 1921, at Dolny Kubin at the age of 72 of natural causes. He is buried in the city cemetery at Dolny Kubin in Slovakia. His life and works have been posthumously celebrated ever since his passing. His life and work are displayed in the literary wing of the Orava Museum in Dolny Kubin. A newly re-constructed town square, *Hviezdoslavovo námestie* (Hviezdoslav Square) was named after him and boasts the National Opera House, among other attractions. In the Pantheon Hall of the Czech National Museum—which pays homage to Czech history, culture and science—there is a bronze bust of Hviezdoslav, which was added to the collection of statues and busts of contributors to the culture in 1930. A commemorative stamp with his face on it was issued January 28, 1998, and a commemorative silver coin bearing his portrait was issued in 1999 for the 150th anniversary of his birth. The Hviezdoslav Theatre was built from 1943 to 1947 and serves as the theatre of the Slovak National Theatre Company. The first performance in it was Hviezdoslav's *Herodes a Herodias*. The P.O. Hviezdoslav Museum documents in detail the life and works of the famous poet, and the Forester's Lodge—where he wrote Hájnikova zena (The Forester's Wife or The Game—Keeper's Wife)—is open to tourists and boasts the original furniture that Hviezdoslav used while composing the epic.

Books

Cassell's Encyclopaedia of World Literature, Volume Two, William Morrow & Company, Inc., 1973.

Columbia Dictionary of Modern European Literature, Second Edition, Columbia University Press, 1980.

Encyclopedia of World Literature in the 20th Century, Volume 4, St. James Press, 1999.

The Penguin Companion to European Literature, McGraw-Hill Book Company, 1969.

Webster's Biographical Dictionary, G.&C. Merriam Company, Publishers, 1976.

Online

"Bratislava Landmarks," *Spectacular Slovakia,* http://www.spectacularslovakia.sk (December 3, 2003).

"Destination Slovakia," *Lonely Planet World Guide,* http://www.lonelyplanet.com (December 3, 2003).

"Forester's Lodge of Hviezdoslav," *Bielafarma,* http://www.bielafarma.com/english/forester (December 3, 2003).

"Hviezdoslav," *Biography and Genealogy Master Index,* Gale Group, 2003. (December 3, 2003).

"Hviezdoslav Theatre," *Web Classics,* http://www.web.classics.co.uk (December 3, 2003).

"The Pantheon," *Czech National Museum,* http://www.nm.cz/english/building/pantheon (December 3, 2003).

"Pavel Hviezdoslav," *The World's Lawyer Poets,* http://www.wvu.edu (December 3, 2003).

"Pavel Orszagh Hviezdoslav," *It's All Relative,* http://www.iarelative.com (November 11, 2003).

"Pavol Orszagh," *Biography Resource Center Online,* Gale Group, 2003. (December 3, 2003).

"Pavol Orszagh Hviezdoslav," *Dolny Kubin,* http://www.dolnykubin.com (November 11, 2003).

"Pavol Orszagh Hviezdoslav," *Find A Grave,* http://www.findagrave.com (December 3, 2003).

"Personalities—Pavol Országh Hviezdoslav," *Slovak Postal Service,* http://www.telecom.gov.sk (December 3, 2003).

"P.O. Hviezdoslav Museum," *Heart of Europe,* http://www.heartofeurope.co.uk (December 3, 2003).

"Shakespeare in Czech and Slovak," *Shakespeare Translated,* http://www.unibas.ch/shine/translatorsczech (December 3, 2003).

"Silver Coin Commemorating Birth of Pavol Orszagh Hviezdoslav," *National Bank of Slovakia,* http://www.nbs.sk (December 3, 2003).

"Slovak Culture," *Slovakia.org,* http://www.slovakia.org (December 3, 2003).

"Slovak Literature," *Czech and Slovak Literature Resources,* http://users.ox.ac.uk/~tayl0010/czech.html (December 3, 2003).

"Slovak Republic Information," *World Info Zone,* http://www.worldinfozone.com (December 3, 2003). □

Innocent X

Innocent X (1574-1655) was elected pope of the Roman Catholic Church as a compromise candidate between fighting factions, although the significance of his papal reign (1644-1655) remains disputed. While some considered him a shrewd politician as well as a reformer, others questioned how much Innocent was influenced by his self-serving sister-in-law.

The future Pope Innocent X was born Giambattista Pamfili on May 6, 1574 in Rome. He was the son of Camillo Pamfili and Flaminia de Bubalis, and the family resided in the region of Umbria. With the assistance of his uncle, young Pamfili studied law, like many well-bred young men of his day. He graduated from the Collegio Romano at the age of twenty.

Since the eighth century the Catholic Church controlled Rome and the surrounding regions as part of the Papal States; there was no civil government, and all courts were run by the Church. Pope Clement VIII appointed Pamfili to a judgeship on the Rota, a high court in Rome that served as a court of appeals for matrimonial cases. Pamfili served on that court from 1604 to 1621, and then made steady progress up through the ranks of the Catholic hierarchy. Pope Gregory V appointed him nuncio—a permanent official representative of the pope to a foreign government—to Naples, and in 1625 Pope Urban VIII sent Pamfili to France and Spain as a datary—an official who dates documents—under Cardinal Francesco Barberini, who was the pope's nephew.

A gifted politician, Pamfili impressed both the pope and Cardinal Barberini, and was subsequently named nuncio to Madrid. In 1626, at the age of 52, he was created the cardinal-priest of Sant' Eusebio, although he was not formally announced as a cardinal until 1629. In addition, Pamfili was also a member of the congregations of the Council of Trent, the Inquisition, and Jurisdiction and Immunity.

Became Pope

In August of 1644, the conclave of cardinals was held in Rome in order to elect a successor to Pope Urban VIII. The meetings were stormy; Urban had been decidedly pro-French, and the Spanish legation was determined to correct the balance of power within Europe. The French faction, in contrast, made it known that they would not give their vote to a candidate who was a Spaniard or was known to be friendly toward Spain. The Spanish candidate, Cardinal Firenzola, was rejected, as he was considered to be the enemy of France, and negotiations almost reached an impasse.

Eventually, fearing the election of a true enemy of France, the French faction came to a compromise with the Spanish faction, and finally agreed upon Pamfili, even though his sympathy for Spain was well known. When the news of their decision reached France, French Prime Minister Cardinal Jules Mazarin sent a veto, but it arrived after the decision had been reached, and on September 15, 1644, Pamfili was elected pope. To honor his uncle, Cardinal Inocenzo del Bufalo, Pamfili took the papal name Innocent. He was crowned in October of 1644 as Pope Innocent X.

Took Pro-Spain Stance in Foreign Affairs

Innocent quickly revealed to the French court that his sympathies indeed were aligned with those of Spain. One of his first papal acts was to begin an investigation into how the powerful Barberini family had amassed its wealth and property while serving under Pope Urban VIII. As part of this investigation, he took down the very man he had once served, Cardinal Francesco Barberini, and eventually, the Barberini property was seized by the Catholic Church.

Cardinals Antonio and Francesco Barberini fled to France to avoid further punishment, and found a powerful ally in Prime Minister Mazarin. In response, in February of 1646 Innocent issued a Papal Bull declaring that any cardinals leaving the Papal States without his permission and remaining away for more than six months would suffer harsh consequences. The Bull declared that such cardinals could forfeit their benefices and their rank as cardinals. In response, the French Parliament declared the papal ordinances to be null and void, but even this threat did not cause the pope to relent; finally the Bull was withdrawn after Cardinal Mazarin threatened to send troops to Rome.

In *Saints and Sinners: A History of the Popes,* Eamon Duffy explained that "The political helplessness of the papacy became clearer with every pontificate, and particularly so in the relations of the popes with France. Elderly and mistrustful . . . Innocent X was as hostile to France as Urban had been favorable." Duffy added, "France's gain, Innocent considered, was inevitably the Roman Church's loss—'only on Spain could the Holy See rely.'" While Innocent was not

adverse to efforts to achieve a peace between France and Spain, he viewed Spain as less of a threat to the Church, which power France was attempting to erode. This position led Innocent to side with Spain in refusing to recognize the election of Juan IV as king of Portugal in 1648, eight years after Portugal declared its independence from Spain.

In *The Oxford Dictionary of Popes,* J. N. D. Kelly noted that Innocent X "was not immune from nepotism." Like many of his predecessors in the papacy, he placed family and colleagues in positions of merit. However, it must be noted that Innocent named two capable men as Vatican secretary of state, both of whom he chose over his nephew, Cardinal Camillo Pamfili. The second of these men, Fabio Chigi—the future Pope Alexander VII—was chosen in 1651 and was made a cardinal the following year.

In 1648 the Thirty Years' War between France and the Habsburgs of Spain and the Holy Roman Empire came to an end with the Peace of Westphalia. Provoked in part by the spread of Protestantism throughout northern Europe, the Peace of Westphalia was seen as a threat to the Church of Rome. Essentially, the treaty declared that a monarch's subjects must follow his or her religion, which Innocent viewed as harmful to Roman Catholic interests, and he formally denounced the treaty in an 1648 Papal Bull. The Bull was not immediately published and was generally considered ineffective.

Despite his efforts to stop the inevitable diminishment of the Church's power in Europe, Innocent also had some notable accomplishments. Papal relations with Venice, which had been strained under Pope Urban VIII, improved under Innocent. Innocent gave financial aid to the Venetian rulers during their fight against the Turks in the struggle for Candia. On their part, the Venetians allowed Innocent free reign in filling the vacant clergy positions within their territory, a right they had previously claimed for themselves.

Obtained Questionable Confidante

As noted by a *New Catholic Encyclopedia* contributor, Innocent was "a lover of justice and his life was blameless; he was, however, often irresolute and suspicious." Another of his failings, as recorded by history, was his reliance on Donna Olimpia Maidalchini, his widowed sister-in-law. Maidalchini was reportedly avaricious and hungry for power, and she is credited by some with provoking the pope to take entrenched positions on matters where he would have been better served by being more open to alternatives. In *The Oxford Dictionary of Popes,* Kelly described Innocent as "an old man, taciturn and mistrustful, slow in reaching decisions." These traits allowed his "powerful and sinister" sister-in-law the opportunity to greatly influence him.

As the *New Catholic Encyclopedia* contributor noted, "for a short time" Maidalchini's influence gave way to that of another persuasive advisor, "the youthful Camillo Astalli, a distant relative of the pope." Innocent was also influenced by Astalli, and made the young man a cardinal. However, Maidalchini soon regained her influence as confidante to the pope; as the *Catholic Encyclopedia* contributor noted, "the pope seemed to be unable to get along without her, and at her insistence, Astalli was deprived of the purple [—lost his position as a cardinal—] and removed from the Vatican." Although Innocent was respected for his moral character and his loyalty to the Church, his reliance on his sister-in-law ultimately clouded his pontificate. By the close of his reign, Kelly explained, Innocent "took no important decision without consulting her."

Condemned Jansenism

The primary religious challenge of Innocent's reign, and one that grew increasingly controversial in subsequent papal reigns as a result of Innocent's actions, had to do with the spread of Jansenism. Named for its founder, Dutch theologian Cornelius Otto Jansen (1585-1638), Jansenism was a reform movement among Roman Catholics that thrived during the sixteenth and seventeenth centuries due to the efforts of theologians such as Antoine Artaud. As Duffy explained, the controversy first broke out in the French Church in the 1640s "over the teachings of the posthumously published treatise *Augustinus* by a former bishop of Ypres, Cornelius Jansen. Jansen's immense and unreadable Latin treatise was in fact a manifesto for a party of devout Catholics alienated by the worldliness of much Counter-Reformation religion."

Jansenism had many traits in common with Protestant Calvinism due to its central belief in the corrupt quality of human nature. Among the principle beliefs of the movement are predestination and the rejection of the Catholic dogma regarding free will. The Jansen movement stands in marked contrast to the Jesuit doctrine, which holds out to Catholics the chance to redeem one's soul through good works; Jansenism holds that original sin destroyed the chances of all except predestined men and women to obtain salvation. Because of this central conflict, Duffy explained, Jansenists "detested the Jesuits . . . whom they saw as chief culprits in the spread of lax moral and sacramental teaching." Duffy further noted that Jansenists also reject Protestantism and places a strong emphasis on the sacraments and the hierarchy of the traditional Church. In short, it takes "a gloomy view of the average man or woman's chances of salvation." However, due to its conservative slant, "on such matters as the need for a Catholic political alliance against Protestantism, Jansenists were ardent supporters of the papacy."

For several decades Jansenists had been a particular target of the French Church, which attempted to ban the sect. Because of his virulent anti-French stance, Pope Innocent X now found himself embroiled in the political as well as religious aspects of the controversy. In 1651 Innocent appointed a special commission to examine the central five propositions within Jansen's *Augustinus,* and even took part in several of the commission's sessions. In 1653 he issued the bull *Cum occasione,* in which he condemned these five propositions as heretical.

Cum occasione is seen as perhaps the most important act of Innocent's papacy; indeed, it proved to be the most controversial. Ultimately, the papal bull, in supporting the Jesuit doctrine over that of the Jansenists, spoke to the need of the Church to embrace rather than alienate its followers. However, it did little to stem the ongoing controversy surrounding Jansenism that would continue to rage over the next several years due to the work of French mathematician Blaise Pascal, who managed, through clever argument, to maintain an uneasy peace between the Church and the faction through several papal administrations.

Patron of the Arts

Like most popes, Innocent supported the arts and, like his predecessor, was a patron of the sculptor, architect, and painter, Giovanni Lorenzo Bernini. During his reign the interior decoration of St. Peter's Basilica remained ongoing and the Piazza Navona was restored and decorated with the Fountain of the Moor and Bernini's Fountain of the Four Rivers. As Duffy reflected, Innocent X's patronage of Bernini "bore fruit in a series of astonishing projections of the Baroque papacy's self-image." Although, as Kelly added, "a combination of straitened finances and thrift prevented Innocent from embellishing Rome on the scale of his predecessors," during his papacy "the interior decoration of St. Peter's was completed."

Innocent's Legacy

In addition to improving papal relations with the Venetians, Innocent expanded the authority of the Congregation for the Propagation of the Faith, and elevated Manila's Dominican College to a university. To further the spread of the Catholic doctrine, he also strongly supported the efforts of missionaries attempting to convert the inhabitants of non-Christian regions in the America and Africa. In civil matters, he oversaw the redesign of prisons in the Papal States, instituting cells for living quarters. However, he also instituted a system for criminals to purchase their freedom after being sentenced, and ended the use of Chinese rituals during the liturgy in China.

Pope Innocent X died on January 7, 1655 in Rome. He was buried in St. Peter's Basilica, but in 1730, his remains were taken to his beloved Spain where he was finally laid to rest at the church of Sant' Agnese of Agone in the Piazza Navone. While it has been argued that his conservative stance did little to command respect, Innocent has also been viewed as a canny politician who, during an era fraught with political, social, and religious upheaval, managed to sustain and perhaps even increase the influence of the Vatican.

Books

Bokenkotter, Thomas, *A Concise History of the Catholic Church,* revised and expanded edition, Doubleday, 1977.
Duffy, Eamon, *Saints and Sinners: A History of the Popes,* Yale University Press, 1997.
Kelly, J. N. D., *The Oxford Dictionary of Popes,* Oxford University Press, 1991.
The New Catholic Encyclopedia, McGraw-Hill, 1967-79. □

Lev Ivanov

Dancer, choreographer, ballet master, composer, and teacher Lev Ivanov's (1834-1901) fame was

almost exclusively posthumous. Ivanov received little recognition in his own lifetime. It wasn't until 30 years after his death in 1901 that he started to receive recognition for his work, including the timeless ballet *Swan Lake,* which was up until then thought of as mainly—or only—as Marius Petipa's work, whose shadow Ivanov lived in for the whole of his life. The *International Encyclopedia of Dance* says of Ivanov's *Swan Lake,* it "stood as a monument to Russian and world ballet of the nineteenth century."

Both Ivanov and his work were integral in the development of classic romantic ballet in Russia. He married dance with music, influencing later choreographers, including Michel Fokine. Known for his ability to choreograph for emotional effect, Ivanov is considered the soul of Russian choreography and of Russian ballet of the late nineteenth century.

Loved Ballet From an Early Age

On March 2 (February 18, old style), 1834 in Moscow, Russia, Ivanov was born into an intelligent and affluent (although not upper class) family. His father was a kind and fairly educated merchant, possibly of Georgian origin. His mother, who raised him and several siblings on her own, moved the family around often. Ivanov's childhood has been described as sad, spent between an orphanage (or foundling hospital) and a merchant's family, before he was sent to boarding school.

Ivanov showed interest in ballet at a very young age. His father introduced him to dance and Ivanov witnessed his first performance—several one-act plays and the ballet *Don Juan*—in the company of his father. Ivanov liked the ballet so much he decided then to become a dancer. Ivanov was sent first to Moscow to study at the school of the Imperial Ballet, then to the St. Petersburg Imperial Theatre School when he was ten years old (also said in 1852). In the school, Ivanov showed enough promise after a year to be taken on as a state-supported student.

Entered St. Petersburg Ballet Scene

Studying under such names as Jean-Antoine Petipa (the father of Marius Petipa), Aleksandr Pimenov, Pierre-Frederic Malavergne and Emile Gredlu, Ivanov showed proficiency not only in dance, but also had a natural ear for music. After hearing a ballet, the talented Ivanov could recreate the entire score, by ear, on the piano. Unfortunately, his musical talent was not especially noted.

In 1850, at age 16, and still in the St. Petersburg Theatre School, Ivanov began to dance in the corps of the Imperial Theatres. He was first presented to the public on June 7, 1850, by Jean Petipa in *Le ballet des meuniers,* in which he danced the title pas de deux. He then appeared in such productions as *Catarina, Esmerelda, Mariquita,* and *La Filleule des fees* (The Fairy's Godchild), all staged by Jules Perrot for ballerina Fanny Elssler. Under Perrot, Ivanov worked for most of his career.

Lost in the Fame of Others

In 1852, Ivanov officially joined the corps de ballet of the Imperial Ballet in St. Petersburg. On March 20, 1852, he was admitted to the ballet troupe of St. Petersburg's Bolshoi Theatre, with principal dancers Jules Perrot, Marius Petipa, and Christian Johansson. Often lost in the brilliance of such talent, Ivanov was however noticed by Elena Adnreyanova, who revived *La Chaumiere hongroise* to a new musical score in 1853, and chose Ivanov for the role of the young peasant, Ulrich. In class, Ivanov was also noticed by Russian ballerina Tatiana Smirnova, who partnered with him in *La fille mal gardee.* on November 3, 1853. Ivanov lived up to expectations in this performance and was given the title role in *Le ballet des meuniers* in 1854.

Ivanov soon began substituting for Marius Petipa during illnesses, which was later to define his career. In 1858, he began to teach in the lower school of the Imperial Theatre School. He taught two junior classes for girls. His students included Evgenia Sokolova, Ekaterina Vazem, Olga Preobrazhenskaya.

An Unhappy Marriage

In 1859, Ivanov dedicated his work in composition and choreography to actress, singer, and dancer Vera Lydova (who was accepted straight into the Bolshoi Theatre out of school) and the two were married within the year. Together they had three children and an unhappy marriage. Lydova's short career was to reach incredible heights as a dancer and singer and in 1869, Ivanov applied for a separate residence permit for her. In the March of 1870, she fell ill and died.

Career Ups and Downs

Ivanov continued to move upward as a dancer. By 1869, he was partnering visiting, eminent ballerinas. He was by then a principal dancer (a position he had acquired in 1858), distinguishing himself as a mime and as a character role dancer. He was also distinguished as a docile stand-in for principal dancers (which made him valuable) when he filled in for Petipa on two occasions, without preparation. His memory was unrivaled. Roles in Perrot ballets quickly followed. He became engaged in nearly every ballet in the repertory. And yet, Ivanov was still not renown and poorly paid, lost in stand-in roles for famous dancers.

In the 1860s and 1870s, Ivanov took leading roles in the ballets of Saint-Leon and Marius Petipa. Although prominent, the roles were limited to mime. Then, Ivanov relinquished the position of principal dancer to Pavel Gerdt, who was elegant and well-proportioned and a favorite to partner with the ballerinas. Ivanov was drinking and had stopped training. In 1877, he married dancer Varvara Ivanova (whose stage name was Malchugina), with whom he had three more children.

Composed Music

In 1878, Ivanov composed music for *The Little Humpbacked Horse,* which was danced by Evgenia Sokolova. In 1882, he became regisseur (stage manager) of the Maryinsky Theatre, a post he kept for only three years. He created many ballets in this capacity, but rarely received credit for them because of Petipa's name. In 1883, he won the Gold Medal with the Stanislaus ribbon in recognition of his outstanding services.

Became Petipa's Assistant

In 1885, at the age of 51, Ivanov became the second ballet master (assistant ballet master) when Petipa was appointed chief ballet master. He was demoted to this position because he had loosened discipline among the company members as regisseur. As second ballet master, Ivanov produced the many minor ballets required for the various stages of the Imperial Theatres, including the Kamenyi-Ostrov Theatre and the Krasnoe Selo spa theatre, as well as produced Saint Petersburg ballets and opera dances in St. Petersburg. The partnership proved advantageous for Petipa, who enjoyed an assistant who would take on any assignment and made no assertions of independence. And again, Ivanov's remarkable memory came in handy, in the recreation of older ballets alongside Petipa.

Ivanov's first major staging was of Dauberval's *La fille mal gardee* in 1885. In 1887, he choreographed *The Enchanted Forrest,* a one act ballet, for the graduation performance of the school. *The Enchanted Forest* was well received and went to the Maryinsky Theatre. In October 4 of that year, *The Tulip of Haarlem* premiered, choreographed by Ivanov, and in 1888, he composed and set to the music of various composers a one act ballet *The Beauty of Seville,* which ran for several seasons.

From 1888 to 1891, Ivanov staged a number of ballets and dances for opera at the Tsar's private court theatre at Krasnoye-Selo. In 1890, he composed *Palovtsian Dances* and choreographed *Cupid's Prank.* The next year, he was awarded the Order of Stanislaus, Third Class and choreographed *The Boatman's Festival* with Friedman.

Choreographed *The Nutcracker*

In 1892, Petipa fell ill during the production of *The Nutcracker,* which was his second collaboration with Tchaikovsky (after *Sleeping Beauty*). Ivanov took over choreography. Ivanov was forced to use the advice and directions of Petipa, even though Petipa was at odds with Tchaikovsky's music, failing to develop it as it was intended. On July 24, 1892, *The Nutcracker* appeared on stage, featuring Ivanov's signature "The Dance of the Snowflakes."

Ivanov appeared on the stage for the last time in 1893, in a Spanish dance with Marie Petipa, for a benefit performance. In that same year, he choreographed *Cinderella* and *The Awakening of Flora,* and was awarded the Order of Anne, Third Class. He also produced *The Magic Flute,* a one act ballet to the music of Drigo. *The Magic Flute* was produced for the private stage of the Theatre School, but later became known to the world as part of the repertory of the Pavlova company.

Choreographed *Swan Lake*

After Tchaikovsky's death, Ivanov revived the second act—the "lakeside" act—of *Swan Lake* for a memorial concert. Its success led to the revival—from 1894 to 1895—

under the direction of Petipa. Petipa contributed the first and third acts, allowing Ivanov keep the second and create the fourth (known as the "white acts"), giving him full creative license. *The International Dictionary of Ballet* says about the collaborative effort; "The acts are typical of their respective creators, Ivanov's second and fourth showing his lyrical, elegiac, dreamlike style, keeping within the limits of traditional choreography, and Petipa's first and third glittering with the bravura feats of the Italian school and vivid national dances." Ivanov's second act is viewed as the culmination of nineteenth century Romantic ballet. "The Dance of the Little Swans" is one of his signature pieces. Performed in 1895, it met with blasé press.

In 1896, Ivanov choreographed *Acis and Galatea.* In 1897, he was invited to Warsaw to stage ballets and dances for the opera. In the same year, he produced Petipa's *Le Marche des innocences* and *La halte de la cavalerie* and his own *The Magic Flute.* In March, *The Mikado's Daughter* premiered but closed after a few performances. Around 1900, Ivanov choreographed the "Czardas" dance to music by Litcz. This was his last major performance.

Ivanov remained Petipa's assistant until his death. In 1901, when Ivanov was 67, he was seized with intense fatigue during the production of *Sylvia* with Pavel Gerdt. Ivanov became ill and died on December 11 (24, old style), 1901, in St. Petersburg, Russia.

Obscurity

There are six reasons for Ivanov's obscurity: one, he had an unassuming character (perhaps lacking in self-confidence) and a very even temperament; two, he was a Russian choreographer in a time of foreign artists, brought in from Europe; third, he danced at a time when all attention was on the ballerina; fourth, his choreography was always in the shadow of the renowned Petipa; fifth, he displayed his talent late in his career, when he encountered Tchaikovsky; sixth, his "preferences and taste were ahead of his time," as claimed by the *International Encyclopedia of Dance.*

As www.balletmet.org notes, despite the fact that Ivanov "never truly escaped from under Petipa's wing" and that Ivanov's choreography was always subject to Petipa's approval and corrections (who often changed it), Ivanov's works aged much better than Petipa's. The second "white act" of *Swan Lake* is still performed in much of the same choreography as in Ivanov's original. And Ivanov is now acknowledged as the chief choreographer of the impressive *Swan Lake.* The *International Encyclopedia of Dance* calls him "the assistant and modest shadow of Marius Petipa." He constantly struggled for financial security and was forced to petition for money on more than one occasion. And yet, he is the "soul of ballet."

Marriage of Music and Dance

Ivanov's musical ear was legendary. He composed music for classical dances, ballets, mazurkas and Hungarian czardas, although he never learned to write them in manuscript. Perhaps this is why composers had such a direct influence on his choreography, awakening his imagination. The *International Encyclopedia of Dance* says of Ivanov's creating experience, "Ivanov's imagination as a choreographer depended entirely on the music: it determined the essence of the ballet's image and form, and a success or failure of a performance was directly proportional to the quality of the music."

In 1991, Ivanov was awarded the Order of Stanislaus, Second Class, for his achievements in ballet.

Books

Bremser, Marta, ed., *International Dictionary of Ballet,* Vol. 1, St. James Press, 1993.

Cohen, Selma Jeanne, ed., *International Encyclopedia of Dance,* Vol. 3, Oxford University Press, 1998.
Cohen-Stratyner, Barbara Naomi, ed., *Biographical Dictionary of Dance,* Schirmer Books, 1982.
Merriam-Webster's Biographical Dictionary, Merriam-Webster Incorporated, 1995.

Online

"Lev Ivanov," androsdance.tripod.com/biographies (January 11. 2004).
"Lev Ivanov," reference.allrefer.com/encyclopedia (January 11, 2004).
"Lev Ivanovich Ivanov, Choreographer," www.balletmet.org/Notes (January 10, 2004). □

J

Marie Trautmann Jaëll

The first pianist to perform all of Beethoven's piano sonatas in Paris, Marie Trautmann Jaëll (1846-1925) was a renowned 19th century French composer, teacher, and pedagogue in piano technique. As a child prodigy, she toured Europe and won the prestigious First Prize of Piano at the Paris Conservatoire at the age of 16. A student of Franz Liszt and a teacher to Albert Schweitzer, Jaëll presented herself to 19th century artists with passion toward composition, individuality, and scientific technique. She composed a variety of styles, such as solo piano, quartets, sonatas, waltzes, four-hand pieces, and orchestral. Considered a derivative composer, Jaëll will be remembered for her treatises on the physiological study of piano playing. She wrote scientific studies describing muscle movements of the hand, the sense of touch, and the mental discipline involved in playing piano.

Won the Premier Prix as a Child Prodigy

Jaëll was born on August 17, 1846, in Steinseltz village in the north of Alsace, France, near Wissembourg. Her father, George Trautmann, was mayor of the village, a man committed to modernization. Her mother, Christine Schopfer, a refined woman who appreciated the arts, encouraged her daughter's musical education. At the age of seven, Jaëll first studied piano under professor F. B. Hamma and with Ignaz Moscheles, both in Stuttgart. Only one year later, with her mother managing her performances, Jaëll was playing concerts in France, Germany, and Switzerland.

In 1856, her mother presented her to the Paris Conservatory's renowned piano teacher Heinrich Herz, who tutored her. Due to her young age of 10, she studied with Herz until she was old enough to formally register with the Conservatory in 1862. Meanwhile, she continued to perform publicly in Paris. At 10, she played piano sonatas, accompanied by the 13-year-old violin prodigy Guillaume Bauerkeller, a student of Alard of the Academy of Paris.

Once she was 16, after only four official months at the Conservatory, she won the Premier Prix (First Prize of Piano) out-performing 20 other girls. Her mother collected newspapers clippings that touted her daughter as not only a child prodigy but "a true artist." The *Revue et Gazette musciale de Paris* reported on July 27, 1862, as seen in the Marie Jaëll Exhibit website, that Jaëll "restored freshness and life to the piece . . . She marked it with the seal of her individual nature. Her higher mechanism, her beautiful style, her play deliciously moderate, with an irreproachable purity, an exquisite taste, a lofty elegance, constantly filled the audience with wonder."

Toured Europe with Husband

At age 20, on August 9, 1866, Marie Trautmann married concert pianist Alfred Jaëll, 15 years her senior, in the Church of La Madeleine in Paris. A student of Chopin, Alfred was an internationally recognized piano virtuoso. Husband and wife navigated Europe and Russia concertizing solos, duos, famous works, and works of their own creations. The two interpreted and performed many four-handed piano compositions popular at the time.

189

With the connections afforded to her by her husband's notoriety and musical circles, Jaëll was introduced to Franz Liszt in 1868 who took her as his student. The encounter would have a profound effect, not only on her piano playing and composition, but also on her scientific endeavors later in life. Liszt, too, was impressed with his young protege, an article in *American Record Guide* said Listzt described her as having "the brains of a philosopher and the fingers of an artist." Liszt, in turn, introduced the now-recognized Jaëll to the period's other great musicians, such as Johannes Brahms and Anton Rubinstein. By 1871, Jaëll's piano compositions were being published.

Jaëll's husband died in 1881 when she was 35 years old, but she continued studying composition under special invitation by Liszt in Weimar, Germany, and with César Franck and Camille Saint-Saëns in Paris, France. As recognition of her talent and status, Saint-Saëns introduced Jaëll to the Society of Music Composers, which was an honor for a woman in those days.

Mentored by Franz Liszt

A true admirer of Jaëll, Liszt became her mentor. He premiered her waltz for piano four hands, "Valses pour piano à quatre mains" Op. 8, which was published by F.E.C. Leuckart, Leipzig. Liszt even wrote variations based on the piece, although these variations were not published.

Jaëll spent the years 1883 through 1886 working for Liszt a few months a year in Weimar where she assisted with his correspondences, performed at his musicales, and witnessed piano lessons taught and studied by renowned pianists. Saint-Saëns offered Jaëll advice on her compositions, and he dedicated his first concerto and the "Etude en forme de valse" to her.

During the 1890s, Jaëll's reputation was secure with incredible performances of the masters played in a series of concerts. Her repertory included the primary piano works of Robert Schumann, which she played in six concerts in Salle Erard; and Liszt, with six concerts in Salle Pleyel. She was the first person in France to perform all thirty-two of Beethoven's sonatas in the course of six concerts in Pleyel in 1893.

Although she performed in the top European cities of her day—Bern, Geneva, Heidelberg, and London—Jaëll retained a fond attachment with her hometown of Alsace and sought to honor it. Remembering a happy childhood there, she wrote a composition, "Harmonies of Alsace," and presented a scientific conference in Paris that she titled, "Some observations addressed to the Society of Physics by a musician from Alsace."

Created Romantic, "Derivative" Compositions

Some critics have labeled Jaëll's original compositions as "derivative" and "characteristic." Her style was certainly a product of her times, a mix of the pervasive Romanticism genre and the French music of the late nineteenth century. *American Record Guide* called her music, "romantic in style, with more flavor of the salon than the concert hall."

She never shied from diversity, composing solo piano as well as four-hand pieces, quartets, waltzes, works for violoncello, and orchestral. She put to music the poems of Victor Hugo and Jean Richepin and wrote the symphonic poem *Ossiane* which was performed in Paris in 1879. She wrote *At the tomb of a child* which contained choruses. Her *Runéa* was an opera.

The *New Groves Dictionary of Music and Musicians* noted that Jaëll "composed piano pieces and songs which, though essentially Romantic, reveal an assimilation of the innovations of the time." She absorbed the influences of the most renowned pianists and composers of Europe: Schumann, Brahms, Liszt. Perhaps because of the greatness around her, Alexander Morin, of *American Record Guide,* is kind when he commented that her work "doesn't supply much evidence of a distinct musical personality. But it is all skillfully written and pleasant to hear."

If she lacked in originality, she embraced the passion and intensity of the artist at work, and strove to identify that element and describe it for other performers. She characterized her own approach to music and the piano as written in the Marie Jaëll Association website, "The body and the spirit, the movement and the thought are the same force. The energy of the movement is in connection with the intensity of the mental representation of this same movement."

Researched the Physiology of the Hand

Franz Liszt's music was a revelation to Jaëll. Absorbed by it when she first met him, she had always wanted to not only analyze and reproduce it, but to preserve it for posterity. Beginning in the 1890s, Jaëll dedicated herself to studying the techniques and methodologies of Liszt. As she also suffered bouts of tendonitis that interfered with her playing and garnered unkind reviews of her concerts, she decided to research the physiology of piano playing.

Jaëll benefited from living in the industrial age. The science of physiology was gaining acceptance as people studied the brain and nervous system. Jaëll added to these the study of the hand to create a new pedagogy of the piano. As the Marie Jaëll Exhibit observed, "According to this completely original approach, science was at the service of art." Moreover, the craft of piano making was employing Europe's new technological inventions.

Jaëll immersed herself in her research. During her 40s, she virtually abandoned her successful life of concert pianist to devote herself to her sciences. She read about physiology, anatomy, chemistry, mathematics, physics, and even psychology to help in her understanding of "artistic laws." She wanted to combine the emotional and spiritual act of creating beautiful music with the physiological aspects of tactile, auditive, and visual sensory.

Through observations and experiments, and through consultation with medical doctors, she focused her study on training the brain and nervous system, and on the unique movements of the hand. In the end, she published *The Touch* in 1894, a psycho-physiological treatise on touch. The book, which was translated into German by her pupil, Albert Schweitzer, was well-received.

Worked with Doctor Charles Féré

In the last years of the 19th century, the noted physiologist, Dr. Charles Féré, noticed that Jaëll referenced his scientific work in her "Music and Psychophysiology," published in 1896. Féré, medical superintendent of the psychiatric clinic at the Kremlin-Bicêtre Hospital near Paris, contacted her and began a collaboration between the two that lasted until his death in 1907.

Again profiting from friends who could help in her achievements, Jaëll accepted use of Féré's laboratory. Jaëll and Féré studied the muscle behavior and the sense of touch to analyze the physical act of playing the piano. By learning how keys are struck and how a person perceives sound mentally, they strove for a new approach to playing. They suggested an economy of movement and a replacement of mechanical drilling methods of learning with precise practice steps that took advantage of the anatomy of the hand.

From H. Keiner, "Marie Jaëll, Problèmes d'esthétique et de pédagogie musicales," Paris, 1952, Jaëll noted of her research with Féré, "I sought the right movements, and by these movements, I found the harmony of the touch, the musical memory, the improvement of the ear, all faculties which seem to sleep in each one of us. These movements were unceasingly controlled in experiments at the laboratory of Dr. Féré."

She continued to study the musical quality of sound. She believed that everything from human fingers and our vision to the wood the piano was constructed from influence our perception of musical notes. In all, Jaëll produced 11 books on piano technique, and left 80 compositions for piano, other instruments, and vocals. Jaëll continued to teach in her later years; her more famous pupils were Albert Schweitzer and Eduardo del Pueyo. She died February 4, 1925, in Paris, at age 79.

Today's Remembrances

In 1979, Marielle and Katia Lebèque recorded six of Jaëll's thirteen "Valses" for the Strasbourg Bibliothéque Nationale et Universitaire. In 1998, the first CD entirely devoted to Jaëll's compositions, performed by Alexandre Sorel and Lea Schmidt-Rogers, was released.

The Strasbourg library in France keeps copies of most of Jaëll's correspondence, compositions, books, and articles. The Marie Jaëll Association Foundation, also in Strasbourg, organizes meetings and training sessions on the method of Marie Jaëll.

Books

International Encyclopedia of Women Composers, Books & Music, 1987.
New Grove Dictionary of Music and Musicians, Macmillian Publishers, Ltd., 2001.
Slonimsky, Nicolas, ed., *Baker's Biographical Dictionary of Musicians,* Centennial Edition, Schirmer, 2001.

Periodicals

American Record Guide, September/October 1998.

Online

"Condensed Introduction to the Life and Work of the French Composer Marie Jaëll," *Schmidt-Roger, Lea, Music Teachers' Association of California,* http://www.sdiegomtac.com/Jaëll .htm (December 22, 2003).
Marie Jaëll Association, http://www.marieJaëll.asso.fr (December 22, 2003).
Marie Jaëll Exhibit, http://perso.wanadoo.fr/jc.ingelaere/Jaëll/ (December 22, 2003). □

Nur Jahan

Nur Jahan (1577–1646) was one of the most powerful women in Indian history. A Persian widow who married the weak Indian king Jahangir, Nur Jahan was the true ruler. In a time when women were unseen and rarely heard, she issued orders from behind the curtains of the harem. In addition to inviting court intrigue and power struggles, Nur Jahan also contributed to women's fashion and embroidery, mutual trade with Europeans, coinage, gardens, architecture, and the design of magnificent marble tombs. Some historians called her selfish and opportunistic, others expounded on her generosity.

Married a Persian

Nur Jahan was born Mihrunnissa (meaning "seal of womankind") in India in 1577, although she was the daughter of a Persian emigrant exiled from his homeland. Her father, Mirza Ghiyas al-Din Muhammador, who served in the magnificent court of the Teymourees in India under the name Itimaduddaula ("pillar of the state"), was said to be elegant and cultivated, a prime example of the aristocracy and a good role model of courtly behavior.

Some sources say that Jahan and Sciah Selim (who would become Emperor Jahangir of India) met as adolescents. Jahangir's father, Emperor Akbar, disapproved of the relationship. In any event, Jahan was married at age 17 to a Persian soldier and adventurer named Ali Quli Istunjuloo, who was renamed Sher Akfan after he killed a lion with his word. Sher Akfan secured an administrative post serving the Moghul Empire at Burdwan in Bengal when Jahangir first inherited the throne in 1605. Akfan found himself caught between politics and jealousy: he sided with Jahangir's enemies, and Jahangir coveted his wife.

At this time, Jahan was already lauded as a woman of great beauty as well as intelligence. The legend says that when Jahangir became emperor, he intended to make Jahan his wife. He accused Akfan of "having a tendency to rebellion" and ordered his soldiers to assassinate Akfan in 1607.

Jahan, widowed and burdened with a baby daughter, Ladili Begam, was brought to the Moghul court to serve as a lady-in-waiting to Emperor Akbar's widow, Lady Salima, in the imperial harem in Agra. It took four years, but Jahangir was at last ready to marry Jahan in 1611.

Became the Twentieth Wife

Jahangir loved Jahan beyond all other women, even though she was considered too old to marry at age 34. Although she became his twentieth wife, he made her his principal queen and renamed her Nur Mahal, or "light of the palace." Later, in 1616, he would bestow upon her the new name, Nur Jahan, "light of the world." Jahangir and Jahan had no children together.

As a king, Jahangir curiously demonstrated his disinterest in politics, affairs of the court, and squabbles in the zanana, or women's quarters. Indolent and alcoholic, Jahangir spent his time enjoying the pleasures of food, wine, and daily doses of opium, while Nur Jahan became the undisputed sovereign. In his memoirs (quoted in *A History of India*), Jahangir had written that "Nur Jahan was wise enough to conduct the business of State," while he "only wanted a bottle of wine and a piece of meat to make merry." King and country were now tools in Jahan's hands.

From Jahangir's harem, Jahan ruled with supreme authority. According to *Medieval India under Mohammedan Rule 712–1764*, British Ambassador to India Sir Thomas Roe wrote, "He hath one Wife, or Queen, whom he esteems and favours above all other Women; and his whole Empire is govern'd at this day by her counsel." Nur Jahan is said to never have broken purdah, the Islamic rule of women hiding themselves from men. From behind the curtains of the harem, she issued her orders to trusted male officers and eunuchs in her service. She granted appointments, controlled promotions, and approved orders.

In addition to gaining the love and trust of the emperor, she easily won admiration from her subjects. With her intelligence and courage, she learned about and exploited the power structure prevalent in the Moghul court and was able to bend laws to suit those in need. Nur Jahan was said to have been very generous, giving alms to beggars. She especially helped orphan girls marry well, paying for their dowries with her own money.

Granted Her Family Privilege

Jahan was reportedly ruthless in keeping her interests and alliances at the fore. She cunningly removed from the harem women who could jeopardize her status or affections with the king, and she removed old captains and ministers, replacing them with men loyal to her.

With her nearly absolute power, Nur Jahan was not above bestowing leading positions at the imperial court upon her own family. Her father, Sher Akfan, was promoted to chief minister for Jahangir. Her brother, Asaf Khan, was given the second highest rank in court. She created a triumvirate of power with her issuing the orders, and her father and brother carrying them out.

To add to the soap opera-like intrigue, Nur Jahan tried to secure her family's place in Jahangir's succession by marrying off her daughter, Ladili Begam, from her first husband, to Khusrau, the king's eldest son. When Khusrau

refused, she enticed Prince Khurram (later known as Shah Jahan, "king of the world"), who also refused. Jahan settled on marrying Ladili to Jahangir's youngest son, Prince Shahryar.

Meanwhile, Asaf Khan succeeded in marrying his daughter, Arjumand Banu Begum, to Shah Jahan in 1612. Shah Jahan renamed her Mumtaz Mahal, "jewel of the palace." When Mumtaz Mahal, Nur Jahan's niece, died in childbirth in 1631, Shah Jahan built the Taj Mahal to her memory.

With Ladili married to Shahryar, Nur Jahan began actively to work against Shahryar's brother Shah Jahan as Jahangir's heir to the throne. Some historians said that Nur Jahan's ambition knew no limits. Under her invisible rule and unscrupulous favoritism, the empire succumbed to bitter jealousies, corruption, and rebellion.

Jahangir's Ill Health

Nur Jahan's grasp on the empire only tightened after Jahangir fell ill in 1620. He suffered poor health from his alcoholism, asthma, and opium addiction. Two years later, her father died in 1622. With her brother away from court, Nur Jahan ruled alone from inside the harem. Factions were growing as Shah Jahan gained the support of Asaf Khan, Nur Jahan's brother and Shah Jahan's father-in-law. Nur Jahan urged Jahangir to name a successor, preferably her daughter's husband, Prince Shahryar, known as a handsome fool. Shah Jahan also wanted to be named heir.

When India lost Kandahar to the shah of Persia in 1622, Jahangir ordered Shah Jahan to retake the annexed region. Fearing Nur Jahan's further intrigues at court if he was gone, he refused to leave. Civil war broke out as Shah Jahan gathered a rebel force against Jahangir and Nur Jahan, but it was quashed by capable General Mahabat Khan. Shah Jahan was exiled, attempted to establish his own kingdom, but ultimately surrendered. It was not until 1625 when he reconciled with his father.

Nur Jahan now set her sites on Mahabat Khan, who posed a threat to her power. Fearing for his life and disgusted over the court politics, Mahabat rebelled. When Jahangir was separated from his guard, Mahabat seized the emperor in a surprise attack and imprisoned him. Ever courageous, Nur Jahan escaped the imperial guard and gathered an army made up of supporters to rescue Jahangir.

Tales recount how Nur Jahan led her troops atop an elephant, shooting arrows from behind her curtained howdah enclosure. An arrow penetrated the curtain to wound her granddaughter, Prince Shahryar's daughter, sitting on her lap. Jahan boldly entered Mahabat's camp but was eventually captured and put into prison with her husband. With Nur Jahan in prison, Mahabat's suspicions waned. Nevertheless, she managed to sway supporters even in prison. Soon, king and queen were free, and Mahabat fled to join sides with Shah Jahan.

Widowed Queen Quietly Retired

Jahangir died on October 28, 1627, the opium and extravagant lifestyle finally overtaking him. Nur Jahan and her brother Asaf Khan now found themselves on opposite sides of a succession dispute. Encouraged by Jahan, Shahryar proclaimed himself emperor at Lahore. Yet Shah Jahan, with Asaf's backing, returned from his stay in Deccan. Asaf imprisoned Shahryar, then later killed him by strangulation. Four other princes who stood in Shah Jahan's way were murdered. Shah Jahan was declared emperor at Agra in February 1628.

By comparison, Nur Jahan was fortunate. Used to controlling the court, she now quietly accepted banishment in Lahore and retired into private life. She received a handsome pension of 200,000 rupees per year, and always wore the white robe of mourning for her husband. While maintaining strict seclusion, she spent her time designing magnificent tombs for her husband, father, and herself. Nur Jahan died in 1646.

Excelled in Many Talents

A woman of remarkable talent in a variety of skills, Nur Jahan influenced fashion and cosmetics, encouraged trade with Europeans, designed gardens, wrote poetry, and painted. Even in coinage, her notoriety was such that Jahangir added her name to his on coins of the realm, an unprecedented gesture in Muslim history.

Nur Jahan influenced commerce as well as the court, turning the Moghul capital of Agra into a cosmopolitan city. She had the power to allow or obstruct trade routes and collected duties from the merchants who passed through the empire's lands. The queen carried on her own cloth business, owned ships that took pilgrims to Mecca, and bought luxury goods from Europeans.

From within the zanana, she wielded considerable influence. Fashion trends were swayed by her tastes and creations. She developed new patterns in fabric, embroidery, and dress styles. It is believed that she designed the new styles of turban and clothing of the emperor. Fashions in women's clothing she adopted were still popular at the end of the 16th century. Artistic and creative, she experimented with various perfumes, hair ointment, jewelry, food, silks, and porcelain from different countries. Coming from a literary family, she wrote poetry and encouraged poetry contests among the court women.

Nur Jahan and Jahangir were known for constructing beautiful Persian style gardens used in their summer retreat in Kashmir and for official functions. These public and private gardens were unique in using water to accentuate the layout. Jahangir also presented his queen with paintings and manuscripts that reflected the art of her Persian homeland.

Nur Jahan's architectural achievements have passed the test of time. Some of the mosques, caravansaries and tombs that she built have survived. She designed new architectural features utilized in the Tomb of Itimaduddaula, her father, which sits on the riverbank in Agra. Her own tomb in Lahore is smaller than those of her husband and father, yet it was the first complete marble Moghul structure. Her tomb is located in a garden near Jahangir's tomb.

Books

Danielou, Alain, *A Brief History of India,* Inner Traditions, 2003.
Edwardes, Michael, *A History of India,* Farrar, Straus & Cudahy, 1961.
Hansen, Waldemar, *The Peacock Throne: The Drama of Mogul India,* Holt Rinehart & Winston, 1972.
Jackson, Guida M., *Women Who Ruled,* ABC-CLIO, 1990.
Lane-Poole, Stanley, *Medieval India under Mohammedan Rule 712-1764,* G.P. Putnam's Sons, 1903.

Periodicals

American Historical Review, June 1994, Vol. 99, Issue 3.
Asia Times, June 18, 2003.

Online

''In the Shadow of the Taj,'' http://www.viewsunplugged.com/VU/20030410/reflections_taj.shtml (December 23, 2003).
''Nur Jahan: Power Epitomized,'' http://members.tripod.com/anantmithal/Itihaas/1998/it980202NurJahan.html (December 23, 2003).
''Nur Jahan,'' Women in World History, http://www.womeninworldhistory.com/heroine11.html (December 23, 2003).
''Women of the Mughal Empire: Nur Jahan 'Light of the World','' Skidmore College, http://www.skidmore.edu/academics/arthistory/ah369/Mughal_website2.htm (December 23, 2003). □

Johannes Vilhelm Jensen

Danish author Johannes Vilhem Jensen (1873-1950) was a prolific writer who produced as many as 60 volumes of stories, novels, essays, and poems. A former medical student, his works reflected his interests in science, evolution, and anthropology. In his most important and best-known work, *Den lange rejse* ("The Long Journey"), a six-novel cycle written between 1908 and 1922, Jensen portrayed, in narrative fashion, his ideas on how humans developed in accordance with the theories of Charles Darwin. The lengthy and controversial work earned him the Nobel Prize for Literature in 1944.

Early Life

Johannes Vilhelm Jensen was born on January 20, 1873, in Farsø, Himmerland, a small village located in North Jutland, Denmark. He was the second son of the district veterinary surgeon, Hans Jensen, and Marie (Kirstine) Jensen. His family came from what has been described as old peasant stock. Both his mother and father descended from farmers and craftsmen.

Until he was eleven years old, Jensen was schooled at home by his mother. His formal education began at the Cathedral School of Viborg, from where he graduated in 1893. Jensen then attended the University of Copenhagen

from 1893 to 1898. For three years, he studied medicine and his curriculum included botany, zoology, physics, and chemistry. During his fourth year at the University, his interest turned to writing, and his scientific studies would greatly influence his future literary work. "The grounding in natural sciences which I obtained in the course of my medical studies . . . was to become decisive in determining the trend of my literary work," he wrote in an autobiographical essay when he received the Nobel Prize.

Jensen was able to earn money with his writing and this, he later indicated, put him at a crossroads. He had to choose between continuing his scientific studies or pursuing a writing career. Jensen opted to become a writer instead of a doctor.

Began Writing in College

While still attending the University of Copenhagen, Jensen managed to write two novels: *Danskere* (1896) and *Einar Elkjær* (1898). Like much of his early writings, these works were set in his native province of Himmerland. Jensen's early output also included genre fiction. He wrote romantic stories and turned out a series of detective novels that were published in a weekly periodical under his pen name "Ivar Lykke."

But it was for his stories, or "tales," that Jensen first gained his most favorable attention. Near the turn of the century, he began writing a series of stories that came to be called *Himmerlandshistorier* ("Himmerland Stories"). He produced these stories, which were set in the area of Den-

mark where he was born, between 1898 and 1910. The stories are categorized into three groups: tales from the Himmerland, (his birthplace), tales from his travels in the Far East, and the "Myths" tales. The Himmerland tales provided vivid depictions of the region's environment and people.

During this period of his career, Jensen also worked as a journalist. He spent the summer of 1898 in Spain, working as a war correspondent, reporting on the Spanish-American war for the newspaper *Politken*. With all assignments, the apolitical Jensen worked on a freelance basis. He never joined the staff of any newspaper, nor did he align himself with any political party. But he infused his journalism with his own impressions and attitudes. In writing a series of articles from the World Exhibition in Paris in 1900, he expressed his enthusiasm for the modern and active lifestyle represented by the exhibition and the city. (These writings were collected and published as *Den gotiske renæssance* in 1901.)

As a young writer, Jensen was prolific, turning out more than 100 "Myths," a literary form that he created that include elements of narrative and essay. As he was turning out these pieces, he also wrote what has come to be regarded as the most significant historical novel in Danish literature, *Kongen's fald* ("The Fall of the King"), written in 1900-01. Taking place in the 16th century, the work is a fictional trilogy, both lyrical and realistic, about the life of King Christian II of Denmark, the last ruler of the three Scandinavian countries, and about Mikkel Thøgersen, a student and later mercenary.

Traveled Far and Wide

Along with his writing activities, Jensen also traveled extensively. Like his academic studies, Jensen's travels profoundly influenced his writing. Between his first two novels, Jensen interrupted his university studies to take the first of several trips to the United States. These transatlantic visits exposed him to new technology and the impact it had on the American culture, and they inspired two novels: *Madame d'Ora* (1904) and *Hjulet*, ("The Wheel" [1905]). They also spurred his developing talent and, in turn, influenced the work of his Danish literary peers. "I inspired a change in the Danish literature and press by introducing English and American vigor, which was to replace the then dominant trend of decadent Gallicism," he recalled.

Like fellow writer and countryman Hans Christian Anderson, Jensen traveled a great deal throughout his life. He made a second trip to the United States in 1903. He circled the globe in 1902-03, visited the Far East in 1912-13, and traveled to Egypt, Palestine, and North Africa in 1925-26. His trips to the Far East, which included visits to Malaya and China, and the subsequent writings, earned him the nickname of "Denmark's Kipling."

Other Writings

While producing his myths and novels, Jensen also wrote poetry, plays, and essays. He felt his poetry was a key to understanding his oeuvre. "The essence of my literary work is to be found in my collection of poems, which may be regarded as a reaction against the fastidious style of the day bearing Baudelaire's poisonous hallmark," he wrote. Specifically, Jensen meant that his poems represented a move toward a simpler style and a focus on deserving subject matter. (Charles Baudelaire's poetry, often described as romantic or decadent, was an extravagant commingling of the beautiful with the morbid, evil, or erotic.)

Jensen's poetic influences included Goethe, Heine and the prose poems of the American poet Walt Whitman. Jensen also employed the Old Norse style poetics for his verse. In 1906, he published a volume, *Digte* ("Poems") that contained all the youthful poems. Later in his life, he published *Digte, 1901-43*.

Jensen's essays were characterized by a poetic prose style and were collected—along with animal, travel, and nature sketches—in *Myter* ("Myths" [1907-1944]), which was published in eleven volumes. His essays, in particular, reflected his interest in anthropology and the philosophy of evolution.

Embraced Darwin's Evolution Theory

During the course of his studies and his writing career, Jensen became greatly interested in the work of Charles Darwin and evolution. When he received his Nobel in 1945, Jensen cited Darwin as "a man of science who has drawn a line between two epochs." Further, Jensen pointed out that, to Darwin, "evolution was not only the subject of a life's study but the very essence of life, proof of the inexhaustible richness and wonder of nature, revealed each day and taken to heart." In his vast literary output, one of Jensen's primary goals was to introduce the reader to the philosophy of evolution and to encourage them to think of life and nature in evolutionary terms.

Most importantly to him, Jensen wanted to address Darwinism because he felt it was an important concept that had been seriously misinterpreted and distorted in the 19th century. In particular, he felt Darwinism was used to justify the concept of the *Übermensch* or, more specifically, the distortion of that particular concept into the idea of the "superman." Nietzsche developed the concept of *Übermensch*, or "Overman," to describe philosophically a transcendence over limitations imposed by traditional morality. The "Overman" accepts the idea that "God is dead" (i.e. that is Christian dogmas must be destroyed and that man must separate himself from the idea of God), and then can emotionally and psychologically accept this independence without succumbing to nihilism. The Overman responds by creating his own moral ideals and lives according to the principles of his "Will to Power." The result is complete independence. Nietzsche's concepts were exploited in some quarters to advance the belief in biological superiority, and Darwinism was used as evidence to support this idea. "The concept of the Übermensch had disastrous consequences in that it led to two world wars, and was destroyed only with the collapse of Germany in 1945," wrote Jensen. To counter the damage done by the misconceptions or deliberate distortions, Jensen developed a new interpretation of the theory of evolution and its moral implications,

and he communicated this interpretation in his literary works.

His theories of evolution were delineated in his most important work: a cycle of six novels collectively called *Den lange rejse* ("The Long Journey"), written between 1908 and 1922 and published in a two-volume edition in 1938. A third volume was written between 1922 and 1924. (In all, the cycle included *I: Den tabte land*, (1919); *II: Bræen*, [1908]; *Norne Gæst*, [1919]; *IV: Cimbrernes tog*, [1922]; *V: Skibet*, [1912]; *VI: Christofer Columbus*, [1922]). In the work, Jensen placed an evolutionary interpretation upon biblical legends. The plot follows the emergence of man from the Ice Age and concludes with Columbus' discovery of America. The first book takes place in the pre-Ice Age warm climates and involves a Prometheus-like main character. The second book, a mythic recounting of the genesis of the Nordic race, involves an outcast who rediscovers fire and starts a new civilization. Later books depict the invention of land and sea vessels, the Roman Empire, and the Vikings. The work not only demonstrated his consummate skill as a literary artist but as an amateur anthropologist as well. It was this work that earned him the Nobel Prize. Jensen's own theories of evolution however, were considered questionable and generated some controversy. One of the work's major themes involved the idea that the ideal of an Edenic paradise developed from genetic memory, and paradise represented a longing for a return to the pre-ice age warm world.

Received Nobel Prize

In 1939 Jensen again visited the United States. The following year, the German army invaded Denmark and Jensen was compelled to destroy a great deal of his personal writings, as much of it was critical of Fascism and anti-Semitism. In 1944, he was awarded the Nobel Prize for Literature. In giving the award to Jensen, the Nobel Committee cited the "rare strength and fertility of his poetic imagination with which is combined an intellectual curiosity of wide scope and a bold, freshly creative style." The ceremonies are held in Stockholm, Sweden, but no presentations were made that year because of the war. Jensen received his award the following year.

In his acceptance speech, given at the Nobel Banquet at the City Hall in Stockholm, on December 10, 1945, Jensen cited the impact of Darwin, Alfred Nobel and the Swedish naturalist Carl Linnaeus, the naturalist who has been called "the father of taxonomy." Linnaeus, Jensen said, "gave animals their proper names and, long before anyone had ever dreamt of evolution, classified monkeys, apes, and man under the name of primates. Passion for nature, for all that stirred and breathed, was the driving force in [his] genius. Whenever one reads of the determination of the species, or opens a book on natural science and history, in whatever language, one inevitably comes across the name of [Linnaeus]." Linnaeus, Jensen said, by designating the species as he did, provided the foundation that enabled Darwin to develop his theories on the origin of the species. As a literary influence, Jensen cited Adam Oehlenschläger, another great name in Danish literature that preceded him by a century.

Died in Copenhagen

Jensen's later works included *Eksotiske noveller* (1907-1917), which was based on travels in the Far East, and *Jørgine* (1926), a story of a deceived peasant girl who salvages her life by entering a loveless marriage and becomes a self-sacrificing mother. Selections were translated as *The Waving Rye*, which was published posthumously in 1958.

In 1904, he married Else Marie Ulrik. They had three sons. Jensen died in Copenhagen on November 25, 1950.

Online

Johannes V. Jensen-Autobiography, *Nobel e-Museum,* http://www.nobel.se/literature/laureates/1944/jensen-autobio.html (December 14, 2003)

Johannes V. Jensen - Banquet Speech, *Nobel e-Museum,* http://www.nobel.se/literature/laureates/1944/jensen-speech.html (December 14, 2003)

Johannes Vilhelm Jensen, *Nobel-winners.com,* http://www.nobel-winners.com/Literature/johannes_vilhelm_jensen.html (December 14, 2003)

Johannes Vilhelm Jensen, *wikepedia.org,* http://en.wikipedia.org/wiki/Johannes_Vilhelm_Jensen (December 14, 2003)

Johannes Vilhelm Jensen, *AllRefer Encyclopedia,* http://reference.allrefer.com/encyclopedia/J/Jensen-J.html (December 14, 2003)

Johannes V. Jensen, *Pegasos,* http://www.kirjasto.sci.fi/jjensen.htm (December 14, 2003)

Johannes Vilhelm Jensen, *slider.com,* http://www.slider.com/enc/27000/Jensen_Johannes_Vilhelm.htm (December 14, 2003)

Johannes V. Jensen, *Britannica.com,* http://www.britannica.com/nobel/micro/302_10.html (December 14, 2003)

Johannes V. Jensen, *Britannica.com,* http://www.britannica.com/nobel/micro/302_10.html (December 14, 2003) □

Mordecai Wyatt Johnson

Mordecai Wyatt Johnson (1890–1976) was one of the most highly respected clergymen, educators, and orators of his time. From 1926 to 1960 he was president of Howard University, where he made significant contributions not only to the university, but to the larger community as well.

The son of former slaves, Johnson was born on January 12, 1890, in Paris, Tennessee. His father, Wyatt Johnson, was a preacher and mill worker. He was a strict disciplinarian who set rigorous standards for his son's chores and behavior. His mother was a domestic employed by one of the prominent families in town. She was kind and gentle and demonstrated a keen interest in her son's education.

Johnson's formal education began in a small elementary school in his native town. From there he went to Roger Williams University in Nashville, then to Howe Institute in Memphis, and later transferred to the Atlanta Baptist College (now Morehouse College) where he completed his secondary and undergraduate education. During his college career, he was a member of the debating team and the Glee Club, a star athlete in three sports, and quarterback of the football team. Offered a faculty position at the college upon graduation, he taught English and economics and served a year as acting dean. He maintained a profound interest in economics throughout his career—an interest that was apparent in some of his major addresses. After one year of teaching, he continued his education at the University of Chicago, where he received a second A.B. degree, and at the Rochester Theological Seminary in Rochester, New York, where he earned the B.D. degree. At Rochester he was profoundly influenced by the great "social gospel" advocate, Walter Rauchenbusch. His experiences there made an indelible impact upon his thinking and his entire career.

After a brief stint as secretary of the western region of the Student Young Men's Christian Association (YMCA), in 1917 he became pastor of the First Baptist Church in Charleston, West Virginia, where he served nine years. During that time, he founded a chapter of the National Association for the Advancement of Colored People (NAACP) and a Rochdale Cooperative, from which his parishioners and the community could purchase supplies at reduced prices. In 1921 he took a leave of absence from his church to study for a year at Harvard University Divinity School where he received the degree of master of sacred theology. At his graduation in June of 1922, he was chosen to represent the Graduate School at the university commencement. His speech on that occasion was entitled "The Faith of the American Negro." It resulted in his establishing a close relationship with Julius Rosenwald, the prominent philanthropist who was president of the Sears, Roebuck Corporation. Rosenwald was later to play a substantial role in helping Johnson realize some of his later administrative goals.

Became President of Howard University

At the age of 36, Johnson was elected the 11th, and the first African American, president of Howard University. He took the position in a crucial period in American history and especially in the history of African Americans. It was 1926 and the United States was enjoying the prosperity that had begun with the close of World War I in 1918. Business was booming and the economy was so strong that many thought progress inevitable. What was known as the Harlem Renaissance was in full swing, with the creative talents of African Americans expressed in literature, music, and art.

Ever since the establishment of schools for freedmen by white missionaries from the North following the Civil War, most of these institutions had been headed by Caucasians, as had Howard from its inception in 1867. Johnson's election to the presidency was hailed with pride by the black community at large. But he found an institution that, in many ways, did not measure up to the standards associated with a first-class university.

Financial Stability First

Johnson's first major responsibility was to assure the financial undergirding of the university. Since 1879 Congress had given some subsidies to the school, but the amounts were by no means adequate to the need nor were they assured each year. Encouraged by Johnson's leadership and his vision for the university, Louis C. Cramton, representative from Michigan, and other sympathetic lawmakers pushed through Congress a law providing annual support. This act in 1928 was of monumental significance for the future of the university. In recognition of this development, the NAACP awarded Johnson the Spingarn Medal, its highest honor.

Johnson set out to raise the quality of each of the schools in the university, starting with the medical school, one of only two in the nation to which African Americans were admitted without prejudice based on race. His first financial goal was to raise $250,000 to match a challenge grant by the General Education Board (GEB) toward a new building and endowment for the medical school, and an additional $180,000 for equipment. With help from Rosenwald, the arduous solicitations of alumni, medical faculty members, and an additional grant by the GEB, Johnson was able to announce at his first commencement as president that the campaign had been successful.

Johnson's primary concern, however, was raising the standards of the law school. When he assumed the presidency, it was a night school taught by men whose primary occupation was the practice of law during the day. With the advice of Associate Justice Louis D. Brandeis of the U.S. Supreme Court, Johnson made contact with top law schools for recommendations of their leading African American graduates to recruit for teaching at Howard. Brandeis pointed out that the bases for fighting racial discrimination were already embedded in the Constitution. What was needed, he said, was for lawyers to be prepared to base their arguments before the Court precisely upon the guarantees in the document. This proved to be significant advice not only for the development of the law school at Howard, but for affecting race relations throughout the country.

Johnson appointed Charles Hamilton Houston as dean of the law school. At the law school, attention was given to research and intense analysis of litigation involving civil rights that had been or might be brought before the Court. Johnson was determined to make the Howard Law School the matrix out of which progress in the welfare of African Americans could be achieved. His role in its development was one of his major contributions to American life.

Controversy and Criticism

The first half of Johnson's tenure at Howard was marked by controversy. There were those who felt that it was unconscionable for the board of trustees to select a Baptist preacher who had no terminal academic degree and very little experience as a teacher and administrator in higher education. They maintained that he was not qualified to lead a great university. Johnson's administrative style was a source of animosity exhibited by some of the faculty and staff at Howard. Some accused him of being a dictator, of

having a "messianic complex," and of being unyielding in the positions he took. Indeed, in one of his sermons he expressed the view that God had chosen individuals for certain purposes from the beginning of time. It would not be surprising if he believed that God had chosen him for a special mission. At this point in the development of some segments of higher education, it was not unusual for the charge of dictatorship to be made against college presidents.

Certain faculty and staff members maintained a continuous barrage of derogatory charges against Johnson during the first half of his administration. He persevered without responding. Through all the controversy he had the confidence and support of the trustees in constantly raising the level of support and the standards of the university. He made fruitful contacts with the major foundations, especially the Julius Rosenwald Fund, GEB, and the Federation of Jewish Charities. At the same time, he was able to attract top talent. During his administration, it was said that at Howard was the greatest collection of African American scholars to be found anywhere. Alain Locke, a philosopher and a Rhodes Scholar from Harvard, and Ernest E. Just, the internationally famous cell biologist, were already on the faculty when Johnson came. Added to them were, among others, Ralph Bunche, professor of political science and later a Nobel Laureate; Charles Drew, who perfected the use of blood plasma; Percy Julian, a noted chemist; Rayford Logan, a leading historian and an authority on the Caribbean; Abram Harris, an outstanding economist; and Sterling Brown, professor of English and a noted poet.

Johnson raised millions of dollars for new buildings and for upgrading all of the schools. Each segment boasted a strong curriculum. National honor societies, including Phi Beta Kappa, were established on campus. In addition, salaries were constantly increased and a favorable working environment was established. Johnson prided himself on upholding the standards and principles of academic freedom. During the era of the Communist scare, the House Un-American Activities Committee conducted investigations of certain faculty members and programs. Because Johnson spoke out favorably on certain aspects of the Russian government, there were those who accused him of being a Communist or a sympathizer—an accusation that he firmly denied.

As an Orator

One of the outstanding orators of his time, Johnson had a phenomenal memory and could speak without notes for as long as 45 minutes, yet was able to hold audiences spellbound because of his engaging speaking style and the content of his message. He traveled 25,000 miles a year speaking principally on racism, segregation, and discrimination. Early in his career, he was frequently in demand to lead religious-weeks in colleges. He was the annual speaker on Education Night at the National Baptist Convention, USA, and a regular on the program at the Ford Hall Forum in Boston. In 1951 he was a member of the American delegation to the North Atlantic Treaty Organization (NATO) that met in London. On that occasion he was selected to speak on behalf of his sub-committee at the plenary session of the gathering. He pleaded for the favored nations to consider the plight of the underprivileged and dispossessed people of the world and stressed the need for a sense of justice that the nations should display with those under their domination.

The Later Years

Johnson retired from the presidency of Howard University in 1960 after 34 years of service. He had brought the university a long way from where he found it in 1926. He had greatly expanded the campus, building a library and new structures for several schools within the university. Finances were sound. Enrollment increased from 2,000 in 1926 to more than 10,000 in 1960. In the larger world, some walls of segregation against which he had fought had begun to crumble.

Johnson married Anna Ethelyn Gardner of Augusta, Georgia, in 1916. To them were born five children: Carolyn, Mordecai Jr., Archer, William, and Faith. After her death in 1969, he married Alice Clinton Woodson, and settled in Washington, D.C. He died on September 10, 1976, at the age of 86, in Washington, D.C.

Books

Boulware, Marcus H., *The Oratory of Negro Leaders: 1900–1968,* Negro Universities Press, 1969.

Butler, Jenifier Bailey, ''An Analysis of the Oral Rhetoric of Mordecai W. Johnson; A Study of the Concept of Presence.'' Ph.D. dissertation, Ohio State University, 1977.

Hill, Richard H., *History of the First Baptist Church of Charleston, West Virginia,* 1934.

Locke, Alain, *The New Negro: An Interpretation,* A. and C. Boni, 1925.

Logan, Rayford, *Howard University: The First Hundred Years, 1867–1967,* New York University Press, 1969.

McKinney, Richard I., *Mordecai, The Man and His Message: The Story of Mordecai Wyatt Johnson,* Howard University Press, 1998.

Muse, Clarence L., ''An Educational Stepchild: Howard University and the New Deal,'' Ph.D. dissertation, Howard University, 1989.

Winston, Michael, *Education for Freedom: The Leadership of Mordecai Wyatt Johnson, Howard University, 1926–1960. A Documentary Tribute to Celebrate the Fiftieth Anniversary of the Election of Mordecai Wyatt Johnson as President of Howard University.* Howard University Archives, Moorland–Spingarn Research Center, 1976. □

K

Rudolf Emil Kalman

Hungarian-born U.S. scientist and professor Rudolf Emil Kalman (born 1930) is widely regarded as the creator of modern control theory and system theory. His research reshaped the field of control engineering and placed the groundwork for future research and innovation. His most widely known accomplishment is his development of the Kalman filter, a mathematical method now widely used in navigation, particularly in aviation.

Kalman was born in Budapest, Hungary, on May 19, 1930, the son of an electrical engineer. Early in his life he decided to follow in his father's footsteps, and pursue a career in a field that involved mathematics. Along with his family, he immigrated to the United States in 1943, as World War II raged in Europe, and after high school he studied electrical engineering at the Massachusetts Institute of Technology (MIT) in Cambridge. Kalman received his bachelor's degree in 1953 and his master's degree the next year. From MIT, he continued his studies at Columbia University in New York City, where he received his doctorate of science in 1957. At Columbia Kalman had the good fortune to study under Professor John R. Ragazzini, head of the school's electronics lab and a man noted for his research on ultra-high frequency—or UHF—techniques, analog computers, and control systems.

Focused Research on Control Systems

During his years at MIT and Columbia, Kalman explored his interests in control theory, the study of how to engineer via mathematical applications a controlling device to alter the output of a given data stream or other input to achieve a desired outcome. (The governor installed on some automobile engines, designed to limit the vehicle's top speed, is one example of a mathematically engineered control.) In addition to directing his research toward state variable representations, Kalman also began demonstrating an individualistic approach to research that would characterize much of his later career.

From 1955 to 1957 Kalman was an instructor in control theory at Columbia University, and in 1958, he became an adjunct assistant professor. At the same time, he was employed as a staff engineer at the IBM Research Laboratory in Poughkeepsie, New York. During these years, through his research Kalman developed significant contributions to the design of linear sampled-data control systems and the use of Lyapunov theory for the analysis and design of control systems. Already, he understood how the digital computer would one day become important to his area of research.

In 1958 Kalman moved to Maryland, where he was employed as a research mathematician at the Research Institute for Advanced Studies in Baltimore (RIAS). The Institute was founded by Solomon Lefschetz (1884-1972), an influential mathematician noted for his groundbreaking work in algebraic geometry, algebraic topology, and differential equations. Kalman worked at RIAS until 1964, first as a research mathematician and then as associate director of research. While at the Institute, he focused his work on the search for a unified theory of control. Through lectures and published papers, he helped advance knowledge about modern control theory, which involves programming robotics and machines to respond to constantly changing conditions and still maintain self-control. One application of such control theory is the automatic pilot system installed in airplanes that prevents an unmanned craft from crashing to the ground. In mathematics, control is a time-dependent function that influences a dynamic engineered system, such as an automatic pilot.

Conducted Innovative Research

Kalman's innovative work, which stressed mathematical generality, had an enormous impact within his field. He was involved in research about fundamental systems concepts such as controllability and observability, and he helped develop solid theories on the structural aspects of engineering systems. In addition, he unified the theory and design of linear systems with respect to quadratic criteria; introduced the analytical work of Constantin Caratheodory (1873-1950) in optimal control theory; and added to the understanding of the interrelations between Russian mathematician Lev Pontryagin's maximum principle and the Hamilton-Jacobi-Bellman equation, as well as variational calculus in general. At the time, he was one of the first to employ the digital computer as an important—and inevitable—part of the design process as well as of the control system's implementations.

However, the most important part of Kalman's work at RIAS was the development of the "Kalman filter," which would become his greatest contribution to his field. During his initial research, conducted in late 1958 and early 1959, he acquired solutions to the discrete-time filtering problems associated with discrete time. (Discrete time systems are linear; that is, they are measurements taken in sequence.) Kalman used as the basis of his research the work on filtering already done by Norbert Wiener (Wiener Filtration), Andrey Nikolaevich Kolmogorov (Wiener-Kolmogorov filter), Henrik W. Bode (electric filters and equalizers), Claude Shannon, Vladimir Pugachev and others, applying the modern stage space approach to this existing body of research. Based on utilization of state-space techniques and recursive algorithms, the Kalman filter revolutionized the field of estimation.

Developed the Kalman Filter

The Kalman filter is a set of mathematical equations that provides an efficient computational—or recursive—solution to discrete time data filtering problems, in essence removing extraneous "noise" from a given stream of data. His mathematical filter involves two sets of algebraic equations that solve real-time problems. Kalman's solution to the discrete-time problem led him to tackle the continuous-time problem. He then fully developed the continuous-time version of the Kalman filter with Richard Bucy between 1960 and 1961 and published an important paper discussing the two men's work. Essentially, the paper describes a way to recursively find solutions to the discrete-data linear filtering problem.

One of the driving forces behind the development of the Kalman filter were the needs of the U.S. Air Force, which helped fund Kalman's work. By the late 1950s and early 1960s, aircrafts had advanced to the point where they required advanced flight-control mechanisms, and the Air Force Office of Scientific Research (AFOSR) funded re-

search on control theory as it related to these advanced aircrafts, as well as to space vehicles. The AFOSR sponsored several efforts in this area, including the research done at RIAS by Kalman and Bucy, which the Air Force believed had the potential to alter control applications. As the AFOSR hoped, Kalman and Bucy's work revolutionized the field of estimation and had an enormous impact on the design and development of precise navigation systems. The Kalman filter was a major breakthrough in guidance technology.

Kalman's algorithm also found practical application in the National Aeronautics and Space Administration (NASA) space program. NASA first used the Kalman filter to solve the problems associated with determining satellite orbits. In the 1960s the Kalman filter was used preparing for in the Ranger, Mariner, and Apollo missions, and when the Apollo 11 lunar module landed on the Moon in July of 1969, it was guided by the Kalman filter. The filter would also be used in NASA space shuttles.

The Kalman filter, and its subsequent extensions to solve nonlinear problems, is the most widely applied by-product of modern control theory, and is used in just about every modern military and commercial control system. It is used in navigational and guidance systems, radar tracking algorithms for anti-ballistic missile applications, sonar ranging, and satellite orbit determination. It also has been used in other fields, such as seismic data processing, nuclear power-plant instrumentation, and even socioeconomic systems.

Thanks to the advances in digital computing, the Kalman filter continues to be a focus of a great deal of research and application, particularly in the area of autonomous or assisted navigation; for example, the Global Positioning System or GPS makes use of the Kalman filter.

Reputation and Horizons Widened

Kalman's achievement was a landmark, and the significance of his findings was immediately grasped. His reputation spread to an international scale, and it led to many honors. In 1962 Kalman received the Outstanding Young Scientist of the Year award from the Maryland Academy of Sciences. In 1964 he became a fellow of the Institute of Electrical and Electronics Engineers (IEEE).

In 1964 Kalman moved to California to assume a professorship at Stanford University, where he worked in the departments of electrical engineering, mechanics, and operations research. By this time, he had shifted the focus of his research to issues relating to the realization theory and algebraic system theory. As with his previous research efforts, his contributions helped create a new field of research in modern system theory, as he developed new directions of study. His contributions involved the formulation and study of many fundamental state-space notions, including controllability, observability, minimality, realizability from input/output data, matrix Riccati equations, linear-quadratic control, and the separation principle. His concepts had a far-ranging impact, because he was the first in his field to understand the crucial part such notions play in systems analysis. Kalman's mathematical advances have become part of educational textbooks and monographs relating to engineering and mathematics.

In 1971 Kalman became a graduate research professor and director of the Center for Mathematical System Theory at the University of Florida in Gainesville. In this position he taught and conducted research in the areas of mathematics, electrical engineering, system engineering, and mathematical system theory. During this period, he was instrumental in the introduction of algebraic and geometric techniques into the study of linear and nonlinear control systems. Starting in 1973, he also held the position of chair for Mathematical System Theory at the Swiss Federal Institute of Technology in Zurich, and also served as a scientific consultant to research centers in the École des Mines in Paris, France. Kalman remained at the University of Florida posts until he retired in 1992.

In the 1980s, Kalman focused his research efforts on a system-theoretic approach to the foundations of statistics, econometric modeling, and identification. This direction was a natural outgrowth of his earlier work in the areas of minimality and realizability. In the meantime, his career achievements—specifically his contributions to control theory and to applied mathematics and engineering in general—continued receiving official recognition.

Received IEEE Medals, Kyoto Prize

In 1974 Kalman received the IEEE Medal of Honor, that association's highest award. The IEEE recognized him "for pioneering modern methods in system theory, including concepts of controllability, observability, filtering, and algebraic structures." Other honors he has received include the 1976 Rufus Oldenburger Medal from the American Society of Mechanical Engineers. In 1984 he received the IEEE Centennial Medal.

In 1985 Kalman was among the first four recipients to receive the Kyoto Prize, established that year to recognize "outstanding intellectual or creative activities which have significantly enriched the human experience." Created to honor pioneering research in the fields of basic science, frontier science, and philosophy, the prize is administered through the Inamori Foundation, established to serve as the Japanese counterpart of the Nobel Foundation. Kalman was honored for his development of a control theory to explain the workings of a dynamic system. The next year Kalman was awarded the American Mathematical Society's Steele Prize for his papers on linear filtering published in 1960 and 1961.

In April of 1994 Kalman was one of 60 new members elected to the National Academy of Sciences. In 1997 the American Automatic Control Council presented him with its Richard E. Bellman Prize, given for distinguished career contributions to the theory or application of automatic control. The award is the highest recognition of professional achievement for U.S. control systems engineers and scientists. He has also been the recipient of several honorary degrees.

Active in Promoting Information

By the end of his illustrious career, Kalman was widely recognized as the individual who, first, all but created the field of modern control theory and, second, was instrumental in advancing its widespread application. He greatly influenced numerous researchers through his significant accomplishments, openness and accessibility, and his appearance at numerous lectures. In addition, he published more than 50 technical articles. His major papers included "Nonlinear Aspects of Sampled-Data Control Systems" (1956), "On The General Theory of Control Systems" (1960), "New Results on Linear Filtering and Prediction Theory" (1961), "Mathematical Description of Linear Dynamical Systems" (1963), and "Algebraic Structure of Linear Dynamical Systems" (1965). In 1969 Kalman co-authored the book *Topic in Mathematical System Theory*. In addition, he served on the editorial boards of numerous technical journals.

Kalman, who is married and has two children, also held memberships in a number of professional societies. Along with his memberships in the IEEE and the National Academy of Sciences, he also belongs to the U.S. National Academy of Engineering and is a fellow of the American Academy of Arts and Sciences. In addition, he is a foreign member of the Hungarian, French, and Russian academies of science.

Online

Air Force Research Laboratory Technology Horizons, http://www.afrlhorizons.com/ (December 16, 2003).
"Creating a Moving Picture of the Earth's Climate," *Insights,* http://sdcd.gsfc.nasa.gov/ESS/insights/vol6/climate.htm (December 16, 2003).
IEEE History Center, http://www.ieee.org/organizations/history_center/legacies/ (December 16, 2003).
Inamori Foundation Web site, http://www.inamori-f.or.jp/KyotoPrizes/contents_e/laureates/ (December 16, 2003).
Kalman Filter, http://www.cae.wisc.edu/~ece539/project/presentation/gissel/Kalman.html (December 16, 2003).
Nobel Prize Winners and Famous Hungarians, http://www.hungary.org/~hipcat/sciencemathandtech2.htm (December 16, 2003).
"Rudolf Emil Kalman," http://icel.me.pusan.ac.kr/ResearchArea/kalman/sub/kalmanbiblio.htm (December 16, 2003). □

Raden Ajeng Kartini

Raden Ajeng Kartini (1879-1904) is credited with starting the move for women's emancipation in Java, an island then controlled by Holland as part of the Netherlands Indies (now Indonesia). Born to the aristocracy, Kartini was privileged to be able to attend Dutch colonial schools, but was forced to quit at an early age due to Islamic law at the time. At the age of 24, she was married to a man twice her age who already had three wives. Kartini wrote letters to her friends in Holland protesting the treatment of

women in Java, the practice of polygamy, and of the Dutch suppression of the island's native population. Decades later, the Indonesian state constitution promised gender equality to all its citizens, and Kartini Day continues to be celebrated on April 21 to commemorate Kartini's contribution to women's rights.

Kartini was born on April 21, 1879, in Mayong village near of Jepara, a town located in the center of the island of Java. She was born into the Javanese *priyayi,* or aristocracy; her father was Jepara mayor Raden Mas Adipati Ario Sosroningrat. Kartini was one of 12 children born to Raden's several wives.

Educated at Dutch Schools

As a child, Kartini was very active, playing and climbing trees. She earned the nickname "little bird" because of her constant flitting around. A man of some modern attitudes, her father allowed her to attend Dutch elementary school along with her brothers. The Dutch had colonized Java and established schools open only to Europeans and to sons of wealthy Javanese. Due to the advantages of her birth and her intellectual inclination, Kartini became one of the first native women allowed to learn to read and write in Dutch.

Despite her father's permission to allow her a primary education, by Islamic custom and a Javanese tradition known as *pingit,* all girls, including Kartini, were forced to leave school at age 12 and stay home to learn homemaking skills. At this point, Kartini would have to wait for a man to ask for her hand in marriage. Even her status among the upper class could not save her from this tradition of discrimination against women; marriage was expected of her. For Kartini, the only escape from this traditional mode of life was to become an independent woman.

Promoted Nationalist Movement

Fearful of losing control over their island territory, the Dutch colonialists believed that knowledge of European languages and education could a be dangerous tool in the hands of the native Javanese. Consequently, they suppressed the activities of the native people, keeping them as peasants and plantation laborers, while at the same time counting on the Javanese nobility to support them in their rule over the region. Only a few of the nobility, Kartini's father included, were taught the Dutch language. Kartini believed that once the Europeans introduced Western culture to the island, they had no right to limit the desire of native Javanese to learn more. Clearly, by the late nineteenth century there was talk of independence. With her letters and her egalitarian fervor, Kartini can be said to have started the modern Indonesian nationalist movement.

Kartini was not proud of being set apart from her countrymen as one of the privileged few of the aristocracy. In her writings she described two types of nobility, one of mind and one of deed. Simply being born from a noble line does

not make one great; a person needs to do great deeds for humanity to be considered noble.

Wrote Letters to Holland

From 1900 to 1904 Kartini stayed home from school in according to the dictates of Javanese tradition; she found an outlet for her beliefs in letters she wrote in Dutch and sent to her friends in Holland. Kartini was unique in that she was a woman who was able to write; what set her apart even further was her rebellious spirit and her determination to air concerns that no one, not even men, were publicly discussing.

Kartini wrote to her European friends about many subjects, including the plight of the Javanese citizenry and the need to improve their lot through education and progress. She recounts how Javanese intellectuals were put in their place if they dared to speak Dutch or to protest. She also describes the restrictive world she lived in, rife with hierarchy and isolationism. In 1902 Kartini wrote to one letter, to Mrs. Ovink-Soer, that she hoped to continue her education in Holland so that she could prepare for a future in which she could make such education accessible to all women.

Kartini is most known for writing letters in which she advocates the need to address women's rights and status, and to loosen the oppressive Islamic traditions that allowed discrimination against women. She protests against education restricted to males of the nobility, believing that all Javanese, male and female, rich and poor, have the right to be educated in order to choose their own destiny. Women especially are not allowed to realize their calling. As Nursyahbani Katjasungkana commented in the *Jakarta Post,* "Kartini knew and expounded the concept that women can make choices in any aspect of their lives, careers, and personal matters."

Opened School for Girls

Rather than remaining submissive and compliant, like a good Javanese daughter, the unconventional Kartini often had disagreements with her father, and it is believed that her family was, consequently, eager to marry her off. On November 8, 1903, she obeyed her father and married Raden Adipati Joyoadiningrat, the regent of Rembang. Joyoadiningrat was a wealthy man of age 50 who already had three wives and a dozen children. Kartini—who was, at 24 years of age, considered too old to marry well—found herself a victim of polygamy. She was devastated by the marriage, which ended her dream of studying abroad just as she was awarded a scholarship to study in Europe.

Despite the marriage, in 1903 Kartini was able to take a first step toward achieving women's equality by opening a school for girls. With aid from the Dutch government Kartini established the first primary school in Indonesia especially for native girls regardless of their social standing. The small school, which was located inside her father's house, taught children and young women to read and make handicrafts, dispensed Western-style education, and provided moral instruction. At this time, Kartini also published the paper "Teach the Javanese."

Kartini's enthusiasm at educating Indonesian girls was short lived. On September 17, 1904, at the age of 25, she died while giving birth to her son. Kartini is buried near a mosque in Mantingan, south of Rembang.

Letters Ultimately Published

Kartini's legacy is found in the many letters she wrote to friends in Holland. In 1911 a collection of her Dutch letters was published posthumously, first in Java and then in Holland as *Door Duisternis tot Licht: Gedachten Over en Voor Het Javanese Volk* ("From Darkness to Light: Thoughts about and on Behalf of the Javanese People"). The book was then translated into several languages, including French, Arabic, and Russian, and in 1920 was translated by Agnes Louis Symmers into English as *Letters of a Javanese Princess*. In 1922 Armijn Pane finally translated the book into the Javanese language under the title *Habis Gelap Terbitlah Terang* ("After Darkness, Light Is Born"), which he based on a verse found in both the Bible and the Qur'an in which God calls people out of the darkness and into the light. More recently, Kartini's granddaughter, Professor Haryati Soebadio, re-translated the letters and published them as *Dari Gelap Menuju Cahaya,* meaning "From Darkness into Light."

Kartini's letters spurred her nation's enthusiasm for nationalism and garnered sympathy abroad for the plight of Javanese women. Syrian writer Aleyech Thouk translated *From Darkness into Light* into Arabic for use in her country, and in her native Java Kartini's writings were used by a group trying to gain support for the country's Ethical Policy movement, which had been losing popularity. Many of Kartini's admirers established a string of "Kartini schools" across the island of Java, the schools funded through private contributions.

Kartini's beliefs and letters inspired many women and effected actual change in her native Java. Taking their example, women from other islands in the archipelago, such as Sumatra, also were inspired to push for change in their regions. The 1945 Constitution establishing the Republic of Indonesia guaranteed women the same rights as men in the areas of education, voting rights, and economy. Today, women are welcome at all levels of education and have a broad choice of careers. Kartini's contributions to Indonesian society are remembered in her hometown of Jepara at the Museum Kartini di Jepara and in Rembang, where she spent her brief married life, at the Museum Kartini di Rembang.

Kartini Day Declared National Holiday

In Indonesia, April 21, Kartini's birthday, is a national holiday that recognizes her as a pioneer for women's rights and emancipation. During the holiday women and girls don traditional clothing to symbolize their unity and participate in costume contests, cook-offs, and flower arrangement competitions. Mothers are allowed the day off as husbands and fathers do the cooking and housework. Schools host lectures, parades are held, and the women's organization Dharma Wanita specially marks the holiday.

In more recent years criticism has arisen regarding the superficial observance of Kartini Day. Many now chose not to commemorate it, and it has increasingly been eliminated from school calendars. What saddens historians and activists is that Kartini has become a forgotten figure for the younger generation, who cannot relate to the achievements she wrought in a repressive society that is now almost forgotten. Historians have also debated the role Kartini herself played in promoting women's emancipation. Other than her letters, some have argued that she was a submissive daughter, feminine but not necessarily a feminist.

A Legacy in Film

The film biography *R. A. Kartini* was produced to highlight her efforts to promote women's emancipation and education. Based on her published letters as well as memoirs written by friends, the film presents the two aspects of Kartini's life: her brief public life which had minimal effect, and her letters which, after her death, had profound influence on women all over the world. The film, written and directed by Indonesian filmmaker Sjuman Djaya, recreates Kartini's family life, ambitions, and the historical context of life under Dutch colonialism. Kartini is also remembered through businesses inspired by her vision. Kartini International, based in Ontario, Canada, advocates for women's education and rights, and won the 2000 Canadian International Award for Gender Equality Achievement for its work.

Books

Kartini, R. A., *Letters from Kartini: An Indonesian Feminist, 1900-1904,* Monash Asia Institute, 1994.
———, *On Feminism and Nationalism: Kartini's Letters to Stella Zeehandelaar, 1899-1903,* Monash Asia Institute, 1995.
Palmier, Leslie, *Indonesia,* Walker & Co., 1965.

Periodicals

Jakarta Post, April 21, 2001; April 20, 2002.

Online

Chaniago, Ira, "Raden Ajeng Kartini—A Pioneer of Women's Education in Indonesia," *University of New England Web site,* http://www.une.edu.au/unepa/Gradpost/gp_9.3web.pdf (December 23, 2003).
Discover Indonesia Online, http://indahnesia.com/Indonesia/Jawa/ (December 23, 2003).
Monash Asia Institute Web site, http://www.arts.monash.edu.au/mai/ (December 23, 2003). □

Ali Akbar Khan

Indian musician Ali Akbar Khan (born 1922) is venerated in his homeland as a National Living Treasure, while internationally he is regarded as the greatest living classical Indian musician. A master of the sarod, a 25-stringed Indian instrument, Khan helped introduce and popularize Indian music throughout the Western world.

Khan was born on April 14, 1922, in Shivpur, East Bengal, an area now known as Bangladesh but then part of British-controlled India. He began learning and playing music when he was three years old. He was taught by his father, the late Padma Vibhusan Acharya Dr. Allauddin Khan, who is regarded as the most important figure in North Indian music of his time. The elder Khan played over 200 instruments and lived to be 110 years old. Regarded as both a great musician and teacher, Allauddin Khan attracted a great many aspiring Indian musicians who wanted to learn from the master.

Khan's family followed the rich tradition of North Indian classical music that had developed over 4,000 years and was based on ancient principles of *rag* (melody) and *taal* (rhythm). The family dates its ancestry back to Mian Tansen, a 16th-century court musician to the Mogul Emperor Akbar.

Allauddin Khan, who also mastered Western and African instruments during his career, continued teaching his son right up until his death in 1972. He also taught his daughters, Sharija, Jehanara, and Annapurna, and instructed many other famous musicians, among them the illustrious sitarist Ravi Shankar, flautist Pannalal Ghosh, and Ali Akbar Khan's own son sarodist, Aashish Khan.

Ali Khan's musical training was rigorous. For more than 20 years, starting at age three, he practiced every day for 18 hours a day. In an interview with V. R. Rao posted on the *Cyberabad Web site,* Khan explained that he learned music like a child learns language. "I didn't consciously want to

learn music. It was more like a language that an infant learns," he said.

Khan's early musical education included a variety of string and percussion instruments including the sarod, sitar, sursingar, pakhavaj, rabab, and violin. In addition to the instruction from his father, Khan also learned vocals from his sister Jehanara and percussion from his uncle, Fakir Aftabuddin. Eventually, his father recommended that he focus on the sarod, an ancient steel-clad member of the lute family at least 2,000 years old with 25 strings and played with a bow. The sarod, Khan's father said, could fulfill 200 instruments in one.

Success Came Early

Khan made his first public performance, in Allahabad in 1935, when he was only 13 years old. At the same time, he began composing his own music under his father's direction. His skill was such that, when he was still a teenager, Khan was scheduled to accompany his father on a tour of Europe and America. However, the plans were canceled because Khan did not like the idea of being away from his mother, and he was not practicing his music as much as his father felt he should. The elder Khan cut his tour short and returned to India, to make sure his son practiced 15 to 18 hours a day.

In 1938 Ravi Shankar began studying with Allauddin Khan in Maihar and, in 1941 he married his teacher's daughter, Ali Khan's sister Annapurna, who was then considered to be the premiere player of the surbahar, a deeper-toned, heavier relative of the sitar, which was Shankar's chosen instrument. Ali Khan studied along with his now-brother-in-law Shankar and, thanks to the guidance of Allauddin Khan, the two musicians became highly regarded in Hindustani music circles for their duets.

In 1943, when he was 21, Khan was appointed court musician to the maharaja of Jodhpur. Khan held this position until the maharaja died several years later. The state of Jodhpur bestowed on the young musician the title of "Ustad," or master musician. At first, Khan's father was amused that his son would receive such a high honor at such an early age. However, later in life, Allauddin Khan told his son that he had been extremely proud of him. Then, to show his pleasure and respect, he gave his son the title of "Swara Samrat" or "emperor of melody." Of all the honors that he received in his life, Ali Khan would value that one the most.

During the 1940s Khan also made his first sound recordings, and he began his own career as a teacher, instructing Maharajah Hanumantha Singh. New opportunities opened up when he met world famous violin virtuoso Yehudi Menuhin at a recital in Delhi in 1952. Menuhin, who would call Khan one of the greatest musician in the world, was so impressed that he encouraged the young man to perform in the West. This resulted in Khan's first trip to the United States in 1955, when he appeared in a first-of-its kind concert at the Museum of Modern Art in New York City. In addition, he appeared on Alistair Cooke's *Omnibus* television show, marking the first time Indian music was performed live on television. Khan's appearance had an enormous impact. It opened the door to Western acceptance of Indian music, an acceptance that reached full bloom in the 1960s, due, in large part, to the embracement of Indian music by the so-called "counterculture." However, at that time, Indian music and culture seemed alien to many Americans. "When I came in '55, because I was in Indian dress, people on the street in New York came out of the bars and shops and followed us," Khan remembered in an interview with Neela Banerjee for *Asian Week.* "They asked me, 'Who are you? Where are you from?' When I said 'India,' some of them didn't even know where it was. Or others who knew I was a musician asked funny questions like, 'How can you play music in India with all the tigers and snakes and monkeys you have to fight off?'"

In 1955 Khan also released his first Western recordings of Indian classical music, titled *Music of India* and *Morning and Evening Ragas.* The following year he established the Ali Akbar College of Music in Calcutta, India. During the same decade Khan first began composing music for films, an activity he engaged in throughout his career. He composed his first score in 1953 for *Aandhiyan,* a film by Indian filmmaker Chetan Anand. Later, he would compose music for *Devi* (1960), by internationally acclaimed Indian filmmaker Satyajit Ray; *The Householder,* (1963), the first film directed by the celebrated team of Ismail Merchant and James Ivory; and *Little Buddha,* directed by Bernardo Bertolucci.

Opened Music School

Throughout the 1960s, Khan continued recording music and releasing recordings. In 1963 and 1966 he received the President of India Award. In addition, acting upon the influence of his father, who had taught him the value of teaching music, he established the Ali Akbar College of Music in Berkeley, California, in 1967, and moved the school to a new location in Marin County two years later. For a long time, he had attempted to set up a school in his homeland, with little success. "For thirty years I struggled to establish a teaching institution in Calcutta," he told Rao. "But it wasn't possible. No response."

By the mid-1960s the West was receptive to listening to and learning about Indian music. A large part of the general public had became aware of Indian music due to the interest in the form by popular rock musicians, such as George Harrison of the Beatles and Roger McGuinn of the Byrds, both of whom integrated Indian instrumentation into their own compositions. The essence of Indian music fit well with the times, and many in the youth movement were willing and ready to explore ideas that were either ancient, revolutionary, exotic, or esoteric.

Complex in form, Indian music is also spiritual and contemplative. Although a performer, Khan sees himself more as a listener and as an extension of his sarod, and he can lose his sense of self while performing. Indian music, he explained to Rao, "is like a meditation, like going to temple. Music makes your heart very, very, very clear. You can feel what is peace, what is friendship, what is love, what you can do for others. Even when you hear, it is like fresh air, clean

water—even if you don't understand it, when you hear it, it is pure."

The West Embraced Indian Music

By the mid- to late 1960s classical Indian musicians such as Khan and Shankar were appearing at U.S. and U.K. music festivals, including the ground-breaking Monterey Pop Festival in San Francisco in 1967 and the first Woodstock music festival held in Bethel, New York, in 1969. In fact, Indian music became a staple at such events, while also gaining its largest mass-audience exposure with *The Concert for Bangladesh,* a documentary film of a musical benefit organized by Harrison to raise funds for the starving people of that country. The performing lineup included some of the most famous rock stars of the era including Harrison, Ringo Starr, Bob Dylan, Eric Clapton, and Leon Russell as well as Shankar, who was accompanied for the event by Khan, Alla Rakah, and Kamala Chakravarty. (For his own concerts, Khan was most often accompanied by Pandit Swapan Chaudhuri on the tabla and son Alam on the sarode.)

During this period, Khan's fame on the international circuit was second only to that of Shankar due to Shankar's longer association with the Beatles. While Shankar had by now divorced Khan's sister, Annapurna, Shankar remained a disciple of Allauddin Khan. Shankar and Khan performed together for the final time at Montpellier, France, in July of 1985. Despite many pleas and generous offers, they never performed together again.

Honors and Awards Accumulated

In 1971 Khan received a Gold Disc award for his appearance on the bestselling *Concert for Bangladesh* album. The previous year, he earned a Grammy nomination for the recording *Shree Rag.* In 1973 and 1974 he received doctor of literature degrees from the Rabindra Bharati University in Calcutta, India, and the University of Dacca in Bangladesh, respectively.

In 1979 Khan started his own recording label, Alam Medina Music Productions label, named after his son. Throughout the next decade his recorded output was prolific. He released six albums in 1980, three in 1981, and four in 1982. In 1983, the year he released two more albums, he was again nominated for a Grammy award, this time for *Misra Piloo.* The following year he released four more albums and received a doctor of letters degree from the University of Delhi, India. From 1985 to 1986 Khan released nine more albums.

In addition to recording, Khan invested time in teaching. In 1985 he opened a new branch of his music school in Switzerland. In 1988, the year he produced his first music video, he received the Padma Vibhusan award, which is the highest honor presented to a civilian in India. He continued amassing honors and awards throughout the 1990s, in 1991 alone receiving the Kalidas Sanman award from the Madya Pradesh Academy of Music and Fine Arts as well as an honorary doctorate degree in arts from the California Institute of the Arts. He also became the first Indian musician to receive a MacArthur Foundation fellowship. The following year, he received the Mahatma Gandhi Cultural Award in London. In 1993 he was honored with the titles of Hathi Saropao and Dowari Tajeem during the Jodhpur Palace's Golden Jubilee Celebration, and also received the Bill Graham Lifetime Achievement Award from the Bay Area Music Awards Foundation.

Established Akbar Foundation

In 1994 Khan founded the Ali Akbar Khan Foundation to fund the Baba Allauddin Khan Institute, a library and archive dedicated to the preservation of his own compositions as well as his father's. This large-scale archiving project involves more than 30,000 compositions, including more than 10,000 compositions from the 16th through the 20th centuries. Khan's wife, sons, and students have joined their efforts to convert collections of music from old reel-to-reel tapes to digital master tapes.

In 1997, the year Khan celebrated his 75th birthday, he received the prestigious National Heritage fellowship from the National Endowment for the Arts. The presentation was made at the White House by First Lady Hillary Rodham Clinton. That same year Khan became the second recipient, after filmmaker Satyajit Ray, to receive the Asian Paints Shiromani-Hall of Fame Award. In August of 1997, to celebrate the 50th year of India's independence, Khan performed at the United Nations in New York and at Kennedy Center in Washington, D.C., at the request of the Indian Embassy.

Khan received yet another doctorate degree in 1998, this one from the Viswa Bharati University in Shantiniketan, India. He also received the Indira Gandhi Gold Plaque from the Asiatic Society of Calcutta. That same year, Willie L. Brown Jr., mayor of San Francisco, proclaimed October 18th "Ustad Ali Akbar Khan Day." In 1999 Khan was appointed adjunct professor to the Department of Music at the University of California at Santa Cruz. In this position he gave concerts and conducted classes and workshops. He also advised the Arts Division in developing courses and resources in classical music of India.

In 2002, to celebrate his life and times, Khan performed an 80th birthday concert at the Palace of Fine Arts in San Francisco. He was accompanied by his 20-year old son Alam and tabla player Swapan Chaudhuri. Also that year, he received an honorary degree in musical arts from the New England Conservatory of Music in Boston. Like his father before him, Khan has continued teaching and performing, although he gradually has cut down on his public performances. Also like his father, much of Khan's time is devoted to teaching his son, Alam.

Periodicals

Asian Week, January 11, 2002.

Online

"Ali Akbar Khan," *Indian Classical Music Society Web site,* http://www.icmschicago.org/Artists/ali_akbar.html (December 18, 2003).

"Ali Akbar Khan," *MusicWeb Encyclopedia of Popular Music,* http://www.musicweb.uk.net/encyclopaedia/k/K42.HTM (December 18 2003).

"Ali Akbar Khan—A Musical Giant," *Rancho Vila.com,* http://www.ranchovilasa-spurs.com/aliakbarkhan.html (December 18, 2003)

Official Ali Akbar Khan Home Page, http://www.ammp.com (December 18, 2003).

"Ustad Ali Akbar Khan, Great Indian Sarod Player" (interview), *Cyberbad Web site,* http://cyberabad.hypermart.net/index .htm (February, 1988). □

Keisuke Kinoshita

One of Japan's most popular filmmakers after World War II, Keisuke Kinoshita (1912-1998) was a prolific director, writer, and producer, specializing in sentimental dramas and comedies and the use of innovative, expressionistic sets.

Rarely have any of Kinoshita's fifty or so films been shown outside of Japan, but in that country he was a well-known director who pioneered the use of color in film and repeatedly touched on domestic themes that resonated with Japanese audiences. Despite his conventional plots and subject matter, Kinoshita was often willing to experiment with avant-garde techniques.

Movie Buff

As a child, Kinoshita was a hopeless movie buff. His father was a grocer in the town of Hamamatsu in the Shizuoka prefecture of Japan. His parents wanted him to learn a trade, so he went to a technical high school, but Kinoshita was completely focused on making movies. He enrolled in the Oriental Photography School in order to learn how to become a cinematographer and break into movies.

At first Kinoshita made only halting strides toward attaining his dream. He applied at one of Japan's biggest movie studios, Shochiku, hoping to be an assistant cameraman, but he was hired to work in the lab processing film. It took awhile before he was allowed to become an assistant cinematographer for the director Yasujiro Shimazu.

For three years, Kinoshita served as Shimazu's assistant cinematographer, but he was often so engrossed in watching acting rehearsals that he would not do his job properly. Another assistant, Kozaburo Yoshimura, who would go on to become a famous director himself, recommended that Kinoshita learn to become a director. It took another two years before a position was available as Yomishura's assistant. For six years, Kinoshita worked under Shimazu, learning much about filmmaking but suffering from Shimazu's dictatorial impulses.

First Films

In 1943, Kinoshita's first two directorial efforts were released: *Ikite iru Magoroku (Magoroku Is Alive)* and *Hana*

saku minato (Blooming Port). The latter was a formulaic comedy about a clash between sophisticated urbanites and rural naifs, but it displayed Hinoshita's love for simplicity and honesty. Since World War II was dominating life in Japan, Hinoshita tried to fit in, directing a wartime propaganda film called *Rikugun (Army)*, but it was decried by military censors for being insufficiently doctrinaire.

A prolific director, Kinoshita made 12 more films in the 1940s, focusing mainly on domestic dramas and comedies in efforts like *Osone-ke no ashita (Morning for the Osone Family)* (1946), the first film he produced as well as directed. Despite its clichéd subject matter, the film was unusual because it was shot almost entirely on a set inside a house. Many of his films featured honest, simple women as the central protagonists, including *Onna (Woman)* (1948), which was shot entirely outdoors on a rocky hillside.

In 1950, Kinoshita wrote his first film, *Konyaku yubiwa (Engagement Ring)*, and he wrote most of the subsequent films he directed. His films became popular during the 1950s, and he continued to direct and release an average of two movies a year. His characters were often optimistic and kind.

Kinoshita's *Karumen kokyo in kaeru (Carmen Comes Home)*, which he directed in 1951, was the first feature film in Japan shot entirely in color. This satirical domestic comedy was followed by *Karumen junjo su (Carmen Falls in Love)* (1952), one of many instances in which Kinoshita followed a title character (always a woman) through more than one movie.

Social Dramas

In 1953, Kinoshita abandoned his customary lighthearted fare for a disturbing social drama, *Nihon no higeki (A Japanese Tragedy)*. Its protagonist is a middle-class woman forced by economic straits to offer her household goods and her body on the black market to support her children; now older and estranged from her adult children, she tries to arrange good marriages for them, but is rebuked because of their shame and vanity. On the website *Strictly Film School*, reviewer Acquarello calls the film "a bleak, affecting, and insoluble portrait of postwar existence . . . a relevant and insightful account of the personal toll of war and the slow, agonizing process of recovery. . . . In the end, a lone image of [the protagonist] Haruko in long shot standing at the top of a train station staircase as commuters hurriedly rush past captures the emotional desolation of the individual human struggle against a formidable and unrelenting tide. . ." In this film, one of Kinoshita's best, the director uses newsreel footage, flashbacks, and frequent shots of trains in motion to heighten the realism.

In his next film, *Nijushi no hitomi (Twenty-Four Eyes)* (1954), Kinoshita adapted a popular novel into a heart-rending drama about a teacher and her twelve students, whom she first teaches during a relatively happy time and then again encounters years later during a period of economic depression and strife. Acquarello notes: "Filmed from a low camera angle, and using exquisitely composed crane, long, and medium shots, Keisuke Kinoshita visually conveys a sense of distance that, in turn, reflects the innocence of the children's perspective." He calls it "a haunting, compassionately realized, and profoundly affecting portrait of humanism, innocence, and the personal toll of war." That Kinoshita was able to combine such compelling drama with his successful comedy-dramas and reach mass audiences in Japan is a measure of his range and ability as a master director in touch with his native land and its contemporary problems.

Kinoshita touched on the tradition of Kabuki theater in his 1955 film, *Nogiku no gotoki kimi nariki (She Was Like a Wild Chrysanthemum)*, in which all his characters wear masks. His willingness to experiment with technique is evident in *Narayama Bushiko (Ballad of Narayama)* (1958). He uses a theatrical stage setting, jarring spotlights, vivid colors, and intentionally anachronistic images to adapt a popular novel about family, duty, and custom. Acquarello calls it a ". . . portrait of love and humanity struggling against the rigidity of tradition, obedience, and sense of duty . . . a haunting allegory on the perils of blind allegiance, martyrdom, and repression—a humanist reflection of the profound introspection, cultural erosion, and ideological ambivalence of postwar Japan."

Eventually Acclaimed

Kinoshita's heyday was the 1950s, but during that time critics did not embrace his sentimental style, even though Japanese audiences responded positively. He made nine more films in the 1960s, but none of them were acclaimed, and only five more films in his declining years, from 1976 to

1988. He also produced Akira Kurosawa's worldwide hit *Dodes'ka-den* in 1970.

Eventually Kinoshita was hailed as one of Japan's foremost directors, for his wide range and innovative techniques within the context of popular contemporary films. In 1991, he was awarded an honor from the Japanese government for his contributions to national culture. In 1999, a panel of Japanese critics named Kinoshita's *Nijushi no hitomi (Twenty-Four Eyes)* as one of that country's ten greatest films of all time.

Online

"Keisuke Kinoshita," *All Movie Guide,* http://www.allmovie .com/cg/avg.dll?p = avg&sql = 2:97490~C (January 2, 2004).
"Keisuke Kinoshita," *Internet Movie Database,*" http://us.imdb .com/name/nm0455839/ (January 2, 2004).
"Keisuke Kinoshita," *Strictly Film School,* http://www.filmref .com/directors/dirpages/kinoshita.html (January 2, 2004).
"Keisuke Kinoshita," *Yahoo! Movies,* http://movies.yahoo.com/ shop?d = hc&id = 1800130311&cf = &cfbiog&intl = us (January 2, 2004). □

Teinosuke Kinugasa

One of the fathers of modern Japanese cinema, Teinosuke Kinugasa (1896-1982) used experimental techniques in the 1920s and went on to direct more than 100 movies, including historical spectacles and several films that gained attention worldwide.

Roots in Tradition

B orn in 1896 in Mie, Japan, Kinugasa was originally an actor in Kabuki theater. As a teenager, he had perfected the art of playing an *onnagata,* a male who performed female character roles. In 1917, he broke into movies as an *onnagata,* at a time when most Japanese films were basically cinematic versions of Kabuki plays.

In 1921, Kinugasa directed his first feature film, *Imoto no shi (The Death of My Sister).* Little is known about this or several other films he directed before the 1923 Tokyo earthquake, which destroyed all of Kinugasa's early work.

By the end of 1928, Kinugasa, a prolific filmmaker, had directed an amazing 44 silent movies. The two most significant were the first films that Kinugasa wrote—1926's *Kurutta Ippeji (Page of Madness)* and 1928's *Jujiro (Crossroads or Crossways).*

Page of Madness

Page of Madness broke new ground in Japanese cinema, which was evolving rapidly from the traditional Kabuki-inspired forms to the kind of abstract and surrealistic expressionism most famously embodied in the German silent masterpiece *The Cabinet of Dr. Caligari.* A *Page of Madness* was the Japanese counterpart to *Caligari.* The film

was full of camera angles that distorted the physical plane and engaged other dark, absurdist stylistic touches that were popular with Expressionists.

The 58-minute film concerned an old man's efforts to rescue his wife from an insane asylum, but the wife is afraid to leave the asylum's confines. Kinugasa created a hallucinogenic world of shadows, frightening figures, and fragmented perspectives. The director wrote and financed the film himself, taking a substantial risk with his budding career.

Despite its avant-garde nature, the film was a surprising box-office success in Japan and it made enough money to propel Kinugasa's career forward. The film also received international attention, which gave notice that Japanese cinema was becoming more modern and experimental. The film helped inspire other Japanese directors to continue to produce films that would contribute to a unique national cinematic language.

International Career

Kinugasa's cinematic forays into deep psychological territory exacerbated his chronic depression. He left Japan, searching for his emotional center, and traveled widely throughout Europe. In Russia, he studied briefly for a time under the great director Sergei Eisenstein.

Before leaving Japan, Kinugasa had completed *Jujiro (Crossroads),* a film in which he combined experimental, subjective camera work with a story that used traditional themes and modern situations. The plot centered around a young man's tragic love for an assertive geisha. In a Shakespearean twist, the young man wounds his main rival in a brawl, blinding him.

Kinugasa brought a print of this film on his travels. He managed to convince officials at Berlin's U.F.A. studio to watch it, and they reacted positively toward the work. The studio officials helped to get the film distributed widely in Europe under the title *Shadows of Yoshiwara.* Audiences responded to its avant-garde techniques and dreamlike sequences. It was the first Japanese film to make an impact on European audiences.

On the strength of this showing, Kinugasa became an important international filmmaker. Critics raved over his use of close-ups and inventive camera angles. Eventually Kinugasa returned to Japan with the new status of a top-flight international director.

Turned toward Epics

Back in Japan, Kinugasa became a top studio director, and a productive one at that. In the 1930s he directed 17 more films, and he managed 9 more during the 1940s— despite World War II. In the 1950s, he became even more active with another 24 films to add to his credit.

Because of the international triumph of Japanese director, Akira Kurosawa's film *Rashomon,* Kinugasa and other Japanese filmmakers turned their attention to period dramas and samurai epics. Kinugasa's 1952 film, *Daibutsu kaigen (Saga of the Great Buddha),* followed this trend.

In 1954, Kinogasa had an international hit, the critically acclaimed *Jigokumon* (Gate of Hell), a samurai epic that was shot entirely in Eastman color. Its vivid cinematography and exotic locations made it an audience favorite at the Cannes Film Festival, where it was awarded a Grand Prix as 1954's best film.

Kinogasa had another hit at Cannes in 1959, when *White Heron* won a special mention award. By this time the filmmaker's career was winding down, and he made only a few more films.

As a whole, Kinugasa's impact as a filmmaker was considerable. He helped define the unique voice of Japanese cinema, and sustained both his experimental impulses and his conventional career as a popular director who brought international attention to the films of his native land.

Online

"A Page of Madness," *British Film Institute,* http://www.bfi.org .uk/collections/catalogues/disability/details.php?id=11 (January 3, 2004).

"Crossways," *British Film Institute,* http://www.bfi.org.uk/ collections/catalogues/disability/details.php?id=99 (January 3, 2004).

"Teinosuke Kinugasa," *All Movie Guide,* http://www.allmovie .com/cg/x.dll (January 3, 2004).

"Teinosuke Kinugasa," *Foreign Films.com,* http://www .foreignfilms.com/person.asp?person_id=1227 (January 3, 2004).

"Teinosuke Kinugasa," *Internet Movie Database,* http://us.imdb .com/name/nm0455938/ (January 3, 2004).

"Teinosuke Kinugasa," *Yahoo! Movies,* http://movies.yahoo .com/shop?d=hc&id=1800069397&cf=gen&intl=us (January 3, 2004). □

Alexander Kipnis

Ukrainian–born American operatic bass Alexander Kipnis (1891–1978) enjoyed an illustrious career made infamous by his mastery of German basso roles. His rich voice and thoughtful interpretations left an indelible mark in the hearts of opera patrons around the world.

Early Life

Alexander Kipnis was born February 13 (February 1 by the Julian calendar), 1891, in the village of Zhitomir in the southern Russian Ukraine. He shared a home in a Jewish ghetto with four siblings and his parents. His academic schooling was basic at best, and although no one in his family played or sang music professionally, David Ewen's *Musicians Since 1900* notes one of his early memories, "Once in a while I can remember my mother [Machli] singing as she would be working around the house, and later on I was astonished to recognize what she sang was 'La donna è mobile' or Schubert's *Serenade.* Where she heard them I don't know." It was the folk music of the Russian peasants surrounding his everyday existence that became a motivating influence, as the same interview explains, "I would hear their songs at twilight when they would play and sing for themselves, and by the time I was four or five years old I had learned most of their songs." His father Isaiah Kipnis, a fabric salesman, was a learned man but with no musical background. He died when Kipnis was 12 years old. That same year a juvenile Kipnis ran off briefly with an opera troupe that visited his village. He then earned a little money as a boy soprano singing in local synagogues before his voice began to change, but he returned home to work as a carpenter's apprentice in an effort to help his mother support their family. He began the study of music at the age of 19 in the hopes that mastering two instruments might result in him being drafted into the Russian Army (an inevitability) at the rank of officer. He began by studying the double bass and the trombone.

Education

While a student at the Warsaw Conservatory Kipnis turned his focus to learning the skills of conducting, and graduated as a conductor with honors in 1912 at the age of 21. Once graduated, his efforts to achieve a better military post through musical knowledge paid off, and he served for a time as a military bandmaster. He also sang in Conservatory choirs and took rudimentary voice lessons from an Italian teacher there. He began frequenting operas and became inspired by what he saw and heard, particularly by the Italian singer Mattia Battistini. Once he had served his time in the military, he concentrated on crafting his natural singing ability. He knew that to truly study voice he must go either to Austria or Germany. In an interesting account recorded in *Musicians Since 1900,* Kipnis describes standing "on the railroad station in Warsaw wondering which of these two capitals should become his destination. While he was trying to reach a decision an express train for Berlin rolled in and Kipnis allowed fate to decide for him." He ended up taking vocal lessons with Ernst Grenzebach at the Klindworth—Scharwenka Conservatory, and the heldentenors Lauritz Melchior and Max Lorenz in Berlin. In 1913 and 1914 Kipnis sang in small production operettas in Berlin, but in 1914 at the beginning of the First World War Kipnis was interned as an enemy alien because he was Russian, although they permitted him to continue his musical studies. He was heard singing one day by a German colonel whose brother was the Impresario for the Hamburg Opera. The colonel suggested that Kipnis audition for his brother, and once he had, Kipnis was allowed to continue his study of singing, but under strict police surveillance. When not performing, Kipnis was kept secluded and under police guard. He spent this time alone practicing and building his repertory of roles and parts such as Gurnemanz in Richard Wagner's *Parsifal,* Colline in *La Bohème,* Kezal in Bedrich Smetana's *The Bartered Bride,* Sparafucile and Monterone in *Rigoletto,* Ramfis in Giuseppe Verdi's *Aida,* Bartolo in Wolfgang Amadeus Mozart's *The Marriage of Figaro,* and Ferrando in Verdi's *Il Trovatore.*

Operatic Career

Kipnis's debut was in the role of the hermit in Carl Maria von Weber's *Die Freischütz* with the Hamburg Opera in Hamburg, Germany, in 1915. From 1916 through 1918 he sang as a member of the Wiesbaden Opera. Once the war was over, he toured with the Berlin State Opera, appearing in various roles and venues from 1919 through 1934 when he settled in the United States. He came to the United States for the first time in 1923 as a member of a visiting operatic ensemble the German Opera Company and made his debut in Baltimore on January 31 of that year. On April 7, 1925, Kipnis married Mildred Levy, the daughter of American concert pianist Heniot Levy. They had one son named Igor who, in his own career became an internationally acclaimed harpsichordist. Kipnis made his New York debut in the role of Pogner in Wagner's *Die Meistersinger* on February 12, 1923. Immediately after his debut the Chicago Civic Opera seized him and he sang with them for a total of nine seasons. While in their company he took principle basso roles in French, Italian and German repertories. In 1932 Kipnis left Chicago to return to sing as principle bass for the Berlin State Opera in Germany until 1935. He had success in London, the Bayreuth Festivals, Covent Garden, Glyndebourne, Salzburg and Buenos Aires. During Hitler's rise to power Kipnis left Germany and traveled to Italy to join the Vienna State Opera.

While in Vienna Kipnis sang the roles of Baron Ochs in Richard Strauss's *Der Rosenkavalier,* Boris Godunov in the Modest Mussorgsky opera by the same name, Sarastro in Mozart's *The Magic Flute,* Leporello in Mozart's *Don Giovanni,* and Gurnemanz which had become his signature role. According to *Musicians Since 1900,* he was so popular in Vienna that he "he sold out the large concert hall [there] for two recitals, at each of which he was compelled to repeat every number of the program because of the vociferous audience reaction." During this time he also appeared at the Paris Opera. Kipnis became an American citizen in 1934 at the age of 43, and made the United States his permanent residence in 1938 in part as a renunciation of the activities of the Nazi regime when Austria was annexed that same year.

On January 5, 1940, Kipnis had his much anticipated and surprisingly belated debut at the Metropolitan Opera House in New York city in the role of Gurnemanz. He remained at the Met for the 1940–1946 seasons displaying his formidable talent in the Wagnerian repertory and playing roles such as Boris Godunov, Sarastro, King Mark in Wagner's *Tristan and Isolde,* Baron Ochs, Hermann in Wagner's *Tannhäuser,* Hagen in Wagner's *Die Götterdämmerung,* Arkel in Claude Debussy's *Pelléas and Mélisande,* Fasolt in Wagner's *Das Rheingold,* Rocco in Ludwig van Beethoven's *Fidelio,* Hunding in Wagner's *Die Walküre,* Nilakantha in Leo Delibes's *Lakmé,* and Leporello. Kipnis retired from the opera in 1946. His exit performance at the Met was in the same role as that of his debut, the Gurnemanz he had perfected to such critical adoration.

Kipnis's voice has been described as unusually flexible for his range, and is praised for its high level of refinement and tonal variety. Robin May's *A Companion to the Opera*

notes that critic Steane called him a "miracle among singers" and described his voice as "grandly sonorous." While there are some critics who claim that Kipnis's performances were not unusually inspiring, everyone agrees that his delivery was always technically breathtaking and textbook perfect. Despite his ethnic heritage as a Russian Jew, his training was almost exclusively German, and although he did experiment with the Russian repertory, his fame lay in his mastery of the German roles. The unusual flexibility of his vocal inflection and range that is so often mentioned also allowed him to execute Italian roles as well as German ones, despite the fact that the Italian roles are often more technically challenging. The *International Dictionary of Opera* explains, "Throughout his career he dabbled in Russian repertoire, but he was never considered a Russian singer in style, vocal quality, or instinct. He was, in fact, the finest German–style bass of his epoch. The smooth voice, spacious phrasing, and sheer vocal resource, however, were a marked departure from the accepted German bass school of his time, which emphasized cavernous black sound at the bottom and 'barking' the upper register with disregard for pitch. Instead of black sound Kipnis produced a deep rich velvety sound, never 'barked' the upper register, and was scrupulous in matters of pitch. This vocal culture enabled him to sing the big Italian roles with extraordinary smoothness." The beauty of his voice was matched always with tremendous stage presence, the combination of which catapulted him to international operatic fame.

Lieder Master

In addition to his obvious talents as an operatic singer, Kipnis was also a celebrated and critically acclaimed interpreter and singer of *lieder* (German for "songs"—short, poetic songs referred to in English as "art songs"). Critics quoted in *Musicians Since 1900* called Kipnis "not only one of the greatest contemporary operatic basses but also one of the foremost living masters of the *Lied*" as well as "the greatest male interpreter of Debussy's song literature." The entry on Kipnis in *The Music Makers* states that "His voice had remarkable flexibility and great range, enabling him to perform *lieder* as effectively as opera." His success as a *lieder* soloist was rare for his range, as the entry in *American National Biography* explains, "He was renowned for the ease, nobility, sonority, and security of his voice in all registers throughout a two—octave compass. . . a somewhat rare achievement for a deep—timbred bass singer." He recorded the *Lieder* of Hugo Wolf for a special issue by the Hugo Wolf Son Society, and he regarded it as some of his finest work.

Life After the Opera

Kipnis spent much of his time after retiring from the opera circuit recording his various roles and the songs of the masters. He is one of the most widely recorded singers of his time and his recordings were invaluable to operatic culture. He was surprisingly versatile as a recording artist, and recorded opera, *lieder,* and classical and contemporary vocal works. In 1937 Kipnis was sought out by the Brahms Song Society to sing on both volumes of their special recording of the Brahms repertory. He gave master classes in voice at the

Julliard School of Music, the New York College of Music, and the Berkshire Music Center in Tanglewood. Kipnis died May 14, 1978, in a convalescent home in Westport, Connecticut. His renditions of classic bass roles and his gift for bringing the pleasures of *lieder* to an international audience have secured Alexander Kipnis an exalted place in operatic history and culture.

Books

American National Biography, Volume 12, Oxford University Press, 1999.
Baker's Biographical Dictionary of Musicians, Eighth Edition, Schirmer Books, 1992.
Biographical Dictionary of American Music, Parker Publishing Company, 1973.
A Companion to the Opera, Hippocrene Books, Inc., 1977.
Encyclopedia of the Opera, Hill and Wang, 1963.
The Metropolitan Opera Encyclopedia, Simon and Schuster, 1987.
Musicians Since 1900: Performers in Concert and Opera, H.W. Wilson Company, 1978.
The Music Makers, Harry N. Abrams, Inc., 1979.
The New Grove Dictionary of American Music, Volume 2, Macmillan Press Limited, 1986.
The Oxford Dictionary of Opera, Oxford University Press, 1992.

Online

"Serbian Language Class," *Saint Sava Serbian Orthodox Church of Boston,* http://www.allston.com/st_sava/school (January 2, 2004).
"Serbian Literature," *Vojvodina,* http://www.vojvodina.srbija-info.yu/ingles/kultura/kultura1 (January 2, 2004). □

Olga Korbut

Soviet gymnast Olga Korbut (born 1955) revolutionized the sport of gymnastics with her charm and incredible flexibility. She captured the hearts of millions of television viewers worldwide and brought gymnastics to the forefront of the Olympics.

Early Interest in Gymnastics

Korbut was born May 16, 1955, in the town of Grodno, close to the border of Poland in the former Belorussian Soviet Socialist Republic, which is now Belarus. Her father, Valentin, was an engineer, while her mother, Valentina, was a cook. She was the youngest of four sisters.

One sister, Ludmilla, was involved in gymnastics, and Korbut followed her lead and started training. She was small, but her size made her more determined to succeed. She could run faster and jump higher than all the other children.

When she was eleven, Korbut qualified to attend the Soviet Union's government sports school. More than 500 girls attended the school. She started training with Yelena

Volchetskaya, a gold medal winner from the 1964 Olympics. Volchetskaya saw Korbut's potential and brought her to the attention of the man who ran the school, Renald Knysh. They both were impressed with her determination and fearlessness. She was always willing to try new flips, jumps, and twists.

New Moves

In 1967, Korbut entered the Belorussian junior gymnastics championships. In 1968, she won gold medals in the vault, balance beam, and uneven bars at the Spartakiade school championship, competing against some of the best gymnasts in the Soviet Union.

At her first Soviet national championship in 1969, the age rules were altered to allow the fourteen-year-old Korbut to participate. She performed two new moves that she had been working on with her coaches. The Korbut Salto was a backwards-aerial somersault, launching and then landing back on the four-inch wide balance beam. Even more daring was the Korbut Flip, an unprecedented back flip on the uneven bars. She placed fifth in her first major competition, but controversy surrounded the unorthodox moves. Some officials complained that they were not in keeping with traditional gymnastics. Others were concerned that they were dangerous.

Korbut became the Soviet vault champion at the Soviet national championships in 1970 and took eighth place overall. She was taken along to the 1970 world championships as a reserve competitor. Soviet officials were concerned that she was too young to compete, but they allowed her to travel with the team to gain the experience of an international meet. Although she did not compete, she did perform for a panel of judges, who were very impressed.

In 1971, she placed fourth in the Soviet national championships. She also earned her Master of Sports title, granted to those who attained excellence in sports. At the time, she was the youngest person to be granted the honor. She decided that she had two goals: to win a gold medal at the Olympics and to finish school.

She finished third in the Soviet national championships in 1972. She then participated in the Riga Cup in Latvia, her first international championship, and won. This allowed the Korbut Salto, the Korbut Flip, and a new move, the Korbut Flic-Flac, to earn wider recognition.

1972 Munich Olympics

Korbut completed school and went to the USSR Cup, which was also the selection trial for the Olympics. She was named as an alternate to the Soviet team. When a teammate was injured, Korbut was added to the squad. Her yarn-bound pigtails made her seem much younger than her seventeen years. She was four feet eleven inches tall, weighed 90 pounds, and was the smallest of all the competitors in the 1972 Olympics.

Five days before the team left for Munich, West Germany, Korbut decided to change her musical selection for the floor exercise. Her coaches strongly advised against it, concerned that she would disrupt her peformance, but Korbut was insistent. Her mother's advice to Korbut before she left, according to the book *Comebacks: Heroic Returns,* was: "Be careful, be first, be joyful."

In the first days of the Olympics, Korbut helped the Soviets win the team gold medal. She also captured the attention of television viewers around the world who watched her joyfully fly through her routines. Most of the Soviet competitors were stern, but Korbut was smiling. People tuned in to see her incredible flexibility but also to see her spirit.

Next came the all-around competition, where gymnasts competed in all four exercises: vault, balance beam, uneven parallel bars, and floor exercise. The athlete with the highest combined score wins the gold medal. Korbut vaulted well, scoring a 9.7 out of 10. She then scored a 9.75 on the floor exercise. As she faced the uneven parallel bars, she was in third place, just 0.15 from first place. Then she fell apart. She bobbled on her start, and it seemed to disrupt her rhythm. Then she caught her toe but recovered. She lost her composure and lost her balance, falling off the bars. She completed her performance and headed back to the bench. The television cameras followed her to watch her cry her eyes out. The world watched and sympathized.

The next day, Korbut returned to the arena and made an incredible comeback. She executed a back flip on the balance beam and a back flip on the uneven bars. Her incredibly flexible body performed contortions that amazed everyone watching. She won individual gold medals on the balance beam and the floor exercise and a silver medal on the uneven bars.

Stardom

The world was enamored of Korbut. Within days, she had catapulted to stardom. The press followed her everywhere. People paid attention when she said she liked ketchup. It was news when she told a reporter, "Life is marvelous now because I have a tape recorder." The American Broadcasting Company's "Wide World of Sports" named her Athlete of the Year. In early 1973, the Associated Press conducted on international poll and named Korbut as Athlete of the Year, marking the first time in more than forty years that an athlete from a communist country received the honor.

Following the Olympics, Korbut attracted huge crowds as she toured the United States and Europe. She visited President Richard Nixon at the White House. She also met with the prime minister and the queen of England. She received bags full of fan mail. Some of it was simply addressed to "Olga, Moscow."

Interest in gymnastics exploded around the world. In the United States, there were 15,000 practicing gymnasts prior to the 1972 Olympics. A decade later, there were 150,000.

Korbut returned to Grodno to attend college. In 1975, she was honored by the United Nations Educational, Scientific and Cultural Organization for bringing the world together. They named her the Woman of the Year and awarded her with the "gold tuning fork."

1976 Montreal Olympics

Korbut returned to the Olympics in 1976 in Montreal. Once again, she was a part of a gold-meal-winning Soviet team. She also took an individual silver medal on the balance beam. However, that year there was a new darling of gymnastics. A fourteen-year-old named Nadia Comaneci scored the first perfect 10 in Olympic history.

Officially retiring from gymnastic competition in 1977, Korbut returned home and completed college. She then accepted a position as head coach of the Belorussian team in Minsk. She was the first inductee when the Gymnastics Hall of Fame opened in 1987. She married Soviet rock star Leonid Bortkevich, and in 1979 they had a son, Richard.

Chernobyl

On April 26, 1986, disaster struck the Soviet Union. There was a nuclear disaster at Chernobyl, 180 miles from Korbut's home in Minsk. She and her family could see the radiation cloud, but they were never warned to stay inside. "I was at my home in Minsk when Chernobyl happened, and they didn't tell us for three or four days," *People* reported Korbut as saying. "You in the West knew first. When people began hearing bits of information, they felt panicky. They were afraid to drink the water, breathe the air, afraid of everything. We were all outdoors, because it was close to the May 1 celebrations, and we were planting gardens and enjoying the spring. If they had told us Chernobyl had exploded, we would have stayed inside and maybe avoided those early heavy doses of radiation.'' She was outraged at the government for endangering the lives of so many people.

Korbut and her husband sent their son to live with relatives in New Brunswick, New Jersey, in order to keep him away from any further effects of the radiation. ''Most of the doctors say the biggest thing you can do for kids is take them out of the country. But so many people can't do that,'' she told *People.*

While traveling in the United States in 1989, she found that she had developed thyroid problems, most likely the result of her exposure to the fallout from the nuclear disaster. In 1990, she became the spokesperson for the Emergency Help for Children Foundation, a nonprofit agency set up to help the victims of the Chernobyl disaster.

Life in the United States

Korbut and her husband moved to the United States in 1991, settling with their son in Atlanta, Georgia, where she continued her coaching. Korbut and Bortkevich divorced in 2000. In 2001, an eviction notice was served at the house in Atlanta. Bortkevich had bought out Korbut's interest in the house during divorce proceedings. Korbut had not lived there for some time, but her son was still there. Officials were surprised to find $30,000 in counterfeit bills as well as child pornography. Officials moved everything from the home, including Korbut's Olympic memorabilia. ''She hasn't lived there for two years,'' Andre Gleen, a part owner in the facility where Korbut coached, told *Sports Illustrated.* Korbut was not implicated in the case.

In January 2002, Korbut was arrested for shoplifting $19 worth of food from a Publix grocery store in Atlanta, Georgia. She avoided prosecution by paying a fine and agreeing to take a ''life values'' course. She also agreed never to shop at Publix again.

Despite taking a few tumbles, Korbut once again staged a comeback. She married Alex Voinich. In 2002, she moved to Scottsdale, Arizona, where she trained young gymnasts. She also presented clinics and made motivational speeches. Her legacy remained untarnished. Almost single-handedly, Olga Korbut revolutionized the sport of gymnastics, making it a highlight of the Summer Olympics for many decades.

Books

Bailer, Darice, *Solid Gold: Gymnastic Stars,* Random House, 2000.
Coffey, Wayne, *Olga Korbut,* Blackbirch Press, 1992.
Great Women in Sports, Visible Ink Press, 1996.
Jennings, Jay, *Comebacks: Heroic Returns,* Silver Burdett Press, 1991.

Periodicals

People, March 4, 1991; July 15, 1996.
Sports Illustrated, Fall 1992; February 18, 2002; April 22, 2002.

Online

''Olga Korbut,'' *Olga Korbut,* http://www.olgakorbut.com (January 9, 2004). □

Serge Koussevitzky

One of the most important symphony conductors in the United States during the first half of the twentieth century, Serge Koussevitzky (1874–1951) not only introduced American audiences to the works of modern Russian and European composers, he championed young American composers. In this regard Koussevitzky played a pivotal role in the development of modern American classical music. He was also instrumental as an educator, with probably his most important contribution in this field being the establishment of the Berkshire Music Center in Massachusetts.

Early Musical Training

Serge Alexandrovich Koussevitzky was born in Vishny-Volochok, Russia, a small town about 160 miles northwest of Moscow, on July 26, 1874. He was born into a musical family: his father played either violin or double bass (possibly both), his mother was a pianist, and one of his siblings, Adolf, was a well-known musician, teacher, and conductor in Moscow. Koussevitzky's mother died when he was three years old and he and his siblings were faced with the strict discipline of his father. At age eight Koussevitzky came under the tutelage of a local woman named Maria Fedorovna Ropenberg who not only mitigated the elder Koussevitzky's harshness, but also taught young Serge piano. Soon afterward he began composing music for the local theater and by the time he was twelve years old was touring with the theater troupe (throughout the local district). Legend has it that Koussevitzky ran away from home at age fourteen to study in Moscow, but that is only partly correct. Koussevitzky did take private cello lessons in Moscow but he seldom stayed there more than a night. In Vishny-Volochok and elsewhere—such as on the train to Moscow or on pleasure boats on the Volga River—he took odd jobs as a musician to pay for his studies and the cost of his travel to and from Moscow. In the fall of 1891 he did, however, make his way to Moscow to begin serious musical studies. He was seventeen years old and he may have been preceded to Moscow by his brother Adolf (the records are unclear).

Koussevitzky first applied for admission to study at the Imperial Moscow Conservatory but was told to reapply in the spring. Instead the impatient Koussevitzky applied for admission at the School of the Moscow Philharmonic Society, where he was given the same reply. This time Koussevitzky would not take no for an answer and the strong-willed youth managed to convince the director, Pyotr Adamovich Shostakovsky, of his desire and his merit. Since the penniless Koussevitzky could not afford the tuition he was given the choice to study either trombone or double bass, both of which came with a scholarship and a stipend (since

The exact date of this conversion is unknown, but it was sometime before joining the Bolshoi Theater Orchestra, which barred Jews.

Koussevitzky gave his first solo performance in 1896 in Moscow—though with the double bass, especially at that time, solo was an elastic word. More often than not Koussevitzky was assisted by a tenor. Koussevitzky also performed in chamber groups, either in trio or quartet. When Koussevitzky's old professor, Rambousek, died in March 1901 Koussevitzky not only stepped in to fill his position as leader of the Bolshoi Orchestra bass section, but also began teaching double bass at the Philharmonic School.

The exact date when Koussevitzky married his first wife, ballet dancer Nadezheda Galat, has been lost, though most scholars place the year as no later than 1902. By this time Koussevitzky's reputation had extended to St. Petersburg and he was about to make the leap onto the international stage. On March 27, 1903, he gave his first performance outside of Russia when he performed at Berlin's Singakademie. He gave a second Berlin performance in December 1903 and performed elsewhere in central Europe at this time. Koussevitzky also began to compose music for the double bass, since the repertoire for the instrument was extremely slim. In 1902 he composed a concerto in F-sharp minor, but he did not perform it until February 1905 with the Moscow Philharmonic. By then the force of Koussevitzky's musicianship and personality more than carried the music.

The year 1905 was a momentous one in Koussevitzky's life. Along with the premier of his composition came two major changes, one personal and the other professional. First, he divorced Nadezheda Galat and on September 8, 1905, married Natalya Ushkov in Dresden, Germany. She was the daughter of a prosperous tea merchant whose Moscow mansion was also a salon that Koussevitzky regularly visited. Thereafter Koussevitzky's musical ambition would be realized with the aid of Natalya and her family fortune. Not long after their marriage Koussevitzky resigned from the Bolshoi Theater Orchestra. In a letter to the press—which was first printed in *Russkoye Slovo* (Russian Word) and reprinted in *Muzykalnaya Gazeta* (Musical Gazette)—Koussevitzky outlined his reasons for quitting the orchestra. These included low pay and poor treatment, but worst of all, as quoted by Moses Smith in *Koussevitzky*, he wrote: "The deadening spirit of police bureaucracy, which has penetrated that domain where, it would seem, it should have no place whatever, into the domain of pure art, has converted the artists into artisans and intellectual work into the forced labor of slaves."

Embarked on a Conducting Career

Koussevitzky and his wife then decamped for Berlin where, in one of the great career changes in twentieth-century music, Koussevitzky forsook that of a promising musician (albeit on a "lesser" instrument) to become an orchestra conductor. He initially gave performances in Berlin, Leipzig, and other central European cities, but it was his acquaintance with conductor Artur Nikisch that altered his career. Interestingly, Koussevitzky did not attend Nikisch's

students seldom chose these instruments). Koussevitzky chose the double bass.

Koussevitzky's double-bass professor was Josef Rambousek, a Czech who was the first double-bass player at Moscow's Bolshoi Theater. Within a year Rambousek had pronounced his gifted student a virtuoso; Koussevitzky, in 1892, even performed with Tchaikovsky (on piano) in the latter's rooms. They played the *Andante Cantabile* from Tchaikovsky's first string quartet. While a gifted musician Koussevitzky was less prodigal when it came to musical theory, and this lifelong weakness not only effected his later career as a conductor but gave rise to various negative rumors.

A Virtuoso Double Bassist

Koussevitzky's performing remained unmatchable. Part of the secret of his success he claimed was that he tuned his instrument a tone higher for added clarity. On October 1, 1894, he joined the Bolshoi Theater Orchestra where he performed for both opera and ballet. Soon after this triumph, and while still attending school, Koussevitzky tried out for the position of double bassist for the orchestra of the St. Petersburg's Imperial Opera. He was the first to audition and after he performed half of the other applicants did not even bother to try out. Koussevitzky was awarded the position but refused, ostensibly because he would be performing in opera only. Many have come to believe that the whole episode was merely a prank. A personal aspect of Koussevitzky at this time is that he converted to Christianity.

conducting class. Instead he studied technique by watching Nikisch conducting during concerts; he also studied the techniques of Gustav Mahler and others. He then set about practicing a composition with a piano for accompaniment. Critics and scholars have argued the efficacy of Koussevitzky's method, but he always maintained that that was the only way he could learn the art of conducting.

Koussevitzky's debut as a conductor came on January 23, 1908, in Berlin's Beethoven Hall. He hired the Berlin Philharmonic Orchestra (another benefit of having wealthy in-laws) to perform a program of Russian music: Tchaikovsky's *Romeo and Juliet*; Rachmaninoff's C minor Piano Concerto, with Rachmaninoff as piano soloist; the entr'acte to Taneiev's *Orestes*; and Glière's Symphony in C minor. The debut was by-and-large judged a success by the critics. At this time Koussevitzky continued performing, appearing on stage in Paris, London, Budapest, and Dresden, as well as Berlin. In 1909 Koussevitzky branched out even further when he and his wife founded the Russian Music Publishing House. He also returned to Russia that year.

Koussevitzky spent the years prior to the First World War performing primarily in Moscow and St. Petersburg. He was an advocate of the music of Alexandr Scriabin, whom he had met in 1908 in Geneva. His music publishing company was also on firm ground, and after 1910 he had near exclusive rights to the work of Igor Stravinsky, with the exception of *The Firebird*. In 1910 Koussevitzky went on tour in Berlin, London, and Paris; his conducting had developed to such a degree that even Nikisch was impressed. On his return to Russia Koussevitzky enacted a bold plan to bring music to the provinces. He hired a steamer to sail down the Volga River to the Caspian Sea with a symphony orchestra. This proved so successful that he repeated his Volga tours annually right up until the First World War. Back in Moscow for the 1910–1911 season, Koussevitzky had enormous plans: he was going to organize his own orchestra to offer concerts at prices the masses could afford, he was going to build a concert hall, and nearby that he was going to build apartments to house musicians. Of all that only the orchestra was organized—for the 1911–1912 season—and named the New Symphony Concert Union.

After war broke out in 1914 Koussevitzky traveled between Moscow and Petrograd (as St. Petersburg was then called) and in the summer of 1915 conducted daily performances in Moscow. With the Bolshevik Revolution in October 1918, however, Koussevitzky's days in Russia were numbered. Between the Soviet expropriation of much of the Ushkov fortune and the bureaucratic rules applied to culture, Koussevitzky decided to immigrate first to Germany, then France. He and his wife made a bungled attempt to cross the Soviet border on their own, but by 1920 he had received permission to leave.

Koussevitzky remained in Paris for four years where his stature was as high as it had been in Russia. During the 1923–1924 season he organized the *Concerts Koussevitzky*, introducing the work of Sergei Prokofiev to the West. By then American music critics, especially Olin Downes of the *New York Times*, had begun to take notice of Koussevitzky. After rejecting two offers from U.S. orchestras

he decided to accept the baton of the Boston Symphony Orchestra in 1924. Before leaving France Koussevitzky was awarded the Cross of the Legion of Honor.

Joined the Boston Symphony Orchestra

Koussevitzky was conductor and music director of the Boston Symphony Orchestra (BSO) for 25 years and his impact on the American musical scene was tremendous. He literally transformed the BSO into a world-class orchestra. In 1931, to celebrate the 50th anniversary of the BSO, Koussevitsky commissioned works by Stravinsky, George Gershwin, Maurice Ravel, and others. During Koussevitzky's tenure as conductor the BSO presented 128 world premieres by such giants of twentieth-century music as Aaron Copland, Roger Sessions, Prokofiev, Paul Hindemith, Gershwin, Stravinsky, Lukas Foss, Samuel Barber, and Arnold Schönberg as well as Koussevitzky's own *Passacaglia on a Russian Theme*. Under his guidance the works of American composers such as Copland, Gershwin, Leonard Bernstein, and Walter Piston, to name a few, were showcased. During the years of the Second World War the Koussevitzky Music Foundation commissioned 20 works.

Perhaps Koussevitzky's most lasting contribution to American music was the establishment in 1940 of the Berkshire (now Tanglewood) Music School, to train conductors, musicians, and composers; in the early years Koussevitzky served as instructor for the conductors and his students included Foss and Bernstein. The BSO had been performing at the Berkshire Music Festival since 1936 and Koussevitzky and the orchestra quickly became linked with the summer festival.

Serge Koussevitsky died in retirement on June 4, 1951, in Boston, Massachusetts.

Books

Leichtentritt, Hugo, *Serge Koussevitzky, the Boston Symphony Orchestra, and the New American Music*, AMS Press/Harvard University Press, 1946.
Smith, Moses, *Koussevitzky*, Allen, Towne & Heath, 1947.

Online

"Serge Alexandrovich Koussevitzky (1874–1951)," http://www.classical.net/music/guide/society/krs/koussbio.html (December 22, 2003). □

Miroslav Krleza

Yugoslavian novelist, poet, essayist, playwright, translator, editor, diarist, polemic writer, lexicographer, and cultural and political force Miroslav Krleza (1893–1981) was a major twentieth century literary voice.

Military Years

The son of Miroslav (a city clerk) and Ivanka Krleza, Miroslav Krleza was born on July 7, 1893, in Zagreb, Yugoslavia (or Croatia; a newly-created country which included South Slavic lands of former Hasberg and the kingdoms of Serbia and Montenegro), in the Austro-Hungarian Empire. Krleza completed the lower grades of secondary school in Zagreb. In 1908, he began preparatory military school in Peczuj and was also educated at Lucoviceum military academy in Budapest, Hungary.

In 1912, Krleza defected from the Austro-Hungarian Empire and volunteered for the Serbian army. He was quickly suspected by the Serbs of being an Austrian spy and Serbia kicked him out of the army and forced him to return to Austria-Hungary. The Austrians arrested him. He was then stripped of his officer's rank and sent to the Eastern front of World War I—Galicia—as a common soldier.

Controversy Began

Krleza's literary career began with idealism and romanticism in 1914, when he wrote his early drama *Legenda*. He published other first poems and plays in that same year, when he joined the Austrian Army. At the conclusion of his Austrian army service in 1918, he wrote the drama *Kraljevo* and returned to Zagreb. His writing took on an embitterment and antiwar sentiment, opposing the Yugoslavian anarchist regime and conflicting with freemasons, nationalists, and clerics.

Krleza married Bela Kangrga and, in 1918, became a member of the Communist Party. The following year, he founded a left-wing literary review, *Plamen* (Flame). In 1920, the play *Galicija* was slated to open but was shut down an hour before it began. Krleza was already a controversial figure, with the attention of the authorities.

Writing Career Began

In 1922, Krleza published *Adam i Eva* (Adam and Eve), an experimental, expressionist play. With *Adam i Eva,* as *Pegasos* noted, Krleza completed his "transformation from a young idealist into a socially conscious artist." In 1922, he published *Hrvatski bog Mars* (The Croatian God Mars), a short story collection that depicted the exploitation of peasants and the miserable condition of the Croatian soldier. *Hrvatski bog Mars* proved to be his most notable short story collection. In 1923, Krleza founded the periodical *Knjizevna republika* (Literary Republic). In 1924, he produced the failed *Galicija* as *O logoru* and published *Novele* (Novellas).

Best Writing Years

The late 1920s to the mid-1930s were to see the majority of Krleza's best work. In 1928, he published the dramatic trilogy—considered by some to be his best drama—that began with *Gospoda Glembajevi* (The Glembajs) and *U agoniji* (Death-throes). The trilogy documents the disintegration of the Glembajs, their move from peasantry to affluence while degenerating morally, and the fall of bour-

geois society. All in all, Krleza's dealing with the Glembajs spanned eleven stories and three plays. In 1932, the trilogy was completed with the publication of *Leda*.

In 1932, Krleza published a poetry collection—*Knjiga Lirike* (A Book of Lyric Poetry)—which predicted the victory of Socialism. In 1934, he founded the periodical *Danas* (Today). In 1936, Krleza published *Balade Petrice Kerempuha* (The Ballad of Patricia Kerempuh), written in the Kajkavian (Croatian *kajkavski*) dialect, interspersed with Latin, German, Hungarian, and archaic Croatian highly stylized idiom. The story in *Balade* spanned more than five centuries and is regarded as Krleza's best poetry.

Writing Continued

In 1937, Krleza published the poetry collection, *Pjesme u tmini* (Poems in the Darkness). A year later, he began the blanket-novel *Banket u Blitvi* (Banquet in Blitva), which dealt with the political situation in Europe in the interwar period. *Banket u Blitvi* takes place in a fictional country, Blitvian. The word "Blitvian" was an unflattering play on the Croatian word for Lithuania.

Political Controversy Heightened

Krleza published *Dijalekticki antibarbarus* in 1939, mocking the orthodox Stalinists. For his controversial views on art and intellectual freedom and for his unwillingness to give open support of Stalin's purges, Krleza was expelled from the Communist Party after the publication of *Dijalekticki antibarbarus.* Meanwhile, he founded the periodical *Pecat* (Seal).

During World War II, Krleza remained in Zagreb, but fell silent and was harassed by the pro-Nazi Croatian government. He refused to join the partisans headed by Communist leader Josip Broz Tito—an old friend—for fear of the Communists' brutality and zeal. He refused to cooperate with the Quisling government, putting his life in danger multiple times.

Political Rehabilitation

After the war, Krleza supported a post-war Communist regime. From 1945 to 1946, Krleza founded the periodical *Republika* (Republic) and in 1947 was elected Vice President of the Academy of Science and Art. In 1951, he became Director of Yugoslav Lexicographical Institute in Zagreb, a position he would hold until 1981. As such, he was the editor-in-chief of *Encyclopedia Yugoslavia.*

Introspective Writing

In 1952, Krleza delivered a famous speech at a writer's conference in Ljubljana. In it, he attacked social realism and Stalinist aesthetics and the result was the strengthening of his following among the younger Yugoslavian artists. In that year, he published *Djetinjstvo u Agramu* (Childhood in Zagreb), which documented his growing self-awareness, and in 1956, he published a memoir/diary, *Davni dani,* (Olden Days), which grappled with the world outside himself.

From 1958 to 1961, Krleza served as President of the Writer's Union. From 1962 to 1977, he published *Zastave* (Banners), a six-volume novel that provides a panoramic view of European life between 1912 and 1922, complete with biographical reminiscences. In 1967, he published *Razgovori s Miroslavom Krlezom,* in which he supported Croatian national and cultural claims and aired his skeptical views of democratic progress in the Balkans. In 1977, he published the seven volume *Dvenici* (Diaries), chronicling his impressions on the aesthetic, political, literary, social, personal, and philosophical. Krleza died in Zagreb, Yugoslavia, on December 29, 1981.

A Significant Cultural Figure

Krleza holds a simultaneous position as the shaper of both Croatian culture and the European avant garde movement. The Swarthmore College website asserted that he "is generally considered the most significant figure in Croatian literature in the 20th century." The Yugoslavian government banned most of his work until 1940, and, despite official restrictions, Krleza turned out plays, novels, short stories, poetry, and essays that would draw praise for years to come. By the 1950s—during his lifetime—he had become a driving force in Yugoslavian culture.

Krleza's themes and politics were sometimes ambiguous. His style was baroque and highly eloquent. He wrote with materialistic convictions, strong emotion, Marxist ideals, liberal philosophy, as a socialist, in defense of personal freedom, for radical humanism, and in a highly controversial way. *Pegasos* said about Krleza, "Throughout his life Krleza stood in the forefront of the struggle against petit-bourgeois attitudes and backwardness in general. He wrote with enormous creative energy, and defended his views fiercely and fearlessly."

Publishers Weekly called him a "convinced communist" and a "shrewd observer of man as social animal." He wrote with disdain for the robber-baron capitalism of an inter-war Croatia and rejected his Catholic upbringing for atheistic existentialism. Many of his works proclaimed his constant faith in the power of humanity, his socialist revolutionary ideas, belief in moral and artistic integrity, and his convictions of artistic and intellectual liberty.

Krleza was attracted to Marxist ideas because of his impressions of the Soviet revolution, but he disdained Stalinism and all totalitarian systems. Because of this, he was regarded with suspicion by fellow Marxists. His influences included Arthur Schopenhauer, Friedrich Nietzche, Feuerbach, Karl Marx, Charles Darwin, Vladimir Lenin, Scandinavian drama, French symbolism, and Austrian and German expressionism and modernism. His memberships included the Yugoslav Writers' Union (as president), Yugoslav Academy of Science and Art (as vice president), and the Yugoslav National Assembly (as deputy).

Krleza wrote numerous essays on politics, literary criticism, and other topics, vehemently defending and proclaiming his beliefs. His essays contain both his best and worst work (thanks to the occasional apologetic pro-Communist rhetoric) and are contained in more than 20 collected volumes. *Wicapedia* said about his essays,

"Encyclopedic knowledge and polemical passion inform the meditations on various aspects and personalities of culture . . . , political anatomies of history both contemporary and medieval . . . , vignettes on art and music—all is covered in this veritable anatomy of European history and culture."

Krleza wrote several plays about the hardships of Croatian peasants, contrasted with aristocratic decadence. His plays are "characterized by straightforward dialogue and merciless revelation of social injustice," according to *Pegasos.*

Only a small portion of Krleza's work has been published in English, including *Povratek Filipa Latinovicza* (The Return of Philip Latinovicz), his most highly praised novel; *Cvrcak pod vodopadom* (The Cricket Beneath the Waterfall), six stories about Eastern Europe during the early part of the twentieth century; *Na rubu pameti* (On the Edge of Reason), a first-person narrative; and *Selected Correspondence.*

Books

The Dictionary of Literary Biography, Volume 147, Gale, 1994.

Periodicals

Kirkus Reviews, December 15, 2002.
Publishers Weekly, September 25, 1995.

Online

"Miroslav Krleza," *BiblioMonde,* www.bibliomonde.net (January 10, 2004).
"Miroslav Krleza," *Contemporary Authors Online, Biography Resource Center,* http://galenet.galegroup.com/servlet/BioRC (January 10, 2004).
"Miroslav Krleza," *Pegasos,* www.kirjasto.sci.fi (January 10, 2004).
"Miroslav Krleza," *Swarthmore College,* www.swarthmore.edu (January 10, 2004).
"Miroslav Krleza," *Wikipedia,* en2.wikipedia.org (January 10, 2004). □

Julie Krone

Overcoming gender prejudice, her tiny stature, and a series of debilitating injuries, Julie Krone (born 1963) became thoroughbred racing's top female jockey and the first woman to win a Triple Crown race and be installed in the sport's Hall of Fame.

Krone was not the first woman to compete in the male-dominated world of thoroughbred racing—her entry into the sport came almost a decade after several female pioneers fought difficult battles to become jockeys. But the prejudice against women succeeding as jockeys still remained when Krone started her career. Krone soon proved that female jockeys could be as tough and competitive as men.

Childhood Dreams

Judi Krone was a riding instructor and former Michigan state equestrian champion, and she first put her daughter Julie on a horse when the child was only two. Judi Krone was trying to sell a palomino and hoping to demonstrate the steed's gentle nature. The horse trotted out, and the toddler reached down for the reins, tugged them, and brought the horse back. From then on Julie Krone loved horses and had one driving ambition: to ride in races.

Born in Benton Harbor, Michigan, on July 24, 1963, young Julie learned about horses from her mother. "Mom taught me all the ways to introduce a young horse to bridle and saddle, and how to train a horse to want to please a rider, which ultimately creates a positive experience for both horse and rider," Krone wrote in her autobiography, *Riding for My Life*. When Julie was six, the family moved to a farm in nearby Eau Claire. Julie and her older brother, Donnie, had free rein. "There were no fences to keep us in, no locked doors, rules, or set mealtimes," Krone later wrote in her autobiography. "I was as wild as the animals on the farm, and just as free." Her father, Don, was an art teacher and photographer who liked to take shots of young Julie taking back flips off a horse. Her parents did nothing but encourage her to ride, often recklessly. On one occasion she rode bareback and standing into the barn, ducking her head only at the last minute. She won her first ribbon at a horse show in an 18-and-under event when she was only five.

As a child, her main challenge was a horse named Filly. "Filly was elusive, naughty, and at times downright mean," Krone wrote in *Riding for My Life*. Filly would frequently run away with Julie on her back. "I credit Filly with teaching me to ride well. Just by being her nasty self, she taught me more than any other horse or instructor. . . Everything I did with Filly was an experiment. But by experimenting I learned to ride instinctively. There are some things a rider has to learn by touch, by reaction—lessons no instructor can give." When she later became a jockey, Krone would earn a reputation for having a close, instinctive rapport with her mounts. It all came from her immersion in horse riding and training as a youngster, following the lead of her mother but learning everything by doing it herself.

Krone was not interested in school—the only classes she liked were art and gym. Horses were always uppermost in her mind. Sometimes she slept with her whip, and she often dreamed of riding in races. As a sophomore in high school, she almost joined a circus as a trick rider, but changed her mind at the last minute. When she was 15, shortly after her parents divorced, she wrote in her diary: "I'm gonna be the greatest jock in the world because I think I can. I know I can." A few months later, her mother predated her birth certificate by three months so she could pass for 16 years old and get a job as a groom and exercise rider at Churchill Downs in Louisville, Kentucky. She worked there a few months, then raced that summer in Michigan, Indiana, and Ohio. In her senior year she dropped out of high school and moved to Florida to live with her grandparents and work as an exercise rider at Tampa Bay Downs. When she arrived at the track, officials there mistook her at first for a much younger girl, because she was so small. It took a lot of convincing for them to give her a job. Within five weeks, she had won her first race at that track.

Earned Respect

At an adult height of 4 foot 10 inches and barely weighing 100 pounds, Krone was small even for a jockey (whose average height is 5 foot 3 inches). And although other women had become jockeys starting in 1969, prejudice still lingered against the idea that a female could control a 1,200-pound thoroughbred. Krone not only looked like a pixie, she had a squeaky, high-pitched voice that also made it hard for her to command respect. But she learned to compensate. She developed a bone-crushing handshake, and she earned respect by refusing to give into intimidation by other jockeys and patronizing by owners and track officials. Often, other riders colluded against her, closing gaps and boxing her horse in by the rail. "Men just didn't want to be beaten by a little girl," she later wrote in *Riding for My Life*.

From the start, though, her special command of horses' emotional language set her apart from the rest of the pack. She won by coaxing horses rather than by whipping them, using her hands to communicate with her mounts, as she had done since she was a little girl. "She rode in this tight little ball that a horse hardly seemed to notice on its back," wrote *Sports Illustrated*'s Gary Smith. "Other riders had to yank back on a colt that was chomping to run too soon in a race; she barely had to move her hands. Other riders had to slash the whip 15 times down the stretch; she might get the same acceleration with two.''

Though gentle and patient with horses, Krone could be a terror with people who defied her or tried to subjugate her in any way. For years, she figured she needed to be more macho than the men she competed against just in order to survive. ''I thought if I showed any feelings, they would be taken for weakness,'' she told Smith. After jockey Yves Turcotte hit her horse with his whip during a race in 1982, she shoved him off the scales during the post-race weighing. She punched jockey Miguel Rujano in 1986 after his whip hit her ear during a race, and then she hit him with a lawn chair. She was fined in 1989 for fighting with jockey Joe Bravo. These altercations earned her suspensions, but they also sent notice that she refused to give into pressure or intimidation.

Top Rank and Hard Knocks

By age 25, Krone was acknowledged as the best female jockey in history. She was the first woman ever to win five races in one day at a New York track, the first woman ever to win a riding title at a major track, and one of three jockeys ever to win six races on one card. She had ridden 1,200 winners and won $20 million in purses.

Krone had a wild streak that belied her little-girl voice and appearance. Mercurial and exuberant, but occasionally depressed and broken, she drove a red Porsche and never let personal relationships interfere with horse riding. In 1983—the year she won a second track title at Atlantic City and missed four months with a broken back after coming off a horse during a workout—officials at Pimlico Race Course in Maryland found marijuana in her car; she was suspended for 60 days and went into drug rehabilitation.

Even when she had proven herself a winner, Krone had to fight prejudice. Others picked on her riding style because it was so different—and called her a ''diabolical'' rider. She was always patient during races and sometimes was criticized for hanging back in the pack too long, waiting for an opening. But the horses she rode were so responsive to her gentle touch that her smart, studied riding could be mistaken for passivity. And win or lose, she was always kind to her mounts. ''If I don't need to use the whip, I don't,'' she wrote in her autobiography. ''A horse's trip is more enjoyable if I can coax him forward by pushing gently with my hands. . . . If a horse enjoys his race, he's going to try even harder next time.''

In 1992, Krone became the first woman to ride in the Kentucky Derby. The following year, she became the first female winner of a Triple Crown race, riding 13-to-1 long-shot Colonial Affair to victory in the Belmont Stakes—''showing the patience, intelligence and tactical savvy that have made her one of the nation's leading performers in a game long dominated by men,'' wrote William Nack of *Sports Illustrated.* Two months later, in a race accident at Saratoga Springs, New York, Krone was thrown from her horse and kicked in the chest by another horse, bruising her heart and shattering her ankle. Only a heavy protective vest

saved her life. It took her nine months to recuperate and return to riding. ''I felt powerless,'' she wrote. ''I've always been able to take care of myself, fight for myself, depend on myself.'' But she refused to quit. ''I spent years trying to prove how tough a rider I was, trying to show the world that male or female, I was a talent,'' Krone wrote. ''To show any weakness felt like failure to me.''

In 1995, she married television reporter Matt Muzikar, riding six races at Saratoga the day of the wedding. She was back at the track to ride six more races the next morning.

In January 1996, riding at Florida's Gulfstream Park, she suffered another accident, breaking both her hands. That accident made her lose her nerve, and the facade of toughness she had maintained for so many years shattered completely. After six weeks, she returned to riding but did terribly. ''Horses felt my anxiety, they got weird, they reared up,'' she said, according to Mark Miller in *Salon.* ''I had been given a magical talent to positive-image a loser right into the winner's circle. . . . And then suddenly it was all gone, and I was exhausted.'' Krone became suicidal and was diagnosed by a psychiatrist as having post-traumatic stress disorder. She recovered by taking anti-depressants and finally finished her high-school degree.

Comeback

Krone never regained her top form, but by the time she retired in 1999, she had won 3,545 races and more than $81 million in purse, piloting 17 percent of her steeds to the winner's circle. The year she retired, she and Muzikar divorced. In 2001, she married Jay Hovdey, a racing writer. They lived in Del Mar, California, and she took up surfing.

In November 2002, Krone surprised the horse world by coming out of retirement, and she quickly won 20 more races. Unfortunately, it did not take long for another setback. In March 2003 she was in an accident at the starting gate at Santa Anita; she fractured two backbones and suffered three compressed vertebrae. Three months later, showing her customary grit, she was back racing. In the 2003 Del Mar meeting she rode 49 winners, including the $1 million Pacific Classic. In November 2003, Krone became the first woman to win a race in the prestigious Breeders' Cup, on the back of favorite Halfbridled, steering the horse from far outside the pack to win. In December 2003 Krone suffered two fractured ribs at Hollywood Park where she had been in the lead, but later told *Sports Illustrated* she would be back sometime in February.

Krone was inducted into racing's Hall of Fame in 2000. At her acceptance speech, standing atop a milk carton to reach the microphone, she said: ''I want this to be a lesson to all kids everywhere. If the stable gate is closed, climb the fence.''

Books

Krone, Julie, with Nancy Ann Richardson, *Riding for My Life,* Little, Brown, 1995.

Periodicals

Knight-Ridder/Tribune News Service, August 7, 2000; October 24, 2003.

People, December 6, 1993; June 26, 1995; September 11, 1995.

Sports Illustrated, August 24, 1987; May 22, 1989; June 14, 1993; June 13, 1994; May 21, 2001; November 3, 2003; January 26, 2004.

Online

"Julie Krone," *Salon,* http://dir.salon.com/people/bc/2000/12/19/krone/index.html (December 30, 2003). □

Umm Kulthūm

Egyptian-born vocalist Umm Kulthūm (1904-1975) is considered perhaps the most famous singer in the modern Arab world. Her unique and masterful singing style appealed to her fellow Egyptians as well as to other Arabs due to its great range and virtuosity, and for many her singing was a symbol of the Egyptian national spirit during the period from Egypt's emergence from British colonial rule through the first decades of that country's independence.

Kulthūm was born poor in Tamayet-el-Zahayra, a rural village in Egypt's Nile delta. Her birth year is a matter of some doubt, but is usually set at 1904. Kuthūm's father, al-Shaykh Ibrāhīim al-Sayyid al-Baltājī, led the local mosque, and her mother, Fatma al-Malījī, kept the family's home. As quoted by Virginia Danielson in her *The Voice of Egypt: Umm Kulthūm, Arabic Song, and Egyptian Society in the Twentieth Century,* Kulthūm once wrote of her village: "The greatest display of wealth was the [village leader's] carriage pulled by one horse.... And there was only one street in the whole village wide enough for the . . . carriage." Her village comprised some 280 households.

Studied the Qur'an

Kulthūm entered a local Islamic religious school when she was about five years old. Memorizing the Qur'an and learning Arabic was the course of study, and she learned to enunciate Arabic, an ability that would bear significantly on her future success. To add to the family income, her father, her brother Khalid, and a nephew would sing religious songs at weddings and other events in the surrounding villages, and Kulthūm learned the songs by hearing her father teach them to the boys. Once when Khalid was ill, Kulthūm was allowed to sing in his place. The repertoire was Qur'anic recitation and other religious songs. Only between five and eight years old, she astounded the audience with the strength of her voice, and she was immediately invited to perform in another village. Word spread, and she soon was in great demand, the family traveling by foot to many villages and towns. She would later remark "that it seemed to her they walked the entire Delta before they ever set foot in Cairo." Because crowds were sometimes rowdy or drunk, Kulthūm's father thought it prudent to dress her as a boy.

Entered the Cairo Milieu

In 1919 or 1920 Kulthūm's father arranged for his daughter's first performance in Cairo. She continued to perform in working-class venues there and also in the homes of wealthy patrons. According to Danielson, "By mid-1922, she was an established performer in the city." The family soon moved to Cairo, where audiences, resentful of condescending Western attitudes toward Arabs and Egypt, hailed the teen as an authentically Egyptian performer because of her roots in the Qur'an and the countryside.

By 1928 Kulthūm had altered her dress and appearance, developed her musical skills, and become a major star. A strengthening Egyptian economy also helped the fortunes of entertainers, and entertainment venues proliferated. Kulthūm was one of a number of young female performers who often entertained primarily male audiences. She no longer concentrated on working-class districts, but was booked into music halls and smaller theaters. Still performing with her father and brothers, she also began to add popular songs to her repertoire. In 1923 Kulthūm began recording and by 1926 had released a number of secular recordings. These sold successfully, in part because her rural following wanted to hear her again. As her popularity grew, she raised her fees, a foreshadowing of the hard-nosed business sense she would develop. She also commissioned new religious texts to be set to music for her to perform.

Part of Kulthūm's education in this period included reading and memorizing poetry and analyzing its form. She also developed her vocal flexibility, learned to play a musical instrument, and learned a new type of song involving difficult melodies. She also studied composition. One teacher in particular, al-Shaykh Abu 'l-'Ila Muhammad, helped her master her strong voice and learn skills for harmonizing meaning and sound. It was felt to be a uniquely Arab and Egyptian style. "He taught me to understand the words before I learned the song and sang it," Kulthūm later recalled of the man who coached her until his death in 1927. As Danielson explained, "the extent to which she pursued musical training distinguished her from most of her peers."

Became Established as a Star

The year 1926 proved to be a watershed year for Kulthūm. She began to wear fashionable dresses and sing love songs written specifically for her, and often drew from a repertoire of completely new songs. She also replaced her family accompanists with a professional instrumental ensemble, called a takht. She hired experts with good reputations, bringing a sophisticated, modern tone to her performances. The takht also facilitated a new mode of singing that became her trademark: As described by Danielson, it was "the solo rendition of sophisticated texts shaped in relation to audience response calling for varied repetition of lines and supported by creative but unintrusive heterophonic accompaniment." Kulthūm was a country girl no longer. Before long she was even the object of imitators. She entered the 1930s at the top of Egypt's roster of female performers, and her wise business management insulated her from the hard economic times ahead.

In the 1930s Kulthūm began one of the best-loved traditions of her career when she started to perform on weekly radio broadcasts. Her live Thursday-night sessions "were undoubtedly her best-known venture, and she continued them almost every season of her career until 1973," noted Danielson. Thursday is significant as the eve of the Muslim holy day. Although some criticized the performances initially, Kulthūm persisted, characteristically determined to follow a path she thought would be productive. Furthermore, the ambitious singer took the production of the concerts into her own hands, negotiated with theaters and arranged advertising, all of which increased her profits. The live broadcasts "institutionalized the first Thursday of every month as 'Umm Kulthūm Night,' " explained Danielson. Kulthūm was at the same time seeking and nourishing friendships with influential men and women within elite Egyptian society. She also learned to cultivate a positive relationship with the press, which had criticized her lack of sophistication in earlier years, and she was diligent in controlling what newspapers and magazine journalists wrote about her.

In 1935 Kulthūm began a new career in the motion picture industry, starring in a film with a story line she invented about a loyal singing slave girl of thirteenth-century Egypt. Her next film tapped nationalist sentiments at a time when students were demonstrating for independence from Great Britain. The third film opened in 1940. "In each film," wrote Danielson, "Umm Kulthūm cultivated sophistication and respectability in her public image and styled herself as an elegant exponent of Egyptian romanticism." The singer made a total of six films, and in five of them she starred as a singer. The songs from these films often made their way into her performance repertoire, where she could elaborate on them.

Possessed Remarkable Vocal Ability

Kulthūm's vocal ability was multifaceted. Her diction was remarkably clear and her pronunciation of literary Arabic excellent. Her voice was strong, and during much of her career she had the stamina to sing for hours at a time. She could sing over two octaves in the 1930s—in 1955, she could still reach a high G— and could sustain long phrases. She also mastered coloristic change, a trait her listeners appreciated as characteristically Egyptian. She controlled resonance well and mastered falsetto, vibrato, and trilling, combining all these devices with great sensitivity to text and great subtlety; furthermore, she did so extemporaneously. Danielson described the desired virtuosity of Egyptian vocalists: "The first task was the clear and skillful delivery of the initial segment [such as a line or stanza] of the composition. Depending on audience response, the singer would then repeat that section, introducing variations, or go on to the next section of the piece. In the ideal performance the singer would vary one or more lines upon encouragement

from the audience and thus extend a five-minute song to twenty or thirty minutes or more. The song performance was shaped in this way by singer and audience responding to each other." Not only were her abilities outstanding; they were regarded as specifically Egyptian.

Another important feature of her art was its close association with a live audience. She liked to observe an audience from backstage before going out to perform, in order to gauge its mood. Her first song in a performance often served the same purpose. Her artistry enabled her to tailor a performance to each audience's mood and inclinations. Although she repeated favorite songs in many performances, it is said that "she never sang a line the same way twice."

1940s Proved to Be Golden Age

The 1940s have been referred to in Egypt as "The Golden Age of Umm Kulthūm." They were also a particularly tumultuous time for Egypt and the Middle East. The economy was recovering slowly, and resentment toward Europeans and European-influenced Egyptian leaders was growing. Kulthūm's music became less romantic; instead she chose songs that glorified the Egyptian working classes. Her last two films also reflected this new direction, and were among her most popular, despite her age. Also in the 1940s, she set out in a new musical direction, called neoclassical, and she continued to sing the songs from this period into the 1950s. This shift, explained Danielson, "may be viewed . . . as part of a strong, deep social and political current toward reaffirmation of Islam and classical Arab civilization as the bases for social order." Neoclassical music was firmly rooted in classical poetry and tradition and overlaid with new musical devices. Kulthūm helped choose texts for these songs, called qasa'id, and suggested the musical devices. With the end of World War II, Egypt's demands for the withdrawal of British troops grew louder, and the music of Kulthūm became more and more closely associated with such nationalist feeling. It was in this period that she was called the singer who "taught poetry to the masses." She also introduced simpler songs that drew popular attention to the nobility of the Egyptian peasantry. Both these populist songs and the more complex qasa'id were appreciated as decidedly non-Western. Once admired, the West was coming to represent in many Arab minds a materialistic and ultimately destructive approach to life. Western secularism in particular was gaining in disfavor. Kulthūm's strong association with pro-Arab feeling is reflected in the sentiment expressed by one Egyptian that "if you want to know what Arab music is, listen to Umm Kulthūm."

Kulthūm's health began to decline in the late 1940s, and she had already been troubled with liver and gallbladder problems in the 1930s. Her mother, with whom she had lived all her life, died in 1947. Curiosity about the singer's personal life and her apparent decision not to marry had existed since she came to Cairo, but it was quieted in 1954 when she married one of her doctors.

Became Associated with Nationalism, Nasser

The 1950s began badly for Kulthūm because of illness and also because the region's political instability and civil unrest had led to curfews and canceled concerts. In July of 1952, when Egyptian King Farouk was forced to abdicate, events were set in motion that led to the 1956 election of Gamal Abdel Nasser (1918-1970) as president. When Kulthūm heard of the overthrow of Farouk, she returned from vacation immediately and commissioned a national song. Danielson says that "between 1952 and 1960, Kulthūm sang more national songs than at any other time in her life; they constituted almost 50 percent of her repertory, and roughly one-third of her new repertory after 1960." She also began to speak out on social and political questions, and she developed a friendship with Nasser. According to Danielson, "Both were from the lower classes and had utilized opportunities for upward mobility new in their lifetimes. Both were powerful personalities who became skilled at reaching the Egyptian population." Nasser's popularity in the Arab world remained strong even after his death, partly because of his long association with Kulthūm.

Musically, Kulthūm once again changed course during the 1950s, choosing romantic love songs from a new generation of writers. Songwriters were eager to write for her because the association gave a powerful boost to their careers. Possibly with the encouragement of Nasser, she also began an important association with a noted musician of her own generation, Muhammad 'Abd al-Wahhab. Their first collaboration was an unprecedented success and represented a modernizing trend in Kulthūm's repertoire. During this period, she still performed some songs in older styles and themes, many written by Riyad al-Sunbati, who nevertheless introduced piano and electric guitar into his compositions. Another innovation of this time was a long love song with a long instrumental introduction and instrumental improvisation. Many of her new songs shifted emphasis from their vocal to their instrumental aspects, perhaps because, while her voice remained strong, it had altered with age. At the same time, Nasser's expansion of radio and television broadcasting extended her audience.

Following Egypt's humiliating defeat against Israel in 1967, Kulthūm began a series of concerts to raise money for the national treasury. She took her concert to Paris in No-vember of that year, her one and only performance outside the Arab world. Between 1967 and her death these concerts raised over $2.5 million for the Egyptian government.

A Funeral Larger than Nasser's

In 1971 Kulthūm's health worsened, sometimes causing her to cancel concerts, and she gave her last performance in 1973. Finally her heart failed, and she died on February 3, 1975. Mahmoud Fadl, a contemporary Egyptian musician, attended the funeral and wrote on the *Piranha Web site;* "The whole of Cairo turned out for her funeral procession—even more than when Nasser died.... The police immediately lost control of the coffin.... It was claimed by the masses and touched by tens of thousands of hands as it left the square on a whole new route." Danielson wrote that the crowds bore the coffin "for three hours through the streets of Cairo" before taking it to one of Kulthūm's favorite mosques.

Fadl recalled that Kulthūm's Thursday broadcasts "brought public life to a complete stand-still, not only in Cairo and Egypt but in the whole Arab world from Atlantic and Gulf. On any Thursday ... nobody would, nobody could, even try to compete with her." It is said that Nasser "timed his major political speeches carefully around her broadcasts." Decades after her death, Kulthūm's voice continued to be heard on Arab radio stations; according to Fadl, "In Egypt, it seems, only the Nile, the pyramids and Umm Kulthūm are forever."

Books

Danielson, Virginia, *The Voice of Egypt: Umm Kulthūm, Arabic Song, and Egyptian Society in the Twentieth Century,* University of Chicago Press, 1997.
Rough Guide to World Music, Volume 1: *Africa, Europe, and the Middle East,* Rough Guides, 1999.

Periodicals

Ak-Mashriq, November, 1995.

Online

Fadl, Mahmoud, "Personal Memories from the Funeral of Umm Kalthum," http://www.piranha.de/records/english/all_1470r.htm (December 19, 2003).
"Umm Kulthūm," *All Music Guide,* http://www.allmusic.com/cg/amg.dll (December 23, 2003). □

L

Susan La Flesche Picotte

Susan La Flesche Picotte (1865-1915) was the first Native American woman to become a physician. She served her community tirelessly in this capacity, and in others as well—as a missionary, as a representative of her people in the East and in the nation's capital, and as a politically active temperance advocate.

La Flesche Picotte was born June 17, 1865. She was the daughter of Joseph La Flesche (Insta Maza, or "Iron Eye"), who was half Omaha and half white and had become a chief of the Omahas in 1853. Her mother was Mary Gale (Hinnungsnun, or "One Woman"). Her half-brother, Francis La Flesche, was a noted ethnologist and interpreter.

Both her parents worked closely with Presbyterian missionaries in the region. The Omaha tribe was considered by missionaries to be exemplary of what other tribes could become. The federal government had already begun individual allotment of Omaha tribal lands by the 1870s, a process that did not get started among many tribes until the next century. La Flesche Picotte grew up in a frame house on a plot of land in her father's name. Her family was Christian, influential, and respected, and emphasized the importance of education. La Flesche Picotte attended Protestant missionary schools until she was 13, at which time she followed in the footsteps of her sister Susette La Flesche Tibbles and went off to the Elizabeth Institute, a finishing school for young ladies in New Jersey. In 1882 she returned to teach at a mission school on the reservation.

Education and the Connecticut Indian Association

In 1884 La Flesche Picotte enrolled at Hampton Normal and Agricultural Institute. Hampton had been founded with the goal of educating black freedmen but was experimenting at the time with Indian education as well. During her tenure at Hampton, La Flesche Picotte came into contact with the Connecticut Indian Association, which had been founded in Hartford in 1881 and was a branch of the nationwide Women's National Indian Association (founded in Philadelphia in 1879). This group was one of many Protestant women's organizations of the late nineteenth century dedicated to improving the welfare and morality of Native Americans according to the standards and values of middle-class Protestants.

La Flesche Picotte's Presbyterian background provided her with the qualities that would make her an ideal symbol of a "progressive" Indian—an eager to embrace change for her people along Euro-American lines. In 1886 she graduated from Hampton and gave a speech, reprinted in *Relations of Rescue,* which demonstrates the nature of her sense of mission: "From the outset the work of an Indian girl is plain before her. . . . We who are educated have to be pioneers of Indian civilization. We have to prepare our people to live in the white man's way, to use the white man's books, and to use his laws if you will only give them to us." She went on to underscore her religious beliefs, saying, "the shores of success can only be reached by crossing the bridge of faith."

The Connecticut Indian Association was interested in training "native missionaries" who would foster the development of Christian lifestyles among their own people. La Flesche Picotte seemed a perfect candidate, so they agreed to fund her medical training at the Woman's Medical Col-

223

lege at Philadelphia. She began study there in October 1886, a few months after finishing at Hampton. Throughout medical school she corresponded with her friend Sara Kinney, the president of the Connecticut Indian Association, assuring her that her professional goals were linked to her desire to return to Nebraska and help her people. When not busy studying, she exhibited her community-oriented nature by speaking to church groups and visiting the Lincoln School for Indian children near Philadelphia. Yet despite her time-consuming extracurricular activities, she graduated at the top of her class in 1889.

Soon after graduation La Flesche Picotte departed on a speaking tour to association branches in Connecticut, which added greatly to the group's membership rolls. Then she returned to Nebraska, as promised, and won a government appointment as physician for the Omaha Agency. Since she was the first Native American woman to become a physician, this was the first such post to be occupied by a Native American woman, and among the first to be filled by any Native American. In 1893 she resigned in order to care for her ailing mother.

Marriage and Temperance

La Flesche Picotte herself was suffering from ill health at this time, too. The break from medical practice afforded her the time not only to convalesce and to care for her mother, but also to get married. She had promised her sponsors at the Connecticut Indian Association, who took an active interest in her personal life, that she would delay

getting married until after she had practiced medicine for a few years. This promise she had kept and was married in 1894 to Henry Picotte, a Yankton Sioux who had gained popularity among the Omaha as a good storyteller. Picotte also had a reputation as a heavy drinker, which may be why her family opposed the marriage. The La Flesche family already had ties with the Picottes, because Henry's brother Charles had married Susan's sister Marguerite six years earlier. The couple settled at Bancroft, Nebraska, and had two sons, Caryl and Pierre.

Despite her marriage to a man who was fond of drinking, La Flesche Picotte herself was a teetotaler and was developing a strong dedication to temperance. This probably caused some tension in her marriage, and it certainly created rifts between her and her tribe. Members of the Omaha tribe had been granted citizenship a great deal earlier than other Indians (citizenship for all Indians did not come until 1924), but citizenship carried with it the right to buy alcohol—a right that previously had been closely curtailed.

After citizenship, there was no more government supervision of the sale of alcohol on the reservation and there was no longer enforcement of the prohibitive laws by the tribal police. La Flesche Picotte viewed the increase in drinking on the reservation with trepidation. According to *Relations of Rescue,* in 1914 she looked back on this time and wrote, "Intemperance increased . . . men, women, and children drank; men and women died from alcoholism, and little children were seen reeling on the streets of the town; drunken brawls in which men were killed occurred, and no person's life was considered safe." The drinking affected her in direct personal ways as well. She worried not only about her husband's drinking, but about her brother's, too. She took a direct involvement in the lives of women who faced abuse from drunken husbands.

La Flesche Picotte's vocal and active opposition to the sale and drinking of alcohol on the reservation caused controversy and was resented by other progressive, white-educated Indians, who found her views condescending. They failed to understand why Indians were less capable than whites when it came to exercising their right to use alcohol. La Flesche Picotte felt that such legalistic arguments were out of place in the midst of what she considered a dire social crisis. She exacerbated the division between herself and members of her community by supporting white politicians who, for reasons different from her own, supported prohibition of the sale of liquor to Indians. She boasted of her influence in banning alcohol sales in the newest reservation town of Walthill, Nebraska, by the Bureau of Indian Affairs, a federal office which was of course not universally admired by Indians. While many Omaha leaders were enraged by the brutal treatment of Indians arrested for drunkenness by white officials, she defended the arrests. This kind of controversy was not new to her, though, as her father had also long been an advocate of temperance. In *Relations of Rescue,* she excused the resentment held for her by many of her tribespeople with statements like: "I know that I shall be unpopular for a while with my people, because they will misconstrue my efforts, but this is nothing, just so I can help them for their own good.''

Final Years and New Directions

After her husband died in 1905 of an illness that may well have been related to alcoholism, La Flesche Picotte was appointed by the Presbyterian Board of Home Missions as missionary to the Omaha. In the years following, animosities toward her by some members of her tribe would be eclipsed by her positive work on their behalf. One of her activities was to improve public health by pressing for modern hygienic and preventative standards among the Omaha. In 1913 she realized a lifelong goal and saw the opening of a hospital for the Omaha at her new home in Walthill, Nebraska. But she served her tribespeople in other ways as well. In 1910 she headed a tribal delegation to Washington, D.C., to discuss issues of citizenship and competency—a fuzzy and often abused legal prerequisite for Indian citizenship—with the Secretary of the Interior.

In the years after her husband's death she began to distrust the role of the government in supervising tribal life, a role which she had heretofore always encouraged. Part of her change in attitude resulted from the difficulty she had in assuming control of the inheritance left by her husband for their two sons. Government officials insisted that care of the inheritance should be given to a hard-drinking distant relative who had only visited the children once and lived in another state. Only after submitting references from white friends was she granted the right to supervise the monies. This encounter with government bureaucracy angered her and fueled a major turnaround in the way she viewed the relationship between Indians and the Bureau of Indian Affairs. She had once likened her tribe to "little children, without father or mother." Now she said, as quoted in *Relations of Rescue,* "this condition of being treated as children we want to have nothing to do with . . . the majority of the Omahas are as competent as the same number of white people."

Shortly before her death in 1915, La Flesche Picotte demonstrated her newfound distance from former white mentors (women like Sara Kinney and anthropologist Alice Cunningham Fletcher) by expressing her support for a new Native American religious movement that worried Protestant missionaries: the Peyote Religion, a pro-temperance Christian denomination that later became known as the American Indian or Native American Church.

La Flesche Picotte became a great deal more than the first Native American woman physician. She was a symbol for many marginalized groups who sought empowerment in the nineteenth century. She was a shining light not only for the Indian rights movement, but for the women's movement as well. She was ahead of her time as a Native American activist because she was among the earliest Indian leaders to look beyond the interests of her own tribe and address the broad issues facing Native Americans in general. She never failed to speak her mind in the face of castigation either from fellow tribespeople or from white supporters. Her courage, in concert with a rare physician's compassion, made her a unique and effective leader for her people.

Books

Native American Women, edited by Gretchen M. Bataille, Garland Publishing, 1993.
Pascoe, Peggy, *Relations of Rescue: The Search for Female Moral Authority in the American West, 1874-1939,* Oxford, Oxford University Press, 1990. □

Chuan Leekpai

Thai politician Chuan Leekpai (born 1938) spent a humble childhood as the son of a vegetable seller. In 1992 he became his country's prime minister amidst a crucial transition from a military government to one of democracy.

Born to Law

Chuan Leekpai was born on July 28, 1938, in Trang Province, in the south of Thailand. His father was a vegetable seller, and his mother a Chinese-language teacher. He was the third of nine children. Despite any odds against him getting an education, Leekpai graduated from Thammasat University 1962 with a law degree, practiced law, and became a member of the Thai Bar Association in 1964. His initial intention was to study art. He decided against that in order to make a better living and help support his family. He has also served as a visiting lecturer in forensic medicine at Chulalongkorn University for the medical school.

In 1969 he became a member of Parliament. By the 1970s his interests were turned almost entirely toward politics when the country's students and intellectuals became engaged in confrontation with the military regime and its stronghold over the country. When the military began prosecuting the activists Leekpai left Bangkok and returned to his home town, according to Rahul Jacob and Kim Gooi in an article they published for *Time International* on March 30, 1998. Leekpai wrote a novel and continued with his art, as he did even into mature adulthood and a life in politics. He noted to Jacob and Gooi that he found "by studying faces as an artist I can get to know people better."

By 1975 Leekpai had returned to government when he was named Deputy Minister of Justice, making him the youngest minister official at the age of 37. That post was quickly followed with his position as Justice. The following year he moved into the Prime Minister's Office serving as minister there until 1980, when he returned to the Minister of Justice post. Leekpai continued to become a well-rounded government minister and held varied positions— some of which he held more than once throughout the next decade including Minister of Commerce, 1980; Minister of Agriculture, 1982–83; Minister of Education, 1983–86; Speaker of the House of Representatives, 1986–88; Minister of Public Health, 1988–89; Deputy Prime Minister, 1989–90; and, returned to the Ministry of Agriculture post that

same year. In 1991 he became the leader of the Democratic party. By May 1992 the military regime was back out onto the street, gunning down demonstrators who were vocal in their support of democracy. All state-owned television and radio stations immediately enforced a media blackout on what was going on during the crisis. Only newspapers were able to get news out. The pro-democratic stance that the print media took paid off in influencing many people to join forces to promote a new democratic form of government, and to vote out the pro-military stronghold politicians. The monarchy in Thailand had remained above the law but had no active role in shaping government as it did in 1973 during student protests against the military. In addition, the monarchy intervened by persuading three generals who had been running the country to leave. Because the king so seldom spoke out, or intervened in any way, when he did, it was significant.

With the election on September 13, 1992, came support, if even by a narrow margin, for the four parties who were in support of change to a pro-democracy form of government. The power passed to Leekpai following that election and he became Thailand's new prime minister. And if the victory was slim, it was still enough of a victory to the pro-democracy forces as they prepared to open parliament that September 21. In a country long known for its political leaders to be known as the worst of dishonest and almost criminal-like bullies who were more interested in Bangkok's night life than in the lives of its average citizens, Leekpai was a welcome choice. According to the September 19, 1992, issue of the *Economist,* however, questions

remained whether the new prime minister would succeed. The journal commented that, "He hardly rates as a strong leader, but appears to offer what the public wants. Despite long experience as a minister in several governments, he has a reputation for honesty." Honesty was what a slim majority of the people of Thailand were clearly willing to gamble on.

Faced Challenges of Office

Leekpai served his first term as prime minister focused on legislation that would diminish the power of the military. Yet even though at that time Thailand was enjoyed double-digit growth, the distribution of wealth remained a serious issue. The capital of Bangkok as well as the regional capitals enjoyed the bulk of the wealth. How that might be spread to the rural areas such as Leekpai's home would be an issue. In March 1993, Rodney Tasker wrote for the *Far Eastern Economic Review* that Leekpai was "governing in a subdued and low-key manner based more on achievements rather than showcase projects." Still, Tasker indicated, due to an angry outburst by a member of Parliament, Chai Chidchob, on February 27, observers thought that he and others might be positioning for another military coup. He noted that most Thais did think that seemed unlikely. Leekpai and the army's commander, General Wimol Wongwanich, were known to possess a mutual respect for one another and were thought to be able to work out any differences that might arise. Leekpai's nickname during that first tenure in office was "Chuan Chuengcha," or "Chuan the slow mover," due to the deliberate and plodding manner he had in implementing his programs.

By 1994, the state of Thailand's affairs did not seem as benign as the hope had been during the first year of Leekpai's term. James B. Goodno wrote for the May–June 1994 edition of *Canadian Dimension,* that "1993 should have been a good year for Thais. In May, they marked the first anniversary of a popular uprising that chased a violent military junta from power. They did so with an elected coalition parties that supported the pro-democracy forces controlling the government. The economy continued growing steadily throughout the year. And a series of political intrigues failed to create the disruption the conspirators hoped for." Then Goodno added the snag in the scenario, much due to two tragedies that occurred that spring and summer. A disastrous fire at a toy factory killed 189 workers. Three months later a hotel that had been enlarged illegally, without regard to any safety codes, collapsed and killed more than 130 employees and guests. Social activists claimed that Leekpai's government bore little difference to the right-wing opposition when it came to favoring wealthy business interests. People in Bangkok's Klong Toey slum began to believe that, too. "Life here is very cheap," Goodno quoted a Klong Toey woman as saying. "No one wants to pay attention to these poor people," she noted. Other problems that Goodno and others were highlighting indicated that while the middle class was growing, and industrial and service jobs were plentiful, there was a darker side to the apparent boom. The GNP (Gross National Product) index per capita matched Jamaica, whose economy was long stalled. "Pollution, prostitution, and an out-of-control AIDS epidemic," according to Goodno, were social problems that showed no signs of diminishing soon. He also described the obvious inequitable distribution of wealth even in the capital city. "Disabled beggars sit in front of glitzy department stores. Shantytowns abut gleaming glass towers. A street named for the reigning monarch begins at a small slum, passes over squatters camped beneath bridges, and ends by a Ferrari dealership."

A scandal that implicated Leekpai emerged unexpectedly from a program he instituted that would put property back into the hands of farmers. A high-ranking government official abused the program by giving his friends and allies valuable real estate on the island of Phuket. Leekpai had not been successful in effecting the reforms he had set out to implement. His government was finished after that.

A Second Term and Crisis

Leekpai ended his first term and left the Prime Minister's office in 1995 and began to serve in his capacity as the leader of the opposition. In 1997 he once again joined Parliament as a representative from his native Trang Province. In 1998 he resumed the role of Prime Minister and served as well as the leader of the Democratic Party and the Minister of Defense. It was at this time when the financial markets throughout Asia had collapsed, throwing Thailand into crisis with a consequently shattered economy. *Time International* correspondents Tim Larimer and Terry McCarthy interviewed Leekpai in March 1998 as angry Thais from the rural areas of the country were protesting outside the government house windows in Bangkok. When the reporters asked the Prime Minister if he thought the worst of the economic crisis was over, he responded that, "The lowest point," had passed, even though its effects were lingering. The problems of liquid cash flow, unemployment and increased layoffs were only beginning to be felt and had a long way to go until the recovery began. Leekpai indicated that measures were being taken to save businesses and to address the unemployment situation. But he agreed with the reporters when he said that, "The real problem did not originate from the poor or working classes. But we cannot avoid the impact on all sectors of society. The government has therefore strenuously avoided cutting social welfare among those people in education, in health care, even in milk for schoolchildren. The rich people, they can fend for themselves," he said assessing the management of the crisis. Leekpai reiterated what had always been his trademark of behavior: "I have told my ministers, because of how we came into office, to be honest. We cannot engage in corrupt practices." Despite Leekpai's good intentions, scandal hit him and his government's second tenure much as it had the first. A leading member of his party, the former interior minister, Sanan Kachornprasart, was found guilty under the 1997 reformist constitution that had been written specifically to eliminate government corruption. The Constitutional Court found that he had forged a document for a $1.2 million loan to hide his assets. No such loan had been made, according to the court ruling, and threw into question over how he accumulated his vast wealth. He was not imprisoned but was forced to leave his governments posts first resigning as interior minister, and his seat in parliament,

and then his position as secretary-general of the ruling Democratic Party. With that scandal, and an election forced on Leekpai by the resignation of a group of opposition party members of parliament on the first day of the new session, his government again was facing the end of another run. A telecommunications billionaire, Thaksin Shinawatra became Leekpai's successor in 2002.

Remained Political Voice

Leekpai continued throughout the next years as his party's chief advisor. As with his own administrations, scandals would continue to plague Thaksin as well. And Leekpai was not averse to criticism of the new government, along with others. But despite unrest in the southern region of the country, and an increasing censoring of the media, Thaksin was voted "Person of the Year" for 2003. Leekpai came in second as the outstanding opposition politician of the year, behind Democrat deputy leader Abhisit Vejjajiva. In April of 2003 Leekpai decided to resign as the Democrat's party leader. Instead he would run as a regular member in the general election. Banyat Bantadtan took his place in May as the new Democrat party leader. In August of 2003 Leekpai became the party's new chairman of the advisory board.

Professional and Private Life

Leekpai has served as the vice president of Songkhla University Council. He has received numerous honors and awards throughout his career that have included Knight of the Grand Cross of the Most Noble Order of the Crown of Thailand, 1979 and 1981; Knight of the Grand Cross of the Most Exalted Order of the White Elephant, 1980 and 1982; honorary Ph.D. in Political Science from Srinakharinwirot University, 1985, and from Rhamkamhaeufg University, 1987; Honorary Ph.D. in Letters, National University San Marcos, Lima, Peru, 1999; Grand Companion of the Most Illustrious order of Chula Chom Klao, 1998; Order of the Sun, Republic of Peru, 1999; Grand Cross of the Order of Christ, Portugal, 1999; and, Jose Dolores Estrada, Batalle de San Jacinto, Nicaragua, 2000.

Though he has a common-law wife and son, Leekpai does not live with them, according to Jacob and Gooi reporting in March 1998. He had been living in the same simple house for 20 years that belonged to a law school friend. His location was described as being "on a noisy, cluttered side street beneath one of Bangkok's new expressways. He lived extremely modestly, and listed a net worth for the last major election of $138,000 as compared with the $48 million of his wealthiest cabinet member, and far below the billions of Thaksin.

Leekpai keeps an active political voice regarding Thai government. In 2004, he voiced concern over the continuing situation in the southern provinces. Leekpai criticized the government for not taking the appropriate actions to resolve the unrest. He also accused the government as quoted from *Asia Africa Intelligence Wire*, of "inviting enemies into the country" due to the deportation of troops to Iraq. Many people fled from the south to relatives because of the growing violence. Within about two months around 50 people were killed. Leekpai believed that the parties must communicate in order to progress ahead. As to his active role in the opposition party Leekpai is certain to be heard for many years to come.

Books

The International Yearbook and Statesmen's Who's Who, 48th edition, Bowker Saur, 2001.

Periodicals

Asia Africa Intelligence Wire, April 15, 2003; May 22, 2003; August 18, 2003; August 19, 2003; November 24, 2003; November 28, 2003; December 22, 2003; December 31, 2003; March 3, 2004; May 21, 2004.
Business Asia, June 29, 1998.
Canadian Dimension, May–June 1994.
Economist, September 19, 1992; January 15, 1994; January 16, 1999.
Far Eastern Economic Review, March 18, 1993.
Financial Times Ltd., The America's Intelligence Wire, January 5, 2004.
Forbes, December 21, 1992.
Knight Ridder/Tribune Business News, December 19, 2003.
Presidents and Prime Ministers, September 1998.
Time Asia, March 18, 2002.
Time International, March 30, 1998; August 24, 1998.
World Press Review, March 1993.
Xinhua News Agency, March 9, 2004.

Online

"Chuan Leekpai," *CIDOB Fundacion (CIDOB Foundation) website,* http://www.cidob.org (December 4, 2003).
"Chuan Leekpai good choice for Thailand PM," *Asia Pacific Management News website,* http://www.apmforum.com (December 4, 2003).
"Man in Motion," *Asia Now/Asia Week website,* http://cgi.cnn.com/ASIANOW/ (December 4, 2003).
"Official Tours of SEAMEO Units by the President of SEAMEC 1994," *Southeast Asian Ministers of Education Organization website,* http://www.seameo.org (December 4, 2003).
"Thai minister in corruption scandal," *British Broadcasting Corporation News website,* http://news.bbc.co.uk (January 10, 2004). □

Sugar Ray Leonard

American boxer Sugar Ray Leonard (born 1956) earned an unprecedented six world championship titles in five weight classes during a twenty-year professional career. An Olympic gold medalist while an amateur, Leonard fought in some of the most memorable professional matches in boxing history.

From Singing to Boxing

The future boxing champ was born Ray Charles Leonard on May 17, 1956, in Rocky Mount, North Carolina. His parents, Getha and Cicero Leonard, had seven children. Leonard grew up in Wilmington, North Carolina, and Palmer, Maryland.

His mother named him after the famous singer Ray Charles because she wanted him to become a singer. And he did have vocal talent: he sang in church with his two sisters, and congregants told Getha Leonard that her son sounded like rhythm-and-blues artist Sam Cooke.

By the time Leonard reached his early teens, his interests turned to boxing. During this period, Leonard, a quiet youngster, was living in Palmer, a racially mixed, lower-middle-class suburb of Baltimore. Two local volunteer boxing coaches recognized his natural talents and began training him. As a fighter, Leonard immediately demonstrated skill and finesse in the ring. Later, his smooth approach would contrast with that of the brawlers and sluggers he battled and surpass that of the other stylists he faced. Eventually, he would adopt the same "Sugar" nickname used by legendary boxer Ray Robinson, who is regarded by many as the most skillful technical fighter of all time.

Won Olympic Gold Medal

Only fourteen years old, Leonard entered the amateur boxing ranks and put together an outstanding record, winning 145 of 150 fights. In six years, he won two National Golden Glove championships (1973, 1974), two Amateur Athletic Union championships (1974, 1975), and a gold medal at the 1975 Pan American Games.

Leonard crowned the amateur phase of his career by winning a gold medal in the light welterweight class in the 1976 Olympic games in Montreal. It was a star-making turn. Leonard came into the final match as an underdog facing Cuban knockout specialist Andres Aldama. Even before the match began, Leonard won the hearts of the live crowd and a national television audience by displaying a picture of his son on the side of his boot. During the fight, Leonard, in dramatic fashion, overcame intense pain in both his hands to score a unanimous 5-0 decision.

Turned Pro

After winning the gold medal, Leonard announced his intentions to retire from boxing, claiming he had fulfilled his dream. However, it turned out to be the first of several premature retirements. Initially, Leonard wanted to make money from commercial endorsements and then attend Harvard to become a lawyer. But the plan collapsed when it was revealed that Juanita Wilkinson, the mother of his illegitimate son, had filed a paternity suit in an effort to get food stamps. It was a public relations disaster that killed any hopes for endorsement contracts. In addition, family bills were mounting due to his father's illness, so the 20-year-old Leonard, lured by a $500,000 offer from boxing promoters, decided to turn professional. Immediately aligning himself with the best people, he hired Angelo Dundee, Muhammad Ali's former trainer, to be his boxing manager and attorney Mike Trainer to be his business manager.

In his first fight, televised live on February 5, 1977, Leonard defeated Luis Vega, a tough Puerto Rican boxer, in a six-round decision. It was the first of 25 straight victories for Leonard, who would go on to win a record-breaking six world titles in five weight classes in a career that featured some of the best fights in the history of sports: memorable matches against Wilfred Benetiz, Roberto Duran, Thomas Hearns, and Marvin Hagler.

Throughout his career, Leonard continually confounded doubters who did not think he could beat the likes of Duran, Hearns, or Hagler. He possessed speed, power, and skill, and he was also smart. He knew how to analyze opponents and then develop a strategy to defeat them. Though not a slugger, he was a dangerous boxing artist with fast hands. His quickness enabled him to deliver left hooks, jabs, uppercuts, and crosses with deadly accuracy. His skills coupled with his vibrant personality made him a bright star at a time when the sport needed a new one. The era of Muhammad Ali was coming to an end.

Comparisons to Ali were inevitable and applicable. Famed sportscaster Howard Cosell even called Leonard the "new Muhammad Ali." Like Ali before him, Leonard divided boxing fans into two camps: those who loved him and those that felt he was arrogant. (To some, taking the nickname of "Sugar Ray" seemed the height of hubris.) His followers claimed that Leonard's perceived arrogance was merely confidence because, like Ali before him, Leonard

made good on his boasts. He fought in what has been deemed the greatest era in the history of boxing's welterweight division and emerged as the best.

Won First Boxing Title

Leonard's two-year unbeaten streak of 25 matches (15 by knockout) earned him a title shot against reigning World Boxing Council (WBC) welterweight champion Wilfredo Benitez, who was also undefeated as a pro. On November 30, 1979, at Caesar's Palace in Las Vegas, Leonard scored a 15-round technical knockout (TKO) with only six seconds left in the fight. It was an impressive win. Benitez, a future boxing Hall of Famer, was one of the great defensive fighters of all time. The following year, Leonard married Wilkinson, the mother of his son.

Roberto Duran's "No Mas"

Leonard held the title less than seven months. He lost the belt in his second title defense, on June 20, 1980, when he went up against the tough Panamanian Roberto Duran in the first of their three classic matches. In front of a large crowd at the Olympic Stadium in Montreal, Duran scored a close but unanimous decision, handing Leonard the first loss of his professional career.

The fight, probably the most anticipated non-heavyweight bout in the history of the sport up to that time, was billed as "The Brawl in Montreal," as the fighters disliked each other intensely. Leading up to the match, Duran wickedly taunted Leonard, and boxing observers believed Duran's mental tactics greatly influenced the fight's outcome. Leonard surprised onlookers by abandoning his usually smooth approach and adopting Duran's rough style. The fighters went "toe to toe" in a slugfest, and in the second round Duran stunned Leonard with a left hook that almost dropped the champion. Afterward, the battle went back and forth over the course of 13 rounds, but Duran fought better. Leonard's heroic image was tarnished and his large ego bruised.

"The fight in Montreal was not a boxing match," Leonard later recalled in an interview for *ESPN*. "It was a street brawl. I didn't utilize my skills there. I was determined to stand my ground and fight Duran his way. I don't like Duran's way. He walks around like he owns the world."

Five months later, Leonard got his revenge in one of the most famous and strangest boxing matches ever fought. In a rematch held November 25, 1980, in the Superdome in New Orleans, Louisiana—an event even more anticipated than their first battle—Leonard came back determined to fight his own fight. The plan worked. Through the first six rounds, Leonard outboxed the increasingly frustrated Duran. By the seventh round, Leonard was taunting and goading his ineffective opponent. Finally, with 17 seconds to go in the eighth round, Duran turned away from Leonard, walked back to his corner, threw up his hands, and told the referee *"no mas"* ("no more"). Referee Octavio Meyran, disbelieving, told Duran to continue, but Duran only repeated *"no mas, no mas."* Duran had given up, and that phrase would be forever linked to his otherwise remarkable boxing career. "I was just as befuddled as everyone else and shocked," Leonard recalled in an interview with ABC's "Wide World of Sports" for the show's fortieth anniversary. "But I thought it was a trick. I thought Duran was trying to get me closer. You know, trying to walk away and say, 'Ah, no,' then punch me. In fact the referee had no idea what was going on. And then Duran said, 'No mas, no mas,' and then the referee ended the fight so I walked away. People remember Duran, not because of his great fights with Hagler, Davey Moore, me, or Benitez. They remember, 'No mas, no mas.'" Technically, the fight was scored a knockout, and Leonard was champion once again.

Second Title, Second Retirement

Leonard retained his title with a tenth-round knockout of Larry Bonds. Then, in June 1981, he moved up to the light-middleweight class and scored a ninth-round knockout over World Boxing Association (WBA) title holder Ayub Kalule in Houston. To celebrate winning his second boxing title, Leonard performed a back flip in the ring.

Leonard immediately relinquished the WBA title and, on September 16, 1981, in Las Vegas, he returned to the welterweight division for a title unification match with WBA champion Thomas Hearns, a man who was both his friend and archrival. The match turned out to be a war, a true boxing classic. Both fighters took turns playing the roles of slugger and technical boxer. Hearns, nicknamed the "Hit Man," was a talented and powerful fighter, and he was beating Leonard through twelve brutal rounds. However, Leonard battled back in the thirteenth and, with one eye all but swelled completely shut, he knocked Hearns to the floor twice. Finally, Leonard won the fight in the fourteenth round by a TKO when the referee was forced to stop the fight as Leonard pounded Hearns on the ropes. With the titles now unified, Leonard became the undisputed world welterweight champion.

Leonard successfully defended the title twice. In the meantime, a highly talent fighter had risen to the top of the middleweight ranks. "Marvelous" Marvin Hagler, as he was billed, possessed excellent technical skills, a powerful punch, and a rather surly disposition. It seemed inevitable that Leonard and Hagler would meet. However, before Leonard's next scheduled title defense, doctors discovered that he had a detached retina. Leonard underwent surgery in May 1982 and, six months later, he announced that he was retiring from the ring. This disappointed boxing fans who had eagerly awaited a match-up with Hagler. But Leonard did not want to risk possible blindness in his surgically treated eye.

However, like his previous retirement, Leonard's announcement proved premature. After being inactive for 27 months, he returned to the ring in May 1984 and scored a ninth-round TKO over Kevin Howard. Despite the outcome, Leonard was less than impressive as Howard, a journeyman fighter, knocked him to the canvas for the first time in his career. After the match, Leonard announced yet again that he was retiring.

During his periods of inactivity, Leonard took a job as a boxing commentator with the HBO cable TV network and endorsed products. He also started the short-lived Sugar Ray

Leonard television network from Maryland, which featured 24-hour boxing news, interviews, and fights.

Returned to Face Hagler

In 1986, the boxing world learned that Leonard was training again and considering a match with Hagler. At last the long-awaited fight was scheduled for April 6, 1987. Many ring observers believed that the up-and-coming Hagler, a ruthless fighter, would easily handle Leonard, who had not fought in three years. However, Leonard scored what *Ring* magazine called the "Upset of the Decade" when he beat Hagler on points. The outcome was controversial, as the decision was split among the judges. Nevertheless, Leonard had won the WBC middleweight crown, his third title. No fighter had ever won on his first try back at a world title after such a long layoff. Leonard earned about $12 million for one night of work. Once again he announced his retirement.

Retiring and returning was becoming a matter of routine, it seemed. One of the reasons Leonard made so many comebacks is that he could not handle retirement very well. "He had to change his whole life to be Sugar Ray Leonard," his first wife Juanita said during an interview with ESPN Classic's "SportsCentury" television series. "And still today, down inside, it's Ray Leonard. But Sugar Ray Leonard won't let him out."

Later, it was learned that during his several retirements in the 1980s, Leonard missed the action so much that he began using cocaine and alcohol as adrenaline substitutes. Leonard admitted he used cocaine from 1984 to 1989. He would later kick both habits, but not before the substance abuse irreparably damaged his marriage. He and Juanita divorced in 1990.

Another Comeback, More Titles

In November 1988 Leonard once again came out of retirement. Now weighing 167 pounds, he faced the hard-punching Don Lalonde. The solidly built Canadian knocked Leonard down early in their match, but Leonard battled back to score a ninth-round knockout that garnered him both Lalonde's WBC light heavyweight title and the vacated WBC super middleweight title. Now with six world titles at five weights classes, Leonard became the most crowned fighter in boxing history.

Leonard successfully defended the super middleweight title twice against two old rivals, though his skills were starting to diminish. In a June 1989 rematch in Las Vegas, Leonard and Hearns battled to a twelve-round draw. Twice, Hearns knocked the champ to the floor, and observers said Leonard was lucky to come away with a draw. On December 7, 1989, Leonard and Duran faced each other for the third and final time. The match was a disappointment. Both fighters were past their prime, and the bout was rather uneventful. Leonard boxed cautiously and kept his distance while Duran had trouble catching up with his elusive foe. Leonard earned the twelve-round decision on points.

After the match Leonard again retired. But two years later, at age 34, he staged another return, this time in Madison Square Garden in New York City. He should have stayed home. For this comeback, he challenged WBC super welterweight champion Terry Norris and lost in a one-sided fight. Norris not only dominated the match, he knocked Leonard down twice.

That appeared to be the end of the road for Leonard, and it had been a marvelous ride. After he turned pro, Leonard won 35 of his first 36 fights, with 25 knockouts. Throughout his career, he had always managed to rise above most of the troubles that have plagued the sport and other fighters. He never found it necessary to sign on with the two controversial promoters who ruled boxing, Don King and Bob Arum. He remained an independent contractor who carved out his own career, keeping himself clean from the sport's ubiquitous corruption. However, he could not avoid the one mistake that has tarnished the careers of many great fighters: He could not resist the lure of "one more fight." In 1997, the year he was elected to the International Boxing Hall of Fame, Leonard, 40 years old, tried one more comeback. The results were even worse than before. He fought Hector Camacho, and the "Macho" man embarrassed him by knocking him out in the fifth round.

Leonard finished his career with 36 wins, 3 losses, and 1 draw, and he earned an estimated $100 million in the ring—the most money ever made by a professional boxer up to that point. Despite the downbeat ending to his fighting career, he is still regarded as the best non-heavyweight boxer since his namesake, Sugar Ray Robinson.

Post-Ring Career

Though he remained retired, Leonard kept involved in the sport, working as a promoter. In 2001, at 47, Leonard launched Sugar Ray Leonard Boxing, LLC. As chairman of the board, he provided overall leadership and worked with fighters, promoters, television executives, venues, and boxing commissioners to plan boxing events.

Outside the ring, during various retirements, Leonard also worked as a broadcaster for NBC, ABC, HBO, and ESPN. In addition, he appeared in movies and television shows and served as a spokesperson for companies such as EA Sports, Vartec Telecom, Track Inc., Ford, Carnation, 7-Up, Nabisco, Coca-Cola, and Revlon. In addition to his promotional activities, Leonard presented motivational speeches to many major Fortune 500 companies in the United States and abroad.

He also was involved in community work, serving for many years as the International Chairman of the Juvenile Diabetes Research Foundation's Walk for a Cure. Leonard had four children and lived in Southern California with his second wife, Bernadette.

Online

"Duran Duran," *ABC Sports Online*, http://espn.go.com/abcsports/wwos/leonard/duran2.html (December 22, 2003).

"Sugar Ray Leonard," *CyberBoxingZone*, http://www.cyberboxingzone.com/boxing/leonard.htm (December 22, 2003).

"Sugar Ray Leonard," *Encyclopedia Britannica*, http://multirace.org/celebs/celeb37.htm (December 22, 2003).

"Sugar Ray Leonard," *IBOF.com*, http://www.ibhof.com/srleon.htm (December 22, 2003).

"Sugar Ray Leonard," *infoplease*, http://www.infoplease.com/ipsa/A0109394.html (December 22, 2003).

Sugar Ray Leonard, *MSN Encarta*, http://encarta.msn.com/encyclopedia_761563061/Leonard_Sugar_Ray.html (December 22, 2003).

"Sugar Ray Leonard," *Wikipedia*, www.ezresult.com/article/Sugar_Ray_Leonard (December 22, 2003).

"Sugar Ray Leonard Boxing," *srlboxing.com*, http://www.srlboxing.com/srlboxing/bio_leonard.asp (December 22, 2003).

"Sugar Ray Leonard—Former WBA/WBC welterweight, WBA light-middleweight, WBC middleweight, WBC super-middleweight and WBC light-heavyweight champion," *SecondsOut.com*, http://www.secondsout.com/legends/legends_31481.asp (December 22, 2003).

"The Sugar Ray Leonard-Roberto Duran Trilogy," *saddoboxing.com*, http://www.saddoboxing.com/boxing-article/Sugar-Ray-Leonard-Roberto Duran.ht ml (December 22, 2003).

"Sugar Ray Leonard's Toughest fight," *INC.com*, http://pf.inc.com/magazine/20030601/25524.html (December 22, 2003).

"Sugar Ray was a ring artist," *ESPN Classic*, http://espn.go.com/classic/biography/s/Leonard_Sugar_Ray.html (December 22, 2003). □

Ada Charlotte Mackenzie

Canadian golfer Ada Mackenzie (1891–1973) is considered a pioneering athlete in her sport, winning major tournaments in Canada throughout her long career.

In the early twentieth century, when female golfers were viewed as something of an oddity, Canadian-born Ada Mackenzie was a pioneer in women's sports. In a career that spanned a half-century, she won all her country's top golf honors for women, her final victory coming in 1969 at the Ontario Senior Women's Championship. An energetic athlete into her early 70s, Mackenzie transcended many of the stereotypes that held most women back from athletic competition. She was quoted in *Golf in Canada: A History* as once remarking: "I started golfing when women were supposed to know more about a cook stove than a niblick."

A Natural Athlete

Ada Charlotte Mackenzie was born in Toronto, Ontario, Canada on October 31, 1891. The fact that both her father and mother were passionate about the game of golf hinted at the young girl's future career: she also showed an athletic bent from an early age. As her family was relatively affluent, Mackenzie was sent, at the age of 12, to Toronto's Havergal College, a private school for girls. Havergal, founded in 1894 by Ellen Knox, was dedicated to building a stronger Canada by empowering the nation's young women through education, skill-building, and traditional values, and Mackenzie thrived in the school's challenging environment. Remaining at Havergal from 1903 until she turned 20 in 1911, Mackenzie began to develop her athletic abilities,

joining the school's basketball, cricket, and tennis teams while also engaging in ice hockey and figure-skating events. Contributing to the success of her school in athletic competition, she was also distinguished for her efforts: for three years in a row she was awarded the title of Athlete of the Year and awarded the Havergal Cup. Mackenzie's record at Havergal remains unbroken.

While Mackenzie excelled in many areas of sport, golf remained her favorite. Deciding to remain at Havergal after graduating in 1911, she accepted a position as the school's athletic instructor and remained in that post for three years. When not involved with her young athletes, she devoted herself to improving her game. Although Mackenzie decided to pursue golf seriously, she retained a full-time job until the age of 40, working at the Toronto branch of the Canadian Bank of Commerce from 1914 until 1930.

The Rise of Women's Golf

Mackenzie grew up watching not only her father, but also her mother playing golf. Having the example of an athletic woman was a rarity in the early 20th century, when most adult women were confined to home and hearth, and most young girls were raised to embrace motherhood and marriage rather than follow personal dreams or career goals. However, Mackenzie also was raised in an affluent family, where adults were free to pursue leisure activities; she was exposed to the sport through her parent's interest in following golfing news. By the time she was ten the names Violet Pooley, Florence Harvey, M. Thompson, F. B. Scott and others—top-notch competitive golfers all—also served as inspiration.

Although golf had been around for centuries and women had played the game almost as long—16th-century monarch Mary, Queen of Scots reportedly had a passion for golf—the first all-female tournament was not held until England's Ladies' Golf Union began a championship in 1893. This first all-woman competition met with stiff resistance; as quoted by Rhonda Glenn in *The Illustrated History of Women's Golf,* a British golf official commented, "Constitutionally and physically women are unfitted for golf. They will never last through two rounds of a long course in a day. Nor can they ever hope to defy the wind and weather encountered . . . even in spring and summer. Temperamentally the strain will be too great for them. The first ladies' championship will be the last, unless I and others are greatly mistaken."

However, the Ladies' Golf Union championship was not a one-shot deal. Despite corsets, tight shoes, and heavy clothing that confined their movements, proper Victorian ladies in Great Britain and North America quickly took to the new sport, prompted by articles in such popular magazines as *Ladies' Home Journal* and *Frank Leslie's Popular Monthly.* By 1900 over 1,000 golf courses had popped up worldwide, and the game had become a popular sport for affluent men and, in lesser numbers, women. Canada's first golf course, the Royal Montreal Golf Club, was founded in 1873, and two years later the U.S. Golf Association organized the first U.S. Women's Amateur Championship, held on Long Island, New York, in November of 1895: there were four contestants. The first Canadian Women's Amateur Championship was not far off; it was inaugurated in 1901.

In 1919 27-year-old Mackenzie captured the Duchess of Connaught Gold Cup in honor of the first of her five Canadian Women's Open Amateur championships (in an "open" championship citizenship in the host country is not mandatory; in a "closed" championship it is). During the decade that followed she enjoyed being one of the top players in a sport that was undergoing extraordinary popularity among the upper classes. She took the Canadian Women's Open Amateur title again in 1925 and 1926 after being pushed to second place in 1924. Competing in the U.S. Women's Open Amateur Championship in 1925, Mackenzie narrowly lost to U.S. champion golfer Glenna Collett during the second round; she went on to compete in the U.S. championship's semifinals again in 1927 and 1932. Closer to home, in the Canadian Ladies' Closed Championship competition Mackenzie triumphed in 1926, 1927, 1929, and was runner-up in both 1923 and 1925. She also won the Ontario Ladies' Championship in 1922, 1923, and 1927.

During the 1930s Mackenzie continued to place in the sport's top tier of women athletes. She won the Canadian Open Amateur Championships in 1933, placed a close second in 1934, and then came back a year later to once again take the championship title. In the Canadian Ladies' Closed Championship competition she triumphed in 1931 and 1933 and took the Ontario Ladies' Champion title in 1931, 1933, and again in 1939.

In the early years of the 1940s interest in athletic competition was replaced by other, more pressing concerns as war raged throughout Europe. When women returned to the golf course following the tournament hiatus prompted by

World War II, Mackenzie once again proved herself a top player. In 1946 the 55-year-old golfer won the Ontario Ladies' Championship title, returning to repeat this performance in 1947 and again in 1950. She was also runner up in the Canadian Ladies' Closed Championship in 1950.

Among her other golf victories during her long career, Mackenzie earned top honors in the Bermuda Women's Tournament held in 1937 and also was named Bercanus Tournament champion in 1958. In her hometown of Toronto, she won that city's tournament ten times during her career and placed second on ten occasions at other amateur tournaments in her native Canada. Even at the height of her career, in 1926, Mackenzie did not confine herself to the links; that year she was also named Canadian waltzing champion.

With the emergence of fellow Canadian Marlene Stewart Streit in the mid-1950s, Mackenzie's reign as her country's top woman golfer was over; Streit, who won the Canadian Women's Amateur Championship all but four years during the 1950s, went on to gain international fame, holding titles in U.S., British, and Canadian championships. In 1955, at the age of 64, Mackenzie joined the senior field, winning the first of six successive Canadian Senior Women's Championships she entered. She returned to take the Canadian Senior Women's Championship again in 1952 and 1965; was runner up in 1961, 1963, 1966, and 1967; and took sixth place in 1969 at age seventy-eight. Mackenzie also competed in the Ontario Senior Women's Championships, taking that title in both 1965 and 1969.

As a championship-level athlete, Mackenzie had the opportunity to travel throughout North America, as well as Great Britain and Europe, to compete in her sport and developed close relationships with her fellow athletes. Her love of the game took her to some of the best golf courses in the world, as well as to private clubs. Among her many memories, Mackenzie recalled an invitation she received in 1929 to join the Scottish National Women's Team at the British Ladies' Open, an invitation she regretfully was unable to accept.

Honored for Achievements

Over the course of her high-profile athletic career many off-the-golf-course honors came Mackenzie's way. In 1933 the Canadian Press Corps awarded her its Outstanding Female Athlete of the Year award. During the decades that followed, so did other honors: Richmond Hill, Ontario, includes the Ada Mackenzie Park, and the Ada Mackenzie Trophy is awarded annually to an outstanding participant in the Canadian Ladies' Golf Association Senior Championships. In 1971, at age 80, Mackenzie was inducted into the Canadian Golf Hall of Fame. And the Ada Mackenzie Memorial Foundation, established in her honor, now provides financial aid to outstanding high school and college-level wheelchair athletes competing in championship-level events.

Active and Busy

Throughout her life, Mackenzie remained active in both her sport and her community. In the early 1920s, frustrated by the limitations put on her by her local Toronto course—women, even championship-level players like Mackenzie, were not allowed on the course on weekends— she decided to take the lead of British women. Establishing a stock company, she set about selling shares in what would become the first North American golf club where members, owners, and staff are exclusively women. With $30 000 and additional financial help offered by Toronto sports enthusiast J. P. Bicknell—who would eventually own the Toronto Maple Leaf hockey team—in 1924 Mackenzie founded the 21-hole Ladies Golf and Tennis Club of Toronto on farmland in Thornhill, Ontario. The course, designed by Stanley Thompson, opened on August 23, 1926. Men have been welcomed at the club almost since its founding but have been restricted to playing only during non-prime-time hours. In another effort to encourage more women— especially younger women—to take up the sport of golf, in 1928 Mackenzie established the Ontario Junior Golf Championships.

A savvy woman who enjoyed financial success, Mackenzie transferred some of her energy to business. In 1930, after leaving her job at the Canadian Bank of Commerce, she established Ada Mackenzie Ltd., a clothing store that addressed the needs of women athletes. Mackenzie remained active in operating her store until she sold it in 1959.

Due to her high energy level, her positive outlook, and her robust health gained from many hours walking the golf course, Mackenzie led, by all accounts, a successful life. Despite the pressures of competition, she remained calm, refusing to succumb to the stresses of the sport. She was once quoted as saying in *A Concise History of Sport in Canada:* "Keeping active and busy has to be my key to success. . . . Some people have a tendency to over-indulge in sports. Not me. I treat athletics like recreation." The year 1969 proved to be Mackenzie's last playing golf as a professional; she passed away four years later, in January of 1973, at the age of eighty-one.

Books

Barclay, James, *Golf in Canada: A History,* McClelland and Stewart, 1992.

A Concise History of Sport in Canada, Oxford University Press, 1989.

Glenn, Rhonda, *The Illustrated History of Women's Golf,* Taylor Publishing, 1991.

Kavanagh, L. V., *History of Golf in Canada,* Fitzhenry and Whiteside, 1973.

Online

"Ada Mackenzie," *Celebrating Women's Achievements: Women in Canadian Sport,* http://www.nlc-bnc.ca/2/12/h112-233-e.html (January 12, 2004).

Ada Mackenzie Memorial Foundation Web site, http://www.ammf.org (January 17, 2004).

"Club History," *Ladies' Golf Club of Toronto Web site,* http://www.ladiesgolfclub.com (January 17, 2004). □

John James Rickard Macleod

British physiologist John James Rickard Macleod (1876–1935) shared the 1923 Nobel Prize in Medicine for the discovery of insulin and the studies of its use in treating diabetes. A pioneer in the area of carbohydrate metabolism, Macleod's major published works include *Diabetes: Its Physiological Pathology* (1913) and *Carbohydrate Metabolism and Insulin* (1926). A member of many major professional scientific associations, he served as president of the American Physiological Society from 1921 to 1923.

M acleod was born in Cluny, Scotland, on September 6, 1876, the first child of Robert and Jane (McWalter) Macleod. Due to his father's calling as a minister, the Maclead family eventually moved to Aberdeen, where Macleod received his education. Macleod proved himself to be an excellent student. After attending Aberdeen Grammar School, he went on to Marishchal College of Aberdeen University, where he began the study of medicine. In his first year Macleod won first prize in all his subjects and, in 1898 he graduated with honorable distinction, earning an M.B. and Ch.B. In 1899, thanks to a traveling scholarship, he attended the Physiological Institute in Leipzig, Germany, where he studied physiological chemistry for a year. While at the institute, he published his first scientific paper.

Entered Academia

In 1900 Macleod joined the faculty at the London Hospital Medical School as demonstrator in physiology, serving under noted physiologist Sir Leonard Hill, who headed the department. Macleod collaborated with Hill to study caisson sickness, a condition that affected laborers who worked in the high atmospheric pressure of the submerged caissons used when building underwater tunnels or sinking bridge pylons. If the workers emerged from the water too quickly, without gradual decompression, they suffered the "bends," a problem also frequently experienced by deep-sea divers who rose too rapidly to the surface. The pain that causes the body to bend over in pain is a result of the sudden bubbling up of nitrogen in the blood and tissues as a result of liquid's inability to absorb gas at reduced pressure; the condition can cause agonizing pain and even death. Macleod and Hill collected data on cases of the sickness and then experimented with mice, subjecting the animals to different pressure levels to determine the effects on their physiology. Their work resulted in a series of articles published in 1903.

In 1902 Macleod was appointed lecturer in biochemistry at the London Hospital Medica School. He also earned a diploma in public health from Cambridge University. That same year he received the McKinnon research studentship

of the Royal Society of Medicine. In 1903 the 27-year-old Macleod married Mary McWalter and in August the couple traveled to the United States. Macleod's work and reputation had attracted the notice of officials at Western Reserve University in Cleveland, Ohio, and they offered him the position of chair of their Physiology Department. Macleod continued studying caisson sickness at Western Reserve and he created a compression chamber for laboratory experiments. But, more significantly, he also became interested in carbohydrate metabolism, particularly in relation to diabetes. He built his reputation on this interest, and it would eventually result in a Nobel Prize.

Also in 1903, Macleod was elected a member of the American Physiological Society (APS) and went on to become an important figure in the organization. In 1915 he was first elected to the APS Council and in 1920 he was named to the board of editors of the organization's publication, *Physiological Reviews*. In 1921 Macleod was appointed president of the APS.

Meanwhile, from 1907 to 1910, Macleod wrote and delivered important articles and lectures about diabetes, and in 1913 published *Diabetes: Its Physiological Pathology*. Works such as this established his reputation as an authority on carbohydrate metabolism. Also during this period, Macleod became a member of several other prominent professional organizations and served on the editorial boards of both the *Journal of Biological Chemistry* and the *Journal of Laboratory and Clinical Medicine*. In addition, during World War I, he was kept busy with various war-related duties and, for part of the winter session of 1916, served as a professor of physiology at McGill University in Montreal, Quebec, Canada.

In 1918 Macleod was elected professor of physiology at the University of Toronto, where he also directed the school's physiological laboratory and served as associate dean of the faculty of medicine. He had first been offered the position two years before, in 1916, but had been unable to accept it, and university officials were so eager to obtain his services that they left the position open until Macleod felt confident that he could dedicate sufficient time to his professorial duties. In that same year he published a textbook titled *Physiology and Biochemistry in Modern Medicine* that placed increased emphasis on the importance of chemistry in physiology and eventually became a classroom standard. In addition, under Macleod's direction, members of his department at the University of Toronto researched the behavior of blood sugar in turtles. Macleod further cemented his reputation when he delivered an important paper, "Methods of Study of Early Diabetes," to a diabetes symposium at the May 1921 meeting of the Ontario Medical Association. He soon began receiving job offers from leading medical institutions in the United States and Great Britain, and he was being considered for election to the Royal Academy of Medicine.

Started Collaboration with Bunting

In 1920 when he was 42 years old, Macleod first met the man who with whom he would share his Nobel Prize. Encouraged by Professor F. R. Miller from the Department of Physiology at Western University Medical School in London, Ontario, Fred G. Banting approached Macleod in his office and related his idea about isolating the internal secretion of the pancreas. Macleod was not overly impressed with Banting's presentation. Still, in 1921, he arranged for Banting to come to the University of Toronto. Banting's idea interested Macleod because he had come to believe that the pancreas was involved in diabetes, but he had been unable to determine its exact role. Previously, it had been suggested by other scientists that the organ produced an internal secretion that controlled the metabolism of sugar. In 1916 the research team of Sharpey-Schafer had named this hypothetical substance "insuline," but nobody could prove its existence. Macleod hoped that Banting's ideas would lead to that proof. Macleod provided Banting with laboratory space and dogs, as well as the services of his two of his best students, C. H. Best and E. Clark Noble. Macleod then instructed Banting in the Hodon method of performing a two-stage pancreatectomy on a dog. Then he went home to Scotland for the summer.

When he returned to Toronto in September, Macleod found that Banting and Best had made significant progress. They had managed to isolate the secretion, and Macleod suggested they call it "insulin." After Banting and Best presented their early findings to the Journal Club of the Physiological Society of the University of Toronto in November 1921, they were joined in their experiments by J. B. Collip. After more work, and before the end of the year, the four researchers present their findings at the annual meeting of the American Physiological Society.

Manufacture of Insulin Started

Despite the initial skepticism of fellow scientists, in January 1922, the researchers initiated the first clinical trials involving insulin at the Toronto General Hospital. When word about the studies got out, the press prematurely reported news about a diabetic cure. Macleod became besieged with questions about this "cure." By the end of the month, the research team began conducting research on the manufacture and physiology of insulin, and it grew to include Noble, J. Hepburn, J. K. Latchford, and the Connaught Anti-Toxin Laboratories under the direction of J. G. FitzGerald and R. D. Defries.

In March George H. A. Clowes, director of research at Eli Lilly and Company, a large pharmaceutical manufacturer based in Indianapolis, Indiana, approached Macleod with a proposal. Clowes suggested that Eli Lilly help the researchers develop a method of large-scale insulin production. Macleod first rejected the offer; he wanted his team to do it on its own. However, the researchers made little progress in developing a way to mass-produce insulin, and Macleod recontacted Clowes. In May of 1922, the University of Toronto entered into an agreement with Eli Lilly and Company. By the summer, thanks to the increased amount of insulin now available, more extensive clinical trials involving insulin could be conducted.

This increased activity added to Macleod's administrative responsibilities. From August 1922 to May 1923, Macleod served as official secretary of the insulin committee created by the board of governors of the University of Toronto to deal with patenting and licensing issues. He was also responsible for coordinating the patenting of insulin in Great Britain and the United States, and he was the main contact for both Clowes and Eli Lilly. Proceeds from the patent were given to the British Medical Research Council for the Encouragement of Research. The four researchers gained no profit from their discovery. In 1926 insulin was isolated in pure form by John Jacob Abel, and it eventually it became available as a manufactured product.

Despite what the press had earlier reported, insulin does not cure diabetes. However, it has proved to be crucial in the treatment of the condition and has provided help where none was previously available. Because its use transforms severe cases of diabetes into milder ones and also improves management of the condition by preventing diabetic coma and death, it has been credited as one of the most important medical discoveries of the 20th century.

Awarded the Nobel Prize

In 1923 Macleod received widespread recognition for his work. Early in the year, he was awarded the Cameron Prize by the University of Edinburgh. In May he was elected a fellow of the Royal Society, the independent scientific academy of the United Kingdom dedicated to promoting excellence in science. The most significant recognition came in October, when Macleod and Banting were awarded a Nobel Prize in Medicine for their discovery of insulin. After the announcement, Macleod made a statement indicating he would share his half of the Nobel prize proceeds with Collip; Banting indicated he would do the same with Best.

Macleod spent the next five years at the University of Toronto experimenting on insulin, looking for alternative sources of the drug, and campaigning for the establishment of an international standard for insulin potency. As a member of the League of Nations health committee, he helped establish a biological standard in 1926.

Returned to Scotland due to Failing Health

In 1926 Macleod published a book on diabetes and insulin titled *Carbohydrate Metabolism and Insulin.* The following year, he accepted an position at his alma mater, the University of Aberdeen, as Regius Professor of Physiology. In 1928 Macleod and his wife sailed to Scotland. Back at Aberdeen, he continued to be active in research and experiments. His subsequent work and publications involved a variety of physiological and biochemical topics, including diabetes, carbamates, purine metabolism, the breakdown of liver glycogen, intracranial circulation, ventilation, and surgical shock. That same year he wrote *The Fuel of Life: Experimental Studies in Normal and Diabetic Animals.* In addition, he held the post of consultant physiologist to the Rowett Institute for Animal Nutrition, and he served as the British representative for the APS.

During the 1930s Macleod suffered declining health. Afflicted with severe arthritis, his movements became more painful and limited. Despite his progressive physical debilitation, his mind remained active and he continued many of his editorial duties. In 1932 he returned to conducting experiments on the role of the central nervous system in the causation of hyperglycemia, something he had first become involved in 1908. Through experiments done on rabbits, he concluded that stimulation of gluconeogenesis in the liver occurred by way of the parasympathetic nervous system. In early 1935 Macleod's health worsened to the point where he was finally admitted to a nursing home. Spending two months there, he returned home to Aberdeen shortly before he died, on March 16, 1935.

During his career Macleod produced 11 books and monographs. He was a member of the Royal Societies of Canada, Edinburgh, and London, as well as London's Royal College of Physicians. He served as president of the APS from 1921 to 1923 and of the Royal Canadian Institute from 1925 to 1926. He received honorary doctorates from the universities of Toronto, Cambridge, Aberdeen, and Pennsylvania, as well as from Western Reserve University and the Jefferson Medical College. He was an honorary fellow of the Academia Medica, Rome, and a corresponding member of the Medical and Surgical Society, Bologna, the Societé Medica Chirurgica, Rome, and the Deutsche Akademie der Naturforscher Leopoldina, as well as foreign associate fellow of the College of Physicians, Philadelphia.

Macleod's interests included golf, gardening, and the arts. As an educator, he was described as sympathetic, stimulating, and humble, but also as demanding. As a man, he was described as loyal, engaging, affectionate, and serene.

Online

"Biography of John James Rickard Macleod," *University of Toronto Libraries Web site*, http://eir.library.utoronto.ca/insulin/application/about.cfm?page=macleod (December 19, 2003).

"John James Rickard Macleod," *American Physiological Society Web site*, http://www.the-aps.org/about/pres/introjjm.htm (December 19, 2003).

"Macleod's Compression Chamber," *Dittrick Medical History Center*, http://www.cwru.edu/artsci/dittrick/artifactspages/b-6chamber.htm (December 19, 2003).

Nobel e-Museum, http://www.nobel.se/medicine/laureates/1923/ (December 19, 2003). □

Agnes Campbell Macphail

In 1921, Canadian activist Agnes Campbell Macphail (1890–1954) accomplished the unthinkable when she was elected to the House of Commons, becoming Canada's first female member of parliament. That Macphail even won the election was phenomenal, given that she lived in a time when women were basically expected to stay home. Macphail, however, believed women were equal to men and spent her lifetime trying to prove it. While in office, Macphail pursued a "politics of equality" for all people, regardless of their gender or socio-economic status. During her political career, Macphail's main legislative interests included farm issues, women's equality, prison reform, and peace activism.

Raised in Family of Farmers

Agnes Campbell Macphail was born March 24, 1890, in a primitive, three-bedroom log cabin in Proton Township, Grey County, Ontario, Canada. Her parents, Dougald and Henrietta Campbell Macphail eked out a living as farmers, just as generations of their Scottish ancestors had done before. Likewise, Macphail went on to manage the family farm and household while at home and found the physical labor invigorating. Later in life, when Macphail met U.S. President Calvin Coolidge in 1930, she told him that she had always yearned to meet the man who was slinging hay when elected president. "Your President understands the spiritual value of work with the hands," she told a reporter at the time, according to her obituary in the *New York Times*.

While growing up—and working with her hands—Macphail became acutely aware of the troubles farmers faced. Her passion for this issue would later turn her into a politician. Macphail attended Ontario's Owen Sound Collegiate Institute and earned a teaching certificate from the teachers' college in Stratford, Ontario, in 1910. She spent the next decade teaching in the rural schools of southwestern Ontario and Alberta.

While working in Sharon, Ontario, Macphail joined the United Farm Women of Ontario and soon became a regular at the meetings of the United Farmers of Ontario. As a farmer's daughter, the issues were near and dear to her heart. Macphail became deeply involved in the organization's causes and started stumping for its political candidates. She also wrote a column for the *Farmers' Sun*. The hot-button issues of the time were tariffs and military service. Macphail and the farmers believed industry benefited from the tariffs because they received money from it, while farmers suffered because they were forced to pay higher prices on farm equipment and supplies. World War I proved to be another hot topic as farmers opposed forced recruitment into the armed forces. Macphail gained popularity because she was able to articulate these struggles.

Elected to Parliament

By 1921, Macphail was deeply dedicated to helping improve the plight of the farmer. The year 1921 was also an election year, and it was the first election where all women would be allowed to vote. Energized by the turn of events, Macphail decided to run for the joint United Farmer-Independent Labor nomination to represent South-East Grey. There were about 25 candidates in the field and as they made their speeches, Macphail stood alone—even her parents felt uncomfortable about supporting a woman running for office. However, Macphail's newspaper column and involvement with the United Farmers of Ontario had made her a household name among the rural Grey County farmers, who ultimately handed her the nomination.

In an era where women were considered secondary citizens, Macphail's nomination created a flurry of excitement, according to the *Toronto Star*'s Donald C. MacDonald. A rebellion soon set in, and MacDonald reported that an old farmer from another township exclaimed: "What! Are there no men left in South-East Grey?" The party asked Macphail to resign, but she steadfastly refused.

Macphail faced an uphill battle in an effort to unseat R.J. Ball, who had represented South-East Grey since 1911. Macphail focused on farm and labor issues. She campaigned relentlessly, touring the countryside in her run-down car that repeatedly broke down, forcing her to finish trips on foot. Her message, however, resonated with farmers, who ultimately elected her to the House of Commons on December 6, 1921.

For Macphail, winning the election was not the end of the battle, it was only the beginning. Macphail reported to the House of Commons in March of 1922 and tried to steer her way though the throng of parliament members gathered in front of the legislative chamber. As she attempted to enter, a man stopped her and asked her if she was lost. He told her that she was in the members' lobby and he would be happy to escort her to the spectators' gallery.

Once inside the legislative chamber, Macphail found a bouquet of roses on her desk and was pleased to have been so warmly welcomed. Later, Macphail learned the roses were payoff for a lost bet, sent by an MP (member of parliament) who bet that she would lose the election.

Faced Battle to be Taken Seriously

From the outset, Macphail found herself doubly isolated as a woman and a diehard agrarian. "These ironical roses were emblematic of my reception to a House hitherto sacred to me," Macphail said later, according to the Montreal *Gazette's* Heather Robertson. "I was intensely unhappy. Some of the members resented my intrusion. Others jeered at me. Everything I said was wrong, everything I wore was wrong, everything I did was wrong . . . . The men did not want me in Parliament and the women had not put me there."

Throughout the course of her 20-plus-year political career, Macphail said that she often felt like the bearded lady, with everyone always pointing her out in crowds and gawking at her, simply because she was a woman in politics. Most often, Macphail was portrayed as "mannish" and dismissed as a spinster schoolmarm. Even the press took Macphail to task, poking fun at her sensible shoes, tailored dressed, and horn-rimmed glasses. Her church affiliation was also used against her. Macphail belonged to the Reorganized Church of Jesus Christ of Latter-day Saints, which her enemies conveniently confused with polygamy and Mormonism.

Macphail, however, possessed one great weapon, which was her voice. It was startling, intelligent, and commanding, carrying to every corner of the legislative chamber when she spoke. In an article in the *Toronto Star,* historian Doris Pennington wrote that a *Toronto Telegram* columnist from Macphail's time once noted that the most beautiful thing about Macphail, besides her "shining honesty," was her voice. "Her voice had the quality of a viola, deep and compassionate and heart-catching . . . Agnes Macphail, standing to denounce injustice or deride pettiness from her place in the Commons of Canada, spoke in tones that echo unforgotten across the years."

Macphail was also a witty master at the crushing one-liner. According to the *Toronto Star,* Macphail was once berated by a heckler who repeatedly interrupted her before telling her to get a husband, to which Macphail replied, "How do I know he wouldn't turn out like you?"

Took up Peace Activism

During her years as a politician, Macphail took up many causes, including the subjugation of women, farm and labor issues, peace activism, and prison reform. Her ideas were radical at the time—especially her notion that parties played too much of a role in politics to the detriment of the people. Macphail suggested that the Cabinet be composed of the most outstanding members of Parliament, regardless of their party. She also reminded members that their priorities should be people, not parties. Macphail also was an advocate for the underprivileged and argued for pensions for the old, blind, disabled, and unemployed.

Abhorred by the dreadful conditions in the penitentiaries, Macphail forced the formation of a royal commission in 1936 to examine the issue, and ultimately, reforms were implemented. She founded the Elizabeth Fry Society, which helped women upon their release from prison.

Macphail's interest in the women's movement seems to have sparked her belief in peace activism, for she came to view women as the natural nurturers of life. Macphail was a member of the Women's International League for Peace and Freedom and attended several international peace conferences in the 1920s. She believed in disarmament and frequently called for a reduction in Canada's defense budget. She also urged the government to form a peace department to foster international understanding. She was one of the first female delegates to the League of Nations (forerunner to the United Nations), and the first woman to sit on its disarmament committee. As a former teacher, she denounced textbooks that glamorized war and got into trouble for suggesting that cadet training be banned from schools because it encouraged a military mentality in boys. As World War II began brewing in Europe, she urged Canada to adopt a neutral position and not get involved.

Because of her social-democratic views, considered radical at the time, Macphail was often maligned as a socialist rabble-rouser. The talk may have been mean, but it put her in the spotlight and turned her into a celebrity of sorts. In an early 1930s poll at the University of Toronto, women students noted Macphail as the woman they wanted most to be.

Macphail's tenure in the House of Commons came to an end in 1940 when a blizzard struck on election day and her rural farmer constituents could not get to the polls. Two days after her 50th birthday, Macphail found herself broke and unemployed, having spent her money on various causes. Though she had served many years in the House of Commons, she did not qualify for a pension. Macphail turned to writing again, this time producing a column exploring agricultural issues for the *Globe and Mail.* She also took up public speaking, mainly in Canada and the United States.

Elected to Ontario Legislature

Macphail returned to politics in 1943, winning election to the Ontario legislature to represent York East, becoming one of the first two women to serve there. She lost her seat in 1945 but won re-election in 1948. Naturally, Macphail continued her battle for women's equality and in 1951 introduced Ontario's first equal-pay legislation. Four decades would pass before it became a reality. She lost her seat again in the 1951 election.

Macphail never married but biographies make a point of noting her suitors. Alberta MP and ally Robert Gardiner proposed to Macphail, but she refused to marry him. Rightfully so, Macphail was leery of marriage because she realized it would likely mean an end to her career. During her lifetime, a married woman was not supposed to work outside the home. Furthermore, she was expected to adopt her husband's political ideologies. Marriage, therefore, would have meant resignation from the legislature or likely defeat in the next election.

Toward the end of her life, Macphail was ill and crippled with arthritis. Cerebral blood clots left her partially paralyzed. She suffered a heart attack on February 11, 1954, and died two days later in a Toronto hospital, buried during a snowstorm in the family plot in Priceville, Ontario. At the time of her death, Macphail was being considered for appointment to the Canadian Senate.

For all of her humanitarian efforts, Macphail has earned a somewhat legendary place in Canadian history. A bronze bust of her likeness was installed in the House of Commons after her death. In October 1990, on the 100th anniversary of her birth, a commemorative stamp was issued in her honor. And, in an effort to keep her spirit alive, the New Democratic Party of Ontario established the Agnes Macphail Award in 1999, given for women's activism. Former Canadian Prime Minister John Diefenbaker summed up Macphail's career best; according to the *Toronto Star*, Diefenbaker once said that Canada had produced five great politicians—and Macphail was one of them.

Books

Rappaport, Helen, *Encyclopedia of Women Social Reformers*, ABC-CLIO, 2001.

Periodicals

Gazette (Montreal, Quebec), September 21, 1991.
Guelph Mercury (Ontario, Canada), October 30, 2001.
New York Times, February 14, 1954.
Toronto Star, March 20, 1990; March 16, 1991; March 31, 1993.

Online

"Agnes Campbell Macphail," National Library of Canada/Bibliothéque Nationale du Canada website, http://www.nlc-bnc .ca/2/12/h12-264-e.html (November 30, 2003). □

Bob Marley

Bob Marley (1945–1981) was a Jamaican musician who popularized reggae music worldwide and became one of the most well-known exponents of the Rastafari religion. Marley was also a cultural revolutionary whose music expressed a fervent longing for political freedom, peace, and racial harmony.

Marley and his band, the Wailers, combined elements of ska, rock and roll, and other musical forms into their own version of reggae, a musical form that had its roots in the Jamaican ghetto of Trenchtown, where Marley spent his formative years. Marley's band had hit records in Jamaica for years before becoming more popular worldwide. The popularity of Marley's music and his message continued to expand around the globe for many years after his death, and many musicians of a number of pop genres credited Marley as a major influence on their songs.

Roots in Ska, Doo-Wop

Marley was born Robert Nesta Marley on February 6, 1945, in the Jamaican mountain village of Nine Mile, the child of a white British naval officer, Norman Marley, and a Jamaican woman, Cedellar Booker. His parents divorced when he was young, and in 1957 his mother moved with him to Trenchtown, an impoverished suburb of Kingston. Trenchtown was a housing project built after a 1951 hurricane had destroyed the area's squatter camps. The Rastafari religion combined with radical politics to foment a protest milieu in the ghetto, but those sentiments were unfocused and unorganized. The political repression and economic hardship that residents of Trenchtown experienced helped to inspire Marley's lyrics about the power of ordinary people standing up for their rights.

As a teenager in Trenchtown, Marley soon became friends with Peter Mcintosh, who as Peter Tosh later would inherit Marley's mantle of reggae superstar, and Neville Livingstone, whose stage name would be Bunny Wailer. They formed a band in 1963, a year after Marley auditioned solo for local Chinese-Jamaican businessman Lesley Kong and Kong produced a record, "Judge Not," on his Beverley label. During the same audition session Marley recorded two other numbers, "Terror" and "One Cup of Coffee," released with the name Bobby Martell, a pseudonym Kong had foisted on sixteen-year-old Marley. All three songs were recorded with a background beat of joyful, thumping ska— the latest popular music in Jamaica.

In the group, originally called the Teenagers, then the Wailing Rudeboys, and finally the Wailing Wailers and just the Wailers, Marley wrote music and lyrics and played guitar. But the young men, including a new member, Junior Braithwaite, took turns as vocalists. Their earliest ska recordings mingled a Jamaican proto-reggae style called mento with New Orleans blues.

Rude Boys and Rastafarianism

Record producer Clement Dodd took the group under his wing after it split with Kong. The band originally recorded two songs at Dodd's studio in 1963, "I'm Still Waiting" and "It Hurts to Be Alone." The latter was a hit, but the lead vocalist on it was Braithwaite, who had left Jamaica with his family for Chicago. Dodd insisted that Marley become the group's lead vocalist. Their next single, "Simmer Down," was released on Christmas Day 1963 and rose quickly to the top of the charts in Jamaica. It was recorded with the backing of a group of studio musicians that Dodd had brought in, including jazz trombonist Don Drummond. The song expressed Marley's warning to his fellow "rude boys" not to bring the law down on themselves, while at the same time replying to a letter from his mother, who was in the United States and was expressing concern that her son was falling in with the wrong kind of friends.

Since Marley's mother had left Jamaica to find work, Marley had no home of his own and stayed with friends. Dodd took Marley under his wing, becoming something of a substitute father figure. In exchange for letting Marley live in a back room at the recording studio, Dodd gave Marley several assignments: one was coaching a vocal group called the Soulettes. One of the trio was Rita Anderson, whom Marley would marry in 1966. A day after the wedding, Marley moved to Wilmington, Delaware, to live with his mother, who had moved there a year earlier.

The Wailers recorded several other records for Dodd's Coxsone label, including rebel anthems "Rude Boy," "Rule Dem Rudie," and "Jailhouse." At this point, Marley's music reflected his membership in the subculture of "rude boys," rebellious ghetto youth who frequently clashed with authorities. In 1965, however, Marley recorded an antidote to such militant anthems with "One Love," a song that distilled Rastafarian teachings and called for unity, peace, and love. These would be recurring themes throughout Marley's career: taking to the streets in strong protest against injustice tempered by a philosophy of non-violence and racial unity.

When Marley returned to Jamaica after his first stint in Wilmington, he and the Wailers signed with manager Danny Sims, an American living in Jamaica, and they recorded 80 songs for him between 1966 and 1972. Sims tried to steer Marley away from writing songs influenced by the Rastafari religion. Sims wanted the Wailers to reach the American market with a less radical message, like other reggae musicians he managed, including Jimmy Cliff and Johnny Nash, who made the upbeat U.S. hit record, "I Can See Clearly Now."

Stardom

After some time living back in Trenchtown and recording for Sims, mainly in the genre known as rock steady, Marley returned to Delaware to work on the assembly line. His early career was marked by interruptions and detours because he could not earn enough money to make a living and the band often battled for creative and financial control with record producers and companies. Marley soon fled back to Kingston after receiving a notice he had been drafted to fight in Vietnam.

Upon his return, Marley sought the advice of Rastafarian elder Mortimer Planner and decided to claim his musical independence. He was tired of compromising his message for other producers and did not like the way Sims had been toning down his philosophy to maximize commercial appeal. Marley opened a record shop and started a label, both called Wail 'N' Soul 'M,' named after the Wailers and the Soulettes, the group of singers that Rita Marley belonged to. After releasing a few singles, the venture folded.

In 1970, after meeting record producer Lee Perry, Marley and the Wailers—Tosh, Wailer, and studio drummer Carly Barrett—began experimenting with reggae, a musical style that was first popularized in a 1968 song by Toots and the Maytals, "Do the Reggay." The Wailers' version of reggae included an upfront bass line and the "one drop" beat played by a rhythm guitar. Perry was a major influence on the sound, persuading the Wailers to abandon doo-wop and dive deep into psychedelic reggae, borrowing heavily from American musicians Jimi Hendrix and Sly Stone.

Marley's first authentically reggae songs drew on Caribbean myths, ghetto scenes, Old Testament verses, and radical sentiments. The Wailers had a series of Jamaican hits but did not burst on the international scene until they went to London and signed with Chris Blackwell's new Island Records. Their first recording for Island was *Catch a Fire,* the album that propelled Marley and the Wailers to global stardom. Their second album, *Burnin',* included the popular tracks "Get Up Stand Up" and "I Shot the Sheriff." Eric Clapton's cover of the latter song was a worldwide hit. The Wailers also recorded the influential album *Natty Dread.*

Just as the band's work was finally receiving increasing worldwide recognition, Tosh and Wailer left the group to pursue solo careers. In 1975 the group was rechristened Bob Marley and the Wailers, even though the original Wailers had left and had been replaced with backup from members of the former I-Threes, another vocal trio that included Rita Marley.

Rastafari Prophet

Marley's influence on music was monumental. Reggae captured the emerging, youthful, rebellious, and confident pulse of the Third World, but its infectious beat also captured the attention of youth in the United States and Europe. The dreadlocks Marley wore also became popular with young people in many countries, standing as a cultural symbol of defiance. But Marley's legacy went far beyond his music to include his spiritual and political crusades, which were always interwoven into his songs. The cultural and political aspects of Rastafarianism defined it as a potential threat to the Establishment. These included a belief in black racial superiority, radical nonviolent action, and an endorsement of the spiritual uplifting that could allegedly be attained by smoking marijuana. These threads fit in perfectly with the cultural rebellion of the 1970s, and Marley's songs expressed his commitment to political and social revolution. He became a prophet to downtrodden peoples worldwide, singing of freedom and justice, of fighting for rights and dignity.

Marley did not just sing about social justice; he practiced what he preached. He took on a series of community projects, at one time supporting more than 6,000 people with food, jobs, and housing. He invested in schools and infrastructure in Jamaica. Marley became a powerful political icon in Jamaica and in 1976 survived an assassination attempt by gunmen apparently trying to stop a free concert organized by the ruling People's National Party. After the frightening incident, Marley left for tours of Europe and the United States and produced four new albums that increased his worldwide popularity: *Exodus* (1977), *Babylon by Bus* (1978), *Kaya* (1978), and *Uprising* (1980).

In 1977, Marley bought a home in Miami, and other members of his clan later moved there. That same year, he injured his big toe in a friendly soccer game in France while he was there promoting *Exodus*. It never properly healed, and he refused to have it amputated, saying his Rastafari faith was all the healing he needed. But some believe the infected toe led to cancer that was not identified in stages early enough to be treated.

Marley died of lung, liver, and brain cancer at age 36 on May 11, 1981, in Miami, Florida, shortly after being awarded the Order of Merit by the Jamaican government. Two separate statues of Marley were commissioned; one is in Celebrity Park in Kingston and the other is at the National Gallery of Jamaica.

More Popular after Death

After her husband's death, Rita Marley continued to make music inspired by her husband with her group the Melody Makers. Their son Ziggy later became the group's headliner and lead vocalist. In 1984, Island Records produced Marley's greatest hits compilation, *Legend*, which sold more than 10 million copies in the United States alone.

Marley was inducted into the Rock and Roll Hall of Fame in 1994. His legend and popularity continued to grow after his death. In 1999, a record, *Chant Down Babylon*, was released, pairing Marley's vocals with those of contemporary pop and urban artists. In Kingston, Marley's face is on posters and billboards everywhere. His family runs Tuff Gong International, which gives tours of Marley's birthplace, tomb, mansion, and recording studio, and oversees the Bob Marley Foundation, which supports community projects in Jamaica, and the Rita Marley Foundation, which funds projects in Africa. Marley's sons Ziggy, Stephen, and Julian and daughter, Stephanie, are also reggae musicians carrying on his legacy.

In 2001, journalist Dennis Howard told Knight Ridder/Tribune's Achy Obejas: "In Africa, in Latin America, in China—in the world, he's bigger than the Beatles, he's bigger than everybody. In the 21st century, he'll be the biggest global superstar." Twenty years after his death, Obejas noted, "his deceptively easy, hypnotizing rhythms and his . . . message of love ha[s] traveled the world many times over." Marley's records sold millions of copies yearly worldwide, much more than when he was alive. "In the world, he has iconic status," said Howard, "he's a messianic figure whose impact has been phenomenal. . . ." Eppie Edwards, deputy director of the National Library of Jamaica, told Obejas: "Marley is more popular in death than in life because a lot of his work is still being discovered and recognized. The message of his songs was peace, looking out for the underdog, love. Simple as that."

Periodicals

Africa News Service, May 11, 2001; May 11, 2002; August 7, 2002.
Billboard, February 25, 1995.
Billboard Bulletin, May 7, 2003.
Entertainment Weekly, November 1, 1999; December 8, 2000.
Jet, January 10, 1994.
Knight Ridder/Tribune News Service, May 14, 2001.
Time, November 29, 1999.
Variety, June 8, 1998.

Online

"Bob Marley," *Bob Marley.com,* www.bobmarley.com (December 31, 2003). □

María Montoya Martínez

Pueblo potter María Montoya Martínez (c. 1881–1980) managed in her long career to almost single-handedly return the fast fading art of traditional Pueblo potting to her people. This accomplishment not only revived cultural pride among the Pueblo, but also gave Martínez the opportunity to teach her skills to others, creating resources that would help sustain the Pueblo community for years to come.

Martínez was born María Antonia Montoya in a pueblo community in San Ildefonso, New Mexico, on an unrecorded date between the years of 1881 and 1887. The San Ildefonso pueblo was a small group of adobe houses on the eastern bank of the Rio Grande. After her birth, Martínez was given the Tewa, or Pueblo, name Po-Ve-Ka, or "Pond Lily" by her mother, Reyes Peña, and her father, Thomas Montoya. She was the second eldest of five daughters supported by her father's varied work as a farmer, a carpenter, and a cowboy.

Received Well-rounded Education

Martínez, a self-taught potter, learned by observing her aunt, a talented potter named Nicolasa Peña. According to Corinne T. Field in the *Dictionary of American Biography,* Martínez would watch her aunt "roll coils of clay between her moistened hands to form a tall cylinder that she would then push out into a graceful contour, smoothing the finished product with a round stone. Finally the dried pot would be painted in a variety of clay slips and baked in a wood fire." By the age of seven or eight Martínez was making crude bowls and plates of her own. She also attended a government grammar school and received a rudimentary academic education until 1896. At that time she and her sister Desideria were selected by the Pueblo's tribal council to spend two of their formative years at St. Catherine's Indian School in Santa Fe, New Mexico.

Martínez eventually returned to her pueblo from St. Catherine's and quickly achieved economic independence by mastering the traditional craft of Pueblo pottery, specializing in coil-built bowls and water jars called *ollas.* She worked in close partnership with her husband, artist Julian Martínez, a member of her pueblo whom she married in 1904. She crafted, shaped, and polished pots and her husband painted them. The couple traveled briefly to St. Louis, Missouri, as demonstrators of both pottery and traditional dance for the 1904 World's Fair before settling permanently in San Ildefonso to make a living from their craft. They eventually had four sons, Adam, Juan, Tony, and Philip, and a daughter who died in infancy.

Raised Pottery to Art Form

At the time Martínez was born, pottery was made for utilitarian purposes, crafted whenever it was needed for cooking or carrying and storing food and water. Even the making of this functional pottery was losing importance as manufactured and mass-produced crockery was increasingly more available and convenient via non-native traders. The Martínezes started their career crafting small-scale pieces painted in multiple earth-toned colors and sold them as curios from 1908 until 1912. Julian had been taking extra work as a farmer in 1907 when he met archaeologist Edgar Lee Hewitt, a member of the Museum of New Mexico's anthropology and archaeology department. Hewitt was excavating a site in the Frijoles Canyon that had, at one time, been populated by ancestors of the Pueblo, the Anasazis. He recovered, among other artifacts, ancient pottery shards from the plateau at Pajarito near the San Ildefonso pueblo. Julian Martínez participated as one of the native workers hired to help with the excavation, and María was hired to cook for the team conducting the dig. Hewitt, having heard of María's skill as a potter, approached the couple about reconstructing the prehistoric pottery. Martínez accepted the challenge with great energy, and through careful observation and trial and error, she learned how to mix the appropriate clay base to make the thin, highly polished pots of her ancestors. Thrilled with the outcome, Hewitt bought the replicas and encouraged the couple to make more.

In an effort to learn more about the ancient pottery, both María and Julius Martínez worked for a time at the Museum of New Mexico, where Hewitt was exhibiting his finds. María was hired as a pottery demonstrator and Julian as a janitor. In 1912 they perfected a plain, small-scale version of the blackware that would made them famous, using methods that were popular in the first decade of the 20th century. The discovery of this technique was accidental, according to anthropologist Alice Marriott in *María: The Potter of San Ildefonso:* "The first black pieces produced by Martínez and her husband were the result of an inadvertent smothering of the fire with fine particles of manure toward the end of the burn. The heavy black smoke that was produced penetrated the vessels inside and out, making them a dense black." In 1915 their scale grew and the couple began creating larger black pots. In 1919 they discovered how to produce the silvery black-on-black designs that became their trademark. Julian found that if he painted his design on the polished black pots in slip before they were fired, the result was a shiny black body with muted, black matte designs. The couple provided what many considered to be a perfect balance of craft and art. As an essayist noted in *Notable Native Americans,* María's "classical shapes were perfectly rendered, her new shapes elegantly proportioned. Julian's decorative designs worked in harmony with the shapes and surfaces. He . . . rarely repeated decorative drawings except for his famous *avanyu,* a mythical water serpent, and his feathers, adapted from the prehistoric Mimbres feather designs." In 1921 the Martínezes began teaching others how to make the black-on-black pots, and this sharing of skills and experience created an industry that soon made their pueblo a center for tourism and Native American crafts.

Refined Craft

In 1923 the Martínezes changed their process to reverse the pattern on the pots so that the body of the pot was shiny and the applied design painted in a matte finish on top. That same year at the request of buyers and peers who wanted to be sure they had a true "María Martínez" creation, María began signing her pots despite a Pueblo tradition that viewed works as the result of the efforts of many rather than just one individual. She began by using the anglicized name "Marie," and as time passed the signature changed according to who she was working with. Some were signed "Marie & Julian," others "Poh ve ka," "Marie & Santana," "Maria Poveka," and "Maria/Popovi." The rapid success of the couple's products and the steady influx of non-native tourists and culture introduced Julian to both fame and alcohol, and the pueblo community to increasing tourism. Tragically, Julian Martínex fell victim to alcoholism and died in 1943, leaving his wife to continue potting until well into her late eighties.

The continued popularity of her pottery led eventually to mass production; particularly after Julian's death, family members took up the practice and continued in Martínez's footsteps. Her younger son Tony, who took the Pueblo name Popovi Da, provided the artistic painting for his mother's pots after his father's death. Martínez also collaborated with her older son Adam and his wife, Santana.

Martínez retired from active potting in 1971, and in 1974 her family began providing the non-native public with pottery workshops in the summer months at the Idyllwild campus of the University of Southern California.

A Highly Decorated Potter

Martínez was showered with numerous awards during her lifetime. In 1934 she was given a bronze medal for Indian Achievement by the Indian Fire Council, the first woman to receive this award. She was awarded honorary doctorate degrees by four colleges, including the University of New Mexico and the University of Colorado. She was the recipient of the prestigious 1954 Craftsmanship Medallion bestowed by the American Institute of Architects, and that same year she also received the French Palmes Académiques for her contributions to the artistic world. Martínez was honored with the Minnesota Museum of Art's Symbol of Man Award in 1969 and the New Mexico Arts Commission's First Annual Governor's Award in 1974. She was invited to the White House by four U.S. presidents: Herbert Hoover, Franklin D. Roosevelt, Dwight Eisenhower, and Lyndon B. Johnson. She was even asked by John D. Rockefeller, Jr., an avid collector of her work, to lay the cornerstone for the Rockefeller Center in New York City. Martínez's fame was truly international, a fact that was supported by the efforts of Japanese master potter Shoji Hamada and Hong Kong potter Bernard Leach, both of whom traveled to her pueblo to meet her and observe her techniques.

Life after Death

Martínez died on July 20, 1980, in the same San Ildefonso, New Mexico, pueblo where she was born and where she lived most of her life. She was well into her 90s when she passed away, leaving behind a legacy of both her work and her knowledge to enrich generations to come. In the *Dictionary of American Biography* Field estimated that "The small pieces of black ware which she would have sold at the pueblo for three to six dollars in 1924 brought up to $1,500 in galleries at the time of her death." Martínez's work was continued by her great granddaughter Barbara Gonzales, her grandson Tony Da, her daughter-in-law Santana, and a relative named Blue Corn. Despite the high prices her pots were capable of commanding, Martínez most enjoyed the company of her family and fellow villagers. While her heart may have been tied to her home, her gifts were shared on a much broader level. As Field noted in the *Dictionary of American Biography:* "When Martínez died in 1980, pottery making was the single most important source of income for the pueblos of the Rio Grande. Largely through her sharing of skills and knowledge, San Ildefonso had been transformed from a poor, remote village to a craft center." Indeed, Martínez's talents as a potter brought to light the artistic beauty of Native crafts and sparked a Native American crafts industry that provided thousands of Americans with a vocation. Her own intentions remained humble, however. As she was quoted as saying by Richard Spivey in his book *María:* "My Mother Earth gave me this luck. So I'm not going to keep it. I take care of our people."

Books

American West, edited by Howard R. Lamar, Yale University Press, 1998.

The Cambridge Dictionary of American Biography, Cambridge University Press, 1995.

Dictionary of American Biography: Supplement 10, Simon & Schuster Macmillan, 1995.

Encyclopedia of North American Indians, Houghton Mifflin Company, 1996.

Handbook of American Women's History, Sage Publications, 2000.

The Illustrated Biographical Encyclopedia of Artists of the American West, Doubleday, 1976.

Marriott, Alice, *María: The Potter of San Ildefonso,* University of Oklahoma Press, 1945.

Notable Native Americans, Gale, 1995.

Peterson, Susan, *The Living Tradition of María Martínez,* Kodansha International, 1989.

Spivey, Richard, *María,* Northland Publishing, 1979, revised edition, 1989.

Women Artists: An Historical, Contemporary, and Feminist Bibliography, second edition, Scarecrow Press, 1978.

Online

"María Martínez and San Ildefonso Pottery," *Maria Pottery Web site,* http://www.mariapottery.com/bio/bio (January 14, 2004).

"Susan Peterson on Her Relationship with María Martínez," *WETA Web site,* http://www.weta.org/productions/legacy/legacy/interview_maria (January 14, 2004). □

Mary Magdalene

The woman known in Christian tradition as Mary Magdalene has been a controversial figure, interpreted by New Testament references as a repentant prostitute who found healing at the feet of Jesus, as a watcher at the Cross, as an attendant at Jesus' burial, and as the first person to hear the words of the newly risen Christ.

A beloved figure to many Christians—she is a Catholic saint with a feast day of July 22—Mary Magdalene has suffered at the hands of some historians and been revered by others. While Roman Catholic tradition holds that Mary was a fallen woman who came to accept and revere Jesus and was present at his resurrection, more recent biblical revisionism has given Mary Magdalene a second look. Many historians since the early 20th century—operating in an increasingly more humane, feminist and liberal world view—have given Mary renewed stature by divesting her of the sins of other, minor characters who bear the same name. Interest in Mary Madgalene, the subject of several scholarly works of historical revisionism, became even more widespread with Dan Brown's best-selling murder mystery *The Da Vinci Code,* which popularized the theory she was the wife of Jesus.

The birth and home of the woman known as Mary Magdalene is, like much in the Bible, shrouded in mystery. Many believe her name identifies the place of her birth as Magdala near Tiberias, a village on the west shore of the Sea of Galilee in Jesus' day. Others believe it derives from a Talmudic expression meaning "curling women's hair," implying a woman of loose moral character.

The Biblical Record

New Testament references to a woman named Mary are few, although collectively they comprise the largest reference to a single female, if indeed there is only one Mary. However, scholars have divided these references into three groups: Mary the repentant sinner, Mary of Bethany, and Mary Magdalene.

In Luke 7:37 a woman appears at the home of Simon the Pharisee in Galilee where Jesus is dining; she washes his feet with her tears, dries them with her hair, and anoints them with oils she carries in an alabaster box. This unnamed woman is a sinner, a city-bred woman who is likely a prostitute. Jesus forgives her sins, telling her "Thy faith has saved thee; go in peace." In John 12:3 this woman is identified as Mary and the ointment described as "spikenard, very costly."

In the tenth chapter of the gospel of Luke, the writer identifies one of the women accompanying him in his journey with the twelve apostles, in 8:2 mentioning "Mary called Magdalene, out of whom went seven devils"—the reference to devils perhaps meaning that she was epileptic

and seen as being possessed by evil spirits. Luke does not link this Mary with the woman of chapter 7, the sinner anointing the feet of Jesus. Mary Magdalene is also identified as one of three women present at Jesus' death (John 19:25) and entombment, in Mark 15:40: "who also, when he was in Galilee, followed him, and ministered unto him." Matthew 27:61 has her "sitting over against the sepulchre" after a large stone had been rolled against the opening to protect the body of Jesus.

She is also, according to Matthew 27:55–56 and 28:1, present at the first Sabbath following Jesus' death, when the sepulchre is discovered to be empty. John's gospel goes further into the events surrounding Jesus' resurrection, describing in chapter 20 the details of Mary Magdalene's discovery, in the dark of early morning, that Jesus' tomb has been opened, her efforts to inform the other disciples and her return to the tomb. While weeping alone at the tomb she encounters two angels. "And they say unto her, Woman, why weepest thou? She saith unto them, Because they have taken away my Lord, and I know not where they have laid him" (John 20: 13–14). She then encounters Jesus but does not at first recognize him. He tells her that he is to ascend to his father; she returns and tells the unbelieving disciples "that she had seen the Lord, and that he had spoken these things unto her" (20:18). In the books of Luke and Mark, Mary Magdalene is joined by Mary the mother of Jesus and either Joanna or Salome in discovering the empty tomb.

In Luke 10:38 the writer describes Jesus' visit to the home of Martha, who "had a sister called Mary, which also sat at Jesus' feet and heard his word." Martha's home in "a certain village" is believed to be located in a town outside Galilee, possibly Bethany. Luke does not link this Mary with his other two references to women of that name, although in John's version of events, when this Mary anoints Jesus' feet, she does so in the home of Lazarus of Bethany (John 12:1–3). John is also very careful to point out that Bethany is "the town of Mary and her sister Martha, who were both sisters of Lazarus." ("It was that Mary which anointed the Lord with ointment," according to John 11:1–2.) In Matthew 26:6–13 the event is also said to occur in Bethany—although in the home of "Simon the leper" not Simon the Pharisee of Galilee, as in Luke's first account; of the actions of the woman, who remains unnamed, Jesus remarks: "she hath wrought a good work upon me." (26:10). Mark's account of this incident, recounted in chapter 14 of his gospel, parallels that of Matthew in almost all areas.

Conflicting Views throughout History

The woman clearly identified in the New Testament as Mary Magdalene, a Jew and perhaps an epileptic, was a constant companion of Jesus during his ministry in Galilee and was one of his earliest followers. She was also likely affluent enough to be a self-supporting unmarried woman while aiding in the support of Jesus and his small ministry. Loyal to the last, Mary Magdalene witnessed the crucifixion and the interment of Jesus' body in the tomb; she was also the first recorded witness of the Resurrection. According to John, the resurrected Jesus singles Mary Magdalene out from all others, charging her alone to bring news of his transcendence over death to his disciples. The possible links to a sinful, wanton woman who finally repents to Jesus, as well as to several instances where women named Mary honored their spiritual leader by washing and anointing him, have created centuries of controversy. Rightly or wrongly, they have also done much to create the beloved figure of St. Mary Magdalene, passionate penitent.

Scholars have puzzled over the differences in the accounts of Luke, John, Mark, and Matthew for centuries. Explaining the ambiguities that arise regarding Mary, some have hypothesized that John, who recorded his recollections 85 years after Jesus' death, felt able to expose Mary of Bethany as the same repentant sinner who anointed Jesus' feet because her death had freed him from the need to protect her reputation. Luke's account, written much earlier, might have been written by a diplomatic man who desired no harm to a woman still living. Mark's account raises a possible link between Mary of Bethany and Mary Magdalene through his description of Jesus' gratitude for the woman's actions so close to his death: "she is come aforehand to anoint my body to the burying. Verily I say unto you, Wheresoever this gospel shall be preached . . . this also that she hath done shall be spoken of for a memorial of her" (Mark 14: 8–9). Perhaps in further gratitude, this Mary was one of the few women who stood loyally by, witnessing the death, burial, and rebirth of Jesus, and identified at this point as Mary Magdalene.

The writings of Pope Gregory the Great, who rebuilt the Roman Catholic Church into a controlling force throughout medieval Europe, were the first to establish all biblical references to Mary as referring to a single woman named Mary: a reformed sinner who became the penitent prostitute of Christian tradition. However, many have taken issue with Gregory's position and have seen the conflated view of Mary a strong, resilient woman who achieves redemption by humbling herself before Jesus. Many recent scholars, in the wake of a developing feminist consciousness, have ascribed to Gregory a misogynist tendency they perceived in much Catholic doctrine. Jane Schaberg refers to this in her *The Resurrection of Mary Magdalene* as *harlotization*. In response to such critics, the Catholic Church in 1969 revised its teachings to separate Mary into three unique women.

In the Eastern Orthodox tradition biblical references identify the Mary of Roman tradition as three separate persons: the fallen woman who appears at Jesus' table in Luke 7:36–50; Mary, the sister of Martha and Lazarus, who anoints Jesus in Luke 10:38–42 and John 11 and 12; and the woman clearly referred to in accounts of the death and resurrection as Mary Magdalene. In this interpretation Jesus was anointed with oil on two separate occasions, only once by a woman named Mary.

Protestant historians have put forth the notion of two distinct persons known as Mary, discounting the Roman Catholics' willingness to equate Mary of Bethany with the "sinner" referred to in Luke 7:37. Roman Catholic historians counter that Protestants are unappreciative of Mary's role in illustrating the importance of the forgiveness of sin.

Appearance in Other Texts

During the 19th and 20th century several ancient Christian texts were discovered hidden in Egypt and dating to the second and third centuries. These writings portray Mary Magdelene as not only a woman requested by Jesus to spread the good news of his resurrection to his twelve disciples; they reveal a loyal disciple who was a leader in the early church due to her actual witnessing of Jesus' rebirth.

The *Sophia of Jesus Christ* names Mary Magdelene as one of a small group of men and women entrusted by the risen Jesus with preaching the gospel. In the *Gospel of Philip* she is referred to as Jesus' companion and as one loved more than all other disciples. This work's reference to Jesus kissing Mary on the mouth—a reference that appears in other texts—supports the contention that Mary Magdalene was Jesus' lover as well as his most ardent follower. In the *Dialogue of the Savior* and the *Pistis Sophia* she is cited as an equal among the other disciples, all men.

In the Gnostic *Gospel of Mary*, which dates from A.D. 125, accepted by many as a record of her writings, Mary Magdalene is shown to be resolute in her belief in Jesus as the son of God. Following Jesus' death she takes on the role of spiritual guide, counseling others in Jesus' teachings and inspiring many to join her in the Christian faith. She also reveals her close relationship with the living Jesus and admits experiencing visions in which she receives the teachings of the risen Christ.

The Cult of Mary Magdalene

In the centuries following her death, legends surrounding Mary Magdalene evolved. Speculation has abounded about the relationship between Mary Magdalene and Jesus, some even saying that Mary was pregnant with Jesus' child at the time of his death. According to the writings of Gregory of Tours and Greek Orthodox Church tradition, the saint retired to Ephesus with John and died there, and her body (or relics) was moved in 886 to Constantinople. Other stories hold that she moved to Gaul after Jesus' crucifixion or to a desert to live out her life in isolation.

One French tradition, recounted in Jacobus de Voragine's *The Golden Legend,* and which first surfaced in the ninth century, holds that Mary Magdalene traveled with a small group that included Joseph of Arimethea and Lazarus and his sister Martha, sailing to France and spreading the Christian gospel throughout the area that is now Provence. Retiring to a small home on a hill at Sainte-Baume, she lived as a recluse for several decades until her death. According to this tradition, Mary's body was interred at Villa Lata (later St. Maximin), in Aix-de-Provence. In the 730s and 740s, according to historian Sigebert, fear of Saracen raids prompted the temporary transfer of Mary Magdalene's remains to Vézelay. Many centuries later, in 1279, a Dominican convent was built at Sainte-Baume on orders of King Charles II of Naples, and an ancient shrine was uncovered. In 1600 the remains discovered there were protected by a sarcophagus on order of Pope Clement VIII. Following the Napoleonic wars, the convent at Sainte-Baume was rebuilt and the ancient tomb reconsecrated. Although the site has been a traditional place of pilgrimage, the Roman Catholic Church does not support the contention that the remains at Sainte-Baume are those of Mary Magdalene.

As Lynn Picknett recounted in her book *Mary Magdalene: Christianity's Hidden Goddess,* belief in Mary Magdalene has been so strong that many have been martyred because of it. On St. Mary's feast day of July 22, 1206, for example, every man, woman, and child living in the small French town of Béziers was massacred by crusaders from Rome, because they were unwilling to relinquish their belief that Mary had once been the lover of Jesus.

St. Mary Magdalene has become an icon representing the penitent fallen woman. Paintings of her throughout the ages often depict her as a somewhat lusty woman with the red, unkempt hair that might befit a whore. She is depicted as bathing the feet of Jesus or standing face to face with the risen Christ near Jesus' open tomb. Mary Magdalene also appears in many artistic representations of Jesus' crucifixion and burial. The popular French name Madeleine is derived from the word Magdalene.

Books

Encyclopedia of Women and World Religion, edited by Serenity Young, Macmillan Reference, 1999.
Holy Bible, Authorized King James Version, William Collins & Son, 1839.
Picknett, Lynn, *Mary Magdalene: Christianity's Hidden Goddess,* Carroll & Graf, 2003.
Schaberg, Jane, *The Resurrection of Mary Magdalene: Legends, Apocrypha, and the Christian Testament,* Continuum, 2002.

Periodicals

Time, August 11, 2003.
U.S. Catholic, April 2000.

Online

Catholic Encyclopedia, www.newadvent.org/ (January 26, 2004).
Mary Magalene, http://wwwmagdalene.org/ (January 26, 2004).
☐

Vincent Massey

Vincent Massey (1887–1967) already had a long record of service to his home country of Canada when he was appointed the country's first native-born governor general in 1952. From that point onward only Canadians were named to that honorable position, and the Canadian identity was forever changed from a British protectorate to an independent nation that could stand independently.

Massey was born Charles Vincent Massey on February 20, 1887, the son of Chester D. Massey and Anna Vincent, in Toronto, Canada. He was born into the wealthy Massey family, whose business legacy had been established by his grandfather, Hart Massey, who

had amassed a fortune expanding the business interests of Massey-Harris, the farm-implement company his own father Daniel Massey had begun in 1847. Massey's brother was Hollywood actor Raymond Massey, whose best-known work included his portrayal of President Abraham Lincoln in the movie *Abe Lincoln in Illinois.*

Massey received a bachelor of arts degree from St. Andrew's College of the University of Toronto and went on to earn his master of arts in history at Balliol College, Oxford. He held a post as a lecturer in modern history at the University of Toronto from 1913 to 1915, while acting as the dean of residence of Victoria College. Massey married Alice Stuart Parkin, daughter of Sir George Parkin, a former principal of Upper Canada College and secretary of the Rhodes Trust, on June 4, 1915.

From his last year as an undergraduate in 1910, Massey had the idea that the university needed some form of student center wherein the 4,000 students could have a place to gather that would enhance the college experience. Thanks to money from his grandfather's legacy, he was able to add to the $16,290 that students had managed to raise and the building began by the next year. Progress slowed during the years of World War I, and Massey himself served as a staff officer of Canada's Military District No. 2 from 1915 to 1918. Once the war was over, Hart House—named for Massey's grandfather—was nearly completed. During the early 1920s Massey spent time at the Hart House's student theater as both an actor and director. He also worked in his family's business and was president of Massey-Harris from 1921 to 1925.

No Equal in the Arts

In September of 1925 Massey joined Canadian Prime Minister William Lyon Mackenzie King's cabinet. Honored as a member of the Canadian delegation to the Imperial Conference in London in 1926, he came back to accept a position as the first Canadian minister to the United States, where he served from 1926 until 1930. From 1932 until 1935 he served as president of the National Liberal Federation of Canada, and from 1935 until the close of World War II he moved to London to serve as high commissioner for Canada. England's King George VI honored his excellent service by investing him with the Companion of Honour in 1946, an order limited to the king and only 50 others. Along with his post in England, Massey concurrently held other positions, including that of Canadian delegate to the League of Nations in 1936 and trustee of the National Gallery and the Tate Gallery from 1941 to 1945, also serving the Tate as chair from 1943 to 1945. Between 1948 and 1952 Massey continued his support of the arts in Canada as chair of the National Gallery of Canada. This position overlapped with his six-year appointment as chancellor of the University of Toronto, which occurred 1947 to 1953.

Between 1949 and 1951 Massey was chair of the newly formed Royal Commission on National Development in the Arts, Letters, and Sciences. Massey's own legacy was recognized through the informal designation of the group as the Massey Commission. The commission issued its first report in 1951. Known as the Massey Report, it not only helped create the Canadian Council on the Arts, but also set the groundwork for establishing the National Library of Canada. In *The Imperial Canadian,* Claude T. Bissell would comment that, during the years when he first headed the arts commission to the end of his term as governor general, Massey, "[more] than any other Canadian," was "responsible for the first major movement of the arts and letters from the periphery of national concern towards the centre. It was a notable achievement." During this period Massey also encountered personal tragedy when he suffered the loss of his wife, Alice, in July of 1950.

Became Governor General

On February 28, 1952, Massey was appointed governor general and commander-in-chief of Canada. During his first years in office the position was not a governing post, but one that required Massey to sign Parliament's official acts. As the first native-born Canadian governor general Massey had followed 17 Britons into the office; after his tenure, only native-born Canadians would served.

Massey's love and devotion to the Crown of England—particularly the British tradition of pageantry—were traits he proudly cultivated. One example of that was his revival of the use of the State carriage in 1953 during the Ottawa celebrations for the coronation of Queen Elizabeth II. According to the *Governor General of Canada Web site,* "Amid much pageantry, the carriage brought Vincent Massey and his staff to Parliament Hill under escort by

members of the Royal Canadian Mounted Police. Mr. Massey introduced Her Majesty Queen Elizabeth II's Coronation speech, broadcast in London and around the world." As he did in so many areas, Massey set the precedent for the carriage's continual use on opening day for Parliament and official State visits.

Massey's devotion to the Crown of England in no way diminished his devotion and support of his beloved Canada, and he remained committed to promoting Canada's national identity. His extensive travels throughout the vast expanse of the country have been described as "tireless" as he sought to unify the culturally diverse society, and he used all available means of travel—including canoe and sled-dog team—to reach the country's most remote areas. He believed Canadians should be true to their heritage and learn both English and French. He honored both native and immigrant alike with his attention and acted as the grand host and welcoming committee for all who had come to participate in Canada's cultural wealth.

The period of the 1950s was a remarkable decade for Canada. The census count as of June 30, 1951, due to the post-war baby boom and the influx of record numbers of immigrants, was 14,009,429; in 1901, when Massey was 14, Canada's population had numbered only 5,371,315. During the 1950s the country's gross national product doubled, manufacturing capabilities grew, and petroleum production increased five times from the previous decade, as did iron ore output. The Canadian dollar enjoyed a quality exchange with the U.S. dollar, reflecting Canada's relative prosperity. Massey's influence in the promotion of Canadian arts was considered the catalyst for the development of home-grown Canadian radio, music, and ultimately, television programming.

Because Massey was widowed, his daughter-in-law Lilias served as his official hostess during his tenure in office. Massey had two sons and several grandchildren. In a *Life* profile of the governor general, Lord Salisbury commented on Massey and his elegance. Due to his British schooling and his upper-class background, the ardently Anglophilic Massey was known for his Oxford accent, as well as for his London tailor even though all admitted he was thoroughly Canadian. Salisbury noted that, "Vincent's a fine chap, but he does make one feel like a bit of a savage."

Retired to Family Home

When he left office Massey continued to keep busy, even after retiring to Batterwood, his family home near Port Hope, Ontario. He continued to chair the Massey Foundation as he done since 1926. The two endowments of the fund closest to his heart were Massey College of the University of Toronto and the campus's Hart House.

Innumerable honors fell to Massey throughout his lifetime. In addition to that with which King George VI invested him, Massey also received the Royal Victorian Chain from Queen Elizabeth II on July 22, 1960, for his achievements representing Canada's sovereign. Another honor was the creation in 1961 of the Massey Lectureship, which provides for a public figure or scholar to lecture on any subject of choice. Many Canadians recognize it to be the most important lecture series in Canada. Institutions of higher learning throughout England, Canada, and the United States presented him with honorary degrees throughout his lifetime. Those included both public and private colleges and universities in British Columbia, Alberta, Saskatchewan, California, New York, New Hampshire, Michigan, and Connecticut, as well as schools in his native Ontario. Massey himself created the Massey Medal in 1959 as a way of honoring outstanding work relating to Canada's geography. The medal is administered by the Royal Canadian Geographical Society.

During his lifetime Massey wrote and published several books, including *On Being Canadian* (1948); *What's Past Is Prologue* (1959); and *Confederation on the March* (1965). He has also been the subject of several biographies, and his term as Canada's governor general has come increasingly under the scrutiny of scholars and historians. His papers are collected in several libraries, including Canada's Trent University.

In his book *On Being Canadian,* Massey noted: "I believe in Canada, with pride in her past, belief in her present, and faith in her future." When he died on December 30, 1967, while visiting London, the life of Canada's truest ambassador came to an end. He was given a state funeral in early January of 1968 and was buried in an Anglican cemetery near his Port Hope home.

Books

Bissell, Claude. *The Imperial Canadian: Vincent Massey in Office,* University of Toronto Press, 1986.

———, *Young Vincent Massey,* University of Toronto Press, 1981.

Finlay, Karen A., *Vincent Massey and Canadian Sovereignty,* University of Toronto Press, 2003.

Massey, Vincent, *On Being Canadian,* University of Toronto Press, 1948.

Periodicals

Canadian Business, May 12, 2003.
Life, March 10, 24, 1952.
National Post, September 5, 2000.
University of Toronto Magazine, Autumn 2000; Spring 2002.

Online

"Charles Vincent Massey Collection," *Trent University Web site,* http://www.trentu.ca/ (December 4, 2003).

Hart House Web site, http://www.harthouse.utoronto.ca (December 4, 2003).

"His Excellency The Right Honourable Vincent Massey," *National Library of Canada Web site,* http://www.nlc-bnc.ca/ (December 4, 2003).

"The Right Honourable Charles Vincent Massey," *Governors General of Canada Web site,* http://www.gg.ca/governor_general/history/bios/massey_e.asp (December 3, 2003). □

Roberto Sebastián Antonio Matta Echaurren

Chilean artist Roberto Sebastian Antonio Matta Echaurren (1911–2002) received no formal instruction in the visual arts, yet evolved into one of the most renowned Surrealist painters of all time. Like most Surrealists, the artist, known simply as Matta, dedicated himself to exploring the powerful inner world of the subconscious on canvas. But Matta took the movement one step further, promoting a technique called "automatic painting," in which he attempted to work without thinking. Matta believed that by painting on sheer impulse—with no forethought—he could capture the unconscious mind at work. For Matta, this technique yielded a lifetime of peculiar, often hallucinatory images, whose originality greatly influenced the 20th-century art world.

Studied Architecture

M atta was born into a well-to-do, bourgeois family in Santiago, Chile. There is some confusion, however, surrounding the year of his birth. Later in life, Matta gave his birth date as November 11, 1911, although his birth year has been frequently cited as 1912. What is known for certain is that Matta's family had ties to the Basque region of northern Spain—Echaurren is a Basque surname. His parents, Don Roberto Matta Echaurren and Mercedes Yanez, were of Basque, Spanish and French descent. Matta's father was a landowner, who by some accounts was a distant and awkward father. Matta received a strict Roman Catholic upbringing.

From early on, Matta demonstrated a flair for creative endeavors. Santiago was a close-knit community, and Matta grew up surrounded by countless cousins. As a youngster, Matta constructed his own theater, complete with a curtain and colored sheets for a backdrop. He was known for assembling his cousins and making them perform on his makeshift stage.

Realizing their son had artist talents, Matta's parents encouraged him to become an architect. The Spanish-speaking Matta enrolled at Santiago's Sacré Coeur Jesuit College, where classes were taught in French, adding a European touch to his Latin American life. Matta studied architecture and interior design. Next, he studied at Santiago's French Catholic university and by 1928 was working in interior design. Soon, Matta began to question his worldview. "At the age of twenty-one I began to see everything again for the first time," Matta said, according to Irene Clurman's book *Surrealism and the Painting of Matta and Magritte.*

With this new vision came a yearning for change. By the early 1930s, Matta wanted to leave Chile for Europe. Matta obtained his passage across the ocean by working as a Merchant Marine, docking in Liverpool, England. From there, he headed to his destination of Paris, which at the time flourished as a hangout for aspiring young artists. In Paris, Matta spent two years as an apprentice in the studio of the famed Swiss-born architect Le Corbusier, whose functional architecture impacted modern design. Architecture, however, did not fulfill all of Matta's expectations.

Discovered Surrealism

Matta quit Le Corbusier's studio and traveled around Europe. While visiting Spain in the mid-1930s, Matta befriended writers Federico Garcia Lorca and Pablo Neruda. The two were "Surrealist" writers who strove to capture the unconscious on paper. The idea intrigued Matta and began to alter his worldview.

Through Lorca, Matta met Spanish Surrealist painter Salvador Dali. Through Dali, he met Frenchman and poet André Breton, the founder of the Surrealist movement. It was Breton who introduced the idea to Matta that reality was much more than what the human eye could see. Matta expressed his fascination with Breton this way in an interview with Nancy Miller for a retrospective on his work titled *Matta: The First Decade:* "If I or anyone was fascinated by Breton, it was because Breton was putting his finger on a very important question—that in representing reality solely by the way it appears to the human eye, we are not representing the whole thing."

In time, Matta returned to Paris and again worked as an architectural draftsman, although he was beginning the transformation from architect to artist. He spent more and more time on his drawings, which he referred to as mere "doodles." Deeply intellectual as well as charming, the Paris Surrealists warmly welcomed Matta into their group. The more Matta hung out with the Surrealists, the more his rigid architectural work—disciplined and ordered—began to bother him. Matta became infatuated with the idea of chance and irrationality, which had no place in architecture. He wanted more than to simply design houses. He wanted to know about the people who would live in them and how they would respond to the environment he created.

Began Painting

Encouraged by the Surrealists, Matta turned to oil painting around 1938. He labeled his first paintings "psychological morphologies" and later called them "inscapes" because he was attempting to illustrate the landscapes of his inner mind. "When I started painting, it was through necessity, of trying to find an expression which I call a morphology, of the functioning of one's thinking, or one's feeling," Matta said in the book *Matta: A Totemic World.*

When painting, Matta did not worry about technique. He began most paintings by placing a splotch of paint on the canvas. Next, he would smear the splotch with his fingers, or with paintbrushes and see what image he came up with and what connections he could make from there, hoping he could spontaneously contact his unconscious.

In his interview with Miller for his retrospective, Matta described his method this way: "I invented my own technique rather than learning my technique as a painter." Matta said that he was influenced by Leonardo Da Vinci, who said it was boring to just put lines on paper because then all you are doing is putting down what you already know. Da Vinci encouraged artists to look at a spot on the wall until something appeared through hallucination. Then, they were to follow that image. "That is my technique. If I see in the spot . . . something I know, I erase it and wait until something else comes along. And then I see something which to me is fascinating, because I do not know what it is. What appears is something like man—something of being—which is made of forms which come from the whole life history of the human species. I get amused, I get surprised."

Though he was only a beginner, Matta's paintings were unique enough to warrant exposition at the 1938 international Surrealist exposition at the Beaux-Arts gallery in Paris. *New York Times* writer Michael Kimmelman had this to say about Matta's first paintings: "His early Surrealist works, from the late 1930's and early '40s, were meant to suggest primordial upheaval: he painted gelatinous landscapes and cosmic spaces filled with eerie organic shapes in off-key, fluorescent colors."

Taught, Influenced American Artists

In 1939, after World War II broke out, many of the Paris Surrealists, including Matta, headed for New York City. Of the group, Matta was one of the only ones who spoke English and therefore had a larger impact on the young American artists they met. Matta instructed the American artists in his technique of "automatic painting," which helped give rise to the American Abstract Expressionism movement and its painters who came to the limelight in the 1950s—people like Mark Rothko, Jackson Pollock, Arshile Gorky and Robert Motherwell. According to *Guardian* writer Michael McNay, Matta so greatly influenced Motherwell that 30 years later, Motherwell called Matta "the most energetic, enthusiastic, poetic, charming, brilliant young artist that I've ever met." Around this time Matta also began to paint on huge floor-to-ceiling canvases and held his first one-man show in 1940 at New York's Julien Levy Gallery.

Matta stayed in the United States until 1948, then returned to Paris only to discover that his Surrealist friends had exiled him. Because Matta had had an affair with Gorky's wife, they blamed Matta for Gorky's suicide and would not let him rejoin their circle. Matta decided to move to Italy, but clearly felt displaced. At the time, Matta said, according to the *Independent* of London: "It was as if a tree were asked to walk—I had to pack up all my roots again in a suitcase and head off once more." Matta lived in Rome from 1950 to 1954, and the Mediterranean culture proved productive for his artwork. Matta returned to Paris by 1955 and in 1956 painted a substantial mural at the United Nations Educational, Scientific, and Cultural Organization's (UNESCO) building.

Over the course of his career, Matta's works evolved. After World War II, he seemed to focus on the interactions of robots and mutant creatures, taking a man vs. machine approach to his art. In an article in *Americas*, B. Mujica describes Matta's post-war work this way: "The paintings of this group constitute a condemnation of modern technology," which in Matta's view had dehumanized life. In "Wound Interrogation" (painted in 1948) "the wound is separated from the human being and subjected to the torture of intense examination by heinous machines. The bloody red insides of the wound convey a life striving to exist, while the greys and blacks of the demonic robots remind one of an industrial plant."

Like most Surrealists, Matta aligned himself with left-wing causes and believed art could be revolutionary. In 1968, he was a keynote speaker at the Havana Cultural Congress, held in Cuba. Here, Matta discussed art and revolution. He also produced a number of anti-Vietnam war paintings.

Created Art Until Death

The reach of Matta's art was evident in a 1972 international art world poll, which voted him as one of the world's 10 greatest living painters. His work was in demand, and during his lifetime, Matta's artwork was shown at respectable art houses around the world. Retrospective exhibitions were held at the Museum of Modern Art in New York in 1957, in Stockholm in 1958, in Brussels in 1963, in Berlin in 1970, at London's Hayward Gallery in 1977 and at the Pompidou Center in Paris in 1985.

Matta never quit creating. He was still painting, designing tapestry and drawing into his last years. He split his time between Paris, London, Milan and Tarquinia, Italy, where he had a studio, gallery and pottery school. He died November 23, 2002, at a hospital in Tarquinia.

Over his lifetime, Matta had several children. He and his first wife, Anne Alpert, had twin sons, Sebastian and Gordon Matta-Clark, born in 1943, both of whom became artists. Matta had a second wife named Patricia, who left him for Pierre Matisse, son of the famed artist Henri Matisse. Another artist son, Pablo Echaurren, was born to Matta and Angela Faranda. Federica Matta, also an artist, was born to Matta and Malitte Pope in 1955, followed by a son, Ramuntcho, in 1960. With his last wife, Germana Ferrari Matta, he had a daughter, Alisee, born in 1970.

Though Matta was always more popular in Europe than he was in the United States, his works were still being exhibited in the United States at the turn of the 21st century. "Matta in America," a look at his 1940s art, began traveling the United States in 2001, opening at the Los Angeles Museum of Contemporary Art before it traveled to the Miami Art Museum and the Museum of Contemporary Art in Chicago. His work continues to be shown because it is timeless. The introduction to *Matta: The First Decade* summed up Matta's influence by saying that his work remains important because it continues to challenge public attitudes and opinions, questioning a range of topics from American politics to the nature of man and the universe—questions that still resonate with viewers even today.

Books

Clurman, Irene, *Surrealism and the Painting of Matta and Magritte,* Stanford University, 1970.
Contemporary Artists, edited by Colin Naylor, St. James Press, 1989.
Matta: A Totemic World, Andrew Crispo Gallery, 1974.
Matta: The First Decade, Brandeis University, 1982.

Periodicals

Americas, 1992.
Art in America, January 2003.
Daily Telegraph (London), November 26, 2002.
Guardian (London), November 25, 2002.
Independent (London), November 25, 2002.
New York Times, November 25, 2002.

Online

"A Matta Biography," Matta-Art.com, http://www.matta-art .com/menu.htm (December 12, 2003). □

Paul McCartney

Paul McCartney (born 1942), a member of the famous band The Beatles and later a solo artist, is one

of the most successful rock stars in the history of the genre. His career spans four decades and has garnered him not only several hits but knighthood as well.

The most commercially successful rock star to date, McCartney was born James Paul McCartney in Liverpool, England, on June 18, 1942. His father, Jim, was a bandleader, and his mother, Mary, was a nurse. McCartney was an above-average student, attending school at The Liverpool Institute.

Teen Years Foundation for Future

When McCartney was 14, his mother died of breast cancer. He also wrote his first song that year and learned guitar before age 15. A mutual friend introduced McCartney to John Lennon at a church picnic during the summer of 1957. Lennon was in a skiffle band called the Quarrymen, which McCartney joined soon after they met. Lennon and McCartney began songwriting together at that point, agreeing to share all songwriting credits.

In 1960, the Quarrymen became The Beatles, and McCartney began playing bass guitar. The initial lineup featured John Lennon on guitar and vocals, George Harrison on guitar, and Stuart Sutcliffe on drums. Ringo Starr later replaced Sutcliffe.

The Beatles

The Beatles were signed by EMI in 1962, and Brian Epstein signed on as their manager. George Martin produced their first album. "Love Me Do," their debut single, reached the top 20 in the UK. Their second single, "Please, Please Me" went to number two. When their third single, "From Me to You," went number one in 1963, the Beatlemania craze had hit.

In 1964 "Beatlemania" hit the U.S. "Yesterday," released by The Beatles in 1965, became the most popular song in history, according to *Rolling Stone,* and was played more than six million times on the radio in the U.S. alone. Only a year later, in 1966, the Beatles gave up touring.

A Long-Lasting Romance

Paul met Linda Eastman, an American photographer, in 1967 while engaged to British girlfriend Jane Asher. The engagement was broken off, and McCartney saw Eastman on and off for a couple of years. The two married on March 12, 1969. The marriage was to become one of the most famously stable marriages in the entertainment industry.

Bob Spitz wrote in the *New York Times,* "Of all his accomplishments, McCartney points to his family as his proudest. His 28-year marriage remains one of the sturdiest in a profession littered by broken relationships." The McCartneys raised four children: Heather (born 1963), from Linda's first marriage, is a potter and jeweler; Mary (born 1969), a photographer and animal rights campaigner; Stella (born 1971), a fashion designer; and James (born 1977), a guitarist. The family, for a long time, lived in a two-bedroom home in Scotland.

Beatles Ended, Solo Career Began

In 1968, disagreements began an irreparable rift among The Beatles. When a new business manager was needed for the group, McCartney suggested his wife's father, Lee Eastman, an attorney. His bandmates, however, chose American businessman Allen Klein, creating further tensions within the group. McCartney later pointed to this incident as the principal reason for the group splitting up.

McCartney and the other Beatles began work on solo albums. *McCartney* was released in April 1970, a month before the last Beatles album, *Let It Be,* was released. McCartney played all the instruments; Linda performed backup vocals. The album featured the US number one hit "Uncle Albert/Admiral Halsey," and "Another Day" which went to number two on the UK charts.

On April 10, 1970, McCartney told a magazine he was no longer with The Beatles, but it was not until December 31, 1970, that McCartney sued Klein and the other three Beatles, effectively ending their partnership.

The McCartneys Formed Wings

In 1971, McCartney released the single "Another Day" just prior to the release of his second album, *Ram.* Later that same year, he formed the group Wings with wife Linda on vocals, Denny Laine (formerly of the Moody Blues) on guitar, and Denny Seiwell on drums. The group's first album, *Wildlife,* was released in December 1971.

In 1972, Wings added Henry McCullough, a studio guitarist, and Geoff Britton, drummer, to their lineup. The group toured the UK and then released three singles: "Give Ireland Back to the Irish" (banned by the BBC), "Mary Had A Little Lamb," and "Hi, Hi, Hi"/"C Moon." They followed these in 1973 with the album, *Red Rose Speedway,* featuring the hit single, "My Love." McCullough and Seiwell left the band before the fourth album.

In 1973, *Band on the Run,* recorded by the McCartneys, was considered a great comeback and topped the charts in the United States, eventually selling three million copies. Singles "Band on the Run" and "Jet" were US and UK top 10 hits.

Jimmy McCullough (no relation to Henry) and Joe English on guitar and drums respectively were added to the lineup. The new Wings released 1975's *Venus and Mars,* and 1976's *At the Speed of Sound,* both hit albums. In 1976, the Wings Over the World Tour spawned the live album, *Wings Over America.* In 1978, Wings released *London Town* with the U.K. single, "Mull of Kintyre," which sold a record-setting two million plus copies in Britain. McCullough left the group later in the year, but Wings continued with 1979's hit album, *Back to the Egg.*

On the 1980 leg of the tour supporting *Back to the Egg* in Japan, McCartney was arrested at Narita on January 16 when customs officials found 7.7 ounces of marijuana in his luggage. McCartney spent 10 days in jail, but in the end, the prosecutor did not file charges. At Amsterdam's Schipol Airport on his return trip, McCartney told reporters (as quoted in *The Globe and Mail*) that marijuana "should be decriminalized. Reliable medical tests should be carried out and these would show it's not harmful."

Another Era Ends

Later that same year, on December 8, 1980, Lennon was murdered outside his New York City apartment. A distraught McCartney cancelled the Wings tour. Laine, the only permanent member of Wings other than the McCartneys, quit the band, effectively breaking it up.

During 1980, a solo album, *McCartney II,* was released, featuring the hits "Coming Up" and "Waterfalls." A third solo album, *Tug of War,* produced by George Martin, was released in 1982.

Back to the Top

The early 1980s began a renaissance of sorts for McCartney's flagging career. In 1982, McCartney had a number one hit, "Ebony and Ivory," with Stevie Wonder, featured on his *Tug of War* album, produced by George Martin. He also appeared on Michael Jackson's 1983 single, "The Girl is Mine," on Jackson's *Thriller* album. Jackson contributed vocals to the number one hit single "Say Say Say" on McCartney's 1983 *Pipes of Peace* album.

Two years later, in August 1985, Jackson paid ATV Music $40 million for the publishing rights to the 1964–1970 Beatles catalog, outbidding and angering McCartney.

The two never recorded together again. (McCartney owns many other lucrative rights, however. In the 1970s, MPL Communications, Inc., McCartney's publishing company, purchased the entire catalog of Buddy Holly, as well as the Edwin H. Morris publishing company, thus gaining control of North American rights to musicals like *Hello Dolly, Mame, A Star is Born,* and others. MPL also controls two Beatles songs, "Love Me Do" and "P.S. I Love You.")

In 1984 McCartney branched out with a directorial film debut, *Give My Regards to Broad Street.* Critics panned the film and its accompanying album. The album did spawn a hit single, however: "No More Lonely Nights." And McCartney, not altogether dissuaded, followed up by writing the film score for the 1985 comedy *Spies Like Us.*

In 1986, McCartney worked with guitarist Eric Stewart on *Press to Play.* Three years later, in 1989, he teamed with Elvis Costello on some tracks for *Flowers in the Dirt* and co-wrote a few songs with Costello on the latter's *Spike.*

That same year, McCartney went out on his first world tour in 10 years and broke attendance records in many countries. Music from the tour can be heard on the 1990 live release *Tripping the Live Fantastic.*

A Classical Spin

In 1991 McCartney changed the pace with the *Liverpool Oratorio,* composed in collaboration with Carl Davis. Written on commission from the Royal Liverpool Philharmonic Society, the piece has been performed over 100 times in 20 countries since its premiere. The premiere was recorded live by EMI Classics and released as a double-CD album.

McCartney continued to explore other styles in 1994 when he joined forces with former Killing Joke member Youth to create ambient music. The two called themselves "Fireman" and released an album titled *strawberries oceans ships forest.*

In 1995, EMI released *The Leaf.* The Prelude composed for solo piano was inspired by McCartney's interest in classical music during the three years he was writing the Liverpool Oratorio. A young Russian pianist and gold medal winner at the Royal College of Music, Anya Alexeyev, performed it at St. James' Palace and recorded it for EMI. That same year, the Prince of Wales appointed McCartney Fellow of The Royal College of Music.

Beatles Revisited

While working with BBC producers on a Beatles documentary, McCartney, Harrison, and Starr met and began working with EMI/Capitol to produce never-before-released songs, "Free As A Bird" and "Real Love," from two John Lennon demo tapes. These songs and other unreleased Beatles demos and outtakes were released on the double-album *Anthology* in 1996.

In 1997 McCartney's solo release, *Flaming Pie,* entered the charts at No. 2 in the U.S. and U.K. and was nominated for Album of the Year Grammy in the U.S. The album, produced by Jeff Lynne, featured Steve Miller on three tracks, and McCartney's son James contributed lead guitar to songs like "Heaven on a Sunday."

Knighthood

On March 11, 1997, Queen Elizabeth II knighted McCartney. Bob Spitz of the New York Times wrote, "The promise of knighthood to the former pesky Beatle . . . is a delicious paradox. It was the Beatles, after all, who were anointed gurus of upheaval at a time when the collapse of the Empire was lashed to the decline of a generation's morals."

On a commission from EMI to mark its 100th anniversary, McCartney wrote the classical tone poem Standing Stone and recorded it in the Abbey Road studios with the London Symphony Orchestra. The piece premiered at Royal Albert Hall in October 1997. McCartney won the National Public Radio New Horizon Award for Standing Stone "in recognition of his work in broadening the appeal of classical music."

On April 17, 1998, Linda McCartney died from breast cancer at the family ranch in Arizona. The following year, McCartney produced an album of songs, Wild Prairie, which Linda had written and recorded. Chrissie Hynde, lead singer of the Pretenders and a close friend of the McCartney family, said (according to Business Wire), "The legacy of Paul's music and the Beatles is one thing, but I think his real legacy is the love story he had with Linda."

On March 15, 1999, McCartney was inducted into the Rock and Roll Hall of Fame as a solo artist. The event also marked his first public performance since the death of his wife. McCartney continued to record new material, as well. Later that year, the album Run Devil Run collected McCartney covers of vintage rock songs by Carl Perkins, Larry Williams, and Little Richard. In October of 1999, Working Classical featured three new short orchestral pieces. A Garland for Linda, an album to commemorate the life of his late wife and raise funds for cancer research, was released in January of 2000. The album featured McCartney's original music as well as that of other contemporary composers. For 2001's Driving Rain, McCartney's son James wrote two songs and played guitar. Wingspan (Hits and History) was released the same year, encapsulating Wings' contributions to popular music.

McCartney's former Beatles bandmate,Harrison, died of throat cancer in Los Angeles, California, on November 29, 2001. On the first anniversary of his death, McCartney and Starr reunited for a musical tribute, "Concert for George," at London's Royal Albert Hall.

A New Love

In 2000, McCartney began dating Heather Mills, a former model and anti-land mine advocate. A year later, they were engaged and in June 2002, the couple wed at an Irish castle. On October 30, 2003, Mills gave birth to their daughter, Beatrice Milly. McCartney toured Europe in the spring of 2004. He also produced a DVD titled Paul McCartney: The Music and Animation Collection.

Books

Miles, Barry, Many Years From Now, Henry Holt and Company, Inc., 1997.
Turner, Steve, A Hard Day's Write, Harper Perennial, 1999.

Periodicals

America's Intelligence Wire, February 27, 2004.
Associated Press, August 14, 1985.
Associated Press Newswires, July 3, 1997; April 20, 1998; June 22, 1998.
Billboard, May 15, 2004.
Buffalo News, June 14, 1998.
Business Wire, October 27, 1998.
Canadian Press, November 30, 2002.
Globe and Mail, April 7, 1979; May 22, 1979; January 26, 1980; January 28, 1980; December 10, 1980.
Herald-Sun, December 1, 2001.
Los Angeles Times, August 15, 1985.
Mirror, May 29, 2003.
New York Times, June 15, 1997.
Orange County Register, April 12, 1999.
People, March 29, 1999.
Reuters News, October 18, 1998; October 30, 2003.
Scotland on Sunday, September 28, 1997.
Seattle Times, October 15, 1997.
Times Union, March 12, 1997.

Online

"Music: Paul McCartney Forever," BBC America, http://www.bbcamerica.com (January 6, 2004).
"Paul McCartney," the iceberg.com, http://www.theiceberg.com (January 6, 2004).
"Paul McCartney," Rolling Stone, http://www.rollingstone.com (January 6, 2004).
"Paul McCartney," 46th Grammy Awards, http://www.grammy.com (January 19, 2004). □

Jose Toribio Medina

Jose Toribio Medina (1852–1930) set out at the age of 22 to catalog the manuscripts and histories of his native Chile. Five years before his death he donated to the Chilean National Library a total of 60,000 original forms, 1,668 manuscripts, and 8,659 transcribed documents. His comprehensive works on the Inquisition in Chile, Peru, and the Philippines would represent only a small part of his remarkable legacy.

Jose Toribio Medina was born on October 21, 1852, in Santiago, Chile. His father was a judge, Jose of the Medina Pillar, and his mother, Mariana Zavala, was of Basque ancestry. When he was three years old, Medina's father was named judge of Talca. There Medina attended a private school called Santiago. In 1860 the family was transferred to Valparaiso, but just two years later Medina's father became a quadriplegic when he was only 33 years old. Medina's father was sent to live in Santiago, and his mother

was given a government pension on which to live and support the family. In 1865 Medina entered the National Institute and graduated in 1869, awarded with prizes in Latin and literature. As a law student at the University of Chile, Medina nonetheless continued with his own studies of Natural History and Entomology. In 1853, at the age of 21, he was awarded his law degree. That same year he published his first piece of literary criticism of the novel, *Maria,* by Colombian Jorge Isaac. It appeared in *Sud America* on August 25, 1873.

Chile in the Nineteenth Century

In the middle of the nineteenth century, Chile was "organized political[ly] and institutionally," according to a *PCLA* article by Javier Piñeiro Fernandez, a professor of History of the Media in the Faculty of Sciences of Communication at University Diego Vestibules, Santiago. Fernandez went on to say that, "The Constitution of 1833 governed the destinies of the country, and during thirty years (1831–1861) preservative governments followed one another. The fever of gold of California and Australia stimulated the economy of the country, through the export of wheat and maize, and of the consolidation of the port of Valparaiso like the main one of the Pacific," which was a key location until the building of the Panama Canal. This time for Chile was one not only of some prosperity, but of a cultural blossoming in education and in literature.

Medina received an appointment as secretary of the Chilean legation to Lima, Peru, the same year he graduated

law school. While in Lima he discovered the remarkable National Library under the guidance of its director, Francisco de Paula Rodriguez Vigil. Medina was not partial to diplomatic work, though it enabled him to travel and to saturate himself in the work he came to love as an investigator into the history of Chile through its volumes of documents. By 1875 he published his first volume of documentary history, a 17th century manuscript, *Memories of the Kingdom of Chile and Don Francisco Meneses,* written by Friar Juan de Jesus Maria. His travel became increasingly frequent, both to Europe and to the United States, digging through archives and searching to fill his bibliographies. In 1877 he published a 1,300-page volume titled *History of the Colonial Literature of Chile.*

Neither War nor Work Interfered

When war broke out between Chile and the Peru-Bolivian confederation in 1879, Medina went into military service. He joined the Army and was sent to the city of Iquique, where he served as advisor to the Chilean Army. While he was in Iquique, he was named judge of Letters and was able to continue his investigations.

When the conflict ended in 1883, Medina returned to diplomatic service and joined the Chilean legation as secretary once again, this time going to Spain. In Madrid and Seville, he was able to examine the archives of Indians and those native to his home country, as well as private libraries that included many Chilean documents. He scouted through the National Library, the Library of the Real Palace, the National Historical File, and the libraries of the ministries of the Navy and War, in a collection known as the Hydrographic file, the real Academies of Language and History, and in convents and other military collections. His government gave him the money he needed to buy these works or have them copied. His location in Europe also gave him easier access to the libraries of Vienna, Berlin, Brussels, and London. While in Spain he and his assistants were able to transcribe more than 15,000 document pages and collect books, pamphlets, and maps. His work during this time also enabled him to publish works on the aboriginal tribes of Chile.

Medina returned to Chile in 1885. He married Mercedes Ibáñez Rondizzoni, the daughter of the diplomat Adolph Ibáñez, who was famous for his work defending Chilean interests in the Patagonia. Rondizzoni not only became Medina's wife, but also his secretary. With her help Medina established his own press, *Ercilla,* in 1888. The first publication his press created was the *American Library of 1888,* which was a catalog of 2,928 titles on Latin America and the Philippines. Medina would eventually list approximately 565 titles of books printed in Manila from 1593 to 1810 in his book, *La Imprenta en Manila desde sus origines hasta 1810,* in 1896. Experts considered this the most extensive bibliography of printed matter in the Philippines that had ever been compiled. The year before he established his own press, Medina also began publication of a series regarding the detailed histories of the Inquisition as it was carried out in the Spanish colonies that included Chile,

Mexico, and Peru. That project was not completed until 1905.

Exile After War

In 1891 Chile entered a civil war. Medina was the mayor of Santiago at the time and supported the sitting president, Jose Manuel Balmaceda. Balmaceda was defeated, however, and he committed suicide. As a consequence, Medina himself was accused of using his press for government propaganda. He was forced into exile and first fled to Buenos Aires, Argentina, in 1892. The director of the Museum of the Silver had extended an invitation to him, and he was thus able to continue his work there. By August of that year he published the *History y bibliografia de la imprenta en el antiguo vireinato del Rio de la Plata* (History and Bibliography of printed matter in the Old Virreinato of the River of the Silver). Medina was able to print his work right at the Museum of the Silver. Before returning to Chile in 1895 he traveled to Spain again in the interest of research.

Between 1895 and 1902, Medina and his wife began a new press, the *Elzeviriana,* and also wrote and published. (He did the writing, and she served as editor.) They published almost 73 books and pamphlets, with seven of them printed as re-issues. One of the most monumental works published in 1895 was *Relación,* which was an account of the 1541–42 Amazon expedition of Francisco de Orellana written by Friar Gaspar de Carvajal, the chaplain who accompanied him. Orellana, originally from Trujillo, Spain, became governor of Guayaquil, Ecuador, in 1540. Parts of the transcript had originally appeared in Oviedo's *Historia general de las Indias,* written in 1542 at the journey's conclusion but not published until 1855. According to an article in the *Athena Review,* "Oveido's account is especially valuable because he combined Carvajal's narrative with interviews of Orellana and some of his men." When Medina edited the full version in 1895, it was the first complete publication of the work.

In 1897 Medina published the *Chilean Hispanic Library.* In 1898 he began publishing what would turn into a seven-volume series, *Biblioteca Hispano-americana, 1493– 1810* (Bibliography of Hispanic America, 1493-1810). Publication would take nine years, and the work was completed in 1907. Also in 1897, Medina began a new aspect of his career when he was chosen as an academic member of the Faculty of Philosophy, Humanities, and Arts at the University of Chile. In 1899 he became the first chair of American and Chilean Documentary History.

Before the end of 1902 Medina and his wife were traveling again, to Europe and to America, sent as a commissioner of the Ministry of Public Instruction to study the file layout of libraries. When he returned to Chile he resumed publishing. Between 1904 and 1912 he published 59 books and pamphlets and 14 articles, in addition to publishing some reissued editions. One of the books published during that time was a bibliography of the Mexican Press between 1539 and 1821. When Medina left again for Europe in 1912, as an official commissioner of the government, he was in pursuit of more information on the Araucana, a tribe of peoples native to Chile.

Medina sold his press in 1919 but continued to work. Between 1920 and 1930 he published works that included *History of the Real University of San Felipe of Santiago* and *Colonial Hispanic Cartography of Chile.* Medina died in December 1930 in Chile.

Medina's Legacy

Many of Medina's works are located in the National Library of Chile. In 1925, he presented his personal collection of 2 individual catalogs; 60,000 original forms; 1,668 manuscripts; and 8,659 transcribed documents. A special room named in his honor is home to the collection.

The Jose Toribio Medina Award, created in Medina's honor, was established by the Seminar on the Acquisition of Latin American Library Materials (SALALM). According to the SALALM website, the award is presented to SALALM members for work that "adds to the body of knowledge about or provides access to Latin American library materials, Latin American libraries and librarianship, or the Latin American book trade." Medina was honored by Chile with a stamp in his honor in 1953.

Books

Encyclopedia of Latin America, McGraw-Hill, 1974.

Periodicals

Athena Review, Vol. 1, No. 3, 1996.

Online

"Jose Toribio Medina (1852–1930)," *Biblioteca Nacional De Chile (National Library of Chile) website,* http://www .cervantesvirtual.com (January 2, 2004).

"Jose Toribio Medina and the Press in Latina America: Notes for a Bio-Biographical Study," *PCLA,* Volume 1, number 2, January/February/March 2000, http://www.metodista.br/unesco (January 2, 2004).

"Jose Toribio Medina Award," *Seminar on the Acquisition of Latin American Library Materials (SALALM) website,* http://www.library.cornell.edu (December 14, 2003).

"Jose Toribio Medina Zavala," *Encyclopedia Escolar, icarito La Tercera website,* http://icarito.tercera.cl (January 10, 2004).

"Memoria Chilena, Cronologia Jose Toribio Medina," *Dirrecion de Bibliotecas Archivos Y Museos (dibam) website,* http://www.memoriachilena.cl (January 2, 2004).

"Philippine Bibliographies," *National Commission for Culture and the Arts (Philippines) website,* http://www.ncca.gov.ph (January 2, 2004). □

Nellie Melba

Vocalist Nellie Melba (1861-1931) rose from a childhood in provincial Australia to become a world-renowned opera soprano who performed regularly at London's Covent Garden and the Metropolitan Opera in New York. A diva with a commanding stage presence and a beautiful voice, Melba was the out-

standing coloratura of her era and one of the biggest celebrities of the early 20th century.

I n her day, the sometimes-outlandish, seemingly larger-than-life Melba was famed around the globe for her beautiful singing and her commanding stage presence. She helped popularize opera throughout Europe and the United States in an era where opera stars not only hobnobbed with royalty, but were often treated like royalty themselves. And no one demanded royal treatment more insistently than Melba. So well known was she that her name became attached to several popular foods named in her honor: Melba toast and the dessert, Peach Melba.

Pioneering Spirit

Born in Melbourne, Australia, in 1861 as Helen Porter Mitchell, the future opera star was the third-born and first surviving child of Isabella and David Mitchell. Seven more children would follow. Melba grew up in the country estate of Lilydale, near Melbourne. As a child she loved the animals and landscape of Australia, and when the family rode into the bush—the wilderness areas of Australia—on a stagecoach, she would insist on sitting next to the driver so she could help spot deadly snakes. "From our earliest childhood we were taught to strike and kill," she later said. She had an indomitable will forged from the pioneering spirit of mid-19th-century Australia. It was said that her career was prophesized by the readings of a fortune teller that she and

some friends encountered one day when she was ten. The woman gazed into Melba's hands and said: "I see you everywhere in great halls, crowded with people. And you are always the center of attraction—the one at whom all eyes are directed."

Her entire family was musically inclined, but Melba was the only child who persisted in music. She attended Presbyterian Ladies College in Melbourne, where Peitro Cecchi recognized her singing talent as a powerful and lilting soprano. However, opportunities for her to perform were limited, and Melba put any thoughts she had of a formal career in music on hold.

When she was 21, Melba married an Irish immigrant named Charles Armstrong. They moved to Queensland and had a son, George. But she envisioned languishing there in a rural area where there was no opera at all. Two months after George's birth, she left Queensland and moved to London, looking for a better opportunity to advance her dream career. After getting nowhere in London, she went to Paris and finally attended her first live opera. There, Madame Mathilde Marchesi became her opera teacher and sponsor. For her stage name she took the name Melba, short for Melbourne; Nellie was the family's nickname for her. She made her debut in Brussels in 1887, playing the role of Gilda in *Rigoletto*.

Became Celebrated Diva

The following year, in 1888, Melba made her London debut at Covent Garden, playing the title role in *Lucia di Lammermoor*. Until 1926, she would be a fixture at the famous London opera house. She also debuted in the United States in the role of Lucia, singing at the Metropolitan Opera House in New York City, where she would also perform regularly until she was in her mid-sixties.

Melba's singing style reflected the influence of her teacher, Marchesi. According to critics her vocals were the very definition of coloratura with their high range, precise intervals, clean intonation, and light but exacting attack. Other performers were often awed. As quoted in *Opera News*, Scottish soprano Mary Garden recalled hearing Melba hit a high C at Covent Garden: "The note came floating over the auditorium of Covent Garden, came over like a star and passed us in our box, and went out into the infinite. . . . That note of Melba's was just like a ball of light."

Although Melba performed mostly in Europe and in New York, she occasionally visited her native Australia, returning for the first time in 1902 to a loud and large reception. Australians felt that she was proving that they could be as sophisticated as any nation, and her fans at home admired the way she cultivated culture while never denying her roots. Between 1909 and 1911 she lived in Coldstream, Australia, and opened the Melba Conservatorium of Music in Richmond. She taught at the conservatorium, a training ground for future opera singers.

For most of the nearly four decades of her career, Melba was the greatest diva of her time, even though she was not a great stage actress. Her immaculate, unforced coloratura singing was immortalized in a series of recordings made between 1907 and 1916, including a moving scene from *Hamlet*. At her impressive home she entertained many of Europe's royal families and was a powerful personality and celebrity. When she had an affair with the duke of Orleans in 1900, her husband divorced her. She did not remarry and had no other children. During World War I, she was unstinting in her war work, often performing at benefit concerts, and in 1918 she was made a dame of the British Empire.

So famous was Melba that two foodstuffs were named after her: Melba toast and Peach Melba, the latter created by the chefs at London's Savoy Hotel. A Melba doll also became popular with children. She lived lavishly, buying a house in London and remodeling it to resemble the French palace at Versailles. Her private rail car was always stocked with plover's eggs and fresh caviar, her favorite foods, and decorated with specially scented linens.

Feared and Admired

Melba was as much feared on the opera circuit as she was loved by admirers. The door of her dressing room at Covent Gardens had a sign that admonished: 'SILENCE! SILENCE!'' She ran her career imperiously. In her 1925 autobiography, *Melodies and Memories,* she wrote: ''The first rule in opera is the first rule of life. That is, to see to everything yourself. You must not only sing, you must not only act; you must also be stage manager, press agent, artistic advisor.'' She was always on guard to maintain her top ranking in opera, making sure she was always paid one pound more than the famed Enrico Caruso, and looking out for competitors. ''When you are the diva, you have to be the best always.'' she wrote in her autobiography. She also described her drive for achievement thus: ''If I'd been a housemaid I'd have been the best in Australia—I couldn't help it. It's got to be perfection for me.''

Though relentless in advancing her career and often snobbish, Melba was also bawdy. She consumed as lavishly as she entertained. Though often considered too overweight for certain ingenue roles, she nonetheless pulled them off by the intensity of her singing, enrapturing audiences and fellow performers.

Melba's fans were ardent and spanned several continents. Once, when she was giving out autographs in St. Petersburg, Russia, an adoring man grabbed her pencil, bit it into pieces, and handed them out as cherished souvenirs. Not known for her humility, Melba in her autobiography wrote that the pencil pieces were received ''with a reverence and an excitement which, I should imagine, must have compared favorably with that of the medieval peasants who scrambled for so-called sacred relics.'' According to legend, a dying man in London once heard her singing nearby and said: ''If there is such beauty on earth as that voice, let me live,'' and he recovered. As she recounted in her memoirs, in one country town, people who couldn't get into a crowded hall crawled under the floorboards in order to hear her sing.

Queen of Farewells

Melba bade farewell to her native Australia in 1924, releasing a letter that said: ''I have tried to keep faith with my art . . . to make the big world outside, through me, understand something of the spirit of my beloved country.'' She then made farewell tours and concerts worldwide, so many so, in fact, that a sarcastic expression arose: ''More farewells than Nellie Melba.'' She sang at the opening of the nation's Parliament House in Canberra in 1927, and her final concert in Australia was in 1928. In 1931, refusing to accept her aging, Melba got a facelift, but the operation resulted in a blood infection, and she died in St. Vincent's Hospital in Sydney, the cause of her death not released to the public.

Ever concerned about her public perception, Melba had even orchestrated her funeral in advance. She had had a photograph taken of her portraying the dead Juliet of *Romeo and Juliet,* and after her death she was made up to look like the photo, with her bed strewn with frangipani, before anyone was allowed to see her. The funeral attracted national and international dignitaries to Melbourne, and she was buried at Lilydale Cemetery under a monument that depicts her reported last words: ''Addio! Senzor Rancor''—''Farewell, without bitterness.''

Books

Melba, Nellie, *Melodies and Memories,* 1926, reprinted, Hodder, 1980.
Moran, William, *Nellie Melba: A Contemporary Review,* Greenwood Publishing, 1985.
Murphy, Agnes, *Melba: A Biography,* Da Capo Press, 1977.

Periodicals

Opera News, October 1996; November 2003.

Online

''Dame Nellie Melba,'' *Australian War Memorial Web site,* http://www.awm.gov.au/forging/australians/melba.htm (December 28, 2003).
Dame Nellie Melba Research Centre Web site, http://www.art-technology.com.au/lilyhist/melba.htm (December 28, 2003).
☐

Albert Memmi

Writer, educator, and sociologist Albert Memmi (born 1920) is the author of the novels *Pillar of Salt* and *Strangers,* works praised as among the best fiction published in post-World War II Europe. Not only respected in the world of fiction, Memmi has authored several sociological works, among them *The Colonizer and the Colonized,* that focus on racism and African colonialism, both of which he experienced first-hand as a Jew growing up in a predominantly Muslim Tunisia. Translations of Memmi's works have been published in Israel, Italy,

Germany, England, Spain, Argentina, Yugoslavia, Japan, and the United States, where they have been well received.

Memmi was born on December 15, 1920, in the Tunisian city of Tunis. The son of artisan and saddlemaker François Memmi and his wife Marguerite (Sarfati) Memmi, the boy grew up in a traditional Jewish household, spending a great deal of time in his father's saddle-making shop. The Memmi family lived near Tunis's Jewish ghetto, known as the Hara. During the early 20th century Tunisia, a colony of France, had a thriving Jewish minority that numbered about 50,000 people, although age-old tensions between the country's Jews and its Muslim majority continued to simmer, particularly in Tunis. During Memmi's childhood, Tunisian Jews focused their efforts on assimilating into the French colonial culture of the region.

Roots in Jewish Tunisia

At age four Memmi was sent to Hebrew school and by age seven he began classes at a school run by the Alliance Israelite Universalle. The Universalle was an organization that merged Jewish tradition with modern European education, a system in keeping with the colonialism of the Tunis Jews. At age 12 Memmi began studies at a French lycée in Tunis, graduating in 1939 with the school's top prize in philosophy.

Memmi enrolled at the University of Algiers, but his studies were soon interrupted by the onset of World War II. North African Jews were soon imperiled by the Vichy collaborationist government in France and its support of Nazi Germany's anti-Semitic laws. As a Jew, Memmi was expelled from the University of Algiers and sent to a forced labor camp in eastern Tunisia. Finally released, he returned to the University of Algiers in 1943 and received his licence es philosophie. By this time, he had already begun writing for Jewish newspapers.

Two Novels Critically Acclaimed

In 1946 Memmi moved to Paris, France, intending to continue his academic studies. He also started writing his first novel, and also married a French-Catholic woman named Marie-Germaine Dubach, with whom he would have three children. In 1951 Memmi returned to Tunis with his wife, and got a job teaching at his former lycée. Two years later he published his first novel, *La statue de sel*—translated as *Pillar of Salt*—which is a largely autobiographical account of the 30-year-old author's life. The novel also examines Jewish life in a predominantly Muslim land, and also views circumstances from the point of view of a North African living in Europe. *Pillar of Salt* took the Carthage Prize the year it appeared, and also received the Feneon Prize in 1954. In 1955 the novel appeared in English translation.

Beginning in 1953, Memmi taught high school in Tunis, and continued at this job for three years. From 1953 to 1957 he also served as the director of the city's Center for Educational Research. In 1955 he published his second novel, *Agar—Strangers*—which explores mixed marriages. Highly popular, *Strangers* was shortlisted for the Prix Goncourt, France's top literary honor. Like *Pillar of Salt, Strangers* is also highly autobiographical, and explores similar themes regarding the problems of Jews living in a Muslim society. In Memmi's *La terre interieure—The Interior Land*—he relates an incident from 1857 when a Tunisian Muslim and a Tunisian Jew have a heated argument and the Jew is sentenced to death.

Succeeded in Nonfiction

When the French colonial government left Tunisia in 1956, many Jews also decided to leave the country, fearing reprisals from the predominantly Muslim government that stepped into power. Memmi and his wife immigrated to France, and the following year he published his first nonfiction work, *Portrait du colonise precede du portrait du colinisateur.* Translated in the mid-1960s as *The Colonizer and the Colonized,* the book explores theories of colonization, and its provocative essays caused an immediate stir throughout North Africa and in France. The book caused an upheaval in its author's personal life as well, when writer Albert Camus took affront at an article in the book titled "The Well-meaning Colonialist." Convinced that it was a couched portrait of himself, Camus ended his friendship with Memmi, and his death in 1960 prevented the rift between the two writers from ever being bridged.

The Colonizer and the Colonized proved to be a highly influential—as well as highly controversial—work. Citing colonization as a variant of fascism, Memmi especially reacts to the decolonization of North Africa in 1956, but states that the dynamics are similar in any colonial system. In his view, although minority populations are exploited under colonial governments, once they gain their freedom and gain political and economic power they in turn become the exploiters.

Taught in France

In 1958 Memmi became a researcher for the National Center of Scientific Research based in Paris, France, and remained there until 1960. He also became conference director of the School of Higher Studies in Social Sciences. From 1959 to 1966 he was an assistant professor of social psychology at the University of Paris, Sorbonne. He also began working toward an advanced degree, which he would earn in 1970.

During and after his professorship in Paris, Memmi continued writing. 1962 saw the publication of Memmi's *Portrait d'un Juif—Portrait of a Jew*—a theoretical work which further explores the exploitation of minorities. In 1962 he also published *La liberation d'un Juif,* which was translated as *The Liberation of a Jew.* He made a lecture tour of the United States in 1966, the same year he gained his professorship at the Sorbonne, and in 1968 he published the essay collection *L'homme domine—Dominated Man*—which explores victims of social and psychological oppression.

Continued Penning Fiction and Nonfiction

In 1969 Memmi returned to fiction with the publication of *Le scorpion ou la confession imaginaire,* published in translation in 1971 as *The Scorpion; or, The Imaginary Confession.* This novel, like Memmi's previous fiction, is autobiographical, and also contains commentary, parables, and a fictional storyline. In 1970 Memmi finally completed his doctorate in letters at the Sorbonne, and after receiving his degree decided to move from the city where he had lived for over a decade. He became a professor of sociology at the University of Paris in Nanterre, France, and in 1972 traveled to North America to become Walker Ames Professor at the University of Seattle. In addition to his degree from the Sorbonne, Memmi earned a Ph.D. from the Université de Beer Scheba.

Continuing to publish during the 1970s, Memmi also continued his role as educator. Returning to France, from 1975 to 1978 he served as director of the department of social sciences at the French School of Higher Studies in Social Sciences. In 1977 he became vice president of the French chapter of the International Association of Poets, Playwrights, Editors, Essayists, and Novelists (PEN), which position he retained until 1980. Throughout his writing career Memmi was an active presence in the French chapter of PEN.

Memmi published *La dependance: esquisse pour un portrait de dependant*—translated as *Dependance*—in 1979 and followed it three years later with one of his most noted works, *La racisme: description, definition, traitment.* Published in English translation as *Racism* after it went into a second edition, the book focuses on the issues behind subtle and overt prejudice. Discussing the book in the *Canadian Journal of Sociology,* Sean P. Hier explained that in *Racism* Memmi "argues that racism is a 'lived experience' arising within human situations." Noting that racism is destructive to all human societies, he contends that "the magnitude of racism is contingent on how the concepts of race and difference are generalized and accepted as social knowledge."

Into his seventies Memmi continued to write, publishing *A contre-courants—Against the Tide* in 1993. In this work he warned of the rising tide of fascism he perceived in Western society, and promoted secular humanism as an antidote. In 1994 he was honored with the Prix de Ratoinalist and in 1995 he received the Union Prize of the Magreb Foundation in Noureddine. Memmi's brother, George Memmi, is also a novelist.

Books

Contemporary Black Biography, Volume 37, Gale, 2003.
Contemporary World Writers, second edition, St. James Press, 1993.

Periodicals

African Writers, Volume 2, Charles Scribner's Sons, 1997.
Canadian Journal of Sociology, December-February, 2000.
Research in African Literatures, Volume 1, number 1, 1970. □

Maud L. Menten

A native of Canada, Maud L. Menten (1879-1960) is a little-known scientist who discovered an equation that has been hailed as a foundation in the modern study of enzymology. As a researcher, Menten made many co-discoveries relating to blood sugar, hemoglobin, and kidney functions. She also worked as a professor and pathologist, and enjoyed diverse pastimes, including mountain climbing and the study of foreign languages. Menten was one of the first Canadian women to earn a medical degree.

Menten was born March 20, 1879, in Port Lambton, Ontario, Canada. Little is known about her parents and childhood other than that the Menten family moved to Harrison Mills, where Maud's mother worked as a postmistress. After completing secondary school, Menten attended the University of Toronto where she earned a bachelor of arts degree in 1904 and a master's degree in physiology in 1907. While earning her graduate degree, she worked as a demonstrator in the university's physiology lab.

A talented student, Menten was appointed a fellow at the Rockefeller Institute for Medical Research in New York City in 1907. There, she studied the effect of radium bromide on cancerous tumors in rats. Menten and two other scientists published the results of their experiment, producing the institute's first monograph. After a year at the Institute, Menten worked as an intern at the New York Infirmary for Women and Children. She returned to Canada and began studies at the University of Toronto a year later. In 1911 she became one of the first Canadian women to receive a doctor of medicine degree.

Discovered Michaelis-Menten Equation

In 1912, Menten boarded a ship and traveled to Berlin, Germany, where she worked with Dr. Leonor Michaelis at the University of Berlin. The following year she and Michaelis coauthored a paper on chemical kinetics that was published in *Biochemische Zietschrift.* The paper described the Michaelis-Menten equation, a concept that quickly changed the study of biochemistry and for which Menten as well as her German coauthor earned worldwide recognition.

The Michaelis-Menten equation is a tool for measuring the rates of enzyme reactions. Proteins called enzymes control the chemical reactions which maintain the life of cells. Menten's 1913 formula gave scientists a way to record how enzymes worked. According to *Pittmed,* the University of Pittsburgh School of Medicine magazine, the equation is the standard for most subsequent enzyme-kinetic measurements. The rate is basic knowledge for biochemistry students and is routinely used in research laboratories.

Menten also worked as a research fellow at Western Reserve University with Dr. George Crile. In 1915 she spent a year performing cancer research at the Barnard Skin and Cancer Hospital in St. Louis, Missouri, and in 1916 she added to her academic credits with a Ph.D. in biochemistry from the University of Chicago.

Armed with her doctorate, Menten joined the School of Medicine at the University of Pittsburgh as an instructor in 1918, delivering one-third of the school's daily pathology lectures and attending all lab sections. She remained at the university until her retirement in 1950, and was promoted to full professor in 1948 at the age of sixty-nine.

In addition to her teaching duties at the University of Pittsburgh, Menten also was a pathologist at the Children's Hospital of Pittsburgh from 1926 to 1950. Her work at Children's Hospital involved three positions: surgical pathologist, post-mortem pathologist, and haematologist. In these positions she became familiar with many cases and worked hard on behalf of her young patients. Pediatric residents often sought her advice, and she was always available to them.

Juggling her work as a pathologist, a researcher, and a professor, Menten often worked 18-hour days. A tireless researcher, she had little patience for scientists who had no new ideas. Rebecca Skloot in *Pittmed* reported that Menten said of a famous physician who had won the Nobel prize, "What has he done since?" She is also said to have let loose with a tirade in a lab of scientists who she thought were not working hard enough.

Many Important Discoveries

With her questioning intellect, Menten never ran out of research ideas or problems to tackle. The Michaelis-Menten equation is the best known of her works, but it was not her only important discovery. She authored or coauthored more than 70 research papers throughout her career. Other well-known accomplishments in the lab included Menten's 1924 discovery, with scientific colleague Helen Manning, that salmonella toxins raised blood glucose levels. In 1944 she partnered with Andersch Wilson to use electrophoresis—the use of an electric charge—to separate different proteins, in this case adult hemoglobin from fetal hemoglobin. Although Menten used the electrophoresis technique in 1944, noted scientist Linus Pauling employed it a few years later; through his renown and outspoken position in the scientific community Pawling has been credited with discovering the technique.

In 1944, together with scientists with Junge and Green, Menten discovered the azo-dye coupling reaction, which has since become a routine tool in biological research and diagnostic medicine. Menten's discovery opened up the field of enzyme histochemistry.

Menten published papers on potassium in cells, oxidases, vitamin C, streptococcal toxins, histochemistry of glycogen, and nucleic acids in bone marrow. She also published papers in other disciplines, including physiology, chemotherapy, hematology and pathology.

Woman of Diverse Interests

Skloot portrays Menten as a petite dynamo of a woman who wore "Paris hats, blue dresses with stained-glass hues, and Buster Brown shoes." She drove a Model T Ford through the University of Pittsburgh area for some 32 years and enjoyed many adventurous and artistic hobbies. She played the clarinet, painted paintings worthy of art exhibitions, climbed mountains, went on an Arctic expedition, and enjoyed astronomy. She also mastered several languages, including Russian, French, German, Italian, and at least one Native-American language.

Although Menten did most of her research in the United States, she retained her Canadian citizenship throughout her life. After her retirement from the University of Pittsburgh in 1950, she returned to Canada where she continued to do cancer research at the British Columbia Medical Research Institute. Poor health forced Menten's retirement in 1955, and she died July 20, 1960, at the age of 81, in Leamington, Ontario.

Throughout her career Menten was affiliated with many scientific societies, and in 1998 she was inducted into the Canadian Medical Hall of Fame. She was also honored at the University of Toronto with a plaque and at the University of Pittsburgh with memorial lectures and a named chair.

At Menten's death, colleagues Aaron H. Stock and Anna-Mary Carpenter honored the Canadian biochemist in an obituary in *Nature:* "Menten was untiring in her efforts on behalf of sick children. She was an inspiring teacher who stimulated medical students, resident physicians and research associates to their best efforts. She will long be remembered by her associates for her keen mind, for a certain dignity of manner, for unobtrusive modesty, for her wit, and above all for her enthusiasm for research."

Books

Notable Women Scientists, Gale, 2000.
Ogilvie, Marilyn, and Joy Harvey, editors, *Biographical Dictionary of Women in Science: Pioneering Lives from Ancient Times to the Mid-20th Century,* Routledge, 2000, pp. 882-883.

Periodicals

Pittmed, October, 2000.
Nature, March 25, 1961, p. 965.

Online

"Dr. Maud Menton," *Canadian Medical Hall of Fame Web site,* http://www.cdnmedhall.org/inductees/menten_98.htm (July 12, 2002).
"Maud Leonora Menton," *Who Named It,* http://www.whonamedit.com/dpctpr/cf,2091.html (November 10, 2003). □

Carl Wilheim Emil Milles

One of the foremost Scandinavian artists of the 20th century, Swedish-born Carl Milles (1875-1955) com-

him to come to run a gymnastics school. However, Milles stopped in Paris, France, on the way to Chile and was enthralled with the vibrant, artistic capital.

Paris proved to be a fertile ground for Milles to develop his talent and he decided to remain in Paris, where he spent the next eight years enhancing his art form. He attended the Ecole des Beaux-Arts (School for the Fine Arts) and the Académie Colarossi, while, as Abbe noted, "supporting himself by making coffins, waiting tables and carving furniture." After two years of living hand-to-mouth, Milles had work accepted in 1899 for exhibition at the distinguished Salon and his career began to accelerate. The following year, Milles exhibited again at the Salon, receiving an Honorable Mention. Two years later, in 1902, Milles's entry to the Sten Sture monument competition in Uppsala, Sweden, received fourth place; however, due to popular demand, the award was changed to first place.

Milles met the renowned sculptor Auguste Rodin at the close of the 19th century. He became an assistant to Rodin and his early works, including *The Struggle for Existence, Women in the Wind,* and *American Bison,* are heavily influenced by Rodin's distinctive style. In the *St. Louis Post-Dispatch,* Jeff Daniel observed "But these weren't yet Milles's work, and he realized as much. According to some accounts, he went so far as to destroy many of his earliest sculptures, such was his desire to break free of Rodin and develop something from his own experience, of his own time—and within his own limits of imagination."

Artistic Development in Europe

In 1904, Milles left Paris for Munich, Germany. During his two years in Munich, Milles found inspiration in the works of Adolf von Hildebrand; he also married Austrian portrait painter Olga Granner in 1905. From Munich, Milles spent two years traveling and studying in Rome and Austria before settling again in Sweden in 1908. Milles and his wife purchased a villa on the small island of Lidingö, just outside Stockholm, and spent several years developing works in their studio there. Milles poured so much money into the villa and accompanying grounds that his wife, Olga, quoted on the Millesgården website, once remarked, "We have no forks and no sheets, but pillars, that's something Carl can always afford!"

Milles's sculptures from this era—still showing signs of the influence of Rodin—were frequently publicly commissioned and include a set of bronze doors for the Church of Saltsjöbaden; *Dancers,* a piece inspired by Classical Greek sensibilities; and two fountains called *Susanna;* one in black granite and one in bronze, executed for the grounds of Milles's villa. Milles's works at the 1914 Baltic Exposition in Malmö, Sweden, drew the attention and praise of European critics, encouraging Milles to continue working on the development of his own unique style.

In 1920, Milles was appointed a professor of modeling at the Kongsthögskola (Royal Academy of Art) in Stockholm. During his 11-year tenure, Milles also produced many monumental public sculptures and fountains in his exuberant and sometimes humorous style. Milles won a gold medal at the landmark 1925 *Exposition Internationale des Arts*

bined many of the influences of late 19th and early 20th century sculpture into his trademark eclectic, humorous style. In addition to producing many grand fountains and publicly commissioned statues, Milles taught at the respected Cranbrook Academy of Art for 20 years.

Early Years in Stockholm and Paris

Carl Milles was born Wilhelm Carl Emil Andersson on June 23, 1875, in Lagga, Sweden, near Uppsala to Lieutenant Emil "Mille" Andersson and Walborg Tisell. Mary Abbe recorded in her *Minneapolis Star Tribune* article "Star of the North" that "Milles was a shy, rather sickly child who preferred nature to school." However, from a young age, he showed an aptitude for modeling figures; in *XXth Century Sculptors,* Stanley Casson noted that "His predilection for sculpture showed itself first in the carving of wood"—for in 1892, Milles began his earliest training as an apprentice to a cabinetmaker in Stockholm. Milles then attended the Kungliga Tekniska Högskola (Technical School) in Stockholm from 1895-1897. In 1897, he was awarded a monetary prize for being the best student in his class. This prize enabled him to leave Sweden, initially to travel to Santiago, Chile, where a family friend had asked

Décoratifs et Industriels Modernes à Paris, which set the stage for—and lent its name to—the Art Deco movement.

1926 provided another hallmark of things to come when Milles executed his first major public fountain, *Europa and the Bull,* for the city of Halmstad, Sweden. This neo-classical fountain played on Milles's fascination with ancient Greek and Roman myth, a theme that characterized many of Milles's works during this period. Abbe described the fountain thus: "Lovely Europa veritably floats above the beast's back and leans forward to stroke his outstretched tongue in a gesture that would make Freud blush . . . *Europa* is one of Milles' most successful pieces in its coupling of a powerful beast and a willfully free-spirited woman."

However, perhaps the most notable of these public commissions is *Folke Filbyter,* which Casson described as "a remarkable achievement. The counterpoise of [Folke Filbyter and his horse], the man leaning forwards and gazing down towards his left, the worn and weary horse leaning in the other direction, is one of the best examples of the proper interrelation of masses in a statue that can be found. The reliefs on the panels of the basin shows episodes in the history of the Folkunga dynasty of Swedish kings. The scenes are rendered with quick humor and Gothic freshness in a manner strongly reminiscent of the carving of English bench ends and choir seats of the fourteenth century." This work, opened at the end of 1927, capped off a successful year which also saw Milles's first major exhibition of exclusively his own work outside of Sweden, at London's Tate Gallery.

Successes in America

Milles and his wife made their first visit to the United States in 1929. Within two years, Milles had achieved fame and success in America following a large touring exhibition of his work, which stopped in St. Louis, Cleveland, New York, and Detroit. At this time, Milles was invited to head the sculpture department at the newly founded Cranbrook Academy of Art in Bloomfield Hills, Michigan, a suburb of Detroit. He and his wife settled at Cranbrook, where he taught until 1951. During this time period, Milles's fame as well as critical recognition for his work grew quickly. He was awarded several honors, including an honorary doctorate from Yale University, gold medals from the American Institute of Architecture and the Architectural League of New York, an Award of Merit from the American Academy of Arts and Letters, and a prize at the 1939 Golden Gate Exhibition. In 1945, Milles and his wife became American citizens.

Milles also produced several public installations for American cities during his two decades at Cranbrook. These include sculptures such as the *Swedish Tercentenary Monument* in Wilmington, Delaware (Milles' first commissioned piece in the U.S.); the *Monument of Peace,* a colossal sculpture of a Native American in the St. Paul, Minnesota, City Hall; and *Man and Nature,* in Rockefeller Center, New York City.

However, as throughout his life, Milles was best known for his fountains; Casson commented "In fountains Milles excels. [With one exception] . . . I know of no modern sculptor who has mastered this art that baffled even the Renaissance. . . . The conception of a work of art in which the graceful lines of falling or spurting water were combined with a harmonious arrangement of bronze and stone seems something altogether new." Milles's American fountains can be found in cities such as St. Louis, Missouri; Falls Church, Virginia; Ann Arbor, Michigan; and Kansas City, Missouri. An extensive collection of Milles's pieces, both sculptural and water elements, remained where he produced them on the grounds of Cranbrook Academy, where today nearly 70 of Milles's sculptures are on display—the largest such collection in the United States.

A Productive Later Life

In 1950, Milles celebrated his 75th birthday, remaining an active artist despite his age. The American Academy in Rome, Italy, offered Milles a resident artist position in 1951, and he and his wife returned to Europe, spending the summers in Sweden. (The Milles had turned their villa in Lidingö into a foundation and public museum, Millesgåden, in 1936; however, they continued to maintain a home on the grounds.) These later years saw the creation of more works in Milles's distinctive style. Daniel described one of these in the *Post-Dispatch:* "Yet Milles's most famous later work, and possibly his most realized, is "Hand of God," a literal interpretation that works so well because of a deceptive simplicity. A figure stands on the hand of God, his feet resting on the holy thumb and index finger. This could be Adam, but Milles once pointed out that this figure was instead all of us, looking skyward and precariously balanced, with an ability to rise or fall based in large part upon our own decisions." With copies around the world, *Hand of God,* completed in 1954, is in Detroit, Michigan, a city that also commissioned the *Spirit of Transportation* for its Civic Center in 1952.

Milles died at his home in Lidingö on September 19, 1955—yet his sculptures did not die with him. In fact, the *Encyclopedia Britannica* noted that "[Milles'] *Aganippe Fountain* was set up in the Metropolitan Museum of Art, New York City, shortly after his death." The last piece Milles executed, the *Aganippe Fountain,* or *Fountain of the Muses,* features jets of water shooting among five stylized figures representing a poet, an architect, a musician, a painter and a sculptor, while animals drawn from myth and the goddess Aganippe form the background. The fountain was purchased by Brookgreen Gardens, America's largest outdoor sculpture garden, located in South Carolina.

Milles's Influence on Sculpture

Casson argued that "No . . . sculptor combines so much personal style with so great variety of treatment, so deep an insight with so varied an imagination." The evolution of Milles' style from its earliest, Rodin-influenced roots to its most idiosyncratic zenith is easily discernible in the chronological progression of his sculpture. His themes draw equally on Neoclassicism and mythological figures, on the creatures of and movements in the sea, and on a later fascination with religion, creating what Daniel called a "curious mix of playful fantasy and existential spirituality."

As the art world moves past the minimalist and abstract movements that have dominated artists' works for nearly 50 years, Milles represents a form of art coming back into vogue and influencing modern pieces. As Pierre Volboudt, quoted in the *Dictionnaire critique and documentaire des Peintres, Sculpteurs, Dessinateurs et Graveurs,* said, ''His art, at once sensual and austere, tormented and serene, is animated with the power of the gods.''

Books

A Biographical Dictionary of Artists, ed. Sit Lawrence Gowing, Prentice Hall-Equinox, 1983.

Bénézit, E., *Dictionnaire critique et documentaire des Peintres, Sculpteurs, Dessinateurs et Graveurs,* Librarie Gründ, 1976.

Casson, Stanley, *XXth Century Sculptors,* Oxford University Press, 1930.

Mantle Fielding's Dictionary of American Painters, Sculptors, and Engravers, Glenn B. Opitz, ed., 2nd edition, Apollo Book, 1986.

Prestel Dictionary of Art and Artists in the 20th Century, Prestel Verlag, 2000.

Taylor, Joshua C., *The Fine Arts in America,* The University of Chicago Press, 1979.

Who Was Who in American Art: 1564-1975, Peter Hastings Falk, ed., Sound View Press, 1999.

Periodicals

Minneapolis Star Tribune, February 27, 2000.

St. Louis Post-Dispatch, May 26, 1998.

Online

Encyclopedia Britannica Online, ''Milles, Carl,'' http://search.eb .com/eb/article?eu=54042 (December 8, 2003).

''Millesgården,'' http://www.millesgarden.se (December 10, 2003).

Stare, Jacqueline, ''The Grove Dictionary of Art Online: Milles, Carl (Wilhelm Emil),'' http://www.groveart.com (December 10, 2003).

''Tate Collections: Carl Milles,'' http://www.tate.org.uk (December 8, 2003). □

Mirabai

Immortalized since the 15th century as a Brahmin princess whose love for Krishna compelled her to wander in search of enlightenment, Mirabai (1498-1547) was a Hindi poetess, mystic, Rajput princess, and Bhakti yogini saint whose life was steeped in legend, but whose contribution to Indian culture remains uncontested.

The one thing that is certain about the life of Mirabai is that everything that is currently known about her is conjecture and educated guesswork at best. The details of her life are so obscured by legend that they remain a hotbed of argumentation due to the essential lack of empirical data regarding her history. Usha Nilsson's account of Mirabai's life in her biography *Mira Bai* is based on the best

that previous scholars had to offer, and can be relied on as a respectable source for readers interested in both the facts and the legends that surround Mirabai's story.

Life vs. Legend

Mirabai's birth has been estimated to have occurred in 1498, and her birthplace was Merta. Merta was an independent kingdom with a fortress city created by Mirabai's grandfather, Rao Dudaji, and ruled by her father, Ratan Singh. The political and social climate during Mirabai's lifetime was one of great unrest between the Muslim forces invading northern India and the Hindu population struggling to maintain their livelihoods and culture. Mirabai's mother died when her daughter was a young child of perhaps four or five years old. With her father wrapped up in the responsibilities of war, following the death of her mother Mirabai was sent to live with her grandparents. As a Brahmin and a royal princess of Merta, the girl was educated at home, with particular attention paid to instruction in music. This grounding in music helps to explain the hypnotic simplicity of Mirabai's later songs, which belied a thorough knowledge of musicality.

Mirabai's religious affinities are believed to have their roots in an event that occurred during her childhood with her grandparents. Her grandfather was a committed follower of the god Vishnu, and Mirabai's childhood environment was one of religious piety and early praise of Krishna. Legend states that a traveling mendicant—a religious beggar—was welcomed into the household, having with him a small idol of Krishna. Mirabai was instantly and deeply smitten with the idol, and cried for it once the mendicant had gone on his way. The mendicant was told in a vision to return to the house and give the idol to the little girl, which he did. From that day on, Mirabai is said to have kept the idol with her at all times and thus began her worship of Krishna.

In 1516, at the age of 18, Mirabai was given in marriage, perhaps against her will, to Bhoj Raj, crown prince of Mewar. Bhoj died of fatal battle wounds only five years later, in 1521. Mirabai welcomed widowhood as an opportunity to live as the devoted spouse of her divine lord Krishna. She dedicated her days to worshiping him and singing and dancing his praises. She also devoted her time and energies to caring for the religious poor, an open denial of her caste and her royal position. This activity was considered unbecoming of a highborn princess who was expected to be secluded and aloof and pay homage to the preferred goddess of her late husband's family, the destructive deity Kali. Mirabai considered Krishna to be her divine match. Her religious fervor did not sit well with her in-laws, and when she refused to commit *sati*—the act of a newly widowed woman throwing herself on her late husband's funeral pyre and burning alive—multiple attempts were made on her life. The details of these attempts, while completely obscured in legend, are interesting nonetheless. In one story Mirabai was sent a basket of flowers with a poisonous snake hidden inside. The story related that when she took the basket and looked inside, the snake turned into a religious figurine. At another time her husband's family demanded that she drink a cup of poison in front of them as retribution for disrespecting her dead husband by refusing to commit sati as Rajput princesses were supposed to. Mirabai drank the poison, but remained unharmed. In a third story, when asked by her late husband's family to drown herself, she attempted to do so, but her body floated and did not sink. Still another tale tells of the princess being forced to lie on a bed of nails, but then arising unharmed. Each of these miraculous escapes were attributed to the intervention of Krishna and are believed to be Mirabai's reward for her undying devotion.

Tired of her family's political maneuverings, Mirabai eventually left Mewar and returned to her childhood home of Merta. In Merta, however, the princess found herself facing more persecution, this time by an uncle who had taken control of the kingdom following the death of Mirabai's father in battle. This uncle, like many others, objected to the young widow's public displays of religious ardor and he made life difficult for her. She fled Merta and traveled to Vrindaban, the birthplace of Krishna, where she joined a religious community. It is believed that Mirabai spent her 30s as a wandering mendicant, finally moving to Dwarka—another place with deep connections to the god Krishna—and dying there in 1547.

As with her life, there are also many legends surrounding Mirabai's death. The most famous story is that her late husband's family sent a group of high-ranking Brahmins to bring her back to Rajasthan. When Mirabai refused to return with them, the Brahmins threatened to fast until dead if she did not comply. Not wanting their deaths to be her responsibility, she asked if she might consult her lord Krishna, and disappeared into the temple. It is believed that Krishna allowed Mirabai to merge with him completely, and she became one with his temple statue, never to be seen again.

Authored Spiritual-centered Poetry

Mirabai participated wholeheartedly in the *Bhakti* movement, which consisted of active devotion displayed and expressed through public, ecstatic, religious song and dance. The tolerant nature of this religious movement gave its members the ability to ignore the restrictions of caste, sex, and creed. This, in turn, allowed Mirabai to rise as a poet-saint through her songs. Mirabai's poetry was written in the form of song verses known as *padas* and mystical love poems called *bhajans*. She is credited with creating a unique *raga,* or mode in which her songs were to be sung, that which was named after her: Mira's *Malar.* Mirabai composed her songs in a combination of the Rajasthani and Braj Bhasa languages, but they have since been translated into Hindi, Rajasthani, and Gujarati.

There are anywhere from 400 to 1,300 songs attributed to Mirabai, but scholars believe she most likely composed somewhere between 103 and 200 padas. As a devotee of Krishna, she strove to celebrate her love for her god; to take credit for the composition of songs in his praise would have been considered an act of pride for a woman striving, ultimately, for a state of selflessness. As a result of this dynamic, it is difficult to arrive at a definitive account of

those lyric poems actually written by Mirabai herself, compared to those attributed to her but not composed by her.

Mirabai's works were not recorded in writing for many reasons. As Nilsson explained, ''At the time Mira Bai lived, there were limited means to preserve manuscripts. . . . After the death of her husband and her father-in-law, Mira Bai was continuously persecuted. . . . it was highly unlikely that they would have made an effort to [record] her works. . . . The works of poets like Kabir were preserved by their disciples. . . . But Mira Bai . . . did not have a following of loyal disciples. . . . She was not striving for poetic recognition and probably did not care to leave her songs in writing.'' As Nancy Martin commented in the *Encyclopedia of Women and World Religion,* Mirabai's songs have been ''preserved in the fluid realm of oral tradition,'' despite the lack of any authentic, historical text.

Mirabai worshiped Krishna, one of the most beloved of the human incarnations of the godhead Vishnu, and the content of her songs revolve around variations of her love for her god. They are filled with sensuous images and expressions of intense longing, addressed from a supplicant to her lord. She chose to shed the more traditional themes used within the genre and adopted instead more personal and intimate topics. In some of her songs she casts herself as a *gopi,* one of the many ''milkmaids'' or ''cowherd girls'' that lord Krishna consorted with. The majority of her poems, however, are addressed to Krishna as if from a wife to her husband. She sings of the longing of the individual soul, the *atman,* to join with the *paramatman,* or the soul of the universe as embodied by Krishna. This construct of husband and wife is unlike that of other Bhakti saint-poets who usually wrote from the perspective of a servant to their god. While those within the Bhakti movement exercised great tolerance and acceptance, many of those outside it did not, and many traditionally minded people, including Mirabai's in-laws, viewed her public displays of spiritual singing and dancing as scandalous and inappropriate, particularly for a woman of high birth.

Living in Memory

Mirabai, while not as well known as her contemporaries Kabir, Tulsi Das, and the blind poet Sur Das, was significant in her own right, and her songs of love and devotion for her lord Krishna became a unique contribution to the history of north Indian culture. One of the earliest poets known by name in Hindi literature, she lives in the minds and hearts of many through her songs, but also as a cultural and social dichotomy. Her name is still used to influence women; saying that a woman is like Mirabai means that she is unwomanly and destined for trouble if she does not straighten up and conform to tradition. Others might say that a woman is like Mirabai and mean that she is a free spirit with the strength of character to stand up for what she believes. As quoted on *Sentient.org,* Dhurvadas, writing in the 17th century said of Mirabai: ''Having forgotten her shyness, she worshiped Giridhar (Krishna). She no longer cared for her family honor. She was Mira, known throughout the world; she was a treasure of devotions. In bliss she visited beautiful Vrindaban. She danced with anklebells on her feet, and with castanets in her hands. In the purity of her heart, she met the devotees of God, and realized the pettiness of the world.'' Many may claim Mirabai's essence to support their arguments, but none truly possess her.

Books

Encyclopedia of Women and World Religion, Macmillan Reference USA, 1999.

The Feminist Companion to Literature in English, Yale University Press, 1990.

Nilsson, Usha S., *Mira Bai,* Sahitya Akademi, 1969.

Online

''Meera Bai,'' *SoulKurry.com,* http://www.soulkurry.com/v2culture/article.php3?articleid=352 (December 19, 2003).

''Mirabai,'' *Poetseers Web site,* http://www.poetseers.org/the_poetseers/mirabai (December 19, 2003).

''Mirabai: 1498-1547,'' *Sentient,* http://www.sentient.org/mirabai (December 19, 2003).

''Mirabai: Biography,'' *Manas: India and Its Neighbors,* http://www.sscnet.ucla.edu/southasia/Religions/gurus/Mirabai (December 19, 2003).

Mirabai Mandir Web site, http://www.mirabai.org (December 19, 2003). □

Franco Modigliani

American economist Franco Modigliani (1918–2003) won the Nobel Prize for Economics in 1985 for a career that began in his native Italy when he won a prize for an economics essay during his second year at the University of Rome. With prospects for a bright future dimming under the rise of Fascism in Mussolini's Italy as it began to collaborate with Hitler's Germany, he left Italy and joined his future wife and her parents in Paris. With World War II about to engulf Europe, Modigliani, himself a Jew, decided it best to leave for America. In August 1939, a few days before the war in Europe broke out, they arrived in New York.

Privilege Was No Escape

M odigliani was born on June 18, 1918, in Rome, Italy. His father, Enrico Modigliani, was a prominent pediatrician and his mother, Olga Flaschel Modigliani, was a volunteer social worker. He described himself in his autobiography for the Nobel Prize committee as being a ''good'' student ''though not outstanding.'' When he was 13 his father died unexpectedly due to an operation. Modigliani was traumatized, and for the next three years his performance at school reflected his grief. It was inconsistent at best. He then transferred to Liceo Visconti, considered the best high school in Rome, and there he began to flourish.

Because of his excellent progress, he took the university exam and was able to skip his last year in high school and begin his college career at age 17. Family hopes that he would follow his father's path into medicine did not last for Modigliani, who admitted a low tolerance for suffering and blood. Instead he initially decided on pursuing a law degree which he saw as opening the door to many possibilities in Italy. That plan, too, was about to change.

In his second year at the University of Rome Modigliani entered an economics essay in a contest by a student organization. He won. It was at that moment that he realized his interest was in economics. Prospects for getting a proper education there were not good due to fascism. Economics education was grim. Instead he decided he would continue to study on his own with the assistance of a few economists he knew personally and whom he valued, especially Riccardo Bachi. He began to read the English and Italian versions of the classics in the field. The same organization that had sponsored the prize, *I Littoriali della Coltura,* had also helped put him into contact with other anti-fascists. His political philosophy changed in that direction, as did his involvement with his future wife, Serena Calabi, and her father, Giulio, both anti-fascists.

Modigliani recalled that, ''In 1938 the Italian racial laws were promulgated and at the invitation of my future in-laws, I joined them in Paris, where, in May 1939, Serena and I were married.'' What was a joyful time in his personal life was shadowed by the state of affairs in Europe. He was not impressed with his classes at the Sorbonne in Paris, and spent his time studying on his own at the St. Genevieve Library (Bibliotheque St. Genevieve). In June he had returned briefly to Italy to discuss his thesis and to receive his Doctor of Juris degree from the University of Rome. But with the certainty of war, Modigliani, his wife, and her parents applied for immigration to the United States. They arrived in August 1939, and the war in Europe began a few days later.

New School for a New Life

When it was apparent that Modigliani would not be returning to Europe for quite a long time, he enrolled at the New School for Social Research in New York City and was awarded with a free tuition scholarship by the Graduate Faculty of Political and Social Science. The New School had been newly created and provided an academic haven for many Europeans, especially Jews, who had escaped the persecutions that had come with Hitler and the other fascist dictatorships. He began studies in the fall of 1939 and continued his studies for three years at night, while he sold European books during the day to support his growing family that would eventually include his two sons, Andre and Sergio. In 1941 he began his first teaching job at the New Jersey College for Woman. The following year he became an instructor in economics at Bard College, which was at the time a residential college of Columbia University. In 1944, he received his doctorate in economics from the New School. His first publication, in January 1944, was in *Econometrica,* which, he noted, was essentially his dissertation, entitled, "Liquidity Preference and the Theory of Interest and Money." It was Modigliani's model present in his dissertation that would provide the core of the Neo-Keynesian Synthesis of post-war macroeconomics, according to the New School website page on Modigliani. An explanation of the economics system he proposed noted that, "In sum, Modigliani proposed that with sticky wages money is non-neutral: an increase in the nominal money supply M raises the price level less-then-proportionally, decreases the interest rate and raises employment and output. If money wages are fully flexible, as in the earlier case, then money is neutral it affects neither interest nor employment nor output and increases the price level proportionally. Thus, Modigliani concludes, Keynes' (Economist John Maynard Keynes) theory only works if there is sticky or rigid money wages."

He returned to the New School to become a lecturer and research associate at the Institute of World Affairs. His project was published in *National Income and International Trade.* He also created his first proposal for saving, known as the *Duesenberry-Modigliani hypothesis.*

Modigliani left New York in 1948 to study at the University of Chicago after receiving the nod for the Political Economy fellowship. At the same time he joined the Cowles Commission for Research in Economics as a research consultant. He soon accepted a position as director of a research project at the University of Illinois on "Expectations and Business Fluctuations." In 1952 Modigliani left Chicago to join the faculty at the Carnegie Institute of Technology, now Carnegie-Mellon University, and stayed there

until 1960. While there he completed two important papers that would set the foundation of his "Life Cycle Hypothesis," as well as a collaboration on a book and two essays with another economist, Merton H. Miller. He then spent a year at Massachusetts Institute of Technology (MIT) as a visiting professor. After another year teaching at Northwestern, he returned to MIT and stayed the duration of his career.

With Nobel, Criticism for President

Modigliani was announced as the recipient of the 1985 Nobel Prize for Economics in October 1985, the 13th American to win the prize since its establishment in 1969. David Warsh of the *Boston Globe* broke the story on the local honoree that was more than simply one expressing Modigliani's pleasure in receiving the nod. "After receiving news of the award," Warsh wrote, "he immediately rebuked President Reagan for coining political positions that contradicted virtually all of the findings of Modigliani's 40 years of investigations." Modigliani seemed to be leveling only criticism at the president that first year of his second term for insisting that the growing deficit did nothing to hurt savings. He also criticized the president for doing everything to undermine the economy except to raise taxes. On a lighter note at his press conference that day in Cambridge, Modigliani said that, "I sometimes think that my work on this subject was colored by the savings bank where I was banking at the time when I was working on this. Their motto was, 'Save it when you need it least, have it when you need it most.' " He also mentioned his appreciation of an early collaborator at Illinois. Richard Brumberg was a "brilliant" graduate student, according to Modigliani, who had been working with him as the "Life Cycle Hypothesis" began to unfold. The plan that was outlined in 1953 and 1954 had laid the foundation for the future evolution of the project. Each of them then went to pursue other work: Brumberg to Johns Hopkins to complete his Ph.D. studies, and Modigliani to Carnegie. Brumberg died suddenly in 1955 of a brain tumor. Modigliani's shock and grief over the untimely death prevented him from publishing the second paper until 1980. Paul Samuelson, the first Nobel Economics winner in 1970 and an MIT colleague of Modigliani, reacted to the announcement of his prize as saying, "With many people with respect to the Nobel Prize, it's a question of 'if;' with Franco, it was only a question of 'when.' "

Modigliani's fame in the United States among his peers, students, and the circle of economists was not nearly as great as it was in Italy, where he was actually a celebrity. He wrote for a leading news magazine there, advised politicians and bankers, and sponsored many Italian students to attend MIT. John Bossons, an economist at the University of Toronto, noted at the time of his Nobel that Modigliani was "a very enthusiastic advocate," and had "inspired a lot of people."

Modigliani published prolifically, particularly in economic journals. In 2003 he published an autobiography titled, *Adventures of an Economist.*

Modigliani, a naturalized United States citizen, was a member of the National Academy of Sciences and the

American Academy of Arts and Sciences, and at the time he was honored with the Nobel, the only man to serve as president of both the American Economic Association and the American Finance Association. He also served as president of the American Econometric Society. In addition to advising Italian banks and politicians, Modigliani acted as a consultant to the United States Treasury, the Federal Reserve System, and numerous European banks.

Modigliani died in his sleep on September 25, 2003, at his home in Cambridge, Massachusetts, at the age of 85. When he died, an obituary in the *Economist* related an interesting, and amusing, story. "Serena Modigliani warned her husband not to turn around if someone shouted his name on the streets of Rome. 'Otherwise they'll shoot you,' she said. It was the winter of 1978, and Italy was gripped by political violence and economic chaos. Franco Modigliani, an economist at the Massachusetts Institute of Technology, had returned to the country of his birth to take part in a televised debate, urging unpopular reforms. When Mr. Modigliani left his hotel the next morning, he heard a man behind him call his name. He tried to walk faster, but his pursuer drew nearer, and finally caught him, grabbing his jacket. An assassin? No: a cobbler, in fact, desperate to tell him that, of all the bigwigs on the television the previous night, Mr. Modigliani had been the only one to say, 'anything comprehensible.' "

Periodicals

Boston Globe, October 16, 1985; December 5, 1985.
CFO, The Magazine for Senior Financial Executives, November 2003.
Economist, October 4, 2003.
The Guardian, October 1, 2003.
MIT News, September 25, 2003.
Science, November 7, 1986.

Online

"*Adventures of an Economist,* by Franco Modigliani," *Texere Publishing website,* http://www.etexere.com (January 16, 2004).
"Dining With Nobel Laureate Franco Modigliani," *Massachusetts Institute of Technology (MIT) News website,* http://www-tech.mit.edu (January 16, 2004).
"Franco Modigliani," *New School for Social Research website,* http://cepa.newschool.edu (December 31, 2003).
"Franco Modigliani," *Sloan School of Management, personal home page,* http://www.elsevier.com (January 16, 2004).
"Franco Modigliani Autobiography," *Nobel Museum website,* http://www.nobel.se (December 31, 2003).
"In memory of Franco Modiglian, (Pierleone Ottolenghi)," *Open Democracy website,* http://www.opendemocracy.net (January 16, 2004).
"Neoclassical Keynesian Synthesis," *New School for Social Research website,* http://cepa.newschool.edu (January 16, 2004).
"A Solution to the Social Security Reform," *Massachusetts Institute of Technology web,* http://web.mit.edu/francom/ (January 16, 2004). □

Ismael Montes

Bolivian statesman, lawyer, and military officer Ismael Montes (1861–1933) served two terms as President of Bolivia (1904–09 and 1913–17). A member of the country's Liberal Party, Montes ran an administration of political and social reform. He was instrumental in developing Bolivia's railway system and he fostered development. He also expanded his country's economy by adopting the gold standard and helping to make tin Bolivia's biggest export.

Early Life and Military Career

Ismael Montes Gamboa was born in Corocoro (later known as La Paz), Bolivia, on October 5, 1861. When he was 16, he graduated from the National College of Ayacucho in La Paz. As a young man, he attended the Greater University of Andres to study law.

In 1879, during the administration of Hilarión Daza, he interrupted his legal education to enlist in his country's army to fight against Chile in the War of the Pacific (1879–83), which involved a dispute between Chile and Bolivia over control of a part of the Atacama Desert on the Pacific coast of South America. Though the fighting ended in 1883, territorial issues would continue right up until Montes's first term as president, when the war would "officially" end.

At the heart of the conflict were valuable mineral resources contained on the disputed territory as well as control of the Pacific coast. Previously, the two countries had formed a treaty that recognized the 24th parallel as their boundary and gave Chile the right to share the export taxes on the mineral resources of Bolivia's territories. Later, however, the Bolivian government expressed dissatisfaction with the terms of the agreement because it did not like having to share the taxes. In addition, Bolivia, in danger of becoming a landlocked country, was afraid that Chile would seize control of the important coastal regions. Peru entered the conflict, siding with Bolivia, because it, too, was concerned about control of the Pacific coast. In 1874, the Chilean-Bolivian treaty was revised so that Chile gave up its share of export taxes on minerals shipped from Bolivia. In return, Bolivia agreed not to raise taxes on Chilean business in Bolivia for 25 years. But, in 1878, Bolivia tried to raise taxes on the Chilean Antofagasta Nitrate Company in the port city of Antofagasta. When the Chilean government protested, Bolivia threatened to confiscate the property. On February 14, 1879, Chile responded by sending troops in to occupy the city, causing Bolivia to declare war. Chile responded with its own declaration of war, against both Bolivia and Peru.

While in the army, Montes rose to the rank of captain. In 1884, he left the army to continue his law studies. He finally received his law degree on June 12, 1886. Afterward, he practiced law and worked as a journalist. Also during this period, he began his political career as a national representative from La Paz.

In 1898, Montes resumed his military career during the "Federal Revolution" of the Liberal Party, which sought to oust the Conservative Party that had been ruling the country for two decades. The following year, the Liberals overthrew the Conservatives. The coup, which would eventually lead to Montes's ascendancy to the presidency, was caused by resentments that developed during the long rule of the Conservatives, as well as regionalism and federalism issues. The Liberty Party gained important support from the rich tin-mining entrepreneurs in and around La Paz. The Conservatives had the support of the silver-mining entrepreneurs. The actual revolution was set in motion when the Liberals demanded that the capital be moved from Sucre to the more developed city of La Paz.

After the Liberals took control of the government, Montes became the army's Minister of War, serving under first party President Jose Manuel Pando. In 1900, he took part in the unsuccessful Acre campaign in Brazil, which involved a dispute over 191,000 square kilometers of territory on the Acre River that contained valuable rubber resources. The dispute escalated into armed conflict with the Brazilian rubber gatherers who had encroached into the territory. After three years of fighting, Pando turned the area over to Brazil when he signed the Treaty of Petropolis. Bolivia gave up its claims to the land in return for two areas on the Madeira and the Paraguay rivers totaling 5,200 square ki-

lometers and the use of a railroad to be built near the Madeira river in Brazilian territory.

Afterward, Montes became Chief of the General Staff and began a process of reforming the army.

Elected President of Bolivia

While congressional elections were fairly open, the Liberal Party, like the Conservatives before them, controlled the presidential elections and, in 1904, Montes became President of Bolivia. He governed from the *Palacio Quemado* ("Burnt Palace"), which was the unofficial name given to the rebuilt Palace of Government after it was burned down by a mob in 1875, during one of the country's many civil and political upheavals that marked that historical period. This would be the first of his two terms. His first term lasted until 1909; by the end of his second term, he would become the dominant figure in the era of Liberal Party rule.

After the Liberal Party gained power, its administration's top priority was settling existing border quarrels. When Montes became president, he inherited some substantial territorial issues. Still in dispute were some of the land claims that had initiated the War in the Pacific. In the first year of Montes's first term, Bolivia signed a peace treaty with Chile that officially ended the war. The treaty recognized Chile's possession of the Pacific coast. Bolivia ceded much in the agreement. It gave up its former coastal provinces and would be without a seaport city. Still, the treaty provided Bolivia with some substantial benefits. For giving up its territory, Bolivia received a cash indemnity of US $8.5 million. More importantly, Chile agreed to build a railroad, at its own cost, that would connect the Bolivian capital of La Paz with Chile's port of Arica. Bolivia was guaranteed free transit for its commerce through Chilean ports and territory. The treaty was ratified in 1905.

The treaty generated some opposition in Montes's country. However, Montes felt that a normalization of relations with Chile was essential to Bolivia's continued economic development. Indeed, the treaty brought a period of political and economic stability.

Improved Bolivia's Economy

While in office, Montes adapted Bolivia to the gold standard. His greatest achievement in office is considered to be the expansion of Bolivia's economy, which he fostered through increasing tin imports and obtaining large loans from foreign countries. These loans were later criticized as irresponsible, but they helped him improve Bolivia's railway systems, which had already benefited from the treaty he helped engineer with Chile. During his first term, he strongly supported railroad construction and greatly advanced railway travel in Bolivia. In 1906, he obtained a sizable loan from the National City Bank of New York, which helped him complete Bolivia's internal rail links. That year, he negotiated with the Speyer Contract, which established the Bolivia Railway Company with the funds obtained from the National City Bank. The company laid down 416 miles of track in a system that linked Bolivian cities and mining centers with the Peruvian network. By

1920, most major Bolivian cities were connected by rail. However, the construction had cost Bolivia $22 million, and the government could not pay off the debt. The British Antofagasta and Bolivia Railway Company then gained control of the rail system.

During his administration, Montes also began an ambitious public works program that included new urban construction, creation of new roads, and the installation of telegraph lines.

Also in his first term, embracing his party's Liberal policies, Montes helped bring about a period of political and social reforms. The army was reorganized under a French military mission, while the educational system was reformed by a Belgian Pedagogical Mission. Many Bolivian teachers were sent overseas for training. The nature of the church and state relationship was changed, too. Liberal Party policies were anti-clerical, and the special privileges that had been officially granted to the Roman Catholic Church were canceled. This created conflicts with the Church. In 1905, Montes legalized public worship by other faiths.

The Liberal Party itself practiced laissez-faire economic policies, which meant that it interfered as little as possible in the marketplace. Tin entrepreneurs and wealthy landowners paid only minimal taxes. When the government seized remaining lands belonging to native communities, it turned them over to private landholders. Montes himself took ownership of some of the most valuable properties. In another major development, the Liberal administration moved the seat of national government to La Paz, which became Bolivia's capital.

In 1909, Montes was succeeded by Dr. Heliodoro Villazón. Montes engineered the election.

Became President for a Second Term

In the years between his two terms, Montes served as a Bolivian diplomat in France and England. In 1913, he secured his own reelection and became president once again. During his second term, Montes continued to increase railroad construction, and he fostered the development of mining. The Liberal era was highlighted by the rise in tin production. During Villazón's administration, tin exports increased dramatically. By Montes's second term, tin became Bolivia's main export, surpassing silver and other products.

Also during his second term Montes continued his first-term policies of development. But a severe economic recession in 1913–14 curtailed his spending. The recession resulted from a drop in international trade that preceded World War I as well as severe droughts that negatively affected national agricultural production. The weakened Bolivian economy led to some civil strife, which gave rise to Liberal opposition in the form of the new Republican Party in 1914.

During most of its period in power, the Liberal Party had been able to rule without significant opposition. The overthrown Conservative Party had been greatly weakened. But the downturn in the economy and a continued loss of

national territory increased support for the Republican Party, who charged the Liberals with abuses of power. In particular, the dissidents charged that Montes's second election was fraudulent.

However, a small economic recovery quelled some of the dissatisfaction, and Montes was able to finish out his second term. In 1917, he handed the reins of the government over to his successor, Jose Gutierrez Guerra.

End of an Era

Guerra's presidency would be the last of the Liberal administration. The Republicans seized power in a bloodless coup in 1920, which brought to an end one of the most stable periods in Bolivia's turbulent history.

After he had finished his second term, Montes was appointed minister to Great Britain and France, acting as Bolivia's delegate to the League of Nations. After the Republican revolution, he decided to live in exile in Paris, France.

He returned to Bolivia in 1928, during the presidency of Republican Hernando Siles Reyes (1926–30). When Daniel Salamanca became President in 1931, Montes was appointed Minister of the Military. Salamanca was a former Liberal who had left the party to become a Republican. When Siles was overthrown, in large part because of conditions resulting from the Great Depression of 1929, Salamanca led a Republican-Liberal coalition and was elected President.

Salamanca was an unpopular president who governed during a period of economic hardship, and he repressed political opposition. During his administration, he renewed past hostilities with Paraguay over disputed territory in the Chaco region. This led to the Chaco War, which turned out to be a disaster for Bolivia, as it resulted in thousands of casualties and only worsened the economic conditions. On November 27, 1934, Salamanca was deposed by a group of Bolivian generals.

During the Chaco War, Montes served as the Major General of the Army of Bolivia, and he supported the war until his death on November 18, 1933, in La Paz.

Montes's Legacy

Today, Montes is regarded by many to have been one of Bolivia's best presidents. He reigned during a period of civil and economic stability, and he was a progressive leader whose development programs and reformation policies helped lead his country out of a turbulent past.

In 1983, the La Paz newspaper *Última Hor* polled 39 prominent Bolivians on which seven presidents they considered "most significant." Montes placed fifth on the list.

Books

Biographical Dictionary of Latin American and Caribbean Political Leaders, edited by Robert J. Alexander, Greenwood Press, 1988.

Encyclopedia of Latin America, edited by Helen Delpar, McGraw-Hill, 1974.

Henderson, James, Helen Delpar, Maurice Brungardt, and Richard Weldon, *Reference Guide to Latin American History,* M. E. Sharpe, 2000.

Online

"Bollandists," *The 1911 Edition Encyclopedia,* http://79.1911 encyclopedia.org/B/BO/BOLLANDISTS.htm (January 18, 2004).

"Bolivia History," *InfoPlease.com,* http://www.infoplease.com/ ce6/world/A0856958.html (January 18, 2004).

"Bolivia-The Liberal Party and the Rise of Tin," *Country Studies.com,* http://countrystudies.us/bolivia/13.htm (January 18, 2004).

"Ismael Montes," *AllRefer Encyclopedia,* http://reference.all refer.com/encyclopedia/M/Montes-I.html (January 18, 2004).

"United States and the Bolivian Sea Coast (Chapter Six)," *BoliviaWeb.com,* http://www.boliviaweb.com/mar/sea/ chapter6.htm (January 18, 2004).

"The War in the Pacific (1879–1884)," *AllWar.com,* http://www .onwar.com/aced/data/papa/pacific1879.htm (January 18, 2004). □

Ann Haven Morgan

Conservationist and educator Ann Haven Morgan (1882-1966) was a woman who enjoyed mucking around in ponds, digging into the earth, and illustrating what wonders she discovered. However, it is her tenure as a teacher—where she established for her students the importance of the study of the natural world, its conservation, and its benefits to humankind—which is her most enduring legacy.

Anna Haven Morgan was a born explorer of nature. Growing up on a farm in Connecticut, Morgan often escaped from her annoying younger sister and brother by wandering through the woods. On these adventures, she waded through ponds and streams, seeking out turtles, crawdads, dragonflies and other creatures of the water.

While attending the Williams Memorial Institute in New London, Connecticut, Morgan struggled to find books about the creatures she had discovered on her childhood adventures. Because there were none, she continued to learn about pond creatures through her own observations. After graduating from Williams, Morgan decided to pursue a degree in zoology at Wellesley College, but found Wellesley to be too strict, and with a dress code that required her to wear tight corsets. For her rebelliousness and aloof manner, Morgan was nicknamed "The New England Refrigerator." Not surprisingly, she left Wellesley and, in 1904, began her studies anew at Cornell University.

Became Lifelong Student of Nature

At Cornell, Morgan flourished. While taking entomology and zoology classes, she met her first mentor, teacher Anna Botsford Comstock. An intelligent woman working

within a field dominated by men, Comstock demonstrated to Morgan that a woman could succeed by studying and teaching science. Graduating from Cornell in 1906 with a degree in zoology and inspired by Comstock's example, Morgan searched for a job in teaching. She began her career in education as an assistant to Cornelia Clapp, the head of the zoology department at Mount Holyoke College, an all-girl's college in South Hadley, Massachusetts.

While assisting Clapp, Morgan discovered that she was not alone in her passion for scientific discovery. Mount Holyoke and Clapp had as much dedication to nature as did Morgan herself, and in Clapp she found a mentor on par with Comstock. With her captivating personality, Clapp taught Morgan that nature is the best teacher, not books.

During the summers of 1907 and 1908, Morgan once again became a student. She returned to Cornell University where she worked with aquatic biology professor James Needham. A well-known "water wizard," Needham taught Morgan how to "see things in water," as Elizabeth D. Schafer explained in *American National Biography Online.* Needham also helped Morgan become a member of the Entomological Society of America, a rare honor for women at that time.

Focusing on aquatic biology, Morgan began her doctoral study research. For this research, she chose to study her favorite insect, the mayfly. Because she was so enthusiastic about this research, students nicknamed her "Mayfly Morgan." Through detailed drawings, Morgan carefully documented the habits of mayflies, as well as making a new discovery regarding the insect's evolution: adaptation. While collecting specimens, she observed that mayflies whose natural habitat was a muddy bank looked different from those whose natural habitat was a river rapid. How these adaptations helped each mayfly survive became Morgan's research question for her dissertation, titled *A Contribution to the Biology of May-flies.* Although earning a doctorate degree was the result of Morgan's research, she also became an expert at catching trout. Morgan was not a fisherman, but because she had studied and exactly illustrated the mayfly, she could create such real-looking fake flies—the trout's favorite food—that her fisherman friends who used her flies caught more fish.

Nicknamed "Electric Professor"

In 1912, after shortening her name to "Ann," Morgan returned to Mount Holyoke College to teach. She formed strong bonds with fellow teacher and former mentor Clapp as well as with her students. Even though some students found her demanding, Morgan mesmerized them with her boundless energy. Throughout the 1920s she continued teaching her students how nature creates its own environment and how within that environment species can survive. However, she also added a new idea to her class curriculum: conservation. Through the field trips she took with her students to rural, unspoiled habitats, Morgan clearly showed her feeling regarding conservation by allowing students to realize that no one could study and learn if what they studied no longer existed.

In 1926 Morgan traveled to British Guiana in South America to study the stump-legged mayfly. There, she finally discovered the answer to a nagging question that had been left unanswered in her doctoral studies: Why do mayflies retain some characteristics of infancy, such as longer front legs, while other body parts disappear? Morgan discovered that adult male mayflies retain their long front legs because they use them to grasp the female of the species during mating. Since the other body parts are not needed for reproduction, through adaptation, they have simply vanished.

Authored Three Books

In 1930 Morgan published her first book, *Field Book of Ponds and Streams: An Introduction to the Life of Fresh Water.* With this volume Morgan wrote the book she had wanted to read when she was a curious child, but never found. "This book began in ponds where frogs sat on lilypads and by swift brooks from which mayflies flew forth at twilight. I hope that it may be a guide into the vividness and variety of their ways," wrote Morgan in the preface to her book. However, *Field Book of Ponds and Streams* turned into more than a guide; it inspired people all over the world to become better observers of nature. Morgan received many letters of thanks from readers who finally had the knowledge they needed to understand and appreciate the natural world.

Published in 1939, Morgan's second book, *Field Book of Animals in Winter,* focuses on the "ways in which animals meet the crises and depressions of winter," commented Schafer. This book was significant as one of the first books to focus on how and why animals hibernate. On its author's part, Morgan discovered an admiration for the animals, who had "persistence which must hearten any human being to contemplate," as Schafer quoted from the volume. Like her first book, *Field Book of Animals in Winter* also became an international best seller, impressing the editorial board of the *Encyclopedia Britannica,* which requested Morgan's permission and assistance in developing an educational film based on her work.

During the 1940s, with World War II raging, Morgan and her students joined many Americans in sending care packages to Allied soldiers. However, Morgan wanted to do more. So, in 1944, in her capacity as Massachusetts State aquatic biologist, she began a new study focusing on the ecosystems of the state's lakes. During war times, food shortages are common. Morgan reasoned that, if fish have no food to eat, they die. If their food supply is depleted, more fish will die, and in turn, the supply of fish for human consumption will also decline. Morgan's study of fish not only spotlighted the need for conservation as a way to sustain fish populations, but also discovered the means to provide more food for people to eat. During this project Morgan also earned another nickname, the "Big Fish Lady."

In 1947 Morgan retired from teaching, but she continued to study and to write, as well as present pubic workshops on conservation. Her third book, *Kinships of Animals and Man: A Textbook of Animal Biology,* published in 1955, reflects Morgan's increasing concern for the environment. As Schafer quoted the ecologist, Morgan wrote that "humanity is facing two very old problems, living with itself and living with its natural surroundings." Through her work she offered an solution: "Conservation is one way of working out these problems, an appreciation and intelligent care of living things and their environment. It is applied Ecology."

For Morgan, the survival of humankind depended upon the survival of animal-kind; she believed that "every creature had its place and function within the natural world," according to Marcia Myers Bonta in *Women in the Field: America's Pioneering Women Naturalists.* For her efforts as an inspiring and enthusiastic teacher and a dedicated field researcher, as well as for her work in public education and conservation, Morgan is remembered.

Books

Bonta, Marcia Myers, *Women in the Field: America's Pioneering Women Naturalists,* Texas A. & M. University Press, 1991.
Hutchinson Dictionary of Scientific Biography, McGraw Hill, 1999.

Online

American National Biography Online, http://www.ang.org/articles/13/13-01171.html (December 31, 2003).
"Ann Haven Morgan Papers," *Mount Holyoke College Archives and Special Collections Web site,* http://www.mtholyoke.edu/lits/library/arch/col/msrg/mancol/ms0764r.htm (January 5, 2004). □

Jelly Roll Morton

American musician Jelly Roll Morton (1885–1941) was America's first great jazz composer and one of the foremost contributors to American music. A pioneering jazz musician and leader as well, Morton claimed to have invented the term jazz and the musical style itself at the height of the Swing Era in 1902 while he performed in New Orleans. Morton was also an influential composer; his works were widely recorded, reaching a vast audience.

Although an important and respected innovator in the transitional period from early to orchestral jazz, Morton had a predilection for embellishing the truth about himself. Because of this, the validity of his claim that he invented the term "jazz" is uncertain. With a penchant for the ostentatious, Morton was known for his colorful clothing and the diamond in his front tooth. Morton's vast output of work was recorded in 1938 at the Library of Congress during a series of several interviews. The resulting eight hours have been called by the *Biographical Dictionary of Afro-American and African Musicians,* "perhaps the most important oral history of jazz ever issued."

Much of the information about Morton's early life is uncertain, due in no small measure to his tendency to invent facts about himself. He was born Ferdinand Joseph La Menthe, on either September 20, 1885, or October 20, 1890, and probably in Gulfport, Louisiana, or Gulfport, Mississippi. Morton's creole father, E.P. Le Menthe (or LaMothe), was a carpenter. La Menthe was also a classically-schooled trombonist and took young Morton to the French Opera House in New Orleans. But La Menthe abandoned the family when Morton was very young. After Morton's mother married Willie Morton, the boy lived in Biloxi and Meridian, Mississippi, and then in New Orleans, mostly under the care of his aunt and godmother, Eulalie—or "Lallie"—Echo.

Learned Several Instruments at Early Age

Morton's Aunt Lallie took him everywhere, including saloons and even jail. But it was in jail, when he heard the inmates singing, that Morton found his first musical inspiration. His first musical instrument, though made of a tin pan and two chair legs, sounded to him like a symphony. Soon Morton learned to play other, more traditional instruments. By age five he could play the harmonica and at age six he had mastered the Jews' harp. Morton was an accomplished guitarist by age seven. He studied the guitar and was soon playing in street bands. He then learned the trombone, which he played in the houses of the red light district in New Orleans known as Storyville. By the time he was a teenager, he also played the piano, which he learned after hearing a concert at the opera house. His aunt sent him to study for a time with a black university professor of music. Morton's mother died when he was 14 or 15, but his aunt was by far the greatest influence in his life. A firm believer in voodoo, his aunt kept glasses of water around the house from which Morton believed he heard voices echoing in the night. Morton also heard chains rattling and the sewing machine running. He would forever be influenced by voodoo and always kept holy water near his bed.

Morton began to earn money—$20 in tips on his first night—as a pianist and gambler in the red light district of New Orleans. Morton's family had great respect for opera, but any other type of music was considered inappropriate, so when his aunt found out where the money for Morton's new clothes was coming from, she threw him out of the house so he would not corrupt his younger sisters.

Discovered Jazz

In 1902, Morton met famous ragtime pianist and composer Tony Jackson. Morton began meeting with Jackson and other musicians in back rooms after all the nightclubs closed, playing until the afternoon. Morton claimed that jazz was born there and that the word was his invention. About this time, he wrote "New Orleans Blues" and "King Porter Stomp," among other early tunes.

When he left his aunt's house, Morton also left New Orleans, never to return. He wandered the country, spending time in Tulsa, Oklahoma, and Chicago in 1904, and in Mobile, Alabama, in 1905. He found work as a musician, a pool shark, and a gambler. Morton even worked as a vaudeville comedian in Memphis, Tennessee, in 1908, and three years later he toured with McCabe's Minstrel Troubadours in St. Louis and Kansas City.

In 1911, Morton arrived in New York City sporting a diamond in his front tooth. It was there that he first played ''Jelly Roll Blues,'' which was published for orchestra in Chicago in 1915, making it perhaps the first jazz orchestration ever published. Several more Morton orchestrations would follow.

Success in the 1920s

The 1920s were Morton's most productive years. He was offered a job in Los Angeles in 1917, where he worked as a bandleader and in other entertainment areas. He also traveled a great deal, performing anywhere from Alaska to Tijuana, Mexico. While in Los Angeles, he began a relationship with Anita Johnson (or Gonzales), a girlfriend from New Orleans. Johnson had owned a saloon in Las Vegas but moved to Los Angeles and bought a small hotel. Morton often referred to her as his wife, although there is no record of their marriage. Johnson was musically inclined herself, and she wrote the lyrics for Morton's ''Dead Man Blues.'' Johnson had a good singing voice, as well, but Morton never allowed her to perform. She also traveled with him when he went on tour, mainly because Morton was intensely jealous of her and did not want her out of his sight.

By this time, Morton owned several small businesses. He was making money and establishing a name for himself. Morton was not above being ostentatious and boastful. He sometimes showed friends a trunk full of money, and his diamond-studded apparel and teeth were well known. Yet, there was no denying his distinctive personality. He was part showman and part sideshow barker. In an age when musicians all wore tuxedos, Morton preferred white trousers and shoes, a wine-colored jacket, and diamonds on his tie and his socks. But he was a dedicated composer, often waking up at night to scribble ideas and later demanding that the band musicians followed his compositions to the note.

In 1922 or 1923, Morton left Johnson and Los Angeles, returning to Chicago. For the next five years, he was the staff arranger for the Melrose Publishing House. A great number of his compositions were recorded during this period, including influential pieces on the Gennett label. He recorded ''London Blues,'' ''Grandpa's Spell,'' and ''The Pearls.'' He also spent some time with a group of white musicians known as the New Orleans Rhythm Kings. Morton was one of the first blacks to play in a mixed band.

Morton reached the height of his popularity between 1926 and 1930. He formed a band called the Red Hot Peppers and produced several classic recordings for the Victor label, both in Chicago and New York. The classics ''Kansas City Stomp,'' ''Sidewalk Blues,'' ''The Chant Mournful Serenade,'' and ''Ponchatrain Blues'' were released during this period. Morton's Chicago recordings also featured some of the best sidemen from New Orleans, such as Kid Ory on the trombone and Baby Dodds on the drums. He also found time to tour with W.C. Handy and played piano with Henry Crowder's band.

While at the Plantation Club in Chicago in 1927, Morton first met Mabel Bertrand, a creole dancer who had been raised in a convent after her parents died and who had

entertained in Europe. They were married in 1928 and traveled together in Morton's Lincoln, while the rest of the band rode in a colorful bus proclaiming, ''Jelly Roll Morton and His Red Hot Peppers.'' In 1928, Morton spent two months at Harlem's Rose Danceland in New York City. The following year he led an all-girl revue in Chicago, and in 1931 he was back in Harlem with his own ensemble. He became the house pianist in Harlem's Red Apple Club in 1934.

The Depression Took Its Toll

By this time, the Depression was taking its toll on the recording industry. Big bands with such colorful figures as Louis Armstrong were coming into fashion, and Morton did not adapt to this new style. Due to his failure to adapt, Morton's success and prestige were dwindling. His fall in popularity as a bandleader had also nearly collapsed his financial empire when he moved to Washington, D.C. in 1935 for a long engagement at a the Jungle Club.

One night at the club in 1939, Morton admonished and then slapped a rowdy club patron. The man attacked Morton with a knife, slicing Morton in the head and chest. He never fully recovered from the incident, which only aggravated other existing health problems. In order to survive, Morton began accepting small weekly checks from Catholic Charities.

For a short time in 1938, Morton established a music publishing company in New York. With his recordings, he took advantage of public interest once again focused on the New Orleans jazz style. But his health was failing. Morton returned to Los Angeles in 1940, leaving his wife behind, although he kept in touch with her. While in Los Angeles, he renewed his relationship with Anita Johnson. Hoping that the California climate would restore his health, Morton formed a new band. Before long, his failing strength made it impossible to work.

In May of 1941, Morton checked into Los Angeles County General Hospital. On June 10, at the age of fifty, Morton died in Johnson's arms. The cause of death was heart failure resulting from chronic high blood pressure. A high mass was sung for Jelly Roll Morton in St. Patrick's Cathedral in New York City. His pallbearers included Kid Ory and other members of his band. Morton's will did not mention his wife. Whatever he had of value, including royalties, was bequeathed to Anita Johnson.

Morton's Legacy

George C. Wolfe's 1992 Broadway musical, *Jelly's Last Jam*, was loosely based on Morton's life. Recognized as the first great composer of jazz, he was an excellent pianist and an intelligent innovator who changed the early ragtime style into a new form. Morton's early works have become collector's items. Perhaps no jazz musician from the early days is now so completely recorded on disc. Morton's great legacy is found in the eight hours of recordings and interviews collected together by Alan Lomax in 1938 and released to the public ten years later.

Books

Logan, Rayford W., and Michael R. Winston, eds., *Dictionary of American Negro Biography*, Norton, 1982.

Online

"A History of Jazz Before 1930," *The Hot Jazz Archive*, www .redhotjazz.com. □

Alva Myrdal

Nobel Prize-winning Swedish diplomat and social reformer Alva Myrdal (1902-1986) worked to revolutionize her country's social welfare system, as well as to end the proliferation of nuclear weaponry in the second half of the twentieth century.

S wedish educator and diplomat Alva Myrdal was one of the most influential social reformers of the 20th century. Seeking to end inequalities among all peoples, she addressed these inequalities beginning with their root in education. In the 1930s she authored several books focusing on education, women's rights, and the role of the state in promoting human welfare, broadening her focus in the 1950s to encompass nuclear disarmament among the world's superpowers. Winner of the 1982 Nobel Peace Prize for her work as part of the U.N.-led disarmament talks in Geneva, Switzerland, during the 1960s, Myrdal's most esteemed book, 1977's *The Game of Disarmament: How the United States and Russia Run the Arms Race,* proved influential with its forward-looking view of the proliferation of nuclear weapons, and its strident argument for world peace.

Alva Reimer Myrdal was born January 31, 1902, in Uppsala, Sweden, one of five children born to middle-class parents Albert and Lova (Larsson) Reimer. Her father, a building contractor involved in local politics, was a staunch social democrat whom Myrdal admired; her relationship with her rigid, tradition-minded mother was more complex. From both her parents she gained a desire to contribute to the betterment of society.

An intelligent child, Myrdal fought with her mother to attend Uppsala's gymnasium, even offering to pay the costs with her own money. She won that battle, and went on to attend the University of Stockholm, where she earned her B.A. in Scandinavian languages and literature and the history of religion in 1924. That same year she married Karl Gunnar Myrdal, a freshly minted economist who would win the Nobel Prize in Economics in 1974. Alike in intellect and socialist leanings, the Myrdals would have three children— son Jan and daughters Sissela and Kaj—although their marriage was not an easy one due to Gunnar's demanding job and Alva's desire to be both responsible mother and supportive wife.

Promoted State-sponsored Childrearing

In 1929 the Myrdals traveled to the United States on Rockefeller fellowships, and Alva Myrdal pursued her interest in education by studying the nation's experimental schools, particularly a program of early education administered by Yale University professor Arnold Gessel. She returned to Sweden a year later inspired to study further, and from 1930 to 1931 attended the University of Geneva, ultimately transferring her credits toward a master's degree in social psychology at the University of Uppsala. Graduating from Uppsala in 1934, Myrdal worked as a teacher in Stockholm. Then, in 1932, she got a job as an assistant psychologist at the city's central prison. Returning to teaching three years later, she established a preschool teachers' training college, the Social Pedagogical Institute, which she directed until 1948, and through which she promoted her progressive theories regarding child care.

Myrdal believed strongly that the state should play a responsible role in the raising of Sweden's young, and that teachers of young children should be not only disseminators of facts; they should be trained in developmental and behavioral psychology. Opposed to punishment of any kind, Myrdal believed discipline and good habits could be instilled through repetition. She incorporated many of the methods used by Maria Montessori to achieve the latter goal.

As a noted educator, Myrdal found herself in a position to make changes in her country's educational policies, and the Myrdal home became a place where major intellectuals of the day would often gather to discuss such issues. Although she was an effective speaker, she more frequently put her thoughts into book form, a habit she would continue throughout her life. 1934's *Kris i befolkinsfrägen* (*Crisis in the Population Question*) addresses Gunnar and Alva's joint concerns over housing, poverty, and education prompted by Sweden's shrinking birth rate; the book was influential in directing the course of national welfare programs throughout Scandinavia. Her 1941 book *Nation and Family* would prove equally influential in the United States.

While continuing her role as director of the Social Pedagogical Institute, Myrdal broadened her concerns by the end of the 1930s, responding to the war advancing through Europe as well as a result of her exposure to new ideas at Columbia University, where she and her husband lectured due to Gunnar's receipt of a Carnegie grant from 1937 to 1942. A brief return to Sweden in 1940 left the Myrdals concerned over the pro-Nazi sentiment that was beginning to influence their country, and they wrote frequently on their concerns in an effort to counteract this fascist tide.

Developed Unique Feminist Viewpoint

The late 1940s found Myrdal increasingly active and influential in the diplomatic realm. The first woman to be awarded a high-level position at the United Nations, Myrdal was appointed principal director of the U.N.'s department of social affairs in 1949. For the first time she recognized that her job was as important as that of her husband, and she made the temporary move to New York alone. Two years later she moved from New York City to Paris to serve as director of the United Nations Educational, Scientific, and Cultural Organization (UNESCO)'s department of social sciences. Among her colleagues at the United Nations, Myrdal gained respect as a skilled, well-reasoned negotiator, a skill that stood her in good stead throughout her diplomatic career. She also gained an ever-greater appreciation of the problems faced by working mothers, particularly poorer, undereducated women, through her work in New York and Paris. In 1956 she would crystallize her thoughts on the changing role of women in her book *Women's Two Roles,* coauthored with British psychologist Viola Klein.

Women's Two Roles takes its title from Myrdal's belief, shared with Klein, that women in modern society are living, in essence, "two lives." Basing their argument on studies showing that the average life span of a woman in 1854 was only 45 years, most of that time spent raising six children; a century later women lived for 75 years, had three children, and gained approximately 30 years of quality life in which they could undertake a productive second career. Her theories connected with her earlier work as an educator, where she had realized that a revolution in child-rearing practices had the potential to free all women from a life of domesticity. While the book's controversial theories were at odds with those of American feminists, who did not view motherhood as the crucial task Myrdal believed it to be, as well as others who viewed a "second life" as a possibility only for educated, affluent women, *Women's Two Roles* was translated into several languages.

Resolute Advocate of World Peace

Returning to her native Sweden in 1955, Myrdal was appointed ambassador to India and minister to Ceylon until 1962, beginning a decade of ambassadorial positions that took advantage of her skills as a negotiator. While in India, she met the country's prime minister, Jawaharlal Nehru, whose pacifist philosophy greatly influenced Myrdal to extend her efforts beyond Sweden and work for world peace. While she was sometimes criticized for her positions on universal compulsory community service in place of a military draft as well as her oft-quoted opinion that peace marches are used only by those who lack political power— which not surprisingly angered many politically active college students of the day—Myrdal persuaded many in adopting her own belief that in order to achieve world peace rhetoric was not enough: peace would only come through negotiation and the development of well-reasoned, concrete plans for action.

After leaving India in 1962, she served as minister to Burma from 1955 to 1958 and ambassador to Nepal in 1960. In 1961 the 59-year-old diplomat began a five-year stint as Sweden's ambassador-at-large. Returning home to Sweden, she requested an appointed special assistant on disarmament affairs, developing her expertise on the subject. As her expertise grew, so did her fear over the proliferation of nuclear weaponry. In 1961 Myrdal gave her first speech asking the superpowers to implement a nuclear test ban, and from that point on she was an outspoken critic of the cold-war policies of the United States and the Union of Soviet Socialist Republics (USSR), policies which by then had them aiming nuclear weapons at cities around the globe. Also elected to the senate of the Swedish Parliament in 1962, disarmament became one of Myrdal's central concerns in representing her constituency.

Nominated as a member of Sweden's delegation to the U.N. General Assembly between 1962 and 1973, Myrdal represented her country's delegation to the disarmament conferences held in Geneva, Switzerland. While in Geneva she spoke out, in representing the unaligned nations of the world, against the threat of destruction posed by nuclear aggression. As minister in charge of disarmament after 1966, she also chaired the 1972 U.N. committee on disarmament and development. When she retired a year later, many of her colleagues expressed their appreciation for her many years of tireless service in public tributes.

Following her retirement, Myrdal devoted her time to publishing work in the area of disarmament. In her 1977 work *The Game of Disarmament: How the United States and Russia Run the Arms Race* she accuses the two world superpowers of fueling the arms race because of self-interest rather than world safety, and strongly criticizes their unwillingness to disarm. Other books include 1977's *Wars, Weapons, and Everyday Violence,* and *Dynamics of European Nuclear Disarmament,* published in 1981. Widely praised, Myrdal's books were distributed throughout North America, Britain, and Europe in their English, French, German, Italian, Japanese, and Spanish translations.

Won Nobel Peace Prize

Myrdal was awarded the Nobel Peace Prize in 1982 for her advocacy of world disarmament; she shared the Prize with Mexican diplomat Alfonso García Robles. Among her many other awards were the West German Peace Prize, the Albert Einstein Peace Prize, and the People's Peace Prize.

Retiring from diplomatic service at the age of 70, Myrdal returned to the field of education, and taught sociology at a number of U.S. schools, among them the Massachusetts Institute of Technology, Wellesley College, and the University of Wisconsin, Madison. In her writings she went beyond national aggressions to focus on the roots of social violence. Her belief in science as a source of understanding led to her promotion of social science and psychological research in this area prompted her to help in the establishment of the Stockholm International Peace Research Institute. She also supported the work of the Myrdal Foundation in its additional efforts in this area. ''The ruin of the planet is there for all to contemplate,'' she wrote in her preface to the 1982 of *The Game of Disarmament*. ''But so, too, is its potential richness if we learn to cooperate.''

An active, energetic woman, Myrdal enjoyed many hobbies during her eventful life, among them traveling, walking, and bicycling. She also enjoyed cooking and often attending the theatre with her husband. Throughout her life she read extensively in international affairs as well as enjoying fiction and poetry, which she read in the original English, French, German, and Spanish. Myrdal died in Stockholm in February of 1986; her husband died the following year.

Books

Bok, Sissela, *Alva Myrdal: A Daughter's Memoir,* Addison-Wesley, 1991.

Carlson, Allan C., *The Swedish Experiment in Family Politics: The Myrdals and the Interwar Population Crisis,* Transaction Publishers, 1990.

Feminist Writers, St. James Press, 1996.

Myrdal, Alva, *The Game of Disarmament: How the United States and Russia Run the Arms Race,* Manchester University Press, 1977, revised edition, Pantheon, 1982.

Periodicals

American Journal of Sociology, November 1957.

Boston Globe, February 3, 1986.

Bulletin of the Atomic Scientists, April 1986.

Change, November 1999.

New York Review of Books, March 5, 1992.

People, August 11, 1980.

Online

Alva Myrdal Conference Web site, http://www.pcr.uu.se/conferences/myrdal/alvapapers.html (March 6-8, 2002).

Nobel Museum Web site, http://www.nobel.se/peace/laureates/1982/myrdal-bio.html. □

N

Jean Negulesco

In a career that spanned more than 30 years, Jean Negulesco (1900-1993) was one of Hollywood's most versatile directors and an early master of Cinemascope, the wide-screen technique pioneered in the 1950s.

Negulesco directed 72 films, nearly half of them short subjects, and served as producer, screenwriter and second-unit director on numerous others. Negulesco is best remembered for such classic films as *The Mask of Dimitrios, Humoresque, Johnny Belinda, Road House, How to Marry a Millionaire* and *Daddy Long Legs.* These and many of his other features contribute to a body of work whose wide appeal is testament to Negulesco's broad aesthetic interests.

Early Interest in Painting

Jean Negulesco was born in Craiova, Romania, on February 26, 1900, the son of a hotelkeeper. Art was Negulesco's first love, and by his mid-teens he was a precocious painter. When composer Georges Enesco visited the military hospital where Negulesco worked during the First World War, the youthful Negulesco drew a portrait of him, and Enesco bought it. Encouraged by this, Negulesco decided he wanted to become a painter.

He went to Paris, where he met fellow expatriate artists Konsantin Brancusi, Jules Pascin and Amodeo Modigliani. Brancusi served as his mentor. During the 1920s Negulesco's artistic reputation grew, and in his late 20s he began to work as a stage designer. In 1927, an exhibition of his work was put on in New York, and Negulesco also began working for Paramount Studios in New York. His early work for the studio involved sketching the opening montage of *Tonight We Sing* and as technical advisor on the controversial *The Story of Temple Drake,* based on William Faulkner's novel, *Sanctuary.* Later the Western Association of Museums gave him a one-man exhibition in Los Angeles as its "foreign painter of the year."

Turned to Film Career

After his one-man show, art critic Elie Faure, who reportedly hadn't even seen the exhibition, advised Negulesco to quit painting and throw himself into film, even though as an artist Negulesco had a following on both sides of the Atlantic. Negulesco remained in Los Angeles and debuted as a director with a self-financed experimental film titled *Three and a Day.* The star of *Three and a Day,* fellow expatriate Mischa Auer, helped Negulesco gain entrance into the big studios.

In 1932 Negulesco was second-unit director for Paramount's film *A Farewell to Arms* and technical director for *This Is the Night.* In 1934 he served as associate director for *Kiss and Make Up,* a comedy starring Cary Grant. In the late 1930s Negulesco worked primarily as a studio writer. He wrote the screenplay for the 1937 film, *Expensive Husbands,* and worked on the stories of other movies.

His work at Paramount and later Universal brought him to the attention of the short subjects department at Warner Brothers. That studio offered him a job as a director of shorts, which in those days were an essential part of movie theater's bills.

Negulesco's first studio directorial effort was the 1940 ten-minute short, *Joe Reichman and His Orchestra.* That same year he directed *Alice in Movieland,* another musical

Grandmother's Follies. These followed his second feature, *The Conspirators,* starring Hedy Lamarr and Paul Henreid and again featuring Greenstreet and Lorre. *The Conspirators* is a World War II film with noir aspects about a group of underground anti-Nazi conspirators in Lisbon, one of whom is a Nazi double agent.

In 1946 Negulesco teamed with Greenstreet and Lorre for the third and final time when he directed *Three Strangers,* a drama about fate and those who attempt to alter it. That same year Negulesco teamed up with actor John Garfield. He first directed Garfield in *Nobody Lives Forever,* a film noir that addressed the plight of returning World War II serviceman. The protagonist is a New York gambler who gets involved with a gang of grifters in California. Negulesco exhibited a firm grasp of noir conventions and in some places modifies them to heighten the film's irony. *Humoresque,* written by Clifford Odetts, was the second collaboration between Negulesco and Garfield; it also starred Joan Crawford as a predatory fan of Garfield's character, a concert violinist. In this film, Negulesco, who had made so many musical shorts, proved what he could do when he was on familiar ground. He followed up with *Deep Valley* (1947), a crime melodrama starring Ida Lupino. Negulesco's next project was to have been *The Adventures of Don Juan,* but artistic differences with Errol Flynn, the film's star, caused studio boss Jack Warner to remove him from the project. The resilient Negulesco bounced back from that setback in 1948, when he directed the film considered to be his greatest artistic achievement.

That film was *Johnny Belinda,* starring Jane Wyman and Lew Ayres. It was the apex of Negulesco's career. He was nominated for an Academy Award for best director (he lost to John Huston), and Wyman won the Oscar for best actress. By the time of the awards ceremony, however, Negulesco was no longer employed at Warner Brothers. Warner disliked *Johnny Belinda* so much that he fired Negulesco after seeing the film's preview.

Master of Different Styles

Negulesco went to Twentieh Century Fox, where he directed film noir staples Lupino, Cornel Wilde and Richard Widmark, as well as Celeste Holm, in *Road House* (1948). This was Negulesco's most solid noir offering, and it capitalized well on his painterly and set-designer background through the use of unreal scenery that mirrors the characters' physical and psychological situations. Negulesco scored another hit in 1950 when he teamed with writer Nunally Johnson for *Three Came Home,* about women in a Japanese prisoner-of-war camp in Borneo. He followed this with *Phone Call from a Stranger* (1952) and *Titanic* (1953). The former featured Bette Davis in a cameo role while the latter starred Clifton Webb and Barbara Stanwyk.

In the five years after he left Warner Brothers, Negulesco's style and his choice of scripts softened. He and Johnson teamed up again for the studio's second CinemaScope feature, *How to Marry a Millionaire.* This was the first of several Negulesco films about women searching for happiness. The others were *Three Coins in the Fountain* (1954), a popular film about three women in Rome that is

short written by Ed Sullivan. Over the next four years Negulesco directed numerous short subjects for Warner Brothers, mostly musicals and many featuring second-caliber big bands. He also worked on the crew that filmed two short dance pieces by Leonid Massine: "Gaiete Parisienne" (released in 1941 as *The Gay Parisian*) and "Capriccio Espagnol," *Spanish Fiesta,* released in 1942.

Feature Director

Negulesco soon started being considered for feature films. He was credited with directing the 1941 melodrama, *Singapore Woman,* although he may have been pulled off the project before completion. Prior to that film he was chosen to direct *The Maltese Falcon,* the movie that would be a big hit for Humphrey Bogart, but he was replaced by John Huston.

Negulesco's real break in Hollywood came in 1944, more than 14 years after he decided to switch careers, when he directed the noir film *The Mask of Dimitrios* starring Sydney Greenstreet and Peter Lorre, both of whom had appeared in *The Maltese Falcoln.* The style was an interesting challenge for the urbane Negulesco, but Greenstreet and Lorre were experienced noir actors and Negulesco pulled off the film's recreations of various European settings. While some critics have argued that *The Mask of Dimitrios* is not first-rate noir, in its time the film was successful enough to lift Negulesco out of the Warner Brothers short subject department. He did direct two more shorts for Warner Brothers in 1944: *Listen to the Bands* and not critically acclaimed; *Woman's World* (1954), an illustration of the adage "behind every successful man is a woman"; and *The Best of Everything* (1959), a film that is the polar opposite of *Woman's World,* in which three women struggle to make it to the top in a New York publishing company.

During his stay at Twentieth Century Fox Negulesco had the opportunity to direct some of the Hollywood's biggest stars, including Fred Astaire (in *Daddy Long Legs,* 1955); Lauren Bacall, Betty Grable, and Marilyn Monroe (in *Millionaire*); Richard Burton and Lana Turner (*The Rains of Ranchipur,* 1955); Irene Dunne (*The Mudlark,* 1950); Sophia Lauren and Alan Ladd (*Boy on a Dolphin,* 1957), and Joan Crawford (*Woman's World*). Yet despite all this star power Negulesco's films in the 1950s were not groundbreaking. Their popularity was largely due to the actors' followings and gimmicks like CinemaScope.

Later Years and Retirement

Negulesco made only four films in the 1960s, and one of them, *The Pleasure Seekers* (1964), was a remake of *Three Coins in the Fountain,* this time set in Madrid. Another project was an uncredited effort for *The Greatest Story Ever Told,* released in 1965. George Stevens was given sole directorial credit, but David Lean and Negulesco also worked on the film. His final directorial effort was 1970's *Hello-Goodbye.*

After 1970 Negulesco worked sporadically. He appeared in three films: *Un officier de Police sans Importance* (1973), *L'Arriviste* (*The Thruster*) in 1976, and *Le Jupon rouge* (*Manuela's Loves*) in 1987. In retirement in the south of France Negulesco invested in real estate and returned to his first love, painting. In 1985 Negulesco published his autobiography, *Things I Did . . . and Things I Think I Did.* In his review of the book for the *New York Times,* John Houseman wrote that Negulesco was "a true man of the world," yet one of his "attractive qualities [was] his modesty."

Negulesco appeared on television twice, both times as himself. In a 1960 episode of *This Is Your Life* he was one of the guests who surprised Italian actor Rossano Brazzi. He also appeared posthumously in the 1997 documentary *The Reality Trip,* which celebrated the centenary of film. As a producer Negulesco sheparded the televising of the 27th Academy Awards ceremony in 1955. In 1962 he produced and codirected the made-for-TV film *Jessica.*

Negulesco was married twice. His first marriage ended in divorce soon after he arrived in the United States. His second marriage was to model Dusty Anderson in 1946. Negulesco had a son, Julian (also a film director), and two adopted daughters. Negulesco died of heart failure on July 18, 1993 in Marbella, Spain.

Books

Silver, Alain and Elizabeth Ward, eds., *Film Noir: An Encyclopedic Reference to the American Style,* The Overlook Press, 1979.

Periodicals

Guardian, July 23, 1993.
Independent, July 22, 1993.
New York Times, February 24, 1985.
Times (London), July 22, 1993.

Online

"Jean Negulesco," http://us.imdb.com/name/nm0624535 (December 9, 2003). □

Vladimir Nemirovich-Danchenko

A dominant figure in early twentieth-century Russian theater, Vladimir Nemirovich-Danchenko (1858-1943), together with Konstantin Stanislavsky, founded the Moscow Art Theatre and helped usher naturalism in theatrical performance and writing.

Vladimir Ivanovich Nemirovich-Danchenko was born in Ozurgety (now Makharadze), Georgia, on December 11, 1858. During the mid-1800s Georgia was annexed to Russia; falling to communist control during the Russian Revolution, in 1922 it would join the Union of Soviet Socialist Republics. From an early age Nemirovich-Danchenko exhibited a love of the theater. By age 13 he was acting and directing amateur theatricals and already trying out different stage techniques and effects. However, at age 18 he set aside his theatrical interests and went to Moscow, where he studied physics and mathematics at the Moscow State University from 1876 to 1879. Theater remained his first love, however, and during this time Nemirovich-Danchenko continued his involvement in the stage as a critic. After leaving school, he put increased effort into his work as a theater critic. Ultimately, while his criticism was much admired, Nemirovich-Danchenko's creative urges sought release in play-writing and fiction, balancing the analytical side of his personality.

Early Theatrical Success

In the 1890s Nemirovich-Danchenko became a well-known figure in Moscow and St. Petersburg as a result of his plays and his fiction. His first theatrical success, translated as *The New Undertaking* or *New Business,* premiered in St. Petersburg in 1890. Despite the early misgivings of some of the cast, and those of Nemirovich-Danchenko himself, the play proved a hit with the most important critic of the day, Flerov-Vassiliev. Nemirovich-Danchenko was awarded Russia's Griboyedov prize—named for 19th-century playwright Aleksandr Sergeyevich Griboyedov—as author of the best play of the season by the Russian Society of Dramatists. Nemirovich-Danchenko's other plays included *Gold,* produced in 1895, which had the distinction of being the first play to hold a dress rehearsal in the history of Russian theater, and *The Worth of Life,* produced in Moscow in

1896. *The Worth of Life* was also awarded the Griboyedov prize, beating out Anton Chekhov's *The Seagull*. Nemirovich-Danchenko, who had encouraged Chekhov to write his play, tried to convince the award judges to reverse their decision, but with no success. Nemirovich-Danchenko's plays were produced at the Maly (''small'') Theater in Moscow, the Alexandrinskii Theater in St. Petersburg, and on stages throughout the Russian provinces.

In 1891 Nemirovich-Danchenko used his success with the play *The New Undertaking* as a springboard for furthering his career in the theater. On the recommendation of acting instructor Aleksandr Yuzhin, he was offered the post of instructor in dramatic art at the Moscow Philharmonic Society. The post was considered a humble one; the Philharmonic's school was considered second compared to the Moscow Imperial school, and there was little prestige in teaching lower-level courses. However, on the strength of Yuzhin's recommendation, as well as Nemirovich-Danchenko's theater criticism and his play, it was viewed as a coup that a non-actor was hired to teach acting. However, as he later wrote in his autobiography *My Life in the Russian Theatre*, translated by John Cournos, Nemirovich-Danchenko admitted not only that the school had a ''bad reputation,'' but also that ''there was among the pupils a terrible lot of riffraff.... The majority came here to be taught in the speediest manner possible how to act, so that they might be given good roles in a graduation play. The educative aim of the school was wholly ignored.'' It was dealing with these manner of students that Yuzhin had to intercede on Nemirovich-Danchenko's behalf, as the students objected to being taught by someone who did not act. To his students Nemirovich-Danchenko stressed the need for longer, better-organized rehearsal and a more flexible acting style. At first the playwright regretted his decision to teach acting, but as he began to weed out the nonserious students and as his principles took hold, the graduation performances at the Moscow Philharmonic Society drama school soon rivaled those of the Imperial School.

During the years he taught at the Philharmonic School Nemirovich-Danchenko published, in addition to plays, a book on acting translated as *Drama behind the Scenes* (1896), as well as two works of fiction: 1896's *The Governor's Inspection* and 1898's *Dreams*. *Dreams* would be Nemirovich-Danchenko's last work of fiction, as by the time it was published his career had already begun to take a new, historic turn.

The Moscow Arts Theater

Recognizing the dreadful state of Russian theater at the turn of the 20th century, Nemirovich-Danchenko arranged to meet with independent-minded stage director Konstantin Sergeyevich Stanislavsky. In 1897 the legendary meeting took place in the restaurant of the Slavyansky Bazaar hotel. The two men discussed the state of Russian theater, their disappointment in contemporary drama, and their hopes for a new style. They soon began to sketch out a plan, and in doing so the two like-minded men—in his autobiography Nemirovich-Danchenko declared that he and Stanislavky did not once disagree during their meeting—brought forth

the seminal ideas for the Moscow Art Theatre. The two men remained at the restaurant long enough to have lunch and dinner there, then left for Stanislavsky's home to continue their discussion. In all, the meeting lasted an incredible 17 hours, but in that time the blueprint for the Moscow Art Theatre was drawn up.

Originally known as the Moscow Popular Art Theatre and the Moscow Academic Art Theatre, the Moscow Art Theatre drew its actors from the best of two groups: Nemirovich-Danchenko's students at the Moscow Philharmonic School, where he remained until 1898, and from the Society of Art and Literature, which Stanislavsky had cofounded in 1888. The influence of the Moscow Art Theater on Russian and world theater in the late 19th and early 20th centuries cannot be exaggerated. Not only did the theater revolutionize the style of acting, leading theater from the mannered to the natural, but in producing the plays Nemirovich-Danchenko chose, it signaled a quantitative leap into modernism. While Nemirovich-Danchenko, in his autobiography, clarified that the theater's birth was nowhere near as smooth as the meeting that inspired it, Nemirovich-Danchenko and Stanislavsky did manage to adhere to a strict division of labor between them. While Stanislavsky had complete control in staging the productions—which subsequently increased his reputation at Nemirovich-Danchenko's expense—Nemirovich-Danchenko served as producer and dramaturg. As dramaturg the playwright was in charge of selecting new plays for production; he also advised Stanislavsky on interpretation and staging.

The first production of the Moscow Art Theatre occurred on October 14, 1898. The play was the 1868 historical drama *Tsar Fyodor*, by Aleksey Konstantinovich Tolstoy. *Tsar Fyodor* went through some 70 rehearsals before the staging, and while the critics gave it good reviews Stanislavsky was disappointed in the performance, declaring that the actors were imitating his directions rather than truly acting. The fledgling theater struggled through three more productions before gaining a firm foothold in the Moscow theater world: *They Who Take the Law into Their Own Hands, The Merchant of Venice,* and *Antigone.* But all during this time Nemirovich-Danchenko was determined to right a wrong, and for the theater's fifth production he engaged Chekhov's *The Seagull,* which had not only lost out on the Griboyedov prize to Nemirovich-Danchenko's own play but had also received bad notices from the critics. It was with their production of *The Seagull* that the Moscow Art Theatre achieved its first real success. The play starred Vsevolod Meyerhold, who would himself become an influential director, and Olga Knipper, who would eventually become Chekhov's wife. Nemirovich-Danchenko had always encouraged Chekhov's theatrical aspirations, and he was the perfect playwright for the theater's philosophy. Thus began a long collaboration between Chekhov and the Moscow Art Theater that would see acclaimed productions of *Uncle Vanya, The Three Sisters,* and *The Cherry Orchard.* In 1904 Nemirovich-Danchenko also staged an independent production of Chekhov's *Ivanov.*

Besides Chekhov's plays, Nemirovich-Danchenko also chose to present a production of William Shakespeare's

Julius Caesar, which was hailed as a masterpiece of psychological theater. He also produced *Lonely Lives* in 1899, a play by Gerhart Hauptmann, whom Chekhov admired, as well as work by Maurice Maeterlinck. Another playwright whom Nemirovich-Danchenko championed was Henrik Ibsen. In the 1890s, while he was the drama instructor at the Moscow Philharmonic School, Nemirovich-Danchenko had been the first director to successfully stage Ibsen's work in Russia when he produced *A Doll's House.* Now, at the influential Moscow Art Theatre, he produced Ibsen's plays in succession: *When We Dead Awaken* in 1900, *Pillars of Society* in 1903, *Brand* in 1906, *Rosmersholm* in 1908, and *Hedda Gabler.*

During the early years of the 20th century Nemirovich-Danchenko also began nurturing the young playwright Maxim Gorky. Gorky had already written a number of short stories and novels when he turned to writing for the stage. His first produced play was *Smug Citizens,* which was eventually banned and for which Nemirovich-Danchenko had to intercede to perform even occasionally. Meanwhile Nemirovich-Danchenko and Stanislavsky urged Gorky to write a play about the downtrodden. What resulted was *The Lower Depths,* a play whose power still held more than a century after its 1902 production at the Moscow Art Theatre. The Moscow Art Theatre also produced Gorky's *Children of the Sun.*

By the 1910s theatrical realism began to seem old-fashioned, although among the many plays Nemirovich-Danchenko produced during this period were Aleksandr Ostrovsky's *Even a Wise Man Stumbles* (1910), Saltykov-Shchedrin's *The Death of Pazukhin* (1914), and two adaptations of Dostoevsky's novels: *The Brothers Karamazov* and *Nikolai Stavrogin,* the latter based on the novel *The Possessed.* Symbolist writers such as Bely, Blok, and Bryusov had already made deep inroads in the Russian aesthetic, and futurists such as Mayakovsy and Meyerhold also came forth to challenge the tenets of realism. In time Nemirovich-Danchenko came to seem conservative, particularly in his choice of plays for production, although he was considered no less influential.

Obtained Soviet Patronage

Following the October 1917 Russian Revolution both Vladimir Lenin, leader of the Russian Soviet army, and Anatoly Lunacharsky, the new Soviet commissar of culture, gave their crucial support to the Moscow Art Theatre. This in turn allowed the theatre troupe to travel abroad and give performances in Europe and the United States. This tour lasted from 1922 to 1924, during which time the Moscow Art Theatre gained widespread international acclaim. Nemirovich-Danchenko and Stanislavsky were now as well known abroad as they were in Mother Russia.

Nemirovich-Danchenko also was interested in musical theater, and as an adjunct to the Moscow Art Theatre he founded the allied Moscow Art Musical Studio in 1919. In 1926 the school's name was changed to the V.I. Nemirovich-Danchenko Musical Theatre and still later to the Stanislavsky-Nemirovich-Danchenko Musical Theatre. Among the works he produced or supervised at the Musical Theatre were Giuseppi Verdi's *La Traviata,* Dmitry Shostakovich's *Katerina Izmailova* (also known as *Lady Macbeth of Mtsensk*), and *Carmencita and the Soldier,* which is based on Georges Bizet's opera, *Carmen.*

In the late 1920s and 1930s Nemirovich-Danchenko worked within the confines of Soviet-promoted socialist realism. His productions included the works of Soviet playwrights, notably Leonid Leonov's *The Orchards of Polovchansk,* adaptations of Tolstoy's novels *Resurrection* and *Anna Karenina,* as well as Russian classics such as Ostrovsky's *The Storm* (1935) and Griboyedov's *Woe from Wit* (1938). Particularly praised during his later career were the Moscow Art Theatre's stagings of Gorky's *Enemies* (1935) and Chekhov's *Three Sisters* (1940). Nemirovich-Danchenko worked with the Moscow Art Theatre right up until its evacuation during World War II. His autobiography was translated into English in 1936 as *My Life in the Russian Theater.*

In addition to the Griboyedov prizes Nemirovich-Danchenko was awarded the State Prize of the USSR in 1942 and 1943, the Order of Lenin, and the Order of the Banner of Red Labor. He died in Moscow on April 25, 1943.

Books

Great Soviet Encyclopedia, third edition, Macmillan, 1978.

Nemirovich-Danchenko, Vladimir, *My Life in the Russian Theatre,* translated by John Cournos, Little, Brown, 1956. □

O

Dositej Obradović

Serbian writer, translator, and educator Dositej Obradović (circa 1740-1811), usually considered the father of modern Serbian literature, dedicated his life and talents to building and celebrating the culture of his people.

Early Life

Dositej Obradović was born Dimitrije Obradović around 1740 in the village of Cakovo near the present-day city of Timisoara in Romania. He was one of four children. His father, Djuradj Obradović, was a furrier and a merchant who died when Obradović was very young. Once widowed, his mother, Kruna Paunkić, took Obradović and his siblings to the home of her family in the nearby village of Semarton. Kruna died when he was nine or ten years old, leaving him orphaned. He was separated from his siblings and returned to Cakovo to live with an uncle on his father's side.

While living with his uncle Obradović discovered a passion for books and learning. He read Serbian and Romanian texts and studied Greek language and literature. His uncle wanted him to become a village priest, so Obradović was exposed to various religious readings. He absorbed the religious literature quickly and longed to become a saint. He made multiple attempts to run away with visiting abbots. Disturbed by these escapes, his uncle sent him to Timisoara as an apprentice to a quilt maker, hoping that learning a trade would make him abandon his grandiose religious aspirations.

But instead of making quilts, in 1757 Obradović left his uncle's household for good and took shelter in the monastery of Hopovo at Fruska Gora. The abbot there, Teodor Milutinović, took Obradović in as his disciple because he was impressed by the young man's reading and writing abilities.

Life as a Monk

Obradović spent the next three years at the monastery reading and studying spiritual literature. He was a serious and devoted pupil. In one of the books he studied he left this inscription: "I, sinful Dositej of Hopovo, an unworthy deacon, finished reading this soul-benefiting book on November 8, 1759." Obradović balanced his reading with secular texts, the most influential of which was a collection of *Aesop's Fables.*

In 1758 he was tonsured, a ceremony that made him officially into a cleric, and given the name Dositej. He was later ordained as a deacon but soon found himself dissatisfied with the rigidly circumscribed nature of his educational material. He fled the monastery in 1760 with the intention of traveling to Kiev to broaden his mind. But Obradović didn't make it to Russia, and instead spent a year in Zagreb studying Latin. He took teaching positions to support himself financially and to save money for his trip to Russia.

Traveling Scholar

In 1763 he headed to Greece to visit Mount Athos, but fell ill and went instead to Montenegro, where he worked for a time as a schoolteacher. It was at this time, while traveling among his own people and teaching in various institutions, that Obradović recognized his culture's need for development. He felt his people were backwards and he wanted to raise their awareness of literature and culture. He began translating great works of other cultures into conversational Serbian.

In 1765 in Smyrna, he studied theology, philosophy, Greek literature, rhetoric, and song as a pupil of the master teacher Hierotheos Dendrinos. This gave him a classical education that few of his countrymen could obtain.

In 1768 Obradović went to Hormovo, Albania to study the Albanian language, worked in Corfu for a time as a student of Andreas Petritsopolos, and then returned to Dalmatia to continue teaching. He was a voracious reader, consuming books in Italian, Greek, and the Slavic languages while simultaneously writing and publishing his own moral works.

In 1771 he traveled to Vienna, and there for the first time he came into contact with the ideas and works of the Western Enlightenment movement. He supported himself by tutoring students in Greek and set about learning French, Latin, and German. He studied logic and metaphysics and tutored students in French and Italian once he had mastered those languages. He also studied French and English literature. In 1777 he took a position tutoring the nephews of Vidak, Archbishop of Karlovac, in Modra, near Bratislava.

Next, in 1779, he traveled to Trieste, continuing through Italy to the island of Chios. While there he taught Italian in a local school, then visited Constantinople briefly but had to leave because of plague outbreaks. He went next to Moldavia, where he spent a year tutoring for a wealthy family. By 1782 he had saved enough money to make a trip to Halle, Germany, where he enrolled in a university to study physics and philosophy. During this time he composed and published his autobiography, a manifesto for his intended educational program titled *Pismo Haralampiju* (1783), and the moral advice book *Sovjeti zdravago razuma* (Counsels of Common Sense, 1784). The morals book advocated coeducation for boys and girls.

In 1784 he spent a year in Europe translating fables and studying English literature. He tutored for the next few years and by 1787 had saved enough money to take his long-desired trip to Russia. He spent six months in Sklov, reading Russian literature and writing the second half of his autobiography.

In 1789 Obradović settled in Vienna. He stayed there for twelve years, writing and printing both original works and translations. In 1802 he traveled back to Trieste because a printing press there was publishing Serbian works. While there he heard of the Serbian uprising against the Turks, and Obradović raised money and donated funds of his own to the cause. He went to work for the victorious Karadjoedje administration in 1806.

At more than sixty years of age, Obradović became a champion of the effort to educate his people. He settled in liberated Belgrade in 1807, and in September 1808 he opened the *Velika skola* (Great School), later the University of Belgrade. His health started to decline in 1809, and he died on March 28, 1811, shortly after being appointed Secretary of Education.

Publishing Pioneer

Obradović's most substantial contribution to the education of his people lay in his dedicated use of the Serbian popular language. In his lifetime, the Serbs were divided into three linguistic camps: the educated few who spoke and wrote in Russian Church Slavonic (a language of prestige), other educated people who spoke and wrote in *slavenoserbski* (a hybrid of Russian Church Slavonic, Old Church Slavonic, Russian, and local Serbian vernacular), and the masses, mostly illiterate, who spoke the local Serbian vernacular. As the *Dictionary of Literary Biography* explains, "Dositej considered the introduction of vernacular elements into the literary idiom necessary because he believed that only one in ten thousand people understood *slavenoserbski* well, whereas the language of the people was understood by all, peasants and educated people alike. With minor dialectal differences, the spoken language was the same in all the areas populated by the Serbs. If books were printed in the language of the people, they would reach broad segments of [the] population."

His work consisted mainly of translations, the most famous of which were his 1788 translations of some of *Aesop's Fables*. Obradović included corresponding moral instructions with each of the fables, as well as Serbian folk proverbs and popular expressions to help the reader relate to the message of each fable. His goal was to help the Serbian public realize their need for significant cultural enhancement.

During the Serbian uprisings he established the first Serbian school of higher learning. His most notable original work is his autobiography titled *Zivot i prikljucenija Dimiteÿa Obradovića, narecenoga u kaludjerstvu Dositej, n'im' istim' spisan' I izdat'* (1793), which was translated in 1953 as *The Life and Adventures of Dimitrije Obradović Who as a Monk Was Given the Name Dositej*. It is believed to be the first book ever published in the Serbian popular language.

Cassell's Encyclopaedia of World Literature describes Obradović's writings as "permeated by enlightened common sense and sane patriotism, sincerity and integrity, keen intellectual curiosity and wide erudition." *Cassell's* states that Obradović's "influence on the development of Serbian literature has proved both far-reaching and constructive." He is considered the chief representative of the Serbian Age of Enlightenment. Through his work the Serbian literary world began to develop its modern literature and culture and to develop a sense of national consciousness.

To this day Obradović is seen as a champion of Serbian culture. In 1911, 100 years after his death, many essays were published in celebration of his life and works. One of the essays imagined Belgrade in the year 2011 with a cultural museum called the Dositej Building, "a magnificent palace, situated in the most beautiful spot in the city centre." Although less grand than imagined in that essay, the Dositej Museum in Belgrade was opened in an old, tiny Turkish home that preserved both Obradović's works and those of language reformer Vuk Karadzic (1787-1864). Obradović remains an admired and much celebrated figure in Serbian literary history.

Books

Cassell's Encyclopaedia of World Literature Volume 2, Funk & Wagnalls, 1954.

Chambers Biographical Dictionary, Chambers Harrap, 1997.

Merriam-Webster's Biographical Dictionary, Merriam-Webster, 1995.

South Slavic Writers Before World War II-Dictionary of Literary Biography, Volume 147, Gale Research, 1995.

Periodicals

Journal of Modern Greek Studies, May 1998.

Online

Fischer, Wladimir, "The Role of Dositej Obradovic in the Construction of Serbian Identities During the 19th Century," *Space of Identity,* http://www.univie.ac.at/spaceofidentity/Vol_3/_HTML/Fischer (January 2, 2004).

"Serbian Literature," *Vojvodina,* http://www.vojvodina.srbija-info.yu/ingles/kultura/kultura1 (January 2, 2004). ☐

Kenzaburo Oe

Japanese novelist Kenzaburo Oe (born 1935) is considered the leading contemporary writer in his language. A 1994 Nobel Prize winner in literature for a body of work that often makes reference to his developmentally disabled son Hikari, Oe has also been a vociferous critic of modern Japanese society and politics. Considered one of Japan's more liberal intellectuals, Oe was described by *Modern Japanese Writers* contributor Dennis Washburn as "a writer driven by an urgent sense of moral and spiritual crisis."

B orn on January 31, 1935, Oe grew up in the village of Ose, located on Shikoku, one of Japan's four main islands. His entry into school coincided with Japan's involvement in the global conflict that became World War II. On August 6, 1945, when Oe was ten years old, U.S. planes dropped the world's first atomic bomb on the Japanese city of Hiroshima; three days later, Nagasaki was also leveled. Japan's Emperor Hirohito surrendered on August 15 in a radio announcement that stunned the country. Oe suddenly quit school a few weeks later. As he explained in a lecture reprinted in *World Literature Today,* "until the middle of that summer, our teachers—who earlier had taught us that the emperor was a god, had made us bow in reverence to his portrait, and had preached that Americans were not human but rather demons or beasts—now started saying things that were quite the opposite, and all too matter-of-factly at that."

After hiding in the forest during the hours he was supposed to be in school for a few weeks, Oe became ill when the rainy autumn weather arrived, and he was nursed back to health by his widowed mother. Resuming his education, he attended high school in Matsuyama, also on Shikoku,

and entered the University of Tokyo in 1954. Initially, he studied science and math, but eventually switched to French literature. He became politically active as well, co-founding the Young Japan Group with a number of other students when the terms of a controversial 1951 U.S.-Japan security treaty were renewed in 1960. The agreement compelled the United States to defend a demilitarized Japan in the event of attack, and in exchange Japan allowed the presence of U.S. military bases, including a large one in the port city of Okinawa. Oe and other Japanese who had come of age during World War II objected to the controversial agreement, for they believed it would draw Japan into a war of aggression against U.S. enemies in Asia.

Literary Acclaim Came Swiftly

In 1957 Oe's first published short story won a school prize. A 1958 novella, *Shiiku* ("The Catch"), also won honors from the Japanese Society for the Promotion of Literature. His first novel, *Memushiri kouchi,* made Oe an overnight literary sensation in Japan. The story—translated as *Nip the Bud, Shoot the Kids*—is set on Shikoku during the war years, and follows the fate of a group of juvenile delinquents sent there. The local residents are hostile to the boys, and when an outbreak of disease comes, the Shikoku villagers flee the island and leave the teens to die. The boys survive, however, and even take into their fold an ostracized Korean boy and an abandoned girl. When the islanders return, they hide their actions from the authorities, and all but one of the boys—the narrator—agree to go along with the lie. Oe's first novel "set the tone for much of his later writing," noted *Financial Times* contributor David Pilling. "While mainstream writers were basking in Japan's miraculous transition to peace and prosperity, Oe was dredging up its filthy past and asking uncomfortable questions about its present."

Oe was still at the University of Tokyo when *Shiiku* was published, and he graduated in 1959 after completing a thesis on the work of French existentialist Jean-Paul Sartre. A year later he married Yukari Itami, the daughter of a well-known Japanese screenwriter, and found himself the youngest delegate in a group invited to Communist China to meet with leader Mao Tse-tung. His next work was the novella *Seventeen* and its sequel, *Death of the Political Youth.* Both novels are based on an actual event that occurred in Japan in 1960 when a 17 year old assassinated the leader of Japan's socialist party, then committed suicide. In Oe's story, the youth is a sexual deviant whose personality disorder makes him an easy target for a right-wing political group. Both Oe and the publisher of the literary journal in which the novellas first appeared consequently received death threats.

Distraught by Birth of Son

During the early 1960s Oe traveled extensively, visiting the Soviet Union and even lunching with Sartre in Paris, after which the two men attended a political demonstration. Oe later said that, despite his early acclaim, he suffered from depression during this period of his life, a condition exacerbated by the birth of his son Hikari in 1963. The boy was born with a large growth on his head and a lesion that exposed his brain tissue. The doctors believed surgery was necessary to save Hikari's life, but told Oe and his wife that it would likely result in severe brain damage. Unable to decide whether to let the infant die or approve the operation, Oe fled to Hiroshima, where he worked on an assignment about the atomic-bomb survivors and the city's anti-nuclear movement. Oe later said that it was his meeting with the head of Hiroshima's Red Cross hospital, Dr. Fumio Shigeto, that changed his life. Shigeto told Oe about a dentist who was filled with despair in the weeks following the atomic catastrophe, when the hospitals were filled with the thousands who had been badly burned or sickened from radiation. "If there are wounded people, if they are in pain, we must do something for them, try to cure them, even if we seem to have no method," Oe recalled Shigeto as saying. Afterward, he said the city "assumed a central place in my work and became a way for me to think about our society, our world—about what it means to be human."

Oe and his wife decided to allow doctors to operate on Hikari, who did suffer brain damage as a result. The experience became the basis for Oe's next novel, *Kojinteki na taiken,* published in 1964 and translated into English as *A Personal Matter* four years later. It is the first of several fictional works from Oe's pen to feature a protagonist whose child is born severely disabled. In the story, a young husband cannot deal with the trauma, and descends into a spiral of alcoholism and infidelity as he waits for his newborn son to die in the hospital. He even spirits the infant away one day and takes him to an abortionist, but undergoes a change of heart. Oe requested that his *Hiroshima Notes* be published simultaneously with the novel, since he felt the two experiences were so intertwined. Pilling, writing in the *Financial Times,* called *A Personal Matter* "arguably the most painful and powerful post-war Japanese novel."

Oe went on to write a number of other prize-winning short stories and novels, some of them touching on the threat of nuclear power while others revisit the author's soul-searching over his severely disabled son. His works were not always well received in Japan, for his literary style eschews the Japanese tendency toward ambiguous language in favor of a far more frank approach. He includes episodes of sexual depravity and violence, and almost always casts a critical eye on Japanese society, politics, and long-held attitudes.

"Those Disgraceful Five Weeks"

Oe's 1983 novel *Rouse Up, O Young Men of the New Age!* once again features a narrator, called "K," who has a disabled son. The boy is entering adulthood, and the father, a scholar and writer, struggles to write a reference book of sorts for his son's upcoming 20th birthday, with definitions of everything in the boy's world. He refers to the boy as Eeyore, after the *Winnie the Pooh* character, and recalls the time just after Eeyore's birth when he wished the boy would die. "No powerful detergent has allowed me to wash out of my life those disgraceful five weeks," the narrator thinks. A group of young social activists criticize the father and the way in which he has centered his life and work around the boy. A student who objects to the narrator/author's politics kidnaps the son, but abandons him in the Tokyo subway. "The novel's artistry lies partly in its structure, each chapter ending with the father taking heart from his son," noted *Guardian* critic Maya Jaggi. "Far from fettering his family, Eeyore brings levity: 'Every day, joy rang out in me at the sight of him,' " Jaggi quoted from Oe's book. "Rescued after the ordeal of his kidnapping, Eeyore 'looked back at me blankly as always, as though unmoved, but tension melted from his face and body and the soft creature that always appeared in this way rose to view with a radiance that was blinding.' "

In *Rouse Up, O Young Men of the New Age!* the father notes that his son is a musical prodigy, and this is indeed what became of Hikari, whose name means "light." Like some autistic children, he was overly sensitive to noise from an early age, but Oe and his wife discovered he had an uncanny ability to recognize bird calls. He spent much of his time listening to music when not in school, and learned to play the piano. By age 13, he began composing music for it, and the first of several CD's containing his work was released in 1992.

Refused to Meet Emperor

After winning the Nobel Prize for Literature in 1994, Oe announced that, since he no longer felt the need to speak for his talented son through his literature, he planned to take a break from fiction. That same year he was also honored with the Bunka Kunsho, or Order of Culture award, bestowed by the Emperor of Japan, but he refused it, thus inciting a minor scandal. To decline it, his detractors said, was an insult to the emperor. Oe explained his reasons in a *Publishers Weekly* interview with Sam Staggs: "I rejected the award because it comes from the Emperor," he said. "One goes to the palace and receives it, but my creed is I don't want to go in front of His Majesty. I want to live like the ordinary people and not make any personal relationship with the Emperor."

A spate of English translations of Oe's early works followed his 1994 Nobel honors, including his debut novel, *Nip the Buds, Shoot the Kids.* Other titles, among them *An Echo of Heaven, A Healing Family,* and *A Quiet Life,* also reached a wider audience. True to his word, Oe wrote no more fiction in 1990s, but then came forward with the first in a trilogy of novels that he claimed would serve as his epitaph. In *Somersault,* published in 2003, an older artist returns to Japan after years away, and becomes fascinated by a local extremist cult not dissimilar to the Aum Shinrikyo group that carried out a deadly sarin gas attack on the Tokyo subway in 1995. As Oe explained in his *Publishers Weekly* interview, critical and commercial acclaim has never been his goal. "I don't write to create beauty," he told Staggs. "I write for the contemporary Japanese. I want to show them how we look. I hope they will say, after reading my books, 'This is us, this is what we look like and how we experience our society.' "

Books

Modern Japanese Writers, Charles Scribner's Sons, 2001.

Newsmakers, Gale, 1997.
Reference Guide to Short Fiction, 2nd edition, St. James Press, 1997.

Periodicals

Antioch Review, Summer 2003.
Billboard, April 1, 1995.
Booklist, August 1996; December 1, 2002.
Christian Century, April 12, 1995.
Financial Times, June 28, 2003.
Guardian (London, England), August 24, 2002.
Lancet, August 22, 1998.
Nation, May 15, 1995.
New Leader, January-February 2003.
Publishers Weekly, August 7, 1995; April 8, 1996; October 7, 1996; October 14, 1996; January 28, 2002.
Review of Contemporary Fiction, Fall 2002; Summer 2003.
Time, October 24, 1994.
World Literature Today, Spring 1996; Winter 1997; Summer 1997; Spring 2002.

Online

Business Week Online, http://www.businessweek.com/ (March 21, 2002). □

Aristotle Onassis

Greek shipping tycoon Aristotle Onassis (1906–1975) earned his fortune by building supertankers that carried oil around the globe, but he also engineered a number of other savvy business deals that gave him a personal wealth estimated to be in the billions when he died in Paris, France, in March of 1975. Sometimes called the "Golden Greek" for his Midas touch in business, Onassis is perhaps best remembered for marrying one of the most elusive woman of the twentieth century, Jacqueline Kennedy, the widow of slain American president John F. Kennedy.

Fled Hometown of Smyrna

Onassis was born on January 15, 1906, in Smyrna, a thriving, ancient port in Turkey that was later renamed Izmir. The city was home to a large Greek population at the time, including his family, and his father, Socrates, was a well-to-do tobacco merchant. Penelope, his mother, died when Onassis was six, leaving him and an older sister; Socrates then remarried and had several more children. An indifferent student, he was ejected from several schools during his teens, and by 1919 was working in his father's office. That year, Greek forces invaded Smyrna, but in August of 1922 the Turks again seized control, and ethnic tensions between the two sides erupted. Several members of Onassis's extended family died, and his father was jailed on charges of conspiring with previous

Greek occupiers. The teen managed to help his family escape to Greece, and arrived there himself with his father's savings taped to his legs.

When Socrates was released and rejoined the family, he treated his son harshly, and Onassis decided to make his fortune elsewhere. He sailed for Argentina in 1923 with some $250 in savings, using a so-called Nansen permit, which allowed a one-way trip for refugees on their way to a country of resettlement. In Buenos Aires, he held a series of menial jobs before finding work as an electrician with the British United River Plate Telephone Company. The boss, he was told, was an Briton who had been stationed in the Greek city of Salonika during World War I, and it was suggested that Onassis say he was from that city to improve his chances of hire. The information made it onto an official application that was used for his Argentine citizenship papers, and would later prove troublesome.

Earned First Fortune in Argentina

Starting out as an electrician at the phone company, Onassis became a night-shift telephone operator for it, and improved his English by listening in on calls made to London and New York. He also overheard information about upcoming business deals, and invested some of his own savings in the ventures. With his first small windfall, Onassis acquired some good suits and joined a posh rowing club to cultivate further contacts in Buenos Aires. He also became romantically involved with Claudia Muzio, an Italian soprano several years his senior. Restoring his relationship with his father, he began a successful tobacco-importing business and earned his first million from it. When a proposed tariff threatened to cut into the business's profits, Onassis brought Greek and Argentine politicians together to hammer out a trade agreement that kept the tax from being imposed. By 1931, his status and influence among the Greek expatriate community in Argentina was so impressive that the Greek government made him its deputy consul in Buenos Aires.

Onassis, however, hoped for greater prestige, and set his sights on the shipping industry. Several Greek names had been dominant over the past century, such as the powerful Livanos clan, but their operations were generally closed to newcomers. After returning to Athens for his father's funeral, he then went to London, where he heard a rumor that several Canadian freighters near Montreal were about to go up for sale. They were owned by the Canadian National Steamship Company, which was in severe financial trouble due to the Great Depression and the worldwide economic repercussions. Onassis struck a deal and bought six of them at the bargain price of $20,000 each. He renamed the first two he put in the water the *Onassis Socrates* and the *Onassis Penelope* in honor of his late parents.

Struck Wartime Deal

The fleet began carrying cargo across the Atlantic, and Onassis divided his time between the London and Buenos Aires offices of Olympic Maritime S.A., as he called his company. His ships were registered under the Panamanian flag, which saved on taxes and soon became common practice for sea-going commercial vessels. Onassis also began an affair with a wealthy heiress to a Swedish shipping fortune, Ingeborg Dedichen, which helped him secure a deal with a Göteborg ship-builder to build a 15,000-ton tanker at its yards, the world's largest at the time. When it was launched in 1938, he named it the *Ariston,* a Greek word for "the best."

Onassis's growing empire was threatened by world war in 1939. Some of his ships were seized by governments of the ports in which they sat, or by governments-in-exile. The following year, his business interests imperiled, he left a London under fire from German Luftwaffe bombs and sailed for New York, sleeping with an attaché case that contained the deeds to all of his vessels. In New York and Washington, he managed to cut deals to save his fleet, and for the rest of the war rented them out to the Allied forces fighting German and Japanese; some were lost at sea, but an agreement he reached with the U.S. government included providing him with war-surplus ships after the end of the conflict at a favorable price.

Wed Shipping Heiress

During the war years, Onassis lived in Centre Island, a village on Long Island, with Dedichen, and spent time in Hollywood, where he dated actresses Veronica Lake and Paulette Goddard. In 1942, he returned to Buenos Aires for business, and on his visa application for re-entry into the United States he used the information on his Argentine passport. Back on Long Island, his romance with Dedichen

disintegrating, Onassis began romancing Athina (Tina) Livanos, the teenage daughter of shipping magnate Stavros Livanos. He competed for her affections with Stavros Niarchos, a young friend and business rival who was the maritime attaché to the Greek Embassy in Washington at the time. The two men would engage in a lifelong rivalry that involved both Livanos daughters—Niarchos wed Tina's sister, Eugenie—and their fleets. Tina's ardor for Onassis overcame her father's objections, and the two were wed in a ceremony at the New York's Greek Orthodox Cathedral on December 28, 1946.

After the war, with the purchase of the surplus American ships, Onassis controlled one of largest privately owned merchant fleets in the world, and press reports began to refer to him as the "golden Greek." Olympic Maritime S.A.'s increasingly immense oil tankers ruled the oceans, and its owner was known for cutting business deals that seemed prescient in their predictions about the next boom or bust in world shipping trends. He ran into trouble in the early 1950s with the U.S. government, which seized some of his ships and launched a Department of Justice investigation. The deal he had cut with the war for the surplus ships required them to be in control of U.S.-based companies, and Onassis skirted the regulations by a series of legal and registry maneuvers; the 1942 visa application, which contained false information about his birthplace, also landed him in trouble. The Federal Bureau of Investigation began compiling a 4,000-page dossier on him, and he eventually paid a $7 million fine for the return of his ships.

Founded Olympic Airways

In 1956, when Egypt seized control of the Suez Canal—a vital shipping channel that brought Middle Eastern oil to the rest of the world—Onassis's immense supertankers carried it instead and he reportedly earned an extra $1 million extra daily during the crisis. He also began dabbling in other non-shipping ventures, including the purchase of a majority stake in Monaco's Société des Bains de Mer de Monte Carlo (SBM), which controlled the posh Monte Carlo casinos and hotels. The deal angered Monaco's Prince Rainier, and a bitter battle between the two endured for several years. Onassis was eventually forced to sell his SBM shares. He had better luck with a deal to operate the Greek national airline, Olympic Airways, which proved a money-losing investment for a number of years; still, the agreement he had reached with the Greek government protected his personal fortune from any financial losses.

Onassis and Tina had two children, Alexander and Christina. They lived lavishly, and commuted to and from their various European homes by means of a fabulously opulent yacht, the *Christina.* The marriage faltered when Onassis began an affair with Greek opera singer Maria Callas, one of the most famous women in the world at the time, and he and Tina divorced in 1960. Callas left her husband as well, but the pair never married; it was said he lost interest when he began courting Jacqueline Kennedy. Onassis met Kennedy in 1963, just months before her husband's assassination. He was friendly with her sister, Lee

Radziwill, and invited both to an Aegean cruise on board the *Christina*. Kennedy had recently suffered the trauma of a difficult childbirth which the infant, a boy they christened Patrick, had not survived, and accepted the invitation.

Family Torn by Strife

Onassis and the former First Lady were wed in October of 1968 on a small chapel on Skorpios, the Greek Island owned by Onassis. The news shocked the world, for Kennedy was a devout Roman Catholic, and as such was forbidden to marry a divorced person under church law. The wedding came just months after the assassination of her brother-in-law, Democratic presidential hopeful Robert F. Kennedy, and it was said that she sought the isolation and safety that only extreme wealth like Onassis's might provide for her and her two young children.

The Onassis-Kennedy union seemed ostensibly happy for the first few years, but rumors circulated that Onassis had resumed his affair with Callas, or that Kennedy-Onassis spent immense amounts of money on clothes and antiques, and sometimes refused to let him stay in her Fifth Avenue apartment when he arrived in New York. Long-simmering family rivalries also played out inside the family: Onassis's children had been devastated when their parents divorced, and were reportedly cool to their new stepmother. Onassis's ex-wife Tina eventually married Stavros Niarchos after the death of her sister Eugenie. Furthermore, Onassis proved intractable regarding the romantic intrigues of his grown children. Onassis objected strenuously to Alexander's romance with Fiona Thyssen, the ex-wife of a steel baron several years his senior, and attempted to thwart it via various means. He had less luck with his Christina's 1971 marriage to Joseph Bolker, a Los Angeles real-estate mogul 27 years her senior—which Tina had encouraged—but the union proved short-lived.

Devastated by Son's Death

Onassis was reportedly planning a divorce from Kennedy-Onassis when his son, Alexander, then age 24, died; the small plane he was piloting crashed on an Athens, Greece, runway. An experienced aviator, Alexander ran a division of Olympic Airways, but he was planning to leave the company, return to earn his university degree, and move in with Thyssen and her children. A father devastated by the loss of his son, Onassis never believed that the crash was an accident, and hinted that either the Central Intelligence Agency or the Greek military junta in power at the time was behind it.

The grief-stricken Onassis rapidly declined in health. He suffered from myasthenia gravis, a muscular disease, and died on March 15, 1975 in Paris, France. His daughter Christina inherited the bulk of his fortune as well as control of the companies, and proved herself an able successor to her legendarily deal-making father. She died, however, in November of 1988 at the age of 37, leaving her three-year-old daughter Athina in the care of her ex-husband, French pharmaceutical heir Thierry Roussel. Athina became the world's wealthiest teenager on her eighteenth birthday in January of 2003, coming into a fortune estimated at $2.7

billion as the last direct descendant of a grandfather she never met.

Books

Davis, L. J., *Onassis, Aristotle and Christina,* St. Martin's Press, 1986.
Evans, Peter, *Ari: The Life and Times of Aristotle Socrates Onassis,* Summit Books, 1986.

Periodicals

Times (London, England), March 17, 1975; January 25, 2003. □

Ernest Oppenheimer

South African business leader Ernest Oppenheimer (1880-1957) established what became the modern diamond industry almost single-handedly in the early decades of the 20th century. By gaining control of the large South African mines from which the costly gemstones came, Oppenheimer created an airtight, lucrative cartel that made his family and heirs immensely wealthy. In the late 1930s he devised a savvy marketing plan promoting the diamond engagement-ring custom in order to create a new, middle-class market for De Beers, the world's largest diamond miner and marketer, which Oppenheimer headed. In the *Guardian,* Dan Atkinson described Oppenheimer as "a legendary figure of astonishing determination."

Oppenheimer was born on May 22, 1880, in Friedberg, Hesse, a state in central Germany. His family was Jewish, and his cigar-maker father, Edward, encouraged Oppenheimer and his brothers to leave Germany and its anti-Semitic tendencies in order to make their fortunes elsewhere. In 1896, when Oppenheimer was 16, he joined his older brother Louis at the London firm of Anton Dunkelsbuhler, a diamond merchant with business interests in South Africa. He first worked in the London office's sorting operations, separating the more flawed stones from the ideal ones, and his talents gained the attention of Dunkelsbuhler himself. After Oppenheimer became a naturalized British citizen in November of 1901, he sailed to South Africa to take over the firm's office in Kimberley, the site of a large diamond mine.

The business empire that Oppenheimer created was linked to the changing political situation in southern Africa and the rapid economic development once that region's tremendous mineral wealth became evident. The diamond rush in southern Africa dated back to the 1870s, and had serious political ramifications both in this part of the continent, where European colonial powers vied for control, and on a more global scale. Foreign settlement in what later became South Africa dated back to 1652, when the Dutch

East India Company established their first outpost in the area, joining the San, Khoikoi, and Bantu indigenous dwellers. Waves of British settlers arrived in the early 19th century after the British took possession of the colony in 1814. Cecil Rhodes, an English èmigrè, secured mining concessions from local tribal leaders once diamond riches were discovered, and in 1888 founded the De Beers Consolidated Mines Company, which had a monopoly on a vast mine in Kimberley. Rhodes, who died in 1902, never managed to make a successful diamond cartel to corner the world market for the gemstones. Part of his failure was due to new competition from discoveries recently made in German South West Africa, which later became Namibia. A stretch of that region's beach, rich with diamonds, became known as the *Sperrgebiet,* or "forbidden zone." There, black workers dug with gags in their mouths to prevent them from swallowing the gems.

Entered Politics

Working in the Kimberley offices, Oppenheimer took copious notes on the new and flourishing diamond trade and quickly rose within the firm. His sharp eye for the ideal gem soon made him one of the most successful diamond traders in Kimberley. He also began to make small investments in gold-mining in the Transvaal as a deal-broker for German investors, a venture that would prove immensely profitable when international politics altered the balance of power in southern Africa. "He was," noted Edward Jay Epstein in *The Rise and Fall of Diamonds: The Shattering of a Brilliant Illusion,* "in many ways the prototype of the

multinational businessman: German by birth, British by naturalization, Jewish by religion, and South African by residence." The merchant was even elected mayor of Kimberley in 1912.

When World War I broke out in Europe in the summer of 1914, Oppenheimer began shuttling between South Africa and London; on one occasion, his ship was torpedoed by German submarines and he had to be rescued from his lifeboat by a British destroyer. The war's danger, however, was offset by a unique series of opportunities that allowed him to gain control of the diamond market. Initially, he sought to create an international corporation that would protect German investors from losing their interest in the Transvaal gold mines. With this in mind, in London in 1917 he founded the Anglo-American Corporation of South Africa with some assistance from his brothers and the house of Morgan, the New York City investment bank. Oppenheimer then moved on to the owners of the Sperrgebiet, which had been occupied by South African troops since 1915. He approached its German investors and offered them shares in Anglo-American in exchange for their holdings. Realizing that, should their side come out the loser in the war, their property would be appropriated by the British-South Africa government anyway, the Germans agreed. Thus Oppenheimer's Consolidated Diamond Mines (CDM) of South West Africa came into existence. The leverage he now held forced the De Beers Company into a bargaining position with him. In exchange for the Namibian properties, he asked De Beers for a share of stock and a seat on the board, and its cornered directors were forced to acquiesce.

Derided on Editorial Pages

The following year, Oppenheimer was knighted by England's King George V for his wartime service, becoming one of a small handful of Jews to receive the honor at the time. Back in South Africa, his Anglo-American Corporation prospered. Because of his prominence, he was sometimes the focus of anti-Semitic jibes in South Africa. He enjoyed a close alliance with the prime minister, Jan Smuts, which helped his business dealings flourish. Smuts led the United South African (Unionist) Party, and was pro-British. The Dutch "Afrikaner"-dominated National Party was known for its harsh attitudes towards non-whites in South Africa—attitudes implemented in a brutal apartheid regime after they won the 1948 elections—and fomented against what it viewed as the collusion of British and Jewish interests exploiting South African resources during this era. Anti-Semitic attitudes were vented in pro-Nationalist newspapers and "represented by a cartoon character called 'Hoggenheimer,' universally identified with Sir Ernest Oppenheimer," explained *New York Times Magazine* writer Joseph Lelyveld.

Over the next few years, Oppenheimer added to his company's increasingly vast holdings. After new diamond riches were discovered in 1927 in Namaqualand and Oppenheimer bought a controlling interest, he was elected chair and managing director of De Beers, which then became part of his Anglo-American Company. In 1929 the U.S. stock market crashed and a global economic depression began. Suddenly, the market for diamonds vanished, and the London diamond-trading syndicate, a successor to the one Rhodes had created, found itself nearly bankrupt by 1931. Via his family connections—three firms were controlled by members of his extended family—Oppenheimer moved to take over the syndicate.

Oppenheimer ordered the Kimberley mine and others in South Africa closed, and the Sperrgebiet area shut down as well. World diamond output was slashed from 2.2 million carats to just 14,000 between 1930 and 1933. He was also forced, however, to buy diamonds that came on the market outside the reach of his companies, mostly from Belgian Congo and Portuguese Angola. The unassailable cartel that endured for decades was formally structured by Oppenheimer in 1934. Its strategy was to keep the supply of diamonds far below the demand, for if large numbers of the gemstones came onto the market the per-carat price would plummet. The cache was kept at De Beers' London offices, and brokers approved by De Beers's Central Selling Organisation (CSO) came every five weeks and met for the day. CSO officials would present to them a box of diamonds for their approval or rejection; the price stated by De Beers was not negotiable.

Devised Engagement-Ring Custom

Diamond sales remained moribund during the 1930s, by 1937 Oppenheimer's De Beers company had stockpiled some 40 million carats, about a 20-years supply. Threatened with bankruptcy, he decided to create a market himself. He first found industrial applications for poor-quality diamonds in manufacturing, and just before the outbreak of World War II Oppenheimer sent his son Harry to New York City to work with Madison Avenue strategists. A campaign touting the four "C's" of diamond perfection—cut, color, clarity, carat—was created, and within two years sales had jumped more than 50 percent. De Beers' ads also began trumpeting the custom of a diamond engagement ring, which was not commonplace at the time at all. The marketing blitz was boosted by De Beers's famous slogan, "a diamond is forever."

The post-World War II years proved hugely profitable for Oppenheimer and De Beers. The company reinvested profit into digging new gold mines in South Africa, and ventured into platinum, steel, paper products, and an array of other industrial holdings. Oppenheimer remained chair and director until 1953, after which he served as board chair only. He was a noted philanthropist, funding the Queen Elizabeth House for Commonwealth studies at Oxford University, and acquiring a priceless collection of art and antiques. His first wife, May Pollack, with whom he had two sons, died in 1934, and his son Frank died after a swimming accident in Madeira in 1935. He underwent a spiritual crisis because of these losses, and converted to Christianity that year. A few months later, he wed Caroline "Ina" Harvey, daughter of an English baron and widow of his nephew Michael, who had died in a 1933 plane crash. Around this same time he founded E. Oppenheimer, a holding company that served to protect his personal fortune. Oppenheimer was, by several millions above his competitors, the richest man in South Africa.

The Oppenheimer Legacy

Oppenheimer suffered one heart attack, and was felled by another one a few months later at his Johannesburg estate on November 25, 1957. Under the leadership of his son Harry, the empire Oppenheimer created continued to thrive, and maintained a legendary level of secrecy. Only Oxford graduates were hired to staff its executive ranks, and the company was rumored to be ruthless in its acquisition of surplus diamonds which found their way onto the world market from mines outside of its control. At one point the CSO and its adjunct, the Diamond Trading Company (DTC) traded 80 percent of the world's diamonds in a business that was estimated to bring in $5 billion annually. The company was often the target of political protests for doing business in South Africa during its brutally oppressive apartheid era; some 250,000 of its black South African employees were restricted by government law to work as only migrant laborers in its mines. They were unable to establish permanent residency in the area where they worked, or to bring their families there to settle. Harry Oppenheimer, who controlled the company and family fortune until his death in 2000, was a surprising advocate of political reform during the 1970s, even supporting the idea of trade-union rights for miners. The Anglo- American Corporation was named in a reparations lawsuit in 2003, a decade after apartheid ended in the country.

By the turn of the 21st century the diamond-trading cartel Oppenheimer created had lost much of its authority. Australia, with its own large and profitable Argyle mine discovered in 1979, dropped out of the DTC cartel in 1996. Still, Anglo-American remained the second largest mining company in the world, and De Beers the largest producer of diamonds, with some 45 percent of the global supply coming from its mines in South Africa. It also had partnerships with the governments of Botswana and Namibia to operate lucrative mines there.

Books

Epstein, Edward Jay, *The Rise and Fall of Diamonds: The Shattering of a Brilliant Illusion,* Simon & Schuster, 1982.
Gregory, Theodore, *Ernest Oppenheimer and the Economic Development of Southern Africa,* Oxford University Press, 1962.
Hocking, Anthony, *Oppenheimer and Son,* McGraw-Hill, 1973.

Periodicals

Economist, July 1, 1989; December 20, 1997.
Guardian (London, England), October 2, 1996.
New York Times Magazine, May 8, 1983.
Time International, July 24, 2000.
Times (London, England), November 26, 1957. □

Ferdinand Leopold Oyono

Ferdinand Leopold Oyono (born 1929) is one of the most renowned anticolonialist novelists of Africa.

Since Cameroon's independence in 1960, he has also served in many diplomatic and government positions. In his novels and his government positions he deals with the place of Africans and their cultures both in Africa and in the world.

Oyono was born in 1929 in south-central Cameroon near Ebolowa, in the Bulu country, and was educated there and in France, where he worked in the theater and on television as well as studying law and administration. In 1956, while a student in Paris, he published his first two novels, *Une vie de boy* (Houseboy) and *Le Vieux Negre et la medaille* (The Old Man and the Medal). In 1960 his third book, *Chemin d'Europe* (Road to Europe), was released. He is recognized as one of the first Francophone novelists and classified with the writers of the Negritude movement. Richard Bjornson, in his translation of *Road to Europe,* called Oyono's first two novels "classics of modern African literature" that are "taught . . . in schools and universities throughout Africa, Europe, and America."

First Novel

In *Houseboy,* perhaps the most widely read of the three novels, Oyono tells the story of Toundi Joseph, a boy from French Cameroon who flees his father's brutality to become the houseboy of a priest at a Catholic mission in a nearby town. Toundi grows up serving the priest and learns to read and write. After the priest dies suddenly, Toundi becomes the houseboy of the French Commandant of the area. When the Commandant's wife arrives, Toundi is smitten with her grace and beauty, but she soon commences a tawdry affair with the colonial prison director, something Toundi cannot help but discover. Later the African mistress of the French agricultural engineer steals the engineer's money and runs away. As Toundi, an innocent acquaintance of the mistress, is taken away in connection with the theft, the Commandant's wife smiles and looks away, happy to triumph over someone who knows of her immorality. Toundi becomes the colonials' scapegoat in the theft, someone with compromising knowledge of the prison official's affair and whom they can punish to disguise their inability to deal effectively with the crime. Toundi's untimely death is the result of their mistreatment. The story is told in the form of Toundi's diary of his years among the French colonials. Although it is sometimes described as humorous, it is really an indictment of colonial rule.

In the work, Oyono showed himself a master of irony, imagery, and keen observation. Toundi's youth and naivete are foils for the evils of the colonials, who dominate the natives. Scholars have found the images of physical destruction to echo the colonials' psychological destruction of the Africans.

Wrote of Tragic Irony

The book, though short, is layered with irony. One commentator notes, for example, Oyono's use of the name Joseph as the priest's name for Toundi, linking it with the Joseph of the Old Testament of the Christian Bible, the

Israelite who, enslaved in Egypt, rises in the estimation of his masters until he is falsely accused of desiring the wife of an Egyptian. It has also been noted that Toundi enters into his relationships with the colonials with frank admiration, accepting the alleged superiority of Western ways and culture until disillusioned by the truth. Not only is Toundi given a Christian name on joining the church and the colonial world; it is practitioners of Christianity who set him on the path that leads to his destruction in spite of his innocence.

Literary analysts have found that *Houseboy* reveals insights into the psychology of oppression. At first dazzled by the education his servitude affords and the loveliness of the Commandant's wife, Toundi is eventually doomed by his close association with the colonials because he learns too much about their real character. Because he knows of the Commandant's wife's indiscretion and of the agricultural engineer's affair, he represents a threat—although his diary reveals no intent to betray anyone. Shortly before his arrest, Toundi writes bitterly of his place in the Commandant's household: "Kicks and insults have started again. He thinks this humiliates me and he can't find any other way. He forgets that it is all part of my job as a houseboy, a job which holds no more secrets for me."

In *The Old Man and the Medal,* Oyono writes about an older African man who has worked closely with the colonials throughout his life and is to receive a medal for his service. He comes to realize how isolated he is from both the native African world and the world of the colonials, who want to bestow an award but do not really want to associate with him beyond a superficial level. In *Road to Europe,* Oyono writes of an African determined to succeed in France. His success costs him his self-regard and does not confer happiness.

Belonged to Negritude Movement

The cruelty, duplicity, and injustice of the colonial system; the dilemma of identity faced by Africans; and the lack of African political and cultural sovereignty are themes in Oyono's novels as well as those of the Negritude literary movement. Negritude is most closely associated with Leopold Sedar Senghor (1906–2001; the first president of Senegal, elected in 1960) and Aime Cesaire (born 1913), from Martinique (who coined the term "Negritude"). It began among African and Caribbean writers in Paris in the 1930s and also drew inspiration from the fountain of African American literary and artistic talent that sprang up in New York City in the 1920s, known as the Harlem Renaissance. In its broadest sense, Negritude sought to celebrate and reclaim black and African culture and values and undo the ravages of slavery and colonialism. It embraced political and economic progress in addition to artistic expression.

Independence Brought Oyono Home

The area now known as Cameroon was first settled by Bantu people, and other groups followed. It became a colony for the first time in 1884, when Germany and various tribal chiefs entered into certain treaties. After Germany's defeat in World War I, France came to control some four-fifths of the area and England the rest; Cameroon was two colonies. After World War II, a gradual progress toward unification and independence began. January 1, 1960, was the official birth of Cameroon as an independent republic. Although both French and English are official in the country today, Cameroon is most closely affiliated with the Francophone world, that is, former colonies of France that still use the French language widely.

Began Diplomatic Career

With his third novel published in 1960, Oyono switched to a diplomatic career. He became newly independent Cameroon's special envoy to Guinea, Mali, Senegal, and Morocco in 1961 and 1962. From 1963 to 1975, he served as ambassador to Liberia, Belgium, Luxembourg, France, Italy, Tunisia, Morocco, and Algeria, after which he chaired the United Nations Security Council, UNICEF (United Nations International Children's Emergency Fund, now known as the United Nations Children's Fund), the Board of the Security Council's Political Committee, and the United Nations Council on Namibia. Between 1984 and 1985 he was Cameroon's ambassador to the United Kingdom. After that he held a series of cabinet posts in Cameroon, culminating in 1998, as he neared the age of seventy, with his appointment as his country's minister of culture.

Promoted Spectrum of Cultural Development

In his capacity as minister of culture, Oyono guided Cameroon's progress in a number of areas. Among the issues before Cameroon in the early part of the twenty-first century are cultural diversity and the threat posed by globalization, viewed by some as promoting cultural uniformity and threatening diversity because it favors domination by large enterprises. The United Nations has affirmed the necessity of preserving cultural diversity as a source of creativity, a socially unifying factor, and a means of economic development. One of Cameroon's relevant cultural undertakings in this area, launched by Oyono, is an inventory of the country's considerable cultural resources, viewed as integral to the identity of the country's people. One is a site inhabited more than 32,000 years ago that lies in the northwestern part of the country. The inventory is viewed as an indispensable prelude to preservation efforts. Another effort is renewing cooperation with an international organization comprising Angola, Cameroon, Central African Republic, Congo Republic, Democratic Republic of the Congo, Comoros, Gabon, Equatorial Guinea, Rwanda, Sao Tome and Principe, and Zambia in documenting and preserving the 3000-year-old Bantu culture, spread over one third of the continent and which some 150 million Africans have in common. The organization promotes intercultural dialog and dissemination of knowledge and appreciation of various aspects of Bantu culture.

Appropriate to his former career as novelist, Oyono promotes reading in his country. He is also involved in efforts to protect the copyrights of musicians. He promotes government subsidies for artists, viewing the arts as a potential source of substantial income for Cameroon. He also seeks to develop cultural tourism and wants cultural development to play an important role in the country's development.

Books

Cartey, Wilfred, *Whispers from the Literature of Contemporary Black Africa,* Random House, 1969.

Harrow, Kenneth W., *Thresholds of Change in African Literature: The Emergence of a Tradition,* Heinemann, 1994.

Oyono, Ferdinand, *Houseboy,* translated by John Reed, Heinemann, 1966.

———, *Road to Europe,* translated by Richard Bjornson, Three Continents Press, 1989.

Periodicals

Research in African Literatures, Spring 2003.

Online

"Cameroon," *Infoplease Encyclopedia,* www.infoplease.com/ita/A01077382.html (January 8, 2004).

"Culture: a vital factor in the development equation," *The Herald,* www.ambafrance-cm.org/html/camero/medias/presse/22072607.htm (January 6, 2004).

"Ferdinand Oyono (Cameroon)," *African Writers Series,* www.africanwriters.com/WritersWriterTop.asp?cPK=OyonoFerdinand2380 (January 6, 2004).

"Literature," *Yahoo! Encyclopedie - Cameroun,* http://fr.encyclopedia.yahoo.com/articles/cl/cl_751_p1.html (January 6, 2004).

Mvogo, Raphael, "Diversite culturelle: question de principes," *Cameroon Tribune,* http://fr.allafrica.com/stories/printable/200306060373.html (January 7, 2004).

Mvogo, Raphael, "Je pense, donc je suis Bantu," *Cameroon Tribune,* http://fr.allafrica.com/stories/printable/200309190654.html (January 7, 2004).

Mvogo, Raphael, "La bantu attitude en marche," *Cameroon Tribune,* http://fr.allafrica.com/stories/printable/200304290876.html (January 7, 2004).

Mvogo, Raphael, "Le livre en lecture simplifiee," *Cameroon Tribune,* http://fr.allafrica.com/stories/printable/200309110695.html (January 7, 2004).

Mvogo, Raphael, "Patrimoine culturel: on fait l'inventaire," *Cameroon Tribune,* http://fr.allafrica.com/stories/printable/200309260567.html (January 7, 2004).

"Oyono, Ferdinand Leopold," *Columbia Electronic Encyclopedia,* http://print.infoplease.com/ce6/people/A0837195.html (January 6, 2004).

Tagne, David Ndachi, "Un milliard pour soutenir la culture nationale," *Cameroon Tribune,* http://allafrica.com/stories/printable/200305300046.html (January 7, 2003).

Tchakam, Stephane, "Aux artistes ce qui est aux artistes," *Cameroon Tribune,* http://fr.allafrica.com/stories/printable/200401060503.html (January 7, 2004). □

P

Panini

Renowned for his writings on classical Sanskrit grammar, Panini (c. 450–350 B.C.E.) established the linguistic rules for the spoken Sanskrit of his day. His treatise *Astadhyayi*, considered the first major work on grammar in any language, was fodder for many later Indian grammarians and is still studied by both Eastern and Western linguists today.

Although it is known that Panini was born in Shalatula, a small town near Attock on the northwestern Indian peninsula in what is now Pakistan, historians remain uncertain as to the exact dates of Panini's birth and death. One theory, supported by internal references that indicate Panini had contact with or was at least aware of Greek civilization, place his life after the year 327 B.C.E., when Macedonian Alexander the Great reached northwestern India. However, historical evidence supports limited contact between the two civilizations as early as the sixth century B.C.E. Commentaries based on Panini's work and written by Indian grammarians Katyayana and Patanjali, who probably lived in the third or fourth and perhaps even in the late second centuries B.C.E., help define Panini's lifespan as well. The natures of these commentaries place Panini well before either Katyayana or Patanjali, causing some scholars to believe Panini to have lived as early as the seventh century B.C.E. As speculation varies wildly, it seems most reasonable to place Panini around the fifth century B.C.E., the midpoint of this wide range. The scant details of Panini's life are, however, completely overshadowed by the importance of his work, a Sanskrit grammatical treatise called the *Astadhyayi*, or "The Eight-chaptered," which is considered to be the most important work in the development of Sanskrit and one of the most important works in the history of any language.

The Birth of a Language

Sanskrit is the classical language of India and the mother tongue of most of the languages currently spoken on the Indian subcontinent. In Sanskrit, the word for grammar means "analysis," reflecting the fact that the Indians of the ancient world considered grammar to be an important field. As Harold G. Coward and K. Kunjunni Raja explained in the *Encyclopedia of Indian Philosophies: The Philosophy of the Grammarians:* "Grammar was recognized from the earliest times in India as a distinct science, a field of knowledge with its own parameters that distinguished it from other sciences such as astronomy, architecture, agriculture, and the like." The impetus to study grammar came from the dominant religion of India: Hinduism. Arthur A. MacDonell described this beginning in *A Sanskrit Grammar for Students* thus: "The first impulse . . . was given by the religious motive of preserving intact the sacred Vedic texts, the efficacy of which was believed to require attention to every letter." The importance of Panini's work on grammar thus lay not only in the linguistic, but also the philosophic realm.

While Panini's treatise dictated the laws that would govern classical Sanskrit, he was not the first grammarian; in the *Astadhyayi*, Panini mentions ten earlier authorities, and scholars believe there were many more. MacDonell commented that, "aided by the great transparency of the Sanskrit language, the ancient Indian grammarians had by the fifth century B.C.E. arrived at scientific results unequaled by any other nation of antiquity." However, as Coward and Raja observed, "no authenticated works of any of these pre-Paninian writers have come down to us, and it is difficult if not impossible to say which, if any, of Panini's rules may have been taken from his predecessors." Regardless of how much or how little Panini derived his work from earlier sources, his *Astadhyayi* is a revolutionary work. Indeed, in his introduction to a modern edition of the *Astadhyayi,* Sumitra M. Katre noted that, because of the book's "importance, all earlier works in this field gradually disappeared. Panini's *Astadhyayi,* in its turn, became the focal point of much critical and explicatory work over the last two millennia." Even subsequent grammatical works, which relied heavily on the *Astadhyayi,* have been largely disregarded by recent Sanskrit scholars in favor of Panini's text.

Format and Content of the *Astadhyayi*

In discussing Panini's work, Katre observed that the *Astadhyayi* "is the earliest extant descriptive grammar of Sanskrit as currently spoken during [Panini's] time . . . in the north-west region of India (now Pakistan). His extraordinary perception of linguistic facts covered, however, a wider region, since he not only refers to the earlier stage of the language as occurring in Vedic literature, but also spreads over the northern and eastern parts of India whose regional variant he also notices in his majestic sweep." MacDonell described Panini's text as "at once the shortest and fullest grammar in the world." Panini sets forth about 4,000 statements regarding the proper composition of Sanskrit in a very brief, almost algebraic format, relying on *sutras,* or terse statements normally intended for memorization. These sutras provided students in Indian societies relying on oral, as opposed to literary, learning with a common way to transmit knowledge. This reliance on oral recitation has caused problems for the *Astadhyayi's* legacy, however. Katre noted that "This was proper as long as the texts were transmitted orally from teacher to pupil in an unbroken line of descent. But this seems to have been broken at some time . . . thus to a large extent the interpretation of each sutra depends largely on the great commentaries." In fact, some scholars believe that even such basic concepts as word meanings were not originally a part of the *Astadhyayi,* but were later added by commentators.

The *Astadhyayi,* for all its brevity, follows a well-defined format. As MacDonell explained: "Book i. contains the technical terms of the grammar and its rules of interpretation; ii. deals with nouns in composition and case relations; iii. teaches how suffixes are to be attached to verbal roots; iv. and v. explain the same process with regard to the nominal stems; vi. and vii. describe the accent and phonetic changes in the formation of words, while viii. treats of words in a sentence." This setup is not, however, stringently adhered to; Panini inserts unrelated rules which typically do follow a related train of thought, or which can be more effectively explained outside the context of the book to which they truly belong. The eight books or chapters referred to in the title of the *Astadhyayi* are further subdivided into quarter-chapters, with each chapter containing a number of sutras. Katre further described this by noting that "Panini has attempted to arrange his sutras under two major headings: [the first] a general rule which encompasses the largest number of linguistic items and [the second] an ex-

ception which covers a smaller group not subject to the general rule." These organizational systems, presumably intended to ease memorization, did not necessarily lend themselves to written clarity, however; thus, there have been many attempts to reorganize Panini's work made by more recent grammarians.

Panini's rules of grammar rely on two simple concepts: that all nouns are derived from verbs, and that all word derivation takes place through suffixes. However, Panini does depart from these guidelines in some instances. Words which do not conform to verbal derivation he collected and incorporated into a separate list. MacDonell commented that such words "were often forcibly derived from verbal roots by means of a number of special suffixes. . . . Panini refers to all such words as ready-made stems, the formation of which does not concern him." To the extent that the *Astadhyayi* addresses word meanings, Panini also chooses to accept the dictates of common usage over those of strict derivation. Raja recorded that the grammarian "says that the authority of the popular usage of words . . . must supersede the authority of the meaning dependent on derivation. The meanings of words (the relations between word and meaning) are also established by popular usage." Panini's preference for examining the language as it was truly spoken, instead of adhering completely to intellectually defined rules, exemplifies the innovation of his work.

Later Commentators Added to Panini's Work

Ancient commentators provide us with important perspectives on the *Astadhyayi.* Katre commented that "nearly a thousand treatises have been produced during two millennia since . . . [the *Astadhyayi*] was composed by Panini." The two seminal treatises on the *Astadhyayi* are Katyayana's *Varttikas* and Patanjali's *Mahabhashya.* These two texts are closely linked, despite having being written over a century apart—as mentioned earlier, Katyayana lived in the third or fourth century B.C.E., while Patanjali lived during the second half of the second century B.C.E. In *India's Past,* Mac-Donell noted that Patanjali's commentary, the *Mahabhashya,* "does not discuss Panini's rules, but Katyayana's varttikas . . . are short criticisms on about one-third of Panini's sutras." Despite the lack of specific discussion, Patanjali's work is generally considered to be the finest ancient commentary on the *Astadhyayi.*

More recent treatises on Panini include Vamana and Jayaditya's *Kasika,* which, unlike the *Mahabhashya,* addresses the full text of the *Astadhyayi* and dates from around the seventh century; Ramacandra's 15th-century *Prakriya-kaumudi,* or "Moonlight of Method," which reorganizes Panini's text into a more understandable format; and Bhattoji's 17th-century *Siddhanta-kaumudi,* or "Moonlight of Settled Conclusions," which also attempts to simplify Panini's format. Another important seventh-century work that draws on Panini, the *Vakyapadiya* by Bhartrihari, "regrouped all previous ideas . . . developing a whole theory of language from the point of view of semantics, psychology, and symbolism," according to Alain Danéilou in *A Brief History of India.* MacDonell commented in *A Sanskrit*

Grammar for Students that "A belief in the infallibility of Panini . . . has often led . . . interpreters, from Patanjali onwards, to give explanations of Panini's rules." These explanations have more often seemed more akin to justifications, as the brevity of the *Astadhyayi* has sometimes obscured Panini's true intent or led to muddled interpretation.

A Monumental Work

The preeminence of the *Astadhyayi* in the development of not only Sanskrit, but of the grammar of all languages, cannot be denied. As Katre observed, "In a work of such magnitude which covers every aspect of the author's speech community . . . there is indeed much scope to find some overstatements as well as understatements. But none of this takes away from the credit which is due to Panini who, in this astounding work, has set up a model which is fully adequate to cover every aspect of the language described." J. N. Mohanty argued in *Classical Indian Philosophy* that "It is possible that no other Hindu intellectual achievement has been able to surpass Panini." Predating even the early Greek's examination of language, Panini's work continues to exert influence in the realm of linguistics 2,000 years after its composition.

Books

Coward, Harold G., and K. Kunjunni Raja, *Encyclopedia of Indian Philosophies: The Philosophy of the Grammarians,* Princeton University Press, 1990.

Daniélou, Alain, *A Brief History of India,* translated by Kenneth Hurry, Inner Traditions, 2003.

Kulke, Hermann, and Dietmar Rothermund, *A History of India,* third edition, Routledge, 1998.

MacDonell, Arthur A., *A History of Sanskrit Literature,* Motilal Banarsidass Publishers, 1900.

———, *A Sanskrit Grammar for Students,* third edition, Oxford University Press, 1927.

———, *India's Past,* Oxford University Press, 1927.

Mohanty, J. N., *Classical Indian Philosophy,* Rowman & Littlefield, 2000.

Panini, *Astadhyayi,* translated by Sumitra M. Katre, University of Texas Press, 1987. □

Andrzej Panufnik

One of Poland's foremost musical figures, Andrzej Panufnik (1914–1991) remains one of the 20th century's most respected composers and conductors. He served as music director with Krakow and Warsaw Philharmonics in Poland and later with the City of Birmingham Symphony Orchestra in his adopted homeland of England. Panufnik's defection from Poland under the Soviet regime provides an arresting study of the desire for artistic and personal freedom.

A Musical Childhood

Panufnik was born in Warsaw on September 24, 1914. His father was an engineer and respected violin maker; his mother was a talented violinist, although she did not play professionally. Panufnik was thus exposed to music from birth; in his autobiography *Composing Myself,* Panufnik commented that "in my early years I never consciously listened to my mother's playing, but it was constantly in my ears, a background music, part of the fabric of my life . . . This music was an intrinsic part of my existence, like cleaning my teeth, eating my meals, even breathing." Panufnik began composing at age nine, inspired by a young musician who visited his home to take down Panufnik's mother's melodies, but did not begin formal musical training until his late teens.

Studied at Home and Abroad

In 1932, Panufnik entered the Warsaw Conservatoire to study percussion, but he transferred shortly after into theory and composition courses. As part of his studies at the Conservatoire, Panufnik composed his first recognized work, the Piano Trio. Panufnik graduated in 1936 and planned to travel to Vienna, a city he was drawn to because of its rich musical history and modern reputation for innovation. This plan was delayed, however, and Panufnik was forced to wait until the following year to commence his instruction in Austria. In Vienna, he studied conducting at the State Academy under the highly respected Felix von

Weingartner, conductor of the Vienna Philharmonic and Vienna Opera. In early 1938, the Nazi German army occupied Austria, Panufnik's classes at the Academy were temporarily canceled, and the atmosphere in Vienna changed drastically. Weingartner was removed from his teaching post and Panufnik, as he related in his autobiography, "realized that I would henceforth be wasting my time in Vienna." He returned to Warsaw, but stayed only a short time before leaving for Paris.

With the intention of studying French music, something Weingartner had not focused on, Panufnik sought out conductor Philippe Gaubert in Paris. He studied with Gaubert briefly, describing these lessons as "few but incomparably valuable," and then decided to work more seriously on his own composition skills. Panufnik began composing his first symphony and spent much of his time attending concerts featuring pieces by other modern composers, which he described as "both instructive and useful in my search for my musical self." This time proved a formative and fruitful one for Panufnik; but after about six months in Paris, he crossed the English Channel to visit London. Despite being somewhat unimpressed by the current British musical climate, Panufnik enjoyed his time in London during the spring and summer of 1939. However, he believed his musical future lay in Poland; in spite of the turmoil brewing in Central Europe, Panufnik returned to Warsaw in late summer 1939, his reputation as a composer and conductor having begun to grow formidably.

Wartime Years

Shortly following Panufnik's arrival in Warsaw, Poland was invaded by the German army. Panufnik remained in Warsaw during the years of war that followed, despite the heavy restrictions placed on the Polish arts community and the danger inherent in living in an occupied city. Primarily performing as a pianist with friend and fellow composer Witold Lutoslawski in small, underground concerts, Panufnik also composed and conducted several works, including two major symphonies. Following the liberation of Poland by the Russians, all the scores of Panufnik's early works were accidentally burnt, practically erasing the output of ten years. Grove Music reported that "after the war, Panufnik reconstructed several of these lost scores;" however, the majority of these early pieces remain lost to this day. The Polish Music Center noted that of the two-piano pieces composed and performed by Panufnik and Lutoslawski during the war, "only Lutoslawski's "Paganini Variations" remain from this bulk of music."

Growth and Repression Under the Soviets

Panufnik spent the years directly following World War II as a conductor. Moving to Krakow in 1945 was a relief after war-torn Warsaw, Panufnik commented that "to arrive in Krakow was like returning from Hades." Krakow—the former capital of Poland and still a major city—had become the artistic hub of the country. Panufnik quickly found a niche there, as the conductor of the Krakow Philharmonic Orchestra. The new Soviet government, however, was no

more accommodating of artistic freedom than the Nazis had been; Panufnik encountered resistance to a short film he had produced which showed the recent destruction of Warsaw. With this censorship, Panufnik began to feel the stirrings of frustration would ultimately lead him to defect. Also during this time, Panufnik reconstructed three of his lost pieces; through his work with the new State Music Publishers, he had his second symphony, *The Tragic Overture*, published using his own, clearer musical notation system, which would be adopted by several other modern composers.

Following his successful conductorship of the Krakow Philharmonic, Panufnik was appointed Music Director at the Warsaw Philharmonic in 1946. The concert hall in Warsaw had been destroyed during the war, and the orchestra itself lacked both musicians and support staff, making his title more hopeful than practical. Panufnik delighted at the challenge, however, and promptly began rebuilding the orchestra to its previous level of excellence. He recruited musicians from throughout Poland, traveled to France to acquire new music for the orchestra, and attempted to secure a new permanent location for the orchestra to perform. Yet, after only a few performances with the orchestra, Panufnik received disappointing news from the government: the apartments promised for his musicians were delayed, with no word on when they might become available. Disheartened, in 1947 Panufnik resigned his post with the Warsaw Philharmonic.

Panufnik, suddenly freed of his duties as Music Director, found time to return to the composition he had neglected for the past five years. He also spent much time traveling internationally to conduct other major symphonies and to act as a representative of the Polish music community. Over the next several years, Panufnik composed some of his best-known works, including the *Sinfonia Rustica,* which won first prize at the Chopin Competition in 1949, and the *Symphony of Peace*. However, Panufnik continued to have run-ins with the Soviet government over issues ranging from artistic freedom to fair housing allocation. He married a British woman, Marie Elizabeth O'Mahoney, and the couple had a daughter in 1952. The infant died tragically in May 1953 and Panufnik was devastated, all the more so because he was serving on a delegation in Beijing at the time. He quickly returned home to Warsaw, but felt artistically empty; in his autobiography, he claimed that he "was just a stuffed dummy of a composer." Yet, as the leading Polish composer, Panufnik continued to be loaded with requests from his government, and his frustration level continued to rise. Panufnik decided the time had come for him to leave Poland permanently.

Defection to England

In *Tempo*, Harold Truscott noted that "after conducting a concert in Zurich in July, 1954, [Panufnik] was ordered to return to Poland. Instead, he came to England, requested, and was granted, political asylum." In fact, this process was not nearly so simple. Panufnik had been planning his defection some time. His wife had previously left the country; while he awaited an opportunity to join her, she made contacts with officials in Britain to aid her husband's defection. When Panufnik was invited to conduct a concert of Polish music in Switzerland, his opportunity arrived. Panufnik packed only a few things and bid farewell to his homeland. In Zurich, he undertook the recording of his *Sinfonia Rustica,* all the while worrying that his plans to defect had been discovered. After the recording was finished, a friend drove him to the airport where he boarded a plane for London and began his new life on July 14, 1954.

The Polish government denounced him strongly and officially erased all of his works, banning any mention of them—or of him—from any printed materials. In the eyes of Poland, Panufnik ceased to exist. Panufnik and his wife struggled financially for several months before he found a patron and his works began to be performed again both in England and internationally. Famed conductor Leopold Stokowski led performances of Panufnik's symphonies in Detroit and Houston, raising awareness of Panufnik in the United States. After a few years in England, Panufnik secured the position of Music Director with the City of Birmingham City Orchestra (CBSO) commencing in 1957 and left London, a move that also dissolved his marriage.

An Active Musical Maturity

Panufnik's time at the CBSO was full; he conducted approximately 50 concerts during the performance season, managed orchestra personnel, and served as a public face for the orchestra. His first season was marked by continual disputes with Norris Stanley, the orchestra's concertmaster—the head of the first violin section and a figure of some authority to the musicians—which led to Stanley's dismissal at the end of the season. In the *Birmingham Post,* Terry Grimley commented that "this does seem to have been personal in that . . . Stanley believed [Panufnik] to be a Communist . . . despite the fact that he was a refugee that had given up an honored position under a Communist government to scratch a living in the West Midlands." Panufnik's second season included four of his own works, a programming selection the orchestra management requested but which he found somewhat embarrassing. At the end of this season, Panufnik's contract expired and he returned to London in 1959, hoping to focus on composing.

Panufnik composed several important works over the coming years, including the *Sinfonia Sacra* and *Autumn Music.* The *Sinfonia Sacra* was particularly well-received, winning first prize in a music competition in Monaco, but was banned by the BBC—the irony of which Panufnik found amusing. Panufnik also began a relationship with a young English photographer, Camilla Jessel, and the two married in 1963. After so many years of upheaval, Panufnik finally settled into a calmer, productive life in Twickenham, a suburb of London. He composed an array of music, including more symphonies, several concertos for many different instruments, choral pieces—indeed, Panufnik composed modern-sounding works in practically every standard format of classical music, a dichotomy which set his works apart. This mixing of tradition and innovation perhaps reached its peak in 1979, when Panufnik composed a piece for the London Symphony Orchestra that required no conductor.

Later Years and Achievements

In 1977, Panufnik's *Universal Prayer* was performed at the Warsaw Autumn Festival, the first time his music had been heard in Poland for over 30 years. After this, his pieces began to appear in the repertoires of orchestras throughout Poland, although Panufnik himself remained officially odious until the fall of the Soviet government. Throughout the 1980s, Panufnik continued to compose and conduct, including a concert on his 70th birthday with the London Symphony. Panufnik returned to his native country in 1990 to conduct the European premiere of his tenth and last symphony. In 1991, Queen Elizabeth II knighted Panufnik. Only months later, he died on October 27, 1991, at the age of 77.

Panufnik's tumultuous life is crowned by his achievements. Considered the most important Polish composer of the 20th century, his works laid the groundwork for essentially all the works of his contemporaries and current followers. Despite the general lack of interest in writing symphonies over the last century, Panufnik composed 12, including the two that were destroyed during the Warsaw Uprising. Many of his pieces drew from the traditional folk songs of his homeland, making his music uniquely Polish. In addition to his musical legacy, his brilliance as a conductor cannot be denied; one of the most respected conductors of his day, Panufnik worked with practically every major symphony throughout the world. Truscott, writing again for *Tempo* only a few years before Panufnik's death, called him "a world artist." A man with a remarkable life and notable talents, Panufnik seems assured to maintain his stature as one of Poland's foremost musical figures well into the future.

Books

Panufnik, Andrzej, *Composing Myself,* Metheun London, 1987.
Panufnik, Andrzej, *Impulse and Design in My Music,* Boosey & Hawkes, 1974.

Periodicals

Musical Opinion, September 1991.
The Musical Times, April 1991.
Tempo, December 1987.
Tempo, September 1984.
Tempo, Spring 1968.
Tempo, Spring 1971.
Tempo, Winter 1960.

Online

Boosey & Hawkes, "Andrzej Panufnik," http://www.boosey .com/pages/cr/composer/composer_main.asp?composerid =2706 (January 9, 2004).
Encyclopedia Brittanica Online, "Panufnik, Sir Andrzej," http://search.eb.com/eb/article?eu=1102 (January 9, 2004).
Grove Music Online, "Panufnik, Sir Andrzej" http://www .grovemusic.com/data/articles/music/2/208/20837 .xml?section=music.20837.1 (January 9, 2004).

Polish Music Center, "Andrzej Panufnik," http://www.use.edu/
    dept/polish_music/composer/panufnik.html (January 9,
    2004). □

C. Northcote Parkinson

When British historian and satirist C. Northcote Parkinson (1909–1993) published his observations from working as a British army staff officer during World War II in *Parkinson's Law, and Other Essays*, in 1957, he might not have realized that its basic premise "work expands to fill the time available for its completion" would become a standard mantra describing modern business practices.

Cyril Northcote Parkinson was born on July 30, 1909, at Barnard Castle, Durham, England. His father, William Edward Parkinson, was an artist, and his mother was Rosemary (Curnow) Parkinson. He attended school at St. Olave's and St. Peter's schools in York, England, from 1916 until 1929, when he entered Emmanuel College, Cambridge. Parkinson received his bachelor of arts degree from Cambridge and then went on to King's College, University of London, where he earned a Ph.D. in history in 1935. Parkinson returned to Emmanuel College as a fellow and taught from 1935 until 1938, then left for a position as senior history master at Blundell's, a private school for boys located in Tiverton, Devon. When Great Britain entered World War II in 1939, Parkinson enlisted in the Royal Navy College at Dartmouth, England. It was during his wartime service, working in training and administration for the British War Office and the Royal Air Force, that his inspiration for Parkinson's Law was born. During the war he attained the rank of major as a member of the Queen's Royal Regiment of the British Army.

Law Inspired by Military Bureaucracy

In an obituary in the *New York Times,* at Parkinson's death in March 1993, Richard W. Stevenson recalled a comment Parkinson once made to the London *Times* regarding his tenure in the British military: "I observed, somewhat to my surprise, that work which could be done by one man in peacetime, was being given to about six in wartime." He added that he thought that "this was mainly because there wasn't the same opportunity for other people to criticize" such a lack of economic efficiency, adding that, in the event of such criticism, someone would likely retort: "Don't you know there's a war on?"

Following the war, Parkinson became a lecturer of naval history at the University of Liverpool, where he stayed until 1950. At that point he left for Singapore to become Raffles Professor of History at the University of Malaya. Parkinson stayed in Singapore until 1958 during which time he produced his now-famous essay, which was first published in the British magazine *Economist* in 1955, submitted by its author as an anonymous essay. When he left Singa-

pore, Parkinson traveled to the University of Illinois at Urbana, where he served as Visiting George A. Miller Professor of History for two years. In 1960 he took on another visiting professorship, this one a year-long position at the University of California, Berkeley. While he was living in California, Parkinson had by now become noted for his creation of *Parkinson's Law,* and California Governor Ronald Reagan asked the British professor to lecture "on the precise reasons why the San Francisco-Oakland Bay Bridge's original repainting crew of 14 members grew to 72 once a labor-saving paint sprayer had been introduced," recalled Francis X. Clines in his interview with of Parkinson for the *New York Times*.

Writing to Fill the Time

In addition to his career as a professor of history, Parkinson was a prolific writer and published a number of books prior to releasing *Parkinson's Law, and Other Essays,* in 1959. His expertise in naval history translated into the bulk of that work, and he was highly regarded as one of the foremost naval historians in Great Britain and throughout the fading British Empire. Some of Parkinson's early writings included *Edward Pellew, Viscount Exmouth* (1934), *Trade in the Eastern Seas, 1793–1813* (1937), *The Trade Winds* (1948), *The Rise of the Port of Liverpool* (1952), *A Short History of Malaya* (1954), and *Heroes of Malaya* (1956), the last volume with his second wife, Elizabeth Parkinson.

The publication of *Parkinson's Law, and Other Essays,* by Houghton Mifflin in 1957 marked a somewhat new direction for the historian. That the book was initially displayed in bookstores in the "Law," "Humor," or "Politics" sections never ceased to delight its author, as well as baffle him. In addition to his *Economist* essay on bureaucratic inefficiency, Parkinson also includes writings on such topics as why driving on the left side of the road—as is the habit in Great Britain—is natural. In his interview with Clines, Parkinson offered a brief chronicle of what the publicity of *Parkinson's Law, and Other Essays* did for his career—in essence imbuing the academic with celebrity status for life. Clines noted that the then-78-year-old Parkinson, by the time of his *New York Times* interview living at Onchan, on the Isle of Man, was attempting to retire from the spotlight and quipped that his role as an "authority" on business practices following the publication of Parkinson's Law was a continuing source of humor to him.

Parkinson also recalled his mentor and hero, G. K. Chesterton, who had given him advice when he was a young man. At the time of his meeting with the British writer, Parkinson was slowly building his new law during lecture invitations, and as he traveled and observed people and their motivations. He found direction in Chesterton's example as a "literate Englishman and practicing essayist" who was active in English letters for much of his life. Parkinson recalled to Clines: "I met Chesterton when I was a young man and he was old, and it was from him that I derived the whole idea of conveying serious thoughts in the form of a joke. The humor made the whole thing more digestible and gave it great publicity."

Life after the "Law"

After formulating his primary "law," Parkinson continued to be inspired to formulate expansions on his central theme, among them *Mrs. Parkinson's Laws,* which addresses the issues of household management in a similar way to those Parkinson addressed in business. By the late 1980s he was developing a new law, which he revealed to Clines as follows: "The chief product of a highly automated society is a widespread and deepening sense of boredom." As Clines explained, "Parkinson has been studying a new generation busy with glyphs and dreams at their work computers, a tool which he declines to pick up." Parkinson cited as "proof" of his new law the example of of one resident of the Isle of Man, an office worker who had "measured an average work week of 56 hours, but found [himself] . . . happier for having to typically do three jobs: farming, carpentry, plus some tourism labors." Parkinson suggested that two days of manual labor in addition to the ever-increasing computer workload was the best preventive for boredom. He suggested that people are happiest when they are doing some kind of physical work.

Parkinson wrote over 60 books during his life, with the majority of those nonfiction. However, he also used his humor and his background in naval history to set the literary world on end again when he published his "Richard Delancey" seafaring mystery novels, telling the story of the quick-witted Delancey's adventures when he enters the disorderly world of the Royal Navy. Throughout the popular six-book series readers have the opportunity to travel with

Delancey to the Mediterranean, the East Indies, the Netherlands, and beyond and follow his remarkable adventures.

Fictional Seafarer Biographies Proved Popular

Two of Parkinson's novels, both fictional "biographies," followed somewhat the same path after publication as did *Parkinson's Law, and Other Essays.* Both *The Life and Times of Horatio Hornblower* and *Jeeves: A Gentleman's Personal Gentleman* were shelved in bookstores in the "Biography" or, in the case of the Hornblower "biography," the "History" section, when in fact they are works of fiction.

When Parkinson published *The Life and Times of Horatio Hornblower* in 1970, he based the book on the fictional 19th-century naval hero created by author C. S. Forester. Forester based his Hornblower character on actual reports from a variety of naval officers of the period and made him so realistic that many readers believed him to be a real person—in fact, the British National Maritime Museum often encountered visitors looking for the "Hornblower Papers." Similarly, *Jeeves: A Gentleman's Personal Gentleman* is based on the fictional butler created by popular British humorist P. G. Wodehouse and who is featured in a series of Wodehouse's novels.

Parkinson's other books included another work of nautical fiction, 1990's *Manhunt.* In the area of naval history, he also authored *Samuel Waters, Lieut. R.N.* (1949), *Britannia Rules* (1977), and *Gunpowder, Treason, and Plot* (1978). Others books by Parkinson, which ranged from cultural commentary to more overt satire, include *The Evolution of Political Thought* (1958), *The Law and the Profits* (1960), *In-Law and Outlaws* (1962), *Left Luggage* (1967), and *The Law of Delay* (1970).

Parkinson married three times during his life. His first wife was Ethelwyn Edith Graves, whom he married in 1943; that marriage was dissolved. Journalist and author Elizabeth Ann Fry became his second wife in September of 1952; and at the time of his death he was married to Iris Hilda Waters, his wife since 1985. Parkinson's children from his first marriage are Alison Barbara and Christopher Francis Graves; those from his second marriage are Charles Nigel Kennedy, Antonia Patricia Jane, and Jonathan Neville Trollope.

A *Contemporary Authors* contributor once noted of Parkinson: "Typical of his tongue-in-cheek satire on managerial bureaucracy is his estimation that the managerial ranks inevitably increase between 5.7 and 6.56 percent annually." "Other observations," the contributor added, "include his statement that the difference between a senior and a junior businessman is the time it takes for each to arrive at his office." Also described was Parkinson's insistence that he was really a satirist rather than a humorist. "A humorist," Parkinson explained, " . . . writes about wildly improbabl[e] things; but the whole point about me is that whatever I write is true. Nothing is dreamt up. It's how the world is actually organized."

Parkinson enjoyed a busy life of travel, writing, and teaching. He also found time for leisure activities, such as painting, theater, listening to radio, and watching television, and also enjoyed investigating castle ruins. He died on March 10, 1993, at a clinic near his home in Canterbury, England.

Books

Contemporary Authors, Gale, 1969.

Periodicals

Law Gazette, September 9, 2002.
New York Times, June 11, 1971; September 25, 1987; March 12, 1993. □

Dolly Parton

American singer and songwriter Dolly Parton (born 1946) was born into poverty but used her talent and determination to become one of the best known women in country and pop music. Her business insight has made subsequent expansion ventures into an empire.

D olly Rebecca Parton was born in Locust Ridge, Sevier County, Tennessee, on January 19, 1946. She was the fourth of twelve children born to Robert Lee and Avie Lee Parton. Her father was a sharecropper, farming someone else's land in return for a share of the crop, and the family was very poor. The family moved to a new house when Parton was five years old. The house was rundown and required a lot of work, but Robert Parton was proud to own it. Parton's grandfather was a preacher in a Pentecostal church and the family all played music and sang in the church.

Parton began writing music and playing the guitar when she was seven years old. She would sing everywhere she went, always trying to get her siblings to sit in front of her while she performed. She would even occasionally perform for the chickens, pigs, and ducks. "They didn't applaud much, but with the aid of a little corn, they could be counted on to hang around for a while," she wrote in her autobiography, *Dolly: My Life and Other Unfinished Business.* Sometimes she got to sing in front of real audiences when the Parton girls would sing at area churches.

Started Singing Professionally

Parton's uncle, Billy Earl Owens, recognized her musical talent early in her life. He taught her to play the guitar and songwriting. In 1956, he brought her to the attention of Cas Walker. Walker owned a grocery store chain and used a show on the radio to promote his stores. When she was ten years old, Parton sang on the show in front of a live audience in Knoxville, Tennessee. The crowd cheered. "At that very moment I fell in love with the public. This was what I had always wanted—no, needed. It was the attention I had longed for. I knew what they were giving me. Now I had confidence in what I had to give them," she wrote.

Parton desperately wanted to sing at the Grand Ole Opry, but it was difficult to get a spot on the program. Then, when she was twelve years old, Jimmy C. Newman gave her his spot, and she got her chance.

Henry Owens, Parton's uncle, was in the service in Lake Charles, Louisiana, and lived next door to Gold Band Records recording studio. He became friends with the owner and arranged for Parton to come down and make a recording. In 1960, she recorded two songs that she had written with her Uncle Bill, "Puppy Love" and "Girl Left Alone."

Parton became determined to find success. One day, when she was sixteen years old, she and her Uncle Bill waited all day at Tree Publishing until someone would see them. The waiting paid off, and when they got their appointment that evening, they signed a deal and Parton got a recording session with Mercury Records. She recorded "It May Not Kill Me (But It's Sure Gonna Hurt)" and "I Wasted My Tears (When I Cried Over You)." She was thrilled when she heard it play on WIVK, the Knoxville radio station.

Parton began to create her image. "I always wanted to be prettier," she said, according to *People.* "I got to fixin' myself up. I wanted my clothes tight, my makeup bright, my nails long, my lips red. I got into it."

Moved to Nashville

In 1964, Parton was the first person in her family to graduate from high school and the very next day she headed for Nashville, Tennessee. "Early next morning I boarded a

Greyhound bus with my dreams, my old guitar, the songs I had written, and the rest of my belongings in a set of matching luggage—three paper bags from the same grocery store. I had asked whatever relatives could afford to give me a graduation gift to please make it cash. I didn't want any additional baggage, and I knew I would need the money for a grub stake until I became a star. I genuinely thought that would happen before my little bit of money ran out," she wrote.

Parton rented a tiny apartment over a laundromat called the Wishy Washy. Soon after she moved in, she was outside, waiting for her clothes to dry, when a man drove by and stopped to chat. His name was Carl Thomas Dean. He stopped by several more times and finally asked her out on a date. On their first date, he took her to his parents' house for dinner. He told his mother, "Fix this girl a plate," wrote Parton. "She's the one I'm going to marry."

Parton got her first big break with Fred Foster who signed her and her Uncle Bill to a deal. Foster invested in Parton, buying her clothes and promoting her career by securing appearances on *American Bandstand* and at a jukebox convention in Chicago.

Parton and Carl decided to get married, but Foster warned against it, thinking she might have more record-buying appeal if she was single. Parton told Foster she would wait, but then she and Carl secretly got married in Ringgold, Georgia, on May 30, 1966, at the Ringgold Baptist Church. They kept it a secret for a year.

Made It Big

In 1967, Parton's hit "Dumb Blonde" made it into the top ten on the country charts. This caught the attention of Porter Wagoner, who had a country music show on television. He asked Parton to sing on his show for $60,000 a year. Parton knew that she had found success.

Parton's relationship with Wagoner was tumultuous. He taught her a lot about entertaining and was generous with information. "I could sing when I met Porter. After knowing him, I knew how to perform," wrote Parton in her book. However, she also resented Wagoner's need to control her career, pushing her uncles out of the way. He also pressured her to leave Monument Records and sign with RCA, which she eventually did. Despite the rocky relationship, Parton stayed with Wagoner through 1974, and Wagoner did a lot to launch her career. He continued to produce her records until 1977.

In 1970, Parton released "Joshua," which was a big hit. In 1971, both "Joshua" and "Old Time Preacher Man" won Broadcast Music, Inc. (BMI) Awards. "I have since won many awards and honors, but those still stand out as special," Parton wrote in her book.

In 1973, Parton released "Jolene," and in 1974, she released "I Will Always Love You" and "Love is like a Butterfly." Along with "Joshua," these hit number one on the country charts. Between 1968 and 1972, she released an amazing 21 albums and each of those years she was nominated by the Country Music Association as Female Vocalist of the Year. After this success, the time had come to leave Wagoner. She received the same nomination every year from 1974 to 1979. Two songs were written with Porter Wagoner in mind. "I Will Always Love You" was written in appreciation of all he had taught her. "Light of a Clear Blue Morning" was written when she finally made her decision to go out on her own.

Crossed Over To Pop

Parton put together the Traveling Family Band, made up mostly of family members, and headed out to face the world. She did find success, but she also found that although she made a lot of money, it was not enough to meet all her staff expenses. Therefore, she started her own publishing company, increased her public relations, started considering movie roles, and searched for songs with the potential to cross over from country into pop.

In 1975, Parton released *The Best of Dolly Parton*, which went RIAA Gold in August of 1978. In 1977, she released *Here You Come Again*, which included both country and pop music. This also went gold and then platinum in 1978.

In 1976, Parton started her own television show, "Dolly!" The show was not very successful, but a few good things did come out of it. First, one of the shows featured Emmy Lou Harris and Linda Ronstadt. "The three of us really got comfortable with just us, our voices and guitars. The result was some of the most unspoiled, pure country music I have ever been a part of. It was a forerunner of our *Trio* album," Parton wrote. Kenny Rogers also appeared on the show, and he and Parton later worked together on several other projects.

In 1980, Jane Fonda sent Parton a script for the movie *Nine to Five*. Initially, she was reluctant to take it since she did not have any training in acting. Her agent, Sandy Gallin, and Fonda both encouraged her to take it. She enjoyed it and received an Oscar nomination for writing the title song, as well as two Grammys for Best Country Song and Best Female Country Vocal Performance.

In conjunction with starring in *The Best Little Whorehouse in Texas* in 1982, Parton re-released "I Will Always Love You." She was the first performer to hit number one twice with the same song. In 1983, she starred in *Rhinestone* and received a Grammy nomination for the song "Tennessee Homesick Blues." She starred in *Steel Magnolias* in 1989.

In 1986, Parton founded Dollywood, a theme park near her hometown. Then, in 1988, just outside of Dollywood, she opened the Dixie Stampede & Dinner Show. The Dixie Stampede & Dinner Show was such a success that she proceeded to open additional locations in Branson, Missouri (1992); Myrtle Beach, South Carolina (1995); and Orlando, Florida (2003).

In 1996, Parton started a literacy program in her hometown called the Imagination Library. It provided one book each month to children from birth to their fifth birthday. The program quickly spread throughout the nation. In 2000, the Association of American Publishers (AAP) presented Parton with one of its first AAP Honors and Awards, which is presented to someone outside the industry for promoting books and authors.

In 1999, Parton became a member of the Country Music Hall of Fame. In 2003, Parton was honored by other country music stars with a tribute CD entitled "Just Because I'm a Woman: The Songs of Dolly Parton," sung by female country and pop stars including Melissa Etheridge, Shania Twain, and Norah Jones. In 2004, Parton was honored by the Library of Congress with The Living Legend award. Parton has no plans of retiring. As quoted in *America's Intelligence Wire* Parton said, "I'll be like Bob Hope, touring when I'm 100."

Books

American Decades CD-ROM, Gale Research, 1998.
Contemporary Musicians, Gale Group, 1999.
Emery, Ralph, *50 Years Down a Country Road,* HarperCollins Publishers, Inc., 2000.
Newsmakers 1999, Gale Group, 1999.
Parton, Dolly, *Dolly: My Life and Other Unfinished Business,* HarperCollins Publishers, Inc., 1994.

Periodicals

America's Intelligence Wire, April 5, 2004; April 14, 2004.
Business Wire, November 3, 2003.
People, November 10, 2003.
Publisher's Weekly, July 4, 1994; January 6, 2003.

Online

"Biography for Dolly Parton," *Internet Movie database,* http://www.imdb.com/name/nm0000573/bio (January 8, 2004).
"Country Music Awards," *Country Music Awards website,* http://www.cmaawards.com/2003/search_artists/view_artist_17.htm (January 8, 2004).
"Grammy Awards," *Grammy Awards website,* http://www.grammy.com/awards/search/index.aspx (January 8, 2004). □

Eric Partridge

New Zealand-born lexicographer Eric Partridge (1894–1979) was one of the twentieth century's leading experts on American, English, and Australian slang.

His most enduring works include *A Dictionary of Slang* (1937), *A Dictionary of the Underworld* (1950), and *Origins: A Short Etymological Dictionary of Modern English* (1958). At the time of Partridge's death, *Meanjin* contributor Ralph Elliott wrote: "He made a contribution to the historical study as well as to the practical use of the English language so substantial and so individual in its scholarship, breadth, imagination and wit that his name is now a household word in every country where English is spoken and studied."

Early Life and Education

The son of John Thomas and Ethel Norris Partridge, Eric Partridge was born in February 1894 on a farm near Gisborne, North Island, New Zealand. His family later moved to Brisbane, Australia, and he attended local schools there, winning a scholarship to study classics at the University of Queensland.

However, his studies were interrupted with the outbreak of the First World War in August 1914, and Partridge joined the Australian Imperial Forces. An infantryman from 1915 to 1919, he fought in the battle of Gallipoli and later saw action along the Western Front. Partridge's memoirs of the war years were later published as *Frank Honeywood, Private: A Personal Record of the 1914–1918 War* (1929) and included together with those of R. H. Mottram and John Easton in *Three Men's War: The Personal Records of Active Service* (1930).

Partridge returned to the University of Queensland in 1919 and completed his degree in 1921. He pursued graduate work in England as a traveling fellow, earning both a master's degree in English poetry from Queensland and a degree in comparative literature from Oxford University in 1923. Remaining in England, Partridge worked as a grammar school teacher and lecturer in English at universities in Manchester and London from 1925 to 1927 and during this time married Agnes Dora Vye-Parmenter.

His academic work was issued by the Parisian publisher Champion in 1924 as *Eighteenth Century English Romantic Poetry; A Critical Medley: Essays, Studies, and Notes in English, French and Comparative Literature* and *The French Romantics' Knowledge of English Literature (1820–1848).* During this time he also edited a volume of poems by Cuthbert Shaw and Thomas Russell and produced the biographical and critical study *Robert Eyres Landor* in 1927.

At this point, however, Partridge abandoned his academic career in favor of publishing and founded the Scholartis Press in London in 1927, a commercial venture that specialized in high-quality editions of eighteenth and nineteenth century works and issued new works on literature and language. Among the reissues was Francis Grose's 1785 compilation *A Classical Dictionary of the Vulgar Tongue,* to which Partridge added a preface and biographical sketch. Partridge contributed *Pirates, Highwaymen and Adventurers* and *The Three Wartons,* a selection of poetry by Thomas Warton, the elder, and his sons Joseph and Thomas Warton. He also published fiction, including the autobiographical novel *Glimpses* (1928), under the pseudonym Corrie Denison.

Classics on Words and Slang

In 1931, Scholartis failed because of the global Depression, and from that time on Partridge earned his living as a freelance writer and compiler of lexicographical works. During the 1930s he began his association with the publishing firm Routledge with such volumes as *Slang Today and Yesterday* (1933), which included a historical sketch and covered English, American, and Australian slang. In it Partridge identified some of the reasons people have developed slang, including the desire to be different, to identify with a certain school or social group, and to be secretive.

The first edition of the work for which he became best known, *A Dictionary of Slang and Unconventional English,* was published in 1937. According to its subtitle, it included "the language of the underworld, colloquialisms and catch-phrases, solecisms and catachreses, nicknames, vulgarisms and such Americanisms as have been naturalized." In the introduction he wrote that the *Dictionary* "should be of interest to word-lovers, but it should also be useful to the general as well as the cultured reader, to the scholar and the linguist." By 2004, more than two decades after Partridge's death, his dictionary was still in print, a recognized classic of its kind, and a two-volume ninth edition was being prepared for release. In the *Guardian* John Mullan called the original work an "extraordinary one-man dictionary" and noted that though much of its content now seems anti-quated modern reference books nevertheless "owe much to [Partridge's] largely solitary endeavours." Writing in the *Times* in 1984, Philip Howard called the volume "a rich treasury of extraordinary and shady language recorded no-where else."

Other works by Partridge in the 1930s include *Words, Words, Words!* (1933), *Name This Child: A Dictionary of English (and American) Christian Names* (1936), the anthol-ogy *A Covey of Partridge* (1937), and *The World of Words: An Introduction to Language in General and to English and American in Particular* (1939).

Enduring Works on Usage

Partridge returned to military service during the Second World War, serving in the British Army Education Corps from 1940 to 1941 and in the Royal Air Force from 1942 to 1945. His wartime experiences provided the inspiration for works on military slang, including his collaboration with John Brophy published as *Songs and Slang of the British Soldier: 1914–1918* (1930) and *A Dictionary of RAF Slang* (1945). Quoted on the Australian National Dictionary Cen-tre website, Partridge's introduction to the 1945 work notes, "In the Services, the men live—or should live—a more exciting life; they deal with equipment and various weap-ons; do things they've never done before—and pretend they never want to again; many of them visit strange countries; many become engaged in a service that is actually instead of nominally active; all of them mingle in such a companion-ship as they have never had before they enlisted and will never again have, once they quit the Service. Such condi-tions inevitably lead to a rejuvenation of language—to vividness—to picturesqueness—to vigour; language be-comes youthful, energetic, adventurous. And slang is the easiest way to achieve those ends."

In peacetime Partridge became a fixture at the British Museum Reading Room, where he worked researching his books, and in 1946 he published the essay collection *Journey to the Edge of Morning: Thoughts upon Books, Love, Life.*

Partridge produced a number of his best-known works during and after the war, including *A Dictionary of Cliches* (1940), *Usage and Abusage: A Guide to Good English*

(1942), and *Shakespeare's Bawdy: A Literary and Psycho-logical Essay and Comprehensive Glossary* (1947). The Shakespeare book provided a key for understanding the ribald humor of numerous images, puns, allusions, and double entendres that would have been apparent to seven-teenth-century theatergoers but which modern audiences fail to comprehend.

Partridge's *Dictionary of Cliches* comprises a list of stock phrases that careful writers should avoid. In the guide-book *Usage and Abusage* he outlined proper grammar and word choice and did so with humor, discussing such sub-jects as ambiguity, jargon and puns. Reviewing Janet Whitcut's 1995 update of *Usage and Abusage,* Tom Hoyt in the journal *Technical Communication* called the volume an "ideal" handbook and concluded that "In this age of Web pages, usability testing, and distance learning, we still need to remember that good, solid writing is at the core of all excellent technical communication. Partridge's book helps writers and editors focus on this important fact."

Love of Common Language

In 1950, Partridge produced *A Dictionary of the Underworld, British and American, Being the Vocabulary of Crooks, Criminals, Racketeers, Beggars and Tramps, Con-victs, the Commercial Under-World, the Drug Traffic, the White Slave Traffic, and Spivs,* one of the first major works to apply scholarly methods to the study of street language. Terms covered include short-hand names for jails, prisons and run-ins with the law, the jargon of criminal activities, including prostitution and narcotics dealing, and the color-ful language of itinerants, such as "alberts," the Australian tramps' name for rags they used to wrap their feet when they lacked the money for socks, or "alley apple," an early twentieth-century American term for a brick or piece of pavement that could be thrown during a street fight.

In addition to *Usage and Abusage,* Partridge produced other guide books, including *You Have a Point There: A Guide to Punctuation and Its Allies* (1953) and *Notes on Punctuation* (1955). He examined the origin, development and nature of the so-called "shaggy dog" story in a 1953 study, and his etymological dictionary *Origins* was pub-lished in 1958. It demonstrated his vast knowledge of word derivations and the development of the English language and became a favorite of logophiles.

His own love of language led to such celebrations as *A Charm of Words* (1960), *Adventuring among Words* (1961), and *The Gentle Art of Lexicography as Pursued and Experi-enced by an Addict* (1963). The slight work *Comic Alpha-bets,* first published in 1961, included such examples of Cockney punning as "A for 'orses," "Q for a bus," and "Y for husband." Commenting on this work in *Eric Partridge: In His Own Words,* Anthony Burgess wrote: "What fascinated Eric . . . was the anonymous human brilliance of this fan-tasy, and it was the creativity of humble users of language which, of course, inspired him to that lifelong devotion to slang and catch phrases which produced the great dictio-naries." Among Partridge's later works, the *Dictionary of Catch Phrases British and American, from the 16th Century to the Present* traces the history of "back to square one," "the bee's knees," "believe you me," "bright-eyed and bushy-tailed" and numerous other familiar terms.

A gentleman scholar, Partridge was well known in England as a cricket and tennis enthusiast, and he occasionally wrote journalistic pieces offering his commentary on competitive events in these sports. He once told *Contemporary Authors,* "In all work, whether lexicographical or expository (or even slight and light-hearted), my aim has been to conceal erudition and to be readable to students and general public alike, and to humanize the subjects treated by not forgetting that one's readers are—most of them—human beings."

Partridge died June 1, 1979, in Devonshire, England. The posthumously published volume *Eric Partridge: In His Own Words* was favorably reviewed in the London *Times* by Philip Howard, who noted that Partridge "was seldom dull, never obscure, and always good-humoured; and he always demonstrated the connexion between clear thinking and clear writing." In an obituary tribute published in that volume Randolph Quirk commented that "In almost any aspect of humane letters—literature, languages, book-craft, and of course word-study—[Partridge] . . . not only had a staggeringly wide knowledge: he had a limitless capacity for sharing it." Howard concluded: "His best work will last as long as there are those around in love with English."

Books

Contemporary Authors, New Revision Series, Volume 3, Gale, 1981.
Crystal, David, ed., *Eric Partridge: In His Own Words,* Macmillan, 1980.

Periodicals

Critical Quarterly, Autumn 1998.
Encounter, February 1985.
Meanjin, 4, 1979.
Technical Communication, August 1996.
Times (London), December 4, 1980.

Online

Australian National Dictionary Centre, http://www.anu.edu.au/ANDC/WWI/Intro.html (January 8, 2004).
"Guide to Print Collections: Eric Partridge Collection," *University of Exeter,* http://www.ex.ac.uk/library/special/books/collections/partridge.html (January 8, 2004). □

Annie Smith Peck

Annie Smith Peck (1850–1935) was an American mountain climber who held the record for reaching the highest altitude in the Americas after her arduous ascent of Peru's Mt. Huascarán in 1908 at age 58. A suffragist, Peck was determined to prove that women were on equal footing with men in all realms. "When she first started mountaineering a man advised her to 'go home where you belong,' " her New

York Times obituary reported. "Peck was as stubborn as she was intrepid."

Competitive Urge

Peck came from an affluent, socially prominent family in Providence, Rhode Island, where she was born on October 19, 1850. Her father, George Bachelor Peck, was an attorney, and Peck was the youngest child and only surviving daughter. Her older brothers disdained her attempts to play alongside them, and that instilled in her a lifelong competitive urge to prove her stamina was equal to that of a man's.

Peck was schooled at Dr. Stockbridge's School for Young Ladies, Providence High School, and the Rhode Island State Normal School. She went on to earn both bachelor's and master's degrees in Greek at the University of Michigan and returned to Providence to teach school. She also taught for a time at Saginaw High School in Michigan, Bartholomew's School for Girls in Cincinnati, and a Montclair, New Jersey high school. In 1881, the year she turned 31, she took a job as Purdue University's Latin instructor.

In 1884, Peck went abroad to study language and music in Hanover, Germany. She applied to and was accepted at the American School of Classical Studies in Athens the following year, making her the first woman ever enrolled there. En route from Germany to Greece, however, Peck came across a sight that changed the direction of her academic career: the majestic Matterhorn in the Alps, on the border of Switzerland and Italy. Awed by it, she vowed to climb it some day, though it had only been scaled for the first time only twenty years before. And Matterhorn expeditions usually ran to about $50 a day, making them affordable only for the independently wealthy.

Earned Living on Lecture Circuit

Back in the United States after her stint in Athens, in 1866 Peck took a post at Smith College, a prestigious school for women in Northampton, Massachusetts. There she taught Latin, classical art, and archaeology and began climbing peaks during her spare time. In 1895 she became only the third woman to scale the Matterhorn.

Eventually Peck decided that lecturing on Greek archeology would be a better way to finance her hobby than teaching, but she failed to earn enough on the lecture circuit and switched to speaking about her mountain-climbing experiences, which proved far more novel a lure for audiences. The sport dated back only to the 1780s and had gained widespread appeal in the 1850s, though women were a relative rarity and subject to much derision for their attempts.

Peck liked to gather scientific data on her climbs and learned how to use a hypsometer, which could calculate an altitude by determining the boiling point of water. Most of her ascents were done without oxygen, and she skirted the outcry against women wearing pants—which was considered a daring flaunting of convention in her day—by wearing practical tunics and knickerbockers.

A committed campaigner for a constitutional amendment that would grant American women the right to vote, Peck hoped to prove that men and women could achieve equality in all fields, and she decided to set a women's record for altitude. She settled on Mt. Orizaba (also called Citlaltépetl) in eastern Mexico's Cordillera de Anáhuas, after obtaining a sponsor, the *New York World* newspaper. Her 1897 ascent to its 18,700-foot-high summit set the women's altitude record, and she also conquered Popocatepetl, another inactive volcano in Mexico, that same year.

Climbs in South America

After scaling the Fuenffingerspitze, in the Italian Dolomites, in 1900, Peck decided to try to climb a mountain that had not yet been scaled by any climber. She settled on a legendary peak in Bolivia, Mt. Illampú, which at the time was believed to be South America's highest peak. She arrived in La Paz in July 1903 with an American geology professor she had invited to come along, and she hired some local guides. The Bolivians proved untrustworthy, however, and the professor disliked the rigors of the climb and succumbed to altitude sickness, which forced the party to turn back at 15,350 feet. She recounted the experience in a lengthy report that appeared in the *New York Times* the following year, in which she noted that in La Paz "a few eatables were added to our store of soups, tea, chocolate, grape nuts [etc.], brought from New York; especially three

bags of coca leaves for our own use as well as the Indians, and valuable indeed they proved, I might say indispensable for us all."

Back in New York, Peck drummed up new sponsorship for a second Illampú attempt, and departed on June 21, 1904. She carried with her a precious, practical suit made from animal skins that had been given to her by the American Museum of Natural History. The Arctic explorer, Robert Peary, had brought it back from one of his expeditions and donated it to the museum. This time Peck also brought an experienced Alpine climber, an Austrian man, but both he and her guides tired easily and forced her to turn back once more, this time after reaching 18,000 feet.

Then Peck learned about Mt. Huascarán, another peak in the Andes. Located outside of Lima, Peru, Huascarán was rumored to be taller than Illampú. This time, Peck took along on her climb an American miner she met at the town near the base, but the two disagreed on the best route, and she went her own way with her own guides, reaching a 19,000-foot ledge that overlooked the glacier that gave Huascarán its distinctive double peaks. On her way down, the party narrowly avoided an avalanche.

Undaunted, Peck returned to New York and planned a second attempt, this time with a $600 advance a magazine had given her to write a story about her trip. That climb and two 1906 attempts were also unsuccessful, but since the editors liked her stories, they were willing to finance her repeated efforts to scale Huascarán. Finally, in 1908 she took along two Swiss men who were able Alpine guides, Rudolf and Gabriel. Despite the combined experience of all three, it was still a perilous climb that nearly cost them their lives.

The Summit At Last

On the way up Huascarán, the wonderful Peary snowsuit was lost because of a guide's carelessness. Finally, they made camp near the peak and started their ascent at eight o'clock on the morning of September 2, 1908. Because of the loss of the Peary suit, Peck later wrote in an account reprinted in David Mazel's *Mountaineering Women*, "I was wearing every stitch of clothing that I had brought:—three suits of light weight woollen underwear, two pairs of tights, canvas knickerbockers, two flannel waists, a little cardigan jacket, two sweaters, and four pairs of woollen stockings; but as most of the clothing was porous it was inadequate to keep out the wind." To protect against the cold, she also wore a woolen hat and mask bought in La Paz that had a painted mustache, as well as a pair of vicuña mittens.

It took Peck and her two Swiss guides seven hours to reach the final peak, tied to one another's waists and hacking out footholds in the ice. But Rudolf lost one of her vicuña mittens and, near the top, "I suddenly realised that my left hand was insensible and freezing," Peck wrote, as recounted in Mazel's book. "Twitching off my mittens, I found that the hand was nearly black. Rubbing it vigorously with snow, I soon had it aching badly, which signified its restoration."

Gabriel suggested they stop to take measurements with the hypsometer, fearing that the wind might be too strong at the summit, and Rudolf untied himself. Peck and Gabriel tried to light the match for the hypsometer but could not find Rudolf, who was needed to shield the wind with a heavy Andean poncho they had brought along. They gave up, and "Rudolf now appeared and informed me that *he* had been on to the summit, instead of remaining to assist with the hypsometer," Peck wrote. "I *was* enraged. I had told them, long before, that, as it was my expedition, I should like, as customary, to be the first one to place my foot at the top. . . . The disappointment may have been trivial. Of course it made no real difference to the honour to which I was entitled, but of a certain personal satisfaction, long looked forward to, I had been robbed."

"A Horrible Nightmare"

Peck did reach Huascarán's north peak, which at 21,812 feet gave Peck her long-awaited record for the highest altitude reached by any climber in the Americas. At three o'clock, they began their arduous descent to camp, but night soon fell and much of the trip down had to be done in the dark. Exhausted, they were buffeted by high winds, and because the Peary suit was gone, Peck had to wear the poncho to stay warm. "The cold and fatigue, the darkness and shadow, the poncho blowing before me, the absence of climbing irons, the small steps, the steep glassy slopes, presented an extraordinary combination of difficulties," she wrote. "I tried to comfort myself with the reflection that accidents do not run in our family. . .but also I was aware that people do not generally die but once."

The grades they descended they estimated to be about 40 to 60 degree in steepness, and the poncho caused her to lose her footing on several occasions. Only the rope and her guides' sheer force in gripping it kept them from tumbling to their deaths. "My recollection of the descent is as of a horrible nightmare, though such I never experienced," she wrote later, recounting that "after these slips my terror increased. Several times I declared that we should never get down alive. I begged Gabriel to stop for the night and make a cave in the snow, but, saying this was impossible, he continued without a pause." Rudolf then lost his own mittens, and by the time they arrived at camp at 10:30 p.m. his hand was frostbitten. He later underwent surgery in Lima to have a finger, part of his hand, and half of his foot amputated.

The Peruvian government honored Peck with a medal, and the north peak of Huascarán was named Cumbre Aña Peck in recognition of her achievement. Her recollections were taken from a memoir published in 1911, *A Search for the Apex of America*. She next scaled Mt. Coropuna in Peru, and on its 21,079-foot summit placed a "Votes for Women" banner. Later, she traveled extensively through South America and wrote a guidebook and also traveled the continent by airplane using all available commercial routes at the time, an experience she chronicled in *Flying Over South America: Twenty Thousand Miles by Air.*

At the age of 84, indefatigable, Peck planned a trip around the world. She departed in January 1935, but while climbing the Acropolis in Athens became exhausted and was forced to return to New York, where she died at her home in the Hotel Monterey on July 18, 1935 of bronchial pneumonia.

Books

Explorers and Discoverers of the World, Gale, 1993.
Great Women in Sports, Visible Ink Press, 1996.
Mountaineering Women, edited by David Mazel, Texas A&M University Press, 1994.
Notable Women Scientists, Gale, 2000.

Periodicals

New York Times, October 9, 1904; July 19, 1935. □

Aristides Maria Pereira

Aristides Maria Pereira (born 1923) fought for the freedom of his people and later became president of Cape Verde.

Searching for Independence

Aristides Maria Pereira was born on November 17, 1923, on Boa Vista, one of Cape Verde's islands. He was the son of Porfirio Pereira Tavares and Maria das Neves Crus Silva. He was educated at the Lycee de Cap-Vert, and he began a career as a radio-telegraphist when he finished his schooling. Pereira rose to the position of head of Telecommunications Services in Bissau, formerly Portuguese Guinea and now known as Guinea-Bissau, across from Cape Verde on the African west coast.

Pereira became an early proponent of independence from Portugal, especially after meeting Amilcar Cabral, a man native to the islands but living in Guinea, as Cabral began a series of radio talks during the summer of 1949. Since 1466, when the first settlers arrived, the Portuguese had ruled Cape Verde, both intermarrying with and brutalizing the native population. Members of more than two dozen African tribes initially were brought to the islands to provide slave labor for the Portuguese.

Famines in the islands earlier in the 1940s "provoked a new trend of thought. There had to be change, there had to be a different future," recalled Pereira. "Many emigrated: not just for jobs but in the search for a way ahead. Some of us went to Portugal, others to Angola, several to Bissau. Yet all of us went with the same notion, the idea of finding a different way ahead."

A Long Struggle

In 1956 Pereira joined Cabral and others to found the *Partido Africano da Independencia da Guine's e Cabo Verde,* a political movement whose acronym was PAIGC. Cabral was a socialist, and both the Soviet Union and Cuba provided support for PAIGC initially. Pereira held various

positions with the PAIGC. He was a member of the Political Bureau's Central Committee, from 1956 until 1970; assistant secretary-general, 1964–1973; and secretary-general, 1973–1981.

Cabral was assassinated in January 1973 by the Portuguese secret police. But Pereira and his comrades did not give up. He became president of newly independent Cape Verde from 1975 until 1991.

Many Obstacles

Pereira's task as the new republic's first president was a daunting one. Physically, the new country suffered from a harsh climate. Disastrous droughts and consequent famines have plagued the islands for centuries. A series of particularly devastating droughts hit the islands throughout the 19th and 20th centuries, each one killing between 10 and 40 percent of the population. Many islanders fled, some of them to the United States.

Agriculture is a challenge due to low annual rainfall and extensive soil erosion. Ninety percent of the country's food must be imported. There are underground reserves of water, but extracting them is too costly.

When the country gained independence it was an extremely poor and largely illiterate culture. Health services and doctors were absent. Roads, if they existed at all, were primitive at best. According to a 2000 article published on *Europa,* the portal site for the European union, "At independence in 1975, there was a certain trepidation as to whether the country could survive. . . . Not just to survive, but to forge an identity as a country with a renowned cultural richness, a stable post-independence period, and good relations with its diverse international partners and neighbours.''

Remarkable Progress

Many nations joined in the effort to support Cape Verde, including the Soviet Union, China, and the United States. The United Nations and its World Food Program helped feed the people. International assistance created a viable infrastructure and a national health service. A program of reforestation was implemented to recover the trees lost to so many droughts and water conservation efforts were put into place.

During his terms as president, Pereira was often criticized for crushing opposing political views. He was known, however, for working to create policies that would help the poor. His alliances with China and Libya were controversial.

The 1991 constitution allowed for the presence of opposing political parties. Pereira was defeated. It was the first time in sub-Saharan Africa that a single-party government was voted out of office.

In July 2002, Cape Verde, along with the Seychelles and Mauritius, both off the eastern coast of Africa in the Indian Ocean, were named the best places to live in Africa by the Human Development Report. Though Cape Verde was listed at number 100 worldwide, the progress in the country was remarkable. Life expectancy at birth had climbed to nearly 70. The literacy rate remained low, as did the per capital income, but improvements were being made. Cape Verde's political stability was considered an important factor in a promising future.

Books

Columbia Encyclopedia, Edition 6, Columbia University Press, 2000.
International Who's Who 2003, 66th edition, Europa Publications, 2002.

Periodicals

Africa News Service, October 28, 2002.
Current Anthropology, August–October 2003.
East African, July 16, 2001.
Footsteps, September 2001.
Monthly Review, December 1998.
Research in African Literatures, Winter 1993.
Review of African Political Economy, Vol. 8, No. 21, Summer 1981.
UNESCO Courier, November 1992.

Online

"Alert Net-Cape Verde,'' *Reuters Foundation AlertNet website,* http://www.alertnet.org (January 5, 2004).
Almeida, Raymond A., "Chronological References: Cabo Verde/ Cape Verdean American,'' *University of Massachusetts Special Programs website,* http://www.umassd.edu (December 9, 2003).
"Aristides Pereira,'' *Wikipedia website,* http://en2.wikipedia.org (December 9, 2003).

"Cape Verde," *Netfirms website,* http://exim.netfirms.com/cv (December 9, 2003).

"Cape Verde," *New Internationalist website,* http://www.newint .org (January 5, 2004).

"Cape Verde," *Tiscali Reference website (Hutchinson Encyclopedia),* http://www.tiscali.co.uk (December 9, 2003).

"Cape Verde," *World Statesmen website,* http://www .worldstatesmen.org (December 9, 2003).

"Cape Verde celebrates its 25th anniversary," *Afrol News website,* http://www.afrol.com (January 5, 2004).

"Cape Verde the struggle for Independence," *University of Massachusetts Special Programs website,* http://www.umassd .edu (December 9, 2003).

"Cape Verdean President to step down in 2005," *Afrol News website,* http://www.afrol.com (January 5, 2004).

"Civil War in Guinnea Bissau," *Conflict Trends, Accord website (Zaire),* http://www.accord.org (December 9, 2003).

"Country Information on Cape Verde," *SOS-Kinderdorf International (SOS Childrens' Villages) website,* http://www.sos-childrensvillages.org (January 4, 2004).

"Country profile: Cape Verde," *BBC News website,* http://newsvote.bbc.co.uk (December 9, 2003).

"Democracy and Governance in Africa, Conclusions and papers presented at a conference of the Africa Leadership Forum, Ota, Nigeria, 29 November-1 December 1991," *Africa Leadership Forum website,* http://www.africaleadership.org (January 5, 2004).

"The History of Cape Verde (Green Cabo)," *Africa Infomarket organization website,* http://africainfomarket.org (January 5, 2004).

"Letter to President Aristides Pereira of Cape Verde on United States Acceptance of the Gift of the Schooner Ernestina," *University of Texas website,* http://www.reagan.utexas.edu (December 9, 2003).

"Ministry of the Finances and Planning," *Cape Verde government website,* http://www.gov.cv (January 5, 2004).

"No fist is big enough to hide the sky: the liberation of Guine and Cape Verde: aspects of an African revolution," *ISBN database website,* http://isbndb.com (December 9, 2003).

"Seychelles, Mauritius and Cape Verde 'best in Africa,' " *Afrol News website,* http://www.afrol.com (January 5, 2004).

"Taking Stock," *Europa (European Union website),* http://europa .eu.int (January 5, 2004). □

Philip

His Royal Highness Prince Philip, duke of Edinburgh (born 1921) has spent over fifty years by the side of his wife, Queen Elizabeth II of Great Britain, and has become known for his outspoken opinions. Distinguishing himself in service to the Royal Navy during World War II, Philip pursued a military career until his duties as consort to his wife required his full attention, and played an active role in promoting the interests of both the royal family and a host of other causes benefitting the British people.

Born Philip Schleswig-Holstein-Sonderburg-Glucksberg, prince of Greece on the island of Corfu, on June 10, 1921, Philip was the youngest child and

only son of Prince Andrew of Greece and wife Alice. Although of Danish and German backgrounds, Philip's parents were members of the Greek royal family. They already had four older daughters when their son arrived almost 20 years into their marriage.

Early Life of Turmoil

In the 1920s Greece was in upheaval. The form of government had changed several times in a short period, and civil war loomed as a threat. Not surprisingly, the royal family soon came under fire and in 1923 Philip's father was put on trial for treason and facing a sentence of death. Desperate to save her husband, Princess Alice appealed to British King George V for help. George V, still haunted by the murder of another relative, Nicholas II of Russia, at the hands of the Bolsheviks in 1917, sent a British cruiser to Greece to rescue the almost destitute family, which included 18-month-old Philip.

Now living in France, Philip's world dramatically changed. By 1930, with all his daughters married off, Prince Andrew abandoned his wife and ten-year-old son and went to live with his mistress. Subsequently, Philip's mother suffered an emotional breakdown. Fortunately, Philip's maternal grandmother stepped in and brought the boy to England. When she died, her oldest son, George, the marquess of Milford Haven, took responsibility for Philip, and upon George's death in 1938, his younger brother, Lord Louis Mountbatten came forward to care for his young nephew.

Philip attended school in France and England, and at the age of 12 attended school in southern Germany. Here Philip fell under the academic guidance of educational pioneer Kurt Hahn, who greatly influenced the boy. A natural athlete, Philip also developed leadership skills at school, where he became a popular student. Unfortunately, his time in Germany was cut short by the rise to power of Adolph Hitler and the Nazi Party in 1933. Within a year Hahn wisely decided to relocate his school to Scotland. He called the new school Gordonstoun, and Philip remembered his time there with such fondness that he educated his sons at Gordunstoun as well.

Began Naval Career

Graduating from Gordonstoun in 1939, 18-year-old Philip joined the Royal Navy just as Great Britain entered World War II. His first naval appointment was as a midshipman to the HMS *Ramillies,* which escorted Allied forces from Australia to Egypt. His leadership skills in evidence, Philip moved up the ranks of the Royal Navy, and in 1941 was mentioned in dispatches for his service in Greece during the battle of Matapan. By the summer of 1942 Philip achieved the rank of lieutenant, quickly followed by promotion to first lieutenant.

Between 1944 and 1946 Philip served aboard the destroyer HMS *Whelp,* stationed in the Pacific. Part of the 27th Destroyer Flotilla, the *Whelp* was anchored in Tokyo bay when the Japanese surrendered following the destruction of Hiroshima and Nagasaki.

Courting the Future Queen

In January of 1946 Philip returned to England, like many of his fellows a changed man. He was now also an experienced naval officer and hero. Before enlisting, Philip had met his distant cousin, Princess Elizabeth of England, then age thirteen; according to some sources, it was Philip's uncle, Lord Mountbatten, who orchestrated the match. He corresponded with Elizabeth throughout the war and a romance developed. Upon his return home Elizabeth invited Philip to visit her family at Balmoral Castle; the couple also got secretly engaged, although both knew there would be family objections.

The Royal Marriages Act of 1772 required that Elizabeth get permission from the reigning monarch in order to marry. Her father, George VI, resisted, believing his 18-year-old daughter was too young to marry. Another obstacle to the match was Philip's Greek citizenship. Lord Mountbatten quickly intervened, and in March of 1947 Philip became naturalized British citizen Philip Mountbatten. At this point the king reluctantly gave his consent, although public announcement of the impending marriage was postponed. On July 8, 1947, a palace spokesman announced the engagement of Princess Elizabeth and Lieutenant Philip Mountbatten, and the pair were married on November 20, at Westminster Abbey. Just prior to his marriage Philip was granted three titles: duke of Edinburgh, earl of Merioneth, and baron Greenwich. He was also appointed a knight of the Garter.

Continuing his career in the Royal Navy, Philip was soon balancing these duties with fatherhood; the couple welcomed their first child, Charles, in November of 1948. For a time, Philip was stationed in Malta and Elizabeth visited like other military wives. In 1950 he was promoted to lieutenant commander and given command of the anti-aircraft frigate HMS *Magpie,* but he resigned his commission in the summer of 1951. The following February George VI died, leaving 26-year-old Elizabeth queen.

A Life of Duty and Diverse Interests

When Elizabeth ascended to the throne in 1952, Philip assumed the role of consort and the duties that went with it. His primary responsibility was the children, which now included Princess Anne (born 1950), Prince Andrew (born 1960), and Prince Edward (born 1964). Their upbringing and education became his primary focus. For his part, he was both a strict disciplinary and a loving father, and he insisted that the children be educated away from the palace.

In 1956 Philip planned a world tour, beginning his journey by attending the opening of the 1956 Olympics in Melbourne, Australia. He also pursued a wide range of personal interests that benefitted both Great Britain and the monarchy over the years. He was interested in science and industry, research and development, and technology. He has also served as patron or president of over 800 organizations, and was the first president of the World Wildlife Fund. He also founded the Duke of Edinburgh's Award Scheme and International Award, which was designed to encourage young people to tackle physical and skills-based challenges and become involved in their community

Philip also served as a chancellor for many universities, learned to fly all kinds of aircraft, and was an avid polo player in his younger days. He also was one of several to push for a rejuvenation of the British monarchy. In *The Lives of the Kings and Queens of England,* an essayist explained that Philip "set himself to modernizing the monarchy, and 'image' is in this instance the appropriate word. Radio, the cinema, and above all, television, has made the presentation of Royalty a exercise in public relations." In 1961 Philip became the first member of the British Royal Family to be interviewed on television. Philip also gained a reputation for speaking his mind, a characteristic that earned him his share of detractors in a country where gossip about the royal family abounds.

Over Fifty Years as Prince Consort

In November of 2003 Philip and Queen Elizabeth II welcomed their seventh grandchild, Lady Louise Mountbatten-Windsor, when their youngest son, Prince Edward, and his wife, had a daughter. The inclusion of the name Mountbatten is a testament to Philip's stature within the royal house of Windsor, as well as a reflection of the respect he has been accorded by his children.

Books

Fraser, Antonia, editor, *The Lives of the Kings and Queens of England,* University of California Press, 1995.

Hall, Unity, *Philip: The Man behind the Monarchy*, St. Martin's Press, 1987.

Heald, Tim, *Philip: A Portrait of the Duke of Edinburgh*, William Morrow, 1991.

Hilton, James, *H.R.H.: The Story of Philip, Duke of Edinburgh*, Little, Brown, 1955.

Periodicals

Biography, February, 2002.

Online

Britain Express Web site, http://www.britainexpress.com/royals/philip.htm (December 4, 2003).

British Monarchy Official Web site, http://www.royal.gov.uk/ (December 4, 2003).

''Fifty Facts about the Duke of Edinburgh,'' *Tiscali: Golden Jubilee Web site*, http://www.tiscali.co.uk/events/2002/goldenjubilee/facts/facts_duke1.html (December 4, 2003).

''Prince Philip, Duke of Edinburgh,'' *HELLO! Magazine Web site*, http://www.hellomagazine.com/profiles/princephilip/ (December 4, 2003).

''Prince Philip, Duke of Edinburgh (1921-),'' *Regiments Web site*, http://www.regiments.org/milhist/biography/royals/1921phil.htm (December 4, 2003). □

Pin-chin Chiang

Regarded as China's most popular female writer of the modern era, Pin-chin Chiang (1904–1986) used the pseudonym Ding Ling in many of her publications. Her best-known writings are the novels *Miss Sophie's Diary* and *The Sun Shines over the Sangaan River* (1951). Persecuted by the Chinese Communist Party for many years and extremely active in political causes, she remained devoted to the Party and produced more than 300 literary works over her lifetime.

Progressive Mother Instilled Feminist Ideals

Pin-chin Chiang was born on September 4, 1904, in Linli County, Hunan Province, China. Her family was wealthy and socially prominent but fell on hard times when her father, Chiang Yufeng (a highly regarded Confucian scholar), died when she was four years old. Pin-chin's mother, Yu Manzhen, was an early female political activist. Her untraditional and progressive views on the place of women in society influenced her headstrong young daughter. Another factor in Pin-chin's political and literary development was the 1919 May Fourth Movement, also known as the ''Chinese Enlightenment.'' This was one of several antiforeign movements that intensified Chinese nationalism and caused some prominent intellectuals to begin studying Marxism as a way to end the foreign aggression that plagued the giant nation.

Pin-chin attended good-quality, progressive schools in Hunan while growing up and watched intently as China's rapid political changes whirled around her. In 1919 she attended school in Changsha, capital of Hunan Province; one of her classmates was Yang Kaihui, who would later become the wife of Chinese Communist leader Mao Zedong. (Mao would command the country beginning in 1949.) She enjoyed reading the modern works of Western authors but was especially captivated by Flaubert's *Madame Bovary*, which she was said to have read at least 10 times.

Pin-chin waged a pitched battle in 1920 with her paternal uncles after they announced their choice of a husband for her. In a move that must have been flabbergasting in its impropriety, Pin-chin told the men that her body was her own and she would do with it what she liked. Taking this stand caused a widening rift in the family, and Pin-chin finally set off on her own. (In fact, Pin-chin was lucky—if she had been born several decades earlier she might have been the victim of footbinding, a tradition in which the parents of wealthy girl children permanently crippled them to indicate that they had no need to work.)

Began True Education

Fleeing Hunan Province for the political and culture center of Shanghai, Pin-chin entered the Common Girls' School there later in 1920. She served as editor of the school's literary journal, the *Women's Voice*, until leaving the school in 1922. She also joined the Anarchist Party in 1920. Pin-chin studied at Shanghai University in 1922, working and writing with many of the people who would soon become the nation's top-ranking Communists, and then left for Beijing in 1923. There she audited classes by Lu Xun, who became her literary idol. Although she was never actually enrolled at the University of Beijing (whether because she did not pass the entrance exam or could not manage to complete the formal enrollment process is unclear), Pin-chin studied with many of the country's most prominent intellectuals at this epicenter of radical Chinese politics.

Meanwhile, in 1924 Pin-chin met a poet, Hu Yuepin, who was as committed as she was to literature and political reform. In 1927-1928, as the Nationalist Party of Chiang Kai-shek and the new Communist Party locked horns in a battle to the death for control of the country, Pin-chin and Hu lived a bohemian life of poverty in Shanghai. She drank excessively, distraught at her perceived lack of achievement so far, and was unfaithful to Hu at least once. However, her misery seems to have prompted her to start writing, because in 1928 she produced and published *Miss Sofie's Diary*.

Began Writing Career

Pin-chin's first work would also be her most famous. Shocking for its extensive use of eroticism, the long story was not strictly autobiographical. However, Pin-chin's readers believed it to be so, and came to see her as the notorious icon of the liberated modern Chinese woman.

Miss Sophie's Diary ignited in Pin-chin a passion for writing. In addition to working as editor of the literary journal *Honghei Congshu* in 1928, she churned out numerous collections of short fiction in which the dominant theme was the problems of Chinese women like her. In 1930 she had her first child, a son, with Hu, but sent the boy to live with her mother in Hunan. She continued her political and literary activities, joining the League of Left-Wing Writers and serving as editor of the communist magazine *Beidou* in 1931. Later that year, Hu and other radical writers were executed by the Nationalist Party, and in 1932 Pin-chin secretly joined the Communist Party—partly as an act of protest. (Her beloved brother, Wang Jianhong, also died at about this point.) The Party did have its appeals, though, since it treated women's issues with respect and gave them importance in the Party platform. Also, by this point, Pin-chin knew many of the Party's leaders, having studied and worked with them earlier.

Pin-chin met and fell in love with a translator, Feng Da, but the couple's new life together was interrupted in 1933 when the Nationalists kidnapped them both and put them under house arrest in Nanjing. During this period, about which very few records exist, Pin-chin's books were banned. She gave birth to a daughter, who was also sent to her mother in Hunan. Despite these hardships, she kept writing, and secretly published *Shui* (Water) and *Muqin* (Mother) in 1933. Feng died of tuberculosis in 1935.

Pin-chin either escaped from her captors or was freed in 1937, when with the help of the Communist underground she fled to the Communist-controlled area of Yanan known as the Red Army Base. To help bolster the morale of the Party members during their struggle, she organized the Northwest Front Service Corps to provide traveling entertainment. She wrote a play for the troupe to perform, the 1938 *Chongfeng* (Reunion). Pin-chin resumed her writing, which gradually came to manifest her disenchantment with what she perceived as a widening split in the Party between practice and theory regarding women's rights and the Party's interest in women's issues. Her most famous work on this theme was the 1941 article "Thoughts on March 8."

Became Leading Figure in Communist Party

By 1942 Pin-chin had become chief speaker for women's issues within the Communist Party and was held in high regard by many of the Party elite. She was also a popular professor at Communist-supported universities and literary editor of the Communist newspaper *Jiefang ribao* until 1942. However, Mao was increasingly losing patience with the writer and her disobedience of his directive (part of his 1942 Rectification Campaign) that all art must serve the Communist revolution in an obvious, direct manner.

Pin-chin came back to toe the Party line when she participated in the early days of the land reform movement in 1946 as the Communist Party began targeting landlords and wealthy peasants and returning their land to "the People." She wrote a critically acclaimed novel about the campaign, *The Sun Shines over the Sangaan River*, in 1948. Mao reportedly loved the book, and sent Pin-chin to serve as a spokesperson for the Party throughout Eastern Europe and the Soviet Union. Pin-chin remained a fixture of the Party's

literary and cultural circles throughout the 1940s and early 1950s and worked as editor of two Party publications, *Wenyo bao* and *Renmin wenxue* from 1950 to 1953. During this time, however, she had fallen out of favor with top Party officials for her continued questioning of its policies. Even her pro-Communist novel had been insufficient to win back their approval.

Expelled from Party and Exiled

In the mid-1950s, Pin-chin found herself becoming further estranged from the Party leadership. Two resolutions of the Writer's Union in 1955 and 1956 led to her being wrongly labeled a "rightist" (one who advocates maintenance of the political status quo, i.e., rule by the Nationalists) and because of this her books were banned from 1957 to 1978. Ultimately, Pin-chin was expelled from the Communist Party in 1958 and sent to live on a farm in the remote northeastern Heilongjiang Province in Manchuria with her husband, Chen Ming, a screenwriter whom she had met in 1942. They spent the majority of two decades there, and were assigned the work of taking care of animals.

Pin-chin's persecution continued into the Cultural Revolution, Mao's all-encompassing reform movement that he initiated in 1965 to eliminate counterrevolutionary elements in the country's institutions and leadership. Characterized by purges of intellectuals, political zealotry, and social and economic chaos, the movement terrified artists like Pin-chin and her husband. Despite her many services to the Communist Party, she was brought back to Beijing in 1970 and publicly humiliated before being put in solitary confinement for the next five years. The Party destroyed her manuscript of *Miss Sophie's Diary*. She later learned that Chen had been next door to her the entire time. Party authorities released Pin-chin from solitary confinement in 1975 only to send her back into exile. Permitted to leave with Chen, the couple were forced to live in Chanxi, a town in Shaanxi Province until 1978.

"Rehabilitated" and Permitted to Return to Literary Life

Upon her return to Beijing in 1978 following the death of Mao and the ascent of reformist Deng Xiaoping, Pin-chin was "rehabilitated" (given back her social standing and good name) in 1979. Reinstated to the prestigious Writers' Union, she was allowed to give interviews to the foreign press and wrote several stories after her release. She traveled to the United States in 1981 to attend a writer's conference in Iowa, but was reportedly confused by the Western version of feminism that she learned about there.

At age 82, still devoted to the Communist Party and its principles—especially that art should support and glorify the Party—Pin-chin died of cancer in Beijing on March 4, 1986. Some historical records indicate that she had never married her early lovers because she believed marriage was a socially condoned form of prostitution.

Books

Commire, Anne, ed., *Women in World History,* Yorkin Publications, 2001.

Online

"Ding Ling," *The Gale Group Biography Resource Center website,* http://galenet.gale.com (January 16, 2004).

"Ding Ling (1904-1986)," *eLibrary website,* http://ask.elibrary .com (December 27, 2003).

"Ding Ling," *The Chinese University of Hong Kong: A Journal of Chinese Literature and Culture,* http://www.renditions.org (December 27, 2003).

"Ding Ling," *The College of Wooster,* http://www.wooster.edu (December 27, 2003).

"Ding Ling," *Indiana University,* http://www.indiana.edu (December 27, 2003).

"Enduring the Revolution: Ding Ling and the Politics of Literature in Guomindang China," *The Greenwood Publishing Group,* http://info.greenwood.com (December 27, 2003). □

William Plomer

When South African writer William Plomer (1903–1973) published his first novel, *Turbott Wolfe*, in 1925, he expressed his vehement anger at the country's policies of racial apartheid. In *I Speak of Africa,* a book of short stories he published two years later, that sentiment was echoed.

William Charles Franklyn Plomer was born on December 10, 1903, in Pietersburg, in South Africa's Northern Transvaal. His father, Charles Plomer, was a magistrate who specialized in native affairs, and his mother was Edythe Waite-Brown Plomer. The family had limited finances, but his parents wanted the best education possible for their son. Charles Plomer's job required a lot of travel, so Plomer's early schooling was entrusted first to a governess, then to his maternal aunt and uncle, Hilda and Telford Haman, who ran a preparatory school at Spondon House, near Derby, England, where he was left by his parents at the age of five. Plomer later recalled that his feelings of isolation and his sense of being a loner stemmed from that early separation. He returned to Africa with his parents and attended St. John's College in Johannesburg. By that time, he had a new brother, Peter. Plomer considered this an idyllic time, as he was free to pursue his interests at the liberal school.

When World War I arrived in Europe, so to did the Plomer family. Initially Plomer was sent to Beechmont, a school he loathed. He later noted that it was probably at Beechmont that he adopted his habit of secrecy. Following this, he went on to the Rugby School where he stayed until 1918, when his family's finances weakened from the war to the point where he could no longer remain there. He finished his education back at St. John's. By this time in his life, Marcel Proust had become Plomer's favorite writer; he now began to consider the possibility of becoming a writer instead of a painter, as he had originally planned.

Became Farmer and Writer

Plomer turned down his father's offer of an Oxford University education and became a farmer, settling in the Stormberg Mountains and joining a local Settler's Association. He also worked as a trader with Zululand. In 1926 Plomer and Roy Campbell founded the satirical magazine *Voorslag* ("Whiplash") and were later joined in the venture by fellow South African Laurens van der Post. Shortly after Plomer published his second book, Afrikaner critics and readers alike dismissed the sentiment of both his books as offensive. At this point, Plomer separated from his friends and fellow writers and ventured to Japan, where he lived for two years, teaching and writing and traveling through the country. His first job was at the Tokyo School of Foreign Language, followed by a post at an exclusive private high school. While in Japan, Plomer immersed himself in the nation's culture and learned everything he could about the exotic country. In his later years, he would talk of Japan as his "university" and recall with appreciation the education that country gave him. Much of Japan's influence can be seen throughout the body of his work.

In 1929 Plomer returned to London by way of Manchuria, Siberia, Russia, and Poland. He had been offered the chair of the department of English literature at Tokyo's Imperial University, but he turned down the offer. After visiting France, Germany, and Italy, he decided to live in Greece, but eventually returned to England. Although he continued to travel, London remained his home base until his death.

During the 1930s Plomer continued to write, especially short stories and poetry; but he became almost as well known for editing the diaries of Francis Kilvert, a Victorian clergyman who was a veritible unknown until Plomer's publication of Kilvert's diaries. Well bolstered by his literary friends as well as part of the socialist Bloomsbury group, Plomer's homosexuality was no secret, particularly after he wrote of his experiences in his poetry collection *The Dorking Thigh.*

World War II and Beyond

During World War II Plomer served the British Admiralty in the Royal Navy Intelligence Division from 1940 until the war's end in 1945. He then returned to a position he had held since 1937 as a literary adviser for Jonathan Cape publishers in London; he would remain at Cape until 1973, the year he died. He also used his writing talents to collaborate with composer Benjamin Britten, penning the librettos for several of Britten's compositions, including, *Gloriana,* a 1953 opera in three acts that was performed during the coronation celebration for Queen Elizabeth II; 1964's *Curlew River;* 1966's *The Burning Fiery Furnace;* and 1968's *The Prodigal Son.*

In 1956 Plomer returned to Johannesburg and the University of the Witwatersrand and worked as visiting lecturer for the academic year. He enjoyed becoming reacquainted with the places in South Africa he loved as a youth but ultimately left once again for England.

Prolific Career in Publishing

As a writer Plomer published numerous volumes of his own writings as well as collaborations with other authors; as an editor he met many other writers and helped to impact their works. In addition to those already noted, his works included the poetry collections *The Family Tree* (1929), *Visiting the Caves* (1936), and *Taste and Remember* (1966); the short-story collections *Paper Houses* (1929), *The Child of Queen Victoria, and Other Stories* (1933), and *A Brutal Sentimentalist and Other Stories* (1969); and the novel, *Sado,* which was first released in 1921 and published the following year in the United States as *They Never Came Back.* Other writings include his memoirs *Double Lives* (1943) and *At Home,* published in 1958; and 1963's *Conversation with My Younger Self.* In 1976 he republished his two volumes of memoirs as *The Autobiography of William Plomer.*

Became Subdued in Age

During his early career Plomer traveled in literary circles that found him rubbing shoulders with some of the most well-known English writers of the early 20th century. In his later years, Plomer lived far more quietly, eventually returning to the Anglican faith in which his mother had raised him. In his mature period, Plomer's "poems became less satirical, more tender and mellow. And he acquired a sympathy with elderly, kindly people who lived in undistinguished bungalows far removed from the worlds that he had known: the immense vistas of Africa, the traditional grace of Japan,

the arrogance of Bloomsbury, and the mingled glitter and squalor of high Bohemian London.''

Plomer's professional life engaged him with several literary and author's groups, including the Royal Society of Literature; the Kilvert Society, which he served as president; the Society of Authors; International P.E.N.; and the Poetry Society, which he also served as president from 1968 to 1971. He was the recipient of several honors, including an honorary doctorate from the University of Durham and the Queen's Gold Medal for Poetry in 1963. Plomer was also made a Commander of the Order of the British Empire in 1968. With Alan Aldridge, in 1973 he won the prestigious Whitbread Award in the Children's literature category for the book, *The Butterfly Ball and the Grasshopper's Feast.* Durham University Library has included within its collection several of Plomer's books, and those he collected, dating between 1870 and 1973. Plomer died on September 21, 1973, in England.

Books

Alexander, Peter, *William Plomer: A Biography,* Oxford University Press, 1989.
Contemporary Literary Criticism, Gale, 1975.
Plomer, William, *The Dorking Thigh and Other Satires,* J. Cape, 1945.
Reference Guide to English Literature, St. James Press, 1991.

Online

"Plomer Collection," *Durham University Library Web site,* http://flambard.dur.ac.uk/ (January 13, 2004). ☐

Alvin Francis Poussaint

Dr. Alvin F. Poussaint (born 1934) is so widely known in the United States for his psychiatric and child-rearing expertise and his groundbreaking consulting role on *The Cosby Show* that John Koch of the *Boston Globe* once told him, "Your name is like a sound bite." His advice is sought on a wide range of topics, including child rearing, the unique challenges faced by African American families, and the effects of racism on African Americans and African American males in particular. In addition to his work in television program production, he writes and speaks and participates often in radio and television talk shows.

Poussaint was born in East Harlem, New York, the next to last of eight children. His mother was Harriet Johnston Poussaint, a homemaker, and Christopher Poussaint, who worked as a printer and typographer, was his father. Alvin Poussaint graduated from Stuyvesant High School in New York, finished Columbia College in 1956, earned an MD from Cornell University in 1960, and received an MS from UCLA in 1964. He interned in 1964 and

1965 at the University of California at Los Angeles Neuropsychiatric Institute, was selected chief resident in 1965, and led the institute's intern training program. He worked in the Civil Rights Movement from 1965 to 1967, serving as Southern Field Director of the Medical Committee for Human Rights in Jackson, Mississippi. In this capacity, he advanced the desegregation of various Southern health facilities as well as serving the medical needs of civil rights workers. He also chaired the board of PUSH (People United to Save Humanity). In 1967 he left Mississippi for Massachusetts to become a member of the Tufts University School of Medicine faculty and director of a community mental health center at Columbia Point housing project. He married Ann Ashmore, and they had a son, Alan.

Poussaint joined Harvard in 1969 and was director of student affairs at Harvard Medical School between 1975 and 1978. In 1984 he became production consultant for *The Cosby Show*, a weekly television situation comedy. Divorced from his first wife, Poussaint married Dr. Tina Inez Young on December 5, 1992, and on November 16, 1999, Poussaint and his wife, an anesthesiologist and neuroradiologist, had a daughter, Alison. Poussaint is presently professor of psychiatry and faculty associate dean for student affairs at the Harvard Medical School and senior associate in psychiatry at Children's Hospital, Boston. He is also director of the media center at Boston's Judge Baker Children's Center, where he is involved in shaping for the better the powerful influence of media on children. He writes, appears on television and radio, and serves on numerous boards. He has received numerous awards and honorary degrees.

Nicknamed "The Brain"

A very early factor in Poussaint's successful life was his mother. "My mother told me I was intelligent," he told a *Boston Globe* reporter. "She nicknamed me 'The Brain.' She made me feel I had something special." When his friends started using the nickname too, "I felt that I had something to live up to."

Other significant threads in his life began when he was 9 and suffered a case of rheumatic fever so severe he was hospitalized and then placed in a convalescent home for several months. In the hospital, he read almost constantly, and, he told one reporter, "I became a study because my case was classic. When the doctors came in with residents and interns, I listened to what they said, the medical phrases they used." To another reporter he related that "when I came out . . . , I wanted to be a doctor, because of my association with the doctors and nurses in the hospital. I felt they had saved me from dying."

Encountered Racism at Age 9

Poussaint's experience in the convalescent home was also energizing, but in a very different way. "I was the only black kid there," he told a *Boston Globe* interviewer. "The white kids got together, pointed at me and sing-songed: 'Nig-ger! Nig-ger!' I was so upset I started to cry and went to the head nurse sobbing. I told her that I wanted to get out of there." But the 9-year-old Poussaint was in for an even more

devastating jolt. When the nurse asked why he wanted to leave and he told her what the children had called him, "She said, 'Well, aren't you a nigger?' I was shocked to discover she felt the same way [that the children did]. I cried even more. I also felt trapped. I felt a terror. Up to that moment I thought the adults in charge of the place would protect me. At that moment, I lost my faith in adults."

The effects of the incident were far reaching. "That was a motivator. I decided to prove to everyone that I was an achiever. Maybe it was a streak of stubbornness. But I decided not to let anything defeat me."

Another significant event came while Poussaint was in junior high school, and he later recalled it with a *Boston Globe* journalist. "A teacher who knew I wanted to be a doctor put a hand on my shoulder and said: 'Have you ever thought of applying to a special science high school?' . . . This quick conversation in a school hallway propelled me to go right into the principal's office to ask for an application form."

Profoundly Influenced by Brother

A uniquely important influence in Poussaint's life was his brother Kenneth. "Athletic, witty, and gifted with an intuitive nature that made him a whiz at sports and card games . . . Kenny was also a leader among his peers," Poussaint writes in the prologue to his most recent book, *Lay My Burden Down*. Poussaint's brother became addicted to heroin at 15. He was eventually able to overcome his addiction, but he also suffered from mental illness, and "He went from being hospitalized to being in prison to being homeless," Poussaint told the *Boston Globe*. Kenneth Poussaint died of meningitis in 1975 at the age of 42. "My brother's situation definitely influenced me to go into psychiatry," Poussaint said in 1986.

Racism Influenced Career Direction

The devastating incident at the convalescent center was not Poussaint's only salient encounter with racism. In college and medical school, he was isolated in predominantly white classes. Later, in Mississippi, a policeman stopped him, addressed him as "boy," and refused to accept that his name was Dr. Poussaint. Pressed by an associate to let the officer call him by his first name, Poussaint felt "demeaned, demoralized, publicly humiliated and powerless." But with the humiliation came a flash of insight: "It was at this moment that I also understood the psychological depths of racism. . . . [and] resolved to fight harder to change the system," Poussaint recalled to an interviewer.

The one-on-one practice of psychiatry hasn't figured prominently in Poussaint's professional life. He once explained to newspaper reporters that "when I left psychiatric training, I realized that one of the most important ways I could help the mental health of black people was not one-on-one therapy. All the segregation and discrimination was damaging their mental health more than anything else, and it was important to fight that. I understood that I had to be political and try to influence the larger society." In his professional life, Poussaint has exerted that influence in several arenas.

Identified as "the preeminent expert on black child-rearing" by the *Boston Globe,* he has written many articles and coauthored *Black Child Care* with James P. Comer, MD, in 1975 (revised and republished in 1992 as *Raising Black Children: Two Leading Psychiatrists Confront the Educational, Social, and Emotional Problems Facing Black Children*). Recognizing that racism in America prevents African Americans from experiencing "a oneness with society and the security that comes from this feeling," the authors say, "Many black parents . . . have mixed feelings about passing on the values and ways of a society that says in so many ways, 'We do not value black men and women, boys and girls, as much as we do whites.' " In addition, Poussaint favors a nonviolent approach to parenting and promotes education in parenting.

Advised *The Cosby Show*

The Cosby Show, starring comedian Bill Cosby, was one effort to overcome negative images of African Americans on television and in American society with positive ones. The show revolved around a physician and a lawyer and their five attractive and talented children. According to *Ebony* magazine, Poussaint "helped make history by advising Bill Cosby on what a father should do and not do on his long-running television show." Poussaint told the *Boston Globe* he edited the scripts to ensure "reality grounding" and to remove " 'subtle but demeaning' humor." He also consulted for *A Different World,* the spinoff of *The Cosby Show,* and has developed a children's program called *Willoughby's Wonders,* fostering teamwork and interaction with stories about an urban, multicultural, coed soccer team. More recently he was a script consultant for Cosby's *Little Bill,* designed for preschool children.

Declared Racism a Mental Disorder

Poussaint is also described on his Harvard Web page as "an expert on race relations in America, the dynamics of prejudice, and issues of diversity." In January 2002 he published an article in the *Western Journal of Medicine* making the case for including extreme racism in the American Psychological Association's *Diagnostic and Statistical Manual of Mental Disorders.* Poussaint says the association views racism as normative in the United States, in other words, as a cultural problem. "To continue perceiving extreme racism as normative and not pathologic is to lend it legitimacy," he argues. "Clearly, anyone who scapegoats a whole group of people and seeks to eliminate them to resolve his or her internal conflicts meets criteria for a delusional disorder, a major psychiatric illness."

He has written articles about dealing with the challenges facing black men and women; black suicide, especially among males; and violence among African Americans. For a 1981 collection of interviews with black leaders titled *Like It Is: Arthur E. Thomas Interviews Leaders on Black America,* he commented that "black men are in a lot of trouble," noting their rising suicide rate, unemployment rate, and disproportionate rate of drug addiction, alcoholism, and incarceration. He pointed out a connection between suicide and the hopelessness that follows from being arrested and jailed and said a similar connection exists between despair and homicide.

Redeems Brother's Suffering

That theme received fuller development in 2000, when Poussaint and journalist Amy Alexander, who lost a brother to suicide, published *Lay My Burden Down: Unraveling Suicide and the Mental Health Crisis among African-Americans.* In it, Poussaint returns to the story of his brother Kenneth, detailing his decline and speculating that it might be viewed as a long, slow suicide (although Kenneth Poussaint died of meningitis, Poussaint writes that "his vital organs [were] defeated by years of drug abuse" as well as his disease). The authors note that "on several levels, [Alexander's brother] Carl Burton and Kenneth Poussaint fit the profile of what has become a growing phenomenon in the United States since the late 1970s: young blacks who self-destruct." They also note that the common lists of suicide warning signs don't always apply to African Americans and speculate that the "high rate of homicide among blacks might be viewed as evidence of a peculiar kind of communal self-hatred, an especially virulent form of anger, self-loathing, and lost hope that leads to a devaluation of the lives of fellow blacks." They also posit that "similar dynamics . . . may account, in part, for the high rates of alcoholism and drug addiction among black people in this society." It is American society's racism, with its message of African American worthlessness, that fosters this self-hatred, and the society's blindness to racism impedes remedies.

At the same time, Poussaint's trajectory reveals that the same society that overwhelmed his brother spurred his own resilience and success, and it is a similar determination and drive in others that Poussaint has sought to foster over the full arc of his career. With his son grown and a young daughter in his life, Poussaint told *Ebony* magazine that as he approaches 70, he is cutting back a bit on his professional activities and enjoying doing some child rearing, and no doubt plenty of esteem building, of his own.

Books

Comer, James P., and Alvin F. Poussaint, *Raising Black Children: Two Leading Psychiatrists Confront the Educational, Social, and Emotional Problems Facing Black Children,* Plume, 1992.
Poussaint, Alvin F., and Amy Alexander, *Lay My Burden Down: Unraveling Suicide and the Mental Health Crisis among African-Americans,* Beacon Press, 2000.
Thomas, Arthur E., *Like It Is: Arthur E. Thomas Interviews Leaders on Black America,* Dutton, 1981.

Online

"Alvin F. Poussaint," *Biography Resource Center,* galenet .galegroup.com/servlet/VioRC?vrsn = 2.0&OP = contains &locID-broward29 & . . . (December 23, 2003).
"Alvin F. Poussaint, M.D.: Biography, Publications, and Titles," www.hms.harvard.edu/orma./poussaint (January 2, 2004).
Beggy, Carol, and Beth Carney, "A Good Start for Baby Girl; From Sam to Bill," *Boston Globe,* nl.newsbank.com/nl-search/we/Archives?p_action = list&p_topdoc = 31 (January 4, 2004).

"Biography, Alvin Poussaint, M.D., and Susan Linn, Ed.D.," *familyeducation.com*, familyeducation.com/bio/0,1379,0-22151,00.html (January 2, 2004).

Christy, Marian, "Bill Cosby's Unflappable Adviser," *Boston Globe Archives*, nl.newsbank.com/nl-search/we/Archives?p_action=print (January 6, 2004).

Koch, "Alvin Poussaint," *Boston Globe Archives*, nl.newsbank.com/nl-search/we/Archives?p_action=print (January 6, 2004).

McCabe, Bruce, "An Off-Camera Psychiatrist," *Boston Globe Archives*, nl.newsbank.com/nl-search/we/Archives?p_action=print (January 6, 2004).

"The Media Center," *Judge Baker Children's Center*, www.jbcc.harvard.edu/media.htm (January 6, 2004).

Norment, Lynn, "Fatherhood at 65," *Ebony*, web4.infotrac.galegroup.com/itw/infomark/342/175/44980592w4/purl=rcl_ITOF_0 . . . (December 23, 2003).

Poussaint, Alvin F., "Is Extreme Racism a Mental Illness? (Point-Counterpoint)," *Western Journal of Medicine*, web7.infotrac.galegroup.com/itw/infomark/990/544/40860498w7/purl=rcl_ITOF_0 . . . (December 23, 2003). □

V. I. Pudovkin

Russian director V. I. Pudovkin (1893-1953) was one of the Soviet Union's leading filmmakers of the 1920s. A master of the montage, or rapid intercutting of images, Pudovkin worked during an era widely considered the golden age of Soviet cinema, when generous government support allowed him and fellow directors like Sergei Eisenstein to make daring cinematic epics that took the fledgling art form to a new level. "Pudovkin made some of the liveliest and most perversely moving films of all," asserted *Guardian* journalist Jonathan Jones, and also termed him "the true ancestor of the modern Hollywood film."

Prisoner of War

The director was born Vsevolod Illiarionovich Pudovkin in Tsarist Russia on February 16, 1893. He was from a manufacturing city in southeast Russia called Penza, and studied physics and chemistry at Moscow University. In 1914, when World War I erupted, he was drafted into an artillery unit of the Russian Army. A year later, he was wounded and taken prisoner, but escaped and was back in Moscow by 1918. By then, a provisional government that ousted the tsar from power was subsequently overthrown by the Bolshevik Party, and Pudovkin's homeland became the world's first Communist state.

Initially, Pudovkin found a job in the new Soviet economy as a chemist in a laboratory, but by chance became acquainted with Lev Kuleshov, a young filmmaker six years his junior. Kuleshov had founded a studio in which he was conducting experiments in film technique and editing.

Pudovkin began taking courses at the State Cinema School around 1920, and was soon working on the government propaganda films that came to be known as "agitprop," part of an effort to further the political goals of the Revolution via works of art and literature. The first film in which he was involved was *Golod . . . golod . . . golod* ("Hunger . . . Hunger . . . Hunger"), a work from 1921 for which he served as co-director and co-scenarist; he also appeared in it. He would also take one of the lead roles in Kuleshov's *The Extraordinary Adventures of Mr. West in the Land of the Bolsheviks*, a 1924 tale of a foreign capitalist who comes to the Soviet Union.

Made Chess Comedy

It was a rewarding time to work in the Russian film industry, for Soviet leader Vladimir Lenin had asserted that the cinema was most important of all the arts for the young Soviet state. Still, filmmakers worked with tight budgets in the early years of Soviet cinema, and were forced to be creative, and from this came ingenious advances in post-production technique. Pudovkin and other filmmakers at Kuleshov's studio, for example, watched a copy of a well-known 1916 American film by D. W. Griffith, *Intolerance*, and were awed by Griffith's filmmaking talents. They took apart the reel and re-edited it themselves, experimenting with the widely differing effects caused by juxtaposing the various shots against one another. Kuleshov's most famous experiment, however, involved an image of an actor's expressionless face. This was intercut with other images, including a bowl of borscht and a woman in a coffin, and though it was the same footage of the performer in every shot, audiences claimed the acting was superb. What became known in contemporary filmmaking as the "Kuleshov effect" asserted that a frame has two elements: the visual reality it presents, and the context it takes when it becomes part of an edited whole.

Though the Soviet Union's greatest filmmaker, Sergei Eisenstein, was also at Kuleshov's experimental laboratory for a time, Pudovkin would become Kuleshov's best protégé, expanding his mentor's ideas in his own extensive writings on film theory, and incorporating them into his own films. The 1925 short *Shakhmatnaya goryachka* ("Chess Fever") is considered Pudovkin's first real work, a comic story of a couple's wedding thwarted because of the groom's passion for the game. The frustrated bride was played by Pudovkin's wife, actress and journalist Anna Zemtsova. Writing in the *Guardian*, Jones called it "a fascinating glimpse of everyday life in Lenin's Moscow."

First of Three Epic Films

In 1926, Pudovkin made a documentary work, *Mekhanikha golovnovo mozga* ("Mechanics of the Brain") with famed Russian scientist Ivan Pavlov. The film depicted Pavlov's important discovery of the principle of conditioned reflexes in humans and animals. Pudovkin's first full-length narrative film, however, was also produced that year: *Mat* ("Mother"), based on a story by Russian writer Maxim Gorky. The tragedy is set during Russia's turbulent 1905 Revolution, and the title character is a simple country woman who despairs over her son's involvement in a trade-union group. She accidentally betrays him to the authorities, and is grief-stricken when he is sentenced to prison in a sham trial. Finally politicized herself, she helps him escape and they take part in a workers' demonstration. At the climax, the son runs from the police and jumps onto an ice floe in a river, whose surface is finally thawing, which the *Guardian*'s Jones called "a piece of pure Marxist poetry."

In Pudovkin's writings, he asserted that it required less emoting from an actor than a work performed on the stage before a live audience. It was the filmmaker, he argued, who gave the finished work its character through editing, which therefore freed the actor to deliver a more subtle performance. Perhaps for this reason, Pudovkin often liked to cast non-actors in his films, which he did in his 1927 epic *Konyets Sankt-Peterburga* ("The End of St. Petersburg"). The film commemorated the tenth anniversary of the 1917 Revolution, and followed the story of a young, naïve peasant who arrives in the city and becomes caught up in the historic events of the time. Pudovkin cast the lead, Ivan Chuvelyov, from the extras that had assembled to play in crowd scenes for reasons that he explained to *New York Times* writer P. Beaumont Wadsworth. "The special qualities that were required for this role were not 'expressed' by this player," Pudovkin said. "He was the part. I doubt now, after having had film experience, whether that young man could give as marvelous a performance in the same role. He is too 'experienced' now."

A Classic of Soviet Cinema

The End of St. Petersburg was first Soviet film ever shown at New York City's largest theater at the time, the Roxy on Broadway. It later became standard viewing in film schools, particularly for the montage sequence that depicts St. Petersburg's gleeful stock-market speculators with images of World War I's carnage. An essay in the *International Dictionary of Films and Filmmakers* termed it "significant in that it is one of the first to satisfactorily blend a fictional scenario into a factual setting. Typically, Pudovkin cast real pre-Revolution stockbrokers and executives as stockbrokers and executives." Decades after it was made, *The End of St. Petersburg* was still occasionally shown at art houses and in retrospectives of Soviet cinema. A 1992 *Nation* review from critic Ben Sonnenberg described its effect as "Homeric-violent and rapid" and a work "ennobled by detestation of privilege, faith in progress, trust in the working class and love for the city of Bely, Dostoyevsky and Pushkin."

Pudovkin made a trio of epic Soviet films during this golden age, and a 1928 work, *Potomok Chingis-khan*, was the last of these three. Titled in English *Storm Over Asia*, it is also called *The Heir to Genghis-Khan*. Pudovkin filmed it in Mongolia, the vast Central Asian land that was once home to a mighty thirteenth-century warrior nation led by Jenghiz Khan. The film's story is set in 1918, during the Russian Civil War, when ousted Russian nobles teamed with Western mercenaries and battled Bolshevik troops for control in the provinces. Pudovkin's plot centers around a Mongol trapper who is cheated out of the price of a precious silver fox fur by foreigners, and his anger leads him into involvement with a

Mongol rebel group. Pudovkin trekked to the region for the first time in his life to make the film, and cast Mongolians in it—many of whom had never before seen a film. "I hope that I have succeeded in revealing Mongolia and the Mongolians to the outer world," he told the *New York Times* in the interview with Wadsworth a year later, "for that, and that alone, was my aim."

Experimented with Sound

In that same article, Pudovkin declared, "I shall not make any more epic pictures," and termed his next project "a simple . . . story of a crisis in the life of a married couple. There will be no great catastrophe, nothing terrible will happen. Only that their happiness is threatened by a sudden, senseless incident. It is like a dream." That movie, *Otchen kharacho dziviosta* ("Life's Very Good"), was revised with new sound technology and re-released two years later in 1932. Pudovkin's first genuine sound picture, *Dezertir* ("Deserter"), came a year later. This work is considered another classic of Soviet cinema, primarily for Pudovkin's use of the new element. The plot centers around labor troubles in a German shipyard that turn violent, and its main character becomes disillusioned with his homeland and moves to the Soviet Union. Its propagandistic message was tempered by several techniques that Pudovkin utilized. "By editing in sound, he contrasted the conversational dialogue of different characters with crowd noises, traffic sounds, sirens, music, and even silence," noted an essay in *International Dictionary of Films and Filmmakers*.

Soviet cinema was becoming a more cautious enterprise during the 1930s, after Josef Stalin succeeded Lenin and became wary of any potential criticism from within. Even Pudovkin joined the Communist Party, but after *Deserter* he was involved in a car accident, and from then on served only as co-director on a number of films from Mosfilm Studios. They include *Pobeda* ("Victory"), *Kino za XX liet* ("Twenty Years of Cinema"), *Pir v Girmunka* ("Feast at Zhirmunka"), and *Amiral Nakhimov*. During this time he also appeared in Eisenstein's 1944 epic, *Ivan Grozny*, a historical drama about Ivan the Terrible that was considered a thinly veiled portrait of Stalin.

Enduring Visionary

After 1935 Pudovkin also taught theoretic studies at the State Institute for Cinematography for a number of years. His last film, for which he received sole director credit, was 1953's *Vozvrachenia Vassilya Bortnikov* ("The Return of Vasili Bortnikov"), a color picture that glorified the mechanization of Soviet agriculture. He died on June 30, 1953, in Riga, Latvia. His writings, among them the essays "The Film Scenario" and "Film Director and Film Material," are standard reading for graduate students in film. His idea that movies are not necessarily created in a scene-by-scene sequence, but rather built in the editing room by the filmmaker, was a pioneering one and taken to new levels by directors such as Francis Ford Coppola in the opening scenes of his 1972 classic *The Godfather*. Though Pudovkin's films are sometimes crude stories carrying a blatant political message, "it's naive to completely separate the cinema of the avant-garde in 1920s Russia from what came afterwards,'' asserted Jones in the *Guardian*. ''They were propagandists, and Pudovkin's emotive editing gets inside you to produce gut responses at odds with any skepticism you might feel about his melodramas of revolution. At the same time, there's a scope and richness that elevates them beyond propaganda and will help them survive as long as cinema itself.''

Books

Contemporary Authors, Gale, 2001.

International Dictionary of Films and Filmmakers, Volume 2: Directors, St. James Press, 1996.

Periodicals

Guardian (London, England), August 31, 2001, p. 8.
Nation, March 9, 1992, p. 311.
New York Times, May 12, 1929, p. X5; May 4, 1930, p. X4.
Times (London, England), July 2, 1953, p. 8.

Online

''Kuleshov and Pudovkin Introduce Montage to Filmmaking, 1927,'' *DISCovering World History,* http://galenet.gale.com (January 16, 2004). □

R

Seewoosagur Ramgoolam

Seewoosagur Ramgoolam (1900–1985) was of Indian heritage and grew up on the island nation of Mauritius when it was still a colony of Great Britain. With a struggle that began in 1936, Ramgoolam took the helm of his country's struggle for independence in 1959. When Mauritius won its freedom, it won a president in Ramgoolam whose first interests would always lie in his homeland.

Son of Immigrants

Ramgoolam was born in the Mauritian town of Belle Rive in the Flacq District, on September 18, 1900. His father was an Indian immigrant who worked as a laborer. His parents affectionately called him by the name, "Kewal." Just as he began his education at the local school where Hindu children were taught their language and culture, his father died. He was seven years old. His early schooling included the Roman Catholic assisted school and then the Bel Air government school where he passed the sixth standard recognition of the completion of the first level of school. He was 12 when a serious accident cost him his left eye an accident that nonetheless did not deter him from continuing his education. He went on to the Curepipe Boys Government School and to the junior Cambridge school at the Royal College of Curepipe. While there he studied science and passed his senior examination for Cambridge. Between the time he left for England for medical studies, he worked as a civil servant for a year.

Ramgoolam set sail for London when he was 21 with plans to study medicine at University College. His first six months there were spent at the Indian Student's Association, an organization that provided support for Indian students who had come to England from abroad. While at India House he came into contact with the Indian leaders of the early twentieth century: Mohandas Gandhi, Jawaharlal Nehru, Subhas Chandra Bose, Lalla Lajpat Raid, and the writer Rabindranath Tagore. Ramgoolam also became a founding member of the Indian Student's Central Association that was located at Knightsbridge in West London. Even though he was a serious student, he continued his political activities on a very intense level. By 1924 he was the president of the London branch of the Indian National Congress. The British Labor Party had come into power under Ramsay MacDonalad as Prime Minister. The political climate of the times encouraged him to join the Fabian Society, a group that promoted the ideas of Fabian Socialism. According to its official website in January 2004, "The Fabian Society had been founded in England in 1884 as a socialist society committed to gradual rather than revolutionary social reform." The name of the group comes from the Roman general Quintus Fabius who was known for the strategy of delaying battle until exactly what he deemed to be the perfect moment. Among the early members of the Fabian Society were the playwright, George Bernard Shaw, and, writer, H. G. Wells. The 1920s in England were a period of a changing landscape recovering from the ravages of World War I, and emerging as a nation as one increasingly eager to enter a modern world where class distinction mattered less, and everyone could partake of the opportunities once enjoyed only by the upper classes.

Ramgoolam was feasting on the ideas that he learned with the Fabian Society, as well as the other political and literary groups he had joined. He was involved in the heart

319

Ile de France, Rodrigues, and the Seychelles. The French-speaking Mauritians were allowed to retain their language. When the British freed the slaves in 1835, they fled to the cities, leaving a gap in the work force on the plantations. Workers from China and especially India were brought in to fill that gap, thus changing the face of the small colony once again, setting the stage for a gradual evolution of culture. When Mahatma Gandhi visited in 1901, he was able to support a greater voice for the Indians who were generally the lowest wage earners by that time. When Ramgoolam successfully organized his people under the banner of the Labor Party, membership increased dramatically, and the party began to grow. He had brought the ideals of his Fabian Socialists to Mauritius.

Slow and Steady

In 1953 Ramgoolam's followers took over the leadership of the Labor Party and won the elections to the Legislative Council. From 1940 until 1953, Ramgoolam had presided as Municipal Councillor, a post he held again in 1956 when he was named Deputy Mayor of Port Louis. In 1950 he rose to the mayor's position. During the time from 1948 until 1959, he also served as a member of the Legislative Council for Pamplemousse-Riviere du Rempart; and then, for Triolet, in 1959; and, for Pamplemousses Triolet from 1967 until his party was defeated, and he stepped down from the Prime Minister's office in 1982. Other government positions Ramgoolam held included that of Ministerial Secretary to the Treasury, 1958; Leader of the House, 1960 onward; Minister of Finance, 1960–68, and Chief Minister from 1961–65. When Mauritius gained independence from England in 1968, Ramgoolam was immediately elevated to the role of Prime Minister. When his party left office, he held the honored yet primarily ceremonial position of Governor General from 1983 until his death in December 1985.

During his years in public service, particularly those as Prime Minister after independence was realized, Ramgoolam created the dreams he had dreamed for his people as a young man. With the University of Mauritius, he offered universal education; he opened hospitals, created village councils; built housing for workers; and instituted old age pensions, along with family allowances, and widows' pensions and a national pension plan. Workers also began to enjoy the benefits of workers in other democratic countries from electricity in their homes to trade unions that moderated wages and employee benefits such as sick leave and holiday pay. He helped oversee the building of banks, hotels, industries, and an airport, that would come to bear his name, honoring him even in death. In an obituary of Ramgoolam for the New York Times, reporter John T. McQuiston discussed how the end of his power came to be. He noted that, "Sir Seewoosagur's difficulties with the electorate grew as the economy of Mauritius fell sharply into decline. By 1981, the buying power of the Mauritian rupee had eroded by two devaluations in two years and it became difficult to arrange commercial credit with Western banks." The support he relied on from the rural Hindi population was overwhelmed by a landslide of the left. They took every seat in Parliament. At the time,

of political life, learning the methods of Parliamentary Democracy. And all of this knowledge was being stored in his mind, as he waited patiently to begin to translate it into the freedom for his own people. When he finished his studies in 1935, he was eager to return to Mauritius. He wanted for his people all the things other free people enjoyed: decent housing, electricity, running water, and the opportunity to establish a democratic form of government so that they could exercise their power in making their own decisions. A lot of work would be necessary before his dream could be realized. In Mauritius, still under British colonial rule, wages were not equitable, there were no pensions or workers' benefits, no health care benefits, no paid leave, and no holiday pay. Until the local people had the right to vote, however, there would be no way to fight for better living conditions. With his help, the Mauritius Labor Party was founded in 1936. By the next year, even through the years of World War II, the party organized worker protests and strikes. In 1937, the right to vote was granted to those over 21 who could sign their names.

Mauritius had been under French control since 1715, five years after the Dutch, who had originally settled the island for the Netherlands and who had named it for their ruler at the time, Maurice, Prince of Orange and Count of Nassau. The Dutch left African slaves, Javan deer, wild boar, tobacco, and sugar cane on the small island. The dodo bird became extinct during their stay of little more than 100 years. Following the Battle of Vieux Grand Port, the British won over Mauritius from the French, and with the Treaty of Paris in 1814 was officially deeded ownership to the islands even the United States was concerned by the election outcome. The island of Diego Garcia, a British-owned island that was claimed by Mauritius, was home to the United States military presence there. During the campaign they had been vocal in their opposition to it.

Ramgoolam had married his wife Sushil in 1939. Their two children were Navin and Sunita. He and his wife moved into the official residence at Le Chateau de Reduit when he became Governor General. It was there that he passed away on Sunday, December 15, 1985. Thousands of mourners came to honor their fallen hero. At his death, the tiny island, which was slightly smaller than Rhode Island, was home to 850,000 people. He was cremated according to Hindi custom, and his ashes were scattered into the Ganges River in India, considered sacred by all Hindi people.

In his lifetime he was presented with many honors that included being Knighted by Queen Elizabeth in 1965. In 2000 Mauritians honored Ramgoolam with a celebration of his birth centenary. He continued to be honored on stamps in death as he had been in life, with his image on the stamp that celebrated the 30th anniversary of Mauritius Independence on March 12, 1998. In his death, as in his life, he was a national hero to his people—a man of slow and deliberate determination who spoke gently and accomplished the move of his tiny nation into the modern world.

Periodicals

Asia Africa Intelligence Wire, Financial Times Ltd., December 1, 2003; December 2, 2003.
Europe Intelligence Wire, Financial Times Ltd., October 8, 2002.
New York Times, December 17, 1985.

Online

''Birth Centenary Celebration of Sir Seewoosagur Ramgoolam,'' *SSR (Sir Seewoosagur Ramgoolam) website, http://ssr.intnet .mu* (December 15, 2003).
''How Mauritius Got a Computer Revolution,'' *allAfrica.com website,* http://allafrica.com (December 23, 2003).
''Mauritius,'' *Lonely Planet Worldguide website,* http://www .lonelyplanet.com (December 23, 2003).
''Mauritius country profile,'' *World Information website,* http://worldinformation.com (December 15, 2003).
''Mauritius Labour Party, Sir Seewoosagur Ramgoolam,'' *Mauritius Labour Party website website,* http://labour.intnet .mu (December 23, 2003).
''Sir Seewoosagur Ramgoolam: Champion of tolerance and social harmony by M. Shaffick Hamuth (London),'' *Mauritius News website,* http://www.mauritiusnews.co.uk (December 15, 2003). □

Dan Irvin Rather

American broadcast journalist Dan Rather (born 1931) is the longest-running anchor of a network news program. For most of his nearly 50 year career, he has been with the Columbia Broadcasting System (CBS), where he has earned the reputation as one of the top figures in American journalism. Since 1981,

he has been the anchor of "CBS Evening News" and has been involved with award-winning programs "60 Minutes," "60 Minutes II," and "48 Hours."

Early Life

For as far back as he could remember, Dan Rather wanted to be a journalist. That single-minded focus took him from his humble beginnings in Texas to great cities all over the world, covering the major events of the latter part of the 20th century to the early part of the new millennium. His career path took him to the top of his profession, into the most important news job of the most respected broadcast journalism organization in the country. His assignments have involved the most crucial events and issues in recent American history (the JFK assassination, the civil rights movements, Vietnam, Watergate, the World Trade Center attacks) and placed him at the hottest spots in the international arena (the Persian Gulf, Afghanistan, Israel, Beijing, Moscow). Interspersed were encounters with the famous and the infamous. He has interviewed every United States president from Dwight D. Eisenhower to Bill Clinton (George W. Bush had not granted an interview with him), and sat down one-on-one with Saddam Hussein and Yasser Arafat. He has been and remains an indefatigable journalist, working simultaneous jobs and often providing marathon coverage of dramatic events such as the 1986 space shuttle tragedy and the horrific disaster of September 11, 2001.

The future news anchor was born Dan Irvin Rather on October 31, 1931 in Wharton, Texas. He grew up with a brother and sister in a tough, working class neighborhood of Houston.

Both his parents liked to read, and they passed their appreciation of the printed word on to their son. His father, who worked as an oil pipeliner, was an avid reader of newspapers, and this especially influenced his son. "I was interested in newspapers because my father, I think, was interested in newspapers," related Rather in a 2001 interview with the Academy of Achievement.

Rather could not remember a time when he didn't want to be a reporter, specifically a newspaper reporter: " . . . at that time and place being a reporter meant being a newspaper person. Why this is I've never quite known, but as far back as I can remember in the mists of my childhood, when somebody asked me what I wanted to be, I always said, 'I want to be a reporter. I want to work for a newspaper,' " he told the Academy.

To achieve his dream, Rather worked his way through college, enrolling at the Sam Houston State Teachers College at Huntsville, Texas, where he would receive a bachelor's degree in journalism in 1953. He had hoped to fund his higher education by securing a football scholarship, but when that plan failed, he took on various jobs that included a three-year, part-time stint at KSAM, a small radio station in Huntsville (1950-53). This turned out to be the start of his broadcast journalism career. He also edited the college newspaper and worked as a reporter for Associated Press (1950) and United Press International (1950-52). After graduating, he spent a year at the college teaching journalism and served a short stint with the U.S. Marine Corps.

In 1954, after leaving the Marines, he landed a job with the *Houston Chronicle* newspaper and its radio affiliate KTRH. In 1956, he became the station's news director. In 1959, he entered television news when he became a reporter for KTRK-TV Houston. In 1961, he began his long association with the Columbia Broadcasting System (CBS) when he became news director at the company's KHOU-TV affiliate. CBS executives were impressed by his coverage of Hurricane Carla and offered him a job as a national news correspondent.

Covered the Kennedy Assassination

In 1961, Rather was appointed head of CBS' southwestern bureau and was responsible for coverage of the South, Southwest, Mexico and Central America. He held the post until CBS promoted him to White House Correspondent in 1964.

Rather earned the promotion because of the work he did in Dallas, Texas on November 22, 1963, the day that President John F. Kennedy was shot. Rather was the first on-the-scene journalist to break the news that Kennedy had died from his bullet wounds. He had to run five blocks to the local CBS affiliate to report the news by phone to CBS radio. The information was relayed to CBS anchor Walter Cronkite, who was covering the story live on the air. It was a journalistic coup for both CBS and Rather.

The round-the-clock coverage of the tragedy proved to be a milestone in broadcast journalism. It would help turn television news into the dominant information source, and Rather had played a pivotal role in this transition. While covering the assassination, he displayed a professionalism that earned him praise in the industry and a reputation as one of the media's finest journalists. In addition to his effective gathering of information, his calm and soothing demeanor helped steady a distraught nation's jangled nerves. CBS rewarded him with the plum White House assignment.

In the 1960s, Rather was on his way to becoming one of the best-known national broadcast journalists, thanks to his coverage of many of that tumultuous decade's biggest stories. Sometimes he became part of the story. In 1968, he covered the Democratic National Convention in Chicago, a turbulent political event where all conflicts and hostilities of an ideologically divided nation seemed to come to a head. Television coverage was highlighted by street riots. The nation watched live broadcasts of Chicago police savagely attacking unarmed demonstrators. Action inside the convention hall was just as riveting. At one point during the live coverage, Rather was attacked by security personnel as he tried to question a delegate who was being forcibly removed from the convention floor.

During the decade, Rather also served as the chief of the CBS London Bureau (1965-66). He returned to his position as White House correspondent in 1966 and remained there until 1974.

Covered the Nixon White House

Rather became even more famous during the early 1970s as a Washington correspondent for the "CBS Evening News with Walter Cronkite," thanks to his unflinching reports about the Richard Nixon presidency and, in particular, the Watergate break-in.

Because of his aggressiveness and effectiveness as a reporter, Rather was not well-liked in the Nixon White house. He was a controversial figure for television viewers, as well. News watchers either loved him or hated him, depending on which side of the political fence they sat. During this period, Rather made news himself thanks to an exchange he had with Nixon during a press conference at a National Association of Broadcasters convention in Houston. When Rather rose to ask a question, colleagues spontaneously reacted by either applauding or booing him. The surprising display caused Nixon to ask him, "Are you running for something?" Rather quickly replied, "No, sir, Mr. President. Are you?" Many saw that as a demonstration of inexcusable arrogance. CBS even considered firing Rather.

Rather remained on board, however, and his star continued to rise. In the mid-1970s he served as the primary anchor for the "CBS Weekend News" and, in 1975, he became correspondent and co-editor of the popular prime time news magazine show "60 Minutes." His investigative style of journalism made him a natural choice for the position, and he helped turn the program into network television's highest-rated show.

In addition, starting in 1977, he began his long-running anchor duties for "Dan Rather Reporting," for the CBS Radio Network.

His best-selling book, *The Palace Guard*, published in 1974, recounted his years covering the Nixon White House. His next book, *The Camera Never Blinks: Adventures of a TV Journalist* (1977), also was a best seller.

Succeeded Conkrite as CBS Anchor

For many years, Walter Cronkite served as the main anchor for the highly respected "CBS Evening News." When he retired in 1981, Rather was the natural choice as his replacement. It was no small responsibility. The nightly broadcast was considered the country's most important news show and Cronkite had established a reputation as "the most trusted man in America."

In 1981, Rather relinquished his position with "60 Minutes" to replace Cronkite. He made his debut on March 9, 1981 and has served as anchor and managing editor ever since. The show initially experienced a drop in ratings. But Rather immediately made an impression and established his own style with his field reporting from the war-torn Afghanistan and with the seven-hour live coverage of Egyptian President Anwar Sadat's assassination. Rather particularly shined during such marathon live coverages. His work during the five-and-a-half-hour broadcast following the explosion of the 1986 Space Shuttle Challenger was especially lauded.

But, for Rather, the 1980s were also marked by controversy and criticism. On September 11, 1987, Rather stalked off the CBS Evening News set to protest the network's decision to cut into the evening news broadcast with its continued coverage of a U.S. Open tennis match. However, the match ended sooner than expected. When the news broadcast began, only two minutes later than expected, Rather couldn't be found. His absence resulted in six minutes of "dead air." The incident was extremely embarrassing and Rather's reputation sustained some serious damage. Most hurtful of all was when Cronkite, a man that Rather greatly respected, told a reporter, "I would have fired him. There's no excuse for it."

In 1988, he was involved in an incident that drew praise from some quarters and criticism in others. During the 1980s, Rather had engaged in some hard-hitting reporting on the Iran-Contra scandal during the Reagan Administration. This led to a famous on-air confrontation in January 1988 with then-Vice President George H. W. Bush. Rather asked Bush some hard questions about contradictory statements he made about his involvement in the scandal. When Bush repeatedly stonewalled, the interview took on a highly volatile tone, with both principals becoming combative. While some praised Rather for only doing his job, others said his approach was disrespectful and inexcusable. Afterward, Bush refused to ever give Rather another interview. His son, George W. Bush, also refused to grant Rather any interviews after he became president in 2000.

In 1988, when Rather became host of another CBS news magazine show, "48 Hours," he became the first network journalist to anchor an evening news broadcast and a primetime news program at the same time.

Chronicled International Events

During the 1990s, Rather cemented his reputation as the hardest working journalist in television news by landing important exclusive interviews and traveling extensively to do field reporting of major news events. In 1990, after Iraq invaded Kuwait, which led to the Persian Gulf war, Rather was the first American journalist to secure an interview with Iraqi leader Saddam Hussein. In 1994, he traveled to Eastern Europe to report on the rise of neo-fascism in the former Soviet Bloc. Also, he went to the Middle East just before the Palestinians moved into Gaza and the West Bank and got interviews with Palestinian leader Yasser Arafat and Egyptian President Hosni Mubarak. The following year, he twice reported from the front line in Bosnia, where American peacekeeping troops were stationed. From Jerusalem, he reported on the assassination of Israeli Prime Minister Yitzhak Rabin.

This decade was not without its own controversies or criticisms, however. In 1993, CBS began an experiment with its "Evening News" broadcast, installing Connie Chung as Rather's co-anchor. Rather was reportedly unhappy with the arrangement. In 1995, CBS discontinued the experiment, and Rather, once again, was the show's only anchor.

In the late 1990s, during President Clinton's second term, critics accused Rather of being biased toward the democratic president, especially during the height of the Monica Lewinsky scandal and the investigation by independent counsel Kenneth Starr, who was appointed to investigate alleged corruption in Clinton's administration. Rather defended Clinton and criticized Starr. Critics pointed to Rather's stance as evidence of a liberal bias in the news media.

Rather's coverage of the Lewinsky scandal and the impeachment of President Clinton by the House of Representatives enabled him to score some more journalistic coups. Working as a correspondent for CBS's "60 Minutes II," which premiered in January 1999, Rather conducted an exclusive interview with President Clinton on March 31, 1999, the president's first since the Lewinsky scandal and the impeachment. Two months later, on May 26, 1999, Rather got an exclusive interview with first lady Hillary Clinton.

Into the New Century

In the early part of the 21st century, Rather's workload remained intensive. Not only did he work on three national television news programs ("CBS Evening News," "48 Hours," and "60 Minutes II"), he also wrote a nationally syndicated newspaper column and recorded the radio program, "Dan Rather Reporting."

In addition, he remained a high-profile journalist doing on-the-spot coverage of major news stories. In 2000, he covered the Russian elections in Moscow and reported on the worsening peace process in Israel.

His marathon coverage during the controversial 2000 presidential election was also praised. Anchoring CBS' "Election Night 2000," he remained on the air from 6:00 p.m. on Tuesday, Nov. 7, to 10:00 a.m. on Wednesday, Nov. 8, especially focusing on events transpiring in Florida. During the broadcast, Rather interviewed both candidates, Al Gore and George W. Bush, about the balloting controversies in Florida.

On September 11, 2001, the day of the terrorist attacks on the World Trade Center and the Pentagon, Rather once again helped steady the nerves of a distraught nation with calming and professional reportage, just as he had 30 years earlier when, as an up-and-coming journalist, he covered the Kennedy assassination. Rather was applauded for his live coverage of the attacks, as well as for his subsequent appearance on the "David Letterman Show," when he delivered an emotional recitation of "America the Beautiful."

Covering the "War on Terrorism" in 2002 and 2003, Rather traveled to Iraq, Kuwait, Afghanistan, Saudi Arabia and Israel. In February 2003, as the United States prepared to attack Iraq, Rather secured an exclusive interview with Saddam Hussein.

No Plans to Retire

In 2001, Rather signed a five-year contract with CBS that runs through 2006. As of 2004, he made no mention of retirement beyond that contract.

In all, Rather has written seven books. Other titles include *The Camera Never Blinks Twice: Further Adventures of a Television Journalist* (1991), *I Remember* (1991) and *Deadlines & Datelines*(1999). Most likely he will continue to write when he retires from broadcasting.

Rather lives in New York City with his wife, the former Jean Goebel. They have two grown children, Dawn Robin and Daniel Martin.

Online

"Dan Rather," *Info Please*, http://www.infoplease.com/ipea/ A0762055.html (January 5, 2003).

"Dan Rather," *Legendary Texans*, http://db1.ledbettersystems .com/legendary/legdetail.asp?Tex_ID=98 (January 5, 2003).

"Dan Rather," *Sciencedaily.com*, http://www.sciencedaily.com/ encyclopedia/Dan_Rather#Biography (January 5, 2003).

"Dan Rather," *TVMuseum.com*, http://www.museum.tv/ archives/etv/R/htmlR/ratherdan/ratherdan.htm (January 5, 2003).

"Dan Rather-Biography," *Academy of Achievement*, http://www .achievement.org/autodoc/page/rat0bio-1 (January 5, 2003).

"Dan Rather-Biography," *CBSNews.com*, http://www.cbsnews .com/stories/2000/04/17/48hours/main185048.shtml (January 5, 2003).

"Dan Rather-Biography," *CBSRadio.com*, http://www.cbsradio .com/features_dan_rather_bios.asp (January 5, 2003).

"Dan Rather-Interview," *Academy of Achievement*, http://www .achievement.org/autodoc/page/rat0int-1 (January 5, 2003).

"Dan Rather-Profile," *Academy of Achievement*, http://www .achievement.org/autodoc/page/rat0pro-1 (January 5, 2003).

"In JKF's death modern TV news was born," *Milwaukee Journal Sentinel*, November 23, 2003, www.azcentral.com/ arizonarepublic/arizonaliving/ articles/1121tvjfk21.html (January 5, 2003).

"That day in Dallas kicked Rather's career into high gear," *Philadelphia Inquirer*, November 19, 2003, http://www .philly.com/mld/philly/entertainment/columnists/gail_ shister/7295520.htm (January 5, 2003). □

Nancy Reagan

First Lady Nancy Reagan (born 1921) has been lauded for her elegance, grace under pressure, "Just Say No" antidrug campaign, and selfless devotion to her husband. Reagan came into the national spotlight as the wife of Ronald Reagan during his governorship of the state of California and his subsequent ascension to the presidency in 1980 and has remained in the public eye ever since. Beginning in 1994, when the former president was diagnosed with Alzheimer's disease, Reagan dedicated herself almost exclusively to her husband's care until his death in 2004.

Born Anne Frances Robbins on July 6, 1921, in New York City, Reagan was known as "Nancy" from an early age. Her mother, Edith "Lucky" Luckett, was an actress, and her father was Kenneth Robbins, scion of a well-to-do New England family that had fallen on hard times. Despite being a Princeton graduate, Robbins "wasn't very ambitious," as Reagan noted in her autobiography *My Turn*, and he earned a living working as a car salesman. The Luckett-Robbins marriage was shaky at best, and after Reagan's birth the couple separated and divorced.

Childhood Unstable until Teen Years

Now a solo parent, Luckett tried for two years to keep her daughter with her, taking the toddler from job to job and theater to theater. Within two years, however, the actress realized that the child needed a more settled environment. She sent Reagan to live with her sister, Virginia Galbraith, and her sister's husband, in Bethesda, Maryland. Although it was "a warm, stable, and happy household . . . and I was treated with great love" as Reagan later recalled, it was still "a painful period" and young Reagan missed her own mother.

In 1929 Luckett married Loyal Davis, a prominent and successful Chicago neurosurgeon. Davis adopted his wife's 16-year-old daughter, and Reagan quickly accepted him as her father. As Mrs. Davis, Luckett abandoned her peripatetic acting career after remarrying, although she continued to work in radio soap operas and maintained frequent contact with her many theater friends. Spencer Tracy, Mary Martin, and Walter Huston, who were frequent guests at the Davis home, proved to be invaluable to Reagan later in her career, and also became lifelong friends.

Reagan was fascinated by her mother's profession from a very early age. "I loved to dress up in her stage clothes, put on makeup, and pretend I was playing her parts," she wrote in her memoir. "I can't remember a time when I wasn't interested in the theater, and in school my main interest was drama. . . . I acted in all the school plays." As a student at Massachusetts' Smith College, she majored in English and theater; she not only acted in several campus plays, but spent her summers as a summer-stock apprentice.

As Nancy Davis, Reagan earned her first professional role in a touring production of *Ramshackle Inn*. She joined the cast in Detroit and traveled with them until the show came to New York, where she decided to remain. A few months later she landed a role in *Lute Song*, starring Yul Brynner and family friend Mary Martin, which would be her only Broadway appearance. Reagan got a few bit parts in theater and on television before going under contract to Metro-Goldwyn-Mayer in 1949. This same year she met Ronald Reagan, a Warner Brothers actor and president of the Screen Actors Guild, the man who would become her future husband.

Met Ronald Reagan

The couple's first meeting came about during the filming of *East Side, West Side,* when Nancy found her name published on a newspaper list of purported communist sympathizers. "In those days I didn't know much about politics, but I knew that my name did not belong on that list," she recalled in her memoir. So she consulted the

politically active Reagan to discuss how best to counter the accusation. Reagan, who had married his first wife, actress Jane Wyman, in 1940 was by now divorced, met Nancy for dinner. "I don't know if it was exactly love at first sight," Reagan later recalled, "but it was pretty close.

Nancy Reagan made 12 films in all but ended her acting career shortly after marriage. The Reagans were married, without family present, on March 4, 1952, and their first child, Patti, was born that October. Although Reagan had decided not to work after becoming a mother, her husband's career had stalled and they needed an income. She made her four last films between 1953 and 1958, among them *Hellcats of the Navy,* a 1957 film that features Nancy and Ronald Reagan as costars. After their second child, Ronald, Junior, was born in 1958, Reagan retired from the movies for good.

In 1954 Ronald Reagan became the host of television's *General Electric Theatre,* a position he held until 1962. His passion for politics, always evident, was increasingly becoming the focus of his attention and his aspiration to hold public office was apparent. He made his political debut in a 1964 fund-raising speech for the presidential campaign of Senator Barry Goldwater; it raised over a million dollars for the Republican Party and put Ronald Reagan at the forefront of the conservative movement. After he announced his candidacy for the California governorship in 1966, he left his role as host of television's popular *Death Valley Days,* after joining the series in 1964.

Propelled into Role of First Lady

When Ronald Reagan was elected governor of California in 1966, he and his family moved to Sacramento. Unfortunately, the governor's mansion made his wife shudder: "that house was so depressing that I just couldn't stand the thought of living there," she recalled in *My Turn.* "It was a tinderbox," Reagan added, "its wooden frame eaten through by dry rot." The Reagans chose instead to lease a house in the suburbs from friends, hoping for a home where their children could have a more normal childhood. This choice, unfortunately, was not positive in terms of Reagan's public image. A *People* contributor noted that the decision made Nancy seem "imperious" to many.

In her role as First Lady of California, Reagan helped oversee the construction of a new governor's mansion, one that would be occupied by their successors. To furnish it, she collected donated furniture and household items. Although she never used the donated furniture, which was placed in storage until construction was complete, Reagan was accused by members of the California state legislature of acquiring items for her own use. "I got so mad that I decided to hold my first press conference," Reagan explained in her memoir. "I answered all questions about the donated furniture . . . anything anyone wanted to ask." Reagan would face similar charges as first lady nearly 20 years later.

Less controversially, Reagan also became involved with Foster Grandparents, a program started by Kennedy brother-in-law and Peace Corps founding director Sargent Shriver. Her efforts helped bring Foster Grandparents branches to all California state hospitals, and the organization went on to take root in other states as well. She also worked with veterans organizations and prisoners of war (POW's), a sensitive topic during the Vietnam era. She organized four state dinners for returning California POW's, calling them "the high point of Ronnie's administration." In 1982 Reagan wrote about the program in *To Love a Child,* a book coauthored with Jane Wilkie; all proceeds were donated to the Foster Grandparents organization.

Life in the Political Fishbowl

As first lady of California, Reagan got her first taste of life in the fishbowl of American politics, even receiving death threats. Although she had realized life would change when the family moved to Sacramento, she could not have imagined the degree to which both she and her husband would come under scrutiny, both by the press corps and by political opponents. Reagan's sensitivity to criticism was already high, and it only increased during her years as a public person.

After Ronald Reagan won the presidency in 1981, the glare of public scrutiny fell on his wife even more heavily. As she noted in her autobiography, "Virtually everything I did during that first year was misunderstood and ridiculed. . . . While I loved being first lady, my eight years with that title were the most difficult years of my life."

When the Reagans moved in to the White House, Reagan found that, while not a firetrap like the California governor's mansion, the presidential residence was also in dire need of repair and renovation: "Some of the bedrooms on the third floor hadn't been painted in fifteen or twenty years!" she recalled in *My Turn.* "The floors hadn't been touched in ages. There were cracks in the walls. The long, wide Center Hall, which runs the entire length of the second floor, was virtually empty."

Reagan and her husband raised private funds to accomplish the needed restoration while declining the $50,000 usually offered by Congress for this purpose. Unfortunately, Reagan wrote, the press "made it look as if the donors were some kind of exclusive, wealthy club, and it wasn't that way at all." The renovations at 1600 Pennsylvania Avenue were just the tip of the iceberg, however. A flap over Reagan's negotiated donation of new china for state dinners—"a symbol of my supposed extravagance," she wrote—was soon overshadowed by criticism over her growing collection of designer gowns, most of which were donated by couturiers. More serious still was the accusation, made by ousted Presidential chief-of-staff Don Regan, that the first lady frequently consulted an astrologer and organized the president's schedule according to his horoscope. In an interview with *Time* magazine, Regan charged that Reagan's meddling "began to interfere with the normal conduct of the presidency." In *My Turn* the former first lady admitted that she had become increasingly reliant on astrological predictions following an attempt on her husband's life in 1981 during which a bullet missed President Reagan's heart by only inches. In her own defense Reagan explained that she influenced the timing of Reagan's schedule, but never his policies. "I knew it might not be the smartest thing to do,

but given my temperament, it was a lot better than just sitting there. If I hadn't taken every step I could think of to protect my husband . . . I would never have been able to forgive myself."

Advocate of Drug Prohibition

As first lady, Reagan sponsored the "Just Say No" crusade against drug abuse, a problem about which she became deeply aware during her husband's first presidential campaign, when she visited the Daytop Village treatment center in New York. During her eight years in the White House, Reagan visited over 60 cities in 33 states, as well as nine foreign countries as part of the "Just Say No" campaign. She made television, radio, and personal appearances and urged parents to become aware of the stresses that lead children to drugs. In 1985 Reagan held a conference at the White House to focus international attention on the problem: First ladies from 17 nations attended.

A popular president, Ronald Reagan easily won reelection in 1984, and by the end of his second term his wife had become inured to the slings and arrows hurled by press and public. "No matter what I said or did, the stories never stopped," she recalled, going on to add: "Over eight years, I never stopped being hurt, although eventually I stopped being very surprised." Public sympathy turned wholly in her favor in October of 1987, when the 66-year-old first lady learned she had breast cancer. Fortunately, Reagan's surgery was successful, and her ordeal raised awareness of the disease for many American women. "The important thing is that every woman should have an annual mammogram," Reagan wrote in *My Turn.* That's the message I want to get out." Tragically, during the same month she was battling cancer, Reagan's mother passed away.

Continued Dedication to Husband

By the end of 1989, as President Reagan prepared to leave office, the Reagans planned to move into a new home outside Los Angeles, California. There the first lady hoped to enjoy retirement, away from public scrutiny and surrounded by family and friends. However, crises continued to erupt. The home they planned to move into was purchased for them, causing a *Time* reporter to quip that "the President and the First Lady have a history of accepting such benefits." Meanwhile, Reagan's habit of "borrowing" designer clothes came under renewed scrutiny when the Internal Revenue Service concluded that $3 million in clothing acquired during her husband's presidency had not been reported as income.

In 1994 Ronald Reagan disclosed to the American public that he had been diagnosed with Alzheimer's disease, a progressive condition that would result in continuing mental and physical deterioration and for which there was no known cure. As his condition worsened, his wife took upon herself the increasing attention to his care, rarely leaving his side. In 1989 she had published *My Turn: The Memoirs of Nancy Reagan, with William Novak* following up an earlier biography, *Nancy,* published in 1980 and cowritten with professional biographer Bill Libby. In 2000 Reagan compiled *I Love You, Ronnie: The Letters of Ronald*

Reagan to Nancy Reagan, a testament to the affection she continued to hold for her husband of many years.

In 2002 Nancy and Ronald Reagan were awarded the Congressional Gold Medal in recognition of their service to the United States. This joint honor was deserved by the former first lady, noted longtime Reagan aide Martin Anderson in congressional testimony transcribed and posted on *NewsMax.com,* because Nancy Reagan was President Reagan's "trusted counselor, someone with superb judgment on policy and people, a rock of support, a loving wife. She was by his side—on the plane and in the hotel rooms on the campaign trail and every single day in the White House." Reagan was awarded the Presidential Medal of Freedom in July of that year by President George W. Bush. The award was given, according to the *White House Web site,* for her devotion "to her family and her country."

In 2003 controversy arose surrounding a miniseries CBS had planned on airing about the Reagans. Conservatives started a boycott of the miniseries claiming it was biased and untruthful. CBS canceled the airing of the miniseries and gave the series to Showtime. CBS claimed that the decision was not based on the controversy about the series, but that it was not happy with the final product.

In 2004 Reagan was honored with a tribute from the Juvenile Diabetes Research Foundation (JDFR) for her endorsement of stem cell research. Reagan believes such research could provide a cure for diseases such as Alzheimer's.

On June 5, 2004, at the age of 93 Ronald Reagan lost his battle with Alzheimer's. He died that afternoon in his Bel Air home in Los Angeles, California, surrounded by Nancy and their two children. Six days of national mourning ensued. Reagan was hailed for her fierce dedication to her husband throughout their life together and, in particular, for her unfaltering devotion to his care during the decade he suffered with Alzheimer's.

Books

Kelley, Kitty, *Nancy Reagan: The Unauthorized Biography,* Simon & Schuster, 1991.

Reagan, Nancy, *I Love You, Ronnie: The Letters of Ronald Reagan to Nancy Reagan,* Random House, 2000.

Reagan, Nancy, and Julia Wilkie, *To Love a Child,* G. K. Hall, 1982.

Reagan, Nancy, and William Novak, *My Turn: The Memoirs of Nancy Reagan,* Random House, 1989.

Periodicals

America's Intelligence Wire, May 9, 2004.
Knight Ridder/Tribune News Service, November 4, 2003.
People, March 13, 2000, June 28, 2004.
PR Newswire, May 9, 2004.
Time, January 14, 1985; April 11, May 16, 1988.

Online

"Award Ronald and Nancy Reagan the Congressional Gold Medal," http://www.newsmax.com/articles/?a = 2000/3/29/220153 (January 12, 2004).

"Bush calls national day of mourning," http://www.cnn.com/2004/ALLPOLITICS/06/06/reagan.main2/index.html (June 11, 2004).

"Nancy Reagan revisits Rotunda," http://www.cnn.com/2004/ALLPOLITICS/06/11/reagan.friday/index.html (June 11, 2004).

"National Cathedral prepares to host state funeral," http://www.cnn.com/2004/US/06/10/national.cathedral/index.html (June 11, 2004).

"President Honors Recipients of the Presidential Medal of Freedom," http://www.whitehouse.gov/news/releases/2002/07/20020709-8.html (January 12, 2004).

"Washington awaits," http://www.cnn.com/2004/ALLPOLITICS/06/09/wed/index.html (June 11, 2004). □

Michael Redgrave

English actor Michael Redgrave (1908-1985), a tall man with an aristocratic bearing, became a major force in British stage and screen during the mid-twentieth century. Part of the generation of classically trained actors that included Laurence Olivier, Peggy Ashcroft, Ralph Richardson and John Gielgud, Redgrave appeared in numerous films, including *Goodbye Mr. Chips, Nicholas and Alexandra* and the first film adaptation of Oscar Wilde's *The Importance of Being Earnest.*

Considered one of the foremost British actors of his generation, Michael Redgrave performed in 35 motion pictures over his long career, although he far preferred the many hours he spent performing in front of a live audience on the London stage. Paired with such noted film directors as Alfred Hitchcock, Fritz Lang, Carol Reed and Anthony Asquith, Redgrave gained particular renown for his performance in films adapted from classic plays and literature, among them *The Importance of Being Earnest* and *The Innocents,* the latter an adaptation of American novelist Henry James's *The Turn of the Screw.* Redgrave was the consummate "actor's actor"; as Nigel Warrington described him in *Theatre Research International,* he was "passionate, literate, industrious, humorous and a model of professional ethics."

A Well-studied Thespian

Michael Scudamore Redgrave was born on March 20, 1908, in Bristol, Gloucestershire, England, the son of George Ellsworth and Margaret (Scudamore) Redgrave. Redgrave's parents were both actors, his father a well-known Australian silent-film star who worked under the name Roy Redgrave.

A bright child, Redgrave seemed at first destined for life as an academic. Attending Clifton College until 1927, he then enrolled at Magdalene College, Cambridge, where he distinguished himself among his classmates as a poet, editor of the school magazine *Venture* and contributor of film reviews to the literary magazine *Granta.*

Having a vague idea of one day becoming a writer, after graduating in 1932 he decided to take the prescribed next step for someone who was not independently wealthy. In 1934 the 25-year-old Cambridge University graduate got a job as a modern-language teacher at England's Cranleigh School. Having been active in theatre as an undergraduate student—he directed a production of *The Battle of the Book* in 1930—Redgrave quickly gravitated to Cranleigh's theatre program.

Inspired to return to his acting roots when his work with young thespians won him praise, Redgrave left Cranleigh and entered the theatre in the mid-1930. He made his stage debut in 1934 in the Liverpool Playhouse production of *Counsellor-at-Law,* and for the next two years he performed, under William Armstrong's direction, in repertory.

He soon came to the attention of noted stage director Tyrone Guthrie, who saw promise in the young man's talent, height and aristocratic bearing. Guthrie asked Redgrave to perform with England's legendary Old Vic company. Jumping at the chance to work with such noted performers as Edith Evans, Olivier, Ashcroft and others, Redgrave moved to London in 1936. At the Old Vic he was soon cast in major roles in various Shakespeare productions, among them *Hamlet.* In 1937 Redgrave moved to the Queen's Theatre, working with Gielgud's repertory company.

In 1938 Redgrave left Gielgud to work with an up-and-coming film director he admired and wound up capturing the heart of film audiences with his role as an eccentric music scholar in Alfred Hitchcock's witty comedy-thriller

The Lady Vanishes. From then on, films would often take precedence over his passion for the stage, even though he professed a certain highbrow disdain for movies throughout his career.

With his work for Hitchcock critically hailed, Redgrave found no trouble tracking down other film roles. Working under British director Carol Reed, he appeared in the 1939 films *Climbing High* and *The Stars Look Down.* He followed these up with the title role in *Kipps,* released in 1941, and as Captain Karel Hasek in the 1946 drama *The Captive Heart,* one of several war-related films Redgrave made after finishing a two-year stint in the Royal Navy during World War II. In 1947 he earned an Academy Award nomination for his performance, opposite American actress Rosalind Russell, in the role of Orin Mannon in the film version of Eugene O'Neill's *Mourning Becomes Electra.*

Brief Tour in Hollywood

By now a well-known matinee idol, Redgrave was tempted by Hollywood, but after arriving in 1947 to work on *Electra* with director Dudley Nichols, he was less than impressed. He remained for only a few more months, completing work with transplanted German director Fritz Lang on the 1948 drama *Secret beyond the Door,* then returned to London.

The early 1950s provided Redgrave with several opportunities to showcase his skills as a comic actor in films. He impressed audiences and critics alike in his portrayal of a repressed schoolteacher in the award-winning film *The Browning Version,* released in 1951. In the part of Jack Worthington (a.k.a. Ernest Worthing) in Anthony Asquith's 1952 film version of Oscar Wilde's classic play *The Importance of Being Earnest,* he demonstrated keen comic timing while starring opposite Joan Greenwood and the indomitable Dame Edith Evans.

While continuing to seek out roles that challenged his natural abilities, Redgrave was a serious student of the craft of acting. He paid special attention to those performers he revered and was known to devote long hours to rehearsing his roles, whether for stage or screen. In addition, he was an adherent of Konstantin Stanislavsky's classic method book *An Actor Prepares.* Though Redgrave stood six feet three inches and was muscular, he often used his gait, stance and body language to depict bookish, ineffectual and vulnerable character types—a testament to his acting ability.

Classified, alongside Olivier and Gielgud, as a "cerebral" actor, Redgrave was often assigned the role of reserved, preoccupied upper-class gentleman, and he performed such roles to critical acclaim in films like *The Browning Version* and *The Loneliness of the Long-Distance Runner,* which was released in 1962. Commenting on the actor's "quite palpable sense of discomfort," a contributor to the *International Dictionary of Films and Filmmakers* added that "few manage better to convey the anguish engendered by having strong feelings but being denied the outlet to express them than Redgrave. . .''

In addition to portraying a brand of constrained nobility, Redgrave was no stranger to more over-the-top performances, as in his role as a lighthouse keeper in the 1942 film *Thunder Rock* and in the highly praised 1945 thriller *Dead of Night,* wherein he took on the role of a ventriloquist driven mad by his sinister dummy. Also noteworthy was his depiction of the cruel and exploitative inquisitor in the 1956 film adaptation of George Orwell's novel *1984,* and the reserved Redgrave seemed frighteningly believable as an alcoholic father in *Time without Pity,* released that same year.

Love of the Stage

Like many of his peers, Redgrave was most at home on the stage and viewed work in films as a necessary but less pleasant part of being an actor. Even in films, he preferred taking on roles derived from plays, such as King Lear, Hamlet and characters created by Anton Chekhov and Eugene O'Neill. In 1948 he made his first Broadway appearance, playing Macbeth.

It came as a surprise to many when he returned full time to the British stage the following year at the urging of director Hugh Hunt. Beginning with the role of Young Marlow in Hunt's 1949 production of *She Stoops to Conquer,* Redgrave went on to perform the lead role in *Hamlet* the following year. His position on the London stage assured, he continued to appear in acclaimed National Theatre productions and was highly praised for his interpretation of leading figures in Shakespearean tragedies—including Prospero, Richard II, King Lear, Shylock and Antony—and for his performances in leading roles in Chekov's *Uncle Vanya* and Heinrich Ibsen's *The Master Builder.*

One of his finest hours on stage came in 1962, in a production of *Uncle Vanya;* his performance in the lead was so impressive that his friend Olivier insisted on immediately directing Redgrave in a film version of the play. The following year Redgrave appeared as Claudius in the National Theatre's first production of *Hamlet,* performing alongside his 20-year-old daughter, Lynn, in her role as a lady in waiting.

Although he was known to the general public predominately as an actor, Redgrave also produced and directed numerous plays. During World War II he staged six plays in London's popular West End and continued to direct sporadically during the next few decades. In 1951 he brought to the Shakespeare Memorial Theatre at Stratford-upon-Avon a production of *Henry IV, Part II.* Later in his career Redgrave also produced and directed operas, music being one of his many interests. He even wrote and published several plays of his own, including 1936's *The Seventh Man* and 1959's *The Aspern Papers,* the latter an adaptation of a story by Henry James that Redgrave produced and starred in on the London stage.

Redgrave Dynasty

Himself the son of actors, Redgrave passed his parent's thespian leanings on. Married to Liverpool Playhouse colleague actress Rachel Kempson in 1935, he fathered three children, Vanessa, Corin and Lynn Redgrave, and all became actors—although Corin Redgrave eventually also pursued a political career. Among Redgrave's grandchild-

ren, Natasha and Joely Richardson, daughters of Vanessa and husband, director Tony Richardson, both established careers as successful actors, as did Jemma Redgrave, daughter of Corin and former wife Deirdre Hamilton-Hill. Another grandson, film director Carlo Gabriel Nero, is the son of Vanessa and *Camelot* costar Franco Nero.

During the peak of his career audiences would not have accepted Redgrave's homsexuality, and it was not acknowledged until Corin Redgrave revealed it in his lovingly penned memoir *Michael Redgrave: My Father.*

Made a Companion of the British Empire in 1952, Redgrave was knighted by Queen Elizabeth II in 1959 for his services to British theater. In addition to his plays, he wrote several books, including the 1959 novel *The Mountebank Tale* and two autobiographies: 1958's *Face or Mask: Reflections in an Actor's Mirror* and 1983's *In My Mind's I: An Actor's Autobiography.* His acting guide, *The Actor's Ways and Means,* collects the lectures Redgrave gave at Bristol University in the early 1950s; it has been praised as a classic introduction to stage acting since its publication in 1953 and was reprinted in a new addition in 1995, with a new introduction by Vanessa Redgrave.

A true professional, Redgrave continued to work into his sixties, acting in films such as *Goodbye, Mr. Chips* (1969) and *Nicholas and Alexandra* (1971). During the early 1970s he was diagnosed with Parkinson's disease, a degenerative illness that made acting increasingly difficult. Redgrave's final film appearance was in a 1976 made-for-television dramatization of Samuel Taylor Coleridge's epic *The Rime of the Ancient Mariner.* His final stage appearance came three years later, when he played a stroke victim in Simon Gray's *The Close of the Play.* By then confined to a wheelchair and finding it almost impossible to memorize sentences of more than a few words in length, the legendary actor had only one line, but his presence on stage was enough. He died six years later, at the age of 77, on March 21, 1985, in Denham, England.

Books

International Dictionary of Film and Filmmakers, Volume 3: *Actors and Actresses,* St. James Press, 1996.

International Dictionary of Theatre, Volume 3: *Actors, Directors, and Designers,* St. James Press, 1996.

Kempson, Rachel, *A Family and Its Fortunes,* 1986.

Redgrave, Corin, *Michale Redgrave: My Father,* Trafalgar Square, 1996.

Redgrave, Michael, *Mask or Face: Reflections in an Actor's Mirror,* Viking, 1958.

Redgrave, Michael, *In My Mind's I: An Actor's Autobiography,* Viking, 1983.

Periodicals

Films and Filming, January-March 1955; December 1955.

Theatre Research International, autumn 1995. □

Ilya Efimovich Repin

The greatest Russian painter of the nineteenth century and the pre-Revolution years, Ilya Repin (1844-1930) painted religious allegories, scenes of searing realism, and portraits of the Russian intelligentsia of the period. Widely admired in his time, Repin's work continued to captivate viewers in the twenty-first century.

Ilya Efimovich Repin was born on July 24, 1844 (August 5, New Style) in the village of Chuguiev, about 45 miles southeast of Kharkov, the second largest city (after Kiev) in Ukraine. Repin's father belonged to the lowly class of peasants known as "military settlers," thus Repin himself was registered as such upon his birth. Since Repin's father, Efim Vasileyvich, did not retire from the army until the early 1850s, Repin's mother, Tatiana Stepanovna, was responsible for Repin's education and that of his older sister, his younger brothers, and some neighborhood children. Tragedy was never far from Repin's family: his sister and one of his brothers died at ages 15 and 10, respectively. On the other hand, Repin's other brother, Vasily, became a respected flutist in St. Petersburg.

In 1855 Repin entered the School of Military Topography in Chuguiev. He had already exhibited artistic talent in painting, drawing and sculpting, and had in fact sold deco-

rated Easter eggs for one and a half rubles to a local merchant. Here he learned drafting and coloring. After the school closed down in 1857 Repin went to study with a local icon painter, Ivan Bunakov. Repin proved such an adept icon painter that he left Bunakov in 1859 to strike out on his own. Repin was able to do this because he had never been Bunakov's apprentice and by age 15 he was already something of a master. Over the next four years Repin accepted commissions from various provincial churches to paint icons and other decorative work. During this time he also painted a self-portrait and portraits of his relatives.

Traveled to St. Petersburg

By 1863 Repin had earned enough money to move to St. Petersburg. That same year he enrolled in the Drawing School for the Society of the Encouragement of Artists so as to meet the requirements of the Imperial Academy of Arts. In January 1864 he passed the drawing examination and began auditing lectures at the Academy while he still attended the Drawing School. Repin was soon befriended by his drawing teacher, Ivan Kramskoi, who was to play a role in shaping Repin's early artistic views. Kramskoi was the founder of Artel, an association of artists that Repin regularly attended. In addition, Repin often sought Kramskoi's advice and approval.

By early September 1864 Repin had passed his general examinations for the Imperial Academy and began matriculating there as a student. In May 1865 the academic council awarded the Minor Silver Medal to Repin. This was the first step in a series that culminated in the Major Gold Medal, which included a stipend to study abroad. The Minor Silver Medal, however, bestowed on Repin the title of "free artist." In November 1865 Repin's work was displayed for the first time at the Imperial Academy of the Arts' annual exhibition: a portrait of a woman and the oil painting *Preparing for Examinations.* Repin's next prize, the Major Silver Medal, came in December 1867. In 1869 Repin was awarded the Minor Gold Medal for *Job and His Friends.*

In 1870 Repin, along with his brother Vasily and some friends, spent three months in the Volga River region. Out of this vacation came one of Repin's greatest works, *Barge Haulers on the Volga,* for which he made studies by the town of Shariayev Buyerak, near Stavropol. By March 1871 Repin submitted a preliminary sketch of "Barge Haulers" to the annual competition of the Society for the Support of Artists. The sketch won first prize. The finished canvas was exhibited in 1873 at the Imperial Academy's exhibition of works to represent Russia at the Vienna International Exhibit. That "Barge Haulers" was chosen as a representative painting was in itself a major accomplishment, because at that time Realism was considered a secondary genre in Russian art. While the conservatives in the Russian art and literary world assailed the painting—though Dostoevsky praised it—it nevertheless gained Repin valued publicity. He would later come to view *Barge Haulers on the Volga* as his first professional painting. It remained one of his greatest.

By the time he exhibited *Barge Haulers on the Volga* Repin had already received the Major Gold Medal, in November 1871, for his painting, *Christ Raising Jarius' Daughter.* In February 1872 Repin married 17-year-old Vera Shevtsova. That spring he and his wife traveled to Moscow.

Sojourn in Paris

Following the initial showing of *Barge Haulers on the Volga* at the Imperial Academy Repin was given a travel scholarship, and he used it to take his family first to Vienna to see the International Exhibition, where "Barge Haulers" was awarded a bronze medal, then on to Rome and Naples. Repin stayed in Italy from June to September 1873. In October 1873 he went to Paris, where he rented a studio in Montmartre. Repin spent nearly three years in Paris, and probably the most important person he met during his time abroad was the Russian millionaire art patron Savva Mamontov. At this time however Mamontov had not yet set up his artists' colony in the Moscow suburb of Abramtsevo.

Meanwhile back in St. Petersburg Repin caused a stir when he exhibited his work at an exhibition of the Society for Traveling Art Exhibitions in January 1874. Being on a travel scholarship, he was forbidden to exhibit in any but Academy-organized shows. Nevertheless, his scholarship was not revoked. In Paris he worked on *Sadko in the Underwater Kingdom,* which he began in 1873 and did not compete until 1876. He exhibited *A Paris Café* at the Salon. He also painted writer Ivan Turgenev's portrait as well as those of others. His immediate circle of Russian expatriates at this time included Turgenev, Alexei Tolstoy, Vasily Polenov, Konstantin Savitsky, and Valentina Serova. His French acquaintances included Camille Saint-Saëns and Emile Zola.

Repin returned to St. Petersburg in July 1876. He completed *Sadko in the Underwater Kingdom,* and in November 1876 was awarded the title of Academician for the painting. In 1878 Repin joined the Society for Traveling Art Exhibitions, with whom he displayed his work that March. At the end of the year he began work on *Tsarevna Sophia in the New Maiden Convent at the Time of the Execution of the Streltsi and the Torture of All Her Servants in 1698.* The painting was displayed, along with a second portrait of Turgenev, in February 1879. At the time Kramskoi called it Repin's second most important work after "Barge Haulers." Repin spent the summer of 1879 at Mamentov's estate, Abramtsevo. There he painted landscapes and drew portraits of Mamentov, his family, and their guests. Repin also painted scenes of peasant life including *The Peasant with the Evil Eye* and *The Timid Peasant* (both 1877), and *Seeing Off the Recruit* (1879). From September 1877 until September 1882 Repin lived and worked primarily in Moscow or its suburb of Abramtsevo.

A Darling of the Intelligentsia

The 1880s was an explosive decade for Russian art. Art criticism was coming into its own, as more journals were published, by the end of the decade Fëdor Bulgakov had published the first reference work on modern Russian painters, *Our Artists.* All of this contributed to a wider appreciation in Russia. This was also the period when Repin gained fame beyond the Imperial Academy, when he was accepted by the intelligentsia (the class of intellectuals and

artists) and others. In 1880, as if to signal this sea of change, no less a personage than Lev Tolstoy visited Repin at his studio. It was also the year Repin began work on *Zaporozhe Cossacks Writing a Mocking Letter to the Turkish Sultan,* though it would be many years before he completed this masterpiece.

In 1881, the same year that Tsar Alexander II was assassinated, Repin painted composer Modest Mussorgsky's portrait while the latter was at the Nikolaevsky Hospital. Later that year Repin began making studies for *Religious Procession in the Province of Kursk,* which he displayed in 1882 in St. Petersburg. Early in 1882, before returning with his family to St. Petersburg, Repin painted a portrait of poet Afanasy Fet.

Repin made another trip to Western Europe-Germany, the Netherlands, France, Spain, and Italy-in the spring of 1883 where he was struck by the paintings of Velázquez and Titian, but unimpressed by the Rembrandts he saw. He returned to Italy in 1887. His most important work of this period was *Ivan the Terrible and His Son, Ivan. 16 November 1581,* displayed in March 1885. After the family's return to St. Petersburg from Moscow, Repin's already tenuous marriage (strained by his infidelity) fell apart completely. Repin and his wife were separated in 1884, though a brief reconciliation was effected in the 1890s.

In March 1891 Repin resigned from the Society for Traveling Art Exhibitions because of the Society's new policy that restricted young artists from joining. The following month he finished a portrait of the Italian actress Eleonora Duse. In the summer he returned to Moscow and Abramtsevo and later visited Tolstoy at his estate, Yasnaya Poliana. In November 1891, 298 of his works were shown in a dual exhibition with Ivan Shishkin. Among Repin's paintings was the finally completed *Zaporozhe Cossacks Writing a Mocking Letter to the Turkish Sultan.* In 1892 a one-man show of his work was exhibited at Moscow's History Museum. In 1894 Repin was appointed an instructor at the Higher Art School, which was attached to the Imperial Academy.

In February 1896 Repin was back in Moscow for the coronation of Nicholas II; he did two compositions for the *Coronation Album.* In August 1896 he exhibited *St. Nicholas of Myra Delivers the Three Innocent Men* at the All-Russian Exhibition at Nizhny-Novgorod. In February 1897 Repin rejoined the Society for Traveling Art Exhibitions. That same month Tolstoy visited his studio again; Repin repaid the visit the following January.

In May 1899 Repin bought an estate at Kuokkala, near St. Petersburg. Repin named the estate Penaty after the Roman household gods, the Penates. At this time Repin's companion was Natalia Borisovna Nordman (1863-1914), who was thought to have exerted a malignant influence over his aesthetic views. At any rate Repin divided his time between Penaty and St. Petersburg, and after he resigned from the Academy in 1907 lived full time at Penaty until his death. Late in 1899 Repin met writer Maxim Gorky (original name Alexei Peshkov), in December 1899. He later illustrated Gorky's *The Notch* as well as Anton Chekhov's *The Peasants.*

Later Years

At this time accolades, both foreign and domestic, were bestowed on Repin. In January 1901 he received the Legion of Honor from France and in 1902 he was elected a member of the Academy of Sciences, Literature, and Fine Arts in Prague. In 1904 Repin was elected an honorary member of the Moscow Literary and Artistic Society. In November 1905, perhaps moved by the political events of that year, Repin resigned from the Imperial Academy of Arts, but he had second thoughts in 1906 and was again teaching a class at the Academy. He resigned for good in September 1907. One effect of resigning from the Academy was that Repin had more time to devote not only to his painting but to writing. In 1909 he wrote an article commemorating the 100th anniversary of the writer Nikolai Gogol. In 1910 Repin wrote two articles–"The Izdebsky Salon" and "In the Caves of the Python"–that were highly critical of modern art. After the death of Nordman, however, Repin softened his stance on modern art. In 1912 Repin turned down the first prize and accompanying medal awarded by the Kuinji Society for *Pushkin on the Lyceum Speech Day, 8 January 1815* because he no longer believed creative work should be judged in terms of prizes.

Repin spent the years of the First World War and the Russian Revolution, 1914 to 1918 at Penaty. A few months prior to the war's outbreak he was visited by opera singer Fëdor Chaliapin and painted his portrait. In 1916 Repin published his memoirs, *Far and Near*. He also painted Gorky's portrait. In 1917 the region where Penaty was located, known as Karelia, became part of Finland and for the rest of his life Repin lived in a "foreign" country. (In 1940, after a brief war, the region reverted to the USSR.) Since the border between Finland and the USSR was closed in 1918, during the Russian Civil War, Repin never returned to Russia, though in his last years Repin maintained close ties with the Finnish artistic community. He donated his collection of Russian paintings to the Ateneumin taidemuseo in Helsinki and even painted artist Axel Gallen-Kallela's portrait. In 1921 he painted his last major work, *Golgotha* (also known as "Cavalry"), though he continued to paint until the end of his life, including a self-portrait. In the 1920s his name and reputation became embroiled in the culture war then raging between the Futurists and those who advocated an aesthetic that eventually became Socialist Realism. Many advocates of the latter movement came to view Repin's work as its precursor. Despite that, the Soviet government never bestowed on him the title of "People's Artist." Ilya Repin died on September 29, 1930 and was buried at the Penaty.

Books

Great Soviet Encyclopedia, trans. of Third Ed., Macmillan, 1979.
Karpenko, Maria, et al., *Ilya Repin,* trans. by Sheila Marnie and Helen Clier, Aurora Art Publishers, 1985.
Valkenier, Elizabeth Kridl, *Ilya Repin and the World of Russian Art,* Columbia University Press, 1990. □

Ralph Richardson

Sir Ralph Richardson (1902–1983) belonged to a small, select cadre of British actors who dominated the profession in their day, and were honored as living legends before their passing. Along with Sir John Gielgud and Lord Olivier, Richardson appeared in dozens of London stage plays, and like his compatriots made the transition to film during the 1940s and '50s. His *Times* of London obituary termed him "the most human of all our great actors. With his ripe face and his excitable voice, his amiable combination of eccentricity and down-to-earth common sense, he was ideally equipped to make an ordinary character seem extraordinary or an extraordinary one seem ordinary."

Lived in Railroad Car

Richardson was born December 19, 1902, in Cheltenham, Gloucestershire, England, and endured hardship and privation as a child as a result of his parents' marital discord. His father, a Quaker, was an art teacher, but Lydia Richardson, a Roman Catholic, left her husband and took her four-year-old son to live in a series of small towns in the south of England. At one point their address was a modest home built from two converted railroad carriages. Richardson was often left alone. "I did a lot of play-acting for my own amusement," *New York Times* obituary writer Albin Krebs quoted him as saying, "dressing up as something or other. Put in a lot of falling dead and rolling over. It was useful practice."

Raised a Roman Catholic, Richardson considered becoming a priest, and was even sent to Jesuit seminary for a time in preparation for his vocation. He chafed at its rules, however, and ran away. He found a job as a low-level assistant at an insurance office in Brighton, and then took art courses at nearby Xaverian College. Brighton was also home to a stage company that used a former bacon factory as its headquarters, and the idea of being on stage seemed appealing to Richardson. He auditioned, but it went so terribly that the company agreed to accept the 18-year-old only if he paid a fee. Put in charge of the sound props for his first job, he had a disastrous debut with the company when he mistook a cue and banged two garbage-can lids together off-stage at the wrong part of the performance.

Made Film Debut with Karloff

Within a year, however, Richardson had graduated from walk-ons to small speaking parts to the lead roles, and soon went on to tour England and Ireland with a Shakespearean repertory company. By 1925, he was married to a fellow thespian, Muriel Hewitt, and joined the respected Birmingham Repertory Theater. He made his London stage debut the following year in *Yellow Sands* at the Haymarket

restoration efforts for the Old Vic Theater, which was badly damaged by German bombing raids on London during the early years of the war. Widowed in 1942, he remarried Meriel ''Mu'' Forbes in 1944, another actress, with whom he had a son born on the first day of 1945. By now Richardson was quite established in his career, and the family lived in a Queen-Anne style home in the posh Hampstead Heath area of London. What has been termed Richardson's greatest stage role came during this era at the Old Vic: as Falstaff in a 1945 production of *Henry IV*. Overwhelmingly assessed by critics as the most compelling performance of his career, it was never filmed and remains lost to posterity. As the rotund, thieving nobleman, Richardson's character ''had wit and innate youthfulness, passion and authority, the eyes rolling majestically under a wild, white halo of hair,'' wrote Nightingale in the *New York Times*.

Richardson was knighted in 1947 for his contributions to British theater, and with the Old Vic decamped to New York for a time in the late 1940s. This led to Hollywood offers, and his first genuine Tinseltown production—not a joint U.S.-British affair, as some earlier ones had been—was William Wyler's *The Heiress* in 1949. In it, Richardson played the father of Olivia de Havilland in the adaptation of the Henry James novel *Washington Square*. His Dr. Austin Sloper railroads his timid daughter into spurning the suitor she loves. A *New York Times* critic, Bosley Crowther, termed Richardson's a ''rich and sleek performance'' and called the movie ''one of the handsome, intense, and adult dramas of the year.'' The actor also won strong praise that same year for his role as the butler in a Graham Greene adaptation, *The Fallen Idol*.

Cowed Audiences into Silence

Known for his self-effacing quips, Richardson was alternately serious and cavalier about his profession. He admitted he was far from the handsome hero, once saying of his face, ''I've seen better-looking hot cross buns,'' according to his *New York Times* obituary. On stage, however, he was intensely dedicated to his craft, and was known to begin a line over and over until he obtained absolute silence from the audience. A *Time* assessment of his career from Richard Corliss noted that in the first half of Richardson's career, ''he was the middle-class Everyman, shuffling toward archetype with good will and capacious common sense. But as he aged, his characters turned imperious and, in spite of their power, ineffectual.'' Corliss believed that Richardson's Dr. Sloper and other parts exemplified ''his ideal role: as the haughty burgher whose tragic flaw lies in realizing too late that he is not quite a tragic figure.''

Richardson suffered some lean career years during the 1950s, as his peers Gielgud and Olivier were gaining increasing stature as Shakespeare interpreters and stage and screen directors, but made an impressive return to the stage in 1957 with *The Flowering Cherry*, a critical hit of the London season that year. Gielgud cast him in several works for the stage that he directed, and filmmaker Otto Preminger gave him the part of a British military officer in the epic *Exodus*, about the founding of the state of modern Israel. American director Sidney Lumet chose him to play the

Theatre, a production that also featured his wife. Over the next decade, he gained increasing renown for his acting talents in such plays as *Sheppey* from W. Somerset Maugham's pen, and the comic melodrama *The Amazing Dr. Clitterhouse*, which had a successful 1936 run at the Haymarket. Richardson also appeared in stagings of Shakespeare plays with London's esteemed Old Vic Company in the 1930s, through which he came to know both Gielgud and Olivier. The trio would become lifelong friends and mentors to one another.

As with his Brighton propmaster job, Richardson made an inauspicious debut in film as well. It came in 1933's *The Ghoul* alongside Boris Karloff. ''I played a parson,'' Richardson recalled with his characteristic dry wit in an interview with *New York Times* writer Benedict Nightingale, ''a very young man with a round innocent face, and the lady of the house liked him, trusted him. But he was getting together firewood all the time to burn the place down! I've never had a more amusing part.'' By 1936, however, Richardson had landed a multi-film deal with producer Alexander Korda, and went on to make several notable films under him, including the cult-classic *Things to Come*, an adaptation of the H. G. Wells science-fiction classic in which Richardson played ''The Boss,'' a dictator in a futuristic world.

The Famous, Vanished ''Falstaff''

Richardson spent World War II in the Fleet Air Arm with Olivier, and reached the rank of lieutenant commander. Both were released early in 1944 to aid in the miserable, alcoholic father in his 1962 adaptation of the Eugene O'Neill classic, *Long Day's Journey into Night,* and Richardson also appeared in the Oscar-winning Russian-revolution drama from director David Lean, *Dr. Zhivago,* in 1965. In 1969, another esteemed British filmmaker, Richard Attenborough, cast Richardson and Gielgud in the *Oh! What a Lovely War,* a re-make of the hit stage musical.

Active Well Into His 80s

It was the hit of the 1970 theater season, however, that established Richardson as the *eminence gris* of British drama. *Home,* a work from playwright David Storey, co-starred him with Gielgud and went on to a successful run on Broadway as well; it was even made into a teleplay. The *New York Times* writer Nightingale termed it another hallmark of a long career for Richardson, particularly the scene "when the mentally damaged old man he was playing stopped his aimless, empty jabber and, his face dark and bunched, began silently to weep." Another outstanding stage work from this era was 1975's *No Man's Land,* a Harold Pinter play that he and Gielgud again reprised for Broadway.

Along the way, Richardson also accepted roles in some less-than-esteemed films that may have provided him with the same sort of scenery-chewing amusement as his 1933 horror-flick debut. These include *Tales from the Crypt* in 1972 and the original *Rollerball* in 1975. Monty Python comedian-turned-director Terry Gilliam cast him as a diffident deity in the 1981 classic *Time Bandits,* which was one of his last roles. Interviewed on the occasion of his 80th birthday by Nightingale in the *New York Times* in 1982, Richardson claimed he could not "afford to retire. I don't know enough. The older you get, the more you realize how little you know. No, I can't afford it, not for my inner self." His last film role was in *Greystoke: The Legend of Tarzan,* the much anticipated modernization of the Edgar Rice Burroughs tale. It was released in theaters in March of 1984, some five months after Richardson's death in London on October 10, 1983. He had been appearing in the tour of a National Theater play, *Inner Voices,* but was forced to withdraw due to a digestive ailment. His wife Meriel died in 2000, two years after their son Charles passed away.

Richardson was a famously recalcitrant interview subject, known for encouraging journalists to drink prodigious amounts of alcohol with him, which seemed not to affect him or ever loosen his tongue. Eccentric well into his senior years, he could sometimes be seen riding around London on his motorcycle, often with Jose, his pet parrot, tucked inside his leather jacket. He also kept a ferret named Eddie for a number of years, an animal he bathed weekly in Lux soap flakes. There remained three trenchant comments that he made about his profession: he told London *Times* writer Ronald Hayman in 1972 that his Roman Catholic upbringing seemed to have influenced his method. "I think basically I must be attracted by ritual, because I believe that there's a kind of religious sense in what I do," he reflected. "I think actors, rather like priests, have a sense of what can be done by ritual." In the *New York Times* interview with Nightingale, when asked how he prepared for a part, he replied "Dig, dig, dig, dig. Find out more and more about the character. What does he eat? What trousers does he wear? What does he do? What does he drink? What is he afraid of?" A much briefer comment about his profession, made to the *New York Herald Tribune* in 1946, revealed Richardson's mordant wit: "Acting," he asserted, "is merely the art of keeping a large group of people from coughing."

Books

International Dictionary of Films and Filmmakers, Volume 3: *Actors and Actresses,* St. James Press, 1996.

Periodicals

Daily Telegraph (London, England), April 28, 2001.
Guardian (London, England), April 17, 2000; March 3, 2001; June 23, 2003.
Independent Sunday (London, England), October 20, 1996.
Mail on Sunday (London, England), July 4, 1999; April 22, 2001.
National Review, February 4, 1983.
New Republic, April 23, 1984.
New York Herald Tribune, May 19, 1946.
New York Times, November 4, 1938; October 7, 1949; December 19, 1982; October 1883.
Observer (London, England), May 28, 2000.
People, April 9, 1984.
Sunday Telegraph (London, England), November 18, 2001.
Time, October 24, 1983; April 2, 1984.
Times (London, England), January 24, 1938; July 20, 1939; March 4, 1952; June 9, 1952; June 11, 1956; July 1, 1972; October 11, 1983. □

Thomas Joseph Ridge

Tom Ridge (born 1946) was appointed by President George W. Bush in October 2001 to serve as assistant to the president for the hastily assembled Office of Homeland Security following the terrorist bombings of New York City's World Trade Center and other targets in September 2001. Ridge was in the middle of his second term as governor of Pennsylvania, but stepped down from the post to accept the new position. Ridge was appointed secretary of the new Cabinet-level Department of Homeland Security in 2002.

Developed Strong Work Ethic

The oldest of three children, Ridge was born in Munhall, Pennsylvania, a small suburb of Pittsburgh in the state's fabled Steel Valley, on August 26, 1946. His father, who was serving in the Navy at the time of his first child's birth, was a veteran who later worked as a traveling meat salesman. Beginning in 1948 the family lived in housing for veterans that the government provided in

Erie, Pennsylvania. As a youth, Ridge was exposed early to politics and rhetoric, since his mother was a staunch Republican and his father an avid Democrat.

Ridge attended the local Roman Catholic schools, serving as an altar boy at church and proving himself both a gifted student and athlete. In particular, he excelled at the art of debate. His work in high school earned him a partial scholarship to Harvard University, and he worked in construction to make up the remainder of his tuition. Ridge graduated with an bachelor of arts degree in government studies and honors in 1967.

Law Career Interrupted by War

Determining that his future lay in the legal profession, Ridge enrolled in Pennsylvania State University's Dickinson School of Law in Carlisle, Pennsylvania. However, he had barely begun his studies there when he was drafted in 1970 to serve in the Army as a staff sergeant in Vietnam. He soon saw combat, and performed his duties with characteristic responsibility and diligence. Ridge was later presented with a Bronze Star for leading an offensive that forced enemy Vietcong from a strategic area. Ridge, like many of his fellow Americans who fought in Vietnam, was a changed man when he returned to the United States after a ruptured appendix ended his tour of duty early. A friend recalled that Ridge seemed more cautious in general.

After his discharge, Ridge returned to the Dickinson School and graduated with his law degree in 1972. He established a small, private practice and then from 1979 to 1981 prosecuted 86 cases serving as an assistant district attorney for Erie County.

Started New Career in Politics

Meanwhile, Ridge had become increasingly active in Republican Party politics. In 1982, he ran successfully for a seat in the U.S. Congress, becoming the first enlisted person who had served in the Vietnam War to be elected to the House of Representatives. He served six consecutive terms there, easily winning each election. Not one to blindly follow the party line, Ridge built a somewhat mixed voting record by backing some liberal causes. These included increasing spending for homeless veterans and more research on post-traumatic stress syndrome, which afflicted so many of the men he fought alongside in the war. In all, he was regarded as a moderate, and garnered a reputation for his ability to charm key people while working quietly behind the scenes. Colleagues in the House later recalled that Ridge had excellent interpersonal skills and a high degree of political aptitude.

Ridge parlayed his popularity and success as a U.S. representative into a 1994 bid to become the forty-third governor of Pennsylvania, winning the contest hands down with a promise to make Pennsylvania "a leader among states" and to cut taxes significantly. He took office on January 1, 1995, and over the course of one-and-a-half terms did indeed cut taxes every year. In addition, many of his supporters—and even some of his detractors—called his electricity deregulation plan a national model for slashing rapidly rising utility rates. Ridge initiated programs to build

the state's advanced computing and life sciences industries to help bring in what he called the "jobs of the future," taking an aggressive stance on technology to foster Pennsylvania's economic, health, education, and environmental advances. His social agenda also included reform of the national welfare system.

Made Name as Moderate Republican

As governor, Ridge enacted the Education Empowerment Act to benefit some 250,000 children in Pennsylvania's poorest-performing schools, and his administration raised by 145 percent the number of children who received low-cost or free healthcare through the state's Children's Health Insurance Program. Ridge also won kudos for his Land Recycling Program and passage of the $650 million "Growing Greener" initiative, which made Pennsylvania the nation's largest environmental investor ever.

Perhaps the most controversial point of Ridge's run as governor was his pro-choice stance on abortion, which surprised many people because of his Catholic upbringing. He also strongly opposed Affirmative Action and spoke out against changes to existing civil rights laws, including the legalization of gay marriage. He was perceived as being tough on crime as well, and held a special legislative session that eventually resulted in a "three-strikes" law and an expedited death penalty process. During his time as governor, Ridge signed more than 200 death warrants—more than five times the total signed by his two successors over the previous 25 years. Two of the warrants were for African American activist and journalist Mumia Abu-Jamal. The governor also passed a bill requiring trigger locks on guns and another making it a felony for a convicted felon to own a gun.

Resigned as Governor to Accept Homeland Defense Leadership

Ridge's tenure as governor of Pennsylvania was cut short by the terrorist bombings of the World Trade Center in New York City on September 11, 2001. As reports continued to flood the media of thousands of people killed and missing, President George W. Bush appointed Ridge assistant to the president for the Office of Homeland Defense. The Office had been quickly created on September 20 in the aftermath of the attacks, and Bush bestowed Ridge with the authority to supervise and coordinate U.S. efforts to prevent any further terrorist threats or actions.

Ridge, who would have been legally required to step down as governor of Pennsylvania after his second term ended in early 2003, accepted the appointment after two days of intense talks with the Bush administration. Following a midnight press conference during which the appointment was announced and Ridge said he would resign as governor on October 5, 2001, he dove into the organization and leadership of what would become the second-largest federal agency after the Pentagon.

Although he had been a popular governor and had won acclaim for many of his programs, Ridge was suddenly more in the national spotlight than he had ever been. He had been rumored to be considering a run for the presidency, and had also been a candidate for Bush's running mate in the 2000 election, although his pro-choice stance on abortion made him unattractive to many right-wingers.

When Bush announced his appointment of Ridge to head the homeland security effort, the president commended him as reported on ABCNEWS.com as "a military veteran, an effective governor, a true patriot, [and] a trusted friend." Bush declared Ridge to be "the right man for this new and great responsibility." Ridge, who moved into his new office on October 8, 2001 with a staff of almost 100 officials and about a dozen of his own employees, had the added benefit of strong friendships with Vice President Dick Cheney and former President George Bush, for whose 1980 election campaign Ridge had volunteered.

In a speech shortly after taking office as homeland security advisor, Ridge said he was "saddened that this job is even necessary. But it *is* necessary, so I will give it everything I have," reported the BBC News Website. The former governor announced his belief that citizens would be much safer with the coordination of local, state, and federal emergency and law enforcement efforts, but cautioned that al Qaeda, the group responsible for the September 11 attacks, and other terrorist groups remained an active threat to the country. Ridge also said he took the attacks personally, since one of the hijacked aircraft, Flight 93, crashed to the ground in Pennsylvania after passengers thwarted the terrorists' apparent plans to destroy the White House with it. Ridge expressed confidence in the country's law enforcement agencies, but warned, "There may be gaps in the system. The job of the Office of Homeland Security will be to identify those gaps and work to close them. The size and scope of this challenge are immense."

Promoted to Secretary of New Department of Homeland Security

On November 25, 2002, Bush (despite his initial opposition to the idea) signed into law a bill creating the Homeland Security Department (HSD), naming Ridge as the first U.S. secretary of Homeland Security-a Cabinet-level position. Congress approved his nomination, and Ridge became responsible for heading the largest reorganization of the government since the Department of Defense was created in 1947. He was sworn in to the position on January 24, 2003 and immediately became one of only a few elite officials who attended top-level daily war council meetings with the president.

Ridge's main task initially was, as he told ABCNEWS .com, "to restructure government in a 21st-century way to deal with the new threat." The scope of the job was staggering: creation of the HSD entailed amalgamating 22 existing government agencies with about $40 billion in combined budgets and 170,000 employees. Such agencies as Border Patrol, the Coast Guard, the Customs Department, the new Transportation Security Administration, and the Immigration and Naturalization Service were to be drawn into the new department, which would also gather information on terrorist threats from the Federal Bureau of Investigation (FBI) and the Central Intelligence Administration (CIA).

Under Ridge's ministrations, the HSD fortified the nation's borders, analyzed massive amounts of intelligence for clues that could prevent terrorist acts or lead to the capture of terrorist leaders, and worked to develop comprehensive response and recovery programs to be implemented in the event of further attacks. However, critics of the department's creation continued to complain that the country could not afford to spend the months—some experts said years—that it would take to complete the organization's setup. Criticism also worsened for the Patriot Act, a key piece of legislation for the HSD that was passed with little input from an American public still in shock, and that Bush had signed into law in October 2001. The administration had hailed the legislation as a means to give law enforcement personnel more access to information that might lead to the apprehension of terrorists, but civil rights advocates condemned the Patriot Act as the legalization of invasive government prying into private civilian matters. One of the most controversial provisions of the act is that bookstore owners and librarians must, if the government can show probable cause, turn over information on an individual's reading and Internet habits.

As leader of the HSD, Ridge also came under fire from numerous quarters in December 2003 when he suggested that the 8-12 million illegal immigrants then living in the United States be permitted to become citizens. His purpose, Ridge's spokesperson later announced, in making the comment was to "acknowledge a practical problem" concerning the huge number of illegal immigrants in the country and to address increasing pressure in Congress to change what many perceived as ineffective ways of dealing with the issue. Ridge's critics denounced the comment and urged the secretary to find ways to enforce existing immigration laws and to deport those who violate them.

Aside from these sticking points, Ridge and the HSD enjoy support from conservative Americans, although many liberals continue to criticize the department and many of its actions. In March 2004, Bush announced that he would triple the department's original 2001 budget to about $30.5 billion. Under Ridge's leadership, one of the HSD's prime goals for the near future is to establish Project BioShield, a program that will help Americans defend against possible terrorist use of bioweapons such as anthrax and smallpox.

Ridge and his wife Michelle (née Moore), a former Erie County Library executive director, married in 1979 and have two adopted children, Tommy and Lesley.

Online

"Bio: Tom Ridge," *Fox News web site,* http://www.foxnews.com (March 12, 2004).

"Biography of Governor Tom Ridge," *Whitehouse web site,* http://www.whitehouse.gov (March 11, 2004).

"Gov. Tom Ridge: Popular Governor and War Veteran Moves into Cabinet to Fight Terrorism," *ABC News web site,* http://www.abcnews.com (March 8, 2004).

"Person of the Week: Tom Ridge," *Time Magazine web site,* http://www.time.com (March 11, 2004).

"President Marks Homeland Security's Accomplishments at Year One," *Whitehouse web site,* http://www.whitehouse.gov (March 11, 2004).

"Profile of Tom Ridge," *Issues2000 web site,* http://www
.issues2000.org (March 6, 2004).

"Ridge Rapped for Immigration Views," *Washington Times web
site,* http://www.washtimes.com (March 9, 2004).

"Secretary: Tom Ridge," *Department of Homeland Security web
site,* http://www.dhs.gov (March 13, 2004).

"The Home Front: Homeland Security Director Tom Ridge,"
National Public Radio web site, http://www.npr.org (March
16, 2004).

"Tom Ridge," *Wikipedia web site,* http://en.wikipedia.org
(March 2, 2004).

"Tom Ridge: 1995-2001," *Pennsylvania Department of General
Services web site,* http://www.dgs.state.pa.us (March 12,
2004).

"Tom Ridge: Head of Homeland Security: First Day as New Anti-
Terror Chief," *ABC News web site,* http://abcnews.go.com
(March 13, 2004).

"Tom Ridge: Homeland Security Secretary," *National Public
Radio web site,* http://www.npr.org (March 16, 2004).

"Tom Ridge: Tough Man for Tough Job," *BBC News Americas
web site,* http://news.bbc.co.uk (March 15, 2004). □

Rozanne Lejeanne Ridgway

**One of the first women to make a large impact in the
United States foreign service, Rozanne Ridgway
(born 1935) was chief negotiator for the five historic
summit meetings between U.S. President Ronald
Reagan and Soviet leader Mikhail Gorbachev in the
1980s. In this and other diplomacy she excelled at
breaking down the barriers between the U.S. and
Soviet blocs during the waning years of the Cold
War.**

Foreign Service Pioneer

Rozanne Lejeanne Ridgway was born in St. Paul,
Minnesota, on August 22, 1935. She was the daughter of Henry Clay Ridgway and Ethel Rozanne Cote
Ridgway. Her father was a gas station attendant, and her
mother was a homemaker who raised three children. She
grew up in a modest home and worked her way through
high school selling Montgomery Ward catalogs. She graduated from Hamline University in St. Paul with a degree in
political science and her sights set on a career in the foreign
service. Her entering class had six women, and Ridgway
was the only one to have a full career within the department.

In 1986, Ridgway, interviewed by Jeff McCrehan for
the *Christian Science Monitor,* reflected on entering the
predominantly male United States foreign service in 1957:
". . . [M]y first years in the service had obstacles in them, but
some of them were credibility obstacles. I was 21 years old.
I wouldn't have asked me to make major foreign policy
decisions, and I think as a young woman who had never
lived overseas, I was seen as someone who might not
seriously understand all of the meaning of a career in diplomacy." After seven years in the service, Ridgway began to
specialize in European political analysis.

Early Diplomatic Successes

In her early career Ridgway was successful in handling
such longstanding issues as fishing rights in Brazil, Peru, and
the Bahamas. In 1975, Ridgway was named deputy assistant
secretary of state for oceans and fisheries. Her job took her
all over the world, and in only 18 months she organized 19
different treaties, including the 200-mile offshore fishing
rights treaty.

She also successfully negotiated the return of U.S. citizens from Czechoslovakia, then still a part of the Soviet-
controlled Eastern bloc. The plan she used was considered a
blueprint for eventually normalizing relations with Cuba.

In 1977, President Jimmy Carter appointed her ambassador to Finland. She was the first female career officer to be
named to a European embassy. In 1980, Ridgway helped
coordinate the Human Rights Conference in Madrid and
assisted in the creation of policy on Poland, which was
beginning its break from Soviet control.

In 1983, she accepted a post as ambassador to West
Germany. While serving there for two years she met and
became involved with Theodore Deming, a Coast Guard
commander who was being sent to an assignment in Alaska.
They managed to work things out despite the distances and
eventually married.

Negotiator at Summits

During the second term of Ronald Reagan's presidency, Ridgway was lead negotiator for all five of the historic summits between Reagan and Soviet leader Mikhail Gorbachev. Officially, her first position was special assistant to the Secretary of State for Negotiations. Next she was named Assistant Secretary of State for Europe and Canada. With Ridgway's careful assistance the two leaders negotiated the first significant reductions in nuclear weapons. Their talks ultimately heralded the end of the Cold War.

When President George H. W. Bush's administration removed Ridgway from her post with European affairs, the decision was criticized widely. *The Economist*, in a May 20, 1989 article, characterized Ridgway as departing "reluctantly" from that post.

After Government Service

When she left government service, Ridgway served as president of the Atlantic Council in Washington D.C. from 1989 through 1992. When she spoke to the Women's National Democratic Club on June 18, 1992, she spoke of the importance of defining the global role of the United States, saying: "Prosperity, security, and freedom is the purpose of our foreign policy. There is a world beyond our borders and it goes on with or without us. It's in our interest to take the lead."

In her interview with McCrehan in 1986, Ridgway noted that she had made 15 moves in her 30 years in government service. Asked what traits the State Department should be looking for in diplomats, Ridgway said "I think what State really needs is a group of people broadly educated. I would say [the Foreign Service needs people grounded in] history, economics, and Shakespeare, individuals who have a sense of integrity and principle which is unshakable."

When asked if she had ever had to compromise her own ethics during high-level negotiations, she recalled that there were times "when I have been a participant in deep and very serious discussions as to which course of action our country should follow . . . when I have found myself centering my preferences around one of those options and the leadership of the government of the time . . . has chosen another. And was in a position in which I had to carry [the decision] out." She said carrying out those decisions never involved a compromise of ethics or integrity.

Ridgway entered the private business world when she left politics. The boards of directors on which she served after 1992 included the 3 M Corporation, RJR Nabisco, Union Carbide Corporation, Bell Atlantic, Citicorp, Citibank, Emerson Electric Company, and Boeing. She has also served as a trustee at her alma mater, Hamline University, and on the board of directors at the Brookings Institution, the American Academy of Diplomacy, the Council on Ocean Law, Partners for Democratic Change, Catalyst, and the Aspen Institute.

In 1998 Ridgway was inducted into the National Women's Hall of Fame. She also served as a member of the Sara Lee Corporation, the New Perspective Fund, and

Emerson Electric Co. after 2002 as well as a trustee for the National Geographic Society, Brookings Institution, and the George C. Marshall Foundation.

Books

Marquis Who's Who of American Women, 19th edition, Reed Reference Publishing, 1995.

Periodicals

Business Journal (Serving Greater Milwaukee), February 27, 2002.
Business Journal (Serving Phoenix and the Valley of the Sun), November 7, 1997.
Christian Science Monitor, November 6, 1986.
The Economist, May 20, 1989; July 7, 1990.
Foreign Affairs, November–December 1995.
PR Newswire, February 26, 2002.
Puget Sound Business Journal, September 3, 1993.
US Department of State Dispatch, April 1, 1991.

Online

"Enrichment Lecture Staff, Ambassador Rozanne Ridgway," *Oninoco River Cruise website*, http://www.nauticom.net (December 9, 2003).
"Hamline University Commencement Ceremonies set for May 24," *Hamline University website*, http://www.hamline.edu (December 9, 2003).
"The 1994 George C. Marshall Lecture," *City of Vancouver, Washington website*, http://www.ci.vancouver.was.us (December 9, 2003).
"U.S. Seeks Ways to Deal with Global Ethnic Conflicts," *North Atlantic Treaty Organization website*, http://www.fas.org (December 9, 2003). □

Augusto Roa Bastos

Augusto Roa Bastos (born 1917) is widely considered to be the finest Paraguayan author of the 20th century. He published his first work, *El ruisenor de la aurora, y otras poemas*, in 1942, but his work was not well known outside his native Paraguay until the 1960s, when the increased attention paid to Latin-American literature highlighted his talent. Although he began by writing poetry, Roa Bastos eventually found that the genre did not allow him to express his social concerns, so he turned to prose. His work, mostly novels, is notable for its blending of myth, fantasy, and realism, and its focus on Paraguay's turbulent military and social history.

B orn in Asuncion, Paraguay on June 13, 1917, Roa Bastos grew up in Iturbe, a provincial city east of Asuncion where his father, Lucio Roa, worked as a manager on a sugar plantation. Lucio Roa was a severe, strict man who came from a old-time Spanish family. Perhaps in response to his father's authoritarian rule over the household, Roa Bastos became preoccupied with thinking

about the evils that could result from power, totalitarianism, and authority; these themes have reoccurred throughout his life's work. He later told Caleb Bach in *Americas* that this theme appeared "whether it manifests itself politically, in a religious form, or in a parental or familial context. Power is a tremendous stigma, a kind of human pride that needs to have control of the will of another. It's an antilogical condition that produces a sick society. . . . Ever since I was very little I felt a need to oppose power, the fierce punishment for little things the basis of which was never conveyed."

Roa Bastos's mother, Lucia Bastos, was of Portuguese descent, and unlike her husband, was cultured and calm. She enjoyed singing and had a small library of books, including a Spanish translation of the tales of English playwright William Shakespeare. This book provided Roa Bastos with his first experience of literature.

When Roa Bastos was eight years old, he was sent to live with his paternal uncle, a priest named Hermenegildo Roa, in Asuncion. He later told Bach, "For me, he was my real father." Hermenegildo Roa paid for the education of all his nephews and nieces, and like Roa Bastos's mother, he had a library of books, including many volumes of philosophy by such authors as Voltaire and Jean-Jacques Rousseau, which were normally forbidden to children. However, the elderly priest told his nephew, "I want you to read these with great care." Roa Bastos's reading of these authors taught him that some ideas, and writers were considered subversive, and that these writers and ideas were the most powerful. For the rest of his life, he would remain interested in French literature, particularly the writers of the Enlightenment era.

Began Writing

In 1932, when Roa Bastos was 13 years old, war broke out between Paraguay and Bolivia regarding control of the barren Chaco region between the two nations. Roa Bastos enlisted as a field hospital orderly. Although he was not involved in combat, the wounded and dying soldiers he saw made a deep emotional impression on him. When the war ended he began working as an apprentice journalist for *El País,* an Asuncion newspaper. When he was not working, the young man wrote his own short stories and poetry. His first novel, which he completed in 1941, was titled *Fulgencio Miranda;* although it was never published, it won a local literary prize. During this period, Roa Bastos read widely among European authors: Rilke, Valery, Cocteau, Eluard, Breton, and Aragon. He also read the work of North American authors such as Faulkner, Hemingway, Hawthorne, and Melville. Roa Bastos told Bach that reading these authors "helped liberate [Latin American writers] from the heaviness of the Hispanic style."

As his work became known, Roa Bastos began to receive recognition. In 1945 he received a travel fellowship from the British Council to travel throughout England and develop program materials on Latin America for the British Broadcasting Corporation. While in England, he continued to write for *El Pais,* focusing on the liberation of France at the close of World War II. Writer Andre Malraux invited Roa Bastos to France, where the journalist managed to get a personal interview with French president Charles de Gaulle. As someone who came from a small town in Paraguay, Roa Bastos looked upon this as an impressive accomplishment.

During this period, Roa Bastos became interested in the history of World War II, particularly the role of the resistance movement in France, in which local people fought against the invasion and rule of their country by Nazi Germany. This was typical of his preoccupation with totalitarianism and rebellion against it. According to Bach, "he came away with the conclusion that the human world is driven by oppositions."

A Life in Exile

In 1946 Roa Bastos returned to Paraguay, but because he had written articles critical of two military governments, he was considered a threat and was forced into exile soon after his return. He fled to the Brazilian embassy, where he hid until he could leave for Buenos Aires, Argentina. There he began a new life.

In Argentina, he worked at various odd jobs: waiter, door-to-door salesperson, proofreader, and insurance salesperson. He also worked for a music publisher, where he translated Guarani folk music into Spanish. Roa Bastos told Bach, "Exile was a permanent school that taught me to see things with greater seriousness. It was also pain, like a death, a state of mourning." He spent the first four or five years in exile enduring depression, and turned to writing, he told Bach, "as a vehicle to recover my human condition, my dignity as an individual."

Roa Bastos wrote a collection of 17 short stories during this period, and it was eventually published as *El trueño entre las hojas* ("Thunder among the Leaves"). The stories, set in Paraguay, deal with themes of political oppression, conflicts between native and foreign cultures, and the human struggle to survive wars and other catastrophes. Argentine director Armando Bo was impressed by the stories, and wanted to make a film based on them. Roa Bastos wrote the script, the first of many screenplays he would write during his career.

Roa Bastos's first novel, *Hijo de hombre* ("Son of Man"), was published in 1960. The novel, set during a time of war, depicts the ruthless exploitation of peasants in the sugar-cane fields and tea plantations. The main character, a peasant, is depicted as a Christlike figure, in opposition to another character, a military officer who is depicted as a Judas. Roa Bastos wrote a film adaptation of one of the novel's chapters. The novel and the film, both of which won awards, attracted wide attention and cemented Roa Bastos's reputation as a fine writer in Buenos Aires. By the mid-1960s he began teaching literature courses at the National University of Rosario, and he was invited to attend international literary conferences in the company of other Latin-American writers. One of these writers was Jorge Luis Borges. Roa Bastos told Bach, "You know, among each people there is an exceptional being who makes up for the deficiencies of the rest. In those moments, when humanity collectively is in a state of decadence, nonetheless there remain those exceptional individuals as a point of reference. Borges was such an individual."

Published *Yo el supremo*

In 1967 Roa Bastos began writing a book about Paraguayan dictator Gaspar de Francia. However, he never completed it, but instead began work on *Yo el supremo* ("I the Supreme"), a complex, many-layered work of fiction that explores the life of a dictator based on Francia. The narrative of the novel reads like pieces of private notebooks written by the dictator, historical fragments, a logbook of his family history, transcriptions of dictations to a secretary, and pieces by an unknown commentator. Composed of many voices and cemented by quasi-academic footnotes that quote invented and real texts, the novel moves through the present, past, and future; the dictator at times even speaks from his grave. Roa Bastos told Bach that the book "reflects a certain insanity I couldn't repeat, and don't want to repeat." He added, "Francia was a terrible dictator, but he had an ambiguous personality. I wanted to show him in his own setting, the dark and the light." He also noted that the structure of the book, with its many voices, reflected the culture of Paraguay, particularly that of the Guarani people, for whom oral history and storytelling are paramount. "My necessity, my defiance as a writer was to rise up against established accounts [of the dictator's life]."

During the six years it took him to write *Yo el supremo* Roa Bastos was supported by a Guggenheim fellowship and by his scriptwriting. Upon its 1974 publication the novel immediately received critical acclaim, and was widely translated, although the English-language version did not

appear until 1986. Carlos Fuentes wrote in the *New York Times Book Review* that the novel is "a richly textured, brilliant book—an impressive portrait, not only of El Supremo, but of a whole colonial society in the throes of learning how to swim, or how best to drown in the seas of national independence." Fuentes also called *Yo el supremo* "one of the milestones of the Latin American novel."

In 1976 Roa Bastos's father died at the age of 95; in that same year, the author suffered a mild heart attack. In addition, the military dictatorship then in power in Argentina put *Yo el supreme* on its list of books banned because they were subversive. Roa Bastos was in danger of being arrested at home, but in France was invited to teach at the University of Toulouse le Mirail. However, one week after he arrived in France, the Argentine police arrived at his apartment in Buenos Aires, intending to arrest him.

In 1980, after being divorced twice, Roa Bastos married Iris Gimenez, another professor at the university who was a specialist in the ancient languages and cultures of Mexico. The couple eventually had a son and two daughters, and his children inspired Roa Bastos to write numerous stories for young people that have been collected in illustrated editions. Also continuing his work for adult readers, in 1984 he published the novel *El Sonambulo* ("The Sleep Walker"), which is about another Paraguayan dictator, Francisco Solano Lopez. Roa Bastos later expanded this into a full-length novel, *El Fiscal* ("The Public Prosecutor"), which was published in 1993. He then published *La vigilia del almirante* (The Admiral's Vigil) a novel about Christopher Columbus. In 1994 he published *Contravida* and in 1996 *Madama Sui*.

Received Cervantes Prize

In 1989, the same year democracy returned to Paraguay, Roa Bastos received the Cervantes Prize, the highest award for literature in the Spanish language. He donated most of the prize money to support impoverished schools in Paraguay and to encourage the publication and distribution of affordable books to poor areas in the interior of the country. He noted that in Paraguay, the cost of a book typically equaled an entire month's pay for a poor agricultural worker.

By the mid-1990s Roa Bastos was able to return to Paraguay one or two times per year, and he began teaching courses for young people during these visits. Although he retired from teaching at the University of Toulouse, he continued to stay in touch with his old colleagues, and he remained in his apartment near the university. He also continued to write. He told Bach, "If there is no room for hope, for anything, for optimism, then the most honest response is suicide. I don't believe in anything more than that I am alive. I think the only way to live is to establish a sense of responsibility. The least I can do is contribute."

Books

Dictionary of Hispanic Biography, Gale, 1996.
Dictionary of Literary Biography, Volume 113: *Modern Latin-American Fiction Writers,* Gale, 1992.
Foster, David, *Augusto Roa Bastos,* Twayne, 1978.

Latin American Writers, Volume 3, Charles Scribner's Sons, 1989.

Periodicals

Americas, November-December, 1996; September-October, 1997.
New Republic, June 15, 1987.
New York Times Book Review, April 6, 1986. □

Rachel Ruysch

Dutch painter Rachel Ruysch (1664–1750) is regarded by many as the best female Dutch artist of the 17th and 18th centuries. A student of artist Willem van Aelst, she mastered the genre of still life, specializing in flower paintings. Her command of technique, her sense of composition, and her use of colors added a compelling vibrancy to her still-life paintings.

Early Life

Ruysch was born in The Hague in the Netherlands in 1664. When she was three years old, she moved with her family to Amsterdam, where she was raised. One of twelve children, she was born into a wealthy and prominent family that provided an artistic pedigree. Her mother's father, Pieter Post, started out as a painter, specializing in landscapes and battle scenes, before becoming an architect who designed buildings in the classical style. In the 1640s, he received an appointment as the court painter and architect for Prince Frederik Hendrik and settled in The Hague. Post's brother Frans also painted landscapes.

More significantly, her father, Frederik Ruysch, was a well-known professor of anatomy and botany. With his trained scientific eye, he observed and recorded nature with a high degree of accuracy, a skill that he instilled in his daughter. This greatly influenced her future artistic output, which would be characterized by realistic, still-life depictions of plants and flowers. In addition, Frederik Ruysch was a talented amateur painter who published textual and graphic descriptions of botanical discoveries. He encouraged Ruysch's own artistic efforts and cultivated her remarkable talent. Her early drawings included scientific studies of insects and flowers.

Further influencing Ruysch's vision and future direction, the Ruysch family lived on Bloemgracht (the "flower canal"). The location was not only naturally beautiful, but it attracted other artists as well. Living nearby was German painter Ernst Stuven, who worked in Holland and had studied under well-known Dutch flower painter Willem van Aelst, who would have a significant impact on Ruysch's career.

Van Aelst, who moved to Amsterdam in 1657, was famous for creating elaborate still-life paintings that featured spiraling compositions and eschewed the convention of symmetrical arrangements of depicted bouquets. Van Aelst's somewhat irregular approach translated itself into the works of his pupils. Among them were Ruysch, Stuven, and Ruysch's younger sister Anna Elisabeth (1666–c. 1741), who also became an artist of recognized merit, although she never attained the stature of her more determined sister.

Studied with van Aelst

In 1679, when she was fifteen years old, Ruysch started an apprenticeship with van Aelst, and she began producing various kinds of still life paintings, mostly flower studies and woodland scenes. Van Aelst taught her the requisite skill of composing a bouquet in a vase but in his less formalized fashion that produced a much more realistic and palpable effect. In their works, some flowers and leaves were allowed to droop over the sides of vases, while others were revealed from the back, which produced a more rounded shape. Ruysch would build upon van Aelst's compositional innovations, which instilled a vitality into her paintings.

It has been speculated that Anna also studied with her sister's teacher. But it is certain that Ruysch taught Anna. Only about ten of Anna Ruysch's signed works survive, and one work in particular—a still life of fruit painted in 1685 when she was nineteen years old—reveals van Aelst's style of composition and also certain unique details that were characteristic of her older sister. (More of Anna's work may survive, but this is somewhat difficult to ascertain, as she didn't sign her work, a practice that was typical of many of her contemporary colleagues. In contrast, about a hundred of her sister's works are known to exist.)

Ruysch studied with van Aelst until he died in 1683, but her earliest paintings began appearing around 1680. By the time she was eighteen she was turning out independently signed paintings and was on her way to establishing a successful career.

Started a Large Family

In 1693, Ruysch married the painter and lace dealer Juriaen Pool. At that time, she was painting large flower pieces for an international circle of patrons. The couple enjoyed a happy marriage and had ten children. Ruysch would continue to work despite her marital and motherly duties. Indeed, even though, as she claimed, she essentially raised her children on her own, her domestic chores coincided with her most creative artistic period. Her large brood seemed in no way to interfere with the quality of her work. In light of her situation, she was fairly productive throughout her lifetime. She finished her final painting in 1747, when she was 83. By the time she died, she had produced more than 250 pictures, an average of about five pictures a year, a considerable number for someone creating flower paintings in painstaking detail.

In 1701, Ruysch and Pool moved to The Hague, where both artists joined the Guild of St Luke, the city's association of painters. In 1708, the couple was invited to Dusseldorf, Germany, to serve as court painters to Johann Wilhelm, the Elector Palatine of Bavaria. Even as a court painter, Ruysch continued meeting the demands of her Dutch patrons. The couple remained in Dusseldorf until the prince's death in 1716, then returned to Holland.

Ruysch remained in Amsterdam for the rest of her life, creating fruit and flower paintings for prominent patrons. Her works were in great demand by prominent noble families.

Baroque Flower Painters

Ruysch practiced her art in the Baroque period of art history. Baroque art was a style that arose in Europe around 1600 as a reaction against the Mannerist style, an intricate and formulaic approach that dominated the late Renaissance period. The Baroque style was less complex and more realistic. Flower painting emerged as part of the movement and was especially popular in the late 17th century. Factors influencing its emergence included the growing and more affluent merchant and middle classes, as well as the growing interest in plants that resulted from the developing science of botany. At the time, northern Europe witnessed the importation of many new and exotic plants. In particular, in Holland, Ruysch's homeland, the Dutch developed a wide variety of flowers and gardening became increasingly popular. Often, gardeners would commission artists to paint pictures of their best or rarest flowers.

Women artists were especially attracted to painting still life. However, artistic painting was considered a male province. The most famous Dutch painter at the time was Rembrandt, who was the leading portraitist in Amsterdam. During the era, artistic efforts were divided into two categories: ''greater'' and ''lesser.'' The greater categories included religious and historical themes. Among the ''lesser'' categories were still life, portraits and landscapes, and these were considered areas appropriate for women. Most other women who were painting in this era were members of noble families or were relatives of well-known male painters, and they painted as a hobby. It was widely believed in those days that women were incapable of artistic genius.

Because of those prevailing attitudes, it is noteworthy that Ruysch, a woman, would come to be such a highly regarded artist. She managed to make her mark in the predominantly male world of the Dutch Old Masters. She was viewed as one of the greatest flower painters of either gender. She stood out from most female contemporaries because she was more ambitious and her paintings were startlingly realistic and, at the same time, symbolic. Only a small number of other women artists shared Ruysch's ambition and talent and were held in high esteem. Among them were Anna Ruysch, Clara Peeters, Judith Leyster, Michaëlina Woutiers and Maria van Oosterwijck

But Ruysch was unique even among the other highly regarded women painters of her time. Her paintings were more than just realistic and scientifically accurate depictions. Ruysch possessed excellent skill and technique. But she enhanced her technique with an artist's sensitivity and sensibility. Like her contemporaries, Ruysch created bouquets that were dramatically lit against dark backgrounds, but Ruysch's backgrounds were more revealing, as they suggested an architectural setting. She used form, color

and textures in ways that were innovative, bold, and dynamic. Moreover, her works displayed a meticulous attention to detail. She paid particular attention to leaves, which she felt were just as important as the flowers.

Her open, diagonal compositions contrasted with the more compact and symmetrical arrangements that the other early 17th century women painters employed. Ruysch's compositions were asymmetrical and much more lively. They featured wildly curving stems that reached high into the air or drooped over the sides of the vase. Her flower arrangements were more loose. They appeared more spontaneous. The arrangements seemed less formalized, but this informality was carefully designed to achieve the ultimate effect. The end result was that her works possessed more energy and created the illusion of immediate realism. A viewer could almost reach out and touch her bouquets.

A representative example of her work is ''Flower Still Life,'' which depicts a large arrangement of flowers that rise and spill over the vase. Each stem and petal is portrayed in intricate detail in bright colors. Against the dark background, the flowers seem almost revealed in a photographic light.

In this way, her works were similar to paintings done by eighteenth-century artists such as Jan van Huysum, Jan van Os and Johan Christiaan Roedig. In fact, with her innovative techniques, Ruysch employed a style that can be seen as a transition from 17th-century to 18th-century flower painting.

Lasting Reputation

Ruysch died in 1750 at age 86. During her lifetime, she was fortunate to gain widespread fame, and her works were highly valued. Among her contemporaries, she was called *Hollants Kunstwonder* (''Holland's art prodigy'') and *Onze vernuftige Kunstheldin* (''Our subtle art heroine''), and the *Onsterflyke Y-Minerf* (''Immortal Minerva of the Amsterdam''). When she died, 11 contemporary poets paid her tribute.

Despite the fact that flower paintings today are regarded as a lesser form of artistic expression, Ruysch's reputation as a great painter remains intact. During the 20th century, there was great interest in her works. Her paintings were featured in major exhibitions in Europe including ''Still Life Paintings from the Netherlands 1550–1720,'' at the Rijksmuseum in Amsterdam in 1999, and ''Each their own Reason: Women Artists in Belgium and the Netherlands 1500–1950'' at the Museum voor Moderne Kunst in Arnhem in 2000.

In January 2000, the art magazine *Kunstschrift* devoted an entire issue to Ruysch and her work, proclaiming, ''When a work by Rachel Ruysch appears on the art market, as still happens from time to time, it creates a sensation.'' Although she produced more than 250 paintings in her life, only about 100 are known to still exist, and most of these are in museums or private collections. When any of her paintings do appear on the market, it makes headlines. For instance, in 1999, a Ruysch still-life painting of flowers with a bird's nest was found behind the door of a country house. The owner of the house and the painting had no idea of the value of the treasure that was stowed away so unceremoniously. Fortunately, the painting was found by an art auctioneer. When it went on sale at an auction at Deauville, Normandy, in January 1999, the painting went for 2.9 million French francs, or the equivalent of $508,000.

Online

''Anna Ruysch's Rabbit Teeth and Fringes,'' *Sotheby's,* http://www.hoogsteder.com/journal/journal4/ruysch/ (January 10, 2004).

''The Baroque Era,'' *Artclypedia,* http://www.artcyclopedia.com/history/baroque.html (January 10, 2004).

''The Feminine Touch,'' *Sotheby's,* http://www.shareholder.com/bid/news/20021204-96443.cfm (January 10, 2004).

''Rachel Ruysch,'' *ArtNet,* http://www.artnet.com/library/07/0747/T074728.asp (January 10, 2004).

''Rachel Ruysch,'' *cartage.org,* http://www.cartage.org.lb/en/themes/Biographies/MainBiographies/r/ruysch/ruysch.htm (January 10, 2004).

''Rachel Ruysch,'' *Sotheby's,* http://www.nmwa.org/collection/Profile.asp?LinkID=388 (January 10, 2004).

''Rachel Ruysch,'' *Web Gallery of Art,* http://www.kfki.hu/~arthp/bio/r/ruysch/biograph.html (January 10, 2004).

''Women Fine Artists Throughout History-The Baroque Period,'' *The Fine Arts Magazine,* http://www.sierra-arts.net/WomenFineArtistsJuly03.html 2004 (January 10, 2004). □

S

Abdus Salam

Pakistani Physicist Abdus Salam (1926-1996) devoted a great deal of research time in the 1950s and 1960s to the study of the relationships between two of the four forces scientists believed governed nature: the electromagnetic force and the weak force. In 1968 he published a paper containing his theory that these two forces may actually be two manifestations of the same fundamental force, the electroweak force. By 1973 additional research had substantiated this theory, and in 1979 Salam was awarded the Nobel Prize for his work. In addition, he helped to found the International Center for Theoretical Physics in Trieste, Italy.

Born on January 29, 1926, in Santokdas, in British India's Western Punjab (now Pakistan), Salam grew up in Jhang, a small, rural town. He was the son of Muhammad and Hajira Hussain, and his father worked for the local department of education. Salam showed an early talent for mathematics, and when he was 16 years old he enrolled at the Government College at Punjab University in Lahore, Pakistan, after earning the highest marks ever recorded at his school. Salam published his first paper, which considered an algebraic problem by noted Indian mathematician Srinivasa Ramanujan, when he was age 17, and in 1946 received his master's degree in mathematics. He was then awarded a scholarship to travel to England to attend St. John's College, Cambridge. At Cambridge Salam worked with theoretical physicist Nicholas Kemmer. At the time, Paul Matthews, another student of Kemmer's, was working

on his Ph.D. in extending renormalization theory from quantum electrodynamics to meson theories. Salam joined Matthews and focused his attention on one of the problems related to this work. He quickly succeeded in solving it, thus establishing his reputation as an outstanding talent in the field. Salam then joined Matthews for a year of study at Princeton University. In 1949, Salam received a bachelor's degree in mathematics and physics, with highest honors.

Return to Pakistan Brought Disappointment

For the next two years, Salam pursued graduate study at Cambridge, but he eventually felt obligated to return to his home country. In Pakistan he took a position as professor of mathematics at the Government College of Lahore, and he also became head of the department of mathematics at Punjab University. However, Salam was disappointed because these positions did not allow him to conduct research. As he told Nina Hall in *New Scientist,* "I learnt that I was the only practicing theoretical physicist in the entire nation. No one cared whether I did any research. Worse, I was expected to look after the college soccer team as my major duty besides teaching undergraduates." In addition to his difficulty in finding a position where he could do research, Salam experienced increasing prejudice due to his membership within the Ahmadiyya sect of Islam. Many Pakistanis were members of a different branch of Islam, which viewed the Ahmadiyya followers as heretics.

Discouraged by these setbacks, Salam returned to Cambridge, where he earned his Ph.D. in theoretical physics in 1952. For the next two years he taught mathematics at Cambridge as a lecturer and fellow. In 1957 he accepted an appointment as professor of theoretical physics at the Imperial College of Science and Technology in London, England.

Salam, who retained his position at the Imperial College, in 1959, at age 33, became the youngest member of the Royal Society, based in London.

Found Unifying Theory

In the mid-1950s Salam began considering a fundamental question of modern physics: whether the various forces that govern everything in nature might actually be manifestations of the same basic force. At the time, scientists knew of four fundamental forces: gravitational force, electromagnetic force, strong force, and weak force. They also believed that if these forces were unified, this unification would not be visible or apparent except at levels of energy vastly greater than the ones humans encounter in the everyday world. These levels of energy exist in cosmic radiation, as well as in the most powerful particle accelerators ever built, so it is difficult for scientists to truly prove if in fact the fundamental forces are unified; most efforts to do so are theoretical exercises that involve complex mathematical formulas and calculations. However, by the 1960s Salam and fellow physicists Steven Weinberg and Sheldon Glashow each independently came up with a mathematical theory that unified two of the four basic forces. All men came up with the same theory, although they started from different beginning points and followed different pathways to their results.

The new theory predicted the existence of new, previously unknown, weak "neutral currents." In 1973 these currents were observed in experiments at the European Cen-

tre for Nuclear Research (CERN) in Geneva, Switzerland, and these experiments were later replicated at the Fermi National Accelerator Laboratory in Batavia, Illinois. The three physicists also predicted the existence of force-carrying particles, called W+, W-, and Z0 bosons. For their work, Salam, Weinberg, and Glashow were jointly awarded the 1979 Nobel Prize in Physics; Salam arrived at the ceremony wearing the traditional Pakistani dress of jeweled turban, baggy pants, scimitar, and curly toed shoes. In 1983 the existence of the force-carrying particles they had predicted was confirmed in experiments at CERN.

Assisted Other Physicists

In addition to his interest in purely theoretical physics, Salam had a lifelong interest in promoting the careers and status of theoretical physicists in developing nations, perhaps because of his own experiences, which had forced him to leave his home in Pakistan. He believed that theoretical physicists in developing countries needed support, encouragement, and instruction, and he decided that a training center should be established to provide this help. In 1964, with the help of the International Atomic Energy Agency, the Italian government, and the city of Trieste, Salam established the International Center for Theoretical Physics (ICTP) in Trieste, Italy; the center invites theoretical physicists from all over the world to lecture and teach students from developing nations. Hall noted that the Center is also a place for theoretical physicists from developing countries to meet and find camaraderie and common ground, "a sort of lonely scientist's club for Brazilians, Nigerians, Sri Lankans, or whoever feels the isolation resulting from lack of resources in their own country." Salam used his share of the Nobel Prize money to support the ICTP and never spent any of it on himself or his family.

Salam was director of the ICTP from its founding until his retirement in 1994. In addition, he served as a member of Pakistan's Atomic Energy Commission from 1958 to 1974 and as a member of Pakistan's Science Council from 1963 to 1978. He was chief scientific advisor to the president of Pakistan from 1961 to 1974, and was chair of Pakistan's Space and Upper Atmosphere Committee from 1962 to 1963. He also served various international groups, From 1964 to 1972 he was a member and later chair of the U.N. Advisory Committee on Science and Technology; served as vice president of the International Union of Pure and Applied Physics from 1972 to 1978, and was a member of the Stockholm International Peace Research Institute from 1970 until his retirement. Salam received over two dozen honorary degrees and many awards, including the Atoms for Peace Award (1968), the Royal Medal of the Royal Society (1978), the John Torrence Tate Medal of the American Institute of Physics (1978), and the Lomonosov Gold Medal of the USSR Academy of Sciences (1983).

A student of Salam's, M. J. Duff, spoke about Salam at a 1996 physics workshop and posted these remarks on the *University of Michigan Center for Theoretical Physics Web site* "Being a student of someone so bursting with new ideas as Salam was something of a mixed blessing: he would allocate a research problem and then disappear on his travels for weeks at a time. . . . On his return he would ask what you were working on. When you began to explain your meager progress he would usually say, 'No, no, no. That's all old hat. What you should be working on is this,' and he would then allocate a completely new problem.'' Duff noted that after experiencing this several times, Salam's students ''began to wise up and would avoid him until we had achieved something positive.''

Personal Life

Even while living in England, Salam continued to fight prejudice against his religious group in Pakistan. In 1974 Pakistani president Zulfikar Ali Bhutto declared that the Ahmadiyya sect was not Muslim. In protest, and to show his solidarity with Islam, Salam grew a beard and adopted the name Muhammad. He also frequently spoke throughout developing countries, but most notably in Islamic countries, and often noted that for several centuries the Arab and Muslim world had been in the forefront of science, far ahead of Europe and other parts of the world. He encouraged the founding of other centers similar to the ICTP, and became the first president of the Third World Academy of Sciences.

Salam was married twice, according to Islamic law, which allows men to marry up to four wives. He had six children: one son and three daughters by his first marriage, and a son and daughter by his second. As he grew older, he suffered from a degenerative neurological disease, progressive supranuclear palsy. This illness made it difficult for him to talk, and to walk, and he began using a wheelchair, while continuing to work as much as he could. Although he was ill, he still made remarkable contributions to research. In 1994 Salam retired from his post as director of the ICTP, and he died at his home in Oxford, England, on November 21, 1996, after a long illness. He was buried in the Ahmadia burial ground in Rabwah, Pakistan. In his honor, the ICTP was renamed the Abdus Salam ICTP. It has continued to help scientists from developing countries conduct research and pursue their careers.

After Salam's death, his reputation as a scientist led a publisher of fine art, Illuminocity, to make him the figurehead in a campaign to promote a positive view of Islam through the construction of a museum devoted to the history of Islamic sciences. The museum, exhibiting a collection of artwork titled ''Heroes of Science,'' housed a painting of Salam by artist Ro Kim, who also painted portraits of President Bill Clinton and the president of Korea.

In a tribute to Salam in the *Australian,* a writer noted, ''Salam was a striking man. Any young scientist who worked closely with him invariably found it to be an exhilarating and character-forming experience. In addition to his intellectual gifts, he had a genuine sense of humor, including that rarest of qualities of being able to laugh at himself. A warm twinkle would often accompany his more unorthodox suggestions as to how exactly the foundation of physics should be revolutionized.''

Books

Building Blocks of Matter: A Supplement to the Macmillan Encyclopedia of Physics, edited by John S. Rigden, Macmillan Reference USA, 2003.
Notable Scientists: From 1800 to the Present, Gale, 2001.
World of Scientific Discovery, second edition, Gale, 1999.

Periodicals

Australian, December 2, 1996.
New Scientist, October 18, 1979; January 27, 1990.

Online

''Abdus Salam: Biography,'' *Nobel e-Museum,* http://www .nobel.se/physics/laureates/1979/salam-bio.html (January 5, 2004).
''Professor Abdus Salam,'' *ICTP Web site,* http://www.ictp .Trieste.it/ProfSalam/index.html (January 5, 2004).
''A Tribute to Abdus Salam,'' *University of Michigan Center for Theoretical Physics Web site,* http://feynman.physics.lsa .umich.edu/~mduff/talks/ (January 5, 2004). □

Hakim Sana'i

A popular and influential poet in the royal court in Ghazna (now in Afganistan) during the late 11th and early 12th centuries, Hakim Sana'i (Abu al-Majd Majdud ibn Adam) (circa 1050–1131) is best known for his classic mystical poem *The Walled Garden of Truth and the Law of the Path.* He is considered one of the finest artists in the Sufi (Islamic mystic) tradition.

Abu al-Majd Majdud ibn Adam is most commonly referred to in historical texts as Hakim Sana'i, which he used as his pen name. The epithet ''hakim'' (''wise one'') was typically reserved for people of great learning. However, he is also referred to variously as Madjdud Sana'i, Adam al-Ghaznawi, Adam Sanai al-Ghaznavi, and simply Sana'i.

Beginnings of a Poet

Sana'i was born in what is now the Afghan city of Ghazna. Most sources give 1050 as the year of his birth, although, like his name, the date varies somewhat. His father was a teacher, but to what extent and in what disciplines Sana'i himself was educated is uncertain.

As a young man, Sana'i seems to have had a talent for enlisting the interest and help of potential patrons from all classes of Ghaznian society. There are records of his interactions with state officials, soldiers, Islamic clergymen, scholars, and artists. Perhaps his most important relationships were with several prominent academics from the Hanafi School of Law.

Sanai's cultivation of numerous patrons and allies, together with his tremendous talent as a poet, led to his appointment as the official court poet of the sultans of

Ghazna. His panegyrics—the lofty, elaborate writings in which he lavishly praised the rulers—made him the darling of the court.

Physical and Spiritual Journey

Sana'i appears to have suddenly abandoned his career as a professional poet after making the acquaintance of a "drinker of dregs" (in modern terms, a drunkard) in about 1114. Whether this person was the reason the poet left his career or not, it is known that Sana'i shortly thereafter left the city of his birth. Records indicate that Sana'i was strongly influenced by the drunkard, who reportedly criticized the poet for writing "in praise of unworthy persons . . . for worldly gains. What will he say to God on the day of the Reckoning when He asks him, 'What have you brought for me?' " Upon hearing this, Sana'i is said to have immediately left the court's service, foreswore writing panegyrics, and embarked upon a spiritual journey.

Sana'i's first stop on his trek was Balkh. From there he reportedly traveled to other cities in Khorasan Province, which is now part of Iran. He eventually found his way to Merv, in modern Turkmenistan, where he dedicated himself to seeking perfection of spirit. He also turned his attention to securing the patronage of the religious class. An influential Hanafi scholar, who was also a *wa'iz* (preacher), took Sana'i under his wing and became the poet's spiritual and professional mentor.

Influential Poem for Sultan

While living in Khorasan, Sana'i became a highly praised writer of religious poetry. Despite his success and popularity in his adopted home, however, Sana'i decided, for reasons that remain unclear, to return to his native city of Ghazna in about 1126. At the time, religious writing was popular among the ruling classes, and the poet soon attracted the attention of the sultan Bharam Shah. The shah quickly became Sana'i's sole patron, encouraging the aging poet to reside with him at the court. Sana'i resisted, determined to maintain his longtime aloofness from worldly matters, but he wrote and dedicated his most important poem to the sultan, indicating that Bharam Shah had a major influence on Sana'i. But the poet did remain in seclusion for the remainder of his life.

For the shah, the now aged Sana'i wrote the first major *mathnawi* (rhymed couplet) in the Dari language. Titled "Hadiqat al-Haqiqah wa shari'at attariqah" ("The Walled Garden of Truth and the Law of the Path"), the poem contained mystical teachings intermingled with proverbs, fables, and anecdotes. The uncommon manner in which Sana'i introduced and explained the esoteric teachings of Sufism—through the medium of poetry—was key to its popularity and lasting value. It is still widely considered by scholars to be the first great mystical poem in Dari, and the work had wide-reaching influence on both Muslim and Persian literature. It became a mainstay of study in the Sufi centers of Multan, Delhi, and Gulbarga.

First to Use Poetic Devices

"The Walled Garden of Truth," which was not translated into English until 1910, is a vast panorama in which Sana'i expresses his thoughts and feelings about God, reason, philosophy, love, and other ideas. Composed of 10,000 couplets, the poem spans ten different sections.

Sana'i was the first poet to use the *mathnawi*, the *qasidah* (ode), and the *ghazal* (lyric) to convey and express the mystical, ethical, and philosophical concepts of Sufism, or Islamic mysticism. Altogether, his collected poetry *(divan)* comprises about 30,000 verses. One of his other better-known works is *The Book of Everything: Journey of the Heart's Desire.* However, despite Sana'i's vow never to write panegyrics again, the presence of mild praise even in some of the poet's religious works indicates that he depended upon his patrons for material, if not spiritual, support.

Died in City of Birth

Sana'i died in Ghazna in about 1131 at a very old age. Scholars believe that he was unable to finish "The Walled Garden of Truth," as we now know it, before his death. Although all of the verses are attributed to Sana'i, historians believe that substantial editorial work by other poets (perhaps commissioned by Bharam Shah) was done to coax the work into its final form.

Because of his great influence on the mystical poetry of Persia, Sana'i was commonly thought to be a prominent Sufi himself. However, because his key patrons were Islamic scholars, that is most likely not the case. In addition, Sana'i's religious poetry praised the Prophet and other great figures of Islam, indicating that his audience was the Muslim community as a whole, rather than merely the elite circle of Sufi adepts.

Books

Bosworth, C. E. et al, *The Encyclopedia of Islam,* Leiden (Brill), 1997.

Online

"Abu al-Majd Majdud ibn Adam," *The Biography Resource Center,* http://galenet.galegroup.com (December 14, 2003).
"Dari Literature during the Ghaznavid Era," *Afghan Magazine,* http://www.afghanmagazine.com (December 14, 2003).
"Hakim Sana'i," *The Storytelling Monk,* http://www.storytellingmonk.org (December 14, 2003).
"Hakim Sana'i of Ghazni," *Afganland.com,* http://www.afghanland.com (December 14, 2003).
"The Mathnavi," *Significant Names in Sufism,* http://www.gulizk.com/significant.html (December 14, 2003).
"Sana'i," *Encyclopedia Britannica,* http://www.britannica.com (December 14, 2003). □

Sonia Sanchez

American poet Sonia Sanchez (born 1934) helped define the mid-twentieth century Black Arts Move-

ment, using the language of the streets to write about the frustrations of Northern urban blacks. As an educator, she pioneered a black studies program at San Francisco State College (later became University).

Sanchez was born Wilsonia Benita Driver on September 9, 1934 in Birmingham, Alabama to Wilson L. and Lena (Jones) Driver. When Sanchez was one year old her mother died trying to deliver twins; the twins perished as well. Sanchez and her sister Pat were raised by their paternal grandmother and relatives until Sanchez was six.

Shaped By Birmingham

[sw-3]Birmingham was a large southern industrial city in the later 1930s and ran under the rules of segregation. When she was a young child, Sanchez experienced an eye-opening incidence of discrimination involving her aunt Pauline. She was riding the bus with her aunt who was on her way to work. At each stop the bus became more crowded with white people who wanted to ride it, the bus driver eventually stopped the bus and told the blacks to get off. Her aunt refused. When the bus driver threatened to throw her off, she spat on him. Her aunt was arrested and taken downtown. The family decided she would have to leave town that evening in order for the rest of them to be able to stay and not be harassed.

Sanchez suffered a huge loss at age six when her grandmother died. It also proved to be a significant turning point in her life. "I began writing when I was a little girl," Sanchez explained to Susan Kelly of the *African American Review,* "and I began stuttering and being tongue-tied. The loss of Mama, my grandmother, made me begin that whole process of writing things down." In 1943, Sanchez and her sister moved to Harlem to live with their father and his third wife. Sanchez began writing poems. "I think writers are born, like mathematicians and scientists," she told David Reich of *UU World* (the magazine of the Unitarian Universalist Association). "What stuttering made me do is write earlier." Sanchez frequented the library and credited one librarian as a significant influence. When Sanchez was 11 or 12 the librarian "gave me an anthology of what at that time was called Negro poetry. . . . I'll never forget this black woman," she told Reich.

Participated in Black Arts Movement

In 1955, Sanchez graduated from Hunter College with a B.A. in political science. She did postgraduate work at New York University in 1958, studying poetry with Louise Bogan. Along with other poets from what became known as the Black Arts Movement, Sanchez formed a writer's workshop in Greenwich Village. Other members included Amiri Baraka (LeRoi Jones) and Askia Muhammad Touré. She performed her first poetry reading in a local bar with this group of poets, because they wanted to reach people that didn't normally hear poetry. Baraka recalled an early impression of Sanchez in his autobiography (as quoted in *The Columbia History of American Poetry*), "[she was] a wide-eyed young woman, quiet and self-deprecating, was herself coming out of a bad marriage and she came to our programs announcing very quietly and timidly that she was a poet." Married and divorced from Puerto Rican immigrant Albert Sanchez, she kept his last name when writing. It was during this workshop that she published her first poem.

By the early 1960s she had joined with Haki R. Madhubuti (Don L. Lee), Nikki Giovanni, and Etheridge Knight, to form the "Broadside Quartet," a group of militant poets. Sanchez published her poetry through the Broadside Press, a newly established black press. "We thought it would be very important to begin our own institution and support our own institution," she told Kelly. "So that's what we did. Many of us turned our royalties back in to that company so they could then continue to publish and survive, and also publish younger writers." Later, she married and divorced Knight. They had three children together— Anita, Morani Neusi, and Mungu Neusi.

The writings of the Black Arts Movement were directly related to the changing environment in which black Americans were living. The civil rights movement was unfolding and Sanchez's personal beliefs were taking shape. She was an integrationist in the early 1960s and supported the philosophy of the Congress of Racial Equality (CORE), but later she embraced the views of Malcolm X and took a separatist point of view, focusing more on her black heritage. "Malcolm articulated all that we thought . . . he gave us his voice," Sanchez told Reich. "That's why many of our poems became so angry at that time - because we picked up on his voice. We said in our poetry what he was saying from stages.'' Sanchez's poetry created a language of its own. Interestingly, because her father was a schoolteacher, Sanchez grew up speaking standard English rather than a Southern or black dialect, but she captured the voices around her. ''Her poetry rejected the language of academia and took on the language of the streets,'' wrote Beth Schneider in *African American Women: A Biographical Dictionary,* ''using lowercase letters, abbreviations, phonetic spellings, and hyphens.''

Developed Early Black Studies Program

In 1965, Sanchez began her career as an educator in San Francisco, sharing her words of revolution which expressed her anger about racial and economic oppression. While at San Francisco State College (now University) she played an integral role in developing some of the first black studies courses in the nation, including a class in black English. She went on to teach at the University of Pittsburgh and became an assistant professor at Rutgers University from 1970-1971. Around this time, Sanchez separated from the ''Broadside Quartet'' and became a poet on her own. She began focusing more on black women in her writing, while her career in academia continued at Manhattan Community College and City College of the City University of New York, and as an associate professor of English at Amherst College in 1972.

It was always clear to Sanchez that her politics had an impact on her career. While at San Francisco State College the FBI pressured her landlord to put her out because she was a radical. After being arrested during a strike at Manhattan Community College in New York City, she felt she was kept from getting other teaching jobs in New York. Yet Sanchez enjoyed a long and distinguished career in academia. She later taught at the University of Pennsylvania and began teaching at Temple University in 1977. By 2003, she had lectured at over 500 universities and colleges in the United States.

Writing Took Off

Sanchez published her first book of poetry, *Homecoming,* in 1969. William Cook wrote in *The Columbia History of American Poetry,* ''her first book of poems reflects thematically and stylistically the Black Arts aesthetic and its focus on the theme of cultural and consciousness development.'' Cook continued, ''Sanchez knows the power of humor and of tenderness, qualities not often associated with Black Arts poetry.'' She followed with *We a BaddDDD People* in 1970, a book that experimented with the use of the black dialect as a poetic medium. Although Sanchez readily acknowledges there was an earlier tradition of using black English by poets such as Sterling Brown who wrote about poor Southern black men and women, she also realized she had broken new ground. ''I took the whole idea of using black English and dealing with it in an urban setting,'' she explained to Kelly, ''incorporating the hipness that was in that black urban setting.''

Sanchez was also writing plays, such as *The Bronx Is Next,* produced in New York in 1970. Sanchez told Kelly, ''[The play's] point was to talk about how destructive Harlem was. Harlem had had its moments, but the kind of Harlem I was beginning to see . . . the change was coming through drugs and decimation.'' The *University of Michigan Black Arts Movement Website* stated that her plays deal ''with characterization of women in [their] work, that make clear the stereotypes that Black women faced in the 1960s and 1970s.''

Sanchez's writing was prolific at this time. In the 1970s she published six more books of poetry and had four more plays produced. She also published three books for children, including her first book of poetry for children, *It's a New Day: Poems for Young Brothas and Sistuhs.* In 1972, she received a $1,000 award from the American Academy of Arts and Letters and a PEN Writing Award. In 1977-78, she received the National Education Association Award. The monetary gift that accompanied it allowed her to continue her creative work. She published *I've Been a Woman* in 1978.

Joined Nation of Islam

Between the years of 1972 and 1976, Sanchez belonged to the Nation of Islam. She has given various reasons for why she left the Nation. In *Black Women Writers at Work,* Sanchez was quoted as saying: ''It was not easy being in the Nation. I was/am a writer. I was also speaking on campuses. In the Nation at that time women were supposed to be in the background. My contribution to the Nation has been that I refused to let them tell me where my place was. I would be reading my poetry some place, and men would get up to leave, and I'd say, 'Look, my words are equally important.' So I got into trouble.'' She added, ''I had to fight a lot of people in and outside of the Nation due to so-called sexism. I spoke up. I think it was important that there were women there to do that.'' However in her interview with Kelly in 2000, she stated: ''I had gone into the Nation because I was raising my children by myself, and the public school situation was really pathetic. The Nation was one of the places to receive a good education at the time. . . . But I was not greeted well in the Nation, because they said I was . . . a revolutionary PanAfricanist and socialist. That was told to me point-blank. So I understood, truly, that my days in the Nation were numbered.'' Sanchez denied to Kelly that she had left the Nation because of feminist issues.

Became Highly-Regarded Poet

Homegirls and Handgrenades won an American Book Award in 1985. Sanchez followed with *Under a Soprano Sky* (1987), then *Wounded in the House of a Friend* (1995). Throughout her writing career, Sanchez tackled the most difficult of subjects, including violence, bigotry, drug abuse, gender issues, and poverty. Her 1997 book *Does Your House Have Lions?* was about her stepbrother who had died of AIDS. It was nominated for both the NAACP Image and the National Book Critics Circle Award. She followed with *Like the Singing Coming off the Drums: Love Poems* (1998). The subject matter of Sanchez's writings was always real life and never shied away from the political. The form of her writing drew equal attention. One notable experiment was her combination of black English and the haiku, as displayed in *Shake Loose My Skin: New and Selected Poems* (1999). Of the last book, which offered a selection drawn from over 30 years of Sanchez's poetry, *Library Journal*'s Ann K. van Buren wrote that it "leaves one in awe of the stretches of language Sanchez has helped to legitimize." *Publisher's Weekly* wrote: "This collection should draw wide attention to the consistency of Sanchez's achievement, and to the success of her formal adaptations."

Made Additional Inroads

In addition to her writing career, Sanchez made occasional recordings of her work as well, including her early books of poetry *Homecoming* and *We a BaddDDD People*. Later came creations such as her 1971 recording *Sonia Sanchez and Robert Bly*, her 1982 recording *IDKT: Captivating Facts about the Heritage of Black Americans*, and *Sacred Ground, with Sweet Honey and the Rock* (1995). She was sought out for her poetry readings, which were impassioned and full of spontaneity. She traveled extensively to such far reaches as Cuba, Africa, the People's Republic of China, Australia, and Norway to read her work.

A contributing editor to *Black Scholar* and *The Journal of African Studies*, Sanchez has also edited two anthologies: *We be Word Sorcerers, 25 Stories by Black Americans* and *360 degrees of Blackness Coming at You*.

Sanchez retired in 1999 from Temple University after they awarded her the Lindback Award for Distinguished Teaching. She began teaching at Temple in 1977 and was their first Presidential Fellow and later became the Laura Carnell professor of English and women's studies. In May 2004 she was awarded an honorary degree from Haverford College.

Sanchez continued to make her home in Philadelphia, writing and taking speaking engagements. She remained committed to social change. "All poets, all writers are political," Sanchez told Reich. "They either maintain the status quo, or they say, 'Something's wrong, let's change it for the better.' That's what my life has really been about." As for her inspiration, she told Kelly: "It is that love of language that has propelled me, that love of language that came from listening to my grandmother speak black English."

Books

African American Women: A Biographical Dictionary, edited by Dorothy C. Salem, Garland Publishing, 1993.
Black Women Writers at Work, edited by Claudia Tate, Continuum, 1983.
The Columbia History of American Poetry, edited by Jay Parini, Columbia University Press, 1993.
"Sonia Sanchez," *Contemporary Black Biography,* Volume 17, Gale Research, 1998.
"Sonia Sanchez," *Contemporary Poets,* 7th ed., St. James Press, 2001.
"Sonia Sanchez," *Major Authors and Illustrators for Children and Young Adults,* 2nd ed., 8 vols., Gale Group, 2002.

Periodicals

African American Review, Winter 2000.
Library Journal, February 1, 1999.
PR Newswire, May 11, 2004.
Publishers Weekly, February 27, 1995; December 21, 1998.
UU World, May/June 1999.

Online

"Lindback Award Winner Sonia Sanchez," *Temple University website,* http://www.temple.edu (January 2, 2004).
"Sonia Sanchez," *Black Arts Movement class at University of Michigan,* http://www.umich.edu (December 16, 2003).
"Sonia Sanchez," *Howard University website,* http://www.founders.howard.edu/reference/sonia_sanchez.htm (December 16, 2003).
"Sonia Sanchez," *The Academy of American Poets website,* http://www.poets.org (December 16, 2003). □

Romy Schneider

Austrian-born actress Romy Schneider (1938–1982) went from playing Bavarian princesses in frothy historical dramas to working with some of the most influential and daring European filmmakers of her era during the 1960s and 1970s. "Elegant and sensuous, she had a striking screen presence," noted Schneider's *Times* of London obituary from 1982, "but despite excellent performances of both comic and dramatic parts, her career did not quite fulfil its early promise."

Schneider was born Rosemarie Magdalena Albach-Retty on September 23, 1938, in Vienna, Austria, and during her early years "Romy" became the shortened version of her given name. She was the third generation in a theatrical family on the side of her father, Wolf Albach-Retty, who regularly appeared with the Vienna Volkstheater. Her paternal grandmother, Rosa Albach-Retty, had been a famous Vienna stage actress of an earlier era. Schneider's mother, meanwhile, was a film actress in Germany during in the 1930s, appearing in the light comedies and toothless historical epics that were part of the Nazi government's propaganda effort. During World War II, Schneider's parents separated, and after the age of four she lived with her mother and maternal grandparents in Berchtesgaden, Germany, where she attended school.

As a teen, Schneider attended a school in Salzburg, Austria, where she performed in plays and participated in several sports. Her ambition was to become a painter, a career idea she jettisoned after her film career was suddenly launched at the age of 15. A director of one of her mother's films offered a part playing the on-screen daughter, and *Wenn der weisse Flieder wieder blüht* (When the White Lilacs Bloom Again) was a box-office success in 1953. Schneider was offered more parts, including a light biopic

about the adolescence of Queen Victoria, *Mädchenjahre einer Königen* (Girlhood of a Queen).

Beloved ''Sissi''

Mädchenjahre einer Königen was written and directed by veteran Austrian filmmaker Ernst Marischka, and its success led to Schneider being cast in 1955's *Sissi,* the first in a trilogy of films about Elisabeth, the wife of Austro-Hungarian Emperor Franz Josef. The film was a huge success in West Germany and Austria at the time and was quickly followed by two sequels that chronicled the beloved princess's 1854 wedding and subsequently tragic personal life. The trilogy's popularity seemed linked to some lingering post-World War II unease in West Germany, maintained critic Ute Schneider. ''Hardly any other 1950s tearjerker film had been more effective in letting the audience sob their heart out,'' she wrote, according to an essay in the *International Dictionary of Films and Filmmakers.* ''It is a pertinent example of the continuing repression of political reality that can be traced in [German] entertainment cinema. Sissi demonstrated yet again the victory of the heart over the 'evil' of politics, the dream of conquering people and countries with no more than a feminine smile and maternal care.''

Fled to Paris

Sissi made Schneider a major new screen star in Europe at the time, but the films proved to have a longevity few expected. ''Unrivalled in their sentimentality, the Sissi films remain a staple of daytime television schedules and occupy

an exalted place in German gay iconography,'' *Guardian* writer Denis Staunton asserted years later. An abridged version of the trilogy was dubbed in English and titled *Forever My Love* for its 1962 release, but overseas audiences were unimpressed. Nor did *Mädchenjahre einer Königen* do particularly well when a dubbed English version was released in 1958 as *The Story of Vickie,* but Schneider did make her first visit to the United States on a small press tour for the release that year.

Schneider later said that her family was still largely in control of her career at the time and were selecting her scripts for her. She was cast in a 1958 movie *Christine,* about romantic intrigues at the 1906 Viennese court, which co-starred her with Alain Delon, one of France's top leading men at the time. The pair fell in love, and upon their engagement Schneider left Germany and settled in Paris with him. The German tabloid press was outraged, as were the studios, directors, and producers who depended on her box-office allure. Despite her fame, she later recalled in an interview with the magazine *Life,* she instead felt like ''an orange that must be pressed to the last drop. Nobody ever thought of me, or ever asked me to shout or be a real human being. People thought, 'How sweet, how lovely, how kind she is!' I wanted to be modern and hard, to be a grown-up woman. I had to run away.''

Taking a break from film for a time, Schneider made an uncredited cameo appearance in *Plein Soleil* (Purple Noon), the first-ever film adaptation of Patricia Highsmith's *The Talented Mr. Ripley* novels, but turned down other parts. She was even offered $200,000 for a fourth *Sissi,* but Schneider was determined to transform herself into a serious film actress, despite the sniping back home that she had given up her career for love. ''I sometimes think I am too true, too honest, too direct,'' she told a writer for *Look* in 1962. ''That was what they thought was wrong with me in Germany.... The German people are now very happy about my new career, and they want me to return. But I will not speak to German film producers because they refused to understand me.''

Multilingual Star

Schneider's return to the screen began with her debut on the Paris stage with Delon in *'Tis Pity She's a Whore,* an Elizabethan drama in translation that required Schneider to play her part in French, which was still unfamiliar to her. The production, in the hands of a famously formidable Italian stage and screen director Luchino Visconti, was a hit with critics and theater-goers, and led Visconti to cast her in *Boccaccio '70.* This was a trilogy of stories involving some salacious romantic intrigues, with Anita Ekberg and Sophia Loren playing the two other roles in segments directed by renowned Italian filmmakers Federico Fellini and Vittorio de Sica. The film was a terrific success across Europe and was released in North America as well. In her story, Schneider played a contessa who discovers that her husband regularly hires costly prostitutes and decides to fool him once herself.

After that point, Schneider made a few films in English, including Orson Welles's lauded adaptation of the Franz

Kafka novel *The Trial.* The 1962 version starred Anthony Perkins as a man who is put on trial for unknown crimes; in an effort to clear his name, he visits the palatial home of the mysterious "Advocate," played by Welles. Schneider was cast as the seductive maid there, Leni. Next, Schneider appeared in *The Victors,* a 1963 Columbia Studios project set during World War II. She also made *The Cardinal* with Otto Preminger, playing a young Viennese woman who falls in love with Tom Tryon's ambitious Roman Catholic priest.

A Few Hollywood Hits

Schneider had a five-picture deal with Columbia, and the most profitable work to come from it was a 1964 farce with Jack Lemmon, *Good Neighbor Sam.* In it, she played a European heiress-to-be who asks her married advertising-executive neighbor to pretend to be her spouse so that she might claim her inheritance. But Schneider disliked working in Hollywood, in part perhaps because of the press she earned for her efforts; a brief *Good Housekeeping* profile from 1965 claimed she "sometimes looks as American as tollhouse cookies; other times, as French as an éclair."

That same year, Schneider's last notable English-language movie was released, *What's New, Pussycat?* The script was written by Woody Allen, the first full-length comedy from him, and featured Peter O'Toole as the fiancé of Schneider's character. He is desperate to curb his infidelities before their impending wedding, but women seem to fall madly in love with him; Peter Sellers played the psychoanalyst who is attempting to cure him, and all parties—including the film's supporting stars, Capucine and Ursula Andress—descend on a country villa for a farcical weekend.

Object of Tabloid Gossip

Schneider went back to France around 1966. Though she continued to appear in the occasional French film with Delon, their romance cooled and he was rumored to have ended it by sending her a single rose. She wed actor and director Harry Meyen-Haubenstock in 1966, with whom she had a son, but they were divorced by 1975, and in Europe's celebrity magazines Schneider was regularly deemed unlucky in love by the press. Her personal life became the subject of tabloid fodder, with even a miscarriage making headlines, but Schneider gave birth to a second child, Sarah, in 1977 with her new husband, photographer Daniel Biasini.

Schneider's career was boosted when director Claude Sautet began casting her with Michel Piccoli in a series of movies, many of which focused on her appeal as an intelligent, sexually modern woman. These included *Les Choses de la Vie* (The Things of Life) in 1970, *Max et les ferrailleurs* (Max and the Junkmen) in 1971, and 1972's *César et Rosalie.* She reprised her "Sissi" role when Visconti made the 1973 period drama *Ludwig,* about the princess's cousin, Prince Ludwig II of Bavaria. This time, however, her Sissi was no sweet ingénue but rather a calculating young woman who views her increasingly unstable cousin Ludwig, who is in love with her, as an unsuitable choice for a spouse.

In 1975, Schneider made a film with Claude Chabrol, *Les Innocents aux mains sales* (Dirty Hands). Its story centered on a woman who plots to kill her husband, played by Rod Steiger, with her lover in Saint-Tropez. In 1977, she appeared in her first German production in nearly two decades, *Gruppenbild mit Dame* (Group Portrait with Lady). The film was a joint French-German effort based on a popular nonfiction book by German writer Heinrich Böll, and it won her the Deutscher Filmpreis for Acting that year. In 1979, she appeared in the Costa-Gavras film *Clair de femme,* following it with a work from director Bertrand Tavernier, *La Mort en direct* (Deathwatch).

A Tragic End

Schneider's health began to fail, and her personal life indeed turned tragic when her 14-year-old son died after climbing over the iron gate of their garden. She underwent a serious kidney operation and died of heart failure in her Paris home on May 29, 1982. Her last film was released in 1981, *La Passante du Sans-Souci* (The Passerby), another French-German co-production in which she co-starred once more with Piccoli. Posthumously, Schneider became an icon in Europe, the symbol of an era when women performers began to take on more daring, provocative roles. There have been several French and German-language biographies of her life and career, and between Vienna and Villach there is even an inter-city train named in her honor that runs twice daily.

Books

International Dictionary of Films and Filmmakers, Volume 3: Actors and Actresses, St. James Press, 1996.

Periodicals

Good Housekeeping, March 1965.
Guardian (London, England), August 15, 1996.
Life, June 14, 1963.
Look, September 11, 1962.
San Francisco Chronicle, January 7, 2000.
Time, December 14, 1962.
Times (London, England), May 31, 1982. □

Tex Schramm

In 2003, the National Football League (NFL) lost one of its greats with the death of Tex Schramm (1920–2003). Not a player, but an owner, a promoter, and an innovator, Schramm created the NFL where the Dallas Cowboys became "America's Team" and football became American fans' sport of choice.

Born in San Gabriel, California, in 1920, and named after his father, not the lone star state, Texas Ernest Schramm ended his football career after high school. The pint-sized-but-almost-150-pound fullback decided that writing about the game was safer than playing it. Attending the University of Texas, Schramm earned a degree in journalism. Then, after a stint in the U.S. Air Force, he began his career as a $30-a-week sportswriter for the *Austin American-Statesman*.

Early Career

In 1947 Schramm entered the arena of football when he was hired as the then Los Angeles Rams' publicity director. During his five-year tenure Schramm hinted at what would become his unwavering commitment to do what was best for the game and its fans. This included forcing an end to discrimination within the team by signing a player from a black college, Tank Younger, in 1949. One year later, the Rams became the first team to draft a black player, running back Dan Towler. Rewarded for his dedication to the team, Schramm was named the Rams' general manager in 1952. Over the next five years he worked, on a broader level, to increase the NFL's popularity. To assist him in accomplishing this goal Schramm hired Pete Rozelle to replace him as the Rams' publicity director. Rozelle would eventually become the commissioner of the NFL.

In 1957 Schramm left his job as the Rams' general manager and returned to journalism, but not as a sportswriter. During the 1950s the major networks were just be-

ginning to realize that sports–football in particular–could be a moneymaker. Schramm also recognized the potential of the new medium to give a boost to football's popularity. By broadcasting games on the television, more people would have access to the sport, effectively increasing the number of football fans, and increased ticket sales would follow. For the next three years Schramm, as an executive for CBS Sports, expanded the media coverage of U.S. football teams, among them a struggling small-market team called the Green Bay Packers. "I cut the Packers a check for $15,000," Schramm later recalled to the *Fort Worth Star-Telegram*. "I threw in more money, thinking it would be good for the network in the long run." Television, however, was not the only means used to increase football's audience. Logically, if the league had more teams, then football would have more fans.

Established Cowboys Dynasty

While expanding the NFL to include more teams has become a common occurrence, in 1960 expansion was a rarity. Schramm resigned from CBS Sports and was hired by Clint Murchison, the founder of the Dallas Cowboys, to become that team's president and general manager before the NFL even approved the Cowboy's existence. Once the NFL gave its approval, however, there was no stopping Schramm. In his plans to grow the team he was helped by what he later called "the most important piece of legislation in the history of sports," as the *Fort Worth Star-Telegram* quoted. That legislation gave all teams in the NFL equal shares of the revenue their televised games generated. The impact of this decision was immediate. No longer would small-market teams like the Packers have to beg Schramm for extra money because their television audience was only a fraction of big-market teams like the Rams. Parity had been created in the NFL.

This new parity helped Schramm and the Dallas Cowboys because the virtually unknown Cowboys now had money to not only attract competent coaches, staff, and players, but also to publicize the fact that a new football dynasty was being built in Texas. As the team's general manager, Schramm spent the team's television money wisely. First, he hired experienced coach Tom Landry and ingenious draft advisor Gil Brant, because he understood that coaching and drafting well would result in an unstoppable team.

For the next five years the Cowboys had a losing record. In 1965 the team began to emerge and reached the .500 mark, and it was clear that the patience required to build the team through drafting was about to pay off. With notable defensive players like Bob Lilly and Mel Renfro as well as wide receiver Boy Hayes, the Cowboys, in 1966, tackled and ran their way into the championship game. Ironically, they lost to the team Schramm once donated money to: the Green Bay Packers.

Merged the NFL and AFL

For a team to become a dynasty, the bar of competition must be raised. However, within the NFL teams competed only against other NFL teams. There was a rival–the American Football League (AFL)–but teams from this league also played only against other AFL teams. What was needed was a merger of the two leagues. In this step the NFL resisted; it saw the AFL as its ugly stepsister, born off its own success. Schramm stepped in and called Lamar Hunt, owner of the AFL's Kansas City Chiefs. Together the two men negotiated a deal where both leagues could benefit. The first benefit of this merger was a championship game where the two top teams from each league competed. It was called the Super Bowl.

Now that the competition had been raised through the successful merger of both leagues, Schramm refocused his efforts on promoting the Cowboys. He wanted his team to be seen not just as just an expansion team, but as a team all football fans would root for, even over their home team. Throughout the 1970s Schramm established what would become the Cowboy's swagger: the unrelenting confidence that no team, no player, no coach was better. To publicize the team he decided to make another merger. Knowing that, on television as everywhere else, sex sells, Schramm hired professional female dancers. These dancers, as the Dallas Cowboy Cheerleaders, toured around the country promoting the Cowboys as well as performing at the team's games. Schramm's highly successfully marketing campaign was not approved by Coach Landry, however. As noted by the London *Times,* Landry referred to the Cheerleaders as "porno queens." Schramm responded by forcing "his coach to watch a real pornographic film." Landry never again negatively commented on Schramm's ideas.

Pushed for More Innovations

Once Schramm had the television audience watching the Cowboys' cheerleaders, he came up with another idea to capture the fan's attention, and this time the focus was on the athletes. He would play the team on a national holiday. The Detroit Lions had already established their presence by playing a morning game on Thanksgiving. That changed when Schramm scheduled the Cowboys to play an afternoon game. Football fans, hungry for something to watch as they ate their turkey dinners, tuned in to the Cowboys. As a result, the team's popularity soared; a new stadium was built with its infamous hole in the dome roof where God could watch his favorite team play; and Texas Stadium's box seats were soon filled with Texas oilmen who would freely spend their money. By 1978 the Cowboys had won two Super Bowls. More importantly to Schramm, the Cowboys had also been named "America's Team" by NFL Films. Fans embraced the team's new name while Schramm conjured up another idea to expand the Cowboy dynasty.

Since its inception, football had been seen as an American sport. As the Dallas Cowboys reigned throughout the 1980s, Schramm knew his team, "America's Team" could become the "World's Team" if only the global audience had the opportunity to see them play-not on television, but live. So, in 1986, Schramm packed up the Cowboys and flew them to Wembley Stadium in London, England for a pre-season game against the Chicago Bears. He called it the American Bowl. His risky idea paid off and the Cowboys

became even more popular. This influenced other teams to travel overseas including to Japan to expand their fan base.

By 1989 Schramm had, as then NFL Commissioner Paul Tagliabue told the *Los Angeles Times,* built "the NFL into America's passion by developing a glamour franchise with national appeal." Yet, this appeal could not stop the decline of the Cowboys. Infamous off-the-field antics and parties that ended in drug busts, as well as on-the-field poor play and the ineffectiveness of Coach Landry eventually overwhelmed "America's Team." New ideas were needed and those ideas came when businessman Jerry Jones bought the Dallas Cowboys. He surprised Schramm by not only firing Landry, but also firing Schramm.

Although no longer affiliated with the team, Schramm remained a fan of the Cowboys and continued working to promote the NFL through his tenure as president and CEO of the World League of American Football (now known as NFL Europe). His efforts led to the NFL being announced over more than 200 radio stations as well as games being broadcasted in Spanish. "Schramm was Barnum and Bailey all rolled into one," former Cowboy Charlie Waters told the *Los Angeles Times.* "He was a great salesman."

In 1991 Schramm was inducted into the Pro Football Hall of Fame, but curiously had not been welcomed into the Cowboy's own Hall of Fame, the Ring of Honor. Jones rarely spoke to his predecessor until 2003, when Schramm's ill health prompted him to announce that Schramm's name would be added to the Ring. "He is going to be recognized as the architect as the man who started and built the Cowboys into America's Team," Jones told the *Los Angeles Times.* "That's as it should be."

Before the induction ceremony could take place, Schramm passed away on July 15, 2003. However, upon first hearing of his induction into the Ring of Honor during a visit to Texas Stadium, he "literally rose to the occasion . . . in stubborn rebellion against infirmity," Frank Luksa wrote in *Texas Monthly,* then "straightened his bent body as best he could and made his way to the stage to bask in forthcoming attention."

Forever Influenced Football

Schramm's influence on football continued after his death. Imagine the game without instant replay, overtimes, microphone-wired referees, the 30-second clock, goal post strips, wild-card playoffs, computerized draft selections, quarterback's wired helmets, and the Super Bowl. All were Schramm's ideas. However, perhaps he will be best remembered for being football's number one promoter who never forgot who mattered most: the fans. Bill "Cowboy" Lamza, president of the Dallas Cowboys Fan Club shared this memory of Schramm with the *Houston Chronicle:* "Tex was always a fan's fan . . . any fan could write a letter to Tex . . . and they'd get a letter back from him, signed personally." This personal touch made fans feel like an important part of the team. However for Schramm it was always the fans, as he once told the *Fort Worth Star-Telegram,* who made him feel great, even after he had been out of the public eye for more than a decade. "When I go somewhere, people always come up and say, 'Tex Schramm? All I want to do is say thank you for a lot of great seasons and great memories.' "

Periodicals

Fort Worth Star-Telegram, December 4, 1998; January 17, 2001.
Houston Chronicle, July 15, 2003.
Los Angeles Times, July 16, 2003.
New York Times, July 16, 2003.
Texas Monthly, September, 2003.
Times (London, England), August 11, 2003.
USA Today, July 16, 2003. □

Richard W. Sears

American merchant Richard W. Sears (1863–1914) possessed one of his era's shrewdest business minds. As the founder of the Sears, Roebuck & Company mail-order powerhouse, Sears revolutionized retailing in a rapidly expanding, increasingly prosperous nation.

"*S*ears had a deep, intuitive feel for the commercial needs and aspirations of the people of rural America," noted *American Heritage* writer John Steele Gordon, "and a genius for writing catalogue and advertising copy that awakened those needs and aspirations."

Early Business Experience

Sears was born on December 7, 1863, in Stewartville, Minnesota. His parents were of English heritage, and his father was a successful wagonmaker who entered into a stock farm venture that failed. After his father died, the teenage Sears was obligated to support his mother and sisters and went to work in the offices of the Minneapolis and St. Louis Railroad in Minneapolis. He worked as a telegraph operator, and then trained to become a station agent.

Relocating to a small burg called Redwood Falls, Sears ran its railroad station and slept in a loft there as well, a berth he got in exchange for keeping the station clean. He supplemented his income by dealing in coal and lumber and by contracting with local Native American communities to ship their venison. In his spare time, he studied the catalogs that came through, comparing the wholesale prices of the merchandise listed on the bills of lading for train freight with the retail prices in the catalogs, and concluded that there was profit to be made in mail-order businesses.

One day in 1886, Redwood Falls's jeweler declined to accept a shipment of watches that arrived at the station. Instead of returning them to the manufacturer, Sears asked for and was given permission to sell them. He then sent out letters to other station agents along the line offering them for sale at $14, two dollars more than what he had paid. The watches had a suggested retail price of $25 and sold quickly. Station agents asked for more, and Sears's first mail-

order company was born. He contracted with the watchmaker for more and took out advertisements in St. Paul newspapers.

After earning $5,000 during his first year in business—a small fortune at the time—he quit his railroad job to devote himself full time to his new business. The R. W. Sears Watch Company catalog started to offer a wider array of jewelry and then silverware, and he decided that relocating to Chicago, a transportation hub, would help keep his shipping costs low. When some of the watches began to come back needing repairs, Sears hired Alvah C. Roebuck, a self-taught watchmaker who had grown up on an Indiana farm.

Bored with Banking

After just three years in operation, Sears decided to sell his mail-order business, and the transaction netted him several thousand dollars. For a time, he ran a bank in rural Iowa but found that he missed the livelier merchandising business. Heading back to Minneapolis, Sears teamed with Roebuck again and put the latter's name on the company. By 1893 both had returned to Chicago and the second venture was thriving under its new name, the Sears, Roebuck and Company.

Sears and Roebuck printed and distributed a free catalog that offered an array of goods, from saddles and guns to baby carriages and blankets. Sears wrote all of its ad copy, but he lacked the organizational skills to keep the company from being constantly inundated with orders—sometimes for goods that were not yet available for shipping. At times, he burned piles of order slips when things became too backed up. He and Roebuck often worked seven days a week, putting in 16-hour days.

Fed up, Roebuck sold his interest around 1894, and Sears scrambled for a new partner with solid managerial experience. He found Aaron Nusbaum, the owner of a pneumatic-tube company who paid a sales call on Sears one day. Sears offered him a partnership, and Nusbaum sold his company to buy into Sears' mail-order firm; he also brought his brother-in-law, Julius Rosenwald, with him. Rosenwald owned a successful Chicago menswear business that had wholesaled suits to Sears and knew the company had vast profit potential.

Earned Enmity of Shopkeepers

Sears' company began a heady period of growth in the late 1890s. Its "audience was rural America, millions of thrifty consumers whose only shopping outlet was the general store, where selection was spares and price markups usually horrendous," wrote Eugene Carlson in the *Wall Street Journal.* The cover of the 1897 Sears catalog urged customers to take it to their local merchants and compare the prices. Inside, its pages offered a vast array of goods, from firearms and ammunition to hats, books and even large-ticket items like pianos that could be purchased on an installment plan. Sears "knew how to talk to flinty, skeptical rural America," noted a *Fortune* profile. "He wrote copy for his catalogue as if he were looking a farmer right in the eye."

Despite his poor managerial skills, Sears had an excellent sense for marketing in addition to his writing talents. The few years he had spent in Iowa as a banker had given him insight into his target customer, and Sears courted German and Swedish immigrants in the Plains states by including ordering instructions in their languages. In another one of his innovative schemes, called the "Iowazation" project, Sears asked his best customers in the state to distribute 24 catalogs among their friends and neighbors; in return, they earned a small percentage of the resulting sales. The program proved so successful that it was used in other states as well.

Within a few years, the Sears catalog was so popular that envious local merchants sometimes paid youngsters to collect them for burning. In other parts of the country, the company was forced to send the catalogs out in brown wrappers, since many local general stores that were losing sales to Sears served as the post offices. Volume sales kept merchandise prices in the catalog low, and a reassuring money-back guarantee won over customers. Sears had copied the "satisfaction guaranteed" idea from the Montgomery Ward catalog, which was already a success by the time he started his company. But Sears' catalog soon surpassed Ward's, and the pair engaged in an intense business rivalry for many years.

Capitalized on Boom Years

When Sears teamed with Nusbaum and Rosenwald in 1895, his company was selling $500,000 worth of goods

annually; five years later, salesr hit $11 million. Sears had found a huge, untapped consumer market in rural America. Some 853,000 Sears catalogs went out in 1900, at a time when the U.S. population of 76 million was classified as three-fifths rural. The catalogs that boasted "We sell everything" were eagerly awaited by households in the rapidly expanding Midwest and West. The women's fashions pages were torn out and taken to small-town dressmakers or copied at home on one of the several models of sewing machines the catalogs sold; customers could even build new homes from kits the catalog offered for sale. The success of the company was helped by fortuitous timing; railroads were expanding across the United States, which helped move freight along more quickly, and the Rural Free Delivery Act, which went into effect in 1896, guaranteed the catalogs would be delivered to every single American home, no matter how remote.

The three partners did not get along well, however. "Nusbaum was a burr under both Rosenwald's and Sears's saddles as a fence sitter who would defer to their decisions but say 'I told you so' if things went wrong," wrote Daniel A. Wren and Ronald G. Greenwood in their book *Management Innovators,* a chapter of which was reprinted in a 1998 issue of the *Journal of Leadership Studies.* Sears eventually delivered an ultimatum: either the brothers-in-law buy out his share of the company, or he and Rosenwald would buy Nusbaum's share. This forced Rosenwald to choose between his family and the company, and he chose the company. Nusbaum was bought out in 1901 for $1.25 million, a massive return on his original investment of $37,500.

Sold Shares in a Huff

By 1906 the Sears catalog enterprise moved into a new Chicago headquarters that made it the largest single-business space in the world at three million square feet. The company was receiving about 20,000 orders daily from its catalog and even boasted the world's first automatic envelope-opening machine; during the leadup to Christmas, about 100,000 orders arrived each day. It was the largest mail-order business in the world.

Rosenwald possessed the managerial genius that helped Sears' marketing vision attain success. He devised a color-coding for order processing and even set up a type of assembly line that enabled them to be filled quickly. An unknown carmaker from Detroit, Henry Ford, visited the Sears headquarters to see the idea in operation and later used it in his first factory. An order could be filled in just 15 minutes from the moment the envelope was opened, but the problem came from orders that had to be filled from multiple departments. Rosenwald created a system under which a department would be fined if it did not fill an order in the targeted time frame.

Sears' lack of business acumen brought his own severance with the company. A 1907 depression caused sales to decline from $49 million in 1906 to $47 million, and Sears argued that the 1908 advertising budget should be increased. Rosenwald resisted, believing it more prudent to reign in expenses during the economic slump, and so Sears sold his shares for $10 million to Goldman, Sachs, the Wall

Street investment banking firm, in 1909. He was given a seat on its board but attended only one meeting.

Sears retired to his farm in the countryside north of Chicago and died in Waukesha, Wisconsin on September 28, 1914. To his wife, Minneapolis native Anna Lydia Meckstroth, and four children he left an estate valued at $25 million. Under Rosenwald and successors, the company that bore Sears' name well into the twenty-first century continued to thrive. It opened its first store in 1925, and the catalog continued to be a staple in American homes until the 1970s.

Sears was buried in an opulent crypt in Chicago's Rosehill Cemetery, where legend has it that near his grave a man in a top hat can be seen walking toward the burial site of Montgomery Ward, Sears' archrival.

Books

Dictionary of American Biography, American Council of Learned Societies, 1928-1936.
Gale Encyclopedia of U.S. Economic History, Gale, 1999.

Periodicals

American Heritage, September 1993.
Fortune, March 23, 1992.
Journal of Leadership Studies, Spring 1998.
Wall Street Journal, February 21, 1989. □

Ruth Porter Crawford Seeger

American composer, music teacher and musicologist Ruth Crawford Seeger (1901–1953) is regarded by many to be the most important American female composer of the 20th Century. She was a crucial figure in the American modernist movement in the 1920s and early 1930s and also played a key part in the American folk music revival. With her husband, composer Charles Seeger, she became a champion of the downtrodden.

Early Years

Seeger was born Ruth Porter Crawford was born July 3, 1901, in East Liverpool, Ohio, the daughter of a Methodist minister and his wife. Because of his religious calling, Seeger's father, a conservative man of humble means, took posts at many different parsonages, and the family moved around a lot. He died in 1914 while the family was living in Jacksonville, Florida.

During Seeger's itinerant childhood, her mother encouraged her interest in music while her father's sermons inspired her to write poetry. Seeger began studying piano when she was 11, and she became an accomplished pianist while still a teenager. After she graduated from high school, she enrolled in Foster's School of Musical Art. When the school relocated to Miami, Seeger moved to Chicago in 1921 to continue her music education. Her mother intended for her to study piano for a year and then return home to teach music.

Began Composing in Chicago

But things didn't go as planned. Chicago opened up a whole new world to Seeger, and at age 19 she entered a period of tremendous personal and artistic growth. She was introduced to orchestral and symphonic music, opera and, later, avant-garde music. She would remain in Chicago until 1929, when she moved to New York.

An important early step in Seeger's increasing sophistication as a musician and an individual came when she began studying musical composition and theory under the hard-driving music teacher Adolf Weidig, whose father had been a pupil of Brahms. The innovative teacher, originally from Hamburg, Germany, encouraged his students to produce original works as part of their education, and that advise greatly influenced Seeger's development as a composer.

Seeger's personal growth took another great leap when she began studying under pianist Djana Lavoie Herz, who was a disciple of Alexander Scriabin, a renowned Russian composer whose deep interests in philosophy and mysticism were evident in his piano sonatas, concertos and symphonies. His later and more complex works exhibited atonality, a method of musical composition that rejects the principles of tonality, harmony and key. Through Herz, Seeger became interested in theosophy, Eastern religions, European modernism and American transcendentalism.

Seeger became part of Herz's circle of musician friends that included avante-garde composers Dane Rudyhar, Aaron Copland, Carl Ruggles, and Henry Cowell. Rudhyar and Cowell encouraged Seeger's leanings toward atonality. Seeger developed a professional relationship with Cowell that had a tremendous impact on her career. Cowell, a highly regarded publisher and promoter of new music, became her most ardent supporter.

Seeger's earliest compositions, created in 1922 and 1923, were unremarkable works created for children. However, her subsequent pieces, produced between 1924 and 1929, represented a quantum leap. Influenced by the new music she was exposed to and by her talented circle of friends, Seeger began developing her own unique compositional style, which became evident in the *Piano Preludes* she created in 1924. At the time, it was a widespread belief among male composers that composition was a task too complex for the female mind, but Cowell recognized Seeger's abilities and would publish and write about her music as well as arrange performances. Concert performances of her work caused a critic to comment that Seeger could "sling dissonances like a man" (according to her daughter Peggy Seeger's website).

Her Chicago work, particularly her nine *Piano Preludes,* showed the influence of Scriabin, with their atonal elements, including dissonance and irregular meters and rhythms. These daring and original pieces reveal an artist at the peak of her form. Other works from this impressive period include *Sonata for Violin and Piano* (1926) and *Suite for Five Wind Instruments and Piano* (1927).

During this time, Seeger worked in folk music as well. She collaborated with poet Carl Sandburg on folk song arrangements, contributing music arrangements to his book *The American Songbag* and, later, music for eight of his poems. She also taught piano to his children. Later in her career, she would return to folk music in a more significant way.

Moved to New York

Cowell had published Seeger's works in a *New Music Quarterly* series, and he convinced Seeger that she had outgrown Chicago. In 1929, acting on Cowell's advice, she moved to New York City. Cowell had arranged for her to study composition with Charles Seeger, an important composer and musicologist, who introduced her to new and more complex musical theories. His teachings greatly affected the way she composed her music.

Initially, it seemed an odd student-teacher coupling. Charles Seeger did not hold a high opinion of women composers, and Seeger found him cold and aloof. However, Charles Seeger soon recognized her tremendous talent, and they entered into a course of intense sessions. Working together, they developed Charles Seeger's theories on dissonance, which would essentially help create a new form of American music that was complex and experimental. Daughter Peggy Seeger relates on her website that her mother later wrote to Charles, saying, "I felt that while you were there I could write symphonies. After a lesson I felt a new power flowing." Soon, Seeger and Charles Seeger realized they were developing strong feelings for each other.

Charles Seeger's influence was so strong that Seeger's work can be divided into two distinctive periods: her Chicago phase and her New York phase. Work from the latter phase is more experimental, as she worked with serial techniques. By 1930, she was regarded as a major talent in American modernism. That year, she became the first woman to receive a Guggenheim fellowship to study in Europe. She visited Berlin and Paris and met famous composers Bela Bartok, Alexander Mossolov, William Walton, Alban Berg, Paul Hindemith, and Josef Rufer.

In Europe, Seeger did more writing than studying. She raised eyebrows when she turned down an opportunity to study with the celebrated Arnold Schoenberg. But she was now confident of her own abilities, and she resented the prevailing Viennese conceit that worthwhile music could not be written beyond the borders of Austria and Germany. While overseas, she wrote some of her best works including "Three Chants," "String Quartet," and "Three Songs." Today, "Three Chants," a wordless text for women's chorus, is considered far ahead of its time.

Before Seeger left for Europe, she and Charles Seeger had admitted their love for each other. In fact, they finally acknowledged their feelings as Charles Seeger was driving her to the Quebec port where she would set sail. They continued their relationship when Seeger returned in 1931,

the year she wrote her most famous work, *String Quartet,* a masterpiece of modernist classical music. In 1960, music critic George Perle, in his pivotal article written for *The Score* ("Atonality and the Twelve-Tone System in the United States"), remarked that the "*String Quartet 1931* of Ruth Crawford is an original and inventive work whose numerous 'experimental' features in no way detract from its spontaneity, freshness, and general musicality."

Hard Times

Today, Seeger's musical reputation is largely built on the works she produced in her New York period, when she was at her most productive and innovative. Her output was severely curtailed after she married Seeger in 1932 and assumed the responsibilities of raising a family. In 1934, she stopped composing music for nearly ten years. Seeger had children from a previous marriage, including Pete Seeger, who would grow up to become a famous folksinger. Two of the Seegers' children, Peggy and Mike, also became well-known folksingers.

During the Depression, the Seegers fell upon hard times. By 1935, the family was poverty stricken, and Charles could find only menial and inconsistent work on farms. But in the autumn of that year, he landed a job with a government relief agency that placed musicians into communities of the poor and displaced. The job required the family to travel to many isolated region across the country. In this way, they were exposed to regional and contemporary American folk music. The Seegers were quite impressed with the music and its creators, and the couple became passionate collectors and transcribers of the music, publishing examples in many songbooks.

Folk Music and Social Causes

Seeger became a driving force in the American folk music revival when she collaborated with two other folk song collectors, John and Alan Lomax. She helped the team edit many songs gathered from actual field recordings. In 1936, the Seegers moved to Washington, D.C. to collect folk songs for the Library of Congress.

The couple's fascination with folk music coincided with their increasing political radicalization, which was due in part to the Depression. Around this time, Seeger began to feel that dissonant music was a bourgeois luxury, and she said that folk music was more in line with her new political beliefs. Indeed, Seeger spent a great amount of time over the next two decades working to bring about social justice and cultural change. In New York City, the couple became deeply involved in the proletarian music movement. Charles Seeger wrote music criticism for the *New York Daily Worker,* while Seeger wrote political songs that addressed contemporary issues and targeted injustices. Typical works included "Sacco, Vanzetti" and "Chinaman, Laundryman." They also became involved with the American Communist Party.

Returned to Teaching and Composing

In the 1940s, Seeger's main interests involved teaching music to children. She gave private piano lessons to many young students at her daughter's nursery school. In 1948, she published *American Folk Songs for Children,* an important work designed for elementary grades that became a standard text in primary music education. Her other folk song collections included *Our Singing Country, American Folk Songs for Children, Animal Folk Songs for Children,* and *American Folk Songs for Christmas.*

In 1950, Seeger began to compose again. She only completed one work, *Suite for Wind Quintet,* in 1952. Appropriately, it combined elements of modernism and folk music. The work demonstrated that her strong compositional powers were still fully intact. By the time she finished the piece, she found out that she had intestinal cancer. She died at the age of 52 on November 18, 1953, in Chevy Chase, Maryland. Charles Seeger was at her side.

Impact

In the years since Seeger's death, her reputation has grown. Many now consider her to be the most important American female composer of the 20th Century, even though the number of works she produced is rather small. Still, what she accomplished in that small but robust body of work helped shape the course of American music as it evolved over the course of the century.

The later part of the century saw a rebirth of interest in her music thanks, in part, to a new movement of American serial composers that emerged in the 1950s and 1960s. In addition, several important reissues and new recordings of her compositions created new excitement about her work. A 1970s reissue of *String Quartet 1931,* in particular, was pivotal in sparking the renewed interest.

Online

" Judith Tick: Ruth Crawford Seeger: A Composer's Search for American Music," *IAWM Journal,* http://music.acu.edu/www/iawm/articles/winter98/Mirchandani.html (January 3, 2004).

"Ruth Crawford (Seeger)," *Classical Composers Database,* http://www.classical-composers.org/cgi-bin/ccd.cgi?comp=crawford (January 3, 2004).

"Ruth Crawford Seeger," *The Guardian,* http://www.pegseeger.com/html/dioguardian.html (January 3, 2004).

"Ruth Crawford Seeger—Bio," *Pegseeger.com,* http://www.pegseeger.com/html/dio.html (January 3, 2004).

"Ruth Crawford Seeger's Different Tunes," *ISAM Newsletter,* http://depthome.brooklyn.cuny.edu/isam/tick.html (January 3, 2004).

"Ruth Porter Crawford," *Virginia Tech Multimedia Music Dictionary,* http://www.music.vt.edu/musicdictionary/appendix/Composers/C/RuthCrawford.html (January 3, 2004).

"Standard Outline of the Life of Ruth Crawford Seeger (1901–1953)," *music.uoregon.edu,* http://music.uoregon.edu/downloads/MUS269/SeegerStandard.pdf (January 3, 2004).

"The World of Ruth Crawford Seeger," *Classical Music Review,* http://www.classical-music-review.org/reviews/JennyLin.html (January 3, 2004). □

Amartya Kumar Sen

Amartya Kumar Sen (born 1933) is the 1998 Nobel prize-winner in economics. He is a well-known economic theorist whose works link ethical questions with economic issues. Jeffrey Sachs wrote in *Time,* "In a lifetime of careful scholarship, Sen has repeatedly returned to a basic theme: even impoverished societies can improve the well-being of their least advantaged members." And although he has spent much of his life outside his native India, his work has always focused on the poverty of India and other developing nations, and how to overcome it.

Born November 3, 1933, in Santiniketan, India, Sen came from an academic family, and actually came into the world on the campus of a small, progressive, coeducational school that was founded by Indian poet and philosopher Rabindranath Tagore. Tagore was in fact a close friend of Sen's maternal grandfather, who taught Sanskrit, the language of Hindu scriptures, at Santiniketan. Tagore helped to name Sen, whose first name means "immortal" in Sanskrit. Sen's father, Ashutosh, was a professor of chemistry at Dhaka University, and his mother, Amita, was a writer who also performed in many dance-dramas that Tagore wrote; she also edited a literary magazine in Bengal, India.

Life-Changing Events

Sen attended the Santiniketan school, which, he told Jonathan Steele in the *Guardian,* was very different from both the English-language schools run by the British, who controlled India at the time, and the Indian nationalist schools. Classes were taught in Bengali, a local language, and the school was deliberately international, emphasizing global culture. However, the school, like others in India, had no room for the poor. When Sen was nine, he had an experience that changed his life. A man, who appeared insane, wandered into the school, and some of the students harassed and teased him. Others, like Sen, wanted to help him. He told Steele, "I got chatting to the man and it became quite clear he hadn't eaten for about 40 days."

Before this encounter, Sen had lived a protected life, blissfully unaware of the vast degree of suffering and hunger among India's poor, despite the fact that a major famine was decimating the country, leading to the deaths of hundreds of thousands of people from starvation. No one in his family was affected by the famine, and he was shocked and upset by it. His grandfather gave Sen a small cigarette tin and said he could fill it with rice and give the rice away, but he could only give away one tinful per family. Sen noted at the time that the effects of the famine depended on social class: only the poor seemed affected, and the wealthier classes had plenty to eat. This memory of widespread death and devastation in the midst of plenty stayed with Sen, and he became preoccupied with issues of poverty and hunger and has continued to be so throughout his career. He later wrote, "Starvation is the characteristic of some people not having enough food to eat. It is not the characteristic of there being not enough food to eat."

Several decades later, in conducting a study of that famine and others in the Sahel, Ethiopia, and China, he noted that the overall production of food in Bengal in 1943, when the famine occurred, was not any lower than production in 1941, when there was no famine. The famine was not caused by a food shortage, but by the fact that the wages paid to poor laborers had not kept up with the rate of inflation, so that poor laborers simply could not afford to buy food even though it was plentiful in the market.

During his teens, Sen received another shock when India's richly diverse culture, made up of many religions and ethnic groups, degenerated into sectarian violence. People began identifying themselves as Hindus, Muslims, or Sikhs, instead of as simply Indian, and killing rampages of one group against another began to occur. One afternoon at Sen's home, a man ran through the gate, bleeding and screaming. Sen's father took him to the hospital. It turned out that the man was a Muslim laborer who had been attacked by Hindus when he began working in a Hindu area in order to make money to buy food for his family. As with the earlier famine, Sen thought deeply about this event, and decided that economic constraints made people vulnerable to serious violations of their rights.

Chose to Become an Economist

By this time, Sen knew that he wanted to follow the path of many members of his family and become an academic. However, he was not sure what he wanted to study, and considered Sanskrit, mathematics, and physics before choosing economics. He attended the Presidency College in Calcutta. At the time, the school was fired up with hot political debates; Sen, like his family, tended to lean toward the left in politics, but, as he told Steele, "I could not develop enough enthusiasm to join any political party." This leeriness of joining any collective group was a trait that would remain with him for his entire life. He was leery of his leftist friends, because although they were committed to egalitarianism, they were not open to new ideas, and were not politically tolerant. He told Steele, "The left didn't take seriously the disastrous lack of democracy in Communist countries." This admiration of democracy remained with him, and he would later point out that no famine had ever occurred in a country with a free press and regular elections.

When Sen was 19, he went to Cambridge, England to study economics at Trinity College. The college was an oasis of tolerance and political diversity, which Sen found refreshing. He felt free to learn from economists as diverse and contradictory as Karl Marx and Adam Smith, as well as many others, without being forced to identify himself as a follower of any one thinker.

In 1960, Sen married Nabaneeta Dev, whom he had met in India. She came to England in 1953, and he proposed to her soon after; they later had two daughters, Antara and Nandana. Antara became a journalist and editor of a literary and political magazine in Delhi, India; Nandana became an actress and film director in New York and Bombay, India.

In 1970, Sen published a groundbreaking book, *Collective Choice and Social Welfare,* which examined the idea held by free-market economists that there was no point in the government interfering in public welfare, and the idea held by statists, who believed that the government should intervene on behalf of the people. Sen argued that it was not necessary to come up with a perfect solution to problems of social welfare, but that poorer and less-assertive citizens should not be ignored.

Sen had developed cancer of the mouth as an undergraduate, and at the time, had been treated with radiation. In 1971, his doctor told him the cancer had returned, and after a fearful and difficult period, this diagnosis turned out to be wrong. However, Sen went through other problems that year when his wife left him. Her career was taking her on another path, and she was tired of following him to the various university campuses where he taught. In addition, according to Steele, she described him as "a good economist but a bad money manager" and "a clumsy father until the children grew old enough to be his students."

Won Nobel Prize in Economics

Sen had married his second wife, Eva Colorni, an Italian economist, in 1978, but she died of cancer in 1985, leaving him with a ten-year-old daughter, Indrani, and an eight-year-old son, Kabir. Sen needed both a change of scene and more money to support his family, so he left England and went to Harvard University, where he worked on the United Nations' Human Development Index. The Index was intended to counter the World Bank's system of ranking countries by such cold factors as savings rates and gross national product; it used more humanitarian indicators. According to Steele, it has since become "the most authoritative international source of welfare comparisons between countries."

In 1988, Sen was awarded the Nobel Prize in economics for his work on the economics of famine. As he had noted during his childhood, famine did not necessarily result from a shortage of food, but from the fact that certain classes of people simply could not afford to buy it. Instead of traditional programs that emphasized getting more food to the famine-stricken areas, Sen noted that cash relief or public works programs might be more effective in restoring people's ability to obtain food. As Alejandro Reuss wrote in *Dollars and Sense,* "Such policies can kick the market into reverse, causing the private food trade to bring food to those in danger, rather than take it away." And Jeffrey Sachs wrote in *Time,* "In a world in which 1.5 billion people subsist on less than $1 a day, this Nobel Prize can be not just a celebration of a wonderful scholar but also a clarion call to attend to the urgent needs of the poor."

After winning the Nobel Prize, Sen was widely honored in India, and was given the prestigious Bharat Rama ("Jewel of India") prize, India's highest civilian award. In keeping with his personal values, he used his Nobel money to set up a trust fund to pay for initiatives to help the poor in India and Bangladesh. The public response to his new fame was sometimes overwhelming; some people began calling him "the Mother Teresa of Economics," and an *Independent* writer reported that shortly after receiving the prize, Sen was walking in Santiniketan when a man came up and put a pen in his hand. Sen, thinking the man wanted him to sign a copy of one of his books, asked the man, "Where is the book?" The man replied, "I do not want your autograph, sir. Just touch the pen and bless it, and I am sure my son will pass his exam."

In addition to his famine studies, Sen is also known for his studies of gender inequalities. He noted that even within classes, some groups are more in danger of famine than others. For example, during the early stages of famine, children are usually given more food, but the elderly are often neglected, and adult men receive more food than adult women. Even in times without famine, in much of the world, women and girls had higher mortality rates than men and boys, because they often received less food and medical care. Sen has also been sharply critical of the Indian government for not working harder to eliminate illiteracy or mass poverty among its citizens.

In 1991, Sen married Emma Rothschild, an economic historian. He taught at Trinity College in Cambridge, England as Master for six years. In January 2004, he went back to his previous position at Harvard as Lamont University Professor of Economics and Philosophy. As quoted from the *Asia Africa Intelligence Wire* Sen said, "I shall still remain a

Fellow of Trinity . . . I intend to continue being active as a member of the Trinity community."

Of Sen's life and work, Steele quoted professor of economics at Oxford Sudhir Anand, who said, "He's very concerned about justice. He's made major contributions not only in measuring poverty but understanding it. To him, poverty is the lack of capability to function, so reducing it is related to positive freedom. What's important to people is to be able to do and be."

Books

Biography Resource Center, Gale Group, 2003.
Debrett's People of Today, Debrett's Peerage, Ltd., 2004.

Periodicals

Asia Africa Intelligence Wire, October 30, 2002.
Dollars and Sense, January-February, 1999.
Europe Intelligence Wire, October 29, 2002.
Guardian (London, England), March 31, 2001.
Independent (London, England), January 24, 1999.
PTI-The Press Trust of India Ltd., December 21, 2003.
Time, October 26, 1988.
Wilson Quarterly, summer, 2001. □

Ramón José Sender

Spanish born novelist Ramón José Sender (1901-1982) survived military service and the political execution of loved ones to become an internationally celebrated author and educator, both in his native Spain and his adopted country, the United States of America.

Sender was born on February 3, 1901, in Chalamera de Cinca, Huesca, a village in Aragon, Spain. His father, José senior, and his mother, Andrea Garcés Laspalas, had 19 children: ten lived to adulthood, of which Sender was the eldest. Sender's relationship with his father was strained from the beginning, with the son resisting the authority and control demanded of his fervently catholic father. Charles King, in his literary biography *Ramón José Sender,* attributes this unrest between father and son as the reason for Sender's lifelong struggle against authority in its many forms.

Education and Pre-War Life

Sender was considered an average student, and began his studies in 1912 when he passed the entrance examinations and began attending the Institute of Zaragoza, a preparatory school. In 1913 12-year-old Sender transferred to the Colegio de San Ildefonso, a boarding school located in Reus, Catalonia. In 1914 he returned to the Institute of Zaragoza and remained there for three years, during which time his literary talent was revealed. At age 15 Sender won first prize in a short-story contest sponsored by Zaragoza's official newspaper. Two years later the Barcelona-based journal *Lecturas* published his novelette titled *A Bonfire at Night,* which was the winning entry in the journal's short novel contest. In 1917, when his family moved to Caspe, Sender chose to move to Alcaniz to work as a clerk in a pharmacy while pursuing his high-school diploma at a local school. The credits he completed in Alcaniz were transferred to the Institute of Teruel, a Catholic college. Sender received his diploma from Teruel in 1918, and immediately enrolled in law school at the University of Madrid.

In 1923 Sender was drafted into the Spanish Army and participated in his country's attempted reconquest of Morocco. Discharged in 1924, he was awarded the Medal of Morocco for his bravery and participation in the war. That same year Sender accepted his first major position within the mainstream, liberal Madrid press, joining the staff of *El Sol* as an editor and literary critic. Targeted by the government as part of a liberal press, in 1927 Sender was arrested and detained in a Madrid jail without trial for three months during the Primo de Rivera dictatorship, the given reason that he was suspected of engaging in revolutionary activity. He was released when the Press Association of Madrid stepped in on his behalf.

Sender remained on staff at *El Sol* until 1930, when he became a freelance journalist. In this capacity he contributed essays and articles, and reviews to various Spanish publications, as well as publishing novels, essays, and plays of his own. Sender married Amparo Barayón on January 7, 1934 when he was 33 years old. They had two children, a son, born in 1935 and named Ramón, and a daughter born in 1936 and named Andrea.

Soldier of the Republic

When the Spanish Civil War broke out in the summer of 1936, 35-year-old Sender enlisted in the communist-backed army of the Republic, and was awarded the Spanish Military Cross of Merit. He sent his wife and infant children to his wife's family in Zamora in 1936, soon after Andrea was born. Tragically, his wife, Amparo, was executed without a trial by monarchic Nationalist forces on October 11, 1936. That same year Sender's brother Manuel was also executed without trial in Huesca, where he had been acting as mayor. Two years later, in 1937, Sender realized that the Republic would inevitably fall to General Francisco Franco and the Nationalist forces; he placed his two children in the care of the International Red Cross in France. Later that year Spain's threatened Republican government sent Sender and other academics on a speaking tour of Europe and the United States in an attempt to raise awareness and support for their failing cause. Sender fled Spain permanently himself in December of 1938 and arrived in France to reclaim his children. He was just in time; Franco's forces captured Madrid in March of 1939 and the Republican government capitulated.

Life in Exile

Sender, by now destitute and with two young children to care for, arrived in New York City in March of 1939. He left his son and daughter in the care of friend and journalist Jay Allen and traveled to Mexico City to join a group of other Spanish exiles that had gathered there. (The children were later adopted by close friend and social worker Julia West and her husband.) Sender spent time traveling and writing in Mexico, and eventually settled in the southwestern United States in 1942 after receiving a Guggenheim fellowship that allowed him to emigrate from Mexico. On August 12, 1943 Sender married Florence Hall, a United States citizen; they divorced 20 years later. Sender became a naturalized U.S. citizen in 1946.

Sender spent the next few years as a visiting lecturer specializing in Spanish literature. He taught at the University of Denver, the University of Colorado, Harvard University, and Amherst College. He served as professor of Spanish literature at the University of New Mexico until 1963. At that juncture he returned briefly to France to reconnect with old friends, and then moved to the Los Angeles area. Serving as a visiting professor of Spanish literature at the University of Southern California from 1965 to 1971, Sender then settled in San Diego. Here he set about writing, in Spanish, about the country he had left in 1938. Sender died at the age of 81, on January 16, 1982, of emphysema.

Prolific and Varied Writing Career

Sender, a prolific author, ranged in his literary efforts from nonfiction and critical essays, to short stories, novels, and poetry. He is credited with at least 102 book titles which include 64 novels, 23 essay collections, five books of plays, two volumes of poetry, and scores of short works of fiction and journalism. In all his writing, whether fiction or nonfiction, he focused on social problems and their effect on the individual. Sender combined realism and fantasy, often inserting subtle propaganda and regularly including within his works autobiographical content. An essay for the *Encyclopedia of World Literature in the 20th Century* suggested that Sender reveals in his work "an abiding faith in man, an implicit but uncompromising protest against social injustice, rare capacity for infusing realistic narrative with a lyrical sense and a metaphysical dimension, and great talent for impregnating ordinary reality with the mysterious and the marvelous." Sender's body of work is often divided by scholars into two groups: life before the Spanish Civil War, and life after Franco's rise to power.

Fiction Contained Political Undercurrents

Sender's 1930 novel *Imán,* translated and published under the title *Pro Patria,* is an anti-war account of the Moroccan campaign of which he was a part. The book's title, which translates as "magnet," reflects its protagonist's seeming characteristic of attracting negative things into his life. Although *Imán* was translated into ten languages, many critics felt it is packed too tightly with horrific descriptions of wartime events, so much so in fact that many reviewers identified it as a journalistic enterprise rather than a work of fiction. Others found it to be brimming with humanity to the extent that the nightmarish qualities produce a lucid picture of human nature that makes it a worthwhile read.

Sender's 1936 novel *Seven Red Sundays* is set in pre-civil war Spain and, like *Imán,* is considered to be closer to a documentary than a work of fiction. Charles King observed that "Sender uses external or ordinary reality . . . as a kind of trampoline from which to launch his leaps to 'higher' realities," and went on to note that "the realism of *Seven Red Sundays* is a strange fusion of ordinary reality with . . . imaginative 'realities' that sometimes add an intellectual dimension, at others a lyrical or metaphysical overtone." It is this experimentation with the various ways in which reality can be perceived that makes Sender's work original as well as educational and challenging to read. His 1937 novel *Mr. Witt among the Rebels,* an historical piece, garnered Spain's highest literary award, the National Literature Prize.

A 1948 novel set in Madrid in the midst of the Spanish Civil War and titled *The King and the Queen* was cited by an essayist for the *Encyclopedia of World Literature in the 20th Century* as Sender's most perfectly structured novel. This work, along with 1943's *Dark Wedding* and 1954's *The Affable Hangman,* were praised by critics as both mystifying and unique in their blend of fantasy and history. Sender's widely praised *Counter-Attack in Spain,* published in 1937, was followed seven years later by *Chronicle of Dawn,* a work defined by the *Encyclopedia of World Literature in the 20th Century* as a "monumental three-volume, nine-part, highly autobiographical novel." The first volume of *Chronicle of Dawn* earned its author Spain's Premio de la Literatura. His next effort, 1949's *The Sphere,* is a dense, philosophical work that, although panned by critics, has been viewed by more recent scholars as Sender's masterpiece. *The Sphere* is the first novel Sender wrote after leaving his country behind; King described it as "an ambitious attempt to fuse into an artistic unity the realistic, the lyrical-metaphysical, the fantastic, and the symbolic." Sender's 1969 novel *In the Life of Ignacio Morel* won him Spain's coveted and lucrative Planeta Prize. While his style is unpretentious and direct, it also embodies both humor and a sharp wit.

Patriot without a Country

During his lifetime Sender had a greater reputation and following abroad than he did in his native Spain because from 1939 through 1962 his work was banned in Spain. Despite the fact that Sender rarely visited Spain following his exile, he has been embraced by his country of birth, and is hailed as one of Spain's most influential and celebrated novelists. Despite his absence, Sender never lost his patriotism and love of Spanish culture, continuing to collect Spanish books and recordings of Spanish folk music throughout his life. As the *Encyclopedia of World Literature in the 20th Century* essayist noted of Sender, "Although uneven in quality, his vast literary output, which was sustained through more than five decades, assures him a permanent place in Hispanic literature."

Books

Columbia Dictionary of Modern European Literature, Columbia University Press, 1980.
Encyclopedia of World Literature in the 20th Century, St. James Press, 1999.
Historical Dictionary of Modern Spain, 1700-1988, Greenwood Press, 1990.
King, Charles L., *Ramón J. Sender,* Twayne Publishers, 1974.
Literary Exile in the 20th Century, Greenwood Press, 1991.
Modern Spanish and Portuguese Literatures, Continuum, 1988.
The Oxford Companion to Spanish Literature, Clarendon Press, 1978. □

Huda Shaarawi

In the Middle East, Egyptian activist Huda Shaarawi (1879–1947) has become a legendary figure. In the early 1920s she was a leader in Egypt's fight for political independence. Turning her attention toward feminism, Shaarawi led the struggle for women's rights in the Middle East, focusing on education, voting rights, and marriage laws. Her act of defiance in removing her veil at the Cairo train station in 1923 marked the first time an Egyptian woman shunned tradition so visibly. From this moment on, increasing numbers of Egyptian women refused the role of silent wife behind the seclusion of the veil.

Shaarawi was born Nur al-Huda Sultan in 1879 on her wealthy family's expansive estate in Minya, Egypt. Her father, Sultan Pasha, was a prosperous landowner and government official who served as inspector-general of Upper Egypt. During this period in history, it was common for upper-class Egyptian men to have both a wife and concubines, or "second" wives, and Shaarawi was born into such an arrangement. She was raised in Cairo in a household that included her unmarried mother, Iqbal Hanim, her father's wife, Hasiba, and her father's other children. Shaarawi lived in an elegant, three-story house, with high ceilings and a sizeable garden filled with fruits and flowering trees. When she was five years old, her father died of kidney disease. Her mother, not yet 25, fell into a state of despair, as did her father's widow, Hasiba.

Educated in Traditional Gender Roles

Shaarawi had a younger brother, Umar Sultan, who was born in 1881, shortly before their father's death. Early on, Shaarawi realized that her status of being the elder child meant nothing in the face of her younger brother's gender. Umar received more attention than she did, and when she asked for a pony like his, she was told that riding was not suitable for girls. Shaarawi often felt jealous, being female in a male-oriented world. However, she was able to voice these frustrations to Hasiba, her father's widow, whom Shaarawi called "Umm Kabira," meaning "Big Mother." Hasiba seems to have understood Shaarawi's discontent.

Writing in her memoirs, published in translation as *Harem Years: The Memoirs of an Egyptian Feminist (1879–1924)* in 1987, Shaarawi described the relationship this way: "I loved Umm Kabira immensely, and she returned that love and showed compassion toward me. She, alone, talked frankly with me on a number of matters. . . . She knew how I felt when people favoured my brother over me because he was a boy. She, too, occasionally fanned the flames of jealousy in me, but without diminishing my love for my brother.''

Coming from a wealthy family, Shaarawi received a private education from tutors and took daily lessons with her brother. She studied Turkish poetry, calligraphy, French, and piano. Before she was ten years old Shaarawi had memorized parts of the Koran, the sacred book of Islam. She was frustrated, however, because she could not understand what she had memorized; no one had taught her Arabic. When Shaarawi requested Arabic grammar lessons, she was refused because girls did not need to know such things. In her memoirs, Shaarawi expressed her aggravation: ''I became depressed and began to neglect my studies, hating being a girl because it kept me from the education I sought. Later, being a female became a barrier between me and the freedom for which I yearned.''

Shaarawi did not neglect her studies for long, however. Soon, she found inspiration in the form of an female itinerant poet named Sayyida Khadija al-Maghribiyya, who often visited her family's house. Sayyida Khadija impressed Shaarawi because the poetess could confidently discuss literary and cultural matters with the men of the household and seemed comfortable in their company, almost like a peer. This surprised Shaarawi because most women she knew were uneducated and were intimidated from speaking directly to men. ''Observing Sayyida Khadija convinced me that, with learning, women could be the equals of men if not surpass them,'' Shaarawi wrote in her memoirs. Inspired by the poetess, Shaarawi bought books from peddlers who came to the door and snuck into her late father's study to gather even more books. She also pilfered her brother's texts.

Betrothed to Older Cousin

As she entered adolescence Shaarawi became increasingly aware of her culture's gender inequalities. She had spent her early years in the close company of boys: her brother, the neighbors, and the sons of family friends. However, when she reached puberty, around age 11, she was forced into the secluded harem life and restricted to the company of girls and women, a common practice in Egypt among the upper and middle classes. Women and men stayed apart, with the females confined to a separate portion of the household called the harem. Even inside the house, if Shaarawi wanted to talk to a man, she was required by tradition to do so from behind a screen. This seclusion followed Shaarawi everywhere; when she went outside, she had to wear a veil that covered her hair and most of her face.

At the time, veiling and seclusion were status symbols. Women in seclusion were guarded by eunuchs, castrated men who were usually slaves from Sudan and who served as intermediaries between the women and the outside world. The transition to harem life was hard for Shaarawi. Separated from the male companions she had known all her life, she was once again frustrated by gender.

Shaarawi's biggest letdown came in 1891 when, at age 13, she was betrothed to an older cousin, Ali Shaarawi, already in his late forties. Shaarawi had always thought of Ali as a father or older brother and did not want to marry him. He already had a wife and three daughters, all of whom were older than Shaarawi. To make things easier for her daughter, in the marriage contract Shaarawi's mother stipulated that Ali Shaarawi had to release his slave-concubine wife and live in monogamy with her daughter. About 15 months into their marriage, Ali Shaarawi's first wife became pregnant with his child. Shaarawi rejoiced that he had broken the marriage contract, and she returned home.

Influenced by Foreign Women

Shaarawi spent seven years separated from her husband, enjoying a life filled with tutors and concerts in a private box at the Khedival Opera House. She also took vacations to the Mediterranean seaport of Alexandria. During these outings Shaarawi came into contact with a number of well-educated foreign women who inspired her to seek change, but whose presence and obvious freedoms also amplified her discontent.

One of the biggest influences in Shaarawi's life was Eugénie le Brun, a Frenchwoman who had married an Egyptian man. Le Brun wrote several books on Egyptian social customs, and in the 1890s she hosted a weekly salon for women at her home. Shaarawi attended, and often the discussions turned to social practices, including veiling. It was Le Brun who suggested to Shaarawi that the veil stood in the way of Egyptian women's advancement. This revelation would later play a role in her public unveiling.

In 1900, facing increasing family pressure, Shaarawi reconciled with her husband. Two children followed, a daughter, Bathna, born in 1903, and a son, Muhammad, born in 1905. Bathna was a sickly child during her first several years of life, often hanging on the cusp of death. Shaarawi lost touch with her female friends while she devoted herself to the care of her children.

Finally, when Bathna had strengthened to the point where she no longer needed her mother's care, Shaarawi began socializing again. She met another Frenchwoman, Marguerite Clement, who was touring the Middle East on a Carnegie endowment. A lecturer, Clement described her travels and public-speaking engagements to Shaarawi, and the two decided Clement should offer a lecture to Egyptian women. With the help of her husband, Shaarawi reserved a university lecture hall for the occasion. The lecture drew a fair crowd and soon became a regular Friday-evening event. The lectures marked a significant turning point in social norms, for it was uncommon for women to leave the seclusion of their homes to gather in a public place. Inspired by this success, Shaarawi formed the Intellectual Association of Egyptian Women in 1914, which worked to improve women's intellectual and social lives.

Involved in Nationalist Movement

At the end of World War I, Shaarawi turned her attention toward nationalism as the Egyptian people demanded independence from Great Britain. In 1919 the Egyptians formed the Wafd party, a political organization aimed at gaining independence. Shaarawi's husband became a leader of the movement and she followed suit. On March 16, 1919, she organized one of the largest protests of the revolution. Calling on the women of Cairo to break social norms, she urged them to leave behind the seclusion of their harems and take to the streets. The crowd faced an army of armed British soldiers, who blocked the path of the march. Shaarawi was ready to step through and defy them, even if it meant giving her life; however, she realized others would probably die, too, and she did not want that. At this point Shaarawi stopped the marchers and instructed them to stand in silent protest for several hours. Over the next several months, such confrontations turned ugly; demonstrations continued, although Eyptians—including women—were sometimes shot or deported.

The nationalist movement forced Egyptian men and women to work together for the first time. In her memoirs, Shaarawi called this period the greatest time of collaboration between herself and her husband. By 1920 the women had formed their own political body, called the Wafdist Women's Central Committee, of which Shaarawi was made president. It was the first political organization for Egyptian women.

In January 1922, Shaarawi held a mass meeting of women at her house. They decided to launch an economic boycott against the British, whereby they would refuse to buy British goods and withdraw their money from British banks. Despite their lack of many rights, women held considerable economic clout because they disposed of the household monies through daily shopping. Also, women inherited money and property in their own name, in accordance with Islamic law. Using their vast network of friends and acquaintances, the women spread the word. The Wafd later credited the women's boycott as one of "the most powerful weapons" in the fight for their nation's independence.

Formed Egyptian Feminist Union

In 1923 Egypt won its independence, although Great Britain retained some rights. Under the new constitution, women found they were not granted suffrage and felt betrayed by the Wafd, which had agreed to grant women the vote. In response, Shaarawi formed the Egyptian Feminist Union (EFU) in early 1923. The main purpose of the group was to attain political, social, and legal equality for women.

In May of 1923 Shaarawi traveled to Rome to attend a conference of the International Alliance of Women. Upon her arrival home, she was greeted at the train station by a group of supporters. Shaarawi now did the unthinkable: she removed her veil in a symbolic act of liberation. For the rest of her life, through this act alone, she became the figurehead of the Egyptian feminist movement.

Shaarawi campaigned to get the minimum marriage age raised so girls were no longer married off at age thirteen. The EFU also worked for other changes, including women's suffrage, the restriction of polygamy, and stricter divorce laws for men. Because she realized that knowledge meant power, Shaarawi also worked to expand the access of girls

and women to education. By 1930 Egyptian universities had admitted their first female student. The EFU also ran a dispensary for women and children.

Shaarawi's work brought her international fame, particularly among the world's suffragists and early feminists. In the late 1930s, when Palestinian women faced a political crisis, they contacted Shaarawi for help. She offered advice on political action, raised funds for them, and helped in the formation of the Arab Feminist Union in 1944. For her service to her own country in its quest for independence, Shaarawi was awarded the Nishan al-Karmal award in 1945. Ironically, even after receiving the highest decoration awarded for service to her country, Shaarawi remained unable to vote in an Egyptian election.

After Shaarawi's death on August 12, 1947, in Cairo, Egypt, the EFU's name was changed to the Shaarawi Society for the Feminist Renaissance, in tribute to the woman who did so much for so many.

Books

Ahmed, Leila, *Women and Gender in Islam: Historical Roots of a Modern Debate,* Yale University Press, 1992.

Opening the Gates: A Century of Arab Feminist Writing, edited by Margot Badran and Miriam Cooke, Indiana University Press, 1990.

Rappaport, Helen, *Encyclopedia of Women Social Reformers,* American Bibliographic Center-Clio, 2001.

Shaarawi, Huda, *Harem Years: The Memoirs of an Egyptian Feminist (1879–1924),* translated by Margot Badran, The Feminist Press, 1987.

Periodicals

Washington Report on Middle East Affairs, July 2001. □

Sheba

A somewhat nebulous figure, the Queen of Sheba (fl. 10th century BCE)—known also as Bilqis and as Makeda—figures prominently in Judaic, Islamic, and Ethiopian traditions. Her legendary voyage to meet Solomon, King of Israel, has inspired centuries of speculation about her kingdom and influence in the ancient world. Modern-day Ethiopians believe her, as the mother of their first Emperor, Menilek I, to be the ultimate maternal ancestor of the dominant Ethiopian royal dynasty.

A Queen of Legend

Little has been verified about the Queen of Sheba's life—in fact, even such basic details as her given name and the exact location of her kingdom remain uncertain. Tradition places her date of birth in the latter half of the 11th century BCE and her death in approximately 955 BCE; although her kingdom is referred to as both to the

two monarchs' exchange of gifts. This brief text forms the basis for later embellishments of the queen's voyage.

Few other direct references to the queen occur in Biblical sources. In Matthew 12:42 (repeated almost exactly in Luke 11:31), Jesus says, "On the Judgment Day the Queen of Sheba will stand up and accuse you, because she traveled all the way from her country to listen to King Solomon's wise teaching." Also, throughout the centuries, the Old Testament book known alternately as the *Song of Songs* and the *Song of Solomon* has been speculated to be a series of love poems sent between Solomon and the Queen of Sheba.

A story that certainly served as inspiration for later Islamic and Ethiopian writers appears in a late paraphrase of the book of Esther explained by C.H. Toy in the *Journal of American Folklore* article "The Queen of Sheba." "On a certain day when [Solomon's] heart was warmed by wine, he . . . invited all the . . . kings of the of the East and the West . . . in order that the kings might see his greatness. All . . . came except the moorcock . . . [who] excused himself by saying that for three months he had been flying over the earth . . . to see if there was any land that did not acknowledge the king's authority." The bird reports he has discovered a fertile land to the east ruled by the Queen of Sheba and Solomon, intrigued, sends the bird back to the queen with a letter requesting her presence at his court. The queen wrote back, sending presents, and undertook the voyage to Jerusalem in three years - although the journey normally required seven years - spurred by her desire to pose riddles to Solomon. Solomon answers correctly, proving his wisdom to the powerful queen.

An Islamic Convert

The Islamic legend of the Queen of Sheba, or Bilqis (alternatively, Balkis) as she is known in the Arabian tradition, stems from these short Jewish narratives. The story of the Queen's appearance at Solomon's court in the Islamic holy text, The Qu'ran, follows a thread similar to that of the Book of Esther. In Chapter 27 of the Qu'ran, a messenger bird declared: "I have come to thee from Saba with sure tidings. I found a woman ruling over all of them; she has been granted everything and she has a wondrous throne. I found her and her worshipping the sun, instead of Allah." The passage further explains that Satan has led the queen and her subjects away from Allah, and Solomon, thinking to test this assertion, sends the bird back to the queen with a letter requesting confirmation of the bird's tale. Upon receiving the queen's response of extravagant gifts, Solomon is not satisfied and writes again, requesting her presence. The queen visits Solomon and, awed by his court, converts to the worship of Allah.

Arabian legends based on the Qu'ran embellish this story to include some speculation about the queen's descent from demons and later, her possible marriage to Solomon. Solomon's advisors inform him that the queen has hairy legs; to discover the truth of this, Solomon constructs a palace with glass floors. The queen, believing the floor to be made of water, lifts her skirts, revealing her legs and feet. As Toy commented, "later Moslem writers interpreted this physical peculiarity as showing that she was of jinn descent;

south and to the east of Israel, scholars generally believe her to have ruled an area in northern Africa roughly equivalent to modern-day Ethiopia, a country which claims her the progenitor of their long-ruling Solomonic dynasty.

The Queen's 10th century BCE visit to the grand court of Solomon, King of Israel and son of the legendary Goliath-slayer David, however, is well-attested in three major ancient sources: the Biblical Old Testament, the Islamic Qu'ran, and the Ethiopian *Kebra Nagast* (Glory of the Kings). These three perspectives on the Queen meld to create a picture of one of the relatively rare, powerful female monarchs of the ancient world.

A Biblical Riddler

The most widespread story of the Queen of Sheba stems from an Old Testament passage describing her journey to Jerusalem to meet with the Jewish king, Solomon, renowned for his wisdom. An account of her stay at Solomon's court appears in I Kings 10:1–14 and in a nearly word-for-word repetition, 2 Chronicles 9:1–12. Both passages begin: "The queen of Sheba heard of Solomon's fame, and she traveled to Jerusalem to test him with difficult questions. She brought with her a large group of attendants, as well as camels loaded with spices, jewels, and a large amount of gold. When she and Solomon met, she asked him all the questions that she could think of. He answered them all; there was nothing too difficult for him to explain." The rest of the tale describes the Queen's awe of Solomon's wisdom, riches, and relationship with God, as well as the they constructed a romantic history of her father's marriage to a jinn maiden." Legends also conjectured that the queen and Solomon wed during her visit to his court and had a son who succeeded to the throne of Sheba.

An Ethiopian Queen

This marriage figures prominently in the Ethiopian accounts of the queen. Drawing on Jewish and Islamic traditions, the Ethiopian story of the Queen of Sheba—identified with Makeda, Queen of Ethiopia—provides the most extensive picture of the Queen. Told in the *Kebra Nagast* (The Glory of Kings), a 14th century compilation of regional oral histories, this version also begins with a voyage to King Solomon's court at Jerusalem. "The Queen was dumbstruck with wonder at the things that she heard from [a traveling merchant], and she pondered in her heart that she would to go to Solomon, the King," related the *Kebra Nagast,* which further details her voyage from Ethiopia bringing lavish gifts to the King. During the queen's stay, Solomon became infatuated with her. Determined to have the virginal queen, Solomon extracts a promise from the queen to take nothing that belongs to him and then orders a grand banquet to be served the night before her departure. As Harold G. Marcus detailed in *A History of Ethiopia:* "He directed his cook to serve the best wines to prepare the spiciest dishes, both of which happily suited Makeda. After having eaten and drunk her fill, the queen fell into a stupor, during which Solomon had jugs of water, labeled as his property, placed strategically around her sofa. When Makeda reawakened, she immediately gulped down some water, an act that permitted King Solomon to satisfy his lust." Solomon, having afterwards dreamt that God was granting him an heir by the queen, requested that the queen send their son to Jerusalem when the boy came of age.

Accordingly, the queen gave birth to a son, Ebna Hakim, who traveled to his father's court as an adolescent. In *Pillars of Ethiopian History,* William Leo Hansberry recorded that "Solomon . . . was overjoyed to see his handsome and noble-minded son. . . . Solomon did his best to persuade Ebna Hakim to remain to Jerusalem, with the intention of making him his successor; but the young prince was deaf to his father's pleas." Solomon thus confirmed his son as the future King of Ethiopia and gathered several of his advisors' sons to return with Ebna Hakim and assist him during his rule. This group refused to leave Jerusalem without the legendary Ark of the Covenant - the chest reputed to contain the original tablets of the Ten Commandments sent to Moses by God, among other religious artifacts - and so, stole the Ark. As Marcus commented, "The larceny was apparently approved by God, who levitated the youths and their holy cargo across the Red Sea before discovery and chase by Solomon's forces." To this day, Ethiopian tradition places the Ark in the northern Ethiopian city Axum.

When the queen died in the mid-10th century BCE, her son rose to the Ethiopian throne as Emperor Menilek I. This Solomonic Dynasty ruled Ethiopia for much of the next 2000 years; the last emperor of Ethiopia, Haile Sellassie, claimed descent from Solomon and the queen through Menilek.

A Lasting Legacy

As these varied accounts show, the Queen of Sheba has fascinated and inspired numerous cultures for nearly 3000 years. The lack of any verifiable details of her life does not seem to inspire doubt about her existence. As Nicholas Clapp commented in *Sheba: Through the Desert in Search of the Legendary Queen,* "Her encounter with King Solomon must have happened . . . because as biblical tales go, it was so dull. She shows up; she's awed; she's crestfallen; she leaves. Nobody is led in or out of temptation, is distraught or gets killed; there is no evident moral message. The story had the earmarks of a day-in, day-out formal court record . . . [this is] reinforced by passages immediately preceding and following the Sheba story, passages that dwell on Solomon's prowess in foreign affairs." Instead of being ignored due to its brevity, the bare narrative given in the Old Testament has served as ample fodder for fanciful stories and modern scholarly and popular speculation about the relationship between the wealthy, intelligent queen and the religious, wise King Solomon. Centuries after her death, the Queen of Sheba still rules over the imaginations of people both within and far beyond the boundaries of her ancient kingdom.

Books

Clapp, Nicholas, *Sheba: Through the Desert in Search of the Legendary Queen,* Houghton Mifflin Company, 2001.

Hansberry, William Leo, *Pillars in Ethiopian History: The William Leo Hansberry African History Notebook,* ed. Joseph E. Harris, Howard University Press, 1974.

Holy Bible, American Bible Society, 1978.

Kebra Negast, trans. Miguel F. Brooks, The Red Sea Press, Inc., 1996.

Marcus, Harold G., *A History of Ethiopia,* University of California Press, 1994.

Munro-Hay, Stuart, *Ethiopia: The Unknown Land,* I.B. Tauris, 2002.

Qu'ran, trans. Muhammad Zafrulla Khan, Interlink Publishing Group-Olive Branch Press, 1997.

Shah, Tahir, *In Search of King Solomon's Mines,* Arcade Publishing, 2002. □

Taras Grigoryevich Shevchenko

Considered the greatest poet of Ukraine and the founder of modern Ukrainian literature, Taras Shevchenko (1814-1861) rose from humble beginnings to the pinnacle of the 19th-century St. Petersburg literary world. His writings draw upon the peasant traditions of his boyhood.

Early Years as a Serf

Taras Grigorievich Shevchenko was born March 9, 1814 into a family of serfs in the village of Morintsy in Ukraine, then part of the tsarist Russian Empire. The Shevchenkos soon relocated to the village of Kirilivka, where Taras grew up. He led an early life of misery. His mother died when he was nine years old, and his step-mother mistreated him and those of his siblings who were still living at home (an older sister, Katerina, had married and moved to another village). His father died when Taras was 12, and he was given over to the care of a local priest, for whom he worked as a shepherd and farmhand.

Shevchenko studied art with numerous local icon painters, but each time his lessons proved short-lived. When Shervchenko was 14, his master, P.V. Engelhardt, took over his training and employed him as a house servant. He was taught to read and write. In 1829 Engelhardt and his wife brought Shevchenko with them to Vilnius, where they lived until 1831. Shevchenko, with Engelhardt's encouragement, enrolled in the Art Academy. In 1831 the Engelhardts moved to St. Petersburg, and Shevchenko became an apprentice to the painter Shirayev, who was primarily a theater decorator. Shevchenko served under Shirayev from 1832 to 1836.

In 1837 Shevchenko met and befriended the Ukrainian artist Ivan Maksimovich Soshenko. The latter quickly recognized Shevchenko's artistic potential and suggested that Shevchenko enroll in St. Petersburg's Imperial Academy of Arts. But as a serf Shevchenko could not do so alone. Fortunately for Shevchenko he had two influential men to champion his cause: the secretary of the academy, V. I. Grigorovich, and the artist and professor K.P. Bryulov. Both sought to obtain Shevchenko's freedom, but Engelhardt demanded 2,500 silver rubles in exchange. Soshenko and the others convinced V.A. Zhukovsky to join Shevchenko's cause. As tutor to the tsarevitch–the Russian crown prince–Zhukovsky traveled in the highest circles in Russia. He consented to have his portrait painted by Bryulov and sold, with the proceeds to go toward Shevchenko's freedom. Shevchenko was granted his freedom in the spring of 1838 and at once enrolled in the academy as Bryulov's pupil.

This was Shevchenko's formative period intellectually. Not only did he study painting, but under Bryulov's influence he became interested in classical antiquity and began to read Ukrainian history and its nascent national literature. Shevchenko started to write poetry during this time, though a few scholars believe he had begun to write before his emancipation. His oldest known poem is "Prychynna" (The Mad Girl).

Growing Nationalism

When a patron who had come to Shevchenko's apartment to have his portrait painted noticed his poems lying about, he asked to borrow them. So enthused was he that he arranged for their publication. Thus, in 1840, *Kobzar* was produced. The title refers to ancient wandering bards who traveled throughout Ukraine singing epic and heroic tales, often playing the stringed instrument, the *kobza*. Though this slim book of eight poems, which were really ballads, was attacked by Russian and Western critics, Ukrininans wholly embraced it. In their view Shevchenko's verse was the next step in the evolution of their national literature, and he was hailed as the successor to Ivan Kotlyarevsky, who had died two years earlier and for whom Shevchenko wrote "To the Eternal Memory of Kotlyarevsky."

In fact Shevchenko's work was far more mature artistically than Kotlyarevsky's. The main complaints against *Kobzar* was that it was peasantlike and thus insignificant. But that tone of the ancient bards was exactly what Shevchenko had set out to achieve. Another major literary influence on *Kobzar* was historical romanticism. Add to this was Shevchenko's growing awareness of Ukrainian nationalism and a newfound desire to see his country independent of Polish domination–just as he himself had gained independence–and the major themes of Shevchenko's work and life are in place. The poems of *Kobzar* include: "Dedication," "Perebendya," "The Poplar," "Dumka," "To Osnovyanenko," "Ivan Pidkova," "The Night of Taras," and "Katerina."

In 1841 Shevchenko published *The Haydamaki*. The longest of his epic poems, *The Haydamaki* recounts a mid-18th-century Ukrainian peasant revolt and the massacre of Poles. It is often seen as the culmination of themes Shevchenko first presented in *Kobzar*. Polish and Russian critics predictably disliked the work, and Ukrainians hailed the poem and Shevchenko. *The Haydamaki* cemented Shevchenko's literary reputation and made him a central figure among St. Petersburg's Ukrainian population. It also transformed him into something of a national hero.

All during this time Shevchenko continued his studies at the Imperial Academy of the Arts, but his painting (mostly portraits) had reached a plateau. After 1841 he received no prizes for his artwork.

In 1843 Shevchenko visited the Ukraine, where he was given a hero's welcome. It was his first time back in his homeland since 1829, when he was a serf. Shevchenko's appeal to the peasants was natural, but the landowners and others of the Ukrainian upper classes also admired him for his nationalism. Many from the Ukrainian upper class commissioned Shevchenko to paint their or their family members' portraits. These commissions renewed Shevchenko's interest in painting, and after a brief side trip to Moscow he returned to St. Petersburg to finish his studies. He graduated from the Imperial Academy of the Arts in December 1845. Before he had even received his diploma Shevchenko had again returned to Ukraine. Though he was now a "free artist of the Academy" it was his literary pursuits that engaged him most.

While finishing his studies at the Academy he wrote the narrative poem "The Dream" (1844), which he subtitled "A Comedy." The subtitle may have been a calculated bit of disingenuousness designed to deceive the censor, for by this time Shevchenko had undergone a political epiphany. He used the narrative device of the dream in order to ward off any charges of sedition for, as he now saw it, Russia, not Poland, was the main oppressor of Ukraine. "The Dream" was the first in a series of poems that addressed this new idea. It follows Shevchenko as he visits, in his dream, Ukraine, Siberia, and St. Petersburg, all the while decrying the deceit, oppression and poverty which the Russian aristocracy has imposed on Ukraine and Russia. At the end of the poem the narrator wakes up. There is a touch of the sacred imbued in the poem, as "The Dream" is prefaced by a quote from the Gospel of St. John: "The Spirit of truth whom the world cannot receive, because it neither sees him nor knows him" (John 14:17).

In 1845 Shevchenko published *Three Years,* a collection of protest poems and impressions written during the years 1843-1845. The poems were sent to friends who later copied them for publication. That year he also published "The Caucasus" and "The Testament." He also wrote two novellas during this period, *The Servant Girl* and *Varnak.*

Arrest and Exile

In 1846 Shevchenko joined the Society of Saints Cyril and Methodius, founded by young progressives in Kiev, the capital of Ukraine. While the dream of this organization was to create a pan-Slavic nation, a republic possibly modeled after the United States, the group was largely theoretical. Its stated goals of education, democracy, and autonomy for each Slavic group and a general Slavic council were seen as a threat by the autocratic Tsar Nicholas I.

During this period Shevchenko brought out a second edition of *Kobzar.* He also sketched the countryside around Kiev and did other painting. In his "Preface" to the second edition of *Kobzar* Shevchenko took a public stand for Ukainian literature. He criticized Kotlyarevsky for vulgarizing Ukrainian literature and opposed those who sought to imitate him. He also took a stand against his contemporary, writer Nikolai Gogol, for forsaking the Ukrainian language for Russian, which Shevchenko considered to be the language of the oppressors. This was Shevchenko's last publication for a while; he was arrested in Kiev on April 5, 1847, after being denounced by a student.

After spending a night in jail in Kiev, Shevchenko was taken to St. Petersburg, where he was interrogated. He denied being a member of the Society of Saints Cyril and Methodius and hedged his associations with some other members who had also been arrested. The interrogators recommended to the tsar that Shevchenko be placed on military duty in Orenburg, in southeastern European Russia. The tsar ordered that Shevchenko could not write or paint. Shevchenko spent ten years in exile and was not released until after the death of Tsar Nicholas I. During the period of his arrest and exile Shevchenko secretly wrote some verse.

Shevchenko disliked army life, but eventually the prohibition against Shevchenko doing any artwork was slightly altered and he was allowed to make government sketches on an expedition to the Sea of Aral. This expedition lasted for a year and a half. In late 1849, having returned to Orenburg, Shevchenko petitioned to be allowed to resume painting. He was supported by his military unit's officers, who allowed him to live in Orenburg and wear civilian clothes. They also turned a blind eye to his portrait painting. However, after a few months of this relative freedom,

Shevchenko was denounced by an officer and rearrested on April 27, 1850. Following a weeklong trial he was exiled to an even more remote outpost-Novopetrovsk on the east coast of the Caspian Sea.

Exile did not stop him from writing, however. In the years between his first and second arrests Shevchenko wrote "In the Fortress" (1847) and "The Tsars" (1848). During his exile Shevchenko wrote the long narrative poem "The Princess," and the shorter poetic works "The Musician," "The Captain's Wife," "The Artist," "Fortune" and "The Muse." In addition to the government sketches Shevchenko's watercolors and drawings done in exile include a series titled *The Parable of the Prodigal Son* and *Running the Gauntlet.*

Last Years

In 1857, Shevchenko was released. He traveled to Ukraine then to Moscow and finally to St. Petersburg. In the years just after his release he wrote "A Pleasant Stroll" and "Not Without a Moral." He published "Fame" in 1858 to complete the trilogy begun with "Fortune" and "The Muse." In 1859 some of his friends published *New Poems of Pushkin and Shevchenko* in Leipzig, and in 1860 he brought out a third edition of *Kobzar.* During this period he wrote his best lyric verse as well as the long, narrative poems "The Neophytes" and "God's Fool" (both written in 1857) and "Mary" (1858).

Shevchenko fell ill late in 1860 and never recovered his health. He died on March 10, 1861. His funeral in St. Petersburg was attended by such literary notables as Saltykov-Shchedrin, Turgenev, Dostoevsky, and Leskov. Herzen published an obituary of Shevchenko, and Nekrasov contributed a poem to mark the occasion. Many of Shevchenko's poems were later set to music by Ukranian and Russian composers including Mussorgsky, Tchaikovsky, and Rachmaninoff.

Books

Great Soviet Encyclopedia, Trans. Of Third Ed., Vol. 29, Macmillan, 1982.

Manning, Clarence A., *Taras Shevchenko: Selected Poems,* Ukrainian national Association, 1945.

Zaitsev, Pavlo, *Taras Shevchenko: A Life,* trans. by George S.N. Luckyj, University of Toronto Press, 1988. □

Esther Shub

Ukrainian film editor Esther Shub (1894-1959) was a pioneer of the "compilation film," editing old footage into new and often brilliant films. As one of the pioneers of the Soviet cinema, she discovered essential principles of editing, which were later developed by other filmmakers.

Esther Shub was born on March 3, 1894 in the Chernigovsky District of the Ukraine, and moved to Moscow as a student. There, she became part of the artistic avant-garde, and soon turned her talents to film. According to Graham Roberts in *History Today,* she later wrote in her memoirs that she saw film as "a method of expressing all that the Great October Revolution had brought," and noted that for her country, "A new life was beginning." A few years before, the bloody upheaval of the Russian Revolution had resulted in the Soviet takeover of the country, and many people were filled with ideological optimism about the new government. Shub applied several times for a job in film, and was refused several times, but she persisted. Eventually she was accepted for a job in the film section of the Commissariat of the Enlightenment.

Created Compilation Film

Shub began working with film in 1922, a few years after the Russian Revolution and the takeover of the Soviet government. At the time, the Soviet Union did not have access to much of the equipment needed for filmmaking. There were few production facilities in the country, and it was difficult for people to get films from other countries. In addition, the new government would only allow films that supported its ideological principles, further cutting down the supply of acceptable material. The Soviet government hired Shub to recut and retitle American films to make them "suitable" for Soviet audiences to watch; this meant that the films had to portray Soviet ideals, not American ones.

Shub took these films from abroad and edited them to conform to Soviet principles. Her first work was a complete re-editing of Charlie Chaplin's 1916 film *Carmen;* it was the first Chaplin film ever to be seen in the Soviet Union. She then edited a wide range of films, from Pearl White serials to the 1916 film *Intolerance.* In her work, Shub was inspired by the earlier work of Dziga Vertov and his wife and collaborator, Elizaveta Svilova. They had developed the style of montage, editing diverse and often seemingly unrelated pieces of film to express a consistent idea or theme. Shub took this style and expanded it, creating the "compilation film," which is completely made up of preexisting film footage. In the process, she discovered principles of editing and intertitling that were used and developed by other filmmakers after her. As the *International Dictionary of Films and Filmmakers* noted, "She brought to [the compilation film] genre far more than her speed, industry, and flair; she brought a positive genius for using all sorts of ill-considered odd bits of old footage as a painter uses his palette, using them as if they had all been especially shot for her."

In addition, Shub eventually began working on the creation of new films, working with famed director Sergei Eisenstein on the shooting script of *Stachka* ("Strike," 1925), *Bronenosets Potemkin* and ("The Battleship Potemkin," 1925). She and Eisenstein enjoyed a collaborative friendship, and Eisenstein was inspired by Shub's work and editing techniques; they influenced one another and shared an interest in documentary techniques.

"The Fall of the Romanov Dynasty"

Working on these films inspired her with the idea to depict events in history by editing and compiling pieces of films from a particular period. She spent three years researching and watching newsreels that had been filmed from 1912 through 1917, Tsar Nicholas II's personal collection of films, footage shot by friends of the imperial family, footage from two official imperial cinematographers, and the long-stored films of wartime cameramen. She even bought some material from sources in the United States. Working with these disparate materials, she compiled *Padeniye dinasti Romanovikh* ("The Fall of the Romanov Dynasty," 1927). She made this film because, surprisingly enough, there was no visual record of the Russian Revolution, which transformed both Russian and world history. The film drew on old sources, but it also included footage that Shub shot in order to make up for gaps in the documentary material. Her studios were not in favor of the project from its inception, and after it was completed, they refused to recognize her rights as author of the film. Graham commented that although few of the pieces she worked with were very long, she turned this potential pitfall into one of the strengths of the film: "Brief scenes are brought together or intercut with bold titles. . . to create a direct, powerful, yet graceful montage form." He added, "Thus a wide range of material could be used effectively to create a single overarching message." That message was that the fall of the Romanov dynasty was inevitable, as was the rise of the Soviet state.

"The Great Road"

"The Fall of the Romanov Dynasty" was followed by *Velikii put* ("The Great Road," 1927). *Velikii put* was drawn from newsreels covering the years 1917 through 1927, and was notable because it incorporated intimate scenes of Soviet revolutionary Nikolai Lenin, the first time these scenes had been seen by Soviet audiences. The film opens with a shot of a Tsarist statue, representing the old empire, followed by a shot of broken statues, showing the shattering of the Tsarist empire at the hands of the revolutionaries. In this debris, a small child, symbol of the new regime, is playing. This is followed by an image of the new government's flag flying over the Kremlin, and shots of massed workers, with the words: "Through their leaders, the proletariat [working people] of all lands are solidly behind the workers' and peasants' revolution." Subsequent scenes show workers in other countries supporting the Russian Revolution.

The second and third reels of the film depict the establishment of the Soviet state and the threats it faced from both external and internal enemies, as well as the new leaders of the state. The fourth reel shows the destruction of Germany resulting from World War I and presents the idea that another revolution is underway there. In the fifth and sixth reels, Shub shows the civil war in Russia from 1918 to 1921. The seventh reel celebrates the leadership of Nikolai Lenin, and the eighth uses footage of Wall Street, the Paris stock exchange, and other symbols of capitalism to present the idea that outside Russia, workers are treated as slaves by capitalist overlords, and that it is only a matter of time before the downtrodden American and European workers rise up against this system in a revolution similar to Russia's.

Graham notes that the film uses techniques that later became Shub's trademarks: the use of text from documents, newspapers, and even statues to anchor her images, and the use of non-Soviet material to make points consistent with the Soviet ideology. As he commented, "Shub can always rely on non-Soviet material that can be manipulated and/or retitled to make pointed criticisms of the actions of industrialists, politicians and anti-Soviet forces in general."

Shub then began work on *Rossiya Nikolaya II i Lev Tolstoy* ("The Russia of Nicholas II and Leo Tolstoy," 1928). This was originally intended to be a biography of writer Leo Tolstoy, but she was unable to find more than a few hundred feet of film about him. Shifting her focus, she wove this material in with film from other sources to create a film about that historical era. Because of her difficulty in finding material for this film, she abandoned the chronological format and instead presented the flavor of the period.

In 1928, Shub also visited the set of Eisenstein's *October* (1928), where they often discussed editing techniques that Eisenstein used in the film. Shub also maintained contact with Dziga Vertov, although they disagreed about whether or not a film should be based on a script. Although both of them emphasized authenticity, Shub believed that a documentary could include both staged events and authentic, historical footage. Vertov, in contrast, believed that there was no room for staged events in a documentary.

Helped Pioneer the Sound Documentary

In 1932, Shub helped to pioneer the sound documentary with *The Komsomol—Sponsor of Electrification* (1932). For this film, she created her own version of the typical "Soviet Hero," a young man who passionately believed in Soviet ideology and who wore the traditional Russian costume of high-necked blouse and leather jerkin. Instead of using her previous technique of editing and combining archival material, she turned to ultra-realism, which, as the *International Dictionary of Films and Filmmakers* noted, predated "by 30 years many of the practices and theories of cinema verité." She deliberately included shots in which people looked directly into the camera, acknowledging that they were in a film; shots that showed the arc-lights illuminating the sets, shots in which people were rendered clumsy or stuttering by the presence of cameras or microphones; and shots which showed the microphones and cameras. She wanted to continually remind the audience that they were watching a film, created by crew and camera. This was a strong contrast to traditional film techniques, which strove to hide the artificiality of filmmaking and make the audience feel that they were part of events and scenes, watching invisibly from the shadows. Perhaps because she was so ahead of her time in doing this, some critics did not understand her motives. According to the *International Dictionary of Films and Filmmakers*, a Soviet critic complained that she was "indulging herself with a contemporary enthusiasm for the future of sound film and with the peculiar cult for film-apparatus."

Despite her skill, in the mid-1930s Shub's films fell into disfavor with the government as Soviet ideology shifted. In her memoirs, she described numerous films that were either never made, or which the government handed to lesser-known but more favored filmmakers. By 1934, according to Graham, she was writing magazine articles titled "I Want to Work," but none of these articles were published. In 1937 she was allowed to make *Strana Sovietov* ("Land of the Soviets"), but only on the condition that she emphasize the heroic role of then-Soviet dictator Josef Stalin.

Ispaniya ("Spain," 1939) incorporated footage from archives, documentary film shot by Roman Karmen, scenes from the film *The Spanish Earth* (1937), and film captured from Fascist forces in the Spanish Civil War to present Spanish Republican principles and ideas. The film also included narrated words and music that were integrated with the images to produce a powerful emotional effect.

In 1940, Shub worked on *Kino za dvadtsat let* ("Twenty Years of Soviet Cinema), and during World War II she worked on more conventional newsreels featuring current events of the war. Over the course of her career, Shub spent over two decades in the Soviet film industry. In the late 1940s and early 1950s, she worked entirely as an editor and wrote her memoirs about filmmaking techniques. In addition, she wrote a script titled *Women* (1933-34), which examined women's roles throughout history. Although this project was never filmed, the script reveals Shub's interest in feminism. Shub died on September 21, 1959, in Moscow.

As the *Oxford Companion to Film* noted, "Shub's accomplished editing, and particularly her use of pre-existing material to create ironic or didactic effects, was influential on later documentary and compilation filmmakers, but perhaps as important was her insistence on the importance of tracing, identifying, and preserving historic film."

Books

Acker, Amy, *Reel Women*, Continuum, 1991.
Barden, Liz-Anne, *Oxford Companion to Film,* Oxford University Press, 1976.
Foster, Gwendolyn Audrey, *Women Film Directors,* Greenwood Press, 1995.
International Dictionary of Films and Filmmakers, Volume 2: Directors, St. James Press, 1996.
Women Filmmakers and Their Films, St. James Press, 1998.

Periodicals

History Today, November, 1997. □

Nina Simone

American jazz singer, songwriter, and pianist Nina Simone (1933–2003), known as the "High Priestess of Soul," used her talent to help shape the Civil Rights Movement of the 1960s. While her overt and sometimes extreme statements and opinions may have overshadowed her music, even critics could

not ignore her soulful voice, which drapes over classically influenced piano lines in a way that defies genre.

Born Eunice Kathleen Waymon, on February 21, 1933, in Tyron, North Carolina, Simone was the sixth of eight children born to John Divine Waymon and his wife Mary Kate, who presided over their family in a house filled with music. "Everything that happened to me as a child involved music," Simone recalled in her autobiography, *I Put A Spell On You.* "Everybody played music. There was never any formal training; we learned to play the same way we learned to walk, it was that natural." While the other Waymon children had a love and talent for music, it became clear that young Eunice had a special affinity, a gift. By the age of six, Simone was the regular pianist at the family's church.

Aspired to Be Concert Pianist

At about the same time, to earn extra money for the family, Simone's mother had begun to clean the house of a white woman named Mrs. Miller who took great interest in the piano talent of Simone. Mrs. Miller suggested that her special talent needed to be fostered with formal training and upon learning the Waymon family could not afford it, offered to pay for Simone's piano lessons herself. Soon, Simone was the pupil of Muriel Massinovitch, an Englishwoman who'd moved to Tyron with her Russian

painter husband and a strict devotee of Bach, a devotion which she passed on to her student. "He is technically perfect," Simone declares in her autobiography. "When you play Bach's music you have to understand that he's a mathematician and all the notes you play add up to something—they make sense. . . . When I understood Bach's music I never wanted to be anything other than a concert pianist; Bach made me dedicate my life to music, and it was Mrs. Massinovitch who introduced me to his world."

Simone then set off to become the first black concert pianist. During her last year of high school she had won a scholarship to the Julliard School of Music in New York for one year. Her plan was to use that year at Julliard to prepare her for the scholarship examination at the prestigious Curtis Institute of Music in Philadelphia, a monumental stepping stone if one wanted to become a concert pianist. The Curtis Institute rejected her application saying her level of piano playing was not good enough. "I just couldn't believe it had happened," Simone recalled, "and all I could think about was what I had given up over the years to get to where I was the day I heard Curtis didn't want me, which was nowhere. It was so hard to understand." Simone resolved to work harder and take the scholarship examination the next year, an idea she abandoned when the perception arose that the reason she did not get in the Curtis Institute was because she was black.

Became Club Performer

Following the disappointment with the Curtis Institute and with her family having migrated from North Carolina to Philadelphia, Simone decided to stay in the Philadelphia area and give piano lessons. When she learned one of her students, a particularly poor student at that, was going to be earning twice as much as she did by playing piano in a bar in Atlantic City for the summer, she decided to do the same. The only problem was Simone's staunchly religious mother—an ordained Methodist minister—would take a dim view of her daughter walking into a bar let alone working in one. To keep her mother from finding out she decided to come up with a stage name. She had loved the way an old boyfriend had often called her Nina, Spanish for "little girl," and she also liked the name Simone from the French actress, Simone Signoret. So there it was: Nina Simone.

The Midtown Bar and Grill was a seedy, Irish bar two blocks from Atlantic City's boardwalk, and in the summer of 1954 served as Simone's introduction to the performing life. For six hours a night—with a fifteen minute break each hour, where she'd sip milk at the bar—Simone first began to blend the genres that influenced her into a fresh synthesis of music. "I knew hundreds of popular songs and dozens of classical pieces," she wrote in her autobiography, "so what I did was combine them: I arrived prepared with classical pieces, hymns and gospel songs and improvised on those, occasionally slipping in a part from a popular tune." On her first night, the owner told her that her playing was fine, but if she wanted to keep the job, she'd have to sing as well. Soon, the drunken regulars had filtered out of the Midtown, replaced by packed crowds of young people enthused by the new style of music they were hearing.

Simone then moved from the Midtown to more upscale supper clubs in Philadelphia where she continued to have success and build an audience. In 1957 Simone hired an agent, Jerry Fields, who put her in contact with the head of New York's Bethlehem Records to do an album. After recording the album, released the next year called Little Girl Blue, Simone unknowingly signed a contract that gave away all her rights—a mistake she estimated that cost her over a million dollars. The first single from the album, a version of George and Ira Gershwin's "I Loves You, Porgy," attracted much attention and set the stage for her first real concert at New York's Town Hall. By this time she was signed to another label, Colpix, who released The Amazing Nina Simone and would also record and release the concert at Town Hall.

Soon Simone was the darling of the Greenwich Village music scene and began to tour America and abroad. While some of her performances were often in jazz clubs, Simone has long resisted the notion that she was a "jazz singer," regarding the term as a racial insult. "To most white people, jazz means black and jazz means dirt and that's not what I play," she declared to Brantley Bardin in a 1997 Details interview. "I play black classical music. That's why I don't like the term 'jazz,' and Duke Ellington didn't like it either—it's a term that's simply used to identify black people." In the early sixties, Simone's feelings of racial oppression merged with the influential friendship of civil rights activist and playwright Lorraine Hansberry. Finding a political voice was not hard for the outspoken Simone, and her songs soon began to merge political thought from the civil rights movement with the blend of classical, blues, and gospel, causing some to label her a protest singer, another term she dismissed.

Activism in the Civil Rights Movement

Inspired by the bombing of a Baptist church in Alabama, which killed four children, and the assassination of civil rights leader Medgar Evers in Mississippi, Simone wrote "Mississippi Goddam," which became an anthem of sorts for the civil rights movement and won her the admiration of such artists and leaders as Stokely Carmichael, Miriam Makeba, Langston Hughes, and James Baldwin.

For the rest of the decade Simone was regarded as the true singer of the civil rights movement and contributed songs like "Sunday in Savannah," "Backlash Blues," and a song declared by the Congress of Racial Equality (CORE) to be the black national anthem, "To Be Young, Gifted, and Black." And while touring, recording, and working for civil rights won Simone praise and notoriety, her home life slowly unraveled.

Married in 1960 to former police detective Andy Stroud, who became her manager, the couple had a daughter, Lisa Celeste, in 1961 and Simone barely saw her grow up. "After Lisa was born I had sworn to keep a check on the pace of my life," Simone wrote in her autobiography, "but in the movement I lived at twice the speed I ever had and music and politics took up my whole life. I didn't have personal ambitions anymore—I wanted what millions of other Americans wanted, and enjoying any private land-

marks was impossible because the outside world always managed to butt in." Simone and her daughter would be periodically estranged from one another for the next thirty years.

Time Spent Abroad

Simone and Stroud divorced in 1970 and Simone began what would be a fifteen-year exile from the United States. Disillusioned by the civil rights movement following the deaths of Martin Luther King, Jr., Malcolm X, Lorraine Hansberry, and Langston Hughes; disturbed by the lack of respect given to her by noisy, talkative audiences; hounded by the Internal Revenue Service who accused her of tax evasion; and fed up with the "pirates" of the record companies who she claimed have never compensated her properly for her records, Simone left. She first went to Barbados, then in 1974, Liberia in Africa.

For some of the time in Liberia, Simone had her daughter with her and when the need for better schooling arose, the two moved to Switzerland in 1976. At this point Simone's career as a singer was virtually nonexistent, and, in an attempt to revive it, she went to London where a con man convinced her he would sponsor her and get her performances. Instead, he robbed and beat her, then abandoned her in London. When the authorities did nothing, Simone attempted suicide by ingesting 35 sleeping pills. She woke up the next day in a London hospital glad to be alive, and hopeful for the future.

Simone spent the next two years playing small dates and then moved to Paris where in 1978 she recorded the album, Baltimore, for a small, independent label. Although the record was well-received, Simone would have another recording drought that would last seven years.

Returned to the United States

In 1985 Simone returned from her self-imposed exile to the United States and played a series of concerts, recorded the album Nina's Back, and even settled into a home in Los Angeles. The response from her fans was gracious and Simone appeared to have mellowed. "I'm ready to accept what the public has to give me," she confessed to Don Heckman of the Los Angeles Times. "And they're giving me a lot. The response I've been getting at all of my programs lately has been fantastic. I wasn't ready for that before, but now I want recognition in this country." Simone also made it clear that she wanted a hit record, telling Alexis DeVeaux of Essence that being a revolutionary is fine, but it does not pay the bills. "Before now, I was always led by whatever was going on politically at the time," she said. "At this point in time, my music is chosen because I want to make a hit record. That's entirely different from the way I chose it before. . . . And it doesn't have anything to do with what's going on in this country. It has to do with what's best for Nina Simone."

Simone would have to wait another two years for a hit and it was an unlikely one at that. For a Chanel perfume commercial in England, the advertising agency chose "My Baby Just Cares For Me," the last song she recorded for the Bethlehem album in 1958. The song was re-released in

Europe in 1987 and became a hit. The hectic pace of America, however, proved too much for Simone and she moved to the Netherlands for a few years before settling in Bouc-Bel-Air in the South of France in 1991. That same year she published her autobiography, *I Put A Spell On You*, which received positive reviews. Two years later, Simone signed to the Elektra label and recorded her first recording for a major label in nearly twenty years, *A Single Woman*. Simone was also featured on the soundtrack of *Point of No Return* in 1993 as her music served to calm the lead character played by Bridget Fonda. She also made a brief appearance in the film. Her music also appeared on the soundtrack for *Ghosts of Mississippi* in 1996.

Simone made some unwanted headlines in 1995, none of which had to do with music or politics. While gardening in her backyard, she was disturbed by the loudness of two teenage boys swimming next door. When they persisted to be loud after she asked them twice to keep it down, Simone responded by shooting a buckshot rifle over the hedge towards the two boys. One of them was slightly injured and Simone was ordered to pay a fine of $4,600 plus damages to the injured boy's family. She was also put on probation for 18 months and forced to undergo psychological counseling where it was discovered that Simone was "incapable of evaluating the consequences of her act." Later that same year Simone was fined $5,000 for causing and leaving the scene of a car accident that occurred in 1993.

From there, the path was brighter for Simone with Verve, Rhino, and RCA all releasing anthology collections of her music in 1996 and 1997. And while she remained outspoken—she openly disliked America—Simone insisted her anger had subsided. "My anger was fire," she told Alison Powell of *Interview* in 1997, "and I was pushing that all that time, but I'm not angry now. I'm philosophical, and I am happy where I am because I can't change the world. I'm getting older and I have no business being out there preaching like I did."

Simone spent the last eight years of her life at her home in Carry-le-Rouet in France. On April 21, 2003, she died of natural causes. Three months after she died, BMG Heritage released a two-disc anthology of her work, running the gamut from her very first recording to her very last.

Books

Gregory, Hugh, *Soul Music A-Z*, Blandford, 1991.
Simone, Nina with Stephen Cleary, *I Put A Spell On You*, Pantheon, 1991.

Periodicals

Africa News Service, April 26, 2003.
Black Enterprise, September 1992.
Details, January 1997.
Downbeat, July 2003.
Ebony, February 1992.
Entertainment Weekly, November 29, 1996.
Essence, October 1985.
Europe Intelligence Wire, April 25, 2003.
Globe and Mail, April 26, 2003.
Interview, January 1997.
Jet, September 4, 1980; April 22, 1985; March 24, 1996; December 10, 2001.
Knight Ridder/Tribue News Service, July 15, 2003.
Los Angeles Times, July 30 1985; January 31, 1987; September 24, 1993.
Musician, November 1993.
New York Times, October 22, 1960; May 8, 1993; August 8, 1993.
New York Times Book Review, April 19, 1992.
Reuter's News Service, July 25, 1995; August 24, 1995.
Rolling Stone, August 10, 1978; November 11, 1993. □

Jessie Carney Smith

American librarian and educator Jessie Carney Smith (born 1930) devoted her life to perpetuating the study of the history and culture of African American people through library science.

I n 1964 Smith became the first African American to earn a Ph.D. in library science from the University of Illinois. Beyond the confines of academia where she found her niche, she is widely known for her written collections that document the culture and achievements of African Americans and of Black people worldwide. Smith has lectured widely and served in a variety of international assignments.

Greensboro Native

Jessie Carney Smith was born Jessie Carney in rural North Carolina on September 24, 1930. One of four children born to James and Vesona (Bigelow), she was the youngest of the brood and the twin sister of Jodie. Raised outside of Greensboro, Smith lived with her family in a home that was situated adjacent to the tobacco farm of her grandparents, John Harvey and Minnie (Lea) Bigelow. Instilled by their parents with a strong work ethic, the Carney siblings spent much of their time helping with their father's business, a gas station and repair shop with a convenience market.

Growing up in the southern United States soon after the onset of the Great Depression, Smith and her family faced the cultural taboos of a segregated society. Regardless, they attended concerts, art exhibits, and other cultural events made available to them in Greensboro. Smith began her formal education in 1935, at age four, as a "primer" student in a four-room schoolhouse in nearby Mount Zion. She proved to be a precocious child and was double promoted from first grade to third grade, continuing at Mount Zion through the seventh grade before attending James B. Dudley High School in Greensboro. Because of segregation, her social contacts and life experience revolved around the African American population. Her primary, secondary, and collegiate education transpired exclusively at segregated schools. Thus she was exposed to history from the vantage point of her African American heritage, a circumstance that influenced her later dedication to the study of African American history and culture.

The Carney children, whose parents were alumni of North Carolina A&T, acquired a great respect for learning and education. Inspired by their parents and other family members, the siblings spent time outside of the classroom in reading the many books—including college texts—which were readily available around the Carney household. In 1946, following up on a youthful aspiration to become a fashion designer, Smith enrolled at North Carolina A&T; she graduated with a B.S. in home economics in 1950.

Smith at this time in her life had not determined to become a teacher; neither had she given consideration to spending her life as an academic in the field of library science. She spent the fall of her college graduation year at Cornell University in Ithaca, New York, where she studied textiles, clothing, and related arts, while becoming increasingly ambivalent about the clothing industry as an option for African Americans. During this time of uncertainty over her career, she married Frederick Douglas Smith on December 22, 1950, in Maryland, before making her way back to Greensboro. After a brief move to the state of Delaware, the couple settled permanently in Nashville, Tennessee.

Dr. Smith

In 1953, disappointed at the limited career opportunities available to her as an African American and a woman, Smith accepted a clerk's job at Fisk University. Holding little aspiration at that time of becoming the head librarian of the university within twelve years, she resumed her education regardless, enrolling at Michigan State University in East Lansing from 1954 to 1955, to earn an M.A. in child development. She returned to Nashville and resumed her clerical position while completing her master's thesis, yet her frustration with the job market persisted. Even with post-graduate work completed, her options for employment were few.

The mother of a young son by now, Smith opted to pursue a curriculum of library science at Nashville's George Peabody College for Teachers (now a part of Vanderbilt University). She earned an M.A. in 1957 and that spring secured a teaching position with the Nashville city schools. Later that year she accepted employment at Tennessee A&I College (now Tennessee State University) in the capacity of head cataloguer and instructor. In 1960, on fellowship from the State of Tennessee, she enrolled in a doctoral program at the University of Illinois, where she worked as a teaching assistant for three years. Having gone through a divorce in April of 1963, Smith returned to Nashville nonetheless in accordance with the terms of her fellowship, which required state service in Tennessee after graduation. She spent two years as assistant professor and coordinator of library services at Tennessee State University.

Upon completion of the graduate program requirements at University of Illinois in 1964, Smith distinguished herself as the first African American ever to earn a doctoral degree in the field of library science from that university. In 1965 she joined the library administration and faculty at Fisk University, succeeding Arna Bontemps as head librarian and establishing a lifelong career.

The 1970s

From her anchor position on the library staff at Fisk, Smith branched out and embarked on a lifelong pursuit of indexing and chronicling the cultural history of African Americans. She spent the 1970s as a part-time lecturer at Peabody Library School and from 1971 to 1973 served as an associate professor and part-time consultant at Alabama A&M University. She spent 1971 through 1974 as the Tennessee representative of the African-American Materials Project, based in North Carolina, and she was a visiting lecturer at the University of Tennessee School of Library Science in 1973–74.

During these years her duties at Fisk were augmented to include a post as director of the federally funded Internship in Black Studies Librarianship, from 1972 to 1975. In that capacity she was charged with overseeing the Mini-institutes in Black Studies Librarianship in the spring of 1975. That same year she served as the director of the school's Research Program in Ethnic Studies Librarianship (also federally funded). In the spring of 1979 she directed the Fisk Institute on Ethnic Genealogy for Librarians.

With the scope of her influence continually expanding, Smith was appointed director of a library study for the Tennessee Higher Education Commission in 1975–76. Likewise, she served on the staff of the Institute in Multicultural Librarianship at the University of Michigan during the summer of 1975. Appointed to a fellowship assignment through the National Urban League, she served in the capacity of Expert to the Library of Congress Processing Department in 1974. In 1976, she served as a consultant to the Oak Ridge National Laboratory Central Research Library, again through the Urban League fellowship program; and from 1974 to 1980 she participated on the visiting team to the American Library Association (ALA) Committee on Accreditation.

African American Historian

As Smith established a niche for herself in the American academic community, she immersed herself in researching the history of the African American people. Armed with enormous pride in her heritage, she increasingly turned toward writing and editing books that detailed the accomplishments of African American individuals throughout history. Likewise she espoused the habit of collecting news items that recorded the achievements of contemporary African Americans in the United States and abroad.

On a mandate to study libraries in Black colleges, through a fellowship from the former Council on Library Resources, Smith completed her first published work in 1977. This publication, *Black Academic Libraries and Research Collections: an historical study,* has been used heavily in determining funding support for these college libraries. By 1980 she had published two dozen educational pieces and bibliographies.

A few years later, encouraged by her colleagues and professional peers, Smith organized a definitive effort to document the lives of notable African American women. The project culminated in the publication of an award-winning volume, called *Notable Black American Women,* in 1992. In these pages, interspersed among the biographies of popular contemporary personalities and renowned individuals from U.S. history, Smith included vignettes of lesser-known African Americans, women whose contributions to American life and society were no less significant than those by more recognizable names. This provocative approach by Smith earned critical acclaim.

With the success of her first collection, Smith embraced yet another mission in life: to document the lives of African Americans, from a variety of unique vantage points. In 1990 her compilation of the *Statistical Record of Black America* was cited among the 30 best references volumes of the year by *Library Journal.* She published *Epic Lives* in 1992, followed in 1994 by the original edition of *Black Firsts,* which was recognized by *American Libraries* as one of the outstanding reference sources of 1995. Smith then reprised the *Notable Black American Women* collection, publishing Volume 2 in 1996. A similar publication, *Notable Black American Men,* appeared in 1999; it too won a number of awards. *Notable Black American Women,* Volume 3, was published in 2003. Her *Powerful Black Women* appeared in 1997, followed by *Black Heroes of the Twentieth Century* in 1998 (re-issued in 2001).

Respected as a reviewer as well as an author and editor, Smith's critiques have appeared in *College and Research Libraries* and in *Journal of Library History.* Her special reports have been commissioned by such bodies as the State of North Carolina, the U.S. Office of Civil Rights, and Oak Ridge National Laboratory. She has lectured at dozens of venues, including the Library of Congress, University of Illinois, Cornell, University of Wisconsin, Jackson State University, Howard, and Savannah State College where she led a faculty workshop and made an appearance as keynote speaker.

Literate in French and German, Smith is well traveled. She lectured worldwide during the 1980s and served in various foreign assignments over a period of three decades. She attended the Pugwash Conference in Nova Scotia in August 1968 and appeared at the University of London in June 1972. In June 1973 she served as director of the librarians' conference workshop in Tokyo, Japan, for the United States Army in the Pacific. She was a book reviewer for the Black Bermudan program at Civic Hall in Hamilton, Bermuda, in May 1980, and spent December 1984 on educational tour to Dakar, Senegal. Among her more notable U.S. projects, in 1984–86 she directed "I've Been to the Mountain Top: A Civil Rights Legacy." For this federally funded lecture program she worked in conjunction with prominent civil rights leaders Coretta Scott King, Lerone Benett, and James Farmer.

Smith has been seen on television talk shows, including *Today in Bermuda* in 1980, Nashville's *Jumpstreet* in 1981, *Black Pulse* in 1982, and on Black Entertainment Television in 1992. She joined Keith Rush on WASP-AM radio in 2001 and Pete Braley on WBSM-AM radio in 2002. Heard on National Public Radio's "Talk of the Nation" in February 2003, she discussed Black firsts with Neal Conan.

Sidelines

Socially active throughout her lifetime, Smith is renowned for her warmth and humanity, traits that she attributes to the example set by her parents and her grandparents. Her memberships include the American Library Association, National Association for the Advancement of Colored People (NAACP), The Links Incorporated, The Metropolitan Nashville Chapter of the Coalition of 100 Black Women, and Alpha Kappa Alpha Sorority. From 1976 to 1977 she presided as president of the national library honor society, Beta Phi Mu, the first black to be so empowered. Central to her message is the importance of keeping open the doors of research and knowledge for upcoming generations of students.

Committed to physical fitness, Smith walks, jogs, works with hand weights, and experiments with low-calorie recipes. Her avocations include flower gardening and reading, especially biographies.

Books

Contemporary Black Biography, Gale Group, 2003.

Other

"Jessie Carney Smith," *AKA Authors,* http://dickinsg.intrasun .tcnj.edu/akaauthors2/Carney.htm (December 16, 2003).
"Vita" (resume of) Jessie Carney Smith, 2003.
(Conversation with) Jessie Carney Smith, January 2004. □

Margaret Jean Smith Court

During her 18-year career, Australian tennis player Margaret Smith Court (born 1942) won more major championships than any other player, male or female, has ever won. She won 62 major titles in singles, doubles, and mixed doubles, including a Grand Slam (the Australian Open, Wimbledon, and the U.S. Open) in 1970.

Born Margaret Jean Smith on July 16, 1942, in the rural town of Albury, Victoria, Australia, Smith Court was one of four siblings. Her father worked in a cheese and butter factory. Neither Smith Court's parents nor her siblings had any interest in tennis, but she was drawn to the game, and she began playing by herself on the road between her house and the nearby Albury tennis courts, using balls that had been hit past the club's hedges. For a racquet, she used a long, thin board she had found; when she was eight, a friend of her mother gave her an old one with a square head, no leather on the grip, and a number of broken strings., and she began using that instead of the board.

In addition to playing in the road, Smith Court and three boys who were her age often sneaked through a hole in the fence at a nearby country club to play when the courts were unoccupied. The courts were partially hidden from the

Championship and made it to the semifinals in the Italian Open and the quarterfinals at Wimbledon and the French Open.

In 1962, Smith Court decided to travel and play independently of the Australian national team. She was more confident and self-reliant, and she won the French and American championships. At Wimbledon, she played newcomer Billie Jean King in the first round and lost in a difficult match. "I had to fight back tears of humiliation," she later said, according to Trent Fayne in *Famous Women Tennis Players*. "That was the start of the personal rivalry between Billie Jean and myself . . . and [it] plunged me into the deepest despondency of my life." Despite this loss, and her emotional reaction to it, she was ranked first in the world at the end of the year. She also received encouragement from huge numbers of fans, as well as from other tennis players.

In 1963, Smith Court played against King again in the finals at Wimbledon. This time she won. In 1964, however, tired from constant play and travel, she had an off year. She won the U.S. Open and made it to the finals at Wimbledon in 1965, and in 1966, feeling that she had missed out on much of the fun she should have had during her teenage years, she decided to retire from tennis.

Grand Slam Winner

Smith Court went back to western Australia, where she opened a boutique. In October 1967 she married wool broker Barry Michael Court. He encouraged her to return to playing tennis, and in 1968 she was back on the courts.

In 1969, she won every Grand Slam tournament except Wimbledon. In 1970, she won all the Grand Slam tournaments, even though she played Wimbledon with a sprained ankle. Playing against King in the Wimbledon finals, Smith Court battled for hours in a record 46 games. Smith Court eventually won 14-12, 11-9. It was only the second time in tennis history that a woman had completed a Grand Slam. About the match, Rex Bellamy wrote in the *Times* of London, "Here were two gloriously gifted players at their best, or so close to it that the margin was irrelevant. They gave us a marvellous blend of athleticism and skill, courage and concentration. They moved each other about with remorseless haste and hit a flashing stream of lovely shots. The match was punctuated throughout by rallies of wondrously varied patterns."

In 1971, Smith Court defended her Wimbledon title and lost to Evonne Goolagong, a rising star. Two weeks later, she played in another tournament and did poorly. After going to her doctor for tests, she found that she was pregnant. Although she continued to play tennis for fun until the seventh month of her pregnancy, she immediately stopped competing. "I would never have played at Wimbledon if I'd known I was pregnant," she told Richard Yallop in the *Australian*. "If anything had happened to the child, I would have regretted it forever." She noted that playing tennis for recreation was far different from playing in international competition, where "The pressure is so great and you drive yourself very hard."

Smith Court took time off to have her baby, but in 1972 she came back to win six tournaments, earning $22,662 in

clubhouse by a thick hedge, but if a ball hit the backstop, it would be visible, so she learned to play while standing at the net and letting the others hit the ball at her from the baseline, cutting off shots so the ball would not hit the backstop. Later, when she became a world-class player and observers praised her volleying, she said it was the first stroke she ever learned.

When she was between the ages of eight and ten, the club owner, Wally Rutter, threw her out so many times that he and his wife eventually decided it would be easier to give her a membership and pay for her to take lessons. The Rutters did not have children, and they took Smith Court under their wing and gave her coaching that her parents could not afford.

Rising Worldwide Star

When Smith Court was a teenager, she moved to Melbourne, where she trained at a club owned by former world champion Frank Sedgman, who told her that he believed she could be the first Australian woman to win a Wimbledon title. To pay for some of the costs of her training, she worked in Sedgman's office as a receptionist. By the time she was 18, she won the Australian Open championship. It was the first of her seven consecutive Australian Open titles and 11 overall.

In 1961, after her second Australian Open win, Smith Court joined the international tour. Her youth and relative inexperience made her nervous on the court and shy when she was not playing, but she won the Kent All-Comers prizes. She then won 16 of the next 18 tournaments she played in, adding $40,000. Confidently, she accepted a challenge from Bobby Riggs to play a singles match and, if she won, to donate the winnings to charity. Smith Court lost that match, but it did not mar her 1973 season. She won 18 of 25 tournaments, including the Australian, French, and U.S. Opens.

Retired from Tennis

Between 1962 and 1973, Smith Court was ranked number one seven times. In 1960 she won her first major championship, and she won her last, the U.S. Open, in 1975. She continued to play until 1977, then quit in order to have more time with her children. In 1979, Smith Court was inducted into the Tennis Hall of Fame. During her career, she also won two ABC Sports Personality of the Year Awards and was made a Member of the British Empire for her services to sport and international relations

Smith Court's life began undergoing a change in 1973, when a friend gave her a religious book. Although she had been raised Catholic, she didn't find that religion touched her very deeply. She decided to become a born-again Christian. After retiring from tennis, she studied at the Word of Faith Bible College in Perth, Australia. She later wrote on the Johnny Lee Clary International website, "The next few years were a real struggle for me dealing with a heart condition, depression and insomnia but what got me through was total devotion to God and . . . the Bible." Smith Court told Louise Perry in the *Australian* that she believed her faith healed her heart condition, and she commented to Jane Cunningham in *ABC Online,* "They said I'd be on medication for the rest of my life and I've never had medication since and been totally healed."

Became a Minister

In 1991, Smith Court was ordained as a minister, and with the help of two other pastors, she founded Margaret Court Ministries, Inc. She turned an abandoned carpet warehouse in an industrial section of Perth, Australia into a church, Victory Life Church, where she preached a Pentacostal ministry. In an interview on *ABC Online,* she told George Negus, "To me, people go to a football match and yell and scream when they're excited about something, or go to a tennis match and enjoy it, and, I mean, that's how church should be." By 2003, 1,500 people were attending the church, where Smith Court often laid hands on members to heal them, and where she usually preached the sermon during the two-hour service. One of her daughters, Marika, worked with her. In 2001, Smith Court announced plans to buy an old hospital and turn it into a home for people with incurable illnesses, drug addicts, unwed mothers, abuse victims, and "any other shipwrecked ship which needs to be fixed," she told Louise Perry in the *Australian.*

Although she no longer played, Smith Court still followed tennis, particularly the Grand Slams. She commented that many women players of the 21st century were "robots," according to John Thirsk in the Surry Hills, Australia *Sunday Telegraph.* She said this was the result of rigid coaching schemes, and also noted that the young women

"lacked hunger because many were simply content to play for a comfortable living rather than chase major honors," according to Thirsk.

Smith Court told Vivienne Oakley in the Adelaide, Australia *Advertiser* that she believed Australia could produce more champions by returning to individual coaching: "I think we put our people into squads too young and champions are very sensitive people. I believe we lose them in the squads at a very early age." She said she never would have become a champion if she had come through the modern coaching system, noting, "I had good mentors. Sometimes I played and won for them, not myself." And, she told Thirsk, "I've seen what happened with some others way back, who had been promising, winning national junior titles. They had individual coaches and because they were good, went into a squad. You've never heard about them again."

Books

Fayne, Trent, *Famous Women Tennis Players,* Dodd, Mead and Co., 1979.
Great Women in Sports, Visible Ink Press, 1996.
Grimsley, Will, *Tennis: Its History, People and Events,* Prentice-Hall, 1971.

Periodicals

Advertiser (Adelaide, Australia), September 6, 2003.
Australian (Sydney, Australia), June 20, 2001; March 18, 2002.
Courier-Mail (Brisbane, Australia), September 8, 2003.
Independent (London), August 23, 2003.
Sunday Telegraph, (Lodnon), January 25, 1998.
Times (London), June 28, 2001, p. 6.

Online

"Court, Margaret Jean," *Australian Women,* http://www.womenaustralia.info/biogs/IMP0179b.htm (January 2, 2004).
"Episode 19: Margaret Court," *ABC Online,* http://www.abc.net.au/ (January 2, 2004).
"Tribute to Margaret Court," *Johnn Lee Clary International,* http://www.johnnyleeclary.com/margaret_court.htm (January 2, 2004). □

Robert Smythson

Robert Smythson (1535-1614), an English architect of the Tudor period, is praised by scholars as the most important architect of his day and a man of independent vision.

In an age where the term "architect" had no meaning, Robert Smythson was the most important designer of English manor houses working during the 16th century. While little is known of his background or personal life, Smythson is known to us through the massive buildings that remain standing throughout England, such as Wollaton Hall, Longleat, and others in middle and northern England. These stately homes, vestiges of a distant past where newly moneyed families attempted to assert their worthiness among the noble class by building impressive estates, still stand, many preserved as historic monuments by British trust and preservation organizations.

An Undocumented Life

In the papers and other documents that have survived the centuries since his birth in 1534, little can be gleaned of the life or professional activities of Robert Smythson. Architectural historians have discovered what little they know about the man from his architectural renderings, from a few letters, and from bills, and other ephemera that have been saved from becoming dust after almost five centuries. Born in 1534 and trained as a stonemason, Smythson first appears on a written record dating from 1566 and relating to the renovation of Longleat, a manor house located in Wiltshire.

During the mid-1500s, as a shift in fortunes and the religious affiliation of many in England created a new ruling class, older manor houses built of wood and plaster were being replaced or renovated using cut stone and brick. In other cases, self-made men from the new Protestant elite bought up rural lands and set about establishing their own dynasty, crowned by a home that reflected their right to vast wealth. The first was the case at Longleat. After an earlier house on the site had been destroyed by fire in April of 1567, Sir John Thynne undertook to construct a more lavish manor house for his family. Working in London at the time, Smythson was contracted by Thynne as principal mason on the building of Longleat. As a master mason, Smythson made his living traveling around England with a crew of masons, and by the time he reached Longleat in March of 1568, at the age of 33, the observant Smythson had likely become well-versed in building design.

In Tudor England during the mid-1500s there was no such term as "architect;" instead the designing of houses was considered a craft–or mechanical as opposed to intellectual art–as it had been since the Middle Ages. While the renaissance ongoing in Europe–out of which would come noted architect Inigo Jones–had produced a new interest in architecture and the arts, such was not the case in England, where tastes were more provincial and Italian influences were reviled as "papish." Due to more pressing concerns, Henry VIII ceased building projects as his differences with the Catholic Church grew, leaving most building in England to wealthy businessmen who aspired to noble status. Consequently, the designer of a house was considered of little importance, as long as his design reflected the wealthy status of its owner.

Master Mason at Longleat

Although by trade a mason, Smythson also possessed recognizable abilities as a designer, perhaps revealed by other projects he had worked on for Thynne's friends. Although he was only one of several people to involve themselves in the design of the house, many of the design features used are characteristic of Smythson's later work: a symmetrical, stately structure with a central hall, the use of many large windows to open the house to the outdoors, and the home's "extroversion"–facing out toward the surround-

ing area rather than curving inward around a central courtyard–were unusual in Tudor homes during the period.

The restrained use of classical elements throughout the portion of the house constructed during this period shows Smythson to have cultivated, educated tastes and a grounding in the design trends in both England and Europe, particularly Italy. His work during this period signals what many historians view as an English Renaissance style that breaks with the Italian classicism that was prevalent on the continent.

Wollaton Hall

Thynne's approval of Smythson's work at Longleat gained the young man the opportunity to design country houses for other members of the landed aristocracy. With work at Longleat finally completed in 1575, Smythson moved on to other projects, in 1570 performing work on Wardour Castle, the home of Sir Matthew Arundell, to transform it into a residence. Other homes which show signs of his work during this period are Corsham Court, in Wiltshire (1575), and Shaw House, in Berkshire.

In 1580 Smythson began work for Arundell's cousin, Sir Francis Willoughby. The sheriff of Nottingham commissioned him to design and supervise the construction of a home and lodge on a hill at Wollaton, Nottinghamshire. This was Smythson's first commission as a professional master surveyor or master artificer, and many historians consider it his most important work. Wollaton Hall now houses the Nottingham Natural History Museum.

Ongoing until 1588, Wollaton Hall contains many of the unique features of Longleat–the house has a central hall and tall, massive second-storey windows along its face that connect it to the surrounding countryside and bath its rooms in light–but these features are more accentuated at Willoughby's home. Although Smythson's design for Wollaton is clearly based on a pattern for Poggio Reale, a house in Naples outlined in Sebastiano Serlio's 1550 work *Libri di arcitectura*, he was also inspired by the work of Jacques Androucet du Cerceau, and incorporates rooms of differing heights, massive corner towers, and other imaginative geometrical elements.

At Wollaton, as elsewhere, Smythson linked his designs to the prevailing fashion set by architects in Italy, but his adaptation was unique. He also drew from renaissance, Flemish, and England's gothic designs, creating an innovative, medievalesque, and romantic style. Elements such as cartouches and strapwork recall the Flemish ornaments of Vredeman de Vries' influential 1563 work *Variae architecturae formae*, while also drawing on ecclesiastical and militaristic design elements.

Settled Permanently in Wollaton

Over the eight years Smythson worked for Sir Willoughby, the two men developed a comfortable working relationship. After the house was finished, Smythson and his family settled in Wollaton permanently, and Smythson worked as a bailiff for Willoughby, collecting rents when not otherwise busy drawing house plans. Much of Smythson's subsequent work was done in this midland region. Among the houses that bear his mark are the Worksop Manor hunting lodge, in Nottinghamshire; Doddington Hall, in Lincolnshire; Welbeck Abbey and Burton Agnes, both in Yorkshire; Chastleton, in Oxfordshire; and Barlborough Hall, in Derbyshire. While documentation tying these homes to Smythson is sometimes scarce, all reflect his unique style, and it is likely that he, at the very least, had a hand in drafting plans for their design.

Smythson's work at Hardwick, Derbyshire, is well documented. Built between 1591 and 1597 by Elizabeth, countess of Shrewsbury, Hardwick Hall was designed to replace an older, smaller home, Hardwick Old Hall, which now lays in ruins on the Hardwick estate. Bess Hardwick was a fascinating woman. Part of a landed family who had lived on this property for six generations, she experienced a downturn in circumstances at age one, when her father died, leaving each of his four daughters 26 pounds, 13 shillings. Working as a servant for a neighboring family as a young teen, she amassed a fortune by outliving four husbands. After the death of her last husband, Lord Shrewsbury, in 1590, 63-year-old Bess was free to buy back her family seat, build a magnificent new home suitable for a woman of her lofty station, and establish a new dynasty. Her sons were the first members of the Cavendish dynasty; the family is now represented by the dukes of Devonshire and live at Chatworth, leaving Hardwick Hall open to the public.

Beth Hardwick was an independent spirit, and she was drawn to Smythson's use of large plates of glass instead of walls. One of the two buildings that sprang from her active collaboration with Smythson—Hardwick Lodge was also build on the property—Hardwick Hall is considered one of the finest examples of Elizabethan architecture in England. Forward looking in its design, it rejects much of the influences of the baroque continental style and prefigures early 17th-century aesthetic sensibilities. At the roofline of the hall is visible a prominently carved set of initials: "E.S.", signifying Bess's station as the Lady Shrewsbury.

The stone used in building Hardwick Hall was quarried nearby, and many of the craftsmen who had built the Old Hall were still alive and took the same care to build the new one. Hardwick's interior, which still contains many of the tapestries and plasterwork that were installed by Smythson, contains elements of medieval chivalric design and Italian classicism. The floor plan is similar, in ways, to that of Italian architect Andrea Palladio's villa Valmarana, built at Lisiera, while the overall structure reflects the same restraint and attention to detail Smythson showed in his work at Longleat.

Among Smythson's other projects is Doddington Hall, Lincolnshire, begun in 1593 and completed in 1600. Still standing, the Hall contains walled gardens, a gatehouse, and a family church. Shireoaks Hall, Derbyshire, was a design commission for the Hewett family; and Thorpe Manor was build for Brian Sandford after an older house was demolished.

Pontefract New Hall and Heath Old Hall, two of Smythson's earliest Yorkshire buildings, have been demolished, but his work can still be seen at Burton Agnes, home to Sir Henry Griffith. Griffith moved to the home in 1599 and began work on the house circa 1601. The house, designed in the traditional Tudor manner around a small internal courtyard, is enhanced by such design elements as bay windows with glass grids, gables, finials, battlements, and strapwork. Smythson modernized the existing house by creating a long gallery on the top floor, complete with carved wainscoting and a highly decorated plaster ceilings. The home's brick gatehouse, built in 1610, is a prime example of its type.

Began Architectural Dynasty

Late in Smythson's career he was joined by his son, John Smythson, who followed in his father's profession. John Smythson's best-known work is at Bolsover Castle, in Derbyshire, a commission undertaken for Bess Hardwick's son, Sir Charles Cavendish. While the plans for Bolsover Castle clearly show the hand of the father, the son remained active on the project during the 30 years it took to complete. In fact, Bolsover hall is credited with employing three generations of the Smythson dynasty: Robert is credited with the renovation plans, son John oversaw the work and designed the interior apartments, while grandson Huntingdon Smythson is credited with designing the adjoining buildings housing Bolsover's riding school, which became famous through the horsemanship of William Cavendish, duke of Newcastle.

Smythson died in Wollaton, England in 1614, and was commemorated by an inscription on his tomb in the town's church that reads: "architect and surveyour unto the most worthy house of Wollaton and divers others of great account."

In his book *Robert Smythson and the Elizabethan Country House* architectural historian Mark Girouard called Smythson a "rough diamond" and described his work as "full of ideas, but full also of . . . conceptions only half worked out." Girouard described Smythson's Wollaton Hall as, "for all its originality, a repulsive building," and Hardwick Hall "a monument of ostentation and pride." Still, Girouard counted Smythson among "the great geniuses of English architecture. As with the Elizabethan age as a whole, along with much that is vulgar, clumsy or hard, there is a boldness in his work that demands admiration and a poetry that can still set the imagination on fire."

Because of John Smythson's respect for his father's work, he saw to the preservation of many of his father's architectural drawings. Influencing the work of not only John Smythson but other English architects as well, Smythson's surviving drawings are now housed in the library of the Royal Institute of British Architects in London.

Books

Friedman, Alice T., *House and Household in Elizabethan England: Wollaton Hall and the Willoughby Family,* University of Chicago Press, 1989.

Girouard, Mark, *Robert Smythson and the Elizabethan Country House,* Yale University Press, 1983.

International Dictionary of Architects and Architecture, St. James Press, 1993.

Summerston, John, *Architecture in Britain, 1530-1830,* Penguin, 1977.

Online

Bolsover Castle Web site, http://www.britcastles.com/bolsover
.htm (December 6, 2003). □

Sobhuza II

Sobhuza II (1899-1982) ruled the African nation of Swaziland for 60 years, first as a British Protectorate and after 1968, when Swaziland gained independence from England, as a sovereign state. During his reign, he regained much, but not all, of the land his people had lost to European colonists under the rule of his grandfather, Mbandzeni.

Born in 1899 in Zombodza, Swaziland, Sobhuza II was the great-great-grandson of Sobhuza I, who founded the Swazi nation, and he inherited a legacy of strife. After being attacked in the early 1800s by Ndwande chief Zwide, Sobhuza I had led his own people, the Ngwane, into the mountains, where they found refuge. Sobhuza I's son, Mswati (c. 1820-68) formed these refugees into a nation-state, called Swazi, and during his reign they became one of the most powerful groups in southern Africa. However, after his death, the nation collapsed into factions which fought each other over who should become Mswati's successor. In 1875, this bitter factional fighting ended in a compromise that resulted in Mbandzeni becoming king.

Gold Brought Europeans

In 1873, gold was discovered in South Africa, and European prospectors flooded into Swaziland, looking for wealth and demanding land from Mbandzeni. In 1876, he granted 36,000 acres in southern Swaziland to two land speculators. Although he made a great deal of money from this transaction, receiving up to 20,000 British pounds per year for the next decade, the opening of land to Europeans ultimately led to a stripping of the country's resources.

When Mbandzeni fell into poor health, various factions in his court battled for control; as a result, several elder councillors, accused of plotting to overthrow Mbandzeni, were executed. When Mbandzeni died in 1889, his son, Bhunu (also known as Ngwane V) succeeded him. Because Bhunu was only 14 at the time, his mother acted as regent. Bhunu held the throne until he died at the age of 24, shortly after the birth of his son, Sobhuza II, in 1899.

Sobhuza's parents initially named him Nkhotfotjeni, which means "Stone Lizard." When his father died five months after his birth, Sobhuza was selected by a royal council to succeed him to the throne; as a mark of this distinction, he was renamed Sobhuza II after his great-great-grandfather. Because Sobhuza was still only an infant when he became king, his grandmother, Labotsibeni, became regent. She ruled Swaziland for the next 20 years.

During Labotsibeni's rule, there was considerable conflict between the Swazi people and the British. The nation came under British control as a protectorate in 1903. As a writer in the *Times* of London explained, this meant that "although the protected country is not a British dominion, its foreign relations are under the exclusive control of the Crown, so that its government cannot hold direct communications with any other foreign Power, nor a foreign Power with its Government." Thus, Swaziland was stripped of its autonomy, and was essentially under British rule.

Four years later, a resident commissioner appointed by the British government arrived in the country. This commissioner settled previous land disputes by ruling that 63 percent of Swazi land belonged to Europeans; as a result, almost half the Swazi people suddenly found themselves living in areas that were no longer part of the now-diminished Swaziland. These people were allowed five years to leave the European-controlled areas. If they did not, they would be forced out. According to an obituary in the *Times*, Sobhuza's father did not fight this, and in fact said, "If I do not give whites rights here, they will take them. Therefore I give when they pay. Why should we not eat before we die?"

"The Lion"

Labotsibeni knew that in order for her country to win back its land, its people would have to deal with the British and that its next leader would have to understand European ways as well as African ones. She sent the young Sobhuza to special primary and secondary schools in Swaziland that had been created especially for him, with teachers she had brought in from South America. From 1916 to 1918, he attended Lovedale College in Cape Province, South Africa. In addition to educating him, Labotsibeni filled Sobhuza with the desire to regain the land his country had lost.

In 1921, Sobhuza became king of Swaziland and received another name, Ngwenyama, which means "The Lion." In 1922, he challenged the 1907 partition of the Swazi lands by the British High Commissioner. To do this, Sobhuza traveled to Britain with a Swazi delegation to meet with King George V and petition him to restore the lands to the Swazi people. King George and his secretary of state for the colonies refused. Sobhuza, undeterred, continued to press his case for the next 15 years, and was repeatedly refused. Eventually, however, King George agreed to help Sobhuza acquire land from white owners and return it to Swazi occupation. As a result, the land held by Swazis increased from 37 percent at the time of the partition to slightly more than 50 percent.

As a result of his education in European ways, Sobhuza was comfortable in both traditional African clothing and settings and in European-style military dress. He often led traditional Swazi rituals and was known by various nicknames, including "The Great Mountain," "The Bull," "The Son of the She-Elephant," and "The Inexplicable." Sobhuza valued his people's traditions, particularly the traditional royal rights to name and dismiss chiefs, to establish courts, to regulate the country's constitution, and to control the Swazi treasury. Another tradition Sobhuza adhered to was polygamy; he married at least 70 wives and had at least 210 children. The custom of taking two new wives each year was believed to preserve the political balance of the kingdom.

However, Sobhuza also freely adopted and used Western technology when it was useful to him or to the Swazi people. In *Who's Who in Africa*, John Dickie noted that Sobhuza once said, "As one of the last countries to achieve independence, we have had the opportunity of learning from nations which have won their independence before us. We have watched them crossing rivers [and] have seen [them] being swallowed by crocodiles. Now that we have seen the crocodile-infested drifts, we shall try to cross through crocodile-free drifts to a peaceful independent Swaziland."

In the 1960s, Sobhuza knew that it would be advantageous for him to align his royal interests with those of his country's white electorate, and he did so. As noted in the *Times*, "The greatest test of his authority was during the maneuvering before independence, but he showed himself to be an adept politician and secured complete control of the national assembly for his traditionally oriented Imbokadvo (Royal) Party. In the nation's 1964 legislative elections, the party won control of all but one seat. When Britain finally granted independence to Swaziland in 1968, Sobhuza became the nation's head of state.

Dissolved Parliament

In 1973, Sobhuza's rule was challenged by political opponents in a legislative election. In response, he suspended the rules of the constitution, which the country had

inherited from England; dissolved the country's parliament; and banned all political parties and trade unions, viewing all these things as threats to his authority. He thus became an absolute ruler, and made all judicial, executive, and legislative decisions, as in a traditional tribal government; his National Council and personal advisors were almost all his close relatives or sons. He continued to rule as an absolute monarch until his death in 1982. His strong rule had the effect of reducing strife among various tribes and maintaining national unity. Unlike many other African nations of the time, Swaziland was a model of political and economic stability.

In 1981, Sobhuza celebrated the Diamond Jubilee of his reign; the ceremony was attended by Princess Margaret on behalf of Queen Elizabeth of England. His last public appearance took place on July 22, 1982, when he celebrated his birthday. He died a month later at the Embo state house, at the age of 83, after reigning 61 years. Although he had regained much of the land his people had lost to the British, he did not live to see his dream of incorporating all of what was once Swaziland under his rule. Two thousand square miles of the former Swazi land still remained part of South Africa.

To show their grief over his death, everyone in the Swazi kingdom, male and female, shaved their heads as a sign of mourning. Sobhuza, like many of his people, had converted to Christianity, and his death ceremonies mingled Christian hymns with the African songs of a traditional tribal funeral, which involved secret rites, such as wrapping the body in the skins of freshly killed oxen. Although his body, dressed in a dark blue military uniform and sitting upright in a wooden casket, was later paraded in a glass-covered casket past more than 25,000 of his subjects, many people refused to believe that their long-reigning monarch was dead. The funeral parade was also attended by massed army bands in natty European dress, as well as hundreds of royal warriors, who wore animal skins and brandished wooden spears. One of Sobuza's senior wives, ceremonially called "The Great She-Elephant," attended in tribal dress: barefoot, wearing animal skins and wearing a headband with a scarlet feather that signified she was a member of the royal clan. The funeral was also attended by many foreign dignitaries, including Prince Michael of Kent, England and the South African foreign minister, Pik Botha.

After Sobhuza's death, Swaziland entered a period of confusion because, in keeping with tradition, no successor to the throne could be designated while the reigning king was alive. Of his many wives and children, one wife had to be selected to rule as queen regent, and one of his great number of sons had to be chosen to ascend the throne; one traditional restriction was that the new king must be an only child. After several years, in 1986, Crown Prince Makhosetive became king, taking the name Mswati III.

Books

Biography Resource Center, Gale Group, 2003.

Dickie, John, and Alan Rake, *Who's Who in Africa,* Africa Buyer and Trader, 1973.

Periodicals

Daily Mail (London), December 14, 2001.
Times (London), April 1, 1926; August 23, 1982; August 24, 1982; September 4, 1982. □

Luang Pibul Songgram

Pibul Songgram (1897-1964) was known as the founder of the modern Thai nation. His political career began in 1932 when he took part in an overthrow that replaced the Thai absolute monarchy with a constitutional regime. He was field marshal and prime minister of Thailand from 1938 to 1944 and from 1948 to 1957.

B orn Plack Khitasangkha on July 14, 1987, Pibul Songgram came from a farming family in the town of Nonthaburi in the Thai province of Nakorn Nayok; he was the second child in a family of four sons and one daughter. His parents considered him difficult, so they gave him up for adoption to the abbot of the Paknam Buddhist temple. This was a common practice among Thais at the time; they believed that if a child was often irritable or difficult, he might be possessed by evil spirits, who would be driven out if the child were given to a respectable, spiritual person such as a monk. Songgram was raised by the monks at the Chumani Temple, and later his parents sent him to study at the Wat Khemaphitaram School in Nonthaburi. In 1909, when he was twelve years old, he went to the Bangkok Infantry Cadet School, and graduated from military training when he was eighteen. He then joined the 7th Artillery Corps in Phitsanulok.

Joined People's Party

In Phitsanulok, he met and married his wife, Thanphuying La-iad, a teacher at a missionary school. In 1919, Songgram went back to Bangkok to undergo four more years of military school; he graduated at the top of his class and earned a scholarship to study artillery in France. He went to France in 1924, studied at Poitier and Fontaineblue, and returned to Thailand in 1927. On his return, he was given the title of Luang Phibunsongkhram and was promoted to captain in the artillery corps. By 1932, he had reached the rank of major and was a supervisor in the ministry of defense.

Also in 1932, Songgram became a member of the "1932 Promoters," later called the People's Party, which had been formed in 1927. This party was dedicated to the overthrow of Thailand's ancient and absolute monarchy. According to Kobkua Suwannathat-Pian in *Thailand's Durable Premier,* however, Songgram "paid little attention to the intellectual side of the revolution and was happy to undertake any operational assignment allocated to him. He demonstrated a refreshing and symbolic naivety in politics by refusing to follow other People's Party leaders in attending the 'begging for His Majesty's forgiveness' ceremony, on the grounds that he was not involved in. . .denouncing the Chakri Dynasty in harsh and disrespectful terms and thus had committed no wrong against the King and the royal family."

Nevertheless, after a successful coup in 1932, Songgram was appointed a minister in the new government, headed by Phraya Mano, and was also named deputy commander of artillery. In June 1933, after a conflict between the progressive wing of the People's Party, which included Phibun, and its conservative wing, Phibun and some allies staged another coup and successfully demanded that Phraya Mano resign. From then on, Songgram continued to become more prominent in both politics and military affairs. By 1934, he was appointed deputy commander-in-chief of the army and minister of defense. In 1934-1935, he also became a group captain of the air force and a naval captain.

Prime Minister of Thailand

In 1938, when Praya Phahon gave up his post as premier of Thailand, the National Assembly chose Songgram to succeed him as both prime minister and commander-in-chief of the army. He presided over a cabinet of twenty-five men, fifteen of whom were members of the military. Within a month, in order to prevent any opposition to his rule, Songgram had forty people arrested on charges of plotting against the government. These included members of the royal family, bureaucratic nobles, elected members of the assembly, and army rivals. After a series of trials, Songgram had eighteen of these people executed, the first political executions in Thailand in more than a century.

In 1939, as part of his efforts to build what he considered a new and modern nation, Songgram changed the country's name from Siam to Thailand. He also began a sweeping series of actions against Chinese settlers in Thailand. The Chinese were considered to be profiting from various businesses that many Thais believed should be theirs, and many Thais resented the Chinese because they were so prosperous. Songgram began a "Thailand for the Thais" campaign and instituted heavy taxes, regulations, and restrictions on non-Thais. At the same time, Thais were encouraged to behave in nationalistic ways, adopting clean and modern clothing, avoiding imported goods, speaking the Thai language instead of local dialects, and staying informed about current affairs. In addition, Songgram made sure that his photograph appeared everywhere, and that his slogans were repeated in newspapers and on billboards and the radio.

New Guidelines for Thai Life

In *Thailand: A Short History,* David K. Wyatt wrote that during Songgram's first premiership, the Thai government "was thoroughly shaped by his power and personality, much as absolute kings had done a generation earlier." However, Wyatt added, this period was also "a period of mass nationalism, not just elite nationalism, a social and political phenomenon that was more nearly egalitarian in its implications than it could have been earlier under a monarchist psychology."

As prime minister, one of Songgram's objectives was to mold the Thai people into what he considered a modern, civilized, and cultured nation, without giving up their essential culture and character, in order to earn respect from other nations. At times, the government's prescriptions of what Thai people should or should not do "overlooked the delicate dividing line between social obligations and individual preference in personal matters," according to Suwannathat-Pian.

A major emphasis of the new guidelines for behavior was personal hygiene, but the guidelines went far beyond cleanliness to specify how people should sit or stand, what they should eat, and when they should sleep, exercise, or rest. In 1939, the government also began a campaign encouraging everyone to maintain a vegetable garden and raise poultry. The intent was to make it possible for even the poorest families to have good food. In addition, contrary to the ancient Thai custom of eating with the hands, which the government considered unclean, people were encouraged to use forks and spoons; if people ate with their hands, they were required to wash them thoroughly first. In addition, many old delicacies were forbidden, and people were told to eat balanced meals of vegetables, meat, eggs, chicken, pork, and fish. Women were told of the proper way they should raise their children, and both men and women were told to behave in a dignified manner in public. Anyone who behaved in a way that would bring shame to the Thai people was punished.

The government also insisted that the people become physically and mentally strong. An individual's day was divided into three parts of eight hours each, for working, for personal activities, and for rest. Each period had certain prescribed activities assigned to it; for example, the encouraged forms of recreation included, according to Suwannathat-Pian, "physical exercise by playing games and undertaking long-distance walks or other such exertions; they were to spend some time in their kitchen gardens and in tending to their poultry; and they were to spend other times in reading, listening to the radio, and attending the religious sermons."

In addition to regulating matters of health and hygiene, the government also regulated the status of men and women. Songgram believed that women were an important part of society, so he decreed that they have equal status at home and on the national level. Husbands who worked for the government were penalized if they did not honor their wives. They were ordered to kiss their wives before going to work and when they came home from work. Also, the government set up a women's corps in the army, as well as a women's cadet academy and a woman's non-commissioned training school.

Songgram also instituted a social welfare state, which took care of its citizens' mental and physical well-being. Unemployed workers were told to report to the authorities, who would find jobs for them. Beggars who could not be employed and who did not have family or friends to care for them fell under the care of the state. It was the first social welfare program ever to exist in Thailand.

As Suwannathat-Pian commented, however, these heavy-handed and controlling changes most often "reflected the authorities' concern for the exterior aspects of Thai society and its positive impression upon foreigners, especially Westerners, rather than the interior or mental strength of the society."

Fell from Power, Returned

In 1941, Songgram became supreme commander of the armed forces, and later that year, after winning the Indo-Chinese war against the French, he became field marshal. As World War II progressed, Thailand's relations with the West deteriorated as it allied itself with Japan.

In 1944, Songgram's first premiership ended with the impending defeat of the Japanese. After the war, Songgram fell from favor; he was arrested and charged with war crimes against the Allied forces. He was also kept under surveillance by the new Thai government. As Wyatt commented, however, "Public opinion on the whole was favorable to Phibun. He was thought to have done the best that could be done to maintain Thai interests in the face of overwhelming Japanese pressure. Phibun and the military were, in effect, exonerated, but they were still reluctant to take an active political role in the face of possible negative reactions from the Western powers on whom Thailand so depended at this point."

In 1947, another coup led by General Phin Chunhawan and others brought Songgram back into power. From April 1948 to September 1957, he was again prime minister of Thailand. He began his rule with another anti-Chinese campaign, and he also came down hard on dissidents and rebels, fearing another coup would topple him. Many potential rivals or opponents were arrested and were tortured and even killed without trial. Newspaper editors who described these events were beaten up and frightened into silence. During this period, Thailand remained a constitutional democracy only on paper. In 1949, elections for government representatives were rigged so that Songgram had a majority in the House of Representatives.

On June 29, 1951, Songgram was attending a ceremony on board an American ship, which the American government was presenting to Thailand, when he was taken by naval officers and their men, who imprisoned him on another ship. By the next day, the government was in chaos, with fierce fighting in Bangkok. The Thai air force eventually bombed the ship holding Songgram, but he managed to swim away as it sank. Eventually he linked up with friendly forces and made a radio appeal to the navy to stop fighting. The coup ended, but with a cost of more than 1,200 fatalities, most of whom were civilians. Following the coup, Songgram cut the navy to one-fourth of its previous strength and arrested many people he suspected of opposing him.

Although the Thai economy improved greatly during the 1950s, Songgram's position remained unstable, as he had many rivals and enemies. By 1955, perhaps sensing this and wanting to seek favor among them, Songgram went on a long tour of the United States and returned professing a deep love for democracy. He began relaxing his previous authoritarian controls on political parties, free speech and the press. However, when an election was held in 1957, it was marred by blatant vote rigging, fraud and tampering. This led to public outrage and a state of national emergency. Songgram was harshly condemned, and on September 13, 1957, was forced out of office.

Songgram went into exile in Cambodia and later in Japan. While in exile, Songgram fulfilled a long-held wish to become a Buddhist monk, which he did at the Buddhagaya Temple in India in August of 1960. Although he wished to return to Thailand, the government there would not allow him to enter the country because they believed that if he did, it might spark another coup, or at the least, a burst of political unrest. He died in Japan on June 11, 1964. His ashes were returned to Thailand with great fanfare and were interred at the Si Mathahat Temple, which he had built as a symbol of the 1932 victory over the conservative wing of the People's Party.

Books

Suwannathat-Pian, Kobkua, *Thailand's Durable Premier,* Oxford University Press, 1995.
Teed, Peter, *Dictionary of Twentieth-Century History, 1941-1990,* Oxford University Press, 1992.
Wyatt, David K., *Thailand: A Short History,* Yale University Press, 1984

Periodicals

Times (London), June 13, 1964. ☐

Bruce Springsteen

Considered by many to be one of the most important musicians to emerge from the 1970s, rock icon Bruce Springsteen (born 1949) tells stories about everyday people in his songs. Whether talking about Vietnam veterans in "Born in the U.S.A.," or reflecting on the aftermath of September 11 in "The Rising," Springsteen makes his characters come alive and touches people.

In his long, successful career, Bruce Springsteen has balanced many roles, including rock star, folk singer, songwriter, cultural icon, and social activist, as well as family man. An award-winning singer and songwriter and a member of the Rock and Roll Hall of Fame, Springsteen is well respected by peers and critics and has always connected with his fans. Writing the introduction for *Bruce Springsteen-The Rolling Stone Files,* Parke Puterbaugh reflected, "Springsteen directly addressed and shaped the dreams of an anxious generation feeling its way through turbulent, uncertain but hopeful times." The *RollingStone.com* website noted that "he is, simply put, the last, true voice of rock and roll."

Jersey Boy

Bruce Frederick Springsteen was born on September 23, 1949 in Freehold, New Jersey. He was the first child and only son of Adele and Douglas Springsteen. Two girls, Ginny and Pam, would follow. Although the Springsteen family name was Dutch, his father was Irish and his mother was Italian.

In his book *It Ain't No Sin to be Glad You're Alive-The Promise of Bruce Springsteen,* Eric Alterman noted that Bruce's mother was a legal secretary whom he has fondly described as "just like Superwoman." Alterman described Bruce's father as "an embittered man who struggled to find a place for himself in the local economy." Dave Marsh, writer of *Bruce Springsteen-Two Hearts-The Definitive Biography, 1972-2003,* added that the Springsteen family "continually struggled to make ends meet" and were "at the poorer end of the American working class."

Alterman wrote that Springsteen's childhood was somewhat "oppressive," and that "his relationship with his father involved little but discipline and rebellion." In addition, Springsteen hated school, and often endured the wrath of the nuns who were his grade school teachers. Music was an escape, and Springsteen was said to be inspired to pursue a career in music after seeing Elvis and the Beatles on *The Ed Sullivan Show.* He taught himself to play the guitar. When he was 16, his mother took out a loan to buy him a guitar for Christmas.

However, both of his parents wanted him to pursue a career other than music, especially his father. This led to more conflict in the house. Springsteen has recalled during his concerts, ''When I was growing up, there were two things that were unpopular in my house: one was me, the other was my guitar.'' But Springsteen kept practicing, never let go of his dream, and began playing in area bands on a regular basis.

New Jersey Music Scene

Springsteen joined his first rock band, the Castiles, in 1965. As noted in *American Decades,* ''When his family moved to California in 1969, Springsteen stayed behind, living along the beaches and boardwalks of Asbury Park [New Jersey] and playing in local bands.'' Those bands included Steel Mill, the Rogues, Dr. Zoom and the Sonic Boom, and the Bruce Springsteen Band. That is how he met many of the musicians who would later become his E Street Band.

Alterman reflected that it was early in his musical career when ''Springsteen first became saddled with the horribly inappropriate nickname 'the Boss.' Springsteen detested the nickname. 'I hate bosses. I hate being called ' ''the Boss,'' ' he has complained.''

In 1972, Springsteen's fortunes improved. At the age of 23, Springsteen signed a deal with fledgling songwriter-producer Mike Appel. This partnership helped Springsteen in the short term and jump-started his career, but the relationship would haunt him. Although Appel dedicated himself to Springsteen's career, he was considered by many to be too abrasive. However, Appel soon arranged for an audition with Columbia Records, and Springsteen impressed the executives and earned a recording contract.

''Born to Run'' Phenomenon

Springsteen released *Greetings From Asbury Park, N.J* in 1973. Sales of the album and radio airplay were minimal. Springsteen was being touted as ''the new Bob Dylan,'' and it has been said that radio disc jockeys were put off by that hype. However, some critics quickly recognized Springsteen's talent. When *The Wild, the Innocent, and the E Street Shuffle* was released later in 1973, more critics took notice, but disc jockeys played the second release even less.

But Springsteen was gaining a reputation as a thrilling live performer. Music critic Jon Landau wrote a review of a Springsteen's show and stated, ''I saw rock 'n' roll's future and its name is Bruce Springsteen.'' The pair met shortly after that review was published and became friends.

Springsteen wanted Landau to produce his next album, a decision that did not sit well with Appel. However, the marketing campaign for *Born to Run,* which was released in 1975, soon took off and worked everyone into a frenzy over Springsteen. He ended up on the covers of both *Time* and *Newsweek* in the same week in October 1975.

The single ''Born to Run'' made Springsteen a star. He told *Entertainment Weekly,* ''with that one I was shootin' for the moon.'' *Rolling Stone* wrote that Springsteen has called ''Born to Run'' his favorite song.

Biographer Marsh noted, ''*Born to Run* was an instant classic. Anyone who loves rock and roll must respond to . . .

the rough and tough music, the lyrics that sum up the brightest hopes - and some of the darkest aspects - of the rock and roll dream.''

Legal Battle Delayed Music

However, Springsteen's success was short-lived. He soon found himself involved in lawsuits with Appel, his manager. As noted on *RollingStone.com,* ''Springsteen fought to break his contract, which not only bound him to Appel, but surrendered complete control of his song catalog.'' Springsteen wanted to have control over his music and finances, and also wanted to work with Landau. Appel countersued, and Springsteen was kept out of the studios for two years.

During the lawsuits, Springsteen had success with other artists recording his music. As noted on the *VH1 Website,* Manfred Mann's Earth Band released a version of his song ''Blinded By The Light'' and Patti Smith recording a cover of his tune ''Because The Night.'' The Pointer Sisters also recorded his material. Ultimately, Springsteen won his case. Landau became his manager and producer, and Springsteen was in control of his catalog and career.

In 1978, Springsteen released his next album, *Darkness on the Edge of Town.* In 1995, in the liner notes of *Bruce Springsteen - Greatest Hits,* Springsteen reflected, ''this was the record, *Darkness on the Edge of Town,* where I figured out what I wanted to write about, the people that mattered to me, and who I wanted to be. I saw friends and family struggling to lead decent, productive lives and I felt an everyday heroism in this.''

The release *The River* followed in 1980 and produced his first top ten hit ''Hungry Heart.'' However, in the St. James Encyclopedia of Popular Culture, it was the title song from *The River* that Springsteen described ''as a breakthrough in his writing.'' The all-acoustic *Nebraska* followed in 1982.

Springsteen worked on songs for *Nebraska* and *Born in the U.S.A.* at the same time. Ultimately, he decided to put his focus on *Nebraska* and completed and released that album first. Frank Stefanko, author and photographer of the book *Days of Hopes and Dreams-An Intimate Portrait of Bruce Springsteen,* noted, ''Springsteen has an unbelievable work ethic. He can work from early morning to late night. For him, it was all about the package, the art. It was all about making it right, and if it wasn't right, he would go back and do it over again until it was. Only then could it be released.''

''Born in the U.S.A.''

Despite Springsteen's popularity with his fans and with the critics, no one was prepared when *Born in the U.S.A.* exploded onto the music scene in 1984 and became a blockbuster hit. As noted on the *Rock and Roll Hall of Fame website,* Springsteen put together most of the album from the 100 songs he had recorded while working on both *Nebraska* and *Born in the U.S.A.*

The album had more mass appeal than Springsteen's earlier work. The *St. James Encyclopedia of Popular Culture* added that ''music video introduced Springsteen to a younger generation'' and boosted sales. The album had had seven Top Ten singles, including the number two hit, ''Dancing in the Dark'' which Springsteen described as ''my big smash . . . teen idol status at 35?!'' The other Top Ten hits were ''Cover Me,'' ''Born in the U.S.A.,'' ''I'm On Fire,'' ''Glory Days,'' ''I'm Goin' Down,'' and ''My Hometown.'' A sold-out world tour followed.

However, many misunderstood some of the songs as patriotic anthems. DiMartino explained, ''Ironically, one of the darkest was the album's title track–which many at the time mistakenly took to be an expression of blind, my-country-right-or-wrong patriotism, when it was anything but.'' Even U.S. President Ronald Reagan claimed to be a big fan of the music, and mentioned Springsteen and his songs in campaign speeches.

Springsteen told Alterman, ''I was not satisfied with the *Born in the U.S.A.* record. I did not think I made all the connections I wanted to make.'' However, Alterman countered, ''Commercially, Springsteen made one of the biggest connections any artist has ever made.'' He concluded, ''By the time he finished the 155 shows of the *Born in the U.S.A.* tour, Bruce Springsteen had become an inescapable icon in American culture.'' When interviewed by *Rolling Stone* reporter James Henke in 1992, Springsteen reflected, ''I really enjoyed the success of *Born in the U.S.A.*, but by the end of that whole thing, I just kind of felt ''Bruced'' out.''

Springsteen met model/actress Julianne Phillips in the summer of 1984, and they married in May of 1985. He participated in the USA for Africa recording of ''We Are the World'' and joined former E Street Band member Steven Van Zandt on the Artists United Against Apartheid song ''Sun City.'' He reached the Top Ten in the United Kingdom with ''Santa Claus Is Coming To Town.'' He also released a 3-CD set *Bruce Springsteen and the E Street Band: Live 1975-1985,* which entered the charts at number one.

Springsteen on His Own

Springsteen released *Tunnel of Love* in 1987 and became romantically involved with backup singer/guitarist Patti Scialfa. The two had known each other for many years from the New Jersey music scene and had begun to work together during the *Born in the U.S.A.* tour. Springsteen and his wife divorced, and he and Scialfa married in June 1991. They had three children: Evan, Jessica, and Sam.

The family settled in Los Angeles, and it would be almost five years before Springsteen released another album. Many eagerly awaited *Human Touch* and *Lucky Town,* two new albums he released in the spring of 1992 without the E Street Band. The albums started strong but quickly fizzled on the charts. Writing for *Entertainment Weekly,* Greg Sandow pondered the ''demise'' of Springsteen's career, calling the two albums ''something that smells like failure, commercial failure.''

However, Springsteen quickly recovered. In 1993, film director Jonathan Demme asked Springsteen to write a song for his latest film, *Philadelphia,* which starred Tom Hanks. The result was the moving ballad ''Streets of Philadelphia,'' which earned Springsteen an Academy Award for best song, as well as four Grammy Awards.

More success followed. He released *Greatest Hits* in 1995, which included three new songs recorded with the E Street Band, whom he hadn't worked with in several years. Also in 1995, he released *The Ghost of Tom Joad,* which earned him a Grammy Award for Best Contemporary Folk Album. He then went on his first solo acoustic tour. Springsteen also made the news when he shocked his former classmates and attended his 30th high school reunion in 1997.

Reunited with Band

In November 1998, Springsteen released the CD box set *Tracks,* which contained 66 songs, 56 of which were previously unreleased. Writing for *Billboard,* Melinda Newman commented, ''*Tracks* is a way to let the listeners into his creative process, a chance to broaden their understanding of how each record was created.'' In addition, rumors of a tour started to swirl.

Springsteen was inducted into the Rock and Roll Hall of Fame on March 15, 1999, and less than a month later, his reunion tour with the E Street Band kicked off in Barcelona, Spain. In July, the U.S. leg of the tour kicked off with the first of 15 sold-out shows at New Jersey's Continental Airlines Arena. Stefanko noted that Springsteen ''explodes on stage. For an entire three-and-a-half hour show, he maintains a constant energy that touches everybody in that theater.''

Controversy surrounded Springsteen in June 2000. As noted on the *VH1 Website,* ''Springsteen unveiled a new song, ''American Skin,'' at a performance at Madison Square Garden [in New York City]. A scathing comment on the police shooting of the unarmed Bronx resident Amadou Diallo, the song prompted calls by the NYPD for a boycott of the singer's concerts.'' The *Knight-Ridder/Tribune News Service* added, ''Springsteen's song has been striking the wrong note with cops since it was released.''

The Rising

New York City and the entire United States experienced major shock and losses when terrorists attacked on September 11, 2001. When it was announced that Springsteen was working on an album inspired by the events of September 11, many were skeptical. Although the *Knight Ridder/Tribune News Service* acknowledged that Springsteen's ''greatest asset has always been his ability to craft anthemic songs about everyday people,'' many had their doubts.

Released in the summer of 2002, *The Rising* met with critical acclaim. Writing for the *Knight Ridder/Tribune News Service,* Brian McCollum called the release ''gracious, stirring and tasteful. It strikes an appropriate balance between mourning and hope, painting narratives of cops, firefighters and widows that ultimately ring universal.'' It was also the first full-length CD by Springsteen and the E Street Band since *Born in the U.S.A.* Springsteen won three Grammy Awards for this work and began another world tour.

Still Going Strong

The year 2003 was a busy year for Springsteen. He received the Les Paul Award at the 19th annual Technical Excellence & Creativity (TEC) Awards, released *The Essential Bruce Springsteen* in November, and in 2004 received a Grammy for "Disorder in the House," his collaboration with the late Warren Zevon. On December 24, the *Pollstar* website announced that Springsteen was the number one concert draw in North America in 2003. The website noted that Springsteen's fans attended his 47 shows in record numbers and "shelled out $115.9 million to 'come on up for the rising.' "

Stefanko noted that Springsteen "remains strong in his commitment to his subject matter. He hasn't sold out in terms of what he's writing or singing about. He maintained everything through honesty- honesty in the music, honesty about his sense of self-worth, and honesty in his dealings with people." He concluded, "He's one of a kind, an original legend."

Books

Alterman, Eric, *It Ain't No Sin to be Glad You're Alive-The Promise of Bruce Springsteen,* Little, Brown and Company, 1999.
"Bruce Springsteen," *American Decades CD-ROM,* Gale Research, 1998.
"Bruce Springsteen," *St. James Encyclopedia of Popular Culture,* 5 vols., St. James Press, 2000.
Contemporary Musicians, Volume 25, Gale Research, 1999.
Cullen, Jim, *Born in the U.S.A.-Bruce Springsteen and the American Tradition,* Harper Collins, 1997.
The Editors of Rolling Stone, Introduction by Parke Puterbaugh, *Bruce Springsteen-The Rolling Stone Files,* Hyperion, 1996.
Marsh, Dave, *Bruce Springsteen-Two Hearts-The Definitive Biography, 1972-2003,* Routledge, 2004.
Sandford, Christopher, *Springsteen-Point Blank,* Da Capo Press, 1999.
Stefanko, Frank, *Days of Hopes and Dreams-An Intimate Portrait of Bruce Springsteen,* Billboard Books, 2003.

Periodicals

Billboard, November 7, 1998.
Billboard Bulletin, June 27, 2003.
Entertainment Weekly, June 5, 1992; June 20, 1997; December 19, 1997; November 1, 1999; February 28, 2003; November 21, 2003;
Knight-Ridder/Tribune News Service, July 29, 2002; August 6, 2002; October 8, 2003.
The Nation, October 6, 1984.
Newsweek, October 27, 1975.
People Weekly, December 4, 1989; April 6, 1992.
The Real Paper, May 22, 1974.
Rolling Stone, September 8, 1988; August 6, 1992;
Time, October 27, 1975.

Online

"Awards for *Philadelphia* (1993)," *IMDB (internet movie database) website,* http://www.imdb.com (December 26, 2003).
"Bruce Springsteen," *VH1.com website,* http://www.vh1.com/artists/az/springsteen_bruce/artist.jhtml (December 20, 2003).
"Bruce Springsteen," *Grammy Awards website,* http://www.grammy.com/awards/search/index.aspx (December 20, 2003).
"Bruce Springsteen," *RollingStone.com website,* http://www.rollingstone.com (December 20, 2003).
"Bruce Springsteen nominated for Grammy Award," *Bruce Springsteen News: BruceSpringsteen.net website,* http://brucespringsteen.net (December 20, 2003).
"Springsteen #1 for 2003," *Pollstar - The Concert Hotwire,* http://www.pollstar.com (December 27, 2003).
"Yahoo! LAUNCH - Bruce Springsteen: Bio," *LAUNCH Music on Yahoo! website,* http://launch.yahoo.com/artist/ (December 20, 2003).
"Welcome to the Rock and Roll Hall of Fame and Museum," *Rock and Roll Hall of Fame and Museum website,* http://www.rockhall.com/ (December 20, 2003). □

Standing Bear

Standing Bear (1829-1908) was a respected leader of the small Ponca Indian tribe that resided for years in northern Nebraska. In the late 1870s, at a crucial point in the tribe's existence, he took heroic action to reverse the wrongs inflicted upon his people at the hands of the U.S. government and its Indian agents. He remains a heroic and symbolic figure in the long struggle for Native American rights.

Nothing is known of Standing Bear's early life, although he is generally assumed to have been born around 1829. He was a member and a chief of the Ponca Indians, a small tribe—apparently never more than 800 or 900 persons strong in the nineteenth century—closely related to the much larger Omaha tribe. Since at least the mid-seventeenth century, the tribe had lived near the region where the Niobrara River enters the Missouri River in what is now northeastern Nebraska.

The Loss of Ponca Land

In a treaty between the U.S. government and the Ponca Indians signed on March 12, 1858, the tribe ceded to the United States all the land they held except for an extensive tract near the mouth of the Niobrara River, which was reserved for the Poncas as their permanent home. In a second treaty, signed on March 10, 1865, the Poncas ceded another 30,000 acres to the federal government, retaining a total of 96,000 acres as their permanent reservation. However, in a separate treaty negotiated with the Sioux Indian tribes three years later, U.S. government negotiators inadvertently included the Poncas' 96,000 acres as part of a much larger reservation granted to the Sioux nation. Since the Poncas had not been consulted in the matter, they continued to occupy the tract. However, the much larger and more warlike Sioux tribes carried out repeated attacks on the Poncas during the next few years, seeking to drive them off land that they regarded as part of Sioux territory. The Indian Bureau in the U.S. Department of the Interior decided in 1876 that the only solution to the problem was to relocate the Ponca tribe

to a new reservation in the Indian Territory, located in the present state of Oklahoma.

Early in 1877, a delegation of ten Ponca chiefs, Standing Bear among them, was escorted by agents of the Indian Bureau to the Indian Territory to survey the land and choose a location for their reservation there. Standing Bear and seven of the other leaders found all the suggested sites unsatisfactory and decided to return to their home in Nebraska; the agents refused to assist them in their return, so the eight chiefs walked the 500 miles from Oklahoma back to Nebraska in 40 days in the late winter of 1877. When they arrived home, they found that their Ponca tribe was already being moved to the Indian Territory under military escort.

About 170 Ponca members had begun the long trek in late April of 1877. Standing Bear and his brother, Big Snake, were briefly imprisoned when they urged that the remainder of the Poncas resist the removal. By May, the remaining 600 or so Poncas—including Standing Bear and his brother—were forced to join in the march, leaving behind their homes, farms, and many of their possessions. Nine persons died in the course of the journey, including a daughter of Standing Bear.

The nine deaths turned out to be a grim prelude to much further hardship and death for the Poncas in their new locale. They suffered from diseases, such as malaria, which afflicted a large number of Indians transported from northern climates to the humid Indian Territory. Estimates of the number of deaths vary greatly, but even Indian Bureau

reports indicate that a sizeable portion of the tribe perished in the course of the first year. Standing Bear and several other leaders went to Washington, D.C., in the autumn of 1877, seeking President Rutherford B. Hayes' approval of their request to return to Nebraska. Hayes reportedly vetoed the request, but allowed the Ponca leaders to select a more desirable location for their reservation within the Indian Territory. Although the Poncas eventually settled on a more favorable site 150 miles away, the ravages of disease and poverty continued. Standing Bear's last living son was among those who had died by 1878.

Standing Bear's Trial

Despair over the situation of the Poncas in Indian Territory, together with the more personal desire to bury his son in the tribe's Nebraska homeland, led Standing Bear to make the move that made him famous—though it cost him the leadership of his tribe. In early January of 1879, he led a small band of Poncas on a return march to Nebraska, determined to resettle on the old land or die in the attempt. Most of the roughly 600 members of the tribe chose to remain in the Indian Territory, but Standing Bear and several dozen followers arrived at the Omaha Indian agency at Decatur, Nebraska, on March 4, 1879. The Omahas welcomed their kinsmen and invited them to settle there; temporarily at least, they did so.

The Indian Bureau had been informed of Standing Bear's flight from the Indian Territory soon after his departure. Secretary of the Interior Carl Schurz ordered General George Crook, commander of the U.S. Army Department of the Platte, at Omaha, to arrest the chief and his followers and return them to the territory in Oklahoma. Schurz and his advisers feared that if Standing Bear and his band were allowed to remain in Nebraska, it would set a precedent for all Native Americans in the Indian Territory to demand a return to their respective homelands.

Although General Crook obeyed the order and arrested Standing Bear and his followers, he is said to have personally sympathized with the Poncas and believed that they had been repeatedly wronged by the government. Crook convinced Thomas Henry Tibbles, an Omaha newspaperman, to undertake a publicity campaign and institute a case in the federal district court to have Standing Bear and his group released.

Tibbles saw to it that the plight of Standing Bear and his followers was well publicized not only in his own Omaha newspaper but in papers nationwide. He also persuaded two young Omaha lawyers to file a writ of *habeas corpus* (a claim of unjust detention) in the federal district court at Omaha for the release of Standing Bear and his group. The trial of *Standing Bear vs. Crook* was held from April 30 to May 2, 1879. The case was of great significance not only as a means of righting the wrongs inflicted on the Ponca tribe, but also because it raised the larger question of Native American citizenship and the rights of Indians to appear in and to sue in the courts of the nation.

The federal district attorney argued that Standing Bear was not entitled to the protection of a writ of *habeas corpus* because he was not a citizen or even a "person" under

American law. Standing Bear spoke briefly but eloquently on his own behalf. Judge Elmer S. Dundy, in the decision he handed down several weeks later, held that an Indian was, indeed, a person within the meaning of the laws of the United States, though he avoided the larger question of what rights of citizenship an Indian might have. He also ruled that the federal government had no rightful authority to remove the Poncas to the Indian Territory by force; Native Americans, he stated, possessed an inherent right of expatriation—that is, a right to move from one area to another as they wished. Dundy therefore ordered the release of Standing Bear and his followers from custody.

Became a Symbol of Human Rights Struggle

Thomas Tibbles and other leaders of the movement for Indian rights hoped to carry the case of Standing Bear to the U.S. Supreme Court in order to secure a more definitive statement on Indian citizenship and rights. Tibbles himself made a tour to Chicago, New York, and Boston in the summer of 1879 to publicize the case and to raise money for the Supreme Court appeal. By October of that year, he had arranged for Standing Bear to lecture in key cities in the eastern United States. As interpreters for the chief, who spoke no English, Tibbles included in the party two Omaha Indians: Susette La Flesche (better known by her Indian name, "Bright Eyes") and her brother, Francis La Flesche, both of whom had been educated in English-speaking schools.

The tour generated great enthusiasm in urban social and literary circles, especially in Boston. Standing Bear, an impressive figure in his full Indian regalia, including feather headdress, related his story and that of his people in simple but emotional terms, while Bright Eyes, also in Indian dress, translated it into poignant English. A good deal of money was raised for the court appeal and for relief of the Poncas, and reform leaders were moved to become active in the cause of Indian rights. Standing Bear and Bright Eyes also testified before committees of Congress in Washington. The tour finally ended in April of 1880.

As it turned out, Secretary of the Interior Schurz was able to quash the proposed appeal of the Ponca case to the Supreme Court. However, the agitation over the affair did lead to both congressional and presidential investigations. On February 1, 1881, President Hayes recommended to Congress that the Poncas be allowed to live where they chose and that they be compensated for lands relinquished and losses sustained during the forced removal to the Indian Territory in Oklahoma. Congress voted the necessary legislation and funds on March 3, 1881.

The majority of the Ponca tribe did in fact remain in the Indian Territory, but Standing Bear and his group lived quietly on the old Nebraska reservation near the mouth of the Niobrara River. Standing Bear died in September of 1908.

Books

Biographical Dictionary of Indians of the Americas, second edition, Newport Beach, California, American Indian Publishers, 1991.

Dockstader, Frederick J., *Great North American Indians,* New York, Van Nostrand Reinhold, 1977.

Green, Norma Kidd, *Iron Eye's Family: The Children of Joseph La Flesche,* Lincoln, Nebraska, Johnson Publishing, 1969.

Mardock, Robert Winston, *The Reformers and the American Indian,* Columbia, University of Missouri Press, 1971.

Mardock, Robert Winston, "Standing Bear and the Reformers," in *Indian Leaders: Oklahoma's First Statesmen,* edited by H. Glenn Jordan and Thomas M. Holm, Oklahoma City, Oklahoma Historical Society, 1979.

Tibbles, Thomas Henry, *Buckskin and Blanket Days: Memoirs of a Friend of the Indians,* Garden City, New York, Doubleday, 1957.

Tibbles, Thomas Henry, *The Ponca Chiefs: An Account of the Trial of Standing Bear,* Lincoln, University of Nebraska Press, 1972.

Periodicals

Mississippi Valley Historical Review, March 1, 1943.
Nebraska History, Fall 1969.
North Dakota Historical Quarterly, July 6, 1932. □

Susan McKinney Steward

Just five years after the Emancipation Proclamation abolished slavery in the United States, Susan McKinney Steward (1847-1918) became the first African-American woman physician in New York and only the third in the country. She practiced homeopathic medicine in Brooklyn most of her life, before moving several times with her second husband. Steward was active in medical societies, and as an abolitionist and suffragist.

Susan McKinney Steward was born Susan Marie Smith in Brooklyn 1847; the exact date is unknown. She was the seventh of ten children born to Sylvanus and Anne S. Smith. Her father was a successful pig farmer. Both of Steward's parents were multi-racial. Her mother was the daughter of a Shinnecock Indian woman and a French colonel. Her father's ancestors included a Montauk Indian and an African who escaped from a slave ship.

A number of events may have motivated Steward to choose medicine as a career. Two of Steward's brothers died during the Civil War. In 1866, Steward witnessed the high death rate from a cholera epidemic that affected Brooklyn. More than 1,200 people died during the epidemic. At one point in her youth, Steward cared for a sick niece. Any of these events may have helped her decide to pursue a career as a physician.

Medicine was an unusual career choice for any woman in the mid-nineteenth century. It was even more unusual for an African-American woman. Male students believed that medical education "unsexed" women. They frequently taunted their female peers. Because women weren't welcome in medical schools, all-female institutions opened up. Steward attended the New York Medical College for Women beginning in 1867. The school was located in Manhattan, where Steward lived with one of her sisters.

Studied Homeopathic Medicine

The New York Medical College for Women was a homeopathic medical school founded by Dr. Clemence Sophia Lozier in 1863. Lozier was a wealthy physician who was sympathetic to African-Americans and hosted anti-slavery meetings in her home. Lozier became Steward's mentor and the two remained close friends until Lozier's death in 1888.

Many women's medical schools specialized in homeopathic medicine. The homeopathic specialty was based on the work of Dr. Samuel Hahnemann, a German physician who was dissatisfied with the medical theories of his day. He conducted experiments and developed treatments that used weak doses of medicine to cure illnesses and conditions. Some traditional doctors dismissed homeopathic medicine as quackery.

Homeopathic students at the New York Medical College for Women were required to study anatomy, physiology, chemistry, materia medica, surgery, obstetrics and medical jurisprudence. Clinical lectures took place at the New York Homeopathic Dispensary and the New York Ophthalmic Hospital. In *Afro-Americans in New York Life & History,* William Seraile explained that when a lack of funds forced the college to send students to Bellevue Hospital for clinic work, the women were greeted by "hisses indecent language, paper balls and other missils," the *Daily Eagle* reported. The paper condemned the students and their faculty for their unruly behavior.

Although her prosperous father could have afforded to pay for her medical school education, Steward paid her own tuition for the three years she attended the New York Medical College for Women. She earned the money teaching music in a colored school in Washington D.C. for two years. Steward graduated from medical school as valedictorian in 1870.

When Steward graduated, she became the first African-American female physician in New York and only the third in the country. Surprisingly, the event did not attract very much attention in most of the city's newspapers. Seraile reported that *The Courier* described her attire at the graduation ceremony as modest and "noted the fact as a good sign of the improvement of the African race." The article went on to say that "Miss Steward belongs to the colored aristocracy in Brooklyn and is a member of the Episcopal church."

Steward had difficulty finding steady work immediately after her graduation, but eventually developed a thriving practice and became known for her ability to treat malnourished children. She maintained offices in Brooklyn and Manhattan and treated a variety of patients regardless of income or ethnicity.

In 1871, Steward married William G. McKinney, an Episcopal minister from South Carolina. The couple lived in Steward's parents' home until 1874, when they moved to a predominantly white area of Brooklyn. McKinney was 17 years older than his wife. The couple had two children: Anna, who became a schoolteacher, and William Sylvanus, who, like his father, became an Episcopal priest. The family lived comfortably in Brooklyn.

In 1890, William McKinney suffered a cerebral hemorrhage and was unable to maintain his normal work schedule. Steward supported the family, as well as six of her relatives who lived in the McKinney home. William McKinney died on November 24, 1895 when Steward was 48.

Active in Medical Societies

Steward was active in many medical societies including Kings County Homeopathic Medical Society and the Homeopathic Medical Society of the State of New York. During the 1880s, she presented two important papers to the New York group. The first was about a pregnant woman who was incorrectly treated. The second paper was about childhood diseases. She served as a delegate to the New Jersey State Homeopathic Society's semi-annual meeting in 1889. She later became a member of the New Jersey society. She was a founding member of the Alumni Association of the New York Medical College for Women and taught at the school in 1882-1883.

Steward was one of the founders of the Brooklyn Woman's Homeopathic Hospital and Dispensary, which was later named Memorial Hospital for Women and Children. She served as a surgeon on the hospital's staff. She was also a physician at the Brooklyn Home for the Aged. She was the only woman in a post-graduate class at Long Island Medical College in 1887-1888.

Steward was also an activist for education, missionary work, women's suffrage and temperance. She was president of the Women's Christian Temperance Union No. 6. She was also active in the Brooklyn Literary Union. She organized many musical programs for the union and sold tickets to many musical events.

Steward had a lifelong love of music. As a child, she took organ lessons from famed organists John Zundel and Henry Eyre Brown. For many years, she served as the organist and choir director for the Siloam Presbyterian and Bridge Street A.M.E. churches. She also contributed to many of the Brooklyn Literary Union's musical programs, often accompanied by her children, who shared her talent.

Two years after her husband William died in November 1894, Steward's 81-year-old mother died of heart disease, senility and hemophilia on the day Steward's daughter, Annie was to be married. The wedding went on since the couple was planning on traveling immediately to Haiti.

Three weeks after her mother's death, Steward married Rev. Theophilus Gould Steward, chaplain of the 25th United States Colored Infantry. Rev. Steward had been Susan Steward's pastor in 1874-1877. He had children, although the exact number is unknown.

Moved From Brooklyn

After having spent her entire life in Brooklyn, Steward and her new family moved several times as Rev. Steward was stationed in various cities. Steward practiced medicine in all the cities in which she lived. Shortly after they were married, the family moved to Montana, where Rev. Steward was stationed at Fort Missoula. From 1898 to 1902, Rev. Steward was in Cuba and the Philippines. Susan Steward became a college physician of Wilberforce University in Ohio. In 1902, Rev. Steward was stationed at Fort Niobrara, Nebraska and his wife joined him there. She was also involved in the Women's Christian Temperance Union. In 1906, the Stewards moved to Fort McIntosh, near Laredo, Texas.

In addition to their frequent moves, the couple traveled extensively. They visited much of the United States, Haiti, Mexico and Europe. In 1897, Steward traveled to Haiti to deliver her first grandson, Louis Holly. In 1911, the Stewards attended a Universal Race Congress in London. The meeting brought together Africans, Asians, Americans and Europeans seeking to improve relationships and cooperation between the East and West. Well-known American author W.E.B. Dubois attended. Steward presented a paper at the conference, titled "Colored American Women." The paper dealt with achievements of famous African-American women including Phyllis Wheatley, Ida Wells Barnett, and Mary Church Terrell.

In 1914, Steward presented a paper on "Women in Medicine" before the National Association of Colored Women's Clubs in Wilberforce, Ohio. Her paper examined the history of women in medicine from Biblical times to 1914. Steward concluded that there was no need for separate medical schools for women, but that they should have equal opportunity for internships.

Steward died suddenly on March 7, 1918 at Wilberforce University. She was 70 or 71 years old. Her body was returned to Brooklyn, where she was buried. She was eulogized by Hallie Q. Brown, a close friend and associate at Wilberforce; Dr. William S. Scarborough, president of Wilberforce University; Dr. W.E.B. DuBois; and Dr. Helen S. Lassen, a white classmate.

Steward's name is not widely known, but during the 1970s and 1980s, efforts were made to honor her. In 1974, her grandson William S. McKinney succeeded in getting the New York Board of Education to name a Brooklyn junior high school the Dr. Susan Smith McKinney Junior High School. During the 1980s, African-American women doctors in New York, New Jersey and Connecticut named their medical society after Steward.

Brown's eulogy included this description of Steward: "She was great in the estimation of those who knew her capacity, her ability, her real worth. She was not a spectacular women. She was modest. A woman absolutely self-reliant, honest to herself and to her friends. She acted upon her own judgment and when she had made up her mind that a thing was right and ought to be done, SHE DID IT. She was one of those generous natures that love peace, order, and harmony. But she could strike, and strike hard, in what she believed to be a righteous cause. With her it was justice on the one side, and injustice on the other."

Books

Brown, Hallie Q., *Homespun Heroines and Other Women of Distinction,* Oxford University Press, New York, 1988.
Notable Black American Women, Book 1, Gale Research, 1992.

Periodicals

Afro-Americans in N.Y. Life & History, July 1985. □

Jackie Stewart

In a short career, Scottish race-car driver Jackie Stewart (born 1939) won 27 Grand Prix races and was world champion status three times on the Formula One circuit. Stewart was also an advocate of driver safety and after his retirement worked as a lively commentator for ABC-TV's "Wide World of Sports."

Often wearing his trademark tartan-patterned racing helmet, Stewart earned his nickname the "Flying Scot" for his speed on the race course and for his meteoric climb to the top of the world Grand Prix racing circuits. Racing for the first time in 1965, Stewart was one of the top drivers on the Formula One circuit into the 1970s. During his career, the sport was revolutionized by design advances that made cars more aerodynamic and much faster. With 27 Grand Prix wins, Stewart combined a natural talent for the sport with a charisma that made him the darling of the media and an effective and outspoken advocate for race course safety.

Racing in His Blood

John Young Stewart was born in Milton in Dumbartonshire, Scotland in 1939. As a child he exhibited exceptional eye-hand coordination, and his father, a former motorcycle racer who owned a garage and sold Jaguars, had hopes that his youngest son would become involved in racing. Stewart grew up around cars and soon became an adept apprentice mechanic. Meanwhile, his older brother, Jimmy Stewart, went from a successful run of local races to qualifying for the British Grand Prix in 1953. Eliminated from the race at Copse after his Ecurie Ecosse car hydroplaned on a wet track, Jimmy Stewart was involved in an even more serious accident while racing at Le Mans, France, forcing him to leave the sport. Stewart's parents, thankful that their oldest son was still alive, discouraged their youngest son, 15-year-old Jackie, from taking up car racing.

Never a promising student, Stewart, who was dyslexic, left school prior to graduation. He soon took up clay target shooting. Competing in shooting tournaments in Scotland, he hoped to qualify to join Great Britain's 1960 Olympic

team. His poor performance during the final round of the Olympic trials on his 21st birthday ended that plan, however, and Stewart returned home, believing he was destined to work at his father's garage.

A Formula Three Natural

In 1963, Barry Filer, a customer of the family garage, approached Stewart, then 24, and asked him to track-test a Formula Three car at England's Oulton Park speedway. His driving impressing several onlookers, and word went out to Cooper's Formula Junior team manager Ken Tyrell. Constantly on the lookout for new talent, Tyrell asked Stewart to come and try out for a position as driver. Taking over the wheel from experienced Formula One driver Bruce McLaren, Stewart held his own in the car, a Cooper F3, and soon matched and even passed McLaren's times around the track. Impressed by the young Scot's lightning-quick reflexes and cool demeanor behind the wheel, Tyrell offered him a place in his Formula Three team, and Stewart accepted.

Formula Three cars such as Tyrell's Cooper are scaled-down versions of Formula One race cars. Aerodynamically designed single-seaters with two-liter racing engines, these cars are designed to run close to the ground, corner on a dime, and attain speeds upwards of 165 miles per hour. Considered a junior version of Formula One racing, Formula Three has been the traditional stepping-up point for many future world champion race drivers, and as someone

with fast reflexes and intense focus, Stewart was no exception.

During his three years on the Formula Three circuit, Stewart won the championship title easily, winning 11 of the 13 races he competed in and finishing a close second once. In 1964 he also won England's *Express & Star* Formula Three championship. He particularly enjoyed working with Tyrell—he would later comment, as quoted on the *Formula Three website* that his "British Formula Three Championship days were the best of my life. . . . It was fantastic winning all those races against some top names, and I think it really sent me on my way." Nonetheless, the Formula One circuit—which included the course in LeMans that had broken his older brother—beckoned. In 1965 the single-minded Scot left Tyrell and joined Graham Hill's BRM Formula One team.

Formula One Experience

Confident after his successes in Formula Three, Stewart traveled to South Africa, where he placed in his first race as a Formula One driver and won his first point toward the coveted world drivers' championship. That race set the pace for the rest of the racing season: during his eighth race for BRM at the Italian Grand Prix at Monza, he got his first win, and by the end of the 1965 season Stewart was ranked third in the world drivers' championships behind Jim Clark and Graham Hill.

Stewart remained with Hill and BRM for two more years, and though his ranking went down he gained experience, including one event that would change his outlook on auto racing forever. The year 1966 held several disappointments, one of which was taking the lead at the Indianapolis 500 only to lose it in the last eight laps due to a scavenge pump malfunction. However, that paled in comparison to Stewart's experiences while competing in the Belgian Grand Prix at Spa. A sudden downpour caused cars to careen off the track, and Stewart was soon among them. Sliding into a ditch, he found himself pinned in his car by the steering wheel, the side of his car crushed inward. Unable to escape, he lay helpless and in pain while fuel began leaking out, soaking his racing suit through to his skin. For twenty-five minutes he lay there, counting every second, while Hill and others in his crew dismantled the steering wheel in order to free him. With no doctors or medical facilities nearby, Stewart was deposited in the bed of a nearby pickup truck and remained there until an ambulance finally arrived. Taken to the track's First Aid center on a stretcher, he was placed on the floor, amid cigarette butts and other garbage, and lay there until yet another ambulance crew picked him up. En route to a hospital in Lié, the ambulance drivers got lost.

During the hours he lay on his stretcher, enduring severe pain, Stewart had a lot of time to reflect on his situation. He had fractured his collarbone, but his injuries could have been more severe. If they had involved internal bleeding, the lack of medical care and the lax emergency transportation would likely have meant his death; if it had been a spinal injury, as many at first feared, he could have suffered permanent disability and the end of his career. He also recalled the deaths of other drivers during the 1960s, casualties of the experiments and advances in Formula One technology.

"Something Sadly Wrong . . . "

After his experience at Spa, Stewart worked with BRM team leader Louis Stanley to campaign vigorously for improved emergency services, better safety barriers around race tracks and the introduction of safety-related devices in race cars. As he was quoted as noting in a biography for the *Grand Prix Hall of Fame website,* "I realized that if this was the best we had there was something sadly wrong: things wrong with the race track, the cars, the medical side, the fire-fighting and the emergency crews. . . . Young people today just wouldn't understand it. It was ridiculous."

Stewart soon recovered from his injury and returned to complete the 1966 season, finishing in seventh place. The following year would be his last with Hill: the redesigned car Stewart was assigned to drive proved useless on the track. Ending 1967 in ninth place, a frustrated Stewart reconnected with Tyrell, who by now had established a Formula One team and quickly signed the Scot to drive his Matra Ford.

Proving that his lackluster performance in the world drivers' championships the previous year had been the result of Hill's BRM car rather than a lack of driver ability, Stewart ended 1968 in second place, despite battling the winding course in Nürbugring, Germany, in the pelting rain and the discomfort caused by a recently fractured wrist.

First Championship Season

Driving a Matra MS80, Stewart won his first world championship for Ken Tyrell's team in 1969; he was also named British Formula One champion. During the season he charted up winning points by taking the trophy in seven out of the fourteen races he entered.

The following year proved to be a disappointment. Problems with the Ford chassis in Tyrell's Matra cars forced Stewart from several races, and the Scot raced for Tyrell in only the Mexican, Canadian, and U.S. Grand Prix that year. Desiring to finish the season out, he raced for March and finished 1970 in fifth place.

By 1971 Tyrell had begun to build his own cars. Stewart gladly returned to the Tyrell fold and won his second world drivers' championship. The following year he was again sidelined because the tension of the track had begun to take its toll on Stewart's health. Plagued by stomach ulcers, he nonetheless persevered, ending in second place despite missing several races.

In 1973, 34-year-old Stewart chalked up his third and final world drivers' championship. His decision to end his career after his 100th race had been made at the start of the racing season. But at the Grand Prix at Watkins Glen, New York, Stewart and Tyrell walked away from the planned final race because his friend and teammate François Cevert was killed in a crash during the race's qualifying round. As Stewart would later comment to March Bechtel of *Sports*

Illustrated, "The key in life is deciding when to go into something and when to get out of it."

With 27 wins in 99 starts, Stewart scored a total of 360 points during his nine-year career, and led at some point in 51 of those 99 races. His record of 27 Grand Prix wins would stand for two decades, until bested by Alain Prost during the 1987 race at Estoril.

A Head for Business

Popular with the press due to his intelligence, easy wit, and charm, Stewart was just as beloved among racing fans, and his advocacy of racetrack safety earned him the respect of many, both in and out of the sport. After his career in Grand Prix racing came to a close, he remained an active presence in the world of Formula One. For the next 14 years his heavy Scottish brogue could be heard in coverage of Formula One Racing on ABC's popular "Wide World of Sports" TV show. He also worked as an engineering consultant for the Ford Motor Company, continuing a relationship that had started on the track, and assisting the automaker in researching and developing new generations of Formula One engines. In later years he added such firms as Goodyear Tire and Rubber Company to his client list.

A beloved figure in his native Great Britain, Stewart was honored by Queen Elizabeth with the Order of the British Empire in 2001. He was also inducted into both the International Motorsports Hall of Fame and the Sports Hall of Fame. Outside the world of racing, Stewart and his wife Helen, whom he married in 1962, raised two sons, Paul and Mark.

Combining his canny business sense with an equally strong sense of civic responsibility, Stewart founded a successful shooting school at Scotland's Gleneagles Hotel in 1985, and held seats on several corporations while also serving as president of the Scottish Dyslexia Trust beginning in 1995.

In 1997, Stewart became chairman of Paul Stewart Grand Prix Racing, a team he founded in partnership with his son Paul and Ford Motor Company. Signing drivers Rubens Barrichello and Jan Magnussen, Stewart managed his team from their first appearance at the 1997 Australian Grand Prix with the same intensity he once showed behind the wheel. Selling Paul Stewart Racing team to Ford in 1999 for 60 million pounds, a year later Stewart retired from active involvement in what was renamed Jaguar Racing, citing the desire to spend time with his family. As of 2003 he retained his role as president of the British Racing Drivers' Club as well as president of the Scottish Dyslexia Trust. He also remained an active role as a Ford Motor Company consultant, acted as trustee for the Scottish International Education Trust, was the Springfield Club's president, and acted as chairman for the Grand Prix Mechanics Charitable Trust. Stewart also was on the board of Moet & Chandon and was a patron of the British Dyslexia Association. He left Formula One auto racing a far safer sport than when he entered it almost four decades before.

Books

Legends in Their Own Time, Prentice Hall General Reference, 1994.

Periodicals

Financial Times, November 29, 2003.
Forbes, May 10, 1993.
Sports Illustrated, February 25, 2002.

Online

Gran Prix Hall of Fame, http://www.ddavid.com/furmula 1/stew-bio.htm.
Official Formula One Web site, http://www.formula1.com/.
Official Formula Three Web site, http://www.fota.co.uk/. □

Maria W. Miller Stewart

American essayist, teacher, and political activist Maria W. Miller Stewart (1803–1879) is thought to be the first American woman to give public lectures. Stewart is known for four powerful speeches, delivered in Boston in the early 1830s—a time when no woman, black or white, dared to address an audience from a public platform.

Stewart was heavily involved with the abolitionist movement, and most of her lectures deal with this topic. More radically, however, she called for black economic progress and self-determination, as well as women's rights. Other recurring themes included the value of education, the historical inevitability of black liberation, and the need for black unity and collective action. Many of her ideas were so far ahead of their time that they remain relevant more than 150 years later.

Despite the fact that she had little formal education, Stewart continually showed her learning in her lectures, referencing the Bible, the U.S. Constitution, and various literary works. She was deeply influenced by a type of sermon developed by Puritan preachers known as the jeremiad, which applied religious doctrines to secular problems. According to Stewart, the way for African Americans to obtain freedom was to get closer to God; conversely, resistance to oppression was the highest form of obedience to God.

Stewart was born free as Maria Miller in 1803 in Hartford, Connecticut. All that is known about her parents is their surname, Miller; their first names and occupations have been lost to history. At the age of five, Stewart was orphaned and forced to become a servant in the household of a clergyman. She lived with this family for ten years, receiving no formal education but learning as much as she could by reading books from the family's library. After leaving the family at the age of fifteen, she supported herself as a domestic servant while furthering her education at Sabbath schools. Specific details about her employment or where she lived at the time are unknown.

On August 10, 1826, at the age of twenty-three, Maria Miller married James W. Stewart at the African Baptist Church in Boston. At her husband's suggestion, Stewart took not only his last name, but also his middle initial as well. James W. Stewart was forty-four years old and a veteran of the War of 1812; after the war, he earned a substantial living by fitting out whaling and fishing vessels. At the time, African Americans made up just three percent of Boston's population, and the Stewarts were part of an even smaller minority: Boston's black middle class.

In December of 1829, just three years after the Stewarts were married, James Stewart died; the marriage had produced no children. Although Maria Stewart was left with a substantial inheritance, she was defrauded of it by his white executors after a drawn-out court battle. Once again, she was forced to turn to domestic service to support herself.

In 1830, partly due to grief over her husband's death, Stewart underwent a religious conversion. A year later, according to her later writings, she made a "public profession of my faith in Christ," dedicating herself to God's service. For Stewart, her newfound religious fervor went hand-in-hand with political activism: she resolved to become a "strong advocate for the cause of God and for the cause of freedom." In the years to come, when she was criticized for daring to speak in public, Stewart would claim that her authority came from God—that she was simply following God's will.

Meanwhile, the abolitionist movement was beginning to gather strength in Boston. In 1831, William Lloyd Garrison, publisher of the abolitionist newspaper the *Liberator,* called for women of African descent to contribute to the paper. Stewart responded by arriving at his office with a manuscript containing several essays which Garrison agreed to publish.

Stewart's first published work, "Religion and the Pure Principles of Morality, the Sure Foundation on Which We Must Build," appeared as a twelve-page pamphlet, priced at six cents, later that year. An advertisement for the pamphlet, which appeared in the *Liberator,* described it as "a tract addressed to the people of color, by Mrs. Maria W. Steward (sic), a respectable colored lady of this city. . . . The production is most praiseworthy, and confers great credit on the talents and piety of its author."

Soon afterward, Stewart began to deliver public lectures. Her first speaking engagement was on April 28, 1832, before the African American Female Intelligence Society of Boston. Aware that she was violating the taboo against women speaking in public, Stewart asserted in her talk that "the frowns of the world shall never discourage me" and that she could bear the "assaults of wicked men." While the main thrust of the speech was to urge African American women to turn to God, she also urged them to stand up for their rights, rather than silently suffer humiliation. "It is useless for us any longer to sit with our hands folded, reproaching the whites; for that will never elevate us," she said.

Six months later, on September 21, 1832, Stewart lectured to an audience of both men and women at Franklin Hall. In that speech, she asserted that free African Americans were hardly better off than those in slavery: "Look at many of the most worthy and most interesting of us doomed to spend our lives in gentlemen's kitchens," she demanded. "Look at our young men, smart, active, and energetic, with souls filled with ambitious fire; if they look forward, alas! What are their prospects? They can be nothing but the humblest laborers, on account of their dark complexions; hence many of them lose their ambition, and become worthless. . . ."

Meanwhile, Stewart continued to submit her writings for publication. In 1832, Garrison published another pamphlet, "Meditations from the Pen of Mrs. Maria W. Stewart." Garrison also printed transcripts of all of Stewart's speeches in the *Liberator;* however, in accordance with the editorial conventions of the day, her contributions were relegated to the paper's "Ladies' Department."

Stewart's third speech, delivered at the African Masonic Hall on February 27, 1833, was titled "African Rights and Liberty." In this speech, she again defended her right to speak publicly, while castigating African American men. "You are abundantly capable, gentlemen, of making yourselves men of distinction; and this gross neglect, on your part, causes my blood to boil within me," she told her audience. "Had the men amongst us, who have had an opportunity, turned their attention as assiduously to mental and moral improvement as they have to gambling and dancing, I might have remained quietly at home, and they stood contending in my place."

Stewart also condemned the colonization movement, a plan to send free blacks as well as slaves back to Africa. In her conclusion, Stewart recounted how whites first drove the native Americans from their land, then stole blacks from Africa and enslaved them, and now wanted to send them back with nothing. Instead, Stewart argued, blacks should remain in the United States and fight for their freedom.

The response to Stewart's speeches—even from those who supported her cause—was overwhelmingly negative; she was roundly condemned for having the audacity to speak onstage. In the words of African American historian William C. Nell, writing about Stewart in the 1850s, she "encountered an opposition even from her Boston circle of friends, that would have dampened the ardor of most women."

Stewart delivered her final Boston speech on September 21, 1833, announcing her decision to leave the city. In the speech, she acknowledged that, by lecturing publicly, she had "made myself contemptible in the eyes of many, that I might win some," which she admitted was "like a labor in vain."

Still, Stewart refused to go quietly, asserting that women activists had divine sanction: "What if I am woman; is not the God of ancient times the God of these modern days? Did he not raise up Deborah, to be a mother, and a judge in Israel? Did not Queen Esther save the lives of the Jews? And Mary Magdelene first declare the resurrection of Christ from the dead?"

In 1835, two years after Stewart had left the city, Garrison published a collection of her speeches, *Productions of Mrs. Maria W. Stewart.* Within a year of its appearance, other women, both black and white, began to follow the path Stewart had opened, lecturing in churches and meeting halls across the country.

Contrary to the prejudices of her day, Stewart had long believed that all African Americans—both male and female—deserved the chance to acquire an education. In her speeches, Stewart had often referred to literacy as a sacred quest at a time when it was a crime to teach slaves to read or write. Now that she had given in to public pressure to cease lecturing, she turned her energy to education.

From Boston, Stewart moved to New York, where she taught in public schools in Manhattan and Long Island. She continued her political activities, joining women's organizations—including a black women's literary society—and attending the Women's Anti-slavery Convention of 1837. She also lectured occasionally, but none of these lectures survive. And while she was affiliated with the radical newspaper *The North Star,* later called *Frederick Douglass' Paper,* none of her work appeared there.

In 1852, Stewart moved to Baltimore, earning a small living as a teacher of paying pupils. "I have never been very shrewd in money matters; and being classed as a lady among my race all my life, and never exposed to any hardship, I did not know how to manage," Stewart later wrote about this period. In 1861, she moved to Washington D.C., where again she organized a school.

By the early 1870s, Stewart had been appointed as matron, or head housekeeper, at the Freedman's Hospital and Asylum in Washington. The facility, established by the Freedmen's Bureau, had room for 300 patients and served not only as a hospital but also as a refugee camp for former slaves displaced by the Civil War. Stewart continued to teach, even as she lived and worked at the hospital.

In 1878, a law was passed granting pensions to widows of War of 1812 veterans. Stewart used the unexpected money to publish a second edition of *Meditations from the Pen of Mrs. Maria W. Stewart.* The book, which appeared in 1879, was introduced by supporting letters from Garrison and others. It also included new material: the autobiographical essay "Sufferings During the War" and a preface in which she once more called for an end to tyranny and oppression.

Shortly after the book's publication on December 17, 1879, Stewart died at the Freedman's Hospital at the age of 76. Her obituary in *The People's Advocate,* a Washington-area black newspaper, acknowledged that Stewart had struggled for years with little recognition: "Few, very few know of the remarkable career of this woman whose life has just drawn to a close. For half a century she was engaged in the work of elevating her race by lectures, teaching, and various missionary and benevolent labors." Stewart was buried in Graceland Cemetery in Washington.

"The emergence of black history and women's studies has reintroduced scholars to the life and work of Maria W. Stewart, but this pioneering black political activist still lacks a critical biographical assessment," wrote Harry A. Reed in *Black Women in America: The Early Years,* which was published in 1983. "Her life and her continuing obscurity illustrate the double pressures of racism and sexism on the lives of black women." Four years later, Indiana University Press published a collected edition of her work, *Maria W. Stewart, America's First Black Woman Political Writer: Essays and Speeches.* While Stewart was criticized and eventually silenced during her lifetime, and her work has been neglected since then, she is finally beginning to be recognized for what she was: a pioneering speaker and essayist.

Books

African-American Orators, edited by Richard W. Leeman, Greenwood Press, 1996.
Black Women in America: The Early Years, 1619–1899, edited by Darlene Clark Hine, Carlson Publishing, 1993.
Bolden, Tonya, The Book of African-American Women, Adams Media Corporation, 1996.
Maria W. Stewart, America's First Black Woman Political Writer: Essays and Speeches, edited by Marilyn Richardson, Indiana University Press, 1987.
Notable American Women, edited by Edward T. James, Harvard University Press, 1971.
Women's Firsts, edited by Caroline Zilboorg, Gale Research, 1997. □

Sylvester I

Very little is known about the early life of Pope Sylvester I (died 335), and for centuries his pontificate was shrouded in legend. The fact that the pontificate coincided with the reign of Roman emperor Constantine I has contributed heavily to such legends. While Sylvester's rule over the Catholic Church has been described as lackluster in some quarters, he nevertheless presided during a period of church-building in Rome. More important from a theological point of view, he was pope during the First Council at Nicea in 325, out of which was established the divinity of Jesus Christ. However it was not the pope, but rather the emperor who was most responsible for these accomplishments.

Separating Fact from Legend

The records declare that Sylvester was born in Rome, the son of Rufinus and Justa, though his parents' identities are also shrouded in legend. At any rate the year of his birth has been lost. Sylvester was ordained by Marcellinus and served as a priest in Rome. He later became attached to the papal court of Pope Miltiades. When Miltiades died in January 314, Sylvester's candidacy as bishop of Rome was put forth, and he succeeded Militiades as pope on January 31, 314. The primary legend surrounding Sylvester's pontificate is that he cured Emperor Constantine of leprosy, and in gratitude the emperor converted to Christianity, bequeathed property to the Church and eventually set up the imperial papacy. The reality was far different.

The Roman emperor Constantine (r. 306-337) in 313 had signed what is known as the Edict of Milan with the eastern, Byzantine co-emperor, Licinius (r. 308-324). This edict formally ended the persecution of Christians in the Roman Empire. There is evidence that Licinius revoked the edict in his territory around the year 320. He promulgated various laws that restricted communication among bishops and limited the ability of Christians to worship. Sylvester was powerless to stop this, but Constantine was not. Although the issue of the treatment of Christians was not the pretext for civil war, Constantine eventually invaded Byzantium and overthrew Licinius.

The First Controversy

At the time of Sylvester's accession to the chair of St. Peter, Christianity was on the verge of enjoying an era of growth and prosperity. However Sylvester inherited an important controversy having to do with the Donatists's request to have the bishop of Carthage removed. Named for their leader, bishop Donatus, the Donatists were extremist separatists who took a hardline view against those Christians who had lapsed from the faith in order to save their lives during the ruthless persecution begun in 303 under the late Emperor Diocletian. A dynamic leader, Constantine overshadowed the pope, and because the office of pope had not yet evolved into the central power of the Church, it was natural that the Donatists would turn to the emperor instead of to Pope Sylvester to resolve their grievances. Constantine convened a council of bishops known as the Synod of Rome that met in 313, during the final months of Miltiades' reign as pope. When the synod ruled against the Donatists, that group again petitioned Constantine, who convened a larger council near present-day Arles.

The second council convened August 1, 314, just six months into Sylvester's papacy. This council, too, decided against the Donatists. It is not known what Sylvester's views were regarding this controversy, though most likely he sided with the majority of his fellow bishops in opposing the radicals. Sylvester, in fact, did not attend the council, but sent two priests and two deacons to represent him. The council sent its decision to the pope, however. Furthermore it was Constantine, not Sylvester or any of the other bishops, who moved to suppress the Donatists. In this the emperor was unsuccessful; the Donatists would flourish in northern Africa through the sixth century.

The Second Controversy

The next major religious controversy that emerged during Sylvester's papacy was far worse in that it involved heresy. The Arian heresy, as it is now known, became widespread about 318. Named for its principal exponent, a priest named Arius, Arianism taught that Jesus was neither eternal nor divine and therefore not the son of God. It conceded that Jesus was the first of God's creatures, and this position made him an intercessor between God and humanity. Arius was denounced by the bishop of Alexandria and, following his excommunication from the Church, he left Alexandria and took refuge at Nicomedia, whose bishop was the influential Eusebius. All during this time Sylvester kept out of the growing debate around Arianism.

The controversy grew so intense that, at Constantine's instigation, another council was convened in May 325, this time at Nicea in Bithynia. More than 300 bishops attended, but only a handful were from the West. Sylvester sent two representatives, the priests Vitus and Vincent. The council's president was most probably Bishop Ossius of Cordova. The Council of Nicea voted overwhelmingly to condemn Arianism—only 17 of the bishops even defended it—yet it managed to create another, this time linguistic, controversy. The most important term of the profession of faith adopted by the council—the first part of which makes up the contemporary Nicene Creed—contains the Greek term *homoousious,* which many of the bishops had not been prepared to accept. Basically meaning "same essence," referring to Jesus as homoousious in effect meant that Jesus was of the same nature as God, and that he in fact was God. While this was a direct rebuke of Arianism it was not the first time this doctrine had been put forth. The second- and third-century ecclesiastical writer Tertullian, for example, had declared essentially the same thing using the Latin term *unius substantiae.*

Despite the misgiving of some of the bishops the term homoousious passed into the article of faith, and the doctrine, along with *heteras ousious,* or "heteroousious" (i.e., different substances or persons), became the basis of the Blessed Trinity. Both of Sylvester's representatives signed the decree, but their names are placed under that of Bishop Ossius, signifying that they bore no great authority as papal legates. While their signatures were seen as Sylvester's confirmation of the decision, the pope nonetheless took no action in later years when Constantine began to favor the Arians.

The fact that Emperor Constantine was a cosigner of the Edict of Milan and that he summoned various Church councils demonstrates his interest in ecclesiastical and theological matters concerning the Church. Most historians believe that his interest dated back to 305, but the story of his ordering his soldiers to paint crosses on their shields and of his subsequent battle victory may be apocryphal. What is also legend is that Sylvester converted the emperor, although it is true that Constantine was baptized on his deathbed.

Constantine erected a number of churches in Rome during Sylvester's papacy. These include the original St. Peter's Basilica, which was on via Ostiensis, as well as the Basilica Constantiniana and its baptistery near the pope's residence. These became known as San Giovanni in Laterano (St. John Lateran), which has remained the pope's cathedral. The basilica of the Sessorian palace was also built, as well as a number of smaller churches to honor the graves of martyrs. Sylvester is particularly connected with the cemetery church built over the Catacomb of Priscilla. Liturgical development also took place during Sylvester's

pontificate, and it is thought that the first martyrology—of Roman martyrs—was drawn up at that time. Sylvester was also involved in the establishment of the Roman school of singing.

Another Legend

The second important legend connected with Sylvester's pontificate concerns the "Donatio Constantini," the Donation of Constantine. This is a forged document, possibly from the ninth century though it may have been written anytime between 750 and 850. The "Donatio" is actually the second part of a larger document titled *Constitutum domni Constantini imperatoris.* The first part of the *Constitutum,* the "Confessio," is a purported memoir by Constantine in which he reveals how Sylvester not only instructed him in Christianity but converted him and cured the emperor of leprosy. The legend of the cure probably dates from the mid-fifth century. The "Donatio" is by far the most important section, helping to extend the pope's influence over medieval Christianity. It was later included in yet another forgery called the False Decretals, which Pope Nicholas I (858-867) employed—without realizing they were forged—to bolster papal authority over recalcitrant bishops.

The Donation of Constantine gave personally to Sylvester—and by extension to succeeding popes—primacy over all the other bishops in the West and over the patriarchs of Antioch, Alexandria, Constantinople, and Jerusalem. The Basilica of St. John Lateran was made the primary church in Christendom; the Lateran palace was given to the pope. The emperor also ceded to the pope the city of Rome, the entire Italian peninsula, and all of the provinces and states of the Western empire, since the emperor had established the new capitol in Constantinople. It attributes the construction of the new capitol city to a desire on Constantine's part to separate the secular empire from the religious one.

By the 15th century the Donation of Constantine was proved to be a forgery. Three important ecclesiastics, Nicholas of Cusa, Lorenzo Valla, and Reginald Pecocke, had each examined the matter and concluded the Donation was false. Aeneas Sylvius Piccolomini, who became Pope Pius II, also questioned the authenticity of the document. However it was not until Baronius proclaimed the forgery of the Donation of Constantine in the *Annales ecclesiastici* that this was universally accepted.

Further legends surrounding Sylvester arose in the fifth and sixth centuries. One of these was intended to rehabilitate Sylvester's reputation vis-à-vis the Council of Nicea. In this version the council was convened by both the emperor and the pope; furthermore, it was Sylvester who designated Bishop Ossius to preside over the council. Another Sylvester legend dating from this period has to do with his association with the Armenian, St. Gregory the Illuminator, whose own legends sometimes parallel those of Sylvester. Like the pope, Gregory was supposed to have converted a monarch—in this case the Armenian king Trdat—although Christianity existed in Armenia long before Gregory's time. A number of letters thought to have passed between Sylvester and Gregory were published in the late 19th century, but these have all been declared forgeries. Nothing is known what influence, if any, Sylvester had in Armenia.

Sylvester's feast day is December 31 and it has been assumed that the date of his death was December 31, 335. Most likely he died a few day earlier and the date given was the date of his burial in the cemetery of Priscilla. The date of his canonization is unknown, though what is remarkable about it is that Sylvester was one of the earliest saints who was not a martyr.

Books

John, Eric, editor, *The Popes: A Concise Biographical History,* Hawthorn Books, 1964.
McBrien, Richard P., *Lives of the Popes: The Pontiffs from St. Peter to John Paul II,* HarperCollins, 1997.

Online

Catholic Encyclopedia, http://www.newadvent.org/ (December 17, 2003).
"Edict of Milan," http://gbgm-umc.org/umw/bible/milan.stm (December 15, 2003). □

T

Vivienne Tam

Chinese-born American fashion designer Vivienne Tam (born 1957) draws inspiration from her Chinese heritage to create distinctive clothing that blends the best of both cultures. After two decades in business, Tam's company enjoyed annual sales in the $40-million-plus range, and she could boast a long roster of celebrity clients devoted to her designs. "When you look at my forms, they're Western, but the embroidery and trims are traditional, based in history," she told a writer for London's *Independent* newspaper. "Combine the two and it becomes a new thing."

Left behind with Grandparents

The second of four children, Tam was born in Guangzhou, China, in 1957, and named Yin Yok, or "jade sparrow." The country's doctrinaire Communist regime was barely a decade old at the time, and there were periodic bursts of official harassment targeted at those considered insufficiently devoted to state-directed socialism. Tam's parents, Tong Tam and Kwan Ngai Lee, owned property, which put them at a severe disadvantage politically for, according to Communist doctrine, the propertied class was the worst of all socio-economic classes. "It was really a difficult time," the designer told *People* writers Sue Miller and Christina Cheakalos about these early years. "Because my father was a landlord, he had to give up all the prop-

erty." Her parents eventually fled China for Hong Kong, taking her brother along with them, and left the infant Tam behind with her grandparents.

Hong Kong was a British colonial possession during the second half of the 20th century. Comprised of a peninsula and islands off mainland China, it emerged as a thriving port and trade center as well as financial hub for Southeast Asia under the British. Thousands of Chinese fled to Hong Kong when Communist leader Mao Zedong came to power in mainland China in 1949 while others, like Tam's family, managed to cross the border later. Tam finally joined her parents when she was three years old, after being taken to Hong Kong by a couple who told authorities she was their daughter.

Earned Design Degree

In bustling, cosmopolitan Hong Kong, Tam attended a Roman Catholic school and took the name Vivienne when she began to learn English in earnest. At home, she still spoke Chinese, and though she was sent to a parochial school, "my family would go to temples," Tam told Francine Parnes in *AsianWeek.com*. "It's a hybrid way of life, where I learned to be more open and accept other people and other cultures." Tam's parents both sewed, and she took it up herself at the age of eight. While growing up, she made her own outfits as well as clothes for her younger brother and sister. Her mother's sharp eye was the first inkling of a design talent in the Tam family, however. "Even though we didn't have much money," Tam told *People*, "my mother would buy scrap fabric and make clothing nobody else had."

Tam also crocheted and did embroidery work, and went on to study fashion design at Hong Kong Polytechnic University. After earning her degree, she moved to London,

but decided to settle in New York City in 1981 in order to launch her business. "My mother supported me," she recalled in an interview with Bergen County *Record* writer Judy Jeannin. "I wanted to learn more—to learn the business, the industry, and the culture. New York is so much like Hong Kong. It is a melting pot and so exciting." Her company officially came into being in March of 1982 as East Wind Code, which connotes good luck and prosperity in Chinese symbolism.

Renamed Label after a Decade

There was a receptive audience waiting for Tam's designs in the early 1980s. She visited buyers at stores like Henri Bendel on the days when they looked at work by new designers, carrying her sample pieces stuffed in a duffel bag, and she also rented a space at the International Fashion Boutique Show that resulted in $100,000 worth of orders. She found a work space on West 38th Street, but her clothes were made in Hong Kong, an international epicenter for garment manufacturing. Her first lines had an avant-garde bent, made from fabrics that included traditional Chinese bedding, which she bleached or dyed. Despite her initial successes, Tam still struggled in her first few years and sometimes took credit-card advances to meet her small staff's payroll.

More and more stores became interested in carrying Tam's line, and she soon found herself shipping to Europe and Africa as well. She eventually cut back and revised her business plan. "The collection wasn't as good then, because

I wasn't focused," she admitted to *Women's Wear Daily* interviewer Maryellen Gordon. "It's not important how big your business is if the collection isn't right." That same year, she changed the name of her label to "Vivienne Tam," and with a $100,000 nest egg she had saved staged her first runway show during New York's biannual Fashion Week, when American designers present their next season's lines to store buyers and fashion journalists.

Tam's clothing was a hit with fashion-forward women, who liked its Asian influence. "The key to her achievement is her ability to design with an eye for East meets West," asserted an essayist in *Contemporary Fashion*. "Bringing these cultural inspirations together in her designs, she is able to design clothing of traditional elements with a modern edge. Her collections are perceived with the idea that each person's personality will bring out different aspects from within each design."

The Mao Controversy

Tam took her Chinese themes to a new level in 1995 after teaming with artist Zhang Hongtu. Together they designed a series of images of Mao, who had died in 1976, for T-shirts and jackets that depicted him sporting pigtails or cross-eyed with a bee perched on the tip of his nose. In Communist China, portraits of Mao had been ubiquitous, and fostered what became a cult of personality that did not immediately end with his death. Some in the Asian American community deemed Tam's cheeky take on the Mao image in poor taste, for countless had died during the periodic waves of political repression during his years in power. Initially she had a hard time finding a Hong Kong manufacturer even willing to take the job, and there was a minor protest outside of her store there one day. Stores in Taiwan, which broke from China after its 1949 Communist revolution, refused to carry the line.

In her defense, Tam contended that Mao was a "fashion czar," as she told *Palm Beach Post* fashion editor Staci Sturrock. The shapeless, drab-colored "Mao suit" had been standard gear for nearly every Chinese person for years. "Where else could one man tell over 1 billion people what to wear?" Tam reflected. Despite the initial fracas, her Mao collection proved to be a hit, and items from it were even added to the permanent collection of the Andy Warhol Museum in Pittsburgh, Pennsylvania, and the museum of New York City's Fashion Institute of Technology.

The Fashion Institute of Technology later invited Tam to present an exhibit, "China Chic: East Meets West," in 1999, where she showed how the rich heritage of her homeland had inspired her vision. Chinese craftsmanship, in particular, continued to play a key role in her designs. As she told Allegra Holch in *Women's Wear Daily,* in the Chinese textile arts there are "all different kinds of techniques for beaded work and crochet work, but unfortunately, they don't always do it in a contemporary way." When her suppliers and manufacturers balked at her ideas sometimes, she noted, she worked hard to win them over. "Sometimes they'll tell me it's impossible, but then they try it and they see it can be done," she enthused.

Adopted Buddha Image

Other collections from Tam's drawing board have continued to find inspiration from Asian culture. Her spring 2001 line was called "Year of the Dragon," and featured another figure ubiquitous is some Eastern lands: that of Buddha. "The Buddha image has always been in the temple, and I wanted to make it more accessible to the people," Tam told Parnes in *AsianWeek.com*. "On clothing, it's like a walking image, not just for the person wearing it, but for the people looking at it. It's a reminder of ourselves, that we have Buddha in our heart."

Tam's success in the 1990s helped her expand her clothing empire. She created a shoe line for Candie's in 1996, and the following year opened her first store in New York City, on Greene Street in the fashionable SoHo district. A Los Angeles address followed, and then Tokyo and Kobe, Japan. She was also invited to design the interior for a new version of General Motors's Alero model, manufactured by Oldsmobile, in 1999. Madonna and Julia Roberts are among Tam's celebrity fans.

"Not Just Cheongsam and Chop Suey"

Tam spent a month in Beijing and Shanghai to interview people for her first book, *China Chic*, which was published in 2000. She co-wrote it with Martha Huang, a scholar of Chinese literature, and the lavish coffee-table tome included a wealth of images from her family's past, including photographs of her parents as newlyweds. Tam's aim, she told the *Palm Beach Post*, was to show Chinese culture in a way that is not filtered through Western biases. "I wanted people to know not just cheongsam and chop suey and chopsticks," she told Sturrock. "I wanted to go deeper." The square shape and red plastic binding of *China Chic* mimicked Mao's famous "Little Red Book" of quotations, but Tam said that the overall design was simply following certain precepts of her culture. "Chinese cosmology is square, it's very grounded," she told *Women's Wear Daily* writer Holly Haber. "Chinese characters are in a square form and so is the architecture. The [Forbidden] Palace is all square forms with symmetric placement of furniture. Everything comes in pairs and a square is totally balanced."

As Tam's business continued to grow, she talked about expanding into other design realms. Asked by *New York Times* journalist Mark Landler if she might eventually head into housewares and become "a Chinese Martha Stewart," Tam said that when she was in the process of writing her book, "I wasn't conscious of trying to do that," she noted. "But towards the end, people began talking about it. It's interesting when you have a label, and other things start coming to you. It's the other things that make it interesting." She ventured into evening and special occasion dresses in 2003, and launched a secondary sportswear and denim line called Red Dragon. She had long been a cautious entrepreneur, however, and was happy that her company remained independent and free of a financial backer, as many designers had been forced to sign with in order to stay afloat in a notoriously tough industry.

Independent Empress

The little sister Tam once dressed as a child now works for her big sister's company. Tam makes her home in New York City, where her company is headquartered, but travels regularly to Hong Kong and China, where factories manufacture her designs. She had made her first visit back to her homeland as a young woman in 1980, just after Mao's successors began to allow foreign visitors across the border again after decades of isolation. She recalled how, during her first visit, people followed her around, intrigued by the padded shoulders of her jackets. During her 1998 sojourn, she was both surprised and slightly uneasy at the changes she found, however. As she told Haber in *Women's Wear Daily*, many she interviewed eagerly expressing a desire for more material wealth. "I feel scared because it is losing its culture and traditional values," Tam said of her native country. She herself remains with feet in both worlds, not entirely immersed in the Western mind-set even after two-plus decades in business. The fashion industry, she told *People*, sometimes makes her feel "like a machine. In this business you feel like you have to produce, but each time you have to produce better."

Books

Contemporary Fashion, second edition, St. James Press, 2002.

Periodicals

Independent (London, England), June 21, 1997.
Interior Design, April 1998.
New York Times, June 21, 1983; December 31, 2000.
Palm Beach Post, November 29, 2000.
People, November 23, 1998.
Record (Bergen County, NJ), November 5, 2000.
Women's Wear Daily, March 29, 1993; January 6, 1994; June 12, 1996; May 23, 1997; November 20, 1997; November 16, 2000; September 6, 2002.

Online

"Vivienne Tam Defines 'China Chic,' *AsianWeek.com*, http://www.asianweek.com/2000_08_10/ae3_viviennetam.html (January 13, 2004). □

Jamsetji Nusserwanji Tata

Jamsetji Nusserwanji Tata (1839–1904) was a pioneer of Indian industrialism as well as a noted philanthropist. In 1858, he joined his father's export firm and established branches in Japan, China, Europe, and the United States. He organized the first large-scale ironworks in India and endowed several scholarships.

Born in Navsari, India, on March 3, 1839, Tata was the only son of five children of Nasarwanji Ratanji Tata, a member of the Parsi religion and a descendant of a priestly family, and Jiverbai Cowasjee Tata. When Tata was thirteen years old, his father opened an export business in Bombay, India. In 1855, when he was sixteen, in accordance with Parsi custom, which encouraged early marriage, he married a ten-year-old girl named Berabai. They would later have a daughter, who died at the age of twelve, and two sons, Sir Dorabij Jamsetji and Ratan Jamsetji.

Expanded Tata & Co. to Asia

Tata attended Elphinstone College in Bombay from 1855 to 1858. He did so well there that the school refunded his fees. After his schooling, his father employed him in the family business. In December of 1859, Tata's father sent him on a business trip to Hong Kong, where he worked to open a branch of his father's firm, and remained until 1863. He established connections and buyers for the business; this was only the beginning of an expansion of the firm, called Tata & Co. and later renamed Tata & Sons. Through Tata's travel and work, the firm would eventually expand its reach to create branches in China, Japan, Paris, and New York, as well as in London.

In 1863, Tata began traveling to England, where he worked to establish an Indian Bank. This venture proved unsuccessful, largely because of bad timing; at the time, a financial crisis was brewing back in India, and the Tata firm was forced to declare bankruptcy. Part of this crisis was the result of the ending of the American Civil War; during the war, the American South did not produce much cotton, so demand for Indian cotton skyrocketed. Once the war was over and American production resumed, demand for the Indian product diminished. However, the Abyssinian war soon brought contracts for army clothing and supplies for the British-Indian Army, and these lucrative contracts allowed the firm to be resurrected. In 1871, Tata began to promote his Central India Spinning, Weaving and Manufacturing Company, Limited.

Adopted Innovations in Factories

In 1872, Tata returned to England to study the cotton industry there, specifically the cotton mills in Lancashire. He was interested in developing the still-primitive cotton industry in India. After examining the Lancashire mills, he decided to site an Indian cotton factory at Nagpur, and he opened his Empress cotton mill there on January 1, 1877; the factory received its name because on the same day, Queen Victoria of England was proclaimed Empress of the British Empire, which at the time included India. Later, Tata bought a troubled mill, the Dharamsi Cotton Mill at Coorla, near Bombay, and made it profitable, renaming it the Swadeshi ("own country") Mill. This mill was named after a political movement, which promoted the use of Indian-made product, as opposed to products imported from Britain, and its founding marked an upsurge in nationalistic feeling among Indians, who wanted to become independent of Britain. The mill was supported by Indian shareholders, and it soon produced cloth that was exported to China, Korea, Japan, and the Middle East.

According to the *Dictionary of National Biography,* Tata's textile mills "were soon recognized to be the best managed of Indian-owned factories." Tata kept a close eye

on the factories, and continually made improvements in order to increase their production as well as to improve the conditions for their workers. Tata, in moves that were far ahead of his time, hired his managers carefully, and instituted policies that gave workers training, guaranteed pensions and tips, medical care, accident compensation, and daycare for women employees who had children. He also devoted his time to improving the quality of the cotton itself. At the time, Indian cotton was rather coarse, so Tata imported different strains of cotton which yielded longer, finer, and softer fibers. One of these types of cotton came from Egypt, and although it was difficult to get the plants to grow in the Indian climate, Tata persisted despite the fact that government agriculturists told him the project was doomed to failure. He eventually succeeded, and even published a pamphlet titled *Growth of Egyptian Cotton in India.* Another pamphlet described how the supply of skilled laborers could be increased.

Tata noted that freight charges for shipping between Bombay and the company's branches in China and Japan were eating into the company's profits. At the time, this shipping route was monopolized by three companies, which kept prices high, so Tata turned to the Japanese Steam Navigation Company (Nippon Yusen Kaisha) for cheaper shipping. As a result, the three monopolizing companies fought back, and Tata spent a great deal of money to prove that their monopoly was hurting Indian trade. He eventually won, and in June of 1896 the freight fees were reduced to a reasonable and competitive level. In addition to fighting for fair freight charges, Tata also opposed taxes placed on Indian cotton products.

Tata realized that the industrial revolution was a key element in industrial success, and he was determined to take advantage of the new advances in technology and methods. At the time, railroads and telegraphs were beginning to be built in order to link various regions of India with one another. Tata incorporated these inventions into his industrial empire, and he also concentrated on enhancing his industries by incorporating the iron and steel industry, electric power generation, and technical education.

Began Iron and Steel Industry

In 1901, Tata turned his attention to the Indian iron industry, which, like the cotton industry, was largely undeveloped; at the time, iron was produced on a very small, local scale, largely by families of craftspeople. He employed English and American surveyors, most notably American Charles Page Perin, who spent years examining the Indian geology for iron deposits. In addition, he traveled to Europe and the United States to get technical advice on the process of making steel. Tata wanted to refine iron ore on a large, factory-based scale, and he invested large sums in the project. Although he would die before this scheme was realized, on August 26, 1907, his sons registered the Tata Iron and Steel Company, sited in Sakchi, about 150 miles west of Calcutta. The manufacturing process drew on coalfields in Bengal, which had rich ore as well as plentiful supplies of water necessary for processing it. The company grew rapidly, and by 1911 included railways connecting the factory to the iron and coal beds, and was producing about 70,000 tons of iron per year. According to the *Dictionary of National Biography,* the entire industry would support 60,000 workers and their dependants.

Another idea Tata was noted for was his suggestion that India make use of the extremely heavy seasonal rainfall that occurred each year in parts of the country to create hydro-electric power that would fuel factories in Bombay. On February 8, 1911, the Governor of Bombay laid the foundation for this project, which involved the creation of several dams to hold the water.

Tata also built the Taj Mahal Hotel in Bombay, which cost a quarter of a million dollars, a huge sum at the time; the hotel was considered the best in India. Tata was not interested in running the hotel; he built it solely to attract visitors to India. On his far-ranging travels, Tata bought many of the hotel's furnishings himself, including the latest European amenities—a soda and ice factory, washing and polishing machines, a laundry, elevators, and an electric generator. The hotel, which opened in 1903, was the first building in Bombay to be lit by electricity.

Became a Philanthropist

Tata also improved the architecture of Bombay, and provided well-built suburban homes for workers. He was generous with his profits, and created scholarships for young students. Although originally these scholarships were open only to Parsis, in 1894 they were broadened to allow young Indians from any background to study in Europe. In September of 1898, he offered the Indian government a large sum, as well as fourteen of his buildings and four land properties, to establish a postgraduate institute for scientific research. Although this plan, like many of his ideas, was not realized during his lifetime, his sons established the Indian Institute of Science at Bangalore, which aimed to apply scientific ideas and methods to Indian arts and industries.

Tata's success in transforming Indian industry went hand in hand with his desire to make India an economically self-sufficient country that was no longer dependent on Britain. As a result, the British government of India felt his success was a threat to their power, and they opposed many of his projects, including his founding of the Indian steel industry and his development of housing in the suburbs of Bombay. This opposition did not stop him from going ahead with his plans.

In the spring of 1904, while visiting Germany, Tata became seriously ill and died in Nauheim, Germany, on May 19. He was buried in the Parsi cemetery in Woking, England. After his death, his sons expanded Tata & Sons into a vast industrial complex, and endowed a cancer research hospital in its name. Tata's brother, who was also involved in the business, endowed social science departments at London University and the London School of Economics.

Far-reaching Imagination and Powerful Insight

Tata was notable for his willingness to adopt innovations and use them to improve not only his business but the lives of Indian people. He also made innovation part of his daily life. He was the first man in India to use rubber tires on his carriage, and the first to drive an automobile in the city of Mumbai. As the *Dictionary of National Biography* noted, Tata characteristically showed "first, a broad imagination and keen insight, next a scientific and calculating study of the project and all that it involved, and finally a high capacity for organization. His personal tastes were of the simplest kind, and he scorned publicity or self-advertisement." His memory is celebrated at the Tata Central Archives, housed in the Tata Management Training Centre in Pune, India. The Archives traces the history of the Tata firm, which is still prominent in India, through documents, photos, medals, and letters. One of his descendants, J.R.D. Tata, wrote on the Tata firm's Web site that the family's business philosophy has not changed: "The wealth gathered by Jamsetji Tata and his sons in half a century of industrial pioneering formed but a minute fraction of the amounts by which they enriched the nation. The whole of that wealth is held in trust for the people and used exclusively for their benefit. The cycle is thus complete: what came from the people has gone back to the people many times over."

Books

Almanac of Famous People, 8th edition, Gale Group, 2003.
Lee, Sidney, ed., *Dictionary of National Biography Supplement, January 1901-December 1911,* Oxford University Press, 1951.
Merriam-Webster's Biographical Dictionary, Merriam-Webster Incorporated, 1995.

Periodicals

Times (London, England), September 4, 1925.

Online

"India's Tryst with Industry Comes Alive at House of Tatas," *Estart.com,* http://www3.estart.com/India/finance/tata.html (January 1, 2004).
"Jamsetji Nusserwanji Tata," *Mumbai/Bombay Pages,* http://theory.tifr.res.in/Bombay/persons/jamsetji-tata.html (January 1, 2004).
"Jamsetji Nusserwanji Tata," *Tata com,* http://www.tata.com/0_b_drivers/jamsetji.htm (January 1, 2004). □

Mildred D. Taylor

In 1977, American children's author Mildred D. Taylor (born 1943) received the prestigious Newbery Medal for *Roll of Thunder, Hear My Cry,* one in a series of books in which Taylor chronicles a close-knit African-American family that survives the indignities of a Southern racist society. Taylor's use of racial epithets in her young-adult novels has met with protest from some quarters, but she has defended them as necessary to telling the ugly but truthful history of racism. A recipient of numerous awards, Taylor was recognized in 1997 with the

ALAN Award for her significant contribution to young adult literature.

Mildred Delois Taylor was born in Jackson, Mississippi, on September 13, 1943, to Wilbert Lee and Deletha Marie (Davis) Taylor. While she had only one sibling, older sister Wilma, Taylor was surrounded by a large family. Her father, who had endured repeated racist assaults, was determined to leave the South and raise his daughters in a less-racist society with more opportunity. The family moved to Toledo, Ohio, when Mildred was only three months old, traveling to their new home in a segregated train. When they arrived in Toledo, the Taylors lived with friends until they were able to buy a duplex. Once every year the family would return to the South to visit relatives, but many of their relatives eventually followed them up North, taking up temporary residence in the duplex until they could afford a place of their own.

Inspired By Family Stories

Storytelling was a big part of Taylor's family and her father was a master storyteller. "By the fireside in our Ohio home and in Mississippi . . . where my father's family had lived since the days of slavery, I had heard about our past," she recalled in a Dial Books biography. "It was not an organized history beginning in a certain year, but one told through stories—stories about great-grandparents and aunts and uncles and others that stretched back through the years

of slavery and beyond." Taylor went on to describe the profound effect storytelling had on her, "Those colorful vignettes stirred the romantic in me. I was fascinated by the stories, not only because of what they said or because they were about my family, but because of the manner in which my father told them. I began to imagine myself as a storyteller." However, Taylor was a shy child, and instead of verbalizing her stories she turned to writing.

At age ten Taylor and her family moved to a newly integrated neighborhood, where she was the only black in her class at school. She was struck by how differently the history of blacks was taught at school versus what she had learned from her family's stories. Textbooks downgraded the contributions of blacks and the injustices they suffered, while she had grown up hearing proud and dignified stories from her family. At times she attempted to share her family's stories in school, but was met with disbelief. Taylor decided to become a writer of truer stories about black families.

Traveled to Africa

Taylor distinguished herself in Scott High School as one of a few African American students to be elected to the National Honor Society, despite the fact almost half of the students at the school were black. She studied hard, was a class officer and editor of the school newspaper. Working to improve her writing, she discovered she was most comfortable writing first-person narratives.

After graduating from high school in 1961, Taylor enrolled at the University of Toledo where she majored in English and minored in history. By age 19 she had written her first novel, *Dark People, Dark World,* the story of a blind white man in Chicago's black ghetto, told in first-person. Although Taylor's novel attracted some interest from a publisher, she disagreed with the editor's call for revisions, so it was never published.

After graduating from college, Taylor entered the Peace Corps for two years. She began by teaching English on a Navajo reservation in Arizona, then traveled to Africa and taught in Yirgalem, Ethiopia. After returning to the United States in 1967, she worked as a recruiter for the Peace Corps and then trained others to become Peace Corps workers.

Taylor eventually resumed her education at the University of Colorado, where she earned a master of arts degree in journalism in 1968. While she was in graduate school she became active in the Black Student Alliance and worked towards the creation of a black studies program. After she graduated she developed a study skills program for the newly formed black studies program, working as its coordinator for the next two years.

Focused on Writing

In 1971 Taylor moved to Los Angeles and spent the next year writing and supporting herself with temporary work such as proofreading and editing. She married Errol Zea-Daly in 1972, but was divorced three years later. Taylor remained steadfast in her determination to become a writer. In 1973 she entered a contest sponsored by the Council on Interracial Books for Children. Her book, *Song of the Trees,* won first prize in the contest's African-American category.

Dial Books published the novella in 1975 and it was listed by the *New York Times* as an outstanding book of the year.

Song of the Trees, set in Mississippi, introduces readers to the Logan family as they endure the hardships caused by the Great Depression as well as racism. Taylor's second book, *Roll of Thunder, Hear My Cry,* continued the family's saga, as told by nine-year-old Cassie Logan. The book was awarded the Newbery Medal in 1977, which awards excellence in books written for children, and secured a permanent place for Taylor in juvenile literature. *Roll of Thunder, Hear My Cry* follows the independent-minded Cassie through a turbulent year in which she is personally confronted with racism and learns the value of being in a family that owns land. A contributor to *Beacham's Guide to Literature for Young Adults,* wrote that the novel "emphasizes family love, determination, pride, and dignified rebellion against racial injustice."

The *New York Times* considered Taylor's next novel, *Let the Circle Be Unbroken,* an outstanding book of the year in 1982. Comparing Cassie Logan with Mark Twain's fictional protagonist Huckleberry Finn, a *New York Times* reviewer also equated the staying power of Taylor's novels with that of Laura Ingalls Wilder's *Little House on the Prairie* books. *Let the Circle Be Unbroken* was nominated for the 1982 National Book Award and received the Coretta Scott King Award in 1983.

Continued Saga of the Logans

The Logan family has served as the subject of most of Taylor's books, including *The Friendship* (1987), *The Road to Memphis* (1990), and *The Well: David's Story* (1995). *The Friendship*—which earned both a *Boston Globe-Horn Book* Award and a Coretta Scott King Award—is set in Mississippi in 1933. In the novel Cassie and her brothers witness a violent betrayal by a white storekeeper of an elderly black man who once saved the storekeeper's life, provoked by the old man's use of the storekeeper's first name in public.

A *Beacham's Guide to Literature for Young Adults* essayist described *The Road to Memphis* as "a bleaker book than some of the earlier Logan stories." Set in 1941, the book tells the story of Cassie at age 17 as she attends school in Jackson, Mississippi, while her older brother Stacey works in a factory. The novel "lets readers see characters from Taylor's earlier books as they are on the verge of becoming adults," the essayist added, noting that Taylor's characters "go on a journey during which they must confront racial hatred directly." With the novella *The Well: David's Story* Taylor turns her focus on the boyhood of Cassie Logan's father David. During a time of drought, the Logan family generously provides water from its well to white families whose wells have run dry. Despite their generosity, family members are treated with disrespect. "Taylor, obviously in tune with these fully-developed characters, creates for them an intense and compelling situation and skillfully delivers powerful messages about racism and moral fortitude," wrote a reviewer in *Publishers Weekly,* adding that *The Well* should "have a special resonance for fans of the series."

Taylor has openly acknowledged that her novels are culled from stories told by relatives and family friends. In fact, *The Road to Memphis* opens with a dedication to Taylor's recently deceased father that reads: "to the memory of my beloved father, who lived many adventures of the boy, Stacey, and who was in essence the man, David." She stated in her Newbery Award acceptance speech, "If people are touched by the warmth of the Logans, it is because I had the warmth of my own youthful years from which to draw. If the Logans seem real, it is because I had my own family upon which to base characterizations."

Taylor's 1987 novel, titled *The Gold Cadillac,* is her most "modern" book. Set in the 1950s, the book is based on Taylor's own childhood experiences. The book follows a black family on a car trip to the South to visit relatives. Taylor vividly remembers the annual trips she took with her family from Ohio to Mississippi. She also recalls the tension she felt as she entered the South and faced segregation, including "Whites Only" bathrooms. In the writing of my books I have tried to present not only a history of my family, but the effects of racism, not only to the victims of racism, but also the racists themselves," Taylor stated in her acceptance speech for the ALAN Award given to *The Gold Cadillac.* "I have recounted events that were painful to write and painful to be read, but I had hoped they brought more understanding." Her book *Mississippi Bridge* presents another departure for Taylor in that it tells its story from the point of view of Jeremy Simms, a white character introduced in earlier *Logan Family* books.

Challenged for Controversial Vocabulary

Although Taylor's books have been almost universally praised for what a *Beacham's* essayist described as "their graceful, poetic style, their superb characterization, and their sensitive treatment of racial conflict in the American South," some have taken issue with her writings. During her acceptance speech for the 1997 ALAN Award she spoke of "those who seek to remove books such as mine from school reading lists . . . because the "n" word is used. There are some who say such events as described in my books and books by others did not happen . . . or who do not want their children to know the past and who would whitewash history, and these sentiments are not only from whites." Taylor continues to defend her choices in writing, noting: "I do not understand not wanting a child to learn about a history that is part of America. . . . My stories may not be 'politically correct,' so there will be those who will be offended, but as we all know, racism is offensive. It is not polite, and it is full of pain."

With this philosophy in mind, Taylor published a Logan family prequel, *The Land,* in 2001. The novel, which took 11 years to complete, begins in the Reconstruction-era South and tells the story of Paul-Edward Logan, a character based on Taylor's own great-grandfather. Paul-Edward is the son of a white plantation owner and an African-Indian mother. While the land had been an important theme in all of Taylor's *Logan Family* books, the reasons are made clear here. As a *Publishers Weekly* contributor explained, "Taylor does not shy away from the complexities of living in a society in which racial lines are clearly drawn and of growing up in a family in which the white patriarch shares his table with his three white sons as well as his mixed-race children and their mother." Taylor told *Booklist* interviewer Hazel Rochman: "I've always been fascinated by my great-grandfather and his story: that he came out of slavery, that he felt allegiance to both sides of this family, that he grew throughout this whole experience and was able to get his own land."

Taylor's experiences, her body of work and her influence on literature has earned her the honor of a "Mildred D. Taylor Day," declared by Governor Haley Barbour, on April 2, in the State of Mississippi. In 2003, she was named the 2003 NSK Laureate for children's literature with a prize of $25,000.

Taylor continued to write at her home in the Rocky Mountains and devote herself to her family. She planned to continue writing about the Logan family. "The last book will take the Logan children, all grown up, through the end of World War II, the years following, and then the beginning of the civil rights movement," she told Rochman, "For the first time, I'll have to weave a part of my own life into the story."

Books

Beacham's Guide to Literature for Young Adults, Beacham Publishing, Volume 2, 1989, Volume 8, 1989.
Contemporary Black Biography, Volume 26, Gale, 2000.
Notable Black American Women, Gale, 1996.
Taylor, Mildred D., The Road to Memphis, Dial Books, 1990.
———, Roll of Thunder, Hear My Cry, Dial Books, 1976.

Periodicals

ALAN Review, Spring 1998.
Booklist, September 15, 2001.
Publishers Weekly, April 13, 1990; January 2, 1995; August 13, 2001; October 22, 2001.
Sacramento Bee, September 16, 2001.

Other

"Barbour Declared Friday Mildred Taylor Day, "*The Daily Mississippian*, http://www.thedmonline.com/vnews/display.v/ART/2004/04/02/406d7becf374f (April 28, 2004).
"Biography of Ethiopia RPCV Mildred Taylor (1943–), "*Peace Corps Web site*, http://peacecorpsonline.org/ (December 18, 2003).
Dial Books for Young Readers publicity material (January 7, 2004).
"Mildred D. Taylor, the 2003 NSK Laureate," *World Literature Today*, http://www.ou.edu/worldlit/NSK/NSK2003Laureate.htm (June 2, 2004). □

Maria Telkes

Known as the "Sun Queen" for her contributions to solar energy research, Hungarian-born American scientist Maria Telkes (1900–1995) was one of the first to research practical ways for people to use solar energy. She spent much of her life researching

solar energy and designed many solar-powered ovens, stills, and generators. She designed the heating system in the first solar-heated home and won numerous awards and honors, including the Society of Women Engineers Achievement Award in 1952 and the Charles Greely Abbot Award from the American Section of the International Solar Energy Society.

Telkes was born in Budapest, Hungary, on December 12, 1900, the daughter of Aladar and Maria Laban de Telkes. She grew up in Budapest and attended high school and college there. She studied physical chemistry at Budapest University, where she earned a B.A. degree in 1920, and she earned a Ph.D. in physical chemistry in 1924. She began her career as an instructor at the University of Budapest.

Began Research on Energy

In 1925, Telkes came to the United States to visit a relative who was the Hungarian consul in Cleveland, Ohio. While in the United States, she was offered a job as a biophysicist at the Cleveland Clinic Foundation to investigate the energy produced by living organisms. She accepted the job and worked there for twelve years under the leadership of scientist George Crile. She and Crile invented a photoelectric mechanism that could record brain waves, and she and Crile also collaborated to write a book, *Phenomenon of Life,* which reported on their findings. Telkes also undertook research to examine the source of this energy, what happens to it when a cell dies, and what changes occur in the energy when a normal cell becomes a cancer cell.

Telkes became an American citizen in 1937. In that same year, she finished her research at the Cleveland Clinic and went to work at Westinghouse Electric as a research engineer. For the next two years, she conducted research and received patents on new thermoelectric devices; these devices converted heat energy into electrical energy.

Designed Several New Solar Projects

Telkes had been interested in solar energy since she was in high school, and in 1939, she joined the Massachusetts Institute of Technology Solar Energy Conversion Project. There, she continued to do research on thermoelectric conversion devices, only in these devices, the heat energy came from the sun.

During World War II, the United States government, noting Telkes's expertise, recruited her to serve as a civilian advisor to the Office of Scientific Research and Development (OSRD). They asked her to devise a portable method of converting salt water into clean drinking water. In the past, the salt water had to be heated until it turned to steam, leaving the salt behind, and then the steam was condensed back into pure water. Telkes designed a solar still, which used the heat of the sun to vaporize the salt water. The still was small enough that it could be used on life rafts to provide drinking water to people waiting for rescue at sea, and it saved the lives of many torpedoed sailors and downed airmen during World War II. The still was also able to be enlarged enough to provide large supplies of fresh water. This system was put into place in the Virgin Islands, which did not have a large, reliable supply of fresh water. For her invention, Telkes received the OSRD Certificate of Merit in 1945.

In 1948, Telkes researched and designed a new solar heating system, which was installed in a solar house built on the estate of sculptor Amelia Peabody in Dover, Massachusetts; the house was designed by architect Eleanor Raymond. This heating system was different from earlier systems, which had stored the solar energy in the form of hot water or heated rocks. Telkes's system converted solar heat into chemical energy through the crystallization of a solution of sodium sulfate. In her system, sunlight passes through a large glass window to heat air that is trapped behind the glass. The heat from the air is then transferred through a metal sheet and into another air space. From this space, fans move the hot air into storage compartments filled with sodium sulfate; these compartments are located inside the walls of the house, so the walls themselves are the heating element for the home. This system proved to be very efficient and cost-effective, even in the cold Massachusetts winter. In addition, during the hot summer months, the chemical stored in the walls drew heat out of the rooms, making them cooler.

In 1953, Telkes went to the College of Engineering at New York University, where she organized a solar laboratory in the College of Engineering. There, she continued to work on solar stills, heating systems, and solar ovens. Her solar ovens were cheap, simple, and easy to build and were used by poor villagers in nations around the world. They could be used to cook any type of cuisine, were safe for children to use, did not burn or scorch foods, and allowed the cook to do other tasks, since the food did not need to be constantly checked or stirred. Her inventions in this area also led to the discovery of a faster way to dry crops. In 1954, the Ford Foundation gave Telkes a $45,000 grant to develop her solar ovens.

Continued to Invent Solar Devices

In 1958 Telkes began working for the Princeton division of the Curtis-Wright company, where as director of research for the solar energy lab, she researched solar dryers and the possible use of solar thermoelectric generators in outer space. During her time there, she also designed a heating and energy storage system for a laboratory building that Curtis-Wright built in Princeton, New Jersey.

From 1961 to 1963, Telkes worked on developing materials that could be used to protect temperature-sensitive instruments. These materials were also used in shipping and storage containers that would be exposed to extreme temperatures in space and undersea applications for the Apollo and Polaris projects. In 1963, she became head of the solar energy laboratory at the MELPAR Company, and again considered the problem of obtaining fresh water from seawater.

In 1969, she joined the Institute of Energy Conversion at the University of Delaware, where she developed materials to store solar energy and designed devices that would transfer heat energy more efficiently. As a result, she received patents in the United States and in other countries for the storage of solar heat. Her methods were used in the construction of an experimental solar-heated building at the University of Denver, known as Solar One.

During the 1970s, Telkes also worked on devising air-conditioning systems that stored nighttime coolness so that it could be used during the heat of the following day. These systems were intended to reduce power demand during times of high heat and to reduce the incidence of power failures and brownouts.

In 1977, Telkes was honored by the National Academy of Science Building Research Advisory Board for her contributions to solar-heated building technology. This put her in the company of innovators such as Frank Lloyd Wright and Buckminster Fuller, who had also received the award. She was named professor emeritus at the University of Delaware in 1978, when she retired from active research. She continued to work as a consultant until about 1992.

Telkes died on December 2, 1995, while making her first visit to her hometown of Budapest, Hungary, in 70 years.

Books

Almanac of Famous People, 8th edition, Gale Group, 2003.
Notable Scientists from 1900 to the Present, Gale Group, 2001.
Stanley, Autumn, *Mothers and Daughters of Invention,* Rutgers University Press, 1993.
Zierdt-Warshaw, Linda, editor, *American Women in Technology,* ABC-CLIO, 2000.

Periodicals

Rocky Mountain News, August 16, 1996. □

Ellen Terry

English actress Ellen Terry (1847-1928) was among the most famous leading ladies of the Victorian era. She won legions of admirers with her grace and golden-haired beauty and is particularly remembered for her interpretations of Shakespearean heroines, including Portia and Beatrice, opposite Henry Irving. At the time of her death a *Times* commentator concluded, "She was a woman of genius; but her genius was not that of the brain so much as of the spirit and of the heart. She was a poem in herself—a being of exquisite and mobile beauty. On the stage or off she was like the daffodils that set the poet's heart dancing."

Early Life and Stage Debut

Terry was born into a theater family, her parents having been actors in a touring company based in Portsmouth. Among her siblings six others performed on the stage, most notably Terry's elder sister Kate, who until her marriage and retirement from the stage in 1867 was one of the most sought after leading ladies in the English theatre. Successive generations followed in the family tradition, including Terry's own children and Kate Terry's grandson Sir John Gielgud, who became one of the twentieth century's most respected actors.

Under the guidance of her father, Terry began training for an acting career at an early age and made her stage debut as Mamillius the child under the direction of Charles Kean in *A Winter's Tale* at the Princess Theater in London on April 28, 1856, with Queen Victoria in attendance. A print made by Martin Laroche capturing her appearance as Mamillius with Kean in costume as Leontes is in the photography collection of the National Portrait Gallery. Although the success of her debut was marred by her unintentionally tripping over a prop wagon, she later played other roles for children, including Prince Arthur in *King John* and Puck in *A Midsummer Night's Dream.* She played comedy and burlesque as well as drama at the New Royalty Theatre in London and at Bristol's Theatre Royal and appeared in a

number of contemporary works as well as *Much Ado about Nothing, Othello,* and *A Merchant of Venice.*

Marriage to G. F. Watts

In 1864, the sixteen-year-old Terry married the well-known painter George Frederick Watts, thirty years her senior, and she retired from the stage. Watts's famous portraits of Terry, including "Choosing" and "Ophelia," were more successful than their domestic affairs, however, and they separated within a year. The famous image in "Choosing" depicts Terry deciding between earthly vanities represented by the showy camellias that she smells and nobler values represented by the violets held in her hand. Together with her sister Kate, Terry is also the subject of Watts's "The Sisters." In 1867 she performed in London in several works by the popular contemporary playwright John Taylor, including *A Sheep in Wolf's Clothing* at the Adelphi Theatre, *The Antipodes* at the Theatre Royal, and *Still Waters Run Deep* at the New Queen's Theatre.

In December 1867 Terry appeared for the first time opposite Henry Irving, with whom she would later develop a long professional association, when she played Katharine in *Katherine and Petruchio,* David Garrick's one-act version of *The Taming of the Shrew* at the Queen's Theatre. However, she ceased performing in 1868 when, separated but not divorced from Watts, Terry eloped with architect and designer Edward William Godwin. The couple took up residence in rural Hertfordshire and had two children, Edith, born in December 1869, and Edward (later the actor, designer, and producer Edward Gordon Craig) born in January 1872. Plagued by mounting debt, Terry returned to the stage in 1874 at the urging of the playwright Charles Reade and appeared in a number of Reade's works, including the roles Philippa Chester in *The Wandering Heir,* Susan Merton in *It's Never Too Late to Mend,* and Helen Rolleston in *Our Seamen.* Terry also performed with the actor/manager Charles Wyndham that same year at London's Crystal Palace as Volante in John Tobin's *The Honeymoon* and as Kate Hardcastle in Oliver Goldsmith's *She Stoops to Conquer.*

Terry's relationship with Godwin ended early in 1875 during preparations for the role that would bring her the highest fame of her career, that of Portia in *The Merchant of Venice,* which she first performed at the Prince of Wales's Theatre in London on April 17, 1875. According to biographer Tom Prideaux, "Her peculiar gift for Shakespeare was evident both in her husky but consummately clear diction and in what appeared to be a temperamental affinity with the poet himself, something akin to his lyric verve and humanity, which made his lines seem to originate in her own mind." While remembered for the sensation caused by Terry's interpretation of her role as well as for the artistry of Godwin's set designs, the production closed after only three weeks. However, those three weeks had been enough to solidify Terry's reputation as an actress of imposing skill and to attract numerous admirers of her beauty, including English poets Oscar Wilde and Algernon Swinburne. Wilde, an Oxford undergraduate at the time, wrote a sonnet describing Terry: "For in that gorgeous dress of beaten gold,/ Which is more golden than the golden sun, / No woman Veronese looked upon / Was half so fair as thou whom I behold." Terry later re-created the role in several touring productions and for numerous engagements from 1879 to her final appearance as Portia at London's Old Vic Theatre in 1917.

Lyceum Years

In late 1878 Terry joined the company managed by Henry Irving who had lately assumed ownership of the Lyceum Theatre. Her association with Irving was to become the most successful of her career, and over the next two decades she played opposite him as many of the great Shakespearean heroines, including Ophelia, Lady Macbeth, Viola, Queen Katherine, Juliet, Cordelia, and perhaps most notably Beatrice in *Much Ado about Nothing,* a role she first performed at the Lyceum in 1882 and later revived in 1884, 1891, and 1893. Over the years she was associated with the Lyceum, Terry appeared in such roles as Pauline in *The Lady of Lyons* by Edward George Bulwer-Lytton (1878), Margaret in *Faust* by William Gorman Wills (1885), Camma in *The Cup* (1880) and Rosamund de Clifford in *Becket* (1893), both by Alfred Tennyson, Jeanette in *The Lyons Mail* by Charles Reade (1883), Guinevere in *King Arthur* by J. Comyns-Carr (1895), and Madame Sans-Gêne in Victorien Sardou and Emile Moreau's play by that name (1897). Also during this period Terry was married to fellow actor Charles Kelly, from whom she had legally separated before his death in 1885.

Having spent most of her career appearing in works that were chosen by leading men to showcase their own talents, in 1903 Terry briefly assumed management of the Imperial Theatre in order to have more control over the material in which she appeared. She mounted a production of Henrik Ibsen's *The Vikings* in 1903 with herself as Hiordis, but the venture was a financial failure. She performed throughout England, including engagements in Nottingham, Liverpool, and Wolverhampton, and appeared in 1905 in J. M. Barrie's *Alice-Sit-by-the-Fire,* with considerable success.

Golden Jubilee Celebration

In 1906 a tribute was produced at the Drury Lane Theatre in celebration of her golden jubilee. Still a popular favorite with audiences, her fans started lining up the previous day for a matinee that included performances by Caruso, Mrs. Patrick Campbell, Eleanora Duse, Lillie Langtry, Herbert Beerbohm Tree, and more than twenty members of the Terry family. According to a contemporary account in the *Times,* "Some thousands of Londoners devoted what was virtually the whole of a working day to a theatrical debauch. From shortly after noon to six o'clock they filled Drury Lane with a riot of enthusiasm, a torrent of emotion, a hurly-burly of excitement, 'thunders of applause.' They cheered 'til they were hoarse, laughed to the verge of hysteria, and sang 'Auld Lang Syne' in chorus, not without tears." The *Times* commentator noted, "For half a century Ellen Terry has been appealing to our hearts. Whatever the anti-sentimentalists might say, that is the simple truth. . . . A creature of the full-blooded, naïve emotions she excites those emotions in us." Her address to the crowd is reprinted by biographer Nina Auerbach, "I will not say good bye. It is one of my chief joys that I *need* not say good bye—*just yet*—but can still speak to you as one who is still among you on the active list—still in your service—if you please."

At the time of the jubilee Terry was appearing at the Court Theatre as Lady Cicely Wayneflete in *Captain Brassbound's Conversion* by Bernard Shaw, one of her most ardent professional and personal admirers. She continued in the part during American and British tours in 1907. While in Pittsburgh she married her co-star, the American actor James Carew. Shaw later assessed her interpretation of Lady Cicely in a letter to Terry written after their return to England and quoted by Prideaux, "At the Court, you were always merely trying to remember your part. But now you have realized you are Lady Cicely. Her history has become your history; and instead of trying to remember somebody else's words, you simply say what is right to say in the situation . . . and there you have the whole thing alive and perfect. It is really a very wonderful performance."

Terry continued to work throughout her sixties and seventies, appearing as Nance Oldfield in a *Pageant of Famous Women* written by her daughter, Edith Craig, and C. Hamilton in 1909. She separated from Carew in 1910. Other notable theatrical engagements of this period include Nell Gwynne in *The First Actress* by Christopher St. John (Christabel Marshall; 1911), and Darling in Barrie's *The*

Admirable Crichton (1916). She also developed a successful career on the international lecture circuit, discussing Shakespearean heroines and interspersing her discussion with recitation. According to a favorable review in *Times*, "She is to English audiences what she is, not merely because she has played nearly all the great Shakespeare heroines, but because she reflects them in her own self and personality. . . . It is a happy thing for England as well as for Miss Terry, now that her acting days are nearly over, that she has found so effective a way of bringing home to Shakespeare's countrymen the inner meaning of his plays and the charm of her own art." During World War I she performed many war benefits.

Although Terry is most associated with the Victorian stage, she remained active into the motion picture era and appeared in several films, including her debut as Julia Lovelace in *Her Greatest Performance* (1917) as well as *The Invasion of Britain* (1918), *Pillars of Society* (1918), *Potter's Clay* (1922), and *The Bohemian Girl* (1922).

In May 1922 Terry received an honorary degree from the University of St. Andrews. She was named a Dame of the British Empire in the New Year's honors list of 1925. She died several days after suffering a heart attack, at home in Smallhythe, near Tenterden, Kent, on July 21, 1928. According to the *Times* obituary, "The death of Dame Ellen Terry . . . has been received with universal sorrow. In the history of the English stage no other actress has ever made herself so abiding a place in the affections of the nation."

Books

Auerbach, Nina, *Ellen Terry: Player in Her Time,* W. W. Norton, 1987.

Prideaux, Tom, *Love or Nothing: The Life and Times of Ellen Terry,* Scribner, 1976.

Shearer, Moira, *Ellen Terry,* Sutton, 1998.

Terry, Dame Ellen, *The Story of My Life,* Schocken Books, 1982.

Periodicals

Journal of European Studies, June-September, 2002.

New Republic, October 12, 1987.

Times (London), June 13, 1906; July 19, 1911; July 23, 1928.

Online

Ellen Terry Biography, http://www.lib.rochester.edu/camelot/terry.html (January 10, 2004).

Ellen Terry Tribute Page, http://www.ellenterry.org (January 12, 2004). □

Rosetta Nubin Tharpe

African American singer-guitarist Rosetta Nubin Tharpe (1915–1973) fused gospel and secular music and overcame a stereotype that women could not play guitars to become one of the most influential women in American music history.

The Little Miracle

Rosetta Nubin Tharpe was born on March 20, 1915, in Cotton Plant, Arkansas. After divorcing the child's father, Katie Bell, Tharpe's mother, a missionary and church choir singer, began traveling and preaching the gospel. When she was six, Tharpe, who had already learned how to play guitar, held her first public performance at a local church, singing "Jesus on the Main Line, Tell Him What You Want." She was so tiny that she had to be "hoisted atop a piano so congregants could get a view of Little Sister Nubin, the 'singing and guitar-playing miracle,'" noted Gayle Wald in *American Quarterly*.

In the late 1920s, Tharpe and her mother moved to Illinois. In Chicago, jazz, not gospel, was the most popular music. Visiting clubs, Tharpe listened and learned from such legendary musicians as King Oliver and Louis Armstrong. Gospel music was her first love, yet she found the church's restrictions on playing other types of music foolish. Lea Gilmore in *Sing Out* described Tharpe's struggle as a "fight with the devil. In the sanctified church, blues and jazz were viewed as the 'devil's music.' No good 'saint' would be seen playing or listening to such." Feeling that secular music like jazz and blues was not "devil's music," Tharpe remained in the church and continued singing gospel. She married a pastor, Pastor Thorpe, whom she later divorced. She changed one letter of his last name and adopted it as her stage name.

Crossed Over to Stardom

By the late 1930s, Tharpe had moved to New York, played in the famous Cotton Club, recorded her first records, and performed at Carnegie Hall. Yet, as she became an entertainment star, the public, especially African Americans, seemed unready for a singer who crossed over from gospel to secular music and back again. "The world offered nothing but sin," Gilmore further explained, " . . . and the church, at least, offered salvation and an assurance that even though life down here may be hard as hell, the next life is where we will reap the spiritual fruit we have sowed."

Yet Tharpe refused to be held back by conventional thinking. She wanted to play all types of music, even if some believed she was making a "mockery of religion," as Darlene Clark Hine commented in *Facts on File Encyclopedia of Black Women in American Music*. In fact, her first popular single, "Rock Me," was a remake of the gospel song "Hide me Thou Bossom," thus "blurring the boundaries between church and night club, Sunday morning and Monday night," noted Wald.

In Tharpe's version, "Rock Me" became not a request for the comforting hand of God, but a cry for the pleasure of a lover's touch. Backed by Lucius "Lucky" Millinder's jazz orchestra, Tharpe "produced a sound that calls forth the spirit even as it calls to mind the pleasures of the flesh," further noted Wald. Once again, many religious believers were upset at her music.

Returned to Gospel

By the 1940s, singers began to appear in "soundies," three-to-four minute performance films. These early music videos put a face to the voice while creating a singer's image. When audiences saw Tharpe in her soundie, "Lonesome Road," they viewed an elegant woman, neatly dressed and primped, singing about the hardships of life as she travels. Although she may have looked understated and restrained, Tharpe's movements suggested otherwise. "Her body language . . . reads like an amalgamation of the Holiness church and Hollywood," commented Wald. Using theatrical gestures like big smiles to play to the camera and to an imaginary audience, Tharpe suggested that being a strong woman who was unafraid of criticism was as important as being a good church congregant.

However, by the late 1940s, perhaps weary of the never-ending criticism as well as her own internal struggle to keep her gospel foundation, Tharpe returned to her roots and started again performing gospel music. But she still played in jazz clubs and theaters and even rearranged chords to put a little rock and roll into her hymns.

In 1947, her recording label, Decca, paired Tharpe with a new teenage singing sensation, Marie Roach Knight. Their duets skyrocketed both Tharpe and Knight into superstardom. One such outstanding duet, "Up Above My Head," capitalized on their complementary voices. Yet, as Knight recalled to Gilmore in *Sing Out!*, "We rarely had rehearsals, because we never did the music the same way. We would trade lead vocals. . . . You cannot do this without the anointing of God."

In 1950, Tharpe and her mother also formed a successful duo. While appearing at the Harlem Apollo, the two presented "Spirituals in the Modern Manner." Even though Tharpe had returned to the church's fold, she could not resist a jab at its narrow viewpoint. As Howard Rye told *American National Biography Online*, just before beginning one song Tharpe mentioned to the audience, "God is as likely to be found at the Apollo as anywhere else; he doesn't stay at church all the time."

Influenced "The King"

By the 1950s and 1960s, listeners had begun to tune out Tharpe in favor of rock and roll legends such as Led Zepplin, the Rolling Stones, and the Who. However, Tharpe found new fans as she toured Europe, most notably with the American Folk, Blues and Gospel Caravan tour in the United Kingdom. One fan, Phil Watson, recalled to Gilmore in *Sing Out!*, "Her guitar playing was a revelation. The electric guitar was highly polished and she used it as mirror to flash lights around the audience." While on tour in 1970, Tharpe suffered a stroke. She never recovered enough strength to perform again and died on October 9, 1973, in Philadelphia, Pennsylvania.

Tharpe's legacy is her lasting influence on music's most popular performers. Elvis Information Network writer Nigel Patterson connected Tharpe's influence to Elvis Presley. Both had drawn criticism for "putting too much motion as well as emotion" into their songs. And their images caused controversy—Tharpe commanded the stage with her "brightly dyed flame-red hair and her guitar slung over her shoulder" while Elvis adopted a similar stance and his famous swiveling pelvis. Yet, the most obvious connection between Tharpe and Elvis was their unflinching dedication to playing all types of music. Both "were musical innovators," Patterson wrote, "who combined diverse musical genres to form a hybrid sound."

A connection can also be made between Tharpe and another performer—Madonna. Both were big on spectacle, on drawing audiences in with their offstage actions. In 1951, much like Madonna's ill-fated and widely publicized wedding to actor Sean Penn, Tharpe married record producer Russell Morrison at Griffith Stadium in Washington D.C. The wedding was billed, as Gilmore stated in *Sing Out!*, "the wedding of the century." Photographs were published in *Ebony* magazine, admission was charged to attend the ceremony, and a gospel concert was held after the exchange of vows.

Although still unfamiliar to most audiences, Tharpe was the Beatles, the Madonna, the In Sync, the Eminem, the 50 Cent of her time. A superstar who never forgot her roots but pushed music past the stigmas of crossover boundaries, Tharpe's "light," as Gilmore further stated in *Sing Out!*, "transcended genre and left a trail of stardust across the musical landscape."

Books

Hine, Darlene Clark, *Facts on File Encyclopedia of Black Women in America: Music*, 1997.

Periodicals

American Quarterly, 2003.
Sing Out!, Winter 2004.

Online

"How Sister Rosetta Tharpe Influenced Elvis," *Elvis Information Network,* http://www.elvis.com/au/en/printer_spotlight_tharpe.shtml (December 28, 2003).
"It's A Girl Thang! Rosetta Tharpe," *BluesLand.net,* http://bluesland.net/thang/tharpe.html (December 26, 2003).
"Tharpe, Sister Rosetta," *American National Biography* http://www.anb.org/articles/18/18-03400.html (December 31, 2003). □

Leon Theremin

Russian scientist Leon Theremin (1896–1993) was the once-forgotten inventor who created the world's first electronic musical instrument. The device that bears his name "produced a strange, undulating, alternately threatening and soothing sound that didn't exist in nature," noted a *New York Times* writer, and when it was first used in classical music compositions during the 1920s, it was hailed as the harbinger of the electronic orchestra of the future.

Russia's Revolutionary Era

Theremin was born Lev Sergeivitch Termen in 1896, in St. Petersburg, Russia. His ancestors may have come to Imperial Russia because of religious persecution in sixteenth-century France. He was fascinated with science as a youngster and took music lessons on the cello as well. Theremin's early life was disrupted by international and domestic political upheavals. Russia was involved in World War I, and in the third year of the conflict, a group of Communists and Socialists seized power, ousted the tsar, and installed the world's first communist state. The events of 1917 ushered in a genuinely revolutionary era in the newly "Soviet" cities of Moscow and St. Petersburg, and its proponents and supporters were determined to rouse Russia from centuries of anti-progressive thought and create the first modern, egalitarian society. Science and rational thinking were heralded as the way to progress, and experiments in all fields, including the arts, were encouraged.

Theremin studied physics and astronomy at the university in St. Petersburg and served in the army during the war years, when he taught electrical engineering at a military school in the city and also continued his cello studies at the St. Petersburg conservatory. By 1920 he was heading the experimental electronic oscillation laboratory at the Institute of Physical Engineering in St. Petersburg. He was particularly interested in the possibilities of vacuum or electron-tube technology, a recent development. He first worked on a government project for an alarm that, using radio technol-

ogy, went off when a person approached, and from those experiments he created the first "theremin." Its sine-wave tones came from a set of oscillators, which worked on the principle of heterodyning. Heterodyning referred to an audio state in which two sets of electronic oscillations are in phase; the device had an electromagnetic field that emitted sounds when a person stepped into it. Thus Theremin found that with a set of horizontal and vertical antennae on the box, he could control a wide range of sounds by simple hand movements, with a degree of sensitivity that was unlike that of any other musical instrument ever created.

Demonstrated for Lenin, Einstein

Theremin originally called his invention the "aetherphon," since it seemed to produce sounds from the air. He gave a performance of it for Soviet premier Vladimir I. Lenin at the Kremlin in Moscow in 1922 and reportedly gave one of the early ones he had built to Lenin as a gift. The device caused a minor sensation in Soviet Russia, still in its heady post-revolutionary modernization fever, and in 1924 it debuted with the Petrograd (St. Petersburg) Philharmonic in the instrument's first public performance. Theremin was hailed as the "Soviet Edison," and further research was encouraged. For a time, he worked on advanced vacuum-tube technology that was instrumental in the development of television, and he took part in a 1926 demonstration at the Leningrad Polytechnic Institute of the first transmission of non-static images onto a screen.

Lenin was eager to show the world the advances that Soviet scientists had made, and Theremin was invited to participate in an international publicity tour. He arrived in western Europe with his theremin in the summer of 1927, giving lectures and demonstrations in Berlin, Paris and London. It caused a sensation everywhere. In Berlin, Albert Einstein was in the audience, and "said it was an experience as significant as that when primitive man for the first time produced sound from a bowstring," according to a *New York Times* report from the era. After a lecture and demonstration at Albert Hall in London, the fascinated *Times* of London critic wrote enthusiastically of Theremin's apparatus. "Particularly striking was one experiment, in which an echo of a series of notes was made to sound as if it had came from the farther side of the hall," the *Times* correspondent noted. After that, the lights in Albert Hall were dimmed, and "the inventor showed by electric lamps that it was possible to change the colour of light with the change in pitch of notes," the *Times* writer testified. "The colour of the electric flame graduated from a deep red through the various colours of the spectrum to bright blue as the notes ascended in the scale."

Celebrity Inventor

Theremin arrived in New York City just before Christmas in 1927. Journalists came aboard his ship before its passengers disembarked in order to interview him. He was described as "a modest and almost diffident physicist and not a world-famous inventor," a *New York Times* journalist reported. "Of course, I hope the apparatus will be manufactured in quantities in the United States," Theremin told the newspaper. "But I am not old enough to worry about the money I may obtain. I am more interested at present in demonstrating my musical discovery, and I hope to test the musical preferences of the American people."

The first American public performance of the theremin took place in the ballroom of the Plaza Hotel in late January 1928. This audience included world-famous conductor Arturo Toscanini and Theremin's fellow Russian, pianist Sergei Rachmaninoff, who expressed a desire to try the instrument. "As it stands now, the instrument is the raw material of music," violinist Joseph Szigeti told the *New York Times* that evening. "What can be done with it remains to be seen. The question is whether it will inspire men of genius. Its future depends on what men of genius do with it." Another *New York Times* article from that week discussed Theremin and his invention at length, with an accompanying illustration and the caption, "The Symphony Orchestra of the Future Will Play Concealed Instruments by the Waving of Hands." "In rapidity and delicacy of response, Theremin's instrument far excels a piano or a violin or any other known musical instrument," the paper's music writer, Waldemar Kaempffert, enthused. "In directness of effect it can be compared only with singing or whistling. . . . Never can the pianist or violinist hope to attain the spontaneity of either the songbird or the opera prima donna. Theremin achieves precisely the same spontaneity by freeing the artist from the necessity of physically touching or grasping. What can be freer than the movement of hands in empty space to produce beautiful sounds?"

Economic Crisis Ended Venture

Thrilled with the reception his apparatus received, Theremin decided to stay in America. He soon met Clara Rockmore, a Russian émigré and renowned violinist, and taught her how to play the challenging instrument, which was proving a bit more difficult for others to master. Rockmore gained fame with her public performances, as did an American, Lucie Bigelow Rosen. In 1929 Theremin was granted a patent for his invention and licensed it to RCA for mass production. The company's advertising campaign touted that the theremin was "Not a radio, not a phonograph! Not like anything you have ever heard or seen!" A thousand were produced by RCA, and a few hundred sold, but then the stock market crashed in October 1929, and the market for any sort of luxury item dwindled significantly.

Theremin, however, was still at work. In 1932, he demonstrated the Terpsitone, a platform on which a dancer's movements produced sounds, at a Carnegie Hall event. There was also the short-lived Theremin Electronic Symphony Orchestra, and at his West 54th Street apartment visitors—who included Einstein with his violin—were stunned to find an array of new musical instruments as well as doors that opened automatically and even a color television. For Sing Sing Prison in nearby Ossining, New York, Theremin also created the world's first electronic security system. But in 1936, when Theremin wed a noted African American ballet dancer named Lavina Williams, he was ostracized by many in his social set. The couple had twin daughters, and one night in 1938, according to Williams, Soviet agents came to their apartment and took Theremin away.

Vanished into Soviet Russia

Back in the Soviet Union, it was later learned, Theremin endured a show trial on charges that included fomenting "anti-Soviet propaganda" and spent time in a notorious Magadan labor camp in Siberia. A German newspaper reported that he had died—life expectancy at Magadan was about a year—and the reports were circulated elsewhere. But Theremin survived by suggesting improvements in the food delivery system in the camp and eventually was removed to Lubyanka, the famed KGB headquarters in Moscow, to work on the world's first "bug," or miniature listening device, for espionage activities during World War II. He was released in 1947 and awarded the Stalin Prize for his work but never again achieved the level of fame and honor he had once enjoyed. He served as a professor of acoustics at the Moscow Conservatory of Music for a time, but was ejected for his work on electronic musical instruments. He was told, according to the *New York Times*, that "electricity is for executing traitors, not making music."

In the West, meanwhile, the theremin slowly fell from favor as well. Lucie Rosen gave a 1950 London performance of Bohuslav Martinu's *Phantasy* for theremin, string quartet, oboe and piano. The evening was reviewed by a *Times* critic who declared that the theremin "sounds like a viola constitutionally and chronically out of tune." It began to be used in film scores, however—after making its soundtrack debut in the 1935 horror classic *The Bride of Franken-stein*—and was most notably deployed in two films from 1945: *The Lost Weekend,* which earned an Academy Award for Ray Milland for his portrayal of an alcoholic as well as the Oscar for best picture, and Alfred Hitchcock's *Spellbound,* in which Gregory Peck's character suffers psychotic episodes, and the theremin sound foreshadows their onset. Hitchcock's music composer for the film, Miklós Róza, won the Academy Award for best music score.

Rock Musicians Revived Interest

In the 1950s, the theremin was used in horror and science-fiction movies, including *The Day the Earth Stood Still* and *It Came from Outer Space.* Youngsters who were fans of the genre grew into the rock music innovators of the 1960s and 1970s, and the inventor of the first synthesizer, Robert Moog, had built his own theremin as a teenager from a how-to kit he bought out of a magazine. The most universally familiar theremin sound, however, remains the introduction to the 1966 Beach Boys hit, "Good Vibrations."

In 1988, the Delos record label released some of Rockmore's concert performances as *The Art of the Theremin,* which led American filmmaker Steven M. Martin to her. Interested in making a documentary about the instrument and its long-lost inventor, Martin was stunned to learn from Rockmore that Theremin was still alive. Martin went to meet him in Moscow in 1990 and brought him back to New Yorl a year later. In Martin's film *Theremin: An Electronic Odyssey,* there are touching images of the elderly Russian awed by the electronically blinking Manhattan cityscape in a city he had not seen since 1938.

Theremin died on November 3, 1993, in Moscow. Despite significant advances in electronic music, his "aetherphon" remains the only musical device that can be played without actual physical contact.

Books

Contemporary Musicians, v. 19, Gale, 1997.

Periodicals

Independent (London), April 13, 1999.
New York Times, December 22, 1927; January 25, 1928; January 29, 1928; August 24, 1993.
Sunday Herald Sun (Melbourne), May 6, 2001.
Times (London), December 13, 1927; December 15, 1927; April 21, 1950. □

Sybil Thorndike

British stage actor Sybil Thorndike (1882-1976) was one of the leading figures in British theatre during the first half of the 20th century. She made her stage debut in a regional company production of *The Merry Wives of Windsor* in 1904, and achieved her greatest success in the title role of *Saint Joan,* a play written for her by George Bernard Shaw in 1924.

Agnes Sibyl Thorndike was born in October of 1882, the daughter of Arthur Thorndike, a canon of Rochester Cathedral, and his wife, Agnes Macdonald Thorndike. As a child she trained as a pianist, taking weekly lessons at the Guildhall School of Music in London, and she gave her first public recital in Rochester in 1899. Compelled by painful hand cramps to abandon her musical aspirations, Thorndike quickly transferred her creative expression to theatre at the suggestion of her younger brother, Russell Thorndike, and made her debut in an 1904 production of a Shakespearean repertory company under the direction of by Ben Greet. Thorndike and her brother traveled throughout the United States with this group, and she gained extensive stage experience during the tour, playing more than 100 minor roles and serving as understudy to several leading roles. She remained with Greet's company until 1907, giving performances as Ceres in *The Tempest,* Viola in *Twelfth Night,* Helena in *All's Well That Ends Well,* and advancing from Lucianus to Gertrude to Ophelia in *Hamlet.*

In 1908 Thorndike and her brother joined Annie Horniman's repertory company based at the Gaiety Theatre in Manchester, and at about this time she met the noted playwright George Bernard Shaw. Understudying the title role in Shaw's *Candida* under the playwright's direction, Thorndike gained valuable instruction and experience. Also during this period she met and married fellow actor and director Lewis Casson. In addition to their interests in theatre and music, Thorndike and Casson shared a concern for leftist social and political causes. They had four children and remained married until Casson's death at age 93 in 1969.

Repertory in Manchester and London

As part of Horniman's company at Manchester's Gaiety Theatre in 1908 and 1909, Thorndike undertook such roles as Mrs. Barthwick in *The Silver Box* by John Galsworthy, Artemis in Gilbert Murray's adaptation of *Hippolytus* by Euripides, Thora in *The Feud* by Edward Garnett, and Bettina in *The Vale of Content* by German dramatist Hermann Sudermann. For a time she joined Charles Frohmann's company in London and appeared in various roles, including Columbine in *The Marriage of Columbine* by Harold Chapin at the Court Theatre, and Winifred in *The Sentimentalists* by George Meredith, and Emma Huxtable in *The Madras House* by Harley Granville Barker, both in 1910 productions at the Duke of York's Theatre.

Thorndike also made her Broadway debut at the Empire Theatre in 1910, playing the role of Emily Chapman in the comedy *Smith* by Somerset Maugham. Touring U.S. theatres in this part throughout 1911, she returned to England and rejoined Horniman's company, going on to perform such roles as Beatrice Farrar in Stanley Houghton's sensational *Hindle Wakes* at London's Aldwych Theatre in 1912, and Ann Wellwyn in John Galsworthy's *The Pigeon* and Lady Philox in Harold Chapin's *Elaine,* both at the nearby Court Theatre. Renewed productions at Manchester's Gaiety Theatre included Portia in Shakespeare's *Julius Caesar,* Privacy in Harley Granville Barker and Laurence Housman's *Prunella,* and Hester Dunnybrig in Eden Philpott's *The Shadow.*

In 1912 Thorndike originated the role of Jane Clegg in St. John Ervine's realistic drama of the same name. Thorndike's portrayal of Jane Clegg, a wife coming to terms with her husband's infidelity and the utter failure of their marriage, became among the best-known roles of her career; she recreated it for London revivals in 1913, 1914, 1922, and 1929, toured internationally with traveling productions of the play, and performed the role for the last time in January of 1967. According to a London *Times* reviewer discussing Thorndike's dual performance of Jane Clegg and Medea at the Wyndham Theatre in 1929, "It is the peculiar power of Miss Thorndike's acting that it can draw to a character just as much sympathy as it deserves and no more. In the quietly felt tragedy of the commercial traveller's wife, no less than in the dreadful and insistent Medean clamour of revenge, this power of shedding a clear, unsentimental light on the complexities of character was equally effective."

In 1914 Thorndike joined Lilian Baylis's Shakespeare company housed at the Old Vic in London. There she distinguished herself in a number of roles, including Lady Macbeth, and became a favorite of audiences. During this time, while many male actors—including Lewis Casson—were serving in the British Army during World War I, Thorndike added a number of male roles to her resumé. Among these were performances as Prince Hal in *Henry IV,* Puck in *A Midsummer Night's Dream,* the Fool in *King Lear,* and Ferdinand in *The Tempest.*

Successes of the 1920s

In the postwar years Thorndike was a fixture of the London theatre season, and appeared in numerous successful productions, including comedies, tragedies, Grand Guignol, modern works, and stage classics. Commenting on the quality of her voice in a 1922 performance of *La Tosca* at the Coliseum, a reviewer in the London *Times* wrote that Thorndike's "wonderful voice could be heard in every corner of the vast theatre, and yet she never seemed to be raising it at all unduly. . . . The whole performance was a signal triumph for one of our most capable actresses. She was recalled time and again before the curtain." Most notable among her roles of this period are her interpretations of Hecuba in *The Trojan Women* and in the title role of *Medea,* both works adapted from the Greek by Gilbert Murray. So successful was Thorndike at portraying these characters that she participated in revivals of these productions until the mid-1950s. Of Thorndike's performance as Medea at London's New Theatre in the fall of 1922, a London *Times,* reviewer faulted Thorndike's vocal style, but concluded that "her performance never falls short of its full tragic effect, and is remarkable, not only for its force but for the intellectual insight it exhibits." In addition to these roles, Thorndike made her film debut in 1921 and assumed management, with Casson, of the New Theatre, London, in 1922.

A resurgence of interest in 15th-century figure Joan of Arc, the French national heroine who led a troop of soldiers in the last phase of the Hundred Years' War, took place in the early 1920s following Joan's canonization as a saint of the Roman Catholic Church. Thorndike originated the role of Joan in Shaw's *Saint Joan,* which debuted at the New Theatre in London in 1924 and ran for 244 performances. The part, which was written specifically for the actress by the 67-year-old Shaw, brought her critical acclaim and became a popular favorite, and Thorndike was called upon to revive her interpretation in revivals at London theatres in 1925, 1926, 1931, and 1941. She also performed the role of Joan before appreciative French audiences at the Théâtre des Champs-Elysées in Paris in 1927, as well as on international touring productions to South Africa in 1928-29, to Australia and New Zealand in 1932, and to the Far East in 1954.

Throughout the ensuing decades Thorndike acted in a wide selection of dramas and comedies both classical and modern. In addition to Shakespearean and Greek heroines, she portrayed leading roles in a number of works by Shaw, Henrik Ibsen, Noel Coward, Emlyn Williams, and Clemence Dane. Thorndike made her television debut in May of 1939 as the Widow Cagle in Lula Vollmer's *Sun Up,* a redemption drama set among the mountain folk of North Carolina in 1917. On the occasion of her 70th birthday in 1952, a drama critic writing in the London *Times* noted that, "As the years have passed there has been no decline in Dame Sybil's art: indeed, it has deepened in feeling and technical assurance, delighted in widened virtuosity."

Witnessed Changing Theatrical Styles

From a perspective of working for over four decades in the theatre, Thorndike commented on the realistic and restrained style of acting that predominated in Britain by the early 1950s in an open letter to the British Actors' Equity Association. As quoted in the London *Times,* Thorndike wrote: "I have seen much that is beautiful in this typically English reticent acting, with its holding back of emotion and feeling bringing under restrained control the passionate throbbing life that is in us. (I think it is a pity that so many of the younger generation copy the restraint, forgetting that there should be some violence to restrain.) This extremely reserved style of playing for which we are famous seems a bit inadequate when it has to serve the plays of our modern poet-dramatists. Where words are important, where phrasing and stylized speech matter more than lighting and *décor,* we may have to resurrect a bit of the stylized speech thrown over long ago—and round the circle again."

Not influenced by such passing fashions in acting style, Thorndike remained true to her heritage, and was applauded for doing so. In a 1953 Green Room Rag performance, Thorndike and Casson re-created the scene in *Henry VIII* in which Queen Katherine receives the two cardinals. According to a London *Times* reviewer, Thorndike's "Queen Katherine is less an interpretation of her own than a true illumination of the text. She adds nothing to the character, as a clever actress of the second rank might do; she is content merely to reveal everything that is there. But it is in simple revelations such as this that the characters of the drama assume for the moment a reality greater than the people about one, and that actors and actresses declare their own greatness."

Golden Jubilee and Later Career

Shakespeare's *Henry VIII* was chosen in 1954 for a special performance in honor of Thorndike's golden jubilee. Fifty years to the day of her first stage appearance, Thorndike, along with fellow actors Casson, Laurence Olivier, John Gielgud, Ralph Richardson, and Robert Donat, performed a version of the play for the BBC Home Service. In addition Thorndike was presented with a commemorative statuette of herself as Joan of Arc.

Thorndike and Casson created new roles in *Eighty in the Shade,* a play written specifically for them by Clemence Dane that premiered at the Globe Theatre in 1959. She continued working through the 1960s, appearing as Lotta Bainbridge in *Waiting in the Wings* by Noel Coward at the Duke of York's Theatre, as Marina in Chekhov's *Uncle Vanya* at the Chichester Festival Theatre, as Abby Brewster in *Arsenic and Old Lace* by Joseph Kesselring at the London's Vaudeville Theatre, and as Mrs. Bramson in a touring production of *Night Must Fall* by Emlyn Williams, among other roles.

In 1969 Her Royal Highness Princess Margaret and Lord Snowdon attended the dedication of the Thorndike Theatre in Leatherhead, outside of London. (The Thorndike has since closed and reopened under new management as The Theatre.) Thorndike's farewell stage appearance was in the Thorndike Theatre's first production, John Graham's

There Was an Old Woman, in which a homeless old woman recalls her life from her optimistic days as an attractive young newlywed through the long struggle of her widowhood and eventual institutionalization. Thorndike, who had been made a Dame of the British Empire in 1931 and a Companion of Honour in 1970, died following a heart attack at her home in south central London in June of 1976.

Books

Casson, John, *Lewis & Sybil: A Memoir,* Collins, 1972.
Morley, Sheridan, *Sybil Thorndike: A Life in the Theatre,* Weidenfeld & Nicolson, 1977.
Sprigge, Elizabeth, *Sybil Thorndike Casson,* Victor Gollancz, 1971.
Thorndike, Russell, *Sybil Thorndike,* Thornton Butterworth, 1929, reprinted, Theatre Book Club, 1950.

Periodicals

Times (London, England), July 4, 1922; October 17, 1922; May 30, 1929; October 24, 1952; December 13, 1952; April 27, 1953; June 10, 1976.

Online

Staples, Siobhan, "Dame Sybil Thorndike," *Retirement Matters Web site,* http://swww.retirement-matters.co.uk/sybthorn.htm (January 6, 2004). □

Susumu Tonegawa

Immunologist Susumu Tonegawa (born 1939) received the 1987 Nobel Prize in Physiology/Medicine for his discovery of the principle under which human genes rearrange to form the antibodies that fight disease. As a graduate student in 1968 he left Japan to earn his Ph.D. in molecular biology at the University of California at San Diego. He then traveled to the Basel Institute of Immunology in Switzerland where he conducted his Nobel winning research. After ten years, he returned to the United States to teach at the Massachusetts Institute of Technology's Center for Cancer Research. In 1998 as an investigator at the Howard Hughes Medical Institute, he used genetically engineered mice to research mechanisms used in learning and memory.

Interest in Chemistry Turned to Biology

Susumu Tonegawa was born in Nagoya, Japan, on September 6, 1939, the son of textile engineer Tsutomu and mother Miyoko. He had two brothers and a sister. His father needed to travel to various textile factories around the rural part of southern Japan, causing the family to move every few years. Staunch believers that parents owe their children a good education, Tonegawa's

parents sent him and his elder brother to live with an uncle in Tokyo so the boys could easily commute to the top-ranking Hibiya High School. In high school, Tonegawa developed an interest in chemistry.

Expecting to pursue chemical engineering in college, Tonegawa took the entrance exams for the Department of Chemistry at the University of Kyoto. Although he failed the first time, he succeeded the second time and was admitted in 1959. At this time, Japan was one year away from re-newing a 10-year defense treaty with the United States. College students rallied in with their opinions and demon-strations, some causing so many disturbances that classes at Kyoto University were often cancelled. When Japan de-cided to renew the treaty, Tonegawa and other students felt a sense of defeat. In this atmosphere, Tonegawa abandoned his original major and decided to pursue the academic life.

In his senior year at Kyoto University, Tonegawa read scientific papers by French biochemists Francois Jacob and Jacques Monod on the operon theory of immunology. So inspired by it was he that he changed his major to molecular biology and wanted to study it as a graduate student. He was accepted into Professor Itaru Watanabe's laboratory at the Institute for Virus Research at Kyoto University, a unique lab where US-trained molecular biologists conducted research. After only two months in the lab, Watanabe suggested that Tonegawa complete his graduate studies in the United States, which had more sophisticated graduate training pro-grams than the ones available in Japan. Watanabe assisted Tonegawa in applications to US universities. In 1963,

Tonegawa graduated from the University of Kyoto with a BS degree in chemistry.

Studied Molecular Biology in California

With Watanabe's help, Tonegawa was awarded a Ful-bright travel grant to attend graduate school in the Depart-ment of Biology at the University of California at San Diego. The department had been newly established by Professor David Bonner in La Jolla, California. At the age of 23, Tonegawa left Japan for the US, and never returned to his native country as a resident. He would spend his scientific and academic career abroad from then on.

Tonegawa served as a research assistant at the Univer-sity of California in 1963, then as a teaching assistant from 1964 to 1968. He also conducted research under the guid-ance of Professor Masaki Hayashi in genetic transcription in bacteriophages. In 1968, Tonegawa earned his Ph.D. in molecular biology.

Tonegawa remained in San Diego as a postgraduate fellow at the Salk Institute. Under the direction of Dr. Renato Dulbecco, the lab hosted a number of international post-doctoral students trained in prokaryotic molecular biology. At the lab, Tonegawa studied the morphogenesis of a phage. His task was aimed at defining the transcripts of SV40 during lytic infection and in transformed cells. Although this was a challenge in the days before experiments with recombinant DNA, Tonegawa was impressed with the excitement of the lab's scientific research and inspired by the stimulating atmosphere.

Proved the Theory of Antibody Diversity

Around the end of 1970, as a recipient of the Fulbright travel grant, Tonegawa could not renew his US visa, which was about to expire. He was required to leave the country for at least two years before re-applying for a visa. Just before he had to leave, Dulbecco sent him a letter from Europe saying that the new Basel Institute for Immunology in Switzerland had opened. Dulbecco suggested that the field of immunology might benefit from someone from a molecular biology point of view and encouraged Tonegawa to apply. Soon, Professor Niels Kaj Jerne in Basel offered Tonegawa a two-year contract to work in Switzerland.

In 1971, Tonegawa became a member of the Basel Institute and stayed for the next ten years. His first year was difficult, as he wanted to continue his work on SV40, but eased into immunology in order to find an interesting sub-ject. The right topic for him was revealed when he learned of a question that had baffled scientists for more than one hundred years—what were the genetic origins of antibody diversity. By now scientists were using the techniques of restriction enzymes and recombinant DNA in molecular biology research, which Tonegawa used to attack the mys-teries of antibodies.

Between 1974 and 1981, Tonegawa thrived at Basel under the direction of Professor Jerne in an atmosphere of freedom and cooperation. With Drs. Nobumichi Hozumi, Minoru Hirama, and Christine Brack, Tonegawa wrestled with two theories on how antibodies, or proteins, in the body fight disease. The "germline" theory hypothesized that all the genes needed to make an antibody were already part of the genetic code. The "somatic mutation" theory said that genes rearrange themselves to create various antibodies so that only a few genes are needed to generate many varieties of antibodies.

Tonegawa wrote an influential paper in 1976 explaining that he was able to scientifically prove the somatic mutation theory. He found that mutating DNA segments were separated by inactive, or noncoding, strands of DNA called introns, which contained a gene control called an enhancer. Antibody diversity was generated by somatic recombination of the inherited gene segments and by somatic mutation. This discovery laid the groundwork for future research in the causes of cancer, specifically blood cancers such as leukemia and lymphoma.

Named Professor at MIT Cancer Center

By the early 1980s, Tonegawa had made his major contribution to immunological research. He was ready to launch a new scientific project and wanted to return to the United States. Selecting from numerous offers, he accepted a position as professor of biology at the Center for Cancer Research at the Massachusetts Institute of Technology (MIT) in Cambridge. Tonegawa credits the assistance of Professor Salvador E. Luria, director of the center.

At MIT, Tonegawa decided to investigate the role of somatic rearrangement in the activation of the rearranged antibody gene and also to extend the research he did in Basel to include the antigen receptor of T cells. Both problems could be addressed if he could discover a tissue-specific transcriptional enhancer in the immunoglobulin heavy chain gene. One important development he made was identifying a gene that led to the discovery of a new T cell receptor, gamma delta, that could be involved in a new type of immunity.

Won Nobel Prize

The news was a surprise to Tonegawa when a reporter called him for his comments on being named 1987's sole winner of the Nobel Prize in Physiology/Medicine. The 48-year-old had not yet been informed by the Nobel committee that he had won. The committee had realized that Tonegawa's key to unlocking the way the immune system functions was the basis for all future research on fighting infectious disease.

The bulk of Tonegawa's work which won the Nobel was done in Switzerland when he discovered how only 10,000 genes in the human body could produce millions of diverse antibodies that fought off disease caused by viruses and bacteria. Tonegawa had used mouse cells to determine that when antibodies are produced, different segments of the gene are combined at random, resulting in a huge number of varying combinations. Tonegawa's research techniques were as notable as his results; they may lead other scientists to make more effective vaccines and to find ways to improve the body's immune system.

Tonegawa's findings had shattered the prevailing belief that genes could not change. He compared the way genes reshuffled to create a variety of antibodies to the way automobiles are built: "It's like when General Motors builds a car that they want to meet the specific needs of many customers. If they custom make each car, it is not economical, so they make different parts, then they assemble it in different ways, and therefore one can make different cars. It's a matter of how you assemble those pieces."

This discovery has implications for improving immunological therapy, treating autoimmune diseases, minimizing graft rejection, and inhibiting adverse reactions during transplantation.

Nancy Hopkins, a biology professor at MIT, commented on the type of scientist Tonegawa is, considering that immunology was not his field: "There are people who are brilliant and come upon things through analysis. He's the kind of person who moves by insight with enormous drive and passion."

Tonegawa himself credited his successful career to mentors and colleagues he met along the way: "When I look back on my scientific career, I am amazed at my good fortune. At every major turn, I met scientists who were not only at the very top in their own fields, but who also gave me insightful advice and generous help."

Investigated Neural Development and Memory

In 1988, Tonegawa was named an investigator at the Howard Hughes Medical Institute where he researched learning and memory. Using genetically engineered mice, he studied neural development and the molecular, cellular, and neuronal circuitry used in memory. His team was also deciphering mechanisms underlying neural activity-dependent development of sensory systems, and looked at specific brain areas to determine which deficits underlie learning, memory, and developmental impairments.

Tonegawa's work at the institute received support from the National Institute of Neurological Disorders and Stroke, the National Institute of Mental Health, the National Institute on Aging, and RIKEN (Institute of Physical and Chemical Research, Japan).

In 1994, he became Picower Professor of Biology and Neuroscience and director of the Picower Center for Learning and Memory at MIT. He holds a professorship at Amgen Inc., is a member of the American Academy of Arts and Sciences, and honorary member of the American Association of Immunologists and the Scandinavian Society for Immunology.

In 2002 at MIT a new complex for neuroscience was underway. The total cost of the new complex was $150 million. MIT received $50 million from a foundation which will go toward the learning and memory center directed by Tonegawa. The new complex will be completed by or before 2005.

In 2004 Tonegawa and his research team made a new discovery regarding memory. They discovered a mechanism in the brain which controls as quoted from Biotech Week, "the formation of lasting memories." They found that MAPK, an enzyme that stands for mitogen-activated protein kinase, was what initiated protein synthesis which is necessary for long-term memory. Memories could not be stored unless MAPK was stimulated first.

Critical of Japan's Educational System

Tonegawa attended the International Forum Commemorating the Centennial of the Nobel Prize held at Tokyo University and in Kyoto in 2002. The event was sponsored by the Science Council of Japan and supported by *The Yomiuri Shimbun* as a forum to discuss the lack of creativity in Japan's educational system.

In Japan, teachers typically ask students test questions that require one simple response, such as a historical date or factual answer, compared to the US where educators engage students in discussions that can yield a variety of views. Tonegawa, one of only five Nobel laureates in science to come from Japan, urged parents and teacher to encourage creativity and independent thought in Japanese children. "Imagination starts from copying," he said. "Creative people attract creative people."

When the 1987 Nobel Prize was given to Tonegawa, who had moved to the US so he could be inspired and free to carry on his research, Japanese academics took notice and some were humiliated. Tonegawa had asserted that if he had remained in Japan, he would have had to spend years courting favor with mentors and dealing with disinterested colleagues, lagging unchallenged and unmotivated, certainly never to attain Nobel laureate. The press labeled the phenomenon as "Tonegawa Shock" which described the actions of similar Japanese scientists, such as Leo Esaki, a 1973 laureate in physics, who left Japan to work at IBM in the US.

Books

Grolier Library of International Biographies, Grolier Educational Corp., 1996.
Notable Scientists: From 1900 to the Present, Gale Group, 2001.
World Book Biographical Encyclopedia of Scientists, Volume 8, 2003.

Periodicals

Asia Africa Intelligence Wire, March 20, 2004.
Biotech Week, April 7, 2004.
Boston Globe, October 13, 1987.
Daily Yomiuri, March 26, 2002.
Lancet, February 12, 2000.
Science, May 17, 2002.

Online

"Learning and Memory in Genetically Engineered Mice," Howard Hughes Medical Institute, http://www.hhmi.org/research/investigators/tonegawa.html (December 23, 2003).
"A New System of University Tenure: Remedy or Disease?," Chubu University Language Center, http://langue.hyper.chubu.ac.jp/jalt/pub/tlt/99/aug/fox.html (December 23, 2003).
Nobel Prize, http://www.nobel.se/medicine/lauretes/1987/tonegawa-autobio.html (December 23, 2003). □

Lee Trevino

Lee Trevino (born 1939) was an innovator in one of the most traditional of sports: professional golf. Born into poverty, he mastered the sport with a home-made club and an unconventional golfing swing, rising in the ranks to become one of the top golfers of his generation.

Mexican American golfer Lee Trevino proved that some of the best golfers are self-taught. After joining the Professional Golfers Association (PGA) tour in 1969, Trevino won many major tournaments, including the U.S. Open, the British Open and the PGA championship title. Trevino's happy-go-lucky, offbeat persona endeared him to many fans. An optimistic, resourceful man, Trevino grew up in poverty and did not begin competing as a professional until age 27.

Humble Roots

Lee Buck Trevino was born in Dallas, Texas, on December 1, 1939, to parents Joseph and Juanita Trevino. He had two sisters and his father left the family at an early age. They lived in four rooms with no running water and no electricity. But with Juanita's pay from her work as a domestic and the help of her father-in-law, Joe Trevino, a gravedigger, the family got by. The house stood in a field and backed up to the fairway of a local Dallas golf course, the Glen Lakes Country Club, and young Lee was fascinated with the world of rolling, finely manicured lawns, spotless putting greens and dapperly clad golfers he saw walking by each day.

Although he was often physically beaten by his grandfather, Trevino was a streetwise kid with an infectious smile and a ready wit who did not resent his family's poverty. Instead, he developed the resourcefulness, drive, and creativity that would characterize his career as a golfer. Using a discarded club cut down to a six-year-old's size, he began developing a golf swing by mimicking what he saw while watching other golfers at a distance. At night he would sneak over the fence and play on the empty course. At age 14 he went to work at Hardy's Driving Range, where he was able to practice his swing with real golf equipment.

Leaving school after seventh grade, Trevino lied about his age and joined the U.S. Marines at 17, serving in Asia from 1956 to 1960 as a machine gunnery sergeant. While in the service, he played golf with the Third Marine Division tournaments in Japan and the Philippines, where he earned a handicap of only four.

Leaving the Marines when his four years were up, he returned to Texas and to Hardy's Pitch-n-Putt, a driving range and par-3 course where he became assistant golf pro. He remained there until 1964, using his off hours to modify his highly original golf swing, and attended the PGA golf school, a requirement for admission to the tour.

Playing golf costs money, even when you work at a course, and the resourceful Trevino soon became known as

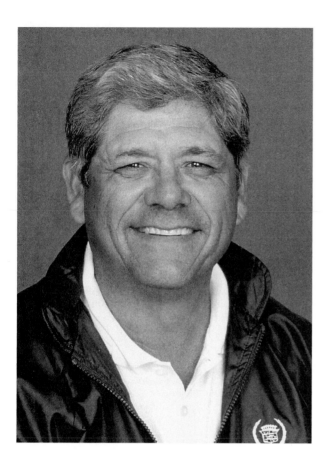

a hustler, betting golfers that he could defeat them using a soft-drink bottle rather than a regulation golf club. Trevino later cited his hustling as good training for staying calm during professional competitions. As he told *Time* magazine, "A $5 bet and only $2 in your pocket—that's pressure."

A Self-Taught Swing

Some have described Trevino's golf swing as resembling a baseball batter's. In their book *The Masters of Golf: Learning from Their Methods,* authors Dick Aultman and Ken Bowden describe his style as "five wrongs" that combine to make "an immaculate right." His stance was open, his grip firm, his shoulders pointing to the left of the point he was aiming for. Standing low over the ball, Trevino reached the top of his swing, his left wrist pushed outward, then he dragged the club down flat to the left. While he battled with a left hook early in his career, he worked for months to counteract it and eventually trained himself to cut the ball to the right.

As his swing improved in accuracy, so did Trevino's reputation among Texas golfers, and with the help of patron Bill Gray, he entered several regional tournaments, including the Texas Open in 1965 and 1966 and the New Mexico Open in 1966. Working as an assistant pro at El Paso's Horizon Hills Country Club, Trevino was earning enough money to support his growing family. He joined the professional tour in 1966 and did well until a discouraging 54th-place finish in the U.S. Open dampened the 26-year-old golfer's aspirations.

Trevino rebounded and returned to the U.S. Open to finish in fifth place in 1967. A total unknown on the national golf circuit, Trevino captured attention with his casual, sunny disposition and his tendency to be unusually talkative in a game that frequently demanded silence.

Leaving his position at Horizon Hills, Trevino officially joined the PGA tour in 1968. Scoring in the 60s in all four rounds at Oak Hill, he tied a record with a score of 275 and beat Jack Nicklaus and Bert Yancey in a touch-and-go finish. He was the first golfer to score under par in all four rounds of the U.S. Open. He earned the PGA Rookie of the Year award and at season's end had official winnings of $125,675 plus endorsements.

With wins at the Amana, Hawaiian and Tucson opens between 1968 and 1969, Trevino continued his winning streak, and in 1969 he gained his first World Cup win. However, 1970 was a different story: over 13 months he entered many tournaments but left without a win.

Trevino rebounded in the spring of 1971. In a playoff round against Nicklaus during the 1971 U.S. Open in Merion, Pennsylvania, Trevino bested him 68-71. That year the PGA named Trevino Player of the Year, one of many awards he would receive for winning the U.S. Open for the second time in four years. Chalking up wins in the British Open and the Canadian Open as well, Trevino became the first to win all three tournaments in a single year; in fact, he won them all in just over three weeks. His second World Cup win was just icing on the cake.

During the early 1970s Trevino was unstoppable, with his second win at the British Open in 1972, and additional victories at the Canadian Open in 1977 and 1979, the Hartford Open in 1972, the Mexican Open in 1973 and 1975, at Colonial National in 1976 and 1978. He won the 1974 World Series of Golf and PGA championships, keeping his name in the news around the world. As a team captain several times throughout the decade and into the mid-1980s, he also gained press for participating in the U.S. Ryder Cup.

Nature Took Aim

By the mid-1970s it seemed as though nothing could stop Trevino, until Mother Nature intervened to slow him down a bit. While out on a golf course in 1975, he was struck by a bolt of lightning, and although he lived to tell—and in typical Trevino fashion, joke—about it, the accident did affect his game. While victories still came Trevino's way, they did not come as easily, and the golfer realized that the problem lay in the way a resulting back problem had altered his golf swing. Adjusting his stance, he aimed less to the right, breaking the unwritten "rules" governing the perfect swing but achieving a championship-winning result.

Trevino won his second PGA championship in 1984, and by the mid-1980s he was one of only three golfers to earn more than three million dollars in tournament prize money. He would laugh about his wealth for years to come, quipping to reporters the oft-quoted comment: "You can make a lot of money in this game. Just ask my ex-wives. Both of them are so rich that neither of their husbands work."

One of Golf's Greatest

Trevino's golfing career was marked by both casual humor and extreme consistency, and he gained a reputation for his proficient swing. On five separate occasions—1970, 1971, 1972, 1974, and 1980—he won the Vardon Trophy, named for British golfer Harry Vardon and awarded each year since 1937 to the touring professional with the lowest stroke average in 60 or more PGA tournament rounds.

Despite his success as a world-class golfer during the 1970s and 1980s, many in the press viewed the down-to-earth Texan as more a showman than a professional athlete. His demeanor was perhaps more unusual in golf than it would be in other sports, because golf had a lengthy history as a sport exclusive to the wealthy and socially refined. However, Trevino reflected a trend that was already under way of golf becoming increasingly popular among younger Americans with time on their hands. "I represent the guy who goes to the driving range, the municipal player, the truck driver, the union man, the guy who grinds it out," he explained to *Time*.

When watching Trevino play, it was not unusual to see him stick his tongue out at a uncooperative golf ball, don a sombrero, or clown around with his caddy, and such antics quickly gained him a group of fans the press dubbed "Lee's Fleas." Off the green, he also developed a reputation for gambling and carousing with friends into the wee hours. "Why go to bed?," he once told a *Time* interviewer. "I like to party because I missed lots of nights when I couldn't afford parties." Because of his quick wit and likeable personality, Trevino was an easy choice when NBC Sports went looking for a golf commentator in 1983.

Seniors Tourney

In 1990 52-year-old Trevino joined the Senior PGA tour and surprised no one when he continued the successful run of his PGA days. During his first year he earned more prize money than the money leader of the regular tour and was both Senior Rookie of the Year and Senior Player of the Year.

Continuing to perform well into the mid-1990s, Trevino became PGA Seniors champion in 1994, but a neck injury forced him to start relaxing a bit. Playing a minimum of 20 tournaments a year, he was in the top ten only three times in 2000, and in 2003 was beaten by an amateur in a People vs. the Pros match in Las Vegas. In 2004 on the Champions Tour, Trevino marked his 16th season, 38 seasons total counting back from 1967 when he first joined the PGA Tour. With age taking its toll, he still worked on his swing, but as he told Bill Fields in *Golf World*, "Usually I go play now and I can tell you how many birds I saw, not how many greens I missed. But it's still a lot of fun."

Trevino married three times and fathered six children. Son Richard Lee, from his first marriage, became a professional golfer. Lesley Ann, Tony Lee, and Troy Liana were from his second marriage to Claudia Lee Fenley, which ended in divorce in early 1983. Trevino wed Claudia Bove, whom he met at the Greater Hartford Open, in December 1983; the couple had two children, Olivia and Daniel.

Part of his role as a golf pro was to help teach others, and Trevino wrote several books about his chosen sport, among them 1971's *I Can Help Your Game* and *Groove Your Golf Swing My Way*, published in 1976. His autobiography, *They Call Me Super Mex*, was published by Random House in 1983. He was also host of the syndicated television program *Golf for Swingers* and remained with NBC as a commentator into the 1990s. Beginning in 1998 golf enthusiasts could play a nine-hole course of his design located at Mexico's El Cid Resort.

Community-minded, Trevino traditionally donated a portion of his winnings to charities. He also served as National Christmas Seal Sports Ambassador in 1971 and was a member of the President's Conference on Physical Fitness and Sports and the National Multiple Sclerosis Society sports committee. Although he lived for several years in Florida at the height of his career, Trevino eventually returned to his Texas roots. He and his family owned a large home only three miles from where the humble, four-room Trevino homestead of his boyhood once stood.

Books

Aultman, Dick, and Ken Bowden, *The Masters of Golf: Learning from Their Methods*, Galahad Books, 1994.

Dictionary of Hispanic Biography, Gale, 1996.

Jackson, Robert M., *Supermex: The Lee Trevino Story*, Hill & Wang, 1973.

Trevino, Lee, with Oscar Fraley, *I Can Help Your Game*, Fawcett, 1971.

Trevino, Lee, with Sam Blair, *They Call Me Super Mex*, Random House, 1983.

——— *The Snake in the Sandtrap, and Other Misadventures on the Golf Tour*, Holt, Rinehart & Winston, 1985.

Periodicals

Golf World, January 19, 2001; July 12, 2002.

Sports Illustrated, December 31, 1971; March 31, 1980; December 4, 2000; December 10, 2001.

Time, July 19, 1971.

Online

"Golf Legend Talks about Favorite Course, Best Shot and His 50-Year-Old Putter," http://golf.about.com/cs/legendsofgolf/a/trevinoqanda.htm (June 2, 2004). □

Trota of Salerno

Trota of Salerno (c. 11th century)—also known as Trotula, Trocta, Trot, Troto, Trotta, Trocula, Truta, and Trutella—was most probably a female physician, obstetrician, and gynecologist who lived in eleventh-century Salerno, a city on the Italian peninsula just south of Naples. By long tradition, she is held to have written the most important and influential texts on women's medicine in medieval Europe and is also alleged to have been the first female professor in the famous school of medicine in

Salerno, a town famed for its wise female healers, known simply as the *mulieres Salernitane*, the Salernitan women. Scholars dispute whether these women were practicing physicians or "merely" midwives and nurses.

Part of Salerno School of Medicine

Reliable biographical information on Trota is scarce—there is very little concrete proof of her existence. She lived in Salerno during the eleventh century, certainly, and was recognized during her lifetime as a remarkable physician. She may have been a member of the noble di Ruggiero family, and some scholars identify her as the wife of Johannes Platearius and mother of Matthias and Johannes the Younger, both medical authors. All four may have been members of the Salerno faculty.

In the medieval era, Salerno's position as a coastal city gave it access not only to culture and commerce but to scientific and medical knowledge from both Europe and Arabia. Even before Trota's day the city was known for the skill of its physicians, and patients came from as far away as England to be treated. Salerno's "school" of medicine was equally famous, although it was not incorporated into anything resembling a modern "university" until the thirteenth century; it, too, attracted students from all over the continent.

During this time, new—or, more properly, newly discovered—Arabic medical texts, based largely on the writings of Galen of Pergamum (A.D. 129–c. 216) began to circulate, competing with the long-established theories of Hippocrates (c. 460–c. 377 B.C.). The Salernitan medical school was the mechanism through which these teachings were incorporated with existing practices, spreading from Italy northward above the Alps and throughout Europe.

Authored Medical Texts

Trota contributed directly to at least three medical texts: *Practica secundum Trotam* (Practical medicine according to Trota), *De egritudinum curatione* (On the treatment of illnesses), and *On Treatments for Women*. The three texts overlap, sharing passages and remedies, proving their common authorship. Although Trota may well have been the principal contributor of these books she was almost certainly not the sole author—at least one book, *De egritudinum curatione,* began as a compendium. All were frequently edited, amended, and otherwise altered by medieval scribes as the works were copied over the centuries. Trota's influence, however, was monumental and her writings remained the foundation of women's medicine in Europe for four hundred years.

Practica secundum Trotam survives in only two manuscripts, and these may be abbreviated versions of what was once a longer work. The book is an assemblage of treatments for everything from toothache to hemorrhoids, with female complaints comprising many of the entries. *De egritudinum curatione,* as noted above, contains writings

from seven Salernitan physicians, Trota included; here her contributions cover remedies for intestinal and ophthalmic disorders.

As the centuries passed and manuscripts were copied, Trota's works were often combined with others to create medical textbooks. One such compilation, which eventually came to be called *De passionibus mulierum* (variously translated as "The sufferings of women" or "The diseases of women"), was the gold standard of gynecology through the sixteenth century. Like most writing attributed to Trota, however, it began its life as separate texts, only one of which (*On Treatments for Women*) could be directly attributed to her. The first compilation appeared at the end of the twelfth century as *Summa que dicitur "Trotula"* (the compendium which is called the "Trotula"). Trotula literally means "little Trota," and the term may have been applied to this manuscript to distinguish it from the longer *Practica secundum Trotam.* Interestingly, of all Trota's works it is the Trotula that has survived best, with twenty-nine extant copies. Variant forms exist as well; by the sixteenth century the Latin Trotula had been translated into most, if not all, European languages—one English version was *The Knowing of Woman's Kind in Childing.* Thus Trota's knowledge was disseminated throughout Europe, influencing both doctors and midwives for centuries.

Medieval Medical Advice

Much of Trota's medical advice strikes modern readers as ludicrous. At this point in history the human body was thought to be dominated by the four elements—hot, cold, wet, dry—and the four humors—blood, red bile, yellow or black bile, and phlegm (although these receive surprisingly little mention). Any systemic imbalances or predominances were detrimental; they not only led to disease but determined its progression and cure. In *Treatments for Women,* quoted in Monica Green's book *The Trotula: A Medieval Compendium of Women's Medicine,* Trota explains the necessity of determining "which women are hot and which are cold" to allow "a succinct exposition on the treatment."

Women who are too cold, Trota claimed, must be treated with "hot" (or supposedly heat-inducing) herbs: pennyroyal, laurel, juniper, hyssop, fleabane, and others. Depending on the condition being treated, this would be done with a bath or even a pessary (tampon) inserted vaginally. Women suffering from excess heat would be given "cold" herbs, such as roses, mallows, and violets. Such treatments, Trota assures her readers in Green's book, will balance the patient's system: "they will be found cleansed from this awful excess and ready for conception."

In *Treatments for Women* Trota discussed many recognizable gynecological and obstetric problems: infertility, difficult births, and uterine prolapse. Others, however, have been invalidated by science. Medieval theory posited that the uterus was an untethered mass that could move inside a woman's body, and "wandering womb" was a commonly diagnosed syndrome; the patient's symptoms depended on the womb's "location." Another condition, "uterine suffocation" (whose symptoms often sound like epilepsy), was thought to be caused by a lack of sexual activity (in married or marriageable women) or a cessation of the menstrual cycle not due to pregnancy. In either case sweet- or foul-smelling substances were among the remedies used to induce the uterus to either "move" to its proper location (i.e. away from the bad smell and toward the good) or to restore its normal function.

Menstruation and its association with fertility was of supreme importance at this time, and many of the cures and medicaments recommended were intended to restore a woman's cycle. "Retention" of menses in a woman who was not pregnant was thought to poison the body, and physicians often encouraged *any* type of bleeding as a substitute, including bloodletting or even a nosebleed. In other instances, herbs were used to bring on menstruation.

Not all of Trota's knowledge was ineffectual, however. Her texts, which gave detailed instructions in how to handle difficult births—including breech, posterior, and other abnormal presentations—told midwives how to turn the infant while still in utero into the proper position. Trota also included sections on how to repair delivery-induced tears with silk thread, and even recommended opiates to dull the pain of labor. This recommendation was notably at odds with Church teaching of the era, which held that women were required to suffer during childbirth as part of their punishment for Eve's sin.

One of the cures described in *Treatments for Women* concerns Trota herself: A young woman, thought to have a ruptured intestine, was about to undergo surgery—a desperate and frequently unsuccessful option in the eleventh century. As a last resort, Trota was summoned and asked for her opinion. Her questioning led her to discount the first diagnosis, and she took the patient to her home. Further examination revealed that the young woman apparently suffered from "wind" in her uterus—yet another now-discounted medieval malady. Trota's treatment of herbal baths and poultices, however, was enough to effect a cure (much to the patient's relief).

Trota also turned her attention to more universal concerns, writing on the treatment of bladder stones, hemorrhoids, and abdominal pain, among other conditions. Treatment depended on the sex of the patient—different remedies were prescribed for men and women. In another departure from accepted medical practice, Trota also devised treatments for male infertility—an interesting speculation in an era when failure to conceive was universally considered the woman's "fault." More mundane medical concerns were also discussed, such as balms for skin that had sunburn or lesions, and salves for chapped lips.

Although the treatments prescribed in Trota's work often seem ineffectual with modern medical knowledge and hindsight, such texts reflect the daily realities of life in the Middle Ages and reveal early (albeit inaccurate) efforts to understand and treat disease. Although it would be centuries before science found causes and treatments for the diseases Trota discusses, books such as hers are windows into an earlier time, when a woman's fertility (whether real or presumed) was frequently the key to her social, financial, *and* physical health.

Modern Discoveries of a Wise Teacher

As time went by and copies (and compilations) of Trota's texts were disseminated, both scribes and readers began to confuse the title with the author. Within a century "Trotula" came to be known as the author, and not simply the title of the work. Modern scholars perpetuated the error, continuing to refer to her as "Trotula of Salerno," and crediting her with authorship of the entire Trotula compendium. Only in the twenty-first century would scholars, particularly Monica Green in *The Trotula: A Medieval Compendium of Women's Medicine,* unearth the truth about Trota, her practice, and her writings.

Like so much of her life, Trota's death remains a mystery. Some sources say she died in 1090, others cite the year 1097, and still others claim she lived into the twelfth century. Whenever she lived, Trota was a unique and formidable *magistra mulier sapiens:* wise woman teacher, even in Salerno, a city noted for its learned females. Her influence on medicine—particularly women's medicine—was profound and lasting.

Books

Alic, Margaret, *Hypatia's Heritage: A History of Women in Science from Antiquity to the Late Nineteenth Century,* The Women's Press, 1986.

Barratt, Alexandra, editor, *The Knowing of Woman's Kind in Childing: A Middle English Version of Material Derived from the Trotula and Other Sources,* Medieval Women: Texts and Contexts 4, Brepols Publishers n.v., 2001.

Green, Monica, *The Trotula: A Medieval Compendium of Women's Medicine,* University of Pennsylvania Press, 2001.

Riesman, David, *The Story of Medicine in the Middle Ages,* Paul B. Hoeber, Inc., 1935.

Online

"Exhuming Trotula, Sapiens Matrona of Salerno," Florilegium (January 19, 2004).

"Social Aspects: Women," Medieval Medicine, http://www .intermaggie.com/med/women.php (January 19, 2004).

"Trotula of Salerno," Malaspina Great Books, http://www .malaspina.com/site/person_1140.asp (January 19, 2004).

"Women Scientists of the Middle Ages & 1600s," Academic Forum Online, http://www.hsu.edu/faculty/afo/2000-01/ merritt1.htm (January 19, 2004). □

V

Agrippina Vaganova

Agrippina Vaganova (1879-1951) was a noted Russian ballet dancer, choreographer, and teacher. She created a new way of teaching ballet, which was named for her, and was the author of a book, *Basic Principles of Classical Ballet* (1934), which is still regarded as a standard in ballet instruction.

Born June 26, 1879, in St. Petersburg, Russia, Agrippina Yakovlevna Vaganova was the daughter of an usher at the Mariinsky Theatre, and thus was exposed to ballet at a very early age. She attended the Mariinsky ballet school, graduating in 1897, and then entered the Mariinsky company of dancers. She performed leading roles in *La Source, Swan Lake, The Little Humpbacked Horse,* and *The Pearl.* She also appeared in *Chopiniana* and *La Bayadére*; her performance in *La Bayadére* is still known as the "Vaganova Variation" today, and she was known as the "Queen of Variations" during her career.

Retired from the Stage to Teach

Despite her talent, Vaganova was overshadowed by contemporaries such as Anna Pavlova, Tamara Karsavina, Olga Preobrazhenskaya, and Matilda Kshesinskaya, and she did not receive the title of Ballerina until 1915, the year before her farewell performance. This lack of recognition was partly because Vaganova was not considered beautiful, as these other performers were, and she also did not have wealthy and influential friends. Perhaps because she did not receive the praise she deserved, Vaganova tended to be critical of herself and her techniques, as well as critical of the systems then used to teach ballet, and she sought to improve both her own dancing and the teaching methods.

Of Vaganova's appearance, Vera Volkova wrote in *Ballet Decade,* "The most remarkable thing about her appearance was her eyes. They were large, blue, unemotional—the eyes of a craftsman rather than of an artist. Her steady gaze seemed always to follow one about, missing nothing. . . . Her large-featured face was the reverse of conventional good looks, but was infused with intelligence."

Vaganova had studied with several well-known French teachers, most notably Nicholas Legat and Paul Gerdt. Their techniques were derived from eighteenth-century French choreographers. Typically, these techniques emphasized soft, graceful movements. For example, the arms were supposed to be beautifully posed, soft, with delicately outstretched fingers. Although this looked beautiful, in this posture the arms could not contribute any power to the dance movements, and this restriction did not allow the dancer to reach a full scope of movement.

Russian ballet was also deeply influenced by Italian instructors, such as Enrico Cecchetti, and performers such as Pierina Legnani, Carlotta Brianza, and Antonietta dell'Era. This influence was particularly strong during the last two decades of the 19th century, when Cecchetti and his Russian students were the main influence on the St. Petersburg ballet stage. Italian ballet emphasized mastering techniques, and dancers were urged to thrill audiences by making moves of extreme technical complexity and difficulty. The lessons were carefully planned, with a set of exercises and study for each day of the week. The Italian style was also known for its emphasis on steadiness, dynamic turns, and strength and endurance in the feet. However, the Italian style was angular rather than graceful;

dancers bent their arms at the elbows and tucked their legs under their bodies when they jumped.

"A New Decisive Turn in Soviet Choreography"

By the time of her early retirement from the stage, Vaganova was already examining these systems and thinking about how they could be improved. From the French style, she took graceful movement. From the Italian style, she adopted the careful plan of study, as well as its steadiness, strength, and endurance. Vaganova also drew on the work of Russian dancers and performers that emphasized spirituality and poetic movement, to create a unique style, which was named for her and which soon became the standard in ballet instruction all over the world. After the upheaval of the 1917 Russian Revolution subsided, she began teaching at the privately owned School of Russian Ballet, which was directed by ballet critic Akim Volynsky. Vaganova's first success was with pupil Marina Semenova, who made a brilliant debut when she graduated from her training in 1925. In *The Soviet Ballet,* Juri Slonimsky commented that Semenova's debut "marked a new decisive turn in Soviet choreography, a resurrection of the classical dance in all its glory and beauty. Semenova's brilliant debut was no accident; it was the result of Vaganova's method of teaching. It goes without saying that had Semenova not possessed real talent her teacher's efforts would have been in vain. It was, however, necessary to unfold, develop and varnish nature's gift. This Vaganova did." Slonimsky also noted that Vaganova had " 'absolute choreographic vision.' The slightest flaw, misstep or manifestation of poor taste are not likely to escape her attention. A rare 'diagnostician' she will at once denote the cause of the failure and suggest the remedy."

Three years later, hearing that the new Soviet Ballet was establishing a school, Vaganova began teaching in the Leningrad Choreographic School. The Vaganova Method, which she refined during the 1920s, was noted for its emphasis on meticulous planning of the teaching process; extremely complex exercises, which were designed to teach students refined techniques; and an emphasis on the dancer's conscious awareness of every movement. Vaganova's innovations, and her stellar students, brought new life to ballet.

The Vaganova Method

Vaganova emphasized dancing with the entire body, promoting harmonious movement among arms, legs, and torso. She believed that the torso was the foundation of all movements, so the dancer's torso had to be strengthened. One exercise she prescribed for this area was that of doing *plies* with the feet in first position; this is a sort of bow, done while the feet are turned sideways. It is difficult for most people to balance and control their movement while doing this, but steady practice led dancers to develop extremely strong abdominal and back muscles, which helped them in all their other moves.

On the *Grinnell College Web site,* Vaganova student Natalia Dudinskaya described the method in this manner:

"A single style, a single dance 'handwriting,' which manifests itself most clearly in the harmonious plasticity of movement and the expressiveness of the arms, in the responsive suppleness and at the same time the iron aplomb of the body, in the noble and natural placement of the head—these are the distinctive traits of the 'Vaganova School.' "

In addition to examining the placement of the dancer's feet, Vaganova paid detailed attention to the placement of arms during movement. She believed a dancer's arms should not simply decorate a movement, but should assist the dancer in high jumps and turns. This method is visible in the technique of Mikhail Baryshnikov, a 20th century dancer who is known for his seemingly impossible leaps high in the air, often with no apparent preparation. Baryshnikov used his arms to create lift in his body without flexing his legs to push off the ground, a trait common to all dancers trained in the Vaganova method.

Rather than relying on intuition and improvising during lessons, Vaganova rigorously planned each session beforehand. Thus, her lessons moved rapidly, taking dancers through difficult and interesting routines. In addition, she made sure to explain the reasons behind each exercise, so that students could not only do the necessary steps, but could also describe the correct form and explain the exercise's purpose. In addition, she often asked students to describe in writing why a step was not correctly performed, which helped them to understand what they were doing wrong and how to correct their faults. Vaganova also fostered creativity among her students by asking them to create new combinations of steps that they had learned in their lessons.

Volkova noted that as a teacher, Vaganova rarely praised a student in words or said that a move was well executed. Instead, she would calmly say, "You are now ready to do that step in public." She was dignified, calm, and quiet at all times, and her manner elicited a natural respect from her students.

Vaganova was head of the State Academic Theatre of Opera and Ballet—formerly the Mariinsky—from 1931 to 1937. She continued to draw on classical tradition, but also introduced innovative choreography, including a completely new version of *Swan Lake.* At the time, traditional ballet was being attacked as too conservative and creatively stagnant, and choreographers strived to work with significant historical themes, dramatic and well-developed plots, and artistically depicted yet realistic characters. Vaganova succeeded, but she did not abandon the classical tradition, maintaining that the new style should draw from the classical exercises, and that dance should flow from and reflect human emotion and behavior. The Russian school of dancing that grew from her influence emphasized rigorously planned classes, virtuoso technique, and conscious awareness of each movement. It also focused on core strength and movements that were complex, agile, diverse, broad, and fast. The arms and head, far from being mere decorative appendages, are integral parts of the movement of the body as a whole, and add to the body's stability, force, life, extension, and appearance.

"One of the Great Ballet Pedagogues of Our Time"

Vaganova's book *The Basic Principles of Classical Ballet* was not translated into English until 1946. Before then, Vaganova was little known in the West, but the book brought her and her methods new attention. In *Ballet Decade,* Vera Volkova wrote that the Russian dancer's book "established her in the Western world as one of the great ballet pedagogues of our time."

In her teaching positions from 1922 until her death, Vaganova trained a great number of talented and successful dancers, including Marina Semenova, Natalia Kamkova, Galina Ulanova, Olga Mungalova, Tatyana Vecheslova, Irina Kolpakova, Olga Lepeshinskaya, Olga Iorden, Feya Balabina, and Natalia Dudinskaya. She also had great influence on male dancers through her book, *Basic Principles of Classical Ballet,* which was published in 1934 and which became the standard for all Soviet ballet teaching.

Vaganova died in Leningrad, on November 5, 1951, but her legacy as a dancer and teacher has remained and continues to influence ballet today. As a teacher, Vaganova was kind and encouraging, but she also demanded precision, attention to detail, concentration, and hard work. She also encouraged her students to learn constantly. In honor of her achievements in ballet, the Leningrad State Ballet School was named after her.

Books

Bremser, Martha, editor, *International Dictionary of Ballet,* volume 2, St. James Press, 1993.
Cohen, Selma Jeanne, editor, *International Encyclopedia of Dance,* Volume 6, Oxford University Press, 1998.
Haskell, Arnold L., editor, *Ballet Decade,* Macmillan, 1951.
Slonimsky, Juri, *The Soviet Ballet,* Da Capo, 1970.

Online

"Agrippina Vaganova and the Vaganova Technique," *Russian Ballet School Web site,* http://www.russianballetschool.com/Agrippa.html (January 1, 2004).
"The Vaganova Method," *Grinnell College Web site,* http://web.Grinnell.edu/ (January 2, 2004). □

Wilma L. Vaught

U.S. Air Force Brigadier General Wilma L. Vaught (born 1930) is one of the most highly decorated women to serve in the United States military. Vaught has led the way for other women to succeed in a career with the U.S. armed forces, and through her efforts as president of the Women's Memorial Foundation board of directors, she has helped to create the Women in Military Service for America Memorial.

Born March 15, 1930, in Pontiac, Illinois, Vaught grew up in the small, rural town of Scotland, Illinois, the oldest of two daughters in a farming family. She grew up working hard, and dreamed of having a tough job that would allow her to be in charge. She attended the University of Illinois and graduated in 1952 with a bachelor of science degree.

Chose a Military Career

Although she quickly found a job in the corporate sector, Vaught found out just as quickly that, at the time, there was no possibility of any real managerial advancement for a woman. After reading a recruiting appeal for the U.S. Army that promised to give all recruits the opportunity to become a manager and supervisor, she decided to join the military, and chose the Air Force. As Vaught recalled to Allison Fabian in *Good Housekeeping,* "I'd always wanted a job that would led me be in charge, so as soon as I found out I could get a direct commission as a second lieutenant, I chose to join."

Vaught was commissioned as a second lieutenant in January of 1957, and completed the Officer's Basic Military Training Course at Lackland Air Force Base in Texas. After this, she spent three months studying at the Statistical Services Officers' Course at Sheppard Air Force Base, also in Texas. In September of 1957, she was assigned to the 805th Air Base Group at Barksdale Air Force Base, Louisiana, as chief of the Data Services branch. She also commanded the Women in the Air Force Squadron Section. From April of 1959 to April of 1963, Vaught served at Zaragoza Air Base in Spain as chief of the Management Analysis Division, 3974th Combat Support Group.

Vaught then returned to the United States and was assigned to the 306th Combat Support Group at McCoy Air Force Base in Florida. There, she served as chief of the Management Analysis Division for the 306th Bombardment Wing. During this period Vaught became the first woman to deploy with a Strategic Air Command operational unit when she served a temporary tour of duty as executive officer and chief of the Management Analysis Division, 4133rd Provisional Bombardment Wing at Andersen Air Force Base in Guam, during Operation ARC Light.

Served in Vietnam

Vaught studied business administration at the University of Alabama in Tuscaloosa from June of 1967 to September of 1968, earning her master's degree. In the following year, she served as a management analyst in the Office of the Deputy Chief of Staff, Comptroller, Military Assistance Command in Saigon, Vietnam. While in Saigon, she experienced rocket strikes that hit less than two blocks from her quarters. Vaught told Fabian that, during the rocket strikes, she did not feel fear. "I'd gone over with the idea that I wouldn't come back alive, and I accepted it."

At the same time she worked near the front lines, Vaught was also caught in a more subtle war zone; as a woman in the military, she was constantly dealing with antagonism, limitations, and doubts about her abilities that were imposed by her male colleagues. Although women's position in the U.S. military had improved through the previous few decades, it still had far to go. Vaught was outspoken about the controversial issue of women serving in the armed forces, telling Fabian, "Women are already in combat, so when people argue about whether they should be permitted to carry weapons, they're really asking whether the military should let women be fired at but not be able to fire back."

In 1967 Vaught and other military women were given new horizons of opportunity when President Lyndon B. Johnson signed into law a measure that allowed women to be promoted to the level of generals and admirals. The new law also removed the quotas that had previously been placed on women to limit the number of servicewomen who could reach other ranks; thus, it allowed women a whole range of new career opportunities in the military.

After completing her year-long tour of duty in Vietnam, Vaught was assigned to Headquarters Air Force Logistics Command at Wright-Patterson Air Force Base in Ohio, as chief of the Advanced Logistics Systems Plans and Management Group. She remained there until July of 1972, and the following month became the first female officer to attend the Industrial College of the Armed Forces.

From July through November of 1977 Vaught served in the Directorate of Management Analysis, Office of the Comptroller, Headquarters U.S. Air Force, in Washington, D.C. She was chief of the Cost Factors Branch and later served as chief of the Security Assistance Division. After this, she was assigned to Air Force Systems Command Headquarters, where she was director of programs and budget in the Office of the Deputy Chief of Staff, Comptroller. She became the deputy chief of staff in this office in March of 1980.

During her career, Vaught also served as chair of NATO's Women in the Allied Forces Committee and was the senior woman military representative to the Secretary of Defense's Advisory Committee on Women in the Service.

Became a Brigadier General

On September 8, 1980, Vaught became the first woman in the comptroller field to become a brigadier general; her father attended the ceremony and pinned the star on her shoulder. In 1982 she was appointed commander of the U.S. Military Entrance Processing Command headquartered at Great Lakes, Illinois.

Vaught retired in 1985, one of only three female generals in the U.S. Air Force and one of seven female generals in the U.S. Armed Forces. During her career she received numerous military honors, including the Defense and Air Force Distinguished Service Medals, the Air Force Legion of Merit, the Bronze Star, and the Vietnam Service Award with four stars. In addition, she was the first woman to command a unit that received the Joint Meritorious Unit Award. Vaught was also the only woman in history ever to serve as president of the board of directors of the Pentagon Federal Credit Union, a position she held from April of 1976 to July of 1982. In 2000 she was inducted into the National Women's Hall of Fame.

Spearheaded Women's Memorial Project

After retiring, Vaught became president of the Women's Memorial Foundation board of directors, and in this position began working on a new project: the establishment of a memorial to honor women in U.S. military service. At the time, many observers doubted that she would be able to raise enough money for the project. However, as Ann Darr wrote in *U.S. News and World Report*, "General Vaught is a determined woman and she vowed to put the memorial in place in time for the remaining WWII veterans to be alive to see it."

The foundation raised over $20 million for the memorial, which was designed and built largely by women. One of its notable features is a computer database that includes names, photographs, biographical information, and career histories and awards of women veterans. Visitors can enter a name into a computer terminal and find information on the military career of a friend, loved one, or historical figure. Although there are about 1.8 military women whose careers could be recorded in the memorial, only a small fraction of them have been entered so far, as the register is open not only to those who have completed their careers, but also to those who are currently serving in the military. Because the foundation itself does not have access to military records, the information must be collected and entered by volunteers. The foundation runs a Web site, where women can register their careers, and also features an "In Search Of" page that holds listings from people looking for information on women veterans they would like to reconnect with. Vaught noted on the organization's Web site that, unfortunately, many women veterans mistakenly believe they are not important enough to be included in the registry: "Most people don't have any idea how many women served in the military," she noted, adding that "Many women have not understood the importance of what they did in the military service until they see something that makes them realize that what they did was really significant."

In addition to creating the memorial, the foundation also created the Margaret Chase Smith Leadership Award, which is given each year to women who open opportunities for women in the American military. The award was created in honor of Margaret Chase Smith, a senator from Maine who introduced legislation that allowed women to participate equally with men in military service.

On October 16, 1997, the Women in Military Service for America Memorial, which now stands at the main gate to the Arlington National Cemetery, was dedicated; the ceremony was attended by generations of women veterans and their supporters. A reporter for the U.S. Army's *Voice* online wrote, "The Women's Memorial stands as a place where the American people and visitors from around the world can learn of the courage and bravery of tens of thousands of women who, like Wilma Vaught, have pioneered the future."

Periodicals

Christian Science Monitor, October 3, 2000.
Good Housekeeping, October 1, 1997.
U.S. News and World Report, November 17, 1997.

Online

"Biography of a Pioneering Woman," *Voice Online,* http://w4 .pica.army.mil/voice2003/030314/4_Comment.html (January 1, 2004).

"Brigadier General Wilma L. Vaught," *Air Force Web site,* http://www.af.mil/bios/bio_7463.shtml (January 1, 2004).

National Women's History Project Web site, http://www.nwhp .org/tlp/biographies/vaught/vaught-bio.html (January 1, 2004).

"Wilma Vaught," *National Women's Hall of Fame,* http://www .greatwomen.org/women.php?action = viewone&id = 160 (June 2, 2004).

Women in Military Service for America Memorial Foundation Web site, http://www.womensmemorial.org/ (December 5, 2003). □

José Garcia Villa

Although José Garcia Villa (1914–1997) is largely known as a Filipino poet, he spent 67 years of his life in the United States. His work has been praised as innovative and talented. A contributor to the ***Dictionary of Oriental Literature*** **observed of Villa that "His craftsmanship and skill remains unchallenged among Filipino poets."**

Born in Manila, Philippines, on August 5, 1914, Villa was the son of Simeon Villa, a doctor who was Army chief-of-staff during the Philippine revolution against Spain, as well as personal physician to revolutionary leader Emilio Aguinaldo; his mother was Guia Garcia, a wealthy landowner. Villa attended the University of the Philippines in 1929. He first studied medicine, and then switched to law, but he was always interested in writing, and as a law student he wrote short stories and poetry. Some of his writing, notably a series of erotic verse titled "Man Poems," was so controversial that the authorities at the University of the Philippines expelled him. In that same year, however, Villa won a prize from the *Philippines Free Press* for the best short story of the year.

Immigrated to United States

Villa moved to the United States in 1930, seeking a more congenial and liberal literary scene. Although he remained a Philippine citizen, he spent the rest of his life in the United States, only rarely returning to his home country. He enrolled in the University of New Mexico, earning a B.A. degree in 1933. While at the University of New Mexico, he founded a literary magazine, titled *Clay,* which published the work of several young American writers who later became famous. Villa attended Columbia University for graduate study in 1942.

Villa began writing short stories while he was still an undergraduate at the University of New Mexico. He published these and his poems in American literary magazines to almost immediate praise. He received far more publicity than his seemingly obscure origins would bring, largely

because of the work of critic Edward J. O'Brien, who saw in Villa an incredible talent. In 1932 O'Brien dedicated his edited collection *Best American Short Stories of 1932* to Villa. Villa also won the Shelley Memorial and Rockefeller awards, received a Guggenheim fellowship for writing, and was given membership in the American Academy of Arts and Letters. Although he was a finalist for a Pulitzer Prize, he did not win, as his work was considered too experimental.

O'Brien was so successful at bringing literary attention to Villa that when a collection of Villa's stories, *Footnote to Youth,* was published in 1933, a reviewer in the *New York Times* was already familiar with Villa's life and reputation. According to Timothy Yu in an article on the *Meritage Press Web site,* the *New York Times* reviewer wrote that "For at least two years the name of Jose Garcia Villa has been familiar to the devotees of the experimental short story. . . . They knew, too, that he was an extremely youthful Filipino who had somehow acquired the ability to write a remarkable English prose and who had come to America as a student in the summer of 1930." This comment points out two streams of commentary on Villa's work that would persist throughout his career: some critics saw him simply as a genius, while others focused on his identity as a speaker, and writer, of English as a second language. This second group of reviewers often seemed surprised that a Filipino could learn to write so well in English, revealing their own prejudices.

Switched from Short Stories to Poetry

After publishing *Footnote,* Villa abandoned short-story writing and turned all his attention to poetry. Between 1933 and 1942 he published very little. Yu speculated that he made the switch from short stories to poetry because most fiction writers are judged by their presentation of the cultures and social settings they are familiar with in their own lives. If Villa had continued to write fiction, he would have been constrained by these expectations to write about the Philippines and, as Yu wrote, "Any attempt by Villa to present 'American' content would likely . . . have been dismissed out of hand. By turning to poetry, he was able to turn his foreignness into an asset, a brand of exoticism that appealed to the orientalist strain in American modernism while still allowing Villa to take his place among the 'great' American writers." Yu noted that another critic, Salvador P. Lopez, had a simpler explanation for Villa's switch from one genre to another: "He is simply a better poet than he is a prose writer." Lopez also implied that "There is simply less competition in the field of poetry, as there may be fewer accomplished Filipino poets writing in English."

In 1942 Villa's first book of poetry to be published in the United States was released. *Have Come, Am Here* introduces a new rhyming scheme, which Villa called "reversed consonance." Babette Deutsch wrote in the *New Republic* that the collection reveals Villa's concern for "ultimate things, the self and the universe. He is also on visiting terms with the world. He is more interested in himself than in the universe, and he greets the world with but a decent urbanity." She noted that, although his range is somewhat narrow, Villa "soars high and plunges deep." British poet

Edith Sitwell wrote in her preface to Villa's later book, *Selected Poems and New,* that when she read *Have Come, Am Here* she experienced "a shock." She described one poem in the collection, "Number 57," as "a strange poem of ineffable beauty, springing straight from the depths of Being. I hold that this is one of the most wonderful short poems of our time, and reading it I knew that I was seeing for the first time the work of a poet with a great, even an astonishing, and perfectly original gift."

Invented "Comma Poems"

In his *Volume Two,* Villa presents a second form of his devise, which he dubs "comma poems." He writes in the preface to the collection, "The commas are an integral and essential part of the medium: regulating the poem's verbal density and time movement: enabling each word to attain a fuller tonal value, and the line movement to become more measures." In these poems, Villa inserts a comma after nearly every word. Some critics were irritated by this technique, viewing it as a gimmick. Leonard Casper wrote in *New Writings from the Philippines* that Villa's use of commas "is as demonstrably malfunctional as a dragging foot" and that ten years later, Villa "still uses the 'commas' with inadequate understanding and skill."

However, Villa's structural approach had many supporters, including Sitwell, who wrote in *The American Genius,* "This poetry springs with a wild force, straight from the poet's being, from his blood, from his spirit, as a fire breaks from wood, or as a flower grows from its soil." Villa's work was also praised by other well-regarded poets, including Marianne Moore, Mark van Doren, Horace Gregory, and Richard Eberhart.

In 1946 Villa married Rosemarie Lamb; they had two sons, Randall and Lance, before divorcing ten years later. He worked as an associate editor at New Directions Publishing in New York from 1949 to 1951 and was director of the poetry workshop at City College of the City University of New York from 1952 to 1960; from 1964 to 1973, he lectured at the New School for Social Research in New York City. Villa also served as cultural attaché to the Philippine Mission to the United Nations from 1952 to 1963, and beginning in 1968, he was advisor on cultural affairs to the president of the Philippines.

"The Anchored Angel," first published in the *Times Literary Supplement* in 1957, serves as the foundation of a collection of about 80 of Villa's "comma poems" published in 2000 as *The Anchored Angel: Selected Writings of José Garcia Villa.* The poem considers the theme of man wrestling with the divine, a recurring interest of Villa's. The commas following each word in the work are intended to "anchor" the reader and focus attention on each word in an almost meditative way. According to Luis Francia in *Asia Week* online, this poem was hailed as Villa's "greatest work."

Turned to Teaching

In the late 1950s Villa decided to stop publishing his poetry, preferring silence to self-repetition, according to Francia. The critic explained that Villa had observed that many other notable poets became repetitious as they achieved fame, and he wanted to avoid that pitfall. After leaving the literary scene, Villa devoted his energies to his teaching in New York. He also held workshops at his apartment, where he critiqued students' poems, repeatedly stating, according to Francia, that real poetry is "written with words, not ideas." He opposed narrative poetry and told his students not to read fiction, so that their poems would not be contaminated by narrative elements.

Villa was highly regarded in his home country, and writers in the Philippines competed to be included in the anthologies of poetry in English that Villa edited. These anthologies were published under the pen name Doveglion, a combination of dove, eagle, and lion.

Villa suffered from ill health as he aged, and in an attempt to hide his condition he saw fewer and fewer visitors, eventually restricting contact with the outside world to a tight circle of students and friends. Discovered unconscious in his New York City apartment in early February of 1997, he was taken to a hospital where he died on February 7, 1997, from complications of pneumonia and stroke. Two years later, *The Anchored Angel* was published and was praised by *Booklist* reviewer Ray Olson, who called Villa's work "a most welcome rediscovery." In *Publishers Weekly,* a reviewer commented that the poems show that Villa was influenced by poets "as diverse as Hopkins, Dickinson, Blake and Cummings."

Villa was instrumental in founding modern writing in English within his native Philippines. As Francia explained in *Asia Week,* "In a world of English-language poetry dominated by British and Americans, Villa stood out for the ascetic brilliance of his poetry and for his national origin." And according to Yu, the Filipino literary critic Salvador P. Lopez described Villa as "the one Filipino writer today who it would be futile to deride and impossible to ignore . . . the pace-setter for an entire generation of young writers, the mentor laying down the law for the whole tribe, the patron-saint of a cult of rebellious moderns."

Books

Casper, Leonard, *New Writings from the Philippines: A Critique and Anthology,* Syracuse University Press, 1966.
Contemporary Authors New Revisions, Volume 12, Gale, 1984.
Encyclopedia of World Literature, St. James Press, 1999.
Prusek, Jaroslav, editor, *Dictionary of Oriental Literature,* Volume II: *South and South East Asia,* Basic Books, 1974.
Sitwell, Edith, *The American Genius,* Lehmann, 1951.
Villa, José Garcia, *Selected Poems and New,* Obolensky, 1958.
———— *Volume Two,* New Directions, 1949.

Periodicals

Booklist, December 1, 1999.
New Republic, October 9, 1942.
Publishers Weekly, February 7, 2000.

Online

"Asian/American Modernisms: José Garcia Villa's Transnational Politics," *Meritage Press Web Site,* http://www.meritagepress.com/yu.htm (January 2, 2004).

"Death Comes to Doveglion," *Asia Week,* http://www.asiaweek
.com/asiaweek/97/0228/feat5.html (January 2, 2004).
"Pinoylit: José Garcia Villa," *Pinoylit,* http://pinoylit.hypermart
.net/filipinowriters/garvilla.htm (January 2, 2004). □

Carlos Raúl Villanueva

**Venezuelan Carlos Raúl Villaneuva (1900–1975)
was the most influential Latin American architect
and community designer of the twentieth century.
He worked in Venezuela for over four decades, and
his concepts, designs, and plans combined European
modernism and the traditions of his native Venezuela to create a unique style that has had wide influence across Latin America and elsewhere. More than
any other architect, he was instrumental in shaping
the development of modern architecture in Venezuela.**

Villanueva was born on May 30, 1900, in Croydon,
Surrey, England. His father was a member of the
Venezuelan diplomatic corps there and also wrote
books on South American history. Villanueva's mother was
French. Although Villanueva was born in England, his nationality was Venezuelan, and he lived most of his life in
that country. His maternal connection to France did, however, have a great influence on his life and work.

Incorporated Traditional and Modern
Forms

Villanueva studied at the Lycee Condorcet in Paris,
France and then received a degree in architecture from the
École des Beaux-Arts in Paris. Thus, he received a strong
grounding in European architectural traditions, particularly
eclecticism. He moved to Caracas, Venezuela in 1928,
where he opened his own office. Although he appreciated
the traditional Venezuelan architecture, which was derived
from colonial Spanish styles, he wanted to renew this tradition and imbue it with a modern flavor. Villanueva served as
architect to the Venezuelan Ministry of Public Works from
1929 to 1939; during this period, he incorporated traditional Spanish/Andalusian designs into his own work,
adapting it to more modern forms and materials, and producing his own unique style.

His earliest work, the Bullring at Maracay, built in
1931, showed that Villanueva was influenced by the work
of other architects, such as Auguste Perret. The bullring was
the first ever built to a contemporary design, and although it
paid homage to historical continuity, it used new materials
and new design elements. One of these new elements was
Villanueva's use of thin, recessed panels between heavy,
load-bearing piers; it was the first time this technique was
used in Latin America. As a writer for the *Encyclopedia of
Modern Architecture* noted, Villanueva "came to a deep
understanding of the new ways of thought in architecture

and devoted himself with a missionary ardor to the spread of
modern architecture in his own land."

In 1933, Villanueva married Margot Arismendi, and
they later had four children: Francisco Raúl, Jose Carlos,
Pavlona, and Carlos Raúl.

In 1935 Villanueva designed the Museo de Los Caobos
in Caracas, Venezuela. The building is notable for its Doric
peristyle, which is very precisely detailed, as well as its
symmetrical arrangement around an open garden courtyard. His use in this building of sculptural elements that are
enhanced by the strong light and deep shadows of the
tropical sun would later become a recurring feature of his
designs. In 1927, he designed the Venezuelan Pavilion at
the International Exposition in Paris, and this building won
first prize for the exposition. Villanueva also won many
other awards and honors during the first ten years of his
career, including a knighthood in the French Legion of
Honor.

Broke from Tradition and Moved to a
Modern Style

Instead of relying on forms that won him these awards,
Villanueva continued to experiment, and introduced new
designs, materials, and ways to use them to Venezuelan and
South American architecture. In 1939, he abandoned tradition entirely when he designed an elementary school, the
Escuela Gran Colombia in Caracas, Venezuela. This was the
first of his buildings without any historical influences; it also
used reinforced concrete, which was the time was considered a new and experimental material by Venezuelan build-
ers and contractors. The building's style was influenced by
Cubism, but was still symmetrical; Villanueva's innovative
design and materials opened the door for other creative
architects who followed him and who also broke from
traditional forms.

After studying at the Institute d'Urbanism of the University of Paris, Villanueva returned to Venezuela in 1940 and
turned his talents to helping with two problems in his country that had been caused by its rapid development and
population growth: an acute housing shortage and extremely poor living conditions for many of its people. Caracas, for example, grew from 163,000 inhabitants in 1936 to
359,000 in 1941, 718,000 in 1951, and by 1964, had
1,300,000 inhabitants; in addition, it was located in a tight
valley, making physical expansion difficult and crowding
worse. Villanueva soon took a position as chief architect
and advisor at the Worker's Bank of Venezuela. The
Worker's Bank, or Banco Obero, was created with the goal
of solving the difficult housing and living conditions that
laborers experienced; it was responsible for launching the
careers of many promising Venezuelan architects, including
Villanueva. For his project, Villanueva worked to redevelop
the worst slum of Caracas, known as El Silencio; it was the
first time any Latin American government had undertaken
such a program. Villanueva's designs provided some of the
best housing in Latin America, as he incorporated cross-
ventilation and glare protection against the strong tropical
sun, as well as noise insulation in each apartment. Every

apartment also had a balcony, which allowed residents to see the sky.

After completing his work in El Silencio, Villanueva worked on a housing project in Maracaibo, Venezuela. For this project, he dropped a previous idea of creating a miniature villa, and emphasized gathering places such as churches, schools, and other gathering places. He also added walkways and gardens to improve the quality of the neighborhood. In another development in Caracas, he sited houses on a hillside so that they formed visually pleasing arrangements; at the same time, they could be naturally ventilated by the cool breezes blowing down the hills. In his "Dos de Diciembre" housing project, Villanueva, in collaboration with José Manuel Mijares, José Hoffman, and Carlos Branco, designed 2,366 houses for 12,744 people. In the "El Paraiso" project, he designed a smaller project, with duplex units in a four-story and a 16-story building. Typically, he made sure to provide social areas and gathering spaces to humanize the communities.

Designed University Buildings

In the 1940s, Villanueva designed the first buildings for the Central University of Venezuela, where he began serving as a founding professor of architecture in 1944. Throughout his career, he continued to design buildings for the university, and characteristically emphasized community design. His walkways and buildings contained murals and sculptures that Villanueva incorporated into the design; the most notable of these is a sculpture by Alexander Calder in the university's auditorium. In 1957, he designed the university's School of Architecture; for his work, he received an honorary doctorate from the university in 1961. The building was nine stories high and quite imposing, and according to Sibyl Moholy-Nagy in *Carlos Raúl Villanueva and the Architecture of Venezuela*, it "imposes on the student the fearful decision to come to terms with the future he/she has chosen."

At this stage in his career, Villanueva's style had these notable characteristics: a dynamism and spontaneity in structural design; a broad assimilation of the work and ideas of many painters and sculptors; a daring use of color; and an ability to work with very large spaces and structures.

Villanueva designed other well-known buildings for the university, including the Olympic Stadium (1950–51), which is notable for its daring use of cantilevered marquees, concrete shell, and exposed ribs. A *Macmillan Encyclopedia of Architecture* contributor wrote, "With breathtaking bravura, the cast concrete form. . . sweeps upward to establish the seating area for 30,000 people and then doubles back dramatically upon itself to soar anew in a daring cantilevered span." Villanueva also designed the Medical Center, Auditorium, and Covered Plaza Cubierta (Covered Plaza and Aula Magna). According to a writer in the *Encyclopedia of Modern Architecture*, the Aula Magna is "one of the most beautiful assembly rooms in the world." It is noted for its white, curved ceiling, which serves as a backdrop for several floating panels designed by artist Alexander Calder; R. Newman, an acoustics specialist, also col-

laborated on the project. According to the *Macmillan Encyclopedia of Architecture* contributor, the artistic and acoustic properties of the building are unified: "Alexander Calder's polychromed "clouds," suspended at varying levels from the ceiling, simultaneously distribute sound evenly throughout the acoustically meticulous auditorium and visually humanize the space."

The building's plain exterior contrasts with and emphasizes the airy openness of the Plaza Cubierto, which is a large, partially enclosed foyer. The Plaza Cubiert features work by such modern artists as Arp, Léger, Vasarely, and others. In all of Villanueva's university buildings, he was careful to identify a theme specific to that building's use, and the theme is carried throughout the building's concrete panels and colored mosaics.

He also designed the Museo de Bellas Artes in Caracas. For this last building he was awarded the Venezuelan National Architecture Prize in 1963. His main interest remained in designing buildings for community development and urban planning. He served as president of the Venezuelan National Board of Historic and Artistic Protection and Conservation and was founder and director of the Venezuelan National Planning Commission. He continued to work until his death in Caracas, Venezuela on August 16, 1975.

In *Carlos Raúl Villanueva and the Architecture of Venezuela*, Sibyl Moholy-Nagy wrote that when Villanueva was asked, "How do you define the architect?" Villanueva replied, "The architect is a highly complex and contradictory personality. The artistic value of his work must be beyond doubt." However, he added, architecture is subject to constraints that don't exist in other forms of art: "The dependence on external, uncontrollable circumstances (client, budget, society, structure, materials) is immeasurably stronger and more coercive than in any other art. Evidently, the architect has a more difficult problem to preserve his freedom of creativity."

Villanueva also spoke of his view of the future of architecture: "The move toward industrialization in building construction will ultimately eliminate hand labor. We shall build with machines. . . . This total industrialization of the building process . . . will raise the level of creative architectural imagination to a global and urban level." He concluded, "Some day, along this path, the entire planet will be free of environmental alienation because the unique talent of the artist-intellectual will make environment again identical with architecture."

Books

Almanac of Famous People, 8th edition, Gale Group, 2003.
Dictionary of Hispanic Biography, Gale Research, 1996.
International Dictionary of Architects and Architecture, St. James Press, 1993.
Moholy-Nagy, Sibyl, *Carlos Raúl Villanueva and the Architecture of Venezuela*, Praeger, 1964.
Pehnt, Wolfgang, editor, *Encyclopedia of Modern Architecture*, Harry N. Abrams, 1964.
Placzek, Adolf K., editor, *Macmillan Encyclopedia of Architecture*, volume 4, Free Press, 1984. □

W

Grete Waitz

Norwegian-born distance runner Grete Waitz (born 1953) has excelled in all forms of running, from track and field to middle-distance road racing to the marathon. She caught the eye of many in the sport in 1975, when she set a new world record for the 3,000 meters, and she caught the imagination of a nation when she won nine New York City Marathons. Waitz is also an Olympic-class runner, having earned a silver medal in the marathon event at the 1984 Olympic Games held in Los Angeles, California.

One of the most versatile female runners of the twentieth century, Norwegian-born Grete Waitz captured two world records in the 3,000 meter, as well as records in the 8-kilometer, 10-kilometer, and 15-kilometer distances and the longer 10-mile, and marathon high-endurance runs. Beginning her career as a track runner, Waitz retired from that specialty in 1978 only to begin a second career as a world-class distance runner following her record-breaking win at the New York Marathon.

The first daughter and youngest of three children born to pharmacist John Andersen and wife Reidun, Grete Andersen was born on October 1, 1953. Waitz grew up in suburban Oslo, Norway. Although she exhibited her athletic abilities at a young age with handball and gymnastics, her older brothers' sports training took precedence, creating a situation wherein young Waitz had to excel competitively in order to be recognized. Inspired by the life of U.S. sprinter Wilma Rudolph, who overcame juvenile polio to earn a bronze medal at the 1956 Olympics, the competitive Waitz began running as a way to keep up with her older brothers. She soon fell in love with the sport for its own sake, and by age eleven had been recruited for a local track team coached by Olympic javelin champion Terje Pedersen. As a teen she got up early in the morning to get in a speedwork session before leaving for school, but realized that her strength lay more in endurance than speed. Developing muscular strength, pacing, and quick foot turnover, she competed in local and regional events, winning the 16-year-old runner national junior titles in the 400 and 800 meters. A year later she set the European junior record in the 1,500 meter with a time of 4:17. This win confirmed Waitz's belief that her future lay in mastering the distance run.

Expanded Opportunities for Women Runners

Her performance in national competition caused Waitz's parents to finally acknowledge their daughter's talent, and they began to support her career as an athlete. After qualifying, she competed in Munich's 1972 Olympics in the 1,500 meter, one of the first women allowed to compete in this event—up until 1960 when the women's 800-meter race was reinstated, women had been barred from any distance longer than 200 meters after two women fainted at the finish line during the 1928 Olympic games. Although she did not place in the event, she received encouragement from her fellow Olympic athletes, and realized that natural talent was not enough; she needed to begin more thorough training. Wisely, she came home to Oslo and began training as a high school physical education teacher; she also started a grueling training regime that included a restricted diet and a running schedule that found her logging an average of 75 miles each week on the track and on the road.

In 1974, four years after winning the Norwegian nationals, Waitz competed in the 1,500 meter at the European championships, taking home the bronze medal in that event. In 1975 she extended her race distance and established a new world record in the 3,000 meter with a time of 8:46.6. During her second Olympic try, in Montreal in 1976, Waitz was eliminated in the 1,500-meter semifinals. In 1977 she won a gold medal in the 3,000 meter at the first World Cup meet, shattering her own record and running a career best of 8:31:75. By the time she was 25, Waitz was the oldest woman on the Norwegian track team, and good naturedly bore up under the nickname ''Grandma.''

A strong runner, Waitz eventually became inhibited by the restrictions of the track. She gradually moved to longer distances on roads and unpaved trails, and won world cross-country titles five times, including in 1978, 1979, 1981, and 1983. Having graduated from teacher's college and now married to former accountant Jack Waitz, Grete balanced her athletic career with a full-time job teaching at Oslo's Bjölsen School. When not teaching, she channeled much of her free time into running the longer distances—up to 13 miles at a time—required of the cross-country runner, while also cross training and following the strict nutritional regimen demanded of an endurance athlete.

Waitz's talent as a runner—her world records of 30:59:8 in the 10,000 meter and 48:01 for the 15,000 meter—while not widely reported in the U.S. press, caught the attention of Fred Lebow, president of the New York Road Runners Club and director of the world-famous New York

City Marathon since its inception in 1970. The New York Marathon, which started as a local race of 55 runners around Central Park, had grown in only a few years into a world-class event with a field of 25,000 that attracted top distance-runners from around the world to its course through the city's five boroughs. In 1978 Lebow contacted Waitz, asking her to come to the United States and race in his November marathon as part of a select group of elite, world-class athletes invited to race each year.

At the urging of her husband, Jack, Grete took Lebow up on his offer, even though she had never run—let alone raced—such a long distance before. What she did not realize, as she later told Peter Gambaccini of *Runner's World Online,* was that Lebow never for a moment believed that Waitz would finish the race. ''He was enthusiastic about having me, but not because he thought I could do a good marathon,'' she explained of the man who would become her distance-running mentor and close friend. ''He thought that with my background as a world class track runner, I would be a good pacesetter for the women's field and lend some international flavor to it, coming from Norway. He thought I'd set a good pace for the women so they could run a fast time, and I would probably drop out.'' On a chilly day in late October, wearing bib number 1173, she followed the course through New York's five boroughs, took the lead at the 18-mile mark, and won the marathon. Completing the first 13.1 miles in one hour 18 minutes, Waitz ran a ''negative split''—she ran faster during the second half of the race—and broke the world record for the women's 26.2-mile event by two minutes with a time of 2:32:30. She also changed the course of her future.

Ironically, Waitz had entered the New York Marathon with the idea of retiring as a professional runner. During the grueling race, as the hours of pounding on New York's unforgiving pavements, exhaustion, and dehydration began to take their toll, by mile 20 she vowed never to run such a long distance again. Within months of her winning finish, however, she found herself embarking on a whole new running career, coached by the tireless Lebow. Leaving her position as a teacher and increasing her weekly training to upwards of 100 miles, running in the New York City Marathon became almost an annual event for Waitz; she went on to win eight more races during the decade that followed—in 1979, 1980, 1982, 1983, 1984, 1985, 1986 and 1988—although she was forced out of the 1981 race due to shin splints. She also continued to challenge the course record, and in 1979 and 1980 upped the world record she had set for the marathon distance in 1978—finishing 104th overall in 1979 with a time of 2:27:33, and in 1980, with a time of 2:25:41, becoming the first woman to complete the 26.2-mile marathon distance in under two and a half hours. Her victories were not hers alone, however; Waitz's performance in 1979 prompted an editorial in the *New York Times* that challenged races around the world to accept women in competition.

In addition to competing in the marathon distance in New York City, Waitz entered the field in 19 other marathons around the world, winning in 13 of these distance events between 1978 and 1988. She tied the world record of

2:25:29 in the London marathon in 1983, a banner year for the Norwegian-born athlete. Competing in the inaugural Women's World Championship Marathon held that same year in Helsinki, Waitz topped the all-female field by three minutes to win the gold, then went on to win the New York Marathon with 2:27:00. Setting a personal record of 2 hours 24 minutes 54 seconds at the London Marathon in 1986, Waitz won her final New York marathon in 1988 with a finish time of 2:28:07.

Encouraged by her triumphant performances in New York, Waitz hoped to qualify for her second Olympic competition in 1980. Unfortunately, that year Norway followed the lead of the United States in boycotting the Moscow Olympic Games. The Union of Soviet Specialist Republics (USSR) had invaded Afghanistan only the year before, and Norway joined several other nations in supporting U.S. President Jimmy Carter's forced withdrawal of all U.S. Olympic teams from the games. Cold War politics may have forced Waitz to put her Olympic dreams on hold, but she rallied and went on to win the international women's cross-country championships for the third year in a row, as well as set several other world records. Four years later, in 1984, she flew to Los Angeles to compete in the first women's marathon offered as part of the historic 1984 Olympics. Excited by the addition of woman's 3,000 meter and marathon distance events to the track portion of the games, Waitz was favored to win the gold based on her stellar performance the previous year at the world marathon championships. However, during the marathon run she was bested by U.S. runner and good friend Joan Benoit, who put in an extraordinary effort to win the gold; Waitz captured the silver medal for Norway.

Beyond Retirement

Although Waitz officially retired in 1991 after suffering a number of running-related injuries, like many distance runners the sport of running remained an important part of her life. Reducing her daily mileage to under ten miles and her weekly mileage to between 35 to 40 miles, she began to invest more time in cross training activities, such as joining her husband, Jack, in Nordic skiing, walking, and biking throughout Germany, Austria, and elsewhere in Europe.

Recognizing early in her career her potential as a role model for others, in 1986 Waitz coauthored the book *World Class,* in which she recounts her own rise in the sport and also provides women of all abilities with training, motivation, and racing advice. She also coauthored the book *On the Run: Exercise and Fitness for Busy People.* Beginning shortly after retirement, she also took on the role of fitness ambassador to women through her participation in the Avon Running Global Women's Circuit, held in major U.S. cities throughout the 1990s. Together with fellow veteran runner Kathrine Switzer—who in 1967, as the genderless K. V. Switzer, became the first registered woman to run the Boston Marathon, then closed to women—Waitz traveled to various races to meet, run, and encourage women of all levels—from walkers to beginners and above—along a 10-K course. She also became an official spokeswoman for Adidas, a running shoe and apparel manufacturer. She con-

tinued to maintain a presence in distance competition, running for five and a half hours alongside former coach Fred Lebow as he completed the New York Marathon course in 1992 while undergoing treatment for the brain cancer that would ultimately take his life.

In 1983, inspired by an all-woman 10-K race she had run in New York City and the encouragement of Lebow, Waitz inaugurated the Grete Waitz Run, a five-kilometer women's-only race through the streets of her hometown of Oslo. Over 3,000 runners turned out for the first race; by 1993 the field had expanded to 40,000, many of whom were inspired to begin running by Waitz. Waitz was honored for her many other contributions to distance running in the United States by the National Distance Running Hall of Fame, which inducted her as its first foreign member. In 1991 *Runner's World* magazine echoed that honor, naming Waitz as female runner of the quarter century. As Peter Gambaccini noted in that magazine, "almost single-handedly" Waitz established "the standard for women's distance running as the sport began to proliferate on American roads."

A modest, down-to-earth woman, Waitz has always been somewhat uncomfortable with her celebrity status. "To suddenly be a hero on a world basis was hard for me to understand," she admitted to *Runner's World* in reflecting on her career. "God gave me a gift. I got the chance to use it. . . . I didn't think I deserved what people were saying. My talent is just more visible than theirs." Continuing her role as ambassador for women's running, Waitz and her husband continue to divide their time between in Oslo and their home in Florida. Continuing her support of personal health and fitness, she donates her time to CARE International and the International Special Olympics. She has also remained active in the New York Marathon organization by acting as chairperson of the group's Women's Foundation, which encouraged running among inner city children. In November of 2003, she once again took to the streets of New York in celebration of the 25th anniversary of her historic win, however this time she was not on foot. As grand marshal, she rode in the woman's lead vehicle, in her accustomed spot at the head of the pack.

Books

Drinkwater, Barbara L., *Female Endurance Athletes,* Human Kinetics, 1986.
Great Women in Sports, Visible Ink Press, 1996.
Waitz, Grete, with Gloria Averbuch, *World Class,* Warner Books, 1986.

Periodicals

New York Times, October 22, 1979.
Runner's World, December, 1991.
Sports Illustrated, October 22, 1979.
Women's Sports, January 1979, March 1980, January 1981.

Online

Amazon.com, http://www.amazon.com/ (June 9, 2004).
DistanceRunning.com, http://www.distancerunning.com/inductees/2000/waitz.html (June 9, 2004).

Runner's World Online, http://www.runnersworld.com/home/
0,1300,1-0-0-2031,00.html (June 9, 2004). □

Florence Sophie Wald

**Florence Wald (born 1917) is credited with starting
the hospice movement in the United States. Wald's
model for hospice care has served as the basis for the
treatment of dying patients and their families.**

Nurse and Yale Dean

Florence Wald was born Florence Sophie Schorske on
April 19, 1917, in New York City. Her parents were
Theodore Alexander Schorske and Gertrude Goldschmidt Schorske. Wald had an older sibling, but little else
is known about her childhood. Wald was raised and educated in Scarsdale, New York, and graduated from Mt. Holyoke College in 1938. She received a master's degree in
nursing from Yale University in 1941.

Wald's first nursing job was as a staff nurse at the
Children's Hospital in Boston in 1941 and 1942. During the
next 15 years, she worked at various nursing jobs in New
York. She worked at the Henry Street Visiting Nurse Service
and held research positions at the cornea research laboratory of the New York City Eye Bank and in the Surgical
Metabolism Unit of the College of Physicians and Surgeons.
During the final stages of World War II, Wald served in the
nursing branch of the Women's Army Corps.

Wald began teaching at Rutgers University School of
Nursing in New Jersey in 1955. In 1957, she became assistant professor of psychiatric nursing at Yale University
School of Nursing. A year later, she was named acting dean
of the nursing school and in 1959 she became Yale's permanent dean. She held the position until 1967. Wald married
Henry Wald, a health facility planner, in 1959. The couple
had two children: Joel David Wald and Shari Johanna Wald.

During Wald's tenure as dean, she initiated many
changes in the nursing curriculum, guiding the program to a
more scholarly approach. One of her concerns when developing the new curriculum was the involvement of the patient, his or her family, and nurses in the patient's care.
Normally in this era, doctors made all medical decisions
and their authority was not questioned.

Met English Hospice Advocate

In 1963, Wald met Dr. Cicely Saunders, an English
physician who was a pioneer in the field of hospice. Saunders, who had been trained as a nurse and physician, visited
the United States to share her ideas about hospice care.
Saunders had worked for two years in clinical trials of
palliative care in St. Joseph's Hospice in London before
establishing her own hospice facility, St. Christopher's, in
London.

Saunders told Yale medical students about her approach to treating terminally ill cancer patients. She advocated easing pain and suffering in the final stages of life so
the patients and their families could concentrate on their
relationships and prepare for death. Saunders's goal was for
patients to discover what they wanted, not yield to doctors'
decisions to prolong life as long as possible. Pain-relieving
drugs were an essential part of hospice care.

Wald described her reaction to Saunders in the essay
"The Emergence of Hospice Care in the United States" in
the book *Facing Death: Where Culture, Religion, and Medicine Meet.* She wrote, "She made an indelible impression
on me, for until then I had thought nurses were the only
people troubled by how a terminal illness was treated. In the
Yale University Nursing School, where I was dean, faculty
and students had found themselves at cross purposes with
doctors when patients asked questions about their illness."

Wald explained that doctors evaded questions about
treatments that failed and rebuffed nurses who tried to intervene on behalf of patients. Nurses were beginning to realize
the importance of patients expressing their thoughts and
feelings about treatment and getting involved in decision-
making. But in the male-dominated medical profession,
nurses could do little more than stand by as patients suffered
through never-ending treatments that did not work.

As dean of the nursing school, Wald sought to revamp
nursing education to focus on patients and their families and
involve them in their medical care. Fortunately, the time
was right for change. During the 1960s, among other social
movements, women were demanding equal rights and opportunities, and institutional authority was generally being
questioned.

The women's movement affected how doctors and
nurses related. Wald explained, " . . . the women's movement gave promise that the gender barrier between doctors
(predominantly men) and nurses (predominantly women)
would be lowered—that doctors would hear what nurses
said and nurses would challenge doctors. The health care
hierarchy was shaken. Nurses became more capable of expressing themselves and began to expect recognition."

Saunders returned to the United States over the next
few years, and the hospice movement attracted more and
more attention. Saunders and Elizabeth Kubler-Ross, an expert on death and dying, traveled around the country giving
lectures on the hospice movement.

Dedicated to Hospice Care

Wald stepped down as dean in 1967 and began working with others who wanted to introduce the hospice concept in the United States. Although she was no longer dean,
Wald continued to work at Yale. She was a research associate from 1969 to 1970 and a clinical associate professor
from 1970 to 1980.

In 1969, Wald served a one-month internship at St.
Christopher's Hospice in London, the hospice founded by
Saunders. When she returned to the United States, she
formed an interdisciplinary team of doctors, clergy and
nurses to study the needs of dying patients. The project was

sponsored by the Yale University Schools of Nursing and Medicine. Funding came from the Nursing Division of the United States Public Health Service and the American Nurses Foundation.

Saunders served as the group's mentor from 1969 to 1971. The team included Wald; another nurse, Katherine Klaus; physicians Dr. Ira Goldenbert and Dr. Morris Wessel; Fathers Don McNeil and Robert Canney, and Pastor Fred Auman. The group worked with terminally ill patients in hospitals, homes and nursing homes. Wald and Klaus provided nursing care and kept diaries of observations, conversations and feelings of patients and their families. The research helped them understand the needs of the patients and their families and where the health care industry fell short in meeting those needs. They studied pain management and learned that it was a very important and little-understood component of hospice care.

Interest in hospice among professionals and the public was "unstoppable," Wald said. In 1974, the interdisciplinary team, along with Henry Wald, founded the country's first hospice, Connecticut Hospice in Branford, Connecticut. Initially, the hospice provided home care only; in 1980 an inpatient facility was added.

In the following years, many hospices opened around the country using the model that Wald created. It called for holistic and humanistic care for patients and required caregivers to understand death and the needs of the dying person and his or her family. *Yale School of Nursing News* quoted Wald, "From the nurse's point of view hospice care is the epitome of good nursing. It enables the patient to get through the end of life on their own terms. It is a holistic approach, looking at the patient as an individual, a human being. The spiritual role nurses play in the end of life process is essential to both patients and families."

Received Many Awards

Wald was recognized for her pioneering efforts in hospice care. She received honorary degrees from Yale, University of Bridgeport and Mt. Holyoke College. She was widely published and earned many honors. She received a Founders Award from the National Hospice Association. She received the American Academy of Nursing's Living Legend Award in 2001. The Connecticut Nurses Association established the Florence S. Wald Award for outstanding contributions to nursing practice in her honor. In 1996, Wald was inducted into the American Nurses Association Hall of Fame. Two years later, she was inducted into the National Women's Hall of Fame and in 1999 the Connecticut Hall of Fame. In April of 2004 she received the Connecticut Treasure Award.

During the 1990s, when Wald was in her 80s, she became involved in prison hospice programs. In an interview in *JAMA: Journal of the American Medical Association,* she explained that the needs of dying prisoners are different because they face death knowing they have not had successful lives. She found that inmates serving as hospital volunteers gained confidence from the situation. "It shows that even in this terrible situation, something good can happen, a sense of possibility emerges."

During the 1990s, Wald expressed her beliefs about health care in America and declared her support for physician-assisted suicide. "There are cases in which either the pain or the debilitation the patient is experiencing is more than can be borne, whether it be economically, physically, emotionally, or socially. For this reason, I feel a range of options should be available to the patient, and this should include assisted suicide."

In JAMA, Wald commented on the role of hospice care and its future. She believed that family, doctors and nurses should all be caregivers and that health maintenance should involve birthing centers, schools, health maintenance organizations, centers for aging and hospices.

"Hospice care for the terminally ill is the end piece of how to care for patients from birth on. It is a patient-family-based approach to health care that belongs in the community with natural childbirth, school-based health care, mental health care, and adult care. . ." she wrote. "As more and more people—families of hospice patients and hospice volunteers—are exposed to this new model of how to approach end-of-life care, we are taking what was essentially a hidden scene, death, an unknown, and making it a reality. We are showing people that there are meaningful ways to cope with this very difficult situation."

Books

Spiro, Howard M., Mary G. McCrea Curnen, and Lee Palmer Wandel, eds., *Facing Death: Where Culture, Religion, and Medicine Meet,* New Haven: Yale University Press, 1996.
Women in World History: A Biographical Encyclopedia, Anne Commire, editor, Yorkin Publications, 1999.

Periodicals

JAMA: Journal of the American Medical Association, May 12, 1999.
M2 Presswire, April 6, 2004.

Online

"Florence Sophie Wald," *Biography Resource Center Online,* Gale Group, 2002.
"Past Yale School of Nursing Dean and Leader in Nursing Research Awarded Title 'Living Legend' by the American Academy of Nursing, *Yale School of Nursing News, Yale University School of Nursing website, 2001,* http://www.info .med.yale.edu/nursing (November 10, 2003). □

Sippie Wallace

Sippie Wallace (1898–1996) ranks among the classic female American blues singers. Her songs "Lovin' Sam," "I'm a Mighty Tight Woman," and "Up the Country" numbered among the most popular blues in the United States during the 1920s, and she went on to gain renewed popularity among subsequent generations of fans.

During the Blues craze of the 1920s, Sippie Wallace took blues audiences by storm, and her strong, rhythmic style reflected her Texas roots and the influences of the best of New Orleans jazz. A woman with incredible charisma onstage due to her upbeat, flamboyant style, she also captivated listeners who never saw her in live performance through the many recordings she made for Okeh. Rising and falling on the wave of the blues craze, Wallace enjoyed a revival in the wake of the Folk Music revival that swept college campuses in the late 1950s and 1960s.

The events of Wallace's life—a mixture of good luck and bad, served as inspiration for her music. The bad— poverty, misguided love, loss, and death—was part of the human condition, particularly that of blacks and women; the good—her ability to translate life's misfortunes into song—was her gift to the world. When Wallace said "I sing the blues to comfort me on," she claimed her music as a personal expression, a catharsis of feelings and emotions uniquely hers and yet reflective of many in her audience.

Wallace was born Beulah Belle Thomas in Houston, Texas, in 1898, the fourth of thirteen children of hard-working George W. Thomas and his wife Fanny, both of whom passed on to her their strong religious beliefs, and grew up in the security of a close-knit family. She gained a love of music while playing the organ and singing at the Shiloh Baptist Church, where her father served as a deacon, and also spent hours listening outside the tent at traveling blues and ragtime shows. She earned her nickname in

elementary school because, as she often explained, "My teeth were so far apart I had to sip everything."

Sippie was not the only Wallace child to possess musical talent: her older brother, George W. Thomas, Jr., went on to become a musician and composer; younger brother Hersal was a composer and pianist, and older sister Lillie was a strong vocalist. Wallace learned from her older siblings—Lillie helped her little sister hone her singing while George Jr. often sat at the piano and improvised melodies to young Sippie's invented lyrics—and worked up an act with pianist Hersal. When George Jr. moved to the Storyville section of New Orleans in 1914 to break into the music business, fifteen-year-old sister Sippie followed, with Hersal in tow. Wallace was enthralled by the life of the entertainers she met there, as well as by a man named Frank Seals whom she soon married.

Wallace's early marriage proved disastrous, and ended in 1917. The following year Wallace returned home to Houston, but her desire to perform quickly overcame her efforts to complete her high school education; she had been out in the world, and her life in Houston could not compete with the stage. She finally got a job as a stage assistant to Madame Dante, who worked as a snake dancer with Philip's Reptile Show, a touring production that traveled throughout Texas. Wallace was soon on stage performing bit parts, performing ballads, or singing and dancing with the troupe chorus, until she met Matthew Wallace, whom she quickly married. Settling in Houston, where her husband's gambling career centered, Sippie linked up with small bands at dances and picnics throughout the state. Because of her smooth, sweet voice, Wallace quickly gained the name the "Texas Nightingale."

Found Recording Career after Move North

In 1920 Wallace joined George in Chicago, where he had become a successful composer and bandleader and had other connections in the ragtime and jazz music industry due to his job at the W. W. Kimball Company. Wallace's husband, Matt, also relocated north, and helped promote his wife's singing career. With Matt's encouragement and George's connections, Wallace formed a trio with brothers George and Hersal and signed a recording contract with Okeh Records in late 1923. Okeh general manager Ralph Peer knew that Sippie and her brothers would prove popular among the African American to which they marketed what was known as "race music." At her first recording session with Okeh, held in New York in May of 1924, she recorded "Leavin' Me Daddy Is Hard to Do," "Stranger's Blues," "Underworld Blues," and "Caladonia Blues." The last two songs were written by Wallace and brother George W. Thomas, Jr. Due to the immediate popularity of these sessions, many other sessions followed, both in New York and Wallace's home town of Chicago, and Wallace soon became one of Okeh's top vocalists.

Okeh recorded Wallace's "Shorty George Blues" in Chicago on October 26, 1924, and the single was successful enough to sell over 100,000 copies. Recognizing Wallace's talent—as a mature singer she developed an earthy, "shouting blues" style influenced by both her native Texas as well as New Orleans and Chicago jazz—and her stage appeal, Okeh promoted her as "The Texas Nightingale . . . with her high-C blues wailing." The record company soon paired her with its top sidemen, among them such soon-to-be jazz greats as Clarence Williams (piano), Louis Armstrong (cornet), Sidney Bechet (soprano saxophone and clarinet), Eddie Heywood (piano), Johnny Dodds (clarinet), King Oliver (cornet), and Perry Bradford (piano). She was also part of the famous Williams Blue Five session, which included Armstrong and Bechet and was taped for Okeh in 1924. Wallace would record over forty sides for Okeh before her contract expired in 1927, including "I'm a Mighty Tight Woman," "Lazy Man Blues," written by brother Hersal Thomas, and "Special Delivery Blues," penned by Wallace herself.

By 1924 Wallace had joined another traveling tent show as a singer, donning the feathered and sequined costumes that she loved and belting out her country-style blues to audiences in many parts of the south. The sidemen who performed with her were top-notch New Orleans jazz musicians, and their shows wowed audiences during the nation's blues craze.

Beset by Personal Tragedies

In 1929 Wallace signed a recording contract with RCA-Victor, but the situation quickly changed. The music industry was on the brink of a downslide due to the onset of the Great Depression of the 1930s, and the Blues craze had abated. In addition, the phenomenal growth of radio took its toll on the record industry, and sales of race records plummeted as a result. At a Chicago session held on February 6, 1929, she recorded four sides. Only two—"You Gonna Need My Help" and a rerecording of the erotically suggestive "I'm a Mighty Tight Woman," one of her most popular songs—were released. With neither the experience nor the guidance from her brother to guide her in refocusing her career, Wallace was unable to adapt her style to changing tastes, and by 1932 she had slipped into the same obscurity as other female blues artists of her era.

After her early successes, Wallace was met with a series of personal tragedies. Hersal had already died, succumbing to food poisoning in 1926 at the age of sixteen. As the years passed, several other close family members died, including her husband Matt in the mid-1930s, her older sister Lillie, and her brother George, Jr., who was tragically run down by a Chicago streetcar in 1928. George's death ended what had been a successful musical collaboration, and Wallace was left without his expert guidance.

Wallace, who moved to Detroit in 1929 and settled on that city's east side, now channeled her energies into her family and her faith. While working as both nurse and choir director/organist at Detroit's Leland Baptist Church, she also served as director of the National Convention of Gospel Choirs and Choruses beginning in the 1930s.; she also wrote gospel choral music. In the early 1950s she also took in the three orphaned children of her niece, Hociel Thomas, also a blues singer.

Rediscovered during Folk Music Revival

Occasional shows at local nightclubs kept Wallace from total obscurity. She recorded occasionally, traveling to Mercury's Chicago studio to join Albert Ammons in a one-day recording session to lay down "Bedroom Blues" in September of 1945, and rejoining Louis Armstrong in 1946, on the Circle and Riverside labels. A 1959 record on Detroit's Fine Arts label convinced friends that her talent was still strong, and they encouraged her to overcome her religious concerns about singing the "Devil's music" and join the growing Folk/Blues festival circuit. In 1966, at the urging of friend and fellow Texan Victoria Spivey, Wallace recorded a series of duets released as *Sippie Wallace and Victoria Spivey,* and performed as part of the American Folk Blues Festival during its European tour. Her strong, earthy sound—Wallace was able to sing over her backup band without the aid of a microphone—was a new sound to younger fans raised on more sophisticated jazz mixes, and together with Spivey, Wallace soon became a popular performer in the United States as well. Her European tour marked the start of Wallace's revival.

Many performances followed, as audiences responded to what *New York Times* writer Jon Pareles dubbed her "earthy and self-assertive" style. 1971 found Wallace on tour with singer Bonnie Raitt who had recorded two of Wallace's songs—the popular "Mighty Tight Woman" and "Women Be Wise, Don't Advertise Your Man"—on her debut album and one more—"You Got to Know How" on her second album. In 1976 Wallace wowed audiences at Ann Arbor, Michigan's Folk and Blues Festival and a year later performed for the first time at New York's Lincoln Center. In 1980 Wallace returned to New York and was featured at Lincoln Center's salute to prominent women of the blues. At 81 years of age, she was the oldest participant. In 1983 she was honored by both her adopted city of Detroit with "Sippie Wallace Day" and by her state as she was inducted into the Michigan Hall of Fame. 1985 marked her first return to a Texas stage in 63 years when she performed at the Austin Music Festival.

During her revival Wallace made several recordings. In 1966 she recorded the solo project *Sippie Wallace Sings the Blues* for the Danish Storyville label. She lay down several blues tracks with the Otis Spann Jim Kweskin Jug Band in 1967, although these session would not be released until the early 1990s by Drive Archive as *Mighty Tight Woman.* With Raitt's help, Wallace signed with Atlantic and recorded *Sippie.* With backing vocals by Raitt, the album was nominated for a 1983 Grammy award for best traditional blues and earned the W.C. Handy Award for best blues album of 1983 the following year. In 1995 Document records released a two-volume *Complete Recorded Works,* which encompasses the years 1924 through the late 1940s.

In the 1970s Wallace's performances were curtailed due to failing health. She suffered a stroke in 1970 that left her temporarily wheelchair-bound and forced her to end her stint as organist of the Leland Baptist Church, but recovered sufficiently to tour with Raitt the following year. In 1983-84 she traveled to Germany to tour with pianist Axel Zwingenberger, returning to that country in the spring of

1986. Despite her failing health, her concerts were highly acclaimed. Fortunately for her fans, many of these performances were recorded, because they would be Wallace's lasting legacy to the blues. Following a concert in Mainz, Germany, in March, she suffered a severe stroke and returned home to Detroit. Wallace passed away on November 1, 1986, her 88th birthday.

Among the top female blues vocalists of her era, Wallace ranked with Ma Rainey, Ida Cox, Alberta Hunter, and Bessie Smith. Most often compared to Rainey, whom she claimed was a strong influence, Wallace's earthy style was uniquely her own: a combination of several elements, including southwestern rolling-bass honky-tonk and the Chicago-based "shouting moan" blues. Her vocal abilities—her strong, smooth voice and excellent articulation, the mournful slides that would become her trademark, her ability to wring a myriad of emotions from a few simple lyrical phrases, and her theatrical sense of timing—gave her music an emotional depth unique in blues performance. In addition, her strong, assertive, even bawdy manner made her music a rallying cry for female audiences, while her religious upbringing gave the good-natured Wallace the perseverance to weather life's ups and downs with grace and dignity. Throughout her long career, Wallace commanded respect, both on stage and off.

Books

Chilton, John, *Who's Who of Jazz: Storyville to Swing Street,* 4th edition, Da Capo Press, 1985.
Contemporary Black Biography, Volume 1, Gale, 1992.
Davis, Angela Y., *Blues Legacies and Black Feminism,* Pantheon Books, 1998.
Harrision, Daphne Duval, *Black Pearls: Blues Queens of the 1920s,* Rutgers University Press, 1988.
Hine, Darlene Clark, editor, *Black Women in America: An Historical Encyclopedia,* Carlson, 1993.
Scribner Encyclopedia of American Lives, Volume 2: *1986-1990,* Charles Scribner's Sons, 1999.

Periodicals

Detroit Free Press Magazine, September 16, 1979.
New York Times, November 4, 1986.

Online

"Sippie Wallace," *Red Hot Jazz Web site,* http://www.redhotjazz.com/ (December 6, 2003).
"Wallace, Beulah Thomas (Sippie)," Handbook of Texas Online, http://www.tsha.utexas.edu/handbook/online/articles (July 23, 2002). □

Vera Wang

After her own unsuccessful search for the perfect wedding dress, American fashion designer Vera Wang (born 1949) created a business plan, started her own company, and filled a void in the bridal gown industry. Perhaps the best known name in bridal fashion, her contemporary yet often simple designs have adorned many brides.

Early Years

Vera Ellen Wang was born in New York City, New York, to Cheng Ching Wang and Florence Wang on June 27, 1949. Her father, who spoke fluent English, was the son of a Chinese general. Her mother was the daughter of a Chinese politician, alleged to be a warlord. The couple had fled China after World War II, eventually marrying and settling in New York City. The Wangs also had a son, Kenneth, who was born 18 months after Vera.

Although Wang's father was the head of a multi-million dollar company which allowed his family an affluent lifestyle, the children were not given a free ride. Wang's parents instilled basic goals and values in their children. They encouraged them to pursue academic and athletic excellence, and to have integrity in what they did.

Wang's mother was considered a beautiful woman with excellent taste. She taught her daughter about style, and they enjoyed going to Paris fashion shows together. As noted on the official Vera Wang website, "Wang's fashion sense . . . came early in life."

Gave Up Skating for Fashion

In addition to clothes and ballet lessons, Wang loved ice skating. After receiving a pair of ice skates one Christmas, she began ice skating lessons at the age of eight. Always the competitor, she won her first regional championship at 12. Wang was usually on the ice by six o'clock in the morning so she could practice before school. Her day usually ended with more practice. As Wang shared in the *A & E Biography* video "Vera Wang: Attention to Detail," "ice skating was the first love of [my] life."

After completing high school, Wang enrolled at the Sarah Lawrence College. However, balancing school and ice skating became too much for her. There was not enough time to study and train, and this led to the greatest disappointment of her life; she chose to give up ice skating. As noted by *A & E Biography,* Wang recalled that after making this decision, she became depressed and moved to Paris. It was there that she seriously considered pursuing a career in fashion. Wang returned to school and earned a degree in art history in 1971, but a career in fashion was her dream.

Paid Dues in Fashion Industry

Wang's first job in fashion was at *Vogue* as an assistant to fashion director Polly Mellen. Wang took the opportunity to study and learn all she could about the fashion industry. Her hard work quickly paid off; Wang was named fashion editor at *Vogue* at the age of 23. She primarily served as "sittings" editor, the person in charge of the editorial fashion spreads that made up the heart of the magazine.

The work and the lifestyle were intense. Wang often worked seven days a week, and had little time for romance. She did enjoy the party scene, and went to Studio 54, a New

York City hotspot in the late 1970s. However, Wang's work was not focused on design, and by the mid-1980s, she was ready for a change. A tired Wang took a leave of absence from *Vogue* and went to Paris for two years. Deciding she wanted to do something different, Wang left *Vogue* after 16 years, and in 1987, went to work for Ralph Lauren, where she was a designer for accessories.

Search for Dress Led to New Business

With a less frenzied pace at Ralph Lauren, Wang had more time for a personal life. She had met her future husband, businessman Arthur Becker, in 1980, at a tennis match. Wang shared with *People Weekly* that soon after they met, Becker started talking marriage, but she wanted to focus on her career. The pair dated off and on in the 1980s and were good friends. However, in the late 1980s, romance blossomed and the couple became engaged. Wang began to plan their wedding.

As Wang shared with *A & E Biography*, she went on a search for a perfect wedding dress and found a "sameness to everything." She told Jane Sharp of *Biography Magazine*, "I wanted something more elegant and subdued, but there wasn't anything. I realized the desire to fill that niche."

Forbes writer Lisa Coleman noted that Wang spent three months "looking for the perfect dress at several department stores and bridal boutiques" but felt the dresses were geared for the younger bride. Coleman continued that eventually, "Wang gave up and hired a dressmaker to create her own gown. The gown cost $10,000." Wang's experience became the inspiration for a new business venture.

However, the business idea had to wait. Wang and Becker married in June of 1989 and, according to *A & E Biography*, the 40-year-old bride began infertility treatments, as the couple wanted to have a baby right away. But soon, the infertility treatments took their toll, and Wang decided to quit her job at Ralph Lauren. The couple eventually adopted two daughters, Cecilia and Josephine, and set up their home in New York City.

Launched Company

In 1990, Wang's father thought the time was right for her to launch her own business and offered financial backing. She began her bridal gown business and opened her shop in the upscale Carlyle Hotel on Madison Avenue in New York City.

According to the official Vera Wang website, "The Vera Wang label quickly took off, earning praise from the fashion elite for its luxurious fabrics, exquisite detailing and modern interpretation of classic lines." *A & E Biography* stated that Wang successfully used colors and innovative ideas in her dresses, adding that she knew how to "attract attention yet still be elegant at the same time." And *Business Leader Profiles for Students* noted that "Wang introduced her trademark use of 'illusion netting' in her gowns, a fabric that gave the illusion of bare skin." However, all this did not translate to immediate profits for her business.

While brides loved Wang's dresses, the fashion press was not so kind. As noted by *A & E Biography,* the fashion press saw her as an insider to the fashion industry who was getting special treatment. Others questioned her family's financial support to the business. Wang retorted, "Nothing replaces hard work."

In the beginning, Wang's success was achieved because of her service to the bride. It did not end with the dress. Wang told Coleman of *Forbes* that she wanted to help the women "that are running around looking for special dresses, looking to have everything taken care of because they have busy lives." Wang's employees discuss many aspects of the wedding with the bride, including jewelry, shoes, hairstyles, and bridesmaids' dresses, just to name a few. Wang concluded, "I'm creating an image, a brand and a name."

Designer to the Stars

Wang's business strategy was to succeed in the bridal gown industry first, then to expand into other areas. She made a splash during the 1992 and 1994 Winter Olympics when American figure skater Nancy Kerrigan wore her costumes. Wang later told *Vogue,* "I felt as though my life had come full circle; I didn't make it to that level of competition, but my clothes did." In 1993, she introduced a line of evening wear.

Wang has also dressed some of the top actresses in Hollywood, including Holly Hunter, Goldie Hawn, Meg Ryan, Whoopi Goldberg, Helen Hunt, Kate Capshaw, and Charlize Theron. In *Business Leader Profiles for Students,* actress Sharon Stone remarked, "Vera's designs are very simple but not boring. Her clothes celebrate the person, they never overwhelm." *A & E Biography* concluded, "Dressing Hollywood was a sound business move for Wang."

In addition, Wang dressed some very famous brides. Singer Mariah Carey wore a dress with a 27-foot train when she married. Karenna Gore, daughter of then-U.S. Vice President Al Gore, and the world famous Barbie doll also wore Vera Wang dresses when they married. Wang also began designing costumes for American figure skater Michelle Kwan.

Company Thrived and Grew

Wang's vision has expanded beyond bridal gowns. Her first book, *Vera Wang on Weddings,* was released in October of 2001. Her first signature fragrance launched in spring 2002, under agreement with Unilever Cosmetics International. She launched the partnering men's fragrance in 2004. Wang opened a second store near her bridal shop that focused on her bridesmaid dress collection. Also in 2002 was the launch of Wang's collection of china and stemware for Wedgwood.

Wang moved on to more new endeavors in 2003. She designed uniforms for the Philadelphia Eagles cheering squad, who debuted their new look on *Monday Night Football* in September. Later that month, American actress Sarah Jessica Parker showed off Wang's new jewelry collection at the Emmy Awards. *Women's Wear Daily* commented, "The beautiful new jewelry underscores Wang's design aesthetic, fusing femininity, sensuality and subtlety.'' Wang launched a Silver and Gifts Collection in 2004 in collaboration with Towle Silversmiths which features barware, flatware, giftware and more.

A & E Biography noted that Wang ''strives to do everything well, which is demanding and adds more pressure.'' She has admitted that she has to work hard to balance her business and family time, but she is excited about what the future will bring, as she challenges herself every day.

Books

Business Leader Profiles for Students, Vol. 1, Gale Research, 1999.
Contemporary Fashion, 2nd ed., St. James Press, 2002.
Newsmakers 1998, Issue 4, Gale Group, 1998.
Notable Asian Americans, Gale Research, 1995.
Wang, Vera, *Vera Wang on Weddings,* HarperResource, 2001.

Periodicals

Biography, June 1998.
Business Wire, October 28, 2003.
Cosmetics International Cosmetic Products Report, November 2003.
Footwear News, September 29, 2003.
Forbes, April 26, 2003.
HFN The Weekly Newspaper for the Home Furnishing Newtwork, July 28, 2003.
People Weekly, February 13, 1995; March 22, 2004.
Vogue, March 2001.
WWD (Women's Wear Daily), February 2, 1994; April 17, 1998; September 8, 2003; September 23, 2003.

Online

''Vera Wang: About Vera,'' Vera Wang official website, http://www.verawang.com (January 1, 2004).

Other

''Vera Wang: Attention to Detail,'' *A & E Biography Video,* 2001.

□

Sarah Frances Whiting

American astronomer, physicist, and educator Sarah Frances Whiting (1847–1927) was a pioneer for women in the world of science. Her work at Wellesley College paved the way for generations of physicists and astronomers to follow in her extraordinary footsteps.

Early Life

Sarah Frances Whiting was born August 23, 1847, in Wyoming, New York. Her parents were Joel Whiting and Elizabeth Lee (Comstock) Whiting; her mother's heritage included seventeenth-century settlers of Connecti-cut and Long Island and her father's lineage traced to pioneers in Vermont. Her father was a highly educated and decidedly enlightened man untainted by the sexist stereotypes of his time. He graduated from Hamilton College and acted as both principle and teacher in various academies in New York state. He taught physics (called Natural Philosophy at the time) and mathematics. Whiting's passion for and interest in science began at an early age. She loved helping her father set up scientific experiments for his classes, and he tutored her at home in experimental science, mathematics, Greek, and Latin. Whiting was a devoted learner and knew Greek at age 8 and Latin by age 10.

Education and Career

The instruction and encouragement of her father prepared her well for her own advanced education. Whiting entered Ingham University in Le Roy, New York, and graduated from that institution with a bachelor's degree at the age of 18 in 1865. She taught the Classics and Mathematics at Ingham for a time and later taught the same subjects at the Brooklyn Heights Seminary for Girls. In her spare time, Whiting attended scientific lectures, demonstrations, and lab exhibitions that chronicled new advances and developments in theories and equipment. Whiting was well-liked and professionally admired as a teacher. *Notable American Women 1607–1950: A Biographical Dictionary* stated, ''She became known as an enthusiastic and effective teacher who showed great ingenuity in improvising apparatus for her lectures and shared with her students her excitement over new discoveries.'' In 1875, Henry F. Durant—the founder of the newly established all-female institution Wellesley College in Massachusetts—approached Whiting about taking a position as the Professor of Physics on Wellesley's all-female faculty. Durant sought her out because her reputation and experience as a scientist was unrivaled by any other woman at that time. She accepted the offer and became Wellesley College's first physics professor in 1876.

In 1877 Durant put Whiting in contact with Professor Edward Pickering, an instructor at the Massachusetts Institute of Technology (MIT) and the director of Harvard College's Observatory. She was invited to MIT to observe the undergraduate physics labs there and to attend physics classes. She visited and observed, attending science classes that were otherwise closed to women, for two years. In 1878 she used the information she had gathered to establish, equip, and operate an undergraduate physics lab at Wellesley, the only one of its kind in the country for women, and second only to the labs she had studied at MIT. Whiting did all the work herself, researching equipment, connecting with manufacturers in Europe to purchase what the lab needed, and finally installing all the equipment without outside assistance.

In 1879 Pickering invited Whiting to visit the Harvard College Observatory and study some of the newest technology being used for astronomical investigations at that time, particularly the field of spectroscopy, which allowed for the observation of the patterns of *spectra* (lines and bands) that form when light is sent through a prism. This experience showed her how to apply theories she had heard when attending a lecture by noteworthy British physicist John Tyndall and inspired her to pursue the integration of astronomy into the Wellesley curriculum. She created and taught the first class in astronomy at Wellesley in 1880 under the heading of "Applied Physics." Teaching the class brought home to Whiting what a necessary and invaluable tool an observatory was. "For two decades," *Notable American Women 1607–1950* noted, "she taught astronomy with only a celestial globe and a 4-inch portable telescope." Ever eager for a new challenge, Whiting set herself the task of having an observatory installed at Wellesley. The funding needs for the project were met by a Wellesley trustee and friend to Whiting, Mrs. John C. Whitin. The Observatory was to be built by converting an organ loft and top story living quarters on the fifth floor of Wellesley's College Hall. Whiting drew up the plans for the facility which, as recorded by *Notable American Women 1607–1950,* "housed a 12-inch refracting telescope with spectroscope and photometer attachment, a transit instrument, and the usual accessories." Once again, as with the undergraduate physics lab, Whiting did most of the work herself. According to the *American National Biography,* Whiting designed equipment herself and also worked with local artisans and traveled throughout New England to order equipment and books. The Whitin Observatory—named after its benefactress and built of white marble to pay homage to the names of the two women who made it happen—was officially opened and established in 1900.

Whiting worked alone for most of her career, although she did receive an assistant for her duties at Wellesley in 1885—much needed considering that she handled everything from purchasing to teaching and administration of the Physics Department. She spent her sabbaticals traveling all over the world to visit scientific facilities and participate in seminars and classes. From 1888 to 1889 she went to Germany and studied briefly at the University of Berlin, followed by time spent in England observing laboratories and visiting noted scientists in her fields. In 1896 she traveled to Scotland and enrolled in the prestigious Edinburgh University—newly opened to women—to study with leading physicist Peter Guthrie Tait. In addition to being a pioneer in the education of women, Whiting also broke new ground by participating in and even founding academic groups and being accepted into all-male scientific societies. She was one of very few female members of the American Astronomical Society and the American Physical Society and was invited to join the New England Meteorological Society as its only female member. This honor led her to introduce a class in meteorology at Wellesley. As *Notable Women in the Physical Sciences* explained, "She purchased an anemometer, thermometers, rain gauges, and other equipment. For ten years there was no weather station in the area, so she became a voluntary observer and her students collected data from the instruments and submitted it to the U.S. Weather Bureau." Whiting was also a forerunner in the study of the newly discovered "X rays." *American National Biography* explained, "In 1895, when American newspapers reported the discovery of X rays, Whiting immediately set up an old Crookes tube and took some of the first photographs in the United States of bones underneath flesh and of coins in a purse."

Retired from Wellesley

While at home teaching at Wellesley, Whiting lived on campus with her unmarried sister Elizabeth P. Whiting. They lived in dormitories and campus housing until 1906 when they moved into Observatory House that was built next to the Observatory facility—thanks to another generous donation compliments of Mrs. Whitin. The Whiting sisters had reputations as warm, gracious hostesses, and Sarah—a stanch prohibitionist and Congregationalist—was very active in the Wellesley College Christian Association's missionary programs. In 1905 Whiting was awarded an honorary doctorate degree from Tufts College, some felt to recognize the caliber of degree that she should have received from Ingham in 1865. She retired from the Physics Department at Wellesley in 1912 to pursue astronomy full time. Four years later, in 1916, she stepped down as director of the Whitin Observatory and spent her remaining years living with her sister in Massachusetts. Whiting died at the age of 80 of arteriosclerosis and nephritis in the home she shared with her sister in Wilbraham, Massachusetts, on September 12, 1927.

Although Whiting was a brilliant researcher and scientist herself, she was most passionately involved in teaching science to others. She was a prolific writer of educational literature, and her collection of scientific exercises titled *Daytime and Evening Exercises in Astronomy* (1912) proved invaluable to future science teachers. She single-handedly instructed and prepared generations of female scientists, most notably the astronomer Annie Jump Cannon, who later became famous in her own right. Scholars and critics agree that Sarah Whiting's contributions to the world of science, and the world of women, have been both significant and long-lasting. *American National Biography* noted, "Whiting's lifelong commitment to teaching women physics and astronomy, her enthusiasm for the experimental method, and her establishment of the first physics laboratory for women in the United States helped generations of women practice and understand science. Through these accomplishments, Whiting stands as one of the pioneers of science education for women."

Books

American National Biography, Volume 23, Oxford University Press, 1999.

American Women in Science, ABC–CLIO, Inc., 1994.

The Biographical Dictionary of Women in Science, Volume 2, Routledge, 2000.

The Continuum Dictionary of Women's Biography, The Continuum Publishing Company, 1989.

A Dictionary of North American Authors Deceased Before 1950, Gale Research, 1968.

Notable American Women 1607–1950: A Biographical Dictionary, Volume 3, The Belknap Press of Harvard University Press, 1971.

Notable Women in the Physical Sciences, Greenwood Press, 1997.

Notable Women Scientists, Gale Group, Inc., 1999.

Who Was Who in America, Volume 1, Marquis Who's Who, Inc., 1966.

The Women's Book of World Records and Achievements, Anchor Press/Doubleday, 1979.

Women's Firsts, Gale Research, 1997.

Online

"Sarah F. Whiting," *4000 Years of Women in Science,* http://www.astr.ua.edu/4000WS/4000WS (January 14, 2004). ☐

Dorothy Maud Wrinch

Dorothy Maud Wrinch (1894-1976), a British mathematician, biochemist, and educator, remains known for her research into unlocking the key to protein structure through the use of mathematical principles. She is best known for developing what came to be called the "cyclol theory" of protein structure. Although the theory was later discredited, the work Wrinch did in this area has contributed to the field of genetics.

Wrinch was born on January 1, 1894, in Rosario, Argentina, a town located north of Buenos Aires on the Parana River. Her parents, Hugh Edward Hart and Ada Minnie Souter Wrinch, were British citizens.

Demonstrated Mathematical Abilities

The Wrinch family relocated to England when Wrinch was still a child, and she grew up in Surbiton, a town in Surrey, England, located near London. She attended Surbiton High, a local public day school, and won a scholarship to attend Girton College at Cambridge University, where Wrinch received her bachelor of arts degree in 1916 and her master of arts degree in 1918. In addition, when Wrinch received her graduate degree in 1918, she earned with it the ranking of wrangler in mathematics, the highest ranking possible on the final examinations in that subject.

On leaving Cambridge, Wrinch accepted a position as a lecturer in mathematics at University College in London, where she received her master of science and doctor of science degrees. She remained at University College until 1921 and then returned to Girton College when she was named a research scholar.

Wrinch went on to teach physics at Balliol College, Oxford. In 1929 she also received her doctor of science degree from the prestigious British university, becoming the first woman to attain such a degree in Oxford's history. She also received a master of arts degree from Oxford.

In 1923, while teaching at Oxford University, Wrinch married John William Nicholson, and together they had a daughter, Pamela, born in 1927. During this period, Wrinch taught mathematics at five women's colleges within communing distance from her home.

Engaged in Varied Collaborations and Associations

As the number and type of her degrees might indicate, Wrinch had a wide range of interests, among which was sociology. In addition, from 1918 to 1932 she published 20 papers on pure and applied mathematics, as well as 16 papers on scientific methodology and on the philosophy of science. During this period Wrinch also was a member of the Theoretical Biology Club founded in the 1930s at Cambridge University by Conrad Hal Waddington, the eminent embryologist and animal geneticist. The club was a multidisciplinary group that embraced the organicist philosophy, which viewed organic life as something to be explained and understood through philosophy as well as the sciences.

Wrinch's interest in the philosophy of science resulted in a productive collaboration with eminent physicist and statistician Sir Harry Jeffreys. Jeffreys (1891-1989), who would later become regarded as the world authority in theoretical geophysics, used probability to deal with problems in the philosophy of science, viewing probability as a degree of reasonable belief. It was Wrinch who introduced him to that notion after she attended a lecture by famed mathematician Walter Ernest Johnson (1858-1931). Together, Wrinch and Jeffreys employed probability to explain induction and to investigate the soundness of various scientific theories, including general relativity. Their collaboration produced the papers "On Some Aspects of the Theory of Probability" (1919), and "On Certain Fundamental Principles of Scientific Inquiry" (1921-23). In 1931 Jeffreys wrote the book *Scientific Inference* in which he summarized and expanded upon his research with Wrinch.

During their years of collaboration, Wrinch and Jeffreys also developed the Simplicity Postulate, which essentially states that "the simplest law is chosen because it is the most likely to give correct predictions." In other words, simpler laws or models have the greater prior probabilities.

In keeping with her interest in sociology, as well as her experiences of motherhood, in 1930 Wrinch published a book on parenting, titled *The Retreat from Parenthood,* under the pen name Jean Ayling. Eventually, she would author or coauthor nearly 200 professional papers and publications.

Wrinch's marriage fell apart in the early 1930s, reportedly as a result of her husband's alcoholism. As a single woman with a child, she was badly in need of money, so she decided to increase her academic credentials to include biology, chemistry, and molecular structure. Her resourcefulness and ambition in this direction paid off, as it enabled her to secure a grant from the Rockefeller Foundation, an organization established in 1913 by John D. Rockefeller to support work in the arts and sciences. The grant would fund her research on the application of mathematics to biological molecular structures.

Developed "Cyclol" Theory

Wrinch's interest in biological molecular structures steered her into the study of genetics, specifically into her investigation into the structure of protein molecules, including egg albumin. She came to believe that protein structure held the secret of life.

In 1935 she came up with an original and controversial theory about globular protein structure. The theory, which would later become known as the "cyclol theory," advanced the concept of the cyclical model of protein structure. Specifically, the theory suggested that the specificity of the gene resides in the amino acid sequences of the gene. Wrinch based her theory on mathematical symmetry concepts and covalent bonding between two adjacent amino acids, drawing a connection between the linear sequence of the gene and the sequence of the amino acids in the polypeptide chain. In the theory, amino acids were hooked together in chains to form a regular pattern of hexagons.

Wrinch was one of many scientists who was busy developing theories about protein structure during the same period. Some colleagues accepted her ideas while others questioned them. The cyclol theory attracted some initial and notable support from Nobel Prize-winning chemist Irving Langmuir (1881-1957). At the same time, prominent physicist John Desmond Bernal (1901-1971) strongly opposed Wrinch's theory, as he favored the hypothesis of the peptide bond, a dehydration synthesis involving a chemical bond formed between two molecules when the carboxyl group of one molecule reacts with the amino group of another. In 1938 Langmuir and Bernal entered into a debate about protein structure. This caused Langmuir to rethink his stance, and he developed the idea of a hydrophobic interaction that determined the three-dimensional structure of proteins. Soon after, Langmuir withdrew his support of Wrinch's cyclol theory.

Clashed with Linus Pauling

A much more heated debate involved Wrinch herself and famous scientist Linus Pauling (1901-1994), who would later win the Nobel Prize in Chemistry in 1954 for his work on chemical bonds, the structure of molecules and crystals, and the development of the alpha helix concept of structure proteins. Their disagreement was noted for its rancor, as it involved the clash of two forceful personalities.

Wrinch has been described as being somewhat caustic and rather aggressive in advancing her theories. She was said to be domineering in conversation and seemingly interested only in her own ideas. Pauling was viewed as being just as egocentric, if not more, and was known for alienating colleagues with his perceived arrogance, abrasiveness, and dogmatism. He was absolutely dogged in defending his work against that of other scientists. Even more, Pauling was keenly determined in his efforts to find errors in the work done by his colleagues, and he would point out these mistakes in both private and public settings.

Pauling's debate with Wrinch took place in the late 1930s, after he became chairman of the Division of Chemistry and Chemical Engineering at the California Institute of Technology. In 1937 he gave the Baker lecture at Cornell University in Ithaca, New York, and spoke about his ideas regarding proteins, which would eventually develop into his alpha helix theory. Soon after, he and Wrinch began their intense disagreement about the soundness of her cyclol theory. They met face to face in Ithaca in 1938, in a meeting that was described as hostile. The following year, Pauling wrote a paper with Carl Niemen titled "The Structure of Proteins" in which he totally discounted Wrinch's cyclol theory. The well-publicized dispute ultimately took its toll on Wrinch's research. Because Pauling continued ridiculing her theories, the result was a cut-off of her funding from the Rockefeller Foundation.

Although it was eventually proven that Wrinch's theory was indeed incorrect for proteins, her work was not in vain. It turned out that the kind of chemical bond she postulated is found in some alkaloids. Used in this new context, her research and published papers have provided valuable contributions to the field of genetics. In 1965 she published her ideas in the book *Chemical Aspects of Polypeptide Chain Structure: An introduction.*

Ironically, Pauling's theory, which involved the alpha helix model, also proved to be wrong. Pauling had based his model on X-ray diffraction data coupled with his experiments, which showed the peptide bond to be two-dimensional. In 1948 he fully set forth his idea that the polypeptide chain was a single-stranded helix, which he called the alpha-helix. It was left up to the famous scientific team of James Watson and Francis Crick to draw the true picture with their double-helix model.

Came to America

In 1939 Wrinch relocated to the United States when she accepted an appointment at Johns Hopkins University in Baltimore, Maryland, as a visiting lecturer in chemistry. In 1941 she accepted a joint position as visiting professor simultaneously at Amherst, Smith, and Mount Holyoke, neighboring colleges located in western Massachusetts. Wrinch remained a visiting professor at Smith College until she retired in 1971.

In the United States, Wrinch focused her new research on the application of mathematical principles to the interpretation of X-ray crystallographic data of complex crystal structures. She wrote about this work in *Fourier Transforms and Structure Factors*, a 96-page book published in 1946 by the American Society of X-ray Diffraction. After retiring from Smith College, Wrinch spent her last years living in Woods Hole, Massachusetts. She died in 1976.

Impact

Throughout her life, Wrinch was a prolific and eclectic writer, publishing books and numerous papers on a variety of subjects, including the interpretation of X-rays studies of crystals and proteins, the structure of protein crystals, mineralogy, scientific methodology, and the philosophy of science, probability, and mathematics. By the close of her career, she had written or co-authored close to 200 articles and publications.

Despite the erroneousness of her cyclol theory, Wrinch had a distinguished career filled with genuine accomplishments and significant recognition. In addition to being the first woman to receive a doctor of science degree from Oxford University, Wrinch was nominated for fellowship in the London Royal Society and for a Nobel Prize, although she did not receive either honor. However, her gender, coupled with her career accomplishments, placed her in unique company during her lifetime. Wrinch was one of a group of pioneering women scientists whose intellectual achievements were influential during the early part of the 20th century. These women worked in theoretical and experimental fields—areas still dominated by men—and they made major discoveries or conducted groundbreaking research. Others in this group included Dame Mary Cartwright (born 1900), the first-ever woman lecturer in mathematics at Cambridge University; crystallographer Kathleen Lonsdale (1903-73) and microbiologist Marjorie Stephenson (1880-1950), who in 1945 became the first women to be elected to the Royal Society; Cecilia Payne Gaposhkin (1900-79), the first woman to become professor of astronomy at Harvard University; and Nobel laureates Marie Curie (1903, 1911), Irene Joliot-Curie (1935), Gerty Radnitz Cori (1947), Maria Goeppert-Mayer (1963), Doro-thy Hodgkin (1964), Rosalyn Yalow (1977), Barbara McClintock (1983), Rita Levi-Montalcini (1986) and Gertrude Elion (1988).

Books

Jeffreys, Harold, *Scientific Inference,* Cambridge University Press, 1931.

Online

''Biographical Snapshots: Dorothy Maud Wrinch,'' *JCE Online,* http://jchemed.chem.wisc.edu/JCEWWW/Features/eChemists/Bios/Wrinch.html (January 4, 2004).

''Dorothy Maud Wrinch (1894-1976),'' *ScienceWorld.Wolfram.com,* http://scienceworld.wolfram.com/biography/Wrinch.html (January 4, 2004).

''Dorothy Maud Wrinch: A Multidisciplinary Researcher,'' *Suite 101.com,* http://www.suite101.com/article.cfm/biographies_scientists/98637 (January 4, 2004).

''Dorothy Wrinch,'' *SJSU Virtual Museum,* http://www2.sjsu.edu/depts/Museum/wri.html (January 4, 2004).

''Harold Jeffreys as a Statistician,'' *University of Southampton Department of Economics Web site,* www.economics.soton.ac.uk/staff/aldrich/jeffreysweb.htm (January 4, 2004).

''Linus Pauling (1901-1994),'' *ScienceWorld.Wolfram.com,* http://scienceworld.wolfram.com/biography/Pauling.html (January 4, 2004). □

Y

Cy Young

In the world of baseball the name of Cy Young (1867-1955) is synonymous with pitching excellence. At the time of his retirement in 1911 Young had amassed more wins and pitched more innings than any other pitcher—and both records have stood into the 21st century. In 1956, to honor his outstanding career, major league baseball named an award in his honor that went to baseball's outstanding pitcher during the previous season. The award was later given to the outstanding pitcher in each league.

Denton True "Cy" Young was born March 29, 1867, in the farming community of Gilmore, Ohio. Except for the fact that Young's formal schooling ended at sixth grade, he seemed to have led the type of all-American life later mythologized by numerous writers: a farm boy who marries the girl next door and enters the wider world where he gains unprecedented success and afterward retires happily to his farm. In fact, Young attributed his success as a pitcher to the strength and stamina he gained while working on his father's farm.

A Star in the National League

In 1890, following a year in which he played third base for the amateur Tuscarawas County team, Young turned professional. He also switched to pitching, compiling a 15-15 record with the Canton team. It was with Canton, so the story goes, that Young acquired the nickname Cyclone. Eager to impress his new boss and teammates, he claimed to

have thrown a baseball against the fence, which tore off a couple of boards from the grandstand. When someone commented that the grandstand looked like a cyclone had hit it, the name stuck. In the beginning newspapers sometimes referred to Young as simply "The Cyclone." Later in 1890 Young signed a $300 contract to pitch for the National League (NL) Cleveland Spiders. He had a 9-7 record for Cleveland that season, the only pitcher on the team with a winning record. For that, and for the potential in his right arm, the Spiders, in 1891, gave Young a raise to $1,400.

The late nineteenth century and the early twentieth century was truly the era of the workhorse pitcher and the strapping Young—in his prime he stood 6 feet, 2 inches and weighed 210 pounds—was no exception. In 1891 he earned every bit of the money Cleveland paid him; he pitched 423 2/3 innings, posting a 27-22 record, with a 2.85 earned run average (ERA). He also recorded two saves. What marred Young's season was that during a six-week period in August and September he won only two of his 13 decisions. He bounced back, however, to win his final six games. He followed that up with an even more spectacular year in 1892: 453 innings pitched, a 36-12 record, and an ERA of 1.93. That season he led the NL in wins, ERA, winning percentage, and shutouts.

Young's season was all the more remarkable because in the months prior to the season the rival American Association went out of business; the NL absorbed four of its teams. Since the Players League had folded two years earlier, at the start of the 1892 season there were 12 major league teams instead of 24, as there had been when three leagues competed against each other for players. Thus, the quality of Young's opposition was far better than in his rookie season.

In 1892 Cleveland finished in first place in the second half of the season, then called the Fall Season. In a championship series they played the Boston Beaneaters who had finished first in the first half, or Spring Season, and had been champions in 1891. Unfortunately for Young and Cleveland Boston proved too strong a rival. They defeated Cleveland five consecutive games in the best-of-nine format; Young started three games and posted an 0-2 record with an ERA of 3.00.

1892 was also the year that Cyclone Young's nickname was shortened to Cy. In his biography of Young, *Cy Young: A Baseball Life,* Reed Browning conjectured that "the consensual acceptance of 'Cy' represents both a typographic abbreviation of 'Cyclone' and a conceptual conflation of stormy speed and rustic roots." In fact, Cy was a common nickname of the time for a naïve farm boy, which Young was in the beginning of his career. On November 8, 1892, Young married Robba Miller, who had been Young's sweetheart since they were teenagers.

Prior to the 1893 season the distance from which the pitcher's back foot rested when he began his pitch was moved from 55 feet 6 inches to 60 feet 6 inches, also the angle at which the pitcher could throw toward the plate was decreased. While these changes certainly favored the batters and ended more than a few pitching careers they did not affect Young. If anything he flourished under the new rules. In all, Young pitched nine seasons for the Cleveland Spiders (1890-1898) and, with the exception of his rookie year he never won fewer than 21 games in a season during that

span. He also led the NL in wins in 1895 (when he won 35 games) and finished second in 1893 with 34 victories. Young's won-loss record with the Spiders was a remarkable 241-135.

In 1899 Young came to play for the St. Louis Perfectos in a very odd, but at that time legal way. St. Louis (then called the Browns) was one of the four American Association teams absorbed by the NL. By the end of the 1890s the team had fallen on hard times and was purchased by the owners of the Cleveland Spiders, the Robison brothers, who retained their ownership of the Spiders. Since Sunday baseball was banned in Cleveland but not in St. Louis, the Robisons essentially transferred the players from one team to the other, hoping that the better Cleveland players would make them more of a profit in a the better baseball town. Thus, Young found himself no longer playing professional baseball in Ohio. Young pitched only two years in St. Louis and his record was 45-35. The 1900 team was especially disappointing. The team badly underachieved and Young himself posted a mediocre 19-19 record. After the season owner Frank Robison criticized the players, singling out Young and a few others for special criticism. Most of Young's teammates felt the criticism of him was undeserved. In fact the episode caused irreparable damage to Young's heretofore good relationship with Robison.

A New League

Complicating all of this was the rise of the American League (AL). In 1900 the Western League, a minor league, changed its name to the American League. The AL soon after announced it was making a bid for major league status. Part of the upstart league's unifying structure was that league president, Ban Johnson, held 51 percent of the stock of each club in the league. The AL then went about placing teams in four Eastern cities: Baltimore, Boston, Philadelphia, and Washington, D.C. With eight teams in place the AL then initiated a bidding war with the NL for those established players who were not under contract. Cy Young was one of these and the Boston team made an offer to him. Meanwhile he served as the St. Louis representative to the February 1901 meeting of the Players Protective Association—an early form of player unionization.

Young signed with the Boston AL team (they were not yet named the Red Sox) in March 1901 for what has been estimated at $3,500. This figure reflects a $500 increase over his 1900 salary, but more important he was offered a three-year contract by the Boston owners rather than the one-year contract that the Robison brothers had presented. Just as important, St. Louis catcher, Lou Criger had already signed with Boston and Young and he would be reunited.

If the Robisons thought Young was past his prime, as he was 34 years old when the 1901 season began, he set out to prove them wrong. This he did by dominating the new league during his first three years with Boston. The 1901 season was one of the finest of Young's career. His record was 33-10-the 33 wins led the league. He also had the lowest ERA, 1.62, in the AL in 1901 and allowed the fewest walks per nine innings while leading the league in strikeouts. He was second in the AL in innings pitched that year with 371 1/3. He followed that up with a season that was only slightly less magnificent. In 1902 Young's record was 32-11. He again led the AL in victories, also innings pitched with 384 2/3. He was second in strikeouts and had the second fewest walks per nine innings in the league. In 1903, at age 36, Young's record was 28-9. Though he recorded five fewer victories than the previous year Young again led the league in that category. He also led the AL in innings pitched, 341 2/3, and fewest walks per nine innings.

At the end of the 1903 season the champions of the AL and the NL played what became known as the World Series. Boston won the AL pennant and faced the Pittsburgh Pirates, winners of the NL pennant. At that time the World Series was a best-of-nine format (it was permanently reduced to its present-day best-of-seven format in 1922). Young vindicated his dismal postseason performance of 11 years earlier by figuring prominently in Boston's victory in the Series. He started three games and pitched in a fourth. His record was 2-1 with an ERA of 1.85. Over the course of his first contract with Boston Young's record was an amazing 93-30, the World Series excluded. He pitched 1097 2/3 innings during which he recorded 494 strikeouts. No other pitcher had recorded more than 58 victories after reaching the age of 34. Young's record after age 34 was 232-155. (The pitcher with the most victories after age 34 was Charley Radbourn, whose record was 58-36.)

Perfect

Young was truly the toast of the town in Boston at the beginning of the 20th century. During the 1904 season the 37-year-old pitched the finest game of his fabled career. It happened in Boston on May 5, 1904, when the Philadelphia Athletics were in town. Young faced Philadelphia's ace and future Hall of Famer, Rube Waddell. It has been estimated that 10,000 people were in the stands to see the two great pitchers square off. Boston won the game 3-0, but more important Young pitched the first perfect game (in which the pitcher gives up neither a hit nor a walk) in AL history. It was also the first perfect game in the major leagues since the pitching distance had been moved back to 60 feet 6 inches. Young also set the then-record of 45 consecutive scoreless innings; and pitched 24 consecutive no-hit innings. At the end of the season Young pitched three consecutive shutouts to clinch the league pennant for Boston. Young's record in 1904 was 26-16. There was no World Series that year because, John Brush and John McGraw, the owner and manager, respectively, of the NL champion New York Giants, refused to let their team play. They still considered the AL inferior despite the fact Boston was the reigning world champion. Later Brush backed down from his unpopular position and tried to schedule a World Series in the spring of 1905 but the idea never took hold.

1904 was Young's last truly great year though he played until 1911. In 1905 he suffered through the first losing season of his career, posting a record of 18-19. In 1906 his record fell to 13-21. He did manage to bounce back his final two years with Boston: his 1907 record was 21-15 and in 1908 he went 21-11. He also pitched two no-

hit games in 1908—the last one nearly a perfect game. Young's record for his eight seasons in Boston was 192-109.

Following the 1908 season Young was traded to Cleveland in the AL. In 1909 his record was 19-15. In 1910 he went 7-10 and for part of the 1911 season he was 3-4. In 1911 Cleveland placed Young on waivers and the Boston Braves in the NL for whom he posted a 4-5 record selected him. His record with Cleveland during two seasons plus was 29-29. For his career he won 511 games and lost 316, both records. He also pitched a total of 7354 2/3 innings. Not surprisingly he also ranks first among pitchers in the number of games started and the number of complete games. Despite the origins of his nickname and his ability to throw hard, Young was a master of control. Fourteen times he led the league in fewest walks per nine innings, including a stretch of nine consecutive years, covering both leagues. He struck out 2,803 batters during his career. In 1937 Cy Young was voted into the baseball Hall of Fame.

When his baseball career ended Young retired to the farm he and his wife had purchased in 1904 and lived another 43 years. In 1913 Young signed to manage the Cleveland Green Sox of the Federal League. He died on November 4, 1955, in Newcomerstown, Ohio. Young played in an era before all-star teams were chosen and postseason awards distributed, but in 1955 he received a singular, posthumous honor. An award for the best pitcher in baseball was instituted and named for him. Since 1967 the Cy Young award has been given to the best pitcher in each league.

Books

Browning, Reed, *Cy Young: A Baseball Life,* University of Massachusetts Press, 2000.

Porter, David L., ed., *Biographical Dictionary of American Sports,* Greenwood Press, 1987.

Online

"Cy Young," Baseball-Reference.com http://www.baseball-reference.com/y/youngcy01.shtml (January 7, 2004). □

Raul Yzaguirre

Raul Yzaguirre (born 1939) is considered a key leader in the U.S. civil rights movement. Dedicating much of his adult life to the advocacy of Hispanic Americans, Yzaguirre spoke out on many issues of contemporary concern as president of the National Council of La Raza from 1996 until 2004.

One of the most high-profile Hispanics in the United States due to his outspoken advocacy of the interests of Mexican-Americans and the creation of a pluralistic society that prides itself on its cultural diversity, Raul Yzaguirre was president of the National Council of La Raza, a Washington, D.C.-based think tank,

for three decades. Representing the interests of his constituents in education, immigration, and in other social policy matters, he devoted his energies to improving the opportunities for Hispanic Americans as that group became a growing and increasingly influential sector of the U.S. population during the late 20th century.

Lifelong Activist

Raul Humberto Yzaguirre was born July 22, 1939, in San Juan, a town in south Texas's Rio Grande Valley. The first son of young parents Ruben Antonio and Eve Linda (Morin) Yzaguirre, Yzaguirre grew up a member of an ethnic group that had battled discrimination for generations. In the late 1800s Hispanics formed mutual aid societies—or *mutualistas* as a way of standing together in the face of the discrimination and violence that was directed toward them. During the Great Depression of the 1930s many Mexican Americans were deported back to Mexico as a way of decreasing unemployment in the southern states; discrimination also existed in areas of education and employment that would not be ended until the civil rights movement of the mid-20th century and beyond. Discrimination also touched Yzaguirre personally. Although his family could trace its Texas ancestry back to the early eighteenth century, due to his Hispanic ethnicity young Yzaguirre carried an identity card so that he was able to prove his status as an American citizen when confronted. This heritage, of being somehow a less-than-valid citizen, coupled with his parents' desire for their son to gain an education beyond their own high school diploma, fostered in Yzaguirre a drive to

succeed. By age 15 he was already active as a community organizer, his first accomplishment an auxiliary of the Hispanic veterans' organization American G.I. Forum called the American G.I. Forum Juniors. Graduating from Pharr San Juan-Alamo high school in 1958, he then enlisted in the U.S. Air Force Medical Corps, where he served for four years and earned certification as a registered medical technologist.

After leaving the Air Force in 1962, the following year Yzaguirre enrolled at the University of Maryland on the G.I. Bill, intending to begin a career in medicine. After one year, however, he decided to transfer to George Washington University, where he became involved in student and community activism in the capitol region. Marrying Audrey H. Bristow during his sophomore year, in 1968 Yzaguirre received his B.S. degree, and began his career in public policy. Going to school in the Washington, D.C. area had inspired Yzaguirre with the changes then going on in the federal government with relation to social justice. During the administration of President Lyndon B. Johnson the president had begun implementation of his "Great Society" program, one of the most notable facets being the 1964 passage of the Economic Opportunity Act. Under this act, the U.S. Office of Economic Opportunity (OEO) was established to serve as a chief actor in Johnson's so-called War on Poverty. Believing that at the federal level of government his efforts would do the most good, Yzaguirre joined the OEO's Migrant Division as a program analyst. In 1969 he founded Interstate Research Associates, a firm specializing in Mexican-American and education-based studies that Yzaguirre built into a highly respected nonprofit consulting firm now based in Washington, D.C.; after serving as the organization's executive director, he left in 1973 to return to Texas.

Growth of La Raza

In 1964, the same year that saw passage of the Economic Opportunity Act, 26-year-old Yzaguirre was working as a community organizer in south Texas. He founded the National Organization for Mexican-American Services (NOMAS) as a small nonprofit organization. NOMAS quickly expanded, and as its focus became more clear during the next four years, Yzaguirre joined with others who envisioned a larger organization, the Southwest Council of La Raza—now called the National Council of La Raza (NCLR). A nonpartisan, tax-exempt umbrella organization established in 1968 and dedicated to reducing poverty and racial discrimination and improving social opportunities for Hispanic Americans, the Washington, D.C.-based NCLR has become a respected voice of Hispanic interests in North America.

The name of Yzaguirre's new organization came after much thought. The term "la raza," while sometimes narrowly translated as "the race," actually has a broader meaning. First coined by early 20th-century Latin-American scholar José Vasconselos, the term translates into English most closely as "the Hispanic people of the New World," a reflection of Vasconselos' realization that Latin Americas are not a race, but rather a union of many old-world races, faiths, and cultures: African, Arab, European, Jew, and Native American. Indeed, by 2000 the U.S. Latino population of 33.5 million people was composed of 66 percent Mexican Americans, 14 percent Central and South Americans, 9 percent Puerto Ricans, and 4 percent Cubans, in addition to Spanish-speaking immigrants from Europe and elsewhere.

During the first years of the NCLR's existence, Yzaguirre assisted the board of directors and the group's executive director, Herman Gallegos. Becoming president and chief executive officer of NCLR in 1974, Yzaguirre charted a new course for the organization, and dedicated his efforts to promote the interests of U.S. Latinos in areas of health care, education, employment, home ownership, and immigration. Boasting 270 affiliates in 40 states as well as Puerto Rico and the District of Columbia by 2000, NCLR grew to become the largest, most influential constituency-based national Hispanic organization in the United States. In addition, with its multimillion-dollar budget and a community network extending to 270 social activist groups across the nation, its efforts touch the lives of over 3.5 million Latinos each year.

While, according to the 2000 U.S. census blacks comprised 13 percent of the U.S. population and whites 69 percent, Hispanics had also become a significant minority group, also ranking at 13 percent of the total U.S. population. In contrast to the black minority, however, Hispanics' advances in this area were recent; during the 1990s alone their population increased by 60 percent. Census data further showed that, with a growth rate greater than that of the U.S. population overall, the Hispanic population was projected to become the largest U.S. minority group by 2005.

High-Profile Social Advocate

The findings of the U.S. census, while encouraging to Hispanics who had long suffered from a low political profile in relation to the vocal black minority, also reflected problems that Yzaguirre had been grappling with for several decades. Although they were the fastest-growing U.S. population segment, Hispanics also showed traditionally low rates of graduation from either high school or college, and most served in jobs that traditionally paid meagre wages: as laborers or in service industries, for example. The median income of an Hispanic family was far below that of whites, and one quarter of all Latinos lived below the so-called "poverty line," according to the census.

While the NCLR worked to combat the problems facing Hispanics on the grassroots level through its network of social-service advocates, Yzaguirre tackled the problem on the federal and organizational level, becoming a figurehead for NCLR concerns. In addition to speaking before organization and university assemblies, he worked to cultivate a media presence as well, and was soon sought out as a commentator on Hispanic concerns by the major television networks, as well as speaking on the *Today* show and on National Public Radio. Widely quoted in the press, his editorials and remarks were picked up in the pages of the nation's most respected newspapers: the *Chicago Tribune*, *Los Angeles Times*, *New York Times*, and *Wall Street Journal* among them.

Deeply involved in immigration issues, he joined the Council on Foreign Relations and in 1979 began a five-year commitment to the Working Commission on the Concerns of Hispanics and Blacks. From 1976 to 1979 he chaired the Forum of National Hispanic Organizations, and became involved within the Common Cause organization as well. In 1977 he cofounded the National Neighborhood Coalition, and was the first Hispanic to serve on the executive committee of the Leadership Conference on Civil Rights. From 1989 to 1990 Yzaguirre also became one of the first Latinos to hold a fellowship at the Institute of Politics at Harvard University's John F. Kennedy School of Government.

Vocal Proponent of Latino Family

Addressing issues of immigration, Yzaguirre believes that the United States has the duty to protect its borders and decide who it should allow within its borders. But he also maintains that the United States must recognize itself as a nation composed of immigrants. The nation's immigration policies, therefore, must reflect its own heritage, as well as its open relationship with neighbors to the north and south. Criticizing the traditional Bracero system that seeks to identify illegal immigrants by allowing them to obtain temporary work permits, he has argued that a truly fair immigration policy would allow taxpaying illegal immigrants—many of whom risk arrest in order to support their families by working in the United States—to earn full legal status as American citizens.

On the controversy regarding bilingual education, Yzaguirre has supported efforts to establish such programs when combined with strong English-language programs. While encouraging Hispanics to treasure the traditions and language of their forbears, he also has exhorted Latinos to learn English as a way of integrating fully in their role as American citizens. Other issues on which Yzaguirre has spoken out include the media's representation of Hispanic Americans and social welfare items as extending food stamps and other benefits to legal immigrants who are not yet citizens of the United States.

Yzaguirre's strongest advocacy has been in the arena of education, which he sees as the key to strengthening the Latino family. In honor of his efforts, Texas's Tejano Center for Community Concerns established charter schools in Houston and Brownsville that bear his name: The Raul Yzaguirre School for Success. Acting within the political arena, during the late 1990s Yzaguirre was appointed chairperson of President Bill Clinton's advisory commission on Educational Excellence for Hispanic Americans, although he left after a year due to differences between himself and the Clinton Administration.

A Life's Work Honored

Yzaguirre has been honored on many occasions for his work, both in and out of the Latino community. He became the first Hispanic to receive Princeton University's Rockefeller Public Service Award for outstanding public service in 1979. Almost two decades later, in 1998, he was awarded both the Hubert H. Humphrey Civil Rights Award by the Leadership Conference on Civil Rights, and the Charles

Evan Hughes Gold Medal Award for courageous leadership in civic and humanitarian affairs, presented to Yzaguirre by the National Conference for Community and Justice. One of the most noted honors of his career came in 1993, when the Mexican government presented Yzaguirre with the Order of the Aztec Eagle, the highest honor awarded by that country to citizens of another nation.

In addition to his work for the NCLR, Yzaguirre has served on a number of boards of directors, including the Salvation Army, the National Democratic Institute, Sears, and the Enterprise Foundation, and during the 1990s was chairperson of the Independent Sector, a large-scale non-profit coalition of foundations, nonprofit corporations, and voluntary organizations. He also founded the Hispanic Association of Corporate Responsibility as a way of encouraging an Hispanic presence in U.S. corporate structure. Other roles include serving as president of the Mexican and American Solidarity Foundation. A strong supporter of his own family as well, Yzaguirre and his wife have raised five children, Regina, Raul Jr., Elisa, Roberto, Rebecca, and Benjamin.

"I believe that we seek power to help this nation fulfill its destiny; to live up to its ideals and to go beyond the sometimes narrow definition of what it means to be an American," Yzaguirre remarked at the 2003 awards ceremony of the Congressional Hispanic Caucus Institute.

Noting that Hispanics will continue to demand equal rights, he went on to state his pluralistic vision of "a nation where people are judged by their actions and not by their accents." While continuing to act as a leader of the Latino community, in January of 2004, at age 65, Yzaguirre stepped down as NCLR president, choosing University of Kansas vice chancellor Janet Murguia to take his place. His appointment was a reflection of a new era for the NCLR as well as for Hispanic Americans, as Latino populations have shifted north and to the Midwest since the 1990s. During the announcement of her appointment Murguia noted to the *Kansas City Star:* "It is not only important that the needs of the Hispanic community be advanced for the sake of our community, but really for the sake of our country. The stakes are very high, and I am humbled by this opportunity."

Periodicals

Americas, June-July, 1980.
Hispanic, July, 1992.
Kansas City Star, January 6, 2004.
Nuestro, March, 1982.

Online

National Council of La Raza Web site, http://www.nclr.org/; profile of Yzaguirre; text of speech before Congressional Hispanic Caucus Institute. □

Z

Natan Zach

Israeli poet, critic, editor and translator Natan Zach (born 1930) is credited with beginning a stylistic revolution within the world of Israeli poetry. He maintains an active role in educating and shaping the poets of the world in his position among the faculty in the Humanities Department at the University of Haifa in Israel.

Beginnings

Zach was born of a German father and an Italian mother on December 13, 1930, in Berlin, Germany and immigrated to Palestine in 1935 when he was five years old. The family soon settled in Haifa, and little is recorded in English regarding his formative years. His first poem was published in 1950, and he was enrolled in various educational institutions from 1952 until he received his BA from the Hebrew University in Jerusalem and Tel Aviv in 1967. From 1968 until 1979 Zach lived in England and did his doctorate work at the University of Essex in England. He was granted his Ph.D. from that institution in 1970. He then returned to Israel to lecture at Tel Aviv University and was later appointed as a professor at the University of Haifa.

Literary Career

Zach was appointed Artistic Co–Director of the Ohel Theatre in Israel in 1960, and stayed with them until 1965. During the same period he served as Lector of the Dvir Publishing House in Tel Aviv for five years from 1959 until 1964. He was an advisor for the Chambre Theater in Tel Aviv in 1967, and served as the London news editor for the Jewish Telegraphic Agency from 1967 through 1979. He has acted as Co–Editor of the Igre Literary Year Book in Jerusalem since 1984, and has worked in Haifa, Israel as a professor of comparative literature since 1993.

Zach is not only a poet, but is also a celebrated translator from English and German into Hebrew. He has translated (among others) the poetry of Else Schüler and Alan Ginsberg. In addition to poetry he wrote a prose piece titled *Death of my Mother,* and his work has been published on its own and in periodicals around the world including *Atlantic Monthly* (U.S.), *Stand* (UK), *Caracters* (France), *Hortulus* (Switzerland), and all major Israeli periodicals.

Activism

Zach has been an ardent civil–rights activist. In 1988 he and fellow literary critic Nissim Calderon were scheduled to head the advisory committee for the International Poetry Festival celebrating Israel's 40th Anniversary, but felt that the festival would not be able to separate itself from the government's military actions at the time on the West Bank, and they feared that supporting one would be supporting the other. In their letter of resignation posted on *The New York Review of Books* website, Zach and Calderon wrote, "A Government . . . [whose acts] may only be described as State Terror. . . no longer merits that poets come to a festivity hosted by it to read there from their poems." Their resignation and inflammatory letter launched a great deal of controversy. The remaining contributors either resigned or expressed their intention to boycott the festival, and as a result it was officially cancelled.

Revolutionary Poet

Zach has been known since the mid–1950s as the leader of the Hebrew Modernistic Revolution. *Contemporary Authors* stated that he is known "for having introduced a sparse, colloquial style of poetry, which broke away from the formal, musical form that was prevalent in Hebrew poetry in the 1930s and 1940s." Yair Mazor, in his 1998 analysis of contemporary Hebrew poetry published in *World Literature Today*, discussed Zach's hand in the birth of what he describes as a "tempestuously esthetic revolution in the territory of modern Hebrew/contemporary Israeli poetry." Mazor discussed the *Likerat* (Toward)—a group of young poets and critics spearheaded by Zach that admired and aspired to the poetic principles of artists such as Ezra Pound, T.S. Eliot, W.H. Auden, William Carlos Williams, Wallace Stevens, and e.e. cummings. Zach's most significant contribution to this movement would be the publication of his 1959 article *Reflections Upon Nathan Alterman's Poetry*, a treatise in which he criticized Alterman's poetics in favor of "a 'poetics of modesty': simplicity in theme, syntax, and diction; understated rhetoric, avoidance of symbolistic intricacy, and flexible rhyme patterns; metrical and rhythmic structures that follow and reflect the flow of conversational language, refraining from lofty, elevated, cerebral, and flashy poetic devices and structures while employing irony in a subtle, distilled fashion; in short, an appealingly simple poetics without undue simplification."

Translation Troubles

Despite having written prolifically since the 1950s, only two of Zach's titles have been released in English: *Against Parting* (1967) and *The Static Element* (1983), which includes selections from *Early Poems* (1955), *Various Poems* (1960), *All the Milk and Honey* (1964) and *North Easterly* (1979). Critic Alan Mintz, in a *New Republic* review of *The Static Element*—Zach's personal responses to World War II which were written between 1955 and 1979—described Zach's belief that "[p]oetry had to be brought back close to the bone of modern consciousness." The style Zach favored was conversational and spare, an aggressive departure from the traditional style of Hebrew poetry.

While Zach is a major Israeli poet, he has never been as well known outside of his native land as his contemporary Yehuda Amichai, who has been extremely popular with the international reading public. Zach is considered by most critics to be a superior craftsman to Amichai, but his reputation has been irreversibly affected by the fact that his work is more difficult to translate from Hebrew into English. The reason for this lies literally in the translations. While Zach's work remains largely un–translated, Amichai made sure that his poems were well–translated and widely available to the international community. He also spent a great deal of time participating in reading tours of the United States and Europe. Mintz explains, "Because Zach's [poetic messages] depend on fine manipulations of tone and idiom, his verse does not go over into English easily." Mintz believes that the popularity of Zach's works will grow in the future as more translations are completed because his poetry is international and modern, rather than exclusively Israeli in both content and style.

Zach's use of colloquial Hebrew set him apart from both his predecessors and his contemporaries, as did his use of secular literary allusions. Despite his general lack of exposure, the *Jewish Virtual Library* records that individual poems from Zach's published works have been widely translated and consumed, making the journey from Hebrew into languages including Arabic, Dutch, English, Portuguese, Russian, Yiddish, Vietnamese, and many others.

Honored Among Many

Zach was awarded the Bialik Prize (Israel's most prestigious literary award) for 1981, and received the Israel Prize (Israel's highest award for excellence in all areas of human effort) in 1995. He also won the Feronia Prize for poetry—an Italian award for international poets issued in Rome.

Books

Cassell's Encyclopaedia of World Literature, Volume 3, William Morrow & Company, Inc., 1973.
Contemporary Authors, Volume 156, Gale Research, 1997.
The International Authors and Writers Who's Who, 10th Edition, Melrose Press Ltd., 1986.
The Reader's Adviser, Volume 2, R.R. Bowker, 1994.

Periodicals

The New Republic, Volume 189, October 1983.
World Literature Today, Volume 72, Number 3, Summer 1998.

Online

''Authors of the 11th Prague Writers' Festival,'' *11th Prague Writers' Festival 2001,* http://www.pwf.pragonet.cz/2001/authorsen/14 (January 2, 2004).

''Because Man is the Tree of the Field,'' *Jewish Heritage Online Magazine,* http://www.jhom.com/topics/trees/zach (January 2, 2004).

''A Letter of Resignation,'' *The New York Review of Books,* http://www.nybooks.com/articles/4406 (January 2, 2004).

''Natan Zach,'' *Israel—Poetry International Website,* http://www.israel.poetryinternational.org/cwolk/view/20207 (January 2, 2004).

''Natan Zach,'' *Jewish Virtual Library,* http://www.us—israel.org/jsource/biography/zach (January 2, 2004).

''Prof. Nathan Zach,'' *University of Haifa—Faculty of Humanities,* http://www.theatre.haifa.ac.il/staff/zach (January 2, 2004). □

HOW TO USE THE *SUPPLEMENT* INDEX

The *Encyclopedia of World Biography Supplement (EWB)* Index is designed to serve several purposes. First, it is a cumulative listing of biographies included in the entire second edition of *EWB* and its supplements (volumes 1-24). Second, it locates information on specific topics mentioned in volume 24 of the encyclopedia—persons, places, events, organizations, institutions, ideas, titles of works, inventions, as well as artistic schools, styles, and movements. Third, it classifies the subjects of *Supplement* articles according to shared characteristics. Vocational categories are the most numerous—for example, artists, authors, military leaders, philosophers, scientists, statesmen. Other groupings bring together disparate people who share a common characteristic.

The structure of the *Supplement* Index is quite simple. The biographical entries are cumulative and often provide enough information to meet immediate reference needs. Thus, people mentioned in the *Supplement* Index are identified and their life dates, when known, are given. Because this is an index to a *biographical* encyclopedia, every reference includes the *name* of the article to which the reader is directed as well as the volume and page numbers. Below are a few points that will make the *Supplement* Index easy to use.

Typography. All main entries are set in boldface type. Entries that are also the titles of articles in *EWB* are set entirely in capitals; other main entries are set in initial capitals and lowercase letters. Where a main entry is followed by a great many references, these are organized by subentries in alphabetical sequence. In certain cases—for example, the names of countries for which there are many references—a special class of subentries, set in small capitals and preceded by boldface dots, is used to mark significant divisions.

Alphabetization. The Index is alphabetized word by word. For example, all entries beginning with *New* as a separate word (*New Jersey, New York*) come before

Newark. Commas in inverted entries are treated as full stops (*Berlin; Berlin, Congress of; Berlin, University of; Berlin Academy of Sciences*). Other commas are ignored in filing. When words are identical, persons come first and subsequent entries are alphabetized by their parenthetical qualifiers (such as *book, city, painting*).

Titled persons may be alphabetized by family name or by title. The more familiar form is used—for example, *Disraeli, Benjamin* rather than *Beaconsfield, Earl of.* Cross-references are provided from alternative forms and spellings of names. Identical names of the same nationality are filed chronologically.

Titles of books, plays, poems, paintings, and other works of art beginning with an article are filed on the following word (*Bard, The*). Titles beginning with a preposition are filed on the preposition (*In Autumn*). In subentries, however, prepositions are ignored; thus *influenced by* would precede the subentry *in* literature.

Literary characters are filed on the last name. Acronyms, such as UNESCO, are treated as single words. Abbreviations, such as *Mr., Mrs.,* and *St.,* are alphabetized as though they were spelled out.

Occupational categories are alphabetical by national qualifier. Thus, *Authors, Scottish* comes before *Authors, Spanish,* and the reader interested in Spanish poets will find the subentry *poets* under *Authors, Spanish.*

Cross-references. The term *see* is used in references throughout the *Supplement* Index. The *see* references appear both as main entries and as subentries. They most often direct the reader from an alternative name spelling or form to the main entry listing.

This introduction to the *Supplement* Index is necessarily brief. The reader will soon find, however, that the *Supplement* Index provides ready reference to both highly specific subjects and broad areas of information contained in volume 24 and a cumulative listing of those included in the entire set.

INDEX

ALAMÁN, LUCAS (1792-1853), Mexican statesman **1** 99-100

ALARCÓN, PEDRO ANTONIO DE (1833-1891), Spanish writer and politician **1** 100-101

ALARCÓN Y MENDOZA, JUAN RUIZ DE (1581?-1639), Spanish playwright **1** 101

ALARIC (circa 370-410), Visigothic leader **1** 101-102

ALA-UD-DIN (died 1316), Khalji sultan of Delhi **1** 102-103

ALAUNGPAYA (1715-1760), king of Burma 1752-1760 **1** 103

ALBA, DUKE OF (Fernando Álvarez de Toledo; 1507-1582), Spanish general and statesman **1** 103-104

AL-BANNA, HASSAN (1906-1949), Egyptian religious leader and founder of the Muslim Brotherhood **1** 104-106

ALBEE, EDWARD FRANKLIN, III (born 1928), American playwright **1** 106-108

ALBÉNIZ, ISAAC (1860-1909), Spanish composer and pianist **1** 108-109

ALBERDI, JUAN BAUTISTA (1810-1884), Argentine political theorist **1** 109-110

ALBERS, JOSEPH (1888-1976), American artist and art and design teacher **1** 110

ALBERT (1819-1861), Prince Consort of Great Britain **1** 110-112

ALBERT I (1875-1934), king of the Belgians 1909-1934 **1** 112

ALBERT II (born 1934), sixth king of the Belgians **1** 112-113

ALBERTI, LEON BATTISTA (1404-1472), Italian writer, humanist, and architect **1** 113-115

ALBERTI, RAFAEL (born 1902), Spanish poet and painter **18** 13-15

ALBERTUS MAGNUS, ST. (circa 1193-1280), German philosopher and theologian **1** 115-116

ALBRIGHT, MADELEINE KORBEL (born 1937), United States secretary of state **1** 116-118

ALBRIGHT, TENLEY EMMA (born 1935), American figure skater **23** 3-6

ALBRIGHT, WILLIAM (1891-1971), American archaeologist **21** 1-3

ALBUQUERQUE, AFONSO DE (circa 1460-1515), Portuguese viceroy to India **1** 118-119

ALCIBIADES (circa 450-404 B.C.), Athenian general and politician **1** 119-120

ALCORN, JAMES LUSK (1816-1894), American lawyer and politician **1** 120-121

ALCOTT, AMOS BRONSON (1799-1888), American educator **1** 121

ALCOTT, LOUISA MAY (1832-1888), American author and reformer **1** 122

ALCUIN OF YORK (730?-804), English educator, statesman, and liturgist **1** 122-123

ALDRICH, NELSON WILMARTH (1841-1915), American statesman and financier **1** 123-124

ALDRIN, EDWIN EUGENE, JR. (Buzz Aldrin; born 1930), American astronaut **18** 15-17

ALDUS MANUTIUS (Teobaldo Manuzio; 1450?-1515), Italian scholar and printer **21** 3-5

ALEICHEM, SHOLOM (Sholom Rabinowitz; 1859-1916), writer of literature relating to Russian Jews **1** 124-125

ALEIJADINHO, O (Antônio Francisco Lisbôa; 1738-1814), Brazilian architect and sculptor **1** 125-126

ALEMÁN, MATEO (1547-after 1615), Spanish novelist **1** 126

ALEMÁN VALDÉS, MIGUEL (1902-1983), Mexican statesman, president 1946-1952 **1** 126-127

ALEMBERT, JEAN LE ROND D' (1717-1783), French mathematician and physicist **1** 127-128

ALESSANDRI PALMA, ARTURO (1868-1950), Chilean statesman, president 1920-1925 and 1932-1938 **1** 128-129

ALESSANDRI RODRIGUEZ, JORGE (born 1896), Chilean statesman, president 1958-1964 **1** 129-130

ALEXANDER I (1777-1825), czar of Russia 1801-1825 **1** 130-132

ALEXANDER II (1818-1881), czar of Russia 1855-1881 **1** 132-133

ALEXANDER III (1845-1894), emperor of Russia 1881-1894 **1** 133-134

ALEXANDER III (Orlando Bandinelli; c. 1100-1181), Italian pope 1159-1181 **24** 12-14

ALEXANDER VI (Rodrigo Borgia; 1431-1503), pope 1492-1503 **1** 134-135

ALEXANDER, SAMUEL (1859-1938), British philosopher **1** 141

ALEXANDER OF TUNIS, 1ST EARL (Harold Rupert Leofric George Alexander; born 1891), British field marshal **1** 135-136

ALEXANDER OF YUGOSLAVIA (1888-1934), king of the Serbs, Croats, and Slovenes 1921-1929 and of Yugoslavia, 1929-1934 **1** 136-137

ALEXANDER THE GREAT (356-323 B.C.), king of Macedon **1** 137-141

ALEXIE, SHERMAN (born 1966), Native American writer, poet, and translator **1** 141-142

ALEXIS MIKHAILOVICH ROMANOV (1629-1676), czar of Russia 1645-1676 **1** 142-143

ALEXIUS I (circa 1048-1118), Byzantine emperor 1081-1118 **1** 143-144

ALFARO, JOSÉ ELOY (1842-1912), Ecuadorian revolutionary, president 1895-1901 and 1906-1911 **1** 144-145

ALFIERI, CONTE VITTORIA (1749-1803), Italian playwright **1** 145-146

ALFONSÍN, RAUL RICARDO (born 1927), politician and president of Argentina (1983-) **1** 146-148

ALFONSO I (Henriques; 1109?-1185), king of Portugal 1139-1185 **1** 148

ALFONSO III (1210-1279), king of Portugal 1248-1279 **1** 148-149

ALFONSO VI (1040-1109), king of León, 1065-1109, and of Castile, 1072-1109 **1** 149

ALFONSO X (1221-1284), king of Castile and León 1252-1284 **1** 150-151

ALFONSO XIII (1886-1941), king of Spain 1886-1931 **1** 151

ALFRED (849-899), Anglo-Saxon king of Wessex 871-899 **1** 151-153

ALGER, HORATIO (1832-1899), American author **1** 153-154

ALGREN, NELSON (Abraham; 1909-1981), American author **1** 154-155

ALI (circa 600-661), fourth caliph of the Islamic Empire **1** 155-156

ALI, AHMED (1908-1998), Pakistani scholar, poet, author, and diplomat **22** 16-18

ALI, MUHAMMAD (Cassius Clay; born 1942), American boxer **1** 156-158

ALI, SUNNI (died 1492), king of Gao, founder of the Songhay empire **1** 158-159

ALIA, RAMIZ (born 1925), president of Albania (1985-) **1** 159

Alicia Alonso Ballet Company Alonso, Alicia **24** 14-17

ALINSKY, SAUL DAVID (1909-1972), U.S. organizer of neighborhood citizen reform groups **1** 161-162

AMOS (flourished 8th century B.C.), Biblical prophet **1** 205

AMPÈRE, ANDRÉ MARIE (1775-1836), French physicist **1** 205-206

AMUNDSEN, ROALD (1872-1928), Norwegian explorer **1** 206-207

AN LU-SHAN (703-757), Chinese rebel leader **1** 239-240

ANAN BEN DAVID (flourished 8th century), Jewish Karaite leader in Babylonia **1** 207-208

ANAXAGORAS (circa 500-circa 428 B.C.), Greek philosopher **1** 208-209

ANAXIMANDER (circa 610-circa 546 B.C.), Greek philosopher and astronomer **1** 209-210

ANAXIMENES (flourished 546 B.C.), Greek philosopher **1** 210

ANCHIETA, JOSÉ DE (1534-1597), Portuguese Jesuit missionary **1** 210-211

ANDERSEN, DOROTHY (1901-1963), American physician and pathologist **1** 212

ANDERSEN, HANS CHRISTIAN (1805-1875), Danish author **1** 212-214

ANDERSON, CARL DAVID (1905-1991), American physicist **1** 214-215

ANDERSON, JUDITH (1898-1992), American stage and film actress **1** 215-216

ANDERSON, JUNE (born 1953), American opera singer **1** 216-218

ANDERSON, MARIAN (1902-1993), African American singer **1** 218-219

ANDERSON, MAXWELL (1888-1959), American playwright **1** 219-220

ANDERSON, SHERWOOD (1876-1941), American writer **1** 220-221

ANDO, TADAO (born 1941), Japanese architect **18** 17-19

ANDRADA E SILVA, JOSÉ BONIFÁCIO DE (1763-1838), Brazilian-born statesman and scientist **1** 221-222

ANDRÁSSY, COUNT JULIUS (1823-1890), Hungarian statesman, prime minister 1867-1871 **1** 222-223

ANDREA DEL CASTAGNO (1421-1457), Italian painter **1** 223-224

ANDREA DEL SARTO (1486-1530), Italian painter **1** 224-225

ANDREA PISANO (circa 1290/95-1348), Italian sculptor and architect **1** 225-226

ANDRÉE, SALOMON AUGUST (1854-1897), Swedish engineer and Arctic balloonist **1** 226

ANDREESSEN, MARC (born 1972), American computer programmer who developed Netscape Navigator **19** 3-5

ANDREOTTI, GIULIO (born 1919), leader of Italy's Christian Democratic party **1** 226-228

ANDRETTI, MARIO (born 1940), Italian/American race car driver **1** 228-230

ANDREW, JOHN ALBION (1818-1867), American politician **1** 230-231

ANDREWS, CHARLES McLEAN (1863-1943), American historian **1** 231

ANDREWS, FANNIE FERN PHILLIPS (1867-1950), American educator, reformer, pacifist **1** 231-232

ANDREWS, ROY CHAPMAN (1884-1960), American naturalist and explorer **1** 232-233

ANDRIĆ, IVO (1892-1975), Yugoslav author **24** 21-24

ANDROPOV, IURY VLADIMIROVICH (1914-1984), head of the Soviet secret police and ruler of the Soviet Union (1982-1984) **1** 233-234

ANDROS, SIR EDMUND (1637-1714), English colonial governor in America **1** 234-235

ANDRUS, ETHEL (1884-1976), American educator and founder of the American Association of Retired Persons **19** 5-7

ANGELICO, FRA (circa 1400-1455), Italian painter **1** 235-236

ANGELL, JAMES ROWLAND (1869-1949), psychologist and leader in higher education **1** 236-237

ANGELOU, MAYA (Marguerite Johnson; born 1928), American author, poet, playwright, stage and screen performer, and director **1** 238-239

ANGUISSOLA, SOFONISBA (Sofonisba Anguisciola; c. 1535-1625), Italian artist **22** 22-24

ANNA IVANOVNA (1693-1740), empress of Russia 1730-1740 **1** 240-241

ANNAN, KOFI (born 1938), Ghanaian secretary-general of the United Nations **18** 19-21

ANNE (1665-1714), queen of England 1702-1714 and of Great Britain 1707-1714 **1** 241-242

ANNING, MARY (1799-1847), British fossil collector **20** 14-16

ANOKYE, OKOMFO (Kwame Frimpon Anokye; flourished late 17th century), Ashanti priest and statesman **1** 242-243

ANOUILH, JEAN (1910-1987), French playwright **1** 243-244

ANSELM OF CANTERBURY, ST. (1033-1109), Italian archbishop and theologian **1** 244-245

ANTHONY, ST. (circa 250-356), Egyptian hermit and monastic founder **1** 246-248

ANTHONY, SUSAN BROWNELL (1820-1906), American leader of suffrage movement **1** 246-248

ANTHONY OF PADUA, SAINT (Fernando de Boullion; 1195-1231), Portuguese theologian and priest **21** 7-9

Anthropological linguistics
see Linguistics

Anthropology (social science)
social
Barbeau, Marius **24** 42-44

Antibodies (biochemistry)
Tonegawa, Susumu **24** 417-420

ANTIGONUS I (382-301 B.C.), king of Macedon 306-301 B.C. **1** 248-249

ANTIOCHUS III (241-187 B.C.), king of Syria 223-187 B.C. **1** 249-250

ANTIOCHUS IV (circa 215-163 B.C.), king of Syria 175-163 B.C. **1** 250

ANTISTHENES (circa 450-360 B.C.), Greek philosopher **1** 250-251

ANTONELLO DA MESSINA (circa 1430-1479), Italian painter **1** 251-252

ANTONIONI, MICHELANGELO (born 1912), Italian film director **1** 252-253

ANTONY, MARK (circa 82-30 B.C.), Roman politician and general **1** 253-254

ANZA, JUAN BAUTISTA DE (1735-1788), Spanish explorer **1** 254-255

AOUN, MICHEL (born 1935), Christian Lebanese military leader and prime minister **1** 255-257

Apartheid (South Africa)
opponents
Breytenbach, Breyten **24** 66-68

APELLES (flourished after 350 B.C.), Greek painter **1** 257

APESS, WILLIAM (1798-1839), Native American religious leader, author, and activist **20** 16-18

APGAR, VIRGINIA (1909-1974), American medical educator, researcher **1** 257-259

APITHY, SOUROU MIGAN (1913-1989), Dahomean political leader **1** 259-260

APOLLINAIRE, GUILLAUME (1880-1918), French lyric poet **1** 260

APOLLODORUS (flourished circa 408 B.C.), Greek painter **1** 261

APOLLONIUS OF PERGA (flourished 210 B.C.), Greek mathematician **1** 261-262

APPELFELD, AHARON (born 1932), Israeli who wrote about anti-Semitism and the Holocaust **1** 262-263

APPERT, NICOLAS (1749-1941), French chef and inventor of canning of foods **20** 18-19

APPIA, ADOLPHE (1862-1928), Swiss stage director **1** 263-264

APPLEBEE, CONSTANCE (1873-1981), American field hockey coach **24** 24-25

APPLEGATE, JESSE (1811-1888), American surveyor, pioneer, and rancher **1** 264-265

APPLETON, SIR EDWARD VICTOR (1892-1965), British pioneer in radio physics **1** 265-266

APPLETON, NATHAN (1779-1861), American merchant and manufacturer **1** 266-267

APULEIUS, LUCIUS (c. 124-170), Roman author, philosopher, and orator **20** 19-21

AQQAD, ABBAS MAHMOUD AL (Abbas Mahmud al Aqqad; 1889-1964), Egyptian author **24** 25-27

AQUINO, BENIGNO ("Nino"; 1933-1983), Filipino activist murdered upon his return from exile **1** 267-268

AQUINO, CORAZON COJOANGCO (born 1933), first woman president of the Republic of the Philippines **1** 268-270

Arabic music
Kulthum, Umm **24** 220-222

ARAFAT, YASSER (also spelled Yasir; born 1929), chairman of the Palestinian Liberation Organization **1** 270-271

ARAGON, LOUIS (1897-1982), French surrealist author **1** 271-272

ARANHA, OSVALDO (1894-1960), Brazilian political leader **1** 272-273

ARATUS (271-213 B.C.), Greek statesman and general **1** 273-274

ARBENZ GUZMÁN, JACOBO (1913-1971), president of Guatemala (1951-1954) **1** 274-276

Arbitration, industrial
see Labor unions

ARBUS, DIANE NEMEROV (1923-1971), American photographer **1** 276-277

ARCHIMEDES (circa 287-212 B.C.), Greek mathematician **1** 277-280

ARCHIPENKO, ALEXANDER (1887-1964), Russian-American sculptor and teacher **1** 280-281

Architecture
Smythson, Robert **24** 378-381
Villanueva, Carlos Raúl **24** 431-432

ARCINIEGAS, GERMAN (1900-1999), Colombian historian, educator, and journalist **24** 27-29

ARDEN, ELIZABETH (Florence Nightingale Graham; 1878?-1966), American businesswoman **1** 281-282

ARENDT, HANNAH (1906-1975), Jewish philosopher **1** 282-284

ARENS, MOSHE (born 1925), aeronautical engineer who became a leading Israeli statesman **1** 284-285

ARÉVALO, JUAN JOSÉ (1904-1951), Guatemalan statesman, president 1944-1951 **1** 285-286

Argentina (Argentine Republic; nation, South America)
migration of Russian Jews to
de Hirsch, Maurice **24** 104-106

Arianism (Christian heresy)
doctrine condemned
Sylvester I **24** 397-399

ARIAS, ARNULFO (1901-1988), thrice elected president of Panama **1** 286-287

ARIAS SANCHEZ, OSCAR (born 1941), Costa Rican politician, social activist, president, and Nobel Peace Laureate (1987) **1** 287-289

ARIOSTO, LUDOVICO (1474-1533), Italian poet and playwright **1** 289-290

ARISTARCHUS OF SAMOS (circa 310-230 B.C.), Greek astronomer **1** 290-291

ARISTIDE, JEAN-BERTRAND (born 1953), president of Haiti (1990-91 and 1994-95); deposed by a military coup in 1991; restored to power in 1994 **1** 291-293

ARISTOPHANES (450/445-after 385 B.C.), Greek playwright **1** 293-294

ARISTOTLE (384-322 B.C.), Greek philosopher and scientist **1** 295-296

ARIUS (died circa 336), Libyan theologian and heresiarch **1** 297-298

ARKWRIGHT, SIR RICHARD (1732-1792), English inventor and industrialist **1** 298

ARLEN, HAROLD (born Hyman Arluck; 1905-1986), American jazz pianist, composer, and arranger **19** 7-9

ARLT, ROBERTO (Roberto Godofredo Christophersen Arlt; 1900-1942), Argentine author and journalist **23** 11-13

ARMANI, GIORGIO (1935-1997), Italian fashion designer **1** 299-301

ARMINIUS, JACOBUS (1560-1609), Dutch theologian **1** 301-302

ARMOUR, PHILIP DANFORTH (1832-1901), American industrialist **1** 302

Arms control
see Nuclear arms control

ARMSTRONG, EDWIN HOWARD (1890-1954), American electrical engineer and radio inventor **1** 302-303

ARMSTRONG, HENRY (Henry Jackson, Jr.; 1912-1988), American boxer and minister **21** 9-11

ARMSTRONG, LANCE (born 1971), American cyclist **23** 13-15

ARMSTRONG, LILLIAN HARDIN (1898-1971), African American musician **23** 15-17

ARMSTRONG, LOUIS DANIEL (1900-1971), African American jazz musician **1** 303-304

ARMSTRONG, NEIL ALDEN (born 1930), American astronaut **1** 304-306

ARMSTRONG, SAMUEL CHAPMAN (1839-1893), American educator **1** 306-307

Army Air Corps
see United States Air Force

ARNAZ, DESI (Desiderio Alberto Arnaz y De Acha; 1917-1986), American musician and actor **21** 12-14

ARNE, THOMAS AUGUSTINE (1710-1778), English composer **1** 307-308

ARNIM, ACHIM VON (Ludwig Joachim von Achim; 1781-1831), German writer **1** 308-309

ARNOLD, GEN. BENEDICT (1741-1801), American general and traitor **1** 309-310

ARNOLD, HENRY HARLEY (Hap; 1886-1950), American general **1** 310-311

ARNOLD, MATTHEW (1822-1888), English poet and critic **1** 311-313

ARNOLD, THOMAS (1795-1842), English educator **1** 313-314

BENJAMIN, JUDAH PHILIP (1811-1884), American statesman **2** 163-164

BENJAMIN, WALTER (1892-1940), German philosopher and literary critic **20** 32-34

BENN, GOTTFRIED (1886-1956), German author **2** 164

BENN, TONY (Anthony Neil Wedgewood Benn; born 1925), British Labour party politician **2** 164-166

BENNETT, ALAN (born 1934), British playwright **2** 166-167

BENNETT, ENOCH ARNOLD (1867-1931), English novelist and dramatist **2** 167-168

BENNETT, JAMES GORDON (1795-1872), Scottish-born American journalist and publisher **2** 168-169

BENNETT, JAMES GORDON, JR. (1841-1918), American newspaper owner and editor **2** 169-170

BENNETT, JOHN COLEMAN (1902-1995), American theologian **2** 170-171

BENNETT, RICHARD BEDFORD (1870-1947), Canadian statesman, prime minister 1930-1935 **2** 171-172

BENNETT, RICHARD RODNEY (born 1936), English composer **2** 172

BENNETT, ROBERT RUSSELL (1894-1981), American arranger, composer, and conductor **21** 32-34

BENNETT, WILLIAM JOHN (born 1943), American teacher and scholar and secretary of the Department of Education (1985-1988) **2** 172-174

BENNY, JACK (Benjamin Kubelsky; 1894-1974), American comedian and a star of radio, television, and stage **2** 174-176

BENTHAM, JEREMY (1748-1832), English philosopher, political theorist, and jurist **2** 176-178

BENTLEY, ARTHUR F. (1870-1957), American philosopher and political scientist **2** 178

BENTON, SEN. THOMAS HART (1782-1858), American statesman **2** 178-179

BENTON, THOMAS HART (1889-1975), American regionalist painter **2** 178-179

BENTSEN, LLOYD MILLARD (born 1921), senior United States senator from Texas and Democratic vice-presidential candidate in 1988 **2** 180-181

BENZ, CARL (1844-1929), German inventor **2** 182-183

BERCHTOLD, COUNT LEOPOLD VON (1863-1942), Austro-Hungarian statesman **2** 183-184

BERDYAEV, NICHOLAS ALEXANDROVICH (1874-1948), Russian philosopher **2** 184-185

BERELSON, BERNARD (1912-1979), American behavioral scientist **2** 185-186

BERENSON, BERNARD (1865-1959), American art critic and historian **20** 34-35

BERG, ALBAN (1885-1935), Austrian composer **2** 186-187

BERG, PAUL (born 1926), American chemist **2** 187-189

BERGER, VICTOR LOUIS (1860-1929), American politician **2** 189-190

BERGMAN, (ERNST) INGMAR (born 1918); Swedish film and stage director **2** 190-191

BERGMAN, INGRID (1917-1982), Swedish actress **20** 35-37

BERGSON, HENRI (1859-1941), French philosopher **2** 191-192

BERIA, LAVRENTY PAVLOVICH (1899-1953), Soviet secret-police chief and politician **2** 192-193

BERING, VITUS (1681-1741), Danish navigator in Russian employ **2** 193-194

BERIO, LUCIANO (1925-2003), Italian composer **2** 194-195

BERISHA, SALI (born 1944), president of the Republic of Albania (1992-) **2** 195-197

BERKELEY, BUSBY (William Berkeley Enos; 1895-1976), American filmmaker **20** 38-39

BERKELEY, GEORGE (1685-1753), Anglo-Irish philosopher and Anglican bishop **2** 197-198

BERKELEY, SIR WILLIAM (1606-1677), English royal governor of Virginia **2** 198-199

Berkshire Music Center (Tanglewood, Massachusetts) Koussevitzky, Serge **24** 213-215

BERLE, ADOLF AUGUSTUS, JR. (1895-1971), American educator **2** 199-200

BERLE, MILTON (1908-2002), American entertainer and actor **18** 37-39

BERLIN, IRVING (1888-1989), American composer **2** 200-201

BERLIN, ISAIAH (1909-1997), British philosopher **2** 201-203

BERLINER, ÉMILE (1851-1929), American inventor **20** 39-41

BERLIOZ, LOUIS HECTOR (1803-1869), French composer, conductor, and critic **2** 203-205

BERMEJO, BARTOLOMÉ (Bartolomé de Cárdenas; flourished 1474-1498), Spanish painter **2** 205

BERNADETTE OF LOURDES, SAINT (Marie Bernarde Soubirous; 1844-1879), French nun and Roman Catholic saint **21** 34-36

BERNANOS, GEORGES (1888-1948), French novelist and essayist **2** 206-207

BERNARD, CLAUDE (1813-1878), French physiologist **2** 208-210

BERNARD OF CLAIRVAUX, ST. (1090-1153), French theologian, Doctor of the Church **2** 207-208

BERNARDIN, CARDINAL JOSEPH (1928-1996), Roman Catholic Cardinal and American activist **2** 210-211

BERNAYS, EDWARD L. (1891-1995), American public relations consultant **2** 211-212

BERNBACH, WILLIAM (1911-1982), American advertising executive **19** 20-22

BERNERS-LEE, TIM (born 1955), English computer scientist and creator of the World Wide Web **20** 41-43

BERNHARDT, SARAH (Henriette-Rosine Bernard; 1844-1923), French actress **2** 212-214

BERNIER, JOSEPH E. (Joseph-Elzéan Bernier; 1852-1934), Canadian explorer **23** 35-37

BERNINI, GIAN LORENZO (1598-1680), Italian artist **2** 214-216 patrons of Innocent X **24** 183-185

BERNOULLI, DANIEL (1700-1782), Swiss mathematician and physicist **2** 216

BERNOULLI, JAKOB (Jacques or James Bernoulli; 1654-1705), Swiss mathematician **23** 37-39

BERNSTEIN, DOROTHY LEWIS (born 1914), American mathematician **2** 217

BERNSTEIN, EDUARD (1850-1932), German socialist **2** 218

BERNSTEIN, LEONARD (1918-1990), American composer, conductor, and pianist **2** 218-219

BERRI, NABIH (born 1939), leader of the Shi'ite Muslims in Lebanon **2** 220-222

BLOCH, FELIX (1905-1983), Swiss/American physicist **2** 328-330

BLOCH, KONRAD (born 1912), American biochemist **2** 330-332

BLOCH, MARC (1886-1944), French historian **2** 332-333

BLOCK, HERBERT (Herblock; 1909-2001), American newspaper cartoonist **2** 333-334

BLODGETT, KATHARINE BURR (1898-1979), American physicist **24** 54-56

BLOK, ALEKSANDR ALEKSANDROVICH (1880-1921), Russian poet **2** 335

BLOOM, ALLAN DAVID (1930-1992), American political philosopher, professor, and author **2** 335-337

BLOOMER, AMELIA JENKS (1818-1894), American reformer and suffrage advocate **2** 337

BLOOMFIELD, LEONARD (1887-1949), American linguist **2** 338

BLOOR, ELLA REEVE ("Mother Bloor"; 1862-1951), American labor organizer and social activist **2** 338-340

BLÜCHER, GEBHARD LEBERECHT VON (Prince of Wahlstatt; 1742-1819), Prussian field marshal **2** 340-341

Blues (music)
Wallace, Sippie **24** 437-440

BLUFORD, GUION STEWART, JR. (born 1942), African American aerospace engineer, pilot, and astronaut **2** 341-343

BLUM, LÉON (1872-1950), French statesman **2** 343-344

BLUME, JUDY (born Judy Sussman; b. 1938), American fiction author **2** 344-345

BLUMENTHAL, WERNER MICHAEL (born 1926), American businessman and treasury secretary **2** 345-346

BLY, NELLIE (born Elizabeth Cochrane Seaman; 1864-1922), American journalist and reformer **2** 346-348

BLYDEN, EDWARD WILMOT (1832-1912), Liberian statesman **2** 348-349

BOAS, FRANZ (1858-1942), German-born American anthropologist **2** 349-351

BOCCACCIO, GIOVANNI (1313-1375), Italian author **2** 351-353

BOCCIONI, UMBERTO (1882-1916), Italian artist **2** 353-354

BÖCKLIN, ARNOLD (1827-1901), Swiss painter **2** 354-355

BODE, BOYD HENRY (1873-1953), American philosopher and educator **2** 355-356

BODIN, JEAN (1529/30-1596), French political philosopher **2** 356-357

BOEHME, JACOB (1575-1624), German mystic **2** 357

BOEING, WILLIAM EDWARD (1881-1956), American businessman **2** 357-358

BOERHAAVE, HERMANN (1668-1738), Dutch physician and chemist **2** 358-359

BOESAK, ALLAN AUBREY (born 1945), opponent of apartheid in South Africa and founder of the United Democratic Front **2** 359-360

BOETHIUS, ANICIUS MANLIUS SEVERINUS (480?-524/525), Roman logician and theologian **2** 360-361

BOFF, LEONARDO (Leonardo Genezio Darci Boff; born 1938), Brazilian priest **22** 69-71

BOFFRAND, GABRIEL GERMAIN (1667-1754), French architect and decorator **2** 361

BOFILL, RICARDO (born 1939), post-modern Spanish architect **2** 362-363

BOGART, HUMPHREY (1899-1957), American stage and screen actor **2** 363-364

BOHEMUND I (of Tarantò; circa 1055-1111), Norman Crusader **2** 364

BOHLEN, CHARLES (CHIP) EUSTIS (1904-1973), United States ambassador to the Soviet Union, interpreter, and presidential adviser **2** 364-366

BÖHM-BAWERK, EUGEN VON (1851-1914), Austrian economist **2** 366

BOHR, NIELS HENRIK DAVID (1885-1962), Danish physicist **2** 366-368

BOIARDO, MATTEO MARIA (Conte di Scandiano; 1440/41-1494), Italian poet **2** 369

BOILEAU-DESPRÉAUX, NICHOLAS (1636?-1711), French critic and writer **2** 369-371

BOK, DEREK CURTIS (born 1930), dean of the Harvard Law School and president of Harvard University **2** 371-372

BOK, EDWARD WILLIAM (1863-1930), American editor and publisher **22** 71-73

BOK, SISSELA ANN (born 1934), American moral philosopher **2** 372-374

BOLEYN, ANNE (1504?-1536), second wife of Henry VIII **18** 47-49

BOLINGBROKE, VISCOUNT (Henry St. John; 1678-1751), English statesman **2** 374-375

BOLÍVAR, SIMÓN (1783-1830), South American general and statesman **2** 375-377

Bolivia, Republic of (nation; South America)
economic development
Montes, Ismael **24** 267-270

BOLKIAH, HASSANAL (Muda Hassanal Bolkiah Mu'izzaddin Waddaulah; born 1946), Sultan of Brunei **18** 49-51

BÖLL, HEINRICH (1917-1985), German writer and translator **2** 377-378

BOLTWOOD, BERTRAM BORDEN (1870-1927), American radiochemist **2** 378-379

BOLTZMANN, LUDWIG (1844-1906), Austrian physicist **2** 379-380

BOMBAL, MARÍA LUISA (1910-1980), Chilean novelist and story writer **2** 380-381

BONAPARTE, JOSEPH (1768-1844), French statesman, king of Naples 1806-1808 and of Spain 1808-1813 **2** 381-382

BONAPARTE, LOUIS (1778-1846), French statesman, king of Holland 1806-1810 **2** 382-383

BONAVENTURE, ST. (1217-1274), Italian theologian and philosopher **2** 383-384

BOND, HORACE MANN (1904-1972), African American educator **2** 384-386

BOND, JULIAN (born 1940), civil rights leader elected to the Georgia House of Representatives **2** 386-387

BONDFIELD, MARGARET GRACE (1873-1953), British union official and political leader **2** 388-389

BONDI, HERMANN (born 1919), English mathematician and cosmologist **18** 51-52

BONHOEFFER, DIETRICH (1906-1945), German theologian **2** 389-391

BONHEUR, ROSA (Marie Rosalie Bonheur; 1822-1899), French artist **19** 29-31

BONIFACE, ST. (circa 672-754), English monk **2** 391

BONIFACE VIII (Benedetto Caetani; 1235?-1303), pope 1294-1303 **2** 392-393

BONIFACIO, ANDRES (1863-1897), Filipino revolutionary hero **2** 393-394

BONINGTON, RICHARD PARKES
(1802-1828), English painter **2**
394-395

BONNARD, PIERRE (1867-1947), French
painter **2** 395-396

BONNIN, GERTRUDE SIMMONS
(Zitkala-Sa; Red Bird; 1876-1938),
Native American author and activist **18**
52-54

BONO (Paul Hewson; born 1960), Irish
musician and activist **24** 56-59

BONO, SONNY (Salvatore Bono; 1935-
1998), American entertainer and U.S.
Congressman **18** 54-56

BONTEMPS, ARNA (Arnaud Wendell
Bontempsl 1902-1973), American
author and educator **21** 47-50

**BONVALOT, PIERRE GABRIEL
ÉDOUARD** (1853-1933), French
explorer and author **2** 396

BOOLE, GEORGE (1815-1864), English
mathematician **2** 396-397

BOONE, DANIEL (1734-1820), American
frontiersman and explorer **2** 397-398

BOORSTIN, DANIEL J. (1914-2004),
American historian **2** 398-400

BOOTH, CHARLES (1840-1916), English
social scientist **2** 400-401

BOOTH, EDWIN (1833-1893), American
actor **2** 401-402

BOOTH, EVANGELINE CORY (1865-
1950), British/American humanist **2**
402-403

BOOTH, HUBERT CECIL (1871-1955),
English inventor of the vacuum cleaner
21 50-52

BOOTH, JOHN WILKES (1838-1865),
American actor **2** 404

BOOTH, JOSEPH (1851-1932), English
missionary in Africa **2** 404-405

BOOTH, WILLIAM (1829-1912), English
evangelist, Salvation Army founder **2**
405-406

BOOTHROYD, BETTY (born 1929), first
woman speaker in Great Britain's
House of Commons **2** 406-407

BORAH, WILLIAM EDGAR (1865-1940),
American statesman **2** 408

BORDEN, GAIL (1801-1874), American
pioneer and inventor of food-
processing techniques **2** 409

BORDEN, SIR ROBERT LAIRD (1854-
1937), Canadian prime minister, 1911-
1920 **2** 409-411

BORGES, JORGE LUIS (1899-1986),
Argentine author and critic **2** 411-412

BORGIA, CESARE (1475-1507), Italian
cardinal, general, and administrator **2**
412-413

BORGIA, LUCREZIA (1480-1519), Italian
duchess of Ferrara **2** 413-416

**BORGLUM, JOHN GUTZON DE LA
MOTHE** (1867-1941), American
sculptor and engineer **2** 416-417

BORI, LUCREZIA (Lucrezia Gonzá de
Riancho; 1887-1960), Spanish
American opera singer **23** 44-45

BORJA CEVALLOS, RODRIGO (born
1935), a founder of Ecuador's
Democratic Left (Izquierda
Democratica) party and president of
Ecuador (1988-) **2** 417-418

BORLAUG, NORMAN ERNEST (born
1914), American biochemist who
developed high yield cereal grains **2**
418-420

BORN, MAX (1882-1970), German
physicist **2** 420-421

Borneo (island)
see Indonesia

BOROCHOV, DOV BER (1881-1917),
early Zionist thinker who reconciled
Judaism and Marxism **2** 421-422

BORODIN, ALEKSANDR PROFIREVICH
(1833-1887), Russian composer **2**
422-423

BORROMEO, ST. CHARLES (1538-1584),
Italian cardinal and reformer **2**
423-424

BORROMINI, FRANCESCO (1599-1667),
Italian architect **2** 424-425

BOSANQUET, BERNARD (1848-1923),
English philosopher **2** 425-426

BOSCH, HIERONYMUS (1453-1516),
Netherlandish painter **2** 426-428

BOSCH, JUAN (born 1909), Dominican
writer, president, 1963 **2** 428-429

BOSE, SIR JAGADIS CHANDRA (1858-
1937), Indian physicist and plant
physiologist **2** 430-431

BOSE, SATYENDRANATH (1894-1974),
Indian physicist **20** 52-54

BOSE, SUBHAS CHANDRA (1897-1945),
Indian nationalist **2** 430-431

BOSOMWORTH, MARY MUSGROVE
(Cousaponokeesa; 1700-1765), Native
American/American interpreter,
diplomat, and businessperson **20**
54-56

BOSSUET, JACQUES BÉNIGNE (1627-
1704), French bishop and author **2**
431-432

Boston Red Sox (baseball team)
Young, Cy **24** 447-449

Boston Symphony Orchestra
Koussevitzky, Serge **24** 213-215

BOSWELL, JAMES (1740-1795), Scottish
biographer and diarist **2** 432-434

Botany (science)
illustrators
Chase, Mary Agnes **24** 79-81

BOTERO, FERNANDO (born 1932),
Colombian artist **24** 59-61

BOTHA, LOUIS (1862-1919), South
African soldier and statesman **2**
434-436

BOTHA, PIETER WILLEM (born 1916),
prime minister (1978-1984) and first
executive state president of the
Republic of South Africa **2** 436-438

BOTHE, WALTHER (1891-1957),
German physicist **2** 438-439

BOTTICELLI, SANDRO (1444-1510),
Italian painter **2** 439-440

BOUCHER, FRANÇOIS (1703-1770),
French painter **2** 440-442

BOUCICAULT, DION (1820-1890), Irish-
American playwright and actor **2**
442-443

BOUDICCA (Boadicea; died 61 A.D.),
Iceni queen **18** 56-58

BOUDINOT, ELIAS (Buck Watie;
Galagina; 1803-1839), Cherokee
leader and author **21** 52-54

BOUGAINVILLE, LOUIS ANTOINE DE
(1729-1811), French soldier and
explorer **2** 443-444

BOULANGER, NADIA (1887-1979),
French pianist and music teacher **20**
56-58

BOULEZ, PIERRE (born 1925), French
composer, conductor, and teacher **2**
444-445

BOULT, ADRIAN CEDRIC (1889-1983),
English conductor **24** 61-64

BOUMEDIENE, HOUARI (born 1932),
Algerian revolutionary, military leader,
and president **2** 445-446

**BOURASSA, JOSEPH-HENRI-
NAPOLEON** (1868-1952), French-
Canadian nationalist and editor **2**
446-447

BOURASSA, ROBERT (born 1933),
premier of the province of Quebec
(1970-1976 and 1985-) **2** 447-449

BOURDELLE, EMILE-ANTOINE (1861-
1929), French sculptor **2** 449-450

BOURGEOIS, LÉON (1851-1925),
French premier 1895-1896 **2** 450-451

transformed the English magazine *Tatler*, then the United States magazines *Vanity Fair* and the *New Yorker* **3** 47-48

BROWN, TONY (William Anthony Brown; born 1933), African American radio personality **24** 68-70

BROWN, WILLIAM WELLS (1815/16-1884), African American author and abolitionist **3** 48-49

BROWNE, SIR THOMAS (1605-1682), English author **3** 49-50

BROWNE, THOMAS ALEXANDER (Rolf Bolderwood; 1826-1915), Australian author **22** 85-87

BROWNER, CAROL M. (born 1955), U.S. Environmental Protection Agency administrator **3** 50-52

BROWNING, ELIZABETH BARRETT (1806-1861), English poet **3** 52-53

BROWNING, ROBERT (1812-1889), English poet **3** 53-55

BROWNLOW, WILLIAM GANNAWAY (1805-1877), American journalist and politician **3** 55-56

BROWNMILLER, SUSAN (born 1935), American activist, journalist, and novelist **3** 56-57

BROWNSON, ORESTES AUGUSTUS (1803-1876), American clergyman and transcendentalist **3** 57-58

BRUBACHER, JOHN SEILER (1898-1988), American historian and educator **3** 58-59

BRUBECK, DAVE (born 1920), American pianist, composer, and bandleader **3** 59-61

BRUCE, BLANCHE KELSO (1841-1898), African American politician **3** 62-63

BRUCE, DAVID (1855-1931), Australian parasitologist **3** 63

BRUCE, JAMES (1730-1794), Scottish explorer **3** 63-64

BRUCE, LENNY (Leonard Alfred Schneider; 1925-1966), American comedian **19** 39-41

BRUCE OF MELBOURNE, 1ST VISCOUNT (Stanley Melbourne Bruce; 1883-1967), Australian statesman **3** 61-62

BRUCKNER, JOSEPH ANTON (1824-1896), Austrian composer **3** 64-65

BRUEGEL, PIETER, THE ELDER (1525/30-1569), Netherlandish painter **3** 65-67

BRÛLÉ, ÉTIENNE (circa 1592-1633), French explorer in North America **3** 67-68

BRUNDTLAND, GRO HARLEM (1939-1989), Norwegian prime minister and chair of the United Nations World Commission for Environment and Development **3** 68-69

BRUNEL, ISAMBARD KINGDOM (1806-1859), English civil engineer **3** 69-70

BRUNELLESCHI, FILIPPO (1377-1446), Italian architect and sculptor **3** 70-72

BRUNER, JEROME SEYMOUR (born 1915), American psychologist **3** 72-73

BRUNHOFF, JEAN de (1899-1937), French author and illustrator **19** 41-42

BRUNNER, ALOIS (born 1912), Nazi German officer who helped engineer the destruction of European Jews **3** 73-74

BRUNNER, EMIL (1889-1966), Swiss Reformed theologian **3** 74-75

BRUNO, GIORDANO (1548-1600), Italian philosopher and poet **3** 75-76

BRUTON, JOHN GERARD (born 1947), prime minister of Ireland **3** 76-77

BRUTUS, DENNIS (born 1924), exiled South African poet and political activist opposed to apartheid **3** 77-78

BRUTUS, MARCUS JUNIUS (circa 85-42 B.C.), Roman statesman **3** 79-80

BRYAN, WILLIAM JENNINGS (1860-1925), American lawyer and politician **3** 80-82

BRYANT, PAUL ("Bear;" 1919-1983), American college football coach **3** 82-83

BRYANT, WILLIAM CULLEN (1794-1878), American poet and editor **3** 83-85

BRYCE, JAMES (1838-1922), British historian, jurist, and statesman **3** 85

Bryn Mawr College (Pennsylvania) Applebee, Constance **24** 24-25

BRZEZINSKI, ZBIGNIEW (1928-1980), assistant to President Carter for national security affairs (1977-1980) **3** 85-87

BUBER, MARTIN (1878-1965), Austrian-born Jewish theologian and philosopher **3** 87-89

BUCHALTER, LEPKE (Louis Bachalter; 1897-1944), American gangster **19** 42-44

BUCHANAN, JAMES (1791-1868), American statesman, president 1857-1861 **3** 89-90

BUCHANAN, PATRICK JOSEPH (born 1938), commentator, journalist, and presidential candidate **3** 90-91

BUCK, PEARL SYDENSTRICKER (1892-1973), American novelist **3** 91-93

BUCKINGHAM, 1ST DUKE OF (George Villiers; 1592-1628), English courtier and military leader **3** 93-94

BUCKINGHAM, 2D DUKE OF (George Villiers; 1628-1687), English statesman **3** 94-95

BUCKLE, HENRY THOMAS (1821-1862), English historian **3** 95-96

BUCKLEY, WILLIAM F., JR. (born 1925), conservative American author, editor, and political activist **3** 96-97

BUDDHA (circa 560-480 B.C.), Indian founder of Buddhism **3** 97-101

BUDDHADĀSA BHIKKHU (Nguam Phanich; born 1906), founder of Wat Suan Mokkhabalārama in southern Thailand and interpreter of Theravāda Buddhism **3** 101-102

BUDÉ, GUILLAUME (1467-1540), French humanist **3** 102-103

BUDGE, DON (J. Donald Budge; born 1915), American tennis player **21** 57-59

BUECHNER, FREDERICK (born 1926), American novelist and theologian **3** 103-105

BUEL, JESSE (1778-1839), American agriculturalist and journalist **3** 105

BUFFALO BILL (William Frederick Cody; 1846-1917), American scout and publicist **3** 105-106

BUFFETT, WARREN (born 1930), American investment salesman **3** 106-109

BUFFON, COMTE DE (Georges Louis Leclerc; 1707-1788), French naturalist **3** 109-111

BUGEAUD DE LA PICONNERIE, THOMAS ROBERT (1784-1849), Duke of Isly and marshal of France **3** 111

BUICK, DAVID (1854-1929), American inventor and businessman **19** 44-45

BUKHARI, MUHAMMAD IBN ISMAIL AL- (810-870), Arab scholar and Moslem saint **3** 111-112

BUKHARIN, NIKOLAI IVANOVICH (1858-1938), Russian politician **3** 112-113

BUKOWSKI, CHARLES (1920-1994), American writer and poet **3** 113-115

BULATOVIC, MOMIR (born 1956), president of Montenegro (1990-1992) and of the new Federal Republic of Yugoslavia (1992-) **3** 115-116

BULFINCH, CHARLES (1763-1844), American colonial architect **3** 116-117

BULGAKOV, MIKHAIL AFANASIEVICH (1891-1940), Russian novelist and playwright **3** 117

BULGANIN, NIKOLAI (1885-1975), chairman of the Soviet Council of Ministers (1955-1958) **3** 118-119

BULOSAN, CARLOS (1911-1956), American author and poet **21** 59-61

BULTMANN, RUDOLF KARL (1884-1976), German theologian **3** 119-120

BULWER-LYTTON, EDWARD (1st Baron Lytton of Knebworth; 1803-1873), English novelist **22** 87-88

BUNAU-VARILLA, PHILIPPE JEAN (1859-1940), French engineer and soldier **3** 120-121

BUNCHE, RALPH JOHNSON (1904-1971), African American diplomat **3** 121-122

BUNDY, McGEORGE (born 1919), national security adviser to two presidents **3** 122-124

BUNIN, IVAN ALEKSEEVICH (1870-1953), Russian poet and novelist **3** 124

BUNSEN, ROBERT WILHELM (1811-1899), German chemist and physicist **3** 124-125

BUNSHAFT, GORDON (1909-1990), American architect **3** 125-127

BUÑUEL, LUIS (1900-1983), Spanish film director **3** 127-128

BUNYAN, JOHN (1628-1688), English author and Baptist preacher **3** 128-129

BURBAGE, RICHARD (c. 1567-1619), British actor **24** 70-72

BURBANK, LUTHER (1849-1926), American plant breeder **3** 129-131

BURCHFIELD, CHARLES (1893-1967), American painter **3** 131-132

BURCKHARDT, JACOB CHRISTOPH (1818-1897), Swiss historian **3** 132-133

BURCKHARDT, JOHANN LUDWIG (1784-1817), Swiss-born explorer **3** 133

BURGER, WARREN E. (1907-1986), Chief Justice of the United States Supreme Court (1969-1986) **3** 133-136

BURGESS, ANTHONY (John Anthony Burgess Wilson; 1917-1993), English author **3** 136-137

BURGOYNE, JOHN (1723-1792), British general and statesman **3** 137-138

BURKE, EDMUND (1729-1797), British statesman, political theorist, and philosopher **3** 138-141

BURKE, KENNETH (born 1897), American literary theorist and critic **3** 141-142

BURKE, ROBERT O'HARA (1820-1861), Irish-born Australian policeman and explorer **3** 142-143

BURKE, SELMA (1900-1995), African American sculptor **3** 143-144

BURLIN, NATALIE CURTIS (Natalie Curtis; 1875-1921), American ethnomusicologist **23** 50-52

BURLINGAME, ANSON (1820-1870), American diplomat **3** 144-145

BURNE-JONES, SIR EDWARD COLEY (1833-1898), English painter and designer **3** 145-146

BURNET, SIR FRANK MACFARLANE (1899-1985), Australian virologist **3** 146-147

BURNET, GILBERT (1643-1715), British bishop and historian **3** 147

BURNETT, CAROL (born 1933), American television entertainer **23** 52-55

BURNETT, FRANCES HODGSON (Frances Eliza Hodgson Burnett; 1849-1924), English-born American author **18** 64-67

BURNETT, LEO (1891-1971), American advertising executive **19** 45-47

BURNEY, FRANCES "FANNY" (1752-1840), English novelist and diarist **3** 147-148

BURNHAM, DANIEL HUDSON (1846-1912), American architect and city planner **3** 148-149

BURNHAM, FORBES (1923-1985), leader of the independence movement in British Guiana and Guyana's first prime minister **3** 149-151

BURNS, ANTHONY (1834-1862), African American slave **3** 151

BURNS, ARTHUR (1904-1987), American economic statesman **3** 151-153

BURNS, GEORGE (born Nathan Birnbaum; 1896-1996), American comedian and actor **3** 153-155

BURNS, KEN (Kenneth Lauren Burns; born 1953), American documentary filmmaker **20** 63-65

BURNS, ROBERT (1759-1796), Scottish poet **3** 155-156

BURR, AARON (1756-1836), American politician, vice president 1801-1805 **3** 156-159

BURRI, ALBERTO (1915-1995), Italian painter **3** 159-160

BURRITT, ELIHU (1810-1879), American pacifist, author, and linguist **3** 160

BURROUGHS, EDGAR RICE (1875-1950), American author **18** 67-68

BURROUGHS, JOHN (1837-1921), American naturalist and essayist **3** 160-161

BURROUGHS, WILLIAM S. (1914-1997), American writer **3** 162-163

BURTON, RICHARD (Richard Jenkins; 1925-1984), British actor **3** 163-164

BURTON, SIR RICHARD FRANCIS (1821-1890), English explorer, author, and diplomat **3** 164-166

BURTON, ROBERT (1577-1640), English author and clergyman **3** 166-167

BUSCH, ADOLPHUS (1839-1913), American brewer and businessman **19** 47-49

BUSH, GEORGE (George Herbert Walker Bush; born 1924), United States vice president (1981-1989) and president (1989-1993) **3** 167-169

BUSH, GEORGE WALKER (born 1946), United States president (2001-) **21** 61-64
Ridge, Thomas Joseph **24** 334-337

BUSH, VANNEVAR (1890-1974), American scientist and engineer **3** 169-171

BUSHNELL, DAVID (1742-1824), American inventor **21** 64-65

BUSHNELL, HORACE (1802-1876), American Congregational clergyman **3** 171-172

BUSIA, KOFI ABREFA (1914-1978), Ghanaian premier and sociologist **3** 172-173

Business and industrial leaders
Austro-Hungarian
de Hirsch, Maurice **24** 104-106
British
Oppenheimer, Ernest **24** 288-290
Greek
Onassis, Aristotle **24** 286-288
Indian (Asia)
Tata, Jamsetji Nusserwanji **24** 402-404
South African
Oppenheimer, Ernest **24** 288-290

Business and industrial leaders, American
bankers (20th century)
Bañuelos, Romana Acosta **24** 40-42

CASALS, PABLO (born Pau Carlos Salvador Casals y Defill; 1876-1973), Spanish cellist, conductor, and composer **3** 348-350

CASANOVA, GIACOMO JACOPO GIROLAMO, CHEVALIER DE SEINGLAT (1725-1798), Italian adventurer **3** 350-351

CASE, STEVE (born 1958), American businessman **19** 61-64

CASEMENT, ROGER (1864-1916), Irish diplomat and nationalist **20** 76-78

CASEY, WILLIAM J. (1913-1987), American director of the Central Intelligence Agency (CIA) **3** 351-353

CASH, JOHNNY (1932-2003), American singer and songwriter **3** 353-355

CASH, W. J. (Joseph Wilbur Cash; 1900-1914), American journalist and author **22** 93-95

CASS, LEWIS (1782-1866), American statesman **3** 355-356

CASSATT, MARY (1845-1926), American painter **3** 356-357

CASSAVETES, JOHN (1929-1989), American filmmaker **22** 96-98

CASSIODORUS, FLAVIUS MAGNUS AURELIUS, SENATOR (circa 480-circa 575), Roman statesman and author **3** 357-358

CASSIRER, ERNST (1874-1945), German philosopher **3** 358-359

CASTELO BRANCO, HUMBERTO (1900-1967), Brazilian general, president 1964-1966 **3** 359-360

CASTIGLIONE, BALDASSARE (1478-1529), Italian author and diplomat **3** 360-361

CASTILLA, RAMÓN (1797-1867), Peruvian military leader and president **3** 361

CASTLE, IRENE and VERNON (1910-1918), ballroom dancers **3** 361-363

CASTLEREAGH, VISCOUNT (Robert Stewart; 1769-1822), British statesman **3** 363-364

CASTRO ALVES, ANTÔNIO DE (1847-1871), Brazilian poet **3** 364-365

CASTRO RUZ, FIDEL (born 1926), Cuban prime minister **3** 365-368

CATHER, WILLA SIBERT (1873-1947), American writer **3** 368-369

CATHERINE OF ARAGON (1485-1536), Spanish princess, first queen consort of Henry VIII of England **18** 85-88

CATHERINE OF SIENA, ST. (1347-1380), Italian mystic **3** 369-370

CATHERINE THE GREAT (1729-1796), Russian empress 1762-1796 **3** 370-372

Catholic Church
see Roman Catholic Church

CATILINE (Lucius Sergius Catilina; circa 108-62 B.C.), Roman politician and revolutionary **3** 372-373

CATLIN, GEORGE (1796-1872), American painter **3** 373-374

CATO, MARCUS PORCIUS, THE ELDER (234-149 B.C.), Roman soldier, statesman, and historian **3** 375

CATO THE YOUNGER (Marcus Porcius Cato Uticensis; 95-46 B.C.), Roman politician **3** 374-375

CATS, JACOB (1577-1660), Dutch poet, moralist, and statesman **23** 64-66

CATT, CARRIE CHAPMAN (1859-1947), American reformer **3** 375-376

CATTELL, JAMES McKEEN (1860-1944), American psychologist and editor **3** 376-377

CATULLUS, GAIUS VALERIUS (circa 84-circa 54 B.C.), Roman poet **3** 377-378

CAUCHY, AUGUSTIN LOUIS (1789-1857), French mathematician **3** 378-380

CAVAFY, CONSTANTINE P. (Konstantinos P. Kabaphēs; 1863-1933), first modernist Greek poet **3** 381-382

CAVALCANTI, GUIDO (circa 1255-1300), Italian poet **3** 382

CAVALLI, PIETRO FRANCESCO (1602-1676), Italian composer **3** 382-383

CAVENDISH, HENRY (1731-1810), English physicist and chemist **3** 383-384

CAVENDISH, MARGARET LUCAS (1623-1673), English natural philosopher **23** 66-67

CAVOUR, CONTE DI (Camillo Benso; 1810-1861), Italian statesman **3** 385-386

CAXIAS, DUQUE DE (Luiz Alves de Lima e Silva; 1803-1880), Brazilian general and statesman **3** 386

CAXTON, WILLIAM (1422-1491), English printer **3** 386-387

CBS
see Columbia Broadcasting System

CEAUSESCU, NICOLAE (1918-1989), Romanian statesman **3** 387-388

CECH, THOMAS ROBERT (born 1947), American biochemist **23** 68-70

CECIL OF CHELWOOD, VISCOUNT (Edgar Algernon Robert Cecil; 1864-1958), English statesman **3** 388-389

CELA Y TRULOCK, CAMILO JOSÉ (1916-2002), Spanish author **3** 389-390

CÉLINE, LOUIS FERDINAND (pen name of Ferdinand Destouches; 1894-1961), French novelist **3** 390-391

CELLINI, BENVENUTO (1500-1571), Italian goldsmith and sculptor **3** 391-392

CELSIUS, ANDERS (1701-1744), Swedish astronomer **3** 392

CELSUS, AULUS CORNELIUS (circa 25 B.C.-A.D. 45?), Roman medical author **3** 393

Central America
see Latin America

CERETA, LAURA (Laura Cereta Serina; 1469-1499), Italian author and feminist **24** 75-77

CEREZO AREVALO, MARCO VINICIO (born 1942), president of Guatemala (1986-1991) **3** 393-395

CERF, BENNETT (1898-1971), American editor, publisher, author, and television performer **22** 98-100

CERNAN, GENE (Eugene Andrew Cernan; born 1934), American astronaut **22** 100-102

CERVANTES, MIGUEL DE SAAVEDRA (1547-1616), Spanish novelist **3** 395-398

CÉSPEDES, CARLOS MANUEL DE (1819-1874), Cuban lawyer and revolutionary **3** 398-399

CESTI, PIETRO (Marc'Antonio Cesti; 1623-1669), Italian composer **3** 399-400

CETSHWAYO (Cetewayo; circa 1826-1884), king of Zululand 1873-1879 **3** 400

CÉZANNE, PAUL (1839-1906), French painter **3** 400-402

CHADLI BENJEDID (born 1929), president of the Algerian Republic (1979-) **3** 402-404

CHADWICK, FLORENCE (1918-1995), American swimmer **19** 64-66

CHADWICK, SIR EDWIN (1800-1890), English utilitarian reformer **3** 404-405

CHADWICK, SIR JAMES (1891-1974), English physicist **3** 405-406

CHADWICK, LYNN RUSSELL (1914-2003), English sculptor **18** 88-90

CHASE, MARY AGNES (1869-1963), American botanist **24** 79-81

CHASE, PHILANDER (1775-1852), American Episcopalian bishop and missionary **3** 472-473

CHASE, SALMON PORTLAND (1808-1873), American statesman and jurist **3** 473-475

CHASE, SAMUEL (1741-1811), American politician and jurist **3** 475-476

CHASE, WILLIAM MERRITT (1849-1916), American painter **3** 476-477

CHATEAUBRIAND, VICOMTE DE (1768-1848), French author **3** 477-479

CHATELET, GABRIELLE-EMILIE (1706-1749), French physicist and chemist **22** 102-103

CHATICHAI CHOONHAVAN (1922-1998), prime minister of Thailand (1988-1990) **3** 479-480

CHATTERJI, BANKIMCHANDRA (1838-1894), Bengali novelist **3** 480-481

CHATTERTON, THOMAS (1752-1770), English poet **3** 481-482

CHAUCER, GEOFFREY (circa 1345-1400), English poet **3** 482-485

CHAUNCY, CHARLES (1705-1787), American Calvinist clergyman and theologian **3** 485-486

CHÁVEZ, CARLOS (1899-1978), Mexican conductor and composer **3** 486

CHAVEZ, CESAR (1927-1993), American labor leader **3** 486-487

CHÁVEZ, DENNIS (1888-1962), Hispanic American politician **3** 488-489

CHAVEZ, LINDA (born 1947), Hispanic American civil rights activists **3** 489-491

CHAVEZ-THOMPSON, LINDA (born 1944), Mexican American businesswoman and labor activist **24** 81-83

CHAVIS, BENJAMIN (born 1948), African American religious leader, civil rights activist, labor organizer, and author **3** 491-493

CHEEVER, JOHN (1912-1982), American short-story writer **3** 493-494

CHEKHOV, ANTON PAVLOVICH (1860-1904), Russian author **3** 494-497
Nemirovich-Danchenko, Vladimir Ivanovich **24** 279-281

CHELMSFORD, 1st VISCOUNT (Frederic John Napier Thesinger Chelmsford; 1868-1933), English statesman **3** 497

Chemistry (science)
chemical structure
Cornforth, John Warcup **24** 92-94
Hauptman, Herbert Aaron **24** 165-167
industrial
Blodgett, Katharine Burr **24** 54-56

CH'EN TU-HSIU (1879-1942), Chinese statesman and editor **3** 501-502

CHENEY, RICHARD B(RUCE) (born 1941), U.S. secretary of defense under George Bush **3** 497-499

CHENG HO (1371-circa 1433), Chinese admiral **3** 500

CHÉNIER, ANDRÉ MARIE (1762-1794), French poet **3** 500-501

CHERENKOV, PAVEL ALEKSEEVICH (1904-1990), Russian physicist **3** 502-503

CHERNENKO, KONSTANTIN USTINOVICH (1911-1985), the Soviet Union general secretary from February 1984 to March 1985 **3** 503-504

CHERNYSHEVSKY, NIKOLAI GAVRILOVICH (1828-1889), Russian journalist, critic, and social theorist **3** 504-505

CHERUBINI, LUIGI CARLO ZANOBI SALVATORE MARIA (1760-1842), Italian-born French composer **3** 505-506

CHESNUT, MARY BOYKIN (1823-1886), Civil War diarist **3** 506-508

CHESNUTT, CHARLES WADDELL (1858-1932), African American author and lawyer **20** 78-82

CHESTERTON, GILBERT KEITH (1874-1936), English author and artist **3** 508-509

CHEVROLET, LOUIS (1878-1941), auto racer and entrepreneur **20** 82-84

CH'I PAI-SHIH (1863-1957), Chinese painter and poet **3** 526-527

CHIA SSU-TAO (1213-1275), Chinese statesman **3** 514-515

CHIANG CHING-KUO (1910-1988), chairman of the Nationalist party and president of the Republic of China in Taiwan (1978-1988) **3** 509-510

CHIANG KAI-SHEK (1887-1975), Chinese nationalist leader and president **3** 510-513

CHIARI, ROBERTO (born 1905), president of Panama (1960-1964) **3** 513-514

Chicago (city, Illinois)
mayors
Daley, Richard M. **24** 102-104

CHICAGO, JUDY (Judith Cohen; born 1939), American artist and activist **3** 515-516

Chicago Legal News (journal)
Bradwell, Myra **24** 64-66

CHICHERIN, GEORGI VASILYEVICH (1872-1936), Russian statesman **3** 516-517

CHICHESTER, FRANCIS (1901-1972), British yachter **24** 83-85

CHIEN-LUNG (Hung-li; 1711-1799), Chinese emperor (1735-1799) **21** 78-79

CHIEPE, GAOSITWE KEAGAKWA TIBE (born 1926), intellectual, educator, diplomat, politician, and cabinet minister of external affairs of Botswana **3** 517

CHIFLEY, JOSEPH BENEDICT (1885-1951), Australian statesman **3** 518

CHIH-I (Chih-k'ai, 538-597), Chinese Buddhist monk **3** 518-519

CHIKAMATSU, MONZAEMON (1653-1725), Japanese playwright **23** 70-72

CHILD, JULIA McWILLIAMS (born 1912), chef, author, and television personality **3** 519-520

CHILD, LYDIA MARIA FRANCIS (1802-1880), American author and abolitionist **3** 520-521

Child development
child rearing
Poussaint, Alvin Francis **24** 313-316

Child psychology
see Child development

CHILDE, VERE GORDON (1892-1957), Australian prehistorian and archeologist **3** 521-522

Children's literature
see Literature for children

CHILDRESS, ALICE (1920-1994), African American dramatist, author, and poet **3** 522-524

Chilean art
Matta Echaurren, Roberto Sebastian Antonio **24** 248-250

Chilean literature
Medina, Jose Toribio **24** 253-255

CH'IN KUEI (1090-1155), Chinese official **3** 524-525

China (nation, East Asia)
• DYNASTIC CHRONOLOGY
207 B.C.-220 A.D. (Han dynasty)
Ban Zhao **24** 38-40

COBBETT, WILLIAM (1763-1835), English journalist and politician **4** 126-127

COBDEN, RICHARD (1804-1865), English politician **4** 127-128

COCHISE (circa 1825-1874), American Chiricahua Apache Indian chief **4** 128

COCHRAN, JACQUELINE (Jackie Cochran; 1910-1980), American aviator and businesswoman **18** 94-96

COCHRAN, JOHNNIE (born 1937), African American lawyer **4** 128-131

COCHRANE, THOMAS (Earl of Dundonald; 1775-1860), British naval officer **20** 91-93

COCKCROFT, JOHN DOUGLAS (1897-1967), English physicist **4** 131-132

COCTEAU, JEAN (1889-1963), French writer **4** 132-133

COE, SEBASTIAN (born 1956), English track athlete **20** 93-95

COEN, JAN PIETERSZOON (circa 1586-1629), Dutch governor general of Batavia **4** 133

COETZEE, J(OHN) M. (born 1940), white South African novelist **4** 133-135

COFFIN, LEVI (1789-1877), American antislavery reformer **4** 135

COFFIN, WILLIAM SLOANE, JR. (born 1924), Yale University chaplain who spoke out against the Vietnam War **4** 135-137

COHAN, GEORGE MICHAEL (1878-1942), American actor and playwright **4** 137-138

COHEN, HERMANN (1842-1918), Jewish-German philosopher **4** 138-139

COHEN, MORRIS RAPHAEL (1880-1947), American philosopher and teacher **4** 139-140

COHEN, WILLIAM S. (born 1940), American secretary of defense **18** 96-98

COHN, FERDINAND (1829-1898), German botanist **20** 95-97

COHN-BENDIT, DANIEL (born 1946), led "new left" student protests in France in 1968 **4** 140-141

COKE, SIR EDWARD (1552-1634), English jurist and parliamentarian **4** 141-142

COLBERT, JEAN BAPTISTE (1619-1683), French statesman **4** 142-143

COLBY, WILLIAM E. (1920-1996), American director of the Central Intelligence Agency (CIA) **4** 143-145

COLDEN, CADWALLADER (1688-1776), American botanist and politician **4** 145-146

COLE, GEORGE DOUGLAS HOWARD (1889-1959), English historian and economist **4** 146-147

COLE, JOHNNETTA (born 1936), African American scholar and educator **4** 147-149

COLE, NAT (a.k.a. Nat "King" Cole, born Nathaniel Adams Coles; 1919-1965), American jazz musician **4** 149-151

COLE, THOMAS (1801-1848), American painter **4** 151-152

COLEMAN, BESSIE (1892-1926), first African American to earn an international pilot's license **4** 152-154

COLERIDGE, SAMUEL TAYLOR (1772-1834), English poet and critic **4** 154-156

COLES, ROBERT MARTIN (born 1929), American social psychiatrist, social critic, and humanist **4** 156-157

COLET, JOHN (circa 1446-1519), English theologian **4** 157-158

COLETTE, SIDONIE GABRIELLE (1873-1954), French author **4** 158-159

COLIGNY, GASPARD DE (1519-1572), French admiral and statesman **4** 159-160

Collective bargaining
see Labor unions

COLLIER, JOHN (1884-1968), American proponent of Native American culture **4** 160-162

COLLINGWOOD, ROBIN GEORGE (1889-1943), English historian and philosopher **4** 162

COLLINS, EDWARD KNIGHT (1802-1878), American businessman and shipowner **4** 162-163

COLLINS, EILEEN (born 1956), American astronaut **4** 163-165

COLLINS, MARVA (born Marva Deloise Nettles; b. 1936), African American educator **4** 165-167

COLLINS, MICHAEL (1890-1922), Irish revolutionary leader and soldier **4** 167-168

COLLINS, WILLIAM (1721-1759), English lyric poet **4** 168-169

COLLINS, WILLIAM WILKIE (1824-1889), English novelist **4** 169-170

COLLOR DE MELLO, FERNANDO (born 1949), businessman who became president of Brazil in 1990 **4** 170-172

Colombia, Republic of (nation, South America)
modern era
Arciniegas, German **24** 27-29

Colombian art
Botero, Fernando **24** 59-61

COLT, SAMUEL (1814-1862), American inventor and manufacturer **4** 172-173

COLTRANE, JOHN (1926-1967), African American jazz saxophonist **4** 173-174

COLUM, PADRAIC (1881-1972), Irish-American poet and playwright **4** 174-175

COLUMBA, ST. (circa 521-597), Irish monk and missionary **4** 175-176

COLUMBAN, ST. (circa 543-615), Irish missionary **4** 176

Columbia Broadcasting System (communications)
Rather, Dan Irvin **24** 321-324

COLUMBUS, CHRISTOPHER (1451-1506), Italian navigator, discoverer of America **4** 176-179

COLWELL, RITA R. (born 1934), American marine microbiologist **4** 179-180

COMANECI, NADIA (Nadia Conner; born 1961), Romanian gymnast **18** 98-100

COMENIUS, JOHN AMOS (1592-1670), Moravian theologian and educational reformer **4** 180-181

COMINES, PHILIPPE DE (circa 1445-1511), French chronicler **4** 181

COMMAGER, HENRY STEELE (1902-1998), American historian, textbook author, and editor **4** 181-183

COMMONER, BARRY (born 1917), American biologist and environmental activist **4** 183-185

COMMONS, JOHN ROGERS (1862-1945), American historian **4** 185

Communist party (China)
and women's issues
Pin-chin Chiang **24** 310-312

COMNENA, ANNA (1083-1148), Byzantine princess and historian **4** 185-186

COMPTON, ARTHUR HOLLY (1892-1962), American physicist **4** 186-188

COMSTOCK, ANNA BOTSFORD (1854-1930), American artist and natural science educator **20** 97-99

COMSTOCK, ANTHONY (1844-1915), American antivice crusader **4** 188-189

CRISPI, FRANCESCO (1819-1901), Italian statesman **4** 310-311

CRISTIANI, ALFREDO ("Fredy" Cristiani; born 1947), president of El Salvador (1989-) **4** 311-313

CRISTOFORI, BARTOLOMEO (1655-1731), Italian musician and inventor of the piano **21** 94-96

Croatian literature
Krleza, Miroslav **24** 215-217

CROCE, BENEDETTO (1866-1952), Italian philosopher, critic and educator **4** 313-314

CROCKETT, DAVID (1786-1836), American frontiersman **4** 314-316

CROGHAN, GEORGE (ca. 1720-1782), American Indian agent and trader **22** 127-129

CROLY, HERBERT DAVID (1869-1930), American editor and author **4** 316-317

CROLY, JANE (Jennie June; 1829-1901), American journalist **21** 96-96

CROMER, 1ST EARL OF (Evelyn Baring; 1841-1907), English statesman **4** 317

CROMWELL, OLIVER (1599-1658), English statesman and general **4** 317-320

CROMWELL, THOMAS (Earl of Essex; circa 1485-1540), English statesman 1532-1540 **4** 320-321

CRONIN, JAMES WATSON (born 1931), American physicist **24** 97-99
Fitch, Val Logsdon **24** 135-138

CRONKITE, WALTER LELAND, JR. (born 1916), American journalist and radio and television news broadcaster **4** 321-322

CROOK, GEORGE (1828-1890), American general and frontiersman **4** 322-323
Standing Bear **24** 388-390

CROOKES, SIR WILLIAM (1832-1919), English chemist and physicist **4** 323-324

CROSBY, HARRY LILLIS (Bing; 1903-1977), American singer and radio and television personality **4** 324-326

Crouching Tiger, Hidden Dragon (film)
Dun, Tan **24** 121-123

CROWLEY, ALEISTER (1875-1947), English author and magician **18** 107-109

CROWTHER, SAMUEL ADJAI (circa 1806-1891), Nigerian Anglican bishop **4** 326

CRUMB, GEORGE (born 1929), American composer and teacher **4** 326-328

CRUZ, CELIA (1925-2003), Cuban American singer **24** 99-101

CRUZ, OSWALDO GONÇALVES (1872-1917), Brazilian microbiologist and epidemiologist **4** 328-329

Crystal structure (cyrstalline)
Hauptman, Herbert Aaron **24** 165-167

CUAUHTEMOC (circa 1496-1525), Aztec ruler **4** 329

Cuban National Ballet
Alonso, Alicia **24** 14-17

CUBBERLEY, ELLWOOD PATTERSON (1868-1941), American educator and university dean **4** 329-331

CUDWORTH, RALPH (1617-1688), English philosopher and theologian **4** 331

CUFFE, PAUL (1759-1817), African American ship captain and merchant **4** 331-332

CUGAT, XAVIER (1900-1990), Spanish musician **23** 81-82

CUGOANO, OTTOBAH (circa 1757-after 1803), African abolitionist in England **4** 332-333

CUKOR, GEORGE (1899-1983), American film director **19** 82-84

CULLEN, COUNTEE (1903-1946), African American poet **4** 333-334

CULLEN, MAURICE GALBRAITH (1866-1934), Canadian painter **4** 334

CULLEN, PAUL (1803-1879), Irish cardinal **20** 100-103

Cultural anthropology (social science)
cultural evolution
Barbeau, Marius **24** 42-44

CUMMINGS, EDWARD ESTLIN (1894-1962), American poet **4** 334-336

CUNHA, EUCLIDES RODRIGUES PIMENTA DA (1866-1909), Brazilian writer **4** 336-337

CUNNINGHAM, GLENN (1909-1988), American track and field athlete **21** 96-99

CUNNINGHAM, IMOGEN (1883-1976), American photographer **19** 84-86

CUNNINGHAM, MERCE (born 1919), American dancer and choreographer **4** 337-338

CUOMO, MARIO MATTHEW (born 1932), Democratic New York state governor **4** 338-339

CURIE, ÈVE (Eve Curie Labouisse; born 1904), French musician, author and diplomat **18** 109-111

CURIE, MARIE SKLODOWSKA (1867-1934), Polish-born French physicist **4** 339-341

CURIE, PIERRE (1859-1906), French physicist **4** 341-344

CURLEY, JAMES MICHAEL (1874-1958), American politician **4** 344-345

CURRIE, SIR ARTHUR WILLIAM (1875-1933), Canadian general **4** 345

CURRIER AND IVES (1857-1907), American lithographic firm **4** 345-346

CURRY, JABEZ LAMAR MONROE (1815-1903), American politician **4** 346-347

CURTIN, ANDREW GREGG (1815-1894), American politician **4** 347-348

CURTIN, JOHN JOSEPH (1885-1945), Australian statesman, prime minister **4** 348-349

CURTIS, BENJAMIN ROBBINS (1809-1874), American jurist, United States Supreme Court justice **4** 349

CURTIS, CHARLES BRENT (1860-1936), American vice president (1929-1932) and legislator **21** 99-100

CURTIS, GEORGE WILLIAM (1824-1892), American writer and reformer **4** 349-350

CURTISS, GLENN HAMMOND (1878-1930), American aviation pioneer **4** 350-351

CURZON, GEORGE NATHANIEL (1st Marquess Curzon of Kedleston; 1859-1925), English statesman **4** 351-352

CUSA, NICHOLAS OF (1401-1464), German prelate and humanist **4** 352-353

CUSHING, HARVEY WILLIAMS (1869-1939), American neurosurgeon **4** 353-354

CUSHMAN, CHARLOTTE (1816-1876), American actress **4** 354-355

CUSTER, GEORGE ARMSTRONG (1839-1876), American general **4** 355-356

CUTLER, MANASSEH (1742-1823), American clergyman, scientist, and politician **4** 356-357

CUVIER, BARON GEORGES LÉOPOLD (1769-1832), French zoologist and biologist **4** 357-359

CUVILLIÉS, FRANÇOIS (1695-1768), Flemish architect and designer **4** 359-360

CUYP, AELBERT (1620-1691), Dutch painter **4** 360-361

CYNEWULF (8th or 9th century), Anglo-Saxon poet **20** 103-104

CYPRIANUS, THASCIUS CAECILIANUS (died 258), Roman bishop of Carthage **4** 361-362

CYRIL (OF ALEXANDRIA), ST. (died 444), Egyptian bishop, Doctor of the Church **4** 362

CYRIL, ST. (827-869), Apostle to the Slavs **4** 362

CYRUS THE GREAT (ruled 550-530 B.C.), founder of the Persian Empire **4** 363-364

D

DA PONTE, LORENZO (Emanuele Conegliano; 1749-1838), Italian librettist and poet **20** 105-106

DAGUERRE, LOUIS JACQUES MANDÉ (1787-1851), French painter and stage designer **4** 365-366

DAHL, ROALD (1916-1990), Welsh-born English author **4** 366-367

DAIGO II (1288-1339), Japanese emperor **4** 367-368

DAIMLER, GOTTLIEB (1834-1900), German mechanical engineer **4** 368

DALADIER, ÉDOUARD (1884-1970), French statesman **4** 369

DALAI LAMA (Lhamo Thondup; born 1935), 14th in a line of Buddhist spiritual and temporal leaders of Tibet **4** 369-371

DALE, SIR HENRY HALLETT (1875-1968), English pharmacologist and neurophysiologist **4** 371-373

DALEY, RICHARD M. (born 1942), mayor of Chicago **24** 102-104

DALEY, RICHARD J. (1902-1976), Democratic mayor of Chicago (1955-1976) **4** 373-375
Daley, Richard M. **24** 102-104

DALHOUSIE, 1ST MARQUESS OF (James Andrew Broun Ramsay; 1812-1860), British statesman **4** 375-376

DALI, SALVADOR (1904-1989), Spanish painter **4** 376-377

DALLAPICCOLA, LUIGI (1904-1975), Italian composer **4** 377-378

Dallas Cowboys (football team)
Schramm, Texas Ernest **24** 352-355

DALTON, JOHN (1766-1844), English chemist **4** 378-379

DALY, MARCUS (1841-1900), American miner and politician **4** 379-380

DALY, MARY (born 1928), American feminist theoretician and philosopher **4** 380-381

DALZEL, ARCHIBALD (or Dalziel; 1740-1811), Scottish slave trader **4** 381-382

DAM, CARL PETER HENRIK (1895-1976), Danish biochemist **4** 382-383

DAMIEN, FATHER (1840-1889), Belgian missionary **4** 383

DAMPIER, WILLIAM (1652-1715), English privateer, author, and explorer **4** 384

DANA, CHARLES ANDERSON (1819-1897), American journalist **4** 384-385

DANA, RICHARD HENRY, JR. (1815-1882), American author and lawyer **4** 385-386

DANDOLO, ENRICO (circa 1107-1205), Venetian doge 1192-1205 **4** 386-387

DANDRIDGE, DOROTHY (1922-1965), African American actress and singer **18** 112-114

DANIELS, JOSEPHUS (1862-1948), American journalist and statesman **4** 387

Danish literature and culture
see Denmark—culture

D'ANNUNZIO, GABRIELE (1863-1938), Italian poet and patriot **4** 388

DANQUAH, JOSEPH B. (1895-1965), Ghanaian nationalist and politician **4** 388-389

DANTE ALIGHIERI (1265-1321), Italian poet **4** 389-391

DANTON, GEORGES JACQUES (1759-1794), French revolutionary leader **4** 391-393

DARBY, ABRAHAM (1677-1717), English iron manufacturer **20** 106-107

DARÍO, RUBÉN (1867-1916), Nicaraguan poet **4** 393-394

DARIUS I (the Great; ruled 522-486 B.C.), king of Persia **4** 394-395

DARROW, CLARENCE SEWARD (1857-1938), American lawyer **4** 396-397

DARWIN, CHARLES ROBERT (1809-1882), English naturalist **4** 397-399

DARWIN, ERASMUS (1731-1802), English physician, author, botanist and inventor **18** 114-116

DARWISH, MAHMUD (born 1942), Palestinian poet **4** 399-401

DAS, CHITTA RANJAN (1870-1925), Indian lawyer, poet, and nationalist **4** 401-402

DATSOLALEE (Dabuda; Wide Hips; 1835-1925), Native American weaver **22** 130-131

DAUBIGNY, CHARLES FRANÇOIS (1817-1878), French painter and etcher **4** 402

DAUDET, ALPHONSE (1840-1897), French novelist and dramatist **4** 402-403

DAUMIER, HONORÉ VICTORIN (1808-1879), French lithographer, painter, and sculptor **4** 403-405

DAVENPORT, JOHN (1597-1670), English Puritan clergyman **4** 405-406

DAVID (ruled circa 1010-circa 970 B.C.), Israelite king **4** 406-407

DAVID, JACQUES LOUIS (1748-1825), French painter **4** 407-409

DAVID, SAINT (Dewi; 520-601), Welsh monk and evangelist **23** 83-85

DAVID I (1084-1153), king of Scotland **4** 407

DAVIES, ARTHUR BOWEN (1862-1928), American painter **4** 409-410

DAVIES, RUPERT (1917-1976), British actor **18** 116-117

DAVIES, WILLIAM ROBERTSON (1913-1995), Canadian author **18** 117-119

DAVIGNON, VISCOUNT (ETIENNE) (born 1932), an architect of European integration and unity through the Commission of the European Communities **4** 410-411

DAVIS, ALEXANDER JACKSON (1803-1892), American architect **4** 411

DAVIS, ANGELA (Angela Yvonne Davis; born 1944), African American scholar and activist **4** 412-413

DAVIS, ARTHUR VINING (1867-1962), general manager of the Aluminum Company of America (ALCOA) **4** 413-414

DAVIS, BENJAMIN O., SR. (1877-1970), first African American general in the regular United States Armed Services **4** 414-415

DAVIS, BETTE (1908-1989), American actress **18** 119-121

DAVIS, COLIN REX (born 1927), British conductor **22** 131-133

DAVIS, ELMER HOLMES (1890-1958), American journalist and radio commentator **22** 133-136

DAVIS, GLENN (born 1925), American football player **21** 101-103

DAVIS, HENRY WINTER (1817-1865), American lawyer and politician **4** 415-416

DAVIS, JEFFERSON (1808-1889), American statesman, president of the Confederacy 1862-1865 **4** 416-418

DAVIS, JOHN (circa 1550-1605), English navigator **4** 419

DAVIS, MILES (1926-1991), jazz trumpeter, composer, and small-band leader **4** 419-421

DAVIS, OSSIE (born 1917), African American playwright, actor, and director **4** 421-422

DAVIS, RICHARD HARDING (1864-1916), American journalist, novelist, and dramatist **4** 422-423

DAVIS, SAMMY, JR. (1925-1990), African American singer, dancer, and actor **4** 423-424

DAVIS, STUART (1894-1964), American cubist painter **4** 424-425

DAVIS, WILLIAM MORRIS (1850-1934), American geographer and geologist **4** 425-426

DAVY, SIR HUMPHRY (1778-1829), English chemist and natural philosopher **4** 426-427

DAWES, HENRY LAURENS (1816-1903), American politician **4** 427

DAWSON, WILLIAM LEVI (1899-1990), African American composer, performer, and music educator **4** 427-428

DAY, DOROTHY (1897-1980), a founder of the Catholic Worker Movement **4** 428-429

DAYAN, MOSHE (1915-1981), Israeli general and statesman **4** 429-431

DAYANANDA SARASWATI (1824-1883), Indian religious leader **4** 431

DE ANDRADE, MARIO (Mario Coelho Pinto Andrade; born 1928), Angolan poet, critic, and political activist **4** 434-435

DE BEAUVOIR, SIMONE (1908-1986), French writer and leader of the modern feminist movement **4** 440-441

De Beers Consolidated Mines (established 1888) Oppenheimer, Ernest **24** 288-290

DE BOW, JAMES DUNWOODY BROWNSON (1820-1867), American editor and statistician **4** 441-442

DE BROGLIE, LOUIS VICTOR PIERRE RAYMOND (1892-1987), French physicist **4** 442-444

DE FOREST, LEE (1873-1961), American inventor **4** 459-460

DE GASPERI, ALCIDE (1881-1954), Italian statesman, premier 1945-1953 **4** 462-463

DE GAULLE, CHARLES ANDRÉ JOSEPH MARIE (1890-1970), French general, president 1958-1969 **4** 463-465

DE GOUGES, MARIE OLYMPE (born Marie Gouzes; 1748-1793), French author **23** 85-88

DE GOURNAY, MARIE LE JARS (1565-1645), French author **23** 88-90

DE HIRSCH, MAURICE (Baron de Hirsch; 1831-1896), Austro-Hungarian financier and philanthropist **24** 104-106

DE KLERK, FREDRIK WILLEM (born 1936), state president of South Africa (1989-) **4** 466-468

DE KOONING, WILLEM (1904-1997), Dutch-born American painter **4** 468-469

DE LA MADRID HURTADO, MIGUEL (born 1934), president of Mexico (1982-1988) **4** 471-472

DE LA ROCHE, MAZO LOUISE (1879-1961), Canadian author **4** 474-475

DE LEMPICKA, TAMARA (Maria Gorska; Tamara Kuffner; 1898-1980), Polish American artist **24** 106-109

DE LEON, DANIEL (1852-1914), American Socialist theoretician and politician **4** 479-480

DE L'ORME, PHILIBERT (1510-1570), French architect **9** 519

DE MILLE, AGNES (1905-1993), American dancer, choreographer, and author **4** 486-488
Alonso, Alicia **24** 14-17

DE NIRO, ROBERT (born 1943), American actor and film producer **21** 103-106

DE PISAN, CHRISTINE (1363-1431), French poet and philosopher **24** 109-111

DE SANCTIS, FRANCESCO (1817-1883), Italian critic, educator, and legislator **4** 505

DE SAUSSURE, FERDINAND (1857-1913), Swiss linguist and author **24** 111-113

DE SICA, VITTORIO (1902-1974), Italian filmmaker **21** 106-108

DE SMET, PIERRE JEAN (1801-1873), Belgian Jesuit missionary **4** 509-510

DE SOTO, HERNANDO (1500-1542), Spanish conqueror and explorer **4** 510-511

DE VALERA, EAMON (1882-1975), American-born Irish revolutionary leader and statesman **4** 514-515

DE VRIES, HUGO (1848-1935), Belgian botanist in the fields of heredity and the origin of species **4** 516-518

DE WOLFE, ELSIE (1865-1950), American interior decorator **20** 107-108

DEÁK, FRANCIS (1803-1876), Hungarian statesman **4** 431-432

DEAKIN, ALFRED (1856-1919), Australian statesman **4** 432-433

DEAN, JAMES (James Byron Dean; 1931-1955), American actor and cult figure **4** 433-434

DEANE, SILAS (1737-1789), American merchant lawyer and diplomat **4** 435-437

DEB, RADHAKANT (1783-1867), Bengali reformer and cultural nationalist **4** 437

DEBAKEY, MICHAEL ELLIS (born 1908), American surgeon **4** 437-438

DEBARTOLO, EDWARD JOHN, SR. and JR., real estate developers who specialized in large regional malls **4** 438-440

DEBS, EUGENE VICTOR (1855-1926), American union organizer **4** 444-445

DEBUSSY, (ACHILLE) CLAUDE (1862-1918), French composer **4** 445-447

DEBYE, PETER JOSEPH WILLIAM (1884-1966), Dutch-born American physical chemist **4** 447-448

DECATUR, STEPHEN (1779-1820), American naval officer **4** 448-449

DEE, RUBY (born Ruby Ann Wallace; born 1924), African American actor **4** 449-452

DEER, ADA E. (born 1935), Native American social worker, activist, and director of Bureau of Indian Affairs **4** 452-454

DEERE, JOHN (1804-1886), American inventor and manufacturer **4** 455

DEERING, WILLIAM (1826-1913), American manufacturer **4** 455-456

DEES, MORRIS S., JR. (born 1936), American civil rights attorney **4** 456-457

DÍAZ DEL CASTILLO, BERNAL (circa 1496-circa 1584), Spanish soldier and historian **4** 536-537

DÍAZ ORDAZ, GUSTAVO (1911-1979), president of Mexico (1964-1970) **4** 537-538

DICKENS, CHARLES JOHN HUFFAM (1812-1870), English author **4** 538-541

DICKEY, JAMES (1923-1997), American poet **19** 87-89

DICKINSON, EMILY (1830-1886), American poet **4** 541-543

DICKINSON, JOHN (1732-1808), American lawyer, pamphleteer, and politician **4** 543-544

DICKSON, LAURIE (William Kennedy Laurie Dickson; 1860-1935), British inventor and filmmaker **20** 112-113

DIDEROT, DENIS (1713-1784), French philosopher, playwright, and encyclopedist **5** 1-2

DIDION, JOAN (born 1934), American author **20** 113-116

DIEBENKORN, RICHARD (born 1922), American abstract expressionist painter **5** 2-4

DIEFENBAKER, JOHN GEORGE (1895-1979), Canadian statesman **5** 4-5

DIELS, (OTTO PAUL) HERMANN (1876-1954), German organic chemist **5** 5-6

DIEM, NGO DINH (1901-1963), South Vietnamese president 1955-1963 **5** 6-7

DIESEL, RUDOLF (1858-1913), German mechanical engineer **5** 7

DIKE, KENNETH (Kenneth Onwuka Dike; 1917-1983), African historian who set up the Nigerian National Archives **5** 7-8

DILLINGER, JOHN (1903-1934), American criminal **5** 9

DILTHEY, WILHELM CHRISTIAN LUDWIG (1833-1911), German historian and philosopher **5** 10

DIMAGGIO, JOE (born Giuseppe Paolo DiMaggio, Jr.; 1914-1999), American baseball player **5** 10-11

DIMITROV, GEORGI (1882-1949), head of the Communist International (1935-1943) and prime minister of Bulgaria (1944-1949) **5** 11-13

DINESEN BLIXEN-FINECKE, KAREN (a.k.a. Isak Dinesen; 1885-1962), Danish author **5** 13-14

DINGANE (circa 1795-1840), Zulu king **5** 14-15

DINKINS, DAVID (born 1927), African American politician and mayor of New York City **5** 15-18

DINWIDDIE, ROBERT (1693-1770), Scottish merchant and colonial governor **5** 18-19

DIOCLETIAN (Gaius Aurelius Valerius Diocletianus; 245-circa 313), Roman emperor 284-305 **5** 19-20

DIOGENES (circa 400-325 B.C.), Greek philosopher **5** 20-21

DIOP, CHEIKH ANTA (1923-1986), African historian **5** 21-22

DIOP, DAVID MANDESSI (1927-1960), French Guinean poet **24** 117-118

DIOR, CHRISTIAN (1905-1957), French fashion designer **5** 22

Diplomats
Cameroonian
    Oyono, Ferdinand Leopold **24** 290-292
Canadian
    Massey, Vincent **24** 246-248
Colombian
    Arciniegas, German **24** 27-29
Swedish
    Myrdal, Alva **24** 274-276
Yugoslavian
    Andrić, Ivo **24** 21-24

Diplomats, American
20th century (in East Germany)
    Ridgway, Rozanne Lejeanne **24** 337-338
20th century (in Finland)
    Ridgway, Rozanne Lejeanne **24** 337-338

DIRAC, PAUL ADRIEN MAURICE (1902-1984), English physicist **5** 23-24

DIRKSEN, EVERETT McKINLEY (1896-1969), Republican congressman and senator from Illinois **5** 24-26

DISNEY, WALTER ELIAS (1901-1966), American film maker and entrepreneur **5** 26-27

DISRAELI, BENJAMIN (1st Earl of Beaconsfield; 1804-1881), English statesman, prime minister 1868 and 1874-1880 **5** 27-29

DIVINE, FATHER (born George Baker?; c. 1877-1965), African American religious leader **5** 29-32

Diving (sport)
Fu Mingxia **24** 149-151

DIX, DOROTHEA LYNDE (1802-1887), American reformer **5** 32-33

DIX, OTTO (1891-1969), German painter and graphic artist **5** 33-34

DJILAS, MILOVAN (1911-1995), Yugoslavian writer **5** 34

DO MUOI (born 1917), prime minister of the Socialist Republic of Vietnam (1988-) **5** 53-55

DOBELL, SIR WILLIAM (1899-1970), Australian artist **5** 34-35

DOBZHANSKY, THEODOSIUS (1900-1975), Russian-American biologist who studied natural selection **5** 35-37

DOCTOROW, EDGAR LAURENCE (born 1931), American author **19** 89-91

DODGE, GRACE HOADLEY (1856-1914), American feminist, philanthropist, and social worker **5** 37-38

DODGE, GRENVILLE MELLEN (1831-1916), American army officer and civil engineer **22** 142-145

DODGE, JOHN FRANCIS (1864-1920) AND HORACE ELGIN (1868-1920), American automobile manufacturers **18** 121-123

DOE, SAMUEL KANYON (1951-1990), Liberian statesman **5** 38-39

DOENITZ, KARL (1891-1980), German naval officer **20** 116-117

DOI TAKAKO (born 1928), chairperson of the Japan Socialist party **5** 39-41

DOLE, ELIZABETH HANFORD (born 1936), American lawyer, politician, and first female United States secretary of transportation **5** 41-43

DOLE, ROBERT J. (born 1923), Republican Senator **5** 43-46

DOLE, SANFORD BALLARD (1844-1926), American statesman **5** 46

DOLLFUSS, ENGELBERT (1892-1934), Austrian statesman **5** 47

DÖLLINGER, JOSEF IGNAZ VON (1799-1890), German historian and theologian **5** 47-48

DOMAGK, GERHARD JOHANNES PAUL (1895-1964), German bacteriologist **5** 48-50

DOMINGO, PLACIDO (born 1941), Spanish-born lyric-dramatic tenor **5** 50-51

DOMINIC, ST. (circa 1170-1221), Spanish Dominican founder **5** 51-52

DOMINO, FATS (Antoine Domino, Jr.; born 1928), African American singer, pianist, and composer **22** 145-147

DOMITIAN (Titus Flavius Domitianus Augustus; 51-96), Roman emperor 81-96 **5** 52-53

DONATELLO (Donato di Niccolò Bardi; 1386-1466), Italian sculptor **5** 55-56

DUBOS, RENÉ JULES (1901-1982), French-born American microbiologist **5** 119

DUBUFFET, JEAN PHILLIPE ARTHUR (born 1901), French painter **5** 119-120

DUCCIO DI BUONINSEGNA (1255/60-1318/19), Italian painter **5** 121-122

DUCHAMP, MARCEL (1887-1968), French painter **5** 122-123

DUCHAMP-VILLON, RAYMOND (1876-1918), French sculptor **5** 123

DUDLEY, BARBARA (born 1947), American director of Greenpeace **5** 123-124

DUDLEY, THOMAS (1576-1653), American colonial governor and Puritan leader **5** 124-125

DUFAY, GUILLAUME (circa 1400-1474), Netherlandish composer **5** 125-126

DUFF, ALEXANDER (1806-1878), Scottish Presbyterian missionary **5** 126-127

DUGAN, ALAN (1923-2003), American poet **5** 127-128

DUGDALE, RICHARD LOUIS (1841-1883), English-born American sociologist **5** 128-129

DUHEM, PIERRE MAURICE MARIE (1861-1916), French physicist, chemist, and historian of science **5** 129

DUKAKIS, MICHAEL (born 1933), American governor of Massachusetts **5** 130-133

DUKE, DORIS (1912-1993), American philanthropist **24** 118-121

DUKE, JAMES BUCHANAN (1856-1925), American industrialist and philanthropist **5** 133-134
Duke, Doris **24** 118-121

DULL KNIFE (born Morning Star; c. 1810-1883), Northern Cheyenne tribal leader **5** 135-136

DULLES, JOHN FOSTER (1888-1959), American statesman and diplomat **5** 134-135

DUMAS, ALEXANDRE (1803-1870), French playwright and novelist **5** 136-138

DUMAS, JEAN BAPTISTE ANDRÉ (1800-1884), French Chemist **5** 138-139

DU MAURIER, DAPHNE (Lady Browning; 1907-1989), English author **18** 125-127

DUN, TAN (born 1951), Chinese American musician **24** 121-123

DUNANT, JEAN HENRI (1828-1910), Swiss philanthropist **5** 139-141

DUNBAR, PAUL LAURENCE (1872-1906), African American poet and novelist **5** 141-142

DUNBAR, WILLIAM (circa 1460-circa 1520), Scottish poet and courtier **5** 142-143

DUNBAR, WILLIAM (1749-1810), Scottish-born American scientist and planter **5** 143-144

DUNCAN, ISADORA (1878-1927), American dancer **5** 144-145

DUNHAM, KATHERINE (born 1910), African American dancer, choreographer, and anthropologist **5** 145-146

DUNMORE, 4TH EARL OF (John Murray; 1732-1809), British colonial governor **5** 147

DUNNE, FINLEY PETER (1867-1936), American journalist **5** 147-148

DUNNING, WILLIAM ARCHIBALD (1857-1922), American historian **5** 148-149

DUNS SCOTUS, JOHN (1265/66-1308), Scottish philosopher and theologian **5** 149-150

DUNSTABLE, JOHN (circa 1390-1453), English composer **5** 150-151

DUNSTAN, ST. (circa 909-988), English monk and archbishop **5** 151-152

DUNSTER, HENRY (circa 1609-1659), English-born American clergyman **5** 152-153

DUONG VAN MINH (born 1916), Vietnamese general and politician **18** 285-287

DUPLEIX, MARQUIS (Joseph François; 1697-1763), French colonial administrator **5** 153

DU PONT, ÉLEUTHÈRE IRÉNÉE (1771-1834), French-born American manufacturer **5** 154

DU PONT, PIERRE SAMUEL (1870-1954), American industrialist **5** 154-155

DU PONT DE NEMOURS, PIERRE SAMUEL (1739-1817), French political economist **5** 155-156

DURAND, ASHER BROWN (1796-1886), American painter and engraver **5** 156-157

DURANT, THOMAS CLARK (1820-1885), American railroad executive **5** 157-158

DURANT, WILLIAM CRAPO (1861-1947), American industrialist **5** 158

DÜRER, ALBRECHT (1471-1528), German painter and graphic artist **5** 159-161

DURHAM, 1ST EARL OF (John George Lambton; 1792-1840), English statesman **5** 161-162

DURKHEIM, ÉMILE (1858-1917), French philosopher and sociologist **5** 162-163

DURRELL, GERALD MALCOLM (1925-1995), British naturalist and conservationist **24** 123-126

DURRELL, LAWRENCE (1912-1990), British author of novels, poetry, plays, short stories, and travel books **5** 163-164

DÜRRENMATT, FRIEDRICH (1921-1990), Swiss playwright **5** 164-165

Dutch art and architecture
genre and portrait painting
Ruysch, Rachel **24** 341-343

Dutch East Indies
see Indonesia—Dutch East Indies

DUVALIER, FRANÇOIS (Papa Doc; 1907-1971), Haitian president 1957-1971 **5** 165-166

DUVALIER, JEAN CLAUDE (Baby Doc; born 1949), president of Haiti (1971-1986) **5** 166-168

DVOŘÁK, ANTONIN (1841-1904), Czech composer **5** 168-169

DWIGHT, TIMOTHY (1752-1817), American educator and Congregational minister **5** 169

DYLAN, BOB (born Robert Allen Zimmerman; b. 1941), American singer, songwriter, and guitarist **5** 170-171

DYSON, FREEMAN JOHN (born 1923), British-American physicist **5** 171-173

DZERZHINSKY, FELIX EDMUNDOVICH (1877-1926), Soviet politician and revolutionary **5** 173-174

E

EADS, JAMES BUCHANAN (1820-1887), American engineer and inventor **5** 175-176

EAKINS, THOMAS (1844-1916), American painter **5** 176-177

EARHART, AMELIA MARY (1897-1937), American aviator **5** 177-179

EARL, RALPH (1751-1801), American painter **5** 179

EARLE, SYLVIA A. (Born Sylvia Alice Reade; born 1935), American marine biologist and oceanographer **5** 180-181

FOX, CHARLES JAMES (1749-1806), English parliamentarian **6** 35-37

FOX, GEORGE (1624-1691), English spiritual reformer **6** 37-38

FOX, VICENTE (born 1942), Mexican president **21** 142-143

FOX, WILLIAM (1879-1952), American film producer **21** 143-144

FOYT, A.J. (born 1935), American race car driver **24** 145-147

FRACASTORO, GIROLAMO (Hieronymus Fracastorius; c. 1478-1553), Italian physician, poet, astronomer, and logician **21** 144-147

FRAENKEL, ABRAHAM ADOLF (Abraham halevi Fraenkel; 1891-1965), Israeli mathematician **23** 109-111

FRAGONARD, JEAN HONORÉ (1732-1806), French painter **6** 38-39

FRANCE, ANATOLE (1844-1924), French novelist **6** 39-40

FRANCIS I (1494-1547), king of France 1515-1547 **6** 40-43

FRANCIS II (1768-1835), Holy Roman emperor 1792-1806 and emperor of Austria 1804-1835 **6** 43-44

FRANCIS FERDINAND (1863-1914), archduke of Austria **6** 44

FRANCIS JOSEPH (1830-1916), emperor of Austria 1868-1916 and king of Hungary 1867-1916 **6** 45-46

FRANCIS OF ASSISI, SAINT (1182-1226), Italian mystic and religious founder **6** 46-47

FRANCIS OF SALES, SAINT (1567-1622), French bishop **6** 47

FRANCIS XAVIER, SAINT (1506-1552), Spanish Jesuit missionary **6** 48

FRANCK, CÉSAR (1822-1890), French composer **6** 48-49

FRANCK, JAMES (1882-1964), German physicist **6** 49-52

FRANCO BAHAMONDE, FRANCISCO (1892-1975), Spanish general and dictator **6** 52-54

FRANCO OF COLOGNE (Franco of Paris; flourished circa 1250-1260), French music theorist **6** 52

FRANK, ANNE (1929-1945), 16-year-old holocaust victim who kept a famous diary **6** 54-56

FRANKENHEIMER, JOHN (1930-2002), American filmmaker **22** 182-185

FRANKENTHALER, HELEN (born 1928), American painter **6** 56-57

FRANKFURTER, FELIX (1882-1965), American jurist **6** 57

FRANKLIN, ARETHA (born 1942), African American singer and songwriter **6** 58-60

FRANKLIN, BENJAMIN (1706-1790), American statesman, diplomat, and inventor **6** 60-64

FRANKLIN, SIR JOHN (1786-1847), English explorer **6** 68-69

FRANKLIN, JOHN HOPE (born 1915), pioneer African American historian **6** 65-67

FRANKLIN, MILES (1879-1954), Australian novelist **6** 68-69

FRANKLIN, ROSALIND ELSIE (1920-1958), British physical chemist and molecular biologist **6** 67-68

FRANKLIN, WILLIAM (circa 1731-1813), American colonial administrator **6** 69-70

FRASER (PINTER), LADY ANTONIA (born 1932), popular British biographer, historian, and mystery novelist **6** 70-71

FRASER, MALCOLM (born 1930), prime minister of Australia (1975-1983) **6** 71-73

FRASER, PETER (1884-1950), New Zealand prime minister 1940-49 **6** 73-74

FRASER, SIMON (1776-1862), Canadian explorer and fur trader **6** 74-75

FRASER-REID, BERT (born 1934), Jamaican chemist **20** 145-146

FRAUNHOFER, JOSEPH VON (1787-1826), German physicist **6** 75-76

FRAZER, SIR JAMES GEORGE (1854-1941), Scottish classicist and anthropologist **6** 76

FRAZIER, EDWARD FRANKLIN (1894-1962), African American sociologist **6** 77

FRÉCHETTE, LOUIS-HONORÉ (1839-1908), French-Canadian poet **6** 77-78

FREDEGUND (Fredegunda, Fredegond; c. 550-597), Frankish queen **20** 146-149

FREDERICK I (1123-1190), Holy Roman emperor 1152-1190 **6** 78-79
and antipopes
  Alexander III **24** 12-14

FREDERICK II (1194-1250), Holy Roman emperor 1215-1250 **6** 79

FREDERICK II (1712-1786), king of Prussia 1740-1786 **6** 81-84

FREDERICK III (1415-1493), Holy Roman emperor and German king 1440-1493 **6** 84-85

FREDERICK WILLIAM (1620-1688), elector of Brandenburg 1640-1688 **6** 85-86

FREDERICK WILLIAM I (1688-1740), king of Prussia 1713-1740 **6** 86-87

FREDERICK WILLIAM III (1770-1840), king of Prussia 1797-1840 **6** 87

FREDERICK WILLIAM IV (1795-1861), king of Prussia 1840-1861 **6** 87-88

FREDHOLM, ERIK IVAR (1866-1927), Swedish mathematician **24** 147-149

FREED, JAMES INGO (born 1930), American architect **6** 88-90

FREEH, LOUIS J. (born 1950), director of the Federal Bureau of Investigation (FBI) **6** 90-91

FREEMAN, DOUGLAS SOUTHALL (1886-1953), American journalist **6** 91-92

FREEMAN, ROLAND L. (born 1936), American photographer of rural and urban African Americans **6** 92-93

FREGE, GOTTLOB (1848-1925), German mathematician and philosopher **6** 93-94

FREI MONTALVA, EDUARDO (born 1911), Chilean statesman **6** 94-95

FREIRE, PAULO (born 1921), Brazilian philosopher and educator **6** 95-96

FRELINGHUYSEN, THEODORUS JACOBUS (1691-circa 1748), Dutch Reformed clergyman and revivalist **6** 96-97

FRÉMONT, JOHN CHARLES (1813-1890), American explorer and politician **6** 97-98

FRENCH, DANIEL CHESTER (1850-1931), American sculptor **6** 98-99

French Cameroon Trust Territory
  see Cameroon Republic

French Guinea
  Diop, David Mandessi **24** 117-118

French literature
  essays
    de Pisan, Christine **24** 109-111
  feminist
    de Pisan, Christine **24** 109-111
  Negritude movement
    Diop, David Mandessi **24** 117-118
  novel (20th century)
    Memmi, Albert **24** 257-259
  poetry (12th-14th century)
    de Pisan, Christine **24** 109-111

French music
piano
Jaell, Marie Trautmann **24** 189-191

FRENEAU, PHILIP MORIN (1752-1832), American poet and journalist **6** 99-100

FRERE, SIR HENRY BARTLE EDWARD (1815-1884), English colonial administrator **6** 100-101

FRESCOBALDI, GIROLAMO (1583-1643), Italian composer and organist **6** 101-102

FRESNEL, AUGUSTIN JEAN (1788-1827), French physicist **6** 102-103

FREUD, ANNA (1895-1982), British psychoanalyst **18** 150-153

FREUD, LUCIAN (born 1922), British painter **20** 149-151

FREUD, SIGMUND (1856-1939), Viennese psychiatrist, founder of psychoanalysis **6** 103-106

FREYRE, GILBERTO (1900-1987), Brazilian sociologist and writer **6** 106-107

FREYTAG, GUSTAV (1816-1895), German novelist, dramatist, and critic **6** 107-108

FRICK, HENRY CLAY (1849-1919), American industrialist and financier **6** 108-109

FRIEDAN, BETTY (Betty Naomi Goldstein; born 1921), women's rights activist and author **6** 109-111

FRIEDMAN, MILTON (born 1912), American economist **6** 111-112

FRIEDRICH, CARL JOACHIM (1901-1984), German-born educator who became a leading American political theorist **6** 113-114

FRIEDRICH, CASPAR DAVID (1774-1840), German romantic painter **6** 114-115

FRIEL, BERNARD PATRICK (born 1929), author, teacher, and playwright from Northern Ireland **6** 115-116

FRIES, JAKOB FRIEDRICH (1773-1843), German philosopher **6** 116-117

FRISCH, KARL VON (1886-1982), Austrian zoologist **6** 117-118

FRISCH, MAX (born 1911), Swiss novelist and dramatist **6** 118-119

FRISCH, OTTO ROBERT (1904-1979), Austrian-British nuclear physicist **6** 119-120

FROBERGER, JOHANN JAKOB (1616-1667), German composer and organist **6** 120-121

FROBISHER, SIR MARTIN (circa 1538-1594), English explorer **6** 121-122

FROEBEL, FRIEDRICH WILHELM AUGUST (1782-1852), German educator and psychologist **6** 122-123

FROHMAN, CHARLES (1860-1915), American theatrical producer **6** 123-124

FROISSART, JEAN (circa 1337-after 1404), French priest, poet, and chronicler **6** 124-125

FROMM, ERICH (1900-1980), German writer in the fields of psychoanalysis, psychology, and social philosophy **6** 125-127

FRONDIZI, ARTURO (1908-1995), leader of the Argentine Radical Party and Argentine president (1958-1962) **6** 127-128

FRONTENAC ET PALLUAU, COMTE DE (Louis de Buade; 1622-1698), French colonial governor **6** 128-130

FRONTINUS, SEXTUS JULIUS (circa 35-circa 104), Roman magistrate, soldier, and writer **6** 130

FROST, ROBERT LEE (1874-1963), American poet **6** 130-133

FROUDE, JAMES ANTHONY (1818-1894), English historian **6** 133-134

FRUNZE, MIKHAIL VASILIEVICH (1885-1925), Soviet military leader **6** 134

FRY, ELIZABETH (1780-1845), British reformer **6** 134-136

FRY, WILLIAM HENRY (1813-1864), American composer **6** 136-137

FRYE, NORTHROP (Herman Northrop Frye; born 1912), Canadian literary scholar **6** 137-139

FUAD I (1868-1936), king of Egypt 1922-1936 **6** 139

FUCHS, LEONHARD (1501-1566), German botanist **20** 152-152

FUCHS, SIR VIVIAN (1908-1999), English explorer and geologist **6** 140

FUENTES, CARLOS (born 1928), Mexican author and political activist **6** 141-142

FUERTES, LOUIS AGASSIZ (1874-1927), American naturalist and artist **24** 152-153

FUGARD, ATHOL (born 1932), South African playwright **6** 142-143

FUGGER, JAKOB (Jacob Fugger; 1459-1525), German banker **21** 147-149

Fugitive slaves
see African American history (United States)

FUJIMORI, ALBERTO KEINYA (born 1938), president of Peru **6** 143-145

FUJIWARA KAMATARI (614-669), Japanese imperial official **6** 145

FUJIWARA MICHINAGA (966-1027), Japanese statesman **6** 145-146

FUKUI, KENICHI (born 1918), Japanese chemist **23** 111-112

FUKUYAMA, FRANCIS (born 1952), American philosopher and foreign policy expert **6** 146-147

FULBRIGHT, JAMES WILLIAM (1905-1995), American statesman **6** 147-149

FULLER, ALFRED (1885-1973), American businessman and inventor **19** 117-118

FULLER, JOHN FREDERICK CHARLES (1878-1966), British soldier and author **22** 185-186

FULLER, META WARRICK (1877-1968), American sculpter **23** 112-114

FULLER, MILLARD (born 1935), American lawyer and social activist **18** 153-155

FULLER, RICHARD BUCKMINISTER (born 1895), American architect and engineer **6** 149-150

FULLER, SARAH MARGARET (1810-1850), American feminist **6** 150-151

FULTON, ROBERT (1765-1815), American inventor, engineer, and artist **6** 151-152

FU MINGXIA (born 1978), Chinese diver **24** 149-151

FUNK, CASIMIR (1884-1967), Polish-American biochemist **22** 187-189

FURPHY, JOSEPH (1843-1912), Australian novelist **6** 152-153

FÜRÜZAN (Fürüzan Selçuk; born 1935), Turkish author and director **22** 189-190

FUSELI, HENRY (1741-1825), Swiss painter **6** 153-155

FUSTEL DE COULANGES, NUMA DENIS (1830-1889), French historian **6** 155

FUX, JOHANN JOSEPH (1660-1741), Austrian composer, conductor, and theoretician **6** 155-156

G

GABLE, WILLIAM CLARK (1901-1960), American film actor **6** 157-158

GABO, NAUM (1890-1977), Russian sculptor and designer **6** 158-159

GABOR, DENNIS (1900-1979), Hungarian-British physicist who invented holographic photography **6** 159-160

GABRIEL, ANGE JACQUES (1698-1782), French architect **6** 160-161

GABRIELI, GIOVANNI (circa 1557-1612), Italian composer **6** 161-162

GADAMER, HANS-GEORG (1900-2002), German philosopher, classicist, and interpretation theorist **6** 162-163

GADDAFI, MUAMMAR AL- (born 1942), head of the revolution that set up the Libyan Republic in 1969 **6** 163-165

GADSDEN, JAMES (1788-1858), American soldier and diplomat **6** 165-166

GAGARIN, YURI ALEXEIVICH (1934-1968), Russian cosmonaut **6** 166-167

GAGE, MATILDA JOSLYN (1826-1898), American reformer and suffragist **6** 167-169

GAGE, THOMAS (1719/20-1787), English general **6** 169-170

GAGNÉ, ROBERT MILLS (born 1916), American educator **6** 170

GAINSBOROUGH, THOMAS (1727-1788), English painter **6** 170-172

GAISERIC (died 477), king of the Vandals 428-477 **6** 172

GAITÁN, JORGE ELIÉCER (1898-1948), Colombian politician **6** 172-173

GAITSKELL, HUGH (1906-1963), British chancellor of the exchequer (1950-1951) and leader of the Labour Party (1955-1963) **6** 173-174

GALAMB, JOSEPH (Jozsef Galamb; 1881-1955), Hungarian American engineer **24** 154-155

GALBRAITH, JOHN KENNETH (born 1908), economist and scholar of the American Institutionalist school **6** 174-177

GALDÓS, BENITO PÉREZ (1843-1920), Spanish novelist and dramatist **6** 177-178

GALEN (130-200), Greek physician **6** 178-180

GALILEO GALILEI (1564-1642), Italian astronomer and physicist **6** 180-183

GALLATIN, ALBERT (1761-1849), Swiss-born American statesman, banker, and diplomat **6** 183-184

GALLAUDET, THOMAS HOPKINS (1787-1851), American educator **6** 185

GALLEGOS FREIRE, RÓMULO (1884-1969), Venezuelan novelist, president 1948 **6** 185-186

GALLO, ROBERT CHARLES (born 1937), American virologist **22** 191-193

GALLOWAY, JOSEPH (circa 1731-1803), American politician **6** 186-187

GALLUP, GEORGE (1901-1984), pioneer in the field of public opinion polling and a proponent of educational reform **6** 187-189

GALSWORTHY, JOHN (1867-1933), English novelist and playwright **6** 189-190

GALT, SIR ALEXANDER TILLOCH (1817-1893), Canadian politician **6** 190-191

GALT, JOHN (1779-1839), Scottish novelist **18** 156-158

GALTIERI, LEOPOLDO FORTUNATO (1926-2003), president of Argentina (1981-1982) **6** 191-193

GALTON, SIR FRANCIS (1822-1911), English scientist, biometrician, and explorer **6** 193-194

GALVANI, LUIGI (1737-1798), Italian physiologist **6** 194-195

GÁLVEZ, BERNARDO DE (1746-1786), Spanish colonial administrator **6** 195-196

GÁLVEZ, JOSÉ DE (1720-1787), Spanish statesman in Mexico **6** 196

GALWAY, JAMES (born 1939), Irish flutist **18** 158-160

GAMA, VASCO DA (circa 1460-1524), Portuguese navigator **6** 196-198

GAMBARO, GRISELDA (born 1928), Argentine author **23** 115-117

GAMBETTA, LÉON (1838-1882), French premier 1881-1882 **6** 198-199

GAMOW, GEORGE (1904-1968), Russian-American nuclear physicist, astrophysicist, biologist, and author of books popularizing science **6** 199-200

GANDHI, INDIRA PRIYADARSHINI (1917-1984), Indian political leader **6** 200-201

GANDHI, MOHANDAS KARAMCHAND (1869-1948), Indian political and religious leader **6** 201-204

GANDHI, RAJIV (1944-1991), Indian member of Parliament and prime minister **6** 204-205

GARBO, GRETA (1905-1990), Swedish-born American film star **6** 205-207

GARCIA, CARLOS P. (1896-1971), Philippine statesman, president 1957-61 **6** 207-208

GARCIA, JERRY (Jerome John Garcia; 1942-1995), American musician **21** 150-152

GARCÍA MÁRQUEZ, GABRIEL (born 1928), Colombian author **6** 208-209

GARCÍA MORENO, GABRIEL (1821-1875), Ecuadorian politician, president 1861-1865 and 1869-1875 **6** 209-210

GARCÍA ROBLES, ALFONSO (1911-1991), Mexican diplomat **23** 117-119

GARCILASO DE LA VEGA, INCA (1539-1616), Peruvian chronicler **6** 210-211

GARDINER, SAMUEL RAWSON (1829-1902), English historian **6** 211

GARDNER, ERLE STANLEY (1889-1970), American mystery writer **22** 193-195

GARDNER, ISABELLA STEWART (1840-1924), American art patron and socialite **21** 152-155

GARDNER, JOHN W. (1912-2002), American educator, public official, and political reformer **6** 211-213

GARFIELD, JAMES ABRAM (1831-1881), American general, president 1881 **6** 213-214

GARIBALDI, GIUSEPPE (1807-1882), Italian patriot **6** 215-217

GARLAND, HANNIBAL HAMLIN (1860-1940), American author **6** 217-218

GARLAND, JUDY (1922-1969), super star of films, musicals, and concert stage **6** 218-219

GARNEAU, FRANÇOIS-XAVIER (1809-1866), French-Canadian historian **6** 219-220

GARNER, JOHN NANCE ("Cactus Jack" Garner; 1868-1967), American vice president (1933-1941) **21** 155-157

GARNET, HENRY HIGHLAND (1815-1882), African American clergyman, abolitionist, and diplomat **24** 155-158

GARNIER, FRANCIS (Marie Joseph François Garnier; 1839-1873), French naval officer **6** 220-221

GARNIER, JEAN LOUIS CHARLES (1825-1898), French architect **6** 221-222

GARRETT, JOHN WORK (1820-1884), American railroad magnate **6** 225

GARRETT, THOMAS (1789-1871), American abolitionist **6** 225-226

GARRETT (ANDERSON), ELIZABETH (1836-1917), English physician and women's rights advocate **6** 222-225

GARRISON, WILLIAM LLOYD (1805-1879), American editor and abolitionist **6** 226-228
abolitionist journalism
Stewart, Maria W. Miller **24** 395-397

GARVEY, MARCUS MOSIAH (1887-1940), Jamaican leader and African nationalist **6** 228-229

GARY, ELBERT HENRY (1846-1927), American lawyer and industrialist **6** 229-230

GASCA, PEDRO DE LA (circa 1496-1567), Spanish priest and statesman **6** 230-231

GASKELL, ELIZABETH (1810-1865), English novelist **6** 231-232

GATES, WILLIAM HENRY, III (''Bill''; born 1955), computer software company co-founder and executive **6** 232-234

GATLING, RICHARD JORDAN (1818-1903), American inventor of multiple-firing guns **6** 234-235

GAUDÍ I CORNET, ANTONI (1852-1926), Catalan architect and designer **6** 235-236

GAUGUIN, PAUL (1848-1903), French painter and sculptor **6** 236-238

GAULLI, GIOVANNI BATTISTA (1639-1709), Italian painter **6** 238-239

GAULTIER, JEAN PAUL (born 1952), French avant-garde designer **6** 239-240

GAUSS, KARL FRIEDRICH (1777-1855), German mathematician and astronomer **6** 240-242

GAVIRIA TRUJILLO, CESAR AUGUSTO (born 1947), president of Colombia **6** 242-243

GAY, JOHN (1685-1732), English playwright and poet **6** 243-244

GAYLE, HELENE DORIS (born 1955), African American epidemiologist and pediatrician **6** 244-245

GAY-LUSSAC, JOSEPH LOUIS (1778-1850), French chemist and physicist **6** 245-246

GE
see General Electric Company

GEDDES, SIR PATRICK (1854-1932), Scottish sociologist and biologist **6** 246-247

GEERTGEN TOT SINT JANS (Geertgen van Haarlem; circa 1460/65-1490/95), Netherlandish painter **6** 248

GEERTZ, CLIFFORD (born 1926), American cultural anthropologist **6** 248-249

GEFFEN, DAVID LAWRENCE (born 1943), American record and film producer **23** 119-122

GEHRIG, LOU (Henry Louis Gehrig; 1903-1941), American baseball player **19** 119-121

GEHRY, FRANK O. (née Goldberg; born 1929), American architect **6** 250-251

GEIGER, HANS (born Johannes Wilhelm Geiger; 1882-1945), German physicist **6** 251-253

GEISEL, ERNESTO (1908-1996), Brazilian army general, president of Brazil's national oil company (Petrobras), and president of the republic (1974-1979) **6** 253-255

GEISEL, THEODOR (a.k.a. Dr. Seuss; 1904-1991), American author of children's books **6** 255-256

GELLER, MARGARET JOAN (born 1947), American astronomer **6** 256-257

GELL-MANN, MURRAY (born 1929), American physicist **6** 257-258

GEMAYEL, AMIN (born 1942), Lebanese nationalist and Christian political leader; president of the Republic of Lebanon (1982-1988) **6** 258-259

GEMAYEL, PIERRE (1905-1984), leader of the Lebanese Phalangist Party **6** 259-261

Gene (biology)
see Genetics

General Electric Company (Schenectady; New York State)
industrial research
Blodgett, Katharine Burr **24** 54-56

GENET, EDMOND CHARLES (1763-1834), French diplomat **6** 261-262

GENET, JEAN (1910-1986), French novelist and playwright **6** 262-263

Genetics (biology)
molecular
Tonegawa, Susumu **24** 417-420
Wrinch, Dorothy Maud **24** 444-446

GENGHIS KHAN (1167-1227), Mongol chief, creator of the Mongol empire **6** 263-265

GENSCHER, HANS-DIETRICH (born 1927), leader of West Germany's liberal party (the FDP) and foreign minister **6** 265-266

GENTILE, GIOVANNI (1875-1944), Italian philosopher and politician **6** 267

GENTILE DA FABRIANO (Gentile di Niccolò di Giovanni di Massio; circa 1370-1427), Italian painter **6** 266-267

GENTILESCHI, ARTEMISIA (1593-1652), Italian painter **22** 195-196

GEOFFREY OF MONMOUTH (circa 1100-1155), English pseudohistorian **6** 268

GEORGE I (1660-1727), king of Great Britain and Ireland 1714-1727 **6** 268-269

GEORGE II (1683-1760), king of Great Britain and Ireland and elector of Hanover 1727-1760 **6** 269-270

GEORGE III (1738-1820), king of Great Britain and Ireland 1760-1820 **6** 270-272

GEORGE IV (1762-1830), king of Great Britain and Ireland 1820-1830 **6** 272-273

GEORGE V (1865-1936), king of Great Britain and Northern Ireland and emperor of India 1910-1936 **6** 273-275

GEORGE VI (1895-1952), king of Great Britain and Northern Ireland 1936-1952 **6** 275

GEORGE, DAN (1899-1981), Native American actor **22** 196-198

GEORGE, HENRY (1839-1897), American economist and social reformer **6** 276

GEORGE, JAMES ZACHARIAH (1826-1897), American politician and jurist **6** 276-277

GEORGE, STEFAN (1868-1933), German symbolist poet **6** 277-278

Georgia Technical University (Atlanta, Georgia)
Heisman, John William **24** 171-174

GEPHARDT, RICHARD ANDREW (born 1941), Democratic majority leader in the House of Representatives **6** 278-280

GÉRICAULT, JEAN LOIS ANDRÉ THÉODORE (1791-1824), French painter **6** 280-281

GERMAIN, SOPHIE (Marie-Sophie Germain; 1776-1831), French mathematician **21** 157-158

GERONIMO (1829-1909), American Apache Indian warrior **6** 281-282

GERRY, ELBRIDGE (1744-1814), American patriot and statesman **6** 282-283

GERSHOM BEN JUDAH (circa 950-1028), German rabbi, scholar, and poet **6** 283-284

GERSHWIN, GEORGE (1898-1937), American composer **6** 284-285

GERSHWIN, IRA (Israel Gershvin; 1896-1983), American lyricist **20** 153-155

GERSON, JOHN (1363-1429), French theologian **6** 285-286

GERSTNER, LOU (Louis Vincent Gerstner, Jr.; born 1942), American businessman **19** 121-124

GESELL, ARNOLD LUCIUS (1880-1961), American psychologist and pediatrician **6** 286-287

GESNER, KONRAD VON (1516-1565), Swiss naturalist **6** 287

GESUALDO, DON CARLO (Prince of Venosa; circa 1560-1613), Italian composer **6** 287-288

GETTY, JEAN PAUL (1892-1976), billionaire independent oil producer **6** 288-290

GHAZALI, ABU HAMID MUHAMMAD AL- (1058-1111), Arab philosopher and Islamic theologian **6** 290-291

GHIBERTI, LORENZO (circa 1381-1455), Italian sculptor, goldsmith, and painter **6** 291-292

GHIRLANDAIO, DOMENICO (1449-1494), Italian painter **6** 292-293

GHOSE, AUROBINDO (1872-1950), Indian nationalist and philosopher **6** 293-294

GIACOMETTI, ALBERTO (1901-1966), Swiss sculptor and painter **6** 294-295

GIANNINI, A. P. (Amadeo Peter; 1870-1949), Italian-American financier and banker **6** 295-297

GIAP, VO NGUYEN (born 1912), Vietnamese Communist general and statesman **6** 297-299

GIBBON, EDWARD (1737-1794), English historian **6** 299-300

GIBBONS, CEDRIC (1893-1960), American film production designer **21** 158-159

GIBBONS, JAMES (1834-1921), American Roman Catholic cardinal **6** 300-301

GIBBS, JAMES (1682-1754), British architect **6** 301-302

GIBBS, JOSIAH WILLARD (1839-1903), American mathematical physicist **6** 302-303

GIBRAN, KAHLIL (1883-1931), Lebanese writer and artist **6** 303-305

GIBSON, ALTHEA (1927-2003), African American tennis player **6** 305-306

GIBSON, BOB (Robert Gibson; born 1935), American baseball player **21** 159-162

GIBSON, WILLIAM (born 1914), American author **6** 306-307

GIDDINGS, FRANKLIN HENRY (1855-1931), American sociologist **6** 307-308

GIDE, ANDRÉ (1869-1951), French author **6** 308-309

GIELGUD, JOHN (born 1904), English Shakespearean actor **6** 310-311

GIERKE, OTTO VON (1841-1921), German jurist **6** 311-312

GIGLI, ROMEO (born 1949), Italian designer **6** 312

GILBERT, SIR HUMPHREY (circa 1537-1583), English soldier and colonizer **6** 313

GILBERT, WALTER (born 1932), American molecular biologist **23** 122-124

GILBERT, WILLIAM (1544-1603), English physician and physicist **6** 313-314

GILBERT, SIR WILLIAM SCHWENCK (1836-1911), English playwright and poet **6** 314-315

GILBRETH, FRANK (1868-1924), American engineer and management expert **21** 162-163

GILBRETH, LILLIAN (born Lillian Evelyn Moller; 1878-1972), American psychologist and industrial management consultant **6** 315-317

GILES, ERNEST (1835-1897), Australian explorer **6** 317-318

GILKEY, LANGDON BROWN (born 1919), American ecumenical Protestant theologian **6** 318-319

GILLESPIE, DIZZY (born John Birks Gillespie; 1917-1993), African American jazz trumpeter, composer, and band leader **6** 320-322

GILLETTE, KING CAMP (1855-1932), American businessman and inventor **21** 163-166

GILLIAM, SAM (born 1933), American artist **6** 322-323

GILMAN, CHARLOTTE ANNA PERKINS (1860-1935), American writer and lecturer **6** 323-325

GILMAN, DANIEL COIT (1831-1908), educator and pioneer in the American university movement **6** 325-326

GILPIN, LAURA (1891-1979), American photographer **6** 326-327

GILSON, ÉTIENNE HENRY (1884-1978), French Catholic philosopher **6** 327-328

GINASTERA, ALBERTO EVARISTO (1916-1983), Argentine composer **6** 328-329

GINGRICH, NEWT (born 1943), Republican congressman from Georgia **6** 329-332

GINSBERG, ALLEN (1926-1997), American poet **6** 332-333

GINSBURG, RUTH BADER (born 1933), second woman appointed to the United States Supreme Court **6** 333-336

GINZBERG, ASHER (Ahad Ha-Am; means "one of the people;" 1856-1927), Jewish intellectual leader **6** 336-337

GINZBERG, LOUIS (1873-1953), Lithuanian-American Talmudic scholar **6** 337-338

GINZBURG, NATALIA LEVI (1916-1991), Italian novelist, essayist, playwright, and translator **6** 338-339

GIOLITTI, GIOVANNI (1842-1928), Italian statesman **6** 339-340

GIORGIONE (1477-1510), Italian painter **6** 340-341

GIOTTO (circa 1267-1337), Italian painter, architect, and sculptor **6** 342-345

GIOVANNI, YOLANDE CORNELIA, JR. (born 1943), African American poet **6** 346-347

GIOVANNI DA BOLOGNA (1529-1608), Italian sculptor **6** 345-346

GIPP, GEORGE (1895-1920), American football player **19** 124-126

GIRARD, STEPHEN (1750-1831), American merchant and philanthropist **6** 347-348

GIRARDON, FRANÇOIS (1628-1715), French sculptor **6** 348-349

GIRAUDOUX, JEAN (1882-1944), French novelist, playwright, and diplomat **6** 349-350

GIRTY, SIMON (1741-1818), American frontiersman **6** 350

GISCARD D'ESTAING, VALÉRY (born 1926), third president of the French Fifth Republic **6** 350-352

GISH, LILLIAN (1896-1993), American actress **20** 155-158

GIST, CHRISTOPHER (circa 1706-1759), American frontiersman **6** 352-353

GIULIANI, RUDOLPH WILLIAM (born 1944), mayor of New York City **6** 353-355

GLACKENS, WILLIAM (1870-1938), American painter **6** 355-356

GLADDEN, WASHINGTON (1836-1918), American clergyman **6** 356-357

GLADSTONE, WILLIAM EWART (1809-1898), English statesman **6** 357-360

GLASGOW, ELLEN (1873-1945), American novelist **6** 360-361

GLASHOW, SHELDON LEE (born 1932), American Nobel Prize winner in physics **6** 361-362

GLASS, PHILIP (born 1937), American composer of minimalist music **6** 362-364

GLASSE, HANNAH (Hannah Allgood; 1708-1770), English cookbook author **21** 166-167

GLEDITSCH, ELLEN (1879-1968), Norwegian chemist **23** 124-126

GLENDOWER, OWEN (1359?-1415?), Welsh national leader **6** 364-365

GLENN, JOHN HERSCHEL, JR. (born 1921), military test pilot, astronaut, businessman, and United States senator from Ohio **6** 365-367

GLIDDEN, JOSEPH (1813-1906), American businessman and inventor **21** 167-170

GLIGOROV, KIRO (born 1917), first president of the Republic of Macedonia **6** 367-369

GLINKA, MIKHAIL IVANOVICH (1804-1857), Russian composer **6** 369-370

Globe Theater (London)
Burbage, Richard **24** 70-72

GLOUCESTER, DUKE OF (1391-1447), English statesman **6** 370-371

GLUBB, SIR JOHN BAGOT (1897-1986), British commander of the Arab Legion 1939-56 **6** 371-372

GLUCK, CHRISTOPH WILLIBALD (1714-1787), Austrian composer and opera reformer **6** 372-374

GLUCKMAN, MAX (1911-1975), British anthropologist **6** 374-375

GLYN, ELINOR (born Elinor Sutherland; 1864-1943), British author and filmmaker **23** 126-128

Gnostic (Gospel of Mary; book)
Mary Magdalene **24** 243-246

GOBINEAU, COMTE DE (Joseph Arthur Gobineau; 1816-1882), French diplomat **6** 375-376

GODARD, JEAN-LUC (born 1930), French actor, film director, and screenwriter **19** 126-128

GODDARD, ROBERT HUTCHINGS (1882-1945), American pioneer in rocketry **6** 376-377

GÖDEL, KURT (1906-1978), Austrian-American mathematician **6** 377-379

GODFREY OF BOUILLON (circa 1060-1100), French lay leader of First Crusade **6** 379

GODKIN, EDWIN LAWRENCE (1831-1902), British-born American journalist **6** 380

GODOLPHIN, SIDNEY (1st Earl of Godolphin; 1645-1712), English statesman **6** 380-381

GODOY Y ÁLVAREZ DE FARIA, MANUEL DE (1767-1851), Spanish statesman **6** 381-382

GODUNOV, BORIS FEODOROVICH (circa 1551-1605), czar of Russia 1598-1605 **6** 382-383

Godwin, Edward W. (1833-1886), British architect
Terry, Ellen **24** 409-411

GODWIN, WILLIAM (1756-1836), English political theorist and writer **6** 383-384

GOEBBELS, JOSEPH PAUL (1897-1945), German politician and Nazi propagandist **6** 384-385

GOEPPERT-MAYER, MARIA (1906-1972), American physicist **6** 385-387

GOETHALS, GEORGE WASHINGTON (1858-1928), American Army officer and engineer **6** 387-388

GOETHE, JOHANN WOLFGANG VON (1749-1832), German poet **6** 388-391

GOGOL, NIKOLAI (1809-1852), Russian author **6** 391-393

GOH CHOK TONG (born 1941), leader of the People's Action Party and Singapore's prime minister **6** 393-395

GOIZUETA, ROBERTO (1931-1997), Cuban American businessman and philanthropist **18** 160-162

GÖKALP, MEHMET ZIYA (1875/76-1924), Turkish publicist and sociologist **6** 395-396

GOKHALE, GOPAL KRISHNA (1866-1915), Indian nationalist leader **6** 396

GOLD, THOMAS (1920-2004), American astronomer and physicist **18** 162-164

GOLDBERG, ARTHUR JOSEPH (1908-1990), U.S. secretary of labor, ambassador to the United Nations, and activist justice of the U.S. Supreme Court **6** 397-398

GOLDBERG, WHOOPI (born Caryn E. Johnson; born 1949), African American actress **6** 398-402

GOLDEN, HARRY (1902-1981), Jewish-American humorist, writer, and publisher **6** 402-403

GOLDIE, SIR GEORGE DASHWOOD TAUBMAN (1846-1925), British trader and empire builder **6** 404

GOLDING, WILLIAM (1911-1993), English novelist and essayist **6** 404-406

GOLDMAN, EMMA (1869-1940), Lithuanian-born American anarchist **6** 406-407

GOLDMARK, JOSEPHINE (1877-1950), advocate of government assistance in improving the lot of women and children **6** 407-408

GOLDMARK, PETER CARL (1906-1977), American engineer and inventor **21** 170-172

GOLDONI, CARLO (1707-1793), Italian dramatist, poet, and librettist **6** 408-409

GOLDSMITH, JAMES MICHAEL (1933-1997), British-French industrialist and financier **6** 409-411

GOLDSMITH, OLIVER (1730-1774), British poet, dramatist, and novelist **6** 411-413

GOLDSMITH, OLIVER (1794-1861), Canadian poet **6** 411

GOLDWATER, BARRY (1909-1998), conservative Republican U.S. senator from Arizona (1952-1987) **6** 413-415

GOLDWYN, SAMUEL (1882-1974), Polish-born American film producer **6** 416

Golf
Mackenzie, Ada **24** 232-234
Trevino, Lee **24** 420-422

GOMBERT, NICOLAS (circa 1500-1556/57), Franco-Flemish composer **6** 416-417

GÓMEZ, JUAN VICENTE (1857-1935), Venezuelan dictator **6** 417-418

GÓMEZ, MÁXIMO (1836-1905), Dominican-born Cuban general and independence hero **6** 418-419

GÓMEZ CASTRO, LAUREANO ELEUTERIO (1889-1965), Colombian statesman, president **6** 419-420

GOMPERS, SAMUEL (1850-1924), American labor leader **6** 420-422

GOMULKA, WLADISLAW (1905-1982), Polish politician **6** 422-424

H

HARRIS, PATRICIA ROBERTS (1924-1985), first African American woman in the U.S. Cabinet **7** 174-175

HARRIS, ROY (1898-1979), American composer **7** 175-176

HARRIS, TOWNSEND (1804-1878), American merchant and diplomat **7** 176-177

HARRIS, WILLIAM TORREY (1835-1909), American educator and philosopher **7** 177-178

HARRISON, BENJAMIN (1833-1901), American statesman, president 1889-1893 **7** 178-179

HARRISON, PETER (1716-1775), American architect and merchant **7** 179-180

HARRISON, WILLIAM HENRY (1773-1841), American statesman, president 1841 **7** 180-181

HARSHA (Harshavardhana; circa 590-647), king of Northern India 606-612 **7** 181-182

HART, GARY W. (born 1936), American political campaign organizer, U.S. senator, and presidential candidate **7** 182-184

HART, HERBERT LIONEL ADOLPHUS (1907-1992), British legal philosopher **22** 218-219

HARTE, FRANCIS BRET (1837-1902), American poet and fiction writer **7** 184-185

HARTLEY, DAVID (1705-1757), British physician and philosopher **7** 185

HARTLEY, MARSDEN (1877-1943), American painter **7** 186

HARTSHORNE, CHARLES (born 1897), American theologian **7** 186-187

HARUN AL-RASHID (766-809), Abbasid caliph of Baghdad 786-809 **7** 188

HARUNOBU, SUZUKI (ca. 1725-1770), Japanese painter and printmaker **7** 188-189

HARVARD, JOHN (1607-1638), English philanthropist **21** 195-197

HARVEY, WILLIAM (1578-1657), English physician **7** 189-190

HASAN, IBN AL-HAYTHAM (ca. 966-1039), Arab physicist, astronomer, and mathematician **7** 190-191

HASKINS, CHARLES HOMER (1870-1937), American historian **7** 191-192

HASSAM, FREDERICK CHILDE (1859-1935), American impressionist painter **7** 192

HASSAN, MOULEY (King Hassan II; 1929-1999), inherited the throne of Morocco in 1961 **7** 194-195

HASSAN, MUHAMMAD ABDILLE (1864-1920), Somali politico-religious leader and poet **7** 194-195

HASTINGS, PATRICK GARDINER (1880-1952), British lawyer and politician **22** 219-221

HASTINGS, WARREN (1732-1818), English statesman **7** 195-196

HATCH, WILLIAM HENRY (1833-1896), American reformer and politician **7** 196

HATSHEPSUT (ruled 1503-1482 B.C.), Egyptian queen **7** 196-197

HATTA, MOHAMMAD (1902-1980), a leader of the Indonesian nationalist movement (1920s-1945) and a champion of non-alignment and of socialism grounded in Islam **7** 197-199

HAUPTMAN, HERBERT AARON (born 1917), American mathematician **24** 165-167

HAUPTMANN, GERHART JOHANN ROBERT (1862-1946), German dramatist and novelist **7** 199-201

HAUSHOFER, KARL (1869-1946), German general and geopolitician **7** 201

HAUSSMANN, BARON GEORGES EUGÈNE (1809-1891), French prefect of the Seine **7** 201-202

HAVEL, VACLAV (born 1936), playwright and human rights activist who became the president of Czechoslovakia **7** 202-205

HAVEMEYER, HENRY OSBORNE (1847-1907), American businessman **22** 222-224

HAWES, HARRIET ANN BOYD (1871-1945), American archeologist **22** 224-225

HAWKE, ROBERT JAMES LEE (born 1929), Australian Labor prime minister **7** 205-206

HAWKING, STEPHEN WILLIAM (born 1942), British physicist and mathematician **7** 206-208

HAWKINS, COLEMAN (1904-1969), American jazz musician **7** 208-210

HAWKINS, SIR JOHN (1532-1595), English naval commander **7** 210-211

HAWKS, HOWARD WINCHESTER (1896-1977), American film director **22** 225-226

HAWKSMOOR, NICHOLAS (1661-1736), English architect **7** 211-212

HAWTHORNE, NATHANIEL (1804-1864), American novelist **7** 212-215

HAY, JOHN (1838-1905), American statesman **7** 215-216

HAYA DE LA TORRE, VICTOR RAUL (born 1895), Peruvian political leader and theorist **7** 216-217

HAYDEN, FERDINAND VANDIVEER (1829-1887), American geologist and explorer **22** 227-229

HAYDEN, ROBERT EARL (1913-1980), African American poet **22** 229-231

HAYDEN, THOMAS EMMET (born 1939), American writer and political activist **7** 217-219

HAYDN, FRANZ JOSEPH (1732-1809), Austrian composer **7** 219-221

HAYEK, FRIEDRICH A. VON (1899-1992), Austrian-born British free market economist, social philosopher, and Nobel Laureate **7** 221-223

HAYES, HELEN (1900-1993), American actress **7** 223-224

HAYES, CARDINAL PATRICK JOSEPH (1867-1938), American cardinal **7** 224-225

HAYES, ROLAND (1887-1977), African American classical singer **7** 225-227

HAYES, RUTHERFORD BIRCHARD (1822-1893), American statesman, president 1877-1881 **7** 227-228

HAYFORD, J. E. CASELY (1866-1903), Gold Coast politician, journalist, and educator **7** 228-230

HAYKAL, MUHAMMAD HUSAIN (born 1923), Egyptian journalist and editor of *al-Ahram*(1957-1974) **7** 230-231

HAYNE, ROBERT YOUNG (1791-1839), American politician **7** 231-232

HAYNES, ELWOOD (1857-1925), American inventor and businessman **22** 231-234

HAYS, WILL (William Harrison Hays; 1879-1954), American film censor **21** 197-199

HAYWOOD, WILLIAM DUDLEY (1869-1928), American labor leader **7** 232-233

HAYWORTH, RITA (born Margarita Carmen Cansino; 1918-1987), American actress **7** 233-235

HAZA, OFRA (1959-2000), Israeli singer **24** 167-169

HAZLITT, WILLIAM (1778-1830), English literary and social critic **7** 235-236

HEAD, EDITH (1898-1981), American costume designer **18** 191-193

I

JOACHIM OF FIORE (circa 1132-1202), Italian mystic **8** 263-264

JOAN OF ARC (1412?-1431), French national heroine **8** 264-265

JOBS, STEVEN (born 1955), American computer designer and co-founder of Apple Computers **8** 265-267

JODL, ALFRED (1892?-1946), German general **18** 210-212

JOFFRE, JOSEPH JACQUES CÉSAIRE (1852-1931), French marshal **8** 267-268

JOFFREY, ROBERT (born Abdullah Jaffa Anver Bey Khan; 1930-1988), American dancer and choreographer **8** 268-270

JOGUES, ST. ISAAC (1607-1646), French Jesuit missionary and martyr **8** 270-271

JOHANAN BEN ZAKKAI (flourished circa 70 A.D.), Jewish teacher **8** 271-272

JOHANNES IV (1836-1889), Ethiopian emperor 1872-1889 **8** 272-273

JOHN (1167-1216), king of England 1199-1216 **8** 274-275

JOHN II (1319-1364), king of France 1350-1364 **8** 275-276

JOHN II (1455-1495), king of Portugal 1481-1495 **21** 223-225

JOHN III (John Sobieski; 1629-1696), king of Poland **8** 276-277

JOHN XXIII (Angelo Giuseppe Roncalli; 1881-1963), pope 1958-1963 **8** 277-280

JOHN, AUGUSTUS EDWIN (1878-1961), Welsh painter **8** 291

JOHN, ELTON HERCULES (Reginald Kenneth Dwight; born 1947), English singer, songwriter and humanitarian **18** 212-214

JOHN, ST. (flourished 1st century A.D.), Christian Apostle and Evangelist **8** 273-274

JOHN CHRYSOSTOM, ST. (circa 347-407), bishop of Constantinople **8** 280-281

JOHN MAURICE OF NASSAU (1604-1679), Dutch governor general of Netherlands Brazil **8** 281-282

JOHN OF AUSTRIA (1547-1578), Spanish general **20** 189-192

JOHN OF DAMASCUS, ST. (circa 680-750), Syrian theologian **8** 282

JOHN OF GAUNT (5th Duke of Lancaster; 1340-1399), English soldier-statesman **8** 282-283

JOHN OF LEIDEN (1509-1536), Dutch Anabaptist **8** 283

JOHN OF PIANO CARPINI (circa 1180-1252), Italian Franciscan monk **8** 284

JOHN OF SALISBURY (1115/20-1180), English bishop and humanist **8** 284-285

JOHN OF THE CROSS, ST. (1542-1591), Spanish Carmelite mystic **8** 285

JOHN PAUL I (Albino Luciani; 1912-1978), Roman Catholic pope (August 26-September 28, 1978) **8** 286-287

JOHN PAUL II (Karol Wojtyla; born 1920), cardinal of Krakow, Poland, and later Roman Catholic pope **8** 287-290

JOHN THE BAPTIST, ST. (flourished circa 29 A.D.), New Testament figure, forerunner of Jesus of Nazareth **8** 290

Johnny Belinda (film) Negulesco, Jean **24** 277-279

JOHNS, JASPER (born 1930), American painter and sculptor **8** 291-293

Johns Hopkins University (Baltimore, Maryland) founded Hopkins, Johns **24** 178-180

JOHNSON, ALVIN SAUNDERS (1874-1971), American economist and editor **8** 293-294

JOHNSON, ANDREW (1808-1875), American statesman, president 1865-1869 **8** 294-295

JOHNSON, BETSEY (born 1941?), American fashion designer **8** 295-296

JOHNSON, CHARLES SPURGEON (1893-1956), African American educator and sociologist **8** 296-297

JOHNSON, EARVIN, JR. ("Magic"; born 1959), popular African American star of the Los Angeles Lakers basketball team **8** 297-299

JOHNSON, GUY BENTON (1901-1991), sociologist, social anthropologist, and archaeologist who was a student of African American culture and an advocate of racial equality **8** 299-300

JOHNSON, HIRAM WARREN (1866-1945), American politician **8** 300-301

JOHNSON, JACK (1878-1946), African American boxer **8** 301-304

JOHNSON, JAMES WELDON (1871-1938), African American author and lawyer **8** 304-305

JOHNSON, SIR JOHN (1742-1830), American loyalist in the American Revolution **8** 305-306

JOHNSON, JOHN HAROLD (born 1918), American entrepreneur and founder of the Johnson Publishing Company **8** 306-308

JOHNSON, JONATHAN EASTMAN (1824-1906), American painter **8** 308

JOHNSON, LYNDON BAINES (1908-1973), American statesman, president 1963-1969 **8** 308-312

JOHNSON, MARIETTA LOUISE PIERCE (1864-1938), founder and 30-year teacher of an Alabama experimental school **8** 312-313

JOHNSON, MORDECAI WYATT (1890-1976), African American educator and minister **24** 196-198

JOHNSON, PAULINE (Emily Pauline Johnson; Tekahionwake 1861-1913), Canadian poet **23** 170-172

JOHNSON, PHILIP (born 1906), American architect, critic, and historian **8** 313-314

JOHNSON, RAFER (born 1935), American decathlete and goodwill ambassador **21** 225-227

JOHNSON, ROBERT (1911-1938), African American musician **23** 172-174

JOHNSON, SAMUEL (1696-1772), American clergyman and educator **8** 314-315

JOHNSON, SAMUEL (1709-1784), English author and lexicographer **8** 315-317

JOHNSON, TOM LOFTIN (1854-1911), American entrepreneur and politician **8** 317

JOHNSON, VIRGINIA E. (born 1925), American psychologist and sex therapist **8** 317-319

JOHNSON, WALTER ("Big Train"; 1887-1946), American baseball player and manager **21** 228-230

JOHNSON, SIR WILLIAM (1715-1774), British colonial administrator **8** 319-320

JOHNSON, WILLIAM (1771-1834), American jurist **22** 268-270

JOHNSON, WILLIAM H. (1901-1970), African American painter of the Black experience **8** 320-322

JOHNSTON, FRANCES BENJAMIN (1864-1952), American photographer **23** 174-177

JOHNSTON, HENRY HAMILTON (Sir Harry Johnston; 1858-1927), English administrator, explorer, and author **8** 322-323

KAUFMAN, GEORGE S. (1889-1961), American playwright **8** 457-458

KAUFMAN, GERALD BERNARD (born 1930), foreign policy spokesman of the British Labour Party **8** 458-460

KAUFMANN, EZEKIEL (1889-1963), Jewish philosopher and scholar **8** 460

KAUNDA, KENNETH DAVID (born 1924), Zambian statesman **8** 460-461

KAUTILYA (4th century B.C.), Indian statesman and author **8** 462

KAUTSKY, KARL JOHANN (1854-1938), German Austrian Socialist **8** 462-463

KAWABATA, YASUNARI (1899-1972), Japanese novelist **8** 463-464

KAWAWA, RASHIDI MFAUME (born 1929), Tanzanian political leader **8** 464-465

KAZAN, ELIA (1909-2003), American film and stage director **8** 465-466

KAZANTZAKIS, NIKOS (1883-1957), Greek author, journalist, and statesman **8** 466-468

KEAN, EDMUND (1789-1833), English actor **21** 237-239

KEARNEY, DENIS (1847-1907), Irish-born American labor agitator **8** 468

KEARNY, STEPHEN WATTS (1794-1848), American general **8** 468-469

KEATING, PAUL JOHN (born 1944), federal treasurer of Australia (1983-1991) **8** 469-470

KEATON, BUSTER (Joseph Frank Keaton; 1895-1966), American comedian **20** 199-201

KEATS, JOHN (1795-1821), English poet **8** 470-472

KEFAUVER, CAREY ESTES (1903-1963), U.S. senator and influential Tennessee Democrat **8** 472-474

KEILLOR, GARRISON (Gary Edward Keillor, born 1942), American humorist, radio host, and author **22** 271-273

KEITA, MODIBO (1915-1977), Malian statesman **8** 474-475

KEITEL, WILHELM (1882-1946), German general **18** 224-226

KEITH, SIR ARTHUR (1866-1955), British anatomist and physical anthropologist **8** 475-476

KEITH, MINOR COOPER (1848-1929), American entrepreneur **8** 476-477

KEKKONEN, URHO KALEVA (1900-1986), Finnish athlete and politician **23** 189-191

KEKULÉ, FRIEDRICH AUGUST (1829-1896), German chemist **8** 477-478

KELLER, GOTTFRIED (1819-1890), Swiss short-story writer, novelist, and poet **8** 478-479

KELLER, HELEN ADAMS (1880-1968), American lecturer and author **8** 479-480

KELLEY, FLORENCE (1859-1932), American social worker and reformer **8** 483-484

KELLEY, HALL JACKSON (1790-1874), American promoter **8** 480

KELLEY, OLIVER HUDSON (1826-1913), American agriculturalist **8** 480-481

KELLOGG, FRANK BILLINGS (1856-1937), American statesman **8** 481

KELLOGG, JOHN HARVEY (1852-1943), American health propagandist and cereal manufacturer **21** 239-242

KELLOR, FRANCES (1873-1952), American activist and politician **8** 481-482

KELLY, ELLSWORTH (born 1923), American artist **8** 482-483

KELLY, GENE (born Eugene Curran Kelly; 1912-1996), American actor, dancer, and choreographer **8** 484-486

KELLY, GRACE (Grace, Princess; 1929-1982), princess of Monaco **19** 174-176

KELLY, PATRICK (1954-1990), African American fashion designer **22** 273-275

KELLY, PETRA (born 1947), West German pacifist and politician **8** 486-487

KELLY, WALT (Walter Crawford Kelly; 1913-1973), American Cartoonist **22** 275-278

KELLY, WILLIAM (1811-1888), American iron manufacturer **8** 487-488

KELSEY, HENRY (circa 1667-1724), English-born Canadian explorer **8** 488

KELVIN OF LARGS, BARON (William Thomson; 1824-1907), Scottish physicist **8** 488-489

KEMAL, YASHAR (born 1922), Turkish novelist **8** 489-491

KEMBLE, FRANCES ANNE (Fanny Kemble; 1809-1893), English actress **8** 491

KEMP, JACK FRENCH, JR. (born 1935), Republican congressman from New York and secretary of housing and urban development **8** 491-493

KEMPIS, THOMAS À (circa 1380-1471), German monk and spiritual writer **8** 493-494

KENDALL, AMOS (1789-1869), American journalist **8** 494

KENDALL, EDWARD CALVIN (1886-1972), American biochemist **8** 495

KENDALL, THOMAS HENRY (Henry Clarence Kendall; 1839-1882), Australian poet **23** 191-194

Kendrake, Carleton
see Gardner, Erle Stanley

KENDREW, JOHN C. (1917-1997), English chemist and Nobel Prize winner **8** 495-496

KENEALLY, THOMAS MICHAEL (born 1935), Australian author **18** 226-228

KENNAN, GEORGE F. (born 1904), American diplomat, author, and scholar **8** 496-498

KENNEDY, ANTHONY M. (born 1936), United States Supreme Court justice **8** 498-500

KENNEDY, EDWARD M. (Ted; born 1932), U.S. senator from Massachusetts **8** 500-502

KENNEDY, JOHN FITZGERALD (1917-1963), American statesman, president 1960-1963 **8** 502-506

KENNEDY, JOHN PENDLETON (1795-1870), American author and politician **8** 506-507

KENNEDY, JOHN STEWART (1830-1909), American financier and philanthropist **8** 507-508

KENNEDY, JOSEPH (1888-1969), American financier, ambassador, and movie producer **19** 176-178

KENNEDY, ROBERT FRANCIS (1925-1968), American statesman **8** 508-509

KENNEDY, WILLIAM (born 1928), American author **19** 178-180

Kenny, Charles J.
see Gardner, Erle Stanley

KENNY, ELIZABETH (Sister Kenny; 1886-1952), Australian nursing sister **8** 509-510

KENT, JAMES (1763-1847), American jurist **8** 510-511

KENT, ROCKWELL (1882-1971), American painter and illustrator **8** 511

KENYATTA, JOMO (circa 1890-1978), Kenyan statesman **8** 512-514

KEOHANE, NANNERL OVERHOLSER (born 1940), American feminist activist and university chancellor **18** 229-230

KEPLER, JOHANNES (1571-1630), German astronomer **8** 514-516

KIPNIS, ALEXANDER (1891-1978), Ukrainian American musician 24 209-211

KIRCH, MARIA WINCKELMANN (1670-1720), German astronomer 20 204-205

KIRCHHOFF, GUSTAV ROBERT (1824-1887), German physicist 9 33-34

KIRCHNER, ERNST LUDWIG (1880-1938), German expressionist painter 9 34-35

KIRKLAND, JOSEPH LANE (1922-1999), American labor union movement leader 9 35-37

KIRKLAND, SAMUEL (1741-1808), American Congregationalist missionary 9 37

KIRKPATRICK, JEANE J. (born 1926), professor and first woman U.S. ambassador to the United Nations 9 37-39

KIRSTEIN, LINCOLN (1906-1996), a founder and director of the New York City Ballet 9 39-41

KISHI, NOBUSUKE (1896-1987), Japanese politician 9 41-43

KISSINGER, HENRY ALFRED (born 1923), U.S. secretary of state and co-winner of the Nobel Peace prize 9 43-45

KITCHENER, HORATIO HERBERT (1850-1916), British field marshal and statesman 9 45-46

KIWANUKA, BENEDICTO KAGIMA MUGUMBA (1922-1972), Ugandan politician 9 46-47

KLEE, PAUL (1879-1940), Swiss painter and graphic artist 9 47-49

KLEIN, A. M. (1909-1972), Canadian journalist, lawyer, novelist, and poet 9 49-50

KLEIN, CALVIN (born 1942), American fashion designer 9 50-52

KLEIN, MELANIE (1882-1960), Austrian psychotherapist 9 52

KLEIST, HEINRICH VON (1777-1811), German author 9 52-53

KLEMPERER, OTTO (1885-1973), German conductor 20 205-207

KLIMA, VIKTOR (born 1947), Austrian chancellor 18 232-234

KLIMT, GUSTAV (1862-1918), controversial Austrian painter 9 53-55

KLINE, FRANZ (1910-1962), American painter 9 55

KLOPSTOCK, FRIEDRICH GOTTLIEB (1724-1803), German poet 9 55-56

KLUCKHOHN, CLYDE (1905-1960), American anthropologist 9 56-57

KLYUCHEVSKY, VASILY OSIPOVICH (1841-1911), Russian historian 9 57-58

KNAPP, SEAMAN ASAHEL (1833-1911), American educator and agricultural pioneer 9 58

KNIGHT, FRANK HYNEMAN (1885-1972), American economist 9 58-59

KNIGHT, PHIL (born 1938), American businessman 19 183-186

KNIPLING, EDWARD FRED (1909-2000), American entomologist 9 59-60

KNOPF, ALFRED A. (1892-1984), American publisher 9 60-61

KNOPF, BLANCHE WOLF (1894-1966), American publisher 9 61-62

KNOWLES, MALCOLM SHEPHERD (1913-1997), American adult education theorist and planner 9 62-64

KNOX, HENRY (1750-1806), American Revolutionary War general 9 64

KNOX, JOHN (circa 1505-1572), Scottish religious reformer 9 65-66

KNOX, PHILANDER CHASE (1853-1921), American statesman 9 66-67

KNUDSEN, WILLIAM S. (1879-1948), American auto industry leader 9 67-68

KOBAYASHI, MASAKI (1916-1996), Japanese film director 23 199-201

KOCH, EDWARD I. (born 1924), New York City mayor 9 68-69

KOCH, ROBERT HEINRICH HERMANN (1843-1910), German physician and bacteriologist 9 69-70

KODÁLY, ZOLTÁN (1882-1967), Hungarian composer 9 71

KOESTLER, ARTHUR (1905-1983), author of political novels 9 71-73

KOHL, HELMUT (born 1930), chancellor of West Germany (1982-1990) and first chancellor of a united Germany since World War II 9 73-74

KOJONG (1852-1919), Korean king 9 74-75

KOKOSCHKA, OSKAR (1886-1980), Austrian painter, graphic artist, and author 9 75-76

KOLAKOWSKI, LESZEK (born 1927), philosopher who wrote on broad themes of ethics, metaphysics, and religion 9 76-77

KOLCHAK, ALEKSANDR VASILIEVICH (1873-1920), Russian admiral 9 77-78

KOLLONTAI, ALEKSANDRA MIKHAILOVNA (1872-1952), Soviet diplomat 9 79

KOLLWITZ, KÄTHE (1867-1945), German expressionist graphic artist and sculptor 9 79-81

KONEV, IVAN STEFANOVICH (1897-1973), Soviet marshal 9 81-82

KONOE, PRINCE FUMIMARO (or Konoye; 1891-1945), Japanese premier 1937-1939 and 1940-1941 9 82-83

KOONS, JEFF (born 1955), American artist 9 83-84

KOOP, C. EVERETT (born 1916), American surgeon general 18 235-237

KÖPRÜLÜ, AHMED (Köprülüzade Fazil Ahmed Pasha; 1635-1676), Turkish statesman and general 9 84-85

KORBUT, OLGA (born 1955), Belarusian gymnast 24 211-213

KORNBERG, ARTHUR (born 1918), Americna biochemist 9 85-87

KORNILOV, LAVR GEORGIEVICH (1870-1918), Russian general 9 87-88

KOSCIUSZKO, TADEUSZ ANDRZEJ BONAWENTURA (1746-1817), Polish patriot, hero in the American Revolution 9 88

KOSSUTH, LOUIS (1802-1894), Hungarian statesman 9 88-90

KOSYGIN, ALEKSEI NIKOLAEVICH (1904-1980), chairman of the U.S.S.R. Council of Ministers and head of the Soviet government (1964-1980) 9 90-91

KOTZEBUE, OTTO VON (1787-1846), Russian explorer 9 91-92

KOUFAX, SANDY (Sanford Braun; born 1945), American baseball player 20 208-210

KOUSSEVITZKY, SERGE (Sergey Aleksandrovich Kusevitsky; 1874-1951), Russian-born American conductor 24 213-215

KOVACS, ERNIE (1919-1962), American comedian 19 186-188

KOVALEVSKY, SOPHIA VASILEVNA (Sonya Kovalevsky; 1850-1891), Russian mathematician 22 280-282

KOZYREV, ANDREI VLADIMIROVICH (born 1951), Russian minister of foreign affairs and a liberal, pro-Western figure in Boris Yeltsin's cabinet 9 92-93

Kramer, Joey (born 1950), American musician Aerosmith 24 4-7

MASON, BRIDGET (Biddy Mason; 1818-1891), African American nurse, midwife, and entrepreneur **22** 312-314

MASON, GEORGE (1725-1792), American statesman **10** 319-320

MASON, JAMES MURRAY (1796-1871), American politician and Confederate diplomat **10** 320-321

MASON, LOWELL (1792-1872), American composer and music educator **10** 321-322

MASSASOIT (1580-1661), Native American tribal chief **10** 322-324

MASSEY, VINCENT (Charles Vincent Massey, 1887-1967), Canadian governor-general **24** 246-248

MASSEY, WILLIAM FERGUSON (1856-1925), New Zealand prime minister 1912-1925 **10** 324

MASSINGER, PHILIP (1583-1640), English playwright **10** 324-325

MASSYS, QUENTIN (1465/66-1530), Flemish painter **10** 325-326

MASTERS, EDGAR LEE (1869-1950), American author and lawyer **10** 326-327

MASTERS, WILLIAM HOWELL (born 1915), American psychologist and sex therapist **10** 327-328

MASUDI, ALI IBN AL- HUSAYN AL- (died 956), Arab historian **10** 328-329

MASUR, KURT (born 1927), German conductor and humanist **20** 246-248

MATA HARI (Margaretha Geertruida Zelle; 1876-1917), Dutch spy **21** 279-282

MATAMOROS, MARINO (1770-1814), Mexican priest and independence hero **10** 329-330

Mathematics
and crystallography
Hauptman, Herbert Aaron **24** 165-167
control theory
Kalman, Rudolf Emil **24** 199-201
direct methods
Hauptman, Herbert Aaron **24** 165-167
integral equation
Fredholm, Erik Ivar **24** 147-149
Kalman filter
Kalman, Rudolf Emil **24** 199-201
system theory
Kalman, Rudolf Emil **24** 199-201

MATHER, COTTON (1663-1728), American Puritan clergyman and historian **10** 330-332

MATHER, INCREASE (1639-1723), American Puritan clergymen, educator, and author **10** 332-333

MATHEWSON, CHRISTY (Christopher Mathewson; 1880-1925), American baseball player **21** 282-284

MATHIAS, BOB (Robert Bruce Mathias; born 1930), American track and field star **21** 284-286

MATHIEZ, ALBERT (1874-1932), French historian **10** 333-334

MATILDA OF TUSCANY (ca. 1046-1115), Italian countess **10** 334-336

MATISSE, HENRI (1869-1954), French painter and sculptor **10** 336-337

MATLIN, MARLEE (born 1965), American actress **19** 228-230

MATLOVICH, LEONARD (1943-1988), American gay rights activist **20** 248-250

MATSUNAGA, SPARK MASAYUKI (1916-1990), Asian American U.S. senator **18** 279-281

MATSUSHITA, KONOSUKE (1918-1989), Japanese inventor and businessman **19** 230-232

MATTA ECHAURREN, ROBERTO SEBASTIAN ANTONIO (Matta, 1911-2002), Chilean artist **24** 248-250

MATTEI, ENRICO (1906-1962), Italian entrepreneur **10** 337-339

MATTEOTTI, GIACOMO (1885-1924), Italian political leader **10** 339-340

MATTHAU, WALTER (Walter Matthow; Walter Matuschanskayasky; 1920-2000), American Actor **22** 314-316

MATTHEW, SAINT (flourished Ist century), Apostle and Evangelist **10** 340-341

MATTHEW PARIS (circa 1200-1259), English Benedictine chronicler **10** 341-342

MATTINGLY, GARRETT (1900-1962), American historian, professor, and author of novel-like histories **10** 342-344

MATZELIGER, JAN (1852-1889), American inventor and shoemaker **19** 232-234

MAUCHLY, JOHN (1907-1980), American computer entrepreneur **20** 250-252

MAUDSLAY, HENRY (1771-1831), British engineer and inventor **21** 286-288

MAUGHAM, WILLIAM SOMERSET (1874-1965), English author **10** 344-345

MAULBERTSCH, FRANZ ANTON (1724-1796), Austrian painter **10** 345

MAULDIN, BILL (1921-2003), cartoon biographer of the ordinary GI in World War II **10** 345-346

MAUPASSANT, HENRI RENÉ ALBERT GUY DE (1850-1893), French author **10** 347

MAURIAC, FRANÇOIS (1885-1970), French author **10** 347-348

MAURICE, JOHN FREDERICK DENISON (1805-1872), English theologian and Anglican clergyman **10** 349-350

MAURICE OF NASSAU, PRINCE OF ORANGE (1567-1625), Dutch general and statesman **10** 348-349

Mauritius (island; Indian Ocean) Ramgoolam, Seewoosagur **24** 319-321

MAURRAS, CHARLES MARIE PHOTIUS (1868-1952), French political writer and reactionary **10** 350-351

MAURY, ANTONIA (1866-1952), American astronomer and conservationist **20** 252-254

MAURY, MATTHEW FONTAINE (1806-1873), American naval officer and oceanographer **10** 351-352

MAUSS, MARCEL (1872-1950), French sociologist and anthropologist **10** 352-353

MAWDUDI, ABU-I A'LA (1903-1979), Muslim writer and religious and political leader in the Indian sub-continent **10** 353-354

MAWSON, SIR DOUGLAS (1882-1958), Australian scientist and Antarctic explorer **10** 354-355

MAXIM, SIR HIRAM STEVENS (1840-1916), American-born British inventor **10** 355-356

MAXIMILIAN I (1459-1519), Holy Roman emperor 1493-1519 **10** 356-357

MAXIMILIAN II (1527-1576), Holy Roman emperor 1564-1576 **10** 357-358

MAXIMILIAN OF HAPSBURG (1832-1867), archduke of Austria and emperor of Mexico **10** 358-360

MAXWELL, IAN ROBERT (née Ludvik Hoch; 1923-1991), British publishing magnate **10** 360-361

MAXWELL, JAMES CLERK (1831-1879), Scottish physicist **10** 361-364

MAYAKOVSKY, VLADIMIR VLADIMIROVICH (1893-1930), Russian poet **10** 364-365

MAYER, JEAN (born 1920), nutritionist, researcher, consultant to government and international organizations, and president of Tufts University **10** 365-366

MAYER, LOUIS BURT (Eliezer Mayer; 1885-1957), American motion picture producer **19** 234-235

MAYNARD, ROBERT CLYVE (1937-1993), African American journalist and publisher **10** 366-367

MAYO, WILLIAM J. (1861-1939) and CHARLES H. (1865-1939), American physicians **10** 367-369

MAYOR ZARAGOSA, FEDERICO (born 1934), Spanish biochemist who was director-general of UNESCO (United Nations Educational, Scientific, and Cultural Organization) **10** 369-371

MAYO-SMITH, RICHMOND (1854-1901), American statistician and sociologist **10** 371-372

MAYR, ERNST (born 1904), American evolutionary biologist **10** 372-374

MAYS, BENJAMIN E. (1894-1984), African American educator and civil rights activist **10** 374-376

MAYS, WILLIE (William Howard Mays, Jr.; born 1931), African American baseball player **10** 376-379

MAZARIN, JULES (1602-1661), French cardinal and statesman **10** 379-380

MAZEPA, IVAN STEPANOVICH (circa 1644-1709), Ukrainian Cossack leader **10** 381

MAZZINI, GIUSEPPE (1805-1872), Italian patriot **10** 381-383

M'BOW, AMADOU-MAHTAR (born 1921), director general of UNESCO (United Nations Educational, Scientific, and Cultural Organization) **10** 383-384

MBOYA, THOMAS JOSEPH (1930-1969), Kenyan political leader **10** 384-385

MCADOO, WILLIAM GIBBS (1863-1941), American statesman **10** 385-386

MCAULIFFE, ANTHONY (1898-1975), American army officer **19** 236-239

MCAULIFFE, CHRISTA (nee Sharon Christa Corrigan; 1948-1986), American teacher **20** 254-257

MCCANDLESS, BRUCE (born 1937), American astronaut **23** 243-246

MCCARTHY, EUGENE JOSEPH (born 1916), American statesman **10** 386-388

MCCARTHY, JOSEPH RAYMOND (1908-1957), American politician **10** 388-389

MCCARTHY, MARY T. (born 1912), American writer **10** 389-391

MCCARTNEY, PAUL (James Paul McCartney; born 1942), British musician **24** 250-253

MCCAY, WINSOR (Zenas Winsor McKay; 1871?-1934), American cartoonist and animator **21** 288-291

MCCLELLAN, GEORGE BRINTON (1826-1885), American general **10** 391-392

MCCLELLAN, JOHN LITTLE (1896-1977), U.S. senator from Arkansas **10** 392-393

MCCLINTOCK, BARBARA (1902-1992), geneticist and winner of the Nobel Prize in physiology **10** 393-394

MCCLINTOCK, SIR FRANCIS LEOPOLD (1819-1907), British admiral and Arctic explorer **10** 394-395

MCCLOSKEY, JOHN (1810-1885), American cardinal **10** 395

MCCLUNG, NELLIE LETITIA (1873-1951), Canadian suffragist, social reformer, legislator, and author **10** 396-397

MCCLURE, SIR ROBERT (1807-1873), English explorer and navy officer **10** 398-399

MCCLURE, SAMUEL SIDNEY (1857-1949), American editor and publisher **10** 398-399

MCCORMACK, JOHN WILLIAM (1891-1980), U.S. congressman and Speaker of the House **10** 399-400

MCCORMICK, CYRUS HALL (1809-1884), American inventor, manufacturer, and philanthropist **10** 400-401

MCCORMICK, ROBERT RUTHERFORD (1880-1955), American publisher **10** 401-402

MCCOSH, JAMES (1811-1894), Scottish-American minister, philosopher, and college president **10** 402-403

MCCOY, ELIJAH (1843-1929), American engineer and inventor **19** 239-241

MCCOY, ISAAC (1784-1846), American Indian agent and missionary **10** 403

MCCOY, JOSEPH GEITING (1837-1915), American cattleman **10** 403-404

MCCULLERS, CARSON (Lula Carson Smith; 1917-1967), American novelist and playwright **18** 281-283

MCCULLOCH, HUGH (1808-1895), American banker and lawyer **10** 404-405

MCDANIEL, HATTIE (1898-1952), African American actress **10** 405-408

MCDUFFIE, GEORGE (1790-1851), American statesman **10** 408

MCENROE, JOHN PATRICK, JR. (born 1959), American tennis player **10** 408-411

MCGILL, RALPH EMERSON (1898-1969), American journalist **10** 411-412

MCGILLIVRAY, ALEXANDER (circa 1759-1793), American Creek Indian chief **10** 412

MCGOVERN, GEORGE STANLEY (born 1922), American statesman **10** 412-414

MCGUFFEY, WILLIAM HOLMES (1800-1873), American educator **10** 414-415

MCINTIRE, SAMUEL (1757-1811), American builder and furniture maker **10** 415

MCKAY, CLAUDE (1890-1948), African American poet and novelist **10** 416

MCKAY, DONALD (1810-1880), American ship builder **10** 416-417

MCKIM, CHARLES FOLLEN (1847-1909), American architect **10** 417-418

MCKINLEY, WILLIAM (1843-1901), American statesman, president 1897-1901 **10** 418-420

MCKISSICK, FLOYD B., (1922-1991), African American civil rights leader **10** 420-422

MCLEAN, JOHN (1785-1861), American jurist and politician **10** 422-423

MCLOUGHLIN, JOHN (1784-1857), Canadian pioneer and trader **10** 423-424

MCLUHAN, MARSHALL (Herbert Marshall McLuhan; 1911-1980), Canadian professor of literature and culture **10** 424-426

MCMASTER, JOHN BACH (1852-1932), American historian **10** 426-427

MCMILLAN, TERRY (born 1951), African American novelist and short story writer **10** 427-428

MCMURRAY, BETTE CLAIR (1924-1980), American inventor and businesswoman **10** 429

MCNAMARA, ROBERT S. (born 1916), U.S. secretary of defense and president of the World Bank **10** 429-431

MCNAUGHTON, ANDREW (1887-1966), Canadian soldier and diplomat **10** 431-432

MCNEALY, SCOTT (born 1954), American businessman **19** 241-243

MILK, HARVEY BERNARD (1930-1978), American politician and gay rights activist **11** 19-21

MILKEN, MICHAEL (born 1946), American businessman **19** 247-249

MILL, JAMES (1773-1836), Scottish philosopher and historian **11** 21

MILL, JOHN STUART (1806-1873), English philosopher and economist **11** 21-23

MILLAIS, SIR JOHN EVERETT (1829-1896), English painter **11** 23-24

MILLAY, EDNA ST. VINCENT (1892-1950), American lyric poet **11** 24-25

MILLER, ARTHUR (born 1915), American playwright, novelist, and film writer **11** 25-26

MILLER, GLENN (Alton Glenn Miller; 1904-1944), American musician **19** 250-251

MILLER, HENRY (born 1891), American author **11** 26-27

MILLER, JOAQUIN (1837-1913), American writer **11** 27-28

MILLER, PERRY (1905-1963), American historian **11** 28-29

MILLER, SAMUEL FREEMAN (1816-1890), American jurist **11** 29-30

MILLER, WILLIAM (1782-1849), American clergyman **11** 30-31

MILLES, CARL WILHELM EMIL (1875-1955), Swedish sculptor **24** 260-263

MILLET, JEAN FRANÇOIS (1814-1875), French painter **11** 31

MILLET, KATE (born 1934), American feminist author and sculptor **11** 31

MILLIKAN, ROBERT ANDREWS (1868-1953), American physicist **11** 33-35

MILLS, BILLY (Makata Taka Hela; born 1938), Native American runner and businessman **19** 251-253

MILLS, C. WRIGHT (1916-1962), American sociologist and political polemicist **11** 35-36

MILLS, ROBERT (1781-1855), American architect **11** 36-37

MILNE, ALAN ALEXANDER (A.A. Milne; 1882-1956), British author **19** 253-254

MILNE, DAVID BROWN (1882-1953), Canadian painter and etcher **11** 37-38

MILNER, ALFRED (1st Viscount Milner; 1854-1925), British statesman **11** 38-39

MILOSEVIC, SLOBODAN (born 1941), president of Serbia **11** 39-40

MILOSZ, CZESLAW (born 1911), Nobel Prize winning Polish author and poet **11** 40-42

MILTIADES (circa 549-488 B.C.), Athenian military strategist and statesman **11** 42-43

MILTON, JOHN (1608-1674), English poet and controversialist **11** 43-46

MIN (1851-1895), Korean queen **11** 46-47

MINDON MIN (ruled 1852-1878), Burmese king **11** 47

MINDSZENTY, CARDINAL JÓZSEF (1892-1975), Roman Catholic primate of Hungary **11** 47-49

MINK, PATSY TAKEMOTO (1927-2003), Asian American congresswoman **18** 287-289

MINTZ, BEATRICE (born 1921), American embryologist **11** 49-50

MINUIT, PETER (1580-1638), Dutch colonizer **11** 50

MIRABAI (Meera Bai; 1498-1547), Indian poet and mystic **24** 263-265

MIRABEAU, COMTE DE (Honoré Gabriel Victor de Riqueti; 1749-1791), French statesman and author **11** 51-52

MIRANDA, FRANCISCO DE (1750-1816), Latin American patriot **11** 52-53

MIRÓ, JOAN (1893-1983), Spanish painter **11** 53-54

MISHIMA, YUKIO (1925-1970), Japanese novelist and playwright **11** 54-55

MISTRAL, GABRIELA (1889-1957), Chilean poet and educator **11** 55-56

MITCHELL, BILLY (1879-1936), American military officer and aviator **20** 269-272

MITCHELL, EDGAR DEAN (born 1930), American astronaut **22** 318-320

MITCHELL, GEORGE JOHN (born 1933), Maine Democrat and majority leader in the United States Senate **11** 56-58

MITCHELL, JOHN (1870-1919), American labor leader **11** 58-59

MITCHELL, JONI (Roberta Joan Anderson; born 1943), Canadian American singer **23** 246-248

MITCHELL, MARGARET (Munnerlyn; 1900-1949), American author of Gone With the Wind **11** 59-60

MITCHELL, MARIA (1818-1889), American astronomer and educator **11** 61

MITCHELL, WESLEY CLAIR (1874-1948), American economist **11** 61-62

MITRE, BARTOLOMÉ (1821-1906), Argentine historian and statesman, president 1862-1868 **11** 62-63

MITTERRAND, FRANÇOIS (born 1916), French politician and statesman and president (1981-1990) **11** 63-66

MIZOGUCHI, KENJI (1898-1956), Japanese film director **23** 248-250

MIZRAHI, ISAAC (born 1961), American designer **11** 66-67

MLADIC, RATKO (born 1943), Bosnian Serb military leader **11** 68-69

MOBUTU SESE SEKO (Joseph Désiré Mobuto; 1930-1997), Congolese president **11** 69-71

MODEL, LISETTE (nee Lisette Seyberg; 1906?-1983), American photographer and educator **19** 254-256

MODERSOHN-BECKER, PAULA (1876-1907), German painter **11** 71-72

MODIGLIANI, AMEDEO (1884-1920), Italian painter and sculptor **11** 72-73

MODIGLIANI, FRANCO (1918-2003), Italian American economist **24** 265-267

MOFFETT, WILLIAM ADGER (1869-1933), American naval officer **21** 299-301

MOFOLO, THOMAS (1876-1948), Lesothoan author **11** 74

MOGILA, PETER (1596/1597-1646), Russian Orthodox churchman and theologian **11** 74-75

Mogul empire
see India—1000-1600

MOHAMMAD REZA SHAH PAHLAVI (1919-1980), king of Iran **11** 75-76

MOHAMMED (circa 570-632), founder of Islam **11** 76-78

MOHAMMED V (Mohammed Ben Youssef; 1911-1961), king of Morocco **11** 79-81

MOHAMMED ALI (1769-1849), Ottoman pasha of Egypt 1805-1848 **11** 81-82

MOHOLY-NAGY, LÁSZLÓ (1895-1946), Hungarian painter and designer **11** 82-83

MOI, DANIEL ARAP (born Daniel Toroitich arap Moi; born 1924), president of Kenya **11** 83-86

Molecular biology
see Biology, molecular

Molecule (chemistry)
Hauptman, Herbert Aaron **24** 165-167

MUSIL, ROBERT EDLER VON (1880-1942), Austrian novelist, dramatist, and short story writer **11** 268-269

MUSKIE, EDMUND SIXTUS (1914-1996), United States senator and Democratic vice-presidential nominee **11** 269-271

MUSSET, LOUIS CHARLES ALFRED DE (1810-1857), French poet, dramatist, and fiction writer **11** 271-272

MUSSOLINI, BENITO (1883-1945), Italian Fascist dictator 1922-1943 **11** 272-274

MUSSORGSKY, MODEST PETROVICH (1839-1881), Russian composer **11** 274-276

MUSTE, ABRAHAM JOHANNES (1885-1967), American pacifist and labor leader **11** 276-277

MUTESA I (circa 1838-1884), African monarch of Buganda **11** 277

MUTESA II (1924-1969), Monarch of Buganda **11** 277-278

MUTIS, JOSÉ CELESTINO (1732-1808), Spanish-Colombian naturalist **11** 278-279

MUTSUHITO (a.k.a. Meiji; 1852-1912), Japanese emperor **11** 279-282

MUYBRIDGE, EADWEARD (1830-1904), English photographer **21** 305-308

MWANGA (circa 1866-1901), Monarch of Buganda **11** 282-283

MYDANS, CARL (born 1907), American photojournalist **11** 283-284

MYRDAL, ALVA (1902-1986), Swedish social reformer and diplomat **24** 274-276

MYRDAL, KARL GUNNAR (1898-1987), Swedish economist and sociologist **11** 284

MYRON (flourished circa 470-450 B.C.), Greek sculptor **11** 285

Mysticism (religion)
Hindu
Baba, Meher **24** 35-38
Mirabai **24** 263-265
in literature
Sana'i, Hakim **24** 346-347

MZILIKAZI (circa 1795-1868), South African warrior leader **11** 285-286

N

NABOKOV, VLADIMIR (1899-1977), Russian-born American writer, critic, and lepidopterist **11** 287-288

NABUCO DE ARAUJO, JOAQUIM AURELIO (1849-1910), Brazilian abolitionist, statesman, and author **11** 288-289

NADELMAN, ELIE (1882-1946), Polish-American sculptor and graphic artist **11** 289-290

NADER, RALPH (born 1934), American lawyer and social crusader **11** 290-291

NADIR SHAH (born Nadir Kouli; 1685-1747), Emperor of Persia **20** 278-281

NAGEL, ERNEST (1901-1985), American philosopher of science **11** 291-292

NAGUMO, CHUICHI (1887-1944), Japanese admiral **19** 263-266

NAGURSKI, BRONKO (Bronislaw Nagurski; 1908-1990), Canadian football player **21** 309-311

NAGY, IMRE (1896-1958), prime minister of Hungary (1953-55, 1956) **11** 292-293

NAHMANIDES (1194-1270), Spanish Talmudist **11** 293-294

NAIDU, SAROJINI (1879-1949), Indian poet and nationalist **11** 294-295

NAIPAUL, V. S. (born 1932), Trinidadian author of English-language prose **11** 295-296

NAISMITH, JAMES (1861-1939), Canadian inventor of basketball **21** 311-313

NAJIBULLAH, MOHAMMAD (born 1947), Soviet-selected ruler of the Republic of Afghanistan **11** 296-298

O

QUISLING, VIDKIN (1887-1945), Norwegian traitor **20** 304-306

R

RABEARIVELO, JEAN JOSEPH (1901-1937), Malagasy poet **12** 523-524

RABELAIS, FRANÇOIS (circa 1494-circa 1553), French humanist, doctor, and writer **12** 524-526

RABI, ISIDOR ISAAC (1898-1988), American physicist **12** 526-527

RABIN, YITZCHAK (1922-1995), Israeli statesman **12** 527-529

Race car drivers
Foyt, A.J. **24** 145-147
Stewart, Jackie **24** 392-395

RACHMANINOV, SERGEI VASILIEVICH (1873-1943), Russian composer, pianist, and conductor **12** 531-532

RACINE, JEAN BAPTISTE (1639-1699), French dramatist **12** 532-535

Racism (United States)
psychological effects of
Poussaint, Alvin Francis **24** 313-316

RADCLIFFE-BROWN, A(LFRED) R(EGINALD) (1881-1955), English anthropologist **12** 535-536

RADEK, KARL BERNARDOVICH (1885-1939), Russian Communist leader **12** 536-537

RADHAKRISHNAN, SARVEPALLI (1888-1995), Indian philosopher and statesman **12** 537-538

RADIN, PAUL (1883-1959), American anthropologist and ethnographer **12** 538-539

Radio (communications)
Egypt
Kulthum, Umm **24** 220-222
personalities
Brown, Tony **24** 68-70
Cosell, Howard **24** 94-97
sportscasters
Cosell, Howard **24** 94-97

RADISSON, PIERRE-ESPRIT (circa 1636-1710), French explorer **12** 539-540

RAFFLES, SIR THOMAS STAMFORD (1781-1826), English colonial administrator **13** 1-2

RAFINESQUE, CONSTANTINE SAMUEL (1783-1840), French naturalist **21** 359-361

RAFSANJANI, AKBAR HASHEMI (born 1934), president of Iran **13** 3-4

RAHNER, KARL (1904-1984), German Catholic theologian **13** 4-5

RAI, LALA LAJPAT (1865-1928), Indian nationalist leader **13** 5-6

Railroads
Latin America
Montes, Ismael **24** 267-270

RAINEY, MA (Gertrude Pridgett; 1886-1939), American singer **19** 306-308

RAINIER III, PRINCE OF MONACO (born 1923), ruler of the principality of Monaco **18** 335-337

RAJAGOPALACHARI, CHAKRAVARTI (1879-1972), Indian nationalist leader **13** 6-7

RAJARAJA I (985-1014), Indian statesman **13** 7

RAJNEESH, BHAGWAN SHREE (Rahneesh Chandra Mohan; 1931-1990), Indian religious leader **13** 7-9

RALEIGH, SIR WALTER (or Ralegh; circa 1552-1618), English statesman, soldier, courtier, explorer, and poet **13** 9-11

RAMA KHAMHAENG (circa 1239-circa 1299), king of Sukhothai in Thailand **13** 11

RAMAKRISHNA, SRI (1833-1886), Indian mystic, reformer, and saint **13** 11-13

RAMAN, SIR CHANDRASEKHAR VENKATA (1888-1970), Indian physicist **13** 13-14

RAMANUJA (Ramanujacarya; c. 1017-1137), Indian theologian and philosopher **21** 361-362

RAMANUJAN AIYANGAR, SRINIVASA (1887-1920), India mathematician **13** 14-15

RAMAPHOSA, MATEMELA CYRIL (born 1952), general secretary of the National Union of Mineworkers (NUM) in South Africa and secretary general of the African National Congress **13** 15-16

RAMAZZINI, BERNARDINO (1633-1714), Italian physician **21** 362-364

RAMEAU, JEAN PHILIPPE (1683-1764), French music theorist and composer **13** 17-18

RAMGOOLAM, SEEWOOSAGUR (1900-1985), president of Mauritius **24** 319-321

RAMOS, FIDEL VALDEZ (born 1928), president of the Philippines (1992-) **13** 18-19

RAMPAL, JEAN-PIERRE LOUIS (1922-2000), French flutist **22** 362-364

RAMPHAL, SHRIDATH SURENDRANATH (born 1928), Guyanese barrister, politician, and international civil servant **13** 19-20

RAMSAY, DAVID (1749-1815), American historian **13** 21

RAMSAY, SIR WILLIAM (1852-1916), British chemist and educator **13** 21-22

RAMSES II (ruled 1304-1237 B.C.), pharaoh of Egypt **13** 22-23

RAMSEY, ARTHUR MICHAEL (1904-1988), archbishop of Canterbury and president of the World Council of Churches **13** 23-25

RAMSEY, FRANK PLUMPTON (1903-1930), English mathematician and philosopher **13** 25

RAMSEY, NORMAN FOSTER, JR. (born 1915), American physicist **13** 25-27

RAMUS, PETRUS (1515-1572), French humanist, logician and mathematician **13** 27-28

RAND, AYN (1905-1982), American author and philosoher **20** 307-309

RANDOLPH, A. PHILIP (1889-1979), African American labor and civil rights leader **13** 28-29

RANDOLPH, EDMUND (1753-1813), American statesman **13** 29-30

RANDOLPH, JOHN (1773-1833), American statesman **13** 30

RANDOLPH, PEYTON (1721-1775), American statesman **18** 337-339

RANDS, BERNARD (born 1934), American musician **23** 324-326

RANGEL, CHARLES B. (born 1930), Democratic U.S. representative from New York City **13** 31-32

RANJIT SINGH (1780-1839), ruler of the Punjab **13** 32-33

RANK, OTTO (1884-1939), Austrian psychotherapist **13** 33

RANKE, LEOPOLD VON (1795-1886), German historian **13** 33-35

RANKIN, JEANNETTE PICKERING (1880-1973), first woman elected to the U.S. Congress **13** 35-37

RANNARIDH, PRINCE NORODOM (born 1944), first prime minister of Cambodia **13** 37-39

RANSOM, JOHN CROWE (1888-1974), American poet and critic **13** 39-40

RAPHAEL (1483-1520), Italian painter and architect **13** 40-42

RAPP, GEORGE (1757-1847), German-American religious leader **13** 42-43

RASHI (1040-1105), French Jewish scholar and commentator **13** 43

RICHTER, CONRAD MICHAEL (1890-1968), American novelist and short-story writer **13** 148-149

RICHTER, GERHARD (born 1932), German artist **23** 338-340

RICHTER, HANS (Johann Siegried Richter; 1888-1976), German-born film director **13** 149-150

RICHTER, JOHANN PAUL FRIEDRICH (1763-1825), German humorist and prose writer **13** 150-151

RICIMER, FLAVIUS (died 472), Germanic Roman political chief **13** 151-152

RICKENBACKER, EDWARD VERNON (1890-1973), World War I fighter pilot and airline president **13** 152-153

RICKEY, WESLEY BRANCH (1881-1965), innovative baseball executive **13** 153-155

RICKOVER, HYMAN GEORGE (1900-1986), U.S. Navy officer **13** 155-157

RICOEUR, PAUL (born 1913), French exponent of hermeneutical philosophy **13** 157-158

RIDE, SALLY (born 1951), American astronaut and physicist **13** 158-160

RIDGE, JOHN ROLLIN (Yellow Bird; 1827-1867), Native American author **22** 373-375

RIDGE, THOMAS JOSEPH (born 1946), American governor of Pennsylvania and first secretary of the Department of Homeland Security **24** 334-337

RIDGWAY, MATTHEW BUNKER (1895-1993), American general **13** 160-161

RIDGWAY, ROZANNE LEJEANNE (born 1935), American diplomat **24** 337-338

RIEFENSTAHL, LENI (1902-2003), German film director **13** 161-163

RIEL, LOUIS (1844-1885), Canadian rebel **13** 163-164

RIEMANN, GEORG FRIEDRICH BERNARD (1826-1866), German mathematician **13** 164-165

RIEMENSCHNEIDER, TILMAN (1468-1531), German sculptor **13** 166

RIENZI, COLA DI (or Rienzo; 1313/14-1354), Italian patriot, tribune of Rome **13** 166-167

RIESMAN, DAVID (1909-2002), American sociologist, writer, and social critic **13** 167-168

RIETVELD, GERRIT THOMAS (1888-1964), Dutch architect and furniture designer **13** 169

RIIS, JACOB AUGUST (1849-1914), Danish-born American journalist and reformer **13** 169-170

RILEY, JAMES WHITCOMB (1849-1916), American poet **13** 170-171

RILKE, RAINER MARIA (1875-1926), German lyric poet **13** 171-172

RILLIEUX, NORBERT (1806-1894), American inventor **20** 309-311

RIMBAUD, (JEAN NICOLAS) ARTHUR (1854-1891), French poet **13** 172-174

RIMMER, WILLIAM (1816-1879), American sculptor, painter, and physician **13** 174

RIMSKY-KORSAKOV, NIKOLAI ANDREEVICH (1844-1908), Russian composer and conductor **13** 174-175

RINGGOLD, FAITH (Faith Jones; born 1930), African American painter, sculptress, and performer **13** 175-177

RIO BRANCO, BARÃO DO (José Maria da Silva Paranhos; 1845-1912), Brazilian political leader **13** 177

RIORDAN, RICHARD JOSEPH (born 1930), American politician; mayor of Los Angeles **13** 177-179

RIPKEN, CAL, JR. (Calvin Edwin Ripken, Jr.; born 1960), American baseball player **18** 346-349

RIPLEY, GEORGE (1802-1880), American Unitarian minister and journalist **13** 179-180

RITSCHL, ALBRECHT BENJAMIN (1822-1889), German theologian **13** 180

RITTENHOUSE, DAVID (1732-1796), American astronomer and instrument maker **13** 180-181

RITTER, KARL (1779-1859), German geographer **13** 181-182

RIVADAVIA, BERNARDINO (1780-1845), Argentine independence leader, president 1826-27 **13** 182-183

RIVAS, DUQUE DE (Angel de Saavedra; 1791-1865), Spanish poet, dramatist, and statesman **13** 398

RIVERA, DIEGO (1886-1957), Mexican painter **13** 183-184

RIVERA, FRUCTUOSO (circa 1788-1854), Uruguayan statesman **13** 184-185

RIVERA, JOSÉ EUSTACIO (1888-1928), Colombian novelist **13** 185-186

RIVERS, LARRY (Yitzroch Loiza Grossberg; 1923-2002), American artist **13** 186-187

RIVLIN, ALICE M. (born 1931), American economist and political advisor **18** 349-350

RIZAL, JOSÉ (1861-1896), Philippine national hero **13** 187-189

ROA BASTOS, AUGUSTO (born 1917), Paraguayan author **24** 338-341

ROBARDS, JASON (Jason Nelson Robards, JR.; 1922-2000), American Actor **22** 375-378

ROBBE-GRILLET, ALAIN (born 1922), French novelist **13** 189-190

ROBBIA, LUCA DELLA (1400-1482), Italian sculptor **10** 19-20

ROBBINS, JEROME (Rabinowitz; 1918-1998), American director and choreographer **13** 190-192

ROBERT I (1274-1329), king of Scotland 1306-29 **13** 192-194

ROBERT II (1316-1390), king of Scotland 1371-90 **13** 194

ROBERT III (circa 1337-1406), king of Scotland 1390-1406 **13** 194-195

ROBERT, HENRY MARTYN (1837-1923), American engineer and parliamentarian **21** 367-370

ROBERT, SHAABAN (1909-1962), Tanzanian author who wrote in the Swahili language **14** 128-129

ROBERTS, FREDERICK SLEIGH (1st Earl Roberts of Kandhar, Pretoria, and Waterford; 1832-1914), British field marshal **13** 195-196

ROBERTSON, SIR DENNIS HOLME (1890-1963), English economist **13** 196

ROBERTSON, MARION G. (Pat Robertson; born 1930), television evangelist who founded the Christian Broadcasting Network and presidential candidate **13** 196-198

ROBERTSON, OSCAR (born 1938), African American basketball player **20** 311-313

ROBESON, ESLANDA GOODE (born Eslanda Cardozo Goode; 1896-1965), African American cultural anthropologist **23** 340-342

ROBESON, PAUL LEROY (1898-1976), American singer, actor, and political activist **13** 198-199

ROBESPIERRE, MAXIMILIEN FRANÇOIS MARIE ISIDORE DE (1758-1794), French Revolutionary leader **13** 199-201

ROBINSON, EDDIE (born 1919), African American college football coach **18** 351-352

SPAATZ, CARL (1891-1974), American army and air force officer **19** 352-355

Spain (Spanish State; nation, Europe)
• MONARCHY and REPUBLIC (1492-1939)
papal relations
Clement XI **24** 90-92

Spain, Colonial Empire of
• LATIN AMERICA AND ASIA
El Salvador
Delgado, José Matias **24** 115-117

SPALLANZANI, LAZZARO (Abbé Spallanzani; 1729-99) Italian naturalist **14** 360-361

Spanish America
see Latin America

Spanish literature
modern
Sender, Ramón José **24** 361-363

Spanish Succession, War of the (1701-1714)
papacy and
Clement XI **24** 90-92

SPARK, MURIEL SARAH (born 1918), British author **14** 361-362

SPARKS, JARED (1789-1866), American historian **14** 363

SPARTACUS (died 71 B.C.), Thracian galdiator **14** 363-364

SPAULDING, CHARLES CLINTON (1874-1952), African American business executive **14** 364-365

SPEER, ALBERT (1905-1981), German architect and Nazi **19** 355-356

SPEKE, JOHN HANNING (1827-1864), English explorer **14** 366-367

SPELLMAN, CARDINAL FRANCIS JOSEPH (1889-1967), Roman Catholic archbishop **14** 367

SPEMANN, HANS (1869-1941), German experimental embryologist **14** 368-369

SPENCE, CATHERINE HELEN (1825-1910), Australian author and activist **23** 374-375

SPENCER, HERBERT (1820-1903), English philosopher **14** 369-370

SPENDER, STEPHEN HAROLD (born 1909), English poet and critic **14** 370-371

SPENER, PHILIPP JAKOB (1635-1705), German theologian **14** 372

SPENGLER, OSWALD (1880-1936), German philosopher **14** 372-373

SPENSER, EDMUND (circa 1552-99), English poet **14** 373-376

SPERANSKI, COUNT MIKHAIL MIKHAILOVICH (1772-1839), Russian statesman and reformer **14** 376-377

SPERRY, ELMER A. (1860-1930), American inventor **14** 377-379

SPIELBERG, STEVEN (born 1947), American filmmaker **14** 379-381

SPINOZA, BARUCH (Benedict Spinoza; 1632-77), Dutch philosopher **14** 381-383

SPITZ, MARK (born 1950), American swimmer **23** 376-378

SPOCK, BENJAMIN McLANE (1903-1998), American pediatrician and political activist and author of *Baby and Child Care* **14** 383-385

Sports
see Athletes, American

Sportscasters Hall of Fame, American
Cosell, Howard **24** 94-97

SPOTSWOOD, ALEXANDER (1676-1740), British general and colonial governor **14** 385

SPRAGUE, FRANK JULIAN (1857-1934), American electrical engineer and inventor **14** 385-386

SPRINGSTEEN, BRUCE (Bruce Frederick Springsteen; born 1949), American musician **24** 385-388

SQUIBB, EDWARD ROBINSON (1819-1900), American physician and pharmacist **21** 390-392

SSU-MA CH'IEN (145-circa 90 B.C.), Chinese historian **14** 388-389

SSU-MA HSIANG-JU (circa 179-117 B.C.), Chinese poet **14** 389-390

SSU-MA KUANG (1019-1086), Chinese statesman **14** 390-391

STAËL, GERMAINE DE (1766-1817), French-Swiss novelist and woman of letters **14** 391-392

STAËL, NICOLAS DE (1914-1955), French painter **14** 392

STAHL, GEORG ERNST (1660-1734), German chemist and medical theorist **14** 392-393

STALIN, JOSEPH (1879-1953), Soviet statesman **14** 393-396

STANDING BEAR (1829-1908), Native American tribal leader **24** 388-390

STANDISH, MYLES (circa 1584-1656), English military adviser to the Pilgrims **14** 396-397

STANFORD, LELAND (1824-1893), American railroad builder and politician **14** 397-398

STANISLAVSKY, CONSTANTIN (1863-1938), Russian actor and director **14** 398-399
Nemirovich-Danchenko, Vladimir Ivanovich **24** 279-281

STANLEY, SIR HENRY MORTON (1841-1904), British explorer and journalist **14** 399-400

STANLEY, WENDELL MEREDITH (1904-1971), American virologist **14** 400-401

STANTON, EDWIN McMASTERS (1814-1869), American statesman **14** 401-402

STANTON, ELIZABETH CADY (1815-1902), American feminist and reformer **14** 402-403

STARHAWK (Miriam Simos; born 1951), theoretician and practitioner of feminist Wicca (witchcraft) in the United States **14** 403-404

STARLEY, JAMES (1831-1881), British inventor and businessman **21** 392-393

STARZL, THOMAS (born 1926), American surgeon **21** 393-395

State, U.S. Secretaries of
see Statesmen, American—Executive (secretaries of state)

Statesmen, American
• EXECUTIVE (CABINET)
secretaries of homeland security
Ridge, Thomas Joseph **24** 334-337
• LEGISLATIVE
representatives (20th century)
Ridge, Thomas Joseph **24** 334-337
• STATE and LOCAL
mayors (20th century)
Daley, Richard M. **24** 102-104

Statesmen, Bolivian
Montes, Ismael **24** 267-270

Statesmen, Canadian
governor generals
Massey, Vincent **24** 246-248
members of Parliament
Macphail, Agnes Campbell **24** 237-239

Statesmen, Cape Verdean
Pereira, Aristides Maria **24** 306-308

Statesmen, English
king consorts
Philip **24** 308-310

Statesmen, Ethiopian
Sheba **24** 365-367

Statesmen, Indian (Asian)
queens
Jahan, Nur **24** 191-193

Statesmen, Mauritian
Ramgoolam, Seewoosagur **24** 319-321

Statesmen, Salvadoran
Delgado, José Matias **24** 115-117

STILL, WILLIAM GRANT (born 1895), African American composer **14** 455-456

STILWELL, JOSEPH WARREN (1883-1946), American general **14** 456-457

STIMSON, HENRY LEWIS (1867-1950), American lawyer and statesman **14** 457-458

STIRLING, JAMES (1926-1992), British architect and city planner **14** 458-459

STIRNER, MAX (1806-1856), German philosopher **14** 459-460

STOCKHAUSEN, KARLHEINZ (born 1928), German composer **14** 460-461

STOCKTON, ROBERT FIELD (1795-1866), American naval officer and politician **14** 461-462

STODDARD, SOLOMON (1643-1728/29), American colonial Congregational clergyman **14** 462-463

STOKER, BRAM (Abraham Stoker; 1847-1912), Irish author **14** 463-464

STOKES, CARL B. (1927-1996), African American politician **14** 464-465

STOLYPIN, PIOTR ARKADEVICH (1862-1911), Russian statesman and reformer **14** 465-466

STONE, EDWARD DURRELL (1902-1978), American architect, educator, and designer **14** 466-468

STONE, HARLAN FISKE (1872-1946), American jurist; chief justice of U.S. Supreme Court 1914-46 **14** 468-470

STONE, I. F. (Isador Feinstein; 1907-1989), American journalist **14** 470-471

STONE, LUCY (1818-1893), American abolitionist and women's suffrage leader **14** 471-472

STONE, OLIVER (born 1946), American filmmaker **14** 472-475

STONE, ROBERT ANTHONY (born 1937), American novelist **14** 475-476

STOPES, MARIE (1880-1958), British scientist and birth control advocate **14** 476-478

STOPPARD, THOMAS (Thomas Straussler; born 1937), English playwright **14** 478-479

STORM, THEODOR (1817-1888), German poet and novelist **14** 479-480

STORY, JOSEPH (1779-1845), American jurist and statesman **14** 480-481

STOSS, VEIT (circa 1445-1533), German sculptor **14** 481-482

STOUFFER, SAMUEL A. (1900-1960), American sociologist and statistician **14** 482-483

STOUT, JUANITA KIDD (1919-1998), African American judge **23** 382-384

STOVALL, LUTHER McKINLEY (born 1937), American silkscreen artist **14** 483-484

STOWE, HARRIET ELIZABETH BEECHER (1811-1896), American writer **14** 484-485

STRABO (circa 64 B.C.-circa A.D. 23), Greek geographer and historian **14** 485-486

STRACHAN, JOHN (1778-1867), Canadian Anglican bishop **14** 486-487

STRACHEY, GILES LYTTON (1880-1932), English biographer and critic known for his satire of the Victorian era **14** 487-488

STRACHEY, JOHN (Evelyn John St. Loe Strachey; 1901-1963), British author and politician **20** 352-354

STRADIVARI, ANTONIO (circa 1644-1737), Italian violin maker **14** 488-490

STRAFFORD, 1ST EARL OF (Thomas Wentworth; 1593-1641), English statesman **14** 490-491

STRAND, MARK (born 1934), fourth Poet Laureate of the United States **14** 491-493

STRAND, PAUL (1890-1976), American photographer **19** 369-371

STRANG, RUTH MAY (1895-1971), American educator **14** 493-494

STRASBERG, LEE (Israel Strasberg; 1901-82), American acting instructor, director, and founding member of the Group Theatre **14** 494-495

STRAUS, ISIDOR (1845-1912), American merchant **14** 496

STRAUSS, DAVID FRIEDRICH (1808-1874), German historian and Protestant theologian **14** 496-497

STRAUSS, FRANZ JOSEF (1915-1988), West German politician **14** 497-498

STRAUSS, JOHANN, JR. (1825-1899), Austrian composer **14** 498-499

STRAUSS, LEO (1899-1973), German Jewish Socratic political philosopher **14** 499-500

STRAUSS, LEVI (Loeb Strauss; 1829-1902), American businessman **20** 354-356

STRAUSS, RICHARD (1864-1949), German composer and conductor **14** 500-501

STRAUSS, ROBERT SCHWARZ (born 1918), Democratic fundraiser and strategist **14** 501-502

STRAVINSKY, IGOR FEDOROVICH (1882-1971), Russian-born composer **14** 502-506

STRAWSON, SIR PETER FREDRICK (born 1919), English philosopher **14** 506-507

STREEP, MERYL LOUISE (born 1949), American actress **23** 384-387

STREETON, SIR ARTHUR ERNEST (1867-1943), Australian landscape painter **14** 507-508

STREISAND, BARBRA (Barbara Joan Streisand; born 1942), American entertainer **18** 386-388

STRESEMANN, GUSTAV (1878-1929), German statesman and diplomat **14** 508-509

STRINDBERG, AUGUST (1849-1912), Swedish author **14** 509-511

STROESSNER, ALFREDO (born 1912), Paraguayan statesman **14** 511-512

STRONG, JOSIAH (1847-1916), American clergyman and social activist **14** 512-513

STRUSS, KARL (1886-1981), American photographer and cinematographer **21** 398-399

STRUVE, FRIEDRICH GEORG WILHELM VON (1793-1864), German-born Russian astronomer and geodesist **14** 513

STUART, GILBERT (1755-1828), American painter **14** 513-515

STUART, JAMES EWELL BROWN (Jeb; 1833-64), Confederate cavalry officer **14** 515-516

STUDENT, KURT (1890-1978), German general **20** 356-358

STUDI, WES (born Wesley Studie; born circa 1944), Native American actor **15** 1-2

STURGES, PRESTON (Edmund Preston Biden; 1898-1959), American playwright, screenwriter, director, and businessman **19** 371-374

STURLUSON, SNORRI (1179-1241), Icelandic statesman and historian **14** 310-311

STURT, CHARLES (1795-1869), British officer, explorer, and colonial administrator **15** 2-3

STURTEVANT, A. H. (Alfred Henry Sturtevant; 1891-1970), American geneticist **15** 3-5

T

Tabano, Ray American musician Aerosmith **24** 4-7

TABARI, MUHAMMAD IBN JARIR AL- (839-923), Moslem historian and religious scholar **15** 69-70

TABOR, HORACE AUSTIN WARNER (1830-1899), American mining magnate and politician **15** 70

TACITUS (56/57-circa 125), Roman orator and historian **15** 70-72

TAEUBER-ARP, SOPHIE (1889-1943), Swiss-born painter, designer, and dancer **15** 73-74

TAEWON'GUN, HŬNGSON (1820-1898), Korean imperial regent **15** 74-75

TAFAWA BALEWA, SIR ABUBAKAR (1912-1966), Nigerian statesman, prime minister 1957-1966 **15** 75

TAFT, LORADO (1860-1936), American sculptor **15** 75-76

TAFT, ROBERT ALPHONSO (1889-1953), American senator **15** 76-78

TAFT, WILLIAM HOWARD (1857-1930), American statesman, president 1909-1913 **15** 78-81

TAGORE, RABINDRANATH (1861-1941), Bengali poet, philosopher, social reformer, and dramatist **12** 529-531

TAHARQA (reigned circa 688-circa 663 B.C.), Nubian pharaoh of Egypt **15** 81-82

TAINE, HIPPOLYTE ADOLPHE (1828-1893), French critic and historian **15** 82-83

T'AI-TSUNG, T'ANG (600-649), Chinese emperor **15** 83-84

TAKAHASHI, KOREKIYO (1854-1936), Japanese statesman **15** 84-85

TAL, JOSEF (Josef Gruenthal; born 1910), Israeli composer, pianist, and professor of music **15** 85-86

TALBERT, MARY MORRIS BURNETT (1866-1923), American educator, feminist, civil rights activist, and lecturer **15** 86-88

Tallarico, Steven (born 1948), American musician Aerosmith **24** 4-7

TALLCHIEF, MARIA (born 1925), Native American prima ballerina **15** 88-89

TALLEYRAND, CHARLES MAURICE DE (Duc de Tallyrand-Périgord; 1754-1838), French statesman **15** 89-90

TALLIS, THOMAS (circa 1505-85), English composer and organist **15** 91

TALON, JEAN (1626-1694), French intendant of New France **15** 91-92

TAM, VIVIENNE (Yin Yok Tam; born 1957), Chinese American designer **24** 400-402

TAMARA (Tamar; 1159-1212), Queen of Georgia (1184-1212) **23** 388-390

TAMBO, OLIVER REGINALD (1917-1993), serves as acting president of the African National Congress **15** 92-94

TAMERLANE (1336-1405), Turko-Mongol conqueror **15** 94-95

TAMIRIS, HELEN (Helen Becker; 1905-1966), American dancer and choreographer **23** 390-392

TAN, AMY (born 1952), American author **15** 95-96

TANAKA, KAKUEI (1918-1993), prime minister of Japan (1972-1974) **15** 96-98

TANEY, ROGER BROOKE (1777-1864), American political leader, chief justice of U.S. Supreme Court **15** 98-99

TANGE, KENZO (born 1913), Japanese architect and city planner **15** 99-101

Tanglewood Music Center (Tanglewood, Massachusetts) Koussevitzky, Serge **24** 213-215

TANGUY, YVES (1900-1955), French painter **15** 101

TANIZAKI, JUNICHIRO (1886-1965), Japanese novelist, essayist, and playwright **15** 101-102

TANNER, HENRY OSSAWA (1859-1937), African American painter **15** 102-103

T'AO CH'IEN (365-427), Chinese poet **15** 104-105

TAO-AN (312-385), Chinese Buddhist monk **15** 103-104

TAO-HSÜAN (596-667), Chinese Buddhist monk **15** 105

TAPPAN BROTHERS (19th century), American merchants and reformers **15** 105-106

TAQI KHAN AMIR-E KABIR, MIRZA (circa 1806-52), Iranian statesman **15** 106-107

TARBELL, IDA MINERVA (1857-1944), American journalist **15** 107-108

TARDE, JEAN GABRIEL (1843-1904), French philosopher and sociologist **15** 108-109

TARKINGTON, NEWTON BOOTH (1869-1946), American author **15** 109

TARKOVSKY, ANDREI ARSENYEVICH (1932-1986), Russian film director **23** 392-395

TARLETON, SIR BANASTRE (1754-1833), English soldier; fought in American Revolution **15** 110

TARSKI, ALFRED (1902-1983), Polish-American mathematician and logician **15** 110-111

TARTAGLIA, NICCOLO (1500-1557), Italian mathematician **15** 111-112

TARTINI, GIUSEPPE (1692-1770), Italian violinist, composer, and theorist **15** 112-113

TASMAN, ABEL JANSZOON (circa 1603-59), Dutch navigator **15** 113-114

TASSO, TORQUATO (1544-1595), Italian poet **15** 114-116

TATA, JAMSETJI NUSSERWANJI (Jamshedji Nasarwanji Tata; 1839-1904), Indian businessman **24** 402-404

TATE, ALLEN (1899-1979), American poet, critic and editor **15** 116

TATLIN, VLADIMIR EVGRAFOVICH (1885-1953), Russian avant garde artist **15** 117-118

TATI, JACQUES (Jacques Tatischeff; 1908-1982), French actor and director **22** 410-412

TAUSSIG, HELEN BROOKE (1898-1986), American physician **15** 118-120

TAWNEY, RICHARD HENRY (1880-1962), British economic historian and social philosopher **15** 120-121

TAYLOR, BROOK (1685-1731), English mathematician **15** 121-122

TAYLOR, EDWARD (circa 1642-1729), American Puritan poet and minister **15** 122-123

TAYLOR, EDWARD PLUNKET (1901-1989), Canadian-born financier and thoroughbred horse breeder **15** 123-124

TAYLOR, ELIZABETH ROSEMUND (born 1932), American film actress **15** 124-125

TAYLOR, FREDERICK WINSLOW (1856-1915), American industrial manager and production engineer **21** 400-402

TAYLOR, JOHN (1753-1824), American politician and political theorist **15** 126

TAYLOR, MAXWELL (1901-1987), American soldier-statesman-scholar **15** 126-127

WATSON, THOMAS J. JR. (1914-1993), American businessman **19** 408-410

WATSON-WATT, SIR ROBERT ALEXANDER (1892-1973), British scientific civil servant **16** 140-141

WATT, JAMES (1736-1819), British instrument maker and engineer **16** 141-143

WATTEAU, ANTOINE (1684-1721), French painter **16** 143-144

WATTLETON, FAYE (Alyce Faye Wattleton, born 1943), African American women's rights activist **18** 405-407

WATTS, ALAN WILSON (1915-1973), naturalized American author and lecturer **16** 144-145

WATTS, J.C. (Julius Caesar Watts, Jr.; born 1957), African American politician **18** 407-409

WAUGH, EVELYN ARTHUR ST. JOHN (1903-1966), English author **16** 145-147

WAUNEKA, ANNIE DODGE (1910-1997), Navajo nation leader and Native American activist **18** 409-410

WAVELL, ARCHIBALD PERCIVAL (1st Earl Wavell; 1883-1950), English general, statesman, and writer **16** 147-148

WAYLAND, FRANCIS (1796-1865), American educator and clergyman **16** 148-149

WAYNE, ANTHONY (1745-1796), American soldier **16** 149-150

WAYNE, JOHN (Marion Mitchell Morrison; 1907-79), American actor **16** 150-151

WEAVER, JAMES BAIRD (1833-1912), American political leader **16** 151-152

WEAVER, PAT (Sylvester Laflin Weaver, Jr.; 1908-2002), American television executive **19** 410-413

WEAVER, ROBERT C. (1907-1997), first African American U.S. cabinet officer **16** 152-153

WEBB, BEATRICE POTTER (1858-1943), English social reformer **16** 153-154

WEBB, SIDNEY JAMES (Baron Passfield; 1859-1947), English social reformer, historian, and statesman **16** 154-155

WEBBER, ANDREW LLOYD (born 1948), British composer **16** 155-156

WEBER, CARL MARIA FRIEDRICH ERNST VON (1786-1826), German composer and conductor **16** 156-157

WEBER, MAX (1864-1920), German social scientist **16** 157-160

WEBER, MAX (1881-1961), American painter **16** 160

WEBERN, ANTON (1883-1945), Austrian composer **16** 160-162

WEBSTER, DANIEL (1782-1852), American lawyer, orator, and statesman **16** 162-164

WEBSTER, JOHN (circa 1580-circa 1634), English dramatist **16** 164

WEBSTER, NOAH (1758-1843), American lexicographer **16** 164-166

WEDEKIND, FRANK (Benjamin Franklin Wedekind; 1864-1918), German dramatist, cosmopolite, and libertarian **16** 166-167

WEDGWOOD, CICELY VERONICA (1910-1997), British writer and historian **16** 167-168

WEDGWOOD, JOSIAH (1730-1795), English potter **16** 168-169

WEED, THURLOW (1797-1882), American politician **16** 169-170

WEEMS, MASON LOCKE (1759-1825), American Episcopal minister and popular writer **16** 170

WEGENER, ALFRED LOTHAR (1880-1930), German meteorologist, Arctic explorer, and geophysicist **16** 170-171

WEI HSIAO-WEN-TI (467-499), Chinese emperor **8** 5

WEI JINGSHENG (born 1950), Chinese human rights activist **18** 410-412

WEI YÜAN (1794-1856), Chinese historian and geographer **16** 180-181

WEIDENREICH, FRANZ (1873-1948), German anatomist and physical anthropologist **16** 171-172

WEIL, SIMONE (1909-1943), French thinker, political activist, and religious mystic **16** 172-174

WEILL, KURT (1900-1950), German-American composer **16** 174-175

WEINBERG, STEVEN (born 1933), Nobel Prize-winning physicist **16** 175-177

WEINBERGER, CASPER WILLARD (born 1917), U.S. public official under three presidents **16** 177-178

WEISMANN, AUGUST FREIDRICH LEOPOLD (1834-1914), German biologist **16** 178-180

WEISSMULLER, JOHNNY (Peter John Weissmuller; 1904-1984), American swimmer and actor **21** 425-427

WEIZMAN, EZER (born 1924), Israeli air force commander and president of Israel (1993-) **16** 181-182

WEIZMANN, CHAIM (1874-1952), Israeli statesman, president 1949-52 **16** 183-184

WELCH, JACK (John Francis Welch, Jr.; born 1935), American businessman **19** 413-415

WELCH, ROBERT (1899-1985), founder of the John Birch Society **16** 184-185

WELCH, WILLIAM HENRY (1850-1934), American pathologist, bacteriologist, and medical educator **16** 185-186

WELD, THEODORE DWIGHT (1803-1895), American reformer, preacher, and editor **16** 186

WELDON, FAY BIRKINSHAW (born 1931 or 1933), British novelist, dramatist, essayist, and feminist **16** 186-188

WELENSKY, SIR ROY (1907-1991), Rhodesian statesman **16** 188

WELK, LAWRENCE (1903-1992), American bandleader and television host **22** 420-422

WELLES, GIDEON (1802-1878), American statesman **16** 188-190

WELLES, ORSON (1915-1985), Broadway and Hollywood actor, radio actor, and film director **16** 190-191

WELLES, SUMNER (1892-1961), American diplomat **16** 191-192

WELLESLEY, RICHARD COLLEY (1st Marquess Wellesley; 1760-1842), British colonial administrator **16** 192-193

Wellesley College (Wellesley, Massachusetts)
Whiting, Sarah Frances **24** 442-444

WELLHAUSEN, JULIUS (1844-1918), German historian **20** 397-400

WELLS, HERBERT GEORGE (1866-1946), English author **16** 195-196

WELLS, HORACE (1815-1848), American dentist **16** 196

WELLS, MARY GEORGENE BERG (born 1928), American businesswoman **16** 197-198

WELLS-BARNETT, IDA B. (1862-1931), American journalist and activist **16** 198-199

WELTY, EUDORA (born 1909), American author and essayist **16** 199-201

WEN T'IEN-HSIANG (1236-1283), Chinese statesman **16** 203